THE ROUTLEDGE HANDBOOK OF NORTH AMERICAN LANGUAGES

The Routledge Handbook of North American Languages is a one-stop reference for linguists on those topics that come up the most frequently in the study of the languages of North America (including Mexico). This handbook compiles a list of contributors from across many different theories and at different stages of their careers, all of whom are well-known experts in North American languages. The volume comprises two distinct parts: the first surveys some of the phenomena most frequently discussed in the study of North American languages, and the second surveys some of the most frequently discussed language families of North America. The consistent goal of each contribution is to couch the content of the chapter in contemporary theory so that the information is maximally relevant and accessible for a wide range of audiences, including graduate students and young new scholars, and even senior scholars who are looking for a crash course in the topics. Empirically driven chapters provide fundamental knowledge needed to participate in contemporary theoretical discussions of these languages, making this handbook an indispensable resource for linguistics scholars.

Daniel Siddiqi is Professor of Linguistics, Cognitive Science, and English at Carleton University in Ottawa. His research focuses on stem allomorphy, metatheory and grammatical architecture, and non-standard English phenomena. Beyond editing this volume, he has edited *The Routledge Handbook of Syntax* and *Benjamins' Morphological Metatheory*. Professor Siddiqi is also the co-editor of the *Canadian Journal of Linguistics/Revue canadienne de linguistique*.

Michael Barrie is a syntactician at Sogang University in Seoul, whose work also includes the syntax-semantics interface and the syntax-prosody interface. Much of his work is based on extensive fieldwork on Northern Iroquoian languages as well as some work on Algonquian languages. Outside of North America, Barrie has also worked on Cantonese, Korean, and Romance.

Carrie Gillon is the co-founder of Quick Brown Fox Consulting and the co-host of *The Vocal Fries*, the podcast about linguistic discrimination. In a previous life, she researched the syntax and semantics of understudied languages, mainly Indigenous languages of Canada. She wrote the book *The Semantics of Determiners: Domain Restriction in Sḵwx̱wú7mesh*, co-authored *Nominal Contact in Michif*, co-edited the Sḵwx̱wú7mesh-English bilingual dictionary, wrote or co-authored eight articles and three book chapters, and co-edited three volumes of *University of British Columbia Working Papers in Linguistics* and a special edition of the *Canadian Journal of Linguistics* on noun phrases.

Jason D. Haugen is Associate Professor of Anthropology at Oberlin College. His research focuses on the morphosyntax and historical linguistics of Uto-Aztecan languages.

Éric Mathieu is Professor of Linguistics at the University of Ottawa. He completed his PhD in 2002 at University College London. His research focuses on French (Modern and Old) and Ojibwe (an Algonquian language). He has published in *Linguistic Inquiry*, *Natural Language and Linguistic Theory*, *Syntax*, *International Journal of American Linguistics*, *Journal of Linguistics*, *Lingua*, *Probus*, *Studia Linguistica*, and *Linguistic Variation*. He is also the author of numerous chapters in books (with Oxford University Press, Cambridge University Press, John Benjamins, Routledge, and Springer, among others) and co-author of several books, a monograph on island effects entitled 'The syntax and semantics of split constructions', a special edition of *Lingua* on noun incorporation, an edited volume on Romance languages, *Variation Across and Within Languages*, and a forthcoming book on plurals.

ROUTLEDGE HANDBOOKS IN LINGUISTICS

Routledge Handbooks in Linguistics provide overviews of a whole subject area or sub-discipline in linguistics, and survey the state of the discipline including emerging and cutting edge areas. Edited by leading scholars, these volumes include contributions from key academics from around the world and are essential reading for both advanced undergraduate and postgraduate students.

THE ROUTLEDGE HANDBOOK OF LANGUAGE AND DIALOGUE
Edited by Edda Weigand

THE ROUTLEDGE HANDBOOK OF LANGUAGE AND POLITICS
Edited by Ruth Wodak and Bernhard Forchtner

THE ROUTLEDGE HANDBOOK OF LANGUAGE AND MEDIA
Edited by Daniel Perrin and Colleen Cotter

THE ROUTLEDGE HANDBOOK OF ECOLINGUISTICS
Edited by Alwin F. Fill and Hermine Penz

THE ROUTLEDGE HANDBOOK OF LEXICOGRAPHY
Edited by Pedro A. Fuertes-Olivera

THE ROUTLEDGE HANDBOOK OF DISCOURSE PROCESSES, SECOND EDITION
Edited by Michael F. Schober, David N. Rapp, and M. Anne Britt

THE ROUTLEDGE HANDBOOK OF PHONETICS
Edited by William F. Katz and Peter F. Assmann

THE ROUTLEDGE HANDBOOK OF VOCABULARY STUDIES
Edited by Stuart Webb

THE ROUTLEDGE HANDBOOK OF NORTH AMERICAN LANGUAGES
Edited by Daniel Siddiqi, Michael Barrie, Carrie Gillon, Jason D. Haugen and Éric Mathieu

Further titles in this series can be found online at www.routledge.com/series/RHIL

THE ROUTLEDGE HANDBOOK OF NORTH AMERICAN LANGUAGES

Edited by
Daniel Siddiqi, Michael Barrie, Carrie Gillon, Jason D. Haugen and Éric Mathieu

NEW YORK AND LONDON

First published 2020
by Routledge
605 Third Avenue, New York, NY 10017
4 Park Square, Milton Park, Abingdon, Oxon OX14 4RN

First issued in paperback 2022

Routledge is an imprint of the Taylor & Francis Group, an informa business

Library of Congress Cataloging-in-Publication Data
A catalog record for this book has been requested

ISBN 13: 978-1-03-247520-2 (pbk)
ISBN 13: 978-1-138-62874-8 (hbk)

DOI: 10.4324/9781315210636

Typeset in Times New Roman
by Apex CoVantage, LLC

Dedicated to the speakers of the Indigenous languages of North America – past, present, and future. And to the activists and documentarians working to preserve, maintain, and revitalize them.

And to our beloved colleague Jane Hill, whose contribution to the study of Indigenous American languages is immeasurable. Her absence from the field will be felt for a long time.

CONTENTS

CONTRIBUTORS

Mark C. Baker is Distinguished Professor of Linguistics and Cognitive Science at Rutgers University. He received his PhD in Linguistics in 1985 from MIT. He taught at McGill University in Montreal for 12 years before moving to Rutgers in 1998. He specializes in the syntax and morphology of less-studied languages, particularly those of the Americas, Africa, and Asia, seeking to bring together generative-style theories, data collected from fieldwork, and typological comparison in a way that illuminates all three. He has written five research monographs, as well as numerous journal articles, and one book for a popular audience, *The Atoms of Language* (2001).

Heather Bliss has been working with Siksika and Kainai community members since 2003 on Blackfoot linguistic research and language documentation projects. Her 2005 MA thesis and 2013 PhD dissertation both focus on issues related to Blackfoot's inverse system. She is Lecturer in Linguistics at Simon Fraser University, and Adjunct Professor at the University of British Columbia and University of Calgary, researching a diverse range of topics around Indigenous language revitalization, syntactic theory, articulatory phonetics, and second language pronunciation. She is the editor and curator of the Blackfoot Oral Stories Database.

George Aaron Broadwell (PhD 1990, UCLA) is Elling Eide Professor of Anthropology at the University of Florida. He is a specialist in Native American languages of the southeastern United States and Oaxaca, Mexico, with a special focus on Choctaw, Timucua, several varieties of Zapotec, and Copala Triqui. He is interested in the issues of integrating language description and documentation with contemporary work in linguistic theory. He is also committed to working with Native American communities to provide dictionaries, texts, and other materials that are useful in language revitalization and maintenance.

Eugene Buckley is Associate Professor of Linguistics at the University of Pennsylvania. His main research interests are syllable and metrical structure, and the role of explanation in phonological theory. Much of his work has focused on Kashaya, a Pomoan language of northern California, as well as other Native languages of California and Oregon.

Livia Camargo Souza is a PhD student at Rutgers University with a background in Generative Syntax and Language Documentation. She coordinated the Yawanawa language documentation project between 2011 and 2013, and she continues to be involved in Panoan linguistics in the Brazilian

Amazon, currently as the team leader of the language documentation project of the recently contacted Xinane people (both projects funded by Museu do Índio, Brazil, and UNESCO). Her work has focused on different aspects of Panoan syntax, especially case and switch-reference, as well as syntax-semantics interface phenomena in both Panoan languages and Brazilian Portuguese.

Lauren Clemens is Assistant Professor in the Program of Linguistics and Cognitive Science in the Department of Anthropology at the University at Albany, State University of New York. She received her PhD in 2014 from Harvard University. Her research work brings prosodic evidence to bear on problems related to syntactic constituency. She draws heavily on data from Mesoamerican languages, including Ch'ol (Mayan) and Copala Triqui (Otomanguean). In addition to bringing data from minoritized languages to linguistic theory, she collaborates in community-engaged language documentation with those who speak their language in diaspora.

Richard Compton is Associate Professor in the Department of Linguistics at the Université du Québec à Montréal. He received his PhD in 2012 from the University of Toronto and then spent one year as a postdoctoral fellow at McGill University. His research interests include agreement, polysynthetic word formation, and lexical categories in varieties of the Inuit language, particularly Inuktitut and Inuinnaqtun. His co-edited dictionary of Kangiryuarmiut Inuinnaqtun with Emily Kudlak was published by Nunavut Arctic College Media in 2018. He holds a Canada Research Chair in Transmission and Knowledge of the Inuit Language.

Henry Davis is Professor of Linguistics at UBC. He specializes in languages of northwest North America, including those of the Salish, Tsimshianic, and Wakashan families. Most of his research is on syntax and its interfaces with semantics and morphology, but he has also worked extensively on the collection, transcription, and translation of texts, dictionary compilation, and the construction of pedagogical materials.

Andréia de Souza is a PhD student in Linguistics at the Université du Québec à Montréal. Her research interests are phonology and its interaction with morphology and phonetics, and second language acquisition. She is currently working on projects related to syllabic structure, stress, and the distribution of rhotics in major Iberian languages. She teaches Portuguese as a foreign language at the Université du Québec à Montréal.

Jane H. Hill was Regents' Professor of Anthropology and Linguistics (Emerita) at the University of Arizona. Her work on Uto-Aztecan languages includes fieldwork on Cupeño, Nahuatl, and Tohono O'odham. At the time of her death in 2018, she held the Viking Fund Medal in Anthropology, the Franz Boas Prize of the American Anthropological Association, and was a Fellow of the American Association for the Advancement of Science, the American Academy of Arts and Sciences, and the Linguistic Society of America.

Marianne Huijsmans is a PhD candidate at the University of British Columbia. Her work focuses on the semantics and syntax of ʔayʔaǰuθəm (Comox-Sliammon), a highly endangered Coast Salish language. She is also collaborating with the Tla'amin, Homalco, Klahoose, and Comox First Nations on a dictionary of ʔayʔaǰuθəm. Her current research focuses on a diverse set of second-position clitics that includes mood/force markers, subject clitics, modals/evidentials, tense markers, and discourse particles.

Alessandro Jaker is a Postdoctoral Fellow at the University of Toronto, and is also affiliated with the Alaska Native Language Center in Fairbanks, Alaska. He has worked with the Yellowknives Dene First Nation since 2005, working with both of their traditional languages, Wıìlıìdeh (a dialect of Tłı̨chǫ Yatıì) and Tetǫ́t'ıné (a dialect of Dëne Sų̨łıné). His interests are phonetics, phonology, morphology, and the development of teaching materials for Dene languages.

Alana Johns was Professor of Linguistics at the University of Toronto until 2017. She taught syntax and morphology and conducted research on Inuktut grammar and dialects, with a focus on verb paradigms, complex predicates, ergativity, noun incorporation, and language revitalization. As Professor Emeritus, Johns is currently lead investigator in a SSHRC-funded project, Sinâni, which involves the collection and transcription of Inuttut oral audio/video materials for linguistic analysis and as a community resource.

Brook Danielle Lillehaugen is a linguist who specializes in Zapotec languages, spoken in Oaxaca, Mexico. She is Associate Professor of Linguistics at Haverford College and co-director of Ticha, a digital text explorer for Colonial Zapotec texts (http://ticha.haverford.edu). She received her PhD in Linguistics in 2006 from the University of California, Los Angeles and has been doing fieldwork with speakers of Zapotec languages since 1999. Lillehaugen's research profile includes technical grammatical description as well as collaborative language documentation and revitalization projects.

Lisa Matthewson is Professor of Linguistics at the University of British Columbia. Her research focuses on formal semantics with a cross-linguistic perspective. The primary languages she investigates are St'át'imcets (Salish), Gitksan (Tsimshianic), and Niuean (Austronesian). She has worked on a range of areas including determiners, quantifiers, pronouns, adverbs, lexical categories, tense, aspect, modals, mood, evidentials, discourse particles, and presupposition. Her research also focuses on methodologies for semantic fieldwork.

Kumiko Murasugi is Associate Professor of Linguistics and Cognitive Science at Carleton University in Ottawa. Her research areas include theoretical and applied linguistics, Inuit languages, language documentation, and linguistic cartography. She is currently developing an online cybercartographic atlas of the Inuit language in Canada in partnership with the Geomatics and Cartographic Research Centre at Carleton, linguistic and applied linguistic collaborators, and Inuit partner organizations.

Sarah E. Murray is Associate Professor in Linguistics at Cornell University, as well as a member of the graduate fields of American Indian and Indigenous Studies, Cognitive Science, and Philosophy. She earned her PhD in Linguistics from Rutgers University in 2010. Her research brings together language documentation with cross-linguistic formal semantics and pragmatics. Every summer since 2006, she has worked with speakers on the Northern Cheyenne Indian Reservation in Montana. She is currently working with Chief Dull Knife College, the Northern Cheyenne tribal college, on a project to create a database of Cheyenne language texts.

Heather Newell is Associate Professor in the Linguistics Department at the Université du Québec à Montréal. She obtained her PhD at McGill University in 2009. She is the editor of the *Canadian Journal of Linguistics/Revue canadienne de linguistique* and has been involved in the organization of the Canadian Linguistics Olympiad. She has published in *Lingua*, *The Routledge Handbook of Phonology*, *The Oxford Encyclopedia of Morphology*, and *Morphological Metatheory* and has published in and co-edited the volume *The Structure of Words at the Interfaces* in the Oxford Studies in Theoretical Linguistics Series.

Carolyn O'Meara is Associate Research Professor in the Department of Indigenous Languages in the Philological Research Institute at the National Autonomous University of Mexico. She is interested in the relationship between language, culture, and cognition. Her research has a particular focus on the domains of landscape and spatial reference and how concepts lexicalized in these domains differ cross-linguistically. She conducts fieldwork on Indigenous languages of Mexico, with a particular focus on the language isolate Seri.

Will Oxford is Associate Professor of Linguistics at the University of Manitoba. His research focuses on the morphosyntax of the Algonquian languages from comparative and theoretical perspectives.

Gabriela Pérez Báez is Assistant Professor in the Linguistics Department, University of Oregon, and co-director of the National Breath of Life Archival Institute for Indigenous Languages. Gabriela has served as Curator of Linguistics at the National Museum of Natural History, Smithsonian Institution, and in its Recovering Voices initiative. Her research centers on Zapotec languages and she has published on migration and language vitality, verbal inflection and derivation, semantic typology, and language and cognition. Gabriela is the compiler of two dictionaries of Isthmus Zapotec within a participatory and interdisciplinary model. She holds a PhD in Linguistics from the University at Buffalo.

Keren Rice is University Professor in the Department of Linguistics at the University of Toronto. She has worked with speakers of Dene languages for many years, with a focus on phonology and morphology as well as language revitalization and the ethics of fieldwork. She was the editor of the *International Journal of American Linguistics* from 2003 until 2013, and served as president of the Society for the Study of Indigenous Languages of the Americas in 2017 and 2018.

Elizabeth Ritter is Professor in the Linguistics Division of the School of Languages, Linguistics, Literatures and Cultures of the University of Calgary. She has been conducting research on Siksika and Kainai Blackfoot since 2004, and has explored a range of topics, including clause structure, animacy, person and tense, direct-inverse marking, and number marking. Much of her research has been conducted in collaboration with linguists Heather Bliss, Martina Wiltschko, Sara Thomas Rosen, and Kyumin Kim, and with her Blackfoot teachers and consultants, Rachel Ermineskin, Noreen Breaker, Brent Prairie Chicken, and Sandra Many Feathers.

Bettina Spreng is Assistant Professor at the University of Saskatchewan. Her research focuses on the interface between morphosyntax and semantics, especially with respect to the interaction of tense and aspect semantics with case and agreement alternations. Her fieldwork focuses on the description and analysis of understudied languages, primarily Canadian Inuktitut and nonstandard German dialects.

Hiroto Uchihara is Assistant Research Professor in the Institute of Philological Research at the National Autonomous University of Mexico. He received his PhD in Linguistics from the University at Buffalo, State University of New York in 2013, and published his dissertation, *Tone and Accent in Oklahoma Cherokee*, with Oxford University Press in 2016. His research focuses primarily on the phonology and morphology of Native American languages in North America, particularly Cherokee and Otomanguean languages (especially Zapotec, Tlapanec, and Mixtec) from both a synchronic and diachronic perspective.

Suzanne Urbanczyk is Associate Professor of Linguistics at the University of Victoria. Her research focuses on non-concatenative morphology of Salish and Wakashan languages.

Nicholas Welch is Assistant Professor in the Department of Linguistics at Memorial University of Newfoundland. He has worked on the syntactic structure of Tłı̨chǫ and Tsúùt'ínà since 2006, focusing on nonverbal predication and temporal grammar. His work on language revitalization with the Tłı̨chǫ and Tsúùt'ínà First Nations since 2007 has centered on lexicography, curriculum design, and the building of IT tools for pedagogy.

Martina Wiltschko is ICREA Research Professor at Universitat Pompeu Fabra (UPF). She holds a PhD from the University of Vienna. Her main area of interest is syntactic theory and how it is to be modeled in light of language variation. She has conducted fieldwork on several First Nations languages indigenous to North America (Halkomelem, Blackfoot, Ktunaxa) and published on various issues relating to the universality and variation associated with functional categories along the nominal and the clausal spine.

EDITOR'S NOTE

Daniel Siddiqi

In 2015, I attended a wonderful conference called "Gender, Class, and Determination" hosted by Éric Mathieu and the University of Ottawa. Most of the editors of this volume and a number of the contributors were there participating. During a talk, a speaker offhandedly threw out that "Everyone knows Blackfoot is the weird Algonquian language". Everyone agreed. My first thought was "Wait a second. Everyone knows this? I don't know this! How do I not know this?" It struck me as a very real possibility that I was the only person in the room that had not one clue about why Blackfoot is an exceptional Algonquian language. Eventually ". . . except Blackfoot" became a bit of a refrain at the conference. It always drew laughs. I tried to hide in the back of the room.

Then Michif came up. It turns out that Michif is famous for being a mixed language with the NP of French and the VP of Cree. Again, everyone in the room knew this fact, and I did not.

This experience began to repeat itself. At small local workshops. At larger conferences. If I was at a conference in North America, there was always a shared knowledge about Indigenous American languages that I just didn't have. I took a moment to reflect on this and realized it wasn't limited to my conference-going experience. The particular subset of the field I work on, Distributed Morphology, is saturated with data from North American languages. Indeed, many of my co-authors, including Heidi Harley, Jason Haugen, and Brandon Fry, specialize in some Indigenous language. I clearly needed to know the generalizations about North American languages. It was increasingly obvious to me that my ability to function as a contemporary linguist was dependent on my understanding the broad strokes of Indigenous American languages, even if I were content to continue to specialize on European languages in my own work (not that I should be so content).

So, of course, I set out to learn as much as I could about North American languages. Marianne Mithun's 2001 book was great, but it wasn't really couched in contemporary theory the way I needed it to be. What I needed was a handbook. Linguistics is swimming in handbooks. It should have been easy enough to find one that surveys North American languages.

I didn't find one.

So, I sent a note to my colleagues, Jessica Coon and Éric Mathieu, and asked them if they knew of a handbook on North American languages. I told them it seemed to me that this really ought to be a thing that exists. I assumed I couldn't be the only linguist whose education didn't include familiarity with North American languages. I couldn't be the only linguist who needed to catch up on the hot data everyone is talking about. They told me that there wasn't such a thing. Then Éric said, "You should do one".

So, I did. And you're reading it.

What Mike, Carrie, Jason, Éric, and I attempted to do with this volume is create a one-stop reference for linguists to find most of the topics that come up most frequently in the study of North American languages. Following in the footsteps of other handbooks in this series, such as *The Routledge Handbook of Syntax*, we compiled a great list of contributors from across many different theories and at different stages of their careers, all of whom are well-known experts in North American languages. We broke this volume into two distinct parts: the first part surveys the types of phenomena most frequently discussed in the study of North American languages, and the second part surveys the most frequently discussed language families of North America. The consistent goal of each contribution is to couch the content of the chapter in contemporary theory so that the information is maximally relevant and accessible for graduate students, young new scholars, and even senior scholars, like me, who are looking for a crash course in the topics primarily being discussed in the literature and conferences of North American linguistics.

Despite my humor, the challenge of putting together a handbook of this type, which has not been done before, is not something we as editors took lightly. The handbook we set out to create is different from the lion's share of linguistics handbooks in circulation. Besides the normal responsibility we have to our audience and the ideas we are setting out to summarize, we have the additional responsibility to the speakers of these languages. The languages documented in this volume are all endangered. For much of our audience, this handbook will be their first in-depth exposure to these languages and will lay the foundations of how they regard these languages. Thus, we had a responsibility to do this absolutely right – to take seriously the important documentary role such a handbook has, even though we are not presenting original documentary research. We have tried our best to live up to that responsibility.

The first part of this book comprises the 14 topics across the major subfields that we thought were most necessary for the emerging scholar to know in order to dive into contemporary linguistic study in North America. The chapters are roughly organized from smallest linguistic constituent to largest (or sounds to clausal semantics, as it were). The contributors have focused primarily on North American data for examples of the phenomena, but we have also made an effort to also include data from and applicability to other linguistic areas. Because of this, we also feel like the first 14 chapters make up a sort of Pocket Handbook of Frequently Studied Linguistic Phenomena. We have prioritized the types of phenomena that are typically not found in the European languages that dominate the literature and thus tend to dominate linguistic handbooks. Thus, we have chapters dedicated to ergativity, polysynthesis, evidentials, and inverse systems.

While the first part of the book focuses on describing particular phenomena cross-linguistically, the second half of the book focuses on describing the North American language families that a budding linguist is most likely to encounter. Again, we have put an effort into couching the description of the languages in contemporary theory in order to maximize the content's accessibility and applicability to our audience's research needs. We have organized the language families from south to north, starting with Otomanguean and Mayan in Mexico and ending with Na-Dene and Eskimo-Aleut in Alaska and Canada. We have also included two special chapters in this section that we think will be especially valuable to our readers. Chapter 23 focuses on proposed long-distance genetic relationships using Uto-Aztecan and Plateau Penutian as an example. Chapter 24 uses the languages of California to exemplify linguistic areas where unrelated languages share systematic common properties as a function of their geographic proximity. What we have created with these ten chapters, we hope, is something akin to a Pocket Handbook of North American Language Families.

I have had the unique experience of being the lead editor of this volume and part of its target audience. Over the course of the last year and a half, it has been my great pleasure to work with the contributors of this volume who have taken very seriously the content of this volume and its importance both to the linguistic theory community and to the various Indigenous communities in North America that it represents. As a person who would benefit from learning the content of this book, I feel confident in thinking this book has made me a better linguist, better able to engage in the literature and discussion generated in North American linguistics, and better able to serve the communities we study. It was our hope in developing this handbook that this will be a shared experience across our audience. I hope you find this volume as helpful as it was to me. I speak for all the editors when I say that we are very proud of the volume we have put together.

PART I

Common Phenomena in North American Languages

1
PHONOLOGICAL INVENTORIES

Keren Rice

1. Introduction

One of the first things that is often done in examining the sound system of a language is to determine the inventories of consonants, vowels, and, if present, tones of the language. This can be done in various ways, but the basic assumption is that it is possible to come to a phonemicization of a language, identifying the distinctive sounds and fitting each into a chart such as that used for presenting the International Phonetic Alphabet (IPA). There may be disagreements around phonemicization: for instance, it might be controversial to determine whether a sound is truly contrastive or is an allophone of some other sound; it might be difficult to determine what should be considered the phoneme and what should be considered the allophone. Nevertheless, there is something important about the notion of inventory, the topic of this chapter. Phonological inventories provide information about the distinctive sounds of a language and about the patterning of those sounds, and, as Maddieson (1984: 1) writes, generalizations about "the content and structure of phonological inventories has been a significant objective of recent work in linguistics".

This chapter examines characteristics of consonant and vowel inventories of languages indigenous to North America. I begin by identifying some of the challenges inherent in such work, and then turn to a study of inventories, considering contrasts and how inventories grow, taking vertical (sound change) and horizontal (borrowing) effects into account. I then address positional inventories, phonological patterning and inventories, and inventories and orthography.

2. Some Challenges

While establishing the phonological inventory of a language is an early step in the analysis of a sound system, it can be a challenge in many ways.

2.1. Perception and Underdetermination

Perception plays a large role in establishing an inventory. The linguist who does the transcription of a language that they do not speak fluently may miss a contrast. For instance, Buckley (2007) writes that Alsea (Alsean) most likely had ejective sonorants as well as obstruents, but that the transcriptions (Frachtenberg 1917; 1920) are difficult to interpret, and he does not include them in the inventory. Thus, it is likely that the Alsea consonant inventory was underdetermined by Frachtenberg.

2.2. Analysis and Possible Overdetermination of Inventories

It might be that two sounds are in complementary distribution, but they are treated as distinctive. For example, Golla (1996: 366) analyzes Hupa (Dene) as having six phonemic vowels, /i, a, o, e:, a:, o:/, noting allophones. Goddard (1905: 7), on the other hand, includes more vowels: i, e, a, o, i:, a:, o:, u:. Goddard does not give a phonemic analysis, but his inventory can be interpreted as including allophones as well as phonemes.

Central Alaskan Yupik (Eskimo-Aleut) presents another example. One version of the consonant inventory is shown in (1).[1]

(1) Central Alaskan Yupik consonant inventory

p	t	ts/tʃ		k		q	
f	ɬ	s		x	xʷ	χ	χʷ
v	l	z	j	ɣ	ɣʷ	ʁ	ʁʷ
m	n			ŋ			
m̥	n̥			ŋ̊			

(Jacobson 1990: 277; Dorais 2003: 22)

Compton (2008: 31) proposes the smaller inventory in (2), with some of the consonants in (1) being allophonic, and thus predictable in distribution.

(2) Central Alaskan Yupik consonant inventory: reanalysis

p	t	ts/tʃ	k	q
f	ɬ	s	x	χ
v	l	z	ɣ	ʁ
m	n		ŋ	

(Compton 2008: 31)

Beyond allophones, other decisions must be made about what to include in an inventory. Are sounds from loanwords and special types of vocabulary to be included? Are infrequent sounds? For example, Golla (1996: 383) lists Hupa sounds that occur in sound symbolism. I use Golla's transcription in (3).

(3) Hupa sound symbolism

Normal sound	*Replacement in affectionate forms*
w	b
W	s (or ʃ)
ǯ	ʒ
čʷ	c
č'	c'
gʸ	g (or ɢ)
kʸ	k
k'ʸ	k' (or q')

(Golla 1996: 383)

Golla notes that b, š, g, k, k' exist only in sound symbolism, and he does not include these in the Hupa consonant inventory.

Similar questions arise in many languages. For instance, Chafe (1996: 553–554) does not include labials in the Seneca (Iroquoian) inventory, saying that they occur only in nicknames and expressive vocabulary. Uchihara (2016: 43), on the other hand, notes that /m/ is marginal in Cherokee

(Iroquoian), found in just a handful of native words and loanwords and not patterning with other consonants in terms of clusters, but he nevertheless includes it in the inventory. Li (1946: 399) includes /m/ in the Dene Sųłiné (Dene; also called Chipewyan) inventory, but writes that in his material it occurred in only one word.

Considering loanwords, Haas (1946: 338) includes /b, d, g, f/ in the consonant inventory of Tunica (isolate), but states that they occur "only in a few isolated words (of foreign or probably foreign) origin". Hill (2005) includes sounds found only in loanwords for Cupeño (Uto-Aztecan). Some do not include such sounds in the inventory. For instance, Moore (2002: 322) does not include /p/ in the inventory of Kaska (Dene) consonants but gives a loanword with /p/. Boudreault (2009: 23–25) partitions the Sierra Popoluca (Mixe-Zoquean) inventory into native phonemes and restricted phonemes, with the latter occurring in ideophones, lexicalized expressions, borrowings, and stylistic alternations.

2.3. *Phonemes vs. Sequences?*

There is debate about whether something is best analyzed as a single sound or as a sequence. Li (1946: 398) includes labialized velars /gʷ, kʷ, kʷ', xʷ, ɣʷ/ (his transcription) in the consonant system of Dene Sųłiné, while Cook (2004: 3) treats these as deriving from *Cu* sequences. The inventories presented by Cook and Li for the same language thus differ.

Montgomery-Anderson (2015: 20) includes aspirated resonants (sonorants written /hw, hy, hn/) in the inventory in Cherokee (Iroquoian), while Uchihara (2016: 37) treats them as clusters of /h/ followed by a resonant. Uchihara (2016: 38) and Montgomery-Anderson (2015: 20) include /ts, kw, tl/ in the inventory; Cook (1979: 5) treats these as sequences for a different Cherokee variety. Zuni (isolate) is considered by some to have ejectives /ts' tʃ' k' k'ʷ/ (Walker 1964), while others analyze these as sequences of /C+ʔ/ (Newman 1965: 16).

2.4. *Variation and Phonemicization*

There may be variation between sounds, with a decision made about which to include in the inventory. In Plains Cree (Algonquian), and other languages, variation is found between [s] and [ʃ] and between [ts] and [tʃ] (Wolfart 1996: 430). Wolfart writes these as /s/, /ts/ (his symbol *c*), not including the variant in the consonant chart, a decision that might be interpreted as being about phonemicization.

2.5. *Other Challenges*

Transcription conventions vary, with different symbols used for the same sound and the same symbol used for different sounds. For instance, older sources often use ' for aspiration; this is not common today. '*c*' might be used for an alveolar affricate, an alveopalatal affricate, or a palatal stop. The same author may use different symbols for the same sound at different times. For instance, Golla (1996: 368) uses /gʸ/ for the Hupa front velar voiceless unaspirated stop, and /ġ/ for what he calls a back velar voiceless unaspirated stop; while Golla (2011: 82) uses /k̑/ for the voiceless unaspirated front velar and /q/ for the voiceless unaspirated back velar (uvular). In the Dene literature generally, symbols *d, g*, etc., are used for what are usually identified as voiceless unaspirated stops and *t, k*, etc., for voiceless aspirated stops.

Terminology changes over time. For example, for Dene Sųłiné, Li (1946: 398) uses the term 'guttural' where Cook (2004: 9) uses 'velar', and Li distinguishes fricatives with 'surd' and 'sonant' where Cook (2004: 7) uses 'voiceless' and 'voiced'. 'Resonant' is commonly used in some language families (e.g., Salish), while 'sonorant' is used in others.

Inventories may differ by where a sound is placed in a phonemic chart. For instance, Haas (1946: 338) includes /y/ (IPA /j/) under semivowels in Tunica, while Li (1946: 398) includes it with the sonant (voiced) fricatives in Dene Sų̨łiné. /w/ is variably treated as a labial, a velar, or a labiovelar consonant depending on the source. See also §6.2.

Considering vowels, the symbol *e* might be used for a phonetically lax vowel if there is no contrast between tense and lax vowels in a language. Maddieson (2013b) includes discussion of the types of factors used to determine the size of vowel inventories, including the challenges of length, nasalization, and diphthongs. For example, a distinction might be considered as primarily featural (e.g., tense/lax) by some, and as involving timing (long/short) by others.

2.6. *Summary*

Comparison of inventories must be done carefully, ascertaining that assumptions underlying the choice of symbols and the composition of inventories are shared. While it is important to be aware that assumptions might differ, nevertheless, inventories are worthy of study.

3. Factors Determining Inventory Shapes

Gordon (2016) provides an overview of accounts of the typology of inventory shapes, including phonetic (perception, articulation), phonological, and historical factors. Dispersion (pressure for segments to be maximally dispersed throughout the available phonetic space), perceptual distinctness, articulatory simplicity, feature economy, featural robustness, and symmetry have been argued to play important roles in shaping inventories. See Gordon (2016), Hall (2011), and Mielke (2009) for overviews and references. We will see some unusual features in inventories of languages of North America, given these factors.

As a preview, in this section I review expectations of consonant inventories based on typological studies. Gordon (2016), building on Maddieson (1984), chapters in Dryer and Haspelmath (2013), and others, investigates common cross-linguistic characteristics of inventories. While languages indigenous to North America meet many of these, some properties are present that stand out as unusual. The 20 cross-linguistically most common consonants are, according to Maddieson (1984), given in (4) (Gordon 2016: 45):

(4) Consonants with highest cross-linguistic frequency

p	t	tʃ	k	ʔ
b	d		g	
f	s	ʃ		h
m	n	ɲ	ŋ	
w	l, r	j		

(Maddieson 1984; Gordon 2016)

A number of North American languages lack common sounds. For instance, labials, or at least labial obstruents, are missing in several languages including many Dene and Iroquoian languages. Maddieson's (1984) survey and PHOIBLE (an online repository of cross-linguistic phonological inventory data; Moran et al. 2014) show that over 80% of the languages surveyed have /p/ and over 90% /m/, so this absence is striking. Nasals are missing phonemically in several languages (e.g., Quileute [Chimakuan], Pawnee [Caddoan]). Again, this absence is unusual. In Maddieson's survey, almost 100% of the languages have /n/ (81% of the languages in PHOIBLE have /n/).

There are also uncommon sounds. Some Salishan languages have pharyngeal consonants. Maddieson (2013c) notes that pharyngeal consonants occur in only 4.1% of the languages surveyed (PHOIBLE, approximately 2%). Maddieson (2013c) also notes that dental/alveolar non-sibilant fricatives are rare, occurring in 7.6% of the languages surveyed (PHOIBLE, 4%); a number of

North American languages include /θ/ (e.g., Karuk [isolate], Arapaho [Algonquian]). Lateral affricates are rare – according to PHOIBLE, /tɬ/ occurs in 14 of 2,155 languages surveyed (1%); all but three are in North America. The ejective lateral affricate occurs in 24 of the PHOIBLE languages, with all but three in North America. The uvular stop /q/ occurs in many languages of North America but in only 9% of the languages in PHOIBLE. See also Mithun (1996: 137; 1999: 15–20) for discussion of unusual sounds in North American inventories.

Some languages exhibit rare sounds to the exclusion of ones that might be expected. In general, the presence of an ejective stop/affricate implies the presence of its non-ejective counterpart. A number of languages have an ejective lateral affricate but lack its non-ejective counterpart (e.g., Patwin [Wintun]; Lawyer 2015: 225). Popti' (Mayan; Day 1973: 9) has an ejective uvular stop without a plain uvular stop. Ktunaxa (isolate; Morgan 1991: 15) has an uvular fricative /χ/ but lacks a velar fricative; PHOIBLE finds that 18% of languages have /x/ while 6% have /χ/. Languages tend to have plain coronal stops and nasals: Ch'ol (Mayan; Vázquez Álvarez 2011: 35) has palatalized coronals /tʲ, tʲ', ɲ/ but not non-palatalized coronals.

There are North America languages with very small and very large consonant inventories. The small inventories are reasonably similar, although they can differ. While the small inventories surveyed for this work contain some of the sounds that are most common according to the surveys – /t/, /k/, /j/ – the highly frequent /n/ is not present in all small inventories, nor are labials. Inventories increase in size through the introduction of contrasts in place of articulation, particularly in obstruents, and through the introduction of laryngeal contrasts. While generally these contrasts appear in obstruents before sonorants, this is not always the case. Large inventories too can lack common sounds – large inventories are found without nasals and without labials, for instance.

4. Consonant Inventories

Maddieson (2013a) classifies languages by the size of consonant inventories: small (6–14); moderately small (15–18); average (19–25); moderately large (26–33); and large (34+). He notes that smaller-than-average consonant inventories are concentrated in the eastern part of North America, while larger-than-average inventories "are most spectacularly concentrated in the northwest of North America". In this section I review some of these inventories, organized from small to large in Maddieson's classification, to give a taste of what inventories of various sizes are like, focusing on the kinds of contrasts that are present in inventories of different sizes.

4.1. Small Inventories (6–14 Consonants)

Caddoan languages tend to have small consonant inventories. For instance, Pawnee has the inventory in (5).

(5) Pawnee consonant inventory

p	t	ts	k	ʔ
		s		h
	r		w	

(Parks 1976: 13)

The absence of nasals stands out.

Iroquoian languages have small consonant inventories. Seneca has the inventory in (6). Mithun (1999: 15) identifies the same inventory for Mohawk, with a single liquid /l/ or /r/, depending on variety.

(6) Seneca consonant inventory

t		k	ʔ
s			h
n			
r	j	w	

(Chafe 1996: 553)

Chafe notes that more consonants occur phonetically. He also remarks on the presence of labials in nicknames and expressive vocabulary (1996: 554) but does not include them in the inventory.

Algonquian languages tend to have small consonant inventories. Wolfart (1996) proposes the inventory in (7) for Plains Cree.

(7) Plains Cree consonant inventory

p	t	ts~tʃ	k	
		s~ʃ		h
m	n			
w		j		

(Wolfart 1996: 430)

This small inventory has a basic obstruent/sonorant contrast, with stops/affricates, fricatives, nasals, and glides, but no liquid.

Some Uto-Aztecan languages have small inventories. An example is Shoshone, with a labiovelar.

(8) Shoshone consonant inventory

p	t	ts	k	kʷ
		s		
m	n			
w		j		

(Miller 1996: 694)

Charney (1993: 10) gives a similar inventory for Comanche (Uto-Aztecan), adding /ʔ h/. Again note the absence of liquids, a property that is not typical of Uto-Aztecan languages.

Dorais (2010) presents the inventory in (9) for Inuktitut (Nunavik dialect, Eskimo-Aleut). This inventory has an uvular stop.

(9) Inuktitut consonant inventory

p	t		k	q
	s			
v	l	j/r	ɣ	ʁ
m	n		ŋ	

(Dorais 2010: 67)

Many Siouan languages have small inventories. Mixco (1997) gives the inventory in (10) for Mandan. He remarks that /tʃ/ occurs in only one morpheme, and he mentions the absence of nasals, saying that they occur as allophones of /w/ and /r/ in some environments.

(10) Mandan consonant inventory

p	t	(tʃ)	k	ʔ
	s	ʃ	x	
w	r			h

(Mixco 1997: 6)

Hidatsa (Siouan), too, has a small inventory (Park 2012: 19), differing from Mandan largely by the presence of a nasal /n/ and /ts/ instead of /tʃ/.

Some Muskogean languages have below average inventories. Koasati (Gordon et al. 2015: 94) and Alabama (Hardy 2005: 82) have the inventory in (11). Martin (2011: 47) does not include /b/ in the Creek inventory, but otherwise it is identical to that of Koasati.

(11) Consonant inventory for two Muskogean languages: Koasati and Alabama

p	t	tʃ	k	
b				
f	s, ɬ			h
m	n			
	l			
w		j		

San Miguel Cimalpa Zoque (Mixe-Zoquean) has a small inventory.

(12) San Miguel Cimalpa Zoque consonant inventory

p	t	ts	k	ʔ
		ʃ		h
m	n		ŋ	
		j	w	

(Johnson 2000: 26)

Faarlund (2012: 6) gives a similar inventory for Chiapas Zoque. Johnson notes that if loanwords, sound symbolism, and derived consonants are considered, the inventory is larger, with voiced stops, /f, s/, /tʃ/, and /l, r/. Wichmann (1995: 21) notes an almost identical inventory for South Highland Zoque, but writes that most of the consonants have palatalized counterparts.

To summarize, small inventories have much in common. They have stops, including a coronal and a velar, and most, but not all, have a labial stop. Many have an affricate, either /ts/ or /tʃ/. Many have /s/. Many have a liquid, either /r/ or /l/, and glides. Many have laryngeal consonants. Distinctions in phonation type are generally absent, at least phonologically, although they may be present phonetically. The presence of /b/ in Koasati and Alabama stands out – Gordon et al. (2015: 287) note, based on Haas (1947), that Koasati and Alabama /b/ is a reflex of Proto-Muskogean *k^w (in Creek, *k^w developed as /k/ or /p/). Thus, essential to small inventories is a place contrast in stops, an overall lack of phonation contrasts, and a manner distinction between obstruents and sonorants. Within sonorants, nasals, while common cross-linguistically, may be absent phonologically, although there may be nasal allophones.

4.2. Moderately Small Inventories (15–18 Consonants)

Several families with languages with small inventories also have languages with moderately small inventories. These languages tend to expand their inventories in a few ways: additional places of articulation or laryngeal contrasts in stops/affricates.

Muskogean languages were introduced earlier. In some, the inventory has an additional consonant, glottal stop. Gordon et al. (2000: 380) give the Koasati inventory (11) for Chickasaw, with the addition of /ʃ/ and /ʔ/, as does Broadwell (2006: 15) for Choctaw.

While some Uto-Aztecan languages have small inventories (§4.1), others fall in the moderately small category. Dedrick and Casad (1999) give the inventory in (13) for Yaqui.

(13) Yaqui consonant inventory

p	t	tʃ	k	ʔ
bʷ				
	s			h
β/v				
m	n			
	r, l			
w		j		

(Dedrick & Casad 1999: 21)

In addition to the same consonants as in Shoshone (8), Yaqui has laryngeal consonants and two liquids. Additional consonants occur in Spanish loanwords.

Miwok languages have moderately small inventories, as illustrated by Sierra Miwok. This inventory occurs in all the languages of the family except for Lake Miwok (§4.6.2). Note the extended coronal places of articulation in stops/affricates.

(14) Sierra Miwok consonant inventory

p	t	ʈ	tʃ	k	ʔ
	s		ʃ		h
m	n			ŋ	
	l				
w			j		

(Golla 2011: 161)

Totonac languages tend to have moderately small inventories, as illustrated by Misantla Totonac.

(15) Misantla Totonac consonant inventory

p	t	ts		tʃ	k	q	ʔ
		s	ɬ	ʃ			h
m	n						
w			l	j			

(MacKay 1994: 370)

Karuk (isolate) has several places of articulation in fricatives.

(16) Karuk consonant inventory

p	t	tʃ	k	ʔ
f	θ	ʃ	x	h
v				
m	n			
	r	j		

(Golla 2011: 86, from Bright 1957)

Tonkawa (isolate) has labiovelars.

(17) Tonkawa consonant inventory

p	t	ts		k	k^w	ʔ
		s		x	x^w	h
m	n					
	l		j		w	

(Hoijer 1946: 290)

Seri (isolate) has many fricatives, including uvulars.

(18) Seri consonant inventory

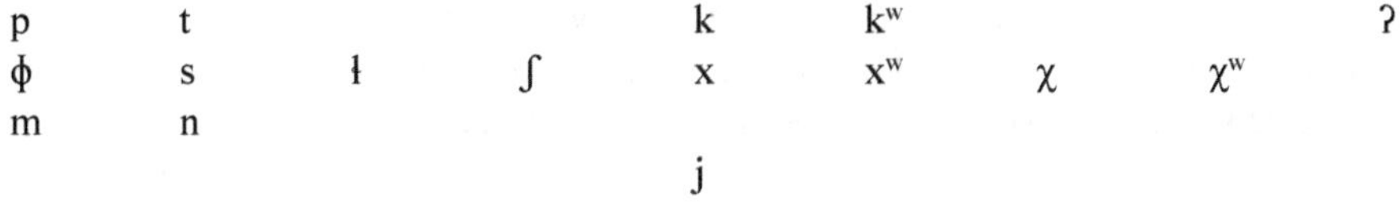

p	t			k	k^w			ʔ
ɸ	s	ɬ	ʃ	x	x^w	χ	$χ^w$	
m	n							
				j				

(Marlett 1988: 246)

Northeastern Maidu (Maiduan) has voiceless unaspirated, ejective, and voiced stops and voiceless unaspirated and ejective affricates.

(19) Northeastern Maidu consonant inventory

p	t	ts		k	ʔ
p’	t’	ts’		k’	
b	d				
	s				h
m	n				
w	l		j		

(Golla 2011: 139, from Shipley 1964)

Chitimacha (isolate) contrasts voiceless unaspirated and ejective stops and affricates.

(20) Chitimacha consonant inventory

p	t	ts	tʃ	k	ʔ
p’	t’	ts’	tʃ’	k’	
		s	ʃ		h
m	n				
w			j		

(Brown et al. 2014: 428)

Natchez (isolate) distinguishes voiced and voiceless sonorants, but has no laryngeal contrast in obstruents.

(21) Natchez consonant inventory

p	t	ts		k	k^w	ʔ
			ʃ			h
m	n	l	j		w	
m̥	n̥	l̥	j̊		w̥	

(Kimball 2005: 392)

In summary, at the small end of moderately small inventories, some Muskogean languages have two additional consonants to those presented in §4.1, /ʔ/ and /ʃ/, but an inventory that is, in spirit, like that of smaller inventories. Yaqui is not too different from Uto-Aztecan languages with small inventories, adding /β~v/ and /bʷ/. Miwok languages extend small inventories through the introduction of a retroflex place of articulation for stops and a velar nasal. Karuk, Tonkawa, and Seri have more places of articulation. Northeastern Maidu, Chitimacha, and Natchez have additional phonation types; they differ in that the first two distinguish these in stops and affricates, and the latter contrasts voiced and voiceless sonorants.

4.3. Average Inventories (19–25 Consonants)

Inventories of average size build on small inventories by extending places of articulation, especially in coronals and in fricatives, and by extending phonation contrasts.

Mutsun (Costanoan) contrasts coronal places in stops/affricates.

(22) Mutsun consonant inventory

p	t	tʲ	ts	ʈ	tʃ	k	ʔ
	s	sʲ					h
m	n	nʲ					
w	l	lʲ		r	j		

(Golla 2011: 167)

Jamul Tipai (Yuman) has extended coronals, labialized velars, and additional sonorants.

(23) Jamul Tipai consonant inventory

p	t	ʈ	tʃ	k	kʷ	ʔ
	s		ʃ	x	xʷ	
m	n		ɲ			
w		r	j			
		l	lʲ			
		ɬ	ɬʲ			

(Golla 2011: 123, from Miller 2001)

Some languages have increased places of articulation for obstruents. Golla (2011) gives the inventory in (24) for Cahuilla (Uto-Aztecan), noting that it has the smallest inventory of the languages of its subgroup. /r/ is rare in non-Spanish words.

(24) Cahuilla consonant inventory

p	t	tʃ	k	q	qʷ	ʔ
	s	ʃ	x		χʷ	h
β						
m	n	ɲ	ŋ			
	l (r)	lʲ				
w		j				

(Golla 2011: 184, from Bright 1965)

Adding phonation contrasts is another strategy for increasing inventory size. Kiowa (Kiowa-Tanoan) has a four-way laryngeal contrast in stops and a two-way contrast in affricates and fricatives.

(25) Kiowa consonant inventory

p	t	ts		k
p^h	t^h			k^h
p’	t’	ts’		k’
b	d			g
		s		
		z		
m	n			
	l		j	

(Watkins, with McKenzie 1984: 4)

Patwin (Wintuan), too, introduces phonation contrasts in stops/affricates and has an ejective lateral affricate but not a non-ejective one.

(26) Patwin consonant inventory

p	t		tʃ	k	ʔ
p^h	t^h			k^h	
p’	t’	tɬ’	tʃ’	k’	
b	d				
	s	ɬ			h
m	n				
w	r	l	j		

(Lawyer 2015: 225)

Languages also introduce laryngeal contrasts in sonorants. Yuki (Yuki-Wappo) adds a retroflex place of articulation, as well as ejective stops, affricates, nasals, and a lateral (27). The first coronal column is dental and the second alveolar. The parenthesized consonants are considered marginal.

(27) Yuki consonant inventory

p	t	ṭ	tʃ	k	
p’	t’	ṭ’	tʃ’	k’	ʔ
		s	ʃ		h
		(s’)			
m	n				
m’	n’				
	l				
	l’				
w			j		
(w’)			j’		

(Balodis 2016: 39, based on Sawyer & Schlichter 1984: 10)

Ktunaxa (isolate) has ejective nasals.

(28) Ktunaxa consonant inventory

p	t	ts			k	q	q^w	ʔ
p’	t’	ts’			k’	q’	q^{w}’	
		s	ɬ			χ	$χ^w$	
m	n							
m’	n’							
				j	w			

(Morgan 1991: 15)

Proto-Mayan has been reconstructed as in (29).

(29) Reconstructed consonant inventory for Proto-Mayan

*p	*t	*ts	*tʃ	*k	*q	*ʔ
	*t'	*ts'	*tʃ'	*k'	*q'	
*ɓ						
		*s	*ʃ		*χ	*h
*m	*n			*ŋ		
	*l, *r					
			*j	*w		

(Campbell & Kaufman 1985: 191)

Interesting here is the implosive /ɓ/ while other places of articulation have ejectives.

As a final example, E. Campbell (2014) presents the inventory in (30) for Zenzontepec Chatino (Zapotecan).

(30) Zenzontepec Chatino consonant inventory

p	t	t^{j}	ts	tʃ	k^{j}	k	k^{w}	ʔ
			s	ʃ				h
m	n	n^{j}						
	l, r	l^{j}						
β				j			w	

(Campbell 2014: 39)

Campbell remarks that the labials are rare. Note the contrasting plain and palatalized coronals.

Overall, languages in the sample with average inventories tend to have additional place contrasts (coronal contrasts, velar-uvular contrast) to those in languages with smaller inventories. They may have more fricative contrasts, creating greater symmetry in place of articulation in obstruents. They also may have contrasts of phonation type in stops, affricates, and sonorants.

4.4. Moderately Large Inventories (26–33 Consonants)

As inventories get larger, they tend to add obstruent place and phonation contrasts.

Wiyot (Algic) has the consonant inventory in (31), with more approximants than in smaller inventories.

(31) Wiyot consonant inventory

p	t	ts		tʃ	k	k^{w}	ʔ
p^{h}	t^{h}	ts^{h}		tʃ^{h}	k^{h}	k^{wh}	
		s	ɬ	ʃ			h
β					ɣ		
m	n						
w		r, ɾ	l	j			

(Golla 2011: 64, based on Teeter 1964)

Sahaptin (Sahaptian), too, has a large number of places of articulation in obstruents, as well as ejective stops/affricates.

(32) Sahaptin consonant inventory

p	t	ts	tɬ	tʃ	k	kʷ	q	qʷ	ʔ
p’	t’	ts’	tɬ’	tʃ’	k’	kʷ’	q’	qʷ’	
		s	ɬ	ʃ	x	xʷ	χ	χʷ	h
m	n								
			l						
w				j					

(Hargus & Beavert 2002: 318)

Nuxalk (formerly called Bella Coola; Salish) has many contrastive places of articulation for obstruents and a two-way laryngeal contrast for stops/affricates. Bagemihl (1991: 591) notes syllabic sonorants, with predictable distribution; /h/ is marginal.

(33) Nuxalk consonant inventory

p	t	ts		k	kʷ	q	qʷ	ʔ
p’	t’	ts’	tɬ’	k’	kʷ’	q’	qʷ’	
		s	ɬ	x	xʷ	χ	χʷ	(h)
m	n		l	j	w			

(Bagemihl 1991: 591)

As in some other languages, there is an ejective lateral affricate without a non-ejective one.

Wintu (Wintuan) has a number of places of articulation for obstruents, and, strikingly, up to a four-way laryngeal contrast in stops/affricates. As in several other languages, the single lateral affricate is ejective.

(34) Wintu consonant inventory

p	t		tʃ	k	q	ʔ
pʰ	tʰ					
p’	t’	tɬ’	tʃ’	k’	q’	
b	d					
	s	ɬ		x	χ	h
m	n					
w	r	l	j			

(Golla 2011: 146, from Pitkin 1984)

Southern Pomo (Pomoan) has both extensive place and laryngeal contrasts in stops/affricates.

(35) Southern Pomo consonant inventory

p	t̪	t	ts	tʃ		k	ʔ
pʰ	t̪ʰ	tʰ		tʃʰ		kʰ	
p’	t̪’	t’	ts’	tʃ’		k’	
b		d					
			s	ʃ			h
m		n					
w		l			j		

(Walker 2013: 42)

Dene (Athabaskan) languages have moderately large to large inventories. They achieve this primarily through laryngeal contrasts available to stops/affricates and places of articulation available to obstruents. Navajo (Diné Bizaad) has the typical organization of a Na-Dene inventory. The labialized velars are considered rare.

(36) Navajo (Diné Bizaad) consonant inventory

p	t	ts	tɬ	tʃ	k	k^{w}	ʔ
	t^{h}	ts^{h}	tɬ^{h}	tʃ^{h}	k^{h}	k^{wh}	
	t’	ts’	tɬ’	tʃ’	k’		
		s	ɬ	ʃ	x		h
		z	l	ʒ	ɣ		
m	n						
w				j			

(McDonough 2003: 4)

Some Siouan languages show a different pattern. Shaw (1980) presents inventories for varieties of Dakota, including Teton, shown in (37).

(37) Teton consonant inventory

p	t	tʃ	k	ʔ
p^{h}	t^{h}	tʃ^{h}	k^{h}	
p’	t’	tʃ’	k’	
b				
	s	ʃ	x	h
	s’	ʃ’	x’	
	z	ʒ	ɣ	
m	n			
	l			
w		j		

(Shaw 1980: 16)

Striking are the phonation contrasts in fricatives as well as in stops/affricates. The presence of glottalization with fricatives offers another way of extending the size of an inventory.

In the moderately large inventories presented so far, the inventory size is due predominantly to extended places of articulation and laryngeal contrasts in obstruents. Some languages extend their inventories through introducing glottalized sonorants.

Yana has ejective nasals and approximants.

(38) Yana consonant inventory

p	t	ts		k	ʔ
p^{h}	t^{h}	ts^{h}		k^{h}	
p’	t’	ts’		k’	
		s		x	h
m	n				
m’	n’				
w	r	l	j		
w’		l’	j’		

(Golla 2011: 102, from Sapir 1922)

Golla (2011) gives the inventory in (39) for Ventureño Chumash (Chumashan), with a full set of ejective sonorants as well as stops/affricates.

(39) Ventureño Chumash consonant inventory

p	t	ts	tʃ	k		q	ʔ
pʰ	tʰ			kʰ		qʰ	
p’	t’	ts’	tʃ’	k’		q’	
		s	ʃ		x		h
					x’		
m	n						
m’	n’						
w	l		j				
w’	l’		j’				

(Golla 2011: 198, from Whistler 1981)

Gitxsan (Tsimshianic), too, has ejective sonorants.

(40) Gitxsan consonant inventory

p	t	ts			k	kʷ	q	ʔ
p’	t’	ts’	tɬ’		k’	kʷ’	q’	
		s	ɬ		x	xʷ	χ	h
m	n							
m’	n’							
			l	j		w		
			l’	j’		w’		

(Brown et al. 2016: 368)

Other languages with moderately large inventories and phonation contrasts in sonorants as well as obstruents include Salinan (isolate; Golla 2011: 117, from Turner 1980); Nez Perce (Sahaptian; Aoki 1994: xi–xii); and Achumawi (Palaihnihan; Golla 2011: 99, from Nevin 1998). Haida (isolate; Enrico 2003: 9) has ejective nasals and an ejective lateral but only plain approximants. Washo (isolate; Yu 2005: 439) has a two-way contrast in sonorants, voiced and voiceless (ŋ̊ is absent, /m̥, n̥, w̥, l̥, j̊/ are present).

Summarizing, languages with moderately large inventories tend to show phonation distinctions in stops/affricates, and sometimes in fricatives. They commonly have extended contrasts in place of articulation in coronals and often have a velar-uvular contrast. Several languages also introduce laryngeal contrasts in sonorants; in the sample, these are found only when there are laryngeal contrasts in obstruents.

4.5. *Large Inventories (34+ Consonants)*

Not unexpectedly, languages with large consonant inventories (34 or more consonant contrasts) have contrasts on place, laryngeal, and manner dimensions. Such languages are found largely on the west coast, particularly in the Pacific Northwest; see §4.6.2.

Kashaya (Pomoan) has the consonant inventory in (41).

(41) Kashaya consonant inventory

p	t	ṭ	tʃ	k	q	ʔ
pʰ	tʰ	ṭʰ	tʃʰ	kʰ	qʰ	
p’	t’	ṭ’	tʃ’	k’	q’	
		s	ʃ			h
		s’				
m		n				
mʰ		nʰ				
m’		n’				
w		l	j			
wʰ		lʰ	jʰ			
w’		l’	j’			

(Buckley 1994: 13)

Buckley’s inventory differs from that proposed by Oswalt (1961), who treats ejective and aspirated sonorants as sequences rather than as single segments and includes /b/ and /d/, corresponding to /m’, n’/ in (41). See §2.3 on segment vs. sequence analysis, and on issues in choosing underlying forms.

Yokuts (Yokutsan) has a number of places of articulation and phonation contrasts in sonorants as well as obstruents. The parenthesized nasals are present in a few Yokuts varieties.

(42) Yokuts consonant inventory

p	t	ʈ	ts	tʃ	k	ʔ
pʰ	tʰ	ʈʰ	tsʰ	tʃʰ	kʰ	
p’	t’	ʈ’	ts’	tʃ’	k’	
	s	ʂ			x	h
m	n				(ŋ)	
m’	n’				(ŋ’)	
w	l			j		
w’	l’			j’		

(Golla 2011: 154–156, from Newman 1944)

Oowekyala is typical of a Northern Wakashan language (Howe 2000: 21), with many places of articulation in obstruents and phonation contrasts in stops/affricates and sonorants. Howe also includes long resonants m:, n:, l:.

(43) Oowekyala consonant inventory

p	t	ts	tɬ	k	kʷ	q	qʷ	ʔ
p’	t’	ts’	tɬ’	k’	kʷ’	q’	qʷ’	
b	d	dz	dl	g	gʷ	ɢ	ɢʷ’	
		s	ɬ	x	xʷ	χ	χʷ	h
m	n		l	j	w			
m’	n’		l’	j’	w’			

(Howe 2000: 21)

Salish languages typically have large consonant inventories, with an elaboration of places of articulation which is particularly striking in the post-velar area, phonation contrasts in stops/affricates, and ejective sonorants. Lushootseed has the inventory in (44). Bates et al. (1994) note that nasals m, m', n, n' appear in certain special words and speech styles, but they do not include them in the inventory.

(44) Lushootseed consonant inventory

p	t	ts		tʃ	k	k^{w}	q	q^{w}	ʔ
b	d	dz		dʒ	g	g^{w}			
p'	t'	ts'	tɬ'	tʃ'	k'	k^{w}'	q'	q^{w}'	
		s	ɬ	ʃ		x^{w}	χ	$χ^{w}$	h
			l						
w				j					
w'				j'					

(Bates et al. 1994: xiii)

The absence of nasals is notable, as are the number of obstruent places of articulation.

Another Salish language, St'át'imcets (Lillooet) has a number of places of articulation, pharyngeal consonants, ejective resonants (often with a fricative-like quality), and a lateral ejective affricate without a non-ejective one. The underdot indicates retraction.

(45) St'át'imcets consonant inventory

p	t	ts	tṣ		k	k^{w}	q	q^{w}		
p'		ts'		tɬ'	k'	k^{w}'	q'	q^{w}'		
		s	ṣ	ɬ	x	x^{w}	χ	$χ^{w}$		
m	n									
m'	n'									
				l ḷ						
				l' ḷ'						
		z	j		ɣ		ʕ	$ʕ^{w}$	h	w
		z'	j'		ɣ'		ʕ'	$ʕ^{w}$'	ʔ	w'

(van Eijk 1997: 3)

San Mateo Huave (isolate) has a large consonant inventory, with a pervasive non-palatalized/palatalized contrast, a voicing contrast, and prenasalized stops and affricates.

(46) San Mateo Huave consonant inventory

p	p^{j}	t	t^{j}	ts	ts^{j}		k	k^{j}	k^{w}	k^{jw}	
b	b^{j}	d	d^{j}				g	g^{j}			
				^{n}ts	$^{n}ts^{j}$						
^{m}b	$^{m}b^{j}$	^{n}d	$^{n}d^{j}$				^{ŋ}g	$^{ŋ}g^{j}$	$^{ŋ}g^{w}$	$^{ŋ}g^{jw}$	
				s	s^{j}						h h^{j}
m	m^{j}	n	n^{j}								
		r	r^{j}			j			w	w^{j}	
		ɾ	$ɾ^{j}$								
		l	l^{j}								

(Noyer 2013: 4)

Languages with large inventories tend to have expanded obstruents, with multiple places of articulation and phonation contrasts in stops and affricates. There are often phonation contrasts in sonorants as well, and some of the languages have pharyngeal consonants.

4.6. Historical Changes: Shifts, Mergers, Splits

Within a family, inventories can differ in size, and in this section I briefly review some of the factors involved in changing sizes. Changes can be vertical, or internally motivated, and horizontal, with inventories shifting due to contact.

4.6.1. Vertical Change

Languages can both shift sounds in quality, maintaining contrasts, and merge sounds. Dene (Athabaskan) languages show both shifts and mergers. The reconstructed inventory is given in (47).

(47) Reconstructed consonant inventory for Proto-Dene

	*t	*ts	*tɬ	*tʃ	*tʃr	*kʲ	*q	*ʔ
	*tʰ	*tsʰ	*tɬʰ	*tʃʰ	*tʃrʰ	*kʲʰ	*qʰ	
	*t'	*ts'	*tɬ'	*tʃ'	*tʃr'	*kʲ'	*q'	
		*z	*l	*ʒ		(*j)	*ʁ	
		*s	*ɬ	*ʃ		*xʲ	*χ	
*m	*n			*ɲ				
*w				*j				

(Leer 2005: 284)

Daughter languages display shifts and mergers in places of articulation. For instance, considering places of articulation of plosives in root-initial position, in Hän the Proto-Dene system is essentially intact, with shifts *ts > tθ, *tʃ > ts, *tʃr > tsr, *kʲ > tʃ, and *q > k – shifts in place of articulation of a series but with the number of contrastive places maintained. Other languages merge places of articulation; for instance, Koyukon mergers led to a system with /p, t, tɬ, ts, k (tʃ), q/, with the following shifts and mergers of series: *ts > tɬ, *tʃ > ts, *tʃr > ts, *kʲ > k, *q > q. In Witsuwit'en, *ts, *tʃ, *tʃr series merged to /ts/ (Hargus 2007: 738–740). (See Krauss & Golla 1981: 72). The Pacific Coast Dene languages are often missing sounds found in related languages due to mergers resulting in neutralization. Mattole, for example, has lateral consonants /l, ɬ, tɬ'/, with /ɬ/ as a reflex of *ɬ, *tɬ, *tʰ (Li 1930: 14). Many Oregon Dene varieties lack voiceless unaspirated and aspirated affricates at lateral, dental, and retroflex places of articulation due to mergers (Golla 2011: 75).

While Algonquian languages generally have small inventories, their more distant relations within Algic, Yurok and Wiyot, have larger inventories. Yurok has a moderately large inventory (Blevins 2003: 372).

(48) Yurok consonant inventory

p	t	tʃ	k	kʷ	ʔ
p'	t'	tʃ'	k'	kʷ'	
	s [ʂ]	ʃ	x		
	ɬ				
m	n				
m'	n'				
w	l, r	j	ɣ		
w'	l', r'	j'	ɣ'		

(Blevins 2003: 372)

Proulx (1984: 178) proposes a Proto-Algic reconstruction with voicelesss unaspirated, aspirated, and ejective consonants, and various mergers in Algonquian languages.

Northern Wakashan languages have large inventories (§4.5), while Southern Wakashan inventories, illustrated with Ditidaht in (49), are smaller.

(49) Ditidaht consonant inventory

p	t	ts	tɬ	tʃ	k	q		ʔ
p’	t’	ts’	tɬ’	tʃ’	k’			
b	d							
b’	d’							
		s	ɬ	ʃ	x	χ	ʕ	h
w	l			j				

(Sylak-Glassman 2013)

Sylak-Glassman includes /m, m’, n, n’/ in parentheses, noting that they are marginal (he also includes q’ as marginal), with nasals generally shifting to voiced stops. Other mergers occur (for instance, voiced consonants merge with voiceless ones; Fortescue 2007: 8), yielding a smaller inventory than in Northern Wakashan languages.

Inventories can increase in size in various ways as well. I illustrate two: reanalysis of sequences into single segments and splits.

While Caddoan languages have inventories with voiceless unaspirated stops, laryngeals, fricatives, and sonorants (see (5)), Caddo has ejective consonants as well. Chafe (1979: 223–224) suggests that these likely arose through coalescence of a stop with a glottal stop (although he notes that they might have been present in the proto-language, with simplification in Northern Caddoan languages). In a study of Seneca (Iroquoian), Chafe (2015: 10) remarks that Proto-Iroquoian is reconstructed with two stops, *t, *k; in modern Seneca, clusters *th, *kh have been reanalyzed as single aspirated segments, yielding a larger inventory.

What is reconstructed as a single phoneme may split through sound change into two (or more). For instance, Langdon and Munro (1980: 126) propose that Proto-Yuman *l split into Proto-Delta-California Yuman *l and ɬ; Miller (2018: 393) further proposes that Proto-Yuman *t and *n split into Proto-Delta-California Yuman *t/*n and *ṭ/*ṇ, likely a result of sound symbolism.

Algonquian languages are generally analyzed as having small inventories (§4.1), but some are treated as having moderately small inventories. Valentine (2001) gives the inventory in (50) for Nishnaabemwin, adding that /h/ occurs in a few adverbs.

(50) Nishnaabemwin consonant inventory

p	t	tʃ	k	
b	d	dʒ	g	ʔ
	s	ʃ		
	z	ʒ		
m	n			
w		j		

(Valentine 2001: 41–42)

Proto-Algonquian is reconstructed with *p, *t, *tʃ, *k, *θ, *s, *ʃ, *h, *m, *n, *r, *w, *j; the nature of *θ is uncertain (Thomason 2006: 191). The Nishnaabemwin inventory includes a voicing distinction in stops; this is treated as involving length rather than voicing in some of the languages, and Valentine notes that voiceless stops are longer than voiced stops. This might be a case of an inventory that increased in size through a split; it is also possible that the different analytic assumptions are involved about segments vs. sequences; see §2.3.

4.6.2. Horizontal Change

Changes in inventories can be externally motivated, attributable to contact. Such changes occurred in Lake Miwok. The Sierra Miwok inventory in (14) is typical of Miwok languages, with voiceless unaspirated stops, two fricatives, nasals, and approximants. Lake Miwok has a larger system. Sounds found in only a small number of words, usually loanwords, are omitted (g, f, θ).

(51) Lake Miwok consonant inventory

p	t	ts		tʃ	ʈ	k	ʔ
pʰ	tʰ				ʈʰ	kʰ	
p’	t’	ts’	tɬ’	tʃ’	ʈ’	k’	
b	d						
		s	ɬ		ʂ		h
m	n						
w	l			j	(r)		

(Callaghan 1963: 20)

Lake Miwok has phonation contrasts and affricates not present in related languages. It is generally assumed that these arose through contact with Hill Patwin and Southeastern Pomo (Golla 2011: 161; Callaghan 1964). Active contact involving borrowing words with new sounds can thus increase the size of inventories.

Inventories may also lose consonants due to contact. Campbell (1997: 331) remarks on the absence of labial stops in Aleut, following Leer (1991) in suggesting that this may be due to contact with other languages of the area including Dene languages, Eyak, and Tlingit, all of which lack labial obstruents. Kinkade (1985) identifies another areal effect, the shifting of consonants. The absence of nasals in Quileute (Chimakuan), Lushotseed and Twana (Salish), and Makah and Ditidaht (Wakashan) represents a shift from nasals to voiced obstruents, an effect he attributes to contact.

4.7. Summary

North American languages span from having very small consonant inventories to very large ones. Several interesting features stand out, including the absence of labial obstruents, even in some very large inventories (e.g., Tanacross [Dene; Holton 2000: 24] has a labial [m] but no other labials, and a large inventory); the absence of nasals, even in large inventories; the presence of lateral affricates; and the presence of ejective affricates in the absence of non-ejective affricates. Many large inventories exhibit a two- or three-way phonation contrast between voiceless unaspirated, voiceless aspirated, and ejective stops and affricates, lacking a voicing contrast. Many languages, even some with average-size inventories, have phonation contrasts in sonorants. The continent thus has languages that are typologically unusual, regardless of inventory size.

5. Vowels

As Mithun (1996: 137) remarks, vowel systems in North American languages are generally relatively simple. In presenting vowel systems, I follow Maddieson (2013b), focusing on quality. Maddieson does not count long and short variants of the same vowel, nor does he count nasalized vowels if there is a non-nasalized counterpart: he focuses on contrasts in qualities of height, backness, and roundness, identifying inventories that are small (2–4 vowel qualities), average (5–6 qualities), and large (7–14 qualities).

As with consonants, there are challenges in phonemicizing vowels. It can be difficult to interpret what symbols mean, with a symbol like *i* representing different phonetic values. Some authors count vowels found only in loanwords, while others do not. The status of schwa can be controversial, with debates about whether it is underlying, epenthetic, or both in a language. Nevertheless, a brief introduction to vowels is worthwhile.

I list inventories by number of vowels; indicating if there are length (L) and nasalization (N) contrasts. Vowels often show variation in quality, and there is some arbitrariness in the choice of symbols.

Three vowel systems are found in languages across North America and are phonemicized in a variety of ways.[2]

i a u. Aleut (L); Alsea; Caddo (L); Nuxalk (L); Misantla Totonac (L, laryngealized)
i a o. many Muskogean languages (L); Blackfoot (L); Hupa (L e: a: o:)
i e o. Arapaho (L)
e a o. Cheyenne
i e a. Wichita (L, overlong)[3]

Several languages have four vowel systems.

i a u ə. Central Alaskan Yupik; Jamul Tipai; Oowekyala (L except /ə/)
i e u a. Pawnee (L); Cahuilla (L); Cupeño (L)
i e o a. Klamath (L); Navajo (L, N); Proto-Algonquian (L)
i e a o. Nishnaabemwin (all L; short i, a, o); Plains Cree (all L; short i, a, o)
i ɨ u a. Sahaptian (L except ɨ, Sahaptin, Umatilla)

Many languages have five vowel systems.

i e a o u. Arikara (L); Chimariko; Siouan languages (Dakota, Chiwere L, nasal i a u + L; Tutelo N i, a, o plus L); Eastern Pomo (L); Kashaya (L); Esselen (L); Patwin (L); some Southern Wakashan (L no o:); Maricopa (L); Spokane (epenthetic ə); Takelma (L); Wappo (L); Wintu (L); Yana (L); Yokuts (L most varieties); Zuni (L); Achumawi (L); Mutsun (L); Huehuetla Tepehua (L); Tataltepec de Valdés Chatino (L; nasalized ĩ ẽ ã õ + L); Tz'utujil (L); Huastec (L); Popti'; Yalálag Zapotec (laryngealized a'a e'e i'i o'o)
i: e: a: o: u:. Karuk (short i a, u); Hidatsa (short i, a, u)
i ø ɯ a u. Ute (L)
i æ a o u. Nez Perce (L)
i e a o ə. Delaware (Munsee, Ontario) (L i: e: o: a:)
i a ə o u. Yuki
i e a o ɔ. Kiowa (L, N; [u] only after velars)
i e ə a u. Lower Rogue River Athabaskan; Tolowa (L, N i, a, u +LN); Wiyot (allophonic L except ə)
i e a o ə̃. Tuscarora (L in one variety; tense/lax in other)

Several languages have six vowel systems.

i e æ a o u. Mandan (L, N i, a, u + LN)
i, ï u e a o. Washo (L); Northeastern Maidu; Sierra Miwok (L); Tubatulabal (L); Chumash languages; Shoshoni (L); Western Mono (L)
i e ə̃ a o u. Cherokee (L)
i, e/ɛ a ə̧ ɔ u. Yurok (L no e:)

i e ə a o u. Chitimacha (L except ə); Sekani (L except ə); Witsuwit'en; Haisla (L i: a: u:); San Miguel Chimalapa Zoque
i ɛ a ɨ ɔ u. Sierra Popoluca (L)
i e ɛ a o u. Tanacross
i ɛ ö a o. Hopi (L)
ɨ e i a o u. Coatzospan Mixtec (L, N except o, creaky)

The largest inventories that I found have seven vowels.

i e ɨ ə a o u. Plains Miwok (L)
i e ɛ a ɔ o u. Tunica

The five most common vowels in the world's languages are not surprising – *i, e, a, o, u* (Gordon 2016: 49), with *i, a, u* most common. The variety of three-vowel inventories proposed for North American languages is interesting, as are the combinations of vowels in five vowel systems, all having /a/ but varying with respect to other vowels. Larger inventories do not necessarily include all the five most common vowels. Careful study of vowel inventories, looking at phonological patterning as well as phonetic realization, might lead to a different understanding of these inventories.

6. Inventories and Phonological Patterning

While inventories are of interest in and of themselves, there are questions that cannot be answered through the study of inventories alone, divorced from phonological patterning. This section addresses a few interesting questions, including inventories and morphological analysis, variation in analysis of what appears to be the same sound, phonological activity, and abstractness.

6.1. Positional Inventories and Morphological Analysis

While generally a single inventory is proposed for a language, there are often several inventories, with constraints on what can appear in positions such as root/stem-initial vs. affix-initial.[4] Roots often host more contrasts than do affixes, aiding in morphological analysis.

Dene languages have restrictions on inventories, as illustrated by Witsuwit'en. The root-initial inventory is given in (52).

(52) Witsuwit'en consonant inventory for roots

p	t	ts	tɬ	c	kʷ	q	
pʰ	tʰ	tsʰ	tɬʰ	cʰ	kʷʰ	qʰ	
p'	t'	ts'	tɬ'	c'	kʷ'	q'	ʔ
		s	ɬ	ç	xʷ	χ	h
		z	l	j	w	ʁ	
m	n						

(Hargus 2007: 19–20, 604–607)

Hargus (2007: 20) notes that the number of consonants is reduced in affixes: in non-lexical affixes, the following consonants appear: ɬ, l, t, s, c, n, xʷ, w, z, h, tʰ, c' (one morpheme), p (one morpheme), ts'/z (one morpheme). Thus, root-initial position hosts a wider range of contrasts than prefix-initial position, aiding the listener in identifying the root.

Tohono O'odham (Uto-Aztecan) has the consonant inventory in (53), with several consonants absent in affixes – p, tʃ, dʒ, g, s, w, l. As in Witsuwit'en, the richer stem-initial inventory provides clues to morphological structure.

(53) Tohono O'odham consonant inventory

p	t		tʃ	k	ʔ
b	d	ɖ	dʒ	g	
	s	ʂ			h
m	n		ɲ		
w	r, l		j		

(Bybee 2005: 178; Urbanczyk 2011: 2498)

O'Hara (2015) argues that while Klamath has the four-vowel inventory /i u e a/ and long counterparts, the full inventory is allowed only in privileged positions; /e/ in verbs is found only in word-initial syllables and raises to [i] or deletes elsewhere, yielding a three-vowel system in non-initial syllables of verbs.

An inventory often represents an amalgam, with morphological (and phonological) constraints on what can occur where, with positional inventories giving clues to word structure.

6.2. Same Sound, Same Status?

Another interesting issue involves the phonological patterning of sounds. How does the phonetics of a sound match its phonological patterning? The IPA chart gives a place to every sound, yet in studying inventories as presented in phonological sketches and grammars, the organization may look quite different from that of the IPA chart. For instance, as noted in §2, /j/ is treated as a sonorant in Tunica, and as a voiced fricative in Dene Sųłiné.

I focus first on /l/, a sound that is generally classified as a sonorant. In many languages it patterns as a sonorant. Klamath (Barker 1964: 39–40; Blevins 1993: 238), for instance, has triplets of sonorants (nasals, laterals, glides) – voiced, voiceless, and ejective. These are distinct from fricatives, where no laryngeal contrasts exist. In other cases, a voiceless lateral fricative and /l/ are found, but no voiced fricatives, suggesting that /l/ is a sonorant and /ɬ/ a fricative (e.g., Wiyot, Golla 2011: 64, based on Teeter 1964). In these languages, /l/ is grouped with sonorants.

However, /l/ does not always pattern as a sonorant. In many Dene languages, this sound is paired with a voiceless lateral, /ɬ/, and, along with fricatives, enters into voicing alternations, as illustrated for stem-initial fricatives in Tanacross (Dene). The accents represent tones and the hyphen before the stem indicates that the noun is possessed.

(54) Voicing alternations with stem-initial fricatives in Tanacross

Non-Possessed Form	Possessed Form	
θέθ	**-ðέðʔ**	'skin'
se:x	**-zě:ɣʔ**	'saliva'
ʃiʔ	**-ʒíʔi**	'food'
xeɬ	**-ɣě:l**	'pack'
ɬu:g	**-lŭ:gʔ**	'fish'

(Holton 2001: 400)

Laterals also participate in the so-called D-Effect, in which a prefix called D combines with certain stem-initial consonants including fricatives. In Tanacross, D combines with a stem-initial fricative, including the lateral, to create stops/affricates at the same of articulation (Holton 2001: 174). In addition, while voiceless sonorants do not occur stem-initially, voiced and voiceless laterals do, as do voiced and voiceless fricatives (Holton 2001: 398). The evidence suggests that the voiced lateral is phonologically a fricative. In presenting inventories of Dene languages, /l/ is placed in the same row as voiced fricatives.

Another language that suggests the importance of language-internal phonological factors in determining the place of sounds in an inventory is Lillooet (St'at'imcets). Van Eijk (1997: 4) divides the consonant inventory into obstruents and resonants, with obstruents including plain and ejective stops/affricates and voiceless fricatives. Resonants include nasals, liquids, and glides in plain and glottalized forms. Listed under glides are /z z' ɣ ɣ' ʕ ʕ' ʕʷ ʕʷ' h ʔ/ as well as /j j' w w'/. Most of the former are generally classed as fricatives rather than sonorants, but their patterning, illustrated by pairings, suggests sonorant status; van Eijk (1997: 4) also notes phonotactic evidence for this classification.

While it is tempting to hear a sound and, based on hearing it, place it in a sound chart, in fact what is judged to be the same sound phonetically may pattern differently in different languages.

6.3. Inventories and Phonological Activity

This section builds on observations in §6.2 and briefly examines a perspective on inventories based on phonological activity, focusing on vowels. As just discussed, what appears to be the same sound can differ in phonological patterning between languages. The discussion is framed in the theory of Modified Contrastive Specification; see, for instance, Dresher (2009) and Hall (2011). This theory of feature specification has bearing on how we view inventories, with phonemes specified only for contrastive features. The contrastive status of a feature is defined based on phonological activity, and expressed as a hierarchy. For instance, the inventory /i, a, u/ could be specified in different ways; two possibilities are shown in (55), using the features [low] and [back]; see Hall (2011: 13).

(55) Contrasting feature specifications for a three-vowel inventory

a. [low] > [back]

	i	a	u
[low]	–	+	-
[back]	–		+

b. [back] > [low]

	i	a	u
[back]	–	+	+
[low]		+	a

In (55a), [low] is selected first, dividing the inventory into /a/ vs. /i u/. The plus value is interpreted as active phonologically, while the minus value is, essentially, default; the expectation is that [+low] could be active in the phonology while [−low] would not be. Next, [back] is selected; [+back] could be active phonologically in the non-low vowels, with no role in the non-low vowels, where it has no specification. In (55b), [back] is selected first, with /i/ [−back]. /u a/ are then distinguished by [low], and [low] is not a relevant feature for /i/. The result is that two inventories that are phonemicized identically are phonologically distinct, with different features, and different patterning is expected. The language learner determines the features based on exposure to the language.

I compare two inventories with four vowels (plus long vowels). Proto-Algonquian, as reconstructed by Bloomfield (1946), had the inventory *i, *ɛ, *a, *o and their long counterparts. Oxford (2015) proposes the following analysis. I omit the feature [long] that he uses in his analysis. Summarizing evidence for the features, the vowel /i/ triggers palatalization, and thus has a feature to give; Oxford calls this feature [coronal]. The sequence */wɛ/ coalesces to */o/; Oxford suggests the feature [labial]. Oxford (2015) proposes the hierarchy in (56); I use plus/minus features whereas he uses privative features.

(56) Proto-Algonquian vowel feature hierarchy
[labial] > [coronal] > [low]

	[labial]	[coronal]	[low]
o	+		
a	–	–	
ɛ	–	+	+
i	–	+	–

(Oxford 2015: 322)

Klamath has a similar vowel inventory (Barker 1964; Blevins 1993; O'Hara 2015), with four short and four long vowels. I consider only short vowels. O'Hara proposes that /a/ is unmarked, adducing evidence from epenthesis. He further proposes that /e/ is marked: in verbs it occurs only in privileged positions and neutralizes to [i] otherwise. Blevins (1993: 239) discusses variation in vowel quality: /a/ varies between [a] and [ə]; /e/ between [æ] and [ɛ]; /i/ between [ɪ] and [i]; and /o/ between [ɔ] and [u]. One way of capturing this patterning is through a feature hierarchy with [coronal] > [low] > [labial].

(57) Klamath vowel feature hierarchy)
[coronal] > [low] > [labial]

	[coronal]	[low]	[labial]
e	+	+	
i	+	–	
o	–		+
a	–		–

(O'Hara 2015)

/e/ is the most marked vowel (only plus values), and /a/ the least marked (only minus values). While /o/ can vary in height from low to high, its front counterpart /i/ does not show the same range of variation as it is contrastive with the [+low] /e/. /a/ too shows some variation in height.

Phonological activity demonstrates that the inventories of Proto-Algonquian and Klamath are different despite their superficial similarities, further suggesting that IPA-type charts that assume a particular organization of sounds have limitations in predicting phonological patterning.

6.4. Abstract Inventories

Sections 6.2 and 6.3 point to the need to examine phonological activity in individual languages to understand the inventory of the language at a deep level. In some cases, small surface inventories can be misleadingly small when phonological activity is considered.

Compton and Dresher (2011) present a detailed study of palatalization across Inuit dialects. Proto-Inuit is reconstructed with four vowels: *i, *a, *u, *ə. Compton and Dresher demonstrate that languages that maintain four vowels show the effect of palatalization by /i/. Some languages merge /i/ and /ə/ to [i], yielding a surface three-vowel inventory. Yet in some of these languages, [i] from *i continues to trigger palatalization, while [i] from *ə does not. In these cases, they argue, the four-vowel system is maintained, despite the surface three-vowel system.

Similar neutralization is found in other languages. Frantz (2017: 1–2) proposes the Blackfoot (Algonquian) vowel inventory /i a o/. However, in discussion of phonological processes he gives a four-vowel inventory, /i I o a/, with /i/ and /I/ neutralizing to [i]. Primary evidence is from variable patterning of [i]: it triggers different processes. Some [i] trigger breaking (/k/ becomes [ks] before the vowel) and other [i] instead change /t/ to [ts] (Frantz 2017: 34–35). If Blackfoot has a phonological three-vowel inventory, it is difficult to account for the different activities of [i]. This different patterning suggests that Blackfoot is similar to Inuit languages with a fourth underlying vowel. See Oxford (2015) for discussion of the development of vowel inventories in Algonquian languages.

Similar discrepancies exist with consonants. For instance, in the Fort Good Hope variety of Sahtú Dene (Rice 1989), there are regular voicing alternations in fricatives.[5]

(58)

NON-POSSESSED	POSSESSED	
sa	-zá	'sun, month'
ʃɛ̨	-jɛ́nɛ́	'song'

Some fricatives are always voiceless, even in the environment where voicing is expected.

(59)

NON-POSSESSED	POSSESSED	
sɛ	-sɛ́	'firewood'
ʃo	-ʃórɛ́	'feather'

If non-alternating voiceless fricatives are treated as voiceless unaspirated affricates /ts, tʃ/, the historical source of these non-alternating voiceless fricatives and sounds that are generally absent from the surface inventory, then both the failure of voicing and the surface gaps can be explained. There is additional evidence for such an analysis, including variation in casual speech.

6.5. Summary

Phonological inventories as determined by surface contrasts alone are useful but can be misleading: the same apparent sound can pattern differently in different languages, and the same apparent surface inventory can show different phonological patterning in different languages. Moreover, the surface inventory alone may mask contrasts that are apparent as phonological activity is considered. Care must be taken in working with inventories as there is not a one-to-one relationship between sound and patterning. The importance of patterning has long been recognized; this is why, for instance, grammars of some languages place sounds such as [j] and [l] as sonorants, and grammars of other languages treat these same sounds as voiced fricatives. A challenge for analysts is to be able to explain these differences; see, for instance, Mielke (2008) and Dresher (2009).

7. Orthography

Linguists sometimes think that if the inventory of a language is understood, then it should be straightforward to develop a writing system for the language – simply use that inventory. While this is perhaps sometimes the case, many factors, both linguistic and social, challenge this assumption; see Sebba (2007) and articles in Cahill and Rice (2014) and Jones and Mooney (2017), for instance. Hinton (2014), writing about Yurok, notes that speakers and learners chose to include symbols for sounds that are not phonemic in Yurok but are in English. Chafe (1996: 553) analyzes Seneca as having two stops, /t k/, but says that "such an orthography obscures the manner in which the language is actually pronounced and is much disfavored by Seneca speakers", who use, for instance, <t, th, d> instead of just <t>. (Note that the angled brackets are used for orthographic representations.) Munro (2014) presents a Tongva (Uto-Aztecan) example, with vowels /i: e: a: o: u:, e a o/. While this phonemicization is adequate from a linguistic perspective, it did not work well for learners trying to understand what appear to be idiosyncratic patterns of reduplication, and it was decided to write short vowels <i u> as well although their distribution is predictable. It is important to keep in mind that the linguistic principles by which inventories are determined are not necessarily the best principles for orthographies, perhaps particularly when literacy in another language exists.

8. Conclusion

A study of phonological inventories introduces many fascinating questions. What inventories are possible? What are the reasons why there are many common properties of inventories cross-linguistically? How can both cross-linguistic commonalities and variation that is found be accounted for? There remains much to understand. The reader, especially those interested in typological generalizations, should take care to consult original sources, as there is much room for debate in the construction of an inventory, with different assumptions leading to different sizes and shapes.

Further Reading

For readings on inventories in languages of North America generally, see Mithun (1996; 1999). For languages of California, Golla (2011) is an excellent source. Suarez (1983) is a good source on languages of Mexico. Maddieson (1984), together with his chapters in WALS (Dryer & Haspelmath 2013), provides information about inventories. Databases of inventories include PHOIBLE (Moran et al. 2014) and LAPSYD (Lyon-Albuquerque Phonological Systems Database). For theoretical work on inventories, see Clements (2003; 2009), Dresher (2009), Gordon (2016), Hall (2011), Mielke (2009), and references therein.

Notes

1. I use IPA symbols unless otherwise noted. The first line shows stops and affricates, with lines below showing stops/affricates of different phonation types. The next lines have fricatives, then nasals, then other sonorants. See §6 for further discussion.
2. Sources for vowel inventories are as follows: Achumawi (Golla 2011); Aleut (Taff et al. 2001); Alsea (Buckley 2007); Arapaho (Cowell & Moss 2008); Arikara (Parks et al. 1979); Blackfoot (Frantz 2017); Caddo (Chafe 1979); Cahuilla (Golla 2011); Central Alaskan Yupik (Jacobson 1990); Cherokee (Cook 1979; Montgomery-Anderson 2015; Uchihara 2016); Cheyenne (Leman 2011); Chimariko (Golla 2011); Chitimacha (Brown et al. 2014); Chiwere (Greer 2016); Chumash languages (Golla 2011); Coatzospan Mixtec (Gerfen 1999); Cupeño (Hill 2005); Dakota (Shaw 1980); Delaware (O'Meara 1996); Eastern Pomo (Golla 2011); Esselen (Golla 2011); Haisla (Wehrle 2010); Hidatsa (Park 2012); Huastec (Larsen & Pike 1949); Huehuetla Tepehua (Kung 2007); Hupa (Golla 2011); Jamul Tipai (Miller 2001); Karuk (Golla 2011); Kashaya (Buckley 1994); Kiowa (Watkins, with McKenzie 1984); Lower Rogue River Athabaskan (Golla 2011); Mandan (Mixco 1997); Maricopa (Gordon 1986); Misantla Totonac (MacKay 1994); Muskogean languages (Mithun 1999); Mutsun (Golla 2011); Navajo (McDonough 2003); Nez Perce (Aoki 1994); Nishnaabemwin (Valentine 2001); Northeastern Maidu (Golla 2011); Nuxalk (Bagemihl 1991); Oowekyala (Howe 2000); Patwin (Lawyer 2015); Pawnee (Parks 1996); Plains Cree (Wolfart 1996); Plains Miwok (Golla 2011); Popti' (Craig 1977); Proto-Algonquian (Bloomfield 1946); Sahaptin (Hargus and Beavert 2002); San Miguel Chimalapa Zoque (Johnson 2000); Sekani (Hargus 1988); Shoshone (Miller 1996); Sierra Miwok (Golla 2011); Sierra Popoluca (Boudreault 2009); Southern Wakashan (Wehrle 2010); Spokane (Carlson & Esling 2000); Takelma (Golla 2011); Tanacross (Holton 2000); Tataltepec de Valdes Chatino (Sullivant 2015); Tolowa (Golla 2011); Tubatulabal (Golla 2011); Tunica (Haas 1946); Tuscarora (Rudes 1999); Tz'utujil (Dayley 1985); Umatilla (Rude 2014); Ute (Givón 2011); Wappo (Golla 2011); Washo (Golla 2011); Western Mono (Golla 2011); Wichita (Rood 1996); Wintu (Golla 2011); Wiyot (Golla 2011); Yalálag Zapotec (Avelino 2004); Yana (Golla 2011); Yokuts (Golla 2011); Yuki (Golla 2011); Yurok (Golla 2011); Zuni (Newman 1965).
3. By Maddieson's criteria, this inventory would have two contrasts, height and backness. Other analyses posit an additional vowel, /o/ or /u/.
4. Syllable-based constraints on distribution of sounds exist as well, and these can intersect with morphologically based constraints. This section examines only morphological restrictions.
5. [ʝ] is the voiced counterpart of [ʃ]. The acute accent represents high tone; the hook is nasalization.

References

Aoki, Haruo. 1994. *Nez Perce dictionary*. University of California Publications in Linguistics 122. Berkeley: University of California Press.

Avelino, Heriberto. 2004. *Topics in Yalálag Zapotec, with particular reference to its phonetic structures*. Los Angeles: University of California Los Angeles. (Doctoral dissertation.)

Bagemihl, Bruce. 1991. Syllable structure in Bella Coola. *Linguistic Inquiry* 22. 589–646.

Balodis, Uldis. 2016. *Yuki grammar. With sketches of Huchnom and Coast Yuki*. University of California Publications in Linguistics 151. Berkeley: University of California Press.

Barker, M. A. R. 1964. *Klamath grammar*. University of California Publications in Linguistics 32. Berkeley and Los Angeles: University of California Press.

Bates, Dawn & Hess, Thom & Hilbert, Vi. 1994. *Lushootseed dictionary*. Seattle: University of Washington Press.

Blevins, Juliette. 1993. Klamath laryngeal phonology. *International Journal of American Linguistics* 59. 237–279.

Blevins, Juliette. 2003. The phonology of Yurok glottalized sonorants: Segmental fission under syllabification. *International Journal of American Linguistics* 69. 371–396.

Bloomfield, Leonard. 1946. Algonquian. In Hoijer, Harry & Bloomfield, L. & Haas, M. R. & Halpern, A. M. & Li, F. K. & Newman, S. S. & Swadesh, M. & Trager, G. L. & Voegelin, C. F. & Whorf, B. L. (eds.), *Linguistic structures of Native America*. Viking Fund Publications in Anthropology 6. 85–129. New York: Johnson.

Boudreault, Lynda. 2009. *A grammar of Sierra Popoluca (Soteapanec, a Mixe-Zoquean language)*. Austin: University of Texas. (Doctoral dissertation.)

Bright, William. 1957. *The Karok language*. University of California Publications in Linguistics 13. Berkeley: University of California Press.

Bright, William. 1965. The history of the Cahuilla sound system. *International Journal of American Linguistics* 31. 241–244.

Broadwell, G. Aaron. 2006. *A Choctaw reference grammar*. Lincoln: University of Nebraska Press.

Brown, Cecil & Wichmann, Søren & Beck, David. 2014. Chitimacha: A Mesoamerican language in the Lower Mississippi Valley. *International Journal of American Linguistics* 80. 425–474.

Brown, Jason & Davis, Henry & Schwan, Michael & Sennott, Barbara. 2016. Gitksan. *Journal of the International Phonetic Association* 46. 367–378.

Buckley, Eugene. 1994. *Theoretical aspects of Kashaya phonology and morphology*. Stanford: Center for the Study of Language and Information.

Buckley, Eugene. 2007. Vowel-sonorant metathesis in Alsea. *International Journal of American Linguistics* 73. 1–39.

Bybee, Joan. 2005. Restrictions on phonemes in affixes. A crosslinguistic test of a popular hypothesis. Linguistic Typology 9. 165–222.

Cahill, Michael & Rice, Keren. 2014. *Developing orthographies for unwritten languages*. Dallas: SIL International.

Callaghan, Catherine. 1963. *A grammar of the Lake Miwok language*. Berkeley: University of California Press. (Doctoral dissertation.)

Callaghan, Catherine. 1964. Phonemic borrowing in Lake Miwok. In Bright, William (ed.), *Studies in Californian linguistics*. University of California Publications in Linguistics 34. 46–53. Berkeley and Los Angeles: University of California Press.

Campbell, Eric. 2014. *Aspects of the phonology and morphology of Zenzontepec Chatino, a Zapotecan language of Oaxaca, Mexico*. Austin: University of Texas. (Doctoral dissertation.)

Campbell, Lyle. 1997. *American Indian languages. The historical linguistics of Native America*. New York and Oxford: Oxford University Press.

Campbell, Lyle & Kaufman, Terrence. 1985. Mayan linguistics: Where are we now? *Annual Review of Anthropology* 14. 187–198.

Carlson, Barry F. & Esling, John H. 2000. Spokane. *International Journal of the International Phonetic Association* 30. 97–102.

Chafe, Wallace. 1979. Caddoan. In Campbell, Lyle & Mithun, Marianne (eds.), *The Languages of Native America: Historical and comparative assessment*, 213–235. Austin: University of Texas Press.

Chafe, Wallace. 1996. Sketch of Seneca, an Iroquoian language. In Goddard, Ives (ed.), *Handbook of North American Indians. Vol. 17, Languages*, 225–253. Washington, DC: Smithsonian Institution.

Chafe, Wallace. 2015. *A grammar of the Seneca language*. Berkeley: University of California Press.

Charney, Jean. 1993. *A grammar of Comanche*. Lincoln: University of Nebraska Press.

Clements, G. N. 2003. Feature economy in sound systems. *Phonology* 20. 287–333.

Clements, G. N. 2009. The role of features in phonological inventories. In Raimy, Eric & Cairns, Charles (eds.), *Contemporary views on architecture and representations in phonological theory*, 19–68. Cambridge, MA: MIT Press.

Compton, Richard & Dresher, B. Elan. 2011. Palatalization and "Strong *i*" across Inuit dialects. *Canadian Journal of Linguistics/Revue Canadienne de linguistique* 56. 203–228.

Compton, Richard. 2008. *Contrast in Inuit consonant inventories*. University of Toronto. (Doctoral Generals Paper).

Cook, Eung-Do. 2004. *A grammar of Dëne Sųłiné (Chipewyan)*. Winnipeg: Algonquian and Iroquoian Linguistics.

Cook, William Hinton. 1979. *A grammar of North Carolina Cherokee*. New Haven, CT: Yale University. (Doctoral dissertation.)

Cowell, Andrew & Moss Sr., Alonzo. 2008. *The Arapaho language*. Boulder: University of Colorado Press.

Craig, Colette. 1977. *The structure of Jacaltec*. Austin: University of Texas Press.

Day, Christopher. 1973. *The Jacaltec language*. Bloomington: Indiana University.

Dayley, Jon P. 1985. *Tzutujil grammar*. Berkeley: University of California Press.

Dedrick, John M. & Casad, Eugene H. 1999. *Yaqui language structures*. Tucson: University of Arizona Press.

Dorais, Louis-Jacques. 2003. *Inuit Uqausiqatigiit – Inuit languages and dialects.* Iqaluit: Nunavut Arctic College.

Dorais, Louis-Jacques. 2010. *The language of the Inuit: Syntax, semantics, and society in the Arctic.* Montreal & Kingston: McGill-Queen's University Press.

Dresher, B. Elan. 2009. *The contrastive hierarchy in phonology.* Cambridge: Cambridge University Press.

Dryer, Matthew S. & Haspelmath, Martin (eds.). 2013. *The world atlas of language structures online.* Leipzig: Max Planck Institute for Evolutionary Anthropology. (http://wals.info) (Accessed 2018-03-16.)

Enrico, John. 2003. *Haida syntax.* Lincoln: University of Nebraska Press.

Faarlund, Jan Terje. 2012. *A grammar of Chiapas Zoque.* Oxford: Oxford University Press.

Fortescue, Michael. 2007. *Comparative Wakashan dictionary.* Munich: LINCOM Europa.

Frachtenberg, Leo J. 1917. Myths of the Alsea Indians of northwestern Oregon. *International Journal of American Linguistics* 1. 64–75.

Frachtenberg, Leo J. 1920. Alsea texts and myths. Washington, DC: Bureau of American Ethnology, Bulletin 67.

Frantz, Donald. 2017. *Blackfoot grammar.* 3rd edn. Toronto: University of Toronto Press.

Gerfen, Chip. 1999. *Phonology and phonetics in Coatzospan Mixtec.* Studies in Natural Language and Linguistic Theory 48. Dordrecht: Kluwer Academic.

Givón, Talmy. 2011. *Ute reference grammar.* Amsterdam/Philadelphia: John Benjamins Publishing Company.

Goddard, Pliny Earle. 1905. *Morphology of the Hupa language.* University of California, Publications in American Archaeology and Ethnology. Berkeley: University of California Press.

Golla, Victor. 1996. Sketch of Hupa, an Athapaskan language. In Goddard, Ives (ed.), *Handbook of North American Indians*, vol. 17, *Languages*, 364–389. Washington, DC: Smithsonian Institution.

Golla, Victor. 2011. *California Indian languages.* Berkeley, Los Angeles, and London: University of California Press.

Gordon, Lynn. 1986. *Maricopa morphology and syntax.* University of California Publications in Linguistics 108. Berkeley: University of California Press.

Gordon, Matthew. 2016. *Phonological typology.* Oxford Surveys in Phonetics and Phonology. Oxford: Oxford University Press.

Gordon, Matthew & Martin, Jack & Langley, Linda. 2015. Some phonetic structures of Koasati. *International Journal of American Linguistics* 81. 83–118.

Gordon, Matthew & Munro, Pamela & Ladefoged, Peter. 2000. Some phonetic structures of Chickasaw. *Anthropological Linguistics* 42. 366–400.

Greer, Jill D. 2016. Baxoje-Jiwere grammar sketch. In Rudin, Catherine & Gordon, Bryan J. (eds.), *Advances in the study of Siouan languages and linguistics*. 183–229. Berlin: Language Science Press.

Haas, Mary. 1946. A grammatical sketch of Tunica. In Hoijer, Harry & Bloomfield, L. & Haas, M. R. & Halpern, A. M. & Li, F. K. & Newman, S. S. & Swadesh, M. & Trager, G. L. & Voegelin, C. F. & Whorf, B. L. (eds.), *Linguistic structures of Native America.* Viking Fund Publications in Anthropology 6, 337–366. New York: Johnson.

Haas, Mary. 1947. The development of Proto-Muskogean *kw. *International Journal of American Linguistics* 13. 135–137.

Hall, Daniel Currie. 2011. Phonological contrast and its phonetic enhancement: Dispersedness without dispersion. *Phonology* 28. 1–54.

Hardy, Heather. 2005. Alabama. In Hardy, Heather & Scancarelli, Janine (eds.), *Native languages of the Southeastern United States*, 75–113. Lincoln: University of Nebraska Press.

Hargus, Sharon. 1988. *The lexical phonology of Sekani.* New York: Garland Publishing Co.

Hargus, Sharon. 2007. *Witsuwit'en grammar: Phonetics, phonology, morphology.* Vancouver: UBC Press.

Hargus, Sharon & Beavert, Virginia. 2002. Predictable vs. underlying vocalism in Yakima Sahaptin. *International Journal of American Linguistics* 68. 316–340.

Hill, Jane. 2005. *A grammar of Cupeño.* University of California Publications in Linguistics. 136. Berkeley: University of California Press.

Hinton, Leanne. 2014. Orthography wars. In Cahill, Michael & Rice, Keren (eds.), *Developing orthographies for unwritten languages*, 140–168. Dallas: SIL International.

Hoijer, Harry. 1946. Tonkawa. In Hoijer, Harry & Bloomfield, L. & Haas, M. R. & Halpern, A. M. & Li, F. K. & Newman, S. S. & Swadesh, M. & Trager, G. L. & Voegelin, C. F. & Whorf, B. L. (eds.), *Linguistic structures of Native America.* Viking Fund Publications in Anthropology 6, 289–311. New York: Johnson.

Holton, Gary. 2000. *The phonology and morphology of the Tanacross Athabaskan language.* Santa Barbara: University of California Santa Barbara. (Doctoral dissertation.)

Holton, Gary. 2001. Fortis and lenis fricatives in Tanacross Athapaskan. *International Journal of American Linguistics* 67. 396–414.

Hopi Dictionary Project (University of Arizona Bureau of Applied Research in Anthropology). 1998. Kenneth C. Hill (Editor in Chief, Project Director), Emory Sekaquaptewa (Cultural Editor), Mary E. Black (Associate Editor), Ekkehart Malotki (Senior Contributing Editor), Michael Lomatuway'ma (Contributing

Editor). *Hopi Dictionary: Hopìikwa Lavàytutuveni: A Hopi–English dictionary of the Third Mesa dialect with an English-Hopi finder list and a sketch of Hopi grammar*. Tucson: University of Arizona Press.

Howe, Darin. 2000. *Oowekyala segmental phonology*. Vancouver: University of British Columbia. (Doctoral dissertation.)

Jacobson, Steve. 1990. Comparison of Central Alaskan Yup'ik Eskimo and Central Siberian Yupik Eskimo. *International Journal of American Linguistics* 56. 264–286.

Johnson, Heidi. 2000. *A grammar of San Miguel Chimalapa Zoque*. Austin: University of Texas. (Doctoral dissertation.)

Jones, Mari & Mooney, Damien. 2017. *Creating orthographies for endangered languages*. Cambridge: Cambridge University Press.

Kimball, Geoffrey. 2005. Natchez. In Hardy, Heather & Scancarelli, Janine (eds.), *Native languages of the Southeastern United States*, 385–453. Lincoln: University of Nebraska Press.

Kinkade, Dale. 1985. More on nasal loss on the Northwest Coast. *International Journal of American Linguistics* 51. 478–480.

Krauss, Michael & Golla, Victor. 1981. Athabaskan languages of the Subarctic. In Helm, June (ed.), *Handbook of North American Indians*, volume 6: *Subarctic*, 67–85. Washington, DC: Smithsonian Institution.

Kung, Susan Smythe. 2007. *A descriptive grammar of Huehuetla Tepehua*. Austin: University of Texas. (Doctoral dissertation.)

Langdon, Margaret & Munro, Pamela. 1980. Yuman numerals. In Klar, Kathryn & Langdon, Margaret & Silver, Shirley (eds.), *American Indian and Indoeuropean studies: Papers in honor of Madison S. Beeler*, 121–135. The Hague: Mouton.

Larsen, Raymond S. & Pike, Eunice Victoria. 1949. Huasteco intonations and phonemes. *Language* 25. 268–277.

Lawyer, Lewis. 2015. Patwin phonemics, phonetics, and phonotactics. *International Journal of American Linguistics* 81. 221–260.

Leer, Jeff. 1991. Evidence for a Northern Northwest Coast language area: Promiscuous number marking and periphrastic possessive constructions in Haida, Eyak, and Aleut. *International Journal of American Linguistics* 57. 158–193.

Leer, Jeff. 2005. How stress shapes the stem-suffix complex in Athabaskan. In Hargus, Sharon & Rice, Keren (eds.), *Athabaskan prosody*, 278–318. Amsterdam: John Benjamins.

Leman, Wayne. 2011. *A reference grammar of the Cheyenne language*. 4th edition. Morrisville, NC: Lulu Press.

Li, Fang-Kuei. 1930. *Mattole, an Athabaskan language*. Chicago: University of Chicago Press.

Li, Fang-Kuei. 1946. Chipewyan. In Hoijer, Harry & Bloomfield, L. & Haas, M. R. & Halpern, A. M. & Li, F. K. & Newman, S. S. & Swadesh, M. & Trager, G. L. & Voegelin, C. F. & Whorf, B. L. (eds.), *Linguistic structures of Native America*. Viking Fund Publications in Anthropology 6. 398–423. New York: Johnson.

MacKay, Carolyn. 1994. A sketch of Misantla Totonac phonology. *International Journal of American Linguistics* 60. 369–419.

Maddieson, Ian. 1984. *Patterns of sounds*. Cambridge: Cambridge University Press.

Maddieson, Ian. 2013a. Consonant inventories. In Dryer, Matthew S. & Haspelmath, Martin (eds.), *The world atlas of language structures online*. Leipzig: Max Planck Institute for Evolutionary Anthropology. (http://wals.info/chapter/1) (Accessed 2018-03-12.)

Maddieson, Ian. 2013b. Vowel quality inventories. In Dryer, Matthew S. & Haspelmath, Martin (eds.) *The world atlas of language structures online*. Leipzig: Max Planck Institute for Evolutionary Anthropology. (http://wals.info/chapter/2) (Accessed 2018-03-12.)

Maddieson, Ian. 2013c. Presence of uncommon consonants. In Dryer, Matthew S. & Haspelmath, Martin (eds.), *The world atlas of language structures online*. Leipzig: Max Planck Institute for Evolutionary Anthropology. (http://wals.info/chapter/19) (Accessed 2018-03-12.)

Marlett, Steve. 1988. The syllable structure of Seri. *International Journal of American Linguistics* 54. 245–278.

Martin, Jack, with the assistance of Margaret McKane Mauldin. 2011. *A grammar of Creek (Muskogee)*. Lincoln: University of Nebraska Press.

McDonough, Joyce. 2003. *The Navajo sound system*. Studies in Natural Language and Linguistic Theory. Dordrecht: Kluwer Academic Publishers.

Mielke, Jeff. 2008. *The emergence of distinctive features*. Oxford: Oxford University Press.

Mielke, Jeff. 2009. Segment inventories. *Language and Linguistics Compass* 3. 700–718.

Miller, Amy. 2001. *A grammar of Jamul Tipay*. Berlin: Mouton de Gruyter.

Miller, Amy. 2018. Phonological developments in Delta-California Yuman. *International Journal of American Linguistics* 84. 383–433.

Miller, Wick. 1996. Sketch of Shoshone, a Uto-Aztecan language. In Goddard, Ives (ed.), *Handbook of North American Indians*, volume 17, *Languages*, 693–720. Washington, DC: Smithsonian Institution.

Mithun, Marianne. 1996. Overview and general characteristics. In Goddard, Ives (ed.), *Handbook of North American Indians*, volume 17, *Languages*, 137–157. Washington, DC: Smithsonian Institution.

Mithun, Marianne. 1999. *The languages of Native North America*. Cambridge: Cambridge University Press.
Mixco, Mauricio. 1997. *Mandan*. Munich: LINCOM EUROPA.
Montgomery-Anderson, Brad. 2015. *Cherokee reference grammar*. Norman, OK: University of Oklahoma Press.
Moore, Patrick. 2002. *Point of view in Kaska historical narratives*. Bloomington: Indiana University. (Doctoral dissertation.)
Moran, Steven & McCloy, Daniel & Wright, Richard (eds.). 2014. PHOIBLE Online. Leipzig: Max Planck Institute for Evolutionary Anthropology. (http://phoible.org) (Accessed 2018–03–12.)
Morgan, Lawrence. 1991. *A description of the Kutenai language*. Berkeley: University of California. (Doctoral dissertation.)
Munro, Pamela. 2014. Breaking rules for orthography development. In Cahill, Michael & Rice, Keren (eds.), *Developing orthographies for unwritten languages*, 169–106. Dallas: SIL International.
Nevin, Bruce E. 1998. *Aspects of Pit River phonology*. Philadelphia: University of Pennsylvania. (Doctoral dissertation.)
Newman, Stanley. 1944. *Yokuts language of California*. New York: Viking Fund Publications in Anthropology.
Newman, Stanley. 1965. *Zuni grammar*. Albuquerque: University of New Mexico Press.
Noyer, Rolf. 2013. A Generative phonology of San Mateo Huave. *International Journal of American Linguistics* 79. 1–60.
O'Hara, Charlie. 2015. Vowel raising and positional privilege in Klamath. (Talk presented at the Society for the Study of Indigenous Languages of the Americas, Portland, Oregon, 11 January 2015).
O'Meara, John. 1996. *Delaware-English English-Delaware dictionary*. Toronto: University of Toronto Press.
Oswalt, Robert. 1961. *A Kashaya grammar (Southwestern Pomo)*. Berkeley: University of California. (Doctoral dissertation.)
Oxford, Will. 2015. Patterns of contrast in phonological change: Evidence from Algonquian vowel systems. *Language* 91. 308–357.
Park, Indrek. 2012. *A grammar of Hidatsa*. Bloomington: Indiana University. (Doctoral dissertation.)
Parks, Douglas. 1976. *A grammar of Pawnee*. New York: Garland Publishing.
Parks, Douglas R. & Beltra, Janet & Waters, Ella P. 1979. *Introduction to the Arikara language*. Bismarck, ND: Mary College.
Pitkin, Harvey. 1984. *Wintu grammar*. University of California Publications in Linguistics 84. Berkeley and Los Angeles: University of California Press.
Proulx, Paul. 1984. Proto-Algic I: Phonological sketch. *International Journal of American Linguistics* 50. 165–207.
Rice, Keren. 1989. *A grammar of Slave*. Berlin: Mouton de Gruyter.
Rood, David S. 1996. Sketch of Wichita, a Caddoan language. In Goddard, Ives (ed.), *Handbook of North American Indians. Vol. 17, Languages*, 225–253. Washington, DC: Smithsonian Institution.
Rude, Noel. 2014. *Umatilla dictionary*. Seattle: Confederated Tribes of the Umatilla Indian Reservation in Association with the University of Washington Press.
Rudes, Blair A. 1999. *Tuscarora-English/English-Tuscarora dictionary*. Toronto: University of Toronto Press.
Sapir, Edward. 1922. The fundamental elements of Northern Yana. *University of California Publications in American Archaeology and Ethnology* 13. 214–234. Berkeley: University of California Press.
Sawyer, Jesse & Schlichter, Alice. 1984. *Yuki vocabulary*. University of California Publications in Linguistics 101. Berkeley: University of California Press.
Sebba, Mark. 2007. *Spelling and society: The culture and politics of orthography around the world*. Cambridge: Cambridge University Press.
Shaw, Patricia. 1980. *Theoretical issues in Dakota phonology and morphology: Outstanding dissertations in linguistics*. New York and London: Garland Publishing, Inc.
Shipley, William. 1964. *Maidu grammar*. University of California Publications in Linguistics 41. Berkeley: University of California Press.
Suarez, Jorge. 1983. *The Mesoamerican Indian languages*. Cambridge: Cambridge University Press.
Sullivant, John Ryan. 2015. *The phonology and inflectional morphology of Chá?knyá, Tataltepec de Valdés Chatino, a Zapotecan language*. Austin: University of Texas. (Doctoral dissertation.)
Sylak-Glassman, John. 2013. The phonetic properties of voiced stops descended from nasals in Ditidaht. (Talk presented at the Linguistic Society of America, Boston, Massachusetts, 3 January 2013.)
Taff, Alice & Rozelle, Lorna & Ladefoged, Peter & Dirk, Moses & Wegelin, Jacob. 2001. Phonetic structures of Aleut. *Journal of Phonetics* 29. 231–271.
Teeter, Karl. 1964. *The Wiyot language*. University of California Publications in Linguistics 37. Berkeley: University of California Press.
Thomason, Lucy. 2006. *Proto-Algonkian phonology and morpho-syntax*. Encyclopedia of Language & Linguistics. 10 (2nd ed.), 190–198. Oxford: Elsevier.
Turner, Katherine. 1980. The reconstructed phonemes of Salinan. *Journal of California and Great Basin Anthropology, Papers in Linguistics* 2. 53–92.

Uchihara, Hiroto. 2016. *Tone and accent in Oklahoma Cherokee*. Oxford: Oxford University Press.
Urbanczyk, Suzanne. 2011. Root-affix asymmetries. In van Oostendorp, Marc & Ewen, Colin & Hume, Elizabeth & Rice, Keren (eds.), *The Blackwell companion to phonology*, 2490–2515. Hoboken, NJ: Blackwell Publishing.
Valentine, J. Randolph. 2001. *Nishnaabemwin reference grammar*. Toronto: University of Toronto Press.
van Eijk, Jan. 1997. *The Lillooet language: Phonology, morphology, syntax*. First Nations Languages Series. Vancouver: UBC Press.
Vázquez Álvarez, Juan Jésus. 2011. *A grammar of Ch'ol, a Mayan language*. Austin: University of Texas. (Doctoral dissertation.)
Walker, Neil Alexander. 2013. *A grammar of Southern Pomo. An Indigenous language of California*. Santa Barbara: University of California Santa Barbara. (Doctoral dissertation.)
Walker, Willard. 1964. *Reference, taxonomy and inflection in Zuni*. Ithaca, NY: Cornell University. (Doctoral dissertation.)
Watkins, Laurel & McKenzie, Parker. 1984. *A grammar of Kiowa*. Lincoln: University of Nebraska Press.
Wehrle, Adam. 2010. *The phonology of Wakashan languages*. Victoria: University of Victoria. (Manuscript.)
Whistler, Kenneth W. 1981. Ventureño dialects. Paper presented to the Group in American Indian Languages, University of California, Berkeley, October 30, 1981.
Wichmann, Søren. 1995. *The relationship among the Mixe-Zoquean languages of Mexico*. Salt Lake City: University of Utah Press.
Wolfart, H. Christoph. 1996. Sketch of Cree, an Algonquian language. In Goddard, Ives (ed). *Handbook of North American Indians*, volume 17, *Languages*, 390–439. Washington, DC: Smithsonian Institution.
Yu, Alan. 2005. Quantity, stress, and reduplication in Washo. *Phonology* 22(3). 437–475.

2
SEGMENTAL PROCESSES

Heather Newell and Andréia de Souza

1. Introduction

A single chapter in a handbook is of insufficient space to discuss the segmental processes of the languages of North America, or to give a complete overview of all existent phenomena. The reader should keep in mind that there are many more segmental processes present in North American languages than can be presented here and must therefore understand if their favorite alternation (or language) does not appear. The interested reader should refer to the citations herein (and within the citations herein) for further details on the alternations discussed. For students and scholars looking for a discussion of a range of common and not-so-common segmental alternations that can be found among the languages of North America, this chapter will give you an indication of the types of phenomena you may find and will hopefully inspire a desire to look further into some of the understudied and threatened languages that evidence the rich variation found in the languages native to North America.

The term *segmental processes* is used here to encompass all phonological operations that target the skeletal level or below, assuming an autosegmental phonological representation as in (1).[1,2]

(1)	C	V	C	C	V	V	C	skeletal tier	
	|	|	|	|	\\	/	|		
	d	i	s	m	á		s	melodic tier	
	d-	ish-		ł-	máás				'to start to roll it'(1P)
	INCP-	∅IMP/1SG-		CL-	IMP.roll				

(Navajo, Na-Dene; McDonough 1996: 244)

Reference to the skeletal tier, or to syllable and foot structure, may be made where relevant, but we remain agnostic here as to whether the latter are structurally represented in the phonology (as in metrical phonology (e.g., Goldsmith 1990; Hayes 1995) or prosodic phonology (e.g., Selkirk 1984; 1986; Nespor & Vogel [1986] 2007) or not, as in CVCV (e.g., Lowenstamm 1996; Scheer 2004; 2012; 2015; Szigetvári 2011), an offshoot of government phonology (e.g., Kaye et al. 1985; 1990; Kaye 1990). We will ignore here all interactions of segments and tone (see Buckley, this volume), but will make some reference to the impact of stress, syllabification, and footing on segmental realization.

In North American languages, as in all languages, segments may be modified, epenthesized, or deleted in particular phonological and morpho-phonological environments. After a general overview of an array of processes, this chapter will briefly focus on the way in which phonological domains within polysynthetic/agglutinative words are picked out by different segmental processes within individual languages (specifically, hiatus resolution strategies in Ojibwe (Algonquian), epenthesis and extrametricality in Cayuga (Iroquoian), and augmentation sensitive to word minimality in Chukchansi (Yokuts)).

2. Segmental Processes Evidenced in North American Languages

This section will focus mainly on segmental processes that should be familiar to anyone who has some knowledge of phonology. We demonstrate here that processes such as assimilation, harmony, epenthesis, deletion, tonic lengthening, and neutralization are commonly found in languages from multiple families across North America, as one expects within any theoretical framework which assumes a common grammatical core to human language. Within these sections, the reader will also find some processes unique to (one or more) North American language(s), which will be presented under the headings of these processes.

2.1. Assimilation

Assimilation, a phonological process where one segment is modified to become (more) similar to an adjacent segment, is generally represented as an autosegmental sharing or matching of features. The types of features that may or must be shared varies according to the language, and sometimes within languages. One common cross-linguistic process is homorganic nasal assimilation. An example of this can be found in the alternations seen in the final nasal segment in 'go' in (2).

(2)	a.	ʔu	k'áát	u	ɓ̥i**m**	**p**áák	'He wants to go (and) weed'.[3]
		he	wants	to	go	weed	
	b.	ʔu	k'áát	u	ɓ̥i**n**	**ʃ**òòk	'He wants to go (and) study'.
		he	wants	to	go	study	
	c.	ʔu	k'áát	u	ɓ̥i**ŋ**	**k**òòl	'He wants to go (to the) milpa.'
		he	wants	to	go	milpa	

(Yucatec, Maya; Straight 1976: 68)

The Yucatec examples evidence preconsonantal nasal assimilation as an example of external sandhi (i.e., a transition between two words), while in the Isthmus Mixe example below, it is an internal sandhi process (i.e., a transition between two morphemes inside of a word). In (3), we see that morpheme-final nasals assimilate to the place of articulation of a following consonant.

(3)	a.	mi**n**	'come!(imp)'
		min	
	b.	mi**mb**	'he is coming'
		min-p	
	c.	mi**ŋg**umbɨ	'he is coming again'
		min-kumpɨ	

(Isthmus Mixe, Mixe-Zoque; Dieterman 2008: 13)

In (4), however, we see that the nasal possessive prefixes in Isthmus Mixe do not undergo the process of assimilation. This phonological behavior is common for prefixes generally, not just in

Mixe-Zoque or North American languages; prefixes often behave as though they are not within the phonological domain of their hosts.

(4) a. **mg**āāgʲ[4] 'your tortilla'
m-kaakʲ
your-tortilla
b. **nb**ɨdō̰ō̰ʃʲ 'my sister'
n-pɨto̰o̰ʃʲ
my-sister

(Isthmus Mixe, Mixe-Zoque; Dieterman 2008: 14)

Place assimilation is not limited to nasals. As we can observe in (5), place assimilation targets coronal consonants in Aivilik Inuktitut (cf. Kivalliq dialect).

(5)

	Kivalliq (W. Canada)	*Aivilik (Repulse Bay)*
tikit- 'arrive' + -puŋa (1SG)	tiki**tp**uŋa	tiki**pp**uŋa
tikit- 'arrive' + -(ŋ)mat (3SG 'because')	tiki**nm**at	tiki**mm**at

(Kivalliq/Aivilik Inuktitut, Eskimo-Aleut; Bobaljik 1996: 333 (data originally from Dorais 1990))

Another common process found in nasal-consonant sequences is nasalization, where a non-nasal consonant assimilates in nasality. In Kangiryuarmiut Inuinnaqtun, spoken in Western Canada, nasalization can be either progressive (left to right) or regressive (right to left). In (6a–b), note that /k/ becomes nasal when it is preceded by a nasal consonant, whereas in (6c–d) and (6e–f), /k/ and /t/ become nasal when followed by a nasal consonant.

(6) a. kamïk 'boot'
boot.SG
b. ka**mŋ**-it 'boots'
boot-PL
c. havik 'knife'
knife
d. havi**ŋ**-**m**un 'with a knife'
knife-INST

(Kangiryuarmiut Inuinnaqtun, Eskimo-Aleut; Bobaljik 1996: 332 (data originally from Lowe 1985))

e. tikitpuŋa
tikit-puŋa
arrive-1SG
f. tikinmat
tikit-(ŋ)mat
arrive-3SG.because

(Kivallik, Eskimo-Aleut: Bobaljik 1996: 333) (data originally from Dorais 1990)

Nasalization is, of course, not confined to consonant-consonant interactions. In the following Mixtec languages, words undergo a process of right-to-left nasal spreading that targets vowels and (some) consonants. An interesting distinction in the pattern of nasalization between the two languages can be seen. In Atatlahuca Mixtec, obstruents block the spread of the feature nasal, while in Ocotepec Mixtec, they do not.[5]

(7)

Atatlahuca	Ocotepec	Underlying Forms and Glosses
sukʷã	sũkʷã	sukʷa^{N} 'thus'
nᵈixẽ	nĩxĩ	nixe^{N}, nixi^{N} 'wing'
nᵈixẽ	nĩxã	nixe^{N}, nixa^{N} 'sandal'
ʒɨkɨ̃	ɲĩkĩ	jɨkɨ^{N}, jiki^{N} 'squash'
ʒuNⁿũ	ɲũtũ	jutu^{N} 'tree'
ʒukʷã	ɲũkʷã	jukʷa^{N} 'there'
ʒaNⁿĩ	ɲãtĩ	jati^{N} 'be near'
ʒaxĩ	ɲãxĩ	jaxi^{N} 'gourd'
ʒukũ	ɲũkũ	juku^{N} 'furrow'

(Marlett 1992: 431)

Another assimilation process found cross-linguistically is palatalization. This process is also common within the languages of North America, being found in the Algonquian (LeSourd 1993), Eskimo-Aleut (Compton & Dresher 2011), Siouan (Shaw 1980), and Athabaskan (Hargus 2010) families, among others. The example in (8) shows a palatalization of alveolars in the Point Barrow subdialect of Alaskan Inupiak.

(8)

	Stem	*Gloss*	*'and an N'*	*'N OBL.PL'*	*'like a N'*	*Proto-Eskimo*
a.	iɣlu	'house'	iɣlulu	iɣlunik	iɣlutun	*əŋlu
b.	iki	'wound'	ikiʎu	ikiɲik	ikisun	*əki
c.	savik	'knife'	saviɣʎu	saviɣɲik	saviksun	*t͡saviɣ
d.	qimmiq	'dog'	qimmiʁʎu	qimmiɲik	qimmisun	*qikmiʁ
e.	ini	'place'	inilu	ininik	initum	* ənə
f.	kamik	'boot'	kamiɣlu	kamiɣnik	kamiktun	*kaməɣ
g.	aiviq	'walrus'	aiviʁlu	aiviʁnik	aiviqtun	*ajvəʁ

(Point Barrow, Eskimo-Aleut; Compton & Dresher 2011: 206 (Proto Eskimo data originally from Fortescue et al. 1994))

(8a) does not contain a trigger for palatalization and allows us to see the underlying forms of the alveolar-initial affixes /lu/, /nik/, and /tun/. In (8b–d), the initial consonants of these affixes palatalize. In (8e-f), they do not. This pattern highlights a distinction between types of synchronic /i/ phonemes in the language. The /i/ in (8b–d) is 'strong' and triggers palatalization, while the /i/ in (8e–f) is 'weak' and does not act as a palatalization trigger. This distinction between 'strong' and 'weak' /i/ is not restricted to dialects of Eskimo-Aleut. Consider the following discussion of Ojibwe.

As pointed out in Buckley (2000), synchronic palatalization in Ojibwe shows interesting effects due to diachronic mergers leading to opacity (data in (9)–(11) originally from Bloomfield 1946; 1957; Kaye 1978; Piggott 1980). Synchronically, there is a palatalization rule in Ojibwe that targets /n/.

(9) a. ki-naan-aa 'you fetch him'
b. ki-naa**ʃ-i**-mi 'you fetch us'

(10) a. ki-miin-aa 'you give him'
b. ki-mii**ʃ-i**-mi 'you give us'

(Ojibwe, Algonquian; Buckley 2000: 7)

N-palatalization is not a process that is common in the languages of the world. In proto-Algonquian, palatalization targeted [t] and [θ]. Historically in (9), the proto-language form of *naan* is

**naaθ*. In the diachrony of Ojibwe, we see that *θ became *l and then *l became /n/ (Buckley 2000: 7). In (10), we see an additional example where an /n/ derived via this diachronic change becomes a palatoalveolar fricative preceding [i] in the synchronic grammar.

A confounding factor affecting palatalization in Ojibwe, like in Point Barrow, is that *e and *i underwent a diachronic process of merger (as [i]). [i]s derived from *i (strong-i) will trigger palatalization (11a), but [i]s derived from *e (weak-i) will not (11b).

(11) a. ki-mii**ʃ-i**-mi 'you give us'
     b. ki-mii**n-in** 'I give you'

(Ojibwe, Algonquian; Buckley 2000: 8)

The merger of a mid vowel with /i/, and therefore a similar opacity in the synchronic application of palatalization, can be seen in many Inuit and Algonquian dialects, as well as in Nez Perce (Sahaptian) (Rigsby & Silverstein 1969; Mithun 2001; among others).

2.2. Harmony

Harmony systems can be seen as a type of assimilation wherein feature-sharing occurs among non-contiguous segments. North American languages contain patterns of both vowel and consonant harmony. While vowel harmony is very well known and commonly found cross-linguistically, consonant harmony is rarer. In his worldwide survey of consonant harmony systems, Hansson (2010) demonstrates that 33% of consonant harmony patterns are found in languages of the Americas, mostly in those spoken in North America.

2.2.1. Vowel Harmony

As pointed out in Mithun (2001: 26), Nez Perce contains one of the best-studied vowel harmony systems among North American languages. Nez Perce vowel harmony is interesting in that it evidences the same type of cross-classification/merger of high front vowels as seen in §2.1. Here they are classified as either dominant or regressive. The complete inventory of vowels in the language can be divided into these two groups – dominant: *i*, *a*, *o*, and regressive: *i*, *e*, *u* – and all vowels in a word will harmonize according to this classification.

(12) a. **wééyik-sene** '(I) went across long ago'
     b. **weyewéèyik-sene** '(I) hurried across long ago'
     c. **wááyik-saqa** '(I) went across recently'
     d. **wayawááyik-saqa** '(I) hurried across recently'

(Nez Perce, Sahaptian; Mithun 2001: 27 (data originally from Aoki 1966))

In Southern Pomo there are multiple vowel interactions that have been described as harmonic in Walker (2013), not all of which are described in (13)–(15). First, [+high] vowels in initial syllables harmonize in height with a subsequent vowel. This harmonization occurs only if the two vowels involved agree for the feature [round]. In (13a–b), we can see [i] lowering to [e] before [e], and in (13c–d), [u] lowering to [o] before [o].

(13) a. **mii**t̪o 'you'
     mii-t̪o
     2SG-PAT

b. **meek**ʰe 'your'
mii-:kʰe[6]
2SG-POSS

(Southern Pomo, Pomoan; Walker 2013: 112)

c. d**u**h**k**ʰe?tʃ'in 'move it towards yourself'
du-hkʰe-tʃitʃ-Vn
by.finger-move-REFL-SG.IMPFV

d. ˈ**dot**':ow 'skinned'
du-t':o-w
by.finger-peel-PFV

(Southern Pomo, Pomoan; Walker 2013: 116)

Second, we see vowel harmony across /ʔ/ within monomorphemic stems (14). Across morpheme boundaries, vowels do not harmonize across /ʔ/ (15a), although the lowering rule seen in (13) may still apply (15b).

(14) a. ts'**i**ʔ:**i**- 'to do; to make'
b. h**e**ʔ:**e** '(head) hair'
c. b**a**ʔ:**a**y 'woman'
d. h**o**ʔ:**o** 'tooth'
e. ts'**uu**ʔ**u** 'arrow'

(Southern Pomo, Pomoan; Walker 2013: 118)

(15) a. ˈm**a**ʔ[:]**e**n 'his fa[ther]'
maH-ʔe-n
3C-father-PAT

b. m**e**ʔ:en 'your father'*
miH-ʔe-n
2SG-father-PAT

(Southern Pomo, Pomoan; Walker 2013: 118, *113)

In Southern Pomo, stress generally falls on the penultimate syllable, and secondary stress may fall on an initial syllable (Walker 2013). Additionally, stress in Proto-Pomo surfaced on the initial syllable of the stem (Moshinsky 1976). Whether the localized harmony seen in the stems in (14) and (15) is related to stress (being restricted to foot-internal sequences) may be an interesting avenue to pursue.

Another case of vowel harmony that has received much attention is rounding harmony in Yowlumne (Newman 1944; Kuroda 1967; Kisseberth 1969; Kenstowicz & Kisseberth 1977; Steriade 1981; Archangeli 1984; 1985; Cole 1987; Cole & Trigo 1988; Kaun 1995; 2004; Archangeli & Suzuki 1997; McCarthy 1998; D 'Arcy 2003; Krämer 2003; Currie-Hall 2007; Jurgec 2013; van der Hulst 2016; 2018). It is especially interesting in that it evidences a pattern that is sometimes opaque on the surface. In (16) we see transparent examples of this harmony pattern. Yowlumne vowels will agree in rounding if and only if they agree in their specification for height: the high unrounded vowel /i/ becomes round after /u/, and the non-high unrounded vowel /a/ becomes round after /o/.

(16) a.
xat-hin 'eats'
bok'-hin 'finds'
xil-hin 'tangles'
dub-h**u**n 'leads by the hand'

b.
xat-al 'might eat'
hud-al 'might recognize'
xil-al 'might tangle'
bok'-**o**l 'might find'

(Yowlumne, Yokutsan; van der Hulst 2018: 235
(data originally from Kenstowicz & Kisseberth 1977: 78))

Yowlumne also has a rule of vowel lowering for long vowels. Interestingly, /uu/ lowers to [oo], while /ii/ lowers to [ee]. The front non-high vowel emerges only in this derived environment.[7] A subsequent rule of vowel shortening in closed syllables means that these lowered vowels are variably long or short in the final surface representation. What is clear from the data in (17) is that rounding harmony must apply before lowering, as these lowered vowels pattern with high vowels on the surface; they trigger the rounding of high vowels, and not of non-high vowels.

(17)	a.	/hiwiit/	'walk'	hiwet-hin	'walks'	hiweet-al	'might walk'
	b.	/c'uum /	'destroy'	c'om-**hun**	'destroys'	c'oom-al	'might destroy'
	c.	/ʔopoot/	'get up'	ʔopot-hin	'gets up'	ʔopoot-**ol**	'might get up'
	d.	/ p'axaat'/	'mourn'	p'axat'-hin	'mourns'	p'axaat'-al	'might mourn'

(Yowlumne, Yokutsan; slightly modified from Curry-Hall 2007: 103 (data originally from Archangeli 1984; D'Arcy 2003))

Data that evidences such opacity continues to be particularly relevant to the ongoing debate about whether phonological derivations are serial (rules/operations apply sequentially), as in Rule-Based Phonology (see Purnell 2017; Vaux & Myler 2017; and Newell 2017a for a recent overview of RBP); or parallel (all rules/operations apply simultaneously), as in classic Optimality Theory (see Iosad 2017; Krämer 2017); or both, as in Stratal Optimality Theory (see Bermúdez-Otero 2017).

2.2.2. *Consonant Harmony*

As mentioned in §2.2, North American languages are an important source of data on consonant harmony systems. The most common type of consonant harmony cross-linguistically involves sequences of coronal consonants. Consider the following example from Tahltan, which has three series of coronal spirants (18) that harmonize regressively (19). In examples (19a–c), we see the default form of the 1sg subject prefix /s-/, and in (19d–h), we see its harmonization with a following coronal sibilant. In (20a–b), we see the default form of the 1du subject prefix /θi(d)-/, and in (20c–e), we see its harmonic form.

(18)	dð	dz	dʒ
	tθ	ts	tʃ
	tθ'	ts'	tʃ'
	ð	z	ʒ
	θ	s	ʃ

(Tahltan, Athabaskan; Mithun 2001: 30 (data originally from Shaw 1991))

(19)	a.	ɛ-**s**-k'ɑɑ	'I am gutting fish'
	b.	nɑdɛdɛɛ-**s**-bɑɑt^{ɬ}	'I hung myself'
	c.	sɛ-**s**-xɛɬ	'I'm going to kill it'
	d.	θɛ-**θ**-ðɛɬ	'I'm hot'
	e.	dɛ-**θ**-k^{w}ʊθ	'I cough'
	f.	hudi-**ʃ**-t^{ʃ}ɑ	'I love them'

g. ya-**ʃ**-$t^{ɬ'}$ɛtᶴ 'I splashed it'
h. noʔɛdɛɛ-**ʃ**-ɬɛdʒi 'I melted it over and over'

(Tahltan, Athabaskan; Odden 1994: 325 (data originally from Shaw 1991))

(20) a. dɛ-**θ**i-gɪ$t^{ɬ}$ 'we threw it'
b. nɑ-**θ**i-bɑɑ$t^{ɬ}$ 'we hung it'
c. i-**ʃ**i-tᶴo$t^{ɬ}$ 'we blew it up'
d. dɛ-**s**i-dᶻɛl 'we shouted'
e. ni-**s**i-t'ɑɑtˢ 'we got up'

(Tahltan, Athabaskan; Odden 1994: 325 (data originally from Shaw 1991))

Importantly, in this type of system non-sibilant coronals do not block harmonization (as in ya-ʃ-$t^{ɬ'}$ɛtᶴ), indicating that although consonant harmony patterns are often coronal, coronality is not a necessary target or blocker of the harmonic process. Consonant harmony systems have motivated two major debates in the literature. The first considers what systems of consonant harmony can tell us about the internal organization of segmental features (Halle & Vergnaud 1981; Archangeli & Pulleyblank 1987; Steriade 1987; Shaw 1991; Odden 1994; Piggott 1996; 1997). The second discusses whether vowel harmony and consonant harmony are representative of the same kind of segmental process (spreading of features), or whether consonant harmony evidences rather an agreement between segments (modification of features without spreading) (see Hansson (2010) for a detailed discussion).

Sibilant harmony has even been shown to override other constraints on coronal consonants in a language. In Samala there is a dissimilation process whereby coronal sibilants are palatalized before coronal [t, l, n]. The 3s morpheme *s-* in the examples below surfaces as [s] when not targeted by dissimilation (/baʔ-s-e/ [baʔse] 'he brought' (McMullin 2016: 10)).

(21) a. **ʃt**epuʔ 'he gambles'
s-tepuʔ
b. **ʃn**iʔ 'his neck'
s-niʔ
c. **ʃl**ok'in 'he cuts it'
s-lok'in
d. ʃi**ʃt**ɨʔ 'he finds it'
s-is-tɨʔ

(Samala, Inseño Chumash, Chumashan; McMullin 2016: 141 (data originally from Applegate 1972))

Samala, like Tahltan, has an anticipatory sibilant harmony system, as seen in (22). As (23) demonstrates, this harmonic assimilation has priority in the language over the dissimilatory operation in (21).

(22) a. k**ʃ**uʃojin 'I darken it'
k-su-ʃojin
b. **s**api**ts**ʰolu**s** 'he has a stroke of good luck'
s-api-tʃʰo-us
c. **ʃ**api**tʃ**ʰolu**ʃ**waʃ 'he had a stroke of good luck'
s-api-tʃʰo-us-waʃ

d. kʃuk'ilimekeke**tʃ** 'I straighten myself up'
k-su-k'ili-mekeken-ʃ

(Samala, Inseño Chumash, Chumashan; McMullin 2016: 140 data originally from Applegate 1972))

(23) a. si**st**isijepus 'they (dual) show him'
s-iʃ-tiʃi-jep-us
b. **sn**etus 'he does it to him'
s-net-us

(Samala, Inseño Chumash, Chumashan; McMullin 2016: 141 (data originally from Applegate 1972))

In addition to the (relatively) common coronal consonant harmony evidenced by Tahltan and Samala (as well as Zoque (Mixe Zoque); Yucatec, Tzeltal (Ts'eltal); Tzotzil (Maya); Wiyot (Algic); Tututni, Tanana, Bear-Lake Slave, Sarcee, Proto-Athapaskan-Eyak, Navajo, Kiowa, Hupa, Chiricahua Apache, (Athapaskan); Tlachichilco Tepehua, Misantla Totonac (Totonacan); Southern Paiute (Uto-Aztecan); and Barbareño Chumash (Chumashan); Hansson 2010), North American languages demonstrate some of the rarer cases of consonant harmony. For one example, see (24)–(26).

(24) a. mí**ɴq**á̰á̰**q**pa**χ**ɛ̰́ʔ 'your shoulder'
min-ka̰a̰k-paqa̰ʔ
b. míŋ**k**á̰á̰**k**tʃa̰a̰n 'your shoulder' [sic!]
min-ka̰a̰k-tʃa̰a̰-nḭ
c. ʔṵ́t ma**q**áʃ**q**ɛ́t 's/he scratches (with hand)'
ut maka-ʃqat
d. ʔṵ́t ma**k**apáʃ 's/he bathes his/her hand'
ut maka-paʃ

(Misantla Totonac, Totonacan; Hansson 2010: 70 (data from MacKay 1999))

(25) a. ʔí̱**k**lá**q**tsa̰**q**a̰ 'I chew [it]'
ik-lak-tsa̰qa̰
b. **k**í̱s**q**ɔjúniɬ 's/he smokes [it] for me'
kin-squ-jan-ni-la(ɬ)

(Misantla Totonac, Totonacan; Hansson 2010: 70 (data from MacKay 1999))

(26) s**q**ɔ**k**ɔ́hɔɬ 'it was smoked'
squ-kuhu-la(ɬ)

(Misantla Totonac, Totonacan: Hansson 2010: 70 (data from MacKay 1999))

According to Hansson (2010), Misantla Totonac evidences one of only five languages containing dorsal harmony patterns, and one of only two (along with the related Tlachichilco Tepehua) to offer evidence of dorsal harmony as an active process rather than a static morpheme structure constraint. Dorsal harmony, or more specifically uvular assimilation, in this language is regressive and constrained to the root and its derivational prefixes. Examples with harmonic body-part prefixes can be seen in (24), the lack of harmonization in inflectional prefixes is shown in (25), and that dorsal does not spread rightward can be seen in (26).

2.3. *Syllabic Effects*

Certain segmental processes can be considered to be controlled by higher prosodic structure (within prosodic phonology) or restrictions on linear segmental relations (government phonology). In the following sections, we will use the term 'syllable' to cover both of these options. The following processes are those that repair the segmental string in a way that brings it in line with the syllabic restrictions of the language in question.

2.3.1. Deletion

Deletion processes target both consonants and vowels. An example of consonant deletion can be found in Dakota in (27) and (28). Dakota has a process of suffixal reduplication in verbal constructions that copies the final syllable of the root. This reduplication can signify plurality of the subject, iterativity of the action, distributivity, or intensification. In this language morpheme final coda consonants are deleted before a complex onset (27). This rule allows for the determination of the status of glottalized and aspirated consonants as simple consonants (as opposed to Cʔ or Ch clusters), as they do not trigger deletion of a preceding coda consonant (28a–b), just as in the case of consonants with plain laryngeal specifications (28c).

(27) a. ksa**ks**apa 'be wise'
ksa**p-ks**ap[8]
b. xlo**xl**oka 'have holes'
xlo**k-xl**ok
c. ptu**pt**uza 'bent over'
ptu**z-pt**uz

(Dakota, Siouan; Shaw 1980: 67)

(28) a. tʔa**xtʔ**aɣa 'rough'
tʔa**ɣ-tʔ**aɣ
b. **tʃʰeptʃʰ**epa 'fat'
tʃʰep-tʃʰep

(Dakota, Siouan; Shaw 1980: 67)

c. na**kn**aka 'twitch'
na**k-n**ak

(Dakota, Siouan; Shaw 1980: 332)

Cluster simplification also targets geminates. As geminate consonants are single melodic items linked to two positions on the skeletal tier, this type of deletion can be either the deletion of a C position on the skeletal tier, or the deletion of the autosegmental line between the melody and one of its skeletal positions. In the following examples from Passamaquoddy, we see that a geminate consonant is maintained when following a vowel (29) and simplified when following a consonant (30).

(29) a. h-kə**pp**-asəka-h-m-ən 'he locks it'
3SG-close-lock-TI-TI-3SG.IN
b. h-kə**ss**e-hl-a-l 'he lets the other in'
3SG-IN-TA-DIR-3SG OBV

(30) a. k**p**-asəka-h-m-on[9] 'lock (sg.) it!'
close-lock-TI-TI-2SG

b. kse-hl-a-t 'if he lets the other in'
in-TA-DIR-3SG AN-(SUBJ)

(Passamaquoddy, Algonquian; LeSourd 1993: 220)

Degemination is also famously evidenced in dialects of Inuit. The process particular to these languages is dubbed the Law of Double Consonants, or Schneider's Law (e.g., Schneider 1972), and has the effect of simplifying a geminate in a syllable that immediately follows a closed syllable. In Labrador Inuttut, all consonant clusters evidence regressive assimilation; after assimilation, they are all phonological geminates (Dresher & Johns 1995). This process is iterative from left to right, resulting in different outcomes depending on the immediate environment of each cluster (Dresher & Johns 1995). Compare (31a) and (31b), where syllable boundaries are indicated by '.'.

(31) a. na.**nuŋ.ŋ**ua.**qaal.l**u.ni 'by first killing a toy bear'
nanu-**ŋŋ**ua(k)-**kq**aa-**ll**uni[10]
bear-toy-do first-by

b. tu**t.t**u.**ŋ**ua**k.q**aa.**l**u.ni 'by first killing a toy caribou'
tuttu-**ŋŋ**ua(k)-**kq**aa-**ll**uni
caribou-toy-do first-by

(Labrador Inuttut; Dresher & Johns 1995: 80 (data originally from Smith 1977))

In Siglitun, a western Inuit dialect, this assimilation process is not active, and we can therefore see that Schneider's Law targets geminates only, and not all CC sequences (Rose et al. 2012).

(32) a. i.qa.**lik.kuaq.t**uaq '(s)he/it went through the window'
iqaliq-**kkuaq-t**uaq
window go.through 3SG.ABS

b. up.**kua.kuaq.t**uaq '(s)he/it went through the door'
up**k**uaq-**kkuaq-t**uaq
door go.through 3SG.ABS

(Siglitun, Inuit; Rose et al. 2012: 4
(data originally from Lowe 1984)

We can see that in (32a), a sequence of two closed syllables is licit, as the second is not closed by the first member of a geminate. Rose et al. (2012) link the non-simplification of heterorganic consonant clusters to a higher faithfulness to Place features in Siglitun, explaining the lack of assimilation and the lack of deletion via the same principle. These authors link Schneider's Law to historical patterns of strengthening and weakening of consonant clusters; although it cannot be linked to metrical patterns synchronically, it appears to be so linked diachronically. Dresher & Johns (1995), however, point out that this kind of sensitivity to syllable weight should show sensitivity to the weight of long vowels in addition to closed syllables, a pattern that they note is not evidenced.

The deletion of vocalic segments is also found throughout the languages of North America. Tonkawa evidences more than one vowel-elision process. Consider the following alternations. In (33) we see constructions all containing the root /notoxo/ 'to hoe'.

(33) a. notxoʔ 'he hoes it'
noto**x**o+oʔ

b. wentoxoʔ 'he hoes them'
we+**n**otox**o**+oʔ

c. notxonoʔ 'he is hoeing it'
notoxo+n+oʔ

d. wentoxono? 'he is hoeing them'
we+**n**o**t**oxo+n+o?

e. notox 'hoe'
notox**o**

(Tonkawa, isolate; Noske 1993: 64–65 (data originally from (Kisseberth 1970)

The first vowel-deletion rule in Tonkawa seen above in (33a–b) is the cross-linguistically very common deletion under hiatus. This is also evidenced in (34a–b) and (35a–c). The second is the deletion of the second vowel of the stem if short, where one prefix – but not two (34c)[11] – may be considered to be stem-internal (33a–d, 34b–c). The third rule in the language deletes word-final vowels (33e).

(34) a. xamco? 'he is broken'
xam**a**c**e**+o?

b. yaxmaco? 'he breaks it'
ya+x**a**mac**e**+o?

c. keyaxmaco? 'he breaks my bones'
ke+ya+x**a**mac**e**+o?

(Tonkawa, isolate; Noske 1993: 67 (data originally from (Kisseberth 1970)

The same rule that deletes the second vowel of the stem if short, shortens long vowels after an initial CV(35a–d). Gouskova (2007) argues that these two rules are due to the weakening of the dependent syllable in an initial trochee (trochees are indicated by bracketing). This latter process can be considered a type of degemination, as described in the discussion of consonant deletion.

(35) a. (xá-**ka**)(nó?) 'he throws it far away'(cf. (a–c))
xa-**kaa**-n**a**-o?

b. (ké-**ja**)(lóo)(nó?) 'he kills me' (cf. (d))
ke-**jaa**loon**a**-o?

c. (ké-**ta**)(nót)(só?) 'he stands with me' (cf. (h))
ke-**taa**-notos**o**-o?

d. (wé.s?**e**)(l?ó?s) 'I scratch them' (cf. (k))
we-s**ee**l-o?s

(Tonkawa, isolate; Gouskova 2007: 371 (data adapted from Hoijer 1946))

Another interesting pattern of vowel deletion as hiatus resolution, alternating with epenthesis, will be discussed in §3 for Ojibwe.

2.3.2. *Epenthesis*

Epenthesis generally has two roles; V-epenthesis breaks up illicit consonant clusters, and C-epenthesis adds onsets to forms that violate language-particular restrictions on hiatus or V-initial sequences. Salishan languages, spoken in the Pacific Northwest, are quite interesting when it comes to V-epenthesis. In particular, these languages allow consonant sequences that are banned in most languages and so are noteworthy in that the epenthesis that they require is minimal to non-existent (at least in the phonology). There is a general agreement that there are two types of schwa in Salishan languages that are not derived from the weakening of an unstressed full vowel; excrescent (phonetic) and epenthetic (phonological) (Montler 1986; Bianco 1994; 1995; Matthewson 1994a; 1994b; Urbancyck 1996; Czaykowska-Higgins & Willett 1997; Kinkade 1998; Shaw & al. 1999; Blake 2000; Shaw 2002; 2004; Leonard 2006; 2007; Parker 2011).

Taking the example of SENĆOŦEN, we can see that root-initial obstruent-obstruent clusters are permitted (36) as long as they do not share place and laryngeal features (37a–b), or consist of a dental fricative-uvular stop (37c) or velar stop-postalveolar fricative cluster (37d).

(36) a. stop-stop
tqep 'saltwater fish trap'
q'p'aχ 'hazel nut'
q'təχ 'rattle'
b. affricate-stop
tʃk'ʷən 'catch a glimpse of'
tʃq'ənˀ 'file'
c. stop-fricative
tsas 'poor'
pxʷeŋ 'Forest Island'
k'ʷsətʃ 'trout
d. fricative-stop
ɬq'it 'any clothes'
χtit 'make/build something'
e. affricate-affricate
ƛ'tʃes 'Discovery Island'
f. affricate-fricative
t'ᶿχit 'pebbles'
tʃ'sey 'Douglas fir'
t**ʃɬ**ət 'thick layer'
g. fricative-affricate
stʃaɬ 'fire wood'
h. fricative-fricative
χɬemˀ 'watch'
xʷθiɬəs 'sidehill'

(SENĆOŦEN, Salishan; Leonard 2006: 22)

(37) a. q'əˈq'iʔ 'guts'
b. ˈqəqəƛ' 'shadow'
c. ˈθəqi 'sockeye'
d. kʷəˈtʃilˀ 'morning'

(SENĆOŦEN, Salishan; Leonard 2006: 24)

Root-initial clusters involving sonorants (resonants) are uniformly disallowed, and schwa is epenthesized to break up such a cluster.

(38) a. resonant-stop
nəˈkʷim 'black'
nəˈqʷey 'yellowish green'
b. stop-resonant
ˈqələχ 'salmon eggs'
ˈk'ʷələwˀ 'skin'
c. resonant-affricate
məˈƛ'el 'pass out'
nəˈt'ᶿexʷ 'once'

d. affricate-resonant
ˈtʃʼələm 'eel grass'
ˈƛʼəwəŋ 'howl'
e. resonant-fricative
ˈŋəsənˀ 'louse'
ˈwəχəs 'march'
f. fricative-resonant
ˈʃələtʃ 'world'
χəylˀ 'lose, die'
g. resonant-resonant
nəˈwˀes 'put inside'
ˈlələtʃʼ 'yellow'

(SENĆOŦEN, Salishan; Leonard 2006: 26)

Root-final clusters may involve resonant-obstruent and resonant-resonant sequences, but they must virtually always obey the sonority sequencing generalization. As can be seen in the examples in (37) and (38), epenthetic schwas may bear stress, confirming their phonological nature. Excrescent schwa, however, never bears stress and arises "optionally . . . between licit consonants (sic) clusters with varying places of articulation or between non-tautosyllabic obstruents and resonants" (Leonard 2006: 20).

Most other languages of the Salishan family demonstrate schwa-epenthesis patterns like the one described above for SENĆOŦEN. The exception to this pattern is argued to be Nuxalk (Bella Coola). This language has been argued to contain only excrescent schwas.

> Excrescent vowels are inserted very late in the phonetic component of the grammar. . . . Its insertion is triggered not by stray (that is, unsyllabified) consonants but rather by the need to mediate a transition between "adjacent articulations requiring some degree of constriction in the oral tract." . . . It is not referred to by any of the phonological rules of the language (Levin (1987: 194)).
>
> (In Bagemihl 1991: 600)

(39) tl̩kʼʷ → təlkʼʷ 'swallow'

(Nuxalk, Salishan; Bagemihl 1991: 599)

Analyses of Nuxalk prosodic structure have ranged from the proposition that the language has no syllables (Newman 1947; Kentowicz & Kisseberth 1979), to the proposition that every consonant in Nuxalk may be syllabic (Hoard 1978). In any case, it is generally agreed that consonant-only words are licit. It is of note, however, that Scheer (2004) questions the validity of these transcriptions, pointing out that

> Languages that are often quoted for having monster sequences of consonants such as the Salish family (native American Northwest languages, e.g. Bagemihl 1991; Bates & Carlson 1992; Czaykowska-Higgins & Willett 1997) suffer from being described, in many instances, with no explicit mention of whether the consonants involved are syllabic or not. For example, Czaykowska-Higgins & Willett (1997: 390) occasionally mention in brackets that words with initial #RəTV-sequences [R=sonorant, T=obstruent] in the Salish language they describe may also be pronounced as #R̩TV. The reader of this article and other sources of Salish cannot be sure that potential candidates for extrasyllabic clustering such

as #RTT-initial words may not occur with a syllabic sonorant, in which case of course there would be no extrasyllabic cluster at all.

(§376)

Some examples of proposed consonant-only words can be seen in (40).

(40) a. p'qʷ 'fine, loose, powdery'
b. ƛ'ɬ 'dry'
c. t'kʷ 'to bleed'
d. c'ktskʷc' 'he arrived'

(Nuxalk, Salishan; Bagemihl 1991: 592–593)

Bagemihl (1991) argues for an intermediate position, where vowels and sonorant consonants may be syllabic, and obstruents may either be syllabified peripherally (as onsets or codas) or may remain unsyllabified. He demonstrates that patterns of reduplication in the language are consistent with the schwas in words like (39) being excrescent, as reduplication treats full vowels and syllabic consonants in a parallel manner, ignoring schwa.

(41) a. CV reduplication
qayt → **qa**qayt-i 'hat' → 'toadstool-diminutive'
tl̩k'ʷ- → **tl̩**tl̩k'ʷ- 'swallow' → 'swallow continuative' * tətəl̩k'ʷ
b. CVC reduplication
yałk → **yał**yałk 'do too much' → 'do too much continuative'
mn̩łkʷa → **mn̩ł**mn̩łkʷ-łp 'bear berry' → 'plant of the bear berry' *mənmənłkʷłp
c. V reduplication
t'ixłala → **ʔi**t'ixłala-y 'robin' → 'robin diminutive'
k'n̩c → **ʔn̩**k'n̩c-i 'sperm whale' → 'sperm whale diminutive' *ʔək'ənc-i

(Nuxalk, Salishan; Bagemihl 1991: 598–599)

Bagemihl argues that excrescent schwa is inserted between any obstruent-sonorant sequence whether they belong to the same syllable or not, marking this process of epenthesis as post-phonological. Studies of epenthesis may thus be used to argue for certain patterns of syllabification within a language. Nuxalk also evidences a process of C-epenthesis, as demonstrated by the insertion of glottal-stops before the word-initial nuclear elements in (41c), arguing for a requirement for syllables to have onsets.

In addition to consonant epenthesis, some languages of North America, like other languages throughout the world, resolve the requirement that syllables have onsets by a process of gliding; spreading the vocalic features of the first vowel in a VV sequence to the intervening onset position. The following data from Dakota (42) exemplify this process.

(42) a. **hu**ˈ**wo**kaxmi 'inner side of knee joint' (leg-corner)
hu%o+kaxmi[12]
b. ˈ**wowi**dake 'to have for a servant'
wa%o+idak
c. **ni**ˈ**ya**te 'your father'
ni+ate
2SG-father[13]
d. **we**ˈ**yo**tʰa 'blood clot'
we%o+tʰa
blood-LOC.-bunch

(Dakota, Siouan; Shaw 1980: 90–91)

To return to V-epenthesis, another very interesting system can be found in Kanien'kéha (Mohawk). As demonstrated by Michelson (1983; 1988; 1989), and subsequently Piggott (1995), there are three different processes of V-epenthesis in the language: i-epenthesis to ensure word minimality (43); e-epenthesis to break up a cluster consisting of a C and an *r*, *n*, or *w* ((43d–e), (44a–b), and (45d)), a C and a word-final ʔ ((43e) and (44c–d)), or a C and a CC cluster "whose first member is any non-syllabic segment except *h* or *s*" (Michelson 1989: 41–42) (44e–f); and a-epenthesis in morphologically determined environments (45).

(43) a. ˈ**i**kyʌs 'I put it'
k-yʌ-s
1SG.AGT-put-HAB

b. ˈ**i**ktats 'I offer it'
k-tat-s
1SG.AGT-offer-HAB

c. ˈ**i**ikeks 'I eat' (153*)
k-eks
1SG.AGT-eat-HAB

d. ˈ**i**s**e**riht 'cook!'
s-riht-∅
2SG.AGT-cook-IMP

e. ˈ**i**t**e**nehr**e**ʔ 'you and I want to' (140*)
t-n-her-ʔ
1INCL-PL-want-HAB

(Kanien'kéha (Mohawk), Iroquoian; Michelson 1983 (*page numbers indicated beside examples); 1989: 45)

We can see that the underlying forms of (43) contain only one vowel, and therefore are monosyllabic. A word-minimality requirement in the language requires that words be bi-syllabic. Piggott argues that i-epenthesis is ordered before stress is assigned, ensuring that epenthetic *i* is always the locus of stress. The Kanien'kéha stress system is composed of moraic trochees. The additional epenthetic vowels in (43) are examples of e-epenthesis. This epenthesis occurs after stress has been assigned, ensuring its invisibility to foot construction in open syllables ((43d–e) and (44a–d)). In (44f), stress falls on the epenthetic vowel. For both epenthetic *e* and *a*, if they surface in closed syllables, they may attract stress.

(44) a. ˈʌk**e**rʌʔ 'I will put it into a container' (41)
ʌ-k-r-ʌʔ
FUT-1SG.AGT-fill into-PUNCT

b. ˈtek**e**riks 'I put them together' (39)
te-k-rik-s
DUA-1SG.AGT-put together, next to each other-HAB

c. ʌˈkaarat**e**ʔ 'I lay myself down' (43)
ʌ-k-arat-ʔ
FUT-1SG.AGT-lay oneself down-PUNCT

d. roˈkuutot**e**ʔ 'he has a bump on his nose' (43)
ro-kut-ot-ʔ
3MASC.SG.PAT-bridge of the nose-stand-STAT

e. k**e**ˈthèèthaʔ 'I pound, am pounding' (42)
k-theʔt-haʔ
1SG.AGT-pound-HAB

f. wa'k**e**nyaks 'I get married' (42)
wak-nyak-s
1SG.PAT-get married-HAB

(Kanien'kéha (Mohawk), Iroquoian; Michelson 1989 (page numbers indicated beside examples))

Epenthetic-a is also inserted to ensure syllabification of illicit consonant clusters but must additionally be specified for insertion to break up clusters at certain morphological boundaries (see Michelson 1989; Piggott 1995).

(45) a. tekaʔ'shaar**a**riks 'I put the knives side by side' (39)
te-k-aʔshar-rik-s
DUA-1SG.AGT-knife-place side by side-HAB

b. ka'naaw**a**ku 'in the swamp' (48)
ka-naw-ku-Ø
NEUT.AGT-swamp-in-STAT

c. wakiʔtuh'kw**a**rhos 'I have a fever' (39)
wak-iʔtuhkw-rho-s
1SG.PAT-flame, fever coat-spread-HAB

d. k**e**'rakwas 'I take it out of something' (48)
k-r-kw-as
1SG.AGT-fill in-undoer-HAB

e. tekahru'w**a**nyu 'many objects put in your path' (48)
te-ka-hruw-nyu-Ø
DUA-NEUT.AGT-put across-DIST-STAT

(Kanien'kéha (Mohawk), Iroquoian; Michelson 1989 (page numbers indicated beside examples))

Piggott argues that the stressing of each of these epenthetic vowels in closed (penultimate) syllables is due to the moraic status of coda consonants in the language. A trochaic foot is built over the final two morae of the word. In the underlying form of a word like *kanawku*, the *w* is unsyllabifiable with any overt vowel in the word, and is therefore considered to sit in the onset of a headless and moraless syllable. The final moraic trochee will therefore be *ka(nawku)*, explaining stress on the antepenultimate syllable in (45b). In the underlying form of a word like *kerkwas*, the *r* and *k* are the onset and coda of a headless syllable. In this case, as the *k* is moraic, the final two morae are footed as in *ke(rkwa)<s>*, where final consonants are extrametrical, leading to stress on the epenthetic vowel in (45d).

2.3.2.1. VOWEL LENGTHENING

The process of vowel lengthening may also be categorized among epenthetic processes. When discussing degemination in §2.3.1, we noted that deletion could target CV slots on the skeletal tier. Epenthesis can also target the skeletal tier, inserting C or V positions. The Kanien'kéha data shown earlier interact with vowel lengthening in an interesting way. In the language, stressed vowels are generally lengthened in open syllables.

(46) a. 'khy**aa**tus 'I write' (53)
k-hy**a**tu-s
1SG.AGT-write-HAB

b. ˈshohktu 'he went back' (135)
s-hro-(a)hkt-u
ITER-MP-go back-STAT

(Kanien'kéha (Mohawk), Iroquoian; Michelson 1988
(page numbers indicated beside examples))

This relationship between stress and vowel-length is by no means specific to Kanien'kéha. The interesting twist here is that the type of epenthetic vowel in the syllable following the stressed vowel has an effect on its ability to lengthen. Stressed vowels may lengthen before epenthetic-*a* (47a), but not before epenthetic-*e* (47b).

(47) a. kaˈ**naawa**ku 'in the swamp' (48)
ka-naw-ku-∅
NEUT.AGT-swamp-in-STAT

b. ˈ**ʌker**ʌʔ 'I will put it into a container' (41)
ʌ-k-r-ʌ-ʔ
FUT-1SG.AGT-fill into-PUNCT

(Kanien'kéha (Mohawk), Iroquoian; Michelson 1989
(page numbers indicated beside examples))

Piggott attributes the above distinction to the fact that the epenthetic-a, being morphologically specified (it has an underlying representation linked to a lexical item), is moraic, while the true epenthetic vowel *e* is moraless. The *a* can therefore give its mora to the stressed vowel, an option that is not available for *e*. Many researchers have proposed, however, that lengthening is the attribution of an extra mora or extra syllabic space by stress itself (e.g., Bye & de Lacey 2008; Ségéral & Scheer 2008). In these types of systems, the distinction in (47) would need an alternate account. A possibility would be the analysis in Kaye (1990), where long vowels need to be governed by a following vowel.[14] If true epenthetic vowels cannot be governors, then length in (47b) would not be able to surface.

2.3.3. Neutralization

A third process that is generally taken to be sensitive to syllabic structure is neutralization. Neutralization is a process whereby segments that are normally contrastive in a language do not contrast in a specific phonological environment. Well-known examples of this process target the laryngeal features of consonants. For example, in German, voiced and voiceless consonants contrast generally in the language but do not do so word-finally; and in Thai, voiced, voiceless, and aspirated consonants are neutralized to their plain voiceless counterparts in syllable-final position. An example of this position-sensitive laryngeal neutralization can be seen in Maidu, a Maiduan (Penutian) language once spoken in California. Maidu stops were either voiced implosive, voiceless glottalized, or plain voiceless, but were neutralized to plain voiceless in coda position. The neutralization of implosives was no longer active in the language at the time the following data was collected (it was evidenced as a morpheme-structure constraint), but synchronic neutralization of glottal stops could still be seen.

(48) a. /hyt'/ 'fat, grease'
ba.tam hy.t'i 'butter'
hy**t**.pe 'fat, obese'

b. /jep'/ 'male'
je**p**.sy 'men'
je.p'im sy.mi 'buck deer'

(Lombardi 1995: 46 (data originally from Shipley 1956; 1963; 1964))

A language of particular interest in the study of positional neutralization is another Penutian language, Klamath. In Klamath, a lenis series of obstruents (with variable amounts of voicing (e.g., g)) contrasts with a fortis series (voiceless with variable aspiration being allophonically determined (e.g., k^h)), and a voiceless glottalized series (e.g., k’). This contrast is neutralized to the lenis series when an obstruent emerges in a position preceding any consonant except a voiced sonorant (Barker 1963; 1964).[15],[16] Kingston (1985) demonstrates that this neutralization may be analyzed as positional. Contrasts are maintained in onset position (49) and are neutralized in coda position (50).

(49) a. as an onset to a syllabic (voiced sonorant)

ma.**k^h**l̩.q^{h}a	‘camps at’
w̩.t^{h}o.**g**l̩.k^{h}i	‘comes to beat someone’
ɢaa.ya.**k’**l̩.gi	‘comes to search for’

(Klamath, Penutian; Kingston 1985: 292 (Data originally from Barker 1963; 1964))

b. as an onset in an obstruent-voiced sonorant cluster

p^{h}ni.ʔaak	‘little wild onion’
ɢlaws	‘sand’
k’loc.kc^{h}a	‘goes to get a fire, torch’

(Klamath, Penutian; Kingston 1985: 263 (Data originally from Barker 1963; 1964))

c. as an onset to a vowel

kt^{h}o.**d**ii.la	‘hits with the fist underneath’
qdoo.**c^h**as	‘rain’
w̩.le.**p’**als	‘lightning’

(Klamath, Penutian; Kingston 1985: 263–264 (Data originally from Barker 1963; 1964))

(50) a. before an obstruent

ʔi**k**.c^{h}ii.ya	‘goes to get plural objects for someone’
ʔi**t**.galt	‘can pick up plural objects’
k^{h}o**p**.k’as	‘torch’

(Klamath, Penutian; Kingston 1985: 274 (Data originally from Barker 1963; 1964))

b. before a voiceless (capitalized here) or glottalized sonorant

q’a**t**.Yaa.w’as	‘species of seagull’
m̩.bo**t**.y’a	‘wrinkle from water’

(Klamath, Penutian: Kingston 1985: 273 (Data originally from Barker 1963; 1964))

c. word-finally

ʔit.gal**t**	‘can pick up plural objects’
q.biwt.gal.wa**pk**	‘will suck out disease’
gan.k^{h}ak.c^{h}a**t**	‘can go hunting’

(Klamath, Penutian; Kingston 1985: 274 (Data originally from Barker 1963; 1964))

d. word-initially before an obstruent (extrasyllabic)

kt^{h}o.dii.la	‘hits with the fist underneath’
qdoo.c^{h}as	‘rain’
qp’al’atk	‘curled up’
ksawalt	‘can lie upon’

(Klamath, Penutian; Kingston 1985: 263 (Data originally from Barker 1963; 1964))

The problem with the analysis of Klamath neutralization as positional is that other phonological rules give evidence against the syllabification seen in (49a–b). For example, the stress rules of the language do not treat the bolded obstruents in (49a–b) as onsets. Stress is weight-sensitive in Klamath, falling on either the rightmost long vowel, on a heavy penult in the absence of a long vowel, and otherwise on the anti-penult (Blevins 1993). The examples in (51) demonstrate heavy penult stress, indicating that the obstruents in a medial obstruent-voiced sonorant cluster (51b–c) must be syllabified as codas, just as the initial consonant in a medial obstruent-obstruent sequence is (51a).

(51) a. či.ˈkač.kis 'species of grasshopper'
b. kep.ˈkap.li 'comes back'
c. saq.ˈpaq'.wis 'a single braid'
(Klamath, Penutian; Blevins 1993: 256–257 (Data originally from Barker 1963))

While Clements & Keyser (1983), Steriade (1983), Kingston (1985; 1990), and Lombardi (1991) argue that the above discrepancy be used as evidence for different syllabification rules at different points in a derivation, Blevins (1993) argues that this cannot be the case and that neutralization in Klamath is sensitive to the linear order of segments rather than to syllable structure. This type of debate has implications for the types and timing of phonological rules that may be active in a language, and therefore for phonological theory in general.

This section has discussed some of the various segmental processes sensitive to syllabic structure that occur in North American languages. The processes of deletion, V-epenthesis, C-epenthesis, gliding, stress-sensitive vowel lengthening, and positional neutralization can all be seen to be active. That said, it is clear that some languages like Nuxalk (analogously to the literature on Berber syllable structure) and Klamath may challenge common theories of syllabification and therefore contain data that is especially important for phonological theories of prosodic structure.

3. Domain Effects

It is of interest for anyone who studies North American languages that they are overwhelmingly polysynthetic. Mithun (2015) discusses this surprisingly uniform areal tendency, which she shows is largely due to a preponderance of head-marking and noun-incorporation in North American languages. The complexity of words in these languages makes them especially interesting for studies at the interface of morpho-syntax and phonology, as well as for studies of word formation and the definition of word-hood. Verbs (especially but not uniquely) in these languages tend to span amounts of syntactic structure represented clausally in more analytic languages, as in the following Inuktitut example (cf. its English translation).

(52) [uqa-limaar-vi-liu(ng)-inna-nngit-tunga $_{CP}$]
speak-all.of-NOM-make-always-NEG-DEC.1SG
'I was not always making libraries.'
(Inuktitut, Eskimo-Aleut; Compton & Pittman 2010: 2168)

The complexity of lexical items like those in (52) in North American languages sometimes gives evidence of sub-domains within the word. This can be seen in the first example given in this chapter from Navajo, repeated below as (53).

(53) dishmáás
d- ish- ł- máás
INCP- ØIMP/1SG- CL- IMP.roll
'to start to roll it'(1P)

(Navajo, Na-Dene; McDonough 1996: 244)

McDonough, expanding on work by Kari (1976) and Young & Morgan (1987), argues that the Navajo word can be separated into two domains, the verb stem domain and the inflectional stem domain. The former includes verb roots and classifier prefixes, and the second includes subject, mode, and qualifier morphemes. This above example can be divided into domains as in (54).

(54) $[\text{d- ish}]_{\text{INFL}}$ $[\text{ł- máás}]_{\text{VERB}}$

In the next example, we can see that in the INFL domain, CC sequences are repaired via epenthesis. The inceptive prefix *d-* shows the variant *di-* before consonants as in (55).

(55) dinishtaał
[d-nish] [l-taał]
QU-nIMP/1SG CL- IMPFV
'I trip him (with foot)'

(Navajo, Na-Dene; McDonough 1996: 245)

Within the verbal domain, we can see that this epenthesis does not occur.[17] We can see, however, that CC clusters are permitted across the INFL-VERB domain boundary. This is the only position in the Navajo verb (discounting clitics) where a CC sequence surfaces. As each C in this sequence is in a different phonological domain, the phonology does not treat them as adjacent, and there is therefore no cluster resolution.

These word-internal sub-domains are found in many languages, and their sizes and behaviors have interesting consequences for theories of grammatical cyclicity and prosodic structure. The main related questions in the literature are (i) why examples like the above contain multiple phonological domains, and (ii) whether they are 'grammatical words'; defined by most authors as "a complex X^0 (syntactic head) realized via head movement", or are (and/or contain) phrasal (XP) material. When discussing the issue of phonological domains, one question is whether these domains are derived procedurally (e.g., through interpretation of morphosyntactic structure in cycles, such as strata or phases), or representationally (e.g., by prosodic structure), or both (see Newell & Scheer 2007; 2017; Bermúdez-Otero & Luís 2009; Scheer 2013 for discussion of the procedural vs. representational debate). We will not argue for or against any side of these theoretical debates here, but we will represent domains in the following discussion in terms of the Prosodic Hierarchy (Selkirk 1984; 1986; Nespor & Vogel 1986/2007) for ease of exposition. We demonstrate some of the relevant patterns by describing analyses of three unrelated languages: Chukchansi (Yokuts), Cayuga (Iroquoian), and Ojibwe (Algonquian). These patterns are not limited to these languages, but it is interesting to see how, in many cases, segmental phenomena are key to demonstrating the complexity of phonological domains within words in North American languages.

3.1. Chukchansi (Yokuts)

Guekguezian (2017) gives evidence that the verbal word in Chukchansi is computed in cycles (phases in the sense of Chomsky 1995), contra Archangeli's (1983) analysis of the language as templatic. In (56), monosyllabic verbs undergo augmentation. It is clear that these modified forms are not caused by general phonotactic repairs (syllables in the language are maximally CVX).

Augmentation occurs only in the presence of trigger affixes (-la or -e); other C-initial and V-initial affixes do not trigger a CVCV:(C) shape on the root. The quality of the long epenthetic vowel in the template is not important here.

(56)

		/_C	/_V	/_trigger
		/-taʔ/ (REM.PAST)	/-it/ (REC.PAST)	/-la, -e/ (CAUS)
/wan/	'give'	[wan.-taʔ]	[wa.n-it]	**[wa.naa**.-la-t]
/tʃiʃ/	'cut'	[tʃiʃ.-taʔ]	[tʃi.ʃ-it]	**[tʃi.ʃaa**.-la-t]
/maax/	'collect'	[max.-taʔ]	[maa.x-it]	**[ma.xaa**.-la-t]
/ʔaml/	'help'	[ʔa.mil.-taʔ]	[ʔam.l-it]	**[ʔa.maa**.l-e-t]
/beewn/	'sew'	[bee.win.-taʔ]	[bew.n-it]	**[be.wee.n**-e-t]

(Chukchansi, Yokuts; Guekguezian 2017: 85)

Interestingly, the template is never imposed upon verbal roots that are already bi-syllabic.

(57)

	/_C	/_V	/_trigger
	/-taʔ/	/-it/	/-la, -e/
/tʃ'edma/ 'think'	tʃ'ed.ma.-taʔ	tʃ'ed.ma-t	**tʃ'ed.ma**.-la-t
/haj'k'it/ 'finish'	haj'.k'it.-taʔ	haj'.k'i.t-it	**haj'.k'it**.-la-t
/joojo/ 'call'	joo.jo.-toʔ	joo.jo-t	**joo.jo**.-la-t
/heweet/ 'walk'	he.wet.-taʔ	he.wee.t-it	**he.wee.t**-e-t

(Chukchansi, Yokuts: Guekguezian 2017: 93)

Guekguezian argues that this distinction is due to prosodic word-minimality constraints in the language. Like in the Kanien'kéha examples in (43), the epenthetic vowels in (56) are inserted to ensure that underlyingly monosyllabic roots may be footed according to the metrical requirements of the language. Where in Kanien'kéha the optimal foot was a moraic trochee, in Chukchansi it is a light-heavy iamb; all augmented roots have this form.

Notably, the word-minimality requirement proposed targets a sub-domain of the total word in the bolded examples in (56), as in (58).

(58) [[**wanaa**] lat]

The splitting of words like (58) into phonological domains is argued to be due to the particular morpho-syntactic status of all of the affixes that trigger templatic forms on their roots. All and only the affixes that condition templatic morphology are sitting in the syntactic head v^0: causative, inchoative, durative, and distributive. In the syntactic literature, the vP is known to be a domain for cyclic operations. For example, the edge of vP is targeted by successive-cyclic WH-movement in the syntax. The cyclic nature of vP is also argued to cause the lower domain of the verb to be interpreted separately in the phonology.[18] This partitioning of the syntactic structure into phonological domains is represented in (59).

(59)

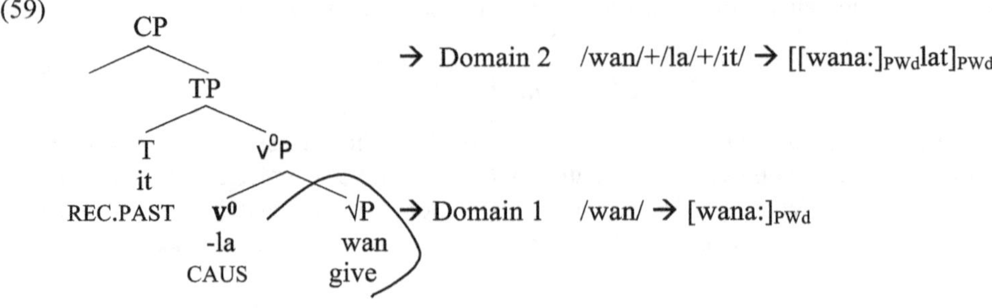

The phonology of Chukchansi, Guekguezian argues, treats Domain 1 in (59) as a prosodic word (PW) and subjects it to word minimality requirements. If it is too small (monosyllabic), it will undergo augmentation as seen in (56). Domain 1 is interpreted as a subpart of Domain 2. As Domain 2 contains Domain 1, it will already be at least as large as a PWd and no further augmentation will take place. If none of the v^0 triggers are present in the morpho-syntax, the entire CP will be interpreted as a single domain. As the CP always contains morphemes that, when added together, are minimally bi-syllabic, word-minimality augmentation will never apply in these cases (see the /_C and /_V columns in (56)).

The Chukchansi data therefore demonstrate that one domain within the verbal word appears to be treated differently by the phonology than another, larger domain. This is not, in fact, the case; word-minimality applies always, but its effects are seen only when the input to the phonology is sub-minimal (monosyllabic); which arises only when the vP is interpreted independently. This type of pattern is pervasive cross-linguistically; where vP or some other syntactically defined domain behaves as special for phonological rule application.

3.2. Cayuga (Iroquoian)

Dyck (2009) argues that the verbal word in Cayuga can be separated into sub-domains and offers segmental and metrical evidence to support this claim. The word in Cayuga may contain pre-pronominal prefixes, pronominal prefixes, an incorporated noun stem, a verb stem, aspectual suffixes, and post-aspectual suffixes among which the pronominal prefixes, verb stems, and aspectual suffixes (in all but the imperatives) are obligatory (Dyck 2009: 594). An example containing all but a post-aspectual suffix can be seen in (60).

(60) tekatnǫh'sahsnyeh 'I am cleaning up the house'
te-k-at-nǫhs-a-hsnye-h
DUAL-1SG.AGT-SRF-house-JOINER-clean.up-HAB

(Cayuga, Iroquoian; Dyck 2009: 582)

That (60) exemplifies a single phonological domain is shown by the behavior of stress placement and epenthesis (among other phenomena). As Dyck demonstrates, stress is generally on the final syllable, unless this syllable is utterance-final. In such a case, stress will fall on the penultimate syllable (61).

(61) a. akaa'khekę[ʔ] 'I saw them'
b. a'heekę[ʔ] 'I saw him'

(Cayuga, Iroquoian; Dyck 2009: 573)

Interestingly, odd-numbered penultimate syllables, as in (61a), will not be stressed if they are closed or if they contain [a]. In such cases, the antepenultimate syllable will emerge as stressed (62).

(62) akatǫh'swe[ʔ]tanih 'I am hungry' (cf. hotǫhsw[ʔ]e'taanih 'he is hungry')

(Cayuga, Iroquoian; Dyck 2009: 574)

Importantly, determining whether a syllable is 'odd' or 'even' is computed from the left edge of the word. As default stress targets the right edge, Dyck has evidence for a single bounded domain in which stress is assigned.

It is in the same domain that epenthesis will apply to break up consonant clusters. Dyck argues that the Cayuga syllable never contains complex margins. Most sequences that contain apparent complex margins contain [h], [ʔ], [w], and [s]. These phonemes may instantiate (i) onsets, (ii) co-articulations of a previous vowel as part of the nucleus ([h] and [ʔ] only when followed by a consonant), or (iii) as a secondary articulation of a following consonant. The joiner vowel seen in (60) (te.kat.nǫh.ˈsahs.nyeh) is one instance of epenthesis triggered by consonant clusters. This is, of course, the same joiner seen in the, related, Kanien'kéha data in §2. An example of e-epenthesis can be seen in (63).

(63) s**e**k.tǫǫ 'examine it!'
s-ktǫǫ
2SG-examine

(Cayuga, Iroquoian; Dyck 2009: 582)

The domain in which stress and syllabification are determined, however, contains smaller domains. Dyck notes that Cayuga does allow for extrasyllabic consonants at the edges of domains. These consonants are those that cannot be included in the syllable to their right. If we consider extrametrical syllables and segments (Hayes 1982), we see that there is often melodic material at the edges of domains that appears to not be incorporated into the adjacent structure. Extrasyllabic consonants in Cayuga may coincide with the domain of stress assignment we have already identified previously.

(64) a. **k.**tak.seˀ 'I am running'
k-takseˀ
1SG.AGT-run.PURP
b. **t.**ka.heeˀ 'it is sitting over there'
t-ka-hee ˀ
CISL-3SG.ZN.AGT-sit.STAT
c. **s.**na.ka.i 'whistle!'
s-nakai
2SG.AGT-whistle

(Cayuga, Iroquoian; Dyck 2009: 585)

As (65) demonstrates, extrasyllabic consonants may also be found at the left edge of incorporated noun stems.[19]

(65) (ęt.**k.**nęę)(t.ˈsʰii)(.neˀ) 'I will lead it by the arm'
ę-t-k-nętsh-ine-ˀ
FUT-DUAL-1SG.AGT-arm-lead-PUNCT

(Cayuga, Iroquoian; Dyck 2009: 587)

As in the discussion of Chukchansi in the previous section, it appears that in Cayuga the CP is parsed as a single domain,[20] but that smaller phonological domains also exist. Dyck argues that the larger domain is a phonological phrase, and the smaller domain is a phonological word. This analysis runs up against a problem of alignment of phonological domains. Notably, feet in Cayuga (66(65)) may contain a PWd boundary (evidenced by the extrasyllabic consonant), which is disallowed within most theories of the Prosodic Hierarchy (Selkirk 1978; 1984; McCarthy and Prince [1986]1999; and Nespor & Vogel [1986]2007).

(66) $[(\text{ęt.}[\textbf{k}\text{.nęę})(\text{t. ˈsh}]_{\text{PWd}}\ \text{ii.})(\text{ne}^{ʔ})]_{\text{PPh}}$

Dyck, however, follows Inkelas (1989; 1993) in assuming that prosodic structure (PWd, PPh. . .) is independent from metrical structure (Syllable, Foot). Although this poses interesting theoretical questions of its own, what is important here is that we again have evidence for nested domains inside of a domain that may be considered a word.[21]

3.3. Ojibwe (Algonquian)

Newell & Piggott (2014), building on much earlier work on Algonquian verb structure (Bloomfield (1946; 1957), Kaye et al. (1971), Piggott & Kaye (1973), Piggott (1980), McGinnis (1995), Déchaine (1999), Brittain (2001), Bruening (2001; 2005; 2009), Valentine (2001), Lochbihler (2008), Lochbihler & Mathieu (2013)) all demonstrate the complex structure of the word in the Odawa dialect of Ojibwe via evidence from footing, stress, and hiatus resolution. Notably, words in Ojibwe may include the verb, inflectional suffixes, an incorporated nominal, preverbal modifiers, tense morphemes, and pronominal morphemes. Newell and Piggott do not examine the phonological structure of incorporated nouns, so we cannot compare their behavior directly with the data on Cayuga in the last section, but they do look at footing. Interestingly, the Ojibwe data contrast with the claim in Dyck that Cayuga feet span the boundaries of phonological words. The smaller prosodic domains inside of the larger verbal (or nominal)[22] word in Ojibwe are also the domains of foot construction.

(67) ˌgiiˈbooˌnimaˌwi 'he stopped crying'
[(ˌgii)[[-(ˈboo)(ˌni)$_{\text{PWd}}$][-(maˌwi)$_{\text{PWd}}$]$_{\text{PWd}}$]$_{\text{PWd}}$]
PAST-stop-cry
(cf. *[(ˌgii)[[-(ˈboo)(ni$_{\text{PWd}}$][-ˌma)(ˌwi)$_{\text{PWd}}$]$_{\text{PWd}}$]$_{\text{PWd}}$])
(Ojibwe, Algonquian; Newell & Piggott 2014: 354)

In (67), there are three separate phonological domains within the largest PWd (Newell & Piggott claim the verbal word is a nested PWd rather than a PPh due to the fact that main stress is found only once in this domain). The first, [gii], is the past tense marker, the second, [booni], is an adverbial modifier, and the third, [mawi], is the verb. As long as each of these domains is bi-moraic (meeting foot-structure, or minimal word requirements), they are footed separately. Footing will never cross the adverbial-verb boundary, but the tense morpheme (and person prefixes that precede the tense morpheme) will be footed within the domain to their right if they are sub-minimal (monomoraic).

(68) (gaˈdaa)(gaˌmo)(ˌsee) 'He will (probably) walk in snowshoes'
ga-aagam-osee-Ø
FUT-snowshoe-walk-FIN
(Ojibwe, Algonquian; Newell & Piggott 2014: 355 (slightly modified))

In (68), *snowshoe* and *walk* are part of the verbal domain. The tense morpheme *ga-*, however, should be footed separately, following the pattern of (67). This prefix, however, is too small to constitute a foot and therefore merges into the verbal domain via a process of Phonological Merger (Newell & Piggott 2014).

(69) Phonological Merger
[X [. . . . PWd]] → [[.. X. . . . PWd]], where X is an affix.
(Ojibwe, Algonquian; Newell & Piggott 2014: 353)

Notably, in the Cayuga example in §3.2, the sequences that merge into an adjacent domain (*ętk* and *tsh*) may also be amenable to a merger-under-sub-minimality analysis.

Linking the Ojibwe data to the discussion of segmental processes, hiatus resolution is bound by the same domains as footing. Consider the following.

(70) a. [ogim**aag**]$_{PWd}$ 'chiefs, leaders'
ogim**aa-ag**
chief-PL

(Ojibwe, Algonquian; Newell & Piggott 2014: 336)

b. [ˈ**gii**]$_{PWd}$ [**a**ˌnoˌkii]$_{PWd}$ 'he worked, hunted'
gii-anokii
PAST-work

(Ojibwe, Algonquian; Newell & Piggott 2014: 338)

c. [gaˈ**daa**gaˌmoˌsee]$_{PWd}$ 'He will (probably) walk in snowshoes'
ga-aagam-osee-Ø
FUT-snowshoe-walk-FIN

(Ojibwe, Algonquian; Newell & Piggott 2014: 355 (slightly modified))

We can see that hiatus resolution is achieved via deletion within the verbal domain, including suffixes (70a) (see Newell & Scheer (2017) for a discussion of the prefix-suffix asymmetry with specific reference to Ojibwe). When two vowels are adjacent but in separate PWds, hiatus is not resolved (70b).[23] In (70c), repeated from (68), we see evidence that any VV-sequence that arises through Phonological Merger is repaired by epenthesis.

As with the discussions of Cayuga and Chukchansi, Ojibwe segmental processes mark sub-domains found within larger domains that are considered words. This line of research has shown similar patterns in Athabaskan languages such as Navajo (Speas 1991; Harley 2010; Travis 2010; Goad & Travis in prep.), Tlingit (Crippen & Dechaine 2016), and Slave (Rice 1993), in Kiowa (Tanoan) (Miller 2015; 2018), Cree (Algonquian), Dakota (Siouan) (Russell 1999), and in other Siouan languages (Rankin et al. 2003), in the Salishan languages Lushootseed (Beck 1999) and Nxaʔamxcín (Czaykowska-Higgins 1997), and in Cup'ik (Eskimo-Aleut) (Woodbury 2003). Note that the recent works cited here discuss word-internal phonological domains through the lens of contemporary theories, but that this work rests on a body of literature cited within each. The wealth of information on phonological domain formation found in the North American languages via the study of segmental, metrical, and prosodic operations cannot be overstated. Work at the phonology-syntax interface has seen renewed interest in the last 20+ years with the introduction of Phases (Chomsky 1995) and realizational theories of morphology such as Distributed Morphology (Halle & Marantz 1993; 1994). These theories contrast with the lexicalist theories of morphophonology (Kiparsky 1982; 1985; Mohanan 1982) in that they propose word formation to occur in the syntax and in a post-syntactic morphological module, while the latter propose word formation to be pre-syntactic. As phonology interprets morphosyntactic structure, the timing of word formation should impact phonological form and phonological domain formation. Words that appear to span clauses offer particularly interesting data with which to tease apart the predictions of theories of word formation and the interface.

4. Conclusion

As stated at the beginning of this chapter, we have not been able to do justice here to the vast literature on the segmental processes evidenced within North American aboriginal languages. What we have done is outline both how these languages are similar in their behavior to languages throughout the world, and unique in ways that are interesting both in and of themselves, and for phonological theory. Notably, North American languages contain a large percentage of the world's data on consonant harmony, intriguing operations like Schneider's Law, rare syllabification patterns like that found in Nuxalk, and a trove of information on the interactions between morphosyntactic structure, segmental processes, and prosodic domains. It is in this latter sphere that we believe will make particularly interesting strides as more data is obtained and more cross-linguistic comparisons are made.

Further Reading

For a discussion of word-hood in many languages (including North American languages), see:

Dixon, R. M. & Aikhenvald, A. Y., eds. 2003. *Word: A cross-linguistic typology*. Cambridge University Press.

For a comprehensive discussion of North American languages, their phonology, morpho-syntax, and genetic relations, see:

Hargus, Sharon. 2010. Athabaskan phonetics and phonology. *Language and Linguistics Compass*, *4*(10), 1019–1040.

Mithun, Marianne. 2001. *The languages of Native North America*. Cambridge University Press.

On crazy rules in North American languages:

Buckley, Eugene. 2000. On the naturalness of unnatural rules. In *Proceedings from the Second Workshop on American Indigenous Languages*: 1–14.

Notes

1. Note that acute and grave accents in this chapter indicate tone. Main stress is indicated by ˈ and secondary stress by ˌ. The segments targeted by phonological operations in the examples are indicated in bold. Abbreviations used herein are: 1SG = first-person singular, 2SG = second-person singular, 3SG = third-person singular, 3C = third-person coreferential, AGT = agent, ABS = absolutive, AN = animate, C = consonant, CAUS = causative, CISL = cislocative, CL = clitic, DEC = declarative mood, DIR = direct, DIST = distributive, DUA = dualic (verb refers to two objects or persons or to a change of state (Michelson 1988: 46)), FIN = final, FUT = future, HAB = habitual, IMPFV = imperfective, IMP = imperative, IN = inanimate, INCL = inclusive, INCP = inceptive, INST = instrumental, ITER = iterative, LOC = locative, MASC = masculine, MP = masculine singular patient, NEG = negative, NEUT = neuter, NOM = nominalizer, OBV = obviative, PAT = patient, PFV = perfective, PL = plural, POSS = possessive, = phonological phrase, PUNCT = punctual, PURP = purposive, QU = qualifier, = phonological word, REFL = reflexive, REC.PAST = recent past, REM.PAST = remote past, SG = singular, SRF = semireflexive, STAT = stative, SUBJ = subjunctive, TA = transitive animate verb, TI = transitive inanimate verb, V = vowel, ZN = zoic-neuter.
2. The example in (1) from Navajo is discussed further in §3.
3. b̥ is a prevoiced stop. Long vowels are indicated in examples as VV (not V:).
4. Here the diacritic over the vowels indicates a fronted allophone.
5. The symbol N^{n} indicates a voiceless nasal with a voiced transition, and ^{N} indicates a floating nasal feature.
6. The /:/ preceding the /k/ in the morpheme /:kʰe/ (seen also in various morphemes in (13)–(15) is a laryngeal increment, and may have varying phonological effects depending on its morphological context. The /H/s in (15) are also laryngeal increments. For a discussion of laryngeal incrementation in Southern Pomo, see §2.2.1 and §2.6.6 of Walker (2013).
7. For a discussion of the implications of the emergence of [ee] for a theory of the featural specifications of Yowlumne vowels, see Currie-Hall (2007).
8. The final [a]s in the surface forms in (27) and (28) are "the epenthetic terminal a̲ by STEM FORM" (Shaw 1980: 330). STEM FORM is a phonological rule (121).
9. "The most frequently encountered schwa/zero alternations in Passamaquoddy are those produced by the deletion of unstressable /ə/ before obstruents" (Lesourd 1993: 167).
10. (k), as with many morpheme-final consonants, is deleted under affixation (Dresher & Johns 1995: 80). Note that in Rose et al. (2012), the 'q's in these examples are transcribed as 'χ' and the morphemes 'nanu' and 'tuttu' both end in /k/.
11. Cf. Gouskova 2007: 373 /ke-we-jamaxa-oo-ka/ (kéw)(jám)(xóo.ka) 'you paint our faces'.
12. The % symbol indicates "the lexical derivation boundary" in Shaw (1980: 35).
13. The morphological glosses are not given for every example in Shaw (1980).
14. 'Government' within the framework of Government Phonology (Kaye et al. 1990) is a lateral relationship between segments. A vowel in this framework has the capacity to govern the vowel in the syllable to its left.
15. Word-finally all consonants are subject to aspiration or frication (Barker 1964: 24; Blevins 1993: 247). This process is independent of neutralization.

16. Neutralization is also evidenced in the sonorant series (voiced, voiceless, glottalized) but displays a different pattern than that of the obstruents. See the references cited in this section for detailed discussions.
17. Phonological interactions between the classifier and the verb root are quite complex. See Sapir & Hoijer (1967), Stanley (1969), and Howren (1971).
18. vP is said in the literature to be a *phase*. See Chomsky (1995), Marantz (2007), and Abels (2012), among others, for discussion of phases and their relation to domains for phonological and syntactic operations.
19. Due to the effects of e-epenthesis, only [k] emerges as extrasyllabic word-internally.
20. Dyck argues that this domain cannot be linked to a particular syntactic constituent due to the fact that not all types of affixes in the verbal template are obligatory. We do not see this as an issue; whatever morphosyntactic structure contained within the clause (CP) will be interpreted as a cohesive phonological domain in Cayuga. Independent nominal domains may also be parsed as phonological domains.
21. Note that there is no universal definition of what a word is. There is no consensus on what a grammatical word is, and phonological words do not always equal morphosyntactic constituents. See Julien (2002), Haspelmath (2011), and Newell (2017b) for discussion.
22. Nominal domains parallel verbal domains in important ways that will not be discussed here due to space limitations.
23. Neither vowel length nor vowel quality are determining factors in hiatus resolution in Ojibwe. Any sequence of vowels within a single PWd will be repaired.

References

Abels, Klaus. 2012. *Phases: An essay on cyclicity in syntax*, vol. 543. Walter de Gruyter.

Aoki, H. 1966. Nez Perce vowel harmony and Proto-Sahaptian vowels. *Language* 42(4). 759–767.

Applegate, R. B. 1972. *Ineseño Chumash grammar*. Berkeley: University of California. (Doctoral dissertation.)

Archangeli, Diana. 1983. The root CV-template as a property of the affix: Evidence from Yawelmani. *NLLT* 1. 347–384.

Archangeli, Diana. 1984. *Underspecification in Yawelmani phonology and morphology*. Cambridge: Massachusetts Institute of Technology. (Doctoral dissertation.)

Archangeli, Diana. 1985. Yokuts Harmony: Evidence for coplanar representations in nonlinear phonology. *Linguistic Inquiry* 16(3). 335–372.

Archangeli, Diana & Pulleyblank, Douglas. 1987. Maximal and minimal rules: Effects of tier scansion. *Proceedings of NELS* 17. 16–35.

Archangeli, Diana & Suzuki, Keiichiro. 1997. The Yokuts challenge. In Roca, Iggy (ed.), *Derivations and constraints in phonology*, 197–226. Oxford: Clarendon.

Bagemihl, Bruce. 1991. Syllable structure in Bella Coola. *Linguistic Inquiry*, 22(4). 589–646.

Barker, M. A. R. 1963. *Klamath dictionary*. UCPL 31. Berkeley and Los Angeles: University of California Press.

Barker, M. A. R. 1964. *Klamath grammar*. UCPL 32. Berkeley and Los Angeles: University of California Press.

Bates, Dawn & Carlson, Barry. 1992. Simple syllables in Spokane Salish. *Linguistic Inquiry* 23. 653–659.

Beck, D. 1999. Words and prosodic phrasing in Lushootseed narrative. In *Amsterdam Studies in the Theory and History of Linguistic Science Series 4*, 23–46. Chicago: John Benjamins.

Bermúdez-Otero, R. 2017. Stratal phonology. In Hannahs, S. J. & Bosch, Anna R. K. (eds.), *The Routledge Handbook of Phonological Theory*, 100–134. Routledge.

Bermúdez-Otero, R. & Luís, A. R. 2009. Cyclic domains and prosodic spans in the phonology of European Portuguese functional morphs. (Workshop on the Division of Labour between Morphology and Phonology & Fourth Meeting of the Network 'Core Mechanisms of Exponence'. Meertens Instituut, Amsterdam (vol. 16)).

Bianco, Violet. 1994. *The role of sonority in the prosody of Cowichan*. Victoria: University of Victoria (MA thesis.

Bianco, Violet. 1995. Stress in Lushootseed – A preliminary analysis. (Working Papers for the 30th International Conference on Salish and Neighbouring Languages, 127–136. Victoria, BC.)

Blake, S. J. 2000. *On the distribution and representation of Schwa in Sliammon (Salish)*. Vancouver: University of British Columbia. (Doctoral dissertation.)

Blevins, Juliette. 1993. Klamath Laryngeal phonology. *International Journal of American Linguistics* 59(3). 237–279.

Bloomfield, Leonard. 1946. Algonquian. *Linguistic structures of Native America* 6. 85–129.

Bloomfield, Leonard. 1957. *Eastern Ojibwa: Grammatical sketch, texts and word list*. University of Michigan Press.

Bobaljik, Jonathan David. 1996. Assimilation in the Inuit languages and the place of the uvular nasal. *International Journal of American Linguistics*, 62(4). 323–350.

Brittain, J. 2001. *The morphosyntax of the Algonquian conjunct verb: A minimalist approach*. Oxford: Routledge. (Outstanding Dissertations in Linguistics.)

Bruening, B. 2001. *Syntax at the edge: Cross-clausal phenomena and the syntax of Passamaquoddy*. Cambridge, MA: MIT. (Doctoral dissertation.)

Bruening, B. 2005. *The Algonquian inverse system is syntax: Binding in Passamaquoddy*. Newark: University of Delaware. (Ms.)

Bruening, B. 2009. Algonquian languages have A-movement and A-agreement. *Linguistic Inquiry* 40. 427–445.

Buckley, E. 2000. On the naturalness of unnatural rules. (*Proceedings from the Second Workshop on American Indigenous Languages*, 1–14.)

Bye, P. & de Lacey, P. 2008. Metrical influences on lenition and fortition. In Brandão de Carvalho, Joaquim & Scheer, Tobias & Ségéral, Philippe (eds.), *Lenition and Fortition*, 173–206. Berlin: Mouton de Gruyter.

Chomsky, N. 1995. *The minimalist program* (Current Studies in Linguistics 28). Cambridge.

Clements, G. N. & Keyser, S. J. 1983. *CV phonology: A generative theory of the syllable*. Cambridge, MA: MIT Press.

Cole, Jennifer. 1987. *Planar phonology and morphology*. Cambridge: Massachusetts Institute of Technology. (Doctoral dissertation.)

Cole, Jennifer & Trigo, Loren. 1988. Parasitic harmony. In van der Hulst, Harry & Smith, Norval (eds.), *Features, segmental structure and harmony processes (Part II)*, 19–38. Dordrecht: Foris.

Compton, Richard & Dresher, B. Elan. 2011. Palatalization and "strong i" across Inuit dialects. *Canadian Journal of Linguistics/Revue canadienne de linguistique*, 56(2). 203–228.

Compton, Richard & Pittman, Christine. 2010. Word-formation by phase in Inuit. *Lingua*, 120(9). 2167–2192.

Crippen, James & Dechaine, Rose-Marie. 2016. How syntax and phonoloherd(e)rive Na-Dene morphology. (Paper presented at the Word & Morpheme Workshop, Berlin.)

Currie-Hall, Daniel. 2007. *The role and representation of contrast in phonological theory*. Toronto: University of Toronto. (Doctoral dissertation.)

Czaykowska-Higgins, E. 1997. The morphological and phonological constituent structure of words in Moses-Columbia Salish (Nxaʔamxcín). *Trends in Linguistics Studies and Monographs* 107. 153–196.

Czaykowska-Higgins, Ewa & Willett, Marie Louise. 1997. Simple syllables in Nxaʔamxcín. *International Journal of American Linguistics*, 63(3). 385–411.

D'Arcy, Alex. 2003. Yowlumne reexamined: A challenge for contrastive specification. *Toronto Working Papers in Linguistics* 20. 21–46.

Déchaine, R.-M. 1999. What Algonquian morphology is really like: Hockett revisited. In Bar-el, L. & Déchaine, R.-M. & Reinholtz, C. (eds.), *Papers from the workshop on structure and constituency in Native American languages*. MIT Occasional Papers in Linguistics 17, 25–72. Cambridge: MIT Working Papers in Linguistics.

Dieterman, Julia Irene. 2008. *Secondary palatalization in Isthmus Mixe: A phonetic and phonological account*. University of Texas at Arlington. SIL International. (Doctoral dissertation.)

Dixon, R. M. & Aikhenvald, A. Y. (eds.). 2003. *Word: A cross-linguistic typology*. Cambridge University Press.

Dorais, Louis-Jacques. 1990. *Inuit Uqausiqatigiit-Inuit languages and dialects*. Iqaluit, NWT: Arctic College.

Dresher, B. Elan & Johns, Alana. 1995. The Law of Double Consonants in Inuktitut. *Linguistica Atlantica* 17. 79–95.

Dyck, C. 2009. Defining the word in Cayuga (Iroquoian). *International Journal of American Linguistics* 75(4). 571–605.

Fortescue, Michael & Jacobson, Steven A. & Kaplan, Lawrence D. 1994. *Comparative Eskimo dictionary with Aleut cognates*. Fairbanks: Alaska Native Language Center.

Goad, Heather & Travis, Lisa. In preparation. *Navajo Verbal Morphology and the Syntax/Phonology Interface*. McGill University. (Ms.)

Goldsmith, John. 1990. *Autosegmental & metrical phonology*. Oxford: Blackwell.

Gouskova, M. 2007. The reduplicative template in Tonkawa. *Phonology* 24(3). 367–396.

Guekguezian, P. A. 2017. Templates as the interaction of recursive word structure and prosodic well-formedness. *Phonology*, 34(1). 81–120.

Halle, M. & Vergnaud, J. R. 1981. Harmony processes. In Klein, Wolfgang & Levelt, Willem (eds.), *Crossing the boundaries in linguistics*, 1–22. Dordrecht: Springer.

Halle, Morris & Marantz, Alec. 1994. Some key features of Distributed Morphology. *MIT Working Papers in Linguistics* 21. 275–288.

Halle, Morris & Marantz, Alec. 1993. Distributed morphology and the pieces of inflection. In Hale, K. & Keyser, S. J. (eds.), *The View from Building 20*, 111–176. Cambridge, MA: MIT Press.

Hansson, Gunnar Ólafur. 2010. *Consonant harmony: Long-distance interaction in phonology*. University of California Publications in Linguistics, 145. Berkeley, CA: University of California Press.

Hargus, Sharon. 2010. Athabaskan phonetics and phonology. *Language and Linguistics Compass* 4(10). 1019–1040.

Harley, Heidi. 2010. Affixation and the mirror principle. In Folli, Raffaella & Ulbrich, Christiane (eds.), *Interfaces in linguistics: New research perspectives*, 166–186.

Haspelmath, M. 2011. The indeterminacy of word segmentation and the nature of morphology and syntax. *Folia linguistica* 45(1). 31–80.

Hayes, Bruce. 1982. Extrametricality and English stress. *Linguistic Inquiry* 13(2). 227–276.

Hayes, Bruce. 1995. *Metrical stress theory: Principles and case studies*. Chicago, IL: University of Chicago Press.

Hoard, J. E. 1978. Syllabication in northwest Indian languages, with remarks on the nature of syllabic stops and affricates. In Bell, A. & Hooper, J. B. (eds.), *Syllables and segments*. North Holland, Amsterdam.

Hoijer, Harry. 1946. Tonkawa. In Hoijer, Harry, Bloomfield, L. & Haas, M. R. & Halpern, A. M. & Li, F. K. & Newman, S. S. & Swadesh, M. & Trager, G. L. & Voegelin, C. F. & Whorf, B. L. (eds.), *Linguistic structures of native America*, 289–311. New York: Viking Fund.

Howren, R. 1971. A formalization of the Athabaskan 'D-effect'. *International Journal of American Linguistics* 37. 96–113.

Inkelas, Sharon. 1989. *Prosodic constituency in the lexicon*. New York: Garland Press.

Inkelas, Sharon. 1993. Deriving cyclicity. In Hargus, Sharon & Kaisse, Ellen M. (eds.), *Phonetics and phonology, vol. 4. Studies in lexical phonology*, 75–110. San Diego, CA: Academic Press.

Iosad, P. 2017. Optimality theory: Motivations and perspectives. In Hannahs, S. J. & Bosch, Anna R. K. (eds.), *The Routledge handbook of phonological theory*, 27–50. Routledge.

Julien, M. 2002. *Syntactic heads and word formation*. Oxford University Press on Demand.

Jurgec, Peter. 2013. Two types of parasitic assimilation. *Nordlyd* 40(1). 108–135. In Blaho, Sylvia & Krämer, Martin & Morén-Duolljá, Bruce (eds.), *A festschrift on the occasion of X years of CASTL phonology and Curt Rice's Lth birthday*. University of Tromsø.

Kari, J. 1976. *Navajo verb prefix phonology*. New York: Garland.

Kaun, Abigail R. 1995. *The typology of rounding harmony: An optimality theoretic approach*. Los Angeles: University of California. (Doctoral dissertation.)

Kaun, Abigail R. 2004. The typology of rounding harmony. In Hayes, Bruce & Kirchner, Robert & Steriade, Donca (eds.), *Phonetically based phonology*, 87–116. Cambridge: Cambridge University Press.

Kaye, Jonathan. 1978. Rule mitosis: The historical development of Algonquian palatalization. In Cook, Eung-Do & Kaye, J. (eds.), *Linguistic studies of Native Canada*, 143–156. UBC Press.

Kaye, Jonathan. 1990. 'Coda' licensing. *Phonology* 7(1). 301–330.

Kaye, Jonathan & Lowenstamm, Jean & Vergnaud, Jean-Roger. 1985. The internal structure of phonological representations: A theory of charm and government. *Phonology Yearbook* 2. 305–328.

Kaye, Jonathan & Lowenstamm, Jean & Vergnaud, Jean-Roger. 1990. Constituent structure and government in phonology. *Phonology* 7(2) (*Phonological Government*). 193–231.

Kaye, Jonathan & Piggott, Glyne & Tokaichi, K. 1971. *Odawa language project: First report*. Department of Anthropology, University of Toronto.

Kenstowicz, Michael J. & Kisseberth, Charles W. 1977. *Topics in phonological theory*. New York: Academic Press.

Kenstowicz, Michael J. & Kisseberth, Charles W. 1979. *Generative phonology: Description and theory*. New York: Academic Press.

Kingston, John. 1985. *The phonetics and phonology of the timing of oral and glottal events*. Berkeley: University of California. (Doctoral dissertation.)

Kingston, John. 1990. Articulatory binding. In Kingston, J. & Beckman, M. (eds.), *Papers in laboratory phonology I: Between the grammar and the physics of speech*. Cambridge: Cambridge University Press.

Kinkade, D. M. 1998. How much does a schwa weigh? In Czaykowska-Higgins, E. & Kinkade, M. D. (eds.), *Salish languages and linguistics: Theoretical and descriptive perspectives*, 197–216. New York: Mouton de Gruyter.

Kiparsky, P. 1982. From cyclic phonology to lexical phonology. *The Structure of Phonological Representations* 1. 131–175.

Kiparsky, P. 1985. Some consequences of lexical phonology. *Phonology* 2(1). 85–138.

Kisseberth, Charles W. 1969. *Theoretical implications of Yawelmani phonology*. Urbana: University of Illinois (Doctoral dissertation.)

Kisseberth, Charles W. 1970. Vowel elision in Tonkawa and derivational constraints. In Sadock, J. & Vanek, A. (eds.), *Studies presented to Robert B. Lees by his students*. Papers in Linguistics, Monograph Series I. Champaign, IL: Linguistic Research, Inc.

Krämer, M. 2017. Current issues and directions in optimality theory: Constraints and their interaction. In Hannahs, S. J. & Bosch, Anna R. K. (eds.), *The Routledge handbook of phonological theory*, 51–81. Routledge.
Krämer, Martin. 2003. *Vowel harmony and correspondence theory*. Berlin: Mouton de Gruyter.
Kuroda, Sige-Yuki. 1967. *Yawelmani phonology*. Cambridge, MA: MIT Press.
Leonard, J. 2006. *Formalising stress in Senćoten*. University of Victoria. (MA thesis.)
Leonard, J. 2007. A preliminary account of stress in SENĆOŦEN (Saanich/North Straits Salish). *Northwest Journal of Linguistics* 1(4). 1–59.
LeSourd, Philip S. 1993. *Accent and syllable structure in Passamaquoddy*. Garland Publishing.
Levin, J. 1987. Between epenthetic and excrescent vowels (or what happens after redundancy rules). In Crowhurst, M. (ed.), *Proceedings of the West Coast Conference on Formal Linguistics* 6. Stanford, CA: Stanford Linguistics Association.
Lochbihler, B. 2008. Person encoding in the Ojibwe inverse system. In Richards, M. & Malchukov, A. J. (eds.), *Linguistische Arbeits Berichte*, vol. 86, 295–315. Universität Leipzig.
Lochbihler, B. & Mathieu, E. 2013. Wh-agreement in Ojibwe relative clauses: Evidence for CP structure. *Canadian Journal of Linguistics/Revue canadienne de linguistique* 58(2). 293–318.
Lombardi, Linda. 1991. *Laryngeal features and laryngeal neutralization*. Amherst: University of Massachusetts. (Doctoral dissertation.)
Lombardi, Linda. 1995. Laryngeal neutralization and syllable wellformedness. *Natural Language & Linguistic Theory* 13(1). 39–74.
Lowe, Ronald. 1984. *Basic Siglit Inuvialuit Eskimo dictionary*. Committee for Original Peoples Entitlement, Inuvik. Quebec: Association Inuksiutiit Katimajiit Inc.
Lowe, Ronald. 1985. *Kangiryuarmiut Uqauhingita Ilihautdjutikhangit* [Basic Kangiryuarmiut Eskimo Grammar]. Inuvik: Committee for the Original Peoples Entitlement.
Lowenstamm, Jean. 1996. CV as the only syllable type. In Durand, Jacques & Laks, Bernard (eds.), *Current trends in phonology. Models and methods*, vol. 2, 419–441. Salford, Manchester: ESRI. WEB.
MacKay, Carolyn J. 1999. *A grammar of Misantla Totonac*. Salt Lake City: University of Utah Press.
Marantz, A. 2007. Phases and words. In Marantz, Alec & Choe, Sook-Hee & Yang, Dong-Wee & Kim, Yang-Soon & Kim, Sung-Hun (eds.), *Phases in the theory of grammar*, 191–222. Dong-In Publishing Co.
Marlett, Stephen A. 1992. Nasalization in Mixtec languages. *International Journal of American Linguistics* 58(4). 425–435.
Matthewson, L. 1994a. Syllable structure in St'at'imcets. In Koskinen, P. (ed.), *Toronto Working Papers in linguistics: Proceedings of the Canadian Linguistics Association*. Toronto: Department of Linguistics, University of Toronto.
Matthewson, L. 1994b. Optimality and syllable structure in St'at'imcets. UBC Generals paper.
McCarthy, John & Prince, Alan. 1999 (1986). Prosodic morphology. In Goldsmith, John A. (ed.), *Phonological theory: The essential readings*, 238–288. Oxford: Blackwell.
McCarthy, John J. 1998. *Sympathy and phonological opacity*. University of Massachusetts, Amherst. ROA #252. (Ms.)
McDonough, J. 1996. Epenthesis in Navajo. In Jelinek, Eloise & Midgette, Sally & Rice, Keren & Saxon, Leslie (eds.), *Athabaskan language studies: Essays in honor of Robert W. Young*, 235–257. Albuquerque: University of New Mexico Press.
McGinnis, M., 1995. Word-internal syntax: Evidence from Ojibwe. In Koskinen, P. (ed.), *Proceedings of CLA Annual Conference Toronto Working Papers in Linguistics*, 337–347.
McMullin, Kevin James. 2016. *Tier-based locality in long-distance phonotactics: learnability and typology*. Vancouver: University of British Columbia. (Doctoral dissertation.)
Michelson, Karin. 1983. *A comparative study of accent in the five nations Iroquoian languages*. Cambridge, MA: Harvard University. (Doctoral dissertation.)
Michelson, Karin. 1988. *A comparative study of lake-Iroquoian accent*. Dordrecht: Kluwer.
Michelson, Karin. 1989, Invisibility: Vowels without a timing slot in Mohawk. In Gerdts, D. & Michelson, K. (eds.), *Theoretical perspectives on native American languages*, 38–69. Albany: SUNY Press.
Miller, T. L. 2018. *The phonology-syntax interface and polysynthesis: A study of Kiowa and Saulteaux Ojibwe*. Newark: University of Delaware. (Doctoral dissertation.)
Miller, Taylor L. 2015. A prosodic analysis of the word in Kiowa. In Wilson, David (ed.), *Penn Working Papers in Linguistics* 21, 1. University of Pennsylvania.
Mithun, Marianne. 2001. *The languages of native North America*. Cambridge University Press.
Mithun, Marianne. 2015. Morphological complexity and language contact in languages Indigenous to North America. *Linguistic Discovery* 13(2). 37–59.
Mohanan, K. P. 1982. *Lexical phonology*. Cambridge: Massachusetts Institute of Technology. (Doctoral dissertation.)
Montler, Timothy. 1986. An outline of the morphology and phonology of Saanich, North Straights Salish. *University of Montana Working Papers in Linguistics* 4.

Moshinksy, Julius. 1976. Historical Pomo phonology. In Langdon, M. & Silver, S. (eds.), *Hokan Studies, Papers from the First Conference on Hokan Languages: Janua Linguarum, Series Practica 181*, 55–75. The Hague: Mouton.

Nespor, Marina & Vogel, Irene. 2007 (1986). *Prosodic phonology: With a new foreword*, vol. 28. Berlin: Walter de Gruyter.

Newell, H. & Scheer, T. 2017. Prosodic domains: Overthrowing the hierarchy. (Paper presented at the 25th Manchester Phonology Meeting, Manchester 25–27 May.)

Newell, Heather. 2017a. The syntax–phonology interface in rule-based phonology. In Hannahs, S. J. & Bosch, Anna R. K. (eds.), *The Routledge handbook of phonological theory*, 197–225. Routledge.

Newell, Heather. 2017b. There is no word. Implications for the phonology-syntax interface. (Paper presented at *GLOW* 40. Leiden, 14 March.)

Newell, Heather & Piggott, Glyne. 2014. Interactions at the syntax – Phonology interface: Evidence from Ojibwe. *Lingua* 150. 332–362.

Newell, Heather & Scheer, Tobias. 2007. Procedural first. (Paper presented at the 38th Poznan Linguistic Meeting, Poznan, 13–16 September.)

Newman, S. 1947. Bella Coola I: Phonology, *IJAL* 13. 129–134.

Newman, Stanley. 1944. *Yokuts language of California*. New York: Viking Fund.

Noske, Roland. 1993. *A theory of syllabification and segmental alternation: With studies on the phonology of French, German, Tonkawa, and Yawelmani*, vol. 296. Walter de Gruyter.

Odden, David. 1994. Adjacency parameters in phonology. *Language* 70(2). 289–330.

Parker, Aliana. 2011. It's that schwa again! Towards a typology of Salish schwa. *Working Papers of the Linguistics Circle of the University of Victoria* 21(1). 9–21.

Piggott, Glyne. 1980. *Aspects of Odawa morphophonemics*. Garland.

Piggott, Glyne. 1995. Epenthesis and syllable weight. *Natural Language & Linguistic Theory* 13(2). 283–326.

Piggott, Glyne. 1996. Implications of consonant nasalization for a theory of harmony. *Canadian Journal of Linguistics/Revue canadienne de linguistique* 41(2). 141–174.

Piggott, Glyne. 1997. Licensing and alignment: A conspiracy in harmony. *Phonology* 14. 437–477.

Piggott, Glyne & Kaye, Jonathan. 1973. *Odawa language project: Second report*. Centre for Linguistic Studies, University of Toronto.

Purnell, T. 2017. Rule-based phonology: Background, principles and assumptions. In Hannahs, S. J. & Bosch, Anna R. K. (eds.), *The Routledge handbook of phonological theory*, 135–166. Routledge.

Rankin, R. L. & Boyle, J. & Graczyk, R. & Koontz, J. E. 2003. Synchronic and diachronic perspective on 'word' in Siouan. In Dixon, R. M. & Aikhenvald, A. Y. (eds.), *Word: A cross-linguistic typology*, 180–204. Cambridge University Press.

Rice, K. D. 1993. The structure of the slave (northern Athabaskan) verb. In Kaisse, Ellen M. & Hargus, Sharon (eds.), *Studies in lexical phonology*, 145–171. Academic Press.

Rigsby, B. & Silverstein, M. 1969. Nez Perce vowels and proto-Sahaptian vowel harmony. *Language*, 45–59.

Rose, Yvan & Pigott, Paul & Wharram, Douglas. 2012. Schneider's law revisited: The syllable-level remnant of an older metrical rule. In *Phonology in the 21st century in honour of Glyne Piggott. McGill Working Papers in Linguistics*, 22(1). Montréal.

Russell, K. 1999. The "word" in two polysynthetic languages. In Hall, Alan T. & Kleinhenz, Ursula (eds.), *Studies on the Phonological Word*, 203–221. Amsterdam: John Benjamins.

Sapir, E. & Hoijer, H. 1967. *The phonology and morphology of the Navaho language*, vol. 50. University of California Press.

Scheer, Tobias. 2004. *A lateral theory of phonology*, vol. 1: *What is CVCV and Why Should it Be?* Berlin: Mouton de Gruyter.

Scheer, Tobias. 2012. *Direct interface and one-channel translation. A non-diacritic theory of the morphosyntax-phonology interface. Vol. 2 of a lateral theory of phonology*. Berlin: Mouton de Gruyter.

Scheer, Tobias. 2013. Why phonology is flat: The role of concatenation and linearity. *Language Sciences* 39. 54–74.

Scheer, Tobias. 2015. *Précis de structure sy labique: accompagné d'un apparat critique*. Lyon: ENS Éditions.

Schneider, Lucien. 1972. *Inukti tuorutit: grammaire purement esquimaude*. Québec: Ministère des Richesses Naturelles.

Ségéral, P. & Scheer, T. 2008. The Coda mirror, stress and positional parameters. In Brandão de Carvalho, Joaquim & Scheer, Tobias & Ségéral, Philippe (eds.), *Lenition and Fortition*, 483–518. Berlin: Mouton de Gruyter.

Selkirk, Elizabeth. 1978. On prosodic structure and its relationship to syntactic structure. In Fretheim, Thorstein (ed.), *Nordic Prosody*, vol. 2, 111–140. Trondheim: TAPIR.

Selkirk, Elizabeth. 1984. *Phonology and syntax: The relation between sound and structure*. Cambridge, MA: The MIT Press.

Selkirk, Elizabeth. 1986. On derived domains in sentence phonology. *Phonology* 3. 371–405.

Shaw, Patricia A. 1980. *Theoretical issues in Dakota phonology and morphology*. Garland Publishing.

Shaw, Patricia A. 1991. Consonant harmony systems: The special status of coronal harmony. In Paradis, Carole & Prunet, Jean-François (eds.), *The special status of coronals: Internal and external evidence*, 125–157. Academic Press.

Shaw, Patricia A. 2002. On the edge: Obstruent clusters in Salish. *Proceedings of WSCLA 7. UBCWPL* 10. 119–136.

Shaw, Patricia A. 2004. Reduplicant order and identity: Never trust a Salish CVC either? In Gerdts, D. & Matthewson, L. (eds.), *Studies in Salish linguistics in honor of M. Dale Kinkade*, vol. 17, University of Montana Occasional Papers in Linguistics. Missoula: University of Montana.

Shaw, Patricia A., Blake, Susan J., Campbell, Jill & Sheperd, Cody. 1999. Stress in hənq̓əmin̓əm̓ (Musqueam) Salish. In *Proceedings of the Workshop on Structure and Constituency in the Languages of the Americas, Dept. of Linguistics, UBC: University of British Columbia Working Papers in Linguistics*, vol. 2.

Shipley, William F. 1956. The phonemes of Northeastern Maidu. *IJAL* 22. 233–237.

Shipley, William F. 1963. *Maidu texts and dictionary*. Berkeley: University of California Press.

Shipley, William F. 1964. *Maidu grammar*. Berkeley: University of California Publications in Linguistics.

Smith, L. 1977. *Some grammatical aspects of Labrador Inuttut (Eskimo): A survey of the inflectional paradigms of nouns and verbs*. Mercury Series No. 37. Ottawa: Museum of Civilization.

Speas, M. 1991. Functional heads and the mirror principle. *Lingua* 84. 181–214.

Stanley, R. 1969. *The phonology of the Navajo verb*. Cambridge, MA: MIT (Doctoral dissertation.)

Steriade, Donca. 1981. *Parameters of metrical vowel harmony rules*. Massachusetts Institute of Technology. (Ms.)

Steriade, Donca. 1983. Syllable templates and syllabification rules. (Lecture delivered at the 1983 Sloan Conference on Phonology, University of Massachusetts, Amherst.)

Steriade, Donca. 1987. Redundant values. *Proceedings of CLS* 23(2). 339–362.

Straight, Henry Stephen. 1976. *The acquisition of Maya phonology: Variation in Yucatec child language*. Garland Publishing.

Szigetvári, P. 2011. The skeleton. In van Oostendorp, Marc & Ewen, Colin J. & Hume, Elizabeth V. & Rice, Keren (eds.), *The Blackwell companion to phonology, vol. 2*, 1263–1284. John Wiley & Sons.

Travis, L. 2010. *Phases and Navajo verbal morphology*. McGill University. (Ms.)

Urbanczyk, S. 1996. *Patterns of reduplication in Lushootseed*. Amherst: University of Massachusetts (Doctoral dissertation.)

Valentine, J. R. 2001. *Nishnaabemwin reference grammar*. Toronto: University of Toronto Press.

van der Hulst, H. 2016. Vowel harmony. *Oxford Research Encyclopedia of Linguistics* (Online). (https://harry-van-der-hulst.uconn.edu/wp-content/uploads/sites/1733/2018/01/157-ORE-Vowel-harmony.pdf)

van der Hulst, H. 2018. *Asymmetries in vowel harmony: A representational account*. Oxford: Oxford University Press.

Vaux, B. & Myler, N. 2017. Issues and prospects in rule-based phonology. In Hannahs, S. J. & Bosch, Anna R. K. (eds.), *The Routledge handbook of phonological theory*, 167–196. Routledge.

Walker, Neil Alexander. 2013. *A grammar of Southern Pomo: An indigenous language of California*. Berkeley: University of California. (Doctoral dissertation.)

Woodbury, A. C. 2003. The word in Cup'ik. In Dixon, R. M. & Aikhenvald, A. Y. (eds.), *Word: A cross-linguistic typology*, 79–99. Cambridge University Press.

Young, R. & Morgan, W. 1987. *The Navajo language*. Revised edn. Albequerque: University of New Mexico Press.

3

STRESS, TONE, AND PITCH ACCENT

Eugene Buckley

1. Introduction

This chapter offers an overview of word-level prominence and pitch in the languages of North America. The diverse languages of this large area show a similarly diverse set of properties, from stress similar to that found in English to complex tonal patterns reminiscent of East Asia or sub-Saharan Africa. Even languages that are fairly close in genetic relation can have quite different prominence patterns. Since it is impossible to discuss every language or every detail, the goal here is to give a sense of the range of possibilities.

Section 2 discusses languages with stress accent, which are best understood with the tools of hierarchical structure and rhythm in metrical phonology. Section 3 deals with languages that can be classified as tonal, and therefore amenable to a direct featural representation of pitch levels such as high and low. Section 4 focuses on the intermediate category of pitch-accent languages that combine properties of these two different kinds of systems; for example, a single main prominence that can be realized by more than one lexically determined tonal representation. Throughout, however, it will be clear that there is often no bright line to be drawn between these categories, and that even languages that largely follow the typology of a prototypical stress or tone language may show some effects of the opposite system, and could easily have been placed in the "pitch accent" category. I have also tended to follow a source's use of the term ACCENT even when it largely follows a metrical stress pattern.

2. Stress

Stress is an abstract representation of prominence, which can be phonetically realized in various ways (especially duration, pitch, and amplitude). Syllables can be classified not only as to whether they are stressed or unstressed, but often crucially as to their relative prominence. This hierarchical relation among prominences is a fundamental property of stress systems (Hayes 1995). As one would expect on this basis, every word will obligatorily bear at least one stress, as its metrical head, a property known as CULMINATIVITY; other prominences will be secondary or tertiary, and they will tend to occur rhythmically on alternating syllables. Their placement might or might not be sensitive to syllable weight, which can be defined differently in different languages, according to vowel length and syllable structure. Some of the languages discussed here are described in the literature as having a single prominence, or as having more than one "primary" stress. Closer analysis may show that just one of these is primary; even if the phonetic realization of the stresses is similar, there may be phonological evidence for one as primary.

The basic description of stress systems involves several left/right parameters. The creation of feet may be oriented to the left or right edge; the main stress (or head foot) of the word may be at the left or right; and a binary foot itself may be left- or right-headed. Another central question is the role of syllable weight, in particular whether the placement of feet is affected by the distribution of heavy syllables, in which case it is quantity-sensitive. Additional properties are relevant to more complex systems, such as whether a syllable at the edge of a domain is skipped by foot structure (extrametricality), and whether feet are always binary or can be unary (nonbranching) or ternary.

The native languages of North America have played quite an important role in the history of research on stress systems and in the development of metrical phonology. A notable characteristic of these languages is the frequency of left-edge iambic footing compared to languages in the world at large.

2.1. Left Orientation

Many languages have main stress that regularly falls on the first or second syllable of a word. Regular initial stress can be attributed to the left-headed feet, also known as TROCHEES, which serve to illustrate the range of parameters. First, consider QUANTITY-INSENSITIVE feet, where syllable weight plays no role. If feet are oriented to the left edge, we will find stress on every odd-numbered syllable. This pattern is very common in some parts of the world, such as among the Pama-Nyungan languages of Australia (Fletcher & Butcher 2014: 114); but it is not especially common in North America, where – as we shall see – sensitivity to syllable weight is more typical. It does match the description of Timucua (isolate; Granberry 1956; 1993), with primary stress on the first syllable and secondary stress on alternating syllables after that (excluding the final), indicating a left-to-right trochaic analysis.[1]

(1) Timucua stress

(ˈti.ra)	‘good’
(ˈa.ki)	‘air’
(ˈwa.ni).hi	‘wolf’
(ˈtʃu.lu).fi	‘bird’
(ˈa.ti)(ˌmu.ku)	‘frost’
(ˈli.ku)(ˌfa.ji)	‘mist’
(ˈti.ra)(ˌku.ku)la	‘best’

(Granberry 1956: 102–103, 105)

There are sometimes disruptions to a strict binary alternation in a way that seems to depend on morphological structure; for example, /ˈuluwaˌtari/, ‘worker’, evidently includes /tari/, ‘work’, although the morphology of the rest of the word is not clear from the sources.

In Tohono O’odham (Uto-Aztecan; Fitzgerald 1997), underived forms are stressed as in Timucua, similarly with no final stress; but morphologically complex forms with an odd number of syllables can include a secondary stress on the final syllable. Here, and throughout this chapter where relevant, roots are shown in bold.

(2) Tohono O’odham stress

(ˈhi.ma)	/**him**-a/	‘the walking’
(ˈta.ta)(ˌdai)	/ta-**tadai**/	‘roadrunners’
(ˈtʃik.pan)(ˌdam)	/**tʃikpan**-dam/	‘worker’
(ˈhai.waɲ)(ˌga.kam)	/**haiwaɲ**-ga-kam/	‘one owning a cow’
(ˈha.hai)(ˌwaɲ.ga)(ˌkam)	/ha-**haiwaɲ**-ga-kam/	‘one owning cows’

(Fitzgerald 1997: 84–91)

Fitzgerald attributes this difference to a requirement that, where possible, every morpheme receives a stress, even if it is final. Note that words with reduplication, as in /ta-tadai/, are morphologically complex.

More frequent is a pattern of left orientation in which the stress falls on the first or second syllable depending on weight. Some languages place stress on the first syllable, whether light (a) or heavy (b), unless the first is light and the second is heavy (c). This includes Tümpisa Shoshone, where syllables with a long vowel are heavy and secondary stresses alternate after the primary (Uto-Aztecan; Dayley 1989).

(3) Tümpisa Shoshone stress

a.	(ˈtu.kum)(ˌpa.na)(ˌpin)	‘sky’
	(ˈnat.tu)(ˌsu.ʔuŋ)(ˌkan.tɨn)	‘doctor’
b.	(ˈpa:)(ˌkan.tɨn)	‘having water’
c.	tɨ(ˈtsɨ:n)(ˌna)	‘to count’
	pih(ˈna:)(ˌwi.tɨn)	‘bee’

(Dayley 1989: 436–438)

Contrast this with the analysis of related Cahuilla by Hayes (1995: 135), where an initial light syllable followed by a heavy is still stressed. By contrast, in Tümpisa, the stress shifts exactly in a light+heavy syllable sequence because there is no way for a MORAIC TROCHEE, a foot consisting of exactly two moras, to include both syllables; the solution is to skip the initial light syllable and build a proper foot over the heavy syllable (as Hayes 1995: 92 finds for unrelated Malayalam).

A word-final monomoraic syllable that would head a degenerate foot is optionally unfooted in phrase-final position, in which case the vowel of that syllable is usually devoiced. Further, initial syllables followed by /s/ or a geminate consonant show variation, and can pattern as either (b) or (c). When that syllable is skipped, it would appear to pattern as extrametrical, since the second syllable need not be heavy and would otherwise have no reason to attract the stress away from the first syllable.

(4) Tümpisa Shoshone stress variation

(ˈtsik.ka)ʔah	~	<tsik>(ˈka.ʔah)	‘cut’
(ˈto.so)(ˌnen.na)	~	<to>(ˈso.nen)(ˌna)	‘to wipe’
(ˈma.su)(ˌtu.hin)(ˌna)	~	<ma>(ˈsu.tu)(ˌhin.na)	‘to rub’

(Dayley 1989: 440)

Not shown here are various phonetic processes including the devoicing of final vowels, which occurs only when unstressed.

Somewhat similar is stress on the second syllable (a) unless the first is heavy (b). This is the classic IAMBIC pattern and is quite common in North America. An example is Hopi (Uto-Aztecan; Jeanne 1978), where the regular pattern follows this generalization.

(5) Hopi stress

a.	(koˈjo)ŋo	‘turkey’
	(tsaˈqap)ta	‘dish’
b.	(ˈpa:)wi.kʲa	‘duck’
	(ˈʔats)ve.wa	‘chair’
	(ˈtsats)qap.ta	‘dishes’

(Jeanne 1978: 33–36)

Two-syllable words consistently take stress on the first syllable, regardless of weight, as in *'ko.ho*, 'wood'; this has been attributed to extrametricality or another principle that prevents stress on final syllables (Hyde 2011). Final stress does occur on some exceptional imperative verbs.

Iambic footing is frequently accompanied by lengthening of stressed vowels that otherwise would be located in light syllables – called RHYTHMIC or IAMBIC LENGTHENING. It occurs in Chickasaw (Muskogean; Munro & Ulrich 1984), with similar but not identical facts for closely related Choctaw. The iambic structure that yields vowel lengthening is not the source of main word prominence, which is pitch accent (§4); thus I mark all foot heads here as secondary stresses.

(6) Chickasaw iambic lengthening

(liˌti:)hah	/**litiha**-h/	'it is dirty'
(saˌli:)(tiˌha:)tok	/sa-**litiha**-tok/	'I was dirty'
(tʃiˌbaʃ)li	/tʃi-**baʃli**/	'he cuts you'

(Munro & Ulrich 1984: 192, 195)

The last example illustrates that lengthening does not apply in closed syllables such as /baʃ/, which are already heavy.

In some languages, including Menominee (Algonquian; Bloomfield 1939), closed syllables count as light, so that footing and iambic lengthening are unaffected by coda consonants such as /h/. Following Hayes (1995: 219), the final consonant is extrasyllabic, indicated by < > brackets; in addition, a leftover light syllable at the right edge is unfooted.

(7) Menominee vowel length

a.	(neˈpɛ:)(maˈtɛ)se<m>	/nɛ-**pɛma:t**-ɛse-m/	'I live'
	(peˈma:)(tɛˈse)<w>	/**pɛma:t**-ɛse-w/	'he lives'
b.	(peˈmo:h)nɛ<w>	/pɛm-**ohnɛ:**-w/	'he walks along'
	(ˈpi:)(tohˈnɛ)<w>	/pi:t-**ohnɛ:**-w/	'he walks hither'

(Bloomfield 1939: 63)

Lengthening in open syllables applies only in the first foot of the word; in later branching feet, there is an unusual pattern in which long vowels are actually shortened in open syllables but lengthened in closed syllables (for discussion, see Hayes 1995; Milligan 2005). A long vowel following another long vowel is also shortened, as seen for the underlyingly long stem vowel in the first word of each pair.

2.2. Right Orientation

The simplest type of right orientation places stress on the final syllable of a word. In Ch'ol (Mayan; Vázquez Álvarez 2011), stress is regularly on the final syllable, in a domain that includes enclitics (8a). The basic pattern also applies in Spanish loanwords that have a different stress in the source word (8b).

(8) Ch'ol final stress

a.	buˈtʃul	/**butʃ**-ul/	'he/she is seated'
	bu.tʃulˈku	/**butʃ**-ul=ku/	'yes, he/she is seated'
	bu.tʃul.tʲo.kuˈla	/**butʃ**-ul=tʲo=ku=la/	'yes, we are still seated'
b.	ka.jeˈtax	< *gaˈlleta*	'cookies'
	tʲe.ʃeˈleʃ	< *tiˈjera*	'scissors'

(Vázquez Álvarez 2011: 44–45)

No alternating stresses are reported, so this pattern could potentially be treated as a single unbounded, right-headed foot.[2]

In Tübatulabal (Uto-Aztecan; Voegelin 1935), stress falls on the final syllable and on alternating light syllables preceding it; long vowels disrupt the count and are always stressed. The footing in (9) follows the analysis of Hayes (1995), where a final stress is required independent of foot structure demands, and preceding trochaic feet consist of exactly two moras.

(9) Tübatulabal stress

to(ˈhat)	/**toha**-t/	'he is hunting'
(ˈto.ha)(ˈki)	/**toha**-ki/	'I am hunting'
(ˈtʃa:)(ˈmin)	/**tsa:mi**-n/	'his acorn gravy'
(ˈtʃa:)mi(ˈla)	/**tsa:mi**-la/	'the acorn gravy (obj.)'
(ˈtʃa:)(ˈmi.ba)(ˈtsu:n)	/**tsa:mi**-batsu:-n/	'away from his acorn gravy'

(Voegelin 1935: 57, 72, 145)

Voegelin calls the final syllable the "main stress" but also states that preceding stresses are equally prominent, so all are here marked as primary.

A branching trochaic foot at the right edge will yield penultimate stress, on the second syllable from the end. This is a common pattern around the world and is found also in many North American languages. For example, this is the most commonly described pattern for Nahuatl varieties (Uto-Aztecan); deviations may be "very rare" as in Tetelcingo (Tuggy 1979). I have added stress marks here to match Tuggy's description, and assume a single trochee at the right edge.

(10) Tetelcingo Nahuatl penultimate stress

kɪ(ˈma.kak)	/kɪ-**maka**-k/	'(he/she) gave him/her'
o.kɪ.ma(ˈka.kɪ)	/o-kɪ-**maka**-k-ɪ/	'(they) gave him/her'
nietʃ.ma.ka(ˈtɪ.ka)	/nietʃ-**maka**-tɪka/	'(he/she) was giving me'

(Tuggy 1979: 23, 112)

Alternating rhythm is not typically mentioned in discussions of Nahuatl, but it is documented for Morelos Nahuatl (Velázquez Patiño 2014); this variety has main stress on the penult and alternating secondary stresses preceding it. The pattern indicates quantity-insensitive trochees from right to left.

(11) Morelos Nahuatl iterative stress

nik(ˌkʷah.kʷal)(ˌtɬaʃ.kal)(ˈma.ka) 'I give him/her beautiful tortillas'

(Velázquez Patiño 2014: 488)

It is possible that additional Nahuatl languages transcribed with just a primary stress will show, on closer examination, evidence for similar iterative footing.

Finally, note that orientation to a particular edge is not necessarily exclusive. For example, in Copainalá Zoque (Mixe-Zoque; Wonderly 1951), the primary stress regularly falls on the penult, but in domains of at least three syllables, a secondary stress falls on the initial syllable. This pattern indicates a trochaic foot at the right edge, and another at the left edge, which is potentially nonbranching. The domain of stress can be either a single word or a "close-knit phrase"; this constituent is not clearly defined, but examples include a verb with an auxiliary or adverb.

(12) Copainalá Zoque stress

(ˈmi.nu)	'he came'
(ˌmin)(ˈgeʔ.tu)	'he also came'
(ˌmin.geʔ)(ˈtu.tih)	'he came again'
(ˌmin.daŋ)geʔ(ˈtu.tih)	'you (pl.) came again'

(Wonderly 1951: 108)

The primary stress has a right orientation, but the secondary has a left orientation. Additionally, if the domain ends in a monosyllabic root, the stress is on the final rather than penultimate syllable; this indicates sensitivity to the morphological structure (see §2.5).

Another way in which both edges are involved can be seen in Creek-Seminole (Muskogean; Tyhurst 1987). Although this system is generally described as a PITCH ACCENT (see §4), it is presented here for its metrical interest. The accent in these closely related dialects falls on either the final or penultimate syllable; but the choice between these two is determined by calculating from the beginning of the word. Iambic feet are built from left to right, and the pitch accent aligns with the head of the rightmost foot.

(13) Oklahoma Seminole accent location

a.	(iˈfá)	'dog'
	(aˈmí)fa	'my dog'
b.	(oˈsá)na	'otter'
	(po.mo)(saˈná)	'our otter'
c.	(a.pa)(taˈká)	'pancake'
	(a.ma)(paˈtá)ka	'my pancake'

(Tyhurst 1987: 163)

Note in particular that although the accent is on one of the last two syllables, its location is shifted when a possessive prefix /am/ or /pom/ is added.

2.3. Ternarity

Languages may show a ternary pattern, with two unstressed syllables before or after a stress, in two basic ways. Fairly uncommon are iterative ternary alternations, which will be discussed below. But more common is EXTRAMETRICALITY, or skipping of a single syllable at an edge – most often the right edge, but sometimes the left. This is ternary in the sense that the stress can fall three syllables from the edge of the word, whereas most languages with bounded stress are restricted to a window of two syllables at either edge.

Combined with a trochee at the right edge, extrametricality can yield ANTEPENULTIMATE stress, i.e., on the third syllable from the end. Fixed antepenultimate stress is rather infrequent typologically (Hayes 1995: 205), but it can occur alongside penultimate stress in various ways. In Natchez (isolate; Kimball 2005), the metrical prominence occurs on the penult if it contains a long vowel (14a), otherwise on the antepenult (14b), or the penult in a disyllable (14c).

(14) Natchez accent

a.	te.kʷeˈpâ:.kĩ	'sit down!'
b.	te.kʷeˈpǎ:.tân.kĩ	'sit down, you two!'
	ˈʔǐ:m̥.ʃal̥.sik	'he agreed, so they say'
	taˈʔáts.pa.tsê: ˈné.tsi.yâ:	'is that man at home?'
c.	ˈkú.n̥a	'the water'
	ˈné.tsa: hû	'he is indeed at home'
	mâ:h ˈʃú.lûh	'look! a spider!'

(Kimball 2005: 396–397)

The prominence is realized as high on short vowels and rising on long vowels (see §4 on pitch accent), except that a falling pitch occurs on the penult in imperatives; this replaces the expected rising tone in (14a), which is the only example given for a long penult. Falling tone also occurs finally on interrogatives and exclamations, as seen in several examples.

Antepenultimate stress also occurs as a limited alternative in languages that normally have a penultimate pattern. Stress in Yokuts (possibly Yok-Utian; Newman 1944) is regularly penultimate but antepenultimate in words containing the durative suffix /xɔ:/ that was formerly a clitic (15a), and in certain three-syllable nouns, especially a particular class of plurals (15b).

(15) Choynimni Yokuts stress

a.	tʃ'eˈtʃ'e:.k'a.xɔʔ	'(it) was getting cold'
b.	ˈtʃ'e:.ʃa.ʃi	'dog (objective)'
	ˈne:.ka.ti	'maternal aunts'

(Newman 1944: 28)

Such examples can be treated as a trochaic foot at the right edge, but with a final syllable that is either extrametrical or excluded from the domain of stress assignment in some other way (for example, if /xɔ:/ can still be treated as a clitic).

In Plains Cree (Algonquian; Wolfart 1996), the main stress falls on the antepenult in words of at least three syllables, but this is accompanied by a secondary stress on the final syllable as well as alternating syllables before the main stress, without regard to vowel length. In disyllables, the stress is on the final syllable. So while the antepenultimate main stress might suggest a trochee with final extrametricality, that makes the final secondary stress surprising; and the full pattern indicates iambic feet from the right, with the complication that in words with at least two feet, the rightmost foot is skipped in determining the location of main stress.

(16) Plains Cree stress

(aˈtim)	'dog'
(ko:ˈnihk)	'in the snow'
(ˈos)(pwa:ˌkan)	'pipe'
(ˈne:)(hiˌjaw)	'Cree Indian'
(e:ˈkwa)(ho:ˌma)	'then this one'
(ˌka:)(toˈtah)(kaˌwa)	'this one told about it'
(ˌpa)(saˌkwa:)(piˈsi)(moˌwin)	'Shut-Eye dance'

(Wolfart 1996: 430–431)

Flynn (2008) proposes that the penultimate foot is selected as the primary stress by grouping the final two feet into a COLON, a constituent of two feet, which in this case is left-headed. He also discusses the fact that these iambs in Plains Cree are counterexamples to theories that predict iambs are always quantity sensitive, and the observation that they are nearly always constructed left to right.

Extrametricality at the left edge, combined with an iambic foot, can yield post-peninitial stress, i.e., on the third syllable. This is the default pattern in Kashaya (Pomoan; Oswalt 1961; Buckley 1994), where the initial syllable is extrametrical unless the word begins with a monosyllabic root. Here the root is /k'il/ 'point' with a prefix indicating action with the finger.

(17) Kashaya extrametricality

<du>(ˈk’il)(muˌc’a:)(laˌme?) /du-**k’il**-muc’-ala-me?/
‘point at each other going down!’
<du>(k’iˈla:)(laˌmuc’)(ˌme?) /du-**k’il**-ala-muc’-me?/
‘point down at each other!’
<du>(k’iˈla:)(laˌme:)c’i /du-**k’il**-ala-mec’-i/
‘point down out of (the window)!’
(Oswalt 1961: 228)

Evidence for secondary stress comes mainly from iambic lengthening; note that lengthening begins on the third syllable, rather than on the second as in Chickasaw, due to extrametricality.

Ternary alternations can occur in an iterative fashion as well, with stresses on every third syllable (barring the effect of syllable weight). This pattern is relatively rare in the world’s languages, but is found in Alutiiq (Pacific Yupik; Leer 1985); in this respect it differs from other Yupik varieties, which are binary. In the Chugach dialect, the first iambic foot places stress on the first or second syllable, but later stresses can skip two light syllables, yielding a ternary pattern of stresses that are marked as equal in prominence. Words are shown here with ternary feet, but another analysis is that the feet are binary with one syllable skipped (Hayes 1995). Note that a binary alternation can also occur if just two light syllables remain at the end of a word.

(18) Chugach Alutiiq iambic feet

(ˈpin)ka ‘mine (pl.)’
(ˈan)(ŋaˈka) ‘my older brother’
(ˈan)(tʃi.kuˈkut) ‘we’ll go out’
(ˈqak)(xʷa.iˈlu:)ni ‘she is winning’
(ˈat)(ma.kuˈtaχ)(tuˈtən) ‘you’re going to hunt’
(paˈla:)yaq ‘rectangular skiff’
(aˈʁi:)(təˈka) ‘my mitten’
(taˈqu:)(ma.luˈni) ‘apparently getting it done’
(uˈlu:)(tə.kuˈna:)ku ‘without watching it’
(maˈŋaχ)(su.quˈta:)(quˈni) ‘if he (refl.) is going to hunt porpoise’
(ˈkum)(la.tʃiˈwi:)(li.yaˈqu:)(ta.quˈni:)ki ‘if he (refl.) is going to undertake constructing a freezer for them’
(Leer 1985 *passim*)

All long vowels in these words are the result of iambic lengthening, which does not apply word-finally. Some complications are omitted, including the patterning of non-initial closed syllables and underlying long vowels.

2.4. Unbounded

The stress systems considered so far are BOUNDED in the sense that stress is never more than two (or three) syllables from a designated edge. Other patterns are UNBOUNDED: stress is sensitive to the location of certain inherently prominent syllables (typically those that are heavy, sometimes just long vowels), and will fall on the leftmost or rightmost heavy syllable regardless of how far from the edge of the word this might be. In the absence of a heavy syllable, stress then falls on the initial or final syllable, which need not correlate with the left or right orientation of the preferred heavy. The combination of these factors yields four basic patterns.

Stress in Mayan languages shows various interactions with syllable weight and word edges (Bennett 2016: 495f; England & Baird 2017: 181). In Huastec (Mayan; Larsen & Pike 1949), stress falls on the rightmost long vowel (19a) and is otherwise initial (19b); some accent marks are added here based on the clearly stated patterns.

(19) Huastec stress

a.	ja:ˈni:l	'many times'
	ˈbi:.nom	'giver'
	ʔe:.la:sˈwa:j	'(they) surely find each other'
	hu:ˈtʃu:k'.tʃik	'blisters'
	ʔa.laˈbe:l	'pretty'
	ˈʔa:ʃuʃ.lom	'field of garlic'
b.	ˈbi.tʃow	'town'
	ˈʔa.t'em	'salt'
	ˈhil.k'o.matʃ	'leftovers'

(Larsen & Pike 1949: 268)

This is a "default to opposite" pattern, since long vowels pull the stress to the right, but the default is at the left.

In Kwakw'ala (Wakashan; Boas 1947; Bach 1975), the reverse pattern holds: stress is on the leftmost heavy syllable (20a–b), otherwise on the final syllable (20c). An interesting aspect of weight in this language is that a non-glottalized sonorant in the coda makes the syllable heavy (20b), but not an obstruent or a glottalized sonorant (20c).

(20) Kwakw'ala stress

a.	ˈqa:.sa	'to walk'
	ˈbi:.bə.gʷa:.nəm	'people'
	ʔaxʷˈso:.le	'hellebore'
	wəl'ˈna:.kʷə.la	'to stop'
b.	ˈan.qa	'to squeeze'
	ˈsən.bənd	'the whole day'
	ˈmən.ya:.yu	'means of measuring'
	məˈxən.χənd	'to strike edge'
c.	bəˈxa	'to cut'
	gasˈxa	'to carry on fingers'
	an'ˈqa	'to put fire among'
	m'ə.kʷəˈla	'moon'

(Boas 1947: 218–219)

Notice the minimal pair of /anqa/ and /an'qa/ based on the presence of glottalization on the nasal consonant.

Other patterns are "default to same". For instance, in Northern Lushootseed (Salish; Hess 1977), stress is on the leftmost "prominent" syllable, otherwise the initial. The prominent syllables are those containing full vowels, i.e., vowels other than schwa. Generally, stress is on the leftmost full vowel (21a–b), but on the first vowel in a word containing only schwas (21c).

(21) Northern Lushootseed stress

a.	ˈtʃa.ləs	‘hand’
	ˈsba.dit	‘mountain’
b.	tʃəˈgʷas	‘wife’
	təˈyil	‘go upstream’
	gʷədˈbi.xʷats	‘blackberry bush’
	k’əˈda.yu	‘rat’
c.	ˈdʒə.səd	‘foot’
	ˈbəʃ.tʃəb	‘mink’

(Hess 1977: 404–405, 411)

Bianco (1995) treats the schwa-containing roots as underlyingly vowelless, with default left stress after epenthesis. Urbanczyk (1996) observes an apparent preference for stress on low /a/ compared to high /i u/, so that prominence might involve the relative sonority of a full vowel as well.

The fourth pattern, with stress on the rightmost heavy, otherwise the final syllable, is reported for Aguacatec (Mayan; McArthur & McArthur 1956). The source does not provide stress-marked examples longer than two syllables, so in practice this means that the stress is final (22a) unless the first syllable has a long vowel and the second does not (22b). A long vowel in the final syllable also attracts the stress (22c).

(22) Aguacatec stress

a.	ʔuˈmul	‘rabbit’
	ʔalˈk’om	‘thief’
	kaʔˈpen	‘day after tomorrow’
	wuˈqan	‘my foot’
b.	ˈha:.luʔ	‘today’
	ˈʔa:.k’ah	‘new’
	ˈʔe:.q’um	‘carrier’
c.	ʔinˈta:	‘my father’
	ʔaˈt̺s̺u:ʔtʃ	‘your milk’

(MacArthur & MacArthur 1956: 73–74)

It is not clear from the data whether word-internal closed syllables are heavy, since in (b) the final consonants could be extrasyllabic. If such syllables are heavy, then (c) illustrates a meaningful instance of “rightmost heavy”. The example /kaˈʃaʔ/ ‘box’, from Spanish *caja* with initial stress, shows that the native pattern is applied to loanwords.

2.5. Morphological and Lexical

In many languages, the placement of stress is sensitive not just to the distribution of particular syllable types, but also to the presence of general MORPHOLOGICAL categories – for example, the root versus the rest of the word, or prefixes versus suffixes – or to the idiosyncratic LEXICAL properties of specific morphemes, whether affixes or roots.

A relatively simple means of assigning stress is by reference to the root of the word. For example, Wappo stress is generally on the first syllable of the root and does not shift when suffixes or prefixes are added (Yukian; Sawyer 1991; Thompson et al. 2006).

(23) Wappo root stress

a.	ˈts'e.seʔ	/**ts'es**-eʔ/	'swim'
	ˈts'es.taʔ	/**ts'es**-taʔ/	'swam'
	ˈts'es.miː.meʔ	/**ts'es**-mimeʔ/	'going swimming right away'
	ˈts'e.sih.yaː.miʔ	/**ts'es**-ih-yaːmiʔ/	'going to go swimming now'
b.	hoˈyo.k'aː.laʔ	/ho-**yok'a**-laʔ/	'(birds) fly around'
	mo.ʔoˈhyo.k'a.kʰiʔ	/moʔo-**yok'a**-kʰiʔ/	'(birds) landed'

(Sawyer 1991: 14, 58, 63)

Some references to Wappo stress have been misled by the statement in Radin (1929: 12) that stress "is practically always on the antepenult". The next sentence makes clear that stress is on "the stem vowel"; the antepenultimate observation is perhaps a coincidence of the typical word length.

In Tahltan (Athabaskan; Alderete & Bob 2005), main stress falls on the first syllable of the stem, and a secondary stress on the prefix string that precedes it. If the prefixes make up just one syllable, the secondary stress will immediately precede the main stress (in a situation of clash). But with two or more syllables, a secondary stress falls two syllables before the primary, indicating a trochaic foot structure that is built from right to left. The basic morphological structure of the word is shown with '-' for more tightly bound CONJUNCT prefixes and # for less tightly bound DISJUNCT prefixes; the root is in bold.

(24) Tahltan stress

(ˌme)(ˈlaʔ)	/me-**laʔ**/	'his/her hand'
(ˌkaː)(ˈts'et)	/kaː#**ts'et**/	'I scratched it out'
(ˌʔes)(ˈθo.ne)	/ʔes-**θone**/	'my star'
(ˌʔu.diŋ̥)(ˈʔuː.da)	/ʔudiŋ̥-**ʔuːda**/	'did you (SG) whistle?'
(ˌme.ʔe)(ˈk'a.he)	/meʔe-**k'ahe**/	'his/her fat'
ʔu(ˌde.θiː)(ˈdlet)	/ʔudeθiː-**dlet**/	'we (DUAL) melted it'
ʔe(ˌdʒi.da)(ˈdaɬ)	/ʔedʒi#da-**daɬ**/	's/he's going hunting'

(Alderete & Bob 2005: 374)

The presence of long vowels does not affect the distribution of feet, which are therefore quantity-insensitive.

This pattern can be contrasted with that of Witsuwit'en, another Athabaskan language that also requires stress on a stem (Hargus 2005). Although the stem requires a stress, the main stress is usually on the leftmost foot of the word, often a prefix.[3]

(25) Witsuwit'en stress

a.	bə(ˈdə.ɢət)	/bə-**dəq**-(ə)t/	'above him'
	(ˈbə.də)(ˌt͡səts)	/bə-də**t͡səs**/	'her fist'
b.	səs(ˈɢuh)	/s-ə-s-**ɢuh**/	'I caught, grabbed it'
	(ˈsəs)(ˌɢuh)	/**səs**/ + /**ɢuh**/	'black bear deadfall trap'

(Hargus 2005: 400)

The last form is a compound of two stems, each of which must be stressed; but when the same sequence /səs/ is prefixal, it is unstressed. That is because Witsuwit'en avoids a foot consisting of a single syllable containing /ə/, and will create one only if necessary to stress a stem. A foot with two such syllables, however, is permitted, as in (*bədə*) in (25a). In fact, more subtle distinctions are necessary: the language shows a preference for stress on long over short vowels; closed over open syllables; and peripheral vowels over central schwa.

In Moses-Columbian (Salish; Czaykowska-Higgins 1993), default stress falls on the rightmost underlying vowel; in words with epenthetic vowels only, stress is on the first syllable (26a–b).[4] This calculation excludes prefixes, even if that is the only source of a full underlying vowel (26c).

(26) Moses-Columbian stress

a.	q'aˈlaχ	/**q'alaχ**/	'fence' (205)
	ha.naˈnik	/**hananik**/	'jackrabbit' (205)
	nq'ə.y'aˈpa.nəʔ	/n-**q'y'**-ap-anʔ/	'branded on the cheek' (215)
b.	ˈxʷə.w'əy'	/**xʷw'y'**/	'fly' (223)
	ˈk'ə.məlqs.txən	/**k'm**-lqst-xn/	'lower leg' (222)
c.	niʔ.wəpˈwə.pəlqs	/niʔ-wp-**wp**-lqs/	'hair in nose' (225)
	ʔatʃˈp'ən.p'ən	/ʔatʃ-**p'n**-p'n/	'windfalls, logs' (225)

(Czaykowska-Higgins 1993; page numbers indicated beside examples)

A possible analysis is that prefixes lie outside the main phonological word that includes the root and suffixes, and therefore outside the domain of stress assignment. Moses-Columbian also has a complex interaction of strong vs. weak roots and dominant vs. recessive suffixes that cannot be covered here.

Many languages have unpredictable stress for a significant number of morphemes, so its location must be lexically listed for those items. In Nez Perce (Sahaptian; Crook 1999), for example, stress is usually penultimate (27a), and most underlyingly long vowels are shortened when not stressed. This leads to shifts in the position of stress when a suffix is added. But nearly a third of nouns have a stress that does not move (27b).

(27) Nez Perce stress

a.	ˈpis.kis	/**piskis**/	'door'
	pisˈkis.ne	/**piskis**-ne/	'door-OBJ'
	ˈwe:p.tes	/**we:pte:s**/	'eagle'
	wepˈte:s.ne	/**we:pte:s**-ne/	'eagle-OBJ'
b.	ˈha:.ma	/**ha̲:ma**/	'man'
	ˈha:.ma.na	/**ha̲:ma**-ne/	'man-OBJ'
	wiˈwi.tseʔ	/**wiwi̲tseʔ**/	'log'
	wiˈwi.tseʔ.ne	/**wiwi̲tseʔ**-ne/	'log-OBJ'
	ˈqo.sa.lat	/**qo̲salat**/	'buck goat'
	ˈqo.sa.lat.na	/**qo̲salat**-ne/	'buck goat-OBJ'

(Crook 1999: 33–35, 319)

The roots that do not follow the regular penultimate pattern have to be marked with an underlying accent or diacritic of some sort to prevent a shift under suffixation, here indicated by underlining.

3. Tone

In a robust tone language, every syllable or mora can bear a distinct tone – unlike in a typical pitch accent language, where there is one locus of tonal contrast in the word. In reality, there may be limitations on tonal distinctions in particular positions, but I include in this section languages that have at least two possible locations of distinctive pitch in the word domain as well as those with a large number of tonal contrasts.

The Athabaskan languages can be divided into three groups: those in which a vowel followed by a glottal stop historically developed a high tone (H); those in which it became a low tone (L); and those that lack lexical tone (Krauss 2005). I give here the example of Dene Sųłiné (Gessner

2005), in which these constricted vowels became H. The tones H and L occur in all combinations in disyllabic words (28a); there are fewer trisyllables in the corpus, but several different patterns are attested, some of them only in morphologically complex words (28b). Note that H tone is marked by an acute accent, and L tone is unmarked. A predictable stress falls on the final syllable.

(28) Dene Sųłiné tone patterns

a.	LL	dɛˈnɛ	'people'
	LH	dʒoˈlɛ́	'ball'
	HL	ʔíˈtu	'jacket'
	HH	θíˈdá	'door'
b.	LLH	ʔɛ.dʒɛˈrɛ́	'cow'
	LHL	sɪ-tθíˈja	'my hair'
	LHH	ʔɛ-ɣéˈgɛ́s	'eggs'
	HLL	θáj.ðəˈrɛ	'death'
	HHL	ná.ðə́ˈrɛ	'alive, living'
	HHH	há.líˈjú	'everybody, all'

(Gessner 2005: 246–247)

Although stress appears to increase the pitch range for tones on that syllable, the distribution of tones themselves does not follow accentual restrictions. Tonal modifications occur in various contexts, including a H tone added in many possessive constructions (Li 1946).

There are three tonal accents in Acoma (Keresan; Miller 1965): high, falling, and glottal (a falling tone with glottal constriction, written here as creaky voice). The high is "unrestricted" and therefore is somewhat like a FREE stress accent that can occur on any syllable of the word; like stress, an accent is obligatory in every word (29a). However, H can be found on more than one syllable (29b), so that it is not culminative.

(29) Acoma high tone

a.	mú.ʃi	'soap'
	ma.jú	'song leader'
	kú:.ku	'winter'
	ja.ʔáí	'sand'
	gá.na.mi	'beans'
b.	dí.ní	'above'
	dá.wá:	'good'
	sbú:.ná	'pottery'
	sk'ú.rú:.ná	'peas'
	k'á.já.má	'chipmunk'

(Miller 1965: 8, 14)

The falling tone is more restricted, and normally occurs only on a nonfinal long vowel or diphthong (30a). However, it can also occur on a short vowel if the next onset is a sonorant and that syllable has a H tone (30b).

(30) Acoma falling tone

a.	sê:.tʃ'a	'I am warm'
	dʲâ:.na	'flour'
	síù.ní	'I know him'
	hí.jâ:.ni	'road'
	k'â:.ka:.t'i	'plaza'

b.	gû.ní	'he knows him'
	dʲâ.wá	'early'
	ʔis.dû.wá	'arrow'

(Miller 1965: 8)

As a falling tone, the glottal accent is subject to the same basic restriction to long nonfinal vowels; exceptions are monosyllables and baby talk words.

(31) Acoma glottal tone

sḛ̂:.tʃ’a	'my tooth'
tʃṵ̂:.dá	'plums'
wá.ʃṵ̂:.zá	'it fits him'
s’í.jṵ̂:.tse	'I took him'

(Miller 1965: 8)

Although the Acoma system is sometimes described as pitch accent, the possibility of several such accents in a word makes it less like the kinds of languages discussed in §4.

The languages of the large Oto-Manguean family of central and southern Mexico have complex tone inventories. For example, in the analysis of Matsukawa (2012), Chicahuaxtla Triqui has five level tones (32a) and several contour tones (32b).[5] Given such complexity, it is conventional to notate the tone levels with numerals, with 1 the lowest pitch and 5 the highest. Contour tones use two numerals to show the starting and ending pitch.

(32) Chicahuaxtla Triqui tonal distinctions

a.	ku^{5}	'bone'
	neʔ^{5}	'we'
	ne^{3}	'to sit, to live'
	ko^{2}	'twenty'
	ne^{1}	'naked'
b.	ne^{32}	'water'
	ne^{31}	'meat'
	jo^{23}	'light'

(Matsukawa 2012: Appendix)

There are certain distributional restrictions – for example, a level 5 tone occurs only on plain (not aspirated) vowels, and contours 31 and 23 occur only on monosyllables – but these contrasts are necessary to capture the attested distinctions.

The tone that occurs on a syllable can change in conjunction with a particular morphological process – in a manner that is more like tone languages than simpler pitch accent languages. A few pairs of words are given here for illustration.

(33) Chicahuaxtla Triqui tone modification

riã^{32}	'face'	riã^{4}=h	'my face' (217)
ku^{5}	'bone'	zi^{32}-kuh^{1} zi^{3}	'his bone' (184)
atʃe^{5}	'to walk'	atʃe^{3}	'she walks' (210)
atʂa^{5}	'sing-CONT'	g-atʂa^{2}	'sing-POT' (168)
ne^{3}	'sit, live-CONT'	ga^{2}ne^{23}	'sit, live-POT' (169)

(Matsukawa 2012; page numbers indicated beside examples)

Note that most polysyllabic roots have distinctive tone only on the final syllable, in which case it is marked only there. This culminativity is reminiscent of pitch accent, but the inventory of tones is considerably larger than one finds in typical pitch accent systems; the simplest view is that there is culminative stress upon which the tonal distribution depends.

In addition to their complex tonal systems, the Chinantecan languages (also part of Oto-Manguean) show intricate changes to the tone on a verb root depending on its place in a paradigm. The following examples illustrate this in Comaltepec (Pace 1990); in this notation, tones are indicated by superscript letters, and the acute accent indicates a BALLISTIC stress, characterized by "an initial surge and rapid decay of intensity" in the syllable, contrasted with more even CONTROLLED stress (with no accent mark); a plausible analysis is that ballistic-stress syllables involve post-vocalic aspiration (Silverman 2006).

(34) Comaltepec Chinantec tone in verb inflection

kó:^{L}	'I am playing'
ni^{L}-**kó:**^{LH}	'I will play'
ka^{L}-**kó**^{M}	'I played'
ko:^{M}-ʔ	'we are playing'
ni^{L}-**kó:**^{H}-ʔ	'we will play'
ka^{L}-**kó**^{H}-ʔ	'we played'

(Pace 1990: 42)

Peñoles Mixtec illustrates the effect of a floating L tone after certain words (Oto-Manguean; Daly & Hyman 2007). Its effect can be observed, for example, in a possessive construction; if the first word has a floating L (written ^{L}), it replaces what would have been a mid (M) tone on the first syllable of the second word, or combines with an existing H tone to create a rising (LH) contour.

(35) Peñoles Mixtec tonal patterns

a.	MM	kɨ.tɨ	'animal'
	MH	di.tó	'uncle'
	HM	kʷé.ɲu	'squirrel'
b.	MM^{L}	ndʒu.ʃi	'chicken'
	HH^{L}	ɲá.ɲá	'coyote'

(Daly & Hyman 2007: 167)

(36) Peñoles Mixtec with MH as second word

a.	MM MH	kɨ.tɨ di.tó	'uncle's animal'
	MH MH	i.dú di.tó	'uncle's deer'
	HM MH	kʷé.ɲu di.tó	'uncle's squirrel'
b.	MM^{L} MH	ndʒu.ʃi dì.tó	'uncle's chicken'
	HH^{L} MH	ɲá.ɲá dì.tó	'uncle's coyote'

(Daly & Hyman 2007: 168)

(37) Peñoles Mixtec with MM^{L} as first word

a.	MM^{L} MM	do.ko kɨ̀.tɨ	'animal's well'
	MM^{L} MH	do.ko ì.dú	'deer's well'
b.	MM^{L} HM	do.ko kʷě.ɲu	'squirrel's well'
	MM^{L} HH^{L}	do.ko ɲǎ.ɲá`	'coyote's well'

(Daly & Hyman 2007: 168)

The last form, /doko ɲǎɲá`/, includes a final floating L tone because it retains the potential to affect a following word in a larger sentence. The M tone behaves in a variety of ways as if it is not present in the tonal representation; as seen here, it is simply replaced by L rather than forming a contour tone as H does. This motivates treating M as unspecified, which is common in languages that have three level tones.

For more discussion of morphological tone in Oto-Manguean, see Palancar (2016) and other papers in the same volume.

3.1. Interactions with Stress

Tone languages may also have relatively salient stress, and this may affect the distribution of tones. For example, as mentioned earlier, in Triqui contrastive tones occur only on the final stressed syllable. In this section I discuss examples in which the location of stress is sensitive to the presence of tones.

In Masset Haida (isolate; Enrico 1991), tone is highly predictable and overlaps considerably with syllable weight; in most cases, syllables ending in a sonorant or containing a long vowel have H tone, whereas short open syllables and those ending in an obstruent have L tone. (Word-final closed syllables do not receive the H tone because of a final L intonational tone not dependent on lexical representations.) There are exceptional cases in which the opposite of the expected tone is found, however, so that syllable weight alone is not a sufficient criterion for predicting tone.

Words containing only low tones have primary stress on the final syllable and alternating secondary stresses before that (38). But the rightmost syllable with H tone attracts the primary stress, and this can be far from the end of the word (39). In that case, alternating secondary stresses are assigned from right to left preceding the H toned syllable, as well as preceding a secondary stress on the final syllable. Following Enrico's analysis, I show iambic foot structure built from right to left, with degenerate feet permitted.[6]

(38) Masset Haida stress with low tones

a. (ˌgu)(diˌsał)(daˈhid)
gudisałda-hid — 'worry-INCEPTIVE'

b. (ˌdla)(dałˌda)(daˈhał)
dladałda-da-hał — 'fall.down-CAUS-DIRECT.that'

c. (dlaˌdał)(daˌga)(daˈhał)
dladałda-ga-da-hał — 'fall.down-into.water-CAUS-DIRECT.that'

(Enrico 1991: 112)

(39) Masset Haida stress with high tones

a. (ˌk'u)(guˈdán)(ˌda)(ʔwaˌgan)
k'ugudan-da-ʔwa-gan — 'taste-CAUS-PLUR-PAST'

b. (giˈnán)(ˌt'sa)(ʔwaˌgan)
ginan-t'sa-ʔwa-gan — 'ask-into-PLUR-PAST'

c. (dlaˈwí:)(gaˌda)(sgaˌhał)
dlawi:-ga-das-ga-hał — 'fall-into.water-CAUS-almost-DIRECT.that'

d. (tsí:ˈgán)(ˌda)(ʔwaˌgan)
tsi:ganda-ʔwa-gan — 'wet.bed-PLUR-PAST'

e. (ˈskán)(ˌt'sał)(daˌgan)
skant'sałda-gan — 'be.lazy-PAST'

(Enrico 1991: 113–114)

Similarly, in Wichita (Caddoan; Rood 1996), primary stresses are assigned to all syllables containing a H tone; or in a L toned word, all syllables containing a long vowel (40b); or failing that, the rightmost voiced vowel bears the primary stress (40c). As in Haida, secondary stresses alternate from the primary stresses, but clash is avoided. I assume quantity-insensitive trochaic foot structure.

(40) Wichita tone and stress

a.	(ˌna.he:)(ˈhá.rih)	'creek'
	(ˌkin.ni:)(ˌt͡sa.ʔak)(ˈʔí:.has)(ˌʔih)	'alfalfa' ("that which does not die out")
	(ˈá.ra)si:(ˈt͡sí.te:)(ˌriw)	'you finished it (put an edge or border on it)'
b.	ni(ˈye:s.ki͡ts)(ˈʔi:s)	'baby' ("unripe child")
	(ˌti.ka)(ˈsi:skʷ)	'he has a beard'
c.	(ˌti.ka)(ˈʔa͡tss)	'he is eating it'
	na(ˌka.ʔa͡tss)(ˈkih)	'the one who is eating it'

(Rood 1996: 582)

There also are certain unexpected occurrences of secondary stresses in clash, which in many cases may be due to deletion of vowels after the assignment of stress.

Oklahoma Cherokee (Iroquoian; Lindsey 1985) has a complex tonal system with six different pitch patterns possible on a syllable, although there are various restrictions on their actual occurrence: low [à], high [á], low-high [ǎ], high-low [â], low fall [ȁ], and superhigh [a̋]. If low-high and high-low are treated as sequences of those simple tones – they occur only on long vowels, hence one tone per mora – we can count four distinct tonal elements (Uchihara 2016).

The following examples illustrate the different tonal patterns on a long vowel. Final vowels are not marked for tone since they are generally deleted, and when they surface they take intonational tones.

(41) Oklahoma Cherokee tones

nò:.ja	'sand'	
á:.ma	'salt'	
skǒ:.ja	'insect'	
tʰâ:.li	'two'	(from /tʰáʔli/)
nə̏:.ja	'rock'	
ő:.sta	'good'	

(Lindsey 1985: 123–124)

Although these words illustrate that Cherokee has some properties of a tonal language, it has accentual properties as well (Uchihara 2016). For example, in several morphosyntactic contexts, including subordinate verbs, adjectives, and derived nouns, an accent is assigned in a manner quite similar to an unbounded stress system (§2.4): a superhigh tone occurs on the rightmost long vowel of the word (42a); and if no long vowel is present, a high tone occurs on the initial syllable (42b). These pairs of words show first one without the accent, then a related word that does have it.

(42) Oklahoma Cherokee tone changes

a.	à.tǎ:.wé:.hi	'magician'	à.tǎ:.wé̋:.hi	'magical'
	tʃù:.kə̀:.wàɬ.ti	'wealth'	tʃù:.kə̋:.wàɬ.ti	'price'
b.	tʃʰà.wà.hi	'buy it!'	tʃʰá.wà.ski	'you are a buyer'
	ùw̥.tóh.ti	'for him to use it'	ákʰ.tòh.ti	'I have to use it'

(Uchihara 2016: 226–227, 238, 250)

This pattern suggests an abstract accented syllable that is determined according to a default-to-opposite metrical principle (Hayes 1995: 296–297), i.e., accent on the rightmost heavy syllable, otherwise the first syllable; and the realization of that accent conforms to the general restriction of superhigh tone to long vowels. Cherokee reinforces the observation that the basic tools of tone and metrical prominence can be deployed in quite complex ways in different languages – leading us to the next topic, pitch accent.

4. Pitch Accent

Researchers have taken different positions on the proper definition of pitch accent, and in particular whether this is a coherent category. Descriptively, pitch accent differs from tone in that there are not typically tones on multiple syllables (or if so, they are quite restricted); but there might be lexically determined tonal contrasts available in that single prominent location, such as level versus falling pitch. Many pitch accent languages – though certainly not all – permit unaccented words, which violates the obligatoriness that is characteristic of stress languages.

This section groups together several "pitch accent" languages as a matter of descriptive convenience. I nevertheless agree with Hyman (2009: 213) that pitch accent is not a formally distinct typological category, because "all one can say is that alleged pitch-accent systems exhibit significant constraints on the distribution of their tonal contrasts". Thus, what has been called pitch accent is often a tonal representation aligned with a prominent position. In this sense, it is a tonal realization of stress accent. Accepting that metrical structure and tonal elements are the basic ingredients of pitch accent, the boundaries between categories will necessarily be somewhat fuzzy, since a particular language may exploit these resources to a greater or lesser degree. In this section I focus on examples that are often described as pitch accent languages, in which a single position is associated with word-level tonal properties, but we will see that they reflect different combinations of metrical and tonal systems.

In addition to rhythmic lengthening similar to that in Chickasaw (§2.1), Oklahoma Choctaw (Muskogean; Ulrich 1986) has a pitch accent system with two basic parts. First, the stem of the word may receive a HL accent from various sources, where the H links to the penult or antepenult, and the L to the following syllable. This is an underlying property of about half the nouns in the language, plus a small proportion of the verbs. It also can arise in particular grades (infixation classes) of verbs, and in nominalizations. Second, word-final accent consists of a H tone linked to the final vowel of a word domain that includes clitics.

The words in (43) illustrate three possible noun patterns: no pitch accent, penultimate, and (rarely) antepenultimate. Phonologically active L tone is marked as an acute accent, but unmarked syllables also surface as L by default, marked with a grave accent. The more abstract stem form is shown in the left column, and the same stem when unsuffixed, with word-final accent and default L tone realization, is shown in the second column.

(43) Oklahoma Choctaw accent in nouns

ką̆ʃ.tih	ą̀ʃ.tíh	'flea'
fá.làh	fá.lăh	'crow'
tį́ʃ.kì.lah	tį́ʃ.kì.láh	'bluejay'

(Ulrich 1986: 69, 71)

The non-final accents could be derived by either metrical or tonal methods: the penultimate and antepenultimate positions are a common metrical locus, to which the HL accent could align; or (as Ulrich proposes), the HL tones could associate from right to left. In either case, antepenultimate accents require that the final syllable be extrametrical or extratonal. What makes Choctaw different from a stress accent language is that there are accentless stems. The word-final accent has some characteristics of an intonational tone, since it aligns with the right boundary. Note in /fálăh/ that the L of the HL accent must be phonologically present, so that addition of word-final H yields the rising LH tone.

Most verbs have no underlying accent, but they acquire a penultimate or antepenultimate accent in the various grades, which also involve infixation of segmental material and changes to segment length. As before, the first column in (44) shows the form before addition of word-final accent; the first line shows the basic form of each verb.

(44) Oklahoma Choctaw accent in verb grades

a.	nok.ʃo:.pah	nòk.ʃò:.páh	'he's scared'
	nok.ʃóh.pàh	nòk.ʃóh.păh	'he just got scared'
	nok.ʃóy.yò.pah	nòk.ʃóy.yò.páh	'he finally got scared'
b.	ta.lo.wah	tà.lò.wáh	'he sang'
	ta.lóh.wàh	tà.lóh.wăh	'he just sang'
	tál.lò:.wah	tál.lò:.wáh	'he finally sang'

(Ulrich 1986: 165, 168, 173–174)

Ulrich (1986; 1989) and Kim (1996) argue that tonal mechanisms yield the best analysis of Choctaw accent. The traditional classification as pitch accent simply reflects the relatively limited use of these tonal resources.

Words in Crow (Siouan; Graczyk 2007) bear one of three pitch accents: simple H on a short vowel, and level H or falling HL on a long vowel (45a). The accent can fall on any vowel of the word, as the set in (45b) illustrates.

(45) Crow pitch accent

a.	bâ:.la:	'winter'
	bá:h.pa	'boulder'
	xa.lá:	'rain'
	a.pâ:	'be cold
b.	í.li.tʃi	'be hit'
	i.lí.tʃi	'odor'
	i.li.tʃí	'hind quarter of animal'

(Graczyk 2007: 20)

Crow accent is overwhelmingly obligatory and culminative, i.e., words bear exactly one accent, with the exception of a few unaccented verb stems such as 'say' and 'exist'; this is similar to a stress accent. Consistent with culminativity is that – with minor exceptions – compounds of two accented morphemes surface with a single accent. On the other hand, the distinction on long vowels between level and falling tone is more like a tonal language. Also very much tonal in nature is a rule that spreads high tone to the leftmost long vowel preceding the accent (including intervening short vowels).

(46) Crow tone spreading

a.la.tʃi.wa.kâ:.u	'church'
am.má:.tʃím.mû:.a	'school'
bá:.í:.hú.lí.ʃó:.pé	'table'

(Graczyk 2007: 21)

Thus, in Crow we see a different combination of characteristics often associated with stress or tone languages, compared to Choctaw, which lacks obligatoriness but has a simpler tonal inventory.

As a third example, consider Arapaho (Algonquian; Cowell & Moss 2011). Here, accent is obligatory, since every word appears to carry at least one high tone; but not culminative, since more than one high tone is possible. The location of the tones in roots is not predictable. On a long vowel, falling tone contrasts with level H tone.

(47) Arapaho pitch accent

a.	bé.nes	'one's arm'
	wo.nóʔ	'one's ankle'
b.	né:.tʃe:	'chief'
	bi:.tʃî:s	'leaf'
	bî:.xú:t	'shirt'

(Cowell & Moss 2011: 24)

Adjacent H tones appear to be prohibited; thus long vowels in adjacent syllables can be HL-HH but not HH-HH. Pitch accent often changes according to the phonological and morphological context, as illustrated by these related verb forms.

(48) Arapaho accent shifts

a.	tʃe.ni:.né.n-o.wo:	'I am putting it down'
	tʃe.ní:.ne.n-óú.ʔu	'they are putting it down'
b.	bé:.ne-no:	'I am drinking'
	be:.ne-nó:.ni	'whenever I drink'
c.	hi:.té.n-oʔ	'he/she has gotten it'
	hí.te.n-o:	'take it!'

(Cowell & Moss 2011: 29, 31)

Many such changes involve accent on the penultimate syllable, or elsewhere within a three-syllable window at the right edge, which is a common pattern in metrical systems.

5. Conclusion

We have seen a wide range of prosodic prominence systems found in the languages of North America. Although some languages can be described strictly in terms of stress or (less often) tone, a consistent theme is that the tools of both theories are necessary, in varying degrees, to account for languages often grouped under the term pitch accent. Even many languages that do not ordinarily go by this name require some involvement of both theories in order for their facts to be analyzed properly.

Further Reading

Rice (2010) gives a thorough survey of accent patterns in North America, organized according language families; languages of Mexico are included when they belong to a family that reaches into the United States. Hulst et al. (2010), in the same volume, cover accent in the languages of Mesoamerica, including the families discussed here for their tonal properties. Herrera Zendejas (2015) includes ten articles on tone, accent, and stress in a range of languages of Mexico. Hayes (1995) discusses the metrical properties of many languages of North America, including stress and pitch accent. Yip (2002) includes a chapter on tonal languages of the Americas. Hyman (2006; 2009) addresses the vexed question of pitch accent, compared to stress accent and tone, using examples from throughout the world.

Notes

1. Here and throughout this chapter, primary stress is marked by [ˈ] and secondary stress by [ˌ] preceding the syllable. Parentheses mark foot structure. Syllable boundaries are indicated by a period [.] when not otherwise shown by stress marks or foot boundaries.
2. Morphologically complex structures may have a secondary stress on the final syllable of a word contained in the larger structure, such as a compound, but this is a matter of cyclicity rather than iterative footing.
3. There is, however, an alternative pronunciation in which the stem takes primary stress; thus the form (*ˈbədə*)(*ˌt͡səts*) can also be stressed as (*ˌbədə*)(*ˈt͡səts*).
4. For simplicity, all epenthetic vowels are written here as schwa, but these vowels take on various qualities depending on the adjacent segments.
5. See Hernández Mendoza (2017) for an analysis with four level tones and six contour tones. The five-level analysis is also discussed in Longacre (1952) and Elliott et al. (2016).
6. Enrico (1991) does not transcribe high tone, but accent marks are added here according to his description.

References

Alderete, John & Bob, Tanya. 2005. A corpus-based approach to Tahltan stress. In Hargus, Sharon & Rice, Keren (eds.), *Athabaskan prosody*, 369–391. John Benjamins Publishing Company.

Bach, Emmon W. 1975. Long vowels and stress in Kwakiutl. *Texas Linguistic Forum* 2. 9–19.

Bennett, Ryan. 2016. Mayan phonology. *Language and Linguistics Compass* 10(10). 469–514.

Bianco, Violet. 1995. Stress in Lushootseed: A preliminary analysis. In *Papers for the 30th International Conference on Salish and Neighbouring Languages*, 127–136. University of Victoria.

Bloomfield, Leonard. 1939. Menomini morphophonemics. In *Etudes phonologiques dédiées à la mémoire de M. le prince N.S. Trubetzkoy*, 105–115. Travaux du Cercle Linguistique de Prague 8. Prague.

Boas, Franz. 1947. Kwakiutl grammar, with a glossary of the suffixes. *Transactions of the American Philosophical Society* 37. 203–377.

Buckley, Eugene. 1994. *Theoretical aspects of Kashaya phonology and morphology*. Stanford, CA: Center for the Study of Language and Information.

Cowell, Andrew & Moss Sr., Alonzo. 2011. *The Arapaho language*. University Press of Colorado.

Crook, Harold David. 1999. *The phonology and morphology of Nez Perce stress*. UCLA. (Dissertation.)

Czaykowska-Higgins, Ewa. 1993. Cyclicity and stress in Moses-Columbia Salish (Nxa'amxcin). *NLLT* 11. 197–278.

Daly, John P. & Hyman, Larry M. 2007. On the representation of tone in Peñoles Mixtec. *IJAL* 73. 165–207.

Dayley, Jon. 1989. *Tumpisa (Panamint) Shoshone grammar*. University of California Publications in Linguistics 115. Berkeley: University of California Press.

Elliott, A. Raymond & Edmondson, Jerold A. & Cruz, Fausto Sandoval. 2016. Chicahuaxtla Triqui. *Journal of the International Phonetic Association* 46(3). 351–365.

England, Nora C. & Baird, Brandon O. 2017. Phonology and phonetics. In Aissen, Judith, England, Nora C. & Maldonado, Roberto Zavala (eds.), *The Mayan languages*, 175–200. Routledge.

Enrico, John. 1991. *The lexical phonology of Masset Haida*. Alaska Native Language Center Research Papers 8.

Fitzgerald, Colleen. 1997. *O'odham rhythms*. University of Arizona. (Dissertation.)

Fletcher, Janet & Butcher, Andrew. 2014. Sound patterns of Australian Languages. In Koch, Harold & Nordlinger, Rachel (eds.), *The languages and linguistics of Australia: A comprehensive guide*, 91–138. De Gruyter.

Flynn, Darin. 2008. Plains Cree and metrical typology. In *Alberta Conference on Linguistics, Banff*, October 25.

Gessner, Suzanne. 2005. Properties of tone in Dene Sųłiné. In Hargus, Sharon & Rice, Keren (eds.), *Athabaskan prosody*, 229–247. John Benjamins Publishing Company.

Graczyk, Randolph. 2007. *A grammar of crow: Apsáalooke aliháau*. Lincoln: University of Nebraska Press.

Granberry, Julian. 1956. Timucua I: Prosodics and phonemics of the Mocama dialect. *IJAL* 22(2). 97–105.

Granberry, Julian. 1993. *A grammar and dictionary of the Timucua language*. University of Alabama Press.

Hargus, Sharon. 2005. Prosody in two Athabaskan languages of northern British Columbia. In Hargus, Sharon & Rice, Keren (eds.), *Athabaskan prosody*, 393–423. John Benjamins Publishing Company.

Hayes, Bruce. 1995. *Metrical stress theory: Principles and case studies*. University of Chicago Press.

Hernández Mendoza, Fidel. 2017. *Tono y fonología segmental en el triqui de Chicahuaxtla*. Universidad Nacional Autónoma de México. (Dissertation.)

Herrera Zendejas, Esther (ed.). 2015. *Tono, acento y estructuras métricas en lenguas mexicanas*. El Colégio de México.

Hess, Thom. 1977. Lushootseed dialects. *Anthropological Linguistics* 19. 403–419.

Hulst, Harry van der & Rice, Keren & Wetzels, Leo. 2010. The languages of Middle America. In Hulst, Harry van der & Goedemans, Rob & Zanten, Ellen van (eds.), *A survey of word accentual patterns in the languages of the world*, 249–311. Berlin: De Gruyter Mouton.

Hyde, Brett. 2011. Extrametricality and non-finality. In Oostendorp, Marc van & Ewen, Colin J., Hume, Elizabeth & Rice, Keren (eds.), *The Blackwell companion to phonology*, chapter 43. Malden, MA: Wiley Blackwell.

Hyman, Larry M. 2006. Word-prosodic typology. *Phonology* 23. 225–257.

Hyman, Larry M. 2009. How (not) to do phonological typology: The case of pitch-accent. *Language Sciences* 31. 213–238.

Jeanne, Laverne Masayesva. 1978. *Aspects of Hopi grammar*. Cambridge, MA: MIT. (Doctoral dissertation.)

Kim, Michael Jinhwa. 1996. *The tonal system of accentual languages*. Chicago, IL: University of Chicago. (Doctoral dissertation.)

Kimball, Geoffrey. 2005. Natchez. In Scancarelli, Janine & Kay Hardy, Heather (eds.), *Native languages of the southeastern United States*, 385–453. Lincoln: University of Nebraska Press.

Krauss, Michael E. 2005. Athabaskan tone. In Hargus, Sharon & Rice, Keren (eds.), *Athabaskan prosody*, 55–136. Amsterdam: John Benjamins Publishing Company.

Larsen, Raymond S. & Victoria Pike, Eunice. 1949. Huasteco intonations and phonemes. *Language* 25. 268–277.

Leer, Jeff. 1985. Prosody in Alutiiq (The Koniag and Chugach dialects of Alaskan Yupik). In Krauss, Michael (ed.), *Yupik Eskimo prosodic systems: Descriptive and comparative studies*, 77–133. Fairbanks: Alaska Native Language Center.

Li, Fang-Kuei. 1946. Chipewyan. In Hoijer, Harry & Bloomfield, L. & Haas, M. R. & Halpern, A. M. & Li, F. K. & Newman, S. S. & Swadesh, M. & Trager, G. L. & Voegelin, C. F. & Whorf, B. L. (eds.), *Linguistic structures of Native America*, 398–423. New York: Viking Fund.

Lindsey, Geoffrey Alan. 1985. *Intonation and interrogation: Tonal structure and the expression of a pragmatic function in English and other languages*. Los Angeles: UCLA. (Doctoral dissertation.)

Longacre, Robert E. 1952. Five phonemic pitch levels in trique. *Acta Linguistica* 7. 62–82.

Matsukawa, Kosuke. 2012. *Phonetics and phonology of Chicahuaxtla Triqui tones*. Albany: SUNY. (Doctoral dissertation.)

McArthur, Harry & McArthur, Lucille. 1956. Aguacatec (Mayan) phonemes in the stress group. *International Journal of American Linguistics* 22. 72–76.

Miller, Wick R. 1965. *Acoma grammar and texts*. University of California Publications in Linguistics 40. University of California Press.

Milligan, Marianne I. 2005. *Menominee prosodic structure*. Madison: University of Wisconsin. (Doctoral dissertation.)

Munro, Pamela & Ulrich, Charles H. 1984. Structure-preservation and Western Muskogean rhythmic lengthening. In Cobler, Mark & MacKaye, Susannah & Wescoat, Michael T. (eds.), *Proceedings of the Third Annual West Coast Conference on Formal Linguistics*, 191–202. Stanford Linguistics Association.

Newman, Stanley. 1944. *Yokuts language of California*. Viking Fund Publications in Anthropology 2.

Oswalt, Robert L. 1961. *A Kashaya grammar (Southwestern Pomo)*. Berkeley: University of California. (Doctoral dissertation.)

Pace, Wanda Jane. 1990. Comaltepec Chinantec verb inflection. In Merrifield, William R. & Rensch, Calvin R. (eds.), *Syllables, tone, and verb paradigms*, Studies in Chinantec Languages 4, 21–62. Arlington: Summer Institute of Linguistics and University of Texas.

Palancar, Enrique L. 2016. A typology of tone and inflection: A view from the Oto-Manguean languages of Mexico. In Palancar, Enrique L. & Léonard, Jean Léo (eds.), *Tone and inflection: New facts and new perspectives*, 109–139. Walter de Gruyter.

Radin, Paul. 1929. *A grammar of the Wappo language*. University of California Press.

Rice, Keren. 2010. Accent in the native languages of North America. In Hulst, Harry van der & Goedemans, Rob & van Zanten, Ellen (eds.), *A survey of word accentual patterns in the languages of the world*, 155–248. Berlin: De Gruyter Mouton.

Rood, David S. 1996. Sketch of Wichita, a Caddoan language. In Goddard, Ives (ed.), *Handbook of American Indians* 17: Languages, 580–608. Washington, DC: Smithsonian Institute.

Sawyer, Jesse O. 1991. *Wappo studies*. Report 7, Survey of California and Other Indian Languages.

Silverman, Daniel. 2006. Chinantec: Phonology. In Brown, Keith & Ogilvie, Sarah (eds.), *Concise encyclopedia of languages of the world*, 211–213. Oxford: Elsevier Ltd.

Thompson, Sandra A. & Park, Joseph Sung-Yul & Li, Charles N. 2006. *A reference grammar of Wappo*. University of California Publications in Linguistics.

Tuggy, David H. 1979. Tetelcingo Nahuatl. In Langacker, Ronald W. (ed.), *Modern Aztec grammatical sketches*, 1–140. Summer Institute of Linguistics.

Tyhurst, James J. 1987. Accent shift in Seminole nouns. In Munro, Pamela (ed.), *Muskogean linguistics*, UCLA Occasional Papers in Linguistics 6. 161–170. Los Angeles: Department of Linguistics, University of California.

Uchihara, Hiroto. 2016. *Tone and accent in Oklahoma Cherokee*. Oxford University Press.

Ulrich, Charles H. 1986. *Choctaw morphophonology*. UCLA. (Dissertation.)

Ulrich, Charles H. 1989. Tone association in Choctaw. *Southwest Journal of Linguistics* 9. 163–174.

Urbanczyk, Suzanne Claire. 1996. *Patterns of reduplication in Lushootseed*. Amherst: University of Massachusetts. (Doctoral dissertation.)

Vázquez Álvarez, Juan Jesús. 2011. *A grammar of Chol, a Mayan language*. Austin: University of Texas. (Doctoral dissertation.)

Velázquez Patiño, Eduardo Patricio. 2014. Intonation patterns of Morelos Nahuatl. In Campbell, Nick & Gibbon, Dafydd & Hirst, Daniel (eds.), *Proceedings of the 7th International Conference on Speech Prosody*, 487–491. Dublin: Science Foundation Ireland.

Voegelin, Charles F. 1935. Tübatulabal grammar. *University of California Publications in American Archaeology and Ethnology* 34. 55–190.

Wolfart, H. Christoph. 1996. Sketch of Cree, an Algonquian language. In Goddard, Ives (ed.), *Handbook of North American Indians*, vol. 17, 390–439. Washington, DC: Smithsonian Institution.

Wonderly, W. L. 1951. Zoque II: phonemes and morphophonemics. *International Journal of American Linguistics* 17. 105–123.

Yip, Moira. 2002. *Tone*. Cambridge University Press.

4

PROSODIC MORPHOLOGY AND REDUPLICATION

Suzanne Urbanczyk

1. Introduction

The Indigenous languages of North America make use of a wide variety of word-formation processes. Reduplication of the root of a word (1a), suffixing to a metrical foot (1b), deletion of a rhyme (1c), expansion of a base (1d), stress shift (1e), reordering consonant and vowel (1f), changing vowel quality (1g), and partial (CV-) reduplication (1h) are all instances in which prosodic structures, such as syllables and feet, help determine the form of a word. The following examples illustrate each of these patterns in turn, where the relevant portions of the word are underlined.[1]

(1) Word-formation processes

a. Nuu-chah-nulth (Wakashan) root reduplication

miitx-miitxaʔiš
RED-mitx-(y)a-ʔiš
RED-to.spin-REP.IT[R]-3S.IND
's/he spins continuously'

(Lee 2013: 3)

b. Ulwa (Musumalpan) third person possessive infix

Stem	*Third Possessive*	*Gloss*
súu.lu	súu-ka-lu	'dog'
kúh.bil	kúh-ka-bil	'knife'
bás.kar.na	bás-ka-kar.na	'comb'
si.wá.nak	siwá-ka-nak	'root'

(McCarthy & Prince 1990: 228)

c. Koasati (Muskogean) plural allomorphy: rhyme deletion

Singular	*Plural*	*Gloss*
pitáf-fi-n	pít-li-n	'to slice up the middle'
akocofót-li-n	akocóf-fi-n	'to jump down'
tiwáp-li-n	tíw-wi-n	'to open s.t.'
simát-li-n	sím-mi-n	'to cut up tanned skin'
ataká:-li-n	aták-li-n	'to hang something'
albití:-li-n	albít-li-n	'to place on top of'
apołó:-ka-n	apół-ka-n	'to sleep with someone'

(Horwood 2001: 1)

d. Cupeño (Uto-Aztecan) habilitative epenthesis

Verb Stem	*Habilitative*	*Gloss*
čál	čáʔaʔal	'husk'
təw	táʔəʔəw	'see'
həlʸə́p	həlʸəʔəʔəp	'hiccup'
kəláw	kəlaʔaʔaw	'gather wood'

(McCarthy & Prince 1990: 234)

e. Upriver Halkomelem (Salish) continuative stress shift

Verb Stem	*Gloss*	*Continuative*	*Gloss*
ts'ɛtɛ́m	'crawl'	ts'ɛ́təm	'crawling'
łɛlqí	'soak'	łɛ́lqi	'soaking'
łəxʷə́łtsɛ	'spit'	łə́xʷəłtsɛ	'spitting'

(Galloway 1993: 56)

f. Island Halkomelem (Salish) imperfective metathesis

Perfective	*Gloss*	*Imperfective*	*Gloss*
pqʷat	'break it (substance)'	paqᵂt	'breaking it'
t̓q̓ʷat	'break it'	t̓aq̓ʷt	'breaking it'
xʷk̓ʷat	'pull it'	xʷak̓ʷt	'pulling it'
sq̓et	'tear/split it'	seq̓t	'tearing/splitting it'

(Hukari & Peter 1995)

g. Island Halkomelem (Salish) imperfective ablaut

Perfective	*Gloss*	*Imperfective*	*Gloss*
č̓ə́kʷx̌	'fry'	č̓ék̓ʷx̌	'frying'
č̓ə́kʷx̌t	'fry it'	č̓ékʷx̌t	'frying it'
sə́wq̓	'seek'	séw̓q̓	'seeking'
ƛ̓ə́px̌t	'sprinkle it (sand)'	ƛ̓épx̌t	'sprinkling it (sand)'
łə́p̓t̓θt	'slurp it'	łép̓t̓θt	'slurping it'

(Hukari & Peter 1995)

h. Island Halkomelem (Salish) imperfective CV- reduplication

t̓íləm	'sing'	t̓í-t̓ələm̓	'singing'
wi̓qəs	yawn	wí-w̓əqəs	yawning
łíc̓ət	cut it	łí-łəc̓ət	cutting it
mél̓q	forget	mé-m̓əl̓q	forgetting

(Hukari & Peter 1995)

The range of ways in which these changes in form express changes in meaning is almost as diverse as the languages spoken in North America. Patterns like those outlined in (1) have occupied the attention of linguists interested in understanding the nature of word formation because not all the patterns are straightforwardly understood as joining up, or concatenating, two meaningful parts. They pose a number of issues to models of word formation that are inherently concatenative. For example, what unit is repeated in (1a) or (1h)? How does the morpheme arrive in the middle of the root in (1b)? What unit is adjoined when there is deletion (1c) or reordering of segments (1f)? Why are some bases expanded more than others in (1d)? Why does stress shift to the first syllable in (1e)? What motivates the change in vowel quality in (1g)?

This chapter examines a range of research in this area, presenting potential answers to these questions. It starts with historical perspectives on how North American languages have been at the heart of discussions of whether morphological models are inherently concatenative or not. This is followed closely by an overview of the tenets of the prosodic morphology research program (§2). The chapter then discusses developments and current issues in Optimality Theory (Prince & Smolensky 1993), regarding reduplication and prosodic morphology (§3). The final section identifies potential directions for further research (§4).

2. Historical Perspectives

Early research on reduplication and prosodic morphology involved documentation and descriptive grammars of languages published in various venues (e.g., Sapir 1915). As linguistic theory evolved, along with concepts like the morpheme (Bloomfield 1933), it became apparent that these patterns of word formation were of particular relevance to understanding the formal properties of models of grammar, especially regarding how morphology and phonology interact and what is considered a 'morph'. The ideal that languages are purely concatenative, in the face of non-concatenative morphology, was discussed by Hockett (1954), which led to a three-way classification of grammatical models, which is where this section begins (§2.1). Advances in nonlinear phonology led to models in which a wide range of non-concatenative morphology can be given a concatenative approach, in the area now referred to as prosodic morphology (§2.2). The last section on historical perspectives ends with a brief discussion of the kinds of patterns that have challenged this non-concatenative ideal (§2.3).

2.1. Hockett's Classification

Much of the debate regarding how "subtractive morphs" as in Koasati (1c) and "replacive" morphs as in Halkomelem (1g) fit into formal models of grammar was highlighted by Hockett (1954), who identified three basic approaches to grammar: Item and Arrangement (IA), Item and Process (IP), and Word and Paradigm (WP). The first is the most straightforward to define: "The essence of IA is to talk simply of things and the arrangements in which those things occur" (Hockett 1954: 387). It is similar to morpheme-based approaches, in which the grammar is primarily concerned with listing morphemes and having general principles for how to combine them. Hockett's paper was in response to a growing body of research that referred to morphological patterns as processes, grouping together a range of phenomena such as suffixing, vowel change, and reduplication. In discussing IP, Hockett notes that this is an older approach and cites Zellig Harris's following description of IP:

> The difference between two partially similar forms is frequently described . . . as a process which yields one form out of the other. Thus, when bases or themes have several vocalic forms, the various forms are said to be the result of vowel-change processes operating upon the base or theme . . . it is merely process through the configuration, moving from one to another or larger part of the pattern.
>
> (Harris 1944: 199)

The pattern in (1g) would be described as a process of vowel change in going from the perfective to the imperfective. Hockett notes that work by Boas, Sapir, and Newman on languages of North America "still stand as examples of IP in action" (Hockett 1954: 386). The oldest framework of the three is WP, which was used traditionally in discussions of languages like Latin, Greek, and Sanskrit. As the label suggests, it is primarily concerned with the word as a basic unit, along with its paradigmatic relationships to other words. There are no additions, modifications, or changes to the words; it is the paradigmatic relationship between words that is fundamental. New words are formed based on analogy with existing patterns (Blevins 2006).

One of the key goals of this type of metatheoretical discussion relates to having principles to classify alternations as phonological or morphological, as well as whether concatenation is the primary morphological operation; this is relevant in determining whether universal grammar should include process-based morphs. This debate was picked up by Thompson and Thompson (1969), who argue that metathesis (e.g., 1f) is a grammatical device in Klallam (Central Salish).

While it can be challenging to align these approaches with current models of morphology, one can roughly categorize the three models as morpheme-based (IA), lexeme-based (IP), and word-based approaches (WP). As will be seen in the ensuing discussion, it is not a straightforward task to classify current theoretical approaches as fitting into one category or another, and many current models are a hybrid involving concatenation of an item as well as a process. The most enduring conceptual framework is IA. So the challenge is to fit non-concatenative morphological patterns into this concatenative ideal.

2.2. Prosodic Morphology

In IA, items are morphemes and the grammar accounts for the arrangement of those items. A key puzzle that reduplication poses for the IA approach is that the reduplicant is a copy, which seems to be inherently process-based. The question that arises is what is the 'item', and what aspect of the grammar is responsible for the copying? Building on work in autosegmental phonology (Leben 1973; Goldsmith 1976) where phonological features like high and low tone can be on separate tiers, McCarthy (1979; 1981) proposed that morphemes can also be on separate tiers, and crucially that morphemes can consist of segmentally empty templates. Universal and language-specific phonological mechanisms ensure that these segmentally empty templates are filled with segments. Marantz (1982) developed this insight into a templatic view of reduplication, in which templates consisted of skeletal C and V slots. Skeletal theory was extended to infixing reduplication, with some interesting proposals regarding the copying mechanism (Broselow & McCarthy 1983). Building on these templatic insights, McCarthy and Prince (1986, et seq.) observed that skeletal templates encoded aspects of prosodic structure, such as whether or not a language permits complex onsets, or how many syllables there are in the reduplicant. They proposed that templates are actual prosodic units, such as syllable and foot. The remainder of this section illustrates the key components of McCarthy and Prince's model.

The theory of Prosodic Morphology (PM), as advanced by McCarthy and Prince (1986; 1990 inter alia) has three key components. The Prosodic Morphology Hypothesis (PMH), as stated in (2a), ensures that templates are authentic units of prosody. The Template Satisfaction Condition (TSC) ensures that the template is filled with segmental content, so that there are no empty prosodic units on the surface (2b). The Prosodic Circumscription of Domains (2c) states that a prosodic unit in the base can be parsed out and can have morphological operations apply to it; it accounts for a number of morphological phenomena that are sensitive to either prosodic structure in the base or the derived output wordform.

(2) Prosodic Morphology Hypothesis

a. **Prosodic Morphology Hypothesis.** Templates are defined in terms of the authentic units of prosody: mora (μ), syllable (σ), foot (F), prosodic word (PW), and so on.
b. **Template Satisfaction Condition.** Satisfaction of templatic constraints is obligatory and is determined by the principles of prosody, both universal and language specific.

c. **Prosodic Circumscription of Domains.** The domain to which morphological operations apply may be circumscribed by prosodic criteria as well as by the more familiar morphological ones. In particular, the MINIMAL WORD within a domain may be selected as the locus of morphological transformation in lieu of the whole domain.

(McCarthy & Prince 1990: 209–210)

The introduction of these three components of the theory led to an expansion of research in this area. By far the most widely accepted concepts were the Prosodic Morphology Hypothesis (PMH) and Template Satisfaction Condition (TSC). An extensive range of analyses were developed, with the gamut of prosodic categories, from mora to phonological word, being proposed and exemplified.

The following illustrates how the PMH and TSC go together for CV- reduplication in Halkomelem (1h). In this derivational model of reduplication, the reduplicative morpheme is a light syllable, as per the PMH. It is prefixed to a base, as in (3a). There is then a copy mechanism, in which only the segmental melody of the base is copied (3b). The TSC ensures that the syllable is filled to its maximal size, as in (3c). Unassociated segments are then deleted and phonological processes of stress assignment and unstressed vowel reduction apply (3d).

(3) Halkomelem (Salish) 'imperfective' reduplication

a. PMH: template is a light syllable

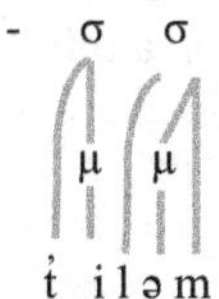

b. Copy stage

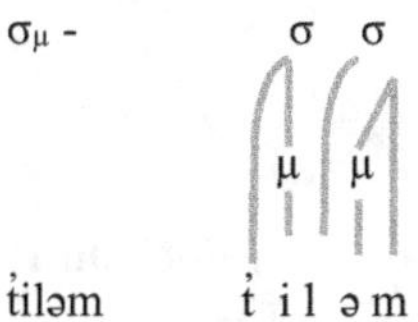

c. TSC: template is filled

d. Deletion of unassociated segments

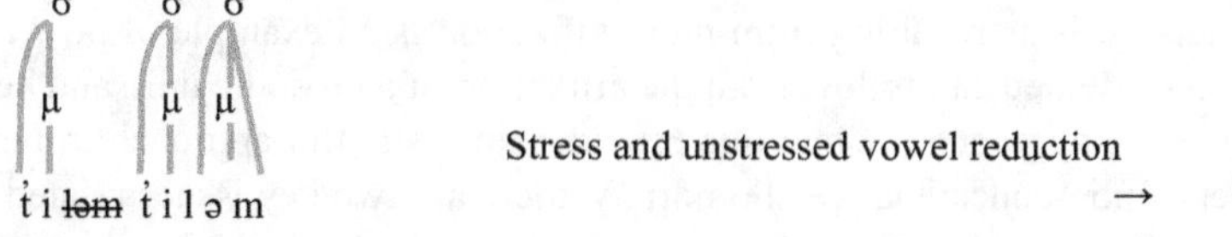

In this approach, reduplicative morphemes are segmentally empty templates, attached to a stem. Segments from the base are copied and associated to the template.

The use of prosodic templates as affixes was also applied to a process-based morphological operation: metathesis. Stonham (1994) accounts for a range of allomorphs in Saanich (Salish) by taking a concatenative approach and arguing against process-based approaches to morphology. The three allomorphs are: CV- reduplication (4a), metathesis (4b), and glottal stop infix (4c).

(4) Saanich dialect of Straits (Salish) 'actual' allomorphy

a.	reduplication			
	t̓ᶿéʔ	'be on top'	t̓ᶿét̓ᶿəʔ	'riding (a horse)'
	s-kʷúl	'school'	s-kʷúkʷəl	'going to school'
	ɬík̓ʷsən	'trip'	ɬíɬək̓ʷsən̓	'tripping'
b.	metathesis			
	sx̣ə́t	'push it'	sə́x̣t	'pushing it'
	θk̓ʷə́t	'straighten it out'	θə́k̓ʷt	'straightening it out'
	tqʷə́t	'tighten it'	tə́qʷt	'tightening it'
c.	glottal stop infix			
	čáq̓ʷəŋ	'sweat'	čáʔq̓ʷəŋ̓	'sweating'
	wéqəs	'yawn'	wéʔqəs	'yawning'
	xʷítəŋ	'jump'	xʷíʔtəŋ̓	'jumping'

(Montler 1986: 114–122)

Stonham proposes that the 'actual' is a segmentally empty mora which is affixed to the root. In his analysis, consonants and vowels are segregated on separate tiers, with consonants on one tier, vowels on a second tier, and the number of moras for each root represented on a third tier, as seen in (5). The separation of moras from segments is used to derive the difference between CCV and CVC roots.

(5) Representation of roots using segregation of C-V-μ

CV	CCV	CVC	CVCVC
⌈ C⌉	⌈CC⌉	⌈CC⌉	⌈CCC⌉
│V│	│V│	│V│	│VV│
⌊1μ⌋	⌊1μ⌋	⌊2μ⌋	⌊3μ⌋

(Stonham 1994: 173)

A segmentally empty mora is added to these representations, increasing the mora count by one for all forms in the 'actual' aspect. The various allomorphs arise by how the moras are filled by the process of linearization. When the mora is affixed to a CVC root, as in (4a), reduplication occurs in order to supply the additional mora with segmental content. When a mora is affixed to a stem that begins with a cluster, as in (4b), the moras are filled by mapping one mora to the vowel and the other mora for the coda, as in (4b); this gives the appearance of metathesis. Bases with an initial open syllable, as in (4c), fill the mora by epenthesizing a glottal stop in the coda.

This approach to metathesis as resulting from mora affixation is an example of how a pattern that appears to be process oriented can follow from the affixation of a prosodic unit, and hence can be given a concatenative IA approach.[2] While this provides an insightful approach to unifying a seemingly disparate set of non-concatenative allomorphy, there are two key issues related to what can fill a mora. First, there is no evidence that coda consonants are moraic in the language (Leonard 2019), so it is not clear how reordering segments so that one can be a coda (4b) or epenthesizing a coda consonant (4c) can fill in a mora.[3] Second, much evidence has been presented that schwa is non-moraic in Central Salish languages (Shaw et al. 1999; Blake 2000), so it is not clear how the metathesized schwa in (4b) fills an empty mora.

The final component of the prosodic morphology hypothesis is the prosodic circumscription of domains. It has been applied to two different morphological phenomena: determining the locus of infixing and the mapping and/or expansion of segments to fill a prosodic template. The following example of infixing in Ulwa illustrates the former. As illustrated in (6), the location of the infix is after an iambic foot, which is right-headed. Comparing the forms in (6a) and (6b) shows that the affix is truly infixed after a heavy syllable. The other foot types found are two light syllables (6c), and the preferred light-heavy structure (6d). Feet are indicated with parentheses.

(6) Ulwa (Misumalpan) infixing 3SG.POSS

a.	al	(ál.)-ka	'man'
	bas	(bás.)-ka	'hair'
	kii	(kíi.)-ka	'stone'
b.	suu.lu	(súu.)-ka.-lu	'dog'
	kuh.bil	(kúh.)-ka.-bil	'knife'
	bas.kar.na	(bás.)-ka.-kar.na	'comb'
c.	sa.na	(sa.ná.)-ka	'deer'
	si.wa.nak	(si.wá.)-ka.-nak	'root'
d.	a.mak	(a.mák.)-ka	'bee'
	sa.paa	(sa.páa.)-ka	'forehead'
	a.naa.laa.ka	(a.náa.)-ka.-laa.ka	'chin'
	ka.ras.mak	(ka.rás.)-ka.-mak	'knee'

(McCarthy & Prince 1990: 228)

Prosodic circumscription locates the infix in Ulwa by identifying an iambic foot as the base and applying the morphological operation of suffixation to that foot. If the operation applies to the base that is parsed out (as with Ulwa), it is referred to as positive prosodic circumscription. If the operation applies to the residue, it is known as negative prosodic circumscription. The latter has been applied to a range of processes such as infixing reduplication in Washo (Hokan; Urbanczyk 1993), infixing in Choctaw (Muskogean; Lombardi & McCarthy 1991), and truncation in Koasati (Muskogean; Lombardi & McCarthy 1991).

In addition to prosodic templates being analyzed as affixes, they have also been used to account for the shape of stems, in which some morphological unit is expanded to a target shape. In these cases, the template is imposed on the base of affixation, rather than on the affix itself. In describing Yowlumne (Yokuts), Archangeli (1991: 232) observes "about half of the 50-odd verbal suffixes impose a syllabic structure on the verb stem itself". The examples in (7) illustrate the effect that the 'consequent adjunctive' suffix has in imposing an iambic shape on underlying CVC roots (a regular process of /uu/ → [oo] occurs in (7a) and (7c)).

(7) Yowlumne

a.	√t̓ul	t̓uloo-ʔuy	lit. 'burn-CONS.ADJ'	
b.	√tan	tanaa-ʔe:y	lit. 'go-CONS-ADJ'	= 'footprint'
c.	√c̓uy	c̓uyoo-ʔoy-nu	lit. 'urinate-CONS.ADJ-INDR.OBJ'	

(Yokuts; Newman 1944: 163, cited in Inkelas 2014: 95)

As one can see, the prosodic morphology research program can account for a wide range of patterns by reference to some type of prosodic template, as affix or base. We now turn to some of the issues that arise with the basic IA approach to morphology.

2.3. Challenges to IA

Challenges to IA approaches have led to the development of alternative models of morphology. As discussed briefly earlier in this chapter, an IP approach is most closely aligned with lexeme-based approaches, in which the item is a stem/lexeme, and a process modifies this base (Anderson 1992; Aronoff 1994). Lexemes are abstract units that, when inflected, result in a wordform. The processes in IP are morphological operations that apply to some stem. IP shares the property with IA of being constructive, as there is some operation to a base that adds some exponent to it. For IA, the process is restricted to the addition of a unit: it is concatenative. For IP, the processes can include affixation as well as other non-concatenative operations which can modify the base, such as deletion, ablaut, and metathesis.

One IP approach is Anderson (1992), in which word-formation rules apply to a stem to produce a new wordform. Anderson (1992, especially Chapter 3) discusses several issues that process-based morphology pose to IA approaches, such as metathesis, subtractive morphology and apophony (vowel changes). For example, in Tohono O'odham, the 'perfective' aspect is formed by deleting the final consonant of the 'imperfective':

(8) Tohono O'odham

	Imperfective	*Perfective*	*Gloss*
a.	má:k	má:	'giving'
b.	hí:nk	hí:n	'barking'
c.	híhim	híhi	'walking (PL)'
d.	gátwid	gátwi	'to shoot object'
e.	nákog	náko	'enduring'

(Uto-Aztecan; Hill & Zepeda 1992; Trommer & Zimmermann 2014: 484)

Anderson notes in particular that if a morphological category is marked by the loss of material, "there is no way to parse the surface form of a word containing this category so that some . . . subpart of its structure constitutes the morph in question" (Anderson 1992: 66). This then opens the door to morphology having processes in addition to affixation. The model Anderson adopts is one in which word-formation rules apply to stems, which he describes as IP for derivation and Word and Paradigm (WP) for inflection. If one considers IP to be an item and a process applying to a base, prosodic circumscription seems to exemplify this with the operation being a process that applies to a base. While some of the operations can involve adding affixes, as with Ulwa *-ka-* '3SG.POSS', there are other operations that do not appear to be straightforwardly concatenative.

In Cupeño (Uto-Aztecan), the 'habilitative' exhibits phonologically conditioned allomorphy, in which segments are epenthesized to reach a prosodic target. For consonant-final stems, as in (9a–c), the habilitative requires stress to fall on the antepenultimate syllable. Because the location of stress is preserved from its verb stem, the 'habilitative' must add a number of syllables to reach that ante-penult target. As one can see, this is done by adding two extra syllables in (9a), one extra syllable in (9b), or no change (9c), if stress already falls on the antepenult. The examples in (9d) show that this process of foot expansion doesn't apply to vowel-final words. The extra syllables are indicated by underlining, separated by dashes.

(9) Cupeño (Uto-Aztecan) habilitative

	Verb Stem	*Habilitative*	*Gloss*
a.	(čál)	čá-ʔaʔa-l	'husk'
	(tə́w)	tə́-ʔəʔə-w	'see'
	hə(lʸə́p)	həlʸə́-ʔəʔə-p	'hiccup'
	kə(láw)	kəlá-ʔaʔa-w	'gather wood'
b.	(páčik)	páči-ʔi-k	'leach acorns'
	(čáŋnəw)	čáŋnə-ʔə-w	'be angry'

c.	(pínəʔwəx)	pínəʔwəx	'sing enemy songs'
	(xáləyəw)	xə́ləyəw	'fall'
d.	čí	číʔ	'gather'
	hú	húʔ	'fart'
	ʔáyu	ʔáyu	'want'

(McCarthy & Prince 1990: 234)

This has been analyzed as circumscribing the stressed foot, indicated by parentheses above, and having an operation insert segments, indicated with *-ʔVʔV-* or *-ʔV-* in (9), within a foot to form a trisyllabic foot (McCarthy & Prince 1990; Crowhurst 1994). The issue that arises here is that trisyllabic feet are not well motivated in metrical theory (see Hayes 1995).[4]

Another pattern that is potentially problematic for some IA approaches is multiple exponence, where one of the exponents is an affix and the other involves some form of stem modification to the base.[5] Wakashan languages have what is referred to as suffix-triggered reduplication. In addition, some Wakashan languages also have a process where vowel length changes co-occur with reduplication as well as suffixation. An example of these morphological patterns is presented in (10). [R] in the gloss indicates that the suffix triggers reduplication of the base. In (10a), the root is 'money' and the reduplicant is CV- shaped with a short vowel, which is triggered by a non-adjacent suffix meaning 'to cry'. In (10b), the reduplicant is a copy of the root 'to spin', triggered by the 'repetitive iterative' suffix. As can be seen in the underlying representation of the root (just below the surface form), both the reduplicant and root surface with lengthened vowels (represented as L in the gloss).

(10) *Nuu-chah-nulth*

a. <u>ta</u>-taanaqayukʔiš
RED-taana-qa-yuk[R]-ʔiš
RED-money-for-to.cry-3S.IND
's/he is pouting for money'

b. <u>miitx</u>-miitxaʔiš
RED-mitx-(y)a-ʔiš
RED-to.spin-REP.IT[R-L]-3S.IND
's/he spins continuously'

(Southern Wakashan; Lee 2013: 63)

In order to account for these patterns, three different types of morphological operations are needed: suffixation, reduplication, and vowel lengthening/shortening. Different affixes trigger different reduplication patterns. In Nuu-chah-nulth, there are approximately 80 suffixes that trigger reduplication, with seven different reduplication patterns identified in terms of how the vowel length changes (Kim 2003; Lee 2013).

In a pure IA approach, the lexical entry of each morpheme would include the suffix and some template for reduplication, an analysis that would be akin to having circumfixes. Kim (2003) proposes that each of the affixes is associated with a syllabic template, to be filled by reduplication. In order to account for the patterns of vowel length adjustments, there is also foot that encodes vowel length in the input. In this way the reduplicated portion occupies the first syllable, while the base occupies the second syllable. The IA approach can account for the basic patterns, by assuming three elements in the input.

2.4. Summary

This section has shown that early approaches have grappled with how to reconcile morphological operations as processes. By far the bulk of research has been in the IA approach, with some work in the IP framework. WP, by contrast, has had little traction in pre-Optimality Theory frameworks. We now turn to how some of the key issues are addressed in Optimality Theory.

3. Current Contributions and Research

Current debates in prosodic morphology and reduplication have arisen from a paradigm shift in phonological theory that occurred with the introduction of Optimality Theory (Prince & Smolensky 1993; henceforth, OT). OT is a constraint-based model of grammar, and many of the key tenets of the PMH research paradigm were recast as constraints on well-formedness (MARKEDNESS) and phonological identity. Early work in OT derived words in parallel, without intermediate stages, and so assumptions about the copying mechanism were recast in several different ways (§3.1). The status of templates has also been called into question and has recently been applied in new and innovative ways (§3.2). Not surprisingly, there seems to be a connection between theoretical proposals regarding the nature of the copy mechanism and how templatic shape is derived. Also included is a section on the issue of segmental identity (§3.3). A final section looks at how infixing has been recast in OT (§3.4).

3.1. Copying Mechanism

A central issue that has emerged in the OT literature on reduplication and prosodic morphology is the nature of the copy mechanism. As was illustrated previously in this chapter, in pre-OT frameworks, reduplication triggers copying of the base, and then associating segments to a prosodic template. This intermediate stage is not available in standard OT models, and so a number of different approaches have arisen. In particular, a common theme now is that there are two different copying mechanisms, depending on the shape or size of the reduplicant. This section briefly outlines the key developments in this area.

One of the earliest models in OT formalized constraints on how morpheme-identity is monitored, known as Correspondence Theory (McCarthy & Prince 1995; 1999). The strings in correspondence can be segmentally specified roots and affixes, with the input being S_1 and the output being S_2. For reduplication, the base serves as S_1 and the reduplicant is S_2. The basic model of reduplication in OT specifies an abstract reduplicative morpheme in the input, which triggers a correspondence relation between base and reduplicant (McCarthy & Prince 1999), with the two correspondence relations as indicated in (11).

(11) Basic Model

Input	/Af_{RED} + Stem/			
		↓↑		*I-O Faithfulness*
Output	R	⇆	B	
		B-R Identity		

(McCarthy & Prince 1999: 232)

In Base-Reduplicant Correspondence Theory (BRCT), there is no copying mechanism per se. Rather, a correspondence relation between base and reduplicant exists and is evaluated by a set of constraints that examine the identity of the strings (FAITHFULNESS). Total reduplication results when every segment in the base is in the reduplicant (i.e., when the constraint MAX-BR is satisfied). Partial reduplication incurs violations of MAX-BR, because some segments of the base are not in the reduplicant. Every candidate is generated with a relation between input and output as well. All aspects of the phonological properties of the reduplicant are evaluated by a set of FAITHFULNESS constraints (BR-FAITH): different FAITHFULNESS constraints relate to the size and segmental quality of the reduplicant. An example of the BRCT analysis of a reduplicated word is illustrated below. The identity of segmentally specified morphemes is evaluated by IO-FAITH.

(12) Halkomelem (Salish) Reduplication under the Basic Model

Input: /RED—t̓iləm /

⇳ *Stem I-O Faithfulness*

Output: t̓í - t̓ələm’

Reduplicant ↔ Base *B-R Faithfulness*

In this basic version of the BRCT model, the input contains an abstract morpheme RED attached to a segmentally specified stem. The output consists of two parts. One part is the reduplicant, with a correspondence relation between base and reduplicant; the other part is the stem, with a correspondence relation between input and output. Each part is evaluated by a set of constraints that examines that part of the word. In the preceding example, MAX-IO is obeyed, because all the segments in the input are in the output. However, only the first two segments of the base have correspondents in the reduplicant, so there are three violations of MAX-BR. In the basic model, there is no direct link between the input and the reduplicant. However, the full model does involve an additional correspondence relation between input and reduplicant.[6]

The BRCT model was proposed to account for a range of segmental identity effects, as identified by Wilbur (1973). The leading idea is that the full range of effects (normal application, over- and under-application, and non-application) could be accounted for by permuting the ranking of BR-FAITH, IO-FAITH, and MARKEDNESS constraints (where the latter penalize marked or less natural phonological patterns). Because constraints on identity can be interspersed with MARKEDNESS constraints, there are several predictions of BRCT, to be discussed in §3.3.

With the advent of Correspondence Theory came research that explored how identity constraints could play a role in triggering prosodically motivated stem modifications as illustrated by Saanich (4) and Koasati (1c). These approaches are inherently word-based, as one needs to compare one word with another, to detect a difference in form with the change in meaning.

In one approach, a general constraint requires a paradigmatically related word to have a different phonological form (Urbanczyk 1999; Kurisu 2001). The choice of what change occurs is based on the ranking of MARKEDNESS and FAITHFULNESS constraints in the language. For example, patterns of non-concatenative allomorphy, such as the Saanich actual (4) and Halkomelem continuative stress shift (1e) were analyzed with this approach. Because these changes are based on the phonological properties of the base, in each case, the correct allomorph is derived. Interestingly, the allomorphs chosen are due to improving the prosodic structure of the word, either by avoiding a stressed schwa (1g), or by having initial stress (1e).

In the second approach, Anti-Faithfulness constraints demand that identity be avoided. This approach was employed to account for patterns of truncation in Koasati (1c). ANTI-MAX constraints ensure that the plural is missing segments from the singular base. In particular, the constraint ¬MAX-V requires the deletion of a vowel. If the stem is vowel-final, no further deletion is required; however, if the stem is consonant-final, the consonant must also be deleted to avoid a sequence of three consonants, thus giving the effect of rhyme deletion (Horwood 2001). Any type of segmental change that is evaluated by FAITHFULNESS is predicted to be a type of morphological marker, including attested patterns like ablaut and insertion.

The powerfulness of Correspondence Theory in terms of its ability to overgenerate potential patterns was critiqued by several researchers, and led to recasting the reduplicative copy mechanism to not invoke BRCT.

Among the models that eschew BRCT, copying is accomplished by two separate mechanisms, depending on the size and other qualities of the reduplicant (Inkelas & Zoll 2005; Saba Kirchner 2013). Generalizing over the specific details, one mechanism involves repetition of a morphosyntactic unit, while the other involves some form of fission, where one input segment corresponds to two output segments (violating the Faithfulness constraint INTEGRITY). Morphosyntactic doubling results in the repetition of a root or stem. The doubled element either stays as it is (total reduplication, as in 1a) or, in one model, it can be truncated to result in the effect of partial reduplication (Inkelas & Zoll 2005). The fission or splitting of one input segment to two output segments is compelled in order to repair a marked phonological representation. The latter is referred to as phonological copying. A brief discussion of the cases in which phonological copying occurs is presented next.

In Spokane (Interior Salish), the repetitive morpheme is analyzed as a vocalic infix *-e-*. When the base begins with a cluster, the vowel is inserted between two consonants, as in (13a). However, when the base begins with a single consonant, the morpheme is prefixed to the base and copying occurs to provide an onset, as in (13b).

(13) Spokane repetitive -e-

a. infix

/-e-, šl̓-n̓-t-ən̓/	š-e-l̓n̓tén̓
REP, chop-CTR-TR-1SGTRS	'I chopped it up repeatedly'
/-e-, lč̓-n̓-t-ən̓/	l̓-e-č̓n̓tén̓
REP, tie-CTR-TR-1SGTRS	'I tied it over and over'

b. phonological copying to provide an onset

/-e-, šl̓/	še-šíl̓
REP, chop	'chopped repeatedly'
/-e-, nič̓-n̓-t-əxʷ/	n̓e-n̓íč̓n̓txʷ
REP, cut-CTR-TR-2SGTRS	'you kept cutting'

(Interior Salish; Bates & Carlson 1992; Inkelas & Zoll 2005: 21)

Another example of phonological copying is from the Kwak'wala (Wakashan) 'distributive'. In this example, segment doubling occurs in order to supply phonological content to a mora affix which co-occurs with a segmentally specified suffix – *m'ut*. If the initial syllable (root) is light, vowel lengthening occurs as in (14a); note that these are light syllables, because obstruent codas are not moraic. If the initial syllable is heavy (has a long vowel or sonorant coda), as in (14b), reduplication occurs (Saba Kirchner 2010; 2013).

(14) Kwak'wala (Wakashan) – m'ut 'distributive'

a. No reduplication with initial light syllable

c̓əx	c̓a:xm̓u:t	'singe'
k̓əxʷ	k̓a:xʷm̓u:t	'suck with whole mouth'
q̓ʷəł	q̓ʷa:łmu:t	'scratch'
t̓əp	t̓a:pm̓u:t	'break'

(Saba Kirchner 2010: §2.2.3)

b. Reduplication with initial heavy syllable

kən	kənkəmu:t	'scoop up'
ma:	ma:məmu:t	'(serpent) crawl'
c̓a:s	c̓a:c̓əsmu:t	'eel grass'
kəmt	kəmkətm̓u:t	'clean berries'

Lengthening occurs in (14a) by straightforward affixation of a mora to a light syllable. The vowel change occurs because there are no long schwas in Kwak'wala. Lengthening is blocked from occurring with heavy syllables in (14b), because Kwak'wala does not permit super-heavy (trimoraic) syllables. This triggers vowel insertion to realize the mora. The initial segment of the root is doubled up, to provide an onset for the syllable; this involves a violation of INTEGRITY.

These multiple copying approaches have arisen to account for correlations between the size of the reduplicant and other phonological properties. Both examples of phonological copying in this section are phonologically conditioned by the prosodic structure of the base, in terms of syllable shape and weight. See Saba Kirchner (2010: 27) and Inkelas (2008) for diagnostics related to determining when the two different copy mechanisms are invoked, as well as for more specific details of each model.

Finally, some approaches go a step further and eschew all manner of correspondence. There is no relation between segments of the base and reduplicant, or between input and output. An interesting shared feature of these models is that they each propose that the general morphological operation is one of affixation of a prosodic unit, in an IA type of approach. A prosodic template is filled either by copying segments of the base in one operation (McCarthy et al. 2012), or by compelling INTEGRITY violation(s) (Bermudez-Otero 2012; Bye & Svenonius 2012; Trommer & Zimmermann 2014). So far, we have seen that the prosodic template plays a crucial role in much of this research. The following section outlines the kinds of evidence that have been presented in favor of and against prosodically defined templates.

3.2. Status of Templates

One of the most widely studied aspects of reduplication and prosodic morphology relates to specifying the shape of morphological units as prosodic units. The three shape properties that are found include: total copy of some morphosyntactic unit; partial reduplication, where the shape is definable as a prosodic unit; and single segment copying, often referred to as atemplatic reduplication. In addition to this, prosodic templates have been proposed to account for phonologically conditioned allomorphy, as was discussed for Saanich. This section reviews recent evidence presented for the role prosody plays in accounting for a range of processes, starting with the earliest instantiation of templatic constraints into OT.

The implementation of templates as constraints in BRCT led to a conundrum first pointed out to McCarthy and Prince by René Kager and Phillip Hamilton. Because constraints on identity can be freely re-ranked, one result of BRCT is that segmental patterns can be "back-copied" onto the base from the reduplicant; if the reduplicant is required to have a certain property, this can also be required of the base in order to preserve identity between base and reduplicant. This accounts for the over- and underapplication patterns to be discussed in Section 3.3. If the templatic pattern is cast as a constraint, like RED=σ_μ, then the base can be truncated to be a light syllable, as well, in order to have total identity between base and reduplicant. The following ranking, with BR-MAX and a constraint on reduplicant shape ranked above IO-MAX, predicts that BR identity will prevail, at the expense of input segments not being parsed in the output.

(15) MAX-BR, RED=σ_μ >> MAX-IO

Interestingly, such a pattern has been found in Guarijío (Caballero 2006). As illustrated in (16), the base word can be disyllabic or trisyllabic; but when reduplicated, the base is truncated to match the single-syllable shape of the reduplicant.

(16) Guarijío 'abbreviated' reduplication

a.	to.ní	'to boil'	to-tó	'to start boiling'
b.	si.bá	'to scratch'	si-sí	'to start scratching'
c.	čo.nó	'to fry (intr)'	čo-čó	'to start frying'
d.	no.gá	'to move'	no-nó	'to start moving'
e.	mu.hí.ba	'to throw'	mu-mú	'to start throwing'

(Uto-Aztecan; Caballero 2006: 278)

Crucially, there is no independent process of truncation in Guarijío; the base is only shortened in this reduplicative construction (Caballero 2006). Further investigation has suggested that this pattern is restricted to around a dozen verbs (Saba Kirchner 2010) and may not be a productive pattern of the language. Nonetheless, language patterns like this exist in other languages and illustrate the reduction of the root to match the syllable form of the reduplication.[7]

In order to avoid the conundrum posed by Kager & Hamilton, researchers posited that there are no templatic constraints per se, but rather that reduplicant shapes emerge as unmarked morpheme shapes in general. This approach is referred to as Generalized Template Theory (GTT; McCarthy & Prince 1999; Urbanczyk 2001; 2006; Downing 2006). In GTT, reduplicative morphemes are segmentally empty morphemes that trigger a BR-Correspondence relation. They are specified for morphological category only, and are not prosodic templates. Constraints that are active in evaluating the shape of morphemes in general are also active in determining the shape of reduplicative morphemes. For example, in Lushootseed, the difference between 'distributive' CVC- and 'diminutive' CV- reduplication is proposed to follow from the former being a root, and permitting coda consonants (17b), while the latter is an affix and hence avoids them, as in (17c) (Urbanczyk 2006). Reduplicative morphemes then illustrate a root-affix asymmetry.

(17) Lushootseed

a.	ʔibəš	'walk, travel or journey over land by any means'
b.	ʔib-ʔibəš	'walk all about (distributive)'
c.	ʔi-ʔibəš-txʷ	'walk a bit (diminutive)'

(Salish; Bates et al. 1994: 15)

Kennedy (2008) takes a different approach to emergent shape by proposing that the patterns follow from where the reduplicative morpheme is affixed, either stem-internal or stem-external. He accounts for two patterns of reduplication in Klamath (Penutian) reduplication by proposing that the 'intensive' is stem-internal, with a closed syllable (18a), while the 'distributive' is stem-external and has an open syllable (18b). The ordering of intensive outside 'distributive' (18c) provides further support for this approach. Klamath has a process of laryngeal neutralization resulting in deglottalization of segments in coda position.

(18) Klamath[8]

a. 'Intensive' reduplication

beq̓	'be bay-coloured'	beq.-beq.-l'i	'INTENSIVE, bay-coloured'
boq̓	'be dusty'	boq.-bo.q̓-a	'becomes dusty, dusty-white'
kesp̓	'pant for breath'	kesp.-kes.p̓-a	'pants for breath'
m̓eč	'be blue'	m̓eč.-m̓eč.-l̓i	'blue'

b. 'Distributive' reduplication

qlin	'choke'	qli.-qlən	'DISTRIBUTIVE-choke'
čonwa	'vomit'	čo.-čən.wa	'DISTRIBUTIVE-vomit'
paga	'barks'	pa-p.ga	'DISTRIBUTIVE-back'
mbeli	'is cross-eyed'	mbe-m.bli	'DISTRIBUTIVE-is cross-eyed'

c. 'Distributive-intensive' reduplication

m̓eč̓	'be blue'	m̓e.-m̓əč.-m̓eč.-l̓i	'DISTRIBUTIVE-blue'
p̓etq	blink	p̓e.-p̓ətq.-p̓et.q̓-a	'DISTRIBUTIVE-BLINK'

(Penutian; Kennedy 2008: 606)

One of the typological cornerstones guiding theories of reduplication was that there is no "syllable-copying" per se (Moravcsik 1978). This observation was crucial to proposing that reduplicative morphemes are segmentally empty templates that are then filled by some mechanism. This point is crucial to supporting reduplication as IA. However, this observation has recently come into question, as the following pattern from Hiaki (Yaqui) 'habitual' reduplication demonstrates (Haugen 2014). The reduplicant shape is the same as the first syllable of the base. If that first syllable is open (19a), the reduplicant is open. If the first syllable is closed, so is the reduplicant (19b).

(19) "Syllable copy" reduplication in Hiaki

a. CV.CVX-initial stems

vu.sa	vu.vu.sa	*vus.vu.sa	'awaken'
či.ke	či.chi.ke	*čik.či.ke	'come one's hair'
ču.pa	ču.ču.pa	*čup.ču.pa	'grow (TRANS)'
he.wi.te	he.wi.te	*hew.he.wi.te	'agree'

b. CVC.CVX-initial stems

vam.se	vam.vam.se	*va.vam.se	'hurry'
čep.ta	čep.čep.ta	*če.čep.ta	'jump over'
čuk.ta	čuk.čuk.ta	*ču.čuk.ta	'cut with a knife or saw'
b^{w}al.ko.te	b^{w}al.b^{w}al.ko.te	*b^{w}a.b^{w}al.ko.te	'soften, smooth'

(Southern Uto-Aztecan; Haugen 2014: 511)

This recently documented pattern uproots the previous motivation for template-filling, where there is a fixed shape that is not dependent on the syllable structure of the base.

Another way that prosodic templates have emerged in an IA type approach is what Bermúdez-Otero (2012) refers to as Generalized-Nonlinear Affixation. Bye and Svenonius (2012) have reworked Stonham's (1994) mora-affixation analysis of metathesis of the Saanich 'actual' allomorphy (represented in (4) above). Each of the allomorphs occurs as a response to how to best provide segmental content to the added mora. Recall that the allomorphs themselves are phonologically conditioned, so there is a direct link between the conditions for the allomorph and the grammar's response to how to fill the prosodic template.

The cognate pattern in Halkomelem has been analyzed as having a morphological foot in the input, to which segments must be mapped (Zimmermann 2013, 2017). This illustrates the role that higher-order prosodic structure can play in accounting for phonologically conditioned suppletive allomorphy. The four allomorphs are: stress shift (20a), vowel lengthening (20b), *h*-epenthesis (20c), and CV- reduplication (20d).

(20) Upriver Halkomelem (Salish) continuative allomorphy

a.	ts'ɛtɛ́:m	crawl	tṡɛ́təm	crawling
b.	ʔíməç	walk	ʔí:məç	walking
c.	mə́qət	swallow	hə́mqət	swallowing
d.	q̇ísət	tie something	q̇íq̇əsət	tying something

(Galloway 1993)

Zimmermann (2013) presents a unified analysis of the patterns of allomorphy as affixation of a morphological trochaic foot. The four different allomorphs arise in order "to avoid a situation where the morphemic foot dominates too much segmental material of the base" (Zimmermann 2013: 13). She proposes that the morphological foot associated with 'continuative' is "integrated in the prosodic structure and 'overwrites' the underlying prosodic structure of the non-continuative base" (Zimmermann 2013: 11).

An innovative application of Generalized Nonlinear Affixation is in its account of morphological truncation (Trommer & Zimmermann 2014). Truncation has long been a classic problem for IA approaches, because this is the opposite of addition, and there is no unit to add (Anderson 1992). Trommer and Zimmermann (2014) account for truncation in Tohono O'odham (Uto-Aztecan), as well as Koasati and related Muskogean languages, by Generalized Mora Affixation. The Tohono O'odham pattern (8) illustrates the deletion of the word-final consonant to indicate perfective aspect. In this approach, a mora is affixed to the base. The mora is filled by segmental content (the final consonant). Abstracting away from the technical details, constraints penalize linking the mora to higher prosodic structure, so that the mora is left hanging, unattached. The failure of the mora to be incorporated into prosodic structure makes it unpronounceable and provides the effect of segment deletion. The segments are parsed into the mora, and the mora is not pronounced. This analysis addresses Anderson's critique of subtraction as not being amenable to an affixational approach.

To summarize, recent work in prosodic morphology and reduplication has been able to account for many patterns by attaching a segmentally empty prosodic unit in the input. Constraints interact with a requirement that the prosodic unit has phonological content, and they ensure that the correct output form is derived. We now look at another key component of reduplication and much of the motivation for BRCT: the (lack of) identity between segments of the base and the reduplicant.

3.3. Segmental Identity

With the advent of Correspondence Theory, attention turned again to issues of segmental identity in reduplication. Motivation for BRCT came from identity effects and Wilbur's (1973) 'mate' relation (McCarthy & Prince 1995; 1999). The 'mate' relation is one in which there is a link between the source segment in the base (X) and its copy in the reduplicant (X′). Wilbur proposed that global rules can apply to both X and X′ to achieve identity. The typology of segmental identity effects that Wilbur (1973) introduced includes overapplication, in which a process applies without the appropriate trigger, and underapplication, in which a process fails to apply, even though it has the appropriate trigger.

These patterns can be seen in (21). In (21a), velar palatalization (/ik +V/ → [ičV]) overapplies because there is palatalized segment without the trigger. In (21b), a regular alternation (/č/ → [š] word-finally or before [-cont]) is suspended (underapplies); note that the affricate is found before [-cont] segments such as /k/. With the free re-ranking of constraints on identity, two further effects can be accounted for. Normal application occurs when phonological patterns are as expected for base and reduplicant (for example, obstruent devoicing in coda position, as in 21c). The emergence of the unmarked (TETU; McCarthy & Prince 1994) occurs when the reduplicant eliminates marked structure from the base. In (21d), coda neutralization of glottalized resonants occurs in the reduplicant only. An extreme case of TETU, called default segmentism, can be seen in (21e), where the contrast in vowels is neutralized in the reduplicant, in favor of the default vowel schwa.

(21) Segmental Patterns in Reduplication

a. Overapplication: Dakota

Underlying Representation	*Surface Form*	*Reduplicated Gloss*
/ wičʰa-ki-kax-RED-ʔiyeya /	wičʰa-ki-čax-čax-ʔiyeya	'he made it for them quickly'
/ nape ki-kos-RED-a /	nape ki-čos-čoz-a	'he waved his hand to him'

(Siouan; Shaw 1980: 193)

b. Underapplication: Luiseño

ča.ráč.ra-š	'torn'
ču.káč.ka-š	'limping'
ča.kúč.ku-š	'crest on a roadrunner'
či.ŋíč.ŋi-š	'aboriginal Luiseño god'

(Uto-Aztecan; Munro & Benson 1973: 18–19)

c. Normal Application: Washo

wét-wedi	'it's quacking'
šúp-šubi	'he's crying gently'
bák-bagi	'he's smoking'

(Hokan; Wilbur 1973: 17)

d. Emergence of the Unmarked: Mainland Comox

t̓əm̓xʷ	'gooseberry'	t̓əm-t̓əm̓xʷ	'gooseberries'
hum̓hum	'blue grouse'	həm-hum̓hum	'blue grouses'
qin̓qin	'duck'	qən-qin̓qin	'ducks'

(Central Salish; Watanabe 2003: 373)

e. Default Segmentism: Mainland Comox

kʷusən	'star'	kʷəs-kʷusən	'stars'
t̓in	'barbecued fish'	t̓ən-t̓in	'lots of barbecued fish'
maθač	'black duck'	məθ-maθač	'black ducks'
ʔimaš	'walk'	ʔəm-ʔimaš	'walk around'

(Central Salish; Watanabe 2003: 372–373)

The identity effects in (21a) and (21b) were straightforwardly analyzed using Correspondence Theory, as having BR-Faith ranked highly. However, as models have moved away from BRCT, these patterns received greater scrutiny, and many of the most well-studied examples seem to be spurious at best. In particular, authentic cases of underapplication have been challenging to find. Saba Kirchner (2010) and McCarthy et al. (2012) both argue that some of the examples of underapplication found are lexically conditioned; therefore, they are not synchronic processes that the grammar should account for.

In addition to the identity effects, it is often the case that a fixed segment is part of the exponent of the reduplicative morpheme; this is referred to as fixed segmentism. Two types of fixed segmentism have been proposed to occur in reduplication (Alderete et al. 1999). In one, an unmarked default segment arises in reduplication (as with schwa in (21e)), in order to avoid marked structure in the reduplicant. The other is where the fixed segment is analyzed as affixal. Lushootseed (Central Salish) illustrates an interesting case of variable default segmentism. When the stem has a full vowel in its base, as in (22a), the vowel is copied. However, when the first vowel is schwa, /i/ is found instead (22b). This vowel has been motivated to avoid a marked stressed schwa (Urbanczyk 2001).

(22) Lushootseed (Central Salish) 'diminutive' reduplication

a. When base has full vowel

čaləs	'hand'	ča-čaləs	'little hand'
s-dukʷ	'bad'	s-dú-ʔ-dukʷ	'riffraff'

b. When base vowel is schwa

tí-təlaw̓il	'run'	tí-təlaw̓il	'jog'
gʷədíl	'sit down'	gʷí-gʷədil	'sit down briefly'

(Bates et al. 1994)

Stressed schwa is avoided in partial reduplication, so this illustrates a pattern referred to as variable default segmentism. This is also analyzed as an extreme case of the emergence of the unmarked, where defaults are the least marked segments of the language.

Other cases of fixed segmentism involve a non-default segment, as in (23a–c), and are analyzed as affixal. Saba Kirchner (2013) analyzes these as having a vocalic affix in the input.

(23) Kwak'wala reduplication patterns

	Meaning	*Form*	*Example*	*Gloss*
a.	Plural	Ci:-	<u>p̓i:</u>p̓əsp̓əyu:	'ears'
b.	Diminutive	Ca:-	<u>ba:</u>bəg^{w}anəm	'little boy'
c.	"Too much"	Cə-	<u>mə</u>mi:χkən	'sleep too much'

(Northern Wakashan; Saba Kirchner 2013: 236)

Because Kwakw'ala lacks prefixes, the vocalic affix is infixed; doubling up of the root-initial consonant (in violation of INTEGRITY) is triggered to supply an onset to the affix.

One finding in support of BRCT is that, when it is combined with GTT, there should be a correlation between the shape and segmental quality of reduplicants. Recall that for GTT there are just general constraints on well-formedness that determine the shape. Also, FAITHFULNESS constraints can evaluate both the size of the reduplicant and the segmental quality. Lushootseed reduplication was shown to exhibit such a correlation, (Urbanczyk 2006), in which segmental and shape properties of three reduplicative morphemes follow from their classification as root or affix. The marked patterns are associated with the classification of the reduplicant as a root (where 'distributive' has a coda and permits stressed schwa: both marked and properties of roots in Lushootseed). While the unmarked patterns (avoiding codas and stressed schwa, as in (22b)) are associated with being morphologically specified as affixes ('diminutive' and 'out-of-control' affixes pattern with other segmentally specified affixes). This correlation between the shape and segmental quality of affixes is predicted by BRCT, but unexpected in other frameworks. Next we look at advances in the typological examination and analysis of infixes.

3.4. Prosodic Domains and Infixing

Recall that one of the applications of the prosodic circumscription of domains was to account for the location of infixes: they can be affixed to a prosodic unit, internal to some morphological unit as in Ulwa (6). There are two general approaches to infixing within Optimality Theory. Yu (2007) refers to these as Phonological Readjustment and Phonological Subcategorization. The former approach analyzes infixes as prefixes or suffixes that must migrate into a base, due to phonological or phonotactic pressure from the language as a whole (McCarthy & Prince 1995). For example, a -VC- shaped prefix is infixed after the first consonant of a root, in order to avoid an onsetless syllable. The Phonological Readjustment occurs in order to satisfy a global constraint of avoiding onsetless syllables. The Phonological Subcategorization approach analyzes infixes as requiring a specific phonological location internal to a root. In Ulwa, the infix subcategorizes to be suffixed to an iambic foot, rather than a morphological unit. Yu argues that the Phonological Readjustment approach cannot be universally applied to infixing because there are several cases in which infixing is non-optimizing (i.e., the location of the infix does not improve the overall phonological structure of the word). He also notes that there are many cases in which the infix has the same shape as a prefix/suffix, so it is still necessary to have some way to distinguish infixes from other types of affixes. In developing the Phonological Subcategorization framework, Yu conducted a typologically balanced survey and found a restricted set of locales for attachment. He proposes the Pivot Theory of infixing, where an affix must be located before or after some salient pivot.

(24) Salient Pivot Hypothesis

Phonological pivots must be salient at the psycholinguistic and/or phonetic level.

(Yu 2007: 68)

Yu found two types of pivots: edge- and prominence-based. The Ulwa infix would be an example of suffixing to a prominence pivot (stressed foot).

(25) Potential pivots of Phonological Subcategorization[9]

Edge Pivots	*Prominence Pivots*
First consonant	Stressed foot
First vowel	Stressed syllable
(First syllable)	Stressed vowel
Last syllable	
Last vowel	
(Last consonant)	

(Yu 2007: 67)

Yu applies his model to Washo infixing reduplication. Observe that the CV- reduplicant is a copy of the stressed syllable, as in (26a). The interesting feature of this pattern is when the stressed syllable is closed, as in (26b). In this case, the reduplicant is non-contiguous, copying the CV- of the following syllable.

(26) Washo (Hokan) plural infixing reduplication

	Singular	*Plural*	*Gloss*
a.	ʔélel	ʔe-lé-lel	'mother's father'
	gúšuʔ	gu-šú-šuʔ	'pet'
	dámal	da-má-mal	'to hear'
	bókoŋ	bo-kó-koŋ	'to snore'
b.	ʔéw.šiʔ	ʔe.-ší-w.šiʔ	'father's brothers'
	nén.t̓uš	ne.-t̓ú-n.tuš-u	'old women (u=nominalizing suffix)'
	mók.go	mo.-gó-k.go	'shoe'

(Jacobsen 1964: 322–325; Winter 1970)

Pivot Theory is able to account for a diverse range of patterns by utilizing a morphological tool that is independently needed: subcategorization. The innovation here is that rather than the base being a purely morphological unit, it can be specified as a psychologically salient phonological unit.

4. Summary: Recommendations and Future Directions

As models of reduplication have evolved alongside theories of phonology and morphology, the prosodic unit/template has emerged as one of the most resilient and adaptable tools to deriving patterns of word formation. A prosodic unit can be an affix or base, or a template to map segments from the base onto. The discussion of shape and copy mechanisms showed that in many current frameworks, there is a connection between prosodic units as affixes and the type of copy mechanism. When the morpheme is a prosodic unit, an explicit correspondence relation between segments of the base and reduplicant is not needed. However, by not having a formal link between segments of the base and reduplicant, the challenge is how to ensure identity (or lack thereof) between these segments, as in cases of overapplication, underapplication, and the emergence of the unmarked.

A further issue is that very little research has been conducted in a word-based approach. However, this is an emerging area of research in morphology (Blevins 2006; Booij 2010), and an examination of the full range of morphological patterns associated with 'imperfective' aspect in Halkomelem has shown several issues that arise when words are constructed by adding elements to a stem (Urbanczyk 2011). This suggests that there may be advances in our understanding by exploring word-based approaches further, and exploiting the inherent connections that exist between reduplicant and base.

Finally, each language is a complex system, with a web of words, connected by shared form and meaning. While we have learned a great deal by looking at a range of patterns, from a typologically diverse set of languages, future research in this area will likely benefit from having an even greater number of very detailed investigations of single languages that have multiple patterns of reduplication and prosodic morphological processes.

Acknowledgments

Many thanks to Khalsa Al-Agbari, Jason Haugen, Keren Rice, Hiroto Uchihara, Eva Zimmermann, and UVic's Researching Indigenous Languages and Linguistics group for very helpful feedback on earlier versions of this chapter. All errors and oversights remain my responsibility.

Further Reading

There is a very large body of literature covering issues in reduplication and other prosodic morphology, both specifically involving the native languages of North America and more generally. These works include: Downing (2006), a monograph outlining universal principles for the prosodic structure of morphemes; the *Graz Database on Reduplication* (Hurch 2005, et seq.), an online database of reduplication patterns and bibliography on works dealing with reduplication; Inkelas and Zoll (2005), a monograph outlining the principles of Morphological Doubling Theory, including many case studies and critiques of BRCT; McCarthy and Prince (1986), a seminal work advancing the prosodic morphology research program, which includes many examples of North American languages that have framed the theoretical debate since its inception; McCarthy and Prince (1999), an introduction to and exemplification of BRCT, including many case studies, discussion and analysis of segmentism and shape; McCarthy et al. (2012), a theoretical approach within OT that provides evidence that prosodic units such as syllable and foot can be copied in reduplication; Mithun (1999), a monograph on languages of North America that includes information about languages known to have reduplication as well as other non-concatenative processes; Saba Kirchner (2010), a doctoral dissertation that proposes two copy mechanisms, including detailed case studies of Kwak'wala and Samala as well as a discussion of recent research on mora affixation; and Trommer and Zimmermann (2014), a theoretical analysis of a number of North American languages that analyzes truncation with the addition of a mora.

Notes

1. The following abbreviations are used: ADJ = adjunctive, BR = base-reduplicant, BRCT = base-reduplicant Correspondence Theory, CONS = consequent, CRT = control transitive, GTT = Generalized Template Theory, IA = Item and Arrangement, IND = indicative, INDR = indirect, IO = input-output, IP = Item and Process, IT = iterative, L = vowel lengthening triggering suffix, MDT = Morphological Doubling Theory, OBJ = object, OT = Optimality Theory, PL = plural, POSS = possessive, R = reduplication triggering suffix, RED = reduplicant, REP = repetitive, S = subject, SG = singular, TETU = the emergence of the unmarked, TR = transitive, WP = Word and Paradigm
2. See Saba Kirchner (2010: 11) for a range of analyses that were proposed to follow from affixing a floating mora in several languages of North America, including Diegueño, Kwak'wala, Proto-Uto-Aztecan, Southern Sierra Miwok, and Washo.
3. Stonham (1994: 178–179) discusses evidence of moraic codas from an analysis of stress in Squamish (a related language) and word minimality. Crucially, there is no evidence that stress is attracted to heavy

syllables. Furthermore, the word-minimality pattern is compatible with a preference that content words are consonant-final in Saanich.

4. This could be explained by assuming a bimoraic foot with an extrametrical syllable (Kager 2012).
5. It is also the case that multiple exponence involves affixes only. See Caballero (2011) and Caballero and Harris (2012).
6. Words like those above – where the reduplicant has a contrast not present in the base – have also been used to argue for a modification in how input-output faithfulness is formalized (see Struijke 1998 for more information on this).
7. English affective reduplication is an example of this: e.g., *police* > *po-po* and *crazy* > *cray-cray*. Thanks to Jason Haugen for sharing this example.
8. Glosses are as found in Kennedy (2008: 606).
9. Yu (2007: 124) notes that the parentheses indicate "convincing patterns of infixation illustrating the need for these pivot points are not very forthcoming".

References

Alderete, J. & Beckman, J. & Benua, L. & Gnandesikan, A. & McCarthy, J. & Urbanczyk, S. 1999. Reduplication with fixed segmentism. *Linguistic Inquiry* 30. 327–364.

Anderson, S. 1992. *A-morphous morphology*. Cambridge, UK: Cambridge University Press.

Archangeli, D. 1991. Syllabification and prosodic templates in Yawelmani. *Natural Language and Linguistic Theory* 9. 231–283.

Aronoff, M. 1994. *Morphology by itself: Stems and inflection classes*. Cambridge, MA: MIT Press.

Bates, D. & Carlson, B. 1992. Simple syllables in Spokane Salish. *Linguistic Inquiry* 23. 653–659.

Bates, D. & Hess, T. & Hilbert, V. 1994. *Lushootseed dictionary*. Seattle, WA: University of Washington Press.

Bermudez-Otero, R. 2012. The architecture of grammar and the division of labor in exponence. In Trommer, J. (ed.), *The morphology and phonology of exponence*, 8–83. Oxford, UK: Oxford University Press.

Blake, S. J. 2000. *On the distribution and representation of schwa in Sliammon (Salish): Descriptive and theoretical perspectives*. University of British Columbia. (PhD thesis.)

Blevins, J. 2006. Word-based morphology. *Journal of Linguistics* 42. 531–573.

Bloomfield, L. 1933. *Language*. New York: Holt, Rinehart & Winston.

Booij, G. 2010. *Construction morphology*. Oxford, UK: Oxford University Press.

Broselow, E. & McCarthy, J. 1983. A theory of internal reduplication. *Linguistic Review* 3. 25–88.

Bye, P. & Svenonius, P. 2012. Non-concatenative morphology as epiphenomenon. In Trommer, J. (ed.), *The morphology and phonology of exponence*, 427–495. Oxford, UK: Oxford University Press.

Caballero, G. 2006. "Templatic backcopying" in Guarijio abbreviated reduplication. *Morphology* 16(2). 273–289.

Caballero, G. 2011. Multiple exponence and the phonology-morphology interface. In Lima, S., Mullin, K. & Smith, B. (eds.), *Proceedings of the North East Linguistics Society 39*. Amherst, MA: GLSA. Paper.

Caballero, Gabriela & Harris, Alice C. (2012). A working typology of multiple exponence. In Kiefer, Ferenc, Ladányi, Mária & Siptár, Péter (eds.), *Current issues in morphological theory: (Ir)Regularity, analogy and frequency. Selected papers from the 14th International Morphology Meeting, Budapest, 13–16 May 2010*, 163–188. John Benjamins.

Crowhurst, M. 1994. Foot extrametricality and template mapping in Cupeño. *Natural Language and Linguistic Theory* 12. 177–201.

Downing, L. 2006. *Canonical forms in prosodic morphology*. Oxford, UK: Oxford University Press.

Galloway, B. 1993. *A grammar of Upriver Halkomelem*. (University of California Publications in Linguistics) Berkeley: University of California Press.

Goldsmith, J. 1976. *Autosegmental phonology*. Cambridge: Massachusetts Institute of Technology. (Doctoral dissertation.)

Harris, Z. S. 1944. Yokuts structure and Newman's grammar. *International Journal of American Linguistics* 10. 196–211.

Haugen, J. 2014. Hiaki (Yaqui) reduplication redux: Morphological and prosodic targets in syllabic reduplication. *International Journal of American Linguistics* 80(4). 507–532.

Hayes, B. 1995. *Metrical stress theory: Principles and case studies*. Chicago: University of Chicago Press.

Hill, J. & Zepeda, O. 1992. Derived words in Tohono O'odham. *International Journal of American Linguistics* 58. 355–404.

Hockett, C. 1954. Two models of grammatical description. *Word* 10. 210–231.

Horwood, G. 2001. *Anti-faithfulness and subtractive morphology*. Rutgers University. (Ms.) ROA: 466–0901-Horwood-0–0.pdf

Hukari, T. & Peter, R. 1995. *Cowichan dictionary*. Duncan, BC: Cowichan Tribes.
Hurch, B. (ed.) in collaboration with V. Mattes. 2005. *Studies on reduplication*. New York: Mouton de Gruyter.
Inkelas, S. & Zoll, C. 2005. *Reduplication: Doubling in morphology*. Cambridge, UK: Cambridge University Press.
Inkelas, S. 2008. The dual theory of reduplication. *Linguistics* 46. 351–401.
Inkelas, S. 2014. *The interplay of morphology and phonology*. Cambridge: Cambridge University Press.
Jacobsen, W. H. J. 1964. *A grammar of the Washo language*. Berkeley: University of California. (Doctoral dissertation.)
Kager, R. 2012. Stress in windows: Language typology and factorial typology. *Lingua* 122. 1454–1493.
Kennedy, R. 2008. Evidence for morphoprosodic alignment in reduplication. *Linguistic Inquiry* 39. 589–614.
Kim, E-S. 2003. *Theoretical issues in Nuu-chah-nulth phonology and morphology*. Vancouver, BC: University of British Columbia. (Doctoral dissertation.)
Kurisu, K. 2001. *The phonology of morpheme realization*. Santa Cruz: University of California. (Doctoral dissertation.)
Leben, W. R. 1973. *Suprasegmental phonology*. Cambridge, MA: Massachusetts Institute of Technology. (Doctoral dissertation.)
Lee, S. 2013. *Multiple exponence in non-inflectional morphology*. Victoria, BC: University of Victoria. (Doctoral dissertation.)
Leonard, J. 2019. *The phonological representation and distribution of vowels in SENĆOŦEN*. Victoria, BC: University of Victoria. (Doctoral dissertation.)
Lombardi, L. & McCarthy, J. 1991. Prosodic circumscription in Choctaw morphology. *Phonology* 8. 37–71.
Marantz, A. 1982. Re reduplication. *Linguistic Inquiry* 13. 435–482.
McCarthy, J. & Prince, A. 1986. *Prosodic morphology*. University of Massachusetts, Amherst & Brandeis University. (Ms.)
McCarthy, J. & Prince, A. 1990. Foot and word in Prosodic Morphology: The Arabic broken plural. *Natural Language and Linguistic Theory* 8. 209–282.
McCarthy, J. & Prince, A. 1994. The emergence of the unmarked: Optimality in prosodic morphology. In Gonzàlez, M. (ed.), *Proceedings of NELS 24*, 333–370. Amherst, MA: GLSA Publications.
McCarthy, J. & Prince, A. 1999. Faithfulness and identity in prosodic morphology. In Kager, R. & van der Hulst, H. & Zonneveld, W. (eds.) *The prosody-morphology interface*, 218–309. Cambridge, UK: Cambridge University Press.
McCarthy, J. 1979. *Formal problems in Semitic morphology and phonology*. MIT (PhD thesis.)
McCarthy, J. 1981. A prosodic theory of nonconcatenative morphology. *Linguistic Inquiry* 12. 373–418.
McCarthy, J. & Kimper, W. & Mullin, K. 2012. Reduplication in harmonic serialism. *Morphology* 22. 173–232.
McCarthy, John & Prince, Alan. 1995. Faithfulness and reduplicative identity. In Beckman, J. N. & Walsh Dickey, L. & Urbanczyk, S. (eds.), *University of Massachusetts Occasional Papers 18, Papers in Optimality Theory*, 249–384. Amherst, MA: GLSA publication.
Mithun, M. 1999. *The languages of native North America*. Cambridge: Cambridge University Press.
Montler, T. 1986. *Morphology and phonology of Saanich*. Missoula: University of Montana Press.
Moravscik, E. 1978. Reduplicative constructions. In Greenberg, J. (ed.), *Universals of human language, vol. 3: Word structure*, 279–334. Stanford, CA: Stanford University Press.
Munro, P. & Benson, P. J. 1973. Reduplication and rule ordering in Luiseño. *International Journal of American Linguistics* 39. 15–21.
Newman, S. S. 1944. *The Yokuts language of California*. The Viking Fund Publications in Anthropology 2. New York: The Viking Fund.
Prince, A. & Smolensky, P. 1993. *Optimality theory: Constraint interaction in generative grammar*. Technical report of the Rutgers University Center of Cognitive Science.
Saba Kirchner, J. 2010. *Minimal reduplication*. Santa Cruz: University of California. (Doctoral dissertation.)
Saba Kirchner, J. 2013. Minimal reduplication and reduplicative exponence. *Morphology* 23. 227–243.
Sapir, E. 1915. Noun reduplication in Comox, a Salish language of Vancouver Island. Canada Department of Mines, Geological Survey, Memoir 63, Anthropological Series, no. 5. Ottawa: Government Printing Bureau.
Shaw, P. A. 1980. *Theoretical issues in Dakota phonology and morphology*. New York: Garland.
Shaw, P. A., Blake, S. J., Campbell, J. & Shepherd, C. 1999. Stress in hun̓q̓əmin̓əm̓ (Musqueam) Salish. In Caldecott, M., Gessner, S. & Kim, E. (eds.), *Proceedings of the Workshop on Structure and Constituency of the Languages of the Americas* 4, 131–164. Vancouver, BC: UBC Working Papers in Linguistics.
Stonham, J. 1994. *Combinatorial morphology* (Current Issues in Linguistic Theory). Amsterdam: John Benjamins.
Struijke, C. 1998. Reduplicant and output TETU in Kwakwala. *University of Maryland Working Papers, vol 7. Papers in Phonology*. 150–178.

Thompson, L. & Thompson, M. 1969. Metathesis as a grammatical device. *International Journal of American Linguistics* 35. 213–219.

Trommer, J. & Zimmermann, E. 2014. Generalized mora affixation and quantity-manipulating morphology. *Phonology* 31. 463–510.

Urbanczyk, S. 1993. Infixing and moraic circumscription. In Sherer, Tim (ed.), *University of Massachusetts occasional papers in linguistics* 16, 319–357. Amherst, MA: Graduate Linguistics Students Association.

Urbanczyk, S. 1999. A-Templatic reduplication in Halq'eméylem. In Shahin, Kimary, Blake, Susan & Kim, Eun Sook (eds.), *Proceedings of West Coast Conference on Formal Linguistics XVII*, 655–669. Stanford, CA: CSLI Publications.

Urbanczyk, S. 2001. *Patterns of reduplication in Lushootseed*. New York: Garland. (Outstanding Dissertations in Linguistics.)

Urbanczyk, S. 2006. Reduplicative form and the root-affix asymmetry. *Natural Language and Linguistic Theory* 24. 179–240.

Urbanczyk, S. 2011. Evidence from Halkomelem for word-based morphology. In Lyon, J. & Dunham, J. (eds.), *International conference on Salish and neighbouring languages* 46, 470–489. Vancouver: UBC Linguistics.

Watanabe, H. 2003. A morphological description of Sliammon, Mainland Comox Salish: With a sketch of syntax. Endangered Languages of the Pacific Rim, Faculty of Informatics, Osaka Gakuin University.

Wilbur, R. 1973. *The phonology of reduplication*. University of Illinois, Urbana-Champaign. (PhD thesis.)

Winter, W. 1970. Reduplication in Washo: A restatement. *International Journal of American Linguistics* 35. 190–198.

Yu, A. 2007. *A natural history of infixation*. Oxford, UK: Oxford University Press.

Zimmermann, E. 2013. Non-concatenative allomorphy is generalized prosodic affixation: The case of Upriver Halkomelem. *Lingua* 134. 1–26.

Zimmermann, E. 2017. *Morphological length and prosodically defective morphemes*. Oxford, UK: Oxford University Press.

5
THE EXPANDED NP
Number, Possessors, Gender, Animacy, and Classifiers

Carrie Gillon

1. Introduction

While North American languages are better known for their complicated verbal structures, the nominal structure of many languages can be nearly as intricate and interesting. In this chapter, I discuss the expanded NP, including number marking (dual, plural, paucal, etc.), possessors and possession marking, gender and animacy, classifiers, determiners and demonstratives, and case marking. The languages of North America vary wildly with respect to the presence or absence of all of these features, as well as their expression. I provide examples from languages across the continent, showing the range of expression for each category. In order to cover all of these topics, the theoretical coverage will necessarily be short; however, I assume a generative framework and a semi-cartographic approach, with functional heads hosting certain kinds of meaning. The syntactic position(s) I assume for each category is briefly mentioned in each subsection.

2. Class Systems

North American languages display a wide range of class systems, mostly based on gender. Some language families make no class system distinctions whatsoever: Chumash (Mithun 1998; Wash 2001) and Eskimo-Aleut (Jacobson 1995; Mithun 1998) both lack class system marking anywhere in their grammar, for example. Some families are mixed between those that display class system marking and those that do not (e.g., Salish). In some languages/language families, class system marking is also found on verbs (e.g., in Algonquian and Iroquoian). In this section, I focus only on class system marking within the nominal domain, which means that some interesting patterns will be missed.

Within a particular class system, there is usually some overlap with nouns in a particular group and some semantic feature (Corbett 2013). This feature is usually biological sex (for gender systems), but it can also be animacy, or other features. Kramer (2015) distinguishes between natural gender/animacy, which are based on semantic features (like biological sex for gender), and grammatical gender/animacy, which are arbitrary. For example, tables have no inherent biological sex, but receive arbitrary feminine gender marking in French.

Within the nominal domain, there are languages that mark gender (masculine/feminine/(neuter)), those that mark animacy, and those with larger class systems. I discuss each in turn, pointing out the semantic vs. arbitrary uses of gender or animacy.

Syntactically, I assume that class marking is hosted in n, following Kramer (2015).

2.1. Gender

There are at least two systems of gender: masculine/feminine and masculine/feminine/neuter.

2.1.1. Masculine/Feminine

In some Salish languages (including Sechelt, Lushootseed, Musqueam, Upper Chehalis, Cowlitz, Nuxalk, Lummi, Saanich, Upriver Halkomelem, Sḵwx̱wú7mesh, and Sliammon), gender is marked on the articles and/or demonstratives. For example, in Sḵwx̱wú7mesh (Squamish), the articles (Table 5.1) and demonstratives (Table 5.2) have masculine[1] and feminine forms.

The feminine determiners are used when the noun phrase refers to female humans or animals; otherwise, masculine determiners are used (Kuipers 1967). There is at least one exception to this: Kuipers (1967) reports that *snexwílh* 'canoe' can also sometimes take the feminine forms. The feminine determiners are also not obligatorily used with female referents, as shown in (1).

(1) Sḵwx̱wú7mesh

Chen	*kw'ách-nexw*	***ta/lha***	*slhánaý.*
1SG.SBJ	look-TR	ART.M/ART.F	woman

'I saw a/the woman.'

(Gillon 2013: 31)

Thus, masculine gender is the default in Sḵwx̱wú7mesh. Feminine gender is usually semantic, with at least one arbitrary use (for canoe).

In Halkomelem, the "feminine gender 'leaks' onto hundreds of inanimate nouns" (Gerdts 2011). For example, *snəxʷəɬ* ('canoe/car') and *lelə́m̓* ('house') can take the feminine form of the determiner (2).

Table 5.1 The Article System of Sḵwx̱wú7mesh[2]

	DEICTIC			*NON-DEICTIC*
	NEUT	*PROX*	*DIST, INVIS*	
M	*ta*	*ti*	*kwa*	*kwi*
F	*lha*	*tsi*	*kwelha*	*kwes*

Source: Adapted from Gillon (2009: 8).

Table 5.2 The Demonstrative System of Sḵwx̱wú7mesh

		NEUT, INVIS	*PROX*	*MED*	*DIST*	
					UNMARKED	*INVIS*
M	#-NEUTRAL	*kwíya*	*tí, tíwa*[a]	*táy'*	*kwétsi*	
	PLURAL	*kwiyáwit*	*iyá(wit)*	*ítsi(wit)*	*kwétsiwit*	*kwáwit*
F		*kwsá*	*tsíwa*	*álhi*	*kwélhi*	

Source: Adapted from Gillon (2009: 8).

[a] The suffix *-wa* is licit only if the referent is human.

(2) Halkomelem

ɬiq̓-t	***θən̓***	*snəxʷəɬ*	*ʔə*	***θə***	*leləm̓.*
move-TR	ART.F.2POSS	canoe	OBL	ART.F	house

'Move your car (F) closer to the house (F)!'

(Gerdts 2011: 419)

Gerdts (2009, 2011) reports that most feminine inanimate nouns refer to buildings, containers, small round objects, flexible objects, fluids or abstract objects. Further, female speakers are more likely to use feminine determiners than male speakers (Gerdts 2011). In Halkomelem, the feminine form has both semantic and arbitrary uses.

Similarly, in Quileute (Chimakuan), demonstratives mark feminine/masculine (Andrade 1933). The demonstratives *yik* and *kiʔ* are used with female referents; *yix̣* and *x̣eʔ* are used with male or neuter referents.

(3) Quileute

a. ***yik*** *áʔč'it-t'*
DEM.F chief-wife
'the chief's wife'

b. ***yix̣*** *áʔč'it*
DEM.M chief
'the chief'

c. ***kiʔ*** *yalôlat*
DEM.F wife
'the wife'

d ***x̣eʔ*** *hé:t́it*
DEM.M husband
'the husband'

e. ***yix̣*** *ƛ̓oťołoót*
DEM.M star
'the star'

(Andrade 1933: 279–282)

In Quileute, masculine is default, and feminine marking is only used semantically.

In Tunica (isolate), nouns take masculine or feminine suffixes (Table 5.3) (Haas 1941: 65). The gender marking is used both semantically and arbitrarily. Female humans or animals take the feminine suffixes; male humans or animals take the masculine suffixes. Most count inanimate nouns are masculine; most mass nouns are feminine.

(4) Tunica

a. *táčɔhaku*
ta-čɔ́ha-**ku**
ART-chief-M.SG
'the chief'

b. *tánisarahč*
ta-nísara-**hči**
ART-young.person-F.SG
'the girl'

c. *tášihkali-**ku***
rock-M.SG
'rock'

d. *tári-**hči***[3]
house-F.SG
'house'

Table 5.3 Gender Suffixes in Tunica

	M	*F*
SG	*-ku*	*-hči*
DU	*-ʔúnima*	*-sínima, sin*
PL	*-sɛ́ma, sɛm*	

Source: Haas (1941: 65).

e. *táwiši-**hči***
water-F.SG
'water'

(Haas 1941: 65)

Heaton and Anderson (2017) argue that the feminine gender is unmarked, partially based on the fact that animals are marked default feminine. Gender is also marked on the pronouns and verbs.

Mayan is usually described as lacking gender marking, but there are a few places where gender is marked. In particular, some nouns take different prefixes depending on the gender of the referent. For example, in Yucatec Maya, the *h-* prefix marks masculine gender and *š-* marks feminine. These can even be found on some proper names (mostly names used by women or girls). Animals are marked via adjectives rather than the prefixes.

(5) Yucatec Maya

a. ***h**-men*
M-shaman
'male medicine maker'

b. ***x**-men*
F-shaman
'female medicine maker'

c. ***X**-Nico*
F-Nicolasa
'Nicolasa'

d. ***H**-Uel*
M-Manuel
'Manuel'

e. ***xibil*** *ceh*
male deer
'stag'

f. ***chupul*** *ceh*
female deer
'doe'

(Bolles & Bolles 2014: 22)

Inanimates are never gender-marked in Mayan. In Mayan, gender marking is purely semantic.

2.1.2. Masculine/Feminine/Neuter

Some languages have a three-way split: masculine, feminine, and neuter. For example, in Kathlamet (Chinookan), all singular nouns have a gender prefix associated with them (Boas 1904). (Plural and dual nouns take only number marking.) If the gender is unknown, speakers use neuter gender (Boas 1911) (6c). This gender marking has both semantic and arbitrary uses. Male humans are marked with masculine gender, female humans with feminine, and humans with unknown gender are marked with neuter. Large animals tend to be masculine, and smaller animals tend to be feminine.

(6) Kathlamet Chinook

a. ***i**-qʔiúqt*
M-old.person
'old man'

b. ***a**-qʔiúqt*
F-old.person
'old woman'

c. ***ɬ**-qʔiuqt*
N-old person
'old person'

d. ***i**-púkua*
M-lynx
'lynx'

e. ***a**-qaɬxíla*
F-crab
'crab'

f. ***ɬ**-cúqua*
N-water
'water'

(Hymes 1955: 90–131)

In Lower Chinook (Chinookan), the gender distinction is sometimes extended to objects to denote size: *i-* represents a larger object, and *u-* represents a smaller one.

(7) Lower Chinook

a. *í-pqunx̣*
M-round.spruce.root.basket
'large round spruce root basket'

b. ***u**-pqunx*
F-round.spruce.root.basket
'small round spruce root basket'

(Boas 1904: 138)

Gender is also marked on the demonstratives and verbs in both Kathlamet and Lower Chinook.

Cayuga (Iroquoian) marks masculine, feminine or neuter genders via a prefix on the noun. There are three unpredictable variants of the neuter gender (*o-*, *ga-*, and *a-*)[4] (Barrie 2016).

(8) Cayuga

a. ***ga**-nǫ́hs-aˀ*
N-house-NSF
'house'

b. ***e**-ksá:ˀ-ah*
F-child-NSF
'girl'

c. ***ha**-ksá:ˀ-ah*
M-child-NSF
'boy'

(Barrie 2016: 366)

This appears to be a completely semantic use of gender marking (inanimates are never marked with feminine or masculine morphology). A more complicated gender system is also found on the verb.

2.2. Animacy

There are at least two different types of animacy marking in North America: a human/non-human distinction and a more general animate/inanimate distinction. Just like with gender marking, animacy has a semantic core that can be extended to arbitrary referents.

2.2.1. Human vs. Non-human

In Coahuilteco (isolate), the demonstratives distinguish between human and non-human referents. The demonstrative system is quite complex, and so I focus here only on the demonstrative stems, which disambiguate between human (singular), human (plural), and non-human (plural). (Singular non-human referents take demonstratives that lack any of these stems; I assume a null stem for singular non-human demonstratives.) The stems can be further modified with deictic information, grammatical role, etc.

(9) Coahuilteco

a. *po:*
DEM.human.SG

b. *pa:*
DEM.human.PL

c. *-Ø-*
DEM.nonhuman.SG

d. *če:*
DEM.non.human.PL

(Troike 1996: 661)

(10) Coahuilteco

a. *kuta:ce* *tu-**po:***
priest NEUT-DEM.human.SG
'the priest'

b. *pi:lam* *a-**pa:***
people PROX-DEM.human.PL
'the people'

c.	*tamo:x*	***tu-če:***	d.	*Hostia*	*ta-**Ø**-x*
	demon	NEUT-DEM.non.human.PL		Host	DIST-non.human.SG-3OBJ
	'demons'				'the Host (of the Mass)'

(Troike 1981: 660–661)

This system appears to be semantic, with no arbitrary uses of human marking on non-human referents.

2.2.2. Animate vs. Inanimate

Animacy is systematically marked in Algonquian[5] languages, in both the nominal and verbal domain, but I focus only on the nominal domain, where it is marked on the demonstratives and number marking. Animate entities, like humans and animals, always receive animate marking and inanimate entities, like rivers, often (but not always) receive inanimate marking. In Meskwaki (Fox), both singular and plural forms encode animacy (Table 5.4) (11)–(12).

(11) Meskwaki

a.	*penêw-**a***	b.	*penêw-**aki***
	turkey-AN.SG		man-AN.PL
	'turkey'		'turkeys'

(Bliss & Oxford 2016: 72)

(12) Meskwaki

a.	*ahte:himin-**i***	b.	*ahte:himin-**ani***
	strawberry-IN.SG		strawberry-IN.PL
	'strawberry'		'strawberries'

(Dahlstrom 1995: 58/62)

In Innu-aimun, only plural forms encode animacy.[6]

(13) Innu-aimun

a.	*mashk[u]*	b.	*mashku-**at***
	bear		bear-AN.PL
	'bear'		'bears'
c.	*shîpu*	d.	*shîpu-**a***
	river		river-IN.PL
	'river'		'rivers'

(Mailhot & MacKenzie 2013: 154/388; Gillon 2015: 136)

In Algonquian, animacy is also marked on the demonstratives.

Table 5.4 Animacy Distinctions in Meskwaki

	SG	PL
AN	*-a*	*-aki*
IN	*-i*	*-ani*

Source: Adapted from Dahlstrom (1995: 55).

(14) Plains Cree

a.	**anima**	maskisin	b.	**ana**	kinosêw
	DEM.IN	shoe		DEM.AN	fish
	'that shoe'			'that fish'	

(Muehlbauer 2007: 174)

In (11)–(14), the distinction is semantic: animals receive animate marking and inanimate objects receive inanimate marking. However, there are cases where animacy marking appears to be arbitrary. For example, in Meskwaki, strawberries receive inanimate marking, while raspberries receive animate marking.

(15) Meskwaki

a.	*ahte:himin-**i***	b.	*ahte:himin-**ani***
	strawberry-IN.SG		strawberry-IN.PL
	'strawberry'		'strawberries'
c.	*wi:tawai:h-**a***	d.	*wi:tawai:h-**aki***
	raspberry-AN.SG		raspberry-AN.PL
	'raspberry'		'raspberries'

(Dahlstrom 1995: 58/62)

The nature of this animate/inanimate distinction has long been debated; some researchers argue that only elements that have 'power' are considered to be animate (Hallowell 1960; Darnell & Vanek 1976; among others), or that this animacy distinction reflects an Algonquian worldview. However, this feature has not been well described and cannot explain the difference between the examples in Table 5.5.

It is unclear why a raisin would have more 'power' than a strawberry, for example. Wolvengrey (2011) lists *kaskitêmin* 'blackberry' as inanimate. What characteristics would blackberries share with animate strawberries, blueberries, and saskatoon berries that they do not also share with inanimate raspberries? It is also unclear why many words for articles of clothing are animate, while *maskisin* 'shoe' is inanimate. (See also the discussion in Dahlstrom 1995 for more examples of arbitrary animacy on some of the words for animal skins and body parts in Meskwaki.)

The "particular worldview" that would be reflected in this gender system is uncertain. Goddard (2002: 200) shows that the word for 'tobacco' is animate in Meskwaki, Cree, Menomini, and

Table 5.5 Plains Cree Animacy

AN		*IN*	
mitâs	'a pair of pants'	*miskât*	'a leg'
astis	'a mitt/glove'	*micihciy*	'a hand'
maskasiy	'a fingernail/toenail'	*mêstakay*	'a hair'
tâpiskâkan	'a scarf/tie'	*nîpiy*	'a leaf'
sôminis	'a raisin'	*mitêhimin*	'a strawberry'
ayôskan	'a raspberry'	*iyinimin*	'a blueberry'
oskâtâsk	'a carrot'	*misâskwatômin*	'a saskatoon berry'
wîhkihkasika	'a cake'	*wîhkwaskwa*	'sweetgrass (pl)'
ospwâkan	'a pipe'	*miskîsik*	'an eye'
asâm	'a snowshoe'	*maskisin*	'a shoe'

Source: Adapted from Ratt (2016: 6, 27).

Ojibwe, while inanimate in Munsee, Unami, and Eastern Abenaki. As Goddard (2002: 201) argues, "the cultural role and status of tobacco differed little among the Algonquian peoples". I therefore assume that animacy marked on, e.g., *ayôskan* 'raspberry' is arbitrary.

Lealao Chinantec (Otomangean) marks animacy via a suffix on adjectives (16a), numerals (16c), and quantifiers (16d). Inanimates are unmarked (16b), and animates are marked via *-y*. This appears to be a true semantic use of animacy marking.

(16) Lealao Chinantec

a.	*dsɨɨ*^{3}	*dxú*^{4}*-y*	b.	*mɨh*^{3}	*dxú*^{4}
	dog	good-AN		clothing	good.IN
	'good dog'			'good clothing'	
c.	*chiú̲*^{3}*-y*	*mɨ*^{1}*-liuh*^{2}	d.	*liáh*^{4}*jɨ*^{3}*-y*	*dsa*^{3}
	four-AN	CLF-little		all-AN	person
	'four children'			'all the people'	

(Rupp 2009: 10, 4, 9)

Animacy is also marked on the verb.

In Southern Tiwa (Tanoan), animates are marked with *-de*, and inanimates remain unmarked.

(17) Southern Tiwa

a.	*sə̀ani-**de***	b.	*kəáʔì-**de***
	man-AN		bear-AN
	'man'		'bear'
c.	*nakáyu*	d.	*p'ién*
	'tortilla'		'mountain'

(Sandia dialect; Brandt 1970: 109)

In the Sandia dialect, anything capable of independent motion is also marked as animate (Brandt 1970: 109). (Perhaps "animacy" is the wrong label; perhaps the real semantic core feature is "independent movement". If so, this is a semantic gender system, with no arbitrary uses.)

(18) Southern Tiwa

a.	*tùmubíli-**de***	b.	*waʔí-**de***	e.	*kànkáruwi-**de***
	automobile-AN		wind-AN		wagon-AN
	'automobile'		'wind'		'wagon'

(Sandia dialect; Brandt 1970: 109)

2.3. Class Systems

There are a few more complicated systems in North America, where nouns are divided into more than the two or three classes that gender or animacy systems have. For example, Yuchi (isolate) has a complex noun class system, which divides nouns into animate and inanimate classes, and further divides the inanimate nouns into vertical, horizontal, and round classes.[7] All animate nouns take the suffix *-nǫ̂*, but are further marked by other suffixes, depending on whether the noun refers to relatives, non-related Yuchis, or other humans/animals; these suffixes also (in most cases) depend on the gender of the speaker. (Female speakers also have a more complicated system than male speakers.) These classes are marked on pronouns, demonstratives, pronominal agreement on the verbs, and on the definite article.

(19) Yuchi

a. ***tála-wə-nǫ̂***
wolf-ART.AN.non.Yuchi-AN
'the wolf'

b. *yá-**fa***
tree-ART.IN.vertical
'the tree'

c. *ya-**'ɛ́***
tree-ART.IN.horizontal
'the log'

d. *tí-**dji***
chair-ART.IN.round
'the chair'

e. *gɔnt'ɛ-**nǫ̂***
man-ART.AN.Yuchi
'the man' (male speaker)

f. *gɔnt'ɛ-**wə-nǫ̂***
man-ART.AN.non.Yuchi-AN
'the non-Yuchi man'

g. *tsowatɛ́-**sɛ-nǫ̂***
sister-ART.AN.relative-AN
'my sister' (male speaker)

h. *dotaonɛ-**s'ɛ́-nǫ̂***
brother-ART.AN.relative-AN
'my brother' (female speaker)

(Wagner 1938: 321)

The Yuchi class system is provided in Table 5.6.

In Ponca (Siouan), the definite articles distinguish between inanimate and animate referents; animate referents are further marked for grammatical role (agent/patient) and whether moving or at rest (Table 5.7). (This last distinction may be a deictic one, rather than a class distinction.)

(20) Ponca

a. *maščįge* ***akʰá*** *paðį* ***ðąkʷá***
Rabbit ART.AN.A.SG.resting Pawnee ART.AN.P.PL.sitting
wéðá *tʰe*
found them
'Maščįge (the Rabbit) detected the Pawnees.'

b. *mį* ***ðą*** *hídexči* *tʰédi, . . .*
sun ART.IN.round at.the.very.bottom when
'When the sun was at the very bottom of the sky. . .'

(Dorsey 1890: 379)

Table 5.6 Yuchi Noun Class Article Suffixes

	MALE SPEAKER	FEMALE SPEAKER
INANIMATE		
VERTICAL INANIMATE OBJECTS	*-fa*	*-fa*
HORIZONTAL INANIMATE OBJECTS	*-'ɛ́*	*-'ɛ́*
ROUND INANIMATE OBJECTS	*-dji*	*-dji*
ANIMATE		
NON-YUCHI(S), ANIMALS	*-wə-nǫ̂*	*-wə-nǫ̂*
YUCHI (EXCEPT CERTAIN FEMALE RELATIVES)	—	—
FEMALE YUCHI (SAME OR DESCENDING GEN)	—	*-sɛ́-nǫ̂*
MALE RELATIVE (SAME OR DESCENDING GEN)	*-nǫ̂*	*-s'ɛ́-nǫ̂*
MALE UNRELATED YUCHI OR MALE RELATIVE (SAME OR DESCENDING GEN)	—	*-ó-nǫ*
MALE RELATIVE (ASCENDING GEN)	—	*-í-nǫ*
FEMALE RELATIVE (SAME OR DESCENDING GEN)	*-sɛ́-nǫ̂*	*-sɛ́-nǫ̂*
FEMALE RELATIVE (ASCENDING GEN)	*-ɛ́-nǫ̂*	*-ɛ́-nǫ̂*

Source: Based on Wagner (1938).

Table 5.7 Ponca Definite Articles[8]

	AGENT	PATIENT
INANIMATE		
HORIZONTAL OBJECT	*kʰe*	*kʰe*
STANDING OBJECT/COLLECTIVE	*tʰe*	*tʰe*
ROUND OBJECT	*ðą*	*ðą*
SCATTERED OBJECT	*ge*	*ge*
ANIMATE		
AT REST SG	*akʷá*	—
IN MOTION SG; AT REST/IN MOTION PL	*amá*	—
STANDING SG	—	*tʰą*
MOVING SG	—	*ðį*
STANDING/MOVING PL	—	*ma*
SITTING SG	—	*ðįkʷé*
SITTING PL	—	*ðąkʷá*

Source: Based on Boas and Swanton (1911: 939–941).

The Tanoan languages also have class systems, but because their systems interact with number marking, I discuss them in §3.

3. Number Marking

North American languages vary widely when it comes to the expression of number within the NP. There are at least a few languages that lack number marking within the NP altogether, e.g., Quiegolani Zapotec (Black 2000) and Chimariko (Dixon 1910). I focus here on languages that have overt expression of number somewhere within the noun phrase.

Syntactically, I assume that plurality can occupy many different positions within the functional domain of the NP, associated with different types of semantics (see, e.g., Butler 2012 for an overview).

3.1. Plural Marking

Many languages have at least some form of plural marking within the noun: some languages only optionally mark it, some obligatorily so.

3.1.1. Optional Plural Marking

Many languages in North America have optional plural marking; the absence of such marking results in a noun with general number (that is, the noun can refer to both atoms and groups of atoms; see Corbett 2000). For example, S<u>k</u>w<u>x</u>wú7mesh (Salish), Piipaash (Maricopa) and Quechan (both Yuman), and Yucatec Maya (Mayan) all mark plurality optionally. In S<u>k</u>w<u>x</u>wú7mesh, plural is productively marked via CVC reduplication on the noun (Kuipers 1967).

(21) S<u>k</u>w<u>x</u>wú7mesh

a.	*push* cat 'cat/cats'	b.	***pesh**-púsh* REDUP-cat 'cats'
b.	*s-lhanay'* NOM-woman 'woman/women'	d.	*s-**lhen**-lhanay'* NOM-REDUP-woman 'women'

(Gillon 2013: 17)

In Piipaash and Quechan, there are a limited number of nouns that can take the plural marking. In Piipaash, the plural form usually involves ablaut (22a–d), but some nouns take *-sh* (22e), *-sh* and <*sh/t*> (22f), ablaut and <*sh/t*> (22g), or ablaut, *-sh*, and <*sh/t*> (22h).

(22) Piipaash

a. *mhay/mh**aa***
boy/boys

b. *mshhay/mshh**aa***
girl/girls

c. *humar/hum**aa**r*
child/children

d. *nchen/nch**ii**n*
older.sibling/older.siblings

e. *akoy/a<**sh**>koy-**sh***
old woman/old women

f. *'iipaa/'iip**a**-**sh***
man/men

g. *kwr'ak/kwr<**sh**>'**aa**k*
old.man/old.men

h. *nkwii/n<**t**>kw**i**-**sh***
uncle/uncles

(Gordon 1986: 29–30)

In Quechan, some nouns can be pluralized by the infix <*c*>. Still others are nominalized pluralized verbs.

(23) Quechan

a. *maxʷá:*
'badger/badgers'

b. *kʷa:nák/kʷa:**c**nák*
hollow, dip (in ground)/hollows

c. *kʷasʔi:đé:*
'doctor'

d. *kʷasʔi:tđ-í-**c***
doctor-ATTR-PL.S
'doctors'
lit: those who are doctors

(Halpern 1946: 209)

In both Yuman languages, plural can be, but does not need to be, marked on the verb instead or in addition to marking on the noun. In Yucatec Maya, an optional plural suffix *-o'ob-* can be added to force a plural reading.

(24) Yucatec Maya

a. *Táan u k'aay le x-ch'úupal-o'*
PROG 3ERG sing DEF F-girl-DIST
(i) 'The girl is singing.'
(ii) 'The girls are singing.'

b. *Táan u k'aay le x-ch'úupal-**o'ob**-o'*
PROG 3ERG sing DEF F-girl-PL-DIST
'The girls are singing.'

(Butler 2011: 52–53)

Plural can also optionally be marked on the verb in Yucatec.

3.1.2. Obligatory Plural Marking

Some languages have obligatory plural marking. This includes most of the Algonquian languages.[9] For example, in Ojibwe, a noun must be marked as plural in the presence of a numeral (other than one).

(25) Ojibwe

a.	*niizh*	*gwiizens-**ag***	b.	**niizh*	*gwiizens*
	two	boy-AN.PL		two	boy
	'two boys'				

(Mathieu 2012: 177)

3.1.3. Multiple Plural Marking

In a few languages, plural may be marked multiple times on the same noun. For example, Gitksan has several different ways of marking plurality: reduplication, prefixation, and irregular morphology (Brown 2007). Two forms of plural marking can be found on the same word simultaneously.

(26) Gitksan

a.	*muxw*[10]	b.	***hu**-muxw*	c.	***g̲a**-muxw*	d.	***g̲a-hu**-muxw*
	ear		PL-ear		DISTRTPL-ear		PL-PL-ear
	'ear'		'ears'		'ears'		'ears'

(Brown 2007)

These plurals are not in complete free variation; however, the details of which lexical item can take which plural form (and whether that item allows stacking of plurals) is not clear (Jason Brown, p.c.).[11]

3.2. Singular Marking

Some Algonquian languages mark singular as well as plural.[12] Meskwaki is an example (11). Zuni (isolate) also has obligatory plural and singular marking (Newman 1965).

(27) Zuni

a.	*ča-**ʔleʔ***	b.	*ča-**weʔ***
	child-SG		child-PL
	'child'		'children'

(Newman 1965: 65)

Some mass nouns are always marked plural (e.g., water, dust, thoughts).

3.3. Dual Marking

A few languages have both dual and plural marking. Inuttut (Labrador Inukitut; Eskimo-Aleut) is one such example. In Inuttut, dual is marked by lengthening of the final vowel, and plural is marked by the suffix *-it*.

(28) Inuttut

a.	*nanuk*	b.	*nanok*	c.	*nanuit*
	nanuk		nanuk		nanu-it
	polar.bear		polar.bear<DU>		polar.bear-PL
	'polar bear'		'two polar bears'		'3+ polar bears'

(Gillon 2012: 215)

Table 5.8 Lower Chinook Demonstratives

	SG			*DU*	*PL*	
	M	*F*	*N*		*NON-HUMANS*	*HUMANS*
PRESENT, VISIBLE						
NEAR 1ST PERSON	*x·ik*	*x·ak*	*x·īLik*	*x·īctik*	*x·ītik*	*x·itikc*
NEAR 2ND PERSON	*x·iau*	*x·au*	*x·īLa*	*x·īcta*	*x·īta*	*x·ītac*
NEAR 3RD PERSON	*x·ix·*	*x·ax·*	*x·ōLa*	*x·ōcta*	*x·ōta*	*x·ōtac*
PAST, INVISIBLE						
NEAR 2ND PERSON	*qiau*		*qēLa*	*qēcta*	*qēta*	*qētac*
NEAR 3RD PERSON	*qix·*	*qax̣*	*qōLa*	*qōcta*	*qōta*	*qōtac*

Source: Boas (1911: 618).

In Tunica, a language isolate, masculine nouns are marked as singular, dual, or plural (Haas 1941: 65), as we saw in Table 5.3. In Lower Chinook, demonstratives and nouns are marked for either gender (if singular) or number (dual or plural) (Table 5.8).

Kathlamet has a similar system. Agreement between the noun, demonstrative, and verb can be seen in examples like (29).

(29) Kathlamet

qust ***i**-kipix̣L* ***i**-ax̣i-ax* ***ik**-i-x-lucx-am*
behold M-sealion M-DEM-EMPH M.ERG-M.ABS-REFL-see-PURP
'Behold, a sealion came to see the dance.'

(Hymes 1955: 304)

There are also a few languages with a "constructed dual" – where the noun is marked as plural, and the verb is marked as singular, resulting in a dual interpretation for the noun. For example, in Zuni, verbs can be marked as plural or singular; when the verb is marked as singular and occurs with a plural marked noun, the noun receives a dual interpretation.

(30) Zuni

ʔa:w-akcek(ʔi) *ʔa:-kya*
PL-boy go-PST
'Two boys went.'

(Corbett 2000: 170)

A dual particle can also be used to enforce a dual interpretation.

(31) Zuni

ʔa:w-akcek(ʔi) ***ʔa:či*** *ʔa:-kya*
PL-boy DU go-PST
'Two boys went.'

(Corbett 2000: 170)

Hopi (Uto-Aztecan) also has a constructed dual, but only with pronouns (Hale 1997), as does Kawaiisu (Uto-Aztecan) (Zigmond et al. 1991).

3.4. Paucal

Paucal number marking marks a small plurality (e.g., 2–6). Very few languages have paucal marking. Koasati (Muskogean) is such an example. First, it has optional plural marking on nouns referring to humans.

(32) Koasati

a.	*ná:ni/ná:ni-**ha***	b.	*tayyí/tayyi-**há***
	man/man-PL		woman/woman-PL

(Kimball 1991: 447)

Some diminutive forms referring to humans may also take a paucal suffix, or both the paucal and the plural suffix.[13]

(33) Koasati

a.	*a:pó:si*	b.	*a:pós-**ki***	c.	*a:pós-**ki**-ha*
	'paternal aunt'		paternal.aunt-PAU		paternal.aunt-PAU-PL
d.	*tá:tasi*	e.	*tátas-**ki***	f.	*tá:tas-**ki**-ha*
	'paternal uncle'		paternal.uncle-PAU		paternal.uncle-PAU-PL

(Kimball 1991: 449)

The paucal form in Koasati is used for a group of 2–6; the paucal plus plural form is used for larger groups.

Hualapai (Yuman) also has a paucal and a plural. Number marking is never obligatory, and most nouns are marked plural via the paucal rather than the 'multiple plural' (Redden 1966).[14]

(34) Hualapai

a.	*pá*	b.	*pá-**č***	c.	*pá-**č**-uv*
	man		man-PAU		man-PAU-PL
	'man'		'a few men, some men'		'several men, many men'

(Redden 1966: 159)

3.5. Inverse Number

The Tanoan languages are infamous for their so-called inverse number, which is often described as "unexpected number". Inverse number appears to be unique to this language family across the world's languages. Kiowa has a class system whereby nouns are divided into four classes. Each class is associated with a different number marking pattern (Table 5.9) (Harrington 1928; Watkins 1984).

The "inverse" or "unexpected number" is found on the plural in Class I, on the singular in Class II, and on both the singular and plural in Class III; no number marking is found on Class IV. The demonstratives are also marked for basic versus inverse number; singular, dual, and inverse are marked on the verb (see Sutton 2010 for further discussion).

(35) Kiowa

a.	***ę́:dè***	*sân*	***Ø**-khóp-dɔ́:*
	this.BAS	child.BAS	3SG-hurt-be
	'This child is sick.'		

Table 5.9 Kiowa Inverse Number

CLASS	SG	DU	PL
I	*tógúl* 'young man'/'two young men'		***tógú:dɔ́*** 'young men'
II	***ɔ̀nsɔ̂y*** 'foot'	ɔ̀nsó: 'feet'	
III	***álɔ̀:bɔ̀*** 'apple'	*álɔ̀:* 'two apples'	***álɔ̀:bɔ̀*** 'apples'
IV	*hóldà* 'dress, dresses'		

Source: Data from Watkins (1984).

Table 5.10 Towa Inverse Number

	SG	DU	PL
I	*hį́* 'person'	*hį́:**míš*** 'people'	
II	*pǫ́:š* 'road/2 roads'		*pǫ́:* '3+ roads'
III	*kʷǫ́:* 'tooth'	*kʷǫ́:š* 'two teeth'	*kʷǫ́:* '3+ teeth'
IV	*p'ǽ̂* 'water'		

Source: Data from Yumitani (1998).

b. ***ę́:dè*** *sân* *ę̀-khóp-dɔ́:*
this.BAS child.BAS 3DU-sick-be
'These two children are sick.'

c. ***ę́:gɔ̀*** *są̂:**dɔ̀*** ***è**-khóp-dɔ́:*
this.INV child.INV 3INV-hurt-be
'These (3+) children are sick.'

(Watkins 1984: 97)

Similarly, in Towa/Jemez, Class I inverse represents dual or plural, Class II inverse represents singular or dual, and Class III inverse represents dual (Table 5.10). (Class IV takes no number marking.)

Class I nouns are mostly animates, Classes II and III are inanimates, and Class IV nouns are mass nouns in Towa/Jemez.

4. Possession

There are two main patterns of possession marking in North America: on the possessed or on the possessor. I discuss each pattern in turn, and then discuss other types of cases, including marking on both the possessed and possessor and (in)alienable possession.

Syntactically, I assume that possessors occupy SpecDP.

4.1. Marking on Possessor (Dependent Marking)

In some languages, possession is marked on the possessor, as in English. For example, in Shoshone (Uto-Aztecan), the suffix *-ng* marks possession on the possessor.

(36) Shoshone

*dênape-**ng*** *kahni*
man-POSS house
'(the) man's house'

(Shaul 2012: 30)

4.2. Marking on Possessed Noun (Head Marking)

In many more languages, possession is marked on the possessed noun. For example, in Acoma Keresan (isolate), the third person possessive marker is found on the possessed noun.

(37) Acoma Keresan

úy'ati *kam'ásdi*
úy'ati **g**-'m'ásdíi
boy 3POSS-hand
'the boy's hand'

(Miller 1965: 148)

Similarly, in Yucatec Maya (Mayan), the possessive marking precedes the possessed noun.

(38) Yucatec Maya

a. ***u*** *ppoc* *Pedro*
POSS hat Peter
'Peter's hat'

b. ***u*** *pek* *le* *palal-ob-o*
3SG.POSS dog DEM child-PL-DIST
'the children's dog'

(Bolles & Bolles 2014: 20)

4.3. Marking on Both Possessor and Possessed Nouns

In some languages, possession marking can be found on both the possessor and possessed nouns. For example, in Southern Sierra Miwok (Miwok-Costanoan), the possessor is marked with genitive case and the possessed noun is marked for person.

(39) Southern Sierra Miwok

*cuku-**ŋ*** *hu·ki-ʔ-**hy·***
dog-GEN tail-EPEN-3SG
'dog's tail'

(Broadbent 1964: 133)

In Inuttut (Eskimo-Aleut), possession is marked on the possessor (via ergative case) and on the possessed.

(40) Inuttut

*inu-**up*** *qimmi-**nga***
person-SG.ERG dog-3.3.SG
'the Inuk's dog'

(Smith 1977: 20)

The marking on the possessed noun agrees with the person and number of the possessor and the number of the possessed noun (Table 5.11).

Table 5.11 Inuttut Absolutive Morphology for Possessives

POSSESSOR / POSSESSED	1			2			3
	SG	DU	PL	SG	DU	PL	
SG	*-ga*	*-vuk*	*-vut*	*-it*	*-tik*	*-si*	*-nga*
DU	*-kka*			*-kkit*			*-gik*
PL				*-tit*			*-ngit*

Source: Data from Smith (1977: 31–37).

Table 5.12 Possession in Crow

		ALIENABLE	INALIENABLE
1	SG	*bas-*	*b-*
	INCL	*baleeis-*	
	EXCL	*bas- . . . -o*	*b- . . . -úua*
2	SG	*dís-*	*d-*
	PL	*dís- . . . -o*	*d- . . .* uua
3	SG	*is-*	*Ø-*
	PL	*is- . . . -o*	*Ø- . . . -úua*

Source: Adapted from Graczyk (2007: 52–53).

This pattern looks like the verbal agreement in Inuttut, which agrees with both the subject and object in ergative/absolutive clauses (see §7).

4.4. *Alienable/Inalienable Possession*

In many languages in North America, there are different patterns of possession marking depending on if the possessed is possessed inalienably or alienably. Inalienable possession refers to possession relations that are always considered to exist between two entities (e.g., relatives or body parts); alienable possession refers to possession relations that are less permanent (e.g., trees are not necessarily owned by anyone). Languages can vary on which nouns count as (in) alienable.

In Crow (Siouan), there are different paradigms for alienable possession vs. inalienable (Table 5.12).[15] Cars are alienable – they do not need to be owned by anyone – and therefore the word for car takes the alienable affixes. Noses are inalienable – they are always attached to an entity, except in horrifying circumstances – and therefore the word for nose takes the inalienable affixes.

(41) Crow

a. ***bas**-íilaalee*
1POSS.INAL-car
'my car'

b. ***b**-apé*
1POSS.AL-nose
'my nose'

(Graczyk 2007: 52–53)

West Greenlandic distinguishes between things you possess for a long time or forever and things that you own for only a short period of time. Temporary possession is marked with an extra suffix *-uti.*

(42) West Greenlandic

a. *savi-**ut**-aa*
knife-POSS-3SG.SG
'the knife he now owns'

b. *savi-a*
knife-3SG.SG
'his knife (an inalienable piece of his hunting equipment)'

(Fortescue 1984: 172)

4.5. More Complicated Systems

Some languages have more than two different systems of possession marking. Superficially, Plains Cree, and Algonquian languages more generally, look like they make an inalienable/alienable distinction. However, Muehlbauer (2007) argues that there are three patterns. First, Plains Cree marks possession on the possessed noun using prefixes (for person) and suffixes (for number) (Table 5.13). The three categories of nouns in Plains Cree according to Muehlbauer (2007) are alienable nouns, relational nouns and inalienable nouns.

(43) Plains Cree

ALIENABLE

a. *minôs*
cat
'cat'

b. *o-minôs-im-a* *Wâpastim*
3-cat-DISJ-OBV Wâpastim
'Wâpastim's cat'

RELATIONAL

c. *okâwîmâw*
o-kâwiy-im-â-w
3-mother-DISJ-IMP-3
'a mother'
(someone has her as a mother)

d. *okâwiya* *Wâpastim*
o-kâwiy-a Wâpastim
3-mother-OBV Wâpastim
'Wâpastim's mother'

INALIENABLE

e. **cihciy*
hand
'hand'

f. *o-cihciy* *Wâpastim*
3-hand Wâpastim
'Wâpastim's hand'

(Muehlbauer 2007: 177, 180)

Table 5.13 Plains Cree Possessive Marking

	PREFIX	SUFFIX
1SG	*ni-*	
2SG	*ki-*	
1EXCL	*ni-*	*-inân*
1INCL	*ki-*	*-inaw*
2PL	*ki-*	*-iwâw*
3SG	*o-*	
3PL	*o-*	*-iwâw*
3'	*o-*	*-iyiw*

Source: Adapted from Ahenakew (1987: 32).

Alienable nouns can always occur on their own without possessive marking. When they are possessed, some nouns are marked with *-im*, but not all.

(44) Plains Cree

a.	*ni-minôs-**im***	b.	**ni-maskisin-**im***
	1-cat-DISJ		1-shoe-DISJ
	'my cat'		intended: my shoe

(Muehlbauer 2007: 176)

The alienable (43b) and relational (43d) nouns require obviation marking (see Wolfart 1996; Oxford, this volume, for discussions of obviation). Inalienable nouns require possessive marking; if they are not possessed, they must be marked with *mi-* (45a). Relational nouns also require possessive marking; if they are not possessed, they must be turned into an impersonal verb (45c).

(45) Plains Cree

a.	***mi**-stikwân*	b.	*****o**-stikwân-im-â-w*
	UP-head		3-head-DISJ-IMP-3
	'a head'		
c.	*okâwîmâw*	d.	**mikâwiy*
	o-kâwiy-im-â-w		**mi**-kâwiy
	3-mother-DISJ-IMP-3		UP-mother
	'a mother'		
	(someone has her as a mother)		

(Muehlbauer 2007: 181, 180)

Most inalienable nouns are body parts, but there are a few "intimate possessions" (Bloomfield 1962; Wolfart 1973) that also pattern like the body parts, taking the prefix *mi-* when not possessed.

(46) Plains Cree

a.	*mi-sôs*	b.	*mi-skotâkay*
	UP-canoe		UP-jacket
	'a canoe'		'a jacket'

(Muehlbauer 2007: 183)

Some languages have vastly more complicated systems. For example, Chichimeca Jonaz (Oto-Manguean) has 12 (and possibly more) possessive classes of nouns, where the classes are "defined broadly as involving tone changes, prefix-like elements, various internal changes, and combinations of these as well as suppletion" (Nichols & Bickel 2011).

(47) Chichimeca Jonaz

1SG	2SG	
námenʔ	*namenʔ*	'face'
suní	*síni*	'lip'
kútún	*utún*	'neck'
túmbiʔir	*nímbiʔir*	'tail'
nahí	*únho*	'friend'
tásócʔ	*kisócʔ*	'belt'
namá	*éMą*	'carrying rack'

kúndí	*kirí*	'water'
nambá	*úngwa*	'hat'
kúmboʔ	*kibóʔ*	'land'
kaʔá	*kanʔa*	'hand'
masų́	*uniʔí*	'wife'
táta	*úngwæ*	'father'

(Lastra de Suárez 1984: 24–25)

5. Classifiers

Some North American languages use classifiers within the noun phrase. Classifiers are usually found with numerals and provide information about the noun. Verbs are also often marked with classificatory elements (e.g., Athabaskan languages), but I focus only on the nouns here. Grinevald (2000) argues that there are three types of nominal classification: numeral, noun, and genitive. Numeral classifiers are found only in the presence of some kind of quantification (e.g., numerals), noun classifiers can be used independently of quantification, and genitive classifiers are used only in possession contexts.

The syntax of classifiers depends on the type of classifier; I remain agnostic as to their positions.

5.1. Numeral Classifiers

Numeral classifiers occur in the context of quantification (such as numerals). Grinevald (2000) distinguishes between true sortal classifiers and mensural ones; not all researchers are so careful, and so I do not always disambiguate here. Some numeral classifiers are free morphemes, and some are bound to the quantificational element. I discuss each in turn here.

5.1.1. Free Numeral Classifiers

Mi'gmaq (Algonquian) has free numeral classifiers. Only numerals above 5 require classifiers (48).[16]

(48) Mi'gmaq

a.	*na'n-ijig*	*ji'nm-ug*	b.	*na'n*	***te's**-ijig*	*ji'nm-ug*
	five-AGR	man-PL		five	CLF-AGR	man-PL
	'five men'					
c.	**asugom-ijig*	*ji'nm-ug*	d.	*asugom*	***te's**-ijig*	*ji'nm-ug*
	six-AGR	man-PL		six	CLF-AGR	man-PL
				'six men'		

(Bale & Coon 2014: 700)

5.1.2. Bound Numeral Classifiers

Many languages have bound classifiers, which are found on numerals and other quantificational elements. For example, S<u>k</u>wx<u>w</u>ú7mesh has different forms of numerals depending on the referent of the noun. Different reduplication patterns are used for numerals referring to animals vs. humans (Table 5.14).[17]

Table 5.14 Numeral Classifiers in Skwxwú7mesh

	OBJECTS	*ANIMALS*	*HUMANS*
'one'	*nch'ú7*	*ní-nch'u7*	*nch'-nch'ú7*
'two'	*án7us*	*án-n7us*	*n-7án7us*
'three'	*chánat*	*chá-ch'n7at*	*chen-chánat*

Source: Adapted from Kuipers (1967: 149).

In Yucatec Maya (Mayan), there are classifiers for humans and inanimate objects.

(49) Yucatec Maya

a. *ka'a-**túul*** *x-ch'úupal-o'ob*
two-CLF.AN F-girl-PL
'two girls'

b, *óox-**p'éel*** *ja'ab-o'ob*
three-CLF.IN year-PL
'three years'

(Blair & Vermont-Salas 1967: 454)

Similarly, Tzotzil (Mayan) has eight sortal classifiers (human, animal, tree, long-rigid, flat-flexible, rectangular-rigid-flat, round-flat, round-3 dimensional), and many more mensural ones. Three of the sortal classifiers are given in (50).

(50) Tzotzil

a. *j-**p'ej*** *k'an-a* *alaxa*
one-CLF.round yellow-ATTR orange
'one round yellow orange'

b. *j-**ch'ix*** *tzaj-al* *kantela*
one-CLF.longish red-ATTR candle
'one longish red candle'

c. *ak'-b-on* *j-**kot*** *le'e*
give-BEN-1A one-CLF.four-legged DEM
'Give me that (animal)'

(De León Pasquel 1988: 68)

Halkomelem (Salish) has lexical suffixes that can appear on numerals to classify the noun. These can be used alone or with the head noun.

(51) Halkomelem

a. *ɬix^{w}=**əqən*** *x̌θəm*
three=container box
'three boxes'

b. *ɬq'ec's=**əmət̓^{θ}*** *šeɬ*
five=long road
'five roads'

c. ***x̌əθi:nə*** *q̓elə̓mi?*
four.people girl.PL
'four girls'

d. *yəselə̓=**nəc*** *k^{w}əmləx^{w}*
two=bottom root
'two roots'

e. *ʔəpan=**əs***
ten=round
'ten dollars'

f. *x̌əθin=**əwəɬ***
four-canoe
'four canoes'

(Gerdts et al. 2002: 153, 155, 156)

The full system is provided in Table 5.15.

Nuu-chah-nulth (Wakashan) has both sortal and mensural numeral classifiers. Some of the sortal classifiers are provided in (52).

(52) Nuu-chah-nulth

a. *ḥayu-**qimɬ*** *maƛimɬ* *šuuk^{w}aa*
ten-unit barrel sugar
'ten barrels of sugar'

Table 5.15 Halkomelem Numeral Classifiers

HUMAN/ANIMAL	*NATURAL ENVIRONMENT*	*MATERIAL CULTURE*	*SHAPE/SIZE*	*CONTAINERS/GROUPS*
ɬxʷ=elə ‘three people’	*s-ɬixʷ=əɬp* ‘three trees’	*ɬixʷ=əw̓txʷ* ‘three houses’	*ɬixʷ=əs* ‘three dollars’	*ɬixʷ=əqən* ‘three containers’
ɬxʷ=ey̓ɬ ‘three children’	*ɬəxʷ=nee* ‘three root plants’	*ɬxʷ=əwəɬ* ‘three canoes’	*ɬxʷ=aləs* ‘three loops’	*ɬixʷ=əl̓eʔc* ‘three loads’
ɬxʷ=iws ‘three ducks’	*ɬxʷ=e:nxʷ* ‘three plant parts’	*ɬxʷ=e:l̓wəs* ‘three paddles’	*ɬixʷ=əy̓əs* ‘three coils’	*ɬxʷ=əmat* ‘three pieces, piles’
ɬixʷ=aʔqʷ ‘three fish (heads)’	*ɬxʷ=əɬcəp* ‘three pieces of firewood’	*ɬxʷ=əlwət* ‘three garments’	*ɬxʷ=als* ‘three spheres’	
ɬxʷ=elqɬ ‘three pieces of game’	*ɬxʷ=ənəp* ‘three plots of land’		*ɬixʷ=əmet̓ᶿ* ‘three long thin objects’	
			ɬixʷ=t̓ᶿeʔ ‘three strands’	
			ɬixʷ=aʔqʷ ‘three heads/ spherical things’	

Source: Adapted from Gerdts et al. (2002: 157).

b. *n̓up-**c̓iqs**-ʔi* *miʕaat*
one-long-DEF sockeye.salmon
‘one sockeye salmon’

c. *suu-**ḥtayuk*** *ḥiixʷaa*
five-strings dentalia
‘five strings of dentalia’

d. *ʔaƛ-**p’iił**-ʔi* *ʕicsy̓in*
two-many.long.obj-DEF spine
‘the two spines’

(Yiu & Stonham 2002: 422, 425c)

Chol also has bound numeral classifiers (Bale & Coon 2014). Only the traditional numerals require a classifier, whereas the borrowed Spanish numerals do not (53). This is true even with Spanish-derived nouns (53e–f).

(53) Chol

a. *ux-**p’ej*** *yumuty*
three-CLF egg
‘three eggs’

b. **ux* *tyumuty*
three egg

c. **nuebe-**p’ej*** *tyumuty*
nine-CLF egg

d. *nuebe* *tyumuty*
nine egg
‘nine eggs’

e. *ux-**p’ej*** *mansana*
three-CLF apple
‘three apples’

f. *nuebe* *mansana*
nine apple
‘nine apples’

(Bale & Coon 2014: 701–702)

5.2. Noun Classifiers

Noun classifiers are much rarer than numeral classifiers, and are perhaps found only in Mesoamerica. They are found independently from quantification. For example, in Jakaltek Popti' (Mayan), the classifier for woman *ix* is used with *malin* 'Marie' and the classifer for corn *ixim* is used with *wah* 'tortilla'. This classifier can also be used in a response to a question without the main noun.

(54) Jakaltek Popti'

a. *swatx'e* ***ix*** *malin* ***ixim*** *wah?*
made CLF.woman Marie CLF.corn tortilla
'Did Mary make the tortillas?'

b. *ho'* *swatx'e* ***ix*** ***ixim***
yes made CLF.woman CLF.corn
'Yes, she made them.'

(Grinevald 2016: 277)

Similarly, in Coatzoquitengo Mixtec (Otomanguean), the classifier for woman *ñá* is used with *Maria* and the classifier for animal *ti* is used with *xuhu*, 'goat'.

(55) Coatzoquitengo Mixtec

xáhni ***ñá*** *Maria* ***ti*** *xuhu*
kill.PST CLF.woman Mary CLF.animal goat
'Mary killed the goat.'

(De León Pasquel 1988: 153)

5.3. Genitive Classifiers

In some languages, certain classifiers are only found in possessive contexts. For example, in Yucatec Maya, there are many classifiers that are used only in possession.

(56) Yucatec Maya

a. *in* ***w-àalak'*** *kàax-o'b-a'*
1SG.POSS EPEN-CLF.domestic chicken-PL-PROX
'my chickens'

b. *u* ***pak'al*** *lol'-o'b*
3POSS CLF.planted flower-PL
'his flowers'

(Lehmann 2002: 65)

Most of the genitive classifiers in Yucatec Maya are verbal nouns, and this process is productive (Lehmann 2002). Thus the verb for 'round', *wolis-*, can be made into a genitive classifier, *woliskunah*.

(57) Yucatec Maya

a. *t-in* *wolis-kun-t-h* *le* *che'-a'*
PST-1SG.SBJ round-FACT-TR-COMPL DEF tree-PROX
'I bent this branch round.'

b. *le* *he'l-a'* *in* ***wolis-kun-ah*** *che'*
DEF PRSV-PROX 1SG.POSS round-FACT-INTR tree
'this is the branch that I bent round'

(Lehmann 2002: 67)

6. Determiners/Demonstratives

Many languages lack overt articles, but all have demonstratives (Chilton 2014). In this section, I describe a few article systems, languages with bare nouns, and a very large demonstrative system.

Syntactically, I assume that demonstratives occupy SpecDP and that articles can occupy functional heads, like D.[18]

6.1. Languages With Overt Articles

Many Salish languages have overt articles; most of those that do have articles that encode deixis (Matthewson 1998; Gillon 2013). For example, S<u>k</u>w<u>x</u>wú7mesh (Table 5.1) and Upriver Halkomelem (Table 5.16). Upriver Halkomelem articles distinguish between gender, number, common and proper, and distance.

Wakashan articles also encode deictic features. For example, Kwak̓wala articles mark case, (non-)specificity, and distance (Table 5.17). The pre-NP articles encliticize to the previous word, and the NP-internal articles encliticize to the first word within the NP.

(58) Kwak'wala

a. *Digila[=**ga*** — *Maya=**x**]* — *<u>k</u>a'<u>a</u>ns.*
make.tea=SBJ.PROX.NON-SPEC — Maya=PROX.VIS — for.us
'Maya (here) is making tea for us.'

b. *Yum̓[=**u<u>x</u>w*** — *Brendan=<u>x</u>].*
DEM.MED=SBJ.MED.NON-SPEC — Brendan=MED.INVIS
'That's Brendan (around).'

Table 5.16 The Upriver Halkomelem Article System

		PROX	MED, INVIS	DIST, INVIS
#-NEUTRAL	M	*te*	*kwethe*	*kw'e*
	F	*the*	*se, kwse*	*kw'the*
PL		*ye*		
PROPER NAMES		*tl'*		

Source: Adapted from Gillon (2013: 213).

Table 5.17 Kwak'wala Article System[19]

	PRE-NP						NP-INTERNAL	
	SUBJECTS		<u>X</u>-OBJECTS		S-OBJECTS		VIS	INVIS
	NON-SPEC	SPEC	NON-SPEC	SPEC	NON-SPEC	SPEC		
PROX	*-ga*	*-gada*	*-<u>x</u>ga*	*-<u>x</u>gada*	*-sga*	*-sgada*	*-(a)x, -(i)x*	*-ga'*
MED	*-u<u>x</u>w*	*-u<u>x</u>wda*	*-<u>x</u>u<u>x</u>w*	*-<u>x</u>u<u>x</u>wda, -<u>x</u>wa, -<u>x</u>wada*	*-su<u>x</u>w*heru<u>x</u>*wda*	*-(e)x, -(i)x*	*-e'<u>x</u>, -a'<u>x</u>*	
DIST	*-i*	*-ida*	*-<u>x</u>*	*-<u>x</u>a, -<u>x</u>ida, -<u>x</u>ada*	*-s*	*-sa*	*-i, -a, -∅*	*-e', -a', -o'*

Source: Adapted from Nicolson and Werle (2009: 6, 11).

c. *A̲ngwax̲tł[=**ida**]* *g̲anang̲m]?*
called.who=SBJ.DIST.SPEC child
'What is that child's (not around) name?'

d. *T̓sola't[=**sgada*** *k̓adayu=**xw**]* *la[=**x̲ux̲w*** *Mike=**ex̲**]*
give=S.OBJ.PROX.SPEC pencil=PROX to=X̲.OBJ.MED.NON-SPEC Mike=MED.VIS
'Give this pencil to Mike.'

(Nicolson & Werle 2009: 5–6)

See also O'Meara and Pérez Báez (this volume) for further discussion of locational/spatial orientation.

Some languages have only indefinite articles. For example, bare nouns in Diné Bizaad (Navajo; Athabaskan) receive a definite interpretation. The article *łéi'* encodes indefiniteness.

(59) Diné Bizaad

a. *ashkii* *yáálti'*
boy 3SBJ.spoke
'The boy spoke.' (familiar, presuppositional)

b. *ashkii* ***łéi'*** *yáálti'*
boy INDF 3SBJ.spoke
'A/some/a certain boy spoke.'

(Jelinek 2006: 286)

Some languages distinguish between indefinite and definite articles. For example, Lakhota (Siouan) has both types of articles (Table 5.18).

The definite articles also distinguish between a plain definite and an emphatic one. The emphatic definite article is used for referents that have already been mentioned, and sentences involving the emphatic definite are usually translated into past tense (Rood & Taylor 1996). This might mean that the real distinction has to do with tense (see Demirdache 1996 and Matthewson 1998 for discussion of past tense articles in St'át'imcets [Salish]).

(60) Lakhota

a. *šų́ka* ***kį*** *hél* *yųké.*
dog ART.DEF there lie
'The dog is lying there.'

b. *šų́ka* ***kʔų*** *thaló* ***kį*** *thebyé.*
dog ART.AFOREMENTIONED meat ART.DEF eat.up
'The aforementioned dog ate up the meat.'

(Rood & Taylor 1996: 455)

Table 5.18 Lakhota Article System[20]

	DEF		*INDEF*	
	PLAIN	*EMPHATIC*	*REAL*	*HYP*
SG	*kį*	*kʔų*	*wą*	*wąži*
PL			*eyá*	*etą́*

Source: Rood and Taylor (1996: 455–456).

The indefinite articles distinguish between number and real vs. hypothetical referents. This is perhaps a specific/nonspecific distinction.

(61) Lakhota

a. *Iyéčhịkiyąke* **wą** *ophéwathų.*
car ART.INDF.REAL I.buy.it
'I bought a car.'

b. *Iyéčhịkiyąke* **wąži** *ophéwathų* *kte.*
car ART.INDF.HYP I.buy.it FUT
'I'm going to buy a car.'

(Rood & Taylor 1996: 456)

6.2. Bare Noun Languages

Many languages lack articles altogether. For example, in Innu-aimun (Algonquian) and Inuttut (Eskimo-Aleut), bare nouns can be used freely.

(62) Innu-aimun

a. ***Atîk***^{u} *pimût-eu.*
caribou walk.AI-3
'A caribou was walking.'

b. *Upa-u* ***pineshîsh.***
take.off.AI-3 bird
'The bird is flying.'

(63) Inuttut (Gillon 2013: 243)

Tuttuk *takujaga.*
tuttuk takuk-jaga
caribou.ABS.SG see-PART.1SG.3SG
'I saw a/the caribou.'

(Gillon 2011: 30)

Demonstratives are used extensively in these languages, and often are used in ways similar to articles (see, for example, Cyr 1993, who argues that Innu-aimun/Montagnais demonstratives are used like definite articles).

6.3. Demonstrative Systems

Many languages have large demonstrative systems (see Table 5.2, for example). The largest system might be Blackfoot's (Algonquian). The basic system is fairly simple: demonstratives distinguish between singular, plural, animate, inanimate, and proximity to first or second person (Table 5.19).

Table 5.19 Basic Blackfoot Demonstrative System

		PROX1	*PROX2*	*DIST*
SG	AN	*amo*	*anna*	*oma*
	IN		*anni*	*omi*
SG	AN	*amoksi*	*anniksi*	*oomiksi*
	IN	*amostsi*	*annistsi*	*omistsi*

Source: Adapted from Wiltschko (2014: 193).

However, the demonstratives can be expanded upon using the template given in (64).

(64) Blackfoot demonstrative template (Wiltschko 2014: 194; adapted from Bliss 2013)
Root + (diminutive) + (restricted) + (inflection) + (post-inflection) + (?? suffix)

This produces 900 forms.

7. Case

There are languages with many different case endings, such as Inuktitut, with ergative, absolutive, oblique, allative, ablative, locative, vialis, and similaris.

(65) Inuttut[21]

a. *nuna-**up***
land-ERG.SG
'the land'

b. ***nunak***
land.ABS.SG
'the land'

c. *nuna-**mik***
land-OBL.SG
'the land'

d. *nuna-**mut***
land-ALL.SG
'to the land'

e. *nuna-**mit***
land-ABL.SG
'from the land'

f. *nuna-**mi***
land-LOC.SG
'in, on the land'

g. *nuna-**kkut***
land-VIAL.SG
'through the land'

h. *nuna-**tut***
land-SIM.SG
'like the land'

(Labrador Inuktitut; Smith 1977: 28)

For the rest of this section I focus only on participant role marking (e.g., marking on subjects and objects) rather than other types of case marking. I also discuss only participant role marking within the NP; some languages also or instead mark participant roles on their verbs.

Syntactically, I assume case occupies K.

7.1. Nominative/Accusative Alignment

Many languages have nominative/accusative marking within clauses. For example, Lake Miwok (Yok-Utian) marks nominative via *=n* and accusative is marked via *=u*.

(66) Lake Miwok

a. *kuku=**n*** *intíkkit* *mékuh*
flea=NOM forehead sit
'A flea is sitting on your forehead.'

b. *káac=**u*** *úe*
fish=ACC saw
'He saw the fish.'

(Callaghan 1963: 91)

7.2. Ergative/Absolutive Alignment

A number of languages display some kind of ergative/absolutive alignment somewhere in their grammar. However, there is usually some kind of split: some clauses have ergative/absolutive marking, while others appear to be nominative/accusative (or absolutive/null or absolutive/oblique) (see Spreng, this volume, for more detail). For example, in Sm'algyax (Tsimshian), ergative/absolutive marking is dependent on tense/aspect. Case is marked on the articles (which are encliticized to whatever precedes them in the clause). Intransitive subjects are marked with the absolutive form of the article. For common nouns, this is *=a* (67a). Transitive subjects (in some tenses/aspects) are marked with the ergative form of the article. For common nouns, this is *=da*. When the subject is marked ergative, the object is marked absolutive (67b).

(67) Sm'algyax

a. *Yagwa* *hadiks=**a*** *üüla.*
PRS swim=ABS.COMMON seal
'The seal is swimming.'

b. *Yagwa=t* *huum=**da*** *duus=**a*** *hoon.*
PRS=3ERG smell=ERG.COMMON cat=ABS.COMMON fish
'The cat is sniffing the fish.'

(Mulder 1988: 32)

In some tenses/aspects, the case alignment is instead absolutive/null. If the transitive subject is marked as absolutive, the object is unmarked (68).

(68) Sm'algyax

Nah *xbeexs=**as*** *Dzon* ***lak*** *da* *ha-xbeexsg=a-hooy-d.*
PRF cut=ABS.PROPER John wood OBL.COMMON INS-saw=ABS.COMMON-use-3
'John has cut the wood with a saw.'

(Mulder 1988: 41)

In Inuktitut, clauses can be ergative/absolutive or absolutive/oblique, depending on the transitivity of the verb (Spreng 2012). If the verb is transitive (evidenced by the mood marking on the verb), the subject is marked ergative (*-up*) and the object is marked absolutive (unmarked). If the verb is marked intransitive, then the subject is marked absolutive (unmarked) and the object is marked oblique (*-nit*).

(69) Inuktitut

a. *arna-**up*** *niri-janga* ***aapu***
woman-ERG.SG eat-DEC.3SG.3SG apple(ABS.SG)
'The woman is eating the apple.'

b. ***Alana*** *niri-juq* *paurngar-**nit***
Alana(ABS.SG) eat-DECL.3SG berry-OBL.PL
'Alana is eating berries.'

(Compton 2012: 11)

Further, some verbs are suffixal and require either an incorporated noun or a dummy prefix *pi-*. These verbs have one fewer argument than the non-suffixal version: *niri-* 'eat' has two possible arguments (ergative subject and absolutive object) and *-tur-* has one (absolutive subject) (see Barrie & Mathieu, this volume, for more detail).

(70) Inutktitut

a. *Palasi-**p*** ***niqi*** *niri-vaa*
minister-ERG.SG meat.ABS.SG eat-INDIC.3SG.3SG
'The minister eats/ate the meat.'

b.	***Palasi***	*niqi-tur-puq*
	minister.ABS.SG	meat-eat-3SG.INDIC

'The minister eats/ate meat.'

(Allen 1988: 6)

7.3. Agent/Patient Alignment

A few languages have an agent/patient alignment (also known as active/inactive alignment). For example, in Southern Pomo (Pomoan), animate agents can be distinguished from animate patients (Walker 2012). (Case marking is optional in Southern Pomo; Walker 2012.) Kinship nouns have a slightly different pattern from all other nouns; I provide only the non-kinship pattern here (see Walker 2012 for details). Agents can be marked with the clitic *=yey* (71a–b). Patients can be marked with the clicic *=yčon*, as in (71a) and (71c). Intransitive subjects can be marked as agents or patients, depending on the type of verb they occur with (71b–c).

(71) Southern Pomo

a.	*kʰaʔbéyey*	*čú:maṭ'čon*	*ʔóh:ow*	*ʔaṭ:í:kʰe*	*c̓u:ʔu*
	kʰaʔbe=**yey**	ču:maṭ'=**yčon**	ʔoh:o-w	ʔat:i-:kʰe	c̓u:ʔu
	rock=A	gray.squirrel=P	give-PERF	3.SG-POSS	arrow

'Rock handed his arrow to Squirrel.'

b.	*kʰaʔbéyey*	*hó:liw*
	kʰaʔbe=**yey**	ho:li-w
	rock=A	leave-PERF

'Rock went off.'

c.	*hamini(:)ba*	*kʰaˀbéyčon*	*sí:ma*	*mí:ṭiw*
	hamini(:)-ba	kʰaˀbé=**yčon**	sí:ma	mi:ṭi-w
	and.then-S.SEQ	rock=P	sleep	lie-PERF

'Having done so, Rock [Man] went to sleep.'

(Walker 2012: 221, 360)

Alongside this alignment, there is a set of articles that encode a nominative/accusative alignment – these are not sensitive to animacy. The agent/patient marking cannot be used simultaneously with the nominative/accusative marking. Inanimate nouns can use only this set of articles (which are optional, like the agent/patient case marking); animate nouns can use either system, but only one or the other (or neither). All four articles appear to mark definiteness; one set is used for 'aforementioned' referents (72b) (Walker 2012).

(72) Southern Pomo

a.	*čú:maṭ'wám:u*	*hoʔ:ówi*	*biʔk̓ik̓:iw*	*šiʔmiʔwan*
	ču:maṭ'=**wam:u**	hoʔ:o=wi	biʔk̓i-k̓:i-w	šiʔmi=**ʔwan**
	gray.squirrel=DEF.NOM	teeth=INS	gnaw-ITER-PERF	bow=DEF.ACC

'The Squirrel gnawed it with his teeth, the bow.'

b.	*ma:*	*nupʰ:é*	*baʔ:áy:o:mu*	*k̓as:ísiʔyowan*	*dóṭ':ow*
	ma:	nupʰ:e	baʔ:ay=**yo:mu**	k̓as:isi=**ʔyowan**	do-ṭ':o-w
	DEM	striped.skunk	woman=DEF.NOM	elk=DEF.ACC	by.finger-skin-PERF

'This Skunk woman skinned the Elk.'

(Walker 2012: 389)

Northern Pomo has a similar system, but it is found only on proper names (Walker 2012).

Yuki (Yuki-Wappo) distinguishes between three types of arguments: agents, patients, and datives (Balodis 2016). Transitive clauses display either agent/patient or patient/dative alignment. I focus here only on the agent/patient alignment. In Yuki, agents are unmarked (73a–b). Patients are also unmarked (73a), unless they are human (73c), or personified animals (as in myths) (73d).

(73) Yuki

a.

sǫ́ˀey	***yím***	*yą:hišti*	*nąwímil*	***hulk'ǿˀi***
sǫ=ˀi	yim	yąh-s-t	nąw=mil	hulk'oˀi
SAME=HSY1	fire	blaze-CONT-INTR	see=FIN	Coyote.A

'And Coyote saw the fire blazing up.'

b.

saˀ	*kʰoˀoyik*
sak	koˀ-y=k
child.A	go-PROG=DECL

'The baby's coming.'

c.

sikiṭ	*hálǰa*	*ho:ṭ*	*yí:kilpaˀ*[22]
si=kiṭ	halč=**ą**	hoṭ	yiˀ-k-il-paˀ
NEW=then	children=P	large	play-PNCT-MPSV-FUT

'children also shall be playing much.'

d.

síkiṭ	*či:mítą*	*móṣ*	*čí:mit*	*mípa*
si=kiṭ	čimit=**ą**	moˀos	čimit	mih-paˀ
NEW=then	bird=P	2PL.A	bird	be-FUT

'And to the (small) birds: "You shall be birds." '

(Balodis 2016: 91, 106, 108, 110)

7.4. Tripartite Case

At least two languages have tripartite case: Nez Perce and Sahaptin (Sahaptian). Tripartite case is rare in the world's languages – possibly found only in these two languages of North America. It involves a three-way patterning of case marking. In Nez Perce, intransitive subjects are unmarked (74a), and transitive subjects and objects are both case-marked (74b).

(74) Nez Perce

a.

sík'em	*hi-wlekix-tee'nix*	*háamti'c.*
horse	3SBJ-run-HAB.PL	fast

'Horses run fast.'

b.

*sik'ém-**nim***	*kúnk'u*	*pée-weewluq-se*	*timaanii-**ne**.*
horse-ERG	always	3/3-want-IMPF	apple-OBJ

'The horse always wants an apple.'

(Deal 2010: 74)

In addition, some sentences allow both subject and object to go unmarked.

(75) Nez Perce

ke 'itúu	*hi-wéwluq-se*	*kúnk'u*	***'ceyéeye.***
something	3SBJ-want-IMPF	always	coyote

'Coyote is always wanting something.'

(Aoki & Walker 1989: 417)

Deal (2010) argues that ergative case is dependent on the case of the object: if the object is unmarked, then the subject is too, and if the object is marked with object case, then the subject must receive ergative case. She further argues that unmarked objects must be non-referential; case-marked objects can be referential or non-referential.

8. Conclusion

Although this chapter only skims the surface of some of the properties noun phrases can encode, it is evident that nouns can be marked in a number of different ways to represent a number of different features. They deserve investigation just as much as the verbal domain.

Acknowledgments

Thank you to Mark C. Baker and Heather Bliss for their very helpful comments and suggestions. This chapter was greatly improved because of them. Thank you also to Jason Brown, for discussing Gitksan plurality with me. It is incredibly fascinating, and I wish I could work on it myself. Thank you to Daniel Siddiqi for asking me to co-edit this volume and to write this chapter, and to the other co-editors (Michael Barrie, Jason Haugen, and Éric Mathieu) for the camaraderie. Finally, thanks to all of my collaborators and consultants over the years. You all made my research and writing better.

Further Reading

Boas, Franz. 1911. *Handbook of American Indian languages*, part 1. Washington, DC: Smithsonian Institution.
Boaz, Franz. 1922. *Handbook of American Indian languages*, part 2. Washington, DC: Smithsonian Institution.
Boas, Franz. 1933. *Handbook of American Indian languages*, part 3. New York: Columbia University.
Boas, Franz. 1941. *Handbook of American Indian languages*, part 4. New York: JJ Augustin.
Campbell, Lyle. 1997. *American Indian languages: The historical linguistics of Native America*. New York: Oxford University Press.
Goddard, Ives. 1996. *Handbook of North American Indians* 17, 390–439. Washington, DC: Smithsonian Institution.
Mithun, Marianne. 1998. *The languages of native North America*. (Cambridge Language Surveys.) Cambridge: Cambridge University Press.

Notes

1. Gillon (2009) argues that they are gender-neutral, rather than masculine.
2. Abbreviations in this chapter are as follows: 1 = first person, 2 = second person, 3 = third person, 3' = third person obviative, A = agent, ABL = ablative, ABS = absolutive, ACC = accusative, AGR = agreement, AL = alienable, ALL = allative, ALIEN = alienable, AN = animate, ART = article, ASSOC = associative, ATTR = attributive, AUX = auxiliary, BAS = basic, BEN = benefactive, CLF = classifier, COLL = collective, COMPL = completive, CONJ = conjunct, DEF = definite, DEM = demonstrative, DIR = direct, DISJ = disjoint, DIST = distal, DISTR = distributive, DU = dual, EPEN = epenthetic element, EMPH = emphatic, ERG = ergative, F = feminine, FACT = factive, FIN = finite, FUT = future, GEN = genitive, HYP = hypothetical, IMP = imperative, IMPF = imperfective, IN = inanimate, INAL = inalienable, INDF = indefinite, INS = instrumental, INTR = intransitive, INV = inverse, INVIS = invisible, IRR = irrealis, LOC = locative, M = masculine, N = neuter, NEUT = neutral, NOM = nominative, NSF = noun suffix, OBL = oblique, OBJ = object, OBV = obviative, P = patient, PART = participial, PAU = paucal, PERF = perfective, PL = plural, POSS = possessive, PREV = preverb, PROG = progressive, PROX = proximal, PRS = present tense, PRSV = presentative, PST = past tense, PURP = purposive, Q = question marker, REDUP = reduplicant, REFL = reflexive, SBJ = subject, SIM = similative, SG = singular, SPEC = specific, SS = same subject, TA = transitive animate, TI = transitive inanimate, TR = transitive, UP = unknown possessor, VIAL = vialis, VIS = visible.
3. It is unclear why *tári-* 'house' patterns with mass nouns.
4. The *a-* prefix is underlyingly *wa-* (Michael Barrie, p.c.).
5. Wiltschko (2012) argues that animacy in Blackfoot (Algonquian) is not in fact gender, but instead a form of inner nominal aspect. I do not address that possibility here.

6. This is an oversimplification; singular obviative forms disambiguate between animate and inanimate (Brittain 1993). See Wolfart (1996) and Oxford (this volume) for discussions of obviation.
7. Mixtec (Otomangean) has a similar system, based on sex (masculine/feminine), age/politeness (older, younger, deceased, etc.), supernatural, animal, and inanimate, but it is only marked on pronouns (Macaulay 1996). Age/politeness might be part of a different formality system (cf. Bliss & Ritter 2009), but I am agnostic as to its status in Mixtec.
8. Boas and Swanton (1911: 939–941) also list an indefinite article *wiⁿ*, which can be used for any referent or grammatical role.
9. There are instances where plural is not entirely obligatory, but number marking is much more systematic in most Algonquian languages than in the languages discussed in §3.1.1. One place where number marking is not obligatory is in certain syntactic contexts in Blackfoot; unmarked nouns in those cases have general number (see Kim et al. 2017).
10. Brown (2007) reports that, for at least one speaker, the singular form is not grammatical, *humuxw* is the regular form, *gamuxw* a more regional one, and *gahumuxw* means 'their ears'.
11. Further, in an experiment using nonce words, speakers used almost all of the strategies to pluralize the words (Brown 2008). Thus, there does not appear to be a default pluralization strategy.
12. This is sometimes dependent on obviation; see Wolfart (1996) and Oxford (this volume) for discussion.
13. The paucal only occurs on a small number of nouns, and these nouns do not take the plain plural suffix by itself. Mark C. Baker (p.c.) suggests that paucal might be misleading in this context; however, I can think of no better term for the semantics of this suffix.
14. Watahomigie et al. (1982) describe a very different system of plural marking. I assume dialect difference here. Further, Redden's description might be better thought of as plural and augmentative, rather than paucal and plural.
15. Mark C. Baker (p.c.) suggests that the inalienable forms may be related to the alienable ones; this is beyond the scope of this chapter.
16. According to Bale and Coon (2014), *te's* is akin to the default classifiers in Mandarin.
17. There are also forms for berries, containers, etc., but they do not involve reduplication.
18. The position of the articles can vary from language to language and is likely determined by the meaning of the article. I abstract away from such issues here.
19. This is an incomplete table; possessive forms are not included. Further, a better description of the distal series might be 'non-deictic'. Nicholson and Werle (2009) describe the distal articles as lacking any deictic information.
20. There is also a more complicated system of negative articles, which I do not discuss (Rood & Taylor 1996).
21. Smith uses different terminology for some of these.
22. While this appears to be an unergative verb, and we would expect agent marking on the subject, "patients tend to be affected but not in control of the action expressed by a verb" (Balodis 2016: 107). I infer from this description that children are not considered to have full control of their play.

References

Ahenakew, Freda. 1987. *Cree language structures: A Cree approach*. Winnipeg: Pemmican Publications.

Allen, Shanley E. M. 1988. Noun incorporation in Eskimo: Postpositions and case marking. *Cahiers Linguistiques de McGill* 5(2). 1–39.

Andrade, Manuel. 1933. Quileute. In Boas, Franz (ed.), *Handbook of American Indian languages*, part 3, 149–292. New York: Columbia University.

Aoki, Haruo & Walker, Deward E., Jr. 1989. *Nez Perce oral narratives*. University of California Publications in Linguistics, vol. 104. Berkeley: University of California Press.

Bale, Alan & Coon, Jessica. 2014. Classifiers are for numerals, not for nouns: Consequences for the mass/count distinction. *Linguistic Inquiry* 45(4). 695–707.

Balodis, Uldis. 2016. *Yuki grammar in its areal context with sketches of Huchnom and Coast Yuki*. Oakland: University of California Press.

Barrie, Michael. 2016. Gender mismatches and ellipsis in Cayuga. *Journal of Cognitive Science* 17(3). 361–388.

Black, Cheryl. 2000. *Quiegolani Zapotec syntax: A principles and parameters account*. Dallas: Summer Institute of Linguistics and University of Texas at Arlington.

Blair, Robert W. & Vermont-Salas, Refugio. 1967. *Spoken (Yucatec) Maya*, vol. 2. Chicago, IL: University of Chicago, Dept. of Anthropology.

Bliss, Heather & Oxford, Will. 2016. A microparametric approach to syncretisms in nominal inflection. In Kim, Kyeon-min & Umbal, Pocholo & Block, Trevor & Chan, Queenie & Cheng, Tanie & Finney, Kelli & Katz, Mara & Nickel-Thompson, Sophie & Shorten, Lisa (eds.), *Proceedings of the 33rd West Coast Conference on Formal Linguistics*, 67–76. Somerville: Cascadilla Proceedings Project.

Bliss, Heather & Ritter, Elizabeth. 2009. A typological database of personal and demonstrative pronouns. In Musgrave, Simon & Everaert, Martin & Dimitriadis, Alexis (eds.), *The use of databases in cross-linguistic research*, 77–116. Berlin: Mouton.

Bliss, Heather. 2013. *The Blackfoot configurationality conspiracy: Parallels and differences in clausal and nominal structures*. Vancouver: University of British Columbia. (Doctoral dissertation.)

Bloomfield, Leonard. 1962. *The Menomini language*, edited by Charles F. Hockett. New Haven, CT: Yale University Press.

Boas, Franz & Swanton, John. 1911. Siouan, Dakota (Teton and Santee dialects) with remarks on Ponca and Winnebago. *Bureau of American Ethnology, Bulletin* 40. 875–965.

Boas, Franz. 1904. Vocabulary of the Chinook language. *American Anthropologist*, New Series 6(1). 118–147.

Boas, Franz. 1911. Chinook. In Boas, Franz (ed.), *Handbook of American Indian languages*, part 1, 559–677. Washington, DC: Smithsonian Institution.

Bolles, David & Bolles, Alejandra. 2014. *A grammar and anthology of the Yucatecan Mayan language*. Rev. edn. Foundation for the Advancement of Mesoamerican Studies.

Brandt, Elizabeth. 1970. *Sandia Pueblo, New Mexico: A linguistic and ethnolinguistic investigation*. Dallas, TX: Southern Methodist University. (Doctoral dissertation.)

Brittain, Julie. 1993. *Two valency-increasing processes in Sheshatshit Innu-aimun: Applicative and causative formation*. St John's: Memorial University of Newfoundland. (Master's Thesis.)

Broadbent, Sylvia. 1964. *The Southern Sierra Miwok language*. Oakland: University of California Press.

Brown, Jason. 2007. Doubled plurals and the syntax of words in Gitksan. (Paper presented at the Workshop on Parts and Quantities, Vancouver, November 16, 2007.)

Brown, Jason. 2008. *Theoretical aspects of Gitksan phonology*. Vancouver: University of British Columbia. (Doctoral dissertation.)

Butler, Lindsay. 2011. *The morphosyntax and processing of number marking in Yucatec Maya*. Tucson: University of Arizona. (Doctoral dissertation.)

Butler, Lindsay. 2012. Crosslinguistic and experimental evidence for non-number plurals. *Linguistic Variation* 12. 27–56.

Callaghan, Catharine. 1963. *A grammar of the Lake Miwok language*. Berkeley: University of California. (Doctoral dissertation.)

Chilton, Paul. 2014. *Language, space and mind*. Cambridge: Cambridge University Press.

Compton, Richard. 2012. *The syntax and semantics of modification in Inuktitut: Adjectives and adverbs in a polysynthetic language*. Toronto: University of Toronto. (Doctoral dissertation.)

Corbett, Greville. 2000. *Number*. Cambridge: Cambridge University Press.

Corbett, Greville. 2013. Sex-based and non-sex-based gender systems. In Dryer, Matthew & Haspelmath, Martin (eds.), *The world atlas of language structures online*. Leipzig: Max Planck Institute for Evolutionary Anthropology.

Cyr, Danielle. 1993. Cross-linguistic quantification: Definite articles vs. demonstratives. *Language Sciences* 15(3). 195–229.

Dahlstrom, Amy. 1995. Motivation vs. predictability in Algonquian gender. In Pentland, David (ed.), *Papers of the 26th Algonquian Conference*, 52–66. Winnipeg: University of Manitoba.

Darnell, Regna & Vanek, Anthony L. 1976. The semantic basis of the animate/inanimate distinction in Cree. *Papers in Linguistics* 9(3–4). 159–180.

Deal, Amy Rose. 2010. Ergative case and the transitive subject: A view from Nez Perce. *Natural Language and Linguistic Theory* 28. 73–120.

De León Pasquel, Maria de Lourdes. 1988. *Noun and numeral classifiers in Mixtec and Tzotzil: A referential view*. Ann Arbor: University of Michigan; Brighton: University of Brighton. (Doctoral dissertation.)

Demirdache, Hamida. 1996. The temporal reference of noun phrases in St'át'imcets. (Paper presented at the Linguistic Society of America, San Diego, CA, 4–7 January 1996.)

Dixon, Roland B. 1910. The Chimariko Indians and language. *University of California Publications in American Archaeology and Ethnology* 5. 293–380.

Dorsey, James Owen. 1890. *The Dhegiha language, the speech of the Omaha and Ponka tribes of the Siouan linguistic family of North American Indians*. (Contributions to North American Ethnology.) Washington, DC: Department of the Interior, US Geographical and Geological Survey of the Rocky Mountain Region.

Fortescue, Michael. 1984. *West Greenlandic*. (Croom Helm Descriptive Grammars.) London: Croom Helm.

Gerdts, Donna B. 2009. Women, fire, and not so dangerous things: Explorations in Halkomelem gender. Presidential Address, Annual Meeting of the Society for the Study of the Indigenous Languages of the Americas, San Francisco.

Gerdts, Donna B. 2011. The purview effect: Feminine gender on inanimates in Halkomelem Salish. In Cathcart, Chundra & Chen, I-Hsuan & Finley, Greg & Kang, Shinae & Sandy, Clare S. & Stickles, Elise (eds.), *Proceedings of the 37th annual meeting of the Berkeley Linguistics Society*, 417–426. Berkeley: Berkeley Linguistics Society.

Gerdts, Donna B. & Hinkson, Mercedes Q. & Hukari, Thomas E. 2002. Numeral classifiers in Halkomelem. In Gillon, Carrie & Sawai, Naomi & Wojdak, Rachel (eds.), *Proceedings of the 37th International Conference on Salish and Neighbouring Languages*, UBCWPL 9, 147–179. Vancouver: University of British Columbia Working Papers in Linguistics.
Gillon, Carrie. 2009. Deictic features: Evidence from Sḵwx̱wú7mesh. *International Journal of American Linguistics* 75. 1–27.
Gillon, Carrie. 2011. Bare nouns in Innu-aimun: What can semantics tell us about syntax? In Black, Alexis & Louie, Meagan (eds.), *Proceedings for the Workshop on the structure and constituency of the languages of the Americas* 16, 29–56. Vancouver: University of British Columbia Working Papers in Linguistics.
Gillon, Carrie. 2012. Evidence for mass and count in Inuttut. *Linguistic Variation* 12. 211–246.
Gillon, Carrie. 2013. *The semantics of determiners: Domain restriction in Sḵwx̱wú7mesh*. Newcastle Upon Tyne: Cambridge Scholars Publishing.
Gillon, Carrie. 2015. Innu-aimun plurality. *Lingua* 162. 128–148.
Goddard, Ives. 2002. Grammatical gender in Algonquian. In Wolfart, H. C. (ed.), *Papers of the 33rd Algonquian Conference*. Winnipeg: University of Manitoba Press.
Gordon, Lynn. 1986. *Maricopa morphology and syntax*. Berkeley: University of California Press.
Graczyk, Randolph Jan. 2007. *A grammar of Crow*. Lincoln: University of Nebraska Press.
Grinevald, Collette. 2000. A morphosyntactic typology of classifiers. In Senft, Gunter (ed.), *Systems of nominal classification*, 50–92. New York: Cambridge University Press.
Grinevald, Collette. 2016. The Jakaltek Popti' noun classifier system. In Berez-Kroeker, Andrea L. & Hintz, Diane M. & Jany, Carmen (eds.), *Language contact and change in the Americas: Studies in honor of Marianne Mithun*, 273–296. Amsterdam: John Benjamins.
Haas, Mary. 1941. Tunica. In Boas, Franz (ed.), *Handbook of American Indian languages*, part 4, 1–143. New York: JJ Augustin.
Hale, Kenneth. 1997. Some observations on the contribution of local languages to linguistic science. *Lingua* 100. 71–89.
Hallowell, A. Irving. 1960. Ojibwa ontology, behavior, and world view. In Diamond, Stanley (ed.), *Culture in history: Essays in honor of Paul Radin*, 19–52. New York: Columbia University Press.
Halpern, Abraham. 1946. Yuma III: Grammatical processes and the noun. *International Journal of American Linguistics* 12. 204–212.
Harrington, John. 1928. *Vocabulary of the Kiowa language*. Bureau of American Ethnology, Bulletin 84. Washington, DC: Smithsonian Institution.
Heaton, Raina & Anderson, Patricia. 2017. When animals become humans: Grammatical gender in Tunica. *International Journal of American Linguistics* 83(2). 341–363.
Hymes, Dell. 1955. *The language of the Kathlamet Chinook*. Bloomington: Indiana University. (Doctoral dissertation.)
Jacobson, Steven A. 1995. *A practical grammar of the central Alaskan Yup'ik Eskimo language*. Fairbanks: Alaska Native Language Center.
Jelinek, Eloise. 2006. The pronominal argument parameter. In Ackema, Peter & Brandt, Patrick & Schoorlemmer, Maaike & Weerman, Fred (eds.), *Arguments and agreement*, 261–289. Oxford: Oxford University Press.
Kim, Kyumin & Ritter, Elizabeth & Wiltschko, Martina & Rullmann, Hotze. 2017. 2 + 2 = 3: Number contrasts in Blackfoot. *Glossa: A Journal of General Linguistics* 2(1). 96.
Kimball, Geoffrey. 1991. *Koasati grammar*. Lincoln: University of Nebraska.
Kramer, Ruth. 2015. *The morphosyntax of gender*. Oxford: Oxford University Press.
Kuipers, Aert H. 1967. *The Squamish language: Grammar, texts, dictionary*. The Hague: Mouton.
Lastra de Suárez, Yolanda. 1984. Chichimeco Jonaz. In Edmonson, Munro S. (ed.), *Supplement to the handbook of Middle American languages: Linguistics*, 20–42. Austin: University of Texas Press.
Lehmann, Christian. 2002. *Possession in Yucatec Maya*. Munich: Lincom.
Macaulay, Monica. 1996. *A grammar of Chalcatongo Mixtec*. (University of California Publications in Linguistics, 127.) Berkeley: University of California Press.
Mailhot, José & MacKenzie, Marguerite. 2013. *Innu-English dictionary*. Sheshatshiu: Mamu Tshishkutamashutau.
Mathieu, Éric. 2012. On the mass/count distinction in Ojibwe. In Massam, Diane (ed.), *Count and mass across languages*, 172–198. Oxford: Oxford University Press.
Matthewson, Lisa. 1998. *Determiner systems and quantificational strategies: Evidence from Salish*. The Hague: Holland Academic Graphics.
Miller, Wick. 1965. *Acoma grammar and texts*. Berkeley: University of California Press.
Mithun, Marianne. 1998. *The languages of native North America*. (Cambridge Language Surveys.) Cambridge: Cambridge University Press.
Muehlbauer, Jeffrey. 2007. Evidence for three distinct nominal classes in Plains Cree. *Natural Language Semantics* 15(2). 167–186.

Mulder, Jean. 1988. *Ergativity in Coast Tsimshian (Sm'algyax)*. Berkeley: University of California Press.
Newman, Stanley. 1965. *Zuni grammar*. (University of New Mexico Publications in Anthropology 14.) Albuquerque: University of New Mexico.
Nichols, Johanna & Bickel, Balthazar. 2011. Locus of marking in possessive noun phrases. In Dryer, Matthew S. & Haspelmath, Martin (eds.), *The world atlas of language structures online* (Chapter 24). Munich: Max Planck Digital Library. (http://wals.info/chapter/24) (Accessed 2017-01-20.)
Nicholson, Marianne & Werle, Adam. 2009. An investigation of modern Kwakwala determiner systems. Victoria: University of Victoria. (http://web.uvic.ca/~werle/files/NICOLSON_WERLE_2009.pdf) (Accessed 2017-03-23.)
Ratt, Solomon. 2016. *mâci-nêhiyawêwin/Beginning Cree*. Regina: University of Regina Press.
Redden, James. 1966. Walapai II: Morphology. *International Journal of American Linguistics* 32(2). 141–163.
Rood, David S. & Taylor, Allan R. 1996. Sketch of Lakhota, a Siouan language. In Goddard, Ives (ed.), *Handbook of North American Indians* 17, 440–482. Washington, DC: Smithsonian Institution.
Rupp, James E. 2009. Animacy in two Chinantec varieties. SIL – Mexico Electronic Working Papers #007. (www.sil.org/mexico/workpapers/WP007i-ChinantecAnimacy-cle-chz.pdf) (Accessed 2016-11-12.)
Shaul, David Leedom. 2012. *Survey of Shoshone grammar with reference to Eastern Shoshone*. (www.easternshoshone.org/assets/survey-of-shoshone-grammar1.pdf) (Accessed 2017-05-30.)
Smith, Lawrence R. 1977. *Some grammatical aspects of Labrador Inuttut (Eskimo): A survey of the inflectional paradigms of nouns and verbs*. Mercury Series No. 37. Ottawa: Museum of Civilization.
Spreng, Bettina. 2012. *Viewpoint aspect in Inuktitut: The syntax and semantics of antipassives*. Toronto: University of Toronto. (Doctoral dissertation.)
Sutton, Logan. 2010. Noun class and number in Kiowa-Tanoan: Comparative-historical research and respecting speakers' rights in fieldwork. In Berez, Andrea L. & Mulder, Jean & Rosenblum, Daisy (eds.), *Fieldwork and linguistic analysis in indigenous languages of the Americas*, 57–89. Honolulu: University of Hawai'i Press.
Troike, Rudolph. 1981. Subject-object concord in Coahuileteco. *Language* 57(3). 658–673.
Troike, Rudolph. 1996. Coahuilteco (Pajalate). In Goddard, Ives (ed.), *Handbook of North American Indians*, 17, 664–665. Washington, DC: Smithsonian Institution.
Wagner, Günter. 1938. Yuchi. In Boas, Franz (ed.), *Handbook of American Indian languages*, part 3, 300–384. New York: Columbia University Press.
Walker, Neil. 2012. *A grammar of Southern Pomo: An indigenous language of California*. Santa Barbara: University of California. (Doctoral dissertation.)
Wash, Suzanne. 2001. *Adverbial clauses in Barbareño Chumash narrative discourse*. Ann Arbor: University of Michigan. (Doctoral dissertation.)
Watahomigie, Lucille J., Bender, Jorigine & Yamamoto, Akira Y. 1982. *Hualapai reference grammar*. Los Angeles: American Indian Studies Center, University of California.
Watkins, Laurel. 1984. *A grammar of Kiowa*. Lincoln: University of Nebraska.
Wiltschko, Martina. 2012. Decomposing the mass/count distinction: Evidence from languages that lack it. In Massam, Diane (ed.), *Count and mass across languages*, 146–171. (Oxford Studies in Theoretical Linguistics.) Oxford: Oxford University Press.
Wiltschko, Martina. 2014. *The universal structure of categories: Towards a formal typology*. Cambridge: Cambridge University Press.
Wolfart, H. C. 1973. *Plains Cree: A grammatical study*. Philadelphia, PA: American Philosophical Society Transactions.
Wolfart, H. C. 1996. Sketch of Cree, an Algonquian language. In Goddard, Ives (ed.), *Handbook of North American Indians* 17, 390–439. Washington, DC: Smithsonian Institution.
Wolvengrey, Arok Elessar. 2011. *Semantic and pragmatic functions in Plains Cree syntax*. Utrecht: LOT.
Yiu, Winnie & Stonham, John. 2002. The nature of Nuuchahnulth classifiers. In Gessner, Suzanne & Oh, Sunyoung (eds.), *Papers for the 37th International Conference on Salish and Neighbouring Languages*. Vancouver: UBC Working Papers in Linguistics.
Zigmond, Maurice L. & Booth, Curtis G. & Munro, Pamela. 1991. *Kawaiisu: A grammar and dictionary with texts*. Berkeley: University of California Press.

6

MORPHOSYNTACTIC STRATEGIES IN LOCATIVE DESCRIPTION

Carolyn O'Meara and Gabriela Pérez Báez

1. Introduction

All languages have grammatical means by which speakers can describe the location of objects in space. While there is variation in terms of the morphosyntactic expression of location cross-linguistically, there appear to be loci of how this category is encoded grammatically. In this chapter we present an overview of some of the ways in which North American languages express location at the morphosyntactic level.

The topic of spatial reference is not new to the literature. In fact, numerous volumes focusing on spatial language begin by mentioning the Kantian tradition of treating space as a cognitive primitive (Hickmann & Robert 2006; Levinson & Wilkins 2006; inter alia). Many recent studies on the language of spatial description have largely focused on topics in semantics (e.g., Levinson & Wilkins 2006; Ameka & Levinson 2007) and the intersection between language, cognition, and culture (e.g., Landau & Jackendoff 1993; Landau 2016). In particular, the work of the Language and Cognition Group at the Max Planck Institute for Psycholinguistics is remarkable in its efforts to study, by means of semantic typology, the domain of spatial description. Levinson and Wilkins (2006: 3) divide the spatial domain into three parts: topological description, motion description, and frames of reference.[1] These three groupings make a distinction between stasis (topological description and frames of reference) and kinesis (motion description). We follow this distinction here and focus on stasis, looking primarily at descriptions that do not require a frame of reference for their interpretation. In other words, we focus primarily on locative descriptions and exclude the discussion of motion event descriptions, although at times it is inevitable to mention the latter.[2]

Generally, in locative descriptions speakers tend to provide the location of a "moving or conceptually movable entity" termed FIGURE, with respect to a reference object termed GROUND (Talmy 2000: 184). For example, in the sentence *The cup is on the table*, *the cup* is the phrase with the noun that refers to the figure and *the table* is the phrase with the noun that refers to the ground. The information related to the cup's location with respect to the table is provided by the preposition *on*. Adpositions, however, are not the only grammatical resource used to fulfill this function, as we see in the text that follows.

In descriptions that locate one object with respect to another, a spatial frame of reference is often required for its successful interpretation. Frames of reference are spatial coordinate systems that are used in interpreting the spatial relations between objects. For instance, in the example *New Mexico is east of Arizona*, a coordinate system based on cardinal directions (north, south, east, west) is required for its interpretation, and in *My glass is to the right of the wine bottle*, the left and right axes of our body provide a coordinate system to interpret the utterance. Frames of reference are of interest to linguists, psycholinguists, and cognitive scientists and have proven to be somewhat controversial in the literature (see Levinson et al. 2002; Li & Gleitman 2002; Majid et al. 2004; Li et al. 2005). Yet, few studies look at spatial frames of reference use in languages of North America, with the exception of studies conducted on languages in and around Mesoamerica (see, e.g., O'Meara & Pérez Báez 2011).

This chapter provides a survey of the morphosyntactic strategies employed in descriptions locating an object in space across the languages of North America and is based on an extensive review of the literature, mostly grammars, of 22 different North American language families. These include four language families spoken in the Mesoamerican cultural area – Mayan, Otomanguean, Mixe-Zoquean, and Totonac-Tepehua – as well as the Uto-Aztecan family, whose languages are distributed along the northwest region of the United States and into Mesoamerica. This sample is the result, to a great extent, of the availability of published studies on the morphosyntax of locative descriptions, as well as our areas of expertise. The data presented in this chapter is a selection of the data obtained from this survey.

We begin the chapter by discussing how locative predicates are encoded, primarily as it pertains to verbal predication, and then focus on other grammatical elements that involve or are associated with verbal forms, such as preverbs, verbal particles, adverbs and directionals, as well as different types of stems, such as bipartite stems. We then change focus to areas outside of the verb where location can be marked, in particular by means of phrases headed by adpositions, spatial relational nouns, and locative case markers. Finally, we conclude by mentioning other strategies for the encoding of locative information in languages of North America.

2. Verbal Predicates in Locative Descriptions

As part of a larger discussion of intransitive predication strategies, Stassen (1997: 55) has noted that the natural strategy for encoding locative predicates cross-linguistically is through verbs. Also interested in the types of verbal predicates used in locative constructions, members of the Language and Cognition group at the Max Planck Institute for Psycholinguistics proposed a classification of such verb types based on cross-linguistic variation and convergence in the grammar of spatial reference (Brown 1994; Levinson & Meira 2003; Ameka & Levinson 2007; inter alia). The data showed that information regarding the figure (e.g., shape and orientation), ground (e.g., shape and medium), and the nature of the spatial relation that holds between the two is packaged in different ways cross-linguistically. Additionally, it is distributed throughout constructions and in morphological and lexical forms throughout the clause in different ways across languages (Levinson & Wilkins 2006).

Indeed, there are languages in which locative predication does not involve a verbal predicate. Rather, locative information is expressed through syntactic sequencing of figure and ground-referring clauses, where the ground is part of an oblique marked phrase.[3] This has been reported for Russian, illustrated in (1). Based on our survey, this strategy does not appear to be a tendency among North American languages.[4]

(1) Russian (Indo-European, Slavonic)

Moja	sestrá	v	Moskvé
my	sister	in	Moscow.OBL[5]

'My sister is in Moscow.'

(Fennell 1961: 57; *apud* Stassen 1997: 59)

Rather, in the languages discussed here, a variety of strategies involving the use of verbs to predicate location have been observed, from the use of a single locational or existential verb, discussed in §2.1, to large inventories of roots or stems that encode the posture or disposition of the figure, discussed in §2.2.

2.1. Locative Predication Encoded by a Single Verb

Some languages make use of a copula in locative constructions. English is an example of such a language, e.g., *The dog* ***is*** *in the house*. Another case is found with the Mayan language Jakaltek Popti', which can make use of a single existential copula, *ay*, in existential, possessive and locative constructions.[6] Examples of locative constructions are provided in (2).

(2) Jakaltek Popti' (Mayan)

a. | **ay**-k'oj | no' | wakaxh | pet | san | marcos |
|---|---|---|---|---|---|
| exist-DIR | CL | cow | in | San | Marcos |

'The cows are (across) in San Marcos.'

b. | **ay**-ik-toj | no' | mis | yul | te' | kaxha |
|---|---|---|---|---|---|
| exist-DIR-DIR | CL | cat | in | CL | chest |

'The cat is (inside away) in the chest.'

(Grinevald 2006: 45–46)

The existential copula combines with directional markers in locative constructions, *-k'oj* in (2a) and *-ik-toj* in (2b). The directional markers are derived from motion verbs (Grinevald 2006: 46).

Another Mayan language, Yucatec, has been described as using a single locative verb *yàan* in locative descriptions (Ameka & Levinson 2007; Bohnemeyer & Brown 2007), as in (3).

(3) Yucatec (Mayan)

Le	lùuch-o',	ti'=**yàan**	y-óok'ol	le	mèesa-o'
DEF	cup-D2	LOC=EXIST(B.3.SG)	A.3-on	DEF	table-D2

'The cup, it's there on the table.'

(Bohnemeyer & Stolz 2006: 290)

Yucatec speakers have other options available to describe the location of objects; specifically, they can also use non-positional resultative forms like *kurzàar-nah-a'n* 'be crossed', or *ts'a'-mah* 'have put' (Bohnemeyer & Stolz 2006: 290). Any time a resultative form is used, the existential form could be used in its place, but not vice versa – the choice of which construction to use is determined pragmatically.[7]

2.2. Posture and Disposition in Locative Predicates

There are languages that use posture verbs (e.g., *sit, stand, lie*, and also sometimes *hang*) in locative constructions. The use of posture verbs, in and of itself, is not typologically unusual – Dutch requires the use of posture verbs in locative constructions (Stassen 1997: 61). It is, however, worth noting that the extent to which these posture verbs are used varies across North America. Languages that use posture verbs are found in the southeastern United States and within the Siouan language family (Mithun 1999), as well as further south in Mesoamerica. We present data to show the use of posture verbs in relation to other devices such as copulas or general locative verbs, diversity in the use of posture verbs with animate versus inanimate subjects, and in the inventories of postures that a language may exhibit, and particular phenomena such as suppletion.

To begin, we provide data from Creek, a Muskogean language of the southeastern United States, which uses posture verbs rather than a copula in locative descriptions, as in (4).

(4) Creek (Muskogean)

a. šampat čoka oofan **léékiis.**
basket.SBJ house inside.OBJ sit
'The basket is in the house.'
(Watkins 1976: 21; *apud* Newman 2002: 11)

b. asean spaaskat **ahwii:iis.**
there.OBJ broom.SBJ stand
'The broom's over there.'
(Watkins 1976: 21; *apud* Newman 2002: 11)

Biloxi (Siouan) has an inventory of classificatory verbs including verbs such as *nąki* 'sitting', *mąki* 'reclining, in a horizontal position', and *ne* 'upright', as shown in (5). The inventory is also said to include the verbs *hine* 'walking' and *ande* 'running'. The verbs may be used independently or in combination with other roots.

(5) Biloxi (Siouan)

Éwa n-**yuķě'**-di
there 1PL-stand-DUR
'We were there.'
(Dorsey & Swanton 1912: 135; *apud* Stassen 1997: 138)

The canonical function of posture verbs is to describe the posture of animate entities (Newman 2002: 7), but they can also be used to describe the location of inanimate entities. This is also the case in Biloxi (following Einaudi 1976). The extent to which posture verbs are used with inanimate entities in addition to animate entities in a systematic and possibly classificatory manner differs cross-linguistically.

Posture verbs can describe postures beyond *sit*, *stand* and *lie*. Central Pomo (Mithun 1998: 165; *apud* Newman 2002: 3), for instance, has been reported to have five verbs that describe different kinds of sitting: *čʰá:w* (single person sitting on chair), *bamáw* (group sitting together on a bench), *ʔčʰá:w* (single person sitting on ground), *napʰów* (group sitting on ground), and *cʰóm* (container of liquid on table).

Other languages have large inventories of what have been termed positionals or dispositionals – roots and/or stems that predicate on the relation between a figure and a ground (Bohnemeyer & Brown 2007). Tzotzil, for instance, has been reported to have an inventory of 16 positional roots (Haviland 1992) that describe seated postures. Tseltal has hundreds of positional roots that can be used in locative constructions (in addition to one preposition, *ta*, that is multifunctional and not specific to spatial descriptions) (Brown 1994), as in (6).

(6) Tseltal (Mayan)

waxal-∅ ta ti'-k'jk' p'in
vertical-ABS.3 PREP mouth-fire pot
'The pot is (standing vertical) by the fire.'
(Grinevald 2006: 42)

In some Mayan languages, dispositional or posture predicates are preferred in locative constructions (e.g., Tseltal), requiring speakers to be particularly attuned to the actual posture of an entity or position of the object to be located, including, for instance, whether it is in canonical position. In other languages (e.g., English, Yucatec Maya), this level of specificity is optional.

Overall, Mayan languages, as well as some Otomanguean languages, are known for their sets of positional or dispositional roots in locative constructions which form their own morphological class (Campbell 1997: 346). There are, however, marked exceptions to this trend. Such is the case of the striking example we have already seen in (2) from Jakaltek Popti', a Mayan language that makes only modest and marked use of positionals and rather favors the use of a single existential copula with directionals as satellites (Grinevald 2006).

There are also languages that make use of posture verbs and, in addition, have a general locative verb that does not lexicalize a particular posture or spatial configuration of the figure. This is the case in Seri, a language isolate spoken in northwestern Mexico, which has a general locative verb, *-ahca* 'be', in addition to a set of posture verbs and a verb used to describe the location of flexible objects, *-iih* 'be [flexible item]' Marlett (2017: 459). However, the distinction is not completely transparent, as is shown in (7), where a book's location is described with *-iih* and a nest's location is described with *-ahca*. Note that in Seri, the definite articles are derived from subject nominalized forms of locative verbs, including posture verbs as well as motion verbs.

(7) Seri (isolate)

a. Ha-p-aspoj ha-noocaj tiix hant
SBJ.NMLZ-PAS-write SBJ.NMLZ.PAS-hold DEM land
i-ti i-qu-eaacalca com
3POSS-on 3POSS-UNSPEC.SBJ-OBL.NMLZ.store.possessions DEF.ART.SG.lie
i-yat hac i-ti y-**iih**.
3POSS-on.top DEF.ART.SG.LOC 3POSS-on DP-be
'The book (lit. what is written that is held) is on top of the bookshelf (lit. land on which one stores possessions).'

b. Ziic i-ime hehe cap i-ti
bird 3POSS-nest wood DEF.ART.SG.stand 3POSS-in
c-**aahca** iha.
SBJ.NMLZ-be.LOC DECL
'The nest is in the tree.'

(O'Meara & Guerrero 2015: 292)

c. I-c-aaspoj com hant i-ti
3POSS-UNSPEC.SBJ-write DEF.ART.SG.lie land 3POSS-on
i-c-aaspoj com i-ti moom.
3POSS-UNSPEC.SBJ-write DEF.ART.SG.lie 3POSS-on RP.lie
'The pencil (lit. with which one writes) is on the desk (lit. land on which one writes).'

(O'Meara & Guerrero 2015: 291)

Many Uto-Aztecan languages from the Cahita branch have been described as making use of general locative verbs as well as posture verbs in locative descriptions (O'Meara & Guerrero 2015). This is the case for Yaqui (or Yoeme), Guarijio, and Lower Piman where it appears that, similar to Seri, posture verbs are used to describe the actual or canonical posture of animate entities, and serve a classificatory function for inanimate entities based on their geometric properties (O'Meara & Guerrero 2015). This can be seen with the example in (8a) from Guarijio, where the machete is being described as lying. It is also worth noting that Guarijio has a specific posture verb for entities that stand on four legs (as opposed to two), as is illustrated in (8b).

(8) Guarijio (Uto-Aztecan)

a. Weh-cí po'í macíra=ga.
ground-on be.lying machete=EMPH
'The machete is on the ground.'

b. Ahká=na cuhkú cuhcúri?
where=MODAL be.standing.with.four.feet dog
'Where is the dog?'

(Miller 1993: 70)

Mayo (Uto-Aztecan) differs from other Uto-Aztecan languages in that its speakers use a general locative verb rather than posture verbs to describe the location of animate entities (O'Meara & Guerrero 2015), as in (9).[8] The extent to which speakers of Mayo use posture verbs for inanimate entities requires further research. However, it is worth mentioning this case, along with earlier examples on Mayan languages, to highlight the fact that diversity in the morphosyntax of locative descriptions can be observed even within languages belonging to the same family.

(9) Mayo (Uto-Aztecan)

In pa howa-po a:ne
1POSS father house-in is.LOC
'My father is in the house.'

(Freeze 1989: 80)

One tendency of languages spoken in the southeastern United States that use posture verbs in locative descriptions is suppletion under certain conditions. Such is the case of the six posture verbs in Choctaw shown in Table 6.1. Broadwell (2006: 335), citing Nicklas (1974: 59) and Heath (1980), reports that all six posture verbs in Choctaw show three-way suppletion to mark subject number (singular, dual, and plural), while most verbs in the language do not exhibit alternations of this kind.

Outside the Southeast region, Yaqui (Uto-Aztecan) also shows suppletion in the number marking of posture verbs, as illustrated in (10).

(10) Yaqui (Uto-Aztecan)

a. U kuchu-Ø frajko-po ba'am waiwa **katek.**
DET fish-NOM container-LOC water inside be.sitting.SG
'The fish is inside the water container.'

b. U-me'e chokim mek-jika-t **jo'oka.**
DET-PL star.PL far-up-over be.sitting.PL
'The stars are over there.'

(O'Meara & Guerrero 2015: 301)

While suppletive forms might be limited to certain languages or regions, it is worth noting that this phenomenon appears to occur within this particular class of verbs across unrelated languages.

Table 6.1 Posture Verbs in Choctaw[9]

SINGULAR	*DUAL*	*PLURAL*	*GLOSS*
attah	*ashwah*	*ayyaashah á̱ashah, áshah, má̱yah*	'to sit, dwell'
biniilih	*chiiyah*	*binohlih, binohmá̱yah*	'to sit'
talaayah	*taloohah*	*talohlih, talohmá̱yah*	'to lie, to sit'
hikiiyah	*hiilih*	*hiyohlih, hiyohmáyah*	'to stand'
ittolah	*kahah*	*kahmá̱yah*	'to lie'
takaalih	*takoohah*	*takohlih, takohmá̱yah*	'to hang'

Source: Following Broadwell (2006: 336).

3. Encoding Location in Verb-Related Morphology

North American languages exhibit a variety of forms that express locative or directional information outside of the verb stem, but that are still closely linked to the verb in some way. This section provides examples including stems or prefixes that encode location and direction and constitute rather large inventories, locative agreement on verbs, and spatial preverbs, relative roots and relative preverbs.

We begin with an example in Klamath (Penutian), a language reported to lack adpositions. Instead, locative-directive stems express both information about the ground object and information about the path of the object in motion event descriptions (Barker 1964; DeLancey 2003). These stems are incorporated into a syntactic unit with complex semantic load. The stems, however, are analyzed as specifically encoding the spatial relation between the figure, the old grizzly, and the ground, the fire, as in (11). The locative-directive stem *elwy* can be glossed as 'by the fire, along the edge'. A characteristic of these locative-directive stems is that they constitute a large set of more than 130 stems that encode a diversity of ground and path configurations (DeLancey 2003: 68).

(11) Klamath (Penutian)

s?as?abam'c	qtan-a	ks-**elwy**-ank	loloqs-dat.
Old.Grizzly	sleep-INDIC	living.OBJ-by.fire-PART	fire-LOC

'Old Grizzly slept, lying by the fire.'

(Gatschet 1890: 121–122, *apud* DeLancey 2003: 69)

Cora (CR) and Huichol (HU) have been described as having an extensive inventory of locational and directional verbal prefixes, the likes of which are not found in other Uto-Aztecan languages (Casad 2012). Table 6.2 illustrates correspondences of such prefixes between the two languages. This list is not exhaustive, however, given that there are prefixes unique to each language. Of particular interest here are the prefixes that specify location, like *u-* 'in a specific location', *ye-* 'inside a bounded area', and the cislocative and translocative prefixes.

Navajo (or Diné Bizaad) has locative agreement marking on verb forms when the subject is a locational noun, as in (12). This marker may also be optionally suffixed to the locational noun. As a verbal prefix, it is obligatory unless a direction marker like *yah* 'into' precedes the verb.

Table 6.2 Huichol and Cora Locative (Verbal) Prefixes

HUICHOL (HU)	*CORA (CR)*	*MEANINGS*
e-	*a'-*	ablative or 'out of sight' (HU), 'off yonder' (CR)
a-	*a-*	allative (HU), 'on a surface' (HU, CR)
u-	*u-*	restrictive (HU), 'in specific location' (CR)
ti-	$t^{y}i$-	'up' (HU, CR)
ta-	*ta-*	'straight' (HU, CR)
ka-	*ka-*	'down' (HU, CR)
ye-	*ra-*	'inside a bounded area' (HU), 'face of' (CR)
wa-	*wa-*	'cavity' (HU), 'extensive throughout bounded area' (CR)
ku-	*ku-*	'back and forth', 'around the corner' (HU, CR)
na-	*na-*	cislocative, 'this side of perimeter' (HU, CR)
nu-	*nu-*	translocative, 'far side of perimeter' (HU, CR)

Source: Casad (2012: 63).

(12) Navajo (Na-Dene)

a'áán-góne'	ha-tl'éé'
hole-in	LOC-be.dark

'it is dark in the hole'

(van Riemsdijk & Huijbregts 2007: 358)

Encoding of locative information in Algonquian languages involves what have been called preverbs, defined as "a phonologically independent word that is syntactically part of a compound verb stem" (Goddard 1990: 478).[10] Arapaho is described as having two types of preverbs, not all of which encode location (Cowell & Moss Sr. 2008). The first type includes "grammatical preverbs, which always precede all lexical preverbs but do not participate in the formation of verb stems" (Cowell & Moss Sr. 2008: 205). Examples include the deictic preverbs *cih-* 'to here' and *eh-* 'from here'. The second type are lexical preverbs, an open subset which encode location as well as direction. Cowell & Moss Sr. (2008: 214–216) list over 100 preverbs such as *sii'ih-* 'into water', *inow-* 'out of sight underwater or underground', and *no'oetei-* 'to a river'. These preverbs can combine, resulting in specialized idiomatic meanings.

Some preverbs in Algonquian languages contain a particular type of morpheme that is known as a relative root, which increases the valence of the verb for an argument known as a relative root complement.[11] In some cases, this argument plays a locative role, sharing properties of both true objects and true obliques (Rhodes 2006), suggesting that they share functional properties with adpositional phrases in other languages. In fact, diachronically, the original form of most relative roots were postpositions (Rhodes 2006: 25).

Meskwaki (Algonquian) exhibits a cognate of the same relative root, */taN-/* (and its allomorphs *tan-*, *taš-*, *tah-*; *taši*), shown in (13). To express the location of an event, this preverb is required (Goddard 2007). Its gloss in (13) is presented in curly brackets as per Goddard (2017) to indicate that the gloss is not a literal translation.

(13) Meskwaki (Algonquian)

i·nahi=ne·h	wina	**taši**	pesеše·+wa
that/LOC=too	3SG/EMPH	{somewhere}/PV	listen+3SG/IND

'He was listening there, too.'

(Goddard 2007: 94)

4. Ground Phrase and the Encoding of Location in Relation to Nouns

A ground phrase is the part of the locative construction that contains the ground-denoting nominal (which we refer to simply as 'ground'). Many languages make use of adpositions to express spatial relations (Landau & Jackendoff 1993), so in these languages the ground phrase would be an adpositional phrase where the head of the phrase is the adposition and the ground is its object. However, this strategy is not universal (see, for example, Brown 1994), and, in fact, the larger tendency is for spatial information to be encoded across various elements of the clause, not just in one or two components (Levinson 2003; Grinevald 2006; Levinson & Wilkins 2006). What the ground phrase consists of varies cross-linguistically, but could include a ground plus an adposition, a ground plus a spatial relational noun, a ground plus locative case marking, or simply a ground-denoting noun with no additional morphology, among other options.[12] When a morpheme serving as a spatial relator is indeed present, it exhibits different levels of constituency between it and the ground-denoting nominal. In this section we discuss some of these different options and how they manifest themselves in the languages of North America. This section differs from previous ones in that it focuses on nouns – since the ground is usually expressed as a noun – and the morphosyntactic processes associated with them.

4.1. Locative Case, Affixes, and Adpositions

According to Stassen (1997: 60), spatial relations tend *not* to be encoded in verbal predicates cross-linguistically, but rather as adjunctive (or optional) constituents, indicated by case markers in the form of affixes or adpositions. Ameka and Levinson (2007) present counter-evidence to this claim, as does Brown (1994) with compelling data from Tseltal, a language that lacks a set of contrastive adpositions. This points to significant cross-linguistic diversity in terms of the structure of ground phrases beyond the encoding of locative information in adpositions. Further, the data in the sample of languages analyzed for this chapter shows that the categorial status of morphemes that encode locative information in the ground phrase is often not easily ascertained. Instead, the data suggest a kind of continuum of morphemes that may be either bound or free, obligatory or adjunctive, and/or in the process of becoming grammaticalized. Generally speaking, adpositions correspond to separate phonological words, and inflectional morphology for case is expressed by bound morphemes (Haspelmath 2008). However, descriptions vary widely in how they characterize adpositions or case inflection. Among the languages reported to have adpositions, some descriptions indicate that they are independent phonological words, and in other cases they are suffixes that attach to the ground. Case morphemes are commonly referred to as 'case markers' or 'case particles', and sometimes authors are agnostic with respect to these categories altogether. Nevertheless, the functional role of adpositions is thought to greatly overlap with that of locative case markers (Haspelmath 2008). Finally, the spatial relations that these forms lexicalize can differ within a particular language, as well as across languages, even if closely related.

Let us begin the discussion with adpositions and then transition to other types of locative morphemes. We can think of adpositions as belonging to two different types: core adpositions that mark local categories (and sometimes grammatical categories) and lexical adpositions (with larger semi-open sets) (DeLancey 2003: 63). For an overview of the different semantic concepts that can be lexicalized in spatial adpositions cross-linguistically, the reader is encouraged to consult Levinson and Meira (2003). Here we are primarily concerned with core spatial adpositions (e.g., in English *in*, *on* and *at*). In adpositional phrases, the object of the adposition is the ground-denoting nominal. Such adpositional phrases modify the verb and function as locative adverbs. Finally, adpositions that precede the ground are prepositions (as in English) and ones that follow the ground are postpositions.

Lakhota (Siouan) has two postpositions that indicate general notions of location and direction: *él* and *ektá* (Rood 2003). The difference in their meaning has to do with proximity to speaker's location (*él*) and location or direction away from speaker's location (*ektá*) (Rood 2003: 255), as in (14). In Lakhota, the postpositions appear to be phonologically independent words.

(14) Lakhota (Siouan)

a. Wačhípi **él** wičhóta.
dance at collective.be.large.amount
'There were a lot of people at the dance (and I am remembering it as it was when I was there).'

b. Wačhípi **ektá** wičhóta.
dance at collective.be.large.amount
'There were a lot of people at the dance (but I am thinking about it from here).'
(Rood 2003: 256)

Yaqui (Uto-Aztecan) is described as having various spatial postpositions, including *-po* 'in, inside', *-ku* 'in, on', *-u/-wi* 'toward, to', *-étči* 'on top, on', and *hika* 'on top of' (Dedrick & Casad 1999: 173; see also (10a), where a relational noun, *waíwa* 'inside', further specifies the location of a figure). An example of *-po* is shown in (15). This postposition, however, is not an independent phonological word and attaches as a suffix to the ground nominal. While the majority of the locative postpositions in Yaqui are bound, some postpositions are free. Additionally, various items can serve as the base of these postpositions, including pronouns (e.g., *né-t* 'on me' Dedrick & Casad 1999: 173–174).

(15) Yaqui (Uto-Aztecan)

Empo	kafe-ta	mesa-**po**	chijakta-k.
2SG:NOM	coffee-ACC	table-LOC	sprinkle-PASTP

'You sprinkled the coffee on the table.'

(Guerrero & Van Valin 2004: 292)

Two other Uto-Aztecan languages, Cora and Huichol, have also been analyzed as having postpositions, namely, *-'e* 'in' and *-taa* 'at', respectively. These are shown in (16) and (17). As in Yaqui, these postpositions combine with the ground nominal as suffixes.

(16) Cora (Uto-Aztecan)

y-é-h	n^y^a-ware-**'e**
here-outside-slope	my-back-in

'right here in the small of my back'

(Casad 2012: 82)

(17) Huichol (Uto-Aztecan)

'é-na	ne-wári-**taa**
PROX-LOC	my-back-at

'here at my back, here behind me'

(Casad 2012: 82)

Some languages are reported to have locative markers that function as adpositions. This is exemplified in the Eastern Algonquian language Maliseet-Passamaquoddy, where some studies have described adpositions as adverbial particles (Bloomfield 1962) and others have described them as postpositions (LeSourd 2014). Part of the justification for calling them prepositions is that they take noun phrase complements and the preposition governs the form of the noun phrase, specifying whether it is in the locative case (LeSourd 2014). This is shown in (18).

(18) Maliseet-Passamaquoddy (Algonquian)

Súsehp	wíku	qihìw	{malsan-ikŭwám-**ok** /	*malsan-íkŭwam}.
Joseph	dwell-(3)	near	merchant-building-LOC	merchant-building

'Joseph lives near the store.'

(LeSourd 2014: 222)

Another example is Papantla Totonac (Totonac-Tepehua), which is analyzed as having a locative marker *nak* that heads the ground phrase (19a), but is optional in certain cases (19b) (Levy 1999). Levy describes these phrases as having an adverbial status in the language. The Totonac data serve to illustrate that, as previously mentioned, the categorial status of morphemes that encode locative information is often not easily ascertained. In this case, one can consider an analysis of *nak* as an adposition (as in (19a)). Levy explains that when the ground phrase does not contain *nak*, a spatial relational noun or part term heads the ground phrase (for further information, see Levy 1999).

(19) Papantla Totonac (Totonac-Tepehua)

a.

xa:lu,	**nak**	ix-qí:-n	chiki'	tawila:na
pot	LOC	3POSS-back-NR	house	they.are.sitting

'The pots are behind (at the back of) the house.'

(Levy 1999: 139)

b.

(**nak**)	ix-aqstí:n	chiki'	ya:	chixkú'
LOC	3POSS-roof	house	stand	man

'The man is on the roof of the house.'

(Levy 1999: 140)

Ayutla Mixe (Mixe-Zoque) forms locative noun phrases by attaching a part morpheme to the ground-denoting nominal. As described in Romero Méndez (2008: 248), Ayutla Mixe has a set of 11 part morphemes that are historically derived from body part terms, but are synchronically bound morphemes. Most of these part morphemes may attach to a noun to form a ground-denoting locative phrase.[13] A part morpheme may combine with a locative marker to form a compound suffix. These two strategies are illustrated in (20a) and (20b), respectively.

(20) Ayutla Mixe (Mixe-Zoque)

a. Tama pelota [näxkëx**p**] LOCATIVE PHRASE

ta-m=ja'a	pelot	nääjx-këx**p**
DEIC.M-LOC=DEM.DIST	ball	ground-ON.SURFACE

'There is a ball on the ground.'

b. Tu'uk pelot tyëk [pejkkemyety**py**] LOCATIVE PHRASE

tu'uk	pelot	y-tëk-∅	pejk-kemy-jot-**py**
one	ball	3-enter-DEP	round-fence-inside-LOC

'A ball enters into the fence.'

(Romero Méndez 2008: 278)

Klamath (Penutian) is described as lacking an adposition category altogether (DeLancey 2003: 68). Instead, the functional equivalents are the locative suffixes *-dat* (locative/allative) and *-dal'* (toward), which attach to a ground denoting nominal in motion event and locative descriptions. In Yurok (Algic), nouns are generally marked as locatives to mean 'in' or 'at' by the suffixation of the morpheme *-oł* and less commonly, by the suffixes *-i* and *-ik* (Robins 1958: 24–25). Sherzer (1976) indicates that locative affixes are a common occurrence in Arctic and Subarctic languages. Central Alaskan Yup'ik (Eskimo-Aleut) has a locative case marker that has myriad functions, but its primary function, as its name suggests, is to mark a noun phrase that indicates a location (Miyaoka 2012).

(21) Central Alaskan Yup'ik (Eskimo-Aleut)

ingri-ni	pissur-luni
mountain-LOC.PL	hunt-APP.3R.SG

'(He is) hunting in the mountains.'

(Miyaoka 2012: 780)

4.2. Relational Nouns and Noun-Derived Relators

In some languages, spatial relations can be expressed by relational nouns, defined as "[nouns] expressing locative and related notions" (Campbell et al. (1986: 545). In this section, we are primarily interested in the use of relational nouns as the key constituent encoding locative information, although, as we will show, the categorial status of these constituents can be a matter of debate, especially given the likelihood of ongoing grammaticalization processes that have not been carefully studied. This is very much the case among Otomanguean and, notably, Zapotec languages. Also, making exclusive reference to relational nouns becomes difficult given the diversity of location-encoding strategies cross-linguistically. For instance, in Haida (isolate),[14] locational phrases include what are termed "bare place nouns" (Enrico 2003: 663). Examples of these are *diid* 'up in the woods' and *xiid* 'on the floor/ground'. These bare place nouns encode the spatial relation between a figure and a ground, but also appear to encode the ground itself. In Dëne Sųłiné (Chipewyan, Na-Dene), locative nouns may be used by themselves as locative adverbs, although they may also occur as objects within a postpositional phrase (Cook 2004: 303).

Relational nouns are often called meronyms – lexical items that refer to a part of a whole. Body part terms are prototypical meronyms, as they refer to parts of the body (see Svorou 1994 and Lehmann 2015). This type of meronym is frequently seen as having the function of a spatial relator in languages of the Americas and in Mesoamerica in particular (Campbell et al. 1986). An overview of the semantics of spatial relators in general and of body part-derived relators in Mexican languages is provided in O'Meara et al. (in press). Some of the key literature on the topic for Mesoamerican languages include works on Otomanguean languages such as Zapotec languages (MacLaury 1989; Lillehaugen 2006; Pérez Báez 2012 and chapters in Lillehaugen & Sonnenschein 2012); Chalcatongo Mixtec (Brugman 1983; Brugman & Macaulay 1986) and Copala Triqui (Hollenbach 1987; 1988); for Mayan languages Tseltal (Stross 1976; Levinson 1994) and Tzotzil (de León 1991); as well as for Tarascan (Friedrich 1969; 1970; 1971), Totonac (Levy 1992; 2008), and Cora (Casad 1982). Two basic examples are provided in (22) and (23) of Zapotec and Mayan languages for illustration.

(22) Diidxazá (Otomanguean)

nuǔ	ti	benda	wiini	**ndaani**	ti	gisu	wiini
exist	a	fish	small	stomach	a	pot	small

'There is a small fish inside a little pot'

(Pérez Báez 2012: 119)

(23) Yucatec (Mayan)

Le=lùuch=o',	ti'	yàan	[y=**óok'ol**	le=mesa=o']
DEF=cup=D2	there	EXIST(B3)	A3=top	DEF=table=D2

'The cup, it's there on the table.'

(O'Meara et al. in press)

The observation made earlier that there is cross-linguistic diversity as to the categorial status of morphemes that encode locative information applies to spatial relators, and especially to body part terms that function as heads of ground phrases. Consider the oft-cited case of Zapotec languages. Pérez Báez (2012) shows that body part-derived relators in Diidxazá (Otomanguean) function as relational nouns. In contrast, body part-derived relators in Tlacolula Valley Zapotec are described in Lillehaugen (2006) as having been grammaticalized into prepositions. Hollenbach (1988) describes the case of Copala Triqui (Otomanguean) as somewhat intermediate between the two Zapotec cases: a case where some body part-derived relational nouns are analyzed as having grammaticalized to adpositions, while others continue to function as relational nouns only. These grammaticalized nouns are *man*^{31} 'body of', *ra*^{31} 'head of', *ra*^{41} 'heart of' and *rian*^{32} 'face of, eye of', which is shown in (24). A proposed path for the grammaticalization of these nouns is explained in detail in Hollenbach (1995: 177).

(24) Copala Triqui (Otomanguean)

ta^{lh}	yan^{3h}	**rian**^{32}	me^{3}sa$^{4!}$	a^{32}
is:on:top	paper	face	table	DECL

'The paper is on top [of] the table's **surface**.'

(Hollenbach 1992: 192; *apud* 1995: 178)

It is noteworthy that both Diidxazá and Tlacolula Valley Zapotec are considered to belong to the same branch of Zapotec languages, and the sets of body part-derived relators in question include, for the most part, cognates across these two languages. Copala Triqui is also related to these two Zapotec languages, although less closely, yet still belonging to the Otomanguean stock. Data from these three languages provide a good example of the diversity of strategies of location encoding that can exist even across related languages. The process of grammaticalization that may be behind the differences described in the two aforementioned Zapotec languages seems to be in line with cross-linguistic grammaticalization patterns, the likes of which have been described by Heine (1997) and Lehmann (2015). However, they have yet to be studied cross-linguistically and in detail.

5. Final Remarks

In this chapter we have provided an overview of the diversity of morphosyntactic strategies employed in the languages of North America to encode locative information. The chapter is roughly organized according to existing classifications of the grammar of spatial reference and the morphosyntactic elements they focus on. As such, we have highlighted strategies for encoding locative information in the predicate, as well as morphology associated with verb forms, followed by strategies associated with ground-denoting nominals. There are, of course, other parts of the grammar where locative or, more generally, spatial information can be encoded. This includes, for instance, demonstratives, which frequently encode information regarding the distance of a particular object with respect to participants in the speech act and/or adverbs that can specify the location of a particular event. Further, languages may encode spatial information as part of nominal classification systems, something that does not appear to be a dominant strategy in languages of North America but does in languages of South America (Grinevald 2006). Conversely, morphosyntactic devices that encode locative information may also encode direction of motion and may belong to a particular word class of directionals.

There is therefore much more to say on the topic of the morphosyntax of locative descriptions in North American languages. Nevertheless, this chapter provides a basic understanding of the diversity of strategies employed in encoding locative information, going well beyond the use of locative adpositions. We also find that certain strategies may be frequent within certain language families but rare elsewhere, while others are widely shared across the language families surveyed. Conversely, we find that closely related languages may employ different strategies despite their close genetic affiliation.

Further yet, what emerges from the exploration across the languages of North America is not only diversity but also complexity in the interaction between the various devices that contribute towards conveying locative information. For instance, it is clear that languages may use a variety of strategies all at once in locative descriptions. In other words, different types of locative information may be encoded in different elements of the sentence, even if this leads to redundancy. The scope of the chapter prevents us from going into such detail for such a diverse language sample, but it is important to highlight the language-specific possibilities for combining grammatical strategies in locative descriptions. There are also cases where the information encoded in a given morpheme might change depending on the interaction between elements of a clause or sentence. Such is the case of relative roots and associated preverbs in Algonquian languages. These observations, we hope, should further support the importance of not only depth in language documentation but also breadth.

Countless avenues for research and analysis of the morphosyntax of spatial language in North American languages remain. To begin, the research for this chapter revealed that analytical works on many North American languages are limited to dissertations, which in turn are often now decades old. While their value is not in question, the organizational principles, theoretical priorities, or methods employed in the elaboration of these works may hamper further analysis of the data in the context of contemporary practices and typological endeavors. Efforts to reanalyze, update, or place such works into different theoretical contexts of research and analysis would greatly enhance the contributions that such works could make towards the advancement of typological studies. On the topic of typology, a comparative study of complementary, multiple or redundant encoding of locative information could reveal interesting patterns of interaction across morphemes and within clause and/or sentence structure. We hope that the overview presented in this chapter will foster further research into the morphosyntactic strategies employed in spatial description in the languages of North America (and beyond) and new discoveries on their diversity and complexity. After all, only in doing so will we expand our knowledge of the possible structures that the human language faculty may deploy when describing spatial relations between objects – or any other meaning, for that matter.

Acknowledgments

O'Meara would like to acknowledge support from the Netherlands Organisation for Scientific Research, NWO project 277-70-011, while writing this chapter. The contributions to this chapter by Pérez Báez were made possible by the Recovering Voices initiative of the Smithsonian Institution's National Museum of Natural History.

Further Reading

The following special issue features a semantic typology approach to locative predicates from a cross-linguistic perspective.

Ameka, Felix K. & Levinson, Stephen C. 2007. Introduction. The typology and semantics of locative predicates: Posturals, positionals, and other beasts. *Linguistics* 45(5). 847–872.

The following three books describe from different theoretical perspectives how spatial concepts are expressed in language.

Hickmann, Maya & Robert, Stéphane (eds.). 2006. *Space in languages: Linguistic systems and cognitive categories*. Typological Studies in Language 66. Amsterdam: John Benjamins.

Levinson, Stephen C. & Wilkins, David P. (eds.). 2006. *Grammars of space explorations in cognitive diversity*. Cambridge: Cambridge University Press.

Svorou, Soteria. 1994. *The grammar of space* Typological Studies in Language 25. Amsterdam: John Benjamins.

Notes

1. Note that they treat deixis separately and do not include discussion of it in their volume.
2. The topic of motion has certainly not been excluded from the analyses of languages of North America. See for instance Mithun (1999) on Mohawk, Broadwell (2006) on Choctaw, and Rude (1985) on Nez Perce, which describe the morphosyntactic strategies for the expression of motion towards a speaker (cislocative)

or towards a reference point (translocative). Rood (2003) describes distinctions in Lakhota focused on motion towards or away from a reference point. Strategies for encoding source, goal, and similar concepts often involve the use of prefixes and suffixes. Some of these strategies are described for Nishnaabemwin (Valentine 2001), Hualapai (Watahomigie et al. 2001), Haida (Enrico 2003), Ineseño Chumash (Applegate 1966), and Creek (Martin 2001). Mithun (1999) reports on similar features for Central Pomo, Shasta (from Silver 1966) and Tsimshianic (from Tarpent 1987).

3. Oblique marking with adpositions and locative case is discussed in more detail in §4 regarding strategies used to encode locative information in ground phrases.
4. Although perhaps this is the case in Kalispel (Salish), but more data are needed to verify this pattern.

   (i) *Čin-es-əl'Ɛi*
   1SG-CONTIN-here
   'I am here'
   (Vogt 1940: 69, *apud* Stassen 1997: 143)

5. The following abbreviations are used: A = cross-reference 'Set A' (ergative possessor), ABS = absolutive, ACC = accusative, ART = article, APP = appositional mood, B = cross-reference 'Set B' (absolutive), CL = classifier, CR = Cora, D2 = distal/anaphoric particle, DECL = declarative, DEF = definite, DEIC = adverbial demonstrative, DEM = demonstrative, DEP = dependent aspect-mood, DET = determiner, DIR = directional, DIST = distal, DP = distant past, DUR = durative, EMPH = emphasis, EXIST = existential, HU = Huichol, IND = independent order indicative (unmarked mode), INDIC = indicative, LOC = locative, NMLZ = nominalizer, OBJ = object, OBL = oblique, PART = participle, PAS = passive, PASTP = past participle, PL = plural, POSS = possessive, POT = potential, PROX = proximal, PV = preverb, R = ditransitive recipient, RP = recent past, SBJ = subject, SG = singular, UNSPEC = unspecified.
6. Note that in many Mayan languages this predicate is also a positional root; for example, in Quichean, the existential root *k'o* can also be used locatively (Larsen 1988: 293). Mayan languages are known for having large positional root classes, forms of which can be used in locative descriptions. Tseltal is an example of a language that can use the existential *ay* in locative constructions, but speakers prefer positional roots (Polian 2013: 575).
7. Existential forms appear to be preferred in cases where the figure object is animate and not attached to the ground object (Bohnemeyer & Stolz 2006).
8. Although note that *katek* 'sit' is used with insects and birds (Freeze 1989).
9. Broadwell (2006: 335) indicates that the plural forms of position verbs show two forms that differ in their ending but not in what they encode. Additional description as to the four plural forms listed for the verb 'to sit, dwell' is in Broadwell (2006: 338), which explains that *áashah* and *áyyaashah* may be reduced and unreduced forms of an unattested root *ashah* and involve additional semantic distinctions.
10. We are grateful for Ives Goddard for consulting with us while drafting the text on Algonquian languages. Any errors or lack of clarity are strictly our responsibility as authors of this chapter.
11. The term relative root dates back to Howse's (1844) grammar of Cree (Algonquian), and refer to roots whose meaning is dependent on those of other words with which they co-occur in the same sentence
12. Svorou (1994: 31) has termed "all of these grammatical forms of language which express primarily spatial relations as *spatial grams*", but this term has not persisted in the literature.
13. Other part morphemes may attach as verbal prefixes for other functions.
14. Note that some consider Haida to be a Na-Dene language (Enrico 2004).

References

Ameka, Felix K. & Levinson, Stephen C. 2007. Introduction. The typology and semantics of locative predicates: Posturals, positionals, and other beasts. *Linguistics* 45(5). 847–872.

Applegate, Richard Brian. 1966. *Ineseño Chumash grammar*. Berkeley: University of California. (Doctoral dissertation.)

Barker, Muhammad Abd-al Rahman 1964. *Klammath grammar* (UCPL 32). Berkeley: University of California Press.

Bloomfield, Leonard. 1962. *The Menomini language*. New Haven, CT: Yale University Press.

Bohnemeyer, Jürgen & Brown, Penelope. 2007. Standing divided: Dispositional verbs and locative predications in two Mayan languages. *Linguistics* 45(5). 1105–1151.

Bohnemeyer, Jürgen & Stolz, Christel. 2006. Spatial reference in Yukatek Maya: A survey. With C. Stolz. In Levinson, S. C. & Wilkins, D. P. (eds.), *Grammars of space*, 273–310. Cambridge: Cambridge University Press.

Broadwell, George A. 2006. *A Choctaw reference grammar*. Lincoln: University of Nebraska Press.

Brown, Penelope. 1994. the INs and ONs of Tzeltal locative expressions: The semantics of static descriptions of location. *Linguistics* 32(4/5). 743–790.

Brugman, Claudia & Macaulay, Monica. 1986. Interacting semantic systems: Mixtec expressions of location. Berkeley Linguistics Society 12. 315–327.

Brugman, Claudia. 1983. The use of body-part terms as locatives in Chalcatongo Mixtec. In Schlichter, Alice, Chafe, Wallace L. & Hinton, Leanne (eds.), Studies in Mesoamerican linguistics (Reports from the survey of Californian and other Indian languages No. 4), 235–290. Berkeley: Survey of Californian and Other Indian Languages.

Campbell, Lyle & Kaufman, Terrence & Smith-Stark, Thomas C. 1986. Meso-America as a linguistic area. *Language* 62(3). 530–570.

Campbell, Lyle. 1997. *American Indian languages: The historical linguistics of native America*. Oxford: Oxford University Press.

Casad, Eugene H. 1982. Cora locationals and structured imagery. San Diego: University of California. (Doctoral dissertation.)

Casad, Eugene H. 2012. *From space to time: A cognitive analysis of the Cora locative system and its temporal extensions*. Amsterdam: John Benjamins.

Cook, Eung-Do. 2004. *A grammar of Dëne Sųłiné* (Chipewyan) (Algonquian and Iroquoian linguistics, special Athabaskan number, memoir 17). Winnipeg: Algonquian and Iroquoian Linguistics.

Cowell, Andrew & Moss Sr., Alonzo. 2008. *The Arapaho language*. Boulder: University Press of Colorado.

de León, Lourdes. 1991. Space games in Tzotzil: Creating a context for spatial reference. Cognitive Anthropology Research Group Working Paper no. 4. Nijmegen: Max Planck Institute for Psycholinguistics.

Dedrick, John M. & Casad, Eugene H. 1999. *Sonora Yaqui language structures*. Tucson: University of Arizona Press.

DeLancey, Scott. 2003. Location and direction in Klamath. In Shay, Erin & Seibert, Uwe (eds.), *Motion, direction and location in languages. In honor of Zygmunt Frajzyngier* (Typological Studies in Language 56), 59–90. Amsterdam: John Benjamins.

Dorsey, James O. & Swanton, John R. 1912. *A dictionary of the Biloxi and Ofo languages*. Washington, DC: Government Printing Office.

Einaudi, Paula F. 1976. *A grammar of Biloxi*. New York and London: Garland Publishing, Inc.

Enrico, John. 2003. *Haida syntax*. Bloomington: Indiana University.

Enrico, John. 2004. Toward Proto-Na-Dene. *Anthropological Linguistics* 46(3). 229–302.

Fennell, John. 1961. *The Penguin Russian course*. Harmondsworth, UK: Penguin.

Freeze, Ray A. 1989. *Mayo de los Capomos* (Archivo de Lenguas Indígenas de México 14). Mexico: El Colegio de México.

Friedrich, Paul. 1969. On the meaning of the Tarascan suffixes of space. *IJAL Memoir* 23.

Friedrich, Paul. 1970. Shape in grammar. *Language* 46(2). 379–407.

Friedrich, Paul. 1971. The Tarascan suffixes of locative space. In Voegelin, C. F. (ed.), *Language Science Monographs*, vol. 9. Bloomington: Indiana University Research.

Gatschet, Albert. 1890. *The Klamath Indians of southwestern Oregon* (Contributions to North American Ethnology, vol. II). Washington, DC: Government Printing Office.

Goddard, Ives. 1990. Primary and secondary stem derivation in Algonquian. *International Journal of American Linguistics* 56(4). 449–483.

Goddard, Ives. 2007. *The owl sacred pack: A new edition and translation of the Meskwaki manuscript of Alfred Kiyana* (Algonquian and Iroquoian Linguistics Memoir 19). Winnipeg.

Goddard, Ives. 2017. *A grammar of Meskwaki*. Washington, DC: Smithsonian Institution.

Grinevald, Colette. 2006. The expression of static location in a typological perspective. In Hickmann, Maya & Robert, Stéphane (eds.), *Space in languages: Linguistic systems and cognitive categories*, 29–58. Amsterdam: John Benjamins.

Guerrero, Lilián & Van Valin, Robert. 2004. Yaqui and the analysis of primary object languages. *International Journal of American Linguistics* 70(3). 290–319.

Haspelmath, Martin. 2008. Terminology of case. In Malchukov, Andrej L. & Spencer, Andrew (eds.), *The Oxford handbook of case*, 505–517. Oxford: Oxford University Press.

Haviland, John. 1992. Seated and settled: Tzotzil verbs of the body. *Zeitschrift für Phonetik, Sprachwissenschaft und Kommunikationsforschung* 45(6). 543–561.

Heath, Jeffrey. 1980. Choctaw suppletive verbs and derivational morphology. In *Kansas Working Papers in Linguistics* 5(2). 1–24. Lawrence: Linguistics Graduate Student Association, University of Kansas.

Heine, Bernd. 1997. *Cognitive foundations of grammar*. Oxford: Oxford University Press.

Hickmann, Maya & Robert, Stéphane (eds.). 2006. *Space in languages: Linguistic systems and cognitive categories*. Typological Studies in Language 66. Amsterdam: John Benjamins.

Hollenbach, Barbara E. 1987. Semantic and syntactic extensions of body-part terms in Mixtecan. (Paper presented at the 86th annual meeting of the American Anthropological Association, XXVIth Conference on American Indian Languages, Otomanguean, Chicago.)

Hollenbach, Barbara E. 1988. Semantic and syntactic extensions of Copala Trique body-part nouns. In Guarza Cuarón, Beatriz & Levy, Paulette (eds.), *Homenaje a Jorge Suarez*, 275–296. México: Colegio de México.

Hollenbach, Barbara E. 1992. Parsing relative clauses in Copala Trique. In Hwang, Shin Ja J. & Merrifield, William R. (eds.), *Language in context: Essays for Robert E. Longacre*, 537–551. Summer Institute of Linguistics and the University of Texas.

Hollenbach, Barbara E. 1995. Semantic and syntactic extensions of body-part terms in Mixtecan: The case of "face" and "foot". *International Journal of American Linguistics* 61(2). 168–190.

Howse, Joseph. 1844. *A grammar of the Cree language; with which is combined an analysis of the Chippeway dialect*. London: J. G. F. & J. Rivington.

Landau, Barbara & Jackendoff, Ray. 1993. *What* and *where* in spatial language and spatial cognition. *Behavioral and Brain Sciences* 16(2). 217–238.

Landau, Barbara. 2016. Update on "what" and "where" in spatial language: A new division of labor for spatial terms. *Cognitive Science* 41(2). 321–350.

Larsen, Tom. 1988. *Manifestations of ergativity in Quiché grammar*. Berkeley: University of California. (Doctoral dissertation.)

Lehmann, Christian. 2015. *Thoughts on grammaticalization* (Classics in Linguistics, 1). 3rd edn. Berlin: Language Science Press.

LeSourd, Philip S. 2014. Prepositional phrases in Maliseet-Passamaquoddy. *International Journal of American Linguistics* 80(2). 209–240.

Levinson, Stephen C. & Meira, Sérgio. 2003. "Natural concepts" in the spatial topological domain – Adpositional meanings in crosslinguistic perspective: An exercise in semantic typology. *Language* 79(3). 485–516.

Levinson, Stephen C. & Wilkins, David P. 2006. Background to the study of the language of space. In Levinson, S. C. & Wilkins, D. P. (eds.), *Grammars of space explorations in cognitive diversity*, 1–23. Cambridge: Cambridge University Press.

Levinson, Stephen C. 1994. Vision, shape and linguistic description: Tzeltal body-part terminology and object description. Linguistics 32(4/5). 791–856.

Levinson, Stephen C. 2003. Spatial language. In Nadel, L. (ed.), *Encyclopedia of cognitive science*, 131–137. Macmillan.

Levinson, Stephen C. & Kita, Sotaro & Haun, Daniel B. M. & Rasch, Björn H. 2002. Returning the tables: Language affects spatial reasoning. *Cognition* 84(2). 155–188.

Levy, Paulette. 1992. Body part prefixes in Papantla Totonac. In de León, L. & Levinson, S. (eds.), Spatial description in Mesoamerican languages. *Zeitschrift fur Phonetik, Sprachwissenschaft und Kommunikationsforschung* 45. 530–543.

Levy, Paulette. 1999. From "part" to "shape": Incorporation in Totonac and the issue of classification by verbs. *International Journal of American Linguistics* 65. 127–175.

Levy, Paulette. 2008. Los sustantivos relacionales en el totonaco de Papantla. In Estrada Fernández, Zarina & Munguía Duarte, Ana Lidia (eds.), *Memorias del IX Encuentro Internacional de Lingüística en el Noroeste*, 403–424. Sonora: Universidad de Sonora.

Li, Peggy & Gleitman, Lila R. 2002. Turning the tables: Spatial language and spatial reasoning. *Cognition* 83(3). 265–294.

Li, Peggy & Abarbanell, Linda & Papafragou, Anna. 2005. Spatial reasoning skills in Tenejapan Mayans. In Bara, B. G. & Barsalou, L. & Bucciarelli, M. (eds.), *Proceedings of the twenty-seventh annual conference of the Cognitive Science Society*, 1272–1277. Hillsdale, NJ: Erlbaum.

Lillehaugen, Brook & Sonnenschein, Aaron Huey. 2012. Expressing location in Zapotec: An introduction. In Lillehaugen, Brook & Sonnenschein, Aaron (eds.), Expressing location in Zapotec (LINCOM Studies in Native American Linguistics 61), 1–34. Munich: LINCOM.

Lillehaugen, Brook. 2006. Expressing location in Tlacolula Valley Zapotec. Los Angeles: University of California. (Doctoral dissertation.)

MacLaury, Robert E. 1989. Zapotec body-part locatives: Prototypes and metaphoric extensions. *International Journal of American Linguistics* 55(2). 119–154.

Majid, Asifa & Bowerman, Melissa & Kita, Sotaro & Haun, Daniel B. M. & Levinson, Stephen C. 2004. Can language restructure cognition? The case for space. *Trends in Cognitive Sciences* 8(3). 108–114.

Marlett, Stephen A. 2017. *Cmiique Iitom: The Seri language*. (https://arts-sciences.und.edu/summer-institute-of-linguistics/faculty/marlett-steve/work-in-progress.cfm) (Accessed 2017-12-05.)

Martin, Jack B. 2001. *A grammar of Creek (Muskogee)*. Lincoln and London: University of Nebraska Press.

Miller, Wick R. 1993. *Guarijío de Arechuyvo, Chihuahua* (Archivo de Lenguas Indígenas de México). Mexico: Colegio de México.

Mithun, Marianne. 1998. The significance of diversity in language endangerment and preservation. In Grenoble, Lenore A. & Whaley, Lindsey J. (eds.), *Endangered languages: Language loss and community response*, 163–191. Cambridge: Cambridge University Press.

Mithun, Marianne. 1999. *The languages of native North America*. Cambridge: Cambridge University Press.

Miyaoka, Osahito. 2012. *A grammar of Central Alaskan Yupik (CAY)* (Mouton Grammar Library [MGL] 58). Berlin: De Gruyter Mouton.

Newman, John. 2002. A cross-linguistic overview of the posture verbs "sit", "stand", and "lie". In Newman, John (ed.), *The linguistics of sitting, standing and lying*, 1–24. Amsterdam: John Benjamins.

Nicklas, Thurston D. 1974. *The elements of Choctaw*. Ann Arbor: University of Michigan. (Doctoral dissertation.)

O'Meara, Carolyn & Guerrero, Lilián. 2015. Typological comparison of Seri with nearby Southern Uto-Aztecan languages: The use of posture verbs in locative descriptions. *Amerindia* 37(2). 285–311.

O'Meara, Carolyn & Pérez Báez, Gabriela. 2011. Spatial frames of reference in Mesoamerican languages. *Language Sciences* 33(6). 837–852.

O'Meara, Carolyn & Pérez Báez, Gabriela & Eggleston, Alyson & Bohnemeyer, Jürgen. In press. Space in languages of Mexico. In Wichmann, S. (ed.), *The languages and linguistics of Middle and Central America: A comprehensive guide* (The World of Linguistics.) Amsterdam: de Gruyter Mouton.

Pérez Báez, Gabriela. 2012. Semantics of body part terms in Juchiteco locative descriptions. In Lillehaugen, Brooke & Sonnenschein, A. H. (eds.), Expressing location in Zapotec (Native American Languages 61), 117–136. Munich: Lincom Europa.

Polian, Gilles. 2013. *Gramática del tseltal de Oxchuc*, vol. I & II. Mexico City: Centros de Investigaciones y Estudios Superiores en Antropología Social.

Rhodes, Richard A. 2006. *Clause structure, core arguments and the Algonquian relative root construction* (The Belcourt lecture). Winnipeg: Rupert's Land.

Robins, Robert H. 1958. *The Yurok language* (University of California Publications in Linguistics 15). Berkeley: University of California Press.

Romero Méndez, Rodrigo. 2008. *A Reference Grammar of Ayutla Mixe (Tukyo'm Ayuujk)*. Buffalo: University at Buffalo, the State University of New York. (Doctoral dissertation.)

Rood, David S. 2003. Two Lakhota locatives and the role of introspection in linguistic analysis. In Shay, Erin & Seibert, Uwe (eds.) *Motion, direction and location in languages. In honor of Zygmunt Frajzyngier* (Typological Studies in Language 56), 255–258. Amsterdam: John Benjamins.

Rude, Noel E. 1985. *Studies in Nez Perce grammar and discourse*. Eugene: University of Oregon. (Doctoral dissertation.)

Sherzer, Joel. 1976. *An areal-typological study of the American Indian languages north of Mexico* (North-Holland Linguistic Series). Amsterdam: North-Holland Publishing Company.

Silver, Shirley. 1966. *The Shasta language*. Berkeley: University of California. (Doctoral dissertation.)

Stassen, Leon. 1997. *Intransitive predication* (Oxford Studies in Typology and Linguistic Theory). Oxford: Oxford University Press.

Stross, Brian. 1976. Tzeltal anatomical terminology: semantic processes. In McClaran, M. (ed.), *Mayan Linguistics*, vol. 1. Los Angeles: American Indian Studies Center, University of California.

Svorou, Soteria. 1994. *The grammar of space* (Typological Studies in Language 25). Amsterdam: John Benjamins.

Talmy, Leonard. 2000. *Toward a cognitive semantics*, vol. I. Cambridge, MA: MIT Press.

Tarpent, Marie-Lucie. 1987. *A grammar of the Nisgha language*. Victoria: University of Victoria. (Doctoral dissertation.)

Valentine, Randolph J. 2001. *Nishnaabemwin reference grammar*. Toronto, Buffalo and London: University of Toronto Press.

van Riemsdijk, Henk & Huybregts, Riny. 2007. Location and locality. In Karimi, Simin & Samiian, Vida & Wilkins, Wendy K. (eds.), *Phrasal and clausal architecture: Syntactic derivation and interpretation. In honor of Joseph E. Emonds* (Linguistik Aktuell/Linguistics Today 101), 339–364. Amsterdam: John Benjamins.

Vogt, Hans. 1940. *The Kalispel language*. Oslo: Norske Videnskaps-Akademi.

Watahomigie, Lucille J. & Bender, Jorigine & Watahomigie Sr., Philbert & Yamamoto, Akira Y. & Mapatis, Elnor & Powskey, Malinda & Steele, Josie. 2001. *Hualapai reference grammar*. Rev. and exp. edn. Kyoto: Endangered Languages of the Pacific Rim.

Watkins, Laurel J. 1976. Position in grammar: Sit, stand, lie. *Kansas Working Papers in Linguistics* 1. 16–41.

7

AGREEMENT AND RELATED PHENOMENA IN NORTH AMERICAN LANGUAGES

Richard Compton

1. Introduction

Research on the Indigenous languages of North America has had a considerable influence on our understanding of agreement in human language, in terms of its cross-linguistic variation as well as its theoretical underpinnings. Data from these languages have either formed the basis for a first description or led to more refined theoretical treatments of such phenomena as direct-inverse agreement systems, ergative-absolutive agreement patterns, inverse number, omnivorous number, and so-called "pronominal agreement". This chapter provides an overview of agreement phenomena in North American languages, including a cross-section of the types of agreement systems attested, the set of relevant agreement features – or φ-features – for these languages, the syntactic loci for agreement within the clause, and the morphosyntactic status of the agreement morphology itself.[1]

The definition of agreement used herein will be intentionally broad, covering the marking of the φ-features of arguments on verbs, including those cases that have been traditionally treated as agreement but have more recently been proposed to be pronominal arguments or clitics (in the sense of Jelinek 1984; Nevins 2011; or Preminger 2014), particularly where no consensus as to their status exists. However, this working definition of agreement will not extend to concord between elements in the nominal domain.

Section 2 gives an overview of the types of agreement patterns found in the Indigenous languages of North America, including nominative-accusative, ergative-absolutive, split intransitive patterns (i.e., active-stative or agent-patient), and hierarchical patterns (including direct-inverse marking). Section 3.1 explores the φ-features involved in agreement, with particular focus on less common features and distinctions, such as obviation, (grammaticalized) animacy, and inverse number. Section 3.2 examines proposals from a variety of these languages as to the points in the clausal spine where agreement can occur. Section 3.3 tackles the issue of the morphosyntactic status of agreement morphology itself: as the exponence of the Agree relation on a functional head or as a pronominal clitic. Section 4 concludes.

2. Overview of Agreement Patterns

As one would expect of such a large number of languages and language families, there is a great deal of variation in the organization, richness, and syntactic status of agreement systems in North American languages.

In terms of syntactic alignment, we find systems that pattern as nominative-accusative, with direct objects receiving distinctive marking, while other systems exhibit an ergative-absolutive pattern, whereby transitive subjects receive distinct marking. Still other systems follow an active-stative or agent-patient pattern, roughly marking the theta roles of arguments, even for intransitive verbs. Finally, hierarchical and direct-inverse systems are organized so as to prioritize agreement with certain φ-features, irrespective of grammatical roles of subject and object, yielding an agreement or person hierarchy, sometimes called an "accessibility" or "empathy hierarchy" (see also the chapter by Bliss et al. in this volume). This section gives an overview of these patterns.

2.1. Nominative-Accusative Agreement Patterns

A number of North American languages follow a NOMINATIVE-ACCUSATIVE agreement pattern, grouping together both transitive and intransitive subjects. For example, Mithun (1999: 207–208) describes Barbareño Chumash as having a series of pronominal prefixes that track subjects, as in (1), while a second series of suffixes tracks objects, as illustrated in (2) (showing only singular forms):[2],[3]

(1) Barbareño Chumash

a. *k-ʰutiy* 'I see (it)'
b. *p-kutiy* 'you see (it)'
c. *s-kutiy* 'he/she/it sees (it)'

(Mithun 1999: 207)

(2) Barbareño Chumash

a. *s-kutiy-it* 'he/she/it sees me'
b. *s-kutiy-in* 'he/she/it sees you'
c. *s-kutiy* 'he/she/it sees (it)'

(Mithun 1999: 208)

Transitive and intransitive clauses in this language share the same subject marking (Mithun 1999: 208–209):

(3) ***s**-iy-eqwel-wun* *hi=s-iy-qilqilk'ɨlɨli-ʔ*
3-PL-make-3PL DEP=3-PL-bead.RDP-EMPHATIC
'They make their beads.'

(4) ***s**-exšwey-waš*
3-melt-PAST
'It melted.'

Similarly, Dëne Sųłiné (Dene, aka Athabaskan) agreement follows a nominative-accusative pattern, distinguishing between pronominal prefixes for subjects and direct objects. Cook (2004) identifies different positions in the verbal stem for subject and object marking, with the same subject marking being used on transitive and intransitive verbs:[4]

(5) Dëne Sųłiné

a. *yasti*
ya#**s**-ł-ti
THEME#**1SG**-CL-talk
'I am talking.'

(Cook 2004: 119)

b. *neschá*
ne-**s**-chá
THEME-**1SG**-big
'I am big.'

(Cook 2004: 267)

c. ***nuhe**-ne-**s**-ʔį*
2DU/PL-THEME-**1SG**-look.at
'I look at you (non-singular).'

(Cook 2004: 121)

In (5a–c), the same exponent appearing in the same position tracks a first-person singular subject with an active intransitive verb, a stative verb, and a transitive verb, respectively.

While the alignment of agreement (and case) – i.e., the way transitive subjects, objects, and intransitive subjects are grouped – is often attributed to languages, it is more properly associated with constructions, as individual languages often exhibit more than one alignment. For example, though typically described as ergative-absolutive, Inuit and Yupik branches of the Inuit-Yupik-Unangan (aka Eskimo-Aleut) language family exhibit some constructions that follow a nominative-accusative pattern. For instance, in the antipassive construction in Inuktitut, the verb agrees in person and number with the (absolutive) subject regardless of its theta role or (semantic) transitivity of the verb. Antipassives in Inuit are formally intransitive, lacking the normal agreement with objects found in transitives. The same agreement pattern obtains with intransitives, yielding a nominative-accusative pattern (see Johns 2001).[5]

(6) Nunavik Inuktitut

a. *kapisikainnatuq* *tuktumik*
kapi-si-kainnaq-**tuq** tuktu-mik
stab-AP-PAST-DECL.INTR.**3SG** caribou-OBL.SG
'He stabbed the caribou.'

b. *angutik* *pallatuq*
angutik pallak-**tuq**
man(ABS.SG) fall-DECL.INTR.**3SG**
'The man tripped.'

Other languages with nominative-accusative agreement patterns include Dene (aka Athabaskan) languages, other Chumashan languages (Mithun 1999; 2008), and Washo (Hokan/isolate) (Ryan Bochnak, p.c.). Despite having a tripartite case system, Nez Perce (Sahaptian) agreement follows a nominative-accusative pattern (Deal 2015a; 2015b). Arguably, Kiowa-Tanoan languages also have a nominative-accusative agreement alignment, insofar as the exponence of intransitive agreement reappears in the transitive paradigm to track subjects, although some members of this family also exhibit hierarchical/direct-inverse patterns (Harbour 2017, p.c.). Comanche (Uto-Aztecan), despite having an ergative pattern of suppletive verbal number for some verbs (tracking intransitive subjects and transitive objects), has optional dual and plural marking of (usually) animate subjects on non-suppletive verbs that follows a nominative-accusative pattern (Charney 1993: 113–114, 149–150). Cupeño (Uto-Aztecan) has person and number marking that tracks nominative arguments in the past tense (Hill 2005: 108–109).

2.2. Ergative-Absolutive Agreement Patterns

A number of North American languages exhibit an ERGATIVE-ABSOLUTIVE agreement pattern, either agreeing with absolutive arguments, exhibiting special agreement with ergative subjects, or a combination of the two.

For instance, in Inuit we find the exponents of intransitive agreement often reappear as part of the transitive paradigm to index objects – essentially tracking absolutive arguments. Other exponents co-vary only with the φ-features of ergative subjects. This is illustrated in Kangiryuarmiut Inuinnaqtun (Western Canadian Inuit, Inuit-Yupik-Unangan) in Table 7.1, based on data from Lowe (1985).[6]

Table 7.1 Kangiryuarmiut Inuinnaqtun Declarative Agreement Forms

	ABS								
ERG	1SG	1DU	1PL	2SG	2DU	2PL	3SG	3DU	3PL
1SG	—	—	—	ɣin	ptik	phi	ʁa	kka	tka
1DU	—	—	—	ptitkin	ptik	phi	qquk	vuk	vut
1PL	—	—	—	ptiɣin	ptik	phi	qqut	vuk	vut
2SG	ʁma	ptiɣuk	ptiɣut	—	—	—	n	kkin	tin
2DU	ptinŋa	ptiɣuk	ptiɣut	—	—	—	qtik	tik	tik
2PL	phinŋa	ptiɣuk	ptiɣut	—	—	—	qhi	tik	hi
3SG	aŋa	atiɣuk	atiɣut	atin	atik	ahi	a	ik	it
3DU	anŋa	atiɣuk	atiɣut	atin	atik	ahi	ak	ik	it
3PL	anŋa	atiɣuk	atiɣut	atin	atik	ahi	an	ik	it
INTR	ŋa	ɣuk	ɣut	tin	tik	hi	(q)	k	t

For instance, in the declarative mood (clause type), *-ɣut* occurs with both intransitive 1PL subjects as well as 1PL objects in the transitive. Conversely, the morphemes *-p-* and *-a-* co-vary between local and nonlocal ergative subjects (in forms with local absolutive objects, but crucially the contrast between them is due to the ergative agent). Other morphemes track the number of ergative subjects (particularly with third person objects), such as *-ʁa* versus *-qqu-*. In addition to the exponents of agreement following an ergative-absolutive pattern, the morphosyntactic distribution of agreement is strictly ergative – the transitive agreement forms in Table 7.1 are used only when ergative case is assigned (albeit covertly in the case of pro-drop) (Compton 2017).[7]

Mayan languages also exhibit an ergative-absolutive agreement pattern. In the Mayanist literature, ergative person morphology is called *Set A*, while absolutive marking is called *Set B*. This patterning is illustrated in (7) with data from K'iche' from Coon (2013) (see also Coon 2016 and Aissen et al. 2017 and references therein).

(7) K'iche'

a. *x-at-u-ch'ay-oh*
COM-B2-A3-hit-SUF
'He hit you.'

b. *x-at-war-ik*
COM-B2-sleep-SUF
'You slept.'

(Coon 2013: 4)

In particular, Coon shows that while Ch'ol (Mayan) has been described as having a split intransitive (or split ergative) agreement system, as illustrated in (8), whereby subjects of unergative verbs pattern with transitive subjects and those of unaccusatives pattern with transitive objects, the system is in fact wholly ergative. She demonstrates that constructions previously analyzed as unergative are in fact transitive, as in (8b), thereby explaining the ergative person marking on the verb:

(8) Ch'ol

a. *Tyi* *jul-i-yety.*
PRFV arrive.here-ITV-B2
'You arrived here.'

b. *Tyi* *a-cha'-l-e* *k'ay.*
PRFV A2-do-DTV song
'You sang.'

(Coon 2013: 9)

Table 7.2 Pivoting Ergative Pattern in Tsimshianic

		INDEPENDENT	*DEPENDENT*
ERG	A	II_{affix}	I_{clitic}
ABS	S	$\text{III}_{independent\ word}$	II_{affix}
	O	$\text{III}_{independent\ word}$	II_{affix}

Source: Adapted from Davis and Forbes (2015: 157).

Yet another example of an ergative agreement pattern is found in Tsimshianic languages, which Davis and Forbes (2015) call *pivoting ergative*. There are three sets of pronominal markers: Set I consists of pre-predicative clitics; Set II, post-predicative affixes; and Set III, post-predicative independent words. In both independent and dependent clauses, transitive agents are marked differently from intransitive subjects and objects, but the marking varies between clause types. The Set II affixes (arguably the most likely instantiation of genuine agreement) index ergative arguments in independent clauses and absolutive arguments in dependent ones. This system is summarized in Table 7.2.

While exponents of agreement that instantiate the two patterns differ according to clause type, in both we find an ergative agreement pattern.

Other North American languages with ergative agreement patterns include Chinookan languages, Halkomelem Salish (see Wiltschko 2006), and Zuni (isolate).[8] Although agreement markers in Dene languages follow a nominative-accusative pattern, these languages also show stem suppletion of a subset of verbs (called classificatory verbs) along an ergative pattern.

2.3. Split Intransitive Agreement Patterns

Yet another pattern of agreement called SPLIT INTRANSITIVE or SPLIT-S(UBJECT) differentiates types of intransitive subjects, roughly distinguishing between agents and patients, although the degree to which this is lexicalized by individual verbs varies across languages. Such languages may either use different exponents for more agent-like and patient-like subjects or place these exponents in different positions with respect to the verb.

Such systems go by a number of names which correlate with the observed triggers for the split. Systems labeled *agent-patient* identify the determining factor as the theta role of the intransitive subject. Those called *active-stative* contrast the aspectual properties of the selecting verbs, with active verbs taking agentive arguments and stative verbs taking more patient-like arguments. The term *fluid-S(ubject)* highlights languages where individual verbs permit either agentive or patientive marking with an accompanying effect on interpretation as more or less volitional. Wichmann (2008) uses the cover term *semantic alignment* instead of split intransitive for such systems, on the grounds that labeling them as split implies that they are underlyingly nominative-accusative or ergative-absolutive.

Kanien'kéha (Mohawk), like all Iroquoian languages, exhibits a split intransitive pattern. Intransitive verbs take one of two sets of pronominal prefixes, as illustrated in (9) and (10) with data from Mithun (1996) for the third-person singular masculine. One set of prefixes is associated with more typically agent-like arguments and another with more patient-like ones.

(9) Kanien'kéha agentive prefixes

a. ***ra****tekhwákwas* 'he bites'
b. ***ra****'nikòn:rara'* 'he is careful'
c. ***ra****rákwas* 'he chooses'
d. ***ra****títa's* 'he climbs in'

(Mithun 1996: 165)

(10) Kanien'kéha patientive prefixes

a. ***ro**hterón:ni* 'he fears'
b. ***ro**'nikónhrhens* 'he forgets'
c. ***ro**tshenón:ni* 'he is happy'
d. ***ro**iéshon* 'he laughs'

(Mithun 1996: 165)

Transitive verbs bear yet another set of prefixes, simultaneously indexing both arguments. Mithun (1999: 221), using examples from Tuscarora (Iroquoian), shows that the conditioning factor between prefix sets cannot be reduced to aspect, as there exist both verbs expressing events that take the patientive prefixes and verbs expressing states that take the agentive prefixes, depending on whether their subject "instigated or controlled" the event or state.

Lakhota (Siouan) agreement is organized similarly, having distinct sets of agreement markers for active and stative intransitives. These are illustrated in (11) and (12) with data from Rood and Taylor (1996: 465–467), with only the singular forms (ignoring other agreement patterns involving infixing).[9]

(11) Lakhota active agreement

a. ***wa**hí* 'I came'
b. ***ya**hí* 'you came'
c. *hí* 'he came'

(Rood & Taylor 1996: 466)

(12) Lakhota stative agreement

a. ***ma**hą́ske* 'I am tall'
b. ***ni**hą́ske* 'you are tall'
c. *hą́ske* 'he is tall'

(Rood & Taylor 1996: 465)

As in Iroquoian languages, transitive verbs in Lakhota mark both the subject and the object, with the exponents for object agreement closely resembling the stative intransitive forms.

Woolford (2010), using data from Choctaw and Lakota, argues that such split systems are real insofar as genuine agreement is restricted to indexing external arguments, while additional arguments may be cross-referenced by pronominal clitics.[10]

Other languages exhibiting a split intransitive alignment in their agreement morphology include those of the Iroquoian and Siouan families, Muskogean languages, and Tlingit.[11]

2.4. Hierarchical and Direct-Inverse Agreement Patterns

Another set of languages exhibits agreement patterns that prioritize agreement with particular φ-features or combinations thereof, yielding a HIERARCHICAL AGREEMENT system. Such languages have been described as employing an agreement hierarchy, whereby agreement occurs preferentially with features occurring higher on the hierarchy. Algonquian languages are the most well-known of this type. For instance, in the following examples from Nishnaabemwin (a variety of Ojibwe) (Valentine 2001: 270), first- and third-person arguments trigger the same exponence of first- and third-person agreement on the verb, regardless of the thematic roles of the arguments. See the chapter by Bliss et al. in this volume for more details on hierarchies and direct-inverse systems, and Oxford's chapter in this volume regarding the status of subjects in Algonquian.

(13) Nishnaabemwin hierarchical agreement pattern

a. *nwaabmaag*
ni-waabam-aa-<u>ag</u>
1-see-DIR-3PL
'**I** see <u>them</u>.'

b. *Nwaabmigoog*
ni-waabam-igw-<u>ag</u>
1-see-INV-3PL
'<u>They</u> see **me**.'

(Valentine 2001: 287)

Generally speaking, Algonquian languages exhibit preferential agreement with speech act participants (i.e., first and second persons, also called *local arguments*) over third persons. A further preference for second-person agreement over first-person agreement is exhibited by the person prefix that appears in certain inflectional forms, such as those in (13). In addition, Algonquian languages distinguish two types of third persons; more topical third persons, called *proximate* (labeled 3), and less topical ones, called *obviative* (labeled 3′) (see §3.1.2). Once again, a hierarchical effect is observed, with agreement preferring proximate arguments to obviative ones. Simplifying somewhat, these two criteria combine to yield the following hierarchy for Nishnaabemwin in the independent order (i.e., clause type) (Valentine 2001: 272):[12]

(14) 2 > 1 > 3 > 3′

Similar hierarchies have been proposed for other languages, placing speech act participants above third persons.

A closely interrelated phenomenon also observed in these examples is that of DIRECT-INVERSE marking. A language with a direct-inverse agreement pattern uses a direct marker on the verb when the external argument is higher on the agreement hierarchy than the internal argument, while using an inverse marker when the internal argument is higher than the external. Thus, in (13a), we find a direct marker, since the first-person agent outranks the third-person patient; while in (13b), we find an inverse marker, as it is now the patient that outranks the agent.

While hierarchical agreement and direct-inverse marking are often presented together as a single type of system, the two phenomena are separate insofar as a language could exhibit preferential agreement along a hierarchy of features but lack direct-inverse morphology (Jacques & Antonov 2014: 310). Conversely, a language could conceivably show full agreement with both core arguments or none with either, and nevertheless possess direct-inverse marking based on the respective features of the arguments.[13] However, a direct-inverse system, as described here, will always make reference to a hierarchy (at least descriptively) in order to determine whether the relationship between arguments is direct or inverse.

While such agreement phenomena have been described in terms of accessibility, salience, and person hierarchies, a number of recent approaches in generative syntax have instead sought to explain them as the result of articulated or relativized agreement probes searching for particular features. For example, Preminger (2014), building on Béjar and Rezac's (2009) system of Cyclic Agree, argues that the phenomenon of omnivorous person agreement in K'ichean (Mayan), in which an exponent of agreement may correspond to either the subject or the object (or both), is due to person probes relativized for the PARTICIPANT feature. As such, this probe can match either a subject or object argument with the corresponding feature. Similarly, Oxford (2014a) argues for relativized probes in Algonquian languages, proposing that differences in the features on these probes explain differences in agreement patterns across different clause types and that even direct-inverse morphology itself should be analyzed as agreement morphology (see §3.2.2).

Another language with a more limited direct-inverse system is Ktunaxa (isolate), in which inverse marking only occurs with an obviative third-person subject and proximate third-person object (Dryer 1991; 1994). This language is discussed in detail in the chapter by Bliss et al. in this volume, as are other direct-inverse patterns.[14]

2.5. Languages Without Visible Agreement

Despite encompassing a number of large families renowned for their rich, even intricate, patterns of agreement, there are nevertheless North American languages claimed to be without overt agreement. Languages without agreement are typically isolating, and since the languages in this part of the world are mostly polysynthetic, it is difficult to find examples of languages that uncontroversially lack any form of verbal agreement. This section will review evidence bearing on this question from two languages that have been analyzed as lacking agreement.

One such potential example is the Haida language (isolate). Enrico (2003: 24) states "Haida has no verb agreement" and that "verbs are not inflected for number, person, or gender of any argument". For instance, in (15), exchanging the subject and object yield no change in the form of the form, while in (16), where the interpretation of which argument is the subject is variable, we again find no agreement on the verb (see also Barrie and Mathieu, this volume).

(15) Haida

a. *'laa* *7iitl'* *gu 'laa-gang*
3 1PL like-PRES
'We like him.'

b. *7iitl'* *'la* *gu 'laa-gang*
1PL 3 like-PRES
'He likes us.'

(Enrico 2003: 46)

(16) Haida

dii-7isan *Joe* *gu 'laa-gang*
1SG-too Joe like-PRES
'I too like Joe/Joe likes me too.'

(Enrico 2003: 47)

Although free pronouns have reduced forms when cliticized in Haida, Enrico shows that various elements may intervene between them and the verbal complex, as illustrated in (16), where the clitic leans on the morpheme meaning 'too', suggesting that these forms are not agreement.

Despite Enrico's claim that Haida lacks agreement, there are several possible exceptions, which he addresses. First, some verbs take classifiers, which might be taken to coincide with noun classes, and thus constitute agreement for gender. He contends, though, that the classifiers do not behave like gender, in that there is no one-to-one match between them and nouns. Instead, they co-vary with properties such as shape, cutting across individual nouns based on context.

Another potential counter-example involves a third-person plural marker that can appear inside the verbal complex. However, he notes that the argument it refers to "need not even be a complement of the verb" (Enrico 2003: 24) as illustrated in (17) where it modifies a possessor. This is unexpected of agreement, which normally must refer to arguments of the verb.[15]

(17) Haida

a. *tsiin-ee* *'laangaa* *hl* *dah* *rujuu-**7wa**-gan*
salmon-DEF 3.POSS I buy all-**PL**-PAST
'I bought all their fish.'

b. *tsiin-ee* *'laangaa* *hl* *dah* *rujuu-gan*
salmon-DEF 3.POSS I buy all-PAST
'I bought all his/her fish.'

(Enrico 2003: 24)

However, Leer (1991) describes this as a form of promiscuous number marking, which might ultimately turn out to be genuine agreement (i.e., an instance of omnivorous number, whereby a probe that might otherwise find a singular target is able to continue probing to find a target with marked number features; see Nevins 2011; Preminger 2014; and references therein).

An additional phenomenon in Haida that could be subsumed under agreement is the existence of root/stem changes marking plurality in some verbs. Again, Enrico argues against an analysis of this being agreement, instead treating this phenomenon as a type of derivational morphology. I refer the reader to his grammar for a detailed discussion of both phenomena outlined earlier.

Another language that could prove to lack verbal agreement is Southern Pomo (Pomoan). Walker (2013: 39) states that "Southern Pomo, like some of its sister languages, does not have pronominal affixes on the verb". While the language has clitic pronouns, they are phonologically reduced versions of full pronouns. Walker also identifies two affixes marking first and second person but crucially notes their optionality, suggesting that they are not agreement, but that they are arguably in the process of grammaticalization towards becoming agreement, possibly from an earlier stage where they acted as evidentials.[16] The language also uses affixes and suppletive verb forms to mark pluractionality. According to Newman (2012: 186), the phenomenon of pluractionality "involve[s] (a) plurality in the verb per se, (b) derivation rather than inflectional agreement, (c) ergative-type relations with other arguments in the sentence, (d) reduplication as a common means of formation, and (e) the common appearance of suppletive forms". Newman further states that pluractionals are usually "semantically-endowed derivational forms having nothing grammatically to do with agreement" (2012: 200), but he notes that in some languages they have taken on the properties of agreement.[17]

However, Southern Pomo has imperative markers that distinguish between singular and plural addressees and which Walker analyzes as being affixes, not clitics:

(18) Southern Pomo

a. *ʔapʰ:eč:in*
||ha-hpʰe-aduč-Vn||
/ʔapʰ:e-č:-in/
carry.on.back-DIR-SG.IMP
'carry it away!'

b. *ʔapʰ:edu:le*
||ha-hpʰe-adu č-le||
/ʔapʰ:e-du:-le/
carry.on.back-DIR-PL.IMP
'y'all carry it away!'

(Walker 2013: 56)

These number-sensitive imperative affixes are the most promising traces of agreement in Southern Pomo. The challenge in finding a clear example of a North American language lacking agreement once again underlines the prevalence of polysynthesis and rich agreement systems in this part of the world.

3. Issues Surrounding Agreement in North American Languages

This section gives an overview of theoretical issues of particular relevance to agreement in North American languages. While none of these phenomena or issues are necessarily confined to this set of Indigenous languages, they are of interest insofar as they challenge our understanding of the set of possible φ-features, the status of their exponence in the form of agreement or pronominal clitics, and their location in clause structure.

3.1. Extending the Set of Φ-Features

In addition to the cross-linguistically well-attested set of φ-features – namely person, number, and gender – a number of North American languages show additional contrasts in their agreement systems based on such phenomena as switch-reference, obviation, inverse number, and animacy.

3.1.1. Animacy

Grammaticalized animacy is often treated as a type of gender system (e.g., Goddard 2002), insofar as nouns may be arbitrarily assigned to either the animate or inanimate classes distinct from their ontological animacy. For instance, in Algonquian languages, a subset of nouns referring to non-human, non-animal objects nevertheless pattern as animate. However, in addition to inflectional differences on nouns, this animacy is also reflected on the verb in two ways. First, Algonquian verb stems often exhibit distinct forms that co-vary with both transitivity and the animacy of arguments. Second, as shown in (19) using data from Rhodes (1990), the form of agreement with objects is sensitive to the animacy distinction:

(19) Animacy interacting with object agreement in Ojibwe

a. *zhiwn-**aa**-waad*
take.TA-**3.ANIM.OBJ**-3PL
'that they take **him/her**'

b. *zhiwd-**oo**-waad*
take.TI-**INAN.OBJ**-3PL
'(that) they take **it**'

(Rhodes 1990: 407)

Lochbihler (2012), adopting a feature-geometric approach to the underspecification of person features following Harley and Ritter (2002), proposes that the featural difference between animate and inanimate in Ojibwe (and presumably Algonquian languages more generally) involves the presence or absence of the [PERSON] or π feature (adapted for clarity):

(20) Ojibwe φ-feature geometry for person

a. SECOND PERSON
π/Animate = 3′ (obviative)
|
Proximate = 3 (proximate)
|
Participant = 1
|
Addressee = 2

b. FIRST PERSON
π/Animate = 3′ (obviative)
|
Proximate = 3 (proximate)
|
Participant = 1

c. THIRD-PERSON PROXIMATE
π/Animate = 3′ (obviative)
|
Proximate = 3 (proximate)

d. THIRD-PERSON OBVIATIVE
π/Animate = 3′ (obviative)

e. THIRD-PERSON INANIMATE
Ø = 0 (inanimate)

(Lochbihler 2012: 37)

Arguably, the status of the feature involved and its role in verb agreement in Algonquian could receive a similar treatment to that of gender agreement in other languages. However, as noted in Lochbihler (2012) and Oxford (2014a), the entailment relations between features in these languages are distinct insofar as those for speech act participants entail animacy, whereas speech act participant features in other languages do not generally directly entail any particular gender features, such as masculine or feminine.

3.1.2. Obviation

The feature-geometric analysis by Lochbihler (2012) above also includes the feature [PROXIMATE] to handle the phenomenon of obviation. Setting aside the animacy distinction, Algonquian languages distinguish between two types of third-person arguments: PROXIMATE and OBVIATIVE.[18] This contrast is manifested both in marking on arguments and in the agreement system, as illustrated in (21) and (22) in Oji-Cree:

(21) Oji-Cree obviation contrast on arguments

a. *Awaasihs*
awaasihs-**Ø**
child-PROX.SG
'a/the child.PROX'

b. *awaasihsan*
awaasihs-**an**
child-OBV
'a/the child.OBV'

(Oxford 2017a: 2)

(22) Oji-Cree obviation contrast in verbal agreement

a. *kaa-takohshihk*
kaa-takohshin-k
IC.PAST-arrive-3
'when s/he.PROX arrived'

b. *kaa-takohshininic*
kaa-takohshin-**ini**-c
IC.PAST-arrive-OBV-3
'when s/he.OBV arrived'

(Oxford 2017a: 2)

While neither category corresponds to any particular thematic role, proximate arguments are said to be more salient or topical and each clause allows only one proximate argument.

Oxford (2017a) lays out a number of arguments against using a feature such as [PROXIMATE] to distinguish proximate and obviative arguments and agreement, arguing instead that the distinction is structural, with obviative nominals having a more complex structure than proximate ones. Two problems stem from the predicted entailment relationships of the geometry itself: speech act participants do not pattern as proximate, and proximate arguments can in fact be inanimate. This suggests that being proximate is orthogonal to these other features. Furthermore, he argues that deriving the obviation contrast through a marked [PROXIMATE] feature misses the generalization that it is obviatives that are more marked; for instance, triggering additional agreement morphology. Instead,

Oxford argues for treating proximate arguments as DPs while obviative ones are KPs, meaning that no dedicated φ-feature need be involved. I refer the reader to Oxford (2017a) and Bliss (2017) and references therein for recent discussion and analyses of obviation.

3.1.3. Inverse Number

Kiowa-Tanoan languages exhibit a phenomenon called *inverse number*, which Harbour (2011) characterizes as "number-sensitive suffixation". For instance, in the data in Table 7.3 from Kiowa, the same marker *-dɔ* patterns differently with different noun classes, appearing in the plural for 'fish', in both the singular and the plural for 'tomato', and in only the singular for 'stick'. Descriptively, the bare noun is restricted in the range of cardinalities it can pick out, and the inverse marker occurs with the complementary set of cardinalities.

Such marking is relevant to the discussion of agreement and φ-features insofar as the suffixed forms trigger an unexpected form of agreement on the verb. In (23), we see the expected forms of agreement with bare nouns referring to singular, dual, and plural referents, while in (24), inverse-marked nouns trigger inverse agreement on the verb:[19]

(23) Kiowa expected number agreement

a. *Ɔ́ɔ́pį́į́* *∅-dɔ́ɔ́.*
fish 3SG-be
'It's a fish.'

b. *Ɔ́ɔ́pį́į́/k!ǫ̂n/áá* *ę-dɔ́ɔ́.*
fish/tomato/stick 3DU-be
'It's two fish/tomatoes/sticks.'

c. *Áá* ***gya**-dɔ́ɔ́.*
stick 3PL-be
'It's some sticks.'

(Harbour 2011: 564)

(24) Kiowa special inverse agreement

*Ɔ́ɔ́pį́į́**dɔ́**/k!ǫ̂ǫ**dɔ**/áá**dɔ*** *e-dɔ́ɔ́.*
fish.I/tomato.I/stick.I 3I-be
'It's some fish/a tomato/some tomatoes/a stick.'

(Harbour 2011: 564)

Harbour analyzes the inverse marker on nouns as the exponent of a D head which is sensitive to both the number features of a Number head, which tracks the cardinality of the referent, as well as number features inherent to each noun class – essentially a set of features associated with the noun itself, much like gender, although Harbour argues that Kiowa noun classes are not arbitrary but instead motivated semantically, forming natural classes.

Table 7.3 Inverse Number Marking in Kiowa

NOUN	SINGULAR	DUAL	PLURAL
'fish'	ɔ́ɔ́pį́į́	ɔ́ɔ́pį́į́	ɔ́ɔ́pį́į́-**dɔ́**
'tomato'	k!ǫ̂ǫ-**dɔ**	k!ǫ̂n	k!ǫ̂ǫ-**dɔ**
'stick'	áá-**dɔ**	áá	áá

Source: Harbour (2011: 564).

(25) Syntactic loci of number features in Kiowa

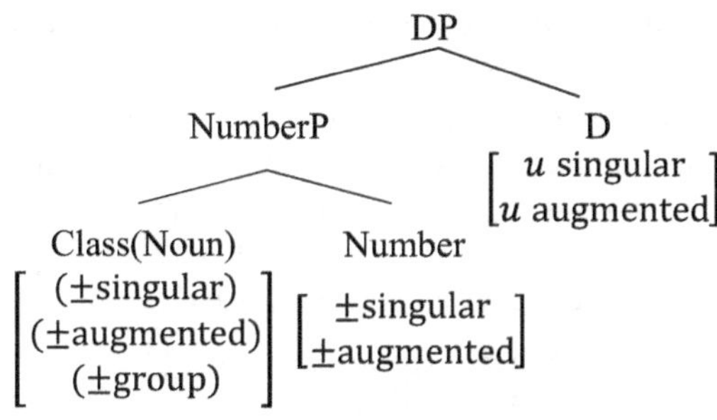

(Harbour 2011: 566)

Harbour uses the features [±singular] and [±augmented] to "generate the number categories singular, dual, plural", while [±group] "characterizes the types of pluralities that nouns form" (2011: 562), including collective plurals and pluralia tantum nouns. According to his proposal, the D head is realized as the inverse marker when the feature values of the noun and Number are in conflict. For instance, if a noun's class is [−augmented], but the cardinality of its referent (and thus the Number) head is [+augmented], these conflicting features will result in inverse marking.

Harbour's analysis of inverse number in Kiowa and the related Jemez language demonstrates the need for three bivalent number features: [±singular], [±augmented], and [±group], showing that privative features would under-generate with respect to the observed system. Crucially, he argues that the proposed features manifest themselves morphologically, combining to pick out the attested noun classes, the distribution of the inverse marker on nouns, the distribution of inverse agreement on verbs, and patterns of verb suppletion on predicates (not shown here), as well as manifesting themselves semantically, corresponding to precise denotations for number and picking out well-defined semantic classes of nouns.

3.1.4. Switch-Reference

Yet another phenomenon that interacts with agreement is switch-reference – a phenomenon whereby languages index arguments (typically subjects) of different clauses as coreferential or disjoint in reference.[20] In Inuit, for instance, switch-reference marking and agreement interact insofar as the language distinguishes *different subject* (DS) and *same subject* (SS) third-person agreement in dependent clause types (i.e., the contingent, conditional, contemporative, incontemporative, and dubitative clause types). These are commonly referred to as third person and fourth person, respectively, in the literature on Inuit-Yupik-Unangan (i.e., Eskimo-Aleut) languages. Interestingly, the exponence of both clause type and number interact with switch-reference marking, in much the same way such features as person, number, gender, and tense interact in other languages. For instance, in the following data from Kangiryuarmiut Inuinnaqtun provided in Table 7.4, the

Table 7.4 Switch-Reference and Agreement in Kangiryuarmiut Inuinnaqtun

	SINGULAR	*DUAL*	*PLURAL*
1	utaqqi**guma**	utaqqi**gumnuk**	utaqqi**gupta**
2	utaqqi**guvin**	utaqqi**guptik**	utaqqi**guffi**
3 SAME SUBJECT	utaqqi**gumi**	utaqqi**gumik**	utaqqi**gumik**
3 DIFFERENT SUBJECT	utaqqi**kpan**	utaqqi**kpangnik**	utaqqi**kpata**

Source: Lowe (1985: 143).

exponence of the CONTINGENT clause type is *-kpa(n)-* for 3DS and *-gu-* elsewhere. Furthermore, the exponence of number differs between 3DS and 3SS, with dual and plural being syncretic for 3SS and marked by *-k*, while the 3DS forms are *-ngnik* and *-ta*, respectively.[21]

In addition to this distinction between coreferential and disjoint (non-coreferential) third-person subjects in subordinate clause types, a further contrast exists in the CONTEMPORATIVE clause type that signals a disjoint subject across all persons – the DIFFERENT SUBJECT marker *-ti(t)-*.[22]

(26) Kangiryuarmiut Inuinnaqtun switch-reference between non-third persons

a. *tupauttaq-**hunga*** *kangiqhi-pkaq-tara*
have.breakfast-CONTEMP.1SG understand-CAUS-DECL.1SG.3SG
'while I was having breakfast, I explained it to him'

b. *tupauttaq-**til-lunga*** *itiq-tuq*
have.breakfast-DS-CONTEMP.1SG enter-DECL.3SG
'while I was having breakfast, he came in'

Insofar as Inuit switch-reference is sensitive to person and affects the exponence of agreement, as well as interacting with clause type, and given proposals that Inuit agreement occurs on C (e.g., Johns 1992; Bittner & Hale 1996; Compton 2016), Mauro (2018) has proposed including a φ-feature [COREF(ERENTIAL)] in the person feature geometry of the language, whose presence can both be targeted by and condition vocabulary insertion rules in the framework of Distributed Morphology.[23]

Similarly, Arregi and Hanink (2017), in their analysis of switch-reference in Washo (Hokan/isolate), have proposed that an uninterpretable INDEX (or ID) feature on C compares the referential indices of matrix and embedded subjects in this language, yielding overt DIFFERENT SUBJECT morphology when these are in conflict (following Harbour's treatment of inverse number). This multiple-agreement approach to switch-reference once again extends the potential inventory of φ-features.

If such approaches are on the right track, they point to expanding the set of φ-features to capture such phenomena as animacy, inverse number, and switch-reference, particularly insofar as these interact with agreement for person and number.

3.2. Loci of Agreement in the Clause

Verbal agreement across many languages is either argued or assumed to be on T (or INFL). And yet, data from Indigenous North American languages suggest that additional loci for agreement may exist within the clause. In particular, both C and *v* are proposed as agreement sites in a number of these languages.

3.2.1. High Agreement on C

While Chomsky (2007; 2008) has proposed that φ-features are transmitted from C to T, some Indigenous languages show evidence of agreement on C. In particular, a number of analyses of case and agreement in Inuit have proposed that agreement occurs on a functional head other than T or INFL. In this vein, Johns (1992: 73) adopts a nominalization analysis of the participial clause type in Eastern Canadian Inuktitut, capitalizing on the fact that participial verbs in the language exhibit a number of nominal properties (including the fact that a portion of verbal agreement morphology originated as possessor agreement on nouns). She posits two agreement projections above what she argues to be a nominalized verb, with ergative agreement on a lower Agr_N head and absolutive agreement on a higher Agr_V head:[24]

(27) *anguti-up* *nanuq* *kapi-ja-a-**Ø*** (Inuktitut)
man-ERG bear(ABS) stab-TR.DECL-3SG.ERG-3SG.ABS
'The man stabbed the bear.'

(Johns 1992: 73)

(28)

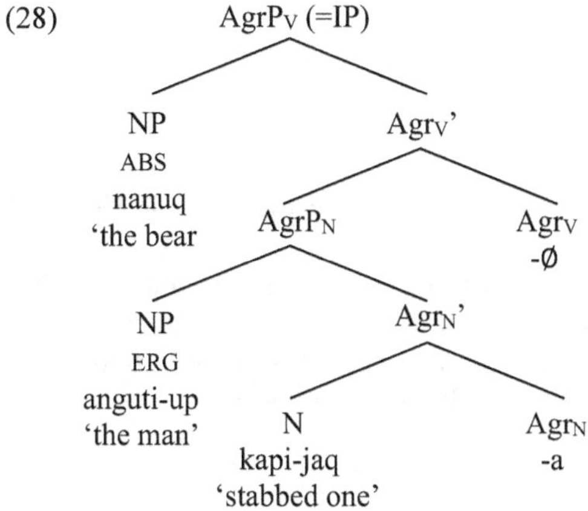

In part, this analysis of the relative position of agreement is based on Johns's observation that transitive verb forms contain an additional agreement morpheme and the fact that it is the outermost morphemes that indexes the absolutive object, with these same morphemes also appearing with intransitives to index absolutive subjects, as seen in the following examples:

(29) Inuktitut transitives

a. *taku-ja-a-nga* 'he sees me'
b. *taku-ja-a-tit* 'he sees you'
c. *taku-ja-a-∅* 'he sees him'
d. *taku-ja-a-tigut* 'he sees us'
e. *taku-ja-a-si* 'he sees you p.'
f. *taku-ja-i-(t)* 'he sees them'

(Johns 1992: 74)

(30) Inuktitut intransitives

a. *pisuk-pu-nga* 'I walk'
b. *pisuk-pu-tit* 'you s. walk'
c. *pisuk-puq-k* 'he walks'
d. *pisuk-pu-gut* 'we walk'
e. *pisuk-pu-si* 'you p. walk'
f. *pisuk-pu-t* 'they walk'

(Johns 1992: 74)

Bittner and Hale (1996) advance a similar proposal for West Greenlandic, arguing that in transitive clauses, nominative (i.e., absolutive) agreement occurs on C and ergative agreement occurs on INFL. In particular, they analyze morphemes typically considered to be dependent clause-type markers (and thus arguably on C) as instead being on INFL. For instance, in the following examples, they treat *-(g) a-* as a tense marker, since its interpretation varies between 'because' or 'when' (in the past):[25]

(31) West Greenlandic

a. *Juuna* *nuannaar-**a**-mi* — *miiqqat*
[Juuna(NOM)$_i$ happy-CONT-3SG.PROX$_i$] pro(ERG)$_i$ children(NOM)$_j$
kunip-p-a-i.
kiss-IND-[+TR]-3SG$_i$.3PL$_j$
'Because Juuna$_i$ was happy, he$_i$ kissed the children.'

b. *Juuna-p* *miiqqat* *taku-**ga**-mi-git* —
[Juuna-ERG$_i$ children(NOM)$_j$ see-CONT-3SG.PROX$_i$-3PL$_j$] pro(NOM)$_i$
nuannaar-p-u-q.
happy-IND-[−TR]-3SG$_i$
'Because Juuna$_i$ has seen the children, he$_i$'s happy.'

(Bittner & Hale 1996: 18)

Compton (2016) argues that both ergative and absolutive agreement in Inuit occurs on C. Evidence for this includes the fact that in Eastern Canadian dialects with obligatory tense marking, agreement morphology is discontinuous from the exponence of T and instead follows both negation and clause-type morphology, the latter of which is normally thought to reside in C.

(32) *Nirikasalauqsimanngimmijara.* (Inuktitut)
niri-kasaq-**lauq**-sima-nngit-mi-ja-**ra**
eat-almost-**DIST.PAST**-PERF-NEG-too-DECL.TR-**1SG.3SG**
'I almost didn't eat it too.'

Furthermore, the exponence of both agreement and clause-type markers condition each other, with agreement being sensitive to clause type and some clause-type markers changing their exponence based on the φ-features involved in agreement. For instance, in (33), the exponence of 2SG:3SG depends entirely on clause type – here an *if*-conditional versus a declarative.

(33). *taku-gu-**viuk*** *ikajuq-langa-ja-**it*** (Inuktitut)
see-COND-**2SG.3SG** help-NEAR.FUT-DECL-**2SG.3SG**
'If you see him/her, you'll help him/her.'

Similarly, Table 7.5 illustrates how the exponence of the interrogative clause type marker is conditioned by agreement morphemes, changing between *-vu*, *-vi*, and *-va*, in contrast with the indicative marker, which is always *-vu*.

Crucially, there is no clear synchronic phonological motivation for such changes. Additional evidence for positing agreement on C in Inuit includes its interaction with switch-reference, as discussed earlier. Since switch-reference is a cross-clausal phenomenon, it is reasonable to assume that it too occurs on C.

Other Indigenous languages of North America that have been argued to exhibit agreement on C include Nez Perce (Deal 2016) and Algonquian (see Oxford 2014a: 270 for references).

Table 7.5 Clause Type Marking Conditioned by Agreement

	INDICATIVE	*INTERROGATIVE*
1SG	taku-vu-nga	taku-vu-nga
2SG	taku-vu-tit	taku-vi-t
3SG	taku-vu(-)q	taku-va
1DU	taku-vu-guk	taku-vi-nuk
2DU	taku-vu-tik	taku-vi-tik
3DU	taku-vu-uk	taku-va-ak
1PL	taku-vu-gut	taku-vi-ta
2PL	taku-vu-si	taku-vi-si
3PL	taku-vu-t	taku-va-t

3.2.2. Low Agreement on v and Voice

A number of North American languages exhibit agreement on a functional projection lower than T, such as light *v* or Voice. For instance, while its position is not argued for explicitly, Béjar and Rezac (2009) assume that the *v* head is responsible for at least some exponents of agreement in Kanien'kéha (i.e., Mohawk, Iroquoian) and Nishnaabemwin (Algonquian). As discussed previously, Algonquian languages exhibit hierarchical agreement, whereby the person features of both the subject and object must be evaluated. Locating the person probe on *v* (and allowing probes to search both into their specifiers and their complements) puts both arguments in the same agreement domain, thereby explaining how either argument can control agreement.

Another such language is Ch'ol (Mayan). Coon (2017) argues that ergative agreement in this language occurs low in the structure, specifically on *v*. In terms of morphophonological evidence, she observes that a CVC template requirement is imposed on roots at the vP phase. As a result, vowel-initial roots are preceded by an epenthetic glottal stop when preceded by proclitics and when occurring word-initially. However, epenthesis does not occur when the root is preceded by an ergative agreement marker, suggesting the marker is present at the vP phase. If agreement were occurring at T, it would be outside of the vP phase and the epenthetic consonant would be expected.

(34) Ch'ol

a. *[ʔil]-añ!*
see-IMP
'Look!'

b. *[ah=ʔil]-k'iñ*
CL=see-festival
'pilgrim'

c. *Tyi [k-il]-ä.*
PRFV 1ERG-see-TV
'I saw it.'

(Coon 2017: 365)

Coon also presents syntactic evidence that ergative agreement is lower than T, showing that in non-finite embedded control clauses that lack TAM marking (and arguably finite T), we nevertheless find ergative agreement. This is expected if it occurs on *v*, as illustrated in (35).

(35) *K-om [k-mek'=ety].*
1ERG-want 1ERG-hug=2ABS
'I want to hug you.'

(Coon 2017: 365)

Both types of evidence converge on ergative agreement occurring at little *v*. Coon also concludes that this language "provides evidence for the existence of true ergative agreement" insofar as it directly targets transitive subjects. It is thus a counter-example to Woolford's (2000) arguments against "covert ergative Case" systems, which she treats as epiphenomenal.

Oxford's (2014a) analysis of agreement in Proto-Algonquian distinguishes between v^0 and Voice^0, treating the former as a category defining head corresponding to the FINALS in the Algonquianist literature, and the latter as the site of object agreement, corresponding to the (object) THEME SIGN. The inverse theme sign is attributed to INFL (Oxford 2014a: 100):

(36)

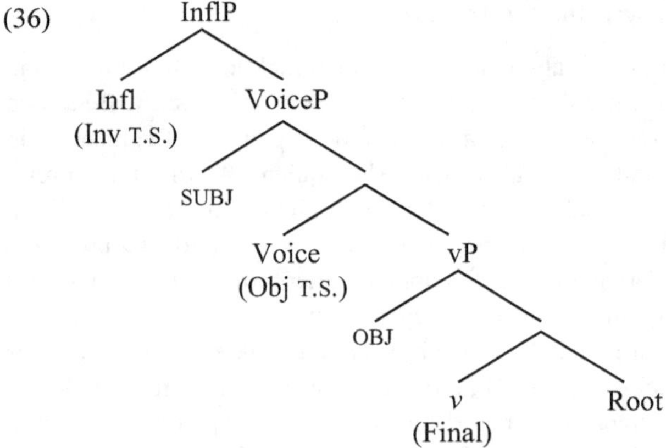

Oxford's arguments for such a division of labor include the fact that while the higher inverse theme sign on INFL must c-command both arguments, in order to yield the direct/inverse pattern, the object theme signs reflect only the features of the object.

3.3. *Differentiating Agreement From Pronominal Clitics*

Given both the degree of variation and complexity found in φ-marking systems in North America, these languages offer rich test cases for distinguishing genuine agreement from pronominal clitics. Once defined in phonological and distributional terms – e.g., Zwicky and Pullum's (1983) criteria of host selectivity, arbitrary gaps, morphophonological and idiosyncrasies, etc. – recent work has questioned the validity of such diagnostics for distinguishing affixes from pronominal clitics. In particular, Nevins (2011) argues that the proper identification of genuine agreement and pronominal clitics must rely on morphosyntactic criteria, insofar as agreement is taken to be the exponence of an Agree relationship on a functional head in the clausal spine between that head and an argument, while a pronominal clitic is a D head. As such, while genuine agreement is expected to be able to interact with other features of the same head, leading to the possibility of tense-variance; for instance, such interactions are unexpected of clitics of category D.[26] Kramer (2014) and Preminger (2014) also propose a number of diagnostics capitalizing on expected syntactic differences between Agree (or some version thereof) and pronominal D^0 clitics, and use these diagnostics to reanalyze several cases of object agreement as in fact being clitics.

A number of North American languages figure prominently in debates on distinguishing agreement and clitics. Notably, many of these languages have been argued or assumed to have pronominal clitics due to Jelinek's (1984) Pronominal Argument Hypothesis (PAH). The PAH asserts that the properties of so-called *non-configurational* languages are due to their (apparent) agreement morphology actually being pronominal arguments with the noun phrase arguments that they index in fact being adjuncts. Reanalyzed in this way, such properties as the variable order of NPs, discontinuous NPs, as well as the possibility of null anaphora are predicted, since the agreement markers are the actual arguments. Notably, Baker's (1996) Polysynthesis Parameter extends this analysis to Kanien'kéha (i.e., Mohawk, Iroquoian), expanding it to account for the properties of noun incorporation in the language. While a PAH-style analysis has also been assumed for a number of Algonquian languages, LeSourd (2006) points out a number of problems for such a treatment for Maliseet-Passamaquoddy, including the presence of secondary object NPs without any corresponding markers on the verb (see references therein for analyses of Algonquian languages adopting the PAH as well as LeSourd's arguments against it).

Table 7.6 Similarity Between Absolutive Agreement and Strong Pronouns in K'ichean

	ABS AGREEMENT MARKER	STRONG PRONOUN
1SG	i(n)-	yïn
1PL	oj-	röj
2SG	a(t)-	rat
2PL	ix-	rïx
3SG	∅-	rja'
3PL	e-	rje'

Source: Preminger (2014: 25).

Preminger (2014), while arguing that agreement should be recast as an obligatory operation that can fail without leading to a crash in the derivation (cf. Chomsky 2000; 2001), provides several diagnostics for differentiating agreement and clitics in the K'ichean branch of Mayan languages. For instance, he observes that first- and second-person absolutive agreement markers exhibit a high degree of similarity with their corresponding strong pronouns, something predicted of clitics as a type of reduced pronoun, but not of agreement (Table 7.6).

Furthermore, he notes that the presence of the approximant *r* in the pronoun forms may be attributable to a determiner, which elsewhere takes the form *ri*. In contrast to the first- and second-person forms, which he concludes are clitics, he argues that the third-person forms are genuine agreement. First, they bear a less striking similarity to the corresponding pronouns (particularly given that *j* represents a voiceless velar fricative). Secondly, he points to evidence that the 3pl agreement form only encodes plurality, not person.

Following Béjar & Rezac's (2009) proposal for Cyclic Agree, Preminger also argues that the cyclic nature of agreement (with person typically thought to probe before number) means that we expect genuine agreement to yield mismatches, with person and number indexing different arguments. Specifically, he proposes the property of coarseness as a test for distinguishing clitics and agreement (Preminger 2014: 51):

(37) The coarseness property of clitic doubling
If CL^0 is the result of clitic doubling of some noun phrase α, then CL^0 will reflect the full set of φ-features on α.

Essentially, clitics are expected to be able to reflect the full set of φ-features of the corresponding arguments. Conversely, he predicts the property of granularity to hold of agreement, since probes for person and number operate separately. For instance, he argues that the agreement probe for number in K'ichean can probe independently of person in search of [PLURAL] in the agent focus construction, yielding omnivorous number-agreement in number with either argument (or, more precisely, the highest plural argument c-commanded by the probe):

(38) K'ichean

a. *ja* *rje'* *x-e/*∅-tz'et-ö* *rja'*
FOC them COM-**3PL/*3SG.ABS**-see-AF him
'It was them who saw him.'

b. *ja* *rja'* *x-e/*∅-tz'et-ö* *rje'*
FOC him COM-**3PL/*3SG.ABS**-see-AF them
'It was him who saw them.'

(Preminger 2014: 40)

A similar effect is found for person in this construction, with first- and second-person (i.e., [PARTICIPANT]) objects controlling agreement when the subject is third person.[27]

Oxford (2014b) takes on the issue of distinguishing agreement and clitics in Algonquian, arguing that the multiple exponence of both subjects and objects mitigates against claims that object agreement is in fact a clitic (e.g., Woolford 2010; Nevins 2011), in part since such a state of affairs would amount to clitic tripling for Algonquian. Other arguments that objects trigger agreement include the position and form of object markers, and their interaction with tense. For instance, in the following Ojibwe example (originally from Valentine 2001: 292), Oxford argues that the outermost prefix and suffix are clitics, while the two inner φ-indexing morphemes are shown to be genuine agreement, with the object and subject in this example, respectively.

(39) Ojibwe

nwābmāsīminābanīg
n=wābm-ā-sī-minā-bany=ag
1=SEE-3-NEG-1PL-PAST=3PL
'we did not see them'

(Oxford 2014b: 337)

Similarly, Compton (2016) argues for the existence of object agreement in Inuit. He observes that while subject/object indexing morphology does not interact with tense, it instead induces clause type variance, with the exponence of clause type markers and of agreement co-conditioning each other, as illustrated in §3.2.1. Such interactions are predicted if φ-marking (for both subjects and objects) is the exponence of the Agree relation on the C head. However, see Yuan (2017) and Johns and Kučerová (2017) for alternative analyses where at least some of these markers are argued to be clitics.

4. Conclusion

In this chapter I have attempted to give an overview of various types of agreement systems found in North American languages, as well as a sample of the phenomena in these languages that bear on the inventory of φ-features, the location of agreement in the clause, and the distinction between genuine agreement and pronominal clitics.

While it is impossible in such a limited space to provide a detailed portrait of agreement in a single language family, let alone across dozens of families, it should be clear to what extent these languages exhibit a rich diversity in agreement systems and agreement phenomena whose proper analysis are relevant to current debates in linguistic theory.

Acknowledgments

Thank you to Michael Barrie, Seth Cable, Jessica Coon, James Crippen, Amy Rose Deal, Daniel Harbour, Will Oxford, Elisabeth Ritter, Leslie Saxon, Neil Alexander Walker, Nicholas Welch, and Andrea Wilhelm for their helpful comments, suggestions, and replies to questions, and pointing me in the right direction. Thank you also to the Inuit speakers who share their language with me. All errors are mine. This work was supported by FRQSC grant 2017-NP-196992.

Further Reading

Aissen, Judith & England, Nora C. & Maldonado, Roberto Zavala (eds.). 2017. *The Mayan languages*. London: Routledge.

Baker, Mark C. 2008. *The syntax of agreement and concord.* Cambridge: Cambridge University Press.
Corbett, Greville G. 2006. *Agreement.* Cambridge: Cambridge University Press.
Dorais, Louis-Jacques. 1988. Tukilik: an Inuktitut grammar for all. *Inuit Studies*, Occasional Papers, no. 2. Association Inuksiutit Katimajit and Groupe d'études inuit et circumpolaires (GETIC).
Drapeau, Lynn. 2014. *Grammaire de la langue innue.* Québec: Presses de l'Université du Québec.
Goddard, Yves (ed.). 1996. *Handbook of North American Indians, volume 17: Languages.* General editor William C. Sturtevant. Washington: Smithsonian Institution.
Harbour, Daniel & Adger, David & Bejar, Susana (eds.). 2008. *Phi-theory: Phi-features across modules and interfaces.* Oxford: Oxford University Press.
Mithun, Marianne. 1999. *The languages of Native North America.* Cambridge: Cambridge University Press.
Oxford, Will. 2014. *Microparameters of agreement: A diachronic perspective on Algonquian verb inflection.* Toronto: University of Toronto (Doctoral dissertation.)
Rice, Keren & Saxon, Leslie. 2005. Comparative Athapaskan morphosyntax: Arguments and projections. In Cinque, G. & Kayne, R.S. (eds.), *The Oxford handbook of comparative syntax*, 698–774. Oxford: Oxford University Press.
Valentine, J. Randolph. 2001. *Nishnaabemwin reference grammar.* Toronto: University of Toronto Press.

Notes

1. Following Adger and Harbour (2008: 2), φ-features are taken to include "those involved in predicate-argument agreement, typically person, number, and gender".
2. Abbreviations: 1, 2, 3 = first, second, third person, 3′ = third-person obviative, 0 = third-person inanimate, A = Set A (ergative/possessive), ABS = absolutive, AF = agent focus, AP = antipassive, B = Set B (absolutive), CAUS = causative; CL = classifier, COM = completive aspect, COND = conditional clause type (in the sense of an antecedent in a hypothetical proposition), CONT = contingent clause type, CONTEMP = contemporative, DA = disjoint anaphor, DECL = declarative, DEF = definite, DEP = dependent, DIR = direct, directional, DIST = distant, DS = different subject, DTV = ditransitive verb suffix, DU = dual, ERG = ergativ, FOC = focus FUT = future I = inverse number, IC = initial change, IMP = imperative, INTR = intransitive, INV = inverse, ITV = intransitive verb suffix, NEG = negative, NOM = nominative; OBJ = object; OBL = oblique; OBV = obviative; PERF = perfect; PL = plural; PRFV = perfective, ROX = proximate, RDP = reduplication; REFL = reflexive; SBJ = subject SG = singular; SJV = subjunctive; SUF = suffix; TA = transitive animate, TI = transitive inanimate, TV = transitive verb suffix. For consistently, glossing has been regularized. Unattributed examples from Inuktitut and Inuinnaqtun were collected by the author.
3. According to Mithun (1999: 207), "two adjacent indentical obstruents merge to an aspirated obstruent, so the sequence *k-k* is pronounced *k*^{h}".
4. The number symbol '#' indicates the boundary between disjunct and conjunct prefixes within the verb.
5. Similarly, switch-reference marking (a phenomenon whereby subjects, prototypically, are marked as being the same or distinct across clauses) in dependent clauses in Inuit can exhibit a nominative-accusative alignment, tracking the logical subjects between clauses, regardless of transitivity (Pittman 2005; Allen 2013). In terms of its relative position in the verbal complex and its sensitivity to clause type, switch-reference in Inuit patterns to some degree like agreement. See also Berge (2011) for a discussion of switch-reference in West Greenlandic.
6. Forms are presented in the IPA. The underlying /ph/ sequences here surface as [ff] and are represented as such in the orthography.
7. Such forms are also found in the possessive marking on nouns, but once again, these are concomitant with ergative marking on possessors (when overt).
8. While Nichols (1997: 10) calls the ergative-absolutive pattern in Zuni epiphenomenal, her reasoning that "prefixal and suffixal agreement can be shown to have different sources and therefore do not reflect a single coherent structural case-marking strategy" seems nevertheless compatible with the phenomenon of ergativity, broadly construed.
9. As is the case in many languages, third-person singular in Lakhota, for both active and stative verbs, is null.
10. Woolford proposes that Optimality-Theoretic constraints limit the exponence of this cross-referencing and set language-specific preferences in terms of their expression as agreement or clitics at PF. She contrasts her approach with two more syntactically oriented explanations of split systems. First, she argues against proposals attributing such splits to abstract case, in which stative verbs assign accusative to their subjects. She states that such a system "does not occur among languages that mark their arguments with morphological case" (Woolford 2010: 2). However, Mithun (1999) provides two examples of languages which at least manifest morphological case distinctions in free pronouns following an active-stative pattern: Haida and Central Pomo. If free pronouns can manifest a split-intransitive pattern, it is not clear that split agreement

patterns must be reduced to PF constraints on the expression of clitics and agreement. The agentive and patientive pronouns in these languages thus point to case and not morphophonological considerations as being responsible for the split. Woolford also argues against an analysis of agreement "that directly targets external and internal arguments" (Woolford 2010: 2). However, as discussed later in this chapter, Coon (2017) provides compelling arguments in favor of agreement on little *v* targeting external arguments in Mayan languages.

11. This list provides only an illustrative sample of languages. Mithun (1999: 213) lists other languages and families as being active-stative or agent-patient, but her classification extends beyond agreement. For instance, she shows that Haida and Central Pomo manifest a split transitive pattern in their choice of free pronouns, as mentioned previously.
12. This hierarchy is a simplified version of the hierarchy presented in Valentine, which includes the 'unspecified actor' in passives above third person (Valentine 2001: 271–272). See Bliss et al.'s chapter in this volume on hierarchies and direct-inverse systems, as well as Oxford (2017b) for a discussion of a number of myths involving agreement in Algonquian.
13. For instance, Murasugi (2017) argues for the presence of a morpheme in the transitive declarative/participial clause type in Inuktitut that corresponds to inverse contexts (i.e., non-local subject and local object), despite the lack of a pattern of preferential agreement along a hierarchy.
14. Jacques and Antonov (2014) also treat the cislocative marker in Nez Perce, which occurs in contexts where second person is acting on first person, as a type of inverse marker. Deal (2015b) treats this as a type of "agreement extension", in an agreement system that is otherwise nominative-accusative.
15. However, as noted by a reviewer, this evidence would be more compelling if we were able to rule out the possibility that this is a case of possessor raising.
16. Walker (p.c.) suggests that the form identified as the (optional) first person marker, -:na, (in Walker 2013) should in fact be analyzed as the imperfective ||-ad(u)|| followed by the performative evidential ||-l:a||, which are then subject to morphophonological changes, including a rule whereby an underlying /d/ can become [:] or [n] in some contexts.
17. Another such language is Shoshone (Uto-Aztecan), which according to Lindsey (2000) and Matsumoto (2015: 86–87) has optional agreement for number and number suppletion for a small closed class of verbs. Matsumoto suggests these could be instances of lexical verbal number, akin to the difference between *kill* and *massacre*.
18. While most Algonquian languages do not show an overt obviation contrast marked on inanimate nouns, Oxford (2017b) and Oxford and Bliss (2017) explain that the contrast nevertheless exists covertly in numerous languages, as evidence by the fact that these inanimates trigger obviative forms of agreement on the verb.
19. Kiowa verbal agreement is considerably more complex than might be suggested by the examples here. For the full set of agreement markers and discussion thereof, see Harbour (2017).
20. A similar phenomenon involving objects is found in Dene languages, whereby third-person objects with disjoint reference with respect to the subject receive special agreement marking (see Saxon 1986; Rice & Saxon 2005). For instance, in the following examples from Tłı̨chǫ Yatiı̀, the third-person object marking distinguishes between (i) disjoint reference with a third-person subject (called "disjoint anaphor" in the literature), (ii) coreference with a third-person subject, and (iii) third-person animate referents with a local subject (Nicholas Welch, p.c., from speaker Archie Wedzin):

    i. *Madlę̀ yaʔı̨.*
    Madlę̀ **ye**-a-ʔı̨
    Madeleine DA-PRFV.3.SBJ-see.PRFV
    'Madeleine saw him/her.'

    ii. *Madlę̀ edeaʔı̨.*
    Madlę̀ **ede**-a-ʔı̨
    Madeleine REFL-PRFV.3.SBJ-see.PRFV
    'Madeleine saw herself.'

    iii. Weehʔı̨.
    we-eh-ı̨
    3.OBJ-PRFV.1SG.SBJ-see.PRFV
    'I saw him/her.'

    This phenomenon may fall outside the definition of switch-reference, which typically involves two or more clauses. Similarly, Inuit possessor marking differentiates between coreference and disjoint reference with clausemate subjects.

21. The contingent clause type, used to mean 'if' or 'when' (in the future), is often (confusingly) called 'conditional' in the literature on Inuit.
22. This clause type receives different names in the literature on Inuit, including "appositional" (Dorais 2003) and "conjunctive" (Lowe 1985). Agreement forms exhibit phonologically and morphologically conditioned allomorphy.
23. Although Pittman (2005) describes switch-reference in Inuktitut as "non-canonical", and on this basis McKenzie (2015) concludes that it lacks (genuine) switch-reference, as he defines it, Mauro (2018) shows that some dialects do in fact have a genuine canonical system of switch-reference, although in other dialects the system is disappearing due to language change, particularly among younger speakers.
24. I use the label *ergative* instead of *relative* for the case found on the agent (and also found on possessors in the language). I have also separated and augmented the glosses for each agreement head. Johns's original glossing labels the morpheme *-ja(q)-* as a passive participle.
25. While the status of this morpheme as a tense marker in West Greenlandic is debatable, its status as a clause type marker in the neighboring dialect of Baffin Inuktitut is supported by existence of dedicated past-tense markers with which it may co-occur. Furthermore, it is compatible with present tense (Nunavut 2000; 2002).

    (i) *qaujima-lau(q)-gama*
    KNOW-DIST.PAST-CONT.1SG
    'because I knew'

    (ii) *qaujima-gama*
    KNOW-CONT.1SG
    'because I know'

26. Nevins (2011) also proposes that the Person-Case Constraint (PCC) and omnivorous number (i.e., a phenomenon whereby number agreement can index a lower argument if the higher argument bears no marked number features) are diagnostics for differentiating agreement and pronominal clitics, but the reasons for which this should obtain appear to be internal to his theory of Multiple Agree.
27. While we might expect the possibility of plural number agreement with a third-person subject and person agreement with a local object, Preminger argues that this is prevented due to there being a single morphological slot available to mark agreement in this construction, with the first- and second-person forms taking precedence over (third-person) plural.

References

Aissen, Judith & England, Nora C. & Maldonado, Roberto Zavala (eds.). 2017. *The Mayan languages*. London: Routledge.

Adger, Daniel & Harbour, Daniel. 2008. Why phi? In Harbour, Daniel & Adger, David & Bejar, Susana (eds.), *Phi-theory: Phi-features across modules and interfaces*, 1–34. Oxford: Oxford University Press.

Allen, Shanley. 2013. The acquisition of ergativity in Inuktitut. In Bavin, Edith L. & Stoll, Sabine (eds.), *The acquisition of ergativity*, Trends in Language Acquisition Research 9, 71–105. Amsterdam: John Benjamins.

Arregi, Karlos & Hanink, Emily. 2017. Switch reference in Washo as multiple agreement (poster), North East Linguistic Society 48. University of Iceland, Reykjavik (October 29).

Baker, Mark C. 1996. *The polysynthesis parameter*. New York: Oxford University Press.

Béjar, Susana & Rezac, Milan. 2009. Cyclic agree. *Linguistic Inquiry* 40(1). 35–73.

Berge, Anna. 2011. *Topic and discourse structure in West Greenlandic agreement constructions*. Lincoln: University of Nebraska Press.

Bittner, Maria & Hale, Ken. 1996. The structural determination of case and agreement. *Linguistic Inquiry* 27(1). 1–68.

Bliss, Heather. 2017. Dependencies in syntax and discourse: Obviation in Blackfoot and beyond. *Working Papers of the Linguistics Circle of the University of Victoria* 27(1). 1–26.

Charney, Jean O. 1993. *A grammar of Comanche*. Lincoln: University of Nebraska Press.

Chomsky, Noam. 2000. Minimalist inquiries: The framework. In Martin, Roger & Michaels, David & Uriagereka, Juan (eds.), *Step by step: Essays on Minimalist syntax in honor of Howard Lasnik*, 89–155. Cambridge, MA: MIT Press.

Chomsky, Noam. 2001. Derivation by phase. In Kenstowicz, Michael (ed.), *Ken Hale: A life in language*, 1–52. Cambridge, MA: MIT Press.

Chomsky, Noam. 2007. Approaching UG from below. In Sauerland, Uli & Gärtner, Hans-Martin (eds.), *Interfaces + recursion = language?: Chomsky's minimalism and the view from syntax-semantics*, Studies in Generative Grammar 89, 1–30. Berlin: De Gruyter.

Chomsky, Noam. 2008. On phases. In Freidin. Robert & Otero, Carlos P. & Zubizarreta, Maria Luisa (eds.), *Foundational issues in linguistic theory: Essays in honor of Jean-Roger Verngaud*, Current Studies in Linguistics, 133–166. Cambridge, MA: MIT Press.

Compton, Richard. 2016. Mutually conditioned mood and object agreement in Inuit. In Hammerly, Christopher & Prickett, Brandon (eds.), *NELS 46: Proceedings of the forty-sixth annual meeting of the North East Linguistic Society, Volume 1*, 241–250. Amherst: GLSA, University of Massachusetts.

Compton, Richard. 2017. Ergativity in Inuktitut. In Coon, Jessica & Massam, Diane & Travis, Lisa deMena (eds.), *The Oxford handbook of ergativity*, 832–850. Oxford: Oxford University Press.

Cook, Eung-Do. 2004. *A grammar of Dëne Sųłiné (Chipewyan)*. Algonquian and Iroquoian Linguistics, Special Athabaskan Number, Memoir 17.

Coon, Jessica. 2013. *Aspects of split ergativity*. New York: Oxford University Press.

Coon, Jessica. 2016. Mayan morphosyntax. *Language and Linguistics Compass* 10(10). 515–550.

Coon, Jessica. 2017. Two types of ergative agreement: Implications for case. In Halpert, Claire & Kotek, Hadas & van Urk, Coppe (eds.), *A Pesky Set: Papers for David Pesetsky*, 361–370. Cambridge, MA: MIT Working Papers in Linguistics.

Davis, Henry & Forbes, Clarissa. 2015. Connect four! the morphosyntax of argument marking in Tsimshianic. In Weber, Natalie & Guntly, Erin & Lam, Zoe & Chen, Sihwei (eds.), *Papers for the international conference on Salish and neighbouring languages 50*, 155–186. Vancouver: UBC Working Papers in Linguistics.

Deal, Amy Rose. 2015a. Interaction and satisfaction in φ-agreement. In Bui, Thuy & Deniz, Özyıldız (eds.), *NELS 45: Proceedings of the forty-fifth annual meeting of the North East Linguistic Society*, 179–192. Amherst: GLSA, University of Massachusetts.

Deal, Amy Rose. 2015b. A note on Nez Perce verb agreement, with sample paradigms. In Weber, Natalie & Guntly, Erin & Lam, Zoe & Chen, Sihwei (eds.), *Papers for the international conference on Salish and neighbouring languages 50*, 389–413. Vancouver: UBC Working Papers in Linguistics.

Deal, Amy Rose. 2016. Cyclicity and connectivity in Nez Perce relative clauses. *Linguistic Inquiry* 47(3). 427–470.

Dorais, Louis-Jacques. 2003. *Inuit uqausiqatigiit – Inuit languages and dialects*. 2nd rev. edn. Iqaluit: Nunavut Arctic College.

Dryer, Matthew S. 1991. Subject and inverse in Kutenai. In Redden, James E. (ed.), *Papers from the American Indian languages conferences*. Occasional Papers in Linguistics 16, 183–202. Carbondale: Southern Illinois University.

Dryer, Matthew S. 1994. The discourse function of the Kutenai inverse. In Givón, T. (ed.), *Voice and inversion*, 65–99. Amsterdam: John Benjamins.

Enrico, John. 2003. *Haida syntax*, vol. 1. Studies in the Anthropology of North American Indians. Lincoln: University of Nebraska Press.

Goddard, Ives. 2002. Grammatical gender in Algonquian. In Wolfart, H. C. (ed.), *Papers of the 33rd Algonquian Conference*, 195–231. Winnipeg: University of Manitoba.

Harbour, Daniel. 2011. Valence and atomic number. *Linguistic Inquiry* 42(4). 561–594.

Harbour, Daniel. 2017. Kiowa-Tanoan languages. *Oxford Research Encyclopedia of Linguistics*. (http://linguistics.oxfordre.com/view/10.1093/acrefore/9780199384655.001.0001/acrefore-9780199384655-e-27) (Accessed 2018-05-24.)

Harley, Heidi & Ritter, Elizabeth. 2002. Person and number in pronouns: A feature-geometric analysis. *Language* 78(3). 482–526.

Hill, Jane H. 2005. *A grammar of Cupeño*, Linguistics Volume 136. Berkeley: University of California Press.

Jacques, Guillaume & Antonov, Anton. 2014. Direct/inverse systems. *Language and Linguistics Compass* 8(7). 301–318.

Jelinek, Eloise. 1984. Empty categories, case, and configurationality. *Natural Language & Linguistic Theory* 2(1). 39–76.

Johns, Alana & Kučerová, Ivona. 2017. On the morphosyntactic reflexes of information structure in the ergative patterning of the Inuit language. In Coon, Jessica & Massam, Diane & Travis, Lisa deMena (eds.), *The Oxford handbook of ergativity*, 397–418. Oxford: Oxford University Press.

Johns, Alana. 1992. Deriving ergativity. *Linguistic Inquiry* 23(1). 57–87.

Johns, Alana. 2001. An inclination towards accusative. *Linguistica Atlantica* 23. 127–144.

Kramer, Ruth. 2014. Clitic doubling or object agreement: The view from Amharic. *Natural Language & Linguistic Theory* 32(2). 593–634.

Leer, Jeff. 1991. Evidence for a Northern Northwest Coast language area: Promiscuous number marking and periphrastic possessive constructions in Haida, Eyak, and Aleut. *International Journal of American Linguistics* 57(2). 158–193.

LeSourd, Philip S. 2006. Problems for the pronominal argument hypothesis in Maliseet-Passamaquoddy. *Language* 82(3). 486–514.

Lindsey, Francis. 2000. Subordinate clauses and ergative patterns in Shoshoni. *Oceanic Linguistics Special Publications* 29. 274–292.

Lochbihler, Bethany C. 2012. *Aspects of argument licensing*. Montreal: McGill University. (Doctoral dissertation.)

Lowe, Ronald. 1985. *Kangiryuarmiut uqauhingita ilihautdjutikhangit – Basic Kangiyuarmiut Eskimo grammar*. Inuvik: Committee for Original Peoples Entitlement.

Matsumoto, Katherine. 2015. *Recent language change in Shoshone: Structural consequences of language loss*. Salt Lake City: University of Utah. (Doctoral dissertation.)

Mauro, Christophe. 2018. *Le statut de la troisième personne en inuktitut*. Université du Québec à Montréal. (MA thesis.)

McKenzie, Andrew. 2015. A survey of switch reference in North America. *International Journal of American Linguistics* 81(3). 409–448.

Mithun, Marianne. 1996. The Mohawk language. In Maurais, Jacques (ed.), *Quebec's Aboriginal languages: History, planning and development*, 159–173. Clevedon, UK: Multilingual Matters.

Mithun, Marianne. 1999. *The languages of Native North America*. Cambridge: Cambridge University Press.

Mithun, Marianne. 2008. The emergence of agentive systems in core argument marking. In Donahue, Mark & Wichmann, Søren (eds.), *The typology of semantic alignment*, 297–333. Oxford: Oxford University Press.

Murasugi, Kumiko. 2017. Direction marking in Inuktitut verbal agreement. (Poster presented at Inuktitut Language and Linguistics Workshop, University of Toronto, May 30.)

Nevins, Andrew. 2011. Multiple agree with clitics: Person complementarity vs. omnivorous number. *Natural Language & Linguistic Theory* 29(4). 939–971.

Newman, Paul. 2012. Pluractional verbs: An overview. In Cabredo Hofherr, Patricia & Laca, Brenda (eds.), *Verbal plurality and distributivity*, 185–210. Berlin: De Gruyter.

Nichols, Lynn. 1997. *Topics in Zuni syntax*. Cambridge, MA: Harvard University. (Doctoral dissertation.)

Nunavut, Legislative Assembly. 2000. *Hansard*, 1st Assembly, 3rd Sess, Day 29 (April 4). (www.inuktitutcomputing.ca/NunavutHansard/). (Accessed 2019-07-30.)

Nunavut, Legislative Assembly. 2002. *Hansard*, 1st Assembly, 6th Sess, Day 14 (May 10). (www.inuktitutcomputing.ca/NunavutHansard/). (Accessed 2019-07-30.)

Oxford, Will. 2014a. *Microparameters of agreement: A diachronic perspective on Algonquian verb inflection*. Toronto: University of Toronto. (Doctoral dissertation.)

Oxford, Will. 2014b. Multiple instances of agreement in the clausal spine: Evidence from Algonquian. In Santana-LaBarge, Robert E. (ed.), *Proceedings of WCCFL* 31, 335–343. Somerville, MA: Cascadilla.

Oxford, Will. 2017a. Proximate DP, obviative KP: Balancing the morphosyntax and pragmatics of obviation. In Monti, Andrew Alexander (ed.), *Proceedings of the 2017 annual Conference of the Canadian Linguistic Association*. Canadian Linguistics Association (http://cla-acl.ca/wp-content/uploads/actes-2017/Oxford_W.2017CLAProceedingsPaper.pdf). (Accessed 2019-07-30.)

Oxford, Will. 2017b. Algonquian grammar myths. *Toronto Working Papers in Linguistics* 39.

Oxford, Will & Heather Bliss. 2017. Patterns of syncretism in nominal paradigms: A pan-Algonquian perspective. In Macaulay, Monica & Noodin, Margaret (eds.), *Papers of the Forty-Sixth Algonquian Conference*, 1–18. East Lansing, MI: Michigan State University Press.

Pittman, Christine M. 2005. Non-canonical switch-reference in Inuktitut. In Gurski, Claire (ed.), *Proceedings of the 2005 annual conference of the Canadian Linguistics Association*, 1–12. Canadian Linguistics Association (http://cla-acl.ca/wp-content/uploads/actes-2005/Pittman.pdf). (Accessed 2019-07-30.)

Preminger, Omer. 2014. *Agreement and its failures*. Linguistic Inquiry Monograph 68. Cambridge, MA: MIT Press.

Rhodes, Richard A. 1990. Ojibwa secondary objects. In Dziwirek, Katarzyna & Farrell, Patrick & Meijas-Bikandi, Errapel (eds.) *Grammatical relations: A cross theoretical perspective*, 401–414. Stanford, CA: CSLI.

Rice, Keren & Saxon, Leslie. 2005. Comparative Athapaskan morphosyntax: Arguments and projections. In Cinque, G. & Kayne, R. S. (eds.), *The Oxford handbook of comparative syntax*, 698–774. Oxford: Oxford University Press.

Rood, David S. & Taylor, Allan R. 1996. Sketch of Lakhota, a Siouan language. In Goddard, Ives (ed.), *Handbook of North American Indians, Volume 17: Languages*, 440–482. Washington, DC: Smithsonian Institution.

Saxon, Leslie. 1986. *The syntax of pronouns in Dogrib (Athapaskan): Some theoretical consequences*. San Diego: University of California. (Doctoral dissertation.)

Valentine, J. Randolph. 2001. *Nishnaabemwin reference grammar*. Toronto: University of Toronto Press.

Walker, Neil Alexander. 2013. *A grammar of Southern Pomo: An Indigenous language of California*. Santa Barbara: University of California. (Doctoral dissertation.)

Wichmann, Søren. 2008. The study of semantic alignment: retrospect and state of the art. In Donahue, Mark & Wichmann, Søren (eds.), *The typology of semantic alignment*, 3–23. Oxford: Oxford University Press.

Wiltschko, Martina. 2006. On 'ergativity' in Halkomelem Salish. In Johns, Alana & Massam, Diane & Ndayiragije, Juvénal (eds.), *Ergativity*. Studies in Natural Language and Linguistic Theory 65, 197–227. Dordrecht: Springer.

Woolford, Ellen. 2000. Ergative agreement systems. *University of Maryland Working Papers in Linguistics* 10. 157–191.

Woolford, Ellen. 2010. Active-stative agreement in Choctaw and Lakota. *ReVEL*, special edition n. 4.

Yuan, Michelle. 2017. Diagnosing object agreement vs. clitic doubling: Evidence from Inuktitut. Manuscript.

Zwicky, Arnold M. & Pullum, Geoffrey K. 1983. Cliticization vs. inflection: English n't. *Language* 59(3). 502–513.

8

INVERSE SYSTEMS AND PERSON HIERARCHY EFFECTS

Heather Bliss, Elizabeth Ritter, and Martina Wiltschko

1. Introduction

The purpose of this chapter is to explore the empirical and theoretical underpinnings of inverse systems and their relation to the person hierarchy. Descriptively, an inverse system can be characterized as a system of argument deployment in the family of – and often compared to – voice constructions including Indo-European passives and Austronesian voice alternations. By way of introduction, consider the examples in (1) from Ktunaxa (aka Kutenai, language isolate).[1]

(1)	a.	wukati	pałkiys	titqat'
		wukati	pałkiy-s	titqat'
		see IND	woman-OBV	man
		'The man$_{\text{PROX}}$ saw the woman$_{\text{OBV}}$.'		
	b.	wukatapsi	titqat's	pałkyi
		wukat-aps-i	titqat'-s	pałkyi
		see-INV-IND	man-OBV	woman
		'The man$_{\text{OBV}}$ saw the woman$_{\text{PROX}}$.' (*or* 'The woman was seen by the man.')		

(Adapted from Dryer 1991: 185 (6)

In these examples, word order and nominal marking (OBVIATIVE *-s*) differ, nevertheless the grammatical relations (subject and object) are identical: in both cases the man functions as the subject, while the woman functions as the object. What distinguishes the two sentences is the verbal morphology: in (1a), the verb is morphologically unmarked, and hence is classified as a *direct* verb; in (1b), the verb is suffixed by *-aps*, which is known as the *inverse* suffix.

The description of the logic of the inverse system provided in Jacques and Antonov (2014: 302f.) is representative. Specifically, inverse systems are viewed as systems of (transitive) person marking with three defining properties. First, agreement markers, if present, do not directly specify grammatical relations. To see this, consider the Blackfoot (Algonquian) examples in (2). The same person prefix *nit-* is used no matter whether the indexed referent (i.e., the speaker) functions as the subject, as in (2a), or as the object, as in (2b).

(2) a. nitsinóáwa
nit-ino-**aa**-wa
1-see.TA-**DIR**-3SG
'I see him/her.'

b. Nitsinóóka
nit-ino-**ok**-wa
1-see.TA-**INV**-3SG
'S/he sees me.'

Second, unlike what happens in the alternation between active and passive voice, the direct/inverse alternation does not involve a change in valency, and the verb is transitive in both direct and inverse clauses.[2] Finally, to encode the relation between the arguments indexed by the agreement markers and their grammatical relations, an obligatory system of verbal affixes is employed on transitive verbs. Direct and inverse marking refers to marking that signals whether there is direct or inverse alignment between the grammatical relations hierarchy given in (3a), and the person hierarchy in (3b). Direct marking – or, in some languages the absence of inverse marking – signals that the two hierarchies are directly aligned, i.e., that the argument that is higher on the person hierarchy also bears the higher-ranked grammatical relation (subject); inverse marking signals that the two hierarchies are inversely aligned, i.e., that the argument that is lower on the person hierarchy maps onto the higher-ranked grammatical relation.

Based on this characterization, a description of the inverse must involve reference to a person hierarchy. Roughly, the person hierarchy ranks speech act participants (first and second person) above non-speech act participants (third person). Moreover, the logic of the inverse dictates that third-person arguments be distinguishable from one another; otherwise, a transitive construction with two third-person arguments would always remain ambiguous. This is where the proximate/obviative distinction observed in (1) comes in: of the two third-person arguments, the proximate third person is ranked higher than the obviative third person, as shown in (3b).

(3) a. Grammatical Relations hierarchy: subject > (in)direct object
b. Person hierarchy (a first pass): 1/2 > 3prox > 3obv

Hence, if the proximate argument functions as the subject, direct marking is deployed; and conversely, if the obviative argument functions as the subject, inverse marking is deployed.

This summarizes the standard description of inverse systems. Obviation marking, famously found in Algonquian languages and referenced in (3b), distinguishes two classes of nominals – those that are proximate and those that are obviative. Obviation is determined by an interplay of syntactic and pragmatic factors, with proximate nominals interpreted as discourse salient (e.g., topics) and/or in a syntactically prominent position. See, inter alia, Bloomfield (1962), Rhodes (1990), Thomason (2003), and Oxford (2014; 2017) for discussion.

The goal of this chapter is to show that neither inverse systems nor the person hierarchy should be viewed as a unified phenomenon, either across languages or within a single language. Instead, we show that there is a range of variation associated with both the hierarchy and the inverse system of argument deployment, which would be hard to capture if we were to treat either of them as a unified phenomenon.

The chapter is organized as follows: In §2, we review in more detail the canonical description of the inverse system. While the main focus is on the logic of the inverse, it is necessary to also treat the logic behind the person hierarchy. In §3, we discuss the empirical variation associated with inverse systems, and in §4, we address some of the analytical variation we observe.

2. The Canonical Picture

2.1. What Is a Person Hierarchy?

Silverstein (1986) developed the hierarchy in (4) to describe the cross-linguistic uniformity and variation in nominal-based split ergativity. The uniformity comes from the observation that in all languages that exhibit this property, nominals at the top of the hierarchy tend to be marked with an accusative case pattern and those at the bottom with an ergative one.[3] The variation comes from the fact that languages differ in the point at which the case-marking split occurs.

(4) 1st/2nd >3rd > proper names > human N >other animate N > inanimate N
ACC --------> <-------ERG
(Adapted from Croft 2003: 130)

This hierarchy is a chain of implicational universals in the following sense: if some type of nominal on the hierarchy is marked with accusative case, then all types of nominals to the left are also expected to be marked accusative. Similarly, if some type of nominal on the hierarchy is marked with ergative case, then all types of nominals to the right are also expected to be marked ergative. See Legate (2014) for discussion and analysis of a range of split systems, and evidence that this is a universal tendency rather than an absolute.

Croft (2003: 130) analyses the hierarchy in (4) as an amalgam of three distinct hierarchies: a person hierarchy (5a), a referentiality hierarchy (5b), and an animacy hierarchy (5c).[4] Given that (4) includes these different components, Croft prefers the term *extended animacy hierarchy*.

(5) a. Person hierarchy: 1st/2nd-person pronoun > 3rd-person pronoun
b. Referentiality hierarchy: pronoun > proper name > common noun
c. Animacy hierarchy: human > animate > inanimate

Other factors such as topicality, discourse prominence, and number specification may be incorporated into language-specific hierarchies. For this reason, Macaulay (2009) adopts the term *prominence hierarchy*. Henceforth, we adopt Macaulay's terminology, as it allows us to avoid privileging one factor over all others.

Macaulay (2009) further observes that prominence hierarchies such as (4) have been used to describe two very different kinds of nominal ranking, which she calls *scalar* and *relative*. We focus here exclusively on relative ranking, which "requires an evaluation of the relative ranking of two arguments against a scale" (Macaulay 2009: 384). Inverse systems exemplify relative ranking in the following sense: if the subject is higher on the prominence hierarchy than the object, then direct morphology is required; if the rankings are reversed, then inverse morphology is required. In the remainder of this chapter, we focus on issues that arise in the application of prominence hierarchies to inverse systems.

The most widely studied inverse systems are found in languages of the Algonquian family. The prominence hierarchy relevant for these languages ranks nominals based on person, animacy, and/or obviation. As Macaulay (2009) observes, there is variation both within and among languages in the relative ranking of first and second person, i.e., speech act participants (SAPs), but they consistently rank above third-person nominals. Moreover, third-person nominals are subdivided by animacy and/or obviation, with animate nominals consistently outranking inanimate ones and proximate nominals consistently outranking obviative ones. A second source of variation arises because languages differ in whether all nominals or only animate ones are specified for obviation. The prominence hierarchy for Menominee (Macaulay 2009: 383) is representative:[5]

(6) SAP > 3rd animate proximate > 3rd animate obviative > 3rd inanimate

While there is no doubt that such hierarchies have proven to be a useful descriptive tool, it is less obvious that they constitute a viable theoretical construct. Certainly, the fact that different languages require different prominence hierarchies to account for their direct/inverse marking properties minimally suggests that the hierarchy is not fixed by Universal Grammar (cf. Newmeyer 2002), although variation is nevertheless constrained. There are also a growing number of theoretical treatments that develop analyses of direct/inverse marking without explicit appeal to prominence hierarchies (e.g., Brittain 1999; McGinnis 1999; Bruening 2005; Oxford 2017; Lewis 2019). Implicit (or sometimes explicit) in such treatments is the assumption that prominence hierarchies are epiphenomenal.

2.2. What Is Inverse?

It is commonly assumed that all human languages distinguish between a system of thematic roles (aka theta roles) and a system of grammatical relations. However, languages vary according to how these two systems relate to each other. In many Indo-European languages, we observe the possibility for isomorphic or non-isomorphic mappings between the two systems (Williams 2003). In an isomorphic mapping, the argument with the highest thematic role (i.e., agent) is mapped onto the highest grammatical relation (i.e., subject): in other words, the agent becomes the grammatical subject. In a non-isomorphic mapping, a lower argument is mapped onto the highest grammatical relation, and typically the highest argument is suppressed (although it is sometimes optionally realized as an adjunct). This is the classic distinction between active and passive voice, illustrated in (7).

(7) A predicate-based active/passive system

a. Active voice (isomorphic mapping)

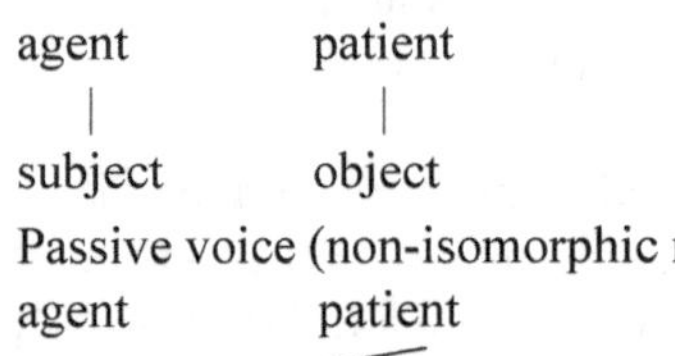

b. Passive voice (non-isomorphic mapping)

agent patient

subject

Inverse has sometimes been described as another instance of passive (LeSourd 1976; Rhodes 1976; 1990; Jolley 1982; Klaiman 1991; Givón 1994; McLean 2001). However, the logic of the inverse is different from that of the passive. Specifically, inverse systems are characterized by morphology that reflects the relative prominence of arguments according to the prominence hierarchy rather than a hierarchy of thematic roles. Hence, the grammatical relations are not aligned with the arguments based on their thematic/semantic relation to the predicate, but instead they are aligned with properties of the nominal arguments themselves. For example, if the agent is first or second person and the patient is third person, a direct mapping will map the higher-ranked argument (first/second person) onto the higher position (subject) and the lower-ranked argument (third person) onto the lower position (object). In contrast, an inverse mapping will map the lower-ranked argument onto the higher position and the higher-ranked argument onto the lower position. This is schematized in (8).

(8) An argument-based inverse system

a. Direct (isomorphic mapping)

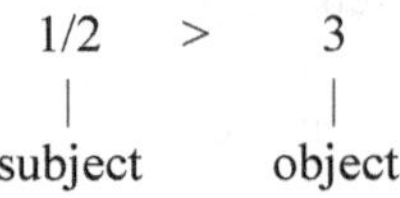

b. Inverse (non-isomorphic mapping)

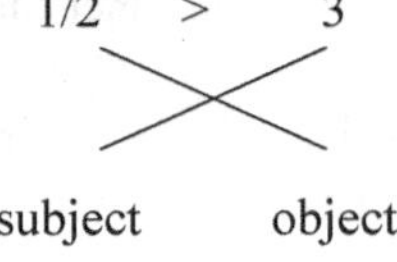

There are (at least) two key aspects along which a predicate-based active/passive system differs from an argument-based direct/inverse system.

First, the active/passive system is not symmetrical, in that the core property of passives is the suppression of the external argument, thus deriving an INTRANSITIVE predicate. Crucially, the agent argument is not mapped onto the lower grammatical role (object); rather, if it is expressed at all, it is realized as an optional adjunct. As a consequence, passivization is not dependent on syntactic transitivity: passivization of intransitive predicates is possible and manifests itself in the form of impersonal passives. This differs from an inverse system, which is always symmetrical in that both direct and inverse predicates are transitive. Hence, inverse is dependent on transitivity: only transitive constructions participate in the inverse system.[6]

The second key difference between active/passive systems and direct/inverse systems has to do with the range of variation we might expect. Given the logic of the predicate-based active/passive system, we expect variation also to be predicate-based. Specifically, the sources of variation concern, on the one hand, whether passivization of intransitive (unergative) predicates is allowed (yes for German, no for English, for example). On the other hand, languages may differ in what type of thematic roles may participate in the passive construction. For example, not all languages allow benefactive arguments to be promoted to subject via passivization.[7]

In contrast, the argument-based direct/inverse systems allow for a greater – and different – range of variation, relating to variation in the deployment of the prominence hierarchy. In §3 we explore some of the variation associated with inverse systems within and across the languages of North America. For example, as noted in the introduction to this chapter, every language in which the inverse system applies to interactions between two third-person arguments has some way of distinguishing between them, e.g., animacy or obviation. However, the thematic role assigned by the predicate is never a consideration in inverse systems, as it is in active/passive systems.[8] Other factors that seem to be irrelevant, at least for the languages under consideration, include mass/count distinctions and masculine/feminine gender distinctions. Whether there is a principled reason for the insensitivity to these properties is beyond the scope of this chapter.

3. Empirical Variation

In this section, we discuss three types of cross-linguistic variation attested in the realization of direct/inverse marking: (i) differences in the contents of the prominence hierarchy that is required to identify the set of nominals to which the direct/inverse system applies (§3.1), (ii) differences in the morphological expression of direct/inverse marking on the verb (§3.2), and (iii) differences in the syntactic structures associated with direct/inverse marking (§3.3).

3.1. Variation in the Hierarchy

We begin by exploring the cross-linguistic variation in the prominence hierarchies that identify the set of nominals that are subject to direct/inverse marking and their relative ranking in the Indigenous languages of North America. Note that in some of these languages, additional variations of these hierarchies are required to describe the relative ranking of nominals for purposes of verb agreement. As our focus in this chapter is on inverse systems, we omit discussion of these language-internal variants.[9] We observe that in all cases, the prominence hierarchy involves distinctions of person and/or animacy and/or obviation. We consider each of these kinds of distinctions in turn.

With respect to person, inverse systems can be broadly divided into three groups: (i) those that apply to all persons, e.g., Blackfoot, Menominee, Cree, Fox, and other Algonquian languages; (ii) those that apply only to third person, e.g., Ktunaxa (isolate), Navajo (Athapaskan), Cherokee (Iroquoian), and Tzotzil (Mayan); and (iii) those that apply only to local (first and second) persons, e.g., Nez Perce (Sahaptian) and Sierra Popoluca (Mixe-Zoquean). Looking specifically at interactions involving local persons, the inverse systems considered here may be subdivided into three subgroups: those that rank first and second persons equally, those that rank first person higher than second person, and those where number plays a role in determining the relative ranking of first and second persons. The first two subgroups represent the most commonly attested rankings of local persons. The last results in a rare exception.

Macaulay (2009) offers a thorough review of the evidence that substantiates the view first espoused by Bloomfield (1962) and Hockett (1966) that local persons are equally ranked in Menominee, and most other members of the Algonquian family, including Cree and Mi'kmaq. Blackfoot, whose direct/inverse marking appears to reflect a ranking of 1 > 2, constitutes a notable exception to this pattern within the Algonquian family (for discussion, see Macaulay 2009; Bliss et al. 2014). The ranking 1 > 2 is also attested in the Sahaptian languages, Sahaptin and Nez Perce (Zúñiga 2006), and in the Kiowa-Tanoan language, Arizona Tewa (Klaiman 1992). Macaulay (1992) demonstrates that Karuk (Hokan) has a more complex hierarchy in which the relative ranking of local persons depends on whether the second-person nominal is singular or plural: 2pl > 1 > 2sg. This last pattern constitutes an exception to the universal tendency for first person to be ranked at least as high as second person.

A broader range of variation can be found in interactions involving third-person nominals, due to the fact that this class of nominals can be further subdivided on the basis of semantic distinctions (animacy) and/or pragmatic distinctions (obviation or discourse prominence).[10] Not surprisingly, both types of properties play a role in languages where direct/inverse marking is restricted to third person, such as Ktunaxa and Navajo. In these languages, pragmatic properties come into consideration only in clauses involving nominals that have the same ranking on the animacy hierarchy (Willie 1991; 2000; Dryer 1994). On the other hand, neither of these properties is relevant for Kiowa, where direct/inverse marking applies only to interactions between a local person and a third-person nominal. Table 8.1 summarizes the attested options.[11]

Table 8.1 Hierarchies Describing Inverse Systems in North American Languages

Person Specification of Arguments That Participate in Inverse System	*Full Hierarchy*	*Language (Family)*	*Sources*
First, second, and third	1/2 > 3prox.anim > 3obv.anim > 3inan	Menominee, Fox, Plains Cree (Algonquian)	Bloomfield (1962: 145), Wolfart (1973), Dahlstrom (1991), as cited in Aissen (1997: 715 footnote 3)
	1/2 > 3	Kiowa (Kiowa-Tanoan), Huastec (Mayan), Jitotoltec (Mixe-Zoquean)	Zavala (1994; 2011), Zúñiga (2006)
First, second, and third	1 > 2 > 3prox.anim > 3obv.anim > 3inan	Blackfoot (Algonquian)	Bliss (2005), Bliss et al. (2014)
	1 > 2 > 3prox > 3obv	Sahaptin (Sahaptian)	Rude (1994), cited in Fadden (2000), Zúñiga (2006)
	1 > 2 > 3	Arizona Tewa (Kiowa-Tanoan)	Klaiman (1992)
First, second, and third	2pl > 1 > 2sg > 3	Karuk (isolate)	Macaulay (2009)
First and second only	1>2	Nez Perce (Sahaptian), Sierra Popoluca and other Gulf Zoquean languages (Mixe-Zoquean)	Zúñiga (2006), Boudreault (2017)
Third only	3prox > 3obv	Ktunaxa (Isolate)	Dryer (1994)
	3prox > 3obv > 3inan	Navajo (Athapaskan)	Willie (1991; 2000)
	human > non-human	Cherokee (Iroquoian)	Scancarelli (1986),
	anim > inan	Columbian, Upper Chehalis (Salish)[12]	Kinkade (1989)

3.2. Morphological Variation

Having identified the types of nominals that trigger direct/inverse marking, we now turn to its morphological expression. Klaiman (1992) asserts that all the North American languages that have inverse systems are head-marking languages. Head-marking languages are those in which verbs are inflected to agree with their arguments, while nouns lack case marking or other markers of grammatical function. Consequently, it is unsurprising that that direct/inverse marking appears on verbs rather than nouns in these languages. The languages differ in the details of verbal marking and can be grouped into two patterns. On the one hand, the verb may have a dedicated set of direct/inverse markers combining with agreement affixes that are insensitive to grammatical function. On the other hand, the verb may have complex agreement markers whose form depends on the φ-features (i.e., person, number, and gender features) and relative prominence of the external and internal arguments.

Algonquian languages illustrate the first pattern: they have overt direct and inverse suffixes, which appear immediately after the transitive verb stem, as well as person agreement prefixes (or proclitics) and number agreement suffixes.

The form of the direct/inverse markers in these languages depends on clause type and on the person, animacy, and obviation status of the external and internal arguments. For the purpose of illustration, consider Table 8.2, which lists the different paradigms for the direct/inverse markers of the Algonquian languages, Blackfoot, and Nishnaabemwin (aka Ojibwe). In the leftmost column, we have indicated the person specification of the two arguments that determine direct/inverse marking, with the number to the left of the colon specifying the person of the subject (and its obviation status if both arguments are third person), and the number to the right of the colon specifying the person of the object (and its obviation status if both arguments are third person).

Cherokee illustrates the second pattern: in this language, verbs have a single pronominal person prefix that indicates the person and number of both the subject and object. When both of these arguments are third person, the form of the pronominal prefix depends primarily on their relative animacy (9). However, if both arguments refer to individuals that have the same animacy status, then syntactic or pragmatic factors come into play. For example, if both arguments are human, and one is questioned or relativized, this will determine the form of the prefix (10). See Scancarelli (1986) for detailed discussion.[13]

Table 8.2 Direct/Inverse Marking on Transitive Animate Verbs in Two Algonquian Languages

	Blackfoot		Nishnaabemwin	
	INDEPENDENT	*CONJUNCT*	*INDEPENDENT*	*CONJUNCT*
1/2 : 3	*-aa*	*-aa*	*-aa*	0 (null)
3 : 1	*-ok*	*-yii*	*-igw*	*-i*
3 : 2	*-ok*	*-yii*	*-igw*	*-iN*
1 : 2	*-o*	*-o*	*-iN*	*-iN*
2 : 1	*-oki*	*-ok-i*	*-i*	*-i*
3PROX : 3OBV	*-yii*	*-aa*	*-aa*	*-aa*
3OBV : 3PROX	*-ok*	*-yii*	*-igw*	*-igw*

Source: Adapted from Bliss, Ritter, and Wiltschko (2014). Nishnaabemwin data from Valentine (2001: 270, 277). Blackfoot data from our own field notes. See also Frantz (2017).

(9) a. Ca:n ki:hl **a:**-hyvthe
John dog **3SG./3SG.DIR**-kicks
'John is kicking the dog.'

b. So:kwili Ca:n **u:**-hyvthe
horse John **3SG./3SG.INV**-kicks
'The horse is kicking John.'

(Adapted from Scancarelli 1986: 225 (3a,b))

(10) a. Ka:kw **k**-v:hniha Ca:ni?
who **3SG/3SG.DIR**-hits John
'Who is John hitting?'

b. Ka:kw **u:w**-a:hniha Ca:ni?[14]
who **3SG/3SG.INV**-hits John
'Who is hitting John?'

(Adapted from Scancarelli 1986: 225 (4))

Note that Klaiman's (1992) generalization regarding the correlation between head-marking and direct/inverse marking is not quite correct, as direct/inverse marking is also found in Sahaptin, a double-marking language with both agreement morphology on its verbs and case morphology on its nominals.[15] According to Zúñiga (2006), Sahaptin has no direct/inverse marking on the verb for mixed interactions involving both a speech act participant and a third-person argument. Rather, the difference between 1/2 : 3 and 3 : 1/2 interactions are realized in the case morphology on the third-person nominal and the form of the third-person agreement on the verb. For clauses with a first- or second-person subject and a third-person object, the verb has the third-person object prefix *á-*, and the object nominal bears objective case – obligatorily for human objects, and optional otherwise. For clauses with a third-person subject and first- or second-person object, the subject is overtly marked with the case marker *-nɨm*, which Zúñiga calls the *inverse ergative* suffix, and the verb is marked with the third-person subject prefix *i-*. The form of the first- or second-person pronominal argument is invariant. In both cases, it is realized as an enclitic on the first word of the clause, as shown in (11).

(11) a. Ín=aš á-tuxnana yáamaš-na
1SG.NOM=1SG 3O-shot mule.deer-OBJ
'I shot a mule deer.'

(Adapted from Zúñiga 2006: 149 (141a))[16]

b. ɨwínš-nɨm=naš i-wyánawi-yawan-a
man-INV.ERG=1SG 3SG.S/A-arrive-DIRTV-PST
'The man came to me (my place).'

(Adapted from Zúñiga 2006: 150 (142b))

In Sahaptin transitive clauses involving two third-person arguments, the case on the third-person nominals and the verbal prefixes reflect the relative discourse prominence of the subject and object. If the subject is proximate and the object is obviative, the former is unmarked for case while the latter is marked with an objective case suffix, and the verb agrees with the subject. However, if the subject is obviative and the object is proximate, the former is marked with the case marker *-in*, which Zúñiga calls the *obviative ergative* suffix, and the verb bears the inverse prefix *pá-*, in place of subject agreement, as shown in (12).

(12) a. ɨwínš i-tuxnana yáamaš-na
man 3SG.S/A-shot mule.deer-OBJ
'The man$_{prox}$ shot a mule deer$_{obv}$.'

b. ɨwínš-in pá-tuxnana yáamaš-na
man-OBV.ERG 3INV-shot mule.deer-OBJ
'The man$_{obv}$ shot a mule deer$_{prox}$.'

(Adapted from Zúñiga 2006: 150 (143))

Finally, in Sahaptin transitive clauses with both a first- and second-person argument, the nature of the morphological expression depends on which speech act participant is the subject and which is the object, and on their number specifications. Significantly, when both are singular, the morphological markers provide clear evidence for the ranking 1 > 2 in this language. As illustrated in (13), when the first-person singular argument is the subject and the second-person singular argument is the object, there is a single portmanteau enclitic whose interpretation is exactly 1SG:2SG. However, when the roles are reversed, the enclitic is specified as second-person singular, and the verb bears the same inverse prefix *pá-* that appears in 3OBV:3PROX clauses.

(13) a. Áw=maš twána-ta
now=1SG.A/2SG.O follow-FUT
'I shall follow you, now.'

b. Níipt=nam pá- ni-ta
two=2SG INV-give-FUT
'You$_{SG}$ will give me two.'
(Adapted from Zúñiga 2006: 151 (144 a, d))

To summarize, inverse systems are most commonly realized on the verb, either in the form of different agreement markers for different combinations of arguments, or in the form of dedicated direct/inverse marking in combination with agreement markers whose form reflects person and/or number, but not grammatical function. Alternatively, we have seen that different nominal case markers can serve this purpose, sometimes in combination with inverse marking on the verb. This survey of different ways of realizing direct/inverse morphology also indicates that languages can be divided into two groups – those that overtly mark both direct and inverse clauses, and those that overtly mark only the inverse.

3.3. Syntactic Variation

What types of syntactic structures can host direct/inverse marking? As discussed in §2, inverse is by definition a phenomenon that is restricted to transitive predications; it requires clauses with (at least) two arguments. Moreover, given the role of the prominence hierarchy in determining whether a given construction is direct or inverse, the two arguments involved must have distinct phi-features (or distinct indices, when both arguments are third person); the predication cannot be reflexive. Beyond these restrictions, there is no a priori reason why a range of different clause types cannot be host to direct/inverse marking; this type of syntactic variation is the focus of this subsection.

In the literature on the inverse, the descriptions and examples tend to be restricted to matrix declarative clauses, and our discussion here reflects this gap; rather than developing any typological generalizations, we simply point to some examples that reflect the range of syntactic variation in the inverse systems of North American languages. We consider two types of variation: (i) matrix versus subordinate clauses, and (ii) illocutionary force, e.g., whether the clause is declarative, interrogative, or imperative.

With respect to the distinction between matrix and subordinate clauses, Algonquian languages encode this distinction via inflectional paradigms typically referred to as *independent* (for matrix clauses) and *conjunct* (for subordinate clauses). As illustrated in Table 8.2, the inverse is found in both independent and conjunct clauses, but with different distributions of the morphological exponents used to mark direct and inverse for each. Table 8.2 highlights two Algonquian languages – Blackfoot and Nishnaabemwin – but to the best of our knowledge, the general pattern of direct and inverse morphemes showing different distributions in independent and conjunct clauses dates back to Proto-Algonquian and extends across the Algonquian language family (Oxford 2014). Like the Algonquian pattern, Olutec (Mixe-Zoquean) uses a different set of inverse markers in matrix and subordinate clauses (Zavala 2007). Another language in which the inverse is found in both matrix and subordinate clauses is Navajo, but unlike the Algonquian languages, the same morphology (direct *yi-* and inverse *bi-*) is used across both types of clauses (Willie 2000). We are not aware of any languages that restrict the inverse to either matrix or subordinate clauses only.

Regarding illocutionary force, again, discussions of the distribution of the inverse are limited; the majority of examples are of declarative clauses. To the best of our knowledge, direct and inverse extends across the entire paradigm of transitive clauses with animate arguments (TA verbs) in Algonquian. Goddard (1994) documents the entire inflectional inventory for the Algonquian language Fox and includes direct and inverse forms for all clause types, including declarative, interrogative, and imperative forms. A notable exception to the general practice of only describing declarative clauses is Macaulay's (1992) discussion of Karuk; she demonstrates that *-ap*, the morpheme she proposes to be an inverse marker, shows variable distribution across positive declarative, negative declarative, and optative (or imperative) clauses. (She does not discuss interrogative clauses explicitly but provides examples of direct interrogative clauses. It is unclear whether the inverse can also appear in interrogative clauses.) Klaiman (1992) notes that the morphology that signals direct and inverse in Arizona Tewa is found on declarative transitive clauses, suggesting that it is not found on interrogative or imperative clauses.

In short, within the range of logical possibilities, there appears to be some variation across languages of North America with respect to the types of clauses that can host inverse constructions. However, the empirical generalizations are not yet well established, as the question of syntactic variation in inverse systems remains largely under-documented.

4. Analytical Variation

The goal of this section is to outline the types of analyses that have been developed for inverse systems of North America. Our aim is neither to reconcile these different analyses nor to comprehensively assess their respective merits and weaknesses. Rather, we describe the types of analytical claims that have been made about inverse systems of North American languages, with a view to highlighting the range of variation. We draw inspiration from Oxford (2014, Chapter 3), who provides a comprehensive review of analytical approaches to Algonquian inverse systems, but our classification schema differs from Oxford's to some degree. Specifically, we classify the approaches as follows: morphological analyses (§4.1), movement analyses (§4.2), case analyses, (§4.3), and agreement analyses (§4.4). We describe each in turn here.

4.1. Morphological Analyses

We define morphological analyses as those that rely exclusively on principles and mechanisms of morphology without referring to any syntactic machinery, such as movement, agreement, or case. Aissen's (1997; 1999) hierarchical alignment approach is one such example. For Aissen, direct and inverse morphemes are of a particular morphological category, *direction*, and they function to signal the alignment or misalignment between two hierarchies: a prominence hierarchy (referred to by Aissen as a *participant hierarchy*), and a relational hierarchy, which ranks participants in an utterance according to their grammatical roles (subject > object). Aissen's analysis is situated within an Optimality Theoretic framework; hierarchical alignment constraints govern the appearance of direct and inverse morphemes. When the two hierarchies are aligned, a direct morpheme is used, and when the two hierarchies are reversed, an inverse morpheme is used. Blain (1997) and Fabri (1996) develop similar analyses for the Plains Cree inverse system. Whereas Blain stipulates alignment conditions that govern the distribution of direct and inverse markers, Fabri develops a feature-based analysis under which the direct and inverse morphemes undergo early insertion based on the alignment of a prominence hierarchy and argument structure. Other more recent works that have adopted a variant of the hierarchical alignment approach include Wolvengrey (2005) and Zúñiga (2006). As noted by Oxford (2014), these types of approaches treat the inverse as a type of derivative of the 'switch' in alignment, and most of them assume the prominence hierarchy to be a grammatical primitive.

4.2. Movement and Role Reversal Analyses

Whether the inverse involves syntactic movement – or the reversal of subject and object roles or positions – varies from language to language. Although this itself is a matter of empirical rather than analytical variation, we have included this discussion here, as the argumentation and analyses used to establish whether a given language's inverse system involves movement or not vary widely. In particular, while some accounts use syntactic diagnostics to demonstrate that the inverse system of a particular language does or does not involve movement (e.g., Bruening 2001; 2009 for Passamaquoddy; Bliss 2013 for Blackfoot; Bliss et al. 2014 for Blackfoot and Nishnaabemwin; Hamilton 2015 for Mig'maq), other accounts simply assume movement (or a lack thereof) either for a particular language or for a group of languages with inverse systems. For instance, as noted in §2.2., there have been numerous attempts to analyze the inverse as a type of passive construction, in which the object moves to a position above the subject (e.g., LeSourd 1976 for Fox; Jolley 1982 and McLean 2001 for Plains Cree). Recall, however, that the inverse differs from canonical passives in that it is fundamentally transitive. An alternative account that retains the insight that the object switches positions with the subject in the inverse is what might be deemed the "grammatical role reversal" account (e.g., Rhodes 1976; 1994; Perlmutter & Rhodes 1988). Under this type of analysis, both direct and inverse constructions are transitive, but the grammatical roles of the participants are switched in the inverse (i.e., the subject becomes the object, and the object becomes the subject). Rhodes (1994) points to a variety of subject/object asymmetries in the Ottawa dialect of Ojibwe that are reversed in the inverse as a way to argue that syntactic role reversal must be involved (See, however, McGinnis 1999 for a morphological account of the same types of data.)

A variant of the role reversal analysis is the A-movement analysis proposed by Bruening (2001) for Passamaquoddy and assumed for other languages (e.g., Bliss 2005 for Blackfoot; Bianchi 2006 for Plains Cree and other languages with inverse; Quinn 2006 for Penobscot). Under this type of analysis, both the subject and the object are generated in theta positions and, when the verb is marked inverse, the object moves to a higher A-position where it scopes over the subject. This account holds promise for some languages, in which c-command relations are reversed in the inverse, but for other languages, the c-command facts suggest that an alternative account is warranted. (See Lochbihler 2008, who argues that the movement analysis alone cannot capture the morphological richness of Ojibwe's inverse.)

4.3. Case Analyses

We define case analyses as those that treat the inverse as functioning analogously to case in other languages, regardless of whether or not it is analyzed as an actual manifestation of case. For example, Déchaine and Reinholtz (1997; 2008) propose that direct and inverse verbs in Plains Cree reflect different organizational patterns for arguments: the direct is associated with nominative/accusative alignment, and the inverse is associated with ergative/absolutive alignment. Others have observed ergative-type patterns in Algonquian (see Oxford 2014, Chapter 7 and references therein) but argue that they are related to the distribution of agreement morphology across transitive and intransitive clauses rather than to the inverse per se. Fabri (1996), meanwhile, develops a morphological analysis for Plains Cree (see §4.1) but suggests that the inverse fulfills the same *linking* functions as case does in other languages: it signals which arguments are associated with which grammatical roles (see Campana 1996, who draws a similar analogy).

Another way in which inverse has been associated with case is in relation to the Person Case Constraint (PCC). The PCC restricts combinations of persons within certain syntactic domains; it is often used to account for the distribution of clitics in accusative-dative pairs in Romance languages (e.g., Bonet 1991). Both Bianchi (2006) and Lochbihler (2007) draw comparisons between PCC effects in Romance and inverse systems in Algonquian, suggesting that the two are derived from the same underlying grammatical principle but differ in their surface manifestations. Quinn (2006) similarly suggests that the inverse in Penobscot matrix clauses can be seen as repair strategy for PCC violations. Others who have noted similarities between the PCC and the inverse include Haspelmath (2004), Anagnostopoulou (2005), Bianchi (2006), and Béjar and Rezac (2009).

4.4. Agreement Analyses

Many researchers have proposed that (at least some) direct and inverse markers are in fact agreement morphemes that signal a syntactic relationship between the verb and its arguments (e.g., Anderson 1992; Halle & Marantz 1993; and Steele 1995 for Potawatomi; Brittain 1999; 2001 for Western Naskapi; Lochbihler 2008; 2012; Béjar & Rezac 2009; and McGinnis 1999 for Ojibwe; Bliss et al. 2014 for Blackfoot; Oxford 2014; 2015 for (Proto-)Algonquian; Hamilton 2015 for Mig'maq). The fine details of these analyses vary, in part due to theory-internal assumptions, but also most likely because the morphology associated with inverse systems varies from language to language. Accordingly, the analyses cannot all be reduced to a single account; the data are too diverse. In what follows, we highlight some of the points of variation in the agreement analyses that have been proposed.

One way in which agreement analyses vary is in terms of which arguments are said to be agreed with. Halle and Marantz (1993), for example, claim that agreement in Potawatomi is always with the non-obviative argument, i.e., the subject with direct verbs and the object with inverse verbs. Brittain (1999; 2001) makes a similar claim, stating that direct morphemes in Western Naskapi agree with the subject, whereas inverse morphemes agree with the object. Conversely, McGinnis (1999) proposes that some of the suffixes typically labeled as direct are object agreement markers, whereas the suffixes typically labeled as inverse are subject agreement. An alternative view is adopted by Béjar and Rezac (2009), who propose that direct and inverse morphemes in Ojibwe agree with both the subject and object via Cyclic Agree. This is a syntactic mechanism whereby the probe (i.e., the verb) seeks out the object for agreement first, and then the subject (see also Lochbihler 2008; 2012). Oxford (2014; 2015) develops an analysis inspired by that of Béjar and Rezac, but in which agreement is primarily with the object, and the inverse suffix surfaces as an elsewhere case when agreement fails (see also Thivierge 2016). A detailed look at the empirical motivations for these competing analyses is beyond the scope of the chapter; we refer interested readers to the sources cited here.

A second point of variation in agreement-based analyses for inverse systems concerns the locus of the direct and inverse morphology. As noted in §3.3, the direct and inverse morphemes of Algonquian languages are suffixes on the verb. However, if one adopts a strictly syntactic view of morphology, the question arises as to the syntactic category of these morphological markers. That is, the syntactic category of a morpheme cannot be straightforwardly determined on the basis of its morphological content and position. Indeed, direct and inverse suffixes have been argued to associate with different syntactic positions. For instance, Lochbihler (2008; 2012), Oxford (2014; 2015), and Hamilton (2015) all associate direct/inverse morphology with *v* or Voice, a functional layer typically assumed to be located immediately above the VP. Brittain (1999) and Bruening (2009), on the other hand, suggest that the direct and inverse morphemes are located higher in the clause, namely in the inflectional layer (Agr or T). Bliss (2013), meanwhile, proposes that direct and inverse morphemes are located in the aspectual layer sandwiched between *v*/Voice and INFL. (See also Bliss et al. 2014, who split the morphemes across *v*/Voice and the aspectual layer.) Empirical support for these analyses varies from morpheme order and morphophonological patterns to restrictions on nominalization and other syntactic properties. Notably, these analyses were developed for different Algonquian languages. Hence, given the empirical variation we have discussed in §3, it is probably not the case that one account is correct and the others are wrong. What is more likely is that they reflect the diversity of empirical phenomena.

4.5. Summary

A number of different types of analyses have been proposed for inverse systems in North American languages. We suggest that, while some of the variation between these analyses is due to differences in theoretical assumptions and analytical argumentation, some of it is also due to variation in terms of the empirical facts: inverse systems do not all behave the same across languages, and therefore should not be subject to the same treatment. As a final case in point, we would like to draw attention to the existence of hybrid-type analyses that acknowledge this heterogeneity by postulating variation within the system, either in a single language or across languages (e.g., Brittain 1999; 2001; Bliss et al. 2014; Hamilton 2015). These analyses speak to the diversity of phenomena that are captured under the umbrella of 'inverse'.

Acknowledgments

Thank you to our Blackfoot and Ktunaxa teachers past and present, including Noreen Breaker, Beatrice Bullshields, Rachel Ermineskin, and Violet Birdstone. Thank you also to Henry Davis and Hiroto Uchichara for helpful reviews of an earlier version of this chapter. This work has been supported by a Banting Postdoctoral Fellowship awarded to H. Bliss and a SSHRC Insight Grant awarded to M. Wiltschko.

Further Reading

Dahlstrom, Amy. (2017). Obviation and information structure in Meskwaki. In Macaulay, M. & Noodin, M. (eds.), *Papers of the forty-sixth Algonquian conference*, 39–54. Albany: State University of New York Press.

Hockett, Charles F. 1996. Voice in Algonquian verbs: A suggestion. In Nichols, John D. & Ogg, Arden C. (eds.), *Nikotwâsik iskwâhtêm, pâskihtêpayih! Studies in Honour of H. C. Wolfart*, 257–261. Winnipeg: Algonquian and Iroquoian Linguistics.

Klaiman, Miriam Holly. 1993. The relationship of inverse voice and head-marking in Arizona Tewa and other Tanoan languages. *Studies in Language* 17. 343–370.

Oshima, David Y. 2007. Syntactic direction and obviation as empathy-based phenomena: A typological approach. *Linguistics* 45. 727–763.

Trommer, Jochen. 2003. Direction marking as agreement. In Junghanns, Uwe & Szucsich, Luka (eds.), *Syntactic structures and morphological information*, 317–339. Berlin: Mouton de Gruyter.

Trommer, Jochen. 2006. Direction marking and case in Menominee. In Kulikov, Leonid & Malchukov, Andrej & de Swart, Peter (eds.), *Case, valency and transitivity*, 91–111. Amsterdam: Benjamins.

Wiltschko, Martina. 2008. Person-hierarchy effects without a person-hierarchy. In D'Alessandro, Roberta & Fischer, Susann & Hrafnbjargarson, Gunnar Hrafn (eds.), *Agreement restrictions*, 281–314. Berlin: Mouton de Gruyter.

Wiltschko, Martina & Burton, Strang. 2004. On the sources of person hierarchy effects in Halkomelem Salish. *Canadian Journal of Linguistics* 49. 51–71.

Zavala Maldonado, Roberto. 2000. *Inversion and other topics in the grammar of Olutec (Mixean)*. Eugene: University of Oregon. (Doctoral dissertation.)

Zúñiga, Fernando. 2008. How many hierarchies, really? Evidence from several Algonquian languages. In Richards, Marc & Malchukov, Andrej L. (eds.), *Scales, Linguistische Arbeitsberichte* 86, 277–294. Leipzig: University of Leipzig.

Notes

1. Unless otherwise cited, examples come from the authors' field notes. Our own examples are given in a four-line format in which the top line represents the phonetic and/or orthographic form. Morphophonological processes such as epenthesis, deletion, pitch accent, etc., that are apparent from the top line are not discussed in this chapter. Abbreviations: 1, 2, 3 = first, second, third person, A = subject of transitive verb, ACC(usative), ANIM(ate), APPL(icative), DIR(ect), DIRTV = directive; ERG(ative), FUT(ure), INAN(imate), IND(icative), INV(erse), NOM(inative), O(bject), OBJ(ective Case), OBV(iative), PL(ural), PROX(imate), PST = past, S(ubject of intransitive verb), SG = singular, TA = transitive animate.

2. In some cases, the verb in both direct and inverse is ditransitive, and the alignment is determined by the relation between the subject and indirect object. Since the choice of direct or indirect object does not affect the discussion in this chapter, we abstract away from this detail.
3. An accusative case pattern consists of accusative case-marked direct objects and (default) nominative case-marking elsewhere, i.e., on subjects of transitive and intransitive verbs; an ergative case pattern consists of ergative case-marked subjects of transitive verbs and (default) absolutive case-marking elsewhere, i.e., on direct objects and subjects of intransitive verbs.
4. As Henry Davis (p.c.) observes, the label *referential hierarchy* may be misleading for (5b) because pronouns may not be more referential than other nominals due to the fact that they may serve as bound variables. What Croft intends here is a hierarchy of nominal types.
5. Bliss (2005) demonstrates that in Blackfoot, both morphological animacy and sentience (semantic animacy) play a role in direct/inverse marking.
6. Although transitivity and reference to a prominence hierarchy are two defining properties of inverse systems, neither of these properties are criterial on their own for distinguishing between active/passive and direct/inverse systems. A more nuanced view of how in/transitivity and hierarchies (person vs. thematic) interact may yield a useful crosslinguistic typology of voice phenomena. This is beyond the scope of this chapter, but we thank Henry Davis for pointing us in this direction.
7. For reasons of space, we omit comparison with Austronesian voice systems, which like direct/inverse systems, are widely seen as different realizations of transitive predicates. See Rackowski (2002), Wouk and Ross (2002), and Pearson (2005), among many others, for discussion.
8. Conversely, passive constructions in some languages (e.g., Straits Salish) can be sensitive to prominence hierarchy effects. Thanks to Henry Davis for this observation.
9. For example, Algonquian languages require one hierarchy for person agreement prefixes, another for number agreement suffixes, and a third for direct/inverse marking on verbs. These three prominence hierarchies encode different options for the relative rankings for Speech Act Participants (2 > 1 > . . . vs. 1 > 2 > . . . vs. 1 = 2 > . . ., respectively). See Hockett (1966), McGinnis (2005), and Oxford (2014), among many others, for discussion. Similarly, in the Mixe-Zoquean language Ocotepec, the second-person marker is used in both 1:2 and 2:1 interactions, suggesting a 2 > 1 ranking in this language (Boudreault 2017).
10. Discourse prominence is one of the determinants of obviation, but syntactic position is also a factor; e.g., in possessed nominals, the possessee is always obviative relative to its possessor.
11. It has been claimed that Lummi (Salish) and Nuu-chal-nulth (Wakashan) also have inverse systems. However, on closer inspection, neither language fits our characterization because in both cases, the inverse is best analyzed as a detransitivizing operation (cf. Jelinek & Demers 1983: 168; Whistler 1985 for Nuuchal-nulth). Similarly, although Aissen (1997) finds striking similarities between Algonquian direct clauses and Tzotzil (Mayan) active ones, we exclude Tzotzil from our sample because "the function of the inverse in Algonquian is carried by the passive in Tzotzil" (Aissen 1997: 722).
12. Kinkade (1989) describes what he calls a topical object marker. Following a suggestion by Henry Davis, we consider this as an inverse marker because it (i) appears only on transitive verbs; (ii) is in complementary distribution with the regular object suffix; and (iii) appears when the object is human and the subject is not. We have not included Lushootseed (Salish) in our table because Kinkade (1989: 27) reports that although it has remnants of a topical object marker with these properties, speakers no longer use it. We have also omitted Cowlitz, Quinault, and Tillamook (Salish) from our table because it is unclear whether their topical object markers should be treated as inverse markers due to the fact that there is either no evidence for, or no information on, a prominence hierarchy that determines the distribution this suffix in these languages (Kinkade 1989: 37).
13. Scancarelli (1986) uses the terms *subject focus* and *object focus*, rather than *direct* and *inverse*. Since we analyze these forms as direct and inverse, respectively, we have modified her glosses to ease comparison with other languages considered here.
14. Thank you to Hiroto Uchihara for alerting us to the fact that the *a:-* prefix in (9a) and the *k-* prefix in (10a) are phonologically and lexically conditioned allomorphs of the same morpheme. Uchihara also suggests that the morphemes glossed here as encoding two participants may in fact just encode one, with *a:-/k-* encoding the actor and *u:-* encoding the goal. We have followed the analysis of Scancarelli in the glosses provided here.
15. Double-marking languages are those in which the verb is indexed with agreement expressing features of the arguments, and the arguments have Case reflecting their grammatical relations (Nichols 1986). In our view, proximate and obviative marking on nouns alongside direct and inverse marking on verbs does not qualify as a double-marking system, as proximate and obviative are properties of the nominals and not a reflex of their relation to the predicate. However, the Mixe-Zoquean language Jitotoltec constitutes a second exception to Klaiman's generalization; like Sahaptin, it has an inverse and is a double-marking language (Boudreault 2017; Zavala 2011).

16. The Sahaptin examples in (11a), (11b), and (12) are originally due to Rigsby and Rude (1996), and (13) is due to Rude (1994), who attributes (13a) to Jacobs (1929: 221: 8) and (13b) to Jacobs (1937, 28:22:2, p. 63). The sources differ slightly in the glosses assigned to the different morphemes. We follow Zúñiga in labeling the verbal prefixes as agreement, rather than case markers, Rigsby and Rude (1996: 676 (13)) in labeling the suffix *-yawan* in (11b) as a directive suffix, and Rude (1994) in labeling the prefix *pá-* in (13b) as inverse. In addition, our glosses have been modified to conform to those used elsewhere in this chapter.

References

Aissen, Judith. 1997. On the syntax of obviation. *Language* 75. 451–485.

Aissen, Judith. 1999. Markedness and subject choice in Optimality Theory. *Natural Language & Linguistic Theory* 17(4). 673–711.

Anagnostopoulou, Elena. 2005. Strong and weak person restrictions: A feature checking analysis. In Heggie, Lorie & Ordoñez, Francisco (eds.), *Clitics and affix combinations: theoretical perspectives*, 199–235. Amsterdam: John Benjamins.

Anderson, Stephen R. 1992. *A-morphous morphology*. Cambridge, UK: Cambridge University Press.

Béjar, Susana & Rezac, Milan. 2009. Cyclic agree. *Linguistic Inquiry* 40. 35–73.

Bianchi, Valentina. 2006. On the syntax of personal arguments. *Lingua* 116. 2023–2067.

Blain, Eleanor. 1997. *Wh-constructions in Nêhiyawêwin (Plains Cree)*. Vancouver: University of British Columbia. (Doctoral dissertation.)

Bliss, Heather & Ritter, Elizabeth & Wiltschko, Martina. 2014. A comparison of theme marking in Blackfoot and Nishnaabemwin. In Valentine, J. Randolph & Macaulay, M. (eds.), *Papers of the 42nd Algonquian Conference*. Albany: SUNY Press.

Bliss, Heather. 2005. *Formalizing point-of-view: The role of sentience in Blackfoot's direct/inverse*. University of Calgary. (MA thesis.)

Bliss, Heather. 2013. *The Blackfoot configurationality conspiracy: Parallels and differences in clausal and nominal structures*. Vancouver: University of British Columbia. (Doctoral dissertation.)

Bloomfield, Leonard. 1962. *The Menomini language*. New Haven, CT: Yale University Press.

Bonet, Eulàlia. 1991. *Morphology after syntax: Pronominal clitics in romance*. Cambridge, MA: MIT. (Doctoral dissertation.)

Boudreault, Lynda. 2017. Introduction, Zoquean narratives. Texts in the *indigenous* languages of the Americas 1. *International Journal of American Linguistics* 83. S1–S23.

Brittain, Julie. 1999. A reanalysis of transitive animate theme signs as object agreement: Evidence from Western Naskapi. In Pentland, David H. (ed.), *Papers of the 30th Algonquian Conference*, 34–46. Winnipeg: University of Manitoba.

Brittain, Julie. 2001. *The morphosyntax of the Algonquian conjunct verb: A minimalist approach*. New York: Garland.

Bruening, Benjamin. 2001. *Syntax at the edge: Cross-clausal phenomena and the syntax of Passamaquoddy*. Cambridge, MA: MIT. (Doctoral dissertation.)

Bruening, Benjamin. 2005. The Algonquian inverse is syntactic: Binding in Passamaquoddy. Manuscript, University of Delaware.

Bruening, Benjamin. 2009. Algonquian languages have A-movement and A-agreement. *Linguistic Inquiry* 40. 427–445.

Campana, Mark. 1996. The conjunct order in Algonquian. *Canadian Journal of Linguistics* 41. 201–234.

Croft, William. 2003. *Typology and universals*. 2nd edn. Cambridge, UK: Cambridge University Press.

Dahlstrom, Amy. 1991. *Plains Cree morphosyntax*. New York: Garland.

Déchaine, Rose-Marie & Reinholtz, Charlotte. 1997. Direct/inverse as case-licensing. In *Third Workshop on the Structure and Constituency of the Languages of the Americas*. Saskatchewan Federated Indian College, Regina.

Déchaine, Rose-Marie & Reinholtz, Charlotte. 2008. Case theory meets linking theory: Algonquian direct/inverse as split case. In *Thirteenth Workshop on the Structure and Constituency of the Languages of the Americas*. Queen's University, Kingston.

Dryer, Matthew S. 1991. Subject and inverse in Kutenai. In Redden, James E. (ed.), *Papers from the American Indian Languages Conferences*, Occasional Papers in Linguistics, 16. 183–202. Carbondale, IL: Dept. of Linguistics.

Dryer, Matthew S. 1994. The discourse function of the Kutenai inverse. In Givón, Talmy (ed.), *Voice and Inversion*, 65–99. Amsterdam: John Benjamins.

Fabri, Ray. 1996. The inverse morphology of Plains Cree (Algonquian). In Booij, Geert and van Marle, Jaap (eds.), *Yearbook of morphology 1995*, 17–41. Dordrecht: Springer.

Fadden, Lorna Marie. 2000. *The inverse continuum*. Burnaby: Simon Fraser University. (MA thesis.)

Frantz, Donald G. 2017. *Blackfoot grammar*. 3rd edn. Toronto: University of Toronto Press.

Givón, Talmy (ed.). 1994. *Voice and inversion*. Amsterdam: John Benjamins.

Goddard, Ives. 1994. *Leonard Bloomfield's Fox lexicon: Critical edition*. Winnipeg: Algonquian and Iroquian Linguistics.

Halle, Morris & Marantz, Alec. 1993. Distributed Morphology and the pieces of inflection. In Hale, Ken & Keyser, S. Jay (eds.), *The view from building 20*, 111–176. Cambridge, MA: MIT Press.

Hamilton, Michael. 2015. *The syntax of Mi'gmaq: A configurational account*. Montreal: McGill University. (Doctoral dissertation.)

Haspelmath, Martin. 2004. Explaining the ditransitive person-role constraint: A usage-based approach. *Constructions* 2. 1–71.

Hockett, Charles F. 1966. What Algonquian is really like. *International Journal of American Linguistics* 32. 59–73.

Jacobs, Melville. 1929. *Northwest Sahaptin texts*. Seattle: University of Washington Press. [*University of Washington Publications in Anthropology* vol. 2, 175–244.]

Jacobs, Melville. 1937. *Northwest Sahaptin texts* (Sahaptin Text). New York: Columbia University Press. [*Columbia University Contributions to Anthropology* vol. 19, part 2.]

Jacques, Guillaume & Antonov, Anton. 2014. Direct/inverse systems. *Language and Linguistics Compass* 8(7). 301–318.

Jelinek, Eloise & Demers, Richard A. 1983. The agent hierarchy and voice in some Coast Salish languages. *International Journal of American Linguistics* 49. 167–185.

Jolley, Catherine A. 1982. On the Plains Cree passive: An analysis of syntactic and lexical rules. In Joseph, B. D. (ed.), *Ohio State University working papers in linguistics* 26, 1–33. Columbus: Ohio State University.

Kinkade, M. Dale. 1989. When patients are topics: Topic maintenance in North American Indian languages. In *Twenty-fourth International Conference on Salish and Neighbouring Languages*, Steilacoom, WA.

Klaiman, Miriam Holly. 1991. *Grammatical voice*. Cambridge, UK: Cambridge University Press.

Klaiman, Miriam Holly. 1992. Inverse languages. *Lingua* 88. 227–261.

Legate, Julie Anne. 2014. Split ergativity based on nominal type. *Lingua* 148. 183–212.

LeSourd, Philip S. 1976. Verb agreement in Fox. In Hankamer, Jorge & Aissen, Judith (eds.), *Harvard Studies in Syntax and Semantics II*, 445–528. Cambridge, MA: Department of Linguistics, Harvard University.

Lewis, Robert E. Jr. 2019. Theme signs in Potawatomi as object agreement and the inverse. In Macaulay, Monica & Noodin, Margaret (eds.), *Papers of the 48th Algonquian Conference*, 123–142. East Lansing: Michigan State University Press.

Lochbihler, Bethany. 2007. The inverse system in Ojibwe: A comparison with the person-case constraint. In Milica Radišić (ed.), *Proceedings of the 2007 annual conference of the Canadian Linguistic Association*. (http://homes.chass.utoronto.ca/~cla-acl/actes2007/actes2007.html)

Lochbihler, Bethany. 2008. Person encoding in the Ojibwe inverse system. In Richards, Marc & Malchukov, Andrej L. (eds.), *Scales, Linguistische Arbeitsberichte* 86, 295–315. Leipzig: University of Leipzig.

Lochbihler, Bethany. 2012. *Aspects of argument licensing*. Montreal: McGill University. (Doctoral dissertation.)

Macaulay, Monica. 1992. Inverse marking in Karuk: The function of the suffix *-ap*. *International Journal of American Linguistics* 58. 182–201.

Macaulay, Monica. 2009. On prominence hierarchies: Evidence from Algonquian. *Linguistic Typology* 13. 357–389.

McGinnis, Martha. 1999. Is there syntactic inversion in Ojibwa? In Bar El, Leora & Déchaine, Rose-Marie & Reinholz, Charlotte (eds.), *Papers from the workshop on structure and constituency in Native American languages*, MIT Occasional Papers in Linguistics 17, 101–118.

McGinnis, Martha. 2005. On markedness asymmetries in person and number. *Language* 81. 699–718.

McLean, Lisa Michelle. 2001. *A passive to inverse reanalysis in Cree*. Winnipeg: University of Manitoba. (MA thesis.)

Newmeyer, Frederick J. 2002. Optimality and functionality: A critique of functionally-based optimality-theoretic syntax. *Natural Language & Linguistic Theory* 20. 43–80.

Nichols, Johanna. 1986. Head-marking and dependent-marking grammar. *Language* 62. 56–119.

Oxford, Will. 2014. *Microparameters of agreement: A diachronic perspective on Algonquian verb inflection*. Toronto: University of Toronto. (Doctoral dissertation.)

Oxford, Will. 2015. Inverse as elsewhere. (Paper presented at the 47th Algonquian Conference. University of Manitoba, Winnipeg.)

Oxford, Will. 2017. Inverse marking as impoverishment. In Kaplan, Aaron et al. (eds.), *Proceedings of the 34th West Coast Conference on Formal Linguistics*, 413–422. Somerville, MA: Cascadilla Proceedings Project.

Pearson, Matthew. 2005. The Malagasy subject/topic as an A′-element. *Natural Language & Linguistic Theory* 23. 381–457.

Perlmutter, David & Rhodes, Richard. 1988. Thematic-syntactic alignments in Ojibwa: Evidence for subject-object reversal. (Paper presented at annual meeting of Linguistics Society of America.)

Quinn, Conor M. 2006. *Referential-access dependency in Penobscot*. Cambridge, MA: Harvard University. (Doctoral dissertation.)

Rackowski, Andrea. 2002. *The structure of Tagalog: Specificity, voice and the distribution of arguments*. Cambridge: MIT. (Doctoral dissertation.)

Rhodes, Richard. 1990. Obviation, inversion, and topic rank in Ojibwa. *Annual Meeting of the Berkeley Linguistics Society* [Online] 16(2). 101–115. Web. 26 July 2017.

Rhodes, Richard. 1994. Agency, inversion, and thematic alignment in Ojibwe. *Annual Meeting of the Berkeley Linguistics Society* [Online] 20(1). 431–446. Web. 26 July 2017

Rhodes, Richard. 1976. *The morphosyntax of the central Ojibwa verb*. Ann Arbor: University of Michigan. (Doctoral dissertation.)

Rigsby, Bruce & Rude, Noel. 1996. Sketch of Sahaptim, a Saptian language. In Goddard, Ives (ed.), *A handbook of North American Indians. Vol 17. Languages*, 666–692. Washington, DC: Smithsonian Institution.

Rude, Noel. 1994. Direct, inverse and passive in Northwest Sahaptin. In Givón, T. (ed.), *Voice and inversion*, 101–120. Amsterdam: John Benjamins.

Scancarelli, Janine. 1986. Pragmatic roles in Cherokee grammar. *Annual Meeting of the Berkeley Linguistics Society* 12. 224–234.

Silverstein, Michael. 1986. Hierarchy of features and ergativity. In Muysken, Pieter & van Riemsdijk, Henk (eds.), *Features and projections*, 163–232. Dordrecht: Foris. (Originally published in Dixon, R. M. W. (ed.). 1976. *Grammatical Categories in Australian Languages*. Canberra: Australian Institutes of Aboriginal Studies.)

Steele, Susan. 1995. Towards a theory of morphological information. *Language* 71. 260–309.

Thivierge, Sigwan. 2016. *Failure to agree in Nishnaabemwin inverse-marking*. Montreal: Concordia University. (Doctoral dissertation.)

Thomason, Lucy G. 2003. *The proximate and obviative contrast in Meskwaki*. Austin: University of Texas. (Doctoral dissertation.)

Valentine, J. Randolph. 2001. *Nishnaabemwin reference grammar*. Toronto: University of Toronto Press.

Whistler, Kenneth W. 1985. Focus, perspective, and inverse person marking in Nootkan. In Nichols, Johanna & Woodbury, Anthony C. (eds.), *Grammar inside and outside the clause*, 227–265. Cambridge, UK: Cambridge University Press.

Williams, Edwin. 2003. *Representation theory*. Cambridge, MA: MIT Press.

Willie, MaryAnn. 1991. *Navajo pronouns and obviation*. Tucson: University of Arizona. (Doctoral dissertation.)

Willie, MaryAnn. 2000. The inverse voice and possessive *yi-/bi-* in Navajo. *International Journal of American Linguistics* 66. 360–382.

Wolfart, H. Christoph. 1973. Plains Cree: A grammatical study. *Transactions of the American Philosophical Society* 63. 1–90.

Wolvengrey, Arok. 2005. Inversion and the absence of grammatical relations. In de Groot, Casper & Hengeveld, Kees (eds.), *Morphosyntactic expression in functional grammar*, 419–446. Berlin: Mouton de Gruyter.

Wouk, Fay & Ross, Malcolm. 2002. *The history and typology of western Austronesian voice systems*. Pacific Linguistics, Research School of Pacific and Asian Studies, the Australian National University.

Zavala Maldonado, Roberto. 1994. Inverse alignment in Huastec. *Funcion* 15/16. 27–81.

Zavala Maldonado, Roberto. 2007. Inversion and obviation in Mesoamerica. In Austin, P. & Simpson, A. (eds.), *Endangered languages*, 267–305. Hamburg: Helmut Buske Verlag.

Zavala Maldonado, Robert. 2011. El jitotolteco: una lengua zoqueana desconocida. (Keynote presentation at the Conference on Indigenous Languages of Latin America VI, October 2011.)

Zúñiga, Fernando. 2006. *Deixis and alignment: Inverse systems in Indigenous languages of the Americas*. Amsterdam: John Benjamins.

9

SWITCH-REFERENCE IN AMERICAN LANGUAGES

A Synthetic Overview

Mark C. Baker and Livia Camargo Souza

1. Introduction

SWITCH-REFERENCE (SR) is a grammatical phenomenon in which one clause is morphologically marked to show whether or not one of its nominal arguments refers to the same entity or entities as a nominal argument of a structurally nearby clause. In the large majority of cases, the nominal arguments in question are the subjects of the clauses involved, in some sense of "subject" to be made precise. Thus the fundamental contrast in switch-reference systems is between SAME SUBJECT (SS) marking and DIFFERENT SUBJECT (DS) marking. (1) shows a canonical pair from Mojave.

(1) Mojave (Yuman)

a. *Nya-isvar-k̲* *i:ma-k.*
when-sing-SS dance-TNS[1]
'When he$_i$ sang, he$_i$ danced.' (The same person did both.)

b. *Nya-isvar-m̲* *i:ma-k.*
when-sing-DS dance-TNS
'When he$_i$ sang, he$_k$ danced.' (Different people did each action)
(Langdon & Munro 1979: 322–323)

The suffixes *-k* and *-m* on the verb 'sing' crucially vary according to whether or not the subjects of the two clauses are interpreted as being the same. These markers are typical in that SR markers are usually outermost affixes or particles on the verb of one of the clauses. SR markers may also express other grammatical notions, such as the temporal or causal relationship between the two clauses, but it is their reference-tracking function that makes them of special interest.

SR phenomena of this sort are found in quite a few North American languages. McKenzie's (2015a) useful survey finds it in some 70+ languages from this region. He shows that the phenomenon is common in the Western United States and adjoining parts of Mexico, but not in other parts of the continent – except perhaps in the Inuit languages of the far North (see §5 in this chapter). SR also qualifies as an areal phenomenon in that it occurs in a wide range of the language families that are represented in this area (Yuman, Muskogean, Uto-Aztecan, Siouan, Kiowa-Tanoan, Pomoan, Yokutsian, etc.) but not in languages from these same families spoken in other regions. SR is by no means unique to this one linguistic area, however. It is also found in several language families of South America, including Quechuan, Jean, Jivaroan, Tukanoan, Takanan, and Panoan languages, to name a few. We include select examples from

Quechuan and Panoan languages in our discussion, for comparative purposes. SR is also found in the Eastern Hemisphere, particularly in New Guinean and Australian languages. Although data from these languages has been important in the literature on SR – especially Roberts's (1987; 1988a; 1988b) studies of Amele and Austin's (1980) survey of SR in Australian languages – they are not included in this discussion, given space restrictions and the focus of this volume. This broader distribution does, however, suggest something significant about the status of SR for general linguistic theory. On the one hand, since the same phenomenon (more or less) is found in different regions of the world, Universal Grammar must naturally allow for it; it cannot be a sui generis phenomenon that arose once as some combination of particular historical factors. On the other hand, the phenomenon is entirely missing in large areas of the world, so Universal Grammar must not require it, either. Furthermore, SR is often pervasive in languages that have it, with reference marking appearing multiple times in almost any page of natural text.

The broad flow of research on SR has been as follows. The first general discussion of SR was Jacobsen's (1967) seminal article from 50 years ago. This work coined the term "switch-reference", brought together material from a variety of languages, and put the topic on the radar of linguists at large. This then became a hot topic for typologists and descriptive linguists in the 1970s and 1980s, as featured in the collection of Haiman and Munro (1983), for example. The first major formal-generative-syntactic theory of SR is that of Finer (1984; 1985), who analyzed it in terms of Chomsky's (1981) government-binding theory as extended by Aoun (1981); for related work, see Broadwell (1990; 1997); Hale (1992 – who builds also on Jeanne 1978, a forerunner to Finer's approach); the minimalist update in Watanabe (2000); and Camacho's (2010) variant built on agreement in case. In the wake of this prominent syntactic analysis, a reaction set in, arguing that SR is more semantic than syntactic. From the semantic viewpoint, SR is primarily concerned with whether or not *events* are closely related, rather than whether subjects are the same or not. Stirling (1993) is the most comprehensive expression of this view, but Mithun (1993) and others are very similar in spirit. The Stirling tradition continues in contemporary work by McKenzie (2012; 2015a; 2015b), who distinguishes SR in adjunct clauses from SR in conjoined clauses and clause chains, claiming that the latter expresses a relationship between (Austinian) situations, not events in the sense of Davidson (1967). Another notable recent contribution is Keine (2013), which takes the further step of saying that most or all SR has the syntactic structure of coordination: SS structures are VP coordinations with a single shared subject, whereas DS clauses are vP/TP coordinations that have two distinct subject positions. Both McKenzie (2015a) and Nonato (2014) dispute this claim, however, McKenzie demonstrating that SR is not inherently tied to any type of connective, and Nonato showing that canonical SS may show up in what is clearly TP coordination. One of the themes that we explore here is that it may be time for the pendulum to swing back from semantic accounts towards the syntactic SR found in embedded clauses.

The rest of this chapter is organized as follows. First we discuss to what extent SR is a syntactic phenomenon or a semantic phenomenon, and indeed whether it is a unified phenomenon in this respect (§2). Then we turn to the important question of what kind of clauses are reference marked in American languages: adjunct clauses, complement clauses, coordinated clauses, even some relative clauses – but not, we claim, nominalized clauses (§3). Then we consider the question of what precisely counts as the subject for same-subject and different-subject marking in various American languages (§4). This is important, because we know that different theoretical principles make use of different senses of subject, so if one can identify what sense(s) of subject are relevant to SR, it could bear on what theoretical principles are at work in SR. Overall, we suggest that there is reason to consider a neo-Finerian syntactic approach, but one that uses principles of agreement and control more than principles of Binding Theory per se.

2. Switch-Reference: How Strict? How Syntactic? How Semantic?

2.1. Arguments for Syntactic SR

As already mentioned, Finer (1984; 1985) presented an analysis of SR that is fundamentally syntactic in nature, attributing it to Binding Theory, the same aspect of linguistic theory that regulates the use of pronouns like *them* and anaphors like *themselves*. One argument that he presented in favor of such a view is that SR marking is obligatory in many languages even when there is no functional pressure to avoid ambiguity. For example, in SR languages like Mojave, Choctaw, and Seri, verbs necessarily agree with their first person subjects. Therefore, in examples like (2a) and (2b), there is no ambiguity as to whether the subjects of the two clauses are coreferential or not: they must be in (2a), and they must not be in (2b). Nevertheless, SS/DS marking is required in (2) as much as it is in (1), where there is potential ambiguity to resolve.

(2) Mojave (Yuman)

a. *ʔinʸeč pap* ***ʔ-əkxi:e-k*** *ʔ-salʸi:-k.*
I potato 1SG-peel-SS 1SG-fry-TNS
'After I peeled the potatoes, I fried them.'

b. *ʔinʸeč pap* ***ʔ-əkxi:e-m*** *Judy-č* ***Ø****-čsalʸi:-k.*
I potato 1SG-peel-DS Judy-NOM 3SG-fry-TNS
'After I peeled the potatoes, Judy fried them.'

(Langdon & Munro 1979: 322; via Finer 1985: 38)

Therefore, if the function of SR is ambiguity reduction, that function has been "grammaticized" here – and grammaticized function is another name for syntax.

Second, Finer points out that SR seems crucially to be marking whether subjects are the same across clauses, not whether topics are the same. This is suggested by an example like (3) from Yavapai (another Yuman language).

(3) Yavapai (Yuman)

*Tokatoka-č Savakyuva u-t-**m**, čikwar-kiñ.*
Tokatoka-NOM Savakyuva see-T-DS laugh-COMPL
'When Tokatoka looked at Savakyuva, he (Savakyuva) laughed.'

(Kendall 1975; via Finer 1985: 37)

Here, the object of the transitive first clause could presumably be the topic (in a suitable context), and it is the same as the only argument of second clause, which is therefore that clause's natural topic. Thus if SS indicated sameness of topic, SS marking should be possible here. Nevertheless, only DS marking can be used. This suggests that the morphology truly is tracking grammatical subjects rather than pragmatic topics (compare also with the Shipibo example in (8b)).

Third, Finer shows that SR depends on a notion of structural (syntactic) closeness, not on, say, linear order. Thus, it is possible in many languages (although not all) for the reference-marked clause to follow the main clause, and SR still works the same way; e.g., see (7). Furthermore, when there are three clauses, the reference marking on the first clause can be determined by either what is the subject of the second clause (the linearly adjacent one), or by what is the subject of the third clause (the nonadjacent one), depending on whether the syntactic embedding structure is [[[S1] S2] S3] or [S1 [[S2] S3]]. This observation has been replicated many times, although it is not always stated in syntactic terms. Gordon (1983) provides a good illustration with the pair of sentences from the Yuman language Maricopa (also known as Piipaash) in (4). In (4a), the DS marking on first clause goes with a syntactic structure in which the first clause is embedded inside the second clause, which in turn is embedded in the third clause ([[[S1] S2] S3]). In contrast, the first clause of example (4b) bears SS marking, indicating a structure in which the first clause is embedded in the third clause, but not in the second clause ([S1 [[S2] S3]]).

(4) Maricopa (Yuman)

a. $[_{S3}\ [_{S2}\ [_{S1}$ *'ayuu* *ny-rav-**m*** $_{S1}]$ *ny-wik-m* $_{S2}]$ *'-wik-pat-k* $_{S3}]$.
   s.t. when.1s-hurt-DS 3s/1o-help-DS 1s-help-again-ASP
   'I helped him [because he helped me [when I was sick]].'

b. $[_{S3}\ [_{S1}$ *'ayuu* *ny-rav-**k*** $_{S1}]$ $[_{S3}\ [_{S2}$ *ny-wik-m* $_{S2}]$ *'-wik-pat-k* $_{S3}]\ _{S3}]$
   s.t. when.1s-hurt-SS 3s/1o-help-DS 1s-help-again-ASP
   'When I was sick, [I helped him [because he helped me]].'

(Gordon 1983)

There are good reasons, then, to treat SR as a syntactic phenomenon, at least in some languages.

In light of facts like these, Finer (1984; 1985) analyzes SR as a binding relation in the sense of Chomsky (1981). Since he assumes that SR relates the subjects of matrix and adjunct clauses, however, the subjects being tracked are not in a c-command relationship. As a result, one subject cannot bind the other directly within Chomskian theory. Finer solves this problem by proposing that it is really the complementizers of the clauses that establish the binding relations: they can be pronominal or anaphoric. In each clause, the subject establishes a relation with the Agr (T) head, which in turn establishes a relation with the complementizer (C) of the clause. The gist of his theory is sketched in (5), with some updates to express it in terms of current generative views about basic clause structure. Once each complementizer is coindexed with its local subject via T, principle A of the Binding Theory forces the lower complementizer to assume anaphoric form (SS) if the subjects are the same, and principle B forces it to assume pronominal form (DS) if the subjects are different. In other words, Finer's SR system achieves indirect binding relations between subjects via their local syntactic relations with functional elements in each clause.

(5)

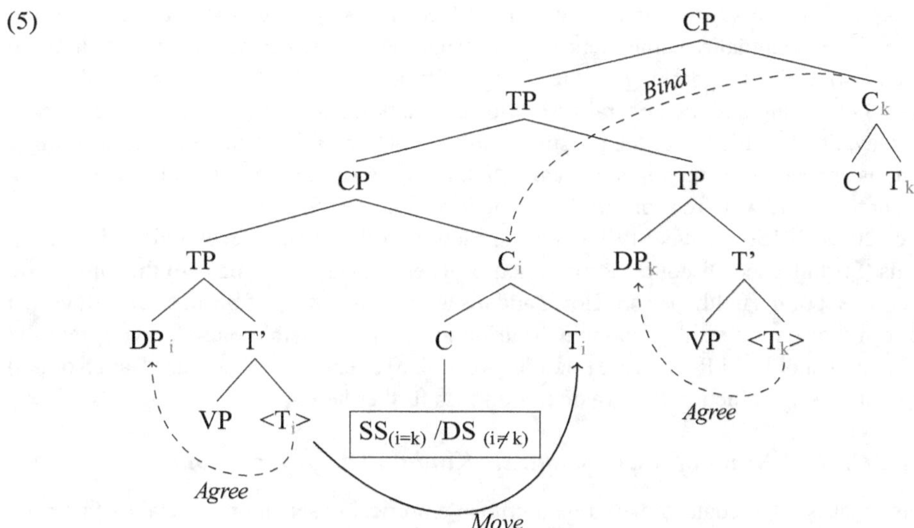

2.2. *Arguments for Semantic SR*

There are also, however, considerations that point away from a predominately syntactic account of SR. Many of these are gathered together by Stirling (1993), who criticizes Finer's approach and discusses many instances of "noncanonical" SR. Her views are inspired by Givón's (1983) notion of SR as a device that operates at the discourse level and tracks topic continuity rather than subject reference per se.[2] For example, in (6a) from Kiowa, SS marking can be used instead of the expected DS marking as long as Kathryn and Esther are part of a unified letter writing campaign – say, to apply political pressure for some cause (from Watkins 1993: 149, via McKenzie 2012). Conversely, in (6b) from Kiowa, DS marking is used despite the subjects being the same because the events are not part of a single coherent situation, but are independent events happening at different times (McKenzie 2012: 154).

(6) Kiowa (Tanoan)

a. *Kathryn* *gʲæ-gúʔ* ***gɔ/nɔ*** *Esther=àl* *gʲæ-gúʔ.*
Kathryn 3SGS/3PLO-write.PFV and.SS/and.DS Esther=too 3SGS/3PLO-write.PFV
'Kathryn wrote a letter and Esther wrote one too.'

b. *Kʰí:dèl* *kˀɔ́e:-tɔ* *ʔéʔ-ʔɔ̃́:m-ẽ́:* ***nɔ*** *é:-hɔ́:-dekʰi.*
yesterday frybread-INV 1PL.EXCL.S/3INV.O-eat.PFV and:DS here-DEF-NOM+day
kí+sɔ̃n é-ʔɔ̃:m-ẽ:.
meat+boil 1PL.EXCL.S-eat.PFV
'Yesterday we made frybread and today we made boiled meat.'

(Watkins 1993: 149; via McKenzie 2012)

Such examples, Stirling says, are too common and consistent within and across languages to be ignored, and they must be integrated into a general theory of SR – a claim often echoed by others (Mithun 1993; McKenzie 2012; Keine 2013). Instead, she claims that SR marking fundamentally expresses a relationship between two eventualities: SS indicates continuity between the eventuality in the marked clause and the eventuality in the context clause, whereas DS indicates some type of discontinuity between the two eventualities (see also Mithun 1993). More specifically, she says that SS is used when the matrix clause does not introduce a new "protagonist" referent that was not already present in the reference-marked clause. Because she defines protagonist as the referent of the *agentive* subject (1993: 64), her characterization of SS allows for some instances of SS marking in which the tracked subjects overlap in reference, but do not strictly have the same reference, as in (20). DS is used when the two eventualities differ in some eventuality parameter, usually (but not necessarily) if the superordinate clause introduces a new protagonist not present in the marked clause. Other eventuality parameters are location, time, and actuality, and changes in these parameters can also justify DS marking, as the change of time does in (6b). Note also that the generalization for SS marking and the generalization for DS marking are not exact opposites of each other. In this way, Stirling allows for the possibility of SS or DS marking being used in seemingly free variation, as appears to happen in some cases, including (6a). Stirling's work has had lasting impact, shifting the field away from primarily syntactic accounts of SR.

McKenzie (2012; 2015b) brings Stirling's basic view into the 2010s, developing it in formal semantic terms (Stirling used Discourse Representation Theory). He makes many of the same basic points, in the context of his fieldwork on Kiowa and his ambitious survey of SR in North American languages. From the semantic side, his main contribution is the plausible one of saying that the morphemes in non-canonical SR cases are relating (Austinian) situations rather than (Davidsonian) events/eventualities – a distinction that we do not discuss further here.

2.3. Two Kinds of SR: A Semantic Kind and a Syntactic One?

McKenzie also makes what could prove to be a crucial empirical observation: he claims that non-canonical switch-reference is quite typical in cases where the clauses seem to be joined by way of conjunction (or clause chaining), but is not found in cases where one clause is subordinated to another as an adjunct or an argument. He demonstrates that this is true internally to Kiowa. The particles *gɔ* and *nɔ* seen in (6) are markers of clausal coordination, and with them non-canonical SR is not uncommon and can be brought out in fieldwork by suitable manipulations of the context. But the same language also has subordinating SR morphemes, including *–tsẽ:/-ẽ:* 'when.SS'/'when.DS', and these give only canonical SR judgments regardless of context. Thus SS marking is categorically rejected with different subjects in (7a), and (7b) cannot have DS marking when the subjects are interpreted as coreferent, regardless of how the relationship between the events is construed.

(7) Kiowa (Tanoan)

a. **Bill* *∅-tsɔ̃́n* [*Sam* *gjà-hó:+ai:-gu=***tsẽ̀:**].
Bill 3S-arrive.pfv Sam 3sg.an/3pl.o-travel+start.off-ipfv=when.ss
'Bill arrived when Sam was leaving.'

b. **Bill* *èm−hâ:* [*ẽ́−bɔ̃́:=***ẽ̀:**].
Bill 3sg-arrive.pfv 3sg.an/1sg.d−see.pfv=when.ds
'Bill$_1$ stood up when he$_1$ saw me.'

(McKenzie 2015b: 21–22)

This suggests that two quite different phenomena may be attested, which have not been clearly distinguished in much of the literature to date. McKenzie (2015a) also claims that his broad cross-linguistic survey supports this generalization: non-canonical SR is attested in cases of coordination and clause chaining, but not with true clausal embedding. Weisser (2012) makes the same point clearly (and at approximately the same time), adding that two Australian languages, Yakanytjatjara and Pitjantjatjara, are very much like Kiowa in showing non-canonical SR in conjoined structures but not in purpose clause adjuncts.

Other hints in the literature also point in this direction. For example, two of the languages that Stirling (1993) discusses in the most detail are Imbabura Quechua (IQ) and Amele. She shows that non-canonical SR is far more prevalent in Amele than in IQ – maybe SR in IQ is only canonical, once one gets the right notion of subject (see §4). This matches with the fact that reference-marked clauses are clearly subordinate clauses in IQ (see §3.1 and examples (27) and (28)), whereas Amele is a quintessential case of clause chaining, arguably a form of coordination (cf. Nonato 2014). There is also good reason to say that reference-marked clauses in the Panoan languages Shipibo and Yawanawa are subordinate clauses, as argued by Camargo Souza (2016), and these languages do not seem to have non-canonical SR: at least, Valenzuela (2003) doesn't mention it, and we have found no clear cases when searching through her many examples, or in our own parsing of texts. Also suggestive on this point are Hale's (1992) remarks on Uto-Aztecan. In Hopi the markers *-t* SS and *-q* DS are clearly attached to the verb in the marked clause as complementizers, and there is no non-canonical SR (as far as Hale 1992 or Jeanne 1978 state, anyway). In contrast, the O'odham cognate to *-t* is *-c*, and this has become separated from the marked clause, now serving as a marker of conjunction. Correlated with this, Hale observes several instances of non-canonical SR in O'odham, different from Hopi. So the McKenzie/Weisser generalization seems very promising, although much remains to be done to confirm it in specific languages – an important area for future research.[3]

If this generalization is correct, it has two important consequences for future research. The first is that SR is not a unified phenomenon, such that we should stop using the same term for both types. We suggest, then, that the term "non-canonical switch-reference" should be replaced with a new term like switch-situation, clearly distinguished from switch-reference proper. The second consequence is that we need a new syntactic approach to switch-reference proper, for the substantial set of constructions in which "same subject" and "different subject" are accurate characterizations. It looks to us – and to Weisser (2012) – like Finer was right that SR is syntactic for a coherent subset of the languages/constructions that have been said to have SR. And whereas McKenzie (2012) makes a contribution to the theory of switch-situation, he has less to say about switch-reference proper.

The Panoan languages Shipibo and Yawanawa have an additional feature that points toward SR being syntactic. In these languages there is actually a three-way contrast in part of the SR paradigm. Perfective/sequential subordinate clauses in Shipibo can be marked SS (*-ax* or *-xon*, depending on the case of the matrix subject; see Camacho 2010), or DS (*-ke-tian*), or with a third marker (*-a*, O=S), which signals that the object of the embedded verb is the same as the subject of the matrix verb.

(8) Shipibo (Panoan)

a. *José-ra* *Rosa* *oin-**ax*** *xobo-n* *ka-ke.*
José-PRT Rosa see-SS.ABS house-LOC go-PFV
'José$_i$, he$_i$ seeing Rosa$_j$, went home.'

b. *José-kan* *Rosa* *oin-**a**-ra,* *xobo-n* *ka-ke.*
José-ERG Rosa see-O=S-PRT house-LOC go-PFV
'When José$_i$ saw Rosa$_j$, she$_j$ went home.'

c. *José-kan* *Rosa* *oin-ke-**tian**-ra,* *(ja)* *xobo-n* *ka-ke.*
José-ERG Rosa see-PFV-DS-PRT s/he home-LOC go-PFV
'When José$_i$ saw Rosa$_j$, he$_m$/she$_k$ (someone else) went home.'

(Valenzuela 2003: 424; Baker 2014: 364)

Although object-equals-subject coreference marking is a rare phenomenon, and challenging for any existing theory, the fact that it is possible provides a hint as to the intrinsic nature of SR. Suppose that we grant to Stirling and McKenzie that (8a) exhibits a continuity of eventualities/situations and (8c) involves discontinuous events/situations because of the introduction of the new agentive subject in the second clause. Where, then, does (8b) fit in? One could say that (8b) is like (8a) rather than (8c) because the second eventuality doesn't introduce a new referent, but then how does one distinguish O=S from SS? Alternatively, one could say that (8b) is like (8c) rather than (8a) in that the two eventualities have different protagonists, but then how does one distinguish O=S from normal DS? Either way, O=S seems to require crucial reference to the syntactic notion of grammatical relations – an expansion of Finer's point concerning examples like (3).

Panoan's three-way distinction also points away from Keine's (2013) view that SR reduces to two different types of coordination, SS being VP conjunction with a single shared subject, and DS being vP conjunction with room for two different subjects, one in each vP. Keine's proposal is summarized in structural form in (9a) and (9b) (based on Keine 2013: 803–804).

(9)

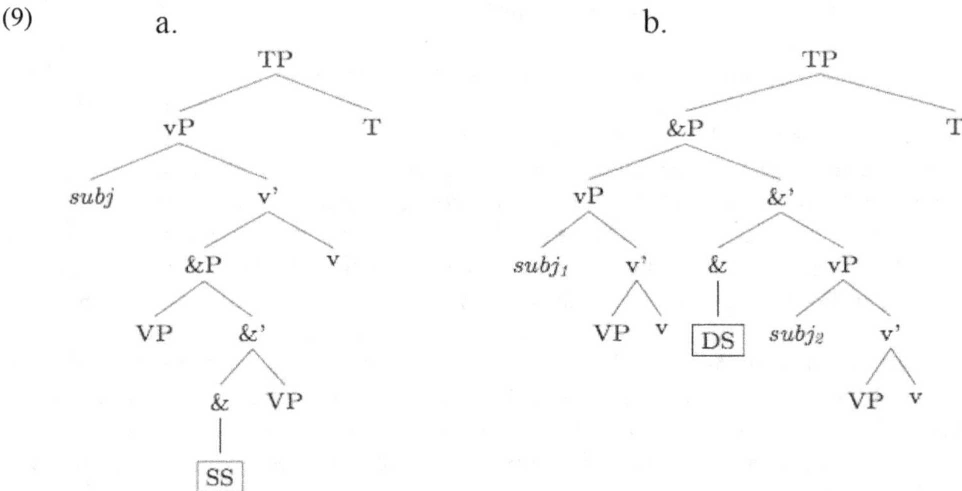

While analyzing SS as VP conjunction in this way has a priori plausibility for some languages, the view could not be generalized to O=S, given normal structural theories of conjunction: there is simply no constituent that contains the subject and the verb but not the object that can be conjoined with a normal VP (cf. English *Chris [[$_{VP}$ came in] and [$_{?P}$ Pat saw]]). In contrast, something like Finer's approach does have prospects for generalizing to this case, given that there are functional heads in the structure of the clause that agree with the object of the clause rather than the subject in some languages. (Indeed, Finer (1985: 52) foresees the possibility of O=S in his system, mentioning Yup'ik as a possible case.) For more on O=S marking in Panoan and its implications for the theory of SR, see Baker and Camargo Souza (in progress).

The tentative conclusion, then, is that there is a syntactic type of switch-reference that involves clausal embedding, and a semantic type that involves clausal conjunction, better called "switch-situation". Although there is recent work that makes progress on the (semantic) theory of switch-situation, there has been less recent attention paid to the theory of switch-reference proper.

3. The Distribution of SR Over Clause Types

We have seen that the distinction between clausal conjunction and clausal embedding seems to be very important for a theory of SR. However, there are also various subtypes of clausal embedding: adjunction, complementation, sentential subjects, adnominal clauses including relative clauses, and so on. Empirically, it seems that languages differ in interesting ways as to how SR distributes over these different kinds of clauses. Theoretically, this distribution may hold hints as to the nature of the phenomenon. For example, Finer's (1984; 1985) theory was originally designed to work for adjunct clauses, and though he originally claimed that SR is not found with complement clauses, he does sketch an account of how SR might work on clausal complements (1984: Chapter 4). In contrast, Keine (2013) takes a strong stand that (one kind of) SR is completely impossible with complement clauses. McKenzie's (2015a) survey brings together quite a bit of data on this topic. He claims that there is no type of clause that cannot be marked for SR in some language or another. He also provides evidence that a kind of implicational hierarchy is at work: SR marking is most common on adjunct clauses (especially temporal and causal adjuncts, but also conditional clauses), as in all the examples so far. It is of intermediate frequency on complement clauses, and it is rare, although attested, on relative clauses. In this section, we consider issues that arise concerning SR on clauses other than adjunct clauses and conjoined clauses.

3.1. SR in Complement Clauses

In accordance with McKenzie's survey, some languages limit SR to adjunct clauses, whereas others extend it to complement clauses. For example, in Shipibo and Yawanawa, SR is usually marked on adjunct clauses; canonical complement clauses are nominalizations that are not reference-marked.[4] This is also the case for Quechua dialects other than IQ, Kiowa, Seri, and Pomoan. The situation in Yuman languages is not entirely clear. and Munro (1976) and Gordon (1983) state that reference-marked clauses in Maricopa and Mojave express clauses that are naturally translated as complement clauses or subject clauses in English, but it is not certain that they are structural complements or subjects in those languages; Munro (1976: 40) provides awkward but conceivable paraphrases in which the reference-marked clauses are adjuncts. Presumably, the matter could be clarified by familiar grammatical tests involving extraction, binding, and scope, but this has not been done systematically. Muskogean languages like Choctaw provide clear examples of reference marking on complement clauses, such as (10).

(10) Choctaw (Muskogean)

a. *John-at* *anokfilli-h* *[pisachokma-**ka-t**].*
John-NOM think-TNS good.looking-COMP-SS
'John$_i$ thinks he$_i$ is good looking.'

b. *John-at* *anokfilli-h* *[pisachokma-**ka**].*
John-NOM think-TNS good.looking-COMP.DS
'John$_i$ thinks he$_k$ is good looking.'

(Broadwell 2006: 269)

Hopi (Uto-Aztecan) also has SR on both adjunct clauses and complement clauses. There the distinction is made salient by the fact that SR marking is morphologically different: adjunct clauses have SS *-t* vs. DS *-q*, whereas complement clauses have SS *-y* vs. DS *-t* (Jeanne 1978; Hale 1992).

IQ provides an interesting contrast with other Quechuan varieties. Most of the Quechuan languages have *-spa/-shpa* (SS) vs. *-pti/-kpi/-jpi* (DS) on temporal, manner, and conditional adjunct clauses, but IQ has innovated an SS-DS contrast on subjunctive clauses as well (Muysken 1977: 70; Cole 1982: 63; van Gijn 2016: 168). These subjunctive clauses can be used as purpose clause adjuncts, but they can also be the complements of verbs like 'want'. In the latter use, they function very much like infinitival complements; compare (15).

(11) Imbabura Quechua (Quechuan)

a. *Muna-y-man* *ñuka* *mama-ta* *riku-**ngapaj*** (SS subjunctive complement)
want-1SG-COND my mother-ACC see-SBJV.SS
'I want that I see my mother; I want to see my mother.'

b. *Muna-ni* *Juzi* *pay-paj* *mama-ta* *riku-**chun*** (DS subjunctive complement)
want-1SG José he-of mother-ACC see-SBJV.DS
'I want José to see his mother.'

(Cole 1982: 37)

Indeed, Keine (2013: 817) accepts IQ as one language for which his deconstruction of SR as conjunction may not apply. See also Assmann (2012) for an analysis of the canonical SR system of Quechua.

As already mentioned, Finer's (1984; 1985) syntactic analysis of SR was initially designed to account for SR on adjunct clauses. This was convenient for him, since it is in these constructions that the C-Agr complex of the lower clause is clearly *locally* c-commanded by the C-Agr complex of the higher clause in the way needed for Binding Theory to apply (see (5)). And inasmuch as SR is most robustly attested in adjunct clauses, it is appropriate for a theory to begin there. But it is now clear that SR can happen in complement clauses, too, so it is important to ask whether a theory of that sort can be extended. It seems like it potentially can be, since the C-Agr complex in an embedded clause is still c-commanded by the C-Agr complex in the matrix clause: see Finer (1984: Chapter 4), Broadwell (1990; 1997), and Hale (1992).

The one potentially serious issue for extending a Finerian account from adjuncts to complements concerns locality: is the reference marker in a complement clause close enough to its antecedent in the matrix clause to have an anaphoric dependency on it? To answer this question, we must reconsider what the antecedent of the SS anaphor really is. Finer and Hale assume that SS anaphors are bound by functional heads (C+T) in the superordinate clause, but an alternative that emerges more clearly with complement clauses in view is that a superordinate nominal could itself be the antecedent of an SS anaphor. Such a model would be reminiscent of a control construction, as we will discuss. Whichever of these is the true antecedent, one would think that the reference marker in a complement clause is close enough to its antecedent, since binding/control-type relations normally are local to a clause, not to smaller constituents.[5] For example, an anaphor in object position can be bound by the subject of the same clause, and one would think that the same could be true for an anaphoric SS marker on a clause in the object position. This seems adequate for examples like (10a) in Choctaw or (11a) in IQ.

However, interesting (challenging) questions now arise for ditransitive verbs that select an object as well as a subject and a reference-marked complement clause. The question here is whether the anaphoric reference marker could take the object of the matrix clause as its antecedent rather than the subject of the matrix clause in this one particular structure, resulting in an S=O relationship. If SR is modeled on reflexive anaphora, we would expect this to be possible in some languages but not others, just as *self*-type anaphors are subject-oriented in some languages (like Norwegian and Japanese) but permit object antecedents in others (like English). If SR is modeled on control, we might even expect the S=O pattern to be the norm, just as transitive verbs with infinitival complements like *persuade* normally have object control (the verb *promise* being a notable exception). In point of fact, however, it seems that reference marking remains strongly subject-oriented even in this situation, as shown in (12a) from Choctaw and (12b) from IQ. These examples must have non-anaphoric DS rather than anaphoric SS marking, even though there is a nearby potential antecedent in the form of the matrix object.

(12) a. Choctaw (Muskogean)

[*Iya-l-aachi̱-h-o̱*] *a̱-maka-tok.*
go-1SG.I-IRR-TNS-PTCP.DS 1SG.III-say-PST
'She ordered me to go.'

(Broadwell 2006: 273)

b. Imbabura Quechua (Quechuan)

Juan-da *kunvinsi-rka-ni* [(*pay*) *Kitu-man* *ri-**chun***].
Juan-ACC persuade-PST-1SG.S he.NOM Quito-to go-SBJV.DS
'I persuaded Juan (that) he go to Quito.'

(Hermon 1985: 123)

This is a challenge for reducing SR fully to the familiar phenomenon of control. Hermon (1985) tries to do so for Quechua, but identifies this as a residue. Similarly, Hale (1992: 67) uses the parallel fact as an argument for distinguishing control from SR/obviation in Hopi and Mismalpan languages. Thinking of this in terms of Binding Theory, one could stipulate that anaphoric SR markers are always subject-oriented anaphors, an existing type of anaphor, but one would like to know why that should be. There is something more to understand here.

3.2. SR and Relative Clauses

McKenzie (2015a) says that SR marking is also possible on relative clauses, although this is rarer than on complements. IQ, for example, does not have this, nor do the Yuman languages, Seri, or the Panoan languages. One notable family that does allow SR on relative clauses is Muskogean; (13) gives an example from Choctaw.

(13) Choctaw (Muskogean)

[*Ofi'* *ipiita-li-k-aash-**ma̱***] *balii-t* *kaniiya-h.*
dog feed-1SG.I-TNS-PREV-D.DS run-PART go:away-TNS
'That dog I fed ran away.'

(Broadwell 2006: 29)

The fact that there could be reference marking on a relative clause is more surprising and potentially problematic from a Finerian perspective: one might very well expect that the relative operator and DP head of the relative clause would disrupt the locality that an anaphoric reference marker needs to have with its antecedent in the matrix clause. But Choctaw actually supports this style of reasoning, as an exception that proves the rule. Relative clauses in Choctaw are crucially internally headed, not externally headed (note that 'dog' is not marked as nominative in (13), as an external head should be). Thus the structure of the matrix subject in (13) may not be [$_{DP}$ DP CP] but just [CP] with DP inside it. Even more strikingly, Broadwell (2006: 300) shows that it is possible to move out of relative clauses in Choctaw, in marked contrast with most other languages, in which relative clauses are islands (the Complex NP Constraint of Ross 1967):

(14) Choctaw (Muskogean)

Kátomma-h	*John-at*	[*ofi'*	*aa-pi̱sa-tok-**at***]	*cho̱pa-tok?*
where-TNS	John-NOM	dog	LOC-see-PST-SS	buy-PST

'What is the place such that John bought the dog that he saw at that place?'

(Broadwell 2006: 300)

Broadwell conjectures that so-called relative clauses in Choctaw are not syntactically DPs, but just CPs in complement position that (somehow) receive a special entity-denoting interpretation in the semantics (see also Gordon & Munro 2017). If so, then it is not surprising that it is precisely this language that also allows reference marking on relative clauses. Overall, the path is open to say that reference marking is subject to syntactic locality, normal headed-relative clause structures disrupt that locality, and reference marking is seen on relative clauses only when they are independently known to have exceptional syntactic structures. Other languages that have SR on relative clauses are Washo (an isolate) and Hopi, possibly for reasons mentioned in the next subsection.

3.3. SR and Nominalization

McKenzie (2015a) says that there is no type of embedded clause that is entirely immune to being reference marked in North American languages, but we think this may not be quite true: nominalized clauses seem (almost) never to be reference marked. This may sound like a terminological quibble, since one can claim that nominalized clauses are not clauses at all, but rather noun phrases. But, in fact, nominalized clauses can have much of the same structure as ordinary clauses; in particular, gerund-like nominalizations in many languages have internal structures that are very similar to clauses in terms of licensing objects, allowing aspect marking, allowing adverbial modifiers, and so on. Often such structures are analyzed as having a single nominal head near the top of a constituent that otherwise consists of a normal verbal/clausal structure; for example, a determiner head might take a VP/vP/AspP complement rather than its usual NP complement (Abney 1987). If this is true, and even gerund-type nominalizations do not involve SR marking, this could tell us something significant about the grammar of SR: that it is category-sensitive and usually involves the very top layer of the clause.

First, we briefly assess the empirical situation. IQ is particularly striking in this respect, since it has a rich range of nominalizations as well as reference marked clauses, and the two can appear in (apparently) the same environments, such as the complement of 'want': compare (15a) with (15b) (cf. also (11a)). Cole (1982), Hermon (1985), and Cole and Hermon (2011) point out that "infinitive" and "nominal" clauses are noun-like in the sense that the clause as a whole is marked for accusative case, and in that the object of the nonfinite clause does not have to be marked for accusative case, as seen in (15a). In contrast, SS clauses like the one in (15b) are not nominal in these respects: they do not bear accusative case themselves, and direct objects inside them must be accusative.

(15) a. Imbabura Quechua (Quechuan)

Aycha-(ta)	*miku-na-**ta***	*muna-ni.* (infinitive)
meat-(ACC)	eat-NMLZ-ACC	want-1SG

'I want to eat meat.'

(Hermon 1985: 25)

b. Imbabura Quechua (Quechuan)

pay-paj *mama-ta* *riku-**ngapaj*** *muna-ni.* (SS subjunctive)
his-POSS mother-ACC see-SBJV.SS want-1SG
'I want that I see his mother; I want to see his mother.'

(Hermon 1985: 30)

There is a systematic complementarity in this: no clause is marked for both SR and morphological case in IQ.

Once we are alert to this issue, we observe the same thing in other languages. For example, in Shipibo, clauses marked with infinitive *-ti* are nominalized in that they can occupy the direct object position and trigger ergative case on the subject, as seen in (16a), and they can themselves be marked for case (oblique), as in (16b). They however show no SS/DS distinction, as can be seen in (16b).[6] In contrast, the embedded clause in (17), although it is functionally equivalent to a complement clause in some Romance languages, is marked SS but is not nominal, as shown by the fact that it does not trigger ergative case on the matrix subject.

(16) Shipibo (Panoan)

a. *E-**n**=ra* *[Rosa* *jo-**ti**]* *onona-ke.*
I-ERG=PRT Rosa come-INF know-PFV
'I know that Rosa will come.'

b. *E-**a**=ra* *keen-ai* *[(mia)* *tee-**ti-nin**]*
I-ABS=PRT want-IPFV (you) work-INF-OBL
'I want (myself) to work', or 'I want you to work.'

(Baker fieldnotes)

(17) Shipibo (Panoan)

*No-**a**=ra* *[-- bewa* *onan-**i**]* *ka-i.*
we-ABS=PRT song learn-SS go-IPFV
'We are going (to school) to learn the song.'

(Baker fieldnotes)

We detect the same negative correlation between nominalization and SR in many other American languages. For example, Choctaw clauses can be in complement position and are reference-marked, but they show no evidence of being nominal, hence case marked. Thus, (10a) has SS marking on the complement clause, which is cognate with nominative marking; it cannot bear accusative case instead (there is a contrast here with internally headed relative clauses, which can be marked with either SR or case although not overtly with both; see Broadwell 2006). In addition, nominalized clauses are clearly not reference-marked in Seri (Marlett 1981: 355) or in Mojave (Munro 1976: 40, 220–222), nor is there any hint of nominalization in SR clauses in the Pomoan languages, judging by McLendon (1975: 89–93) and Mithun (1993). McKenzie (2015a: 63) mentions Ute as having SR with nominalized verbs, but in fact most embedded clauses in Ute do not show an SS-DS distinction (Givón 2011: Chapters 9, 17). The only clauses which have SS forms distinct from DS are *-chi* marked clauses used as purposive adjuncts and as complements of verbs like 'want', and these clauses are less unambiguously nominal than other clauses in Ute, in that they do not bear accusative case marking or have genitive-case marked subjects, as other nominalized clauses do (the subject in *-chi* marked clauses is usually null). It seems, then, that the generalization that SR proper cannot apply to nominalized clauses is quite robust in the Americas.

One exception that proves the rule is Hopi. Jeanne (1978) and Hale (1992) show that what looks like a DS/SS contrast is seen on complement clauses with the nominal head – *qa* (also an ingredient in reference-marked relative clauses). However, Hopi is also special in that it marks ordinary NPs like 'dog' differently if the possessor of the noun is the same as the local subject (*-y*) or if it is different from that subject (*-y-at*). This is not SR per se, although it may be part of some more general theory of "obviation", as Jeanne and Hale suggest. It is thus reasonable to conjecture that Hopi's putative use of SR on nominalized complements is formally an instance of marking anaphoric possessors (=subjects) of NPs, not an instance of true SR marking on clauses. Indeed reference marking on complement clauses in Hopi is cognate with the markers seen on nouns (SS/proximate *-y*, DS/obviative *-t*), and not with the canonical SR markers used on non-nominalized adjunct clauses (SS *-t*, DS *-q*).[7]

3.4. SR as Control of an Operator?

What is the theoretical significance of the observation that SR is largely incompatible with nominalization? We think it suggests that there is a syntactic operator at the edge of the reference-marked clause that is crucially involved in the SR phenomenon. The matrix subject then controls this operator (in some sense), and the C-T morphology in the embedded clause forces the operator to be the same as the subject of the clause in a way akin to what Finer said. This is illustrated in (18), in the context of an adjunction structure.

(18)

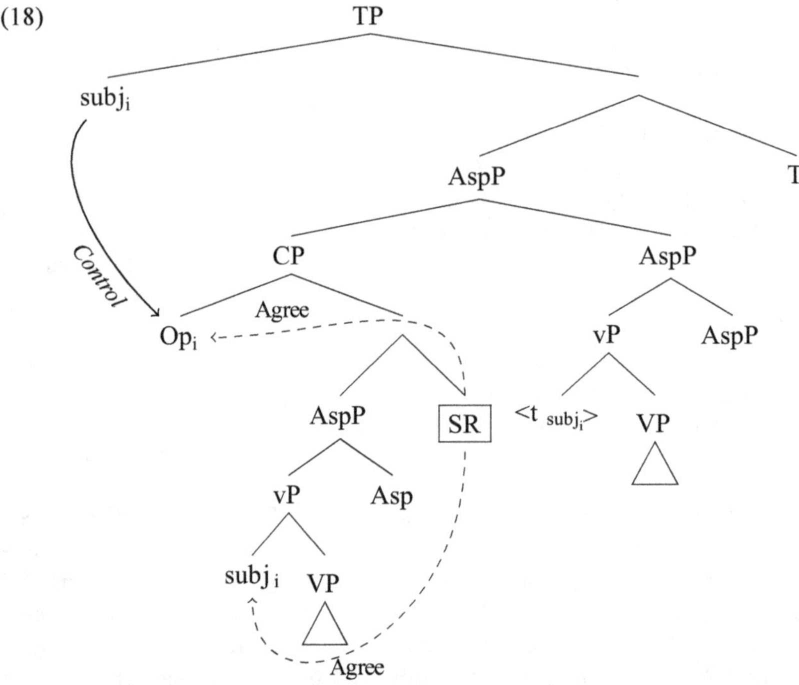

Nominalized clauses are then different from verbal clauses in that they do not allow such operators. That generalization can be independently motivated. For example, it is known that infinitival clauses allow overt *wh-* operators in English but more nominal gerund clauses with *-ing* do not, as seen in (19).

(19) a. Mary remembered to take her medicine.
b. Mary remembers taking her medicine
c. Mary remembered which medicine to take.
d. *Mary remembers which medicine taking.

This also seems to be true for more abstract (phonologically null) operators involved in licensing logophoric pronouns and indexical shift: for example, indexical shift is possible in verbal clauses but not in nominal clauses in Turkic languages such as Uyghur (Shklovsky & Sudo 2014).

Arguably, this follows from a general theory of category distinctions like Baker's (2003), where verbal categories differ from nominal (and adjectival) categories precisely in having the ability to license specifiers – although there is work to be done to generalize this theory from lexical heads to a full range of functional heads. The negative interaction between nominalization and reference marking suggests that SR involves a similar infrastructure of DP operators in the left periphery of the clause.

Positing an operator that mediates between the matrix subject and the embedded clause could contribute to a neo-Finerian account in other respects. First, as already mentioned, an account in terms of control is compatible with the matrix subject being referentially related to SS in a CP complement, whereas an entirely agreement-based theory may not be (see endnote 4 in this chapter).[8] Second, it opens up some new space to think about the fact that SS marking is sometimes possible when the subject of the main clause and the subject of the embedded clause overlap in reference, but one is plural and the other singular. An example is (20) from Mojave (Langdon & Munro 1979: 325; see also Munro 1983); this is also allowed in Maricopa, Kashaya (Oswalt 1983), Washo, and Panoan languages, although not in Muskogean languages, Seri, or Quechua.

(20) Mojave (Yuman)

Town	*ɔ-tayəm-k̲*	*Allen-č i:*	*mattəkʷəha:v*	*tu:raw-m.*
town	1-go.PL-SS	Allen-NOM	shirt	buy-TNS

'We (=Allen and I) went to town and Allen bought a shirt.'

(Langdon & Munro 1979: 325)

This seems problematic for Finer's literal project of explaining SR in terms of Binding Theory, since anaphors cannot generally overlap in reference with their antecedents (**John annoyed ourselves on the family vacation,* trying to mean 'John annoyed a group [e.g., his family] that includes himself and the speaker'). This is also problematic for an unmediated agreement theory, where some head agrees directly with both the matrix subject and the embedded subject, inducing SS (e.g., Camacho 2010), since the two subjects do not agree in person-number-gender features in cases like these.[9] However, control is one linguistic relationship that does sometimes tolerate number mismatches, as in "partial control" examples like (21), studied by Landau (2000, and much subsequent work).

(21) Mary prefers [PRO to meet at 5:00 pm]
(Mary and others – possibly including the speaker – meet)

4. What Counts as the Subject for Reference Marking?

Another important issue is what exactly counts as the "subject" for same-subject and different-subject marking, and what that implies about the constructions. This is an empirically rich area, with an interesting array of facts in different languages, discovered in part by Relational Grammarians constructing arguments that different nominals can be subjects at different levels of representation – see, for example, Marlett (1981) and Farrell et al. (1991) on Seri, Jake (1985) on IQ, and Davies (1986) on Choctaw. It is also theoretically very important for our understanding of what SR is. Earlier, we mentioned controversies about whether SR is really sensitive to subjects (Finer's view), or topics, or Stirling's discourse-based notion of protagonist. A fair question, then, is whether the allegedly syntactic notion of subject is really any better defined than a semantic-pragmatic notion like protagonist, once one looks at the details. More narrowly, within generative terms, it is known that different aspects of grammar operate with overlapping but different senses of subject. For example, dative subjects in Icelandic famously act just like ordinary nominative case subjects for purposes of controlling and being controlled, and for purposes of binding anaphors, but not for purposes of case assignment and agreement (Zaenen et al. 1985). What exactly counts as a subject for SR, then, could provide valuable hints as to what grammatical mechanisms are involved: for example, whether they are mechanisms of binding, or control, or agreement, or a combination.

4.1. Thematic Role and Grammatical Function

First of all, it seems clear that SR is never determined exclusively or even primarily by thematic role, like agent or patient, rather than by grammatical function, such as subject and object. Thus, the theme subjects of unaccusative verbs are generally treated as equivalent to the agent subjects of transitive or unergative verbs for purposes of SS marking. For example, there is SS marking in examples like (22) from Choctaw, where the type of agreement on the verb shows that the first verb is unaccusative (glossed II) whereas the second is unergative (glossed I) (see Davies 1986).

(22) Choctaw (Muskogean)

*Ik-si-abiik-ahi̱la-h-makoo-**sh**,* *iya-l-aachi̱-h.*
N-1SG.II-sick-POT-TNS-CONCESS-SS go-1SG.I-IRR-TNS
'Even if I get sick, I'll go.'

(Broadwell 2006: 294)

Clear examples of this type are also found in Panoan languages, among others.

One might think that passive clauses should behave like unaccusative clauses in this respect, and sometimes they do. For example, the promoted theme of a passive clause counts as the subject for reference marking in (23) from IQ (Jake 1985: 62; see also Hermon 1985: 124–125), just as the theme of 'get sick' does in (22).

(23) Imbabura Quechua (Quechuan)

Wajcha *[jari* *ayuda-shca* *ca-**ngapaj/*chun**]* *caya-rca.*
poor.person man help-PASS be-SS/*DS call-3SG.PST
'The poor person called so as to be helped by the man.'

(Jake 1985: 62)

But subjecthood is a bit more complex with passives than with unaccusatives, because passives have covert agents. These are arguably still present in the syntactic representation, and hence they could also have an influence on reference marking. Indeed, in Seri, it seems to be the covert agent that counts for SR, not the theme. Hence, (24a), which is formally similar to (23) in IQ, must be marked DS, whereas (24b) can be marked SS because the covert agents are coreferential, even though the theme "subjects" are not (Seri; Marlett 1981: 357; Farrell et al. 1991: 434; Keine 2013: 780).

(24) Seri (Isolate)

a. *ʔp-po-a:ʔ-kašni* ***ta**-X* *ʔp-si-o:ʔa* *ʔa=ʔa.*
1SG.S-IRR-PASS-bite DS-UT 1SG.S-IRR-cry AUX=DECL
'If I am bitten, I will cry.'

b. *ʔa:t* *kiʔ* *p-a:ʔ-ka:* ***Ø**-X* *ʔe:pol* *kiʔ* *mos* *s-a:ʔ-ka:*
limberbush the IRR-PASS-look.for SS-UT ratany the also IRR-PASS-look.for
ʔa=ʔa.
AUX=DECL
'If limberbush is looked for, white ratany should also be looked for.'

(Marlett 1981: 357; Farrell et al. 1991: 434; Keine 2013: 780)

In fact, this difference between IQ and Seri seems to be explicable given details about the so-called passive constructions in the two languages. IQ has no so-called "impersonal passive" in which the thematic object fails to become the syntactic subject (Cole 1982: 133), whereas Seri clearly does (Marlett 1981: 314–328). Theme arguments of passives in Seri trigger object agreement rather than subject agreement when they are plural, or when an oblique argument is also present. With this in mind, we can conjecture that Seri does not have a real personal passive construction at all, but rather an "unspecified subject" construction with a featurally defective but syntactically present subject. The theme argument then remains an object grammatically, even though T may agree with it in that position under some circumstances (as is possible in oblique subject constructions in Icelandic and Hindi, for example). Then (24b) has SS because the two unspecified subjects corefer, and (24a) has DS because the unspecified subject of the first clause does not corefer with the subject 'I' of the second clause.[10] Another language similar to Seri in this respect is Central Pomo (Mithun 1993: 123).

Another sort of clause that has a mismatch between the grammatical function of subject and the thematic role of agent is possessor raising clauses, in which the thematic possessor of the subject moves out of the subject DP, perhaps into Spec TP, with the result that it becomes case marked and/or agreed with as if it were itself the subject. This sort of possessor raising is known to feed reference marking, so that SS is used if the subject of one clause is coreferential with the raised possessor of the subject of the other clause. This happens in Choctaw (Broadwell 2006: 308–309), Chickasaw, and Maricopa, as in (25).

(25) Maricopa (Yuman)

a. DS with no Possessor Raising
M-e'e-ny-sh *nyiily-**m*** *m-shhot* *m-lyvii-k.*
2.POSS-hair-DEM-NOM black-DS 2SG-pretty 2SG-be.like-ASP
'You are pretty because your hair is black.'

b. SS with Possessor Raising
Man-sh *m-e'e* *m-nyiily-**k*** *m-shhot* *m-lyvii-k.*
you-NOM 2.POSS-hair 2SG-black-SS 2SG-pretty 2SG-be.like-ASP
'You are pretty because your hair is black (because you are black-haired).'

(Gordon 1983: 85)

Broadwell (1997) uses this as an argument against Stirling's semantic view – correctly, we believe. However, more thorough analyses of the syntax and semantics of possessor raising in the relevant languages would be helpful in confirming this.[11]

4.2. The Impact of Case Marking

One group of languages in which the thematic distinction between agent and patient does seem to affect SR is the Pomoan languages. For example, in Eastern Pomo, according to Stirling (1993: 99–105), two coreferential agents trigger SS, and two coreferential patients trigger SS, but a patient paired with an agent triggers DS, as in the following data (originally from McLendon 1978; see Mithun 1993 for similar data from Central Pomo).

(26) Eastern Pomo (Pomoan)

a. *Háa* *káluhu-**y**,* *Ø* *siimáa* *mérqakiihi.*
1SG.AG went.home-SS 1SG.AG sleep lay.down
'I went home and then went to bed.'

b. *q̀aalalma-**y*** *wí* *míipal* *diiLaqmaya.*
get.sick-SS 1SG.P 3SG.P think.about
'When I get sick, I think about him.'

c. *Háa* *xáaqak̀i-**qan**,* *wí* *q'aalálmaya.*
1SG.AG take.bath-DS 1SG.P get.sick
'Just because I took a bath, I got sick.'

(McLendon 1978)

But this is yet another exception that proves the rule. First, as Stirling herself discusses, one cannot refer *only* to thematic role even in Pomo, since having a patient object in one clause and a patient subject in the other does not license SS marking; for example, (26b) cannot mean 'When *he* gets sick, I think about *him*', with patient subject equated to direct object using SS marking. So it must be a combination of grammatical function and thematic role that determines SR in Pomo. Moreover, it is surely no coincidence that the one family of languages in which agenthood and patienthood seem to be directly relevant for SR is the very family in which agenthood and patienthood seem to be relevant for case marking and number agreement. Thus, the patient nominal bears a different case marking from the agent nominal in (26c) as well (for the full paradigm of Eastern Pomo, see McLendon 1975; for Central Pomo, see Mithun 1993: 121–122). So we would not take Pomo as evidence that semantic distinctions like thematic role can determine reference marking directly; rather, we would take it that morphosyntactic distinctions like case marking can influence reference marking – and case is, rather unusually, influenced by thematic role in Pomoan languages, for reasons to be determined. In other words, our interpretation of (26) is that SS is used in Pomo only if the subjects of the two clauses are coreferential and they bear the same case.[12]

Also interesting are experiencer subjects of verbs like 'be thirsty' or 'be hurting' when those bear a case distinct from that of ordinary agentive subjects in a language. IQ presents relevant examples, where certain experiencer subjects are marked with accusative case and do not trigger subject agreement on the verb. These are perhaps the closest analogs of Icelandic quirky case subject constructions to be found in American languages with SR. The question, then, is whether these experiencers count as subjects for SR, as they do for binding and control in IQ (as in Icelandic; Zaenen et al. 1985), or whether they do not, as they do not for case and agreement (as in Icelandic). Interestingly, Hermon (1985) reports an asymmetry in this respect: accusative experiencers in the matrix clause can count as subjects for SS marking (27a), but accusative experiencers in the embedded clause do not, as seen in (27b) (see also Cole 1982: 112).

(27) Imbabura Quechua (Quechuan)

a. [— *yaku-pi* *ka-**shpa**-ka*] *chiri-wa-rka-mi.*
water-in be-SS-TOP be.cold-1SG.O-PST.3SG-VAL
'When I was in the water, I(ACC) was cold.' (also OK: ka-**jpi**-ka, with DS)

b. *[— *nana-**shpa***] *doktur-pag-man* *ri-rka-ni*
hurt-SS doctor-POSS-to go-PST-1SG.S
'When I(ACC) hurt, I went to the doctor.'
(OK with *nana-**jpi***, DS, Cole 1982: 112) (Hermon 1985: 125, 115)

This potentially surprising asymmetry makes some sense in light of the possibility that SR is mediated by a null operator in Spec CP of the embedded clause, as we proposed in (18). Then the relationship of the matrix subject to the operator is one of control, and its special case-agreement properties are not relevant to that. However, the relationship between the operator and the embedded subject is different: it is arguably coreference enforced by two nominals agreeing with the same head C. Therefore, whether or not the downstairs subject is active for agreement is relevant for that aspect of the construction, and case-marked experiencers are not active in this way. The IQ asymmetry could thus be very instructive for teasing out the primitive syntactic relationships that SR is built out of. It remains to be seen, however, how general this asymmetry will prove to be.[13]

4.3. An Interaction

Finally, IQ also shows a potentially very instructive interaction between the topic of this section, subject choice, and the topic of the last section, types of embedding. Recall that IQ has innovated SR marking on subjunctive clauses in addition to temporal adjuncts. Unlike the temporal clauses, subjunctive clauses can appear in complement (or low-adjunct) positions. Significantly, the two clauses also differ in what counts as a subject in the matrix clause, according to Cole (1983): the covert experiencer of a predicate like 'be good' or 'be heavy' counts for subjunctive clauses, but not for temporal clauses. Hence, SS marking is possible in (28a), in contrast to DS marking in (28b), but the temporal clause in (28c) can have only DS marking.

(28) Imbabura Quechua (Quechuan)

a. *Chay kipi llashaj-mi ka-rka* [(*ñuka*) *apa-**ngapaj***].
that bag heavy-VAL be-3SG.PST I take-SS.SBJV
'That bag was too heavy (for one/me) to carry.'

b. *Chay kipi llashaj-mi ka-rka* [*pay/*ñuka apa-**chun***].
that bag heavy-VAL be-3SG.PST he /*me take-DS.SBJV
'That bag was too heavy for him to carry.'

c. [*Ñuka ñan-pi puri-ju-**jpi**/*shpa*] *chay kipi llashaj-mi ka-rka.*
I road-in walk-PROG-DS/*SS that bag heavy-VAL be-3SG.PST
'When I was walking in the road, that bag was heavy (for me).'

(Cole 1983: 7–8)

We interpret this as follows. Predicates like 'be heavy' have an (often) null experiencer argument, in a position like Spec ApplP that is lower than the syntactic subject but higher than a complement, which can control something in its c-command domain (as in English *That bag is heavy for John* [*PRO to carry*]). The subjunctive clause is a complement, so it is inside the c-command domain of the experiencer and its operator can be controlled by it in (28a). In contrast, the temporal clause is adjoined higher, tentatively to AspP (see (18)), so it is outside the c-command domain of the experiencer in Spec ApplP and cannot be controlled by it, but only by a true subject in Spec TP. This supports the idea that it is the theory of control – and certainly not Agree, since there is no agreement with the covert experiencer – that determines what counts as the "subject" in the matrix clause. (This, however, deepens the mystery of why SS marking never shows that the subject of a complement clause is coreferential with the object of the matrix clause in examples like (12b), even when the embedded clause does seem to be a complement. Perhaps the object never in fact c-commands the embedded clause, but it remains to be understood exactly why that is so.)

5. A Note on the Boundaries of Switch-Reference

Before concluding, we should note that with switch-reference, as with other linguistic phenomena, there are many borderline or less canonical cases. Whether they should be included in the fold depends partly on semi-arbitrary definitions and partly on the results of close analysis of the phenomenon in question.

As an illustrative case in point, we mention Kalaallisut (Greenlandic) and the other Inuit languages. As Richard Compton (p.c.) points out, McKenzie's (2015a) survey does not count these languages as having SR, but most practicing Inuitists claim that they do have SR; see, for example, Bittner (1994: 153) for what looks like a straightforward SR paradigm in Kalaallisut (including a kind of object=subject form) (see also Fortescue (1984) and Bok-Bennema (1991), among others). Indeed, Bittner's examples certainly fit our preliminary definition in that "one clause is morphologically marked to show whether or not one of its nominal arguments refers to the same entity or entities as a nominal argument of a structurally nearby clause". Nevertheless, there are also significant differences between the Inuit phenomenon – traditionally called "fourth person" marking – and canonical SR as we know it from other regions of the Americas. Perhaps the most theoretically important has to do with what counts as a subject for SS marking. Sources agree that in Kalaallisut, the putative SS form can show that the subject of the reference-marked clause is the same as the subject of *any* higher clause (see Bittner 1994: 180; Fortescue 1984: 147–148; Bok-Bennema 1991: 157), not necessarily the immediately superordinate one, as in most other languages (e.g., see

Camargo Souza 2016 for Panoan). Also potentially important is the fact that putative SR marking in Kalaallisut is thoroughly integrated into the language's rich agreement system: SS marking is a special form of agreement (*mi*) with the subject, and O=S marking is a special form of agreement (*ni*) with the absolutive argument. This is why, in traditional Inuit grammatical terminology, these forms are called "fourth person" agreement, which is found side by side with agreement with the usual three persons in inflectional paradigms. Finally, Kalaallisut also has an overt reflexive nominal *immi*, which is used for oblique arguments that are not agreed with (see e.g., Bittner 1994: 147). This overt DP anaphor is morphologically similar to fourth-person marking and is grammatically similar to it in that it must take a subject as its antecedent but it does not necessarily need to be the most local subject – which is rather typical behavior for a morphologically simple, SE-type long-distance anaphor. Therefore, we tentatively assume, roughly along the lines of Bok-Bennema (1991: 154–158), that fourth-person agreement in Kalaallisut is a special form of agreement that licenses a null SE-type anaphor, in contrast to third-person agreement which licenses a null third-person pronoun. If so, then there are both similarities and differences between Inuit fourth person and "standard average" SR. Functionally and pragmatically, they are probably used in discourse in much the same way, but structurally, there is an important difference in whether the lower-tracked argument is linked to the higher one by the principles of nominal anaphora (Inuit), or by a combination of agreement and control, the latter giving a stricter form of locality in canonical SR languages.

More generally, American languages have a rich array of reference tracking devices, of which SR is only one. For example, Algonquian languages famously distinguish two types of third person, proximate and obviative – terminology that is sometimes extended into the domain of SR, especially by Uto-Aztecanists (see Hale 1992: 55). Two arguments in the same domain that are marked proximate must be coreferential, whereas one marked obviative must be disjoint from one marked proximate. This can give an effect analogous to SR in some contexts. However, even arguments in matrix clauses are marked proximate and obviative in these languages, so the phenomenon is not intrinsically about interclausal relationships the way that SR is (although an Algonquian language may have SR marking too: Muehlbauer (2012) claims that the morpheme *-yi* in Plains Cree is a DS marker, even though it has been considered as part of the obviation system in previous work).[14] Similarly, Athapaskan languages like Slave have three different clitic/agreement markers for third-person objects, depending on whether the subject of the clause is first or second person, a third-person coreferential with the object (i.e., a reflexive), or a third-person disjoint in reference from the object (see Rice 1989: Chapter 28 on Slave). Like SR, this seems to be some kind of extension of the pronoun-anaphor distinction into the domain of functional heads, but again, it is not an interclausal relationship per se, the way SR is. Overall, then, the topic of switch-reference may be one important subtopic within the wider topic of anaphora and reference tracking in American languages (and beyond). But mapping out this larger domain and reflecting on what overarching principles might unite it (if any) goes far beyond what we can do here.

6. Conclusion

In this chapter, we have surveyed some of the highlights from the literature on switch-reference in American languages over the last 50 years. We have concentrated on three issues of lasting interest and importance: Is switch-reference determined syntactically or semantically? What range of clause types does it happen in? And, what counts as a subject for marking same subject versus different subject? Our review of these issues suggests that a syntactic approach along the general lines of Finer (1984; 1985) is appropriate for an important subset of SR phenomena, but possibly worked out in terms of control (for identifying the matrix subject) and Agree (for identifying the embedded subject) rather than Binding Theory per se. This approach would not necessarily apply in its entirety to everything that might rightly be called SR, however, such as the phenomenon of fourth-person marking in Inuit languages, or the same-situation marking that is found on conjunctions in Kiowa and other languages.

Further Reading

Finer, Daniel. 1985. The syntax of switch-reference. *Linguistic Inquiry* 16. 35–55.

Jacobsen, William. 1967. Switch-reference in Hokan-Coahuiltecan. In Hymes, Dell & Bittle, William (eds.), *Studies in Southwestern ethnolinguistics*, 238–63. The Hague: Mouton.

McKenzie, Andrew. 2012. *The role of contextual restriction in reference-tracking*. Amherst: University of Massachusetts. (Doctoral dissertation.)

McKenzie, Andrew. 2015a. A survey of switch-reference in North America. *International Journal of American Linguistics* 81. 409–448.

Stirling, Lesley. 1993. *Switch-reference and discourse representation*. Cambridge: Cambridge University Press.

Notes

1. The following abbreviations are used: 1/2/3 = first, second, third person, AN = animate, ABL = ablative, ABS = absolutive, ACC = accusative, AG = agent, ASP = aspect, AUX = auxiliary, CMP = comparative, COMP = complementizer, COMPL = completive, CONCESS = concessive, COND = conditional, D = dual, DECL = declarative, DEF = definite, DEM = demonstrative, DS = different subject, ERG = ergative, EXCL = exclusive, I = agreement class I, II = agreement class II, IPFV = imperfective, IND = indicative, INF = infinitive, INV = inverse number, IRR = irrealis, LOC = locative, N = negative agreement class, NEG = negative, NOM = nominative, O = object agreement, OBL = oblique, O=S = embedded object is the same as matrix subject, P = patient, PASS = passive, PL = plural, PTCP = participle, POSS = possessive, POT = potential, PREV = previous mention, PFV = perfective, PROG = progressive, PRT = second position particle (evidential), PST = past tense, RECIP = reciprocal, S = subject agreement, SBJV = subjunctive, SG = singular, SR = switch-reference, SS = same subject, S.T. = something (unspecified argument), T = temporal, TNS = default tense, TOP = topic, UT = unspecified time, VAL = validator (evidential).
2. See also Woodbury (1983) for a different argument that SR operates in larger discourse units than clauses/sentences. There seems, however, to be a real difference between Eskimoan languages and others in this respect; see §5 for a brief comment on this.
3. In particular, what counts as "clause chaining" is not well defined by McKenzie (or others). We hope that this category can be reduced to either a particular kind of conjunction (as Keine (2013) does for Amele, and Nonato (2014) for Kĩsêdjê), or to a particular kind of subordination, depending on the language (see also Broadwell 1997 for another possible structure). If that is correct, then we need to sort out which instances of clause chaining are which in order to fully evaluate the McKenzie/Weisser empirical generalization. Some potential problems may be lurking here. For example, Mithun (1993) shows that there is non-canonical SR in Central Pomo, and McKenzie classifies this as clause chaining, consistent with his generalization. But if forced to choose between conjunction and subordination, there is some reason to think that most of Mithun's cases may be subordination. For example, three of the four SS markers allow the reference-marked clause to follow the main clause. This suggests that they are subordinate clauses, which often can come before or after the main clause rather freely, in contrast to conjoined clauses, which are usually ordered iconically, matching the sequence of the events they report. So there is important work to be done to clarify this issue.
4. The only complements that might be reference-marked in Shipibo and Yawanawa are the complements of certain auxiliary verbs (e.g., 'go', 'begin', 'be'), where only SS marking is possible; see (17). McKenzie (2015a: 33) shows that similar verb-auxiliary constructions in Yuman languages also mark SS. He analyzes it as a historical vestige of a former SR construction, since these constructions always require SS and there is no second subject to be tracked.
5. The one sort of neo-Finerian theory that might have more trouble generalizing SR to complement clauses is one based purely on Agree relationships, such as Camacho (2010). It is not clear that the C head on a CP inside VP is close enough to the matrix subject to enter into Agree with it, there being a phase head (v) and sometimes a goal object between the two.
6. The matrix subject is not ergative in (16b) because the infinitive complement is marked for oblique case.
7. In addition, the obviation affixes found on nouns are also used to mark SR on relative clauses in Hopi, presumably for the same reason. Another interesting case is Washo (Jacobsen 1964; 1967). Although the DS marker *-š* appears on nominalized complement clauses (and on internally headed relative clauses), Washo is somewhat unusual in that the nominal head/morpheme *-gi/ge* appears outside of the SR marker, and there are no obvious signs of nominalization internal to the clause. This morpheme order is in marked contrast to languages like Choctaw and Hopi, where SR markers are outside of C or NOML morphemes. Following Arregi and Hanink (2018), we could say that a D head takes a full CP complement in Washo, and then there is still room for an operator in Spec CP (cf. 18).

8. Still pending, however, is the question of why the operator is always controlled by the matrix subject, never by the matrix object, as noted in connection with (12). Although this is not a property of canonical control, it is apparently a property of the control of logophoric operators and of complementizer agreement in Bantu languages like Lubukusu (see Diercks 2013). Thus, the principles of control may be somewhat different for subject PROs and for null operators in CP, for reasons that remain to be understood.
9. Note that in (20), the two subjects disagree in person features as well as in number features. Therefore, splitting T into separate person and number probes along the lines of Béjar and Rezac (2009) and Preminger (2014: Chapter 4) and saying that SR is mediated by the person probe only (as suggested to us by Richard Compton) does not help to explain this example. Not all languages that allow SS marking in cases of referential overlap allow it in cases where the subjects do not match in person (Stirling 1993: 38, 82–83), but some do, including Mojave.
10. This account also explains the fact that a passive clause linked to an intransitive clause with the "unspecified subject" marker *ka* can also be marked SS in Seri (Marlett 1981: 357). See Keine (2013) for a somewhat different but related interpretation of these facts.
11. One sometimes sees SS marking if the subject of one clause is coreferential with the possessor of the subject of the other clause, even when there is no independent evidence of possessor raising. Seri (Marlett 1981: 362–363) has one clearly described instance of this. Since all of the examples involve inalienable possession (I = my limbs, my heart, my spirit), it may simply be that an NP that denotes a person can count as coreferential with an NP that denotes a part of the person, as happens with discontinuous constituents in Australian languages like Warlpiri.
12. Case is relevant to SR in Panoan languages too, although in a different way: the form of the SS marker varies depending on whether the matrix subject is ergative or not (Valenzuela 2003; Camacho 2010; Baker 2014). So case features can be picked up by SR markers, and Pomo is presumably a variant of this. See Camacho (2010) for the stronger claim that case is central to the agreement relation that establishes interclausal dependencies in SR constructions. More generally, the relationship of SR to case marking is an important topic that we are unable to discuss systematically here.
13. There is also good evidence that what counts as the object of the embedded clause for O=S reference marking in Panoan is an agreement-theoretic sense of object. See Baker and Camargo Souza (in preparation) for discussion.
14. We thank Richard Compton for pointing out this reference to us.

References

Abney, Steve. 1987. *The English noun phrase in its sentential aspect*. Cambridge: Massachusetts Institute of Technology. (Doctoral dissertation.)

Aoun, Joseph. 1981. *The formal nature of anaphoric relations*. Cambridge: Massachusetts Institute of Technology. (Doctoral dissertation.)

Arregi, Karlos & Hanink, Emily. 2018. Switch reference in Washo as multiple subject agreement. In Sherry Hucklebridge & Max Nelson (eds.), *Proceedings of NELS* 48. 39–48. Amherst, MA: GSLA.

Assmann, Anke. 2012. Switch-reference as interclausal tense agreement: Evidence from Quechua. In Weisser, Philipp (ed.), *Perspectives on switch-reference: Local modeling and empirical distribution*, 41–82. Leipzig: Universität Leipzig.

Austin, Peter. 1980. Switch-reference in Australian languages. In Munro, Pamela (ed.), *UCLA Working Papers in Syntax* 8, 7–47. Los Angeles: University of California.

Austin, Peter. 1981. Switch-reference in Australia. *Language* 57. 309–334.

Baker, Mark. 2003. *Lexical categories: Verbs, nouns and adjectives*. Cambridge: Cambridge University Press.

Baker, Mark. 2014. On dependent ergative case (in Shipibo) and its derivation by phase. *Linguistic Inquiry* 45. 341–379.

Baker, Mark & Livia Camargo Souza. 2019. *Agree without agreement: Switch reference and reflexive voice in two Panoan languages*. Rutgers University (ms.). (http://sites.rutgers.edu/mark-baker/wp-content/uploads/sites/199/2019/07/Agree-without-Agreement-resubmitted.pdf)

Béjar, Susana & Rezac, Milan. 2009. Cyclic agree. *Linguistic Inquiry* 40. 35–73.

Bittner, Maria. 1994. *Case, scope, and binding*. Dordrecht: Kluwer.

Bok-Bennema, Reineke. 1991. *Case and agreement in Inuit*. Berlin: Walter de Gruyter.

Broadwell, George Aaron. 1990. *Extending the binding theory: A Muskogean case study*. Los Angeles: University of California. (Doctoral dissertation.)

Broadwell, George Aaron. 1997. Binding theory and switch-reference. In Bennis, Hans & Pica, Pierre & Rooryck, Johan (eds.), *Atomism and binding*, 31–49. Dordrecht: Foris.

Broadwell, George Aaron. 2006. *A Choctaw reference grammar*. Lincoln: University of Nebraska Press.

Camacho, José. 2010. On case concord: The syntax of switch-reference clauses. *Natural Language and Linguistic Theory* 28. 239–274.
Camargo Souza, Livia. 2016. *Agree as coindexation: The case of switch-reference*. Rutgers University. (Ms.)
Chomsky, Noam. 1981. *Lectures on government and binding*. Dordrecht: Foris.
Cole, Peter. 1982. *Imbabura Quechua*. Amsterdam: North-Holland.
Cole, Peter. 1983. Switch-reference in two Quechua languages. In Haiman, John & Munro, Pamela (eds.), *Switch-reference and universal grammar*, 1–15. Amsterdam: John Benjamins.
Cole, Peter & Hermon, Gabriella. 2011. Nominalization and case assignment in Quechua. *Lingua* 121. 1225–1251.
Davidson, Donald. 1967. The logical form of action sentences. In Rescher, Nicholas (ed.), *The logic of action and decision*, 105–148. Pittsburgh, PA: University of Pittsburgh Press.
Davies, William. 1986. *Choctaw verb agreement and universal grammar*. Dordrecht: Reidel.
Diercks, Michael. 2013. Indirect agree in Lubukusu complementizer agreement. *Natural Language and Linguistic Theory* 31. 357–407.
Farrell, Patrick & Marlett, Steve & Perlmutter, David. 1991. Notions of subjecthood and switch-reference: Evidence from Seri. *Linguistic Inquiry* 22. 431–456.
Finer, Daniel. 1984. *The formal grammar of switch-reference*. Amherst: University of Massachusetts. (Doctoral dissertation.)
Finer, Daniel. 1985. The syntax of switch-reference. *Linguistic Inquiry* 16. 35–55.
Fortescue, Michael. 1984. *West Greenlandic*. London: Croom Helm.
Givón, Talmy. 1983. Topic continuity in discourse: The functional domain of switch-reference. In Haiman, John & Munro, Pamela (eds.), *Switch-reference and universal grammar*, 52–82. Amsterdam: John Benjamins.
Givón, Talmy. 2011. *Ute reference grammar*. Amsterdam: John Benjamins.
Gordon, Lynn. 1983. Switch-reference, clause order, and interclausal relationships in Maricopa. In Haiman, John & Munro, Pamela (eds.), *Switch-reference and universal grammar*, 83–104. Amsterdam: John Benjamins.
Gordon, Lynn & Munro, Pamela. 2017. Relative clauses in Western Muskogean languages. *Glossa* 2. 1–18.
Haiman, John & Munro, Pamela. 1983. Introduction. In Haiman, John & Munro, Pamela (eds.), *Switch-reference and universal grammar*, ix–xv. Amsterdam: John Benjamins.
Hale, Kenneth. 1992. Subject obviation, switch-reference, and control. In Larson, Richard & Iatridou, Sabine & Lahiri, Utpal & Higginbotham, James (eds.), *Control and grammar*, 51–77. Dordrecht: Kluwer.
Hermon, Gabriella. 1985. *Syntactic modularity*. Dordrecht: Foris.
Jacobsen, William. 1964. *A grammar of the Washo language*. Berkeley: University of California. (Doctoral dissertation.)
Jacobsen, William. 1967. Switch-reference in Hokan-Coahuiltecan. In Hymes, Dell & Bittle, William (eds.), *Studies in Southwestern ethnolinguistics*, 238–263. The Hague: Mouton.
Jake, Janice. 1985. *Grammatical relations in Imbabura Quechua*. Garland: New York.
Jeanne, LaVerne. 1978. *Aspects of Hopi grammar*. Cambridge: Massachusetts Institute of Technology. (Doctoral dissertation.)
Keine, Stephan. 2013. Deconstructing switch-reference. *Natural Language and Linguistic Theory* 31. 767–826.
Kendall, Martha. 1975. *Selected problems in Yavapai syntax*. New York: Garland.
Landau, Idan. 2000. *Elements of control: Structure and meaning in infinitival constructions*. Dordrecht: Kluwer.
Langdon, Margaret & Munro, Pamela. 1979. Subject and (switch-) reference in Yuman. *Folia Linguistica* 13. 321–344.
Marlett, Stephen. 1981. *The structure of Seri*. San Diego: University of California. (Doctoral dissertation.)
McKenzie, Andrew. 2012. *The role of contextual restriction in reference-tracking*. Amherst: University of Massachusetts. (Doctoral dissertation.)
McKenzie, Andrew. 2015a. A survey of switch-reference in North America. *International Journal of American Linguistics* 81. 409–448.
McKenzie, Andrew. 2015b. *Austinian situations and switch-reference: The role of context in reference-tracking*. University of Kansas. (Ms.)
McLendon, Sally. 1975. *A grammar of Eastern Pomo*. Berkeley: University of California Press.
McLendon, Sally. 1978. Ergativity, case and transitivity in Eastern Pomo. *International Journal of American Linguistics* 44. 1–9.
Mithun, Marianne. 1993. Switch-reference: Clause combining in Central Pomo. *International Journal of American Linguistics* 59. 119–136.
Muehlbauer, Jeffery. 2012. The relationship of switch-reference, animacy, and obviation in Plains Cree. *International Journal of American Linguistics* 78. 203–238.
Munro, Pamela. 1976. *Mojave syntax*. New York: Garland.

Munro, Pamela. 1983. When "same" is not "not different". In Haiman, John & Munro, Pamela (eds.), *Switch-reference and universal grammar*, 223–243. Amsterdam: John Benjamins.
Muysken, Pieter. 1977. *Syntactic developments in the verb phrase of Ecuadorian Quechua*. Lisse: The Peter De Ridder Press.
Nonato, Rafael. 2014. *Clause-chaining, switch-reference and coordination*. Cambridge: Massachusetts Institute of Technology. (Doctoral dissertation.)
Oswalt, Robert. 1983. Interclausal reference in Kashaya. In Haiman, John & Munro, Pamela (eds.), *Switch-reference and universal grammar*, 267–290. Amsterdam: John Benjamins.
Preminger, Omer. 2014. *Agreement and its failures*. Cambridge, MA: MIT Press.
Rice, Keren. 1989. *Slave*. Berlin: Mouton de Gruyter.
Roberts, John. 1987. *Amele*. London: Croom Helm.
Roberts, John. 1988a. Amele switch-reference and the theory of grammar. *Linguistic Inquiry* 19. 45–63.
Roberts, John. 1988b. Switch-reference in Papuan languages: A syntactic or extrasyntactic device? *Australian Journal of Linguistics* 8. 75–117.
Ross, John. 1967. *Constraints on variables in syntax*. Cambridge: Massachusetts Institute of Technology. (Doctoral dissertation.)
Shklovsky, Kirill & Sudo, Yasutada. 2014. The syntax of monsters. *Linguistic Inquiry* 45. 381–402.
Stirling, Lesley. 1993. *Switch-reference and discourse representation*. Cambridge: Cambridge University Press.
Valenzuela, Pilar. 2003. *Transitivity in Shipibo-Konibo grammar*. Eugene: University of Oregon. (Doctoral dissertation.)
van Gijn, Rik. 2016. Switch-reference: An overview in Western South America. In van Gijn, Rik & Hammond, Jeremy (eds.), *Switch-reference 2.0*: *Typological studies in language*, vol. 114. 153–206. Amsterdam: John Benjamins.
Watanabe, Akira. 2000. Feature copying and binding: Evidence from complementizer agreement and switch-reference. *Syntax* 3. 159–181.
Watkins, Laurel. 1993. The discourse function of Kiowa switch-reference. *International Journal of American Linguistics* 59. 137–164.
Weisser, Philipp. 2012. Is there switch-reference marking in coordinated clauses? In Weisser, Philipp (ed.), *Perspectives on switch-reference: Local modeling and empirical distribution*, 165–190. Leipzig: Universität Leipzig.
Woodbury, Anthony. 1983. Switch-reference, syntactic organization, and rhetorical structure in central Yup'ik Eskimo. In Haiman, John & Munro, Pamela (eds.), *Switch-reference and universal grammar*, 291–315. Amsterdam: John Benjamins.
Zaenen, Anne, Maling, Joan & Thráinsson, Hoskur. 1985. Case and grammatical functions: The Icelandic passive. *Natural Language and Linguistic Theory* 3. 441–483.

10

ERGATIVITY AND ERGATIVITY SPLITS

Bettina Spreng

1. Introduction: Ergativity

Ergativity is a phenomenon where subjects of transitive clauses (A) show contrasting behavior to subjects of intransitive clauses (S) and objects (O).[1] These properties contrast with nominative-accusative alignment where subjects are treated identically (1). Ergativity manifests across unrelated languages and can be found to be variable even within language families. It is less commonly found compared to the more familiar nominative-accusative alignment in languages (Comrie 2013). Among North American language families, it is found in Eskimo-Aleut, Mayan, Salish, Sahaptian, Zoque, Chibchan (Bribri), and Tsimshian.

(1) Ergative and nominative-accusative alignment

	A	S	O
Ergative	ergative	absolutive	absolutive
Nominative-accusative	nominative	nominative	accusative

These contrasts between subjects are most commonly exhibited with respect to case marking, verb agreement, word order, and other surface phenomena. Ergativity is more commonly found in case-marking (Comrie 2013; Siewierska 2013) than in verbal agreement marking.

An example of an ergative language is shown in (2) from Canadian Inuktitut [iku] spoken on Baffin Island, Nunavut, Canada. It shows ergativity in both case marking and agreement.

(2) Inuktitut

a. Transitive

anguti-up	*arnaq*	*kunik-paa*
man-ERG	woman.ABS	kiss-IND.3SG/3SG

'The man kissed the woman'

b. Intransitive[2]

anguti	*niri-vuq*
man.ABS	eat-IND.3SG

'The man is eating'

(Spreng 2001: 161)

In the transitive clause in (2a), the subject of the transitive clause A shows ergative case marking *-up* and O shows absolutive case marking Ø, which is the same case marker used for the intransitive subject S in (2b). In Inuktitut, verb inflection also reflects person and number agreement with ergative- and absolutive-marked arguments. Thus, in basic declarative sentences, we have agreement with both A and O, while in intransitive sentences, agreement is with S.

If a language shows these contrasts in these surface properties, it is considered morphologically ergative (ME). This means that the morphology but not the syntax treats A differently from S and O. Such languages thus show a mismatch between syntax and morphology that may require explanation.

When these alignments are shown in syntactic properties, languages are considered syntactically ergative (Dixon 1979). Syntactic ergativity (SE) means that A is treated differently from O and S in the syntax, too, thus mirroring the morphological alignment. SE is most commonly exhibited in the ergative-marked argument's inaccessibility to Ā-extraction. This assigns the ergative marked noun phrase A a special place compared to S and O. Other factors such as deletion in purpose clauses, conjunction reduction, and other coreference configurations may also indicate SE (Manning 1996).

An ergativity split is a nominative-accusative alignment in a primarily ergative alignment language. While nominative-accusative alignment may serve the function of making A accessible to Ā-extraction, it is not the only trigger for split ergativity. Generally, nominative-accusative alignments are found triggered by verbal properties such as tense, aspect, modality and/or nominal properties triggered by certain persons, animacy, or (in)definiteness (Dixon 1994).

When it comes to the analysis of ergativity in a language, the main questions center around the status of the ergative A argument. Especially in SE patterns, the ergative argument is special in some sense compared to the absolutive. In that case, the morphology reflects something deeper in the syntax.

Another question that needs addressing with respect to splits is whether the O case in splits is in fact equal to a structural accusative or an oblique case like in an antipassive. Antipassives are configurations that are formally intransitive in that the subject behaves like an intransitive subject while still having an O that shows oblique case (Polinsky 2008). The main difference is that O has now a different case from a regular O, and a different case from S and A, which is exactly what nominative-accusative alignment is. Whether that counts as split is treated differently, depending on the languages that are being investigated. For example, Eskimo is not normally taken as a split-ergative language. However, some analyses treat (some) antipassives as nominative-accusative (Bok-Bennema 1991 for West Greenlandic; Spreng 2006 for Inuktitut). The example in (3) shows a fairly typical example of antipassives where the case on O becomes *-mik*, analyzed consistently as accusative in Bok-Bennema (1991), but only for antipassives with overt antipassive morphology (3a) in Spreng (2006).

(3) Inuktitut

a. *anguti* *kunik-si-vuq* *arna-mik*
man.ABS kiss-AP-IND.3SG woman-MIK
'the man kissed a woman '

b. *anguti* *niri-∅-vuq* *niqi-mik*
man.ABS eat-AP-IND.3SG meat-MIK
'the man is eating meat'

(Spreng 2006: 248)

Antipassive markers are generally either homophonic to reflexive markers or aspectual markers (Polinsky 2008; Spreng 2010). Formally, they are treated as less transitive (Hopper & Thompson 1980), but also as triggered by the same properties as ergativity splits (Tsunoda 1981; Spreng 2010). Thus they are often discussed in similar contexts as ergativity splits.

The rest of this chapter is organized as follows.

Section 2 will outline the different representations of ergativity we find in North American languages. Examples from Eskimo-Aleut, Mayan, Salish, Sahaptian, Chinookan, Chibchan, and Tsimshian languages will illustrate the variety of ergativity in North America.

The approaches to the above questions on the status of A in ergative alignment and O in splits will be divided into three major sections. While the two major families of analyses will be presented separately, we will also see that they borrow elements from each other, which is not surprising considering that they are supposed to account for the same or similar phenomena.

Section 3.1 will cover the *ergative=structural case* family of approaches with its variations. Section 3.2 will discuss the approaches that analyze ergative as a non-default case that is dependent on the licensing of a default absolutive/nominative case. Section 3.3 discusses the family of approaches that can be summarized as *ergative=inherent case*. Section 3.4 will address approaches to ergativity splits.

Section 4 closes with a summary on the state of analysis based on the work being conducted on North American languages. It will be concluded that ergativity is not a homogenous phenomenon as evidenced by the variety of properties of ergativity from different languages and proposed accounts.

2. Ergativity in North American Languages

In North America, ergativity is attested in languages of the Eskimo-Aleut, Mayan, Salish, Sahaptian, Tsimshian, Siouan, and Chinookan language families (Mithun 1999).

Outside of North America, ergativity exists in many language families, for example in the Indo-Aryan branch of Indo-European (Butt 1997; Butt & Holloway-King 1998; Altshuler 2014; Ura 2006; Mahajan 2012; Torrego 2012), and in Caucasian (Polinsky & Potsdam 2001; Harris 1976). It is also prevalent in Austronesian (Aldridge 2004, 2008a, 2008b, 2016; Massam 2001; 2006; Otsuka 2006; Herd et al. 2011), Sino-Tibetan (DeLancey 1990), and it famously exists in the isolate Basque (Levin 1983a; Oyharçabal 1992; Uriagareka 1999; Hualde & Urbina 2003; Laka 2006a, 2006b; Preminger 2012; Rezac et al. 2014). It is thus not a defining property of a language family, although it may be more common in some than in others.

Within the context of discussions, descriptions, or analyses of ergativity, we also find discussions of split-S systems.[3] In addition to contrasting the transitive subject A from O and the intransitive S, these systems also show contrasts between subjects of transitive and intransitive unergative (active) verbs on one hand, and the subjects of unaccusative verbs and O on the other. Thus, they show case marking that seems to contrast argument structure positions (Harris 1982; 1990; Dixon 1994) in that internal arguments have one case and external arguments another.

In the Lakota (Siouan) [lkt] example in (4), the agreement marker for first person differs depending on whether the subject is patient S, agent S, or agent A. If that agreement marker targets O (4d), it will be the same marker as for the patient S *ma-* (4b). On the other hand, the marker targeting A (4a) and agent S (4c) show the same marker *wa-*.

(4) Lakota

a.	***wa**psíča*	***wa**hí*
	'I jumped.'	'I came.'
b.	***ma**k^{h}úže*	***ma**xwá*
	'I'm sick.'	'I'm sleepy.'
c.	*a**wá**ʔu*	***wa**ktékte*
	'I bought it.'	'I'll kill him.'
d.	*a**má**ʔu*	***ma**ktékte*
	'He brought me.'	'He'll kill me.'

(Mithun 1991: 514)

Another split-S system is found in Nez Perce (Sahaptian) [nez]. Here, the intransitive S is unmarked (5a). In the transitive, the direct object however gets a marker, thus O (5b) shows different morphology from S, and S also shows different morphology from A.

(5) Nez Perce

a. *háama* *hipáayna*
man he.came
'The man came.'

b. *háama-**nm*** *pée'wiye* *wewúkiye-**ne***
man-ERG he.shot.it elk-DO
'The man shot an elk.'

(Rude 1988: 547–548)

These systems are often included in the discussion of ergativity since the main question as to whether the status of A is different from the status of S is relevant as well.

2.1. Ergativity: Mostly Head and (Some) Dependent Marking

Surface (morphological) ergativity is exhibited in case marking and/or agreement marking. It seems that in North American languages, head marking is more common than dependent marking and ergativity is more often shown in the agreement inflection on the verb (Mithun 1999). In Eskimo-Aleut, ergativity is shown in both case and agreement marking (6). Thus, ergative case is contingent on transitive agreement on the verb as shown in the example from one of the Yup'ik languages.[4] In (6a), we find ergative case on A, while the agreement marker on the verb targets both A and O. In the formally intransitive antipassive in (6b), the third-person singular agreement targets only the absolutive marked S and the former O is marked with an oblique case. Ergativity is thus shown in both head and dependent marking.

(6) Yup'ik

a. *Caanam* *qimugtet tangellrai*
John-ERG doga-ABSP see-PST-IND3S-3P
'John saw the dogs.'

b. *Caanaq* *qimugtenek* *tangellruuq*
John-ABS doga-AMP see-PST-IND3S
'John saw the dogs.'

(Benua 1995: 28)

In Salish, ergativity is only shown in the agreement marker. Third-person transitive subject agreement targets A, but not third-person intransitive S (Gerdts 1982; Jelinek & Demers 1994; Wiltschko 2006), as in the example from Halkomelem Salish [hur] in (7). Only (7a) shows agreement in person and number with the subject, while there is no agreement marker on the verb in the intransitive sentence (7b), thus singling out the transitive subject A for agreement while neither O nor S are targeted by agreement.

(7) Halkomelem Salish

a. *q'ó:y-t-es* *te* *Strang* *te* *sqelá:w*
kill-TRANS-3S DET Strang DET beaver
'Strang killed the beaver.'

b. *í:mex* *te* *Strang*
walking DET Strang
'Strang is walking.'

(Wiltschko 2006: 197)

Chol [ctu], a Mayan language, also shows head marking in that only A is targeted with a prefix *i-* on the predicate as shown in (8a), while S and O are not (8b).

(8) Chol

a. VOS TRANSITIVE

Tyi	*i-ña'ty-ä*	*pañämil*	*kixtyaño.*
PRFV	A3-know-DTV	world	people

'The people understood.' (lit: – 'The people knew the world.') (D.175)

b. VS INTRANSITIVE

Ta-x	*'lajm-i*	*jiñi*	*x-ñek.*
PRFV-already	die-ITV	DET	CL-ñek

'The xñek already died.'3 (D.30)

(Coon 2013b: 4)

In Gitksan [git], a Tsimshian language, ergativity is manifested in the marker *-s* on the verb (analyzed as case in Hunt 1993) as shown on the verb in the transitive (9a), but not in the intransitive sentence (9b). This pattern is found in independent clauses (Hunt 1993).[5]

(9) Gitksan

a. *ga'as dip John t Mary*

kaʔ-ə=s	tip	John	t=Mary
see-ERG=CASE	CN	John	CN=Mary

'John and them saw Mary.'

b. *yee dip John go'ohl Terrace*

ye:	tip	John	quʔ=ɬ	Terrace
go	CN	John	LOC=CN	Terrace

'John and them went to Terrace.'

(Hunt 1993: 28)

In Chinook, we also find ergativity in the agreement marking of the predicate. It cross-references A, S, and O, including IO (indirect object) in the order A-O/S-indirect object for person, number, and gender. There are two series for these pronominal affixes, *unmarked* for S, O, and indirect object, and *ergative* for A (Rezac 2009: 784).

(10) Chinook

(***i-kala***$_i$)	*ga-**č**$_i$-ł$_j$-(a)š$_k$-l-u-√łada*	*((i)ł-šqwa$_j$)*	*((i)š-Gagilak$_k$)*
3SM-man	RPT-**3SME**-3N-3DU-APPL-DIR-threw	3N-water	3DU-woman

He (the man) threw it (the water) at the two of them (at the two women).

(Silverstein 1976: 130;[6] cited from Rezac 2009: 784)

2.2. Splits: No Ergative Alignment

Nominative-accusative alignment in ergative or split-S languages is triggered by certain verbal and/or nominal properties. This means that under certain conditions, subjects are treated equally while contrasting with O.

Contrasting properties between ergative and nominative-accusative alignment are often shown in the verbal TAM system and in nominal properties such as person and definiteness. Nominative-accusative/non-ergative alignment in ergative languages is consistently shown in the contrasting values displayed in (11). This means if a split is conditioned by TAM, we never find ergative alignment with non-past tenses when there is nominative-accusative alignment with past tenses. Thus, if there is nominative-accusative alignment with past tense, then the nominative-accusative alignment is triggered by something other than tense, and we also find past and non-past tense with both types of alignment.

(11) Conditions for splits

		Ergative alignment	*Nominative-accusative alignment*
a.	Tense	Past	Non-past
b.	Aspect	Perfective, telic	Imperfective, atelic
c.	Mood	Indicative, realis	Subjunctive, irrealis
d.	Main/dependent clause	Main	Dependent
e.	Definiteness of object	Definite	Indefinite
f.	Specificity of object	Specific	Nonspecific
g.	Person of arguments	Third person	First and second person
h.	Full DP	Full DP	Pronoun
i.	Wide scope	Absolutive DP	Nominative DP

Some of these conditions may be contingent on each other or may be unified as a cluster of conditions. For example, subjunctives or irrealis moods (11c) are often expressed in dependent clauses, which may explain the tendency to have non-ergative alignment with dependent clauses (11d) (Anderson 1976). With respect to DP properties, since full DPs are third person and pronouns are always definite, we may expect a language to exhibit a person contrast such as (11g) together with a full DP/pronoun contrast (11h). A definiteness contrast (11e) may occur in conjunction with a pronoun/full DP contrast (11h), and possibly a person contrast (11g).

The split according to DP types was summarized in Silverstein (1976) as a person/animacy hierarchy whereby nominals higher on the animacy hierarchy (e.g., first- and second-person pronouns) are more likely to be marked with accusative, whereas those lower in the hierarchy are more likely to be marked with ergative case. The nominal hierarchy outlined in Dixon (1994: 85) similarly specifies that the likelihood of ergative alignments decreases towards DPs that are closer to first and second person, while third-person common nouns appear at the other end of this continuum. Thus, since first- and second-person pronouns are always specific/definite/animate, third-person nouns and pronouns show a wider variability since they may show animacy/definiteness contrasts that do not exist for first- and second-person pronouns.

(12)
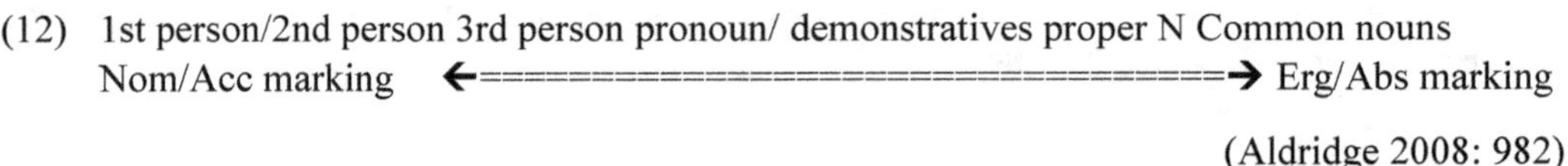

(Aldridge 2008: 982)

In addition to the splits conditioned by nominal contrasts, we also find splits conditioned by verbal properties that are consistent across languages. Ergative alignment corresponds to past-type tenses, perfective, bounded, telic aspects, and indicative, realis type moods and nominative-accusative alignment occurs with non-past tenses, imperfective, unbounded aspects, and subjunctive/irrealis type moods. More recent work has actually shown that the splits based on tense are more likely due only to aspect splits (Salanova 2007), and the apparent tense contrasts are due to overlaps of tense and aspect in the verbal inflection. For example, past tense marking may coincide with perfective aspect reading when the language has no separate perfective aspect marking, such as in English.

What is interesting to note about this type of split is that imperfective aspect tends to correspond to non-default alignments not only in primarily ergative-alignment languages, but also in primarily nominative-accusative alignment languages (Spreng 2012; Kratzer 2004).[7] This provides some further support for the idea that these "splits" are nothing but epiphenomena of different structural configurations for case assignment (Coon 2013b; Baker 2015) and are not a phenomenon typical only for primarily ergative alignment languages.

Splits are not necessarily exhibited as nominative-accusative alignment. For example, in Nez Perce, we find a "split" in a construction where all case marking ceases both in intransitive and transitive constructions (Deal 2010). In (13b), the A and O arguments are case marked in the transitive construction.

(13) Nez Perce

a. Intransitive: Subject unmarked

sík'em *hi-wleke'yx-tee'nix* *háamti'c*
horse 3SUBJ-run-HAB.PL fast
'Horses run fast.'

b. Transitive: Subject marked, object marked
*'ip-**ním*** *pée-qn'i-se* *qeqíi-**ne***
3SG-**ERG** 3/3-dig-IMPERF edible.root-OBJ
'He digs qeqíit roots.'

(Crook 1999: 238)

In line with the unusual ergative pattern in Nez Perce, where S, A, and O have different case morphology, the "split" is not exactly a nominative-accusative alignment, but the subject and the objects have no case markers at all (14), thus sharing some of the properties of intransitive configurations with no case marker on S (13a).

(14) Nez Perce
'ipí *hi-qn'íi-se* *qeqíit*
3SG 3SUBJ-dig-IMPERF edible.root
'He digs qeqíit roots.'

(Crook 1999: 238)

A more common example of a person-based split is exhibited in the split-S language Bitsbi (Pomo). Subject pronouns in transitive and volitional intransitive clauses are marked identically, thus exhibiting nominative-accusative alignment. On the other hand, intransitive subjects of clauses with non-volitional predicates show the same marker as O in transitive clauses. The system thus shows a split-S system, i.e., case marking aligning with argument structure positions and split ergativity in that depending on the underlying argument position, it either follows an ergative pattern (non-volitional in (15a) and (15c)) or a nominative-accusative pattern (volitional in (15a) and (15b)).

(15) Bitsbi

a. *mi'p'* *mip-al* *sak'a.*
he.NOM he-ACC killed
'He killed him.'

b. *mip'kaluhuya.*
'He went home.'

c. *mi'p-al* *xa* *bakut ma.*
he-ACC water fell
'He fell in the water.'

(Delancey 1981: 651)

Tsimshianic languages show ergativity splits along the lines of clause types, TAM, and noun types (Mulder 1994; Peterson 2006). While there are different types of splits and different pronominal systems within the languages that seem to correlate in a rather complex manner (see the summary in Mulder 1994:

111), the split along the lines of person and argument type discussed in Forbes (2017) are persistently present along with the other factors. With respect to clause type and TAM, the language family patterns similarly to others. However, TAM is always subject to the overarching conditioning factor of proper vs. common nouns and the indicative vs. subjunctive factor. Thus, there is a propensity for splits being determined by clause type and noun type, which puts it closer to the splits exhibited in Salish.

(16) Coast Tsimshian (Sm'algyax)

a. *Yagwa* *hadiks-a* *üüla*
PRES swim-CN seal
'The seal is swimming.'

b. *Yagwa-t* *huum-da* *duus-a* *hoon*
PRES-3 smell-CN cat-CN fish
A PRED PRED
'The cat is sniffing the fish.'

(Mulder 1994: 32)

As mentioned earlier in this section, a very common trigger for splits is imperfective aspect. Chibchan [cba] is one of the more heterogeneous language families of the Americas both with respect to the number of languages and their morphosyntactic surface properties (Pache 2015). With respect to ergativity and ergativity splits, we find splits triggered by aspect as shown in (17).

(17) Chibchan

a. *ie'-r* *i* *bikéitse* *tö . . .*
3SG-ERG 3SG.ABS think that
'She thinks that. . .'

b. *ie'tso'* *i* *bikéits-uk.*
3SG.be 3ABS think-INF
'She is thinking.'

(Quesada 1999: 32)

We also find aspect-triggered splits with Mayan languages, as discussed for Chol in Coon (2013a). Perfective aspect corresponds to ergative alignment (18), while nominative-accusative alignment corresponds to imperfective aspect (19).

(18) Chol perfective

a. *Tyi* *k-mek'-e-yety.*
PRFV 1ERG-TV-hug-2ABS
'I hugged you.'

b. *Tyi* *wäy-i-yety.*
PRFV sleep-ITV-2ABS
'You slept.'

(Coon 2013a: 181)

(19) Chol imperfective

a. *Choñkol* *k-mek'-ety.*
PROG 1.ERG-hug-2.ABS
'I'm hugging you.'

b. *Choñkol* *a-wäy-el.*
PROG 2.ERG-sleep-NML
'You're sleeping.'

(Coon 2013a: 182)

Another facet to splits triggered by aspect are antipassives. While formally intransitive, they do tend to look like nominative-accusative configurations with a case on O that is distinct from the subject case. As we have seen with Nez Perce, for example, splits are not necessarily tied to nominative-accusative if we allow for the view that any non-ergative alignment is triggered by comparable properties while the outcome is not necessarily the same cross-linguistically.

What supports the idea that antipassives and nominative-accusative configurations may be treated similarly in some languages is that the conditions for splits and antipassives are similar cross-linguistically (Tsunoda 1981), at least for splits triggered by aspect (Tsunoda 1981; Spreng 2010). One of the issues that needs resolving for any language thus is whether the case on O is what we would consider structural accusative, or whether we take it only as accusative because it has a different case from regular O and S.

2.3. *Syntactic Ergativity*

The preceding two sections have discussed morphological, or surface ergativity. In this section, I discuss deep or syntactic ergativity, which goes beyond morphological ergativity in distinguishing the ergative marked argument from the absolutive marked arguments.

Syntactic ergativity (SE) is evidence of the syntactic "reality" of ergativity, where we find that syntactic processes after case assignment treat the ergative A differently from O and S. The most common of these is Ā-movement. Ergative marked noun phrases tend to not be accessible for Ā-extraction (Dixon 1994).

For example, West Greenlandic (Kalaallisut) does not allow two-argument relative clauses where the gap would correspond to ergative marked A. In (20a), the gap in the relative clause corresponds to O, and its head in the main clause is S, thus both are absolutive. In the ungrammatical (20b), the gap represents the agent of the two-argument relative clause, A is thus not acceptable with the intended meaning. To make that possible, the relative clause must be made antipassive (20c), as shown in the intransitive agreement on the verb in the relative clause, the oblique case *-mik* on O, and the antipassive marker *-si* on the verb.

(20) West Greenlandic

a. *miiqqa-t* [*Juuna-p* *paari-sa-i*[8]] *sinip-p-u-t*
[child-ABSPL [J.-ERG look.after-REL(+TR)-3SG.PL] ABS] sleep-JND-LRJ-3PL
'The children that Juuna is looking after are sleeping.'

(Bittner 1994: 55)

b. * *angut* [*aallaat* *tigu-sima-sa-a*]
[man(ABS) [ERG gun(ABS) take-PRF-REL(+TR)-3SG.3SG]
('the man who took the gun')

c. *angut* [*allaam-mik* *tigu-si-sima-su-q*
[man(ABS) [ABS gun-INS take-AP-PRF-REL(-TR)-3SG]]
'the man who took the gun'

(Bittner 1994: 58)

While Eskimo languages thus show some properties of SE languages in prohibiting Ā-extraction of ergative arguments in some types of relative clauses, *wh*-extraction in interrogatives is not consistently SE. While *wh*-words may be absolutive, ergative, and accusative (Gillon 1999), there are some restrictions for A on some other Ā-extraction phenomena (Sherkina-Lieber 2004).

Thus, not all types of Ā-extraction are subject to SE, and languages allow for considerable variation (Rill 2017). The definition of SE may thus include more than this restricted definition.

An even wider definition of SE includes other coreference relations between two noun phrases that may or may not include movement, such as in binding, raising, control, NP deletion in conjunctions, or coreference in purpose clauses (Kazenin 1994; Manning 1996; Dixon 1994).

Another example on the restriction of Ā-extraction of A can be found in Mayan. The following example is from Q'anjob'al. If S is extracted, it moves the *wh*-word overtly to the beginning (21).

(21) Q'anjob'al

a.

Max	*way[-i]*	*naq*	*winaq.*
ASP	sleep-ITV	CLF	man

'The man slept.'

b.

Maktxel$_1$	*max*	*way-i*	$_1$?
who		ASP	sleep-ITV

'Who slept?'

(Coon et al. 2014: 192)

In (22), while the reading representing O-extraction is grammatical (22b), the reading representing A-extraction is not (22c) and can only be interpreted as O-extraction. This blocking of Ā-extraction of A extends to relativization or third-person focus movement (Coon et al. 2014).

(22) Q'anjob'al

a.

Max	*y-il[-a']*	*naq*	*winaq*	*ix*	*ix.*
ASP	3.ERG-see-TV	CLF	man	CLF	woman

'The man saw the woman.'

b.

Maktxel$_1$	*max*	*y-il[-a']*	*naq*	*winaq* ___$_1$?
who	ASP	3.ERG-see-TV	CLF	man

'Who did the man see?'

c. *

Maktxel$_1$	*max-Ø*	*y-il[-a']* ___$_1$	*ix*	*ix?*
who	ASP-3ABS	3.ERG-see-TV	CLF	woman

intended: 'Who saw the woman?'
(grammatical as: 'Who did the woman see?')

(Coon et al. 2014: 192–193)

SE does not seem to be common in North American languages. Kroeber (1997) notes that there is no distinction between grammatical functions or argument positions for the gaps in Thompson River Salish. Davis (2010), in an article on the six different relativization strategies in St'át'imcets (aka Lillooet, Northern Interior Salish), outlines the problems in determining whether there is raising or matching in the different relative clause types.

SE with respect to all Ā-movement and other diagnostics seems to be rare in the world's languages, and the most common ones mentioned tend to be Dyirbal (Dixon 1994) and Basque (Levin 1983b). Even for those languages, SE is not a phenomenon to be applicable for every instance of A (Rezac et al. 2014). A broader view on syntactic ergativity contrasting A from S and O includes phenomena regarding coreference relations such as in control, conjunctions, binding, and quantifier float (Dixon 1994; Kazenin 1994; Manning 1996).

Features that show SE form an implicational hierarchy, as shown in (23), indicate how common SE is with respect to properties other than Ā-extraction. Thus, if a language has SE under purpose clause formation, it will also exhibit SE for conjunctions and relative clause formation. Thus, we should find SE most commonly in relative clause formation, and if absent there, then it is unlikely to be found with the properties lower on the hierarchy.

(23) Syntactic ergativity

Relativization > conjunction reduction > purpose clause formation

(Kazenin 1994; Manning 1996)

Tsimshian has a rather elaborate system of ergativity splits, but none of them seem to be motivated by an inaccessibility of A to Ā-extraction (Mulder 1994; Peterson 2006).

An example of SE based on conjunction deletion is illustrated here from Yidin (Pama–Nyungan, Australia) [yii]. Conjunction deletion in Yidin targets S and O or A. This happens only if they are all third person, since first- and second-person arguments follow nominative-accusative alignment (Kazenin 1994). O and S are conjoined in (24a) and both are third person. In (24b), A and S pattern together since A is first person, thus allowing for nominative-accusative alignment. It is, however, flexible in also allowing O and S patterning. In (24c), the only possible interpretation is the one where A and S pattern together. First and second person thus control conjunction deletion only if they are A or S (24a–b), but not when they are O (24c), thus following a nominative-accusative pattern.

(24) Yidin

a. *dama:riŋgu* *bama* *band,a:r* / *wanda: ŋ*
Damari:ERG man follow:PST fell:PST
'Damari followed the man and the man fell down'. (O, S)

b. *ŋayu* *bama* *band,a:r* / *wanda:ɲ*
1SGS/A man follow:PST fell:PST
'I followed the man and fell down' (A, S)
(or 'I followed the man and the man fell down'.) (O, S)

c. *ŋaɲaɲ* *buna:ŋ wawa:l* / *yarŋga:ŋ*
1SG.O woman:ERG see:PST frighten:PST
'The woman saw me and was frightened'. (A, S)
(not 'The woman saw me and I was frightened'.)

(Dixon 1977: 390–391)

Polinsky (2017) argues that inclusion of so many varied features to type languages as SE cannot be done adequately, except in an in-depth analysis. For example, while relative clause extraction behavior can be described consistently as a gap left behind[9] by the ergative marked argument or not, other Ā-movements for topicalization or *wh*-movement might not require Ā-movement consistently.

Another problem is deciding whether examples such as conjunction deletion apply to the equivalent grammatical function in one language or in another. Polinsky (2017) notes that even in a well-known language like English, determining whether A is excluded from conjunction deletion is not always easy to determine. For example, when a passive and an active sentence are conjoined (25), it is not at all clear whether we are dealing with VP or clausal conjunction and thus whether the diagnostic applies.

(25) a. The students worked hard and were rewarded with high grades.
b. The student was found and wrote the paper later.

Ā-extraction blocking alone, however, remains a fairly robust phenomenon to be addressed across typologically unrelated languages despite the language-specific variations exhibited based on the type of Ā-extraction to be found (Aldridge 2008a; Legate 2012). We can thus see variations of syntactic ergativity based on what kind of Ā-extraction blocking of A a language exhibits.

3. Approaches to Ergativity

Three major approaches to ergativity in formal linguistics will be discussed in the next three subsections. The main difference between them is how they treat case assignment. The first two treat ergative case as structural case primarily while the third and arguably most common approach treats ergative case as inherent case. Of the first two types of approaches, the first one focuses on case licensing based on functional heads, while the second one, the dependent/default case approach, considers case licensing based on the configuration two arguments are to each other. In the last subsection, I briefly address recent ideas on how to treat ergativity splits.

3.1. Ergative Case Is Structural Case

This family of approaches centers around the idea that ergative-case marked DPs are either surface subjects (Levin & Massam 1985; Bobaljik 1993; Chomsky 1993; Bittner & Hale 1996a; Bobaljik & Branigan 2006) or direct objects (Wunderlich 1997; Ura 2006; also Davison 2004 for some references). Analyzing the ergative marked argument as subject thus requires some explanation as to how and why the transitive subject is marked differently from the intransitive subject.

One type of analysis divorces agreement from case assignment and argues for different procedures of case assignment, either based on Agree for absolutive case or movement to subject position triggered by an EPP feature for the ergative case. As discussed for Hindi/Urdu in Ura (2006), ergative case is assigned by its theta assigning head, but is moved to subject position Spec of TP because of an EPP feature. Agreement with T does not play a role here. On the other hand, absolutive case is licensed via agreement with T, and this noun phrase moves to subject position only when there is no other argument blocking this movement.

This type of approach requires that A and S share surface subject properties, most commonly the ability to control the missing DP in purpose clauses. For Hindi, supporting evidence for agreement-based case assignment by T to the lower merged theme to get absolutive case is also supported by Hindi having object agreement (Mahajan 2012; Torrego 2012). This is not crucial for an analysis of ergative as structural, however.[10] This approach thus has in common with inherent case approaches that variation between ergative alignment and nominative-accusative alignment revolves around the case assignment properties of *v*.

This approach allows for the ergative marked DP to raise to subject position, while this is not an option with inherent-case approaches. Thus, this approach accounts for subject-like behaviors of the ergative DP and works well for such languages where these behaviors are prevalent (Massam 2001). However, it cannot work for languages where agreement with the ergative is based on agreement with T, or the ergative case marked argument has few typical subject properties. Most of the approaches that analyze ergative case marked arguments as subjects still show that *v* is involved in some way in licensing ergative case. They have this in common with many approaches that take ergative case to be inherent case.

Another family of approaches roots the differences in case/agreement alignment in a difference in structural configurations at the level of argument structure. Ergativity is thus based on a difference in argument structure, where ergative alignment languages may have the argument that ends up with ergative case as an internal argument instead of an external argument (Marantz 1984), effectively making ergative and accusative case equal. This kind of approach works well for languages where ergative DPs show very few subject-like behaviors, but ergative case still shows properties reflecting structural case. Since this family of approaches falls under the view that ergative case is structural case, it is built into the framework that argues that languages vary in whether their surface subjects are also underlying subjects (Levin 1983a; Marantz 1984). Variation with respect to ergativity across languages is thus due to differences in argument structure between ergative and nominative-accusative languages.

This kind of approach is relatively uncommon by now, since many formal approaches to case and agreement think of argument structure as universal and thus not subject to variation (Hale & Keyser 1993; 2002).

A combination of these approaches can be found in the work of Legate (2008) that argues that ergative alignment systems differ with respect to how absolutive case is licensed. Legate (2008) proposes two types of ergative-alignment languages. In the first, absolutive case is equal to nominative case and thus is consistently licensed by T in a finite clause, both in transitive and intransitive clauses. Ergative case is argued to be licensed by *v* and thus is equal to accusative case. In the second type of ergative system, absolutive is considered default case, and ergative case may be licensed by varying means (Legate 2017). In both systems, ergative case is licensed primarily in the lower part of the clause in *v*P. While the methods of licensing and properties of the ergative marked argument may vary across languages, the conclusion here is that ergative case is not associated with subjecthood except at the level of argument structure.

3.2. *Ergative As Non-Default Case*

This family of accounts for ergativity is now better known as the dependent case theory approach (Marantz 2000; Bittner & Hale 1996a, 1996b; Baker 2015; Baker & Bobaljik 2017). The idea behind this approach is that case is not contingent on the position of a DP with respect to a functional head, but contingent on its position relative to another DP in a syntactic domain.

This family of approaches accounts for variation in taking a view that ergative languages and nominative-accusative languages vary with respect to which case is the default case, i.e., if absolutive or nominative is chosen for the O argument based on its position with respect to another argument. It therefore locates language variation initially within variation in the argument structure. It is thus a further development of the ergative as structural case approach (Levin & Massam 1985; Marantz 2000; Bobaljik 1993) that argues ergativity is based on differences in argument structure.

Ergative-alignment and nominative-accusative alignment languages differ in that if the second DP is lower than the default DP, it is marked accusative, and when the second DP is higher than the default DP, we get ergative case. Languages differ with respect to which of the two DP's is marked by default, and how they are marked, allowing for further alignment types other than the classical dichotomy of ergative vs. accusative alignment.

Different case systems are thus the result of choosing different arguments to be assigned default nominative/absolutive case, i.e., unmarked case. Ergative and accusative are then only assigned when there is a second, i.e., non-default case to be assigned within a domain. Depending on the functional head and general configuration under which that happens, we find differences in whether these second cases may be structural or not (Baker 2015). Thus, a second source of variation is built into the system in that in addition to where the non-default case is licensed, it may also differ in the type of functional head that licenses the non-default case. For example, splits would thus be the result of different configurations for non-default case assignment. Thus, the dependent case theory makes the following predictions:

1. Ergative case is structural in that it is not tied to a particular case assigning head nor is it associated with one theta role. This means that derived subjects should allow for ergative case.
2. Ergative case may be licensed only if there is a second argument DP within a syntactic domain. This domain is usually associated with a phase or a small clause. Languages discussed within that approach are Chuckchi, Shipibo, Kalaallisut, and Yup'ik. Derived constructions for evidentiary support are most importantly applicatives.

3.3. *Ergative Case Is Inherent Case*

Arguably, the most common approach to ergativity is to analyze ergative case as an inherent case of some sort (Nash 1996; Anand & Nevins 2006; Laka 2006a; Massam 2006; Woolford 2006; Aldridge 2008a; Legate 2008, 2012; Mahajan 2012; Coon 2013b). While non-structural case is traditionally considered just one type, most recent analyses on the ergative follow the distinction between lexical and inherent non-structural case as discussed in Woolford (2006). The former is idiosyncratic and based on lexical requirements of heads such as V or P, and the latter is tied to specific theta roles and thus to theta-assigning heads such as *v* (Chomsky 2000), a head with both theta-assigning and case/agreement properties (Chomsky 2008). This family of analyses thus can account for the fact that ergative case marked arguments tend to be agents or causers and rarely experiencers, which aligns it with the properties assigned to inherent case since ergative case does not occur with internal arguments (Woolford 2006: 115).

Another piece of support for this type of approach is that ergative case morphology often serves other functions in many languages, while absolutive case morphology is used exclusively for O and S grammatical functions. In some Australian languages (Anderson 1977; Dixon 1979), it also serves as the case marker for instruments and locatives, and in Eskimo-Aleut it is used for possessors (Johns 1987; 1992). So, while ergative case on core arguments commonly serves as inherent case, it may be used for lexical and possibly structural cases. An analysis as lexical for such languages will thus also serve since it is not unusual that the same case morphology may be used for different types of case licensing, as is well known for dative or even accusative case in Germanic (McFadden 2004).

In the inherent case type of approach, ergative case is thus assigned in its theta position in most recent minimalist accounts by a version of *v* to its specifier position. *v*, for some reason or another does not assign structural accusative case to the internal argument. Many approaches thus revolve around the properties of the functional head that is responsible for case assignment. They have this in common with an approach as in Legate (2008; 2017) and some approaches that take ergative to be structural (see §3.1). The *ergative=inherent* approach thus makes the following predictions:

1. Ergative case will occur only on core arguments with certain types of theta roles, such as external agents, causers, possibly experiencers, but never with theme-type theta roles.
2. Ergative case is also available for non-core arguments such as possessors.
3. Ergative case will not appear on derived subjects. Thus, there should be no ergative subjects in passives, antipassives, unaccusative verbs, raising, or ditransitive constructions.
4. Ergative might not occur on every externally merged argument. This may mean that it occurs independently of transitivity, counter to views in Woolford (2006), Massam (2006), and Legate (2012), and may occur without a second argument in the absolutive.

One type of account to syntactic ergativity in this family of approaches argues that a movement triggering EPP feature on ergative assigning *v* attracts the absolutive argument to an external Spec of *v*P, thus trapping the ergative DP to be inaccessible for Ā-extraction (Aldridge 2004; 2008a; 2008b; Coon et al. 2014; Erlewine 2016).

A parametrized approach to ergativity within the ergative=inherent approach is discussed in Sheehan (2017) as shown in (26).

(26)

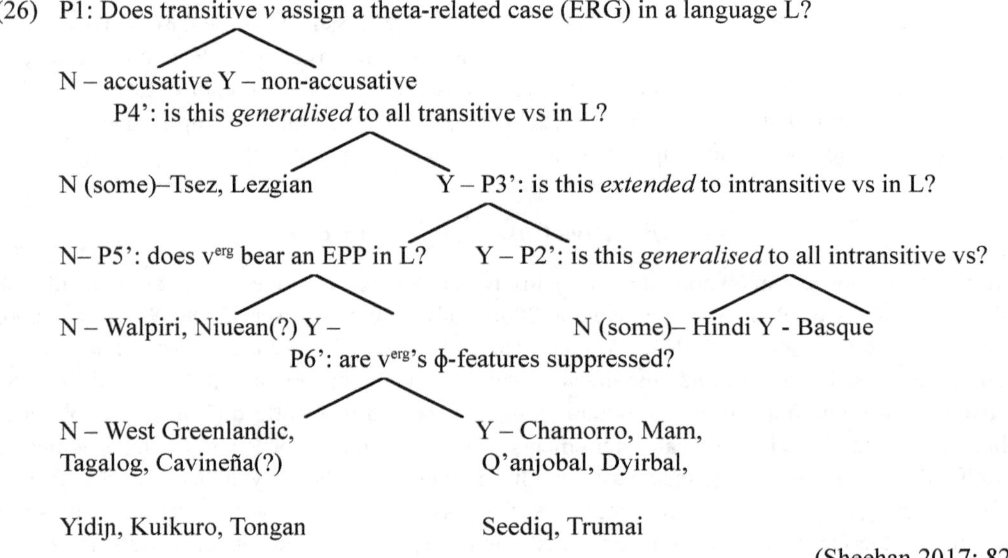

(Sheehan 2017: 82)

It incorporates some of the proposals from the ergative=structural approach in that case licensing is subject to variation depending on agreement (P6'). It also allows for split-S systems (P3'). The main prediction is that all ergative systems have ergative case as theta-related case.

Many approaches thus treat ergative case simply as inherent case. Some approaches take the ergative as a complement of a preposition, accounting for the blocking of Ā-extraction of ergative DPs in SE languages (Polinsky 2016) in this way.

A similar line of analyses that treats ergative as a non-structural case for subjects or objects is found in Coon (2013b). In Mayan, ergative case is in fact genitive and 'transitive' constructions are in fact nominalizations. It is known from other languages that ergative case marking is morphologically identical to genitive case such as in Eskimo-Aleut (Johns 1992; Jacobson 2001), Nez Perce (Rude 1991). In fact, Eskimo linguistics has a longstanding tradition to treat the transitive construction as nominal (Thalbitzer 1930; Hammerich 1951).

In that vein, Johns (1987, 1992) argues for Inuktitut that the agreement inflection in transitive clauses is in fact a passive participle, effectively treating the verb as a derived nominal, which thus becomes unable to assign a theta role. This has the effect of transferring the internal theta role to the absolutive argument in transitive sentences. The original agent is thus merged in a nominal projection and receives genitive case.

3.4. Approaches to Splits

If ergative case is inherent in some way, then a change to a nominative-accusative alignment is like a promotion of that argument to subject status; in other words, it seems like a reverse passive with the agent argument in a more foregrounded role. The cause may lie within the triggers for splits. Legate (2012) argues that splits based on nominal type are purely morphological and have no syntactic consequences. Within this family of approaches, it highly depends on what the focus of triggering properties is for the split. If the split in a language is triggered based on properties of the verb, then splits are generally attributed to changing case assignment capabilities of *v*. Regular ergative case is assigned by *v*, while when there is a split, no ergative is assigned by *v* and accusative case is licensed instead by *v* or another functional head.

Splits in the approach with ergative being part of a PP are somewhat of a non-issue since a DP that is a complement of an adposition will never get subject case. This proposal thus predicts that these languages will not exhibit any splits in the traditional sense, while languages with ergative arguments being simply DPs marked with inherent case should exhibit a split.

Some more recent approaches to ergativity splits argue that these are not in fact actual splits between ergative and nominative-accusative alignment (Laka 2006b). Apparent nominative-accusative structures are shown to be intransitive structures or smaller-clause structures with structural differences from ergative alignment structures. What is common to this family of approaches is that nominative-accusative alignments seem to be due to structures that are more complex than ergative structures (Laka 2006b). It has been argued that seemingly nominative-accusative configurations are due to additional aspectual structure between TP and *v*P that is absent in ergative structures (Nash 2017), or object shift that creates more complex structures (Bittner & Hale 1996a; 1996b). Thus, the "split" is epiphenomenal, not limited to ergative languages (Coon 2013b), and there is no actual split between different case-agreement alignments. What supports this family of approaches is that aspectual alternations, object shift, or person restrictions on O, which are all common triggers for splits, are phenomena that exist also in languages with primarily nominative-accusative alignment and do not trigger any ergative alignment splits in those languages. For example, we find aspectual contrasts due to different object case marking configurations in both ergative and nominative-accusative languages (Spreng 2010), which can often be traced back to different structural configurations (Kratzer 2004).

4. Summary

As becomes apparent from the previous, albeit short discussion of ergativity, it is not a phenomenon easily characterized. Languages may have ergative alignment patterns under certain conditions, show ergativity only on the surface, and show partial syntactic ergativity in the head marking or dependent marking while also showing non-ergative alignment under contrasting conditions. As the more recent approaches to ergativity have shown, analyses of the phenomenon need to be able to accommodate this rather vast variety. As many of these analyses are not necessarily approaches exclusive to ergativity but must also be able to accommodate non-ergative alignment, it becomes more and more noticeable that ergativity is not a uniform specific phenomenon in contrast to nominative-accusative alignment that types languages neatly into two contrasting groups but more of a continuum of possible variations on case/agreement configurations that are possible in languages. Current and future approaches thus need to be able to account for the variation but need to be restrictive enough not to allow patterns not found in language. Therefore, the study of less-studied languages is of such significant importance.

Further Reading

Some other overviews on ergativity and split ergativity can be found in DuBois (1987), Garrett (1990), Moure (1995), Abraham (1996), Johns et al. (2006), McGregor (2009), Polinsky (2016), and Coon et al. (2017).

Some examples of work on ergativity in other languages and other frameworks can be found in DeLancey (1990), Mithun (1994), Quizar (1994), Adelaar (1996), Quesada (1999), and Aldridge (2016).

Notes

1. Abbreviations A, S, and O are based on Dixon (1994).
2. Gloss: ERG = ergative case; ABS = absolutive case; IND = indicative mood, PART = participial mood. The mood marker is an obligatory part of the verbal agreement inflection and these function as declarative moods. See Johns (1987, 1992) and Yuan (2017) for detailed discussion.
3. Also known as active, active-neutral, active-inactive, active-static, stative-active, agentive, agent-patient, and split intransitive patterns (Mithun, 1991). I will use the term *split-S*.
4. Except for when it is used as possessor case (Johns 1987) and in some recently emerging passive constructions (Spreng 2012).
5. Dependent clauses do not show ergativity in this way.
6. Indices from Rezac (2009: 784). Ergative cross-reference bolded here for emphasis. RPT: recent past.
7. Kratzer (2004) proposes an analysis based on this view for Finnish and German.
8. Gaps with the corresponding case added by this author.
9. Although see Davis (2010) for an appreciation of the complexities analyzing relative constructions in more unfamiliar languages.
10. Torrego (2012) and Mahajan (2012) argue for an inherent case analysis of ergative.

References

Abraham, Werner. 1996. The aspect-case typology correlation: Perfectivity triggering split ergativity. *Folia Linguistica* 30. 5–34.

Adelaar, K. Alexander. 1995. Problems of definiteness and ergativity in Embaloh. *Oceanic Linguistics* 34(2). 375–409.

Aldridge, Edith. 2004. *Ergativity and word order in Austronesian languages*. Ithaca, NY: Cornell University (Doctoral dissertation.)

Aldridge, Edith. 2008a. Generative approaches to ergativity. *Language and Linguistics Compass* 2. 966–995.

Aldridge, Edith. 2008b. Absolutive case in Tagalog. *Proceedings from the Annual Meeting of the Chicago Linguistic Society,* vol. 42. No. 2. *Chicago Linguistic Society*, 2006. 1–15.

Aldridge, Edith. 2016. Ergativity from subjunctive in Austronesian languages. *Language and Linguistics Compass* 17. 27–62.

Altshuler, Daniel. 2014. A typology of partitive aspectual operators. *Natural Language and Linguistic Theory* 32. 735–775.

Anand, Pranav & Nevins, Andrew. 2006. The locus of ergative case assignment: Evidence from scope. In Johns, Alana & Massam, Diane & Ndayiragije, Juvenal (eds.), *Ergativity: Emerging issues*, 3–25. Dordrecht: Springer.

Anderson, Stephen R. 1977. On mechanisms by which languages become ergative. In Li, C. (ed.), *Mechanisms of syntactic change*, 317–363. Austin: University of Texas Press.

Anderson, Stephen. 1976. On the notion of subject in ergative languages. In Li, C. (ed.), *Subject and topic*, 1–24. New York: Academic Press.

Baker, Mark C. 2015. *Case: Its principles and its parameters*. Cambridge: Cambridge University Press.

Baker, Mark C. & Bobaljik, Jonathan David. 2017. On inherent and dependent theories of ergative case. In Coon, Jessica & Massam, Diane & Travis, Lisa DeMena (eds.), *The Oxford handbook of ergativity*, 111–134. New York: Oxford University Press.

Benua, Laura. 1995. Yup'ik Antipassive. In Dainora, Audra (ed.), *Papers from the 31st regional meeting of the Chicago Linguistic Society, I: The main session; II: The parasession on clitics* I. 28–44. Chicago, IL: Chicago Linguistic Society.

Bittner, Maria. 1994. *Case, scope, and binding*. Dordrecht: Springer.

Bittner, Maria & Hale, Ken. 1996a. The structural determination of case and agreement. *Linguistic Inquiry* 27(1). 1–68.

Bittner, Maria & Hale, Ken. 1996b. Ergativity: Toward a theory of a heterogeneous class. *Linguistic Inquiry* 27(4). 531–604.

Bobaljik, Jonathan David. 1993. On ergativity and ergative unergatives. *MITWPL* 19. 45–88.

Bobaljik, Jonathan David & Branigan, Phil. 2006. Eccentric agreement and multiple case checking. In Johns, Alana & Massam, Diane & Ndayiragije, Juvenal (eds.), *Ergativity: Emerging issues*, 47–77. Dordrecht: Springer.

Bok-Bennema, Reineke. 1991. *Case and agreement in Inuit*, vol. 38: Studies in Generative Grammar. Berlin and New York: Foris Publications.

Butt, Miriam. 1997. *Aspectual complex predicates, passives and disposition/ability*. Edinburgh LAGB handout. (Ms.)

Butt, Miriam & Holloway-King, Tracy. 1998. *Licensing semantic case*. Utrecht. (Ms.)

Chomsky, Noam. 1993. A minimalist program for linguistic theory. In Hale, Kenneth & Keyser, Samuel Jay (eds.), *The view from building 20: Essays in linguistics in honor of Sylvain Bromberger*, 1–52. Cambridge, MA: MIT Press.

Chomsky, Noam. 2000. Minimalist inquiries: The framework. In Martin, Roger (ed.), *Step by step: Essays on minimalist syntax in honor of Howard Lasnik*, 89–156. Cambridge, MA: MIT Press.

Chomsky, Noam. 2008. On phases. In Freidin, Robert & Otero, Carlos P. & Zubizarreta, Maria Luisa (eds.), *Foundational issues in linguistic theory: Essays in honor of Jean-Roger Vergnaud*, 133–166. Cambridge, MA: MIT Press.

Comrie, Bernard. 2013. Alignment of case marking of full noun phrases. In Dryer, Martin S. & Haspelmath, Martin (eds.), *The world atlas of language structures online*, Leipzig: Max Planck Institute for Evolutionary Anthropology. (http://wals.info/chapter/98) (Accessed 2018-04-20.)

Coon, Jessica. 2013a. TAM Split Ergativity, Part 1. *Language and Linguistics Compass* 7/3. 171–190.

Coon, Jessica. 2013b. *Aspects of split ergativity*. Oxford: Oxford University Press.

Coon, Jessica & Massam, Diane & deMena Travis, Lisa. 2017. *The Oxford handbook of ergativity*. Oxford University Press.

Coon, Jessica & Pedro, Pedro Mateo & Preminger, Omer. 2014. The role of case in A-bar extraction asymmetries: Evidence from Mayan. *Linguistic Variation* 14. 179–242.

Crook, Harold David. 1999. *The phonology and morphology of Nez Perce stress*, Los Angeles: UCLA (Doctoral dissertation).

Davis, Henry. 2010. A unified analysis of relative clauses in St'át'imcets. *Northwest Journal of Linguistics* 4. 1–43.

Davison, Alice. 2004. Structural case, lexical case, and the verbal projection. In Dayan, Veneeta & Mahajan, Anoop (eds.), *Clause structure in South Asian languages*, 199–225. Dordrecht: Springer.

Deal, Amy Rose. 2010. Ergative case and the transitive subject: A view from Nez Perce. *Natural Language & Linguistic Theory* 28. 73–120.

Delancey, Scott. 1981. An interpretation of split ergativity and related patterns. *Language* 57. 626–657.

DeLancey, Scott. 1990. Ergativity and the cognitive model of event structure in Lhasa Tibetan. *Cognitive Linguistics (includes Cognitive Linguistic Bibliography)* 1. 289–322.

Dixon, R. M. W. 1977. *A grammar of Yidiny*. Cambridge: Cambridge University Press.

Dixon, R. M. W. 1979. Ergativity. *Language* 55. 59–138.

Dixon, R. M. W. 1994. *Ergativity*. Cambridge, MA: Cambridge University Press.

DuBois, John W. 1987. The discourse basis of ergativity. *Language* 63. 805–855.

Erlewine, Michael. 2016. Anti-locality and optimality in Kaqchikel agent focus. *Natural Language & Linguistic Theory* 34. 429–479.

Forbes, Clarissa. 2017. Persistent ergativity and split absolutive agreement in Gitksan. In Lamont, Andrew & Tetzloff, Katerina (eds.), *Proceedings of the 47th Annual Meeting of the North East Linguistic Society* 2, GLSA, 11–24.

Garrett, Andrew. 1990. The origin of split ergativity. *Language* 66. 261–296.

Gerdts, Donna Blanche. 1982. *Object and absolutive in Halkomelem Salish*. Princeton, NJ: Princeton University. (Doctoral dissertation.)

Gillon, Carrie. 1999. *When Wh-words move and why: A case study in Inuktitut*. University of Toronto. (MA thesis.)

Hale, Kenneth & Keyser, Samuel-Jay. 1993. On argument structure and the lexical expression of syntactic relations. In Hale, Kenneth & Keyser, Samuel-Jay (eds.), *The view from building 20: Essays in linguistics in honor of Sylvain Bromberger*, 53–109. Cambridge, MA: MIT Press.

Hale, Kenneth L. & Keyser, Samuel-Jay. 2002. *Prolegomenon to a theory of argument structure*, vol. 39: Linguistic Inquiry Monograph. Cambridge, MA: MIT Press.

Hammerich, Louis Lenor. 1951. Kleinschmidt Centennial I: The cases of Eskimo. *International Journal of American Linguistics* 17.1. 18–22.

Harris, Alice C. 1976. *Grammatical relations in modern Georgian*. Cambridge, MA: Harvard University. (Doctoral dissertation.)

Harris, Alice C. 1982. Georgian and the unaccusative hypothesis. *Language* 58(2). 290–306.

Harris, Alice C. 1990. Georgian: A language with active case marking: A reply to BG Hewitt. *Lingua* 80. 35–53.

Herd, Jonathon, Macdonald, Catherine & Massam, Diane. 2011. Genitive subjects in relative constructions in Polynesian languages. *Lingua* 121(7). 1252–1264.

Hopper, Paul J. & Thompson, Sandra A. 1980. Transitivity in grammar and discourse. *Language* 56. 251–299.

Hualde, Jose Ignacio & de Urbina, Jon Ortiz (eds.). 2003. *A grammar of Basque*. Berlin: Mouton de Gruyter.

Hunt, Katherine. 1993. *Clause structure, agreement and case in Gitksan*. Vancouver: University of British Columbia. (Doctoral dissertation.)

Jacobson, Steven A. 2001. *A practical grammar of the St. Lawrence Island/Siberian Yupik Eskimo language*. 2nd edn. University of Alaska, Fairbanks: Alaska Native Language Center.

Jelinek, Eloise & Demers, Richard A. 1994. Predicates and pronominal arguments in Straits Salish. *Language* 70. 697–736.

Johns, Alana. 1987. *Transitivity and grammatical relations in Inuktitut*. Ottawa: University of Ottawa. (Doctoral dissertation.)

Johns, Alana. 1992. Deriving ergativity. *Linguistic Inquiry* 23. 57–88.

Johns, Alana & Massam, Diane & Ndayiragije, Juvenal. 2006. *Ergativity: Emerging issues*, vol. 65. Studies in Language and Linguistic Theory. Dordrecht: Springer.

Kazenin, Konstantin I. 1994. Split syntactic ergativity: Toward an implicational hierarchy. *STUF – Language Typology and Universals* 47.2. 78–98.

Kratzer, Angelika. 2004. Telicity and the meaning of objective case. In Guéron, Jacqueline & Lecarme, Jacqueline (eds.), *The syntax of time*, 389–423. Cambridge, MA: MIT Press.

Kroeber, Paul. 1997. Relativization in Thompson River Salish. *Anthropological Linguistics* 39. 376–422.

Laka, Itziar. 2006a. On the nature of case in Basque: Structural or inherent? In van Riemsdijk, Henk C. & Corver, Norbert & Broekhuis, Hans & Huybregts, Riny & Kleinhenz, Ursula & Koster, Jan (eds.), *Organizing grammar: Linguistic studies in honor of Henk van Riemsdijk*, 374–382. Berlin & New York: Mouton de Gruyter.

Laka, Itziar. 2006b. Deriving split ergativity in the progressive: The case of Basque. In Johns, Alana & Massam, Diane & Ndayiragije, Juvenal (eds.), *Ergativity: Emerging issues*, 173–195. Dordrecht: Springer.

Legate, Julie Anne. 2008. Morphological and abstract case. *Linguistic Inquiry* 39. 55–101.

Legate, Julie Anne. 2017. The locus of ergative case. In Coon, Jessica & Massam, Diane & deMena Travis, Lisa (eds.), *The Oxford handbook of ergativity*, 135–158. New York: Oxford University Press.

Legate, Julie Anne. 2012. Types of ergativity. *Lingua* 122. 181–191.

Levin, Beth Carol. 1983a. Unaccusative verbs in Basque. In Sells, Peter (ed.), *Proceedings of ALNE 13/NELS 13*. 129–144. Amherst, MA: University of Massachusetts.

Levin, Beth Carol. 1983b. *On the nature of ergativity*. Cambridge, MA: MIT. (Doctoral dissertation.)

Levin, Juliette & Massam, Diane. 1985. Surface ergativity: Case/theta relations reexamined. In Berman, Steven (ed.), *Proceedings of NELS* 15. 286–301. Amherst, MA: University of Massachusetts.

Mahajan, Anoop. 2012. Ergatives, antipassives and the overt light v in Hindi. *Lingua* 122. 204–214.

Manning, Christopher. 1996. *Ergativity: Argument structure and grammatical relations*. Stanford, CA: CSLI Publications.

Marantz, Alec P. 1984. *On the nature of grammatical relations*, vol. 10: Linguistic Inquiry Monographs. Cambridge, MA: MIT Press.

Marantz, Alec P. 2000. Case and Licensing. In Reuland, Eric (ed.), *Explaining Burzio's generalization*, 11–30. Amsterdam: John Benjamins.

Massam, Diane. 2001. On predication and the status of subjects in Niuean. In Davies, William D. (ed.), *Objects and other subjects: Grammatical functions, functional categories and configurationality*, 225–246. Dordrecht: Springer.

Massam, Diane. 2006. Neither absolutive nor ergative is nominative or accusative: Arguments from Niuean. In Johns, Alana & Massam, Diane & Ndayiragije, Juvenal (eds.), *Ergativity: Emerging issues*, 27–46. Dordrecht: Springer.

McFadden, Thomas, 2004. The Position of Morphological Case in the Derivation: A Study on the Syntax-Morphology Interface. Philadelphia: University of Pennsylvania. (Doctoral dissertation.)

McGregor, William B. 2009. Typology of ergativity. *Language and Linguistics Compass* 3. 480–508.

Mithun, Marianne. 1991. Active/agentive case marking and its motivations. *Language* 67. 510–546.

Mithun, Marianne. 1994. The implications of ergativity for a Philippine voice system. In Fox, Barbara (ed.), *Voice: Form and function*, 247–277. Amsterdam: Benjamins.

Mithun, Marianne. 1999. *The Languages of Native North America*. Cambridge Language Surveys. (CaLaSu). Cambridge: Cambridge University Press.

Moure, Teresa. 1995. Typological gradations: Evidence of ergativity in accusative languages. *Verba* 22. 397–428.

Mulder, Jean Gail. 1994. *Ergativity in Coast Tsimshian (Sm'algyax)*, vol. 124. University of California Publications in Linguistics. Berkeley: University of California Press.

Nash, Léa. 1996. The internal ergative subject hypothesis. In Kusumoto, Kiyomi (ed.), *Proceedings of the North East Linguistic Society 26*, 195–210. Amherst: GLSA.

Nash, Léa. 2017. The structural source of split ergativity and ergative case in Georgian. In Coon, Jessica & Massam, Diane & Lisa DeMena Travis (eds.), *The Oxford handbook of ergativity*, 175–200. Oxford: Oxford University Press.

Otsuka, Yuko. 2006. Syntactic ergativity in Tongan: Resumptive pronouns revisited. In Johns, Alana, & Massam, Diane & Ndayiragije, Juvenal (eds.), *Ergativity: Emerging issues*, 79–107. Dordrecht: Springer.

Oyharçabal, Beñat. 1992. Structural case and inherent case marking: Ergaccusativity in Basque. In Lakarra, Joseba A. & de Urbina, Jon Ortiz (eds.) *Anuario del Seminario de Filología Vasca "Julio de Urquijo"*. 309–342. San Sebastian, Spain: Julio Urkixo Euskal Filologi Mintegi-Institutuak (JUMI).

Pache, Matthias. 2015. Morphosyntactic properties of Chibchan verbal person marking. *Linguistic Discovery* 13.2. 80–95.

Peterson, Taylor. 2006. Issues of morphological ergativity in the Tsimshian languages. In Kulikov, Leonid & Mal'chukov, A. L. & de Swart, Peter (eds.) *Case, valency and transitivity*, 65–90. Amsterdam and Philadelphia: John Benjamins Publishing Company.

Polinsky, Maria. 2008. Antipassive constructions. In Dryer, Martin S. & Haspelmath, Martin (eds.), *The world atlas of language structures online*. Munich: Max Planck Digital Library. (http://wals.info/chapter/108) (Accessed 2018-04-20.)

Polinsky, Maria. 2016. *Deconstructing ergativity: Two types of ergative languages and their features*. New York: Oxford University Press.

Polinsky, Maria. 2017. Syntactic ergativity. In Everaert, Martin, van Riemsdijk, Henk C. (eds.), *The Wiley Blackwell companion to syntax*, 2nd edn, 1–37. Oxford: Wiley-Blackwell.

Polinsky, Maria & Potsdam, Eric. 2001. Long-distance agreement and topic in Tsez. *Natural Language & Linguistic Theory* 19. 583–646.

Preminger, Omer. 2012. The absence of an implicit object in unergatives: New and old evidence from Basque. *Lingua* 122(3). 278–288.

Quesada, J. Diego. 1999. Ergativity in Chibchan. *STUF-Language Typology and Universals* 52.1. 22–51.

Quizar, Robin. 1994. Split ergativity and word order in Ch'orti'. *International Journal of American Linguistics* 60. 120–138.

Rezac, Milan. 2009. On the unifiability of repairs for the person case constraint: French, Basque, Georgian and Chinook. *Anuario del Seminario de Filología Vasca" Julio de Urquijo"* 43(1–2). 769–789.

Rezac, Milan & Albizu, Pablo & Etxepare, Ricardo. 2014. The structural ergative of Basque and the theory of case. *Natural Language & Linguistic Theory* 32. 1273–1330.

Rill, Justin. 2017. *The morphology and syntax of ergativity: A typological approach*. Newark: University of Delaware. (Doctoral dissertation.)

Rude, Noel. 1988. Ergative, passive, and antipassive in Nez Perce: A discourse perspective. In Shibatani, M. (ed.), *Passive and voice*, 547–560. Amsterdam: Benjamins.

Rude, Noel. 1991. On the origin of the Nez Perce ergative NP suffix. *International Journal of American Linguistics* 57. 24–50.

Salanova, Andres. 2007. *Nominalizations and aspect*. Cambridge, MA: MIT. (Doctoral dissertation.)

Sheehan, Michelle. 2017. Parametrizing ergativity: An inherent case approach. In Coon, Jessica & Massam, Diane & Travis, Lisa DeMena (eds.), *The Oxford handbook of ergativity*, 59–85. New York: Oxford University Press.

Sherkina-Lieber, Marina. 2004. Focus fronting in Wh-questions in Inuktitut. *Toronto Working Papers in Linguistics* 23. 119–132.

Siewierska, Anna. 2013. Alignment of verbal person marking. In Dryer, Martin S. & Haspelmath, Martin (eds.), *The world atlas of language structures online*, Leipzig: Max Planck Institute for Evolutionary Anthropology. (https://wals.info/chapter/100) (Accessed 2018-04-20.)

Silverstein, Michael. 1976. Hierarchy of features and ergativity. In Dixon, R. M. W. (ed.), *Grammatical categories in Australian languages*, 112–171. Canberra: Australian Institute of Aboriginal Studies.

Spreng, Bettina. 2001. Little *v* in Inuktitut: Antipassive revisited. *Linguistica Atlantica* 23. 155–190.

Spreng, Bettina. 2006. Antipassive morphology and case assignment in Inuktitut. In Johns, Alana & Massam, Diane & Ndayiragije, Juvenal (eds.), *Ergativity: Emerging issues*, 247–270. Dordrecht: Springer.

Spreng, Bettina. 2010. Conditions on antipassives. *Language and Linguistics Compass* 4. 556–575.

Spreng, Bettina. 2012. *Viewpoint aspect in Inuktitut: The syntax and semantics of antipassives*. Toronto: University of Toronto. (Doctoral dissertation.)

Thalbitzer, William. 1930. The Absolutive and the Relative in Eskimo. In Bøgholm, Niels & Aage Brusendorff & Bodelsen, Carl Adolf (eds.), *A grammatical miscellany offered to Otto Jespersen on his seventieth birthday*, 319–329. Copenhagen: Levin and Munksgaard.

Torrego, Esther. 2012. The unaccusative case pattern of Hindi and auxiliary be. *Lingua* 122. 215–224.

Tsunoda, Tasaku. 1981. Split-case marking patterns in verb-types and tense/aspect/mood. *Linguistics* 19. 389–438.

Ura, Hiroyuki. 2006. A parametric syntax of aspectually conditioned split-ergativity. In Johns, Alana & Massam, Diane & Ndayiragije, Juvenal (eds.), *Ergativity: Emerging issues*, 111–141. Dordrecht: Springer.

Uriagareka, Juan. 1999. Minimal restrictions on Basque movements. *Natural Language and Linguistic Theory* 17. 403–444.

Wiltschko, Martina. 2006. On 'ergativity' in Halkomelem Salish: And how to split and derive it. In Johns, Alana & Massam, Diane & Ndayiragije, Juvenal (eds.), *Ergativity: Emerging issues*, 197–227. Dordrecht: Springer.

Woolford, Ellen B. 2006. Lexical case, inherent case, and argument structure. *Linguistic Inquiry* 37.1. 111–130.

Wunderlich, Dieter. 1997. Cause and the structure of verbs. *Linguistic Inquiry* 28.1. 27–68.

Yuan, Michelle. 2017. Decomposing transitive agreement in Inuktitut. In *Annual Meeting of the Linguistic Society of America*. Austin, TX (Ms).

11

NOUN INCORPORATION AND POLYSYNTHESIS

Michael Barrie and Éric Mathieu

1. Introduction

This chapter discusses the complex morphosyntax of polysynthetic languages of North America. We begin with a discussion of the kinds of concepts that are encoded morphologically in various languages of North America, including tense, aspect, agreement, causation, noun incorporation (NI), and several other inflectional and derivational concepts. Many of these concepts are discussed in detail in other chapters in this volume, so we touch on these only briefly here. We do include an in-depth discussion of NI, however. We discuss the origin of the typological term *polysynthesis* and the kinds of analyses that have been proposed to account for it. Section 1 covers the origin of the notion of polysynthesis since Humboldt, how it has changed since the time of Humboldt, and how it is understood today. Section 2 discusses morphological aspects of polysynthesis, including the kinds of features that are expressed morphologically in polysynthetic languages. Section 3 discusses noun incorporation and how it varies in languages across North America. Section 4 discusses recent theoretical discussions of polysynthesis. Finally, Section 5 summarizes and discusses the outlook for future research.

2. Polysynthesis

The term *polysynthesis* was added to the repertoire of morphological typology by Humboldt (1825; 1836) to describe languages in which individual words typically contain several morphemes. This is the essence of polysynthesis – the tendency for a large number of morphemes to exist on a single word. In the Humboldtian tradition, languages occupy one of four typological categories, which are treated as ends of a spectrum (isolating versus incorporating, and inflecting versus agglutinating). Inflecting languages are also called fusional, and incorporating languages are also called polysynthetic. The notion of incorporation is discussed later in this chapter. For more details on the typological classification of language within the context of the languages of North America, the reader is referred to Liedtke (1997). We note, however, that polysynthetic languages are found in every continent in the world, and that not all languages indigenous to North America are polysynthetic. Indeed, many are not. This is an important point we come back to in the analysis of polysynthesis and noun incorporation.

Precise definitions of polysynthesis are hard to come by; however, Comrie (1989: 45) offers the following working definition:

> Polysynthesis, however, refers simply to the fact that, in a language of this type, it is possible to combine a large number of morphemes, be they lexical or grammatical, into a single word, often corresponding to a whole sentence in English.

Comrie does distinguish between combining lexical roots into a larger word structure (incorporation) versus combining functional morphology into a larger word structure (polysynthesis) but uses the term *polysynthesis* as a cover term for the two concepts. We will use the term *narrow polysynthesis* when required to refer to polysynthesis to the exclusion of incorporation. As we will see in Baker's discussion, incorporation and narrow polysynthesis are intimately linked in his Polysynthesis Parameter; however, as far back as Brinton (1886) the link between the two was noticed. We hasten to point out, however, that there are polysynthetic languages that do not have NI and that there are languages with NI that are not polysynthetic, a point touched on as far back as Sapir (1911: 250) with the following quote.

> In the first place so-called pronominal incorporation and noun incorporation stand in no necessary relation to each other.

We continue our discussion with some examples of polysynthesis. The following examples illustrate some extreme cases of polysynthesis in North Baffin Inuktitut [iku] (Eskimo-Aleut), (1a), Mohawk [moh] (Iroquoian), (1b), and Wichita [wic] (Caddoan), (1c), respectively.

(1) a. North Baffin Inuktitut

annulaksi-kkanni-nginna-jualu-gasu-lauqsima-guma-nngit-tsiaq-galuaq-tunga
imprison-again-really-a.lot-try-ever-want-NEG-EMPH-EMPH-1SG.INTR.DECL
'I would never ever even want to try to end up in jail ever again even for a bit.'
(Johns 2007: 564)

b. Mohawk

Tha'tewakatonnhatierónnion
tha'-te-wak-at-onnh-at-ier-onni-on
CONTR-DUC-1SG.PAT-SRFL-life-SRFL-do-DIST-STAT
'My life was really quite strange.'
(Mithun 2014: 5)

c. Wichita

kiya: ki-riwa:c-7aras-a-ri-kita-7a-hi: rik-s
EVID.AOR:3-big-meat-COLL.U-TR-top-come-ITER-IMPF
'by making many trips, he carried the large (quantity of) meat up into it [the tree]'
(Rood 1976: 75)

2.1. Classifying Polysynthesis

Mattissen (2017) builds on the distinction between incorporation and affixation introduced earlier to classify polysynthetic languages into distinct types. She offers the following definition of polysynthesis:

> Languages qualify as polysynthetic if they have complex, polymorphemic verbal units which necessarily integrate productively non-root bound morphemes with "lexical" and grammatical meanings, especially local ones, and optionally allow concatenation of lexical roots within a verbal wordform.
>
> (Mattissen 2017: 72)

She furthermore postulates the following parameters distinguishing subtypes of polysynthesis, which we review in succession. Note that we have adapted Mattissen's original wording of the parameters for the sake of space.

(2) Parameter 1: Word-Formational Type: The verbal complex allows one of the following options.

i. One lexical root and various affixes
ii. More than one lexical root and various affixes
iii. One lexical root, various affixes, and a small number of fossilized forms indicative of noun incorporation or verb serialization that may have once been productive

Examples of languages of the first type include Greenlandic [kal] and Navajo/Diné Bizaad [nav], and examples of the second type include Wichita and Nez Perce [nez]. Noun incorporation is discussed in detail later in this chapter, but we give examples here to illustrate the concept. As an example of the first type, Compton (2012) gives the following Inuktitut example. The only lexical root in this example is *iglu* ('house'). See Compton for discussion on this point.

(3) Inuktitut

iglu-liu-tuinna-ruma-junga
house-make-only-want-DECL.1SG
'I just want to make houses/igloos.'

(Compton 2012: 10)

For the second type, Mattissen notes that forms with two lexical roots include not only NI but also verb-root serialization and adverb incorporation. Here is an example from Lakota.

(4) Lakota

a-čhą́-kozA
LOC-wood-wave
'to swing clubs on someone'

(de Reuse 1994: 213)

As an example of the third type, Mattissen offers Maskoke [mus] (Muskogean). Consider the following examples.

(5) Maskoke

a.	***nok**-sómk-i:*	b.	*ca-**nók**-wa*
	throat-get.lost-part		1sg-neck-suf
	'hoarse'		'my neck'

(Haas 1941: 312)

The lexical root *nok* ('neck/throat') appears as a frozen form in a small number of Maskoke verb forms, but no longer undergoes productive incorporation.

(6) Parameter 2: Internal Organization: The order of the morphemes is dictated in one of the following ways.

i. The morphemes are ordered by a strict template.
ii. The morphemes are ordered by semantic scope, with no discernable template.
iii. The order of the morphemes is a combination of the above.[1]

Navajo/Diné Bizaad is an example of the first type. As this type of language follows a strict template, we show the template here (Young & Morgan 1987: 38).

(7) Position of verbal morphemes from left to right:

0	Direct object of postposition. Possessive prefix with nouns.
Ia	Null postposition
Ib	Adverbial – Thematic ('postpositional stems')
Ic	(Reflexive)
Id	(Reversionary)
Ie	(Semeliterative)
II	(Iterative)
III	(Distributive Plural)
IV	Direct Object Pronouns
V	Deictic Subject Pronouns
VIa	Adverbial – Thematic
VIb	Adverbial – Thematic
VIc	Transitional/Semelfactive Aspect markers
VII	Modal – Aspectival Conjugation markers
VIII	Subject Pronouns
IX	'Classifier'
X	Stem

Greenlandic is an example of the second type. Mattissen gives the following minimal pair.

(8) Greenlandic

a. *Kaalat* *tiki-nngik-kallar-puq*
Kaalat arrive-NEG-yet/still-IND.3SG
'Kaalat has not yet arrived.'

b. *Kaalat* *tikik-kallan-nngi-laq*
Kaalat arrive-yet/still-NEG-IND.3SG
'Kaalat has still not arrived.'

(Mattissen 2017: 80–81, citing Fortescue 1984: 137)

As an example of the last type, Mattissen (2017) gives the following Southern Sierra Miwok [skd] (Utian) example, citing Broadbent (1964: 39–40). Observe the difference in order between the causative (CAUS) and the form for *ready* in the following examples. The difference in morpheme order relates to the difference in meaning. We infer from Mattissen's discussion that the remainder of the affixes are ordered according to a template. We also refer to reader to Rice (2000) for an in-depth discussion of morpheme order and semantic scope in Athapaskan.

(9) Southern Sierra Miwok

a. *ʔetal-nuk'u-lumhu-'*
return-CAUS-ready-PRS.IMPF.3SG
'He is ready to take him home.' (lit: 'He is ready to make him go home.')

b. *ʔetla-lamhy-nuk'u-'*
return-ready-CAUS-PRS.IMPF.3SG
'He is making him ready to return home.'

(Mattissen 2017: 81, citing Broadbent 1964: 39–40)

(10) Parameter 3: Participant Encoding: A polysynthetic language may encode participants in one of the following three ways.

i. Polypersonalism: encoding at least two participants on the verb
ii. Monopersonalism: encoding only one participant on the verb
iii. Apersonalism: encoding no participants on the verb

While polypersonalism is typically regarded as a hallmark property of polysynthetic languages, Mattissen suggests that it is not a necessary characteristic. Greenlandic and Mohawk are examples of polypersonal languages in which a maximum of two participants are encoded on the verb. Southern Tiwa permits up to three participants; see (11). Wintu [wnw] was an example of a monopersonal language. Agreement is discussed below and in Compton (this volume), but we give some relevant examples here. Southern Tiwa, as mentioned, is a polypersonal language. Here is a Southern Tiwa example that references three arguments.

(11) Southern Tiwa

ka-'u'u-wia-ban *ĩ-'ay*
1SG.AG.2SG.RECIP.3ANIM.SG.PAT-baby-give-PST 2SG-to
'I gave the baby to you.'

(Allen et al. 1984: 303)

Mattissen (2017, citing Harrington (1921), gives the following Chimariko [cid] (possibly Hokan) examples to illustrate monopersonality.

(12) Chimariko

a. *qh-uk'o-ˀna-n*
2PL.AG-talk-APPL-ASP
'You (guys) talked to him.'
b. *qha-k'o-ˀna-n*
2PL.PAT-talk-APPL-ASP
'He talked to you (guys).'

(Mattissen 2017: 70, citing Harrington 1921)

Finally, Haida [hai] (isolate, possibly Dene–Yeniseian) is an example of an apersonal language. Mattissen (2017), citing Swanton (1911), gives the following example.

(13) Haida

ɢien *l'* *L-gī'gî'l-gAn*
then 3SG shave.of.man-swim-landward-PST
'Then he swam landward.'

(Mattissen 2017: 70, citing Swanton 1911: 255)

(14) Parameter 4: Evolutionary Path: The structure of the verb form [what we call here the *verbal complex*] is historically derived in one of the three following ways.

i. Onion type: verbal complex is not expandable and consists of a central core in which morphemes are added to the outside
ii. Sandwich type: verbal complex is internally expandable
iii. Burdock type: verbal complex is expandable, and formed by the coalescence of adjacent free forms

The onion type languages include Navajo, Blackfoot, Wichita, and Cherokee. Many examples can be seen in this and other chapters. Here is a Mohawk example, repeated from (1b).

(15) Mohawk

Tha'tewakatonnhatierónnion
tha'-te-wak-at-onnh-at-ier-onni-on
CONTR-DUC-1SG.PAT-SRFL-life-SRFL-do-DIST-STAT
'My life was really quite strange.'

(Mithun 2014)

The sandwich type languages include Greenlandic, Washo, and Nez Perce. An example of this type is shown for North Baffin Inuktitut in (1a), repeated here as (16). Observe that adverbial and other typically optional material can be freely added to the verbal complex. This contrasts with the Mohawk example in (15). Although the Mohawk example contains many concepts, it cannot be expanded as the Greenlandic example can. For instance, to express the idea of 'wanting to do something' in Mohawk, two separate verbal complexes must be used.

(16) Greenlandic

annulaksi-kkanni-nginna-jualu-gasu-lauqsima-guma-nngit-tsiaq-galuaq-tunga
imprison-again-really-a.lot-try-ever-want-NEG-EMPH-EMPH-1SG.INTR.DECL
'I would never ever even want to try to end up in jail ever again even for a bit.'

(Johns 2007)

The burdock type languages include Muskogean, Klamath, and Takelma. Mattissen provides the following Klamath example, which is quite telling of the evolutionary pathway she suggests. Observe specifically the historical transition of *nannwi* 'as soon as' from a free form to a bound form (note the timeline of the sources: 1890 and 1964). This example underscores Mattissen's treatment of this parameter as a categorization of polysynthetic properties as a historical process.

(17) Klamanth

a. . . . qtanc'an nannwi sq'ol-lG-o:t-a-k
fall.asleep as.soon.as SG.lie.down-while-IND-EMPH
'(He) fell asleep as soon as he lay down.'

(Gatschet 1890: 113)

b. qtan-c'n-nannwi-ank
sleep-just.do.and.no.more-right.away/at.once-PST.PTCL
'having gone right to sleep.'

(Mattissen 2017, citing Barker 1964: 158)

In brief, no standardly accepted definition of polysynthesis exists because the division of languages into discrete categories is far from straightforward. The legacy of the Humboldtian tradition holds that polysynthesis is the extreme end of a spectrum along which languages may vary. Mattissen's investigation has revealed that polysynthetic languages exhibit a great deal of internal variation. In §4 we will revisit the issue of whether polysynthesis constitutes a unitary phenomenon when we explore Baker's Polysynthesis Parameter, but for now we will discuss some of the empirical properties associated with polysynthetic languages. We begin with an investigation of the various kinds of affixal morphology found on verbs followed by a discussion of noun incorporation.

2.2. Affixal Morphology

Polysynthetic languages encode an extremely wide variety of concepts on their verbs, as suggested by the examples in (1). Common, if not nearly universal concepts encoded on verbs include agreement, tense/aspect, mood, and applicatives. Other less common concepts include iteration, location, distributivity, pluractionality, evidentiality, and illocutionary force, just to name a few. We begin with a discussion of the common features, followed by a description of some of the less common features.

Agreement is a hallmark of polysynthetic languages, though see the discussion of Mattissen's Parameter 3 in §2.1. (See also Compton, this volume, for more discussion on agreement in the languages of North America.) Baker's Polysynthesis Parameter is motivated by the idea that all arguments are morphologically referenced on the verb. Languages vary tremendously in how arguments are referenced on the verb. Iroquoian languages reference only human arguments and are restricted to a maximum of two referents (Lounsbury 1949; Lounsbury 1953; Abbott 2000; Barrie 2015b). Algonquian languages also reference only two arguments but do so in a complex way involving the use of *theme signs* (Oxford, this volume). Southern Tiwa (Tanoan) references up to three arguments. Consider the following Southern Tiwa example. The agreement prefix *tam* references the subject (first person), the direct object, which is also incorporated, and the indirect object.

(18) Southern Tiwa

a. *'Uide tam-musa-wia-ban*
child 1SG.AG:3PL.TH:3SG.RECIP-cat-give-PST
'I gave the cats to the child.'

b. *Kam-musa-wia-ban*
1SG.AG:3PL.TH:2SG.RECIP-cat-give-PST
'I gave the cats to you.'

(Rosen 1990: 670, ex (3) and (10b), respectively)

The expression of person and number is sometimes expressed by distinct morphemes. Although agreement in Iroquoian often exhibits a great deal of portmanteau morphology, in first and second person, number agreement is expressed by separate and distinct morphemes. Consider the following Seneca examples. The first two examples show that person and number are separate. The last two examples illustrate portmanteau morphology.[2] See Barrie and Uchihara (this volume) for the full paradigm of agreement morphology in Iroquoian languages.

(19) Seneca

a. *sni:awiʔ*
s-**ni**-awi-ʔ
2-**DU**-carry-HAB
'You two are carrying something.'

b. *ʔakwátheʔthaʔ*
ʔa-**k**-**wa**-theʔt-haʔ
EXCL-**1**-**PL**-pound-HAB
'We (excl.pl) are pounding something.'

c. ***shako**-yɛt-haʔ*
3SG.M.AG:3SG.F.PAT-hit-HAB
'He's hitting her.'

d. ***hakʌ**-yɛt-haʔ*
3SG.M.AG:3PL.PAT-hit-HAB
'He's hitting them.'

(Chafe 1960: 225 and 230)

Algonquian languages show this more clearly, as the person and number affixes are not adjacent. Consider the following Ojibwe examples. Note that there is allomorphy in the form of the plural marker; see Rhodes (1976) and Oxford (this volume) for discussion.

(20) Ojibwe

a. *gwi:nizi*
g-w:in-izi-**mw**
2-dirty-TH.VAI-**PL**
'You are dirty.'

b. *gwi:nizimi*
g-wi:n-izi-**min**
2-dirty-TH.VAI-**PL**
'We (INCL) are dirty.'

c. *nwi:nizimi*
n-wi:n-izi-**min**
1-dirty-TH.VAI-**PL**
'We (EXCL) are dirty.'

(Rhodes 1976: 82)

Many polysynthetic languages mark reflexives morphologically on the verb rather than with a reflexive pronominal (such as *myself* in English). Mohawk exhibits both reflexives and middle voice (called *semireflexive* in Iroquoianist literature). Consider the following examples. The reflexive is used in typical situations expressing reflexivity. The middle voice is used with verbs of grooming and inherently reflexive events, among others. Lounsbury (1949), as far as we know, was the first to note the similarity between the Iroquoian middle voice and Romance SE.

(21) Mohawk

a. *wahontatié:nawa'se'*
wa-hon-**atat**-ienawa's-e'
FACT-3PL.AG-**REFL**-help-PUNC
'They helped themselves.'

b. *k-**at**-konhs-óhare-s*
1SG-**MID**-face-wash-HAB
'I wash my face.'

(Mithun 2006: 202, 205)

Garifuna [cab] marks reflexives both synthetically on the verb and analytically with a separate but etymologically related pronoun.

(22) Garifuna

a. *w-aséfuru-b-on gurúyara*
1.PL-save-FUT-3.F canoe
'We are going to save the canoe.'

b. *n-asáfura-**gu**-nya n-ún-**gwa***
1.SG-save-**REFL**-PROG 1.SG-to-**REFL**
'I am saving myself.'

(Haurholm-Larsen 2016: 118)

Upriver Halkomelem [hur] has an optional reflexive marker on the verb. It is not required to give rise to a reflexive interpretation, but if it is present a reflexive meaning holds (Wiltschko 2004: 108).

(23) Upriver Halkomelem

a. *q'óy-**thet*** *te* *swíyeqe*
kill-**REFL** DET man
'The man killed himself.'

b. *q'óy-t-es* *te* *swíyeqe*
kill-TRANS-3ERG DET man
= 'The man killed himself.'
= 'The man killed him.' (where he ≠ the man)

(Wiltschko 2004: 108)

Iteration or repetition is another property encoded by verbal morphology in some polysynthetic languages. Consider the following Upper Necaxa Totonac [tku] data (Beck 2008: 32).

(24) Upper Necaxa Totonac

a. *namín*
na-min-Ø
FUT-come-IMPF
'He will come.'

b. *namimpalá*
na-min-**pala**-Ø
FUT-come-**RPT**-IMPF
'S/he will come again.'

(Beck 2008: 32)

Polysynthetic languages typically have valency changing morphology of one sort or another. Causatives and benefactives are typically found in grammatical descriptions of many polysynthetic languages. We illustrate with an example of a causative from Nuu-chah-nulth.

(25) Nuu-chah-nulth

haʔukˈaps
haʔuk **-'ap** -s
he.eats **-CAUS** -1SG
'I make him eat.' 'I serve him a meal.'

(Nakayama 2001: 123, ex (330))

Caballero (2014) notes that Choguita Rarámuri exhibits valence stem allomorphy. Table 11.1 shows some of her data (p. 734).

Tense, aspect, and mood (TAM) are also commonly expressed morphologically in North American languages. Iroquoian languages have complex TAM systems, which are described in this volume (Barrie & Uchihara). Choctaw [cho] has a series of TAM suffixes. Broadwell (2006: 169ff.) gives the following examples, showing irrealis mood (IRR), past tense (PST), and non-past tense (TNS). The reader is referred to Broadwell (2006) for more details.

Table 11.1 Valence Stem Allomorphy in Choguita Rarámuri

INTRANSITIVE	*TRANSITIVE*	*APPLICATIVE*	*GLOSS*
suwí	suwá	suwé	'run out'
wirí	wirá	wiré	'stand'
uku	–	uké	'rain'

(26) Choctaw

a. ***O̱b-aachi̱-h***
rain-**IRR-TNS**
'It's going to rain.'

b. ***Ip-aachi-tok***
eat-**IRR-PST**
'He was going to eat.'

c.

John-at	*Mary*	*pi̱sa-**tok***
John-NOM	Mary	see-**PST**

'John saw Mary.'

(Broadwell 2006: 169ff.)

Direction and location are commonly expressed in polysynthetic languages. Central Pomo has an extensive array of locative suffixes to express a variety of location and direction types. Consider the following forms for the verb *run* (Mithun 2010: 687).

(27) Central Pomo suffixes

čá-w	'run' (one)
čá-:la-w	'run down'
čá-:qač'	'run up (as up a hill)'
čá-č'	'run away'
čá-way	'run against hither, as when a whirlwind came up to you'
čá-:'w-an	'run around here and there'
čá-mli-w	'run around it (a tree, rock, house, pole etc.)'
čá-mač'	'run northward'
čá-:q'	'run by, over (along on the level), southward'
čá-m	'run over, on, across (as bridge)'

Jany (2017), citing Jany (2009: 135), gives the following example with combined directional markers in the extinct language Chimariko [cid].

(28)

*ye-čuču-**tap**-mu-n*	*hiṭiytew*	*y-u'cu*ˀ*-**tamu**-n*
1SG.AG-?-**dir(out)**-DIR(towards.there)-ASP	fence	1SG.AG-?-**DIR**-ASP

'I dodged, I jumped over the fence.'

(Jany 2017, 279) [Chimariko]

Iroquoian languages also exhibit locative prefixes (called *translocative* and *cislocative*), which express movement (see Barrie & Uchihara, this volume, for more details).

Distributivity and pluractionality are expressed morphologically in several languages of North America. Pluractionality is somewhat vaguely defined. It refers to some plurality of actions, either in number of participants, number of events, place of events, or the like (Lasersohn 1995; Newman 1980: 13n23). Here are two examples from Onondaga, where the term *distributivity* is used to refer to this concept.

(29) Onondaga

a. *waˀgne:nohgwayęthwáhęˀ*

waˀ-	k-	nenohkw-	a-	yęthwa	**-hę**:	-ˀ
FACT-	1SG.AG-	potato-	JOIN-	plant	**-DIST**	-PUNC

'I planted several potatoes.'

b. *hagáedǫnyǫk*
ha- káetǫ **-nyǫ** -k
3.SG.M.AG- tell.stories **-DIST** -HAB
'He tells many stories.'

(Barrie 2015b)

Some languages exhibit verbal root suppletion to express pluractionality. Consider the following Navajo data (Young & Morgan 2000). This is not simple number agreement, as these forms indicate that event of going or walking takes place in a group.

(30) 'go, walk'
-yá- 'go.SG'
-'ash- 'go.DU'
-áál- 'go.PL'

Instrumental affixes have two functions. On the one hand, they can function as part of a bipartite root (a root composed of two identifiable parts, both of which are necessary for a well-formed word), indicating how an action is undertaken. On the other hand, they can function as an applicative, introducing an instrumental argument into the event. Consider first the following Karuk data (Macaulay 1993). These exemplify bipartite roots with an instrumental component.

(31) a. *im 'involving fire or heat'
impat 'to become broken due to heat'
imcak 'to get burnt'
imcax 'to be hot'
impuk 'to be warm'
imnis 'to cook'
b. *ʔak 'with the hand'
ʔdkiO 'to handle a soft mass'
ʔaknup 'to thump'
ʔakrap 'to slap'
ʔaktuv 'to pluck at'
ʔakxarap 'to scratch'

Consider now the following Muskogee [mus] data, which show an instrumental affix used as an applicative to introduce an additional instrumental argument (Martin 2011: 192–193). Martin notes that 'binoculars' (INSTR-see-INF) can appear with the non-subject case clitic (NON.SUBJ.CASE).

(32) Muskogee
a. *Bill* *sókha-n* *hi:c-ís*
Bill hog-NON.SUBJ.CASE see-IND
'Bill is looking at a hog.'
b. *Bill* *sókha-n* ***ís**-hi:c-ís*
Bill hog-NON.SUBJ.CASE **INSTR**-see-IND
'Bill is looking at a hog (with something).'
c. *Bill* *is-hic-íta* *sókha-n* ***ís**-hi:c-ís*
Bill INSTR-see-INF hog-NON.SUBJ.CASE **INSTR**-see-IND
'Bill is looking at a hog with binoculars.'

(Martin 2011: 192–193)

Many polysynthetic languages can incorporate evidential, epistemic, and evaluative morphology. Mithun (2016) gives the following Yup'ik examples illustrating scope interactions in the last two examples.

(33) Yup'ik

a. *Quyayuumiitrepuyugnargua*
quya-yuumi-ite-llru-**yugnarqe**-u-a
thankful-yearn-NEG-PAST-**probably**-INTR.IND-1SG
'I guess I didn't want to be thankful.'

b. *Taiciqsugnarqnillruuq*
tai-ciq-**yugnarqe**-ni-llru-u-q
come-FUT-**probably**-claim-PST-INTR.IND-3SG
'He said he would probably come.'

c. *Taiciqnillruyugnarquq*
tai-ciq-ni-llru-**yugnarqe**-u-q
come-FUT-claim-PAST-**probably**-INTR.IND-3SG
'He probably said he would come.'

(Mithun 2016: 151)

In some polysynthetic languages the lexical root is not identified by a single morpheme but is discontinuous. Consider the following Western Apache [apw] examples.

(34) Western Apache

a. *k'enádadihidléh*
k'e-ná-**da**-Ø-d-(h)-id-d-**léh**
TH-ITER-**PL**-3.OBJ-TH-PEG?-1NONSG.SUBJ-TH-**SFO.IT**
'We (more than two) plant it usually.'

b. *k'edishłēē*
k'e-Ø-**d**-Ø-sh-Ø-**lēē**
TH-3.OBJ-**TH**-CM-1.SUBJ-CL-**SFO.IMPERF**
'I am planting it.'

(de Reuse 2017: 528f.)

The meaning of plant here arises from the combination of the two thematic elements, *k'e* and *d/da* along with the element marked SFO (slender flexible object), which varies with respect to aspect. De Reuse states that "[the thematic elements (TH)] function somewhat like the *cran-* and *boysen-* in *cranberry* and *boysenberry*". From this, we infer that these morphemes cannot appear on their own.

Finally, polysynthetic languages may possess adverbial elements that modify the predicate. These can be either an incorporated adverb or an affix on the verb. In some cases, it may not be easy to distinguish between the two possibilities, although we do not discuss possible diagnostics here. The following Plains Cree example and subsequent Inuktitut example are relatively straightforward, though. Consider the Plains Cree example first.

(35) *sakih -iso **-si** -hkaso -ski -w* [Plains Cree]
love -REFL **-DIM** -pretend -HAB -3SG.IND
'He's in the habit of pretending to love himself a little bit.'

(Dahlstrom 1991: 135, ex (24))

The gloss suggests that *si-*, which gives rise to the meaning of *a little bit*, is an affix, possibly the head of a functional projection in or around the *v*P layer. Consider again the Inuktitut example in (1a), repeated here as (36).

(36) *annulaksi-**kkanni-nginna-jualu**-gasu-**lauqsima**-guma-nngit-tsiaq-galuaq-tunga*
imprison-**again-really-a.lot**-try-**ever**-want-NEG-EMPH-EMPH-1SG.INTR.DECL
'I would never ever even want to try to end up in jail ever again even for a bit.'

Here, a number of adverbial elements appear inside the verbal complex. In (36), the gloss suggests that these may be incorporated lexical elements (see the next section for incorporation). We come back to this point in the conclusion. This contrasts with (35), where the putative adverbial element, glossed as DIM, does not appear to be a lexical root, but rather a functional element.

3. Noun Incorporation

Noun incorporation (NI) in North American languages has been discussed in the literature since at least Kleinschmidt (1852; see also Cuoq 1866; Brinton 1886; Kroeber 1909; Sapir 1911). Debates as to the proper characterization and analysis of NI have figured prominently for over 100 years (Kroeber 1910; Sapir 1911). Debates on the analysis continue to this day (Sadock 1980; 1986; Mithun 1984; 1986; Baker 1988; 1996; 2009; 2014; Rosen 1989; Baker et al. 2005; Barrie 2015c; Barrie & Mathieu 2016). While we touch on these debates, the goal of this section is to describe the variety of NI constructions found in the languages of North America.

Defining the term *noun incorporation* is not straightforward, and disagreements as to what does and does not count as noun incorporation span a century. We eschew an in-depth discussion of this dissent and, indeed, a precise definition of noun incorporation in favor of a brief discussion on the consensus of the set of properties that most researchers take to characterize noun incorporation. We discuss various morphological, syntactic, and semantic properties of noun incorporation.

Before getting to the details of NI, we very briefly touch on one issue in the debates on NI, which can be traced back to Kroeber (1910) and Sapir (1911). For a relatively modern debate on this matter, the reader is referred to Mithun (1984; 1986) and Sadock (1986). The issue centers on the identity of the incorporated element. Given the label noun incorporation, it stands to reason the incorporated element should be a noun. In Onondaga (and Northern Iroquoian in general) this is reasonably clear as many incorporated forms contain nominalizers; see (39). In Salish, it is less clear. Wiltschko (2009) argues that the incorporated element is a bare lexical root and not a noun. Does it still count as noun incorporation? As mentioned, we do not take a stand on these issues, but rather present the facts as known and leave it to the reader to consult the references cited here for more details.

Noun incorporation prototypically consists of a verbal compound consisting of a verbal root and a nominal root. Often, the incorporated noun is morphologically impoverished compared to its unincorporated counterpart. Consider the following Onondaga example. *Nakt* 'bed' in (37b) is a reduced version of *ka-nakt-aˀ* in (37a).

(37) Onondaga

a. *waˀkhnínú: neˀ ganakdaˀ*

waˀ-	k-	hninu-	:	neˀ	ka-nakt-aˀ
FACT-	1.SG-	buy-	PUNC	NE	NOM.PREF-bed-SUF

'I bought the/a bed.'

b. *waˀgenakdahnínú:*

waˀ-	k-	**nakt-**	hninu-	:
FACT-	1.SG.AG-	**bed-**	buy-	PUNC

'I bought a bed.'

(Gloria Williams, Nora Carrier, speakers)

Languages vary in how much morphological material may appear on the incorporated noun. Salish languages typically allow only a bare root as an incorporated noun. Consider the following Halkomelem example. Wiltschko shows that nothing other than the lexical root can appear in NI constructions. Note in this example that the incorporated form for *dish* is a suppletive form of the freestanding root for *dish*.

(38) *th'éxw-**wíl**-t-es* *te* ***ló:thel*** [Halkomelem]
wash-**dish**-TR-3SG DET **dish**
'He washed the dish.'

(Wiltschko 2009: 211)

Northern Iroquoian languages can incorporate bare nominal roots or nominalized verbal roots, in which an overt nominalizer is present (see Barrie & Uchihara, this volume, for further information on NI in general for Iroquoian). Consider the following Onondaga example, in which a verbal root appears with a nominalizer and is then incorporated into the larger verbal complex.

(39) *agatgų'tshé:hwih* [Onondaga]
ak- **[atkų-'tshR]**- ohw -ih
1.SG.PAT- **[be.poisonous-NZLR]**- put.in.water -STAT
'I have poisoned it with liquid poison.'

(Woodbury 2003: 278)

Finally, Algonquian languages can incorporate much larger structures (see Barrie & Mathieu 2016 for extended discussion). Consider the following Ojibwe example. The incorporated noun, contained in square brackets, is internally complex. See Compton (2013) for similar effects in Inuit.

(40) *gii-naajibakwezhgane* [Ojibwe]
gii- naad -i -**[bakwezhi-ge-an]** -e
PST- fetch -EPEN -**[cut-VAI-NZLR]** -VAI
'He/she went after some bread.'

(Barrie & Mathieu 2016: ex (19a))

Noun incorporation also provides a trigger for root allomorphy in some languages. Consider the following Halkomelem data (Wiltschko 2009, citing Galloway 1980).

(41)

a. nominal suffixes	b. regular nouns
-as -face	s'ó:thes face
-tses -hand	chálex hand
-awtx -building	lálém house
-ilep -ground	téméxw earth, land
-elcep -firewood	siyólh firewood
-als -fruit/round	sth'í:m berry, fruit
-(e)wi:l(s) -dishes	ló:thel dish

Some of the incorporated forms (nominal suffixes) resemble the non-incorporated forms (regular nouns), but in most cases they represent full suppletion.

Another property of noun incorporation that varies is the interaction between noun incorporation, on the one hand, and argument structure and agreement on the other. Rosen (1989) identifies two kinds of noun incorporation: classifier and compounding. This distinction still informs investigations into noun incorporation to this day. In short, classifier incorporation does not affect the argument structure of the verb, while compound incorporation does. Thus, classifier incorporation permits an incorporated noun that is linked with a non-incorporated full nominal. The full DP is virtually always more specific than the incorporated noun. Thus, if the direct object is incorporated, a full nominal direct object can still appear. Rosen discusses several aspects of noun incorporation that fall out from this contrast, but we focus only on this aspect here. See Barrie (2015c) for more recent discussion. See also Mithun &andCorbett (1999) for a discussion on the lexical aspects of noun incorporation and its effect on transitivity. Consider the following Mohawk example. Observe that the incorporated noun *tsy* ('fish') is doubled by a full nominal phrase ('eight bullheads').

(42) *Tohka* *niyohserá:ke* *tsi nahe'* *sha'té:ku* *nikú:ti*
several so.it.year.numbers so it.goes eight of.them
rabahbót *wa-hu-**tsy**-ahní:nu* *ki* *rake'níha.*
bullhead FACT-3SG.M-**fish**-bought this my.father
'Several years ago, my father bought eight bullheads.' [Mohawk]

(Mithun 1984: 870)

By contrast, compound noun incorporation involves the suppression of an argument by incorporation. Once the object is incorporated, a full nominal that is linked with the incorporated noun cannot appear. Rosen discusses only Polynesian languages in the context of compound noun incorporation; however, de Reuse's (1994: 234) discussion of noun incorporation in Lakota [lkt] suggests it has the same properties as Rosen's compound noun incorporation. Since de Reuse does not specifically mention Rosen's work, a full comparison cannot be made. Nevertheless, consider the following example. Despite the orthographic space between the noun and the verb, *look.for*, de Reuse contends this is an example of a "syntactic compound". De Reuse also notes in the same example that the full form for 'child' is *hokšíla* and appears with an article.

(43) ***hokší*** *okìle* *pi* *škhé?* [Lakota]
child ST.S0.A0.poss-look.for PL QUOT-DECL
'. . . they looked for the child (seriously) . . .'

(de Reuse 1994: 234)

De Reuse goes on to note (p. 219) that, unlike Iroquoian languages, Lakota does not strand determiners or modifiers. Stranding is a hallmark property of classifier incorporation, suggesting Lakota is not a classifier incorporating language. As de Reuse notes, however, further research is needed into the syntactic properties of noun incorporation in Lakota.

4. On the Analysis of Polysynthesis

This section reviews some of the major treatments of polysynthesis in the literature, presenting the outlook for future research. We present Baker's (1996) macroparametric approach, couched within a generative framework. We also present Mithun's (1983) functional approach to polysynthesis. We end by touching on parameter hierarchies as proposed by Roberts (2016).

Baker (1996) offers a comprehensive Polysynthesis Parameter that distinguishes polysynthetic languages such as Mohawk from non-polysynthetic ones, such as English. This theory is couched within a general framework that makes use of macroparameters, which has, of course, come under much scrutiny recently (Boeckx 2011; Kayne 2013; Roberts 2016). An updated version of the Polysynthesis Parameter is offered in Baker et al. (2005), but we present only Baker's original (1996) theory here. This macroparameter is captured by the Morphological Visibility Condition (MVC).

(44) MVC: A phrase X is visible for theta role assignment from a head Y only if it is coindexed with a morpheme in the word containing Y via:

i. an agreement relationship, or
ii. a movement relationship
Yes: Mohawk, Nahuatl, Rembarrnga. . .
No: English, French, Chichewa. . .

In short, for Baker, in a language such as English, the verb assigns its theta roles to the relevant arguments, which are separate words. In a language such as Mohawk, however, the verb assigns its theta roles to *morphemes* inside the verb. Thus, the polysynthetic nature of Mohawk, Nahuatl, and other such languages falls out from the fact that all theta roles are assigned word-internally, necessitating several morphemes in the verb.

The explanatory adequacy of the macroparametric approach lies in its ability to account for a large number of properties. To show that the Polysynthesis Parameter is explanatorily adequate, Baker shows that it accounts for a large number of properties beyond noun incorporation and rich agreement. He offers the following list of properties of polysynthetic languages in the macroparametric sense. That is, the following properties are argued to fall out from the MVC.

(45) a. syntactic noun incorporation
b. obligatory object agreement
c. free pro-drop
d. free word order
e. no NP reflexives
f. no true quantifiers
g. obligatory *wh*-movement
h. noun agrees with R arguments
i. no true determiners
j. noun agrees with possessor
k. restricted morphological causative
l. noun incorporation or agreement in PP
m. CP arguments only if nominal
n. no infinitives

Baker, by and large, shows that the properties in (45) generally hold in the languages he investigates. While he investigated Mohawk in depth to confirm these properties, he relied on published sources for the other languages he analyzed. Those languages of North America include Nahuatl, Tanoan languages, and Wichita. While a short survey chapter is no place to examine all the properties above, we do discuss a few here. The first two properties were addressed directly with the MVC. In addition to the MVC, Baker also assumes that heads do not assign case to argument positions. Thus, no full NP can appear in argument position without violating the case filter. As such, all overt NPs are adjoined clause-peripherally, along the lines of Jelinek (1984). As adjuncts, the overt NPs can be freely ordered or omitted if recoverable from the discourse, accounting for properties c and d. Furthermore, since reflexives and quantifiers must appear in argument position for proper interpretation at LF, Baker contends that they cannot appear in polysynthetic languages. The Garifuna data in (22) are of interest here, as this language appears to have overt pronominal reflexive pronouns. Finally, since *wh*-phrases must leave a variable in argument position for proper interpretation at LF, it follows that *wh*-movement is obligatory in polysynthetic languages.

We leave the discussion of Baker's Polysynthesis Parameter here. Although this proposal has had its share of criticism, as is natural for any bold proposal, (Spencer 1995; Kaiser 1996; MacSwan 1998; Nordlinger & Saulwick 2002; Haugen 2016),[3] it continues to inform our theoretical understanding of polysynthesis. We briefly mention some of the criticism here. These critiques all target the list of polysynthetic properties in (45). According to the Polysynthesis Parameter, a polysynthetic language should exhibit all the properties in this list. Kaiser (1996) argues that while Ainu is a typical polysynthetic language, it lacks crucial properties in (45). Specifically, word order in Ainu is much more rigid than in Mohawk, *wh*-phrases remain in situ, and morphological causatives can be formed from unergatives. Likewise, MacSwan (1998) and Haugen (2016) argue that Southeast Puebla Nahuatl and Classical Nahuatl, respectively, both fairly typical polysynthetic languages, also lack the same free word order that Mohawk has. He also argues that it has non-referential quantified NPs (i.e., true quantifiers). Nordlinger and Saulwick (2002) show that Rembarrnga has infinitives. Finally, Spencer (1995) argues that the incorporation non-objects (such as adverbs, obliques such as instruments and temporal expressions). Spencer's arguments do not impinge on the Polysynthesis Parameter per se, but are problematic for Baker's syntactic analysis of NI.

As mentioned earlier, Baker et al. (2005) update the approach above to take into account cross-linguistic variation in the availability of agreement with noun incorporation. Specifically, they discuss noun incorporation in Southern Tiwa, in which agreement is obligatory with the incorporated noun and compare it with Mapudungun [arn], where agreement is impossible with the incorporated noun. Finally, Roberts (2010) proposes a novel analysis of head movement, briefly addressing the issue of noun incorporation and the properties of polysynthesis in (45). We leave the reader to explore these references.

We move next to Mithun's (1983) discussion of the functional properties of polysynthesis. She notes that polysynthetic properties of languages typically exist alongside analytic counterparts. For instance, noun incorporation is often not an obligatory process but is optional. Consider the pair of sentences in example (37) again, repeated here as example (46).

(46) [Onondaga]

a. *waˀkhnínú: neˀ ganakdaˀ*

waˀ-	k-	hninu-	:́	neˀ	ka-nakt-aˀ
FACT-	1.SG-	buy-	PUNC	NE	NOM.PREF-bed-SUF

'I bought the/a bed.'

b. *waˀgenakdahnínú:*

waˀ-	k-	**nakt-**	hninu-	:́
FACT-	1.SG.AG-	**bed-**	buy-	PUNC

'I bought a bed.'

(Gloria Williams, Nora Carrier, speakers)

She also notes that synthetic causatives and locatives exist alongside their analytic counterparts. The same observation has been made by Nakayama (2001) for Nuu-chah-nulth. Both of these authors contend that polysynthesis plays a functional role in languages where they are found. Note that this contrasts with the formal analysis Baker proposed; nevertheless, the two are not entirely incompatible. Specifically, Mithun and Nakayama propose that polysynthesis gives rise to several functional possibilities not found in non-polysynthetic languages (or at least not found to the same degree). The items in Table 11.2 are extracted from Mithun (1983).

Table 11.2 Functional Properties of Polysynthesis

Property	*Functional Effect*
Agreement	Word order based on information structure rather than grammatical role
Causative	Expression of a single event
Instrumental and Locative	To background instrument or location in discourse
Noun Incorporation	To background discourse participant or to name a recurring or habitual activity

We cover only a couple of the properties discussed by Mithun, starting with causatives. Mithun offers the following Lakota examples.

(47) [Lakota]

a. *Sab-wá-ye*
black-1SG-CAUS
'I blackened it.'

b. *Sápa* *wa-káye.*
black 1SG-make
'I made it black.'

(Mithun 1983: 224, ex (9))

Mithun reports that a Lakota speaker would use the first sentence to refer to the event of polishing a shoe and would use the second sentence to refer to an event of hanging a kettle too close to a fire, the result of which is that the kettle became black. She relates this to the event structure of the two constructions. The synthetic causative in (47a) refers to a single event (the act of polishing the shoe), while the analytic causative in (47b) refers to two events (placing the kettle near the fire, and the kettle becoming black).

Turning to noun incorporation, Mithun argues that the noun in the incorporated construction loses its referential status (though this is disputed by Baker et al. 2005) and, together with the verb, names a habitual activity or, in Mithun (1984), an institutionalized activity. She gives the following Comanche examples.

(48) [Comanche]

a. *wana-roh-peti*
cloth-by.force-throw
'to gamble'

b. *waa-hima*
cedar.tree-take
'to celebrate Christmas'

(Mithun 1984: 855)

Finally, Roberts (2016) and earlier work offers a novel approach to understanding cross-linguistic variation. He proposes that parameters are structured in hierarchies, rather than being all or nothing. In short, his proposal reconciles the problems raised by the fact that a strict macroparametric approach has trouble dealing with exceptions, and that denying any kind of parameterization leaves well-known Greenbergian generalizations a mystery (such as the strong correlation between OV order and postpositions). While this research program is ongoing, he offers the following parameter hierarchy related to word structure. Only the portion of the hierarchy of interest to us is shown. The hierarchy refers to a *probe*, which is a theoretical device in generative syntax to trigger head movement – roughly, the movement of individual words in a sentence.

(49) Do some probes trigger head movement?

N: analytic Y: Do all probes trigger head movement?

Y: polysynthetic N: does [+V] trigger head movement?

For Roberts, then polysynthesis results from specific parametric choices made at the top of the parameter hierarchy. Specifically, all heads trigger head movement in the sense of Roberts (2010). Few details are offered in the discussion, leaving the exact implementation of our understanding of polysynthesis, not to mention the variation found within polysynthetic languages, to future research. Crucially, Roberts's hierarchy, like Baker's Polysynthesis Parameter, seems to allow only two choices: polysynthetic/non-polysynthetic. Mattissen's discussion earlier in this chapter suggests that more choices are needed under the 'polysynthetic' node in (49). The difference between Baker's approach and Roberts's approach, then, is that Baker's Polysynthesis Parameter inherently does not afford any option for variation, whereas Roberts's microparametric approach does. Specifically, additional microparameters can be proposed that hang off of the 'polysynthetic' node in (49).

5. Summary and Outlook

This chapter began with a discussion on the definition of polysynthesis, of which no clear, precise definition can be found, the formal definition of Baker notwithstanding. Rather, it is merely a tendency for a high degree of morphological complexity on the verb. We have reviewed several morphosyntactic aspects of polysynthetic languages, dividing the discussion into affixal morphology and noun incorporation. We discussed several properties that can be encoded on the verb, some common, some rare. We also discussed general properties of noun incorporation in polysynthetic languages of North America.

In the third section we discussed some theoretical aspects of polysynthesis, including some of the analyses of Baker, Mithun, and Roberts. Baker's formal analysis is arguably the most well-known, although it is not without its problems. The crux of his Polysynthesis Parameter is the parametric choice between a verb assigning theta roles word-internally or word-externally. All other properties of polysynthetic languages fall out from this choice. As noted, though, some authors have described polysynthetic languages that deviate from the expectations of the Polysynthesis Parameter. Mithun's functional analysis contrasts the functional differences of synthetic and analytic constructions, although see Harley (2012) for a detailed discussion of the semantic properties of lexical decomposition. The remarks on Roberts's parameter hierarchies were sketchy, given the programmatic nature of this framework. Again, future studies should address the variation found among polysynthetic languages, rather than treating them as a monolithic entity. In this regard, Haugen's (2016) discussion of cross-linguistic variation in Uto-Aztecan, including his discussion of the historical development of the Uto-Aztecan languages would be an excellent place to apply a microparametric analysis along the lines Roberts has proposed.

We end this section with a brief discussion of some possible outlooks for future research. A notable property of polysynthetic languages is that it is the verbs that display such a high degree of morphological complexity. The nouns, while exhibiting some morphology, are virtually always more simple. Given the hypothesis that the extended nominal projection mirrors the extended verbal projection (Grimshaw 1990; Ogawa 2001; Megerdoomian 2008), this asymmetry calls for an explanation. We have roughly defined polysynthesis as extreme morphological complexity, either by the appearance of numerous functional affixes or the incorporation of lexical material into the verbal complex. One issue we touched on in this chapter is that it is not always clear whether a given morpheme is a functional affix or incorporated lexical material. This point was brought to light in the discussion on adverbial elements at the end of §2. An avenue for future research is developing diagnostics to distinguish between these two possibilities. Namely, are the adverbial elements in the Inuktitut example lexical or functional? Compton (2012; 2013) addresses these issues for Inuit; however, the question requires further examination for other polysynthetic languages. Finally, the last section discussed theoretical aspects of polysynthesis. It is still an open question whether polysynthesis can be defined formally, as Baker does. In other words, is there a macroparametric setting distinguishing polysynthetic languages from non-polysynthetic ones? Or is there a series of microparameters that is better able to capture the cross-linguistic variation?

Further Reading

For further reading of polysynthesis in general, the reader should consult the papers in Fortescue et al. (2017). Murasugi (2014) provides an excellent overview of many of the same concepts here from a different perspective. There are also several relevant survey articles on noun incorporation (Gerdts 1998; Massam 2009; Barrie 2015a).

Notes

1. Mattissen actually splits this category into two subgroups. We have conflated them here to keep the discussion brief.
2. Although Iroquoianists largely agree that the agreement morphology in Iroquoian is generally portmanteau, Chafe (1960) gives an attempt of full decomposition with significant allomorphy. See Barrie and Uchihara (this volume) and the other references cited here for more details.
3. One criticism of Baker (1996) we do not address here is Koenig and Michelson (2015). This is because Koenig and Michelson do not directly address the issue of polysynthesis, so it is out of place to discuss it in detail here. Nevertheless, they offer a strong and important critique of Baker (1996), both empirically and theoretically, and their discussion impinges a great deal on the study of polysynthesis. The core of their claim is that overt NPs are never selected by the verb but are rather syntactically adjoined to the verb. They claim that lexical words in Northern Iroquoian are "functionally complete", thus obviating the need for selection of any kind, lambda-abstraction, and phrase structure (be it X-Bar Theory or Bare Phrase Structure).

References

Abbott, Clifford. 2000. *Oneida*. Munich: Lincom Europa.

Allen, Barbara Jane & Gardiner, Donna & Frantz, Donald. 1984. Noun incorporation in Southern Tiwa. *International Journal of American Linguistics* 50. 292–311.

Baker, Mark C. 1988. *Incorporation: A theory of grammatical function changing*. Chicago, IL: University of Chicago Press.

Baker, Mark C. 1996. *The polysynthesis parameter*. Oxford: Oxford University Press.

Baker, Mark C. 2009. Is head movement still needed for noun incorporation? *Lingua* 119. 148–165.

Baker, Mark C. 2014. Pseudo noun incorporation as covert incorporation: Linearization and crosslinguistic variation. *Language and Linguistics* 15.

Baker, Mark C. & Aranovich, Roberto & Golluscio, Lucía A. 2005. Two types of syntactic noun incorporation: Noun incorporation in Mapudungun and its typological implications. *Language* 81. 138–76.

Barker, Muhammad Abd-al-Ramhan. 1964. *Klamath grammar*. Berkeley: University of California Press.

Barrie, Michael. 2015a. Generative approaches to noun incorporation. In Shin, S.-Y. & Wang, H.-S. & Chung, H. & Cheon, J.-Y. & Park, J.-U. & Barrie, M. & Chung, I. & Kang, B.-G. (eds.), 언어 현상과 언어학적 분석 [*Linguistic phenomena and linguistic analysis*]. Seoul: Language and Information Society.

Barrie, Michael. 2015b. *A grammar of Onondaga*. Berlin: Lincom.

Barrie, Michael. 2015c. Two kinds of structural noun incorporation. *Studia Linguistica* 69. 237–271.

Barrie, Michael & Mathieu, Éric. 2016. Noun incorporation and phrasal movement. *Natural Language & Linguistic Theory* 34. 1–51.

Beck, David. 2008. Variable ordering of affixes in Upper Necaxa Totonac. (Paper presented to the Twelfth Workshop of Structure and Constituency in Languages of the Americas, Vancouver, BC.)

Boeckx, Cedric. 2011. Approaching parameters from below. In Di Sciullo, A. M. & Boeckx, C. (eds.), *The biolinguistic enterprise*, 205–221. Oxford: Oxford University Press.

Brinton, Daniel G. 1886. On polysynthesis and incorporation as characteristics of American languages. *American Philosophical Society* 23. 48–86.

Broadbent, Sylvia M. 1964. *The southern Sierra Miwok language*. Berkeley: University of California Press.

Broadwell, George Aaron. 2006. *A Choctaw reference grammar*. Lincoln and London: University of Nebraska Press.

Caballero, Gabriela. 2014. Uto-Aztecan. In Lieber, R. & Štekauer, P. (eds.), *The Oxford handbook of derivational morphology*, 724–742. Oxford: Oxford University Press.

Chafe, Wallace. 1960. Seneca morphology III: Expanded pronominal prefixes. *International Journal of American Linguistics* 26. 224–233.

Compton, Richard. 2012. The syntax and semantics of modification in Inuktitut: Adjectives and adverbs in a polysynthetic language. University of Toronto.

Compton, Richard. 2013. Word-internal XPs and right-headedness in Inuit. (Paper presented at the 31st West Coast Conference on Formal Linguistics, Arizona State University.)

Comrie, Bernard. 1989. *Language universals and linguistic typology*. Oxford: Basil Blackwell.

Cuoq, Jean-André. 1866. *Etudes philologiques sur quelques langues sauvages*. Montreal, QC: Dawson Brothers.

Dahlstrom, Amy. 1991. *Plains Cree morphosyntax*. New York: Garland Publications.

de Reuse, Willem. 2017. Western Apache, a southern Athabaskan language. In Fortescue, M. & Mithun, M. & Evans, N. (eds.), *The Oxford handbook of polysynthesis*, 517–535. Oxford: Oxford University Press.

de Reuse, Willem J. 1994. Noun incorporation in Lakota (Siouan). *International Journal of American Linguistics* 60. 199–260.

Fortescue, Michael. 1984. *West Greenlandic*. London: Croom Helm.

Fortescue, Michael & Mithun, Marianne & Evans, Nicholas (eds.). 2017. *The Oxford handbook of polysynthesis*. Oxford: Oxford University Press.

Galloway, Brent. 1980. *The structure of Upriver Halkomelem, a grammatical sketch and classified word list for Upriver Halkomelem*. Sardis, BC: Coqualeetza Education Training Center.

Gatschet, Albert S. 1890. *The Klamath Indians of southwestern Oregon*, vol. 2. Washington, DC: Department of the Interior.

Gerdts, Donna B. 1998. Incorporation. In Spencer, A. & Zwicky, A. M. (eds.), *The handbook of morphology*, 84–100. Malden, MA: Blackwell.

Grimshaw, Jane. 1990. *Argument structure*. Cambridge, MA: MIT Press.

Haas, Mary R. 1941. Noun incorporation in the Muskogean languages. *Language* 17. 311–315.

Harley, Heidi. 2012. Lexical decomposition in modern syntactic theory. In Hinzen, W. & Werning, M. & Machery, E. (eds.), *Handbook of compositionality*, 328–350. Oxford: Oxford University Press.

Harrington, John P. 1921. Chimariko field notes on microfilm, Reels 20–1. National Anthropological Archives, Smithsonian Institution (https://anthropology.si.edu/naa/harrington/harrington_mf2.html)

Haugen, Jason D. 2016. Configurationality in classical Nahuatl. (Paper presented at the Workshop on Structure and Constituency in the Languages of the Americas 20, University of Arizona.)

Haurholm-Larsen, Steffen. 2016. *A grammar of Garifuna*. University of Bern. (Doctoral dissertation.)

Humboldt, Wilhem von. 1825. *Über das Entstehen der grammatischen Formen und ihren Einfluß auf die Ideenentwicklung*. Berlin: Königlische Preussische Akadamie der Wissenschaften.

Humboldt, Wilhem von. 1836. *Über die Kawi-sprache auf der Insel Java. Vol I. Über die Verschiedenheit der menschlichen Sprachbaues*. Berlin: Königlische Preussische Akadamie der Wissenschaften.

Jany, Carmen. 2009. *Chimariko grammar: Areal and typological perspective*. Berkeley: University of California Press.

Jany, Carmen. 2017. The Northern Hokan area. In Fortescue, M. & Mithun, M. & Evans, N. (eds.), *The Oxford handbook of polysynthesis*, 260–283. Oxford: Oxford University Press.

Jelinek, Eloise. 1984. Empty categories, case, and configurationality. *Natural Language & Linguistic Theory* 2. 39–76.

Johns, Alana. 2007. Restricting noun incorporation: Root movement. *Natural Language and Linguistic Theory* 25. 535–576.

Kaiser, Lizanne. 1996. Ainu: Evidence against the polysynthesis parameter. In Green, A. D. & Motapanyane, V. (eds.), *Proceedings – Eastern States Conference on Linguistics (ESCOL)*, 13, 170–181. Ithaca, NY: Cornell University.

Kayne, Richard. 2013. Why are there no directionality parameters? In Biberauer, T. & Sheehan, M. (eds.), *Theoretical approaches to disharmonic word order*, 219–244. Oxford: Oxford University Press.

Kleinschmidt, Samuel. 1852. *Grammatik der grönländischen Sprache mit theilweisem einschluss des Labradordialects*. Berlin: Reimer.

Koenig, Jean-Pierre & Michelson, Karin. 2015. Invariance in argument realization: The case of Iroquoian. *Language* 91. 1–47.

Kroeber, Alfred L. 1909. Noun incorporation in American languages. (Paper presented at the XVI. Internationaler Amerikanisten-Kongress, 2nd, Vienna and Leipzig.)

Kroeber, Alfred L. 1910. Noun incorporation in American languages. (Paper presented at the XVI. Internationalen Amerikanisten-Kongress, 2nd, Vienna and Leipzig.)

Lasersohn, Peter. 1995. *Plurality, conjunction, and events*. Dordrecht: Kluwer.

Liedtke, Stefan. 1997. *The languages of the 'First Nations': Comparison of Native American languages from an ethnolinguistic perspective*. Munich: Lincom Europa.

Lounsbury, Floyd Glenn. 1949. *Iroquoian morphology*. New Haven, CT: Yale University. (Doctoral dissertation.)

Lounsbury, Floyd Glenn. 1953. *Oneida verb morphology*. New Haven, CT: Yale University.

Macaulay, Monica. 1993. Reduplication and the structure of the Karuk verb stem. *International Journal of American Linguistics* 59. 64–81.

MacSwan, Jeff. 1998. The argument status of NPs in southeast Puebla Nahuatl: Comments on the Polysynthesis Parameter. *Southwest Journal of Linguistics* 17. 101–114.

Martin, Jack. 2011. *A grammar of Creek (Muskogee)*. Lincoln and London: University of Nebraska Press.

Massam, Diane. 2009. Noun incorporation: Essentials and extensions. *Language and Linguistics Compass* 3. 1076–1096.

Mattissen, Johanna. 2017. Sub-types of polysynthesis. In Evans, N., Mithun, M. & Fortescue, M. (eds.), *The Oxford handbook of polysynthesis*. Oxford: Oxford University Press.

Megerdoomian, Karine. 2008. Parallel nominal and verbal projections. In Freidin, R. & Otero, C. P. & Zubizarreta, M. L. (eds.), *Foundational issues in linguistic theory: Essays in honor of Jean-Roger Vergnaud*, 73–103. Cambridge, MA: MIT Press.

Mithun, Marianne. 1983. The genius of polysynthesis. *University of Oklahoma Papers in Anthropology* 24. 221–242.

Mithun, Marianne. 1984. The evolution of noun incorporation. *Language* 60. 847–894.

Mithun, Marianne. 1986. On the nature of noun incorporation. *Language* 62. 32–37.

Mithun, Marianne. 2006. Voice without subjects, objects or obliques: Manipulating argument structure in agent/patient systems. In Tsunoda, T. & Nishimitsu, Y. & Kageyama, T. (eds.), *Voice and grammatical relations*, 195–216. Amsterdam: John Benjamins.

Mithun, Marianne. 2010. Contact and North American languages. In Hickey, R. (ed.), *Handbook of language contact*, 673–694. Oxford: Blackwell.

Mithun, Marianne. 2014. Morphological complexity and language contact. (Paper presented at the Diachronic Stability of Complex Verbal Morphology, Adam Mickiewicz University, Poznań.)

Mithun, Marianne. 2016. Affix ordering: Motivation and interpretation. In Hippisley, A. & Stump, G. (eds.), *The Cambridge handbook of morphology*, 149–185. Cambridge: Cambridge University Press.

Mithun, Marianne & Corbett, Greville G. 1999. The effect of noun incorporation on argument structure. In Mereu, L. (ed.), *Boundaries of morphology and syntax*, 49–71. Amsterdam: John Benjamins.

Murasugi, Kumiko. 2014. Noun incorporation, nonconfigurationality, and polysynthesis. In Carnie, A. & Siddiqi, D. & Sato, Y. (eds.), *The Routledge handbook of syntax*, 283–304. London and New York: Routledge.

Nakayama, Toshihide. 2001. *Nuuchahnulth (Nootka) morphosyntax*. Berkeley and Los Angeles: University of California Press.

Newman, Paul. 1980. *The classification of Chadic within Afroasiatic*. Leiden: Universitaire Pers Leiden.

Nordlinger, Rachel & Saulwick, Adam. 2002. Infinitives in polysynthesis: The case of Rembarrnga. In Evans, N. & Sasse, H. J. (eds.), *Problems of polysynthesis*, 185–201. Berlin: Akademie Verlag.

Ogawa, Yoshiki. 2001. *A unified theory of verbal and nominal projections*. Oxford: Oxford University Press.

Rhodes, Richard A. 1976. *The morphosyntax of the central Ojibwa verb*. Ann Arbor: University of Michigan. (Doctoral dissertation.)

Rice, Keren. 2000. *Morpheme order and semantic scope: Word formation in the Athapaskan verb*. Cambridge: Cambridge University Press.

Roberts, Ian. 2010. *Agreement and head movement: Clitics, incorporation, and defective goals*. Cambridge, MA: MIT Press.

Roberts, Ian. 2016. Some remarks on parameter hierarchies. In Eguren, L. & Fernández-Soriano, O. & Mendikoetxea, A. (eds.), *Rethinking parameters*, 170–199. Oxford: Oxford University Press.

Rood, David S. 1976. *Wichita grammar*. New York: Garland.

Rosen, Carol. 1990. Rethinking Southern Tiwa: The geometry of a triple-agreement language. *Language* 66. 669–713.

Rosen, Sara Thomas. 1989. Two types of noun incorporation: A lexical analysis. *Language* 65. 294–317.

Sadock, Jerrold. 1980. Noun incorporation in Greenlandic: A case of syntactic word formation. *Language* 56. 300–319.

Sadock, Jerrold. 1986. Some notes on noun incorporation. *Language* 62. 19–31.

Sapir, Edward. 1911. The problem of noun incorporation in American languages. *American Anthropologist* 13. 250–282.

Spencer, Andrew. 1995. Incorporation in Chukchi. *Language: Journal of the Linguistic Society of America* 71. 439–489.

Swanton, John R. 1911. Haida. In Boas, F. (ed.), *Handbook of American Indian languages, Part 1. Bureau of American ethnology bulletin 40*, 205–282. Washington, DC: Government Printing Office.

Wiltschko, Martina. 2004. Reflexives in Upriver Halkomelem. *International Journal of American Linguistics* 70. 101–127.

Wiltschko, Martina. 2009. √Root incorporation: Evidence from lexical suffixes in Halkomelem Salish. *Lingua* 119. 199–223.

Woodbury, Hanni. 2003. *Onondaga-English/English-Onondaga dictionary*. Toronto: University of Toronto Press.

Young, R. W. & Morgan, W. 1987. *The Navajo language*. Albuquerque: University of New Mexico Press.

Young, R. W. & Morgan, W. 2000. *The Navajo language: A grammar and colloquial dictionary*. Salina Bookshelf.

12
ANTIPASSIVES

Kumiko Murasugi

1. Introduction

Cooreman (1994: 50) defines the antipassive as "a construction typical for ergative languages . . . [that] occurs along with ergative constructions as a morphosyntactic alternative for the same proposition". Shown in (1) are sentences from Inuktitut, a dialect of the Inuit language spoken in Canada; (1a) is an intransitive sentence, (1b) is a transitive ergative sentence, and (1c) is an example of an antipassive structure.[1]

(1) Inuktitut

a. Intransitive
Piita *pisik-tuq.*
Peter(ABS) walk-PART.3SG
'Peter is walking.'

b. Ergative
Anguti-up *arnaq* *kunik-taa.*
man-ERG woman(ABS) kiss-PART.3SG/3SG
'The man kissed the woman.'
(Spreng 2006: 253)

c. Antipassive
Anguti *kunik-si-vuq* *arna-mik.*
man(ABS) kiss-AP-IND.3SG woman-mik
'The man kissed a woman.'
(Spreng 2006: 248)

The ergativity of Inuktitut is revealed in its case pattern, where the intransitive subject in (1a) and the object in (1b) have the same absolutive case, while the transitive subject in (1b) has a different case, ergative. The antipassive construction in (1c) is an alternate syntactic construction for the transitive ergative proposition in (1b). However, it differs from the ergative in the case on the subject and object, and verbal agreement. Sentence (1c) has the four key features of a prototypical antipassive construction: the verb agrees only with the subject, like an intransitive verb; the subject

Table 12.1 Differences Between Antipassive and Ergative Structures

	Antipassive	*Ergative*
Agreement	Single (subject) agreement	Single or double agreement
Case on subject	Absolutive	Ergative
Case on object	Oblique	Absolutive
Morphology	AP morpheme (overt or null)	No AP morphology

is marked with absolutive case, like an intransitive subject; the object appears in an oblique case, modalis in this example; and the verb appears with the antipassive morpheme *-si*. Morphosyntactic differences between antipassive and ergative structures are shown in Table 12.1.

The antipassive construction is found in ergative languages of the Americas such as Eskimo-Aleut languages (e.g., Yup'ik, Iñupiaq, and Inuktitut), Mayan languages (e.g., K'iche', Tz'utujil, Mam, and Akatek), Halkomelem Salish, Nez Perce (Sahaptian), Gitxsan (Tsimshian), Lakhota (Siouan), Katukina-Kanamari (Katukinan), Kuikúro (Carib), and Matses (Panoan). It is also found in languages of other geographical regions, for example: Dyirbal, Warrungu, and Kalkatungu (Australia); Embaloh (Malayic; Indonesia); Tagalog (Philippines); Chamorro (Northern Marianas); Päri (Africa); Japhug (Sino-Tibetan; China); Puma (Kiranti; Nepal); and Chukchi (Siberia). While the antipassive is normally associated with ergative languages, it is not found in all languages that have ergative properties. Furthermore, this construction is claimed to exist in non-ergative languages as well (see §5).

In §2 we describe the structural properties of the antipassive, including case, agreement, verb transitivity, and the antipassive morpheme. It will be shown that there are variations in the antipassive properties listed in Table 12.1 as well as in the interpretation of the defining features of an antipassive. Given that the antipassive is an alternate form for a transitive ergative sentence describing the same event, a key question is: What determines the choice of one structure over the other? The answer to this question is explored from two perspectives: functional (§3), and structural (§4). Section 5 discusses cases of the antipassive in non-ergative (i.e., accusative) languages.

2. Structural Properties

2.1. Subject and Object

The subject in an antipassive construction is aligned morphologically and syntactically with an intransitive subject. In case-marking ergative languages the antipassive subject appears with absolutive case, the same case found on intransitive subjects, as shown earlier in (1a) and (1c) for Inuktitut. This is found to be remarkably consistent across languages.

Much more variation is found in the properties of the antipassive object. Languages vary, for instance, in whether the object is optional (Inuktitut, Spreng 2006) or not permitted (Lakhota; Van Valin 1980; Matses, Fleck 2003). The oblique case marking the non-core status of antipassive objects differs among languages: e.g., dative in Chukchi, modalis/instrumental in Inuit. Furthermore, the oblique antipassive case often has other uses as well. As an example, the *-mik* case in Inuktitut is also found on the patient of double object constructions, in applicatives, and on modifiers of incorporated nouns (Johns 2001; 2006).

Analyses differ in their assumptions about what constitutes a valid antipassive object. For some, any object of an intransitive verb is considered to be an antipassive object, although they may be classified in different ways, such as zero (or absolutive), oblique/demoted, or incorporative. Such classifications have been used in Mayan languages (Smith-Stark 1978; Coon 2016) and Katukina-Kanamari (Queixalós 2012). In other analyses, the defining property of an antipassive is the demotion of the object from direct object to oblique. This allows for many types of antipassive structures that share object demotion, but where the object and the verb do not have the properties typically associated with antipassives (see, for example, Kozinsky et al. 1988 for Chukchi).

2.2. Antipassive Verb and Morpheme

The antipassive verb is considered to be syntactically intransitive. Two ways that intransitivity can be observed is through verbal agreement and intransitive affixes. In many languages agreement on antipassive verbs corresponds to agreement found on regular intransitive verbs, e.g., Inuktitut; see (1a) and (1c), Salish (Kroeber 1986), Nez Perce (Rude 1986), K'iche' (Davies & Sam-Colop 1990), and Yup'ik (Payne 1982). Antipassive verbs may also appear with affixes normally reserved for intransitive verbs, such as the tense suffix *-nyu* in Dyirbal (Dixon 1972) or the perfective infix *-um-* in Tagalog (Aldridge 2012). While verbal morphology supports the intransitivity of the antipassive verb, the antipassive clause is "semantically transitive" as it involves both subject and object participants (Cooreman 1982).

There are cross-linguistic differences in the number of antipassive morphemes a language may possess. Some, like Nez Perce, have no overt morpheme (Rude 1986), Halkomelem has two (plus a null morpheme) (Gerdts & Hukari 2000), while Kalaallisut and Iñupiaq can have up to four, in addition to a null form (Bittner 1987; Nagai 2006). Distinct forms of the antipassive morpheme may reflect semantic differences (e.g., aspect), phonological requirements, or lexical restrictions (Sadock 1980; Bittner 1987; Kozinsky et al. 1988; Gerdts & Hukari 2000; Nagai 2006).

There is also variation on whether a language has a dedicated antipassive marker, or whether the morpheme has other uses besides marking the antipassive (Polinsky 2013). The most common alternative use for an antipassive morpheme is to mark reflexivity, aspect or modality. For example, the verbal prefix *t-* in Kuikúro (Carib) often codes reflexivity or possessive reflexivity in addition to the antipassive (Franchetto 1990). The middle suffix *-m* that marks antipassives in Halkomelem Salish is used in numerous other constructions as well, "including logophoric reflexives, personal reflexives, main-clause passives, and various monadic intransitive constructions, including verbs of motion and body care" (Gerdts & Hukari 2000: 52). Jacques (2014) identifies five origins of the antipassive morpheme cross-linguistically: reflexive, benefactive/malefactive, reciprocal/coparticipation, indefinite, generic argument, and verb *make* or *get*. It is thus not surprising that the antipassive morpheme is currently used for some of these functions as well.

3. Functions of the Antipassive

In this section we present functional explanations for the antipassive construction. The antipassive has been associated with many functions both within and across languages (Heath 1976; Comrie 1978; Tsunoda 1988; Cooreman 1994). The main functions discussed in the literature are related to semantic properties such as the indefiniteness or low identifiability of the object and imperfective aspect of the predicate, or to syntactic functions such as the realignment of the subject from transitive to intransitive, and topic chaining.

3.1. Semantic Functions

One of the most common correlates with the use of the antipassive is the low degree of identifiability of the object (Cooreman 1994). Objects with low identifiability have been characterized in a number of ways, including indefinite, non-referential, nonspecific, generic, unknown, and undisclosed; essentially, their identity is not considered an important part of the discourse (Heath 1976; Givón 1984; Dixon & Aikhenvald 1997). Languages with antipassive objects exhibiting these types of properties include K'iche', Chamorro, Nez Perce, and Kalaallisut (Cooreman 1994); other examples are Kuikúro (Franchetto 1990), Puma (Bickel et al. 2007), Japhug (Jacques 2012), and Matses (Fleck 2003).

However, not all antipassive objects exhibit low identifiability, underscoring the non-uniformity of antipassive functions across languages. For example, while earlier studies on Inuit languages claimed that the antipassive object was indefinite and the absolutive object definite (e.g., Sadock 1980; Fortescue 1984), Bittner (1987) showed that the object could be a proper name, pronoun, or definite description and could be modified by determiners, all of which are associated with definite meaning (see also Manga 1996). In a different approach, Bittner (1987; 1994) and Bittner and Hale (1996a, 1996b) claim that the difference between objects of ergative and antipassive clauses in Kalaallisut is not definiteness but scope: antipassive objects take narrow scope with respect to sentential operators such as negation, tense and aspect, and modals, while transitive objects obligatorily take wide scope. Similar results are presented in Wharram (2003) for objects in Inuktitut.[2]

(2) Inuktitut

a. Antipassive object (narrow scope)
Akittiq *iqalung-mik* *taku-∅-nngit-t-u-q*
Akittiq(ABS) fish-MOD[MIK] see-AP-NEG-PART-[-TR]-3SG.ABS
i. Akittiq didn't/doesn't see (even) a single fish.
ii. #There is a (particular) fish that Akittiq doesn't/didn't see.

b. Absolutive object (wide scope)
Taqqialu-up *tuktu* *taku-lau-nngit-t-a-(ng)a*
Taqqialuk-ERG caribou(ABS) see- PAST-NEG-PART-[+TR]-3SG.ERG.3SG.ABS
i. #Taqqialuk didn't see a (single) caribou.
ii. There is a (certain) caribou that Taqqialuk didn't see.

(Wharram 2003: 39)

The antipassive is also associated with verbal aspect: the antipassive verb signals an event or state of affairs that is incomplete or non-punctual, with no perceptible onset or conclusion. Cooreman (1994) discusses many languages with antipassive verbs that are iterative, distributive, habitual, progressive, or continuous: Tz'utujil and Kalallisut, also Chamorro, Chukchi, Circassian, Dyirbal, and Warrungu. In Kalaallisut, the antipassive morpheme can mark various kinds of aspect including imperfective, frequentative, inceptive and progressive (Blake 1976; Bittner 1987; Nagai 2006).

The correlation between imperfective aspect and low object identifiability is explained as follows (Cooreman 1994: 69):

> in events which have no discernable point of beginning or end, the focus of attention tends to be more on the process, or the activity itself . . . rather than on its effect on the object, or even on the identity of the object.

Consequently, objects of incomplete activities often also exhibit a low degree of affectedness.

3.2. Syntactic Functions

The main syntactic function of the antipassive is to satisfy constraints on coreferencing across subordinated or coordinated clauses. The best known example of this is from Dyirbal (Dixon 1972; 1979; 1994), where interclausal coreferencing requires both arguments to be absolutive. In example (3), the (null) transitive subject of the second clause must become an intransitive absolutive subject through antipassivization if it is to be coreferenced with the absolutive object *ŋuma* of the first clause.

(3) Dyirbal

ŋuma	*jaja-ŋgu*	*ŋamba-n*	*bural-ŋa-nʸu*	*yabu-gu*
father.ABS	child-ERG	hear-NONFUT	see-AP-NONFUT	mother-DAT

'The child heard father and he (father) saw mother'

(Dixon 1994: 162)

This syntactic constraint may apply to relative clauses as well, for example in Inuktitut (Creider 1978; Smith 1984; Johns 1992; Bok-Bennema 1991). In sentence (4a) the man, being the subject of a transitive relative clause, cannot be interpreted as the one doing the stabbing. However, this interpretation is possible in (4b), as the man is the subject of an antipassivized relative clause. (For a similar constraint in Mayan, see §4.2.)

(4) Inuktitut

a.

anguti-up	*nanuq*	*kapi-ja-a*	*ani-juq*
man-REL	bear(ABS)	stab-PASS.PART-3S	go out-INTR.PART.3SG

*'The man who stabbed the bear left.'

b.

angut	*nanur-mik*	*kapi-si-juq*	*ani-juq*
man	bear-MOD	stab-ANTIPASS-INTR.PART.3SG	go out-INTR.PART.3SG

'The man who stabbed the bear left.'

(Johns 1992: 72)

Another syntactic function of the antipassive is to realize coreference between a subject and the possessor of a direct object, as in the Nez Perce example in (5). While Nez Perce antipassives exhibit no overt markers such as an antipassive morpheme or oblique object, they also bear no markers of transitivity, such as an ergative case-marked subject or transitive prefixes on the verb.

(5) Nez Perce

hi-wéwluq-se	*c'oláakstimt*	*x̣áx̣aac*
3NOM-want-ASP	hand-drum	grizzly

'Grizzly wants his hand-drum'

(from Phinney 1934, cited in Rude 1986: 130)

Cooreman (1994) observes several differences between the antipassive structures used for semantic/pragmatic purposes and those used to satisfy structural constraints. The object is obligatory in the structural antipassive but is optional or obligatorily absent in the semantic/pragmatic antipassive; there is more freedom in the case assigned to the antipassive object in the structural antipassive; and it is the properties of the object that motivate the semantic/pragmatic antipassive, while it is the subject that necessitates antipassivization in the structural antipassive (see also Foley & Van Valin 1984: 171). Cooreman (1994) proposes that the semantic/pragmatic antipassive was co-opted to fulfill syntactic functions, evidenced by the existence of many languages that have only the semantic/pragmatic antipassive, but no language that has only the structural one.

3.3. Discourse Functions

Discourse context is a key factor in the use of the antipassive (Givón 1984; Cooreman 1994). The semantic properties of the antipassive, in particular the low identifiability of the object and imperfective aspect, can be subsumed under the more general discourse notion of object backgrounding. Backgrounding can refer to the unimportance of the object to the discourse, shown by its indefinite, generic or non-referential property, or its absence altogether.

Elements that are not backgrounded have a central role in the discourse as topics. Two quantitative measures of topicality – referential distance and topic persistence (see Givón 1983) – were applied to ergative and antipassive sentences in Nez Perce (Rude 1986). The antipassive object was far less topical than the subject, while in ergative clauses, both subject and object were equally topical. In another study, Berge (2011: Chapter 3) examined texts in Kalaallisut and found that in the few antipassive constructions that appeared in the texts, the object was nontopical and of peripheral importance in the narrative. In contrast, the absolutive object in ergative structures was identified as the primary topic.

The topic status of an argument is also related to whether it is introducing new or given information in the discourse (Cooreman 1982). As previously observed by Kalmár (1979), nontopical antipassive objects introduce new information, revealed by their tendency to be indefinite and exhibit high referential distance, i.e., not to be repeated later in the discourse (Cooreman 1982; Deal 2010; Berge 2011: 112). On the other hand, since new information can in fact be definite, antipassive objects are not always non-referential and indefinite but could be a proper noun, for example. Unlike antipassive objects, the antipassive subject normally provides given rather than new information, especially when it is used to link an argument to a preceding clause (Dixon 1972: 81).

4. Structural Analyses of the Antipassive

In this section we discuss structural analyses of the antipassive construction. Most early descriptions of the antipassive assumed they were derived from the more basic ergative form, e.g., Silverstein (1972), Rigsby (1975), Heath (1976), Dixon (1979; 1994), Hewitt (1982), Quizar and Knowles-Berry (1988), and Dixon and Aikhenvald (1997). Arguments for the derivational approach were based on the markedness of the antipassive compared to its transitive ergative counterpart: the verb carries an additional morpheme; and the antipassive form occurs less frequently than the transitive form, has a specialized syntactic function, exhibits syntactic gaps, and can have specialized aspectual/modal meaning (Tsunoda 1988). Formal analyses of the derivational approach considered antipassivization to be a grammatical function changing operation, demoting the object from a direct to oblique or deleted object, either in the syntax (Woodbury 1977; Smith 1982; Davies & Sam-Colop 1990) or in the lexicon (Grimshaw & Mester 1985).

One of the first researchers to argue against a derivational approach, Kalmár (1979), claimed that antipassive clauses consist of a subject and direct object just like their ergative counterparts. This is now the standard theoretical approach to the antipassive, with the ergative and antipassive being alternate derivations of verbs with similar argument structures. The rest of this section presents structural analyses of the antipassive from a generative perspective, concentrating on three North American language families for which a substantial amount of literature is available: Inuit, Mayan, and Nez Perce.

4.1. Inuit

Structural analyses of Inuit antipassivization can be classified into three categories: lexical, incorporation, and verbal. We focus here on their accounts of case on the object and the structure and function of the antipassive morpheme. In lexical analyses, adding an antipassive morpheme to the verb in the lexicon affects theta role and case assignment to the arguments. An example of an early lexical analysis is Marantz (1984: Chapter 4), who proposes that in ergative languages, including Inuit, the antipassive affix combines with a verb in the lexicon to yield a derived verb. The intransitive feature of the affix makes the derived verb intransitive as well, resulting in oblique rather than absolutive case on the object. Similarly, for Jensen and Johns (1989), the Inuit antipassive morpheme is a nominalizing affix that attaches to the verb. This affix prevents the verb from assigning a thematic role (rather than case, as in Marantz's theory) to the object. The morpheme assigns the agent role to the subject, causing the theme to be lexically realized as an oblique. More recently, Beach (2011) analyzes antipassivization as a lexical rule that adds an antipassive affix to a verb. This affix determines the case that appears on its arguments based on whether the input is an [intransitive] or [transitive] verb stem.

In an incorporation analysis, the antipassive morpheme is considered a nominal argument that incorporates into the verb, accounting for the verb's intransitivity. In Baker's (1988) theory, the antipassive morpheme is the D-structure internal argument that obligatorily incorporates into the verb. This bound morpheme absorbs the theta role normally assigned to the object, and transmits it to the oblique adjunct object with which it is coindexed. For Bittner and Hale (1996b), the complement of the verb is an NP headed by the antipassive N, which in turn takes the antipassive object as its complement. The antipassive N incorporates into the verb, yielding the proper structural configuration for the verb to assign oblique instrumental case to the antipassive object.

In the third approach, the antipassive morpheme is a verbal element that projects in the syntax. Bok-Bennema (1991) was the first to propose that the AP morpheme is a verbal element, claiming it to be an auxiliary verb. In her analysis, the case assigned to the antipassive morpheme is not an oblique case, but is structural accusative case, the same case assigned to objects of transitive verbs in non-ergative languages. Similarities in case and agreement between the antipassive construction and transitive sentences in non-ergative languages have been noted: the subject has the same case found on intransitive subjects (nominative/absolutive), the object has a different case (accusative/instrumental, etc.), and the verb agrees only with the subject (see Kalmár 1979; Johns 2006). This relation is further explored in Spreng (2010), who observes similarities in the triggers for the antipassive and the accusative side of split ergativity.

For Bok-Bennema (1991), accusative case assignment is a property of the verb. The antipassive auxiliary verb has a [+ACC] feature and, combining with transitive verbs lacking this feature, assigns accusative case to their objects. In her analysis, verbs like *niri* 'eat', which appear in the antipassive without overt morphology (which she calls 'ambiguous' verbs), alternate freely between ergative-absolutive (6a) and nominative-accusative (6b) structures, depending on whether they appear with a [−ACC] or [+ACC] feature, respectively.

(6) Inuktitut

a. Ergative

anguti-up	*niqi*	*niri-vaa*
man-ERG	meat(ABS)	eat-IND.3SG/3SG

'the man is eating meat'

b. Antipassive

anguti	*niri-vuq*	*niqi-mik*
man(ABS)	eat-IND.3SG	meat-MIK

'the man is eating meat'

(Spreng 2006: 253)

Subsequent analyses make use of the split VP structure and adopt the upper *v* as the locus of the antipassive morpheme (e.g., Johns 2006; Spreng 2006; Basilico 2012). For Spreng (2001; 2006) the antipassive morpheme *-si* is a verbal element in *v* that agrees with the object argument, thus licensing structural accusative *-mik* case. Investigating further the properties of verbs that appear with *-mik* objects, she proposes that the distribution of *-si* correlates with a verb's argument structure: it occurs only with verbs that have an external argument, either by being inherently transitive (e.g., *kapi* 'stab' and *kunik* 'kiss') or due to causativization (e.g., *surak* 'break' in *Piita surak-si-juq anautar-mik* 'Peter broke the stick'). Verbs like *niri* 'eat' in (6) that appear without an overt antipassive morpheme (which she calls object-permitting verbs) are like unergatives in having an external argument in *v*P, but differ in allowing an optional object. According to Spreng (2010), the object that appears with such verbs is not an argument; thus it receives lexical *-mik* case from *v*. Both Spreng and Bok-Bennema reject the existence of a null antipassive morpheme in cases like (6b). While a null morpheme is required by analyses that associate the antipassive morpheme with *-mik* case (e.g., Bittner & Hale 1996b), since for Spreng and Bok-Bennema, case is assigned or licensed by the verb and not the antipassive morpheme, there is no need to assume a null allomorph of *-si*.

Johns (2001) investigates differences in the use of the ergative and antipassive in Western and Eastern Canadian dialects from the perspective of language change. She proposes that the status of *-mik* case is undergoing a change from oblique to structural across Inuit dialects: it is an independent oblique case in the western dialects, and a less complex structural case in the eastern dialects. This analysis is further developed in Johns (2006) as a difference in the syntactic AGREE relation between *v* and the *-mik* case.

Other analyses account for the semantics of the object and/or antipassive verb in addition to their syntax. In Benua's (1995) analysis of Yup'ik (Eskimo-Aleut), the telicity of the antipassive verb and the semantic interpretation of the object depend on the location of the object inside or outside the VP at s-structure. If the object remains in the VP, the antipassive predicate has an irresultative or non-completive reading; but if it raises to ASPP, it triggers a telic or accomplishment reading. Definite and indefinite objects differ in their raising requirements. Definite objects obligatorily raise at LF, escaping Existential Closure and getting a specific interpretation, while indefinite objects may remain inside the VP at LF. If they do not raise, they get a nonspecific reading, but if they do raise (at LF), they get a specific reading.

In other analyses, the features and structural position of the antipassive morpheme in *v* determine semantic properties such as aspect and indefiniteness. Johns (2006), following Spreng (2006), recognizes two *-si* morphemes in Inuktitut: antipassive and inceptive aspect. She proposes that both morphemes contain the features of an indefinite quantifier, but these features have different interpretations depending on their structural position. When located outside the *v*P, the features are interpreted as inceptive aspect. When located in *v*, they result in an imperfective, atelic interpretation. In both cases, the indefinite quantity features of the antipassive morpheme is the link between the antipassive and indefinite objects observed in many ergative languages.

Spreng (2016) further investigates aspect contrasts in Inuktitut, concluding that there is only one *-si* morpheme. This morpheme can be added to both transitive and intransitive verbs to indicate inceptive aspect. It can also be used to enable an imperfective viewpoint aspect reading for achievement verbs such as *aqtuq* 'touch' or *kapi* 'stab' (providing the meaning of 'stroke' and 'poke', respectively). Furthermore, this inceptive *-si* is required with transitive achievement verbs in antipassive constructions to enable the imperfective reading. By assuming only one *-si* morpheme, rather than an aspectual one and a "meaningless detransitivizing antipassive *-si*" (p. 227), Spreng provides an account of why *-si* is the most common antipassive marker across the Eskimo languages, why it has been assumed that there is homophony between the antipassive and the inceptive marker, and why antipassives are cross-linguistically interpreted as imperfectives.

Finally, for Basilico (2012), the difference between antipassive and ergative verbs lies in the interpretation of the verb root as an event or result component. In an antipassive structure the root merges with the *v* head *-si* and is interpreted as a manner verb, with the oblique object providing the path or scale for the event. It is the event and not the result state that is highlighted, accounting for the incompleteness and non-punctuality of the antipassive event as well as the optionality of the object. Similar to analyses such as Bok-Bennema (1991) and Spreng (2001; 2006), case to the oblique object is assigned by *-si*. Basilico proposes that creation/consumption verbs, which include *sana* 'build' and *niri* 'eat' (see (6b)), do not require an antipassive suffix in their intransitive form because the oblique-marked object functions as an extent path or scale. In contrast, in an ergative structure the verb root, which combines with a verbalizing *v*, supplies the result state; the object is assigned an Undergoer theta role, resulting in the completiveness of the event and the affected nature of the object.

4.2. Mayan

In many Mayan languages a transitive subject is prohibited from undergoing A-bar extraction, i.e., being questioned, focused, or relativized. In order to undergo these processes, it must become an intransitive subject either through antipassivization or another strategy known as agent focus (or focus antipassive) (Smith-Stark 1978; Dayley 1981; England 1983; Stiebels 2006; Coon 2016). While the two constructions may be used for the same syntactic function, given the many differences between them, the consensus is that agent focus is not a form of antipassive (Smith-Stark 1978; Ayres 1983; Stiebels 2006; Coon et al. 2014). Coon et al. (2014) note the following differences between the two constructions: in agent focus the object is an obligatory core (non-oblique) argument and is cross-referenced on the verb with absolutive agreement, while in the antipassive the object is oblique and optional, and the verb shows absolutive agreement with the subject. Furthermore, the agent focus construction is possible only when the transitive subject undergoes A-bar extraction, whereas the antipassive is not restricted to extraction environments.

(7) Q'anjob'al

a. Agent Focus

Maktxel	*max-ach*	*il-on-i?*
who	ASP-2ABS	see-AF-ITV

'Who saw you?'

b. Antipassive

Maktxel	*max-Ø*	*il-waj[-i]*	*[$_{OBL}$ h-en] ?*
who	COM-3ABS	see-AP-ITV	2ERG-RN

'Who saw you?'

(Coon et al. 2014: 215)

Stiebels (2006) observes further differences between the antipassive and agent focus structures: the subject moves to the preverbal focus position in agent focus, and there are semantic restrictions on the object of the antipassive that do not apply in agent focus clauses. She claims that agent focus was originally restricted to 3–3 settings in order to avoid ambiguities, but was then extended to all object-subject settings, leading to competition between agent focus and antipassive in some Mayan languages. Stiebels (2006) also observes similarities between the antipassive and agent focus constructions in languages such as Q'eqchi', where the agent focus verb agrees with the subject and has an oblique object, and the agent focus and antipassive markers have merged completely. Examining the properties of the antipassive and agent focus in a range of Mayan languages, she presents a language hierarchy showing the degree to which the two constructions have merged. Stiebels's (2006) goal is to account for morphosyntactic differences in agent focus constructions across Mayan languages, and she does so within the framework of Lexical Decomposition Grammar, basing her analysis on a system of lexical features and faithfulness and markedness constraints.

While much of the theoretical literature on Mayan languages focuses on the agent focus rather than antipassive construction, we present here two studies that discuss antipassives in specific Mayan languages. In her work on split ergativity and transitivity in Chol, Coon (2012; 2013) classifies both unergative and antipassive stems as "complementless", i.e., lacking an internal argument (antipassive objects are not permitted in Chol). Following her generalization that all verbs obligatorily assign absolutive case to a DP complement, Coon argues that unergative and antipassive stems cannot be verbs; rather, they are nominal complements of the transitive light verb *cha'l* 'do', as shown with an antipassive in (8).

(8) *Tyi* *k-cha'l-e* *wuts'-oñ-el*
PRFV A1-do-TV wash-AP-NML
'I washed.' (lit.: 'I did washing.')

(Coon 2012: 244)

It is the light verb that assigns the external theta role and absolutive case to the subject, inflects as a verb, and takes the transitive suffix *-e*.

Aissen (2011) "resurrects a version of the antipassive analysis" (p. 8) for agent focus structures in K'iche', claiming that agent focus is more closely related to intransitive incorporative antipassives than to transitive ergative clauses. All three structures take two obligatory arguments, but while transitive verbs index them both on the verb (with Set A and Set B markers), agent focus and incorporative antipassives display only Set B markers. Furthermore, the latter two structures appear with the same voice morpheme, while the morpheme for transitives has a different form.

Aissen proposes the same basic *v*P structure for all three constructions, but with different heads: v_{act} for transitives, and v_{nt} (neutral) for incorporative antipassives and agent focus. Each *v*P has an external argument in its specifier, and a *tv*P complement consisting of the *tv* stem and the object. v_{act} licenses ergative case to the external argument, realized as Set A affixes on the verb; the object is case-licensed by finite I and is associated with nominative case. The v_{nt} head in antipassives has no case-licensing properties. The subject is case-licensed by finite I, and the object, being a bare N, does not require case (see (9)).

(9) *ch'u'k* *k-at-b'iinisa-n* *ch'iich'.*
wrecklessly [sic] ICP-B2SG-drive-AP car
'you car-drive wrecklessly [sic].'

(Mondloch 1981: 250, in Aissen 2011)

The v_{nt} head in agent focus clauses is augmented with a [FOC] feature, resulting in a different case structure from the antipassive. More specifically, the [FOC] feature allows the head to license case to the external argument in its specifier. Finite I licenses case to the object (rather than the subject as in the antipassive), since the external argument is case-licensed separately by v_{nt}. This is shown in (10), where the object is indexed on the verb with the Set B affix associated with nominative case.

(10) *jachin* *x-at-to'-wik?*
who CP-B2SG-help-AF-SS_{IV}
'who helped you?'

(Mondloch 1981: 70, in Aissen 2011)

4.3. Nez Perce

Nez Perce has a three-way case-marking system, where intransitive subjects are unmarked for case, and transitive subjects and objects are marked with ergative and objective case forms, respectively (Rude 1986; Deal 2010).

(11) Nez Perce

a. Intransitive
sík'em *hi-wleke'yx-tee'nix* *háamti'c*
horse 3SUBJ-run-HAB.PL fast
'Horses run fast.'

(Deal 2010: 74)

b. Transitive

sik'ém-nim *kúnk'u* *pée-wewluq-se* *timaaníi-ne*
horse-ERG always 3/3-want-IMPERF apple-OBJ
'The horse always wants an apple.'

(Deal 2010: 75)

Subjecthood and transitivity are important notions in Deal's (2010) analysis of ergative case. While it had previously been claimed that transitivity in Nez Perce is determined by the presence of a direct object (e.g., Rude 1986), Deal (2010) argues that it is object agreement that is the determinant of transitivity, and therefore of ergative case. The transitive subject is the "agreeing subject of a clause with an agreeing object" (Deal 2010: 114), i.e., it agrees with a higher T but originates in a lower *v*P containing fully-valued φ-features. Ergative case, which appears on transitive subjects, is the morphological spell-out of subject and object agreement.

Antipassives exhibit another case pattern found in transitive clauses, where both the subject and object are unmarked for case. These clauses, which Deal calls *caseless clauses*, consist of antipassives and extended reflexives. We focus here on antipassives (see (12) from Deal 2010: 85).

(12) Context: One house in Lewiston is red, and yesterday, John found that house.

a. *Cáan-nim* *páa-'ya'x-na* *'iníi-ne*
John-ERG 3/3-find-PERF house-OBJ
'John found the house.'

b. *Caan* *hi-'yáa'x-na* *'iníit.*
John 3SUBJ-find-PERF house
'John found a house.'

Comment: "It's not referring to the red house or anything, it's just that he found a house he's been looking for."

Antipassive structures provide evidence in support of Deal's (2010) analysis. Despite having two arguments, they do not have ergative case, because while they agree with the subject, they lack object agreement. Deal's account of the absence of object agreement centers on the semantic properties of the antipassive object: such objects are property-denoting NPs rather than referential DPs, as indicated by their interpretation as weak indefinites, their inability to scope over the distributive quantifier *wi*, and their restriction to theme arguments. Agreement probes require nominals to project a φP on their edge to make the φ-features accessible outside the NP. In Nez Perce this φ-projection is allowed only when there is a D; since antipassive objects are DPs, agreement is not possible.

5. Antipassive in Accusative Languages

Whether or not the antipassive exists in non-ergative (i.e., accusative) languages depends on the interpretation of what constitutes an antipassive construction. If it is the counterpart of a transitive ergative construction, as assumed in Cooreman (1994), then it cannot exist in non-ergative languages. For Cooreman, the English sentence *The man hit at the cat* is not an antipassive but a "parallel detransitivized construction" that exhibits the same functional properties as an antipassive, with a prepositional object marked as lower in identifiability or affectedness than the direct object in *The man hit the cat*. Dixon (1979; 1994) claims that the antipassive is found mainly in ergative languages because its primary function is to feed an S/O[3] pivot constraint on clause combining. In an accusative language, which has an S/A pivot, there is no need to place an A into S. When necessary, the passive will place an O into the S role to satisfy the S/A pivot.

On the other hand, when the antipassive is defined more generally as a structure that demotes the patient of a transitive verb and places the subject in the role of intransitive subject, it will be found in accusative languages as well (Heath 1976; Givón 1984: 165; Tsunoda 1988). The literature on antipassives in non-ergative languages mainly focuses on languages outside of North America, such as Slavic languages and Bantu. Janic (2013) discusses antipassives in Slavic languages, which exhibit overt verbal morphology and have the identical semantics as their transitive counterpart. She claims that all Slavic languages, including Polish and Russian, have an antipassive morpheme that evolved from the reflexive via the middle.

Based on the properties of antipassives listed in Table 12.1, Bostoen et al. (2015) claim that the antipassive is found in at least 12 Bantu languages, including Cilubà, Kirundi (see Ndayiragije 2006), Kikamba, Kinyarwanda, and Ikalanga. They classify the languages in several ways: whether the antipassive morpheme is a dedicated antipassive marker or is polysemous with the reciprocal/associative marker; whether antipassive verbs are productive or restricted to a limited set of verbs; and whether the antipassive always deletes the object, or deletes it only in monotransitive clauses. They claim, moreover, that in the Bantu languages the antipassive developed from the reciprocal/associative meaning through reanalysis.

Despite their syntactic and functional similarities, the antipassive in ergative and accusative languages differ in one major respect: in accusative languages there is no change in the case of the subject when the object is demoted or deleted (Givón 1984: 165; Tsunoda 1988). While the object appears with an oblique case or is deleted, the subject remains nominative in both transitive and antipassive structures, making the structure less conspicuous in accusative languages.

6. Conclusions

As an alternative construction for transitive ergative clauses, the antipassive has been investigated from both functional and theoretical perspectives. Earlier studies such as Dixon (1972), Heath (1976), Tsunoda (1988), and Cooreman (1994) focused on functional and structural descriptions of the antipassive. Interest in this structure for linguistic theory emerged with the Minimalist Program (Chomsky 1991; 1995), where the introduction of new functional categories expanded the possibilities for case assignment to subject and object arguments. This led to a surge in research on ergativity (e.g., Johns 1992; Murasugi 1992; 1997; Bobaljik 1993; Bittner & Hale 1996a; 1996b; Manning 1996; Woolford 1997), which has continued to this day (see §4 and the Further Reading section in this chapter). While earlier generative approaches focused primarily on case and agreement, later studies incorporated semantic properties of the object and the verb into their analyses as well. Given the prevalence of the antipassive in ergative languages, research on this structure is necessarily linked to issues in ergativity and split ergativity, including case, agreement, argument structure, transitivity, scope, and aspect.

Further Reading

Polinsky's (2017) overview chapter of antipassives includes theoretical analyses as well as associated syntactic phenomena and "antipassive lookalikes". For syntactic analyses of the antipassive in languages outside of North America, see, for example, Bobaljik and Branigan (2006), Aldridge (2012), and Chung (2013). Excellent sources for a comprehensive description of ergativity, including antipassives, are Dixon (1979, 1994) and Comrie (1978). For recent generative approaches to issues in ergativity, see Johns et al. (2006), Woolford (2006; 2015), Legate (2008), Aldridge (2008; 2012), and sources cited in §4.

Notes

1. The following abbreviations are used in the glosses: 3 = third person, A = Set A (ergative/genitive), ABS = absolutive, AF = agent focus, AP/ANTIPASS = antipassive, ASP = aspect, B = Set B (absolutive), COM/

CP = completive, DAT = dative, E/ERG = ergative, HAB = habitual, ICP = incompletive, IMPERF = imperfective, IND = indicative mood, INTR = intransitive, ITV = intransitive verb, MOD = modalis, NEG = negation, NONFUT = nonfuture, NML = nominal suffix, OBJ = objective case, PART = participial mood, PASS = passive, PERF = perfective, PL = plural, PRFV = perfective, REL = relative case (= ergative), RN = relational noun, SG = singular, SS = status suffix, SUBJ = subject, TR = transitive, TV = transitive verb.

2. See Murasugi (2017) for evidence that in Baffin Inuktitut, the antipassive object can be interpreted with wide or narrow scope.
3. A, S, and O refer to transitive subject, intransitive subject, and object, respectively.

References

Aissen, Judith. 2011. On the syntax of agent focus in K'ichee'. In Shklovsky, K. & Pedro, P. M. & Coon, J. (eds.), *Proceedings of FAMLi*. Cambridge, MA: MIT Working Papers in Linguistics.

Aldridge, Edith. 2008. Phase-based account of extraction in Indonesian. *Lingua* 118. 1440–1469.

Aldridge, Edith. 2012. Antipassive and ergativity in Tagalog. *Lingua* 122. 192–203.

Ayres, Glenn. 1983. The antipassive "voice" in Ixil. *International Journal of American Linguistics* 49. 20–45.

Baker, Mark C. 1988. *Incorporation: A theory of grammatical function changing*. Chicago, IL: Chicago University Press.

Basilico, David. 2012. The antipassive and its relation to scalar structure. In Cuervo, M. C. & Roberge, Y. (eds.), *The end of argument structure? Syntax and semantics*, vol. 38, 75–103. United Kingdom: Emerald.

Beach, Matthew. 2011. *Studies in Inuktitut grammar*. Buffalo: State University of New York. (Doctoral dissertation.)

Benua, Laura. 1995. Yup'ik antipassive. In Dainora, A. & Hemphill, R. & Luka, B. & Need, B. & Pargman, S. (eds.), *CLS 31: Papers from the 31st Regional meeting of the Chicago Linguistic Society; Volume I: The main session*, 28–44. Chicago, IL: Chicago Linguistic Society.

Berge, Anna. 2011. *Topic and discourse structure in West Greenlandic agreement constructions*. Lincoln: University of Nebraska Press.

Bickel, Balthasar & Gaenszle, Martin & Rai, Arjun & Rai, Prem Dhoj & Rai, Shree Kumar & Rai, Vishnu S. & Sharma Gautam, Narayan P. 2007. Two ways of suspending object agreement in Puma: Between incorporation, antipassivization, and optional agreement. *Himalayan Linguistics* 7. 1–18.

Bittner, Maria. 1987. On the semantics of the Greenlandic antipassive and related constructions. *International Journal of American Linguistics* 53. 194–231.

Bittner, Maria. 1994. *Case, scope, and binding*. Dordrecht: Kluwer.

Bittner, Maria & Hale, Ken. 1996a. The structural determination of case and agreement. *Linguistic Inquiry* 27. 1–68.

Bittner, Maria & Hale, Ken. 1996b. Ergativity: Toward a theory of a heterogeneous class. *Linguistic Inquiry* 27. 531–604.

Blake, Barry J. 1976. Case mechanisms in Kalkatungu. *Anthropological Linguistics* 18. 287–193.

Bobaljik, Jonathan. 1993. Nominally absolutive is not absolutely nominative. In Mead, J. (ed.), *WCCFL 11: Proceedings of the Eleventh West Coast Conference on Formal Linguistics*, 44–60. Stanford, CA: CSLI.

Bobaljik, Jonathan & Branigan, Phil. 2006. Eccentric agreement and multiple case checking. In Johns, A. & Massam, D. & Ndayiragije, J. (eds.), *Ergativity: Emerging issues*, 47–77. Dordrecht: Springer.

Bok-Bennema, Reineke. 1991. *Case and agreement in Inuit*. Berlin: Foris.

Bostoen, Koen, Dom, Sebastian & Segerer, Guillaume. 2015. The antipassive in Bantu. *Linguistics* 53. 731–772.

Chomsky, Noam. 1991. Some notes on economy of derivation and representation. In Freidin, R. (ed.), *Principles and parameters in comparative grammar*. Cambridge, MA: MIT Press.

Chomsky, Noam. 1995. *The minimalist program*. Cambridge, MA: MIT Press.

Chung, Sandra. 2013. Syntactic identity in sluicing: How much and why. *Linguistic Inquiry* 44. 1–44.

Comrie, Bernard. 1978. Ergativity. In Lehmann, W. P. (ed.), *Syntactic typology: Studies in the phenomenology of language*, 329–394. Sussex: The Harvester Press.

Coon, Jessica. 2012. Split ergativity and transitivity in Chol. *Lingua* 122. 241–256.

Coon, Jessica. 2013. *Aspects of split ergativity*. Oxford: Oxford University Press.

Coon, Jessica. 2016. Mayan morphosyntax. *Language and Linguistics Compass* 10. 515–550.

Coon, Jessica & Pedro, Pedro Mateo & Preminger, Omer. 2014. The role case in A-bar extraction asymmetries: Evidence from Mayan. *Linguistic Variation* 14. 179–242.

Cooreman, Ann. 1982. Topicality, ergativity, and transitivity in narrative discourse: Evidence from Chamorro. *Studies in Language* 6. 343–374.

Cooreman, Ann. 1994. A functional typology of antipassives. In Fox, B. & Hopper, P. J. (eds.), *Voice: Form and function*, 49–87. Amsterdam/Philadelphia: John Benjamins.

Creider, Chet. 1978. The syntax of relative clauses in Inuktitut. *Etudes/Inuit/studies* 2. 95–110.

Davies, William D. & Sam-Colop, Luis Enrique. 1990. K'iche' and the structure of antipassive. *Language* 66. 522–549.

Dayley, Jon P. 1981. Voice and ergativity in Mayan languages. *Journal of Mayan Linguistics* 2. 3–82.

Deal, Amy Rose. 2010. Ergative case and the transitive subject: A view from Nez Perce. *Natural Language and Linguistic Theory* 28. 73–120.

Dixon, R. M. W. & Aikhenvald, Alexandra Y. 1997. A typology of argument-determined constructions. In Bybee, J. & Haiman, J. & Thompson, S. A. (eds.), *Essays on language function and language type: Dedicated to T. Givón*, 71–114. Amsterdam: John Benjamins.

Dixon, R. M. W. 1972. *The Dyirbal language of North Queensland*. Cambridge: Cambridge University Press.

Dixon, R. M. W. 1979. Ergativity. *Language* 55. 59–138.

Dixon, R. M. W. 1994. *Ergativity*. Cambridge: Cambridge University Press.

England, Nora C. 1983. Ergativity in Mamean (Mayan) languages. *International Journal of American Linguistics* 49. 1–19.

Fleck, David William. 2003. *A grammar of Matses*. Houston, TX: Rice University. (Doctoral dissertation.)

Foley, William A. & Van Valin, Robert D. Jr. 1984. *Functional syntax and universal grammar*. Cambridge: Cambridge University Press.

Fortescue, Michael. 1984. *West Greenlandic*. London: Croom Helm.

Franchetto, Bruna. 1990. Ergativity and nominativity in Kuikúro and other Carib languages. In Payne, D. L. (ed.), *Amazonian linguistics: Studies in Lowland South American languages*, 407–427. Austin, TX: University of Austin Press.

Gerdts, Donna B. & Hukari, Thomas E. 2000. Multiple antipassives in Halkomelem Salish. In *International Conference on Salishan and Neighboring Languages 33, UBCWPL*, vol. 3, 95–105.

Givón, T. 1983. Topic continuity in discourse: An introduction. In Givón, T. (ed.), *Topic continuity in discourse: A quantitative cross-language study*, 1–41. Amsterdam/Philadelphia: John Benjamins.

Givón, T. 1984. *Syntax: A functional-typological introduction*, vol. I. Amsterdam and Philadelphia: John Benjamins.

Grimshaw, Jane & Mester, Ralf-Armin. 1985. Complex verb formation in Eskimo. *Natural Language and Linguistic Theory* 3. 1–19.

Heath, Jeffrey. 1976. Antipassivization: A functional typology. In *Proceedings of the 2nd annual meeting of the Berkeley Linguistics Society (1976)*, 202–211. Berkeley: UC Berkeley Linguistics Society.

Hewitt, B. G. 1982. Anti-passive and 'labile' constructions in North Caucasian. *General Linguistics* 22. 158–171.

Jacques, Guillaume. 2012. Argument demotion in Japhug Rgyalrong. In Authier, G. & Haude, K. (eds.), *Ergativity, valency and voice*, 199–225. Berlin/Boston, MA: De Gruyter Mouton.

Jacques, Guillaume. 2014. Denominal affixes as sources of antipassive markers in Japhug Rgyalrong. *Lingua* 138. 1–22.

Janic, Katarzyna. 2013. The Slavonic languages and the development of the antipassive marker. In Chahine, I. K. (ed.), *Current studies in Slavic linguistics*, 61–74. Amsterdam: John Benjamins.

Jensen, John T. & Johns, Alana. 1989. The morphosyntax of Eskimo causatives. In Gerdts, D. B. & Michelson, K. (eds.), *Theoretical perspectives on Native American languages*, 209–229. Albany: SUNY Press.

Johns, Alana. 1992. Deriving ergativity. *Linguistic Inquiry* 23. 57–87.

Johns, Alana. 2001. An inclination towards accusative. *Linguistica Atlantica* 23. 127–144.

Johns, Alana. 2006. Ergativity and change in Inuktitut. In Johns, A. & Massam, D. & Ndayiragije, J. (eds.), *Ergativity: Emerging issues*, 293–311. Dordrecht: Springer.

Johns, Alana & Massam, Diane & Ndayiragije, Juvenal (eds.) (2006). *Ergativity: Emerging issues*. Dordrecht: Springer.

Kalmár, I. 1979. The antipassive and grammatical relations in Eskimo. In Plank, F. (ed.), *Ergativity: Towards a theory of grammatical relations*, 117–143. London: Academic Press.

Kozinsky, Issac Š. & Nedjalkov, Vladimir P. & Polinskaja, Maria S. 1988. Antipassive in Chukchi: Oblique object, object incorporation, zero object. In Shibatani, M. (ed.), *Passive and voice*, 651–706. Amsterdam/Philadelphia, PA: John Benjamins.

Kroeber, Paul D. 1986. Antipassives and the differentiation of progressive aspect in Southern Interior Salish. In Farley, A. M. & Farley, P. T. & McCullough, K.-E. (eds.), *CLS 22 Part 1: Papers from the general session at the twenty-second regional meeting*, 75–89. Chicago, IL: Chicago Linguistic Society.

Legate, Julie Anne. 2008. Morphological and abstract case. *Linguistic Inquiry* 39. 55–101.

Manga, Louise. 1996. Specificity in Inuktitut and syntactic representation. *Études/Inuit/Studies* 20. 63–85.

Manning, Christopher D. 1996. *Ergativity: Argument structure and grammatical relations*. Stanford, CA: CSLI.

Marantz, Alec. 1984. *On the nature of grammatical relations*. Cambridge, MA: MIT Press.

Mondloch, James Lorin. 1981. *Voice in Quiche-Maya*. Albany: State University of New York. (Doctoral dissertation.)

Murasugi, Kumiko. 1992. *Crossing and nested Paths: NP movement in accusative and ergative languages*. Cambridge, MA: MIT. (Doctoral dissertation.)

Murasugi, Kumiko. 1997. Nested paths in syntactically ergative languages. In Mendikoetxea, A. & Uribe-Etxebarria, M. (eds.), *Theoretical issues at the morphology-syntax interface, Supplements of the International Journal of Basque Linguistics and Philology*, 325–357. Zarautz: Itxaropena, S. A.

Murasugi, Kumiko. 2017. Linguistic fieldwork and scientific methodology. In Halpert, C. & Kotek, H. & van Urk, C. (eds.), *A pesky set: Papers for David Pesetsky*. MIT Working Papers in Linguistics 80.

Nagai, Tadataka. 2006. *Agentive and patientive verb bases in North Alaskan Iñupiaq*. Fairbanks: University of Alaska. (Doctoral dissertation.)

Ndayiragije, Juvenal. 2006. The ergativity parameter: A view from antipassive. In Johns, A. & Massam, D. & Ndayiragije, J. (eds.), *Ergativity: Emerging issues*, 271–292. Dordrecht: Springer.

Payne, Thomas. 1982. Role and reference related subject properties and ergativity in Yup'ik Eskimo and Tagalog. *Studies in Language* 6. 75–106.

Phinney, Archie. 1934. Nez Perce texts. *Columbia University Contributions to Anthropology*, vol. 25. New York: Columbia University Press.

Polinsky, Maria. 2013. Antipassive constructions. In Dryer, M. S. & Haspelmath, M. (eds.), *The world atlas of language structures online*. Leipzig: Max Planck Institute for Evolutionary Anthropology. (http://wals.info/chapter/108) (Accessed 2017-23-03.)

Polinsky, Maria. 2017. Antipassive. In Coon, J., Massam, D. & Travis, L.D. (eds.), *The Oxford handbook of ergativity*, 308–331. Oxford: Oxford University Press.

Queixalós, Francesc. 2012. The Katukina-Kanamari antipassive. In Authier, G. & Haude, K. (eds.), *Ergativity, valency and voice*, 227–258. Berlin/Boston, MA: De Gruyter Mouton.

Quizar, Robin & Knowles-Berry, Susan M. 1988. Ergativity in the Cholan languages. *International Journal of American Linguistics* 54. 73–95.

Rigsby, Bruce. 1975. Nass-Gitksan: An analytic ergative syntax. *International Journal of American Linguistics* 41. 346–354.

Rude, Noel. 1986. Topicality, transitivity, and the direct object in Nez Perce. *International Journal of American Linguistics* 52. 124–153.

Sadock, Jerrold M. 1980. Noun incorporation in Greenlandic: A case of syntactic word formation. *Language* 56. 300–319.

Silverstein, Michael. S. 1972. Chinook Jargon: Language contact and the problem of multi-level generative systems, II. *Language* 48. 596–625.

Smith, Lawrence R. 1982. An analysis of affixal verbal derivation and complementation in Labrador Inuttut. *Linguistic Analysis* 10. 161–189.

Smith, Lawrence R. 1984. On the nonergativity and intransitivity of relative clauses in Labrador Inuttut. In Cook, E. D. & Gerdts, D. (eds.), *The syntax of Native American languages*, 289–315. New York: Academic Press.

Smith-Stark, Thom. 1978. The Mayan antipassive: Some facts and fictions. In England, N. C. (ed.), *Papers in Mayan linguistics*, 169–187. Columbia: Curators of the University of Missouri.

Spreng, Bettina. 2001. Little *v* in Inuktitut: Antipassive revisited. *Linguistica Atlantica* 23. 155–190.

Spreng, Bettina. 2006. Antipassive morphology and case assignment in Inuktitut. In Johns, A. & Massam, D. & Ndayiragije, J. (eds.), *Ergativity: Emerging issues*, 247–270. Dordrecht: Springer.

Spreng, Bettina. 2010. On the conditions for antipassives. *Language and Linguistics Compass* 4(7). 556–575.

Spreng, Bettina. 2016. Aspect contrasts in Inuktitut. *Amerindia* 38. 201–232.

Stiebels, Barbara. 2006. Agent focus in Mayan languages. *Natural Language and Linguistic Theory* 24. 501–570.

Tsunoda, Tasaku. 1988. Antipassives in Warrungu and other Australian languages. In Shibatani, M. (ed.), *Passive and voice*, 595–649. Amsterdam/Philadelphia, PA: John Benjamins.

Van Valin, Robert D., Jr. 1980. On the distribution of passive and antipassive constructions in Universal Grammar. *Lingua* 50. 303–327.

Wharram, Doug. 2003. *On the interpretation of (un)certain indefinites in Inuktitut and related languages*. Storrs: University of Connecticut. (Doctoral dissertation.)

Woodbury, Anthony C. 1977. Greenlandic Eskimo, ergativity, and relational grammar. In Cole, P. & Sadock, J. M. (eds.), *Syntax and semantics: Volume 8: Grammatical relations*, 307–336. New York: Academic Press.

Woolford, Ellen. 1997. Four-way case systems: Ergative, nominative, objective, and accusative. *Natural Language and Linguistic Theory* 15. 181–227.

Woolford, Ellen. 2006. Lexical case, inherent case, and argument structure. *Linguistic Inquiry* 37. 111–130.

Woolford, Ellen. 2015. Ergativity and transitivity. *Linguistic Inquiry* 46. 489–531.

13

EVIDENTIALS AND MODALS

Marianne Huijsmans and Sarah E. Murray

1. Introduction

Rich evidential and modal systems are common features of the languages indigenous to North America (Mithun 1999, Aikhenvald 2004). The study of these phenomena in indigenous North American languages has driven much of the theoretical work in these areas. In this chapter, we focus on topics that have been influential in the study of the semantics of evidentials and modals, but we begin by introducing some of the basic distinctions.

Evidentiality is the linguistic expression of source of information, while modality is the linguistic expression of possibility and necessity. Every language has ways to encode this information: English can express evidentiality with parentheticals (1) and adverbs (2) and modality with auxiliary verbs (3) and adverbs (4), among various other constructions.

(1) Sandy won, I hear.

(2) Sandy reportedly won.

(3) Kathy must have won.

(4) Maybe Kathy won.

The notions of evidentiality and modality are not unrelated, and often one linguistic item may encode both an evidential component and a modal component. This has been argued, for example, for English epistemic *must* (3): it is a necessity modal that carries an indirect evidentiality implication (e.g., Kratzer 1991; von Fintel & Gillies 2010; Murray 2014).

In many languages, evidentiality and modality are grammatically encoded (in contrast to lexically, as with English adverbs). This is especially true of the languages indigenous to North America. Consider, for example, Eastern Pomo, a Pomoan language of California, where evidentials are verbal suffixes, as seen in the paradigm in (5); and St'át'imcets, a Salish language of British Columbia, where modals are second-position clitics (6).

(5) Eastern Pomo (PEB, Pomoan)[1]

a. *mí·-p-al*   *pʰa·bé-k-**a***
3SG-MASC-PATIENT   burn-PUNCTUAL-**DIR.EV**
'He got burned' (I have direct evidence)

b. *bi·Yá*   *pʰa·bé-kʰ-**ink'e***
hand   burn-PUNCTUAL-**SENSORY.EV**
'I burned my hand' (I feel the sensation of burning in my hand)

c. *bé·k-al* *pʰa·bé-k-**ine***
3PL-PATIENT burn-PUNCTUAL-**INFR**
'They must have gotten burned' (I see circumstantial evidence – signs of a fire, bandages, burn cream)

d. *bé·k-al* *pʰa·bé-kʰ-·**le***
3PL-PATIENT burn-PUNCTUAL-**HS**
'They got burned, they say' (I am reporting what I was told)

(McLendon 2003: 101–102)

The evidential paradigm shown in (5) illustrates a common pattern of evidential distinctions, with a division between direct evidence (what one personally experiences, typically sensory evidence) and indirect evidence (what is inferred or reported by someone else). In Eastern Pomo, there is a four-way evidential distinction: two direct evidentials (visual (5a) and non-visual sensory (5b)) and two indirect evidentials (inferred (5c) and reported (5d)).

Distinctions commonly grammaticized in modal systems are the type of possibility or necessity referred to, including epistemic (relating to what is known), circumstantial (relating to circumstances), and deontic (relating to laws and obligations) claims. Consider the St'át'imcets modals in (6), which are all grammaticized as second-position clitics.

(6) St'át'imcets (LIL, Salish)

a. Context: His car isn't there.
plan ***k'a*** *qwatsáts*
already INFER leave
'Maybe he's already gone.'

b. *ka-kwís-a* ***kelh*** *ti* *k'ét'h-a*
CIRC-fall-CIRC FUT DET rock-DET
'That stone might drop.'

c. *qwatsáts-kacw* ***ka***
leave-2SG.SUBJ DEON
'(Maybe) you should leave.'

(Rullmann et al. 2008: 321, 326, 328)

Example (6a) makes a claim about what is possibly the case based on available evidence, an epistemic modal claim. Example (6b) makes a claim about what could happen based on current circumstances, a circumstantial modal claim. Example (6c) makes a modal claim based rules or obligations that apply to the addressee, a deontic modal claim. We will see in §2 that deontic modals are considered a subtype of circumstantial modality.

Besides modal markers such as those in (6), modality in the languages indigenous to North America has been described in terms of phenomena such as sentential mood, which encodes sentence type (e.g., declarative, interrogative, imperative), and the realis/irrealis distinction. In this chapter we focus on modal markers of necessity and possibility, like those in St'át'imcets in (6) and English in (3) and (4), since the investigation of these markers is most directly relevant to previous literature on modality and because the detailed semantic work on these markers has had an important impact on semantic theory.

Before we turn to the specific ways in which North American languages have influenced the semantic analysis of modals and evidentials, we would like to give an overview of research that focuses on modals or evidentials in North American languages, including references that do not specifically address the areas that we will focus on in the following sections. This work represents a diverse set of languages from a number of languages families.

Work focused on modality in languages indigenous to North America includes: ʔayʔaǰuθəm (Comox-Sliammon, COO, Salish) (Reisinger 2018), Blackfoot (BLA, Algonquian) (Silva 2009;

Louie 2015), Gitksan (GIT, Tsimshian) (Peterson 2010a; Matthewson 2013), Mohawk (MOH, Iroquoian) (Mithun 2016), Navajo (Diné Bizaad, NAV, Dene-Athabaskan), Nez Perce (NEZ, Sahaptian) (Deal 2011), Nsyilxcen (Okanagan, OKA, Salish) (Menzies 2013), St'át'imcets (Lillooet, LIL, Salish) (Matthewson et al. 2007; Rullmann et al. 2008; Davis et al. 2009), Tlingit (TLI, Dene-Athabaskan) (Burge 2017; Cable 2017), and Washo (WAS, isolate) (Bochnak 2015b). While not specifically investigating modality, Bohnemeyer (2002) discusses the relationship between temporality and modality in Yucatek Maya (YUA, Mayan).

Work on evidentiality in languages indigenous to North America includes: Cheyenne (CHY, Algic) (Murray 2010; 2014; 2016), Eastern Pomo (PEB, Pomoan) (McLendon 2003) Gitksan (GIT, Tsimshian) (Peterson 2010a; 2012; 2018; Matthewson 2013), Kalaallisut (Greenlandic, KAL, Eskimo-Aleut) (Fortescue 2003; Bittner 2008; 2014), Karuk (KYH, isolate) (Brugman & Macaulay 2015), Kashaya (Southwestern Pomo, KJU, Pomoan) (Oswalt 1986), Makah (MYH, Wakashan) (Jacobsen 1986), Meskwaki (Sac and Fox, SAC, Algic) (Dahlstrom to appear), Nuu-chah-nulth (NUK, Wakashan) (Waldie 2012), Patwin (PWI, Wintuan) (Whistler 1986), Piipaash (Maricopa, MRC, Cochim'ı-Yuman) (Gordon 1986), St'át'imcets (Lillooet, LIL, Salish) (Matthewson et al. 2007; Rullmann et al. 2008), Western Apache (APW, Athabaskan) (de Reuse 2003), Wintu (WNW, Wintuan) (Schlichter 1986), and Yucatec Maya (YUA, Mayan) (AnderBois 2017). Works on evidentiality in multiple languages or language families include: Algonquian (Junker et al. 2018), Cree/Montagnais/Naskapi (James et al. 2001; Blain & Déchaine 2007), Northern Iroquoian (Mithun 1986), Jaqi languages (Hardman 1986), Pomoan languages (McLendon 2003), and Uto-Aztecan languages (Thornes 2018).

The remainder of this chapter focuses in on topics that have been influential in the semantics of evidentiality and modality, driven by work on the Indigenous languages of North America. For modality, this is the encoding of modal flavor and strength, and the organization of modal paradigms (§2). For evidentiality, this is the overlap of modality and evidentiality, the kinds of meanings involved in evidential sentences, and how evidentials interact with different sentence types (§3). Section 4 is a conclusion, which is followed by suggestions for further reading.

2. Modals

In this section, we focus on in-depth semantic analyses of modals in North American languages, reflecting on the ways in which investigating these languages has contributed to our understanding of modality. The literature includes work on a small but diverse set of languages belonging to the Salish (St'át'imcets, Nsilxcen, ʔayʔaǰuθəm), Tsimshian (Gitksan), Dene-Athabaskan (Tlingit, Navajo), Algonquian (Blackfoot), Iroquoian (Mohawk), and Sahaptian (Nez Perce) language families, as well as the isolate Washo. We focus in particular on how the study of North American languages has contributed to our understanding of the encoding of modal flavor (§2.2), the encoding of modal strength (§2.3), how paradigms are organized, and the possibility of paradigmatic gaps (§2.4). We begin by providing background on the semantics of modals (§2.1).

2.1. Background

As alluded to in the introduction, modals are used to make claims about possibilities and necessities, claims involving possible worlds (taking into consideration different ways the world could be). Much of the literature on modality assumes a Kratzerian approach to modality (e.g., Kratzer 1981; 1991; 2012), where a modal is interpreted against a conversational background, which has a modal base and an ordering source. These provide the context within which the modal claim is made.

All modal claims are made relative to a context. For instance, recall (3), repeated here as (7a). For the speaker to utter this felicitously, she has evidence indicating Kathy won – perhaps Kathy's family and friends cheering – but did not directly witness the winning event. Consider also (7b): in order to make this modal claim, the speaker has in mind a set of circumstances (modal base), such as Kathy being a student and it being a weekday, and a set of rules (ordering source), according to which Kathy has an obligation to attend school; these provide the context within which the modal claim is made.

(7) a. Kathy must have won.
b. Kathy must go to school.

Formally, the modal base is a function from a world to a set of propositions that are true in that world, either a set of propositions representing circumstances in the world – a circumstantial modal base (as in (7b)) – or a set of propositions representing available evidence – an epistemic modal base (as in (7a)). The set of worlds in which all these propositions are true (the intersection of the set of propositions) is the set of worlds that are accessible from the evaluation world.

The ordering source is a function that assigns to each world a set of propositions that represent notions such as norms, rules, goals, and desires. In (7b), for instance, the modal claim evaluates Kathy's actions in different possible worlds not just according to the circumstances of the world, which include her being a student, but also according to whether she obeys the rules; it is deontic – more precisely, a circumstantial modal with a deontic ordering source. Similarly, (7a) makes a claim about what is stereotypical given the available evidence (Kathy's friends and family could be cheering for someone else, but it is most likely that they are cheering because Kathy won); the modal is epistemic with a stereotypical ordering source. Formally, the ordering source ranks the set of accessible worlds according to how many of the ordering source propositions are true in that world.

The modal then quantifies over the best possible worlds – those that come closest to the ideal provided by the ordering source. Both examples in (7) contain necessity modals, which involve universal quantification over these best possible worlds. In (7b), the speaker makes the strong modal claim that in all the worlds where the propositions in the circumstantial modal base are true (e.g., that Kathy is a student) and where the rules (e.g., that students have an obligation to attend school) are obeyed, Kathy goes to school. In (7a), the speaker makes the strong modal claim that in all possible worlds where the propositions in the epistemic modal base are true (e.g., Kathy's family and friends are cheering) and in which circumstances are stereotypical (e.g., Kathy's family and friend's cheer for Kathy), Kathy won.

Now let us consider some modals in Gitksan. In (8a) the modal base is circumstantial, a set of propositions concerning the circumstances under which berries grow. The weak modal claim involves existential quantification over the worlds in which these propositions hold true, saying that there exists at least one possible world in which berries are growing. The ordering source is empty, since the claim is simply about circumstantial possibility. Example (8b) also involves a circumstantial modal base, but it also has a deontic ordering source, ranking worlds according to whether the rules are obeyed. It claims that there does not exist a world where the relevant circumstances are the same as in the evaluation world, and where if I go outside, the rules are still obeyed – it makes a deontic modal claim. Finally, (8c) involves an epistemic modal base and a stereotypical ordering source. It claims, based on the stereotypical association between the sound of pattering and rain, that there exists a possible world in which the evidence available in the evaluation world also holds (the pattering sound) and where it is raining.

(8) Gitksan (GIT, Tsimshianic)

a. *nee=dii* *wan=hl* *maa'y* *go'osun* *ii* *ap* ***da'a<u>k</u>hlxw*** *dim*
NEG=CNTR sit.PL=CN berries LOC.here and EMPH CIRC.POSS FUT
lim<u>x</u>s-t
grow-3SG.II
'There are no berries around here, but they could grow here.'

b. *ii* *nee=dii* ***anook**-xw* *dim* *xsaw-i'y*
and NEG=CNTR DEON.POSS-MED FUT go.out-1SG.II
'It is not allowed that I go out.'

c. Context: You hear pattering, and you're not entirely sure what it is.
*yugw=**imaa/ima'**=hl* *wis*
IMPF=EPIS=CN rain
'It might be raining.'

(Matthewson 2013: 358, 370, 377)

As will be discussed later in this chapter, the study of North American languages provides important insights about how and whether these components of modality are lexicalized cross-linguistically.

2.2. Specification of Flavor

As laid out in the previous section, there are generally assumed to be two types of modal bases: circumstantial and epistemic.[2] In English, modals can frequently be used with different conversational backgrounds (e.g., Kratzer 1977; 1981). For instance, consider the famous hydrangea example from Kratzer (1991) in (9). Kratzer points out that in order to felicitously utter (9a), one must only believe it is possible for hydrangeas to grow in the location given the quality of the soil and the climate – it is not necessary to believe that there are actually any hydrangeas growing. In (9b), in contrast, one must infer that there could actually be hydrangeas growing, perhaps because hydrangeas grow in other locations nearby or because the vegetation is like the vegetation in other places where hydrangeas are found.

(9) a. Hydrangeas can grow here./Hydrangeas might grow here.
b. There might be hydrangeas growing here.

(Kratzer 1991: 646)

Here, (9a) involves a circumstantial modal base and makes a claim about what is possible given the circumstances; (9b) involves an epistemic modal base and involves an inference based on the available evidence. In English, it is possible to use the same modal *might/may* in both the circumstantial context (9a) and the epistemic context (9b); it is also possible to use *can* in the circumstantial context (which is the modal Kratzer (1991) originally uses when giving this example).

Unlike Indo-European languages where it is common for single modal to be able to express both epistemic and circumstantial modality, it is much less common in languages of North America (van der Auwera & Ammann 2013b). For instance, consider the modal system of St'át'imcets in Table 13.1 (based on Matthewson et al. (2007), Rullmann et al. (2008), and Davis et al. (2009)). All modals are either epistemic or circumstantial with no overlap in usage.

This is further illustrated with the St'át'imcets version (10) of the hydrangea example from (9). In St'át'imcets, there is no option for using the same modal in both contexts. The circumstantial

Table 13.1 Modal System in St'át'imcets

Epistemic	*Circumstantial*
k'a 'inferential'	ka 'deontic'
ku7 'reportative'	kelh 'future'
-an' 'perceived evidence'	ka- -a 'circumstantial'

modality must be expressed with the circumfix *ka- -a*, while the epistemic modality must be expressed with the inferential *k'a*.

(10) St'át'imcets (LIL, Salish)

a. *wa7* ***ka-ríp-a*** *ku* *káwkew* *kents7á*
IPFV CIRC-grow-CIRC DET sagebrush around.here
'Sagebrush can grow around here.'
Consultant's comment: "If somebody brought some seeds it would grow here – it's just a possibility it would grow here."

b. Context: Not only are the climate and soil right, but you have reason to believe that it's actually possible there is some sagebrush.
wa7 ***k'a*** *ri7p* *ku* *káwkew* *kents7á*
IPFV INFER grow DET sagebrush around.here
'Sagebrush may be growing around here.'

(Rullmann et al. 2008: 322)

In fact, of the languages for which there is detailed semantic work, only Washo (Bochnak 2015a; 2015b) has a modal that is used for both epistemic and circumstantial modality. Table 13.2 illustrates this with modals from St'át'imcets (Matthewson et al. 2007; Rullmann et al. 2008; Davis et al. 2009), Nsilxcen (Menzies 2013), ʔayʔaǰuθəm (Comox-Sliammon) (Reisinger 2018; Huijsmans in prep), Gitksan (Peterson 2010a; 2010b; 2012; 2018; Matthewson 2013), Blackfoot (Louie 2015; Silva 2009), Mohawk (Mithun 2016), Nez Perce (Deal 2011), Tlingit (Cable 2017; Burge 2017), Navajo (Bogal-Albritten 2016), and Washo (Bochnak 2015a; 2015b).

2.3. Specification of Force

While English modals such as *might* and *must* are underspecified for conversational background, they are specified for force; *might* expresses existential quantificational force over possible worlds (a weak modal claim) and *must* expresses universal quantificational force (a strong modal claim). Languages of North America show a great deal of variation as to whether the force of modals is specified or modals can vary in the strength they express. For instance, the St'át'imcets inferential *k'a* often expresses universal quantification, as in (11a), but can also express existential

Table 13.2 Modal Flavor in North American Languages

	EPISTEMIC	CIRCUMSTANTIAL
St'át'imcets	ku7, k'a, -an'	ka, kelh, ka- -a
Nsilxcen	mat, cmay, kʷukʷ	cakʷ
ʔayʔaǰuθəm	č̓a, k̓ʷa, qʷayigan	havtə, xʷačam
Gitksan	ima('a), gat	da'a<u>k</u>hlxw, anoo<u>k</u>, sgi
Blackfoot	aahk, aahkam-	aahkama'p-, -ohkott-, -áak-, -sstsina'
Mohawk	-ehr-, -aterien'tar-, particles	-kweni-, -kont-, -aton, -atonhontsiohon, particles
Nez Perce	pay's, páalwit, 'éete, ku'(nu) weet	-o'qa, participial + -(n/t)e's
Tlingit	gwál, shákdé, gíwé	potential mode, prospective mode
Navajo	sha'shin	laanaa, lágo, bee haz'ą́
Washo	-eʔ	
English	must, might	

quantification, as in (11b) (Rullmann et al. 2008). The other modals in St'át'imcets similarly exhibit variable quantificational force (Matthewson et al. 2007; Rullmann et al. 2008; Davis et al. 2009).

(11) St'át'imcets (LIL, Salish)

Context: Jim Hoffmann thought he saw a sasquatch and came running back with huge terrified eyes.

a. *ka-q'us-tum'-á* **k'a** *wi7*
CIRC-frighten(CAUS)-PASS-CIRC INFER EMPH
'It must have really frightened him.'

b. ***k'a*** *lh-zúqw-as* *tu7* *ni7* *na* *múkw-a* *qelhmín* *smúlhats*
INFER COMP-die-3CONJ *lh-* then DEMON DET other-DET old.person woman
k'a *mím'c-as* *tu7* *nka7*
INFER COMP-move-CONJ then where
'Maybe the old woman died or maybe she moved somewhere.'
(Rullmann et al. 2008: 323–324; originally from Matthewson 2005: 61, 418)

The Washo modal *-eʔ*, like the St'át'imcets modals, also has variable quantificational force. Gitksan (Peterson 2010a; 2010b; 2012; 2018; Matthewson 2013), Nsilxcen (Menzies 2013), and Nez Perce (Deal 2011) have both modals with variable quantificational force interpretations and modals with fixed quantificational force. In the case of Gitksan, the difference in the encoding of quantificational force coincides with the split between epistemic and circumstantial modality. Epistemic modals have variable quantificational force, while circumstantial modals have fixed quantificational force. In contrast, Nsilxcen has two epistemic modals, one with fixed quantificational force and one with variable quantificational force. While the modal *mat* with variable force is felicitous both in contexts supporting a strong modal claim and a weak modal claim ((12) and (13)), *cmay* is only felicitous in contexts that support a weak modal claim (13).

(12) Nsilxcen (OKA, Salish)

Context: We are working away and my stomach starts to growl. You think, she must be hungry.

a. **mat** *talí* *ʔilx̌ʷt*
EPIS.MOD very hungry
'She must be hungry.'

b. # ***cmay*** *talí* *ʔilx̌ʷt*
EPIS.MOD very hungry
'She might be hungry.'
Consultant: With *cmay* it means maybe she is hungry. It's like you are asking or curious. You can't say that if you hear her stomach growl.

(Menzies 2013: 24)

(13) Nsilxcen (OKA, Salish)

Context: You don't hear my stomach growling and I'm not in the room. It is supper time and we have been working for a while.

a. **mat** *talí* *ʔilx̌ʷt*
EPIS.MOD very hungry
'She might be hungry.'

b. ***cmay*** *talí* *ʔilx̌ʷt*
EPIS.MOD very hungry
'She might be hungry.'

(Menzies 2013: 24–25)

In contrast, Tlingit (Cable 2017) and Blackfoot (Silva 2009; Louie 2015) modals have only fixed force. However, Burge (2017) argues that the modality of the prospective/future and potential modes in Tlingit comes from the *-g̲* prefix, which does not have specified force; the force is then fixed through combination with other morphemes (resulting in existential quantificational force in the potential mode and universal quantificational force in the future mode). For instance, the verb in (14a) is in the potential mode and the proposition expresses circumstantial possibility, while the verb in (14b) is in the prospective/future mode and expresses circumstantial necessity. The modality in both (14a) and (14b) is nevertheless argued to be contributed by the same *-g̲* prefix.

(14) Tlingit (TLI, Dene-Athabaskan)

a. Potential
gwál k̲wasi.ee
gwál **k̲**-w-x̲a-si-√.ee
gwál ∅-∅-**g̲**-u-x̲a-si-√.i-μ
DUB 3O-∅.CJ-g̲.MD-IRR-1S-CL-√cook-VAR
'Maybe I can cook them.'

b. Prospective
kuk̲asa.ée
k-u-**k̲**-a-sa-√.ée
∅-g-u-**g̲**-x̲-s-√.i-Hμ
3O-g.CJ-IRR-g̲.MD-1S-CL-√cook-VAR
'I will cook it.'

(Burge 2017: 48, adapted from Twitchell 2016)

Table 13.3 summarizes the discussion of modal force, giving paradigms for St'át'imcets (Matthewson et al. 2007; Rullmann et al. 2008; Davis et al. 2009), Washo (Bochnak 2015a; 2015b), Gitksan (Peterson 2010a; 2010b; 2012; 2018; Matthewson 2013), Nsilxcen (Menzies 2013), Nez Perce (Deal 2011), Tlingit (Burge 2017; Cable 2017), and Blackfoot (Silva 2009; Louie 2015).[3] Variable force modals are highlighted in gray. The table illustrates the variability in the specification of force between languages and within the modal systems of individual languages.

For the modals with variable force interpretations, there have been different proposals regarding how to capture these formally. St'át'imcets (Matthewson et al. 2007; Rullmann et al. 2008; Davis

Table 13.3 Modal Force in North American Languages

<table>
<tr><th></th><th></th><th>Strong</th><th>Weak</th></tr>
<tr><td>St'át'imcets</td><td>Epistemic</td><td colspan="2">ku7, k'a, -an'</td></tr>
<tr><td></td><td>Circumstantial</td><td colspan="2">ka, kelh, ka- -a</td></tr>
<tr><td>Washo</td><td>Epistemic
Circumstantial</td><td colspan="2">-eʔ</td></tr>
<tr><td>Gitksan</td><td>Epistemic</td><td colspan="2">=ima('a), =g̲at</td></tr>
<tr><td></td><td>Circumstantial</td><td>sgi</td><td>da'ak̲hlxw, anook̲</td></tr>
<tr><td>Nsilxcen</td><td>Epistemic</td><td colspan="2">mat, k^{w}uk^w</td></tr>
<tr><td></td><td>Circumstantial</td><td></td><td>cmay</td></tr>
<tr><td></td><td></td><td colspan="2">cak^w</td></tr>
<tr><td>Nez Perce</td><td>Circumstantial</td><td colspan="2">-o'qa</td></tr>
<tr><td>Tlingit</td><td>Epistemic Circumstantial</td><td>prospective mode</td><td>participial + -(n/t)e's
dubitative particles
potential mode</td></tr>
<tr><td>Blackfoot[4]</td><td>Circumstantial</td><td>-áak, -ohkott-</td><td>aahkama'p-</td></tr>
</table>

et al. 2009), Nsilxcen (Menzies 2013), and Washo (Bochnak 2015a; 2015b) are argued to have strong modals with the possibility of weaker interpretations if the domain of quantification is more restricted (universal quantification over a narrower domain leads to a weaker claim). Nez Perce and Gitksan are argued to have weak modals with the possibility of strong interpretations. For Nez Perce, Deal (2011) argues that the modal is weak but can be felicitously used in contexts supporting a strong modal claim because there is no strong counterpart and no scalar implicature arises. For Gitksan, Peterson (2010a; 2012) argues that stronger modal interpretations arise when the ordering source narrowly restricts the domain of quantification (existential quantification within a narrower domain leads to a stronger claim). It seems likely that there is variation between languages, as the variable force modals have different default readings in these languages. More robust tests are emerging in the literature to show this more definitively (e.g., Deal 2011 on the interpretation of variable force modals in downward entailing and upward entailing environments). However, there is still work to be done to develop tests that are directly replicable across languages and determine the best way to model variable force and account for variation between languages.

2.4. Paradigmatic Organization and Paradigmatic Gaps

Another realm in which modals in North American languages have provided interesting insights is the realm of paradigmatic organization. As illustrated in Table 13.3, languages may have gaps in their modal system. For instance, Tlingit does not have strong epistemic modals, though it has weak epistemic modals (Cable 2017), while Nsilxcen (Menzies 2013) and Nez Perce (Deal 2011) both have weak modals that are not paired with a strong counterpart but are rather paired with another modal with variable force.

Another way that the paradigms vary is in how the different types of modality are grammaticized. In some languages, both epistemic and circumstantial modality are expressed through similar grammatical means. In St'át'imcets, for instance, both epistemic and circumstantial modality are expressed by second-position clitics (circumstantial modality is also expressed through verbal affixation) (Matthewson et al. 2007; Rullmann et al. 2008; Davis et al. 2009; see (6), (10), (11)). Similarly, Nsilxcen modals are all expressed by particles (Menzies 2013; see (12), (13)) and in Blackfoot modals are all expressed by preverbs (Silva 2009; Louie 2015; see (15)).

(15) Blackfoot (BLA, Algonquian)

a. aahksoowatoom annihkayi po'tstákssin
__aahk__-iowaatoo-m *annihkayi* *po'tstákssin*
must-eat.VTI-3:0 dem.invis sandwich
'He must have eaten the sandwich.'

b. áóhkottsspiyi
á-__ohkott__-ihpiyi-wa
IMPF-able-dance.VAI-3
'He can/is able to dance.'

(Louie 2015: 135, 170)

In other languages, epistemic and circumstantial modality are expressed through different grammatical means. In Nez Perce (Deal 2011) and Tlingit (Cable 2017), epistemic modality is expressed via particles, while circumstantial modality is expressed by verbal morphology (16).

(16) Tlingit (TLI, Dene-Athabaskan)

a. Epistemic possibility
Scenario: We're at a party, and we're looking at our friend across the room. We're wondering what he's eating. Whatever it is, it's white. It looks kind of like herring eggs, which someone did bring to the party. We make the guess that it's herring eggs.

Gwál	*gáax'w*	*ax̲á.*
DUB	herring.eggs	3O.IMPFV.3SGS.eat

'Maybe he's eating herring eggs.'

b. Circumstantial possibility

Scenario: We are at a party. Our friend will be coming later. At the party, they are serving herring eggs. Our friend kind of likes herring eggs. When he shows up later, there's a chance that he'll eat some of the herring eggs.

G̲áax'w	***agaax̲aa.***
herring.eggs	3O.POT.3SGS.eat

'He might eat herring eggs.'

(Cable 2017: 8, 20)

In Gitksan, epistemic modality is expressed with second-position clitics, while circumstantial modality is expressed with modal verbs and the verbal particle *sgi* (Peterson 2010a; 2010b; 2012; 2018; Matthewson 2013) (e.g., (8)). Mohawk also shows an interesting split in organization where both circumstantial and epistemic modality can be expressed with verbal roots and particles, but there are far more particles for expressing epistemic modality (Mithun 2016).

Modals in Yucatek Maya exhibit a different type of paradigmatic puzzle, where a set of markers of temporality and modality seem to be in competition for the same preverbal position. Bohnemeyer (2002), discussing temporal reference in Yucatek Maya, refers to an intriguing paradigm of 13 preverbal aspect-mood markers. The markers are mutually exclusive, yet their contributions are quite varied: six encode modal meanings, including obligation (17a) and desire (17b), while the remaining seven mark aspect or temporal distance (e.g., (17c)).

(17) Yucatek Maya (YUA, Mayan)

a.

Lasséeys-ak-e'	*Pedro-e'*	***yan***	*u*	*bin*	*y-iknal*	*doktòor.*
six.o'clock-ak-TOP	Pedro-TOP	OBL	A.3	go	A.3-at	doctor

'At six, Pedro, he had to go the doctor.'

b.

Pedro-e'	*hach*	*ka'n-a'n,*	***táak***	*u*	*wèen-el.*
Pedro-TOP	really	tire-RES(B.3.SG)	DES	A.3	die-INC

'Pedro, he is really tired, he wants to sleep.'

c.

Táan	*in*	*xok-ik*	*le*	*periyòodiko-o'.*
PROG	A.1.SG	read-INC(B.3.SG)	DEF	newsaper-D2

'I /am/was/will be/ reading the paper.'

(Bohnemeyer 2002: 268, 303, 310)

2.5. Other Topics in Modality

There is not room to discuss all the ways that the study of modals in North American languages has informed our understanding of modals cross-linguistically, but we mention a few additional findings here. Silva (2009) discusses the actuality entailments of the circumstantial possibility modal *ohkott-* in Blackfoot, arguing that these arise through conventional implicature. Louie (2015) investigates the interaction between temporality and circumstantial modality in Blackfoot, finding that *ohkott-* behaves like an eventive predicate, while the other two circumstantial modals *áak-* 'future' and *aahkama'p-* 'might' behave like stative predicates, a distinction she analyzes as stemming from the agentivity requirement on the complement of *ohkott-*. Chen et al. (2017) discuss the temporal orientation and perspective of modals in six North American languages (as well as six languages from other parts of the world). Mithun (2016) discusses grammaticization processes affecting modals in Mohawk, arguing the verbs used to express modality are not just lexical items recruited to express modal meanings but show evidence of grammaticizing as modals. Finally,

Bogal-Albritten (2016) studies the attitude verb *nisin* in Navajo, which determines only the attitude holder, while modals (in some cases covert modal operators) embedded in the subordinate clause determine whether the attitude is 'thinking' or 'desiring'. Additional suggestions are given in the Further Reading section.

3. Evidentials

As with modality, the study of evidentiality in the Indigenous languages of North America has strongly influenced our understanding of the semantics of evidentiality in general. The semantics literature includes work on a diverse sample of language families, including Algonquian (Cheyenne), Eskimo-Aleut (Kalaallisut), Salish (St'át'imcets), Tsimshian (Gitksan), and Wakashan (Nuu-chah-nulth). This section focuses on three topics in particular: the overlap of evidentiality and modality (§3.1), the type of projective content involved in evidential sentences (§3.2), and the interactions with and implications for sentence types (§3.3). Other topics are briefly discussed in §3.4.

3.1. Overlap With Modality

Evidentiality is the linguistic expression of source of information – the encoding of the kind of evidence an individual has for some information (Aikhenvald 2004; Brugman & Macaulay 2015). Direct evidence is what one personally experiences, typically sensory evidence, while indirect evidence is an inference from some evidence or a report. When defined like this, the connection of indirect evidentiality to epistemic modality is clear: are inferential evidentials just epistemic modals? More generally, are all evidentials modals with kinds of evidence as their conversational background?

The question of whether evidentials are modals has a long history, authors coming down on both sides of the issue (see, e.g., de Haan 1999; Matthewson et al. 2007; Matthewson 2015; Murray 2017). There are also semantic analyses of evidentials as modals (e.g., Izvorski 1997; Matthewson et al. 2007; Faller 2011) and analyses where evidentials are not modals (e.g., Faller 2002; Murray 2009; 2014). This section reviews the debate and the crucial influence from North American languages.

There are two issues that should be separated when discussing the overlap of evidentiality and modality: whether evidentials in a particular language are morphosyntactically modals, and whether evidentials (in a particular language or across all languages) must be given a modal analysis. The answer to the former question varies widely – in some languages, evidentials may be modal particles or auxiliaries, while in other languages, they may be independent morphemes or fused with other categories, such as tense or sentential mood. Aikhenvald (2004) discusses at length the different morphosyntactic realizations of evidentiality, from morphological type to whether they are fused with another category.

The semantics literature has been focused on the latter question – whether evidentials must be given a modal analysis. As discussed in §2, modals are typically analyzed as quantifiers over worlds, either existential (possibility, $\Diamond$p) or universal (necessity, $\Box$p), with different conversational backgrounds accounting for different flavors of modality. Though not working with languages indigenous to North America, Izvorski (1997) analyzes evidentials as modals, as in (18), with a necessity modal quantifying over epistemically accessible worlds.

(18) The Interpretation of Ev*p*:

a. Assertion: $\Box$p *in view of the speaker's knowledge state*
b. Presupposition: *Speaker has indirect evidence for* p

(Izvorski 1997: 226)

Table 13.4 Excerpt of the Cheyenne Mood Paradigm

a. Direct evidential *É-néméne-∅.* 3-sing-DIR 'She sang, I witnessed.'	b. Interrogative *Né-némene-**he**?* 2-sing-INT 'Did you (sg.) sing?'
c. Reportative evidential *É-némene-**sėstse**.* 3-sing-RPT.3SG 'She sang, they say.'	d. Imperative *Néméné-**stse**!* sing-IMP.2SG '(You (sg.)) sing (now)!'

Source: Murray (2016).

In (18), the evidential contribution comes from a presupposition about the kind of evidence the speaker has. The status of this evidential proposition will be discussed in §3.2.

Matthewson et al. (2007) argues for a modal analysis of evidentials in St'át'imcets (see Table 13.1), building on Izvorski (1997). The details are different from (18), to account for other features, including the variable quantificational force of the modals, but in general terms evidentials in St'át'imcets are argued to be epistemic modals with an evidential presupposition.

There are other analyses, though, where evidentials are not treated as modals. The seminal work in this vein is Faller (2002) on Cuzco Quechua (a language indigenous to South America), which argues for a speech act operator approach to evidentials. On this analysis, evidentials can modify the different components of a speech act, including the proposition expressed, the illocutionary force, the sincerity conditions, and the degree of strength. Some evidentials, including the direct and the reportative, have no modal component, while inferential evidentials do have a modal component. Similarly, for Gitksan, Peterson (2010a) argues for a modal analysis of certain evidentials and a non-modal analysis of others.

Building on both the modal approach, where evidential contributions are truth conditional, and the speech act operator approach, where evidentials can affect the force of a sentence, Murray (2010) argues that evidentials contribute truth conditional, not-at-issue restrictions and may also compositionally affect sentential force (see also Murray 2009; 2014; 2017). Motivation for this approach comes from Cheyenne, where the evidential system is part of the sentential mood paradigm, shown in Table 13.4, suggesting a semantic connection.

There are also inferential and narrative evidentials in Cheyenne, as well as other sentential moods. A compositional analysis is given in an update semantics, but can be summarized for direct and inferential evidentials in general as in (19).

(19) a. Interpretation of a direct evidential sentence:
i. At-issue content: p
ii. Not-at-issue content: speaker has direct evidence for p
iii. Sentential force: propose to add p to common ground
b. Interpretation of an inferential evidential sentence:
i. At-issue content: p
ii. Not-at-issue content: speaker has inferential evidence for p
iii. Sentential force: propose to add $\Diamond p$ to common ground

(Murray 2014)

On this analysis, every sentence presents a proposition, the at-issue proposition, and sentences may make a range of commitments to that proposition. The evidential contribution is to the not-at-issue content and potentially to the sentential force

As for Faller (2002) and Peterson (2010a), for Murray (2010) some evidentials do not have any modal component to their analysis, while other evidentials may. In Cheyenne, direct, reportative, and narrative evidentials do not have a modal component, while the inferential does (i.e., (19b)). Even for the inferential, though, the modal component is in the sentential force, how the at-issue content relates to the context, not in the at-issue content. This contrasts with St'át'imcets, where evidence supports that there is additionally a modal proposition expressed (Matthewson et al. 2007: §4.5): both the main, at-issue proposition and a modal proposition are directly challengeable, able to be targeted in subsequent discourse with follow-ups like 'that's not true'.[5]

To summarize, the behavior of at least some evidentials can be captured without an analysis as a quantifier over worlds. Evidentiality is the expression of source of information, while modality is the expression of possibility and necessity. Some morphemes may express both meanings, others may not. There are analyses of evidentials as modals as well as non-modal analyses, and differences may exist across languages as well as within a language.

3.2. Projective Content

All of the approaches discussed in the previous section assume there are at least two propositions contributed by sentences with evidentials: a main proposition, what is called the prejacent for modal sentences, and an evidential proposition. This is illustrated with an Eastern Pomo example in (20), a declarative sentence with a reportative evidential.

(20) a. Eastern Pomo (PEB, Pomoan) =(5d)
bé·k-al *pʰa·bé-kʰ-·**le***
3PL-PATIENT burn-PUNCTUAL-**HS**
'They got burned, they say' (I am reporting what I was told)
b. Main proposition: They got burned (= *p*)
Evidential proposition: the speaker has reportative evidence for *p*

The semantic approaches discussed in §3.1 all treat the evidential proposition differently – as a presupposition, a sincerity condition, or a not-at-issue restriction, different varieties of not-at-issue content. What status does the evidential proposition have?

Like a presupposition, the evidential proposition projects when an evidential construction is embedded. However, there are important differences. Consider first a classic case of presupposition projection from English: each of the sentences (21a)–(21d) presupposes that there is a unique present queen of France, (22), triggered by the definite description *the present queen of France* (Chierchia & McConnell-Ginet 1990).

(21) a. The present queen of France lives in Ithaca.
b. It is not the case that the present queen of France lives in Ithaca.
c. Does the present queen of France live in Ithaca?
d. If the present queen of France lives in Ithaca, she has probably met Nelly.

(22) There is a unique present queen of France.

Sentences with this definite description presuppose (22), no matter whether the sentence is embedded under negation (21b), in an interrogative (21c), or in the antecedent of a conditional (21d). The presupposition is said to project through these environments, and so each sentence (21a)–(21d) has the same presupposition (22).

This 'family of sentences' test has been applied to sentences with evidentials in many languages, for example with negation in St'át'imcets (23).

(23) St'át'imcets (LIL, Salish)

aoz	***k'a***	*k-wa-s*	*Sylvia*	*ku*	*xílh-tal'i*
NEG	INFER	DET-IMPF-3POSS	Sylvia	DET	do(CAUS)-TOP

'It is necessarily not Sylvia who did it.' [presupposition: indirect evidence]
≠ 'It is not necessarily Sylvia who did it.' [presupposition: indirect evidence]
≠ 'It is not the case that I have indirect evidence that it was necessarily Sylvia who did it.'
(Matthewson et al. 2007: 218)

In (23), the evidential proposition of indirect evidence does not get negated – it projects, much like the presupposition case in (21b). However, there is an important difference: an evidential sentence and its negation do not have exactly the same implication, as did the presupposition example (21). This is spelled out in (24): (24b) is the negation of (24a), but the evidential proposition in (24b) is different from the one in (24a) (see also Murray 2010).[6]

(24) Cheyenne (CHY, Algonquian)

a. *É-némene-**sėstse*** *Annie.*
3-sing-RPT.3SG Annie
'Annie sang, they say.'
q = that Annie sang
p = that the speaker heard that Annie sang

b. *É-sáa-némené-he-**sėstse*** *Annie.*
3-not-sing-NEG$_{AN}$-RPT.3SG Annie
'Annie didn't sing, they say.'
q' = that Annie **didn't** sing
p' = that the speaker heard that Annie **didn't** sing

(Murray 2017: 30)

In (24b), the evidential proposition projects – it does not get negated, i.e., it isn't that the speaker does not have reportative evidence. The evidential proposition in (24b) is reportative evidence for a negative proposition, unlike in (24a). Evidentials in interrogatives also do not yield the same results as the standard family of sentences test (21c), discussed in §3.3. So while the evidential proposition is a type of projective content, it does not have the same projection behavior as a standard presupposition.[7] This pattern of behavior of evidentials has added to the investigation of different types of projective content, beyond just presupposition (see, e.g., Tonhauser et al. 2013).

3.3. Evidentials and Sentence Types

Another way the study of evidentiality in North American languages has been influential is in the study of sentence types and the interactions with evidentials. Evidentials have been found to have many different possible interpretations in interrogatives. One widely attested interpretation is the "interrogative flip" interpretation, where the anchoring of the evidential flips from the speaker to the addressee. For example, in (25), the person with reportative evidence is the hearer, not the speaker as it was in the declarative (24).

(25) Cheyenne (CHY, Algonquian)

*Mó=' -é-némene-**sėstse*** *Annie?*
Q=EP-3-sing-RPT.3SG Annie
'Given what you heard, did Annie sing?'

(Murray 2016: 512)

This example also illustrates another way the projection of the evidential proposition is unlike standard presupposition projection: in the presupposition example (21), the interrogative (21c) implied the same proposition as the declarative (21a). For (25), the implication is that the addressee has reportative evidence for an answer to the question.

There are a range of other reported interpretations of evidentials in interrogatives. In many languages, the combination of evidentials and interrogatives can yield a statement of uncertainty, as in (26).

(26) St'át'imcets (LIL, Salish)

*lan=as=há=**k'a*** *kwán-ens-as*
already=3.SBJN=YNQ=INFER take-DIR-3.ERG
ni=n-s-mets-cál=a.
DET.ABS=1sg.POSS-NOM=write-ACT=EXIS
'I wonder if she's already got my letter.' 'I don't know if she got my letter or not.'

(Littell et al. 2010: 90)

Littell et al. (2010) calls such constructions "conjectural questions", as they contain a conjectural, or inferential, evidential. Such statement of uncertainty interpretations are also available in Cheyenne for interrogatives with reportatives (Murray 2010; 2017).

Evidentials can also occur with other sentence types, such as imperatives and optatives, as in (27).

(27) Kalaallisut (KAL, Eskimo-Aleut)

Olegooq isirli.
Ole=**guuq** isir-li
Ole=rpt come.in-opt.3sg
i. Let Ole come in, [they] say.
ii. Tell Ole to come in.

(Bittner 2008: 11)

These and more various possible interpretations of evidentials across sentence types have implications both for the semantics of evidentials and for the semantics of mood.

Lastly, evidentials frequently have mirative uses – expressions of surprise (DeLancey 2001; Peterson 2010b; Rett & Murray 2013). Though these may not be separate sentence types, they are interpreted differently from standard declaratives. Consider the example in (28) of a mirative in Gitksan.

(28) Gitksan (GIT, Tsimshian)

a. *bagw* *ńidiit*
arrive.PL 3pl
'They've arrived.'
b. *ńakw=hl* *bagw=diit*
EVID=CND arrive.PL=3pl
'They must've arrived!' 'Looks like they've arrived!'

(Peterson 2010b: 129)

Ńakw in (28b) is an indirect evidential that, in certain contexts, has a mirative interpretation: "When a speaker witnesses an event, *ńakw* can be used to express surprise at a situation, such as the unexpected arrival of guests at a party" (Peterson 2010b: 130). Peterson (2010b) proposes to analyze mirativity as a result of a quantity implicature, one that is a conversational implicature in some languages (languages where evidentials have mirative used) and a conventional implicature in others (languages with dedicated mirative morphemes). Rett and Murray (2013) propose a semantic analysis for mirative uses of evidentials, building on work on the semantics of exclamatives in English.

3.4. Other Topics in Evidentiality

This section has discussed three topics where the study of evidentials in languages indigenous to North America has made a substantive contribution to the general study of the semantics of that topic. There are many other works on the semantics of evidentials, a few of which are mentioned here. Looking at evidentials across the Cree dialects, Blain and Déchaine (2007) argue that evidentials differ according to the syntactic domain where they are introduced, dividing evidentials into ones that are CP-external (with illocutionary force) and ones that are IP-external (with temporal or modal force). Working with both Nuu-chah-nulth and Plains Cree, Déchaine et al. (2017) argues languages might differ typologically as to default illocutionary force. Working with St'át'imcets as well as Nivacle, Gutiérrez and Matthewson (2012) argue that determiners in these languages encode evidential distinctions. Additional suggestions are in the Further Reading section.

4. Conclusion

The study of languages indigenous to North America has enriched our understanding of the ways in which languages express modal and evidential claims. In the realm of modality, we have seen that the modals of North American languages are frequently specified for modal flavor but may express variable quantificational force. This contrasts with modals in well-studied languages like English and German, where modal force is fixed but certain modals may express both epistemic and circumstantial modal claims. The study of North American languages is also contributing to our knowledge about how modal paradigms can be organized, both in terms of how different types of modality are grammaticized and the possibility of paradigmatic gaps.

In the realm of evidentiality, the study of North American languages has been an important influence in the discussion of whether evidentials are epistemic modals and whether this varies between languages. The differences in the behavior of evidentials between languages and even within a single language suggest that there is variability in how evidential claims are grammaticized and whether they involve modality. Another outcome of this investigation is an increased coverage of projective content beyond presupposition. The study of evidentials in North American languages has also uncovered a range of different interpretations that arise through the interaction between evidentials and different sentence types.

There are other areas relevant to the study of evidentiality and modality in North American languages, which we are unfortunately unable to cover here. This includes the connection to mood and the realis/irrealis distinction. For instance, Matthewson (2010) argues that mood in St'át'imcets restricts the conversational background of a governing modal, weakening the force of a modal claim. As mentioned in §3, Cheyenne has a grammatical mood paradigm; Murray (2010; 2014) argues for a semantics for this mood marking that isn't about expressing necessity and possibility but does relate to a body of information, namely the common ground. Suggestions for Further Reading are given at the end of §§2 and 3, as well as general suggestions below.

Acknowledgments

We would like to express our gratitude for all the speakers who contributed to the literature discussed here. Without their resilience and desire to share their knowledge, none of this work would be possible. We would also like to thank Carrie Gillon, Jason Haugen, Lisa Matthewson, and Daniel Siddiqi for their support and helpful comments. Any errors are our own.

Further Reading

Suggestions for readings on evidentials and modals in particular languages and language families can be found in the introduction to this chapter. More general further reading on evidentiality includes books (Aikhenvald 2004; Murray 2017), encyclopedia entries (de Haan 2013a; 2013b), and collections of articles (Chafe & Nichols 1986; Aikhenvald & Dixon 2003; Peterson & Sauerland 2010; Aikhenvald 2018). More general reading on modality includes books (Portner 2009; Kratzer 2012; Nuyts & Auwera 2014), handbook articles (von Fintel 2006; Hacquard 2011; Matthewson 2016), and encyclopedia entries (van der Auwera & Ammann 2013a; 2013b; 2013c; Garson 2018).

Notes

1. All language data is given as in the cited source. The language name is as used by the cited author. In parentheses are alternate names (if used), ISO 639–3 code, and language family according to Ethnologue (Simons & Fennig 2018).
2. Though it is difficult to always distinguish the two (see, e.g., Nauze 2008; Kratzer 2012).
3. Mohawk, Navajo, and ʔayʔaǰuθəm are not included in Table 13.3, either because the research does not explicitly discuss modal force, as for Mohawk (Mithun 2016) and Navajo (Bogal-Albritten 2016), or because the investigation of modal force is still ongoing, as for ʔayʔaǰuθəm (Reisinger 2018; Huijsmans in prep).
4. I do not include Blackfoot epistemic modals in Table 13.3, as Louie (2015) does not provide an analysis of modal strength for the epistemic modals. Also, it should be noted that while *ohkott-* is a strong modal involving universal quantification over possible worlds in her analysis, it is nevertheless weaker than *áak-* in her more finely graded system, since *ohkott-* involves existential quantification over actions, but *áak-* involves universal quantification over actions (see especially Louie 2015: 147–148).
5. The evidential proposition is not directly challengeable across the discussed languages.
6. In Cheyenne, the negation morphologically appears under the reportative, but this does not reflect its semantic scope. In addition, the same pattern in (24) holds for other languages where the negation is morphologically higher.
7. There are further differences with presupposition, including that the evidential proposition is new information. This has led some authors to argue for a status other than presupposition for the evidential proposition (e.g., Faller 2002; Murray 2010, 2017).

References

Aikhenvald, Alexandra Y. 2004. *Evidentiality*. Oxford: Oxford University Press.

Aikhenvald, Alexandra Y. (ed.). 2018. *The Oxford handbook of evidentiality*. Oxfo rd University Press. (http://dx.doi.org/10.1093/oxfordhb/9780198759515.001.0001) (Accessed 2019-08-18.)

Aikhenvald, Alexandra Y. & Dixon, Robert M. W. (eds.). 2003. *Studies in evidentiality* (Typological Studies in Language 54). John Benjamins. (http://dx.doi.org/10.1075/tsl.54) (Accessed 2019-08-18.)

AnderBois, Scott. 2017. An illocutionary account of reportative evidentials in imperatives. In Burgdorf, Dan & Collard, Jacob & Maspong, Sireemas & Stefánsdóttir, Brynhildur (eds.), *Semantics and linguistic theory (SALT)*, vol. 27, 459–479. LSA a nd CLC Publications. (http://dx.doi.org/10.3765/salt.v24i0.2424)

Bittner, Maria. 2008. *Reportative evidentials in Kalaallisut*. F ield Notes, Rutgers. (http://rci.rutgers.edu/~mbittner/) (Accessed 2019-08-18.)

Bittner, Maria. 2014. *Temporality: Universals and variation*. Wiley-Blackwell.

Blain, Eleanor M. & Déchaine, Rose-Marie. 2007. Evidential types: Evidence from Cree dialects. *International Journal of American Linguis tics* 73(3). 257–291. (http://dx.doi.org/10.1086/521728) (Accessed 2019-08-18.)

Bochnak, M. Ryan. 2015a. Underspecified modality in Washo. In Weber, Natalie & Chen, Sihwei (eds.), *Proceedings of the eighteenth and nineteenth workshop on structure and constituency in the languages of the Americas*, 3–17. Amherst, MA: UBCWPL.

Bochnak, M. Ryan. 2015b. Variable force modality in Washo. In Bui, Thuy & Özyıldız, Deniz (eds.), *Proceedings of the forty-fifth annual meeting of the North East Linguistic Society (NELS 45)*, 105–114. Amherst, MA: GLSA.

Bogal-Albritten, Elizabeth. 2016. *Building meaning in Navajo*. Amherst: University of Massachusetts. (Doctoral dissertation.)

Bohnemeyer, Jürgen. 2002. *The grammar of time reference in Yukatek Maya*. München: Lincom Europa.
Brugman, Claudia & Macaulay, Monica. 2015. Characterizing evidentiality. *Linguistic Typology* 19(2). 201–237.
Burge, Heather. 2017. *Prospective aspect in Tlingit*. Vancouver: University of British Columbia. (MA thesis.)
Cable, Seth. 2017. The expression of modality in Tlingit: A paucity of grammatical devices. *International Journal of American Linguistics* 83. 619–678.
Chafe, Wallace & Nichols, Johanna (eds.). 1986. *Evidentiality: The linguistic coding of epistemology*. Norwood, NJ: Ablex Publishing Corporation.
Chen, Sihwei & Hohaus, Vera & Laturnus, Rebecca & Louie, Meagan & Matthewson, Lisa & Rullmann, Hotze & Simchen, Ori & Turner, Claire K. & Vander Klok, Jozina. 2017. Past possibility cross-linguistically: Evidence from 12 languages. In Arregui, Ana & Rivero, María Luisa & Salanova, Andrés (eds.), *Modality across syntactic categories*, 235–287. Oxford: Oxford University Press.
Chierchia, Gennaro & McConnell-Ginet, Sally. 1990. *Meaning and grammar: An introduction to semantics*. Cambridge, MA: MIT Press.
Dahlstrom, Amy. to appear. An overview of Meskwaki evidentiality. In Macaulay, Monica & Noodin, Margaret (eds.), *Papers of the forty-ninth Algonquian Conference (2017)*. East Lansing, MI: Michigan State University Press.
Davis, Henry & Matthewson, Lisa & Rullmann, Hotze. 2009. "Out of control" marking as circumstantial modality in St'át'imcets. *Cross-Linguistic Semantics of Tense, Aspect and Modality* 205–244.
Deal, Amy Rose. 2011. Modals without scales. *Lang uage* 87(3). 559–585. (http://dx.doi.org/10.1353/lan.2011.0060) (Accessed 2019-08-18.)
Déchaine, Rose-Marie & Cook, Clare & Muehlbauer, Jeffrey & Waldie, Ryan. 2017. (De-)constructing evidentiality. *Li ngua* 186–187. 21–54. (http://dx.doi.org/10.1016/j.lingua.2016.10.001) (Accessed 2019-08-18.)
de Haan, Ferdinand. 1999. Evidentiality and epistemic modality: Setting boundaries. *Southwest Journal of Linguistics* 18(1). 83–101.
de Haan, Ferdinand. 2013a. Coding of evidentiality. In Dryer, Matthew S. & Haspelmath, Martin (eds.), *The world atlas of language structures online*. Leipzig: Max Planck Institute for Evolut ionary Anthropology. (http://wals.info/chapter/78) (Accessed 2019-08-18.)
de Haan, Ferdinand. 2013b. Semantic distinctions of evidentiality. In Dryer, Matthew S. & Haspelmath, Martin (eds.), *The world atlas of language structures online*. Leipzig: Max Planck Institute for Evolut ionary Anthropology. (http://wals.info/chapter/77) (Accessed 2019-08-18.)
DeLancey, Scott. 2001. The mirative and evidentiality. *Journal of Pragmatics* 33(3). 369–382.
de Reuse, Willem J. 2003. Evidentiality in Western Apache (Athabaskan). In Aikhenvald, Alexandra Y. & Dixon, Robert M. W. (eds.), *Studies in evidentiality*, 79– 100. John Benjamins. (http://dx.doi.org/10.1075/tsl.54.07reu) (Accessed 2019-08-18.)
Faller, Martina. 2002. *Semantics and pragmatics of evidentials in Cuzco Quechua*. Stanford, CA: Stanford University. (Doctoral dissertation.)
Faller, Martina. 2011. A possible worlds semantics for Cuzco Quechua evidentials. In Li, Nan & Lutz, David (eds.), *Proceedings of semantics and linguistic theory 20*, 660–683. Ithaca: CLC Publications.
Fortescue, Michael. 2003. Evidentiality in West Greenlandic. In Aikhenvald, Alexandra Y. & Dixon, Robert M. W. (eds.), *Studies in evidentiality*, 291–306. John Benjamins. (http://dx.doi.org/10.1075/tsl.54.16for) (Accessed 2019-08-18.)
Garson, James. 2018. Modal logic. In Zalta, Edward N. (ed.), *The Stanford encyclopedia of philosophy*, Fall 2018 edn. (Metaphysics Research Lab). Stanford, CA: Stanford University.
Gordon, Lynn. 1986. The development of evidentials in Maricopa. In Chafe, Wallace & Nichols, Johanna (eds.), *Evidentiality: The linguistic coding of epistemology*, 75–88. Norwood, NJ: Ablex Publishing Corporation.
Gutiérrez, Analía & Matthewson, Lisa. 2012. Evidential determiners: Best (sensory) evidence. In Bogal-Allbritten, Elizabeth (ed.), *Proceedings of SULA 6: The semantics of under-represented languages in the Americas*, 63–79. GLSA.
Hacquard, Valentine. 2011. Modality. In Maienborn, Claudia & von Heusinger, Klaus & Portner, Paul (eds.), *Semantics: An international handbook of natural language meaning*, 1484–1515. Berlin: de Gruyter.
Hardman, Martha James. 1986. Data-source marking in the Jaqi languages. In Chafe, Wallace & Nichols, Johanna (eds.), *Evidentiality: The linguistic coding of epistemology*, 113–136. Norwood, NJ: Ablex Publishing Corporation.
Huijsmans, Marianne. in prep. *Second-position clitics in ʔayʔaǰuθəm*. Ms, UBC.
Izvorski, Roumyana. 1997. The present perfect as an epistemic modal. In Lawson, Aaron (ed.), *Proceedings from semantics and linguistic theory VII*, 222–239. Ithaca, NY: Cornell University.
Jacobsen, William H. 1986. The heterogeneity of evidentials in Makah. In Chafe, Wallace & Nichols, Johanna (eds.), *Evidentiality: The linguistic coding of epistemology*, 3–28. Norwood, NJ: Ablex Publishing Corporation.

James, Deborah & Clarke, Sandra & MacKenzie, Marguerite. 2001. The encoding of information source in Algonquian: Evidentials in Cree/Montagnais/Naskapi. *International Journal of American Linguistics* 67. 229–263.

Junker, Marie-Odile & Valentine, Randolph & Quinn, Conor. 2018. Evidentiality in Algonquian. In Aikhenvald, Alexandra Y. (ed.), *The Oxford handbook of evidentiality*. Oxfo rd University Press. (http://dx.doi.org/10.1093/oxfordhb/9780198759515.013.21) (Accessed 2019-08-18.)

Kratzer, Angelika. 1977. What 'must' and 'can' must and can mean. *Linguistics and Philosophy* 1. 6337–6355.

Kratzer, Angelika. 1981. The notional category of modality. In Eikmeyer, H. J. & Rieser, H. (eds.), *Worlds, worlds, and contexts*, 38–74. Berlin and New York: de Gruyter.

Kratzer, Angelika. 1991. Modality. In von Stechow, A. & Wunderlich, D. (eds.), *Semantics: An international handbook of contemporary research*, 639–650. Berlin: de Gruyter.

Kratzer, Angelika. 2012. *Modals and conditionals*. Oxford and New York: Oxford University Press.

Littell, Patrick & Matthewson, Lisa & Peterson, Tyler. 2010. On the semantics of conjectural questions. In Peterson, Tyler & Sauerland, Uli (eds.), *Evidence from evidentials*, vol. 28, 89–104. (Working Papers in Linguistics). Vancouver: University of British Columbia.

Louie, Meagan. 2015. *The temporal semantics of actions and circumstance in blackfoot*. Vancouver: University of British Columbia Press. (Doctoral dissertation.)

Matthewson, Lisa. 2005. *When I was small – I wan kwikws*. Vancouver: University of British Columbia Press.

Matthewson, Lisa. 2010. Cross-linguistic variation in modality systems: The role of mood. *Semantics and Pragmatics* 3. 1–74.

Matthewson, Lisa. 2013. Gitksan modals. *International Journal of American Linguistics* 79. 349–394.

Matthewson, Lisa. 2015. Evidential restrictions on epistemic modals. In Alonso-Ovalle, Luis & Menéndez-Benito, Paula (eds.), *Epistemic indefinites: Exploring modality beyond the verbal domain*. Oxford University Press.

Matthewson, Lisa. 2016. Modality. In Aloni, Maria & Dekker, Paul (eds.), *The Cambridge handbook of formal semantics*, 525–559. (Cambridge Handbooks in Language and Linguistics). Cambridge University Press. (http://dx.doi.org/10.1017/CBO9781139236157.019) (Accessed 2019-08-18.)

Matthewson, Lisa & Rullmann, Hotze & Davis, Henry. 2007. Evidentials as epistemic modals: Evidence from St'át'imcets. In Van Craenenbroeck, Jeroen (ed.), *Linguistic variation yearbook 2007*, vol. 7, 201–254. John Benjamins.

McLendon, Sally. 2003. Evidentials in Eastern Pomo with a comparative survey of the category in other Pomoan languages. In Aikhenvald, Alexandra Y. & Dixon, Robert M. W. (eds.), *Studies in evidentiality*, 101–129. John Benjamins. (http://dx.doi.org/10.1075/ tsl.54.08mcl) (Accessed 2019-08-18.)

Menzies, Stacey. 2013. *Nsyilxcen modality: Semantic analysis of epistemic modality*. University of British Columbia. (MA thesis.)

Mithun, Marianne. 1986. Evidential diachrony in Northern Iroquoian. In Chafe, Wallace & Nichols, Johanna (eds.), *Evidentiality: The linguistic coding of epistemology*, 89–112. Norwood, NJ: Ablex Publishing Corporation.

Mithun, Marianne. 1999. *The languages of native North America*. Cambridge University Press.

Mithun, Marianne. 2016. Modality and mood in Iroquoian. In Nuyts, Jan & Van Der Auwera, Johan (eds.), *The Oxford handbook of modality and mood*. Oxford University Press.

Murray, Sarah E. 2009. A Hamblin semantics for evidentials. In Cormany, Ed & Satoshi Ito & Lutz, David (eds.), *Semantics and linguistic theory (SALT) 19*, 324–341. Ithaca, NY: CLC Publ ications, eLanguage. (http://dx.doi.org/10.3765/salt.v19i0.2543) (Accessed 2019-08-18.)

Murray, Sarah E. 2010. *Evidentiality and the structure of speech acts*. New Brunswick, NJ: Rutgers University. (Doctoral dissertation.) (www.semanticsarchive.net/Archive/WViOGQxY/) (Accessed 2019-08-18.)

Murray, Sarah E. 2014. Varieties of update. *Semantics and Pragmatics* 7(2). 1–53. (http://dx.doi.org/10.3765/sp.7.2) (Accessed 2019-08-18.)

Murray, Sarah E. 2016. Evidentiality and illocutionary mood in Cheyenne. *International Journal of American Linguistics* 82(4). 487–517. (http://dx.doi.org/10.1086/688604) (Accessed 2019-08-18.)

Murray, Sarah E. 2017. *The semantics of evidentials*. Oxford University Press. (http://dx.doi.org/10.1093/oso/9780199681570.003.0001) (Accessed 2019-08-18.)

Nauze, Fabrice. 2008. *Modality in typological perspective*. Institute for Logic, Language and Computation, Universiteit van Amsterdam. (Doctoral dissertation.)

Nuyts, Jan & Van Der Auwera, Johan. 2014. *The Oxford handbook of modality and mood*. Oxford: Oxford University Press. (www.oxfordhandbooks.com/view/10.1093/oxfordhb/9780199591435.001.0001/oxfordhb-9780199591435) (Accessed 2019-08-18.)

Oswalt, Robert L. 1986. The evidential system of Kashaya. In Chafe, Wallace & Nichols, Johanna (eds.), *Evidentiality: The linguistic coding of epistemology*, 29–45. Norwood, NJ: Ablex Publishing Corporation.

Peterson, Tyler. 2010a. *Epistemic modality and evidentiality in Gitksan at the semantics- pragmatics interface*. Vancouver: University of British Columbia. (dissertation.)

Peterson, Tyler. 2010b. Examining the mirative and nonliteral uses of evidentials. In Peterson, Tyler & Sauerland, Uli (eds.), *Evidence from evidentials*, vol. 28, 129–159. (Working Papers in Linguistics). Vancouver: University of British Columbia.

Peterson, Tyler. 2012. The role of the ordering source in Gitksan epistemic modals. In *Pro- ceedings of semantics of under-represented languages in the Americas 6*, Amherst: GLSA.

Peterson, Tyler. 2018. Evidentiality and epistemic modality in Gitksan. In Aikhenvald, Alexandra Y. (ed.), *The Oxford handbook of evidentiality*. Oxfo rd University Press. (http://dx.doi.org/10.1093/oxfordhb/9780198759515.013.22) (Accessed 2019-08-18.)

Peterson, Tyler & Sauerland, Uli (eds.). 2010. *Evidence from evidentials*. Vancouver: University of British Columbia Working Papers in Linguistics.

Portner, Paul. 2009. *Modality*. New York: Oxford University Press.

Reisinger, Daniel. 2018. Modality in Comox-Sliammon. In Huijsmans, Marianne & Lo, Roger & Reisinger, Daniel & Tkachman, Oksana (eds.), *Papers for the fifty-third International Conference on Salish and Neighbouring Languages*. Vancouver: University of British Columbia Working Papers in Linguistics.

Rett, Jessica & Murray, Sarah E. 2013. A semantic account of mirative evidentials. In Snider, Todd (ed.), *Semantics and linguistic theory (SALT)*, vol. 23, 453–472. Ithaca, N Y: CLC Publications. (http://dx.doi.org/10.3765/salt.v23i0.2687) (Accessed 2019-08-18.)

Rullmann, Hotze & Matthewson, Lisa & Davis, Henry. 2008. Modals as distributive indefinites. *Natural Language Semantics* 16(4). 317–357. (http://dx.doi.org/10.1007/ s11050-008-9036-0) (Accessed 2019-08-18.)

Schlichter, Alice. 1986. The origins and the deictic nature of Wintu evidentials. In Chafe, Wallace & Nichols, Johanna (eds.), *Evidentiality: The linguistic coding of epistemology*, 46–59. Norwood, NJ: Ablex Publishing Corporation.

Silva, Amelia Reis. 2009. Circumstantial modality in Blackfoot. (Paper presented at Chronos 9 at the Université Paris-Diderot).

Simons, Gary F. & Fennig, Charles D. (eds.). 2018. *Ethnologue: Languages of the world*. Dallas, TX: SIL international 21st edn. Online version. (www.ethnologue.com) (Accessed 2019-08-18.)

Thornes, Tim. 2018. Evidentiality in the Uto-Aztecan languages. In Aikhenvald, Alexandra Y. (ed.), *The Oxford handbook of evidentiality*. Oxford University Press. (http://dx.doi.org/10.1093/oxfordhb/9780198759515.013.20) (Accessed 2019-08-18.)

Tonhauser, Judith & Beaver, David & Roberts, Craige & Simons, Mandy. 2013. Toward a taxonomy of projective content. *Language* 89(1). 66–109. (http://dx.doi.org/10.1353/lan.2013.0001) (Accessed 2019-08-18.)

Twitchell, Lance. 2016. *Haa wsineix̲ haa yoo x̲'atángi: Our language saved us*. Goldbelt Heritage Foundation, Alaska Native Language Center.

van der Auwera, Johan & Ammann, Andreas. 2013a. Epistemic possibility. In Dryer, Matthew S. & Haspelmath, Martin (eds.), *The world atlas of language structures online*. Leipzig: Max Planck Institute for Evolutionary Anthropology. (https://wals.info/chapter/75) (Accessed 2019-08-18.)

van der Auwera, Johan & Ammann, Andreas. 2013b. Overlap between situational and epistemic modal marking. In Dryer, Matthew S. & Haspelmath, Martin (eds.), *The world atlas of language structures online*. Leipzig: Max Planck Institute for Evolutionary Anthropology. (https://wals.info/chapter/76) (Accessed 2019-08-18.)

van der Auwera, Johan & Ammann, Andreas. 2013c. Situational possibility. In Dryer, Matthew S. & Haspelmath, Martin (eds.), *The world atlas of language structures online*. Leipzig: Max Planck Institute for Evolutionary Anthropology. (https://wals.info/chapter/74) (Accessed 2019-08-18.)

von Fintel, Kai. 2006. Modality and language. In Borchert, Donald M. (ed.), *Encyclopedia of philosophy*, 2nd edn., 20–27. Detroit: Macmillan.

von Fintel, Kai & Gillies, Anthony S. 2010. Must . . . stay . . . strong! *Natural Language Semantics* 18(4). 351–383. (http://dx.doi.org/10.1007/s11050-010-9058-2) (Accessed 2019-08-18.)

Waldie, Ryan. 2012. *Evidentiality in Nuu-chah-nulth*. Vancouver: University of British Columbia. (dissertation.)

Whistler, Kenneth W. 1986. Evidentials in Patwin. In Chafe, Wallace & Nichols, Johanna (eds.), *Evidentiality: The linguistic coding of epistemology*, 60–74. Norwood, NJ: Ablex Publishing Corporation.

14
QUANTIFICATION

Henry Davis and Lisa Matthewson

1. Introduction

1.1. Overview

North American languages have played a pivotal role in the history of cross-linguistic work on quantification and in the development of quantificational theory. In this chapter we outline the major empirical results and theoretical developments involving quantification in North American languages. We restrict our attention to the nominal domain, for reasons of space and because this reflects the focus of most of the literature. A large part of our discussion is devoted to the debate concerning the existence of generalized quantifiers and of the elements which create them (*D-quantifiers*).

In the remainder of the introduction we provide a brief theoretical background on quantification. In §2 we provide some historical perspective, focusing on the debate over Barwise and Cooper's (1981) NP-Quantifier Universal. Section 3 breaks down this debate into a series of empirical hypotheses, and it surveys evidence for and against each one in North American languages.

1.2. Theoretical Background

Quantification in the nominal domain is illustrated in (1) for English.

(1) a. **All** humans are mortal.
 b. **Every** student passed the exam.
 c. Josie ate **most** of the cupcakes.

The standard view of quantification, which emerged in the formal semantic literature in the 1980s, can be summarized as follows (simplifying for the purposes of exposition). Common noun phrases (CNPs; for example, *humans*) and verb phrases (like *are mortal*) denote sets of individuals. Quantifiers like *all* denote relations between those two sets. For example, the universal quantifier *all* denotes a subset relation, so (1a) is true if and only if the set of humans is a subset of the set of mortal individuals. This is schematized informally for the general case in (2). Following Partee (1991) and Bach et al. (1995), we call noun-phase internal quantifiers like *all* D-quantifiers.

(2) '*all* CNP VP' is true if and only if CNP $\subseteq$ VP

Although the D-quantifier semantically relates the CNP and the VP, syntactically it forms a constituent with its CNP sister. (For example in (1a), *all* semantically relates the set of humans to the set of beings who are mortal, but it forms a syntactic constituent only with *humans*.) Under the assumption that semantic composition reflects syntactic constituency (the Principle of Compositionality), the D-quantifier must take the CNP as its first argument; the entire quantified noun phrase then denotes a function from VP-denotations (sets) to truth values. Quantified noun phrases with these denotations, like *all humans*, denote *generalized quantifiers*; an example is given in (3). See Szabolcsi (2010: Chapter 1 and references therein) for a useful introduction to generalized quantifiers.

(3) a. The generalized quantifier '*all* CNP' denotes that function which takes a VP and returns a proposition which is true if and only if CNP $\subseteq$ VP.
   b. more formally: [[*all* P]] = $\lambda Q.\ P \subseteq Q$

D-quantification as in (1) contrasts with *A-quantification* (Partee 1991, 1995; Bach et al. 1995). A-quantifiers comprise adverbs (4), auxiliaries, affixes, and argument-structure adjusters (Partee 1991: 441).

(4) a. Bill **always** eats pancakes for breakfast.
   b. I'm **usually** at home on Saturdays.

Here we concentrate exclusively on D-quantification: this reflects the primary focus of the literature, both in general and in North American languages. For targeted discussion of quantification in the verbal domain in North American languages, see among others van Geenhoven (2004) and Bittner and Trondhjem (2008).

Another important division within the set of quantifiers is the strong-weak distinction. Weak quantifiers, otherwise known as cardinal, intersective, or existential, are defined as follows by Keenan (2012: 2):

(5) For a quantifier Q and sets A,B, Q(A)(B) is determined by A∩B, the set of As that are Bs.

For example, *some*, *no*, and *three* are intersective because the truth of *some/no/three*(A)(B) depends solely on the size of A∩B (the set of As that are also Bs must have a cardinality of above zero, zero, or three, respectively). This result can be achieved by assigning the quantificational word itself the semantics of a simple cardinality predicate (e.g., Partee 1988). Under such an analysis, intersective quantifiers like *some/no/three* do not actually form generalized quantifiers (functions from CNP-denotations to truth values). Instead, they denote predicates, which pick out sets of individuals of a certain size.

Following Milsark (1974) and others, a standard diagnostic for weak quantifiers is that they are acceptable in existential (*there*-insertion) contexts, as in (6).

(6) There are **some/no/three** hedgehogs in the garden.

In many North American languages, intersective quantifiers may function syntactically as main predicates. This is shown for St'át'imcets (aka Lillooet, Northern Interior Salish) in (7) and for Kwak'wala (Northern Wakashan) in (8). In these sentences, the quantifiers occupy predicative position and take a DP subject. This is a pervasive phenomenon cross-linguistically (see the papers in Bach et al. 1995; Matthewson 2008; Keenan & Paperno 2012; 2017).

(7) ***Nkekelhás/cw7it/k'wík'wena7*** *i=smelhmúlhats=a.*[1]
   three.HUMAN/many/few DET.PL=women=EXIS
   'The women are three/many/few.'

(St'át'imcets)

(8) *ḵinam=ox̱=da* *gi-gukw*
many=MED=DET PL-house
'There are many houses.'
(more literally: 'The houses are many.')
(Kwak'wala; Moewaki 2016: 28)

Strong quantifiers, on the other hand (otherwise known as proportional quantifiers), depend not on the size of the set denoted by the CNP, but crucially on the proportional relation between the CNP and the VP denotation. They thus satisfy the definition in (9), from Keenan (2012: 4).

(9) For a quantifier Q and sets A,B, QAB depends on the proportion of As that are Bs: $|A \cap B|/|A|$.

Notice that universal quantifiers also count as proportional quantifiers. Since a universal quantifier requires that *all* As be Bs, the cardinality of $A \cap B$ (the set of As which are also Bs) must be equal to the cardinality of A, which means that the proportion required ($|A \cap B|/|A|$) is equal to 1.

Proportional quantifiers are generally degraded in existential sentences in English, as shown in (10), and cannot function as main predicates, as shown in (11)–(12). In these respects they contrast with weak/intersective quantifiers, as shown in (6)–(8).

(10) # There are **all/most** hedgehogs in the garden.

(11) ***tákem*** *i=smelhmúlhats=a*
all DET.PL=women=EXIS
'all the women' (not a full sentence)
(St'át'imcets)

(12) ***wi'la****(-m)=ox̱ =da* *gi-gukw*
all(-DISC)=MED=DET PL-house
'all the houses'
Speaker 1 comment: 'I do not know what you want to say.'
Speaker 2 comment: 'It is not a sentence.'
(Kwak'wala; Moewaki 2016: 43)

As discussed extensively in the literature (Milsark 1974; Partee 1988; among others), certain quantifier words are ambiguous between a cardinal and a proportional reading. This is true of English quantifiers like *many* or *few*. There are syntactic reflexes of these two readings, as seen in (13a) vs. (13b).

(13) a. There are **many/few** hedgehogs in the garden. (cardinal)
b. # There are **many/few of the** hedgehogs in the garden. (proportional)

A final important concept is *scope*. Generalized quantifiers are predicted to enter into scopal relations with each other (and with other scope-bearing operators). Different scope readings for English quantifiers are illustrated in (14). In (14a), the subject has wide scope relative to the object, and in (14b) the subject has narrow scope relative to the object.

(14) **Every** child read **most** of the books.
a. For every child x, x read most of the books WIDE SCOPE SUBJECT
b. For most of the books, every child read those books NARROW SCOPE SUBJECT

The discourse context in (15) differentiates the two readings of (14). In this context, the sentence is true under the wide scope subject reading, but false under the narrow scope subject reading.

(15) Context supporting only the wide scope subject reading of (14):

There are three children (A,B,C) and five books (1,2,3,4,5). Each child reads three out of the five books, but a different set of three in each case:

A reads	B reads	C reads
books 1,2,3	books 2,3,4	books 3,4,5

2. Historical Perspectives

Early formal semantic work on generalized quantifiers was almost exclusively based on English data, but the theory was intended to be universally valid. Barwise and Cooper (1981) proposed a set of semantic universals relating to generalized quantifiers, among them (16).

(16) NP-Quantifier Universal

[E]very natural language has syntactic constituents (called 'noun phrases') whose semantic function is to express generalized quantifiers over the domain of discourse.

(Barwise & Cooper 1981: 177)

For a decade, (15) was not subjected to systematic cross-linguistic investigation. That changed with Jelinek's claim that "Straits Salish lacks 'essentially quantificational' DPs" (Jelinek 1995: 487). Jelinek also made the even stronger claim that Straits possesses only A-quantification, lacking D-quantification completely. Similar claims were made for other North American languages by Baker (1995, for Mohawk (Iroquoian)) and Faltz (1995, for Navajo (Athapaskan, aka Diné bizaad) and Lakhota (Siouan)).

The claim that a language lacks generalized quantifiers cannot be evaluated on the basis of superficial syntactic evidence. Thus, it is not immediately obvious from the examples in (17)–(21) how Straits, Mohawk, Navajo, and Lakhota differ in their quantificational strategies from English.

(17) ***mək'ʷ=Ø*** *'əw'* *p'əq* *tsə* *sp'eqəŋ*
all=3ABS LINK white DET flower
'They are all/completely white, the flowers.'

(Straits; Jelinek 1995: 514)

(18) ***mək'ʷ =ɬ*** *'əw'* *ŋa-t-Ø* *cə* *sče:nəxʷ*
all=1PL.SBJ LINK eat-TR-3OBJ DET fish
'We ate all the fish/We all ate the fish/We ate the fish completely up.'

(Straits; Jelinek 1995: 514)

(19) ***Akwéku*** *wa-hoti-yéshu-'.*
all FACT-M.PL.II-laugh-PUNC
'Everybody laughed.'

(Mohawk; Baker 1995: 23)

(20) *Awéé'* ***t'áálá'i néitínígo*** *deíłhozh.*
baby 3=**each** 1SG→3=PL-tickle=PFV
'I tickled each baby.'

(Navajo; Faltz 1995: 293)

(21) *Wakˁaŋyeja* **iyohila** *wayawa* *pi.*
child **each** 3=read PL
'Each child attends school.'
(Lakhota; Faltz 1995: 291)

Nevertheless, Jelinek argues that the Straits quantifier *məkʼʷ* 'all' is syntactically an adverbial and can freely quantify over events as well as entities. Baker shows that the Mohawk universal quantifier *akwéku* necessarily takes plural agreement (for example, the predicate in (19) cannot be replaced with *wa-ho-yéshu-'*, with M.SG.II agreement). He argues that rather than being a true quantifier, *akwéku* merely "emphasizes that the entire referent picked out by the NP is involved" (1995: 24).[2] Finally, Faltz argues that both Navajo and Lakhota lack an NP category altogether and that in examples like (20) and (21), the quantifier does not form a generalized quantifier constituent with the common noun phrase.

These proposals had a triply significant effect: they brought North American quantification data to the attention of the field, they inspired subsequent research on other languages, and they posed the important theoretical question of whether the semantics of noun phrases varies in fundamental ways across languages. In the next section we turn to a critical assessment of the evidence for and against D-quantifiers, and generalized quantifiers, in North American languages.

3. Critical Issues and Topics

The discussion in this section is structured around a set of empirical hypotheses which we have derived from Jelinek's arguments against the existence of generalized quantifiers in Straits Salish. In each subsection, we include a discussion of Salish, responding directly to Jelinek's arguments and reflecting our own areal expertise, as well as a broader (and necessarily less inclusive) discussion of literature on other North American language families.

3.1. Hypothesis I: Weak Quantifiers Can Be Cardinality Predicates

Jelinek's first argument for the absence of D-quantifiers in Straits Salish is that weak quantifiers function as cardinality predicates. This claim is based on data such as (22); the weak quantifier *ŋən̓* is in predicate position.

(22) ***ŋən̓***=*Ø* *cə* *sčeenəxʷ*
big/many=3ABS DET fish
'They are many, the fish.'
(Straits; Jelinek 1995: 519)

It is not surprising, given the discussion in §1.2, that weak quantifiers in Straits can function as main predicates. The same is true in many other North American languages, including St'át'imcets (7), Kwak'wala (8), Passamaquoddy (Algonquian, (23)), Chickasaw (Muskogean, (24)), Gitksan (Tsimshianic, (25)), and Q'anjob'al (Mayan, (26)).

(23) *'Sami* *pihce* ***ktanaqsu-pon-ik*** *motewolonu-wok.*
because long.ago **be.many-PRET-3PL** motewolon-3PL
'because there used to be a lot of *motewolonuwok.*'
(more literally: 'because *motewolonuwok* used to be numerous.')
(Passamaquoddy; Bruening 2008: 72)

(24) *Ihoo-at* ***lawa.***
woman-NOM **be.a.lot**
'There are a lot of women.'

(Chickasaw; Munro 2017:145)

(25) ***Hlibuu****=hl* *gitxsan.*
few=CN Gitksan
'There are few Gitksan.'
(more literally: The Gitksan are few.)

(Gitksan; Bicevskis et al. 2017: 316)

(26) ***Xiwil*** *hon.*
many 1PL.B
'There are many of us.'

(Q'anjob'al; O'Flynn 2017: 728)

We conclude that Hypothesis I is supported by North American languages.[3]

3.2. Hypothesis II: Weak Quantifiers Can Only *Be Cardinality Predicates*

We have seen that weak quantifiers *can* be used as cardinality predicates; Jelinek (1995), however, makes the stronger claim that weak quantifiers in Straits Salish *must* be cardinality predicates. Syntactically, this predicts that quantifiers like Straits *ŋən̓* 'many' cannot either replace or adjoin to the determiner within a noun phrase; semantically, it entails that weak quantifiers do not have strong, or proportional, readings.

Jelinek does not give evidence – either syntactic or semantic – for this claim in Straits. However, Matthewson (1998) investigates the issue in related St'át'imcets; she finds that DP-internal weak quantifiers in this language can appear in a DP-internal pre-determiner position unavailable for ordinary adjectives, and allow *only* proportional readings in this position. Both of these findings are illustrated in (27).

(27) **[*Cw7it*** *i=plísmən=a*] *úxwal'.*[4]
[many DET.PL=policeman=EXIS] go.home
'Many (of the) policemen went home.'

False in context: (*context supporting only the cardinal reading*)
There are 100 policemen (along with a bunch of cooks and teachers) at a party. Twenty-five policemen go home, and 75 stay.

False in context: (*context supporting only the cardinal reading*)
There are 25 policemen (along with a bunch of cooks and teachers) at a party. All the 25 policemen go home.

True in context: (*context supporting the proportional reading*)
There are 30 policemen (along with a bunch of cooks and teachers) at a party. Twenty-five policemen go home, and five stay.

(St'át'imcets; Matthewson 1998: 304–305)

The strong readings of St'át'imcets DP-internal quantifiers are further illustrated in (28). In this discourse context, it is true that a large proportion of policemen are women (80/100), but false that a large proportion of women are policemen (80/500). In this situation, (28a) is judged as true and (28b) as false. These results make sense if the DP-internal weak quantifier *cw7it* 'many' is being interpreted proportionally.

(28) Context: There are 500 women, 100 policemen, and 80 of the policemen are women.

a. *Syáqtsa7=wit* [*i=***cw7ít***=a* *plísmen*].
woman=3PL [DET.PL=**many**=EXIS policeman]
'Many (of the) policemen are women.' (*judged true*)

b. *Plísmen=wit* [*i=***cw7ít***=a* *syáqtsa7*].
policeman=3PL [PL.DET=**many**=EXIS woman]
'Many (of the) women are policemen.' (*judged false*)

(St'át'imcets; Matthewson 1998: 302)

This evidence suggests that Hypothesis II is false for Salish. Matthewson further argues that the proportional readings of elements like St'át'imcets *cw7it* 'many' and *k'wík'wena7* 'few' constitute an argument for generalized quantifiers in Salish.

Looking to other North American languages, it seems to be common for weak quantifiers to appear as modifiers inside DPs. One example of this is Gitksan, where the quantifiers for 'many' and 'few' take the attributive marker when appearing inside DP, just like ordinary adjectives. Note that in (29) and elsewhere, *=hl* (glossed as 'CN' for 'common noun connective'), is an enclitic determiner which forms a prosodic constituent with the preceding word but a syntactic constituent with the following noun phrase.

(29) *Gya'a-'y=hl* ***held-a*** *x̱biist.*
see(TR)-1SG.II=CN **many-ATTR** box
'I saw many boxes.'

(Gitksan; Bicevskis et al. 2017: 311)

Weak quantifiers in post-determiner positions within DP are compatible with a Jelinek-style analysis in which these elements are always intersective modifiers rather than D-quantifiers. However, Bicevskis et al. (2017) show that in DP-internal positions the Gitksan quantifiers *helt* 'many' and *hlibuu* '(a) few' have not only weak/cardinal readings, but also strong/proportional readings. An unambiguously cardinal case of *hlibuu* '(a) few' is illustrated in (30), and an unambiguously proportional reading of the same quantifier is shown in (31).[5]

(30) ***Hlibuu****=hl* *simgigyet=hl* *bagw-it* *g̱o'o=hl* *li'ligit.* *gwalḵ'a* *'nidiit* *si'moogit-xw-u'm.*
few=CN PL.chief=CN PL.come-SX LOC=CN feast all 3PL.III PL.chief-PASS-1PL.II (*context supporting only the cardinal reading*)
'Few chiefs came to the feast. They were all the chiefs we have.'

(Gitksan; Bicevskis et al. 2017: 315)

(31) Context: There are 30 million people in Canada. Ten million voted NDP.

Hlibuu*=hl* *gyet* *en=t* *ksgya'a=hl* *NDP.*
few=CN person AX=3.I choose=CN NDP
'Few people chose the NDP.' (*context supporting only the proportional reading*)

(Gitksan; Bicevskis et al. 2017: 318)

In Chickasaw, weak quantifiers such as *lawa* 'many' pattern syntactically as reduced relative clauses when DP-internal; Munro (2017) does not discuss their interpretation, though the prediction is that they will yield only cardinal readings.

(32) [*Takolo* ***lawa**-ho*] *apa-li-tok.*
[peach **be.a.lot**-FOC.DS] eat-1S.I-PT
'I ate a lot of peaches.' (literally 'I ate the peaches which were many.')
(Chickasaw; Munro 2017: 146)

In Passamaquoddy, *ktanaqsu* 'many' is a verb, but it can appear as "a modifier forming a constituent with the noun", without being inflected as if it were part of a relative clause (Bruening 2008: 72).

(33) *Koluskap neke wiku-ss monihku-k wiciw **ktanaqsu**-wok skicinu-wok,*
K. then.PAST live.3-PRET island-LOC together.with **be.many**-3PL Indian-3PL
'Long ago, Koluskap lived on an island with many Indians.'
(Passamaquoddy; Bruening 2008: 73)

For Pima, Smith (2012) argues that the language has no monomorphemic proportional quantifiers. However, *mu'i* 'many', which does not straightforwardly pattern like a predicate (see note 3), behaves as a 'standard D-quantifier' when inside DP (Smith 2012: 703).

(34) ***Mu'i*** *gogogs 'o tototk*
many PL.dog AUX PL.bark
'Many dogs are barking.'
(Pima; Smith 2012: 703)

To summarize: contra Jelinek, DP-internal weak Qs in Salish languages appear to have *only* strong readings, while in Gitksan, DP-internal weak Qs are ambiguous between strong and weak readings. Evidence is fragmentary elsewhere, because systematic semantic investigation has not been carried out. However, it has yet to be shown in any North American language that DP-internal weak Qs lack a proportional reading. We conclude that Hypothesis II is falsified at least for those North American languages for which data are available.

3.3. Hypothesis III: Strong Quantifiers May Be Expressed as A-Quantifiers

We begin this section by distinguishing two notions of A-quantification and setting one aside. The first involves quantification over events or situations as opposed to over individuals. The second is confined to quantification over individuals, but involves the quantifier being syntactically associated with the predicate rather than with an argument.

These two notions do not necessarily coincide, either in English or in North American languages. The DP-internal use of event-related adjectives such as *occasional* represents a case in point in English (Zimmermann 2000), while in North America, Matthewson (2000) shows that in St'át'imcets, the DP-internal quantifier *pipála7* 'one by one' always quantifies over events, not individuals. For example, the context in (35) is one where it is not true that all the boxes were lifted, but it is true that every sub-event is a temporally separated box-lifting event. In this context, the individual-related universal quantifier *tákem* 'all' is infelicitous (35a), but the event-related universal quantifier *pipála7* is felicitous (35b).

(35) Context: There are four boxes in the room. Rose lifts three of them, one at a time.

a. # *Cát-an'-as s-Rose* [***tákem*** *iz' i=xétsem=a*].
lift-TR-3ERG NMLZ-Rose [**all** those PL.DET=box=EXIS]
'Rose lifted all of those boxes.'

b. √ *Cát-an'-as* *s=Rose* ***[pipála7*** *iz'* *i=xétsem=a*].
lift-TR-3ERG NMLZ=Rose **[one-by-one** those PL.DET=box=EXIS]
'Rose lifted those boxes one by one.'

(St'át'imcets; Matthewson 2000: 104)

We set these cases aside for reasons of space, focusing instead on the second notion: A-quantification over individuals. Here, the primary diagnostics involve demonstrating that a quantificational element does not form a constituent with the CNP that restricts it. This might appear straightforward, but the possibility of syntactic movement (via quantifier 'floating', 'stranding', or incorporation) complicates the diagnosis, as witnessed by the debate in English and French as to whether DP-external *all* and *tous* are stranded by syntactic movement or base-generated as adverbials (see Bobalijk 2003 for an overview).

These debates have counterparts in North America. For example, Bach (1995: 19) claims that in Haisla (Northern Wakashan), "Meanings associated with determiners or generalized quantifiers are restricted to roots and stems", which he takes as evidence that the language lacks D-quantification. An example of a quantificational root is *q'i* 'much, many, a lot', as in (36).

(36) ***q'i-***|*utl* *John* *miai*|*x̄i.*
much-catch John fish-3PL.DEM
'John caught a lot of fish.'

(Haisla; Bach 1995: 17)

Bach rejects a syntactic derivation in which V-associated quantifiers are incorporated from an argument position (thus potentially being D-quantifiers), because that would entail that 'incorporating' verbs like 'catch' were suffixal: they cannot surface without an incorporated element to their left. However, exactly such an analysis has been independently proposed for the Southern Wakashan language Nuu-chah-nulth (Wojdak 2008): there, amongst other evidence, the 'bound verb' hypothesis is supported by the fact that the incorporating element can strand a phrasal remnant in argument position, one of the hallmarks of syntactic incorporation. This is not to say that such an analysis is necessarily right for Haisla, but generally, the existence of a quantificational element in a non-argument position cannot necessarily be taken to indicate it is an A-quantifier.

This argument cuts both ways: just as superficial syntactic properties cannot be taken as evidence for an A-type analysis, they also cannot be taken as evidence for a D-type analysis. For example, in the course of her detailed study of morpheme order and scope inside the verb across the Athabaskan language family, Rice (2000) shows that many Athabaskan languages have a distributive prefix, illustrated in (37) for Beaver (aka Dane-zaa), which can contribute universal quantification over an argument.

(37) ***dà***-*ghə-d-ì-ze*
DISTRIB-HUMAN.PL.SBJ-QUALIFIER-QUALIFIER-STEM
'They each shout.'

(Beaver; Rice 2000: 47)

Although the distributive prefix appears inside the verbal template, Rice shows that it quantifies exclusively over individuals rather than over events; she therefore classifies it as a D-quantifier (in fact, even as a determiner; Rice 2000: 59). However, accounts of distributivity based on the theory of plurality developed by Link (1983) posit a null distributive operator over the *predicate* (see, for example, Cable 2014 on distributive numerals in Tlingit (Na-Dene)), which is exactly where the overt distributive prefix occurs in Athabaskan languages. On such an analysis, the distributive prefix counts as a canonical case of A-type quantification, even though its domain is that of individuals.

With this in mind, let us return to Jelinek's claim that Straits lacks D-quantification. For strong quantifiers, this claim can be broken down into two parts, the first (less radical) part being that strong quantifiers *can* be A-quantifiers. Jelinek's canonical case of a strong quantifier, the universal *mək̓ʷ* 'all', standardly appears in a non-argument position preceding the predicate, so this prediction appears to be borne out (see also (17)).

(38) ***mək'ʷ*** *=ɬ* *'əw'* *ŋa-t-Ø* *cə* *sče:nəxʷ*
all=1PL.SBJ LINK eat-TR-3OBJ DET fish
'We ate all the fish/We all ate the fish/We ate the fish completely up.'
(Straits; Jelinek 1995: 514, as cited in Davis 2013: 218)

However, Jelinek provides no evidence against an analysis in which the quantifier is syntactically displaced from an argument position.[6] This is possible in Salish: in a detailed examination of the syntax of universal quantifiers in Salish, Davis (2013) shows that instances of what he refers to as "quantifier fronting" show standard movement diagnostics. However, Davis also identifies two cases of base-generated pre-predicative universal quantifiers, both of which fail movement diagnostics. In one of these, illustrated in (39), the quantifier is an auxiliary, as demonstrated by its position following other auxiliaries and preceding the main predicate. It therefore represents a canonical case of A-quantification.

(39) *ni* ***mək̓ʷ*** *ʔu-wəwáʔəs* [*kʷθə=sqʷəmqʷəméyʔ*]
AUX **all** LINK-bark [DET=dog(PL)]
'All the dogs barked.'
(Island Halkomelem; Gerdts 1988: 80, as cited in Davis 2013: 237)

Given the close resemblance between the Halkomelem case and its Straits equivalent, we can conclude that pre-predicative *mək̓ʷ* does indeed involve A-quantification, thereby supporting the first part of Jelinek's claim.

Looking further afield in North America, potential cases of A-type quantification over individuals are not hard to come by. While in many of these cases alternative analyses involving syntactic movement have not been conclusively ruled out, there is at least one type where a movement account seems implausible, simply because there is no source in argument position for the putative movement. In Blackfoot (Algonquian), universal quantification involves the bound preverb *ohkan-*, which has no analogue in the argument domain:

(40) *ómiksi* *nínaiksi* *iiht**ohkanáyisstsinimyaa*** *óttowan* *omi* *pisatsskiitaan*
om-iksi ninaa-iksi iiht-**ohkana**-yisstsini-m-yaawa ot-isttowan om-yi pisatskiitaan
DEM-PL man-PL means-**all**-cut.VTI-3:0–3PL 3POSS-knife DEM-0 cake
'Every man$_i$ used his$_{i/j}$ knife to cut the cake.'
(Blackfoot; Louie 2014: 53)

In another set of cases, a syntactic account can be ruled out on the basis of the failure of recognized movement diagnostics. For example, A'-movement in Gitksan has a conspicuous morphological signature in the form of distinct extraction marking for intransitive subjects, transitive subjects, and objects (Bicevskis et al. 2017). In certain cases, movement of a quantified phrase triggers this morphology (41a), but there are also cases of 'Q-float' where no extraction morphology occurs (41b); in these latter cases, we can safely assume that A-quantification is involved, since there is no movement.

(41) a. ***[Gwalk'a*** ***'nit=hl*** ***haanak'*]*=hl*** *miiluxw-**it.***
[**all** **3SG.III=CN** **PL.woman]=CN** dance-**SX**
'All the women danced.'

(Gitksan; Bicevskis et al. 2017: 331)

b. ***Gwalk'a*** *miiluxw(***-it)=hl*** ***haanak'.***
all dance(***-SX)=CN** **PL.woman**
'All the women danced.'

(Gitksan)

To conclude this section, we can confidently say that strong quantifiers over individuals in North American languages are rather frequently expressed by A-quantification strategies. Hypothesis III is therefore upheld.

3.4. Hypothesis IV: Strong Quantifiers Can Only *Be Expressed by A-Type Quantification*

As we saw earlier, Jelinek's claim that Straits employs an A-type strategy for strong quantifiers is supported. However, Jelinek fails to give negative evidence showing that strong quantifiers *cannot* form a DP constituent with their restriction. In fact, it turns out that they can, as shown in (42), an example elicited from one of Jelinek's original consultants; here, the universal quantifier *mək̓ʷ* must be analyzed as part of the post-predicative DP.

(42) *ŋa-t=ł=kʷəʔ* ***[mək̓ʷ*** *ksə=šče:nəxʷ*]
eat-TR-1PL.SBJ=INFER **[all** DET=fish]
'We ate all the fish.'

(Straits; Davis 2013: 221)

The same is true across Salish; Matthewson (1998) shows that in at least the following languages, universal quantifiers form syntactic constituents with argument DPs: St'át'imcets, Secwepemctsín (aka Shuswap, Northern Interior), Upper Chehalis (Tsamosan), Halkomelem (Central), and Sk̲wx̲wú7mesh (Central). No Salish language has been shown to lack such constituents.

Hypothesis IV is thus falsified both in Straits and across the Salish family. Elsewhere in North America, however, the evidence is not as clear-cut. Part of the problem is that showing that a language *lacks* D-quantifiers involves targeted elicitation of negative evidence, and for many languages, this type of evidence is missing. Often the nearest we can get is a weak inference from the absence of DP-internal strong quantifiers in the available data to their ungrammaticality. The problem is more acute in languages that lack overt determiners altogether (which includes members of many major North American language families, including Algonquian, Athabaskan, Eskimo-Aleut, Iroquoian, and Uto-Aztecan), and even more so in those with potentially discontinuous arguments (including Algonquian, Athabaskan, and Iroquoian).[7]

Given this, the best potential candidates for languages without D-quantification are those like Blackfoot where strong quantifiers *only* occupy predicate-related positions. Blackfoot is critically different in this respect from related Algonquian languages such as Cree (Reinholtz 1999) and Passamaquoddy (Bruening 2008), which do allow quantifiers to form constituents with argument phrases.

In short, there *may* be North American languages without D-quantification. However, care needs to be taken to ensure that a quantifier in the predicate domain is not related to an argument position by syntactic movement.

3.5. Hypothesis V: There Are No Quantificational Determiners

Though Jelinek's broad claim that Northern Straits lacks D-quantification is false, there is a narrower sense in which she is correct. As she points out, "Straits entirely lacks Determiners corresponding to *each, every, most, some, few, no*, numbers, etc." (Jelinek 1995: 511). The same is true of every other Salish language: there are no quantificational elements which occupy D position and take common noun phrases as their sister. This means that Salish falsifies another of Barwise and Cooper's proposed universals, given in (43).[8]

(43) Determiner Universal

Every natural language contains basic expressions, (called determiners) whose semantic function is to assign to common count noun denotations (i.e., sets) A a quantifier that lives on A.

(Barwise & Cooper 1981: 179)

This is a significant point of variation between Salish and European languages, which Matthewson (1998) links to another point of variation, namely that Salish languages lack *definite* determiners. Since both definites and strong quantifiers involve presuppositions, and since presuppositions place restrictions on the common ground of the discourse, Matthewson argues that the absence of both definites and quantificational determiners in Salish follows from a general restriction on determiners (rather than a restriction on quantifiers). She proposes that elements in D position in Salish may not encode distinctions which rely on the common ground (Matthewson 1998: 114).[9]

More broadly, the absence of quantifiers that replace determiners and take NPs as their restriction is a recurring theme in many North American languages. For example, in Kwak'wala, both strong and weak quantifiers always co-occur with determiners when inside DPs (Moewaki 2016). The syntactic position of the strong quantifier *wi'la* 'all' is illustrated in (44); the accusative marker is part of Kwak'wala's extremely complex determiner system.

(44) *ha̱'m-x'id=i* *Ruby* [$_{DP}$ ***wi'la*** [$_{DP}$ *=x̱a* [$_{NP}$ *lemon*]].
eat-PFV=DIST Ruby **all** =ACC lemon
'Ruby ate all the lemons.'

(Kwak'wala; Moewaki 2016: 44)

The same is true in Gitksan; Bicevskis et al. (2017: 378) observe that in this language, although there are D-type quantifiers, there is an "absence of quantificational determiners: Gitksan determiners . . . primarily contribute a domain-restricting function, and there are no direct equivalents of English determiners like 'no', 'some' or 'every'". For Pima, Smith (2012) similarly argues that D-quantifiers are adnominal, not in determiner position. Pima quantifiers are frequently floated, but may also appear inside DP following the determiner, or preceding the determiner in a partitive structure.

North American languages which lack (overt) determiners altogether cannot by definition display the pattern where D-quantifiers combine with determiners. In fact, it seems that in languages of this type, quantificational elements might vacuously satisfy the Determiner Universal, since in the absence of determiners, adjoined quantifiers occur directly adjacent to their NP restrictions, as shown below for Passamaquoddy and San Lucas Quiaviní Zapotec (SLQZ):

(45) ***Psite*** *wasis* *kisi-ntu.*
all child PRV-sing
'Every child sang.'

(Passamaquoddy; Bruening 2008: 79)

(46) ***Yra'ta'*** *gyìia'* *nàa* *ncyets*
every/all flower N.be white
'All the flowers are white.'

(SLQZ; Lee 2008: 356)

However, the analysis of such strings turns on the status of bare noun arguments in the relevant languages. There are at least three possibilities. First, they could be of predicative type, like English common noun phrases, in which case the quantifiers would indeed count as (semantic) determiners. Second, they could be of argumental type, as in Chierchia's (1998) account of bare nouns in Chinese, or in the North American context, Wilhelm's (2015) analysis of the Athabaskan language Dëne Sųłiné (Chipewyan). Or alternatively, 'bare' nouns could have silent determiners, in which case their semantics would be that of full DPs (see Gillon 2015 for discussion of diagnostics in this realm).[10]

Lee (2008) argues explicitly for this third possibility for SLQZ. She shows that bare nouns are freely used with both definite and indefinite readings, and with both singular and plural readings, and she argues that "bare noun arguments in SLQZ are DPs with silent determiners" (2008: 371). She further shows that SLQZ quantificational elements "show predicate-like behavior inconsistent with determiner status" (2008: 356).

There is also evidence in Passamaquoddy that quantificational elements do not combine directly with NPs. Bruening observes that in this language, quantifiers may co-occur with demonstratives and may take pronouns as their restrictions. Neither of these is possible for standard quantificational determiners, as shown by the ungrammaticality of English **every that woman*, **no them*. Under the assumption that quantifiers have a uniform semantic type within each language, these data suggest that Passamaquoddy quantificational elements never combine directly with common noun phrases.

(47) ***Psite/peskuwok*** ***nekomaw*** *mokesew-sew-hotu-wok.*
all/some.3PL **3PL** black-dress-PL-3PL
'All/some of them are dressed in black.'

(Passamaquoddy; Bruening 2008: 87)

In short, Hypothesis V holds up well in North America: quantificational determiners are rare to absent, providing evidence against the Determiner Universal.

3.6. Hypothesis VI: Some Languages Lack Generalized Quantifiers

Having seen that many North American languages violate the Determiner Universal, in this section we revisit the NP-Quantifier Universal. The implicational relation between these two notions is as follows: a language which possesses determiner quantifiers in the narrow sense of the Determiner Universal will necessarily have generalized quantifiers, but a language which lacks them could still have generalized quantifiers (henceforth sometimes abbreviated to GQs). This is because there is a distinction between the semantics of an entire quantified noun phrase (what the NP-Quantifier Universal is about) and the internal syntactic composition within that quantified noun phrase (what the Determiner Universal is about).

In this vein, Matthewson (1998) specifically argues that although Salish languages falsify the Determiner Universal, they do not falsify the NP-Quantifier Universal. She argues that the bracketed constituents in (48), where a quantifier word co-occurs with a determiner rather than replacing it, are nevertheless generalized quantifiers.

(48) a. [*Cw7it* *i=tsítcw=a*] *wa7* *tseqwtsíqw.*
[**many** DET.PL=house=EXIS] IPFV red
'Many houses are red.'

(St'át'imcets; Matthewson 1998: 250)

b. *Qwatsáts=tu7* [***tákem*** *i=sk'wemk'úk'wm'it=a*].
leave=then [**all** DET.PL=children=EXIS]
'All the children left.'

(St'át'imcets; Matthewson 1998: 238)

Syntactically, Matthewson shows that quantificational elements form constituents with their restrictions; semantically, she argues that their truth conditions parallel their counterparts in languages like English, including importantly allowing strong/proportional readings, as illustrated in (27) above. Matthewson (2001) provides a compositional analysis of St'át'imcets quantified phrases which assimilates them roughly to English partitives like *all (of) the women*, with a difference in the semantics of determiners between the two languages, but the same semantics for quantified DPs.

A decade later, however, the semantic component of this proposal was put into question by Davis (2010; 2013). Davis argues that quantified DPs in St'át'imcets fail to satisfy one of the core predictions of generalized quantifier theory, that they should participate in scopal interactions. He therefore proposes that St'át'imcets – and by extension, the whole Salish family – lacks GQs after all, as originally conjectured by Jelinek.

To illustrate the argument, let us adopt the simple concrete analyses of the GQ-creating quantifiers *all* and *half* in (49). From this, and allowing Quantifier Raising to give inverse scope, we predict that (50) has the two readings given in (50a) and (50b).

(49) a. $[[all]] = \lambda P.\ \lambda Q.\ \forall x\ [x \in P \rightarrow x \in Q]$
all applies to a CNP and a VP and creates a proposition which is true if and only if all atomic members of the set denoted by the CNP are members of the set denoted by the VP.

b. $[[half]] = \lambda P.\ \lambda Q.\ |\ P \cap Q\ | \geq \frac{1}{2}\ |\ P\ |$
half applies to a CNP and a VP and creates a proposition which is true if and only if the cardinality of the set of individuals who are members both of the set denoted by the CNP and of the set denoted by the VP is greater than half the cardinality of the set of individuals denoted by the CNP.

(50) All the children read half the books.

a. $\forall x\ [\text{child}(x) \rightarrow [|\{z : z \text{ is a book and } x \text{ read } z\}| \geq \frac{1}{2}\ |\{y : y \text{ is a book}\}|]]$
WIDE SCOPE SUBJECT

b. $|\{z : z \text{ is a book } \&\ \forall x\ [\text{child}(x) \rightarrow [x \text{ read } z]\}| \geq \frac{1}{2}\ |\{y : y \text{ is a book}\}|$
NARROW SCOPE SUBJECT

In a scenario with four children and four books, the reading in (50a) requires that each child reads (at least) two books, while (50b) requires it to be the case for (at least) two books (say, books 1 and 2) that every child read them. While the second reading is dispreferred, the general expectation is that both readings will be possible.

Consider now the St'át'imcets sentence in (51). If *tákəm ʔi=šk'ʷúk'ʷmiʔt=a* 'all the children' and *šáq'ʷuɬ ʔi=púkʷ=a* 'half the books' were generalized quantifiers, we would expect the same two scopal readings as in English.

(51) Context: Four children are meant to read four books over the summer holidays.

[***tákəm***	*ʔi=šk'ʷúk'ʷmiʔt=a*]	*paqʷal'ikšt-mín-itaš*	[***šáq'ʷuɬ***	*ʔi=púkʷ=a*]
[**all**	DET.PL=child=EXIS]	read-RED-3PL.ERG	[**half**	DET.PL=book=EXIS]

'All the children read half the books.'

(St'át'imcets; Davis 2010)

Davis establishes that (51) does not allow either of these readings, by showing that the sentence is rejected by speakers in discourse contexts that satisfy the first reading and not the second, as in (52a), and *also* rejected in contexts that satisfy the second reading and not the first, as in (52b).

(52)

	A reads	B reads	C reads	D reads
a.	books 1,2	books 2,3	books 3,4	books 1,4
b.	books 1,2,3	books 1,2,4	books 1,2,3,4	books 1,2

Instead, (51) is acceptable only in contexts which support a *cumulative* reading (Scha 1981): those in which all the children did reading, and a total of two titles were read. Cumulative readings involve a relation between two sets, each having a specified size. They crucially do not involve generalized quantifier interpretations.

How can these results be reconciled with Matthewson's earlier findings that DP-adjoined quantifiers in St'át'imcets have (only) proportional readings? While traditionally, proportional quantifiers have been assumed to form GQs, the St'át'imcets findings suggest that proportionality can exist without scopal interactions. Davis provides an account in which proportional quantifiers impose restrictions on the domains of plural DPs created by choice function determiners (Reinhart 1997; Winter 1997; Kratzer 1998; Matthewson 1999; among others).

If the absence of scopal effects is criterial, St'át'imcets thus represents a language which lacks generalized quantifiers. Though work in this area has not been systematically undertaken for other Salish languages, some research on other North American families indicates that DP-internal (but non-determiner) quantifiers *do* participate in scope interactions. Bruening (2008) argues that in Passamaquoddy direct-marked clauses, quantified subjects always scope over quantified objects, but in inverse-marked clauses, either subject or object may take wide scope. For Gitksan, Bicevskis et al. (2017) show that for at least some speakers and some quantifiers, true scopal interactions are possible. And Moewaki (2016) reports that in Kwak'wala, all logically possible scopal readings are available between two clausemate quantifiers. An example is given in (53). This sentence is accepted by speakers in all four scenarios.[11]

(53)

wi'la-'m=o<u>x</u> =da	*ts'i-ts'<u>a</u>da<u>k</u>*	*dala=<u>x</u>a*	***s<u>a</u>k'a***	*gi-g<u>a</u>ldas*	*la<u>x</u>=i's*	*gukw.*
all=DISC=MED=DET	PL-woman	carry=ACC	**five**	PL-box	PREP=POSS	house

'All the women carried five boxes to her (another woman's) house.'

i. *Collective:* Four women together carried five boxes.
ii. *Distributive:* Four women carried five boxes each (20 boxes total).
iii. *Inverse distributive:* Five boxes were each carried by four women (20 women total).
iv. *Cumulative:* A total of four women carried a total of five boxes, in some combination.

(Kwakw'ala; Moewaki 2016: 111)

Such data seem to confirm that DP-internal quantifiers *can* enter into scopal interactions in Kwak'wala, and by assumption, are GQ-creating.

There is even less data on scopal interactions between DP-internal and DP-external ('A-type') quantifiers, but what there is indicates that there is no difference in scope interactions between these cases and those with two DP-internal quantifiers. For Passamaquoddy, Bruening (2008: 89) explicitly states "I have been unable to find any interpretive differences between split and non-split quantifiers . . . both have the same scopal properties", where 'split' quantifiers feature a pre-predicative quantifier associated with a restriction in a postverbal argument position. For Gitksan, Bicevskis et al. (2017: 334) also claim there is no interpretive difference between 'floated' (adverbial) and DP-internal universal quantifiers.

4. Conclusion: Variation in Quantificational Strategies in Languages of North America

We are now in a position to reassess the quantificational landscape of North American languages. Perhaps unsurprisingly, it is more complex than first imagined.

For Jelinek, a simple binary parameter separates conventional 'D-quantificational' languages like English from 'A-quantificational' languages like Straits Salish: the former have determiner quantifiers, which create generalized quantifiers, while the latter lack both, and instead have adverbial quantifiers, which unselectively quantify over both entities and events.

What we find on closer inspection is a very partial validation of this view. Determiner quantifiers are indeed systematically absent from Straits Salish, Salish more generally, and possibly from North America as a whole; but DP-internal quantifiers are present in Straits and all other Salish languages, and are at least very common in the rest of North America (with some caveats about languages such as Blackfoot where strong quantifiers only appear in the verbal complex). However, this does *not* mean that all these languages have generalized quantifiers, as shown by St'át'imcets: the possibility that strong (proportional) quantifiers are not GQ-creating, as diagnosed by their lack of scope, means that DP-internal position is a necessary but not sufficient condition for a GQ.

On the A-quantification side, the picture is even more complex. Not all A-quantifiers are unselective binders in the original sense of Lewis (1975): in fact, many if not most strong quantifiers in 'adverbial' positions in North American languages are sortally restricted to entities, with event quantification being conveyed by different lexical items. It is tempting for this reason to assimilate them to D-quantifiers via syntactic movement, but A-quantifiers may be base-generated in predicate-related (adverbial and auxiliary) positions. As yet, however, it is unclear what interpretive differences – if any – there are between A-quantificational and D-quantificational instances of entity-related strong quantifiers.

Acknowledgments

We are very grateful to Mike Barrie, Carrie Gillon, Betsy Ritter, and Dan Siddiqi for comments on an earlier version of this chapter.

Further Reading

Bach et al. (1995) is a key reference for the study of quantification in North American languages, containing a number of foundational papers structured around the distinction between A-quantification and D-quantification.

Matthewson (2008) and the two volumes edited by Keenan and Paperno (2012; 2017) contain a number of articles on quantification in North American languages. The Keenan and Paperno volumes are structured around a specific questionnaire in order to allow direct cross-linguistic comparison.

Notes

1. In citing examples, we retain the orthographic representations used in the original sources; however, glossing and formatting have in some cases been updated. Abbreviations which are not in the Leipzig Glossing Rules are as follows: 0 = third person inanimate, ATTR = attributive, B = series B agreement marker

(Mayan), CIRC = circumstantial modal, CN = common noun connective, DISC = discourse marker, DIST = distal invisible, DS = different subject, EXIS = assertion of existence, FACT = factual mode, I,II,III = series I,II,III pronoun, INFER = inferential, INFR = informative, LC = limited control, MED = medial visible, PART = particle, PARTIT = partitive, PRET = preterite, PRV = preverb (which usually has past or perfective interpretation), PT = past/perfective, PUNC = punctual aspect, RED = redirective transitivizer, SX = intransitive subject extraction, TR = transitive, VTI = transitive inanimate (object) verb stem.

2. The same can be – and has been – argued for English *all*: see Lasersohn (1999); Brisson (2003). More broadly, Baker uses three syntactic diagnostics to distinguish 'true' quantifiers like English *every* from *all*-type quantifiers: 'true' quantifiers c-command dependent variables, they show weak crossover effects, and they take singular agreement. In semantic terms, 'true' quantifiers presumably create generalized quantifiers, while *all*-type quantifiers are operators on plural domains.
3. A possible counter-example is provided by Pima (aka Akimel O'odham; Uto-Aztecan), where according to Smith (2012), the quantifier *mu'i* 'many' requires a partitive ending when it acts as a predicate. Compare (i) with (ii):

   (i) ***Mu'i*** *gogogs* *'o* *tototk*
   many PL.dog AUX PL.bark
   'Many dogs are barking.'

   (Pima; Smith 2012: 703)

   (ii) *Totobi* *'o* ***mu'-ij***
   PL.rabbit AUX **many-PARTIT**
   'The rabbits are many.'

   (Pima; Smith 2012: 723)

   However, the translation given for (ii) is not partitive, so further investigation is required into these constructions.
4. This sentence may also be syntactically analyzed with the quantifier in predicate position, taking a headless relative clause as its argument ('The policemen who went home were many'). However, Matthewson (1998) demonstrates that this alternative structure is not always available, due to categorial restrictions on modification. Gillon (2006/2013) provides even stronger syntactic evidence from Sḵwx̱wú7mesh, a Central Salish language closely related to Straits: here, pre-determiner weak quantifiers are freely available in post-predicative positions, where no alternative predicative analysis is possible:

   (i) *Chen* *kw'ach-nexw* [***ḵex̱*** *ta* *sḵwemḵwemay'*].
   1SG.SBJ see-LCT **[many** DET dogs]
   'I saw lots of dogs.'

   (Sḵwx̱wú7mesh; Gillon 2006: 27)
5. The Gitksan cases are complicated by the fact that weak quantifiers in clause-initial position are structurally ambiguous between main predicate and DP-internal uses. See Bicevskis et al. (2017: 313) for ways to distinguish the two structures.
6. Part of Jelinek's argumentation that *mək̓ʷ* is an A-type quantifier is that it unselectively quantifies over entities and events, as suggested by the translations of (38). However, Davis (2013) shows that these translations are misleading. The reason is that in Straits (a) number marking on DPs is optional, and (b) the universal quantifier *mək̓ʷ*, like English *all*, can quantify either over individuals or proper subparts of individuals. There is therefore a reading of (38) in which *mək̓ʷ* quantifies over proper subparts of *ce sče:nəxʷ* 'the fish'; this is truth-conditionally indistinguishable from an event-related 'completely' reading. (The same reasoning applies to the case in (17).) However, it is possible to test specifically for event-related readings by using singular arguments with predicates where proper subpart readings are absurd, as in the St'át'imcets example in (i):

   (i) # ***Takem***=*lhkácw*=*ha* *tsúkw-al'ts?*
   all=2SG.SBJ=YNQ finish-food
   # 'Has all of you (i.e., each proper subpart) finished eating?'
   ≠ 'Have you completely finished eating?'

   (St'át'imcets; Davis 2013: 243)

   The only reading available here is the absurd proper subpart reading, showing that the (pragmatically plausible) event-related reading is unavailable. More generally, Davis concludes that universal quantifiers in Salish are sortally restricted to individuals.
7. 'Determiners' here excludes demonstratives, which have different syntax and semantics from 'true' determiners in many languages; see for example (35), where demonstratives and determiners co-occur in St'át'imcets.
8. The property 'lives on' is otherwise known as conservativity, and states that Q(A)(B) is true if and only if Q(A)(A∩B) is true. The point here is the prediction that all languages have determiners which turn common noun phrases into generalized quantifiers.

9. Lyon (2013) confirms this for Nsyílxcən (Okanagan; Southern Interior Salish), but Gillon (2006/2013) argues against it based on S<u>k</u>wx<u>w</u>ú7mesh. Further afield, Lee (2008) argues that San Lucas Quiaviní Zapotec (Otomanguean) also lacks determiners that access the common ground.
10. Gillon (2006/2013) suggests that the last option may be the case for S<u>k</u>wx<u>w</u>ú7mesh, a language which possesses overt determiners and allows quantifiers to appear either in combination with full DPs, or in structures without an overt D such as in (45)–(46).
11. What Moewaki calls "distributive" and "inverse distributive", we previously called "wide scope subject" and "narrow scope subject", respectively.

References

Bach, Emmon. 1995. A note on quantification and blankets in Haisla. In Bach, Emmon & Jelinek, Eloise & Kratzer, Angelika & Partee, Barbara (eds.), *Quantification in natural languages*, 13–20. Dordrecht: Kluwer.

Bach, Emmon & Jelinek, Eloise & Kratzer, Angelika & Partee, Barbara (eds.). 1995. *Quantification in natural languages*. Dordrecht: Kluwer.

Baker, Mark. 1995. On the absence of certain quantifiers in Mohawk. In Bach, Emmon & Jelinek, Eloise & Kratzer, Angelika & Partee, Barbara (eds.), *Quantification in natural languages*, 21–58. Dordrecht: Kluwer.

Barwise, Jon & Cooper, Robin. 1981. Generalized quantifiers and natural language. *Linguistics and Philosophy* 4. 159–219.

Bicevskis, Katie & Davis, Henry & Matthewson, Lisa. 2017. Quantification in Gitksan. In Paperno, Denis & Keenan, Edward (eds.), *Handbook of quantification in natural languages volume II*, 281–382. Dordrecht: Springer.

Bittner, Maria & Trondheim, Naja. 2008. Quantification as reference: Evidence from Q-verbs. In Matthewson, Lisa (ed.), *Quantification: A cross-linguistic perspective*. (North-Holland Linguistics Series: Linguistic Variation 64), 7–66. Bingley, UK: Emerald Publishing.

Bobaljik, Jonathan David. 2003. Floating quantifiers: Handle with care. In Cheng, Lisa & Sybesma, Rint (eds.), *The second glot international state-of-the-article book*. Berlin and New York: Mouton de Gruyter.

Brisson, Christine. 2003. Plurals, *all*, and the non-uniformity of collective predication. *Linguistics and Philosophy* 26. 129–184.

Bruening, Benjamin. 2008. Quantification in Passamaquoddy. In Matthewson, Lisa (ed.), *Quantification: A cross-linguistic perspective*. (North-Holland Linguistics Series: Linguistic Variation 64), 67–104. Bingley, UK: Emerald Publishing.

Cable, Seth. 2014. Distributive numerals and distance distributivity in Tlingit (and beyond). *Language* 90(4). 562–606.

Chierchia, Gennaro. 1998. Reference to kinds across language. *Natural Language Semantics* 6(4). 339–405.

Davis, Henry. 2010. Salish languages lack generalized quantifiers after all! (Paper presented at SALT 20, University of British Columba, Simon Fraser University).

Davis, Henry. 2013. All about "all" in (some) Salish languages. In Gil, Kook-Hee & Harlow, Stephen & Tsoulas, George (eds.), *Strategies of quantification*, 214–259. Oxford: Oxford University Press.

Faltz, Leonard. 1995. Towards a typology of natural logic. In Bach, Emmon & Jelinek, Eloise & Kratzer, Angelika & Partee, Barbara (eds.), *Quantification in natural languages*, 321–362. Dordrecht: Kluwer.

Gerdts, Donna B. 1988. *Object and absolutive in Halkomelem Salish*. New York: Garland.

Gillon, Carrie. 2006/2013. *The semantics of determiners: Domain restriction in S<u>k</u>wx<u>w</u>ú7mesh*. Vancouver: University of British Columbia. (Doctoral dissertation.) Published 2013 by Cambridge Scholars Publishing, Newcastle Upon Tyne.

Gillon, Carrie. 2015. Investigating D in languages with and without articles. In Bochnak, Ryan & Matthewson, Lisa (eds.), *Methodologies in semantic fieldwork*, 175–203. Oxford: Oxford University Press.

Jelinek, Eloise. 1995. Quantification in straits Salish. In Bach, Emmon & Jelinek, Eloise & Kratzer, Angelika & Partee, Barbara (eds.), *Quantification in natural languages*, 487–540. Dordrecht: Kluwer.

Keenan, Edward L. 2012. The quantifier questionnaire. In Keenan & Paperno (eds.): 1–20.

Keenan, Edward L. & Paperno, Denis (eds.). 2012. *Handbook of quantification in natural language: Volume I*. Dordrecht: Springer International Studies in Linguistics and Philosophy 90.

Keenan, Edward L. & Paperno, Denis (eds.). 2017. *Handbook of quantification in natural language: Volume II*. Dordrecht: Springer International Studies in Linguistics and Philosophy 97.

Kratzer, Angelika. 1998. Scope or pseudo-scope? Are there wide-scope indefinites? In Rothstein, Susan (ed.), *Events in grammar*. Dordrecht: Kluwer.

Lasersohn, Peter. 1999. Pragmatic halos. *Language* 75. 522–551.

Lee, Felicia. 2008. On the absence of quantificational determiners in San Lucas Quiaviní Zapotec. In Matthewson, Lisa (ed.), *Quantification: A cross-linguistic perspective* (North-Holland Linguistics Series: Linguistic Variation 64), 353–382. Bingley, UK: Emerald Publishing.

Lewis, David. 1975. Adverbs of quantification. In Keenan, Edward L. (ed.), *Formal semantics of natural language*, 3–15. Cambridge: Cambridge University Press.

Link, Godehard. 1983. The logical analysis of plurals and mass terms: A lattice-theoretical approach. In Bäuerle, Rainer & Schwarze, C. & von Stechow, Arnim (eds.), *Meaning, use and interpretation of language*, 303–323. Berlin: De Gruyter.

Louie, Meagan. 2014. *The temporal semantics of action and circumstance in blackfoot*. Vancouver: University of British Columbia. (Doctoral dissertation.)

Lyon, John. 2013. *Predication and equation in Okanagan Salish: The syntax and semantics of determiner phrases*. Vancouver: University of British Columbia. (Doctoral dissertation.)

Matthewson, Lisa. 1998. *Determiner systems and quantificational strategies: Evidence from Salish*. The Hague: Holland Academic Graphics.

Matthewson, Lisa. 1999. On the interpretation of wide-scope indefinites. *Natural Language Semantics* 7. 79–134.

Matthewson, Lisa. 2000. On distributivity and pluractionality. In *Proceedings of SALT X*, 99–114. Ithaca, NY: CLC Publications.

Matthewson, Lisa. 2001. Quantification and the nature of cross-linguistic variation. *Natural Language Semantics* 9. 145–189.

Matthewson, Lisa (ed.). 2008. *Quantification: A cross-linguistic perspective*. (North-Holland Linguistics Series: Linguistic Variation 64). Bingley, UK: Emerald Publishing.

Milsark, Gary. 1974. *Existential sentences in English*. Cambridge, MA: MIT. (Doctoral dissertation.) Published by New York: Garland, 1979.

Moewaki, Ayako. 2016. *Quantifiers in Kwakw'ala*. University of British Columbia. (MA thesis.)

Munro, Pamela. 2017. Chickasaw quantifiers. In Keenan, Edward L. & Paperno, Denis (eds.), *Handbook of quantification in natural language: Volume II*, 113–201. Dordrecht: Springer International Studies in Linguistics and Philosophy 97.

O'Flynn, Kathleen Chase. 2017. Quantification in Q'anjob'al. In Keenan, Edward L. & Paperno, Denis (eds.), *Handbook of quantification in natural language: Volume II*, 697–750. Dordrecht: Springer International Studies in Linguistics and Philosophy 97.

Partee, Barbara. 1988. Many quantifiers. In Powers, J. & de Jong, K. (eds.), *Proceedings of the fifth ESCOL*. The Ohio State University.

Partee, Barbara. 1991. Adverbial quantification and event structures. *Berkeley Linguistics Society* 17. 439–456.

Partee, Barbara. 1995. Quantificational structures and compositionality. In Bach, Emmon & Jelinek, Eloise & Kratzer, Angelika & Partee, Barbara (eds.), *Quantification in natural languages*, 541–601. Dordrecht: Kluwer.

Reinhart, Tanya. 1997. Quantifier scope: How labor is divided between QR and choice functions. *Linguistics and Philosophy* 20. 335–397.

Reinholtz, Charlotte. 1999. On the characterization of discontinuous constituents: Evidence from Swampy Cree. *International Journal of American Linguistics* 65(2). 201–227.

Rice, Keren. 2000. *Morpheme order and semantic scope: Word formation in the Athabaskan verb*. Cambridge: Cambridge University Press.

Scha, Renko. 1981. Distributive, collective, and cumulative quantification. In Groenendijk, Jeroen & Janssen, T. & Stokhof, Martin (eds.), *Truth, interpretation, and information* (GRASS 2). Dordrecht: Foris.

Smith, Marcus. 2012. Pima quantifiers. In Keenan, Edward L. & Paperno, Denis (eds.), *Handbook of quantification in natural language: Volume I*. 629–727. Dordrecht: Springer International Studies in Linguistics and Philosophy 90.

Szabolcsi, Anna. 2010. *Quantification*. Cambridge: Cambridge University Press.

van Geenhoven, Veerle. 2004. *For*-adverbials, frequentative aspect, and pluractionality. *Natural Language Semantics* 12(2). 135–190.

Wilhelm, Andrea. 2015. A radically [+arg, -pred] language. In Pasquereau, Jérémy (eds.), *Proceedings of the Eighth Conference on the Semantics of Under-represented Languages of the Americas*, 121–136. Amherst, MA: GLSA.

Winter, Yoad. 1997. Choice functions and the scopal semantics of indefinites. *Linguistics and Philosophy* 20. 399–467.

Wojdak, Rachel. 2008. *The linearization of affixes: Evidence from Nuu-cha-nulth*. (Studies in Natural Language and Linguistic Theory 73). Dordrecht: Springer International.

Zimmermann, Malte. 2000. Pluractional quantifiers: The occasional-construction in English and German. In *Proceedings of SALT X*, 290–306. Ithaca, NY: CLC Publications.

PART II

Selected Language Families and Issues in the Historical Linguistics of North America

15
OTOMANGUEAN LANGUAGES

Brook Danielle Lillehaugen

1. Introduction, Languages, and Locations

Historically stretching from Central Mexico to Costa Rica, the Otomanguean family is the Mesoamerican family with the greatest geographic range and diversity (Kaufman & Justeson 2009: 226), on par with of that of Indo-European (227). The name Otomanguean is a blend of Otomí (the northernmost member of the language family) and Mangue (the southernmost member of the family).[1]

There are over two million speakers of Otomanguean languages (INALI 2015). The exact number of languages within the family is hard to pinpoint. *The Ethnologue* currently catalogs more than 180 Otomanguean languages (Simons & Fennig 2018), but given historical underestimation of diversity within the family, the number may be higher. Rensch (1976) proposed the relatedness of most Otomanguean languages, though there were earlier observations of the relationship between certain Otomanguean languages and many subsequent refinements of the Otomanguean family (e.g., Rensch 1977; Suárez 1986).

The threatened status and limited documentation of many Otomanguean languages create an urgent situation for speakers, language learners, and researchers. Many languages and language varieties within the family are threatened: some have no current speakers, some have only a few, and many are spoken only by adults, with no children currently acquiring the language. Kaufman and Justeson proclaim that "[d]etailed documentation of most surviving Indigenous languages is now a research emergency for Mesoamerican studies" (2009: 221), of which Otomanguean studies is a part.

This introduction section begins with the structure of the Otomanguean family (§1.1), geographic distribution, and level of endangerment of major subgroups within the family (§1.2). I then turn to shared phonological (§2) and morphosyntactic characteristics (§3) of Otomanguean languages in general. Many of these shared features are characteristics shared among languages in the Mesoamerican linguistic area (e.g., Campbell et al. 1986; van der Auwera 1998; Wichmann in press). Given the diversity of the Otomanguean family, it is not possible to discuss subgroups in depth, though each of these subgroups warrant further and deeper discussion; in (§4) I offer some resources for further investigation at the subgroup level. The chapter closes with a section of key historical resources (§5) and conclusions (§6).

1.1. Structure of the Family

The structure of the eight major subgroups of the Otomanguean family is presented in Figure 15.1. Here I follow Kaufman (1988, as cited in Campbell 2017b). The internal structures of

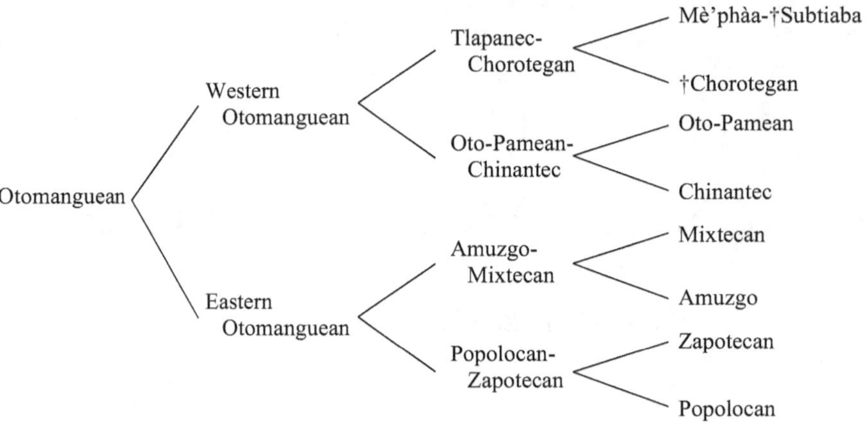

Figure 15.1 Structure of Otomanguean Family
Source: Based on Campbell (2017b); Kaufman (1988).

the subgroups are presented in §4. In many cases, there are significant open questions regarding classification at these levels, including among Mixtecan and Zapotecan languages.

Otomanguean is an old family, with a time depth of approximately 6,000 years (Kaufman 2006: 819). Kaufman and Justeson bemoan the "rudimentary" (2009: 227) extent to which proto-Otomanguean has been reconstructed so far, attributing this gap in part to the time depth of the family. It is, of course, this time depth that makes proto-Otomanguean so critical for understanding human history in Mesoamerica. Kaufman also notes that the failure may in part be methodological:

> Quite a few comparative studies designed to identify cognates and reconstruct ancestral phonology and semantics have been carried out with O[to]M[anguean]. Most have been flawed by a failure to recognize many or most of the now unused word formation processes of earlier stages.
>
> (Kaufman 2006: 822)

Lyle Campbell points out that there is some disagreement here, noting that "[s]ome Otomangueanists believe that Otomanguean reconstruction is so advanced as to rival that of Indo-European (see, for example, Longacre 1968: 333), though this view is not widely shared" (2016: 120). Campbell rates the reconstruction of Otomanguean phonology as "advanced", but calls for further understanding of the difference between inherited aspects of languages as distinguished from those that are borrowed or due to language contact (2016: 125). In addition to work on historical morphosyntax, Campbell also calls for the development of etymological dictionaries (2016: 125).

Table 15.1 lists some reconstructions available for subgroups of proto-Otomanguean, the data for which were compiled from Eric Campbell (2017b), an invaluable resource in understanding the content and relationship of these various works. There are no reconstructions for proto-Mè'phàà-Subtiaba (Campbell 2017b: 3).

1.2. Geographic Distribution and Number of Speakers

All the Otomanguean languages that are currently spoken are Mexican languages, though the family used to extend further south into Nicaragua and Costa Rica. Otomí is the most northern member of the language family, spoken in Central Mexico. Otomanguean languages are found across the entire geographical extent of the Mesoamerican cultural area (Campbell 2000: 157). Kaufman and Justeson attribute most discontinuities in the geographic expanse of Otomanguean to Nahuatl intrusions (2009: 223). An overview of the geographic distribution of Otomanguean languages is

Table 15.1 (Partial) Reconstructions for Proto-Otomanguean Subgroups

proto-Chatino (Upson & Longacre 1965; Campbell & Cruz 2010; Campbell 2013; 2018)
proto-Chiapanec (Fernández de Miranda & Weitlaner 1961; Rensch 1968)
proto-Chinantec (Weitlaner & Smith 1962; Rensch 1989)
proto-Chorotegan (Fernández de Miranda & Weitlaner 1961)
proto-Matlatzinca-Tlahuica (Hasler 1961; Pérez 2007; Pascacio Montijo 2014)
proto-Mazatec (Gudschinsky 1956; 1959; Kirk 1966; 1985)
proto-Mixtecan (Longacre 1955; 1957; Mak & Longacre 1960; Bradley 1981; Bradley & Josserand 1982; Josserand 1983; Kaufman 1983; Dürr 1987)
proto-Otopamean (Bartholomew 1965; 1989; Kaufman 1983)
proto-Otomi (Newman & Weitlaner 1950a; Bartholomew 1959; 1960)
proto-Otomi-Mazahua (Newman & Weitlaner 1950b)
proto-Otomian-Matlatzinca (Weitlaner 1953; Bartholomew 1959)
proto-Popolocan (Fernández de Miranda 1951; Longacre 1962; Veerman-Leichsenring 2000; 2004; Costaouec & Swanton 2015)
proto-Popolocan-Mixtecan (Gudschinsky 1959)
proto-Triqui (Matsukawa 2005)
proto-Zapotecan (Swadesh 1947; Suárez 1973; Benton 1988; 2001; Fernández de Miranda 1995; Kaufman 2016; Beam de Azcona et al. 2018)

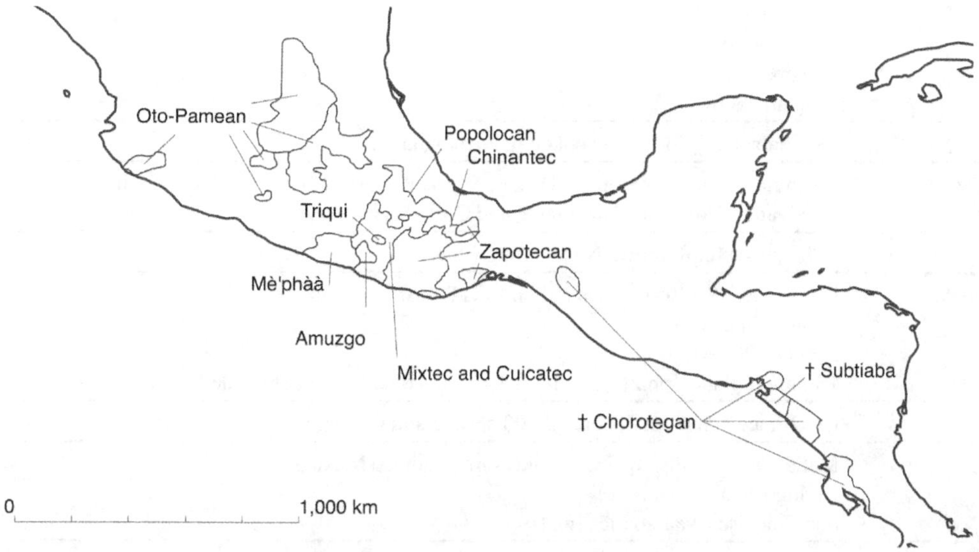

Figure 15.2 Map of Otomanguean Family

Source: Artwork by Jeremy Fahringer; adapted from Kaufman and Justeson (2009: Figure 15.1).

presented in Figure 15.2, which is a modified version of Kaufman and Justeson's map of Mesoamerican languages (2009: 223).

According to the Instituto Nacional de Lenguas Indígenas (INALI 2015), only 11.7% of speakers of Otomanguean languages are monolingual; 88.3% of speakers of Otomanguean languages are reported as being bilingual in Spanish. Diaspora communities of speakers of Otomanguean languages can be found far beyond the borders indicated in Figure 15.2, including in Oaxaca City, Mexico City, Los Angeles, Chicago, North Carolina, and New York. For example, Romero and Sonnenschein (2016) report that there are more speakers of San Bartolomé Zoogocho Zapotec in the greater Los Angeles area than there currently are in Oaxaca. There are, in fact, so many

Oaxacans living in California that the term "Oaxacalifornia" has emerged. It is not uncommon to find restaurants and businesses with names in Otomanguean languages in Oaxacalifornia and elsewhere in diaspora communities. For example, at the time this chapter is being written, there are currently Zapotec-language writings on the walls of the Main Public Library in Los Angeles, as part of a mural created by a Tlacolula de Matamoros-based art collective called the Tlacolulokos. Given this, it is unsurprising that some speakers of Otomanguean languages are multilingual, with Spanish/English as second/third languages.

Table 15.2 presents the location and number of speakers for languages within the eight major subgroups of Otomanguean. Languages are presented along with ISO codes where possible. While ISO codes are not unproblematic, given the multiple alternate names (some of which are presented in parenthesis in Table 15.2), they can aid in identifying language varieties. Some alternate names may be easy to reconcile, such as differences in spelling and use of accents (e.g., Triqui/Trique or Otomi/Otomí), while others are less transparent and require insider knowledge, such as the use of both "Juchiteco" and "Isthmus Zapotec" to refer to the same language (variety). Autonyms for

Table 15.2 Location and Number of Speakers for Major Subgroups

SUBGROUP	LOCATION, NUMBER OF SPEAKERS
Mè'phàà-Subtiaba	Mè'phàà (Tlalpanec), appx. 55,000 speakers, eastern part of the state of Guerrero Azoyù [tpc] Malinaltepec [tcf] Tlacoapa [tpl] Acatepec [tpx] Teocuitlapa [tpx]
	†Subtiaba [sut], formerly spoken in Nicaragua
Chorotegan	†Mangue [mom] (Chorotega, Dirian, Nagranda, Orotiña), formerly spoken in El Salvador, Honduras, Nicaragua, and Costa Rica
	†Chiapanec [cip], formerly spoken in Chiapas
Otopamean[2]	Pame, appx. 7,500 speakers in San Luis Potosí Central Pame [pbs] Nothern Pame [pmq] †Southern Pame [pmz], formerly spoken in Hidalgo and Estado de México
	Chichimec-Jonaz [pei], appx. 2,000 speakers in Guanajuato
	Matlatzinca-Ocuilteco, 750 speakers in Estado de México Atzingo Matlazinca [ocu] San Francisco Matlatzinca [mat]
	Mazahua, appx.100,000 speakers in Michoacán, Estado de México, and Queretero Central Mazahua [maz] Michoacán Mazahua [mmc]
	Otomi, appx. 250,000 speakers in Hidalgo, Veracruz, Puebla, Estado de Mexico, Tlaxcala, Guanajuato, Queretaro, Michoacán Eastern Highland Otomi [otm] Estado de México Otomi [ots] Ixtenco Otomi [otz] Mezquital Otomi [ote] Querétaro Otomi [otq] Temoaya Otomi [ott] Tenango Otomi [otn] Texcatepec Otomi [otx] Tilapa Otomi [otl]

Subgroup	*Location, Number of Speakers*
Chinantec	Appx. 140,000 speakers in Oaxaca, Veracruz Chiltepec Chinantec [csa] Comaltepec Chinantec [cco] Lalana Chinantec [cnl] Lealao Chinantec [cle] Ojitlán Chinantec [chj] Ozumacín Chinantec [chz] Palantla Chinantec [cpa] Quiotepec Chinantec [chq] Sochiapam Chinantec [cso] Tepetotutla Chinantec [cnt] Tepinapa Chinantec [cte] Tlacoatzintepec Chinantec [ctl] Usila Chinantec [cuc] Valle Nacional Chinantec [cvn]
Zapotecan	Zapotec languages, spoken by 450,000 speakers in Oaxaca and Veracruz Aloápam Zapotec [zaq] Amatlán Zapotec [zpo] Asunción Mixtepec Zapotec [zoo] Ayoquesco Zapotec [zaf] Cajonos Zapotec [zad] Chichicapan Zapotec [zpv] Choapan Zapotec [zpc] Coatecas Altas Zapotec [zca] Coatlán Zapotec [zps] El Alto Zapotec [zpp] Elotepec Zapotec [zte] Guevea de Humboldt Zapotec [zpg] Güilá Zapotec [ztu] Isthmus Zapotec [zai] Lachiguiri Zapotec [zpa] Lachixío Zapotec [zpl] Lapaguía-Guivini Zapotec [ztl] Loxicha Zapotec [ztp] Mazaltepec Zapotec [zpy] Miahuatlán Zapotec [zam] Mitla Zapotec [zaw] Mixtepec Zapotec [zpm] Ocotlán Zapotec [zac] Ozolotepec Zapotec [zao] Petapa Zapotec [zpe] Quiavicuzas Zapotec [zpj] Quioquitani-Quierí Zapotec [ztq] Rincón Zapotec [zar] San Agustín Mixtepec Zapotec [ztm] San Baltazar Loxicha Zapotec [zpx] San Pedro Quiatoni Zapotec [zpf] San Vicente Coatlán Zapotec [zpt] Santa Catarina Albarradas Zapotec [ztn]

(Continued)

Table 15.2 (Continued)

SUBGROUP	LOCATION, NUMBER OF SPEAKERS
	Santa Inés Yatzechi Zapotec [zpn]
	Santa María Quiegolani Zapotec [zpi]
	Santiago Xanica Zapotec [zpr]
	Santo Domingo Albarradas Zapotec [zas]
	Sierra de Juárez Zapotec [zaa]
	Southeastern Ixtlán Zapotec [zpd]
	Southern Rincon Zapotec [zsr]
	Tabaa Zapotec [zat]
	Tejalapan Zapotec [ztt]
	Texmelucan Zapotec [zpz]
	Tilquiapan Zapotec [zts]
	Tlacolulita Zapotec [zpk]
	Totomachapan Zapotec [zph]
	Western Tlacolula Valley Zapotec [zab]
	Xadani Zapotec [zax]
	Xanaguía Zapotec [ztg]
	Yalálag Zapotec [zpu]
	Yareni Zapotec [zae]
	Yatee Zapotec [zty]
	Yatzachi Zapotec [zav]
	Yautepec Zapotec [zpb]
	Zaachila Zapotec [ztx]
	Zaniza Zapotec [zpw]
	Zoogocho Zapotec [zpq]
	Chatino, appx. 36,000 speakers in Oaxaca
	Eastern Highland [cly]
	Nopala [cya]
	Tataltepec [cta]
	Western Highland [ctp]
	Zacatepec [ctz]
	Zenzontepec [czn]
Amuzgo	Appx. 52,000 speakers, Costa Chica of Guerrero and Oaxaca
	Guerrero Amuzgo [amu]
	Ipalapa Amuzgo [azm]
	San Pedro Amuzgos Amuzgo [azg]
Mixtecan	Mixtec, appx. 348,000 speakers in Oaxaca, Guerrero, Puebla
	Alacatlatzala Mixtec [mim]
	Alcozauca Mixtec [xta]
	Amoltepec Mixtec [mbz]
	Apasco-Apoala Mixtec [mip]
	Atatlahuca Mixtec [mib]
	Ayutla Mixtec [miy]
	Cacaloxtepec Mixtec [miu]
	Chayuco Mixtec [mih]
	Chazumba Mixtec [xtb]
	Chigmecatitlán Mixtec [mii]
	Coatzospan Mixtec [miz]
	Cuyamecalco Mixtec [xtu]
	Diuxi-Tilantongo Mixtec [xtd]
	Huitepec Mixtec [mxs]
	Itundujia Mixtec [mce]

Subgroup	*Location, Number of Speakers*
	Ixtayutla Mixtec [vmj] Jamiltepec Mixtec [mxt] Juxtlahuaca Mixtec [vmc] Magdalena Peñasco Mixtec [xtm] Metlatónoc Mixtec [mxv] Mitlatongo Mixtec [vmm] Mixtepec Mixtec [mix] Northern Tlaxiaco Mixtec [xtn] Northwest Oaxaca Mixtec [mxa] Ocotepec Mixtec [mie] Peñoles Mixtec [mil] Pinotepa Nacional Mixtec [mio] San Juan Colorado Mixtec [mjc] San Juan Teita Mixtec [xtj] San Miguel el Grande Mixtec [mig] San Miguel Piedras Mixtec [xtp] Santa Lucía Monteverde Mixtec [mdv] Santa María Zacatepec Mixtec [mza] Silacayoapan Mixtec [mks] Sindihui Mixtec [xts] Sinicahua Mixtec [xti] Southeastern Nochixtlán Mixtec [mxy] Southern Puebla Mixtec [mit] Southwestern Tlaxiaco Mixtec [meh] Soyaltepec Mixtec [vmq] Tacahua Mixtec [xtt] Tamazola Mixtec [vmx] Tezoatlán Mixtec [mxb] Tidaá Mixtec [mtx] Tijaltepec Mixtec [xtl] Tlazoyaltepec Mixtec [mqh] Tututepec Mixtec [mtu] Western Juxtlahuaca Mixtec [jmx] Yoloxóchitl Mixtec [xty] Yosondúa Mixtec [mpm] Yucuañe Mixtec [mvg] Yutanduchi Mixtec [mab]
	Cuicatec, appx. 10,000 speakers in the district of Cuicatlán, Oaxaca Tepeuxila Cuicatec [cux] Teutila Cuicatec [cut]
	Triqui (Trique), appx. 31,000 speakers, Oaxaca Chicahuaxtla Triqui [trs] Copala Triqui [trc] San Martín Itunyoso Triqui [trq]
Popolocan	Ixcatec [ixc], a few speakers in Oaxaca
	Popoloca (Ngiwa, Ngigua), appx. 26,000 speakers in Puebla and Oaxaca Coyotepec Popoloca [pbf] Mezontla Popoloca [pbe] San Felipe Otlaltepec Popoloca[pow] San Juan Atzingo Popoloca [poe]

(Continued)

Table 15.2 (Continued)

Subgroup	*Location, Number of Speakers*
	San Luís Temalacayuca Popoloca [pps] San Marcos Tlacoyalco Popoloca [pls] Santa Inés Ahuatempan Popoloca [pca]
	Chocholtec (Chocho, Ngiwa, Ngigua) [coz], 500 speakers, Oaxaca
	Mazatec, appx. 195,000 speakers, Oaxaca, Puebla, and Veracruz Ayautla Mazatec [vmy] Chiquihuitlán Mazatec [maq] Huautla Mazatec [mau] Ixcatlán Mazatec [mzi] Jalapa de Díaz Mazatec [maj] Mazatlán Mazatec [vmz] Puebla and Northeastern Mazatec [pbm] San Jerónimo Tecóatl Mazatec [maa] Soyaltepec Mazatec [vmp]

languages often target the local dialect level: for example, there are many ways to say 'Zapotec' in Zapotec language varieties that all are classified as [zab], Western Tlacolula Valley Zapotec. The ISO codes presented here come from the *Ethnologue* (Simons & Fennig 2018), as are the data for location and number of speakers, unless otherwise indicated. A dagger preceding a language name indicates that that variety is no longer spoken.

Readers should be aware that there is even greater diversity than Table 15.2 might suggest. The level of dialect diversity within what is called a language can be significant; for example, in Western Tlacolula Valley Zapotec [zab], there is micro-diversity of language on a local level where almost every pueblo has a different variety of the language. (The Spanish word *dialecto* has a strongly pejorative meaning, referring to something less than a full or "real" language. When talking about linguistic diversity at this level, it may be prudent to use a different word.) Grammatical differences within what has been designated a language may include differences in pronoun systems, tense/aspect systems, and tone systems. Local varieties of languages are often referenced with the name of the pueblo; for example, San Lucas Quiaviní Zapotec and Teotitlán del Valle Zapotec are both varieties of Western Tlacolula Valley Zapotec [zab] spoken in San Lucas Quiaviní and Teotitlán del Valle, respectively. Because there may be more than one pueblo with the same name, knowing the district is often necessary in determining a location.

2. Phonological Characteristics

2.1. Proto-Otomanguean

Proto-Otomanguean had the following consonant inventory (Table 15.3) according to Kaufman (2006: 821) referencing his unpublished 1988 manuscript.

Table 15.3 Proto-Otomanguean Consonant Inventory

Plosive	p		t		k	kʷ	ʔ
Affricate			ts				
Fricative		θ	s		x	xʷ	h
Lateral			l				
Nasal	m		n				
Glide	w			j			

Source: Kaufman (1988; 2006: 821).

Rensch's (1977) reconstruction of proto-Otomanguean consonants differs in important ways from that of Kaufman. Rensch reconstructs no bilabials, no lateral, and only [s] and [h] as fricatives (p. 68). Kaufman himself notes that "[t]here is little evidence for reconstructing *p, but it seems required for the protolanguage" and "[t]he evidence for *m is better than for *p, but many O[to] M[anguean] languages lack /m/ as a phoneme" (2006: 821).

Kaufman reconstructs the four vowels /i e a u/ and five diphthongs (2006: 821). He posits that proto-Otomanguean had three level tones and may have had a rising and falling tone as well (2006: 821). Rensch, on the other hand, reconstructs four tones for proto-Otomanguean (1977: 68).

Proto-Otomanguean roots are mostly disyllabic roots of the shape CVCV (Kaufman & Justeson 2009: 227). Syllable codas are extremely limited, consisting perhaps of only /n/, /ʔ/, /h/, /nh/, /nʔ/, and /nhʔ/ (Kaufman 2006: 821). There were significantly more options for syllable onsets in proto-Otomanguean, including complex onsets. Kaufman (2006: 821) reconstructs the maximal onset as having four consonants, subject to strict phonotactic constraints.

2.2. Modern Otomanguean Languages

All major branches of Otomanguean have undergone significant phonological changes since proto-Otomanguean. Here, the diversity of the family makes phonological generalizations difficult, but some observations are made in this section.

2.2.1. The Syllable

One such area of change in the phonology of Otomanguean languages since proto-Otomanguean is that of the syllable. While proto-Otomanguean syllables were of the shape CV, there is significant diversity in syllable type for modern Otomanguean languages. Based on their survey of 94 Otomanguean languages, DiCanio and Bennett report that 35% allow only open syllables and 23% allow only a glottal consonant in the coda, leaving a sizable number that permit other coda types (2018: 7). Complex onsets are also now permissible in many Otomanguean languages. For example, while generally syllables are of the shape CV in San Ildefonso Tultepec Otomí [otq], the maximal syllable is CCVCC (Palancar 2009: 11). Considering the status of glottal stop and glides may be important in understanding the syllable, as shown in Marlett and Pickett (1987) for Isthmus Zapotec.

2.2.2. Tone and Phonation

All Otomanguean languages have tone contrasts (DiCanio & Bennett 2018: 2). Most morphemes in Otomanguean languages are specified for tone, and lexical tone has a high functional load (2018: 8). DiCanio and Bennett present an extensive examination of the tone systems in Otomanguean languages based on a survey of all extant phonological literature for Otomanguean languages. They show that about half of Otomanguean languages have small tonal inventories of two or three tonal contrasts and 19% have large inventories utilizing six or more tonal contrasts, with the remaining languages falling somewhere in between (2018: 2). Inventories often also contain contour tones, some derived from sequences of tones within a syllable but others being non-compositional (2018: 3). Examples from each of the four branches of Otomanguean are given as follows.

San Ildefonso Tultepec Otomí (Oto-Pamean-Chinantec) is a language with a small tonal inventory, having three contrastive tones: low, high, and rising. Minimal pairs showing these contrasts are presented in (1).

(1) San Ildefonso Tultepec Otomí [otq]

a.	High tone	*yá* 'already'	*ká* 'in'
b.	Rising tone	*yǎ* 'liver'	*kǎ* 'crow'
c.	High tone	*yó* 'dog'	

d.	Low tone	*yò* 'walk'
e.	Low tone	*pìdi* 'scare'
f.	Rising tone	*pǐdi* 'be thick'

(Palancar 2009: 38)

Acatepec Mè'phàà (Mè'phàà-Subtiaba) also has three tones, in this case all level: low, mid, and high, which are shown in the final syllable in the words in (2).

(2) Acatepec Mè'phàà [tpx]

a.	*mugù*	'lamb'
b.	*guma*	'tortilla'
c.	*dutá*	'coal'

(Cline 2013: 14)

Cline posits that all nine logically possible combinations of tone occur underlyingly in CVCV nouns. However, some of these patterns do not surface phonetically, such as HL, which never surfaces in monomorphic noun roots, though there is evidence it is the underlying tone pattern in some roots, such as 'hill' in (3), where it surfaces as HH.

(3) Acatepec Mè'phàà [tpx]

a.	LL	*sìnù*	'grinding stone'
b.	ML	*mugù*	'lamb'
c.	HL	*kúbá*	'hill' (HL posited to be underlying)
d.	LM	*dùsi*	'bird (sp.)'
e.	MM	*guma*	'tortilla'
f.	HM	*tʃáda*	'sandal'
g.	LH	*dùbú*	'chayote'
h.	MH	*dutá*	'coal'
i.	HH	*gúmá*	'string'

(Cline 2013: 14)

DiCanio et al. (2014: 204) posit four level contrasting tones for Yoloxóchitl Mixtec (Amuzgo-Mixtecan), with 20 possible surface tonal melodies occurring on monosyllabic words, as shown in (4), where 1 marks the lowest tone level and 5 the highest.

(4) Yoloxóchitl Mixtec [xty]

a.	11	*nda*^{1}*a*^{1}	'flat'
b.	13	*ta*^{1}*a*^{3}	'man'
c.	14	*ndo*^{1}*o*^{4}	'sugarcane'
d.	132	*kwe*^{13}*e*^{2}	'linger'
e.	133	*nda*^{13}*a*^{3}	'went up'
f.	134	*tu*^{13}*u*^{4}	'stripped'
g.	1414	*kwi*^{14}*i*^{14}	'is not peeling'
h.	142	*ndi*^{14}*i*^{2}	'pink'
i.	143	*ʃa*^{14}*a*^{3}	'new'
j.	1413	*ndo*^{14}*o*^{13}	'to not stay'
k.	1424	*ka*^{14}*a*^{24}	'does not slip'
l.	32	*nda*^{3}*a*^{2}	'sloping'

m. 33 *ʃa*^{3}*a*^{3} 'fast'
n. 34 *nde*^{3}*e*^{4} 'strong'
o. 342 *ɲũ*^{3}*ũ*^{42} 'night'
p. 414 *kwi*^{4}*i*^{14} 'is peeling'
q. 42 *nda*^{4}*a*^{2} 'where'
r. 44 *nda*^{4}*a*^{4} 'black'
s. 413 *nde*^{4}*e*^{13} 'they enter'
t. 424 *ka*^{4}*a*^{24} 'slips'

(DiCanio et al. 2014: 204)

Chicahuaxtla Triqui has five tone levels, four of which are realized in level tones. All five tone levels are at play in the plethora of contour tones (Elliot 2017). Example (5) illustrates the 15 possible tone contrasts in V: final words.

(5) Chicahuaxtla Triqui [trs]

a. 4 *na:*^{4} 'long ago'
b. 3 *ruʔmã:*^{3} 'hole'
c. 2 *ni:*^{2} 'and'
d. 1 *w:i:*^{1} 'hidden'
e. 53 *joʔo:*^{53} 'dirt'
f. 45 *at͡ʃi:*^{45} 'ask'
g. 43 *ruwa:*^{43} 'inside'
h. 32 *t̪o:*^{32} 'feather'
i. 31 *g*^{w}*i:*^{31} 'people'
j. 23 *n̪d̪a:*^{23} 'until'
k. 21 *nane:*^{21} 'wind'
l. 13 *gat͡si:*^{13} 'white'
m. 353 *w:e:*^{353} 'palm mat'
n. 323 *n:e:*^{323} 'water'
o. 313 *m:ĩ:*^{313} 'bridge'

(Elliot 2017: Table 15.4)

Amuzgo languages have eight contrasting lexical tones, illustrated in the minimal set in (6) from Kim (2016: 202) (1 represents a low tone and 5 a high tone).

(6) San Pedro Amuzgos Amuzgo [azg]

a. ŋ̊ɛ^{5} 'dust'
b. ŋ̊ɛ^{3} 'cheap'
c. ŋ̊ɛ^{34} 'shudder (CPL 3SG)'
d. ŋ̊ɛ^{1} 'grass'
e. ŋ̊ɛ^{12} 'vegetarian'
f. ŋ̊ɛ^{35} 'ripe'
g. ŋ̊ɛ^{53} 'sell (CPL 3SG)'
h. ŋ̊ɛ^{31} 'already'

(Kim 2016: 202)

Otomanguean languages may utilize phonation contrasts in vowels (creaky voice, breathy voice, etc.). Many languages allow both tone and phonation contrasts on vowel, which Silverman refers to as "laryngeally complex" (1997b: 236). Jalapa Mazatec has contrasts between three phonation types as well as between three tones, though there are constraints on which phonation types and tones can co-occur (Garellek & Keating 2011: 186).

The interaction between tone and phonation is a source of debate in some languages, such as for San Lucas Quiaviní Zapotec (Popolocan-Zapotecan). Munro et al. (2007, Vol 1: 53) demonstrate that there are 19 different contrasts that occur on the "key syllable"; these contrasts are analyzed as being phonation contrasts which have corresponding tonal melodies (Munro et al. 1999: 3). Examples of these contrasts are shown in (7), in the practical orthography. The tone melody indicated in the first column applies to the last (or only) syllable in the word provided. Multiple phonation contrasts can occur in a vowel complex: unmarked vowels indicate a modal voice and a grave accent indicates creaky voice. An apostrophe following a vowel marks that the vowel is checked; an <h> following a vowel indicates breathy voice.

(7) San Lucas Quiaviní Zapotec [zab]

a.	High tone	*ri'cy*	'there'
b.	High tone	*wii*	'guava'
c.	High tone	*badiia*	'roadrunner'
d.	Low tone	*zhih*	'day'
e.	Low tone	*bihih*	'air'
f.	Low tone	*rguìiny*	'hit'
g.	Rising tone	*gui'izh*	'city person'
h.	Rising tone	*chi'iinnzh*	'bed bug'
i.	Rising tone	*nnàaan*	'mother'
j.	Falling tone	*zhi'ih*	'nose'
k.	Falling tone	*gahllgui'ihihzh*	'sickness'
l.	Falling tone	*dìi'zh*	'language'
m.	Falling tone	*dàa'ah*	'petate'
n.	Falling tone	*mnìi'iny*	'child'
o.	Falling tone	*garzììi'*	'guts'
p.	Falling tone	*àaa'*	'yes'
q.	Falling tone	*baahlly*	'fire, flame'
r.	Falling tone	*bax:aa't*	'toad'
s.	Falling tone	*bàa'ah*	'earlier today'
t.	Falling tone	*yaàa'*	'up'

(Munro et al. 2007, Vol 1: 53)

While Munro and Lopez et al. (1999) analyze tone as predictable from (the sequence of) phonation type in a vowel (complex), Chávez Peón argues against this, positing that the language does in fact have independent tone and phonation contrasts (2010).

2.2.3. Tonal Morphology

Otomanguean languages exhibit tonal morphology, including morphemes that consist of floating tones associated with segmental material and morphemes that consist of only tonal material. For example, in Southeastern Nochixtlán Mixtec [mxy], the imperfective is marked with a prefix that is a floating high tone (McKendry 2013: 205). Throughout Mixtec languages, according to Palancar et al. (2016: 295), it is "common for tone alone to distinguish the irrealis and the incompletive". In Talapa Otomi [otl], a floating high tone is involved in the marking of the incompletive for some persons (Palancar 2018: 111).

In Sierra Juárez Zapotec, the first person marker triggers local and nonlocal tone changes in a verb (Bickmore & Broadwell 1998: 37), as shown in (8); note that in (8b) and (8d) – the first-person forms – there is an additional high tone near the beginning of the word (1998: 38), due to a floating high tone associated with the first-person marker (Bickmore & Broadwell 1998: 42).

(8) Sierra Juarez Zapotec [zaa]

a.	*gú-xuʔnì-luʔ*	'You will wrinkle.'
	POT-wrinkle-2	(cited from Nellis & Nellis 1983: 110)
b.	*gú-xúʔnì-ʔàʔ*	'I will wrinkle.'
	POT-wrinkle-1	(cited from Nellis & Nellis 1983: 110)
c.	*ru-lábàʔ-luʔ*	'You count.'
	HAB-count-2	(cited from Marks 1976: 78)
d.	*rú-lábàʔ-àʔ*	'I count.'
	HAB-count-1	(cited from Marks 1976: 78)

(Bickmore & Broadwell 1998: 38)

2.2.4. Tone Sandhi

Tone sandhi is an important phonological phenomenon, especially in Eastern Otomanguean, though it is also found in Western Otomanguean languages such as Chinantec (Oto-Pamean-Chinantec). The data in (9) demonstrate this, showing that the underlying low tone in 'chayote' is realized as a high tone when following a rising tone in 'give a chayote'. Likewise, the underlying mid tone in 'money' becomes a high fall (from high to mid) when following a rising tone in 'give money'.

(9) Comaltepec Chinantec [cco]

a. /kwǎ ŋɨ̀h/ → [kwǎ ŋɨ́h] 'give a chayote'
b. /kwǎ ku/ → [kwǎ kû] 'give money'

(Silverman 1997a: 474)

Hollenbach provides the following data, which exemplify the only type of productive tone sandhi process in Copala Triqui: morphologically triggered tone replacement (1984: 266). As she explains, the triggering morphemes are a group of non-third-person pronouns, including the second singular pronoun *zoʔ*^{1}. She demonstrates that when a word of a certain tone pattern is immediately followed by one of these pronouns, the tone of that word is raised, as shown for the words 'come', 'black', and 'quickly' in the bolded forms in (10).[3]

(10) Copala Triqui [trc]

a.	*ʔnaʔ*^{3}	*zoʔ*^{3}	*a*^{32}		'He comes.'
	comes	3SGM	DECL		
b.	***ʔnaʔ***^{4}	*zoʔ*^{1}	*a*^{32}		'You come.'
	comes	2SG	DECL		
c.	*kunu*^{3}	*maru*^{31}	*zoʔ*^{3}	*a*^{32}	'He turned black.'
	became	black	3SGM	DECL	
d.	*kunu*^{3}	***maru***^{4}	*zoʔ*^{1}	*a*^{32}	'You turned black.'
	became	black	2SG	DECL	
e.	*če*^{5}	*yo*^{13}	*zoʔ*^{3}	*a*^{32}	'He walks quickly.'
	walks	quickly	3SGM	DECL	
f.	*če*^{5}	***yo***^{4}	*zoʔ*^{1}	*a*^{32}	'You walk quickly.'
	walks	quickly	2SG	DECL	

(Hollenbach 1984: 267)

2.2.5. Stress

Many Otomanguean languages have stress (DiCanio & Bennett 2018: 3), which is usually fixed to one of the syllables of the root or stem (2018: 4). The DiCanio and Bennett survey found that 70 of the 94 Otomanguean languages considered had a description of stress. Stress and tone may interact in that more contrasts may be available on stressed syllables. This is true for San Lucas Quiaviní Zapotec; the 20 possible phonation contrasts shown in (7) are possible on the key – or stressed – syllable. DiCanio and Bennett report that for the Otomanguean languages in which the phonetic correlates of stress have been studied, which are few, "the main correlate of stress is acoustic duration" (2018: 5), but given the paucity of work in this area, it remains an open question. A non-trivial number of Otomanguean languages (11 out of 94 in DiCanio & Bennett's 2018 survey) have a ballistic/controlled stress distinction, including Comaltepec Chinantec (Silverman 1997b: 239) and other Chinantec languages (DiCanio & Bennett 2018: 5). For more on "ballistic" stress, see Merrifield (1963), Mugele (1982), and DiCanio and Bennett (2018: 5–6).

3. Morphosyntax Characteristics

Otomanguean languages tend to be VSO (§3.1), head-initial, and head-marking. The following orders tend to be observed: adjectives, demonstratives, and relative clauses follow nouns. The possessum precedes the possessor, and a class of nouns (including body parts and some kinship terms) are inalienably possessed (§3.2). Quantifiers precede nouns; the languages have prepositions. Locatives are based on body part terms (§3.3). Lexically, compounding is robust (§3.4) and some languages have productive classifiers (§3.5). Most languages have a base-20 numerical system (§3.6). Verbal inflection is discussed in §3.7.

3.1. Word Order: VSO and Preverbal Focus

Otomanguean languages tend to be VSO, though there are exceptions to this. A verb-initial word order is consistent with the larger areal tendency of Mesoamerican languages to have word orders that are not verb final (Campbell et al. 1986: 547). As would be typologically expected, Otomanguean languages are also more generally head-initial. Exceptions from the more common basic word order of VSO include Otomi, some varieties of Chinantec, and Mazatec.

Comaltepec Chinantec (Chinantec) has a basic word order of VSO, as illustrated in (11), as does San Pedro Amuzgos Amuzgo (Amuzgo), as shown in (12).

(11) Comaltepec Chinantec [cco][4]

V	S	O	
ka^{L}*-kuë̋:n*^{L}	*huan*	*ha:n*^{L}	*kuä*^{LH}
PST-give^C3	John	one	horse

'John gave a horse.'

(Anderson 1989: 36)

(12) San Pedro Amuzgos Amuzgo [azg]

V	S	O
Tuan	*xjöhö'*	*ndiaaso*
washed	sister.my	blanket

'My sister washed the blanket.'

(Buck 2000: 468)

In many Otomanguean languages, arguments and other constituents can appear in preverbal position, usually with a focus reading. This is the case for Azoyú Me'phaa [tpc] (Mè'phàà-Subtiaba), as Wichmann attests: "Tlapanec exhibits a VAO basic word order with the possibility of fronting A or O in a topicalization construction" (2009: 797).

Concepción Pápalo Cuicatec, a variety of Tepeuxila Cuicatec (Mixtecan), also exhibits this pattern. It has a basic word order of VSO (Bradley 1991: 420), as seen in (13). In (13), 'two lions' is focused and appears preverbally; a resumptive pronoun (S(pro)) appears in the prototypical subject position.

(13) Tepeuxila Cuicatec [cux]

	V	S	O		
a.	*xēhē*	*túhú*	*nīnū*		
	CON:eat	chicken	corn		
	'The chicken is eating the corn.'				
	S		V	S (pro)	O
b.	*ūvī*	*īyháyan*	*chīnúū*	*ti*	*īkyahan*
	two	lion	COM:walk	it:AML	forest
	'Two lions were walking in the forest.'				

(Bradley 1991: 420–421)

The examples in (14) exhibit the same pattern in another Mixtecan language, Alacatlatzala Mixtec. The basic word order is VSO (Zylstra 1991: 10), and there is a preverbal focus position. Zylstra notes that "[w]hen the subject is focused, a clitic pronoun copy may also occur in normal subject position following the verb" (Zylstra 1991: 24–25), as we saw above in the Cuicatec example. In (14), the object is focused preverbally, and no such resumptive pronoun occurs.

(14) Alacatlatzala Mixtec [mim]

a.	V	S	O
	kanī	*rā*	*rí*
	COM:hit	he	it:AML
	'He hit the animal.'		
b.	O	V	S
	tīton	*ndísō*	*i*
	firewood	CON:carry.on.back	I
	'I'm carrying firewood (on my back).'		

(Zylstra 1991: 11, 25)

DiCanio et al. (2018: 1) describe how words produced with contrastive focus in Yoloxóchitl Mixtec exhibit a raised pitch and an expanded tonal range.

Broadwell shows that San Dionisio Ocotepec Zapotec (Zapotecan) has a basic word order of VSO, as shown in (15). He states that "any NP or PP may appear in [Spec, CP] when it bears a special discourse function such as contrastive focus or topic" (Broadwell 2001: 3), as seen in (15b) with the preverbal subject 'Juan', in (15c) with a preverbal object 'dog', and in (15d) with the preverbal prepositional phrase adjunct 'with a stick'.

(15) San Dionisio Ocotepec Zapotec [ztu]

	V	S	O			
a.	*Ù-dííny*	*Juààny*	*bèh'cw*	*re'*	*cùn*	*yààg.*
	COM-hit	Juan	dog	that	with	stick
	'Juan hit that dog with a stick.'					

b. *Juáàny* *ù-dííny* *bèh'cw* *cùn* *yààg.*
Juan COM-hit dog with stick
'Juan (TOPIC/FOCUS) hit the dog with a stick.'

c. *Bèh'cw* *ù-dííny* *Juààny* *cùn* *yààg.*
dog COM-hit Juan with stick
'Juan hit the dog (TOPIC/FOCUS) with a stick.'

d. *Cùn* *yààg* *ù-dìny* *Juààny* *bèh'cw.*
with stick COM-hit Juan dog
'Juan hit the dog with a stick (TOPIC/FOCUS).'

(Broadwell 2001: 3–4)

In San Marcos Tlacoyalco Popoloca (Popolocan), the basic word order is VSO, as seen in (16). Stark and Luna Villanueva (2011) explain that subjects of adverbs can appear preverbally, and when they do so, the preverbal element is focused, as in (16).

(16) San Marcos Tlacoyalco Popoloca [pls]

V S O

a. *Anto* *rinao* *José* *ndaxra* *ngataon* *jngui* *jai.*
a.lot want Jose food in field today
'Jose really wants to eat [his] food in the field today.'
(Stark & Luna Villanueva 2011: 16)

b. *José* *anto* *rinao* *ndaxra* *ngataon* *jngui* *jai.*
Jose a.lot want food in field today
'<u>Jose</u> really wants to eat [his] food in the field today.'

(Stark & Luna Villanueva 2011: 17)

In Chiquihuitlán Mazatec, another Popolocan language, the preverbal focused element is "almost always" followed by the morpheme *ne*, which, according to Jamieson (1988: 18), marks the focused order, and which she glosses with a comma in (17).

(17) Chiquihuitlán Mazatec [maq]

Yujme *ne,* *cafehe* *ndetsin.*
corn , 3.arrived market
'The corn arrived at the market.'

(Jamieson 1988: 18)

3.2. Word Order: Possessed NPs

In most Otomanguean languages the possessum precedes the possessor in a possessed noun phrase, which is an areal feature of Mesoamerican languages more generally (Campbell et al. 1986: 545). Moreover, Otomanguean languages show differences in how kinship and body part terms are possessed: often these terms cannot occur without an overt possessor and employ different morphological patterns of possession. This, too, is an areal feature of Mesoamerican languages (Campbell et al. 1986: 549). The kinship and body part nouns that cannot occur without an overt possessor are usually referred to as *inalienable*.

Foreman (2006) demonstrates the difference between inalienable and alienable possession in San Pablo Macuiltianguis Zapotec. As shown in (18a)–(18c), when a noun is inalienable, it is possessed through juxtaposition with the possessor, which immediately follows the possessum, whether than possessor is a NP or a prounoun. When the possessum is alienable, the possessor is preceded by the preposition *què'* 'of' as seen in (18d)–(18f).

(18) San Pablo Macuiltianguis Zapotec [zaa]

	possessum	*possessor*		*[inalienable]*
a.	*ìcchá*	*béccú' =ni*		
	head	dog=PROX		
	'this dog's head'			
b.	*ca xiila*	*Margarita=ni*		
	PL woman's.sister	Margarita=PROX		
	'Margarita's sisters'			
c.	*ca xiila*	*=ya'*		
	PL woman's.sister	=1SG		
	'my sisters'			
	possessum	*què'*	*possessor*	*[alienable]*
d.	*ca béccú' síttsì'*	*què'*	*Felipe=à'*	
	PL dog white	of	Felipe=DIST	
	'Felipe's white dogs'			
e.	*bèyùú'*	*què'*	*Pánfila=ni*	
	man	of	Pánfila=PROX	
	'Pánfila's husband'			
f.	*ca bèyùú'*	*què'*	*=ca=yé=á*	
	PL man	of	=PL=3FG=INVIS	
	'their husbands'			

(Foreman 2006: 212–213)

3.3. Body Part Locatives

Locative relations in Otomanguean languages are expressed through body part locatives, also called "relational nouns". These lexical items are related to nouns for body part words either synchronically or historically and are used to express locative relations. In some languages, such body part locatives may be grammaticized as prepositions. Campbell et al. (1986: 545, 549) list relational nouns as an areal feature shared by nearly all Mesoamerican languages. There is some disagreement as to the grammatical category of body part locatives in particular languages and subgroups, though it is not always clear if these different analyses are due to differences in the morphosyntactic facts, differences in the criteria of categorization (e.g., Lillehaugen & Sonnenschein 2012a; 2012b: 6–9), or in other complicating factors.

Comaltepec Chinantec (Chinantec) also has "a small subset of inalienable nouns . . . which function like locative prepositions" (Anderson 1989: 103). 'Face' is one of these body part locatives, as seen in (19), where it is used as a locative meaning 'on'. This and seven other body part locatives are listed in (19) with their referential and locative meanings.

(19) Comaltepec Chinantec [cco]

a.	*gia^{M}a*	*ni^{LH}*	*mes^{LH}*
	put^P1S	face^3	table
	'I put them on top of the table.'		

(Anderson 1989: 103)

		Referential Meaning	*Locative Meaning*
b.	*ni^{LH}*	'face of'	'on top of'
c.	*tï:^{M}*	'lower leg of'	'at the foot of'
d.	*zí^{LM}*	'heart of'	'inside of'
e.	*ʔo:^{M}*	'mouth of'	'at the mouth of'

f.	*ki*^{L}*ni*^{HM}	'space before'	'in front of'
g.	*ka*^{L}*lú:*^{HM}	'space behind'	'behind, outside of'
h.	*mo*^{L}*gi*^{LH}	'head of'	'at the head of'
i.	*mo*^{L}*koʔ*^{LH}	'back of'	'on the back of'

Buck (2000) provides nearly 20 examples of body part locatives in San Pedro Amuzgos Amuzgo (Amuzgo), some of which are listed in (20). She classifies these as prepositions with nominal origins; additional meanings of these prepositions are demonstrated in Buck (2000), though even in these examples the reader gets a sense of the broad range of meaning of some of these lexical items.

(20) San Pedro Amuzgos Amuzgo [azg]

	Prepositional Phrase (preposition in bold)	*Gloss*	*Nominal Source of Preposition*
a.	***'ndyo** jndaaha'*	'at the edge of the river'	mouth
b.	***naxen'** v'aa*	'behind the house'	back
c.	***ndëë** librohin'*	'in the books'	face (pl.)
e.	***ngiaa'** tsjö'hö'*	'beside the rock'	side
f.	***ngiaa'** tioon'juuhö'*	'behind his corral'	side
g.	***ng'ee** ncüii tyo't'man*	'at the foot of a large hill'	foot
h.	***nnon** tsonmësaha'*	'on the table'	face
i.	***nnon** tyjöhö'*	'to my little brother'	face
j.	***quii'tsiaa'** jnduuhu'*	'under the bed'	belly
k.	***ts'on** natöhö'*	'on the road'	heart
l.	***xquen** v'aaha'*	'above the house'	head
m.	***xquen** tyo'va'*	'at the top of that mountain'	head

(Buck 2000: 468)

Likewise, Hollenbach analyzes body part locatives in eight Mixtec languages as grammatical prepositions (1995: 173). She also lays out clear paths of semantic change through metaphor and metonymy that account not only for the Mixtec languages she considers, but likely for the more general Otomanguean pattern. Hollenbach (1995) discusses these examples from Shields (1988) showing semantically extended uses of *sàʔà* 'foot' in Silacayoapan Mixtec, including as a locative in (21).

(21) Silacayoapan Mixtec [mks]

a.	*na*	*čindúhu*	*ñá*	*xáhma*	*saha*	*yíto*
	COM	COM:put:down	she	cloth	foot	tree

'She put the cloth at the foot of the tree.'

b.	*kándúhu*	*na*	*saha*	*yíto*
	CON:be:lying	they	foot	tree

'They are lying down at the foot of the tree.'

c.	*sákū*	*nā*	*saha*	*ndiī*
	CON:cry	they	foot	dead:person

'They are crying on behalf of the dead person.'

d.	*ndítúhún*	*nde*	*saha*	*ñūū*	*nde*
	CON:discuss	we:EX	foot	town	our:EX

'We are talking about our town.'

(Shields 1988: 317–318)

3.4. Compounding

Otomanguean languages tend to make use of compounding as a strategy in word formation. Compounds are head-initial and often lexicalized, as can be seen in the following examples from Chiquihuitlán Mazatec (Popolocan). For example, (22) is not just any wooden house, but is lexicalized to mean 'jail'. Regarding compound in Chiquihuitlán Mazatec, Jamieson points out, "When two words are joined in this way, they form a compound noun that has a specific meaning, which isn't always evident based on the meaning of the component words" (1988: 31).

(22) Chiquihuitlán Mazatec [maq]

a.	*ndava-ya*	house-wood	'jail'
b.	*chuxin-xtë*	skin-garbage	'huarache (sandals)'
c.	*naxa-haxi*	salt-sweet	'sugar'
d.	*nachja-hani*	banana-red	'mamey'
e.	*nachja-tsjen*	banana-honey	'chicozapote (sapodilla)'

(Jamieson 1988: 31)

Such compounding processes may result in phonological changes including tone changes. Alexander (1980) points out a range of phonological changes that take place in noun-noun compounds in Atatlahuca Mixtec, including regular tone changes and irregular tone changes, some of which may vary on a speaker-to-speaker level (1980: 53). The first noun in the compound may also be shortened, seen in (23).

(23) Atatlahuca Mixtec [mib]

a.	*yɨquɨ yúhu* 'lower jaw bone'	*yɨquɨ* 'bone' + *yuhu* 'mouth'
b.	*ndūyu cāa* 'nail'	*ndūyu* 'pointed stick' + *cāa* 'metal'
c.	*vecāa* 'jail'	*vehe* 'house' + *cāa* 'metal'

(Alexander 1980: 53)

Otomanguean verbs can be formed with a verbal root followed by a nominal root, particularly body parts. Body part incorporation in verbs is "widely attested" in Otomanguean (Kaufman 2006: 822) and is considered a general feature of Mesoamerican languages (Campbell et al. 1986: 551). What follows are examples from Atatlahuca Mixtec (Mixtecan), Miahuatec (Zapotecan), and Coatec (Zapotecan). In the verb 'will push' in Atatlahuaca (24), note that the tone for 'hand' changes when it is part of the verb 'will push'. Beam de Azcona (2017) gives examples of incorporation in two Southern Zapotec languages. In the Miahuatec example (25) 'mud' is incorporated into the verb 'become', yielding a very 'become muddy'. 'Thought' is incorporated into the verb 'do' resulting in the verb 'think', in the Coatec example in (26).

(24) Atatlahuca Mixtec [mib]
chundahá 'will push' (*chuhun* 'will put' + *ndaha* 'hand')

(Alexander 1980: 49)

(25) Miahuatec [zam, zao, ztm, ztp]
ndxáakyop 'become muddy' (*ndxáak* 'become (HAB)' + *yop* 'mud')

(Beam de Azcona 2017: 58)

(26) Coatec [zca, zpo]
ndunbe'y 'think' (*ndun* 'do (HAB)' + *be'y* 'thought')

(Beam de Azcona 2017: 62)

Broadwell notes that in Copala Triqui, there are three different syntactic realizations of what one might call a compound verb, depending on the degree to which the second element (X) forms a constituent with the verb stem. He defines the following types of compound verbs: (i) the incorporation type, where V+X form a single syntactic word; (ii) the adjunction type, where X is adjoined to V to form a larger V; and (iii) a non-constituent type, where V and X do not form a syntactic constituent, but are lexically linked (Broadwell 2014: 11).

3.5. Classifiers

Some Otomanguean languages, including Poplocan, Mixtecan, and Triqui languages (Swadesh 1960: 89), utilize lexical classifiers, which, "in most languages . . . are completely fossilized" (Suárez 1983: 89), though Suárez notes that lexical classifying systems are still "operational in some Mixtec and Chinantec languages" (1983: 89). These classifiers can be realized as free nouns preceding and forming a syntactic unit with the following noun, as in some Mixtecan language. Most typically, lexical classifiers are realized as monosyllabic prefixes, as in Popolocan languages, as exemplified in (27) with just a subset of the classifiers inventoried for Mezontla Popoloca by Veerman-Leichsenring (2004: 416, Table 15.1). (The language is referred to as "Popoloc (Metzontla)" in the original source.)

(27) Mezontla Popoloca [pbe]

classifier — *(related noun)*

a. *ku*^{2}- 'animal, animal-like' (*ku*^{2} 'animal')
exs. *ku-nǯe* 'snake' [nǯe 'soil']
ku^{2}*še*^{3}*Nki* 'whirlwind'

b. *nda*^{3}- 'tree, made of wood' (*nda*^{3} 'tree')
exs. *nda*^{3}*nu*^{2} 'pirul tree'
nda^{3}*thu*^{2} 'gun, rifle'

c. *su*^{3}- 'flower, flower-like' (*chu*^{3} 'flower')
exs. *su*^{3}*čaʔ* 'orchid'
su^{3}*-kha*^{2} 'cock's comb' [*kha*^{2} 'head']

d. *ka*^{3}- 'plant, leaf, vegetal fiber or fiber-like' (*ka*^{3} 'leaf ')
exs. *ka*^{3}*-nǯi*^{3}*a*^{3} 'quelite (kind of herb)' [*nǯi*^{3}*a*^{3} 'house']
ka^{3}*či*^{2}*nga*^{2} 'hat'
ka^{3}*ne*^{3}*ne*^{3} 'wing'

e. *tu*^{3}- 'fruit, spherical' (*tu*^{3} 'fruit')
exs. *tu*^{3}*-sã*^{1} 'orange' [*sã*^{1} 'sour']
tu^{3}*cũ*^{1}*ʔĩ*^{3} 'her breasts'

f. *šu*^{3}- 'stone, stone-like' (*su*^{3}*ʔ* 'stone')
exs. *šu*^{3}*če*^{3}*ʔ* 'grindstone (metate)'
šu^{3}*çi*^{2} 'piece of soap'

g. *nǯe*^{3}- ~ *nǯi*^{3}- 'soil, soil-like' (*nǯe*^{3} 'earth')
exs. *nǯe*^{3}*se*^{3} 'sand'
nǯi^{3}*nda*^{2}*tha*^{2} 'clay'

h. *nda*^{3}*ʔ*- ~ *nda*^{3}- 'liquid' (*nda*^{3}*ʔ* 'water')
exs. *nda*^{3}*-čhĩ*^{3} 'sweat' [čhĩ^{3} 'woman']
nda^{3}*ʔni*^{2}*nǯe*^{3} 'river'
nda^{3}*ʔ-ta*^{3} 'saliva' [*ta*^{3} 'voice']

(Veerman-Leichsenring 2004: 422)

3.6. Vigesimal Numerical Systems

Otomanguean languages have base-20 number systems, a feature which is "pan-Meso-American" (Campbell et al. 1986: 546). Consider the following examples from Chiquihuitlán Mazatec

(Popolocan) in (28) and Colonial Valley Zapotec (Zapotecan) in (29). In both these cases, the numbers 16–19 are built from 15 and the numbers 30 and 50 are built from 20 and 40, respectively.

(28) Chiquihuitlán Mazatec [maq]

a.	*ngu*	1
b.	*jo*	2
c.	*jyan*	3
d.	*ñuju*	4
e.	*hñú*	5
f.	*jyun*	6
g.	*yatu*	7
h.	*jyin*	8
i.	*ñaja*	9
j.	*të*	10
k.	*tyjuhun*	15
l.	*tyjuhunngu*	16 (15+1)
m.	*tyjuhunjo*	17 (15+2)
n.	*tyjuhunjyan*	18 (15+3)
o.	*tyjuhunñuju*	19 (15+4)
p.	*can*	20
q.	*can të*	30 (20+10)
r.	*yachan*	40
s.	*yachan yë*	50 (40+10)

(Jamieson 1988: 67)

Colonial Valley Zapotec is a historical form of modern Tlacolula Valley Zapotec [zab]. The numbers indicated in (29) are just a small portion of the numbers presented in Fray Juan de Cordova's (1578a) grammar of the language. A digital edition with morphological analysis of these and the other numbers presented can be found online (Lillehaugen et al. 2016; https://ticha.haverford.edu/en/texts/cordova-arte/208/original/). In Colonial Valley Zapotec there is a second set of numbers, called the B set, which according to Corodva (1578a: 105v) are used for flat things, like rope and wood. Colonial Valley Zapotec exhibits B set forms for the numbers 1–4, as seen in (29). In most modern Valley Zapotec languages, only the B form for 'one' is still used, and in many cases it is limited to counting tortillas and other breadstuffs, as is the case for San Lucas Quiaviní *chah* 'one (B)' (Munro et al. 1999: 96), though in some varieties the cognate has a slightly broader use and other (flat) things are counted with it, as in San Jerónimo Tlacochahuaya, another Western Tlacolula Valley Zapotec variety. The morpheme *bi-* is used to mean 'and' or 'more' in numbers.

(29) Colonial Valley Zapotec

	Set A		Set B	
a.	*tobi*	1	*chaga*	1(B)
b.	*topa*	2	*cato*	2(B)
c.	*chona*	3	*cayo*	3(B)
d.	*tapa*	4	*taa*	4(B)
e.	*cayo*	5		
f.	*xopa*	6		
g.	*cache*	7		
h.	*xono*	8		
i.	*caa*	9		
j.	*chij*	10		

k.	*chino*	15
l.	*chino-bi-tobi*	16 (15+1)
m.	*chino-bi-topa*	17 (15 + 2)
n.	*chino-bi-chona*	18 (15+3)
o.	*chino-bi-tapa*	19 (15+4)
p.	*calle*	20
q.	*calle-bi-chij*	30 (20+10)
r.	*toua*	40
s.	*toua-bi-chij*	50 (40+10)

(Cordova 1578a: 99r–105r)

In some Otomanguean languages, the modern number system shows influence from Spanish, with some speakers using Spanish borrowings, especially for numbers 15 and higher. For example, in San Lucas Quiaviní Zapotec there are multiple ways to count, with older speakers (around age 55 and older) tending to use the conservative forms and younger speakers (age 55 and younger) tending to use the newer forms borrowed from Spanish. Munro et al. (1999: 67) note that "[s]ome younger speakers use only the first ten native Zap[otec] numbers", counting above ten with numbers borrowed from Spanish. Those ages 30–55 may use a mix of both (Felipe H. Lopez, p.c., 3 February 2018). The newer forms for numbers over ten are presented on the right in (30). Note that *ahb-* is cognate to the Colonial Valley Zapotec *bi-* 'and, more (in numbers)' seen in (29).

(30) San Lucas Quiaviní Zapotec [zab]

a.	*chah*	1B		
b.	*te'ihby*	1		
c.	*tyo'p*	2		
d.	*chòonn*	3		
e.	*tahp*	4		
f.	*gài'*	5		
g.	*x:o'p*	6		
h.	*gàaz*	7		
i.	*x:òon*	8		
j.	*gààa'*	9		
k.	*tsêë'*	10		
l.	*tsèèi'ny*	15	*qui'nseh*	15
m.	*tsèi'ny ahbteeby*	16 (15+1)	*diesiseiz*	16
n.	*tsèi'ny ahbtyo'p*	17 (15+2)	*diesisye't*	17
o.	*tsèi'ny ahbchòonn*	18 (15+3)	*diesyo'ch*	18
p.	*tsèi'ny ahbta'p*	19 (15+4)	*diesinweeb*	19
q.	*gàallyd*	20	*be'enny*	20
r.	*gàally ahbtsêë'*	30 (20+10)	*tre'enny*	30
s.	*tyùùa'*	40	*cware'nn*	40
t.	*tyùa' ahbtsêë*"	50 (40+10)	*sinncwe'nn*	50

(Munro et al. 1999; Munro & Sonnenschein 2007: 3)

3.7. Verbal Inflection

Of the various word classes in Otomanguean languages, verbs are the class that exhibit the most complex morphology. Verbs in Otomanguean tend to be inflected for aspect and mood (rarely, if ever, for tense). Proto-Otomanguean tense/aspect/mood markers have been reconstructed by

Kaufman (1988). These inflections are realized through prefixes, except in Otopamean, which also has suffixes.

In Zenzontepec Chatino a verb minimally consists of a root with aspect/mood inflection, with only a few irregular verbs lacking any overt aspect/mood marking (Campbell 2015: 1396). The verbal template in (31) illustrates the morphology of verbs, which can also optionally exhibit other pre-root morphology such as derivational prefixes (transitivizer/intransitivizer), as well as causative or iterative prefixes (Campbell 2015: 1396).

(31) Zenzontepec Chatino [czn] verbal template
(ASP- AUX)+ ASP- (CAUS/ITER-) (DERV-) root (+stem)* (=ADV)* (=SBJ)
(Campbell 2015: 1396)

In most Otomanguean languages, the valency changing morphology is now mostly unproductive; for examples in Zapotec languages, see chapters in Operstein and Sonnenschein (2015).

Campbell demonstrates the complexity of the aspect/mood prefixes in Zenzontepec Chatino, as shown in Table 15.4. Here we see the forms and allomorphs for the potential (POT), habitual (HAB), progressive (PROG), and completive (CPL) prefixes organized by verb class and subclass.

Otopamean differs from other Otomanguean languages in having more elaborate preverbal inflection, including marking for subject. Acalzulco Otomi even marks "[d]iscourse salient extra-thematic participants" through "(a) cumulative inflectional morphemes that also code TAM and Subject person . . . and (b) consonant and tone mutations in the verb stem" (Hernández-Green 2016: 354).

Tone has a high functional load in verbal inflection in Otomanguean languages (see Palancar 2016). For example, in the verbs in (32) from San Ildefonso Tultepec Otomí, we see that tone (high is marked with an acute accent; low is unmarked) is used to distinguish the incompletive (INCPL) and the irrealis.

(32) San Ildefonso Tultepec Otomí [otq]

a. gí=tso̲t'e
2.INCPL=arrive.there
'You arrive there.'

b. gi=tso̲t'e
2.IRR=arrive.there
'You'll arrive there.'

(Palancar 2016: 113)

In San Pedro Amuzgos Amuzgo [azg], person inflection in intransitive verbs is realized through inflectional aspects as well as "stem alternations in tone, vowel height, and/or glottalization" (Kim 2016: 199).

Table 15.4 Zenzontepec Chatino [czn] Aspect Prefix (Sub-)classes

	CLASS A		*CLASS B*			*CLASS C*	
	Au, Ac	*A2*	*Bc*	*Bt*	*By*	*Ca*	*C2*
POT	*ki-*	*ki-*	*ki-*	*(t → ty)*	*(y → ch)*	*k-*	*k-*
HAB	*nti-*	*nti-*	*nti-*	*n- (t → ty)*	*n- (y → ch)*	*nti-*	*nti-*
PROG	*nte-*	*nte-*	*nte-*	*nte-*	*nte-*	*nch-*	*nch- /ntey-*
CPL	*nka-*	*nkwi-*	*nku-*	*nku-*	*nk(u)-*	*nku-*	*y- /nkay-*

Source: Campbell (2011; 2015: 1397).

4. Major Subgroups and Further Readings

Given the size, time-depth, and diversity of the Otomanguean family, additional characteristics of the grammar of the major subgroups warrant further discussion. Sources providing such discussion are provided here organized by subgroup, beginning with the Western Otomanguean branch (§4.1, Mè'phàà-Subtiaba; §4.2, Chorotegan; §4.3, Otopamean; and §4.4, Chinantecan) and then turning to those of the Eastern Otomanguean branch (§4.5, Mixtecan; §4.6, Amuzgo; §4.7, Zapotecan; and §4.8, Popolocan). I do not repeat references on reconstructions, which are listed in Table 15.1. Historical sources are listed in §5.

4.1. Mè'phàà-Subtiaba

The Mè'phàà-Subtiaba subgroup, also referred to as Tlapanecan, has a time depth of approximately 800 years (Kaufman 2006: 819). There has been some debate as to the classification of languages in this subgroup. Rensch (1976; 1977) demonstrated that Mè'phàà and Subtiaba were Otomanguean. Previous discussions of possible classifications included possible inclusion in Hokan-Coahuiltecan (Sapir 1925) and Macro-Mixtecan (Swadesh 1960: 85), among others. For more on the history of the classification of Mè'phàà-Subtiaba see Campbell (2017b: 3).

4.2. Chorotegan

All Chorotegan language varieties are currently dormant, having no current native speakers. A grammatical sketch of Chiapanec exists (Albornoz 1875), but beyond this, little morphosyntactic information is available. Kaufman puts the time depth of this subgroup at 1,300 years (Kaufman 2006: 819). Tone contrasts in Chorotegan languages may have been eliminated or reduced to a two-way contrast (Kaufman 2006: 823).

4.3. Otopamean

It is not possible to treat the Otopamean subgroup with the detail it deserves in this space. I refer the interested reader to the following sources and provide a few notes here: Bartholomew (1959; 1960); Palancar (2004; 2009; 2018); Perez (2007); Wichmann (2009); and Hernández-Green (2015; 2016).

Otopamean, which has a time depth of approximately 3,600 years (Kaufman 2006: 819) is atypical within the Otomanguean family in a number of ways. Spoken in Central Mexico, it is geographically separate from most Otomanguean languages, defining the northernmost border of the family (Palancar 2018: 98). According to Palancar (2018: 98), Otopamean contains one of the most, if not the most, endangered Otomanguean language variety, namely Tilapa Otomí. The Otopamean subgroup is linguistically divergent as well, including phonologically and morphosyntactically; for example, Otopamean is notable for having a large consonant inventory for an Otomanguean language, as well as for having monosyllabic morphemes (Kaufman 2006: 821) and smaller tonal inventories, as exemplified earlier in (1). Campbell et al. mention that "Some sort of vowel harmony occurs in Mazahua (Amador 1976) and Tlapanec" (1986: 543).

While most Otomanguean languages exhibit a basic word order of VSO (§3.1), Otopamean languages tend not to. For example, Chichimeco Jonaz, spoken in Guanajuato – outside of Mesoamerica – has a basic word order of SOV (Campbell et al. 1986: 548). In Otomí languages, the conservative varieties are verb-initial (Palancar 2018: 105), with VOS being the most common. Northern Otomí languages have become SVO (Palancar 2018: 131). Otopamean langauges also tend to have elaborate TAM systems, such as in Acazulco Otomi (Hernández-Green 2016: 380–381).

Discussion and representation of the internal structure of Otopamean can be found in Palancar (2018: 98), and Campbell (2017b: 5), which is based on Soustelle (1937) and Kaufman (1988).

4.4. *Chinantec*

The Chinantec subgroup is about 1,500 years old (Kaufman 2006: 819). These languages tend to be monosyllabic and animacy plays an important role in the grammar (Campbell 2017b: 6). There is a reported contrast between ballistic and controlled syllables (Merrifield 1963; Mugele 1982; Campbell 2017b: 6). Tone sandhi process are important in Chinantec, as illustrated earlier in (9).

An internal classification for Chinantec can be found in Rensch (1989). Other references include Anderson (1989), Silverman (1997a), and Foris (2000).

4.5. *Mixtecan*

The Mixtecan subgroup dates back to at least 3,700 years ago (Kaufman 2006: 819) and consists of the Cuicatec languages, the Mixtec languages (which can be grouped together into Mixtec-Cuicatecan), and the Triqui languages (Rensch 1976). There are two Cuicatec languages, and these are among the least-studied Otomanguean languages (Campbell 2017b: 8). There are three Triqui languages. Mixtec, however, is a large and complex group of languages, with approximately "2000 years of internal diversification" (Josserand 1983, cited in DiCanio & Bennett 2018: 1). The *Ethnologue* (Simons & Fennig 2018) lists 52 Mixtec languages, which from "at least 18 mutually-unintelligible dialect clusters" (Josserand 1983, cited in DiCanio & Bennett 2018: 1).

In addition to those cited above, other important resources on Mixtecan language include Alexander (1980), Hollenbach (1984; 1995), Bradley and Hollenbach (1988), Shields (1988), Bradley (1991), Zylstra (1991), Macaulay (1996), DiCanio (2008), McKendry (2013), DiCanio et al. (2014), Palancar et al. (2016), Elliot (2017), and Josserand (n.d.).

4.6. *Amuzgo*

Amuzgo languages have eight contrasting lexical tones, as illustrated earlier in (6) (Kim 2016: 202). These languages also have monosyllabic roots (Apóstol Polanco 2014) and semantic alignment (Palancar & Feist 2015: 344). Additional references include Buck (2000), Stewart and Stewart (2000), and Smith Stark and Tapia García (2002).

4.7. *Zapotecan*

The Zapotecan subgroup itself is a complex, highly diversified language family dating back at least 2,400 years (Kaufman 2006: 819). It consists of two branches: Zapotec and Chatino. Both groups have internal complexity, though the Chatino branch is significantly smaller than Zapotec. The Zapotecan subgroup, together with the Popolocan subgroup (§4.8), make up the Popolocan-Zapotecan branch of Eastern Otomanguean.

While the internal structure of the Zapotec language family "is more elaborated . . . than for any other Otomanguean group" (Campbell 2017b: 11), there is no single accepted structure for the Zapotec language family. Several excellent overviews of Zapotec languages exist, and I refer the interested reader to Smith Stark (2007), Broadwell (2015), Beam de Azcona (2016), and Campbell and Broadwell (in press).

There is significant documentary and analytical work on Zapotec languages; a few of these sources are: Marks (1976), Marlett (1993), Munro et al. (1999, 2007), Black (2000), Broadwell (2001, 2015), Smith Stark (2002, 2007), Foreman (2006), Avelino (2004), Beam de Azcona (2004), Lillehaugen (2006), and Black et al. (2009).

Discussion of the internal structure of the Chatino family can be found in Campbell (2013, 2017b: 12) and Sullivant (2016). Important works on Chatino languages include Upson and Longacre (1965), Nellis and Nellis (1983), Rasch (2002), Campbell (2013 2015), Cruz, E. (2011), Cruz, H. (2014), McIntosh (2015), Operstein and Sonnenschein (2015), Villard (2015), and Sullivant (2016).

4.8. Popolocan

Popolocan, also referred to as Mazatecan, has a time depth of at least 2,500 years (Kaufman 2006: 819). Together Popolocan and Zapotecan (§4.7) form the Popolocan-Zapotecan branch of Eastern Otomanguean. Popolocan consists of Chocholtec, Ixcatec, Mazatec, and Popoloca. The word *popoloca* was used in Nahuatl language texts to refer to the speaking of foreign languages more broadly; furthermore, several (unrelated) languages may have very similar sounding names, such as the Popoluca languages (Mixe-Zoquean) spoken in Veracruz, which are not related to Oaxacan Popolocan languages (Swanton 2016: 17–18).

Chocholtec [coz] is extremely endangered, with estimates of number of speakers at around 500 (Swanton 2016: 38). Chocholtec is also referred to as Chocho and with endonyms including Ngiwa and Ngigua, among others. See Swanton (2016: 12–26) for a history and explanation on the various names used for this language. Additional references include Mock (1982) and Stark and Luna Villanueva (2011).

Ixcatec has only a few elderly speakers (M. Swanton p.c., cited in Simmons & Fennig 2018: [ixc]). Resources include Costaouc and Swanton (2015).

Mazatec has nine varieties and Popoloca seven (Simmons & Fennig 2018: [popolocan]). Swanton (2016: 28) described the history of the internal classification of the Popolocan family, pointing to Hamp's (1958) classification as authoritative. Mazatec resources include Gudschinsky (1959) and Jamieson (1988).

5. Key Historical Sources

The Otomanguean family is particularly rich in historic linguistic resources.[5] The representation of Otomanguean languages in pictographic form, including lienzos, codices, and hieroglyphic writing has been, and continues to be, an exciting area of research (e.g., Caso 1965; Smith 1973; Oudijk 2003; 2012; Jansen & Pérez Jiménez 2011). Significant work remains to be done in understanding what pre-colonial Mesoamerican writing can teach us about Otomanguean languages.

In addition to the non-alphabetic representation of language, there are significant materials in Otomanguean languages produced using the Roman alphabet during the Mexican Colonial period. While Kaufman is justified in critiquing the "inadequate" orthography and the "calque[ing]" of the Latin grammatical model (2006: 824) implemented in the dictionaries and grammars, these shortcomings – if we even want to call them that – pale in light of the resources provided in these corpora. In addition to these meta-linguistic resources, the corpus also contains religious texts and administrative manuscripts. The corpus is also diverse in that some of the resources are printed – among the first books to be printed in the Americas – while others are handwritten manuscripts, which themselves can range from less than one page to several hundred pages. Speakers of Otomanguean languages as well as students and researchers are in an enviable position to have such material.

Colonial texts exist in a great number of Otomanguean languages, including Chiapanec, Chinantec, Otomi, Mazahua, Matlatzinca, Mazatec, Mixtec, Zapotec, Popoloca, and Chocholtec, though the size of the colonial corpus that exists for any particular language can vary greatly from just one text (Mazahua; p.c. Michael Swanton) to large, diverse corpora of several hundreds of texts (e.g., Zapotec, Mixtec, Chocholtec). Table 15.5 contains a non-exhaustive list of primary sources, analyzed texts, and other relevant contemporary references.

Table 15.5 Some Resources and References on Colonial Texts in Otomanguean Languages

Chiapanec (Chorotegan)	
	Núñez Perez (1631) (sermons); Barrientos (1690) (doctrine); Albornoz (1691) (grammar)
Chocholtec (Popolocan)	
	Doesburg and Swanton (2008) (doctrine with translation); Swanton (2016) (analyzed texts)
Cuicatec (Mixtecan)	
	Doesburg (2013) (confessional)
Matlatzinca (Otopamean)	
	Castro (1557) (vocabulary); Basalenque (1640; 1644) (grammar and vocabulary); Lastra et al. (2017) (analyzed vocabulary)
Mazahua (Otopamean)	
	Nájera Yanguas (1637) (doctrine); Knapp (2013) (analyzed edition of Nágera Yanguas 1637)
Mixtec (Mixtecan)	
	Hernández (1567) (doctrine);[6] Alvarado (1593) (vocabulary); Reyes (1593) (grammar); Terraciano (2001) (ethnohistorical context, analyzed parts of texts)
Otomi (Otopamean)	
	Vargas (1576) (doctrine); Cárceras (1580) (grammar); Miranda (1759) (catechism)
Popoloca (Popolocan)	
	Roldán (1580) (doctrine); Veerman-Leichsenring (1995); Swanton (2001)
Zapotec (Zapotecan)	
	Feria (1567) (doctrine); Cordova (1578a) (grammar), (1578b) (vocabulary); Oudijk (2008) (analyzed text); Smith Stark et al. (2008) (analyzed texts); Oudijk and Miceli (2015) (digital edition of Cordova 1578b); Lillehaugen et al. (2016) (analyzed texts, including Cordova 1578a); Munro et al. (2018) (analyzed text)

6. Conclusion

The Otomanguean family is a significantly large and diverse family, its diversity stemming from its time depth. This makes understanding the development of Otomanguean key in understanding the early history of people in Mexico and is likely to be key in our further understanding the development of farming practices in the area. Otomanguean language history also relates to the evolution of writing systems. Otomanguean languages have the potential to further inform linguistic theory, including phonology, and especially in the areas of tone and phonation. Grammaticalization theory and linguistic typology will undoubtedly benefit from the continued growth in documentation and analysis of these languages as well. As Otomanguean languages are part of the Mesoamerican linguistic area, documentation and analysis of Otomanguean languages will contribute to our further understanding of this linguistic area and of areal linguistics more broadly.

Given the threat these languages face, it is dangerous to separate the academic study of the grammar of the languages from the well-being of the speakers and their sense of freedom to use their language in as many domains of life as they desire. Linguists studying the structure and use of Otomanguean language may encounter opportunities to partner with or be consulted by local language activists who are resisting the various pressures against language use. Reading and supporting native-speaking writers may be of interest to some readers of this chapter. Bilingual English publications in Otomanguean languages include poetry in varieties of Zapotec (e.g., Terán 2015; Toledo & Sullivan 2015; Lopez & Lillehaugen 2018) and Mazatec (Regino 2015) and short stories in varieties of Mazatec (e.g., Velasco Casimiro 2016) and Triqui (e.g., Camarillo López 2016). Bilingual editions in Otomanguean and Spanish are numerous, and there is a growing number of monolingual works in Otomanguean languages, such as Zavala and Cata (2014), an anthology of short stories translated into Isthmus Zapotec.

Current policies, de facto practices, power structures, and social dynamics create an environment that continues to threaten speakers of Otomanguean languages and the free use of these languages. While in some communities there are only a few elderly speakers, in other pueblos, children are acquiring Otomanguean languages as their first language. While change would not be easy, it is not too late.

Acknowledgments

I owe my thanks to those who read and commented on drafts of (sections of) this chapter, including George Aaron Broadwell, Christian DiCanio, Michael Swanton, an anonymous reviewer, and the editors. I am grateful to Julie Gonzales, Joseph Stein, Emily Drummond, Conor Stuart Roe, Avery A. King, and especially Jaime Metzger for their research and editorial support. All errors are my own.

As always, I am indebted to my Zapotec-language teachers for sharing their knowledge so generously with me. Xtyozën yuad: Dr. Felipe H. Lopez, Moisés Garcia Guzmán, Janet Chávez Santiago, and many others.

Notes

1. The term "Otomi-Mangue" was used as a designation for this family in the early 20th century (Schmidt 1977 [1926], cited in Campbell 2017b: 4) and "Otomanguean" seems to be derived from that (Jiménez Moreno 1962, cited in Campbell 2017b: 4). The language family name is often spelled with a hyphen, "Oto-manguean" or "Oto-Manguean", which is likely an analogy to other family names like Uto-Aztecan. However, because Otomanguean is a blend, I write the name without a hyphen.
2. *Ethnologue* data supplemented with data from Palancar (2018), though there is disagreement between these sources about subgroup internal structure and number of languages.
3. The glossing of the original authors are retained throughout, which means there might be inconsistencies across examples. The following abbreviations are used in glossing: 2 = second person; 3 = third person; AML = animal; COM = completive; CON = continuative; CPL = completive; DECL = declarative; DIST = distal; HAB = habitual aspect; INCPL = incompletive; INVIS = invisible; M = masculine; PL = plural; POT = potential aspect; PROX = proximate; PST = past tense; SG = singular.
4. Anderson marks the completive with C.
5. This section benefited greatly from comments and suggestions from Michael Swanton.
6. Consists of the same doctrine in two different varieties of Mixtec.

References

Albornoz, Fr. Juan de. 1875 [1691]. *Arte de la lengua chiapaneca*. Paris: Ernest Leroux. (https://babel.hathitrust.org/cgi/pt?id=uc1.c3019892;view=1up;seq=7) (Accessed 2018-28-07.)

Alexander, Ruth María. 1980. *Gramática mixetca de Atatlahuaca*. (Serie de gramáticas de lenguas indígenas de México, 2). México: Insituto Lingüístico de Verano.

Alvarado, Francisco de. 1593. *Vocabulario en lengua mixteca*. Mexico City: En casa de Pedro Balli.

Amador Hernandez, Mariscela. 1976. *Gramatica del mazahua de San Antonio Pueblo Nuevo*. Mexico: Escuela Nacional de Antropologia e Historia. (Bachelor's thesis.)

Anderson, Judi L. 1989. *Comaltepec Chinantec syntax*. Dallas: The Summer Institute of Linguistics; Arlington: University of Texas.

Apóstol Polanco, Jair. 2014. *Clases flexivas verbales en el amuzgo de Xochistlahuaca, Guerrero*. México: Centro de Investigaciones y Estudios Superiores en Antropología Social (Master's thesis.)

Avelino Becerra, Heriberto. 2004. *Topics in Yalálag Zapotec, with particular reference to its phonetic structures*. Los Angeles: University of California. (Doctoral dissertation.)

Barrientos, Fr. Luis. 1690. *Doctrina en lengua chiapaneca*. Newberry Library, Ayer MS 1519.

Bartholomew, Doris. 1959. *Proto-Otomi-Pame*. Philadelphia: University of Pennsylvania. (Master's thesis.)

Bartholomew, Doris. 1960. Some revisions of Proto-Otomi consonants. *International Journal of American Linguistics* 26(4). 317–329.

Bartholomew, Doris. 1965. *The reconstruction of Otopamean (Mexico)*. Chicago, IL: University of Chicago. (Doctoral dissertation.)

Bartholomew, Doris. 1989. The proto-Otopamean vowel system and the development of Matlatzinca. In Key, Mary Ritchie & Hoenigswald, Henry M. (eds.), *General and American ethnolinguistics: In remembrance of Stanley Newman*, 345–363. Berlin: Mouton de Gruyter.

Basalenque, Fr. Diego. 1975 [1640, 1644]. *Arte y vocabulario de la lengua matlaltzinga vuelto a la castellana*. (María Elena Bribiesca S., ed.). Mexico City: Biblioteca Enciclopedia del Estado de México.

Beam de Azcona, Rosemary G. 2004. *A Coatlán-Loxicha Zapotec grammar*. Berkeley: University of California. (Doctoral dissertation.)

Beam de Azcona, Rosemary G. 2016. *Zapotecan languages*. (Oxford Research Encyclopedia of Linguistics). Oxford University Press. DOI: 10.1093/acrefore/9780199384655.013.73. Online. (https://oxfordre.com/linguistics/view/10.1093/acrefore/9780199384655.001.0001/acrefore-9780199384655-e-73) (Accessed 2018-28-07.)

Beam de Azcona, Rosemary G. 2017. Spanish infinitives borrowed into Zapotec light verb constructions. In Dakin, Karen & Parodi, Claudia & Operstein, Natalie (ed.), *Language contact and change in Mesoamerican and beyond*, 55–80. Amsterdam and Philadelphia: John Benjamins Publishing Company.

Beam de Azcona, Rosemary, Arellanes, Francisco, Chávez Peón, Mario E., Hernández Luna, Mario, Morales Camacho, Sofía Gabriela, & Wagner Oviedo, Carlos de Jesús. 2018. Umlaut y otros procesos de los sistemas vocálicos de las lenguas zapotecas. In Buenrostro Díaz, Elsa Cristina, Meléndez Guadarrama, Lucero, & San Giacomo Trinidad, Marcela (eds.), *Lingüística histórica de lenguas indomexicanas: hallazgos y discusiones recientes*, 39–84. Mexico City: Universidad Nacional Autónoma de México, Instituto de Investigaciones Antropológicas.

Benton, Joe. 1988. *Proto-Zapotec phonology*. (Ms.)

Benton, Joe. 2001. *A reconstruction of the tone system of Proto Zapotec*. (Ms.)

Bickmore, Lee & Broadwell, George Aaron. 1998. High tone docking in Sierra Juárez Zapotec. *International Journal of American Linguistics* 64(1). 37–67.

Black, Cheryl A. 2000. *Quiegolani Zapotec syntax: A principles and parameters account*. Dallas: Summer Institute of Linguistics International.

Black, Cheryl A., H. Andrew Black & Stephen A. Marlett (eds). 2009. *The Zapotec grammar files*. SIL International. Online. (http://mexico.sil.org/resources/archives/35298) (Accessed 2018-28-07.)

Bradley, C. Henry. 1981. The Proto Mixtec kinship system. In Merrifield, William L. (ed.), *Proto Otomanguean kinship*, 199–212. Dallas: Summer Institute of Linguistics.

Bradley, C. Henry & Hollenbach, Barbara E. (ed.). 1988. *Studies in the syntax of Mixtecan languages. Vol. 1*. Dallas: Summer Institute of Linguistics.

Bradley, C. Henry & Josserand, J. Kathryn. 1982. El protomixteco y sus descendientes. *Anales de Antropología* 19(2). 279–343.

Bradley, David P. 1991. A preliminary syntactic sketch of Concepción Pápalo Cuicatec. In Bradley, C. Henry & Hollenbach, Barbara E. (eds.), *Studies in the syntax of Mixtecan languages*, 409–506. Dallas: Summer Institute of Linguistics; Arlington: University of Texas Publications in Linguistics.

Broadwell, George Aaron. 2001. Optimal order and pied-piping in San Dionicio Zapotec. In Peter Sells (ed.), *Formal and empirical issues in optimality theoretic syntax*, 197–223. Stanford, CA: Center for the Study of Language and Information Publications.

Broadwell, George Aaron. 2014. Syntax from the bottom up: Elicitation, corpus data, and thick descriptions. In Butt, Miriam & Holloway King, Tracy (ed.), *Proceedings of the LFG14 Conference*, 131–157. Stanford, CA: Center for the Study of Language and Information Publications.

Broadwell, George Aaron. 2015. The historical development of the progressive aspect in Central Zapotec. *International Journal of American Linguistics* 81(2). 151–185.

Buck, Marjorie J. 2000. Gramática Amuzga. In Stewart, Cloyd & Stewart, Ruth D. (eds.), *Diccionario amuzgo de San Pedro Amuzgos*. México: Instituto Lingüístico de Verano.

Camarillo López, Eugenio. 2016. The great-uncle and his friend the dog; Cotton Loom. In Moctezuma, Lino Santacruz (ed.), *Potslom: Cuentos de los pueblos indígenas de México*, 345–359. Berlin: Álamos.

Campbell, Eric W. 2013. The internal diversification and subgrouping of Chatino. *International Journal of American Linguistics* 79(3). 395–420.

Campbell, Eric W. 2015. Valency classes in Zenzontepec Chatino. In Malchukov, Andrej & Comrie, Bernard (ed.), *Valency classes in the world's languages. Vol. 2, Case studies from Austronesia and the Pacific, the Americas, and theoretical outlook*, 1391–1426. Berlin: De Gruyter Mouton.

Campbell, Eric W. 2017b. Otomanguean historical linguistics: Exploring the subgroups. *Language and Linguistics Compass* 11(7). 1–23.

Campbell, Eric W. 2018. Una mirada al desarrollo fonológico del protochatino. In Buenrostro Díaz, Elsa Cristina, Meléndez Guadarrama, Lucero, & San Giacomo Trinidad, Marcela (eds.), *Lingüística histórica de lenguas indomexicanas: hallazgos y discusiones recientes*, 15–37. Mexico City: Universidad Nacional Autónoma de México, Instituto de Investigaciones Antropológicas.

Campbell, Eric W. & Broadwell, George Aaron. In press. Zapotecan languages. In Wichmann, Søren (ed.), *The languages and linguistics of Middle America: A comprehensive guide*. Berlin: DeGruyter Mouton.

Campbell, Eric W. & Cruz, Emiliana. 2010. El sistema numérico del proto-chatino. In *Proceedings of the Conference on Indigenous Languages of Latin America-IV*. Austin: AILLA.

Campbell, Lyle. 2000. *American Indian languages: The historical linguistics of Native America*. Oxford and New York: Oxford University Press.

Campbell, Lyle. 2016. Comparative linguistics of Mesoamerican languages today. In Gorrochategui, Joaquín & García Castillero, Carlos & Vallejo, José M. (ed.), *Comparative linguistics today in the field of both Indo-European and other relevant non-Indo-European linguistics families*, 113–134. (Special publication of VELEIA, Revista VELEIA Aldizkaria Instituto de Ciencias de la Antigüedad, Vitoria-Gasteiz, Spain.)

Campbell, Lyle & Kaufman, Terrence & Smith Stark, Thomas C. 1986. Meso-America as a linguistic area. *Linguistics* 62(3). 530–570.

Cárceras, Fr. Pedro de. 1908 [1580]. Arte de la lengua othomi. In León Nicolás (ed.), *Boletín del Instituto Bibliográfico Mexicano*, vol. 6, 38–155.

Caso, Alfonso. 1965. Mixtec writing and calendar. In Wauchope, Robert & Willey, Gordon R. (ed.), *Handbook of Middle American Indians* 3(2). 948–961. Austin: University of Texas Press.

Castro, Fray Andrés de. 1557. *Vocabulario castellano-matlatzinca*. Ms.

Chávez Peón, Mario E. 2010. *The interaction of metrical structure, tone, and phonation types in Quiaviní Zapotec*. Vancouver: University of British Columbia. (Doctoral dissertation.)

Cline, Kevin. 2013. *The tone system of Acatepec Me'phaa*. Grand Forks: University of North Dakota. (Master's thesis.)

Cordova, Fr. Juan de. 1578a. *Arte del idioma zapoteco*. Mexico City: En casa de Pedro Balli.

Cordova, Fr. Juan de. 1987 [1578b]. *Vocabulario en lengua çapoteca*. Mexico City: Ediciones Toledo (INAH).

Costaouec, Denis & Swanton, Michael. 2015. Classification nominale en Ixcatèque. *La Linguistique* 51(2). 201–238.

Cruz, Emiliana. 2011. *Phonology, tone, and the functions of tone in San Juan Quiahije Chatino*. Austin: University of Texas. (Doctoral dissertation.)

Cruz, Hilaria. 2014. *Linguistic poetics and rhetoric of Eastern Chatino of San Juan Quiahije*. Austin: University of Texas. (Doctoral dissertation.)

DiCanio, Christian. 2008. *The phonetics and phonology of San Martín Itunyoso Trique*. Berkeley: University of California. (Doctoral dissertation.)

DiCanio, Christian & Amith, Jonathan D. & García, Rey Castillo. 2014. The phonetics of moraic alignment in Yoloxóchitl Mixtec. In *Proceedings of the 4th tonal aspects of language symposium*. Nijmegen, The Netherlands.

DiCanio, Christian & Benn, Joshua & Castillo Garcia, Rey. 2018. The phonetics of information structure in Yoloxochitl Mixtec. *Journal of Phonetics* 68. 50–68.

DiCanio, Christian & Bennett, Ryan. 2018. Prosody in Mesoamerican languages. In Gussenhoven, Carold & Chen, Aoju (ed.), *The Oxford Prosody handbook*, chapter 28. Oxford: Oxford University Press.

Doesburg, Sebastián van. 2013. Un confesionario en lengua cuicateca de finales de la época virreinal. *Tlalocan* IXX. 249–299.

Doesburg, Sebastián van & Swanton, Michael. 2008. La traducción de la Doctrina ristiana en lengua mixteca de fray Benito Hernández al chocholteco (ngiwa). In López Cruz, Ausencia & Swanton, Michael (ed.), *Memorias del coloquio Francisco Belmar*, vol. 2. 81–117. Oaxaca: Biblioteca Francisco de Burgoa/Fundación Alfredo Harp Helú.

Dürr, Michael. 1987. A preliminary reconstruction of the proto-Mixtec tonal system. *Indiana* 11: 19–61.

Elliot, Raymond A. 2017. Ruhuâ ru'man hio'óogatsii "In the hole of white dirt" legend in Chicahuaxtla Triqui. *International Journal of American Linguistics Texts Online* 2(1). 1–32. (www.americanlinguistics.org/?page_id=2171) (Accessed 2018-28-07.)

Feria, Pedro de. 1567. *Doctrina christiana en lengua castellana y çapoteca*. Mexico City: En casa de Pedro Ocharte.

Fernández de Miranda, María Teresa. 1951. Reconstrucción del protopopoloca. *Revista Mexicana de Estudios Antropológicos* 12. 61–93.

Fernández de Miranda, María Teresa. 1995. *El protozapoteco*. (Piper, Michael J. & Bartholomew, Doris A., eds.). Mexico City: El Colegio de México and Instituto Nacional de Antropología e Historia.

Fernández de Miranda, María Teresa & Weitlaner, R. J. 1961. Sobre algunas relaciones de la familia Mangue. *Anthropological Linguistics* 3(7). 1–99.

Foreman, John. 2006. *The morphosyntax of subjects in Macuiltianguis Zapotec*. Los Angeles: University of California. (Doctoral dissertation.)

Foris, David P. 2000. *A grammar of Sochiapan Chinantec: Studies in Chinantec languages 6*. Dallas: Summer Institute of Linguistics International.

Garellek, Marc & Keating, Patricia. 2011. The acoustic consequences of phonation and tone interactions in Jalapa Mazatec. *Journal of the International Phonetic Association* 41(2). 185–205.

Gudschinsky, Sarah. 1956. *Proto-Mazatec structure*. Philadelphia: University of Pennsylvania. (Master's thesis.)

Gudschinsky, Sarah. 1959. Discourse analysis of a Mazatec text. *International Journal of American Linguistics* 25(3). 139–146.

Hamp, Eric P. 1958. Protopopoloca internal relationships. *International Journal of American Linguistics* 24. 150–153.

Hasler, Juan A. 1961. Reconstrucciones matlatzinca-ocuiltecas. *Anales de Antropología* 13(42). 269–278.

Hernández, Fr. Benito. 1567. *Doctrina en lengua misteca*. Mexico City: Pedro Ocharte.

Hernández-Green, Néstor. 2015. *Morfosintaxis verbal del otomí de Acazulco*. Mexico: CIESAS. (Doctoral dissertation.)

Hernández-Green, Néstor. 2016. Registration versus applicative constructions in Acazulco Otomi. *International Journal of American Linguistics* 82(3). 353–383.

Hollenbach, Barbara Elena. 1984. *The phonology and morphology of tone and laryngeals in Copala Trique*. Tucson: University of Arizona. (Doctoral dissertation.)

Hollenbach, Barbara Elena. 1995. Semantic and syntactic extensions of body part terms in Mixtecan: The case of 'face' and 'foot'. *International Journal of American Linguistics* 61(2). 168–190.

INALI. 2015. *Proyecto de indicadores sociolingüísticos de las lenguas indígenas nacionales*. Instituto Nacional de Lenguas Indígenas. (http://site.inali.gob.mx/Micrositios/estadistica_basica/) (Accessed 2018-28-07.)

Jamieson, Carole. 1988. *Gramática mazateca: Mazateco de Chiquihuitlán de Juárez*. México: Instituto Lingüístico de Verano, A.C.

Jansen, Maarten E. R. G. N. & Pérez Jiménez, Gabina Aurora. 2011. *The Mixtec pictorial manuscripts: Time, agency, and memory in ancient Mexico*. Leiden: Brill.

Jiménez Moreno, W. 1962. Estudios mixtecos. In F. F. de Alvarado (ed.), *Vocabulario en lengua mixteca*, 9–105. México: Instituto Nacional Indigenista e Instituto Nacional de Antropología e Historia S. E. P.

Josserand, Judy Kathryn. 1983. *Mixtec dialect history*. New Orleans, LA: Tulane University. (Doctoral dissertation.)

Josserand, Judy Kathryn. n.d. *MesoAmerican languages collection of Kathryn Josserand. The Archive of the Indigenous Languages of Latin America*. (www.ailla.utexas.org/search/collection.html?c_id=79.) (Accessed 2018-28-07.)

Kaufman, Terrance. 1988. *Otomanguean tense/aspect/mood, voice, and nominalization markers*. (Unpublished monograph.)

Kaufman, Terrance. 2016. *Tlapaneko-Sutiaba, OtoMangean, and Hokan: Where Greenberg went wrong*. (Institute for Mesaoamerican Studies). Albany: University at Albany, State University of New York. (www.albany.edu/ims/PDLMA_publications_new.html) (Accessed 2018-28-07.)

Kaufman, Terrence. 1983. *New perspectives on comparative Otomanguean phonology*. Pittsburgh: University of Pittsburgh. (Master's thesis.)

Kaufman, Terrence. 2006. Oto-Mangean languages. In Brown, Keith (ed.), *Encyclopedia of Language & Linguistics*, 2nd edn., vol. 9, 118–124. Oxford: Elsevier.

Kaufman, Terrance & Justeson, John. 2009. Historical linguistics and pre-Colombian Mesoamerica. *Ancient Mesoamerica* 20. 221–231.

Kim, Yuni. 2016. Tonal overwriting and inflectional exponence in Amuzgo. In Palancar, Enrique L. & Léonard, Jean Léo (ed.), *Tone and inflection: New facts and new perspectives*, 199–224. Berlin: De Gruyter Mouton.

Kirk, Paul L. 1966. *Proto-Mazatec phonology*. Seattle: University of Washington. (Doctoral dissertation.)

Kirk, Paul L. 1985. Proto-Mazatec numerals. *International Journal of American Linguistics* 51(4). 480–482.

Knapp, Michael H. 2013. *Doctrina y enseñanza en la lengua mazahua. Estudio filológico y edición interlineal del texto bilingüe de Nájera Yanguas*. Mexico City: Instituto Nacional de Lenguas Indígenas/Secretaría de Educación Pública,

Lastra, Yolanda & Pascacio, Etna & Valiñas, Leopoldo (eds.). 2017. *Vocabulario castellano-matlatzinca de Fray Andrés de Castro (1557) y vocabulario español-matlatzinca de Roberto Escalante y Marciano Hernández (Circa 1973)*. Mexico City: Instituto de Investigaciones Antropológicas, Universidad Autónoma de México.

Lillehaugen, Brook Danielle. 2006. *Expressing Location in Tlacolula Valley Zapotec*. Los Angeles: University of California. (Doctoral dissertation.)

Lillehaugen, Brook Danielle & Broadwell, George Aaron & Oudijk, Michel R. & Allen, Laurie & Plumb, May & Mike Zarafonetis. 2016. *Ticha: A digital text explorer for Colonial Zapotec*. 1st edn. (http://ticha.haverford.edu/) (Accessed 2018-28-07.)

Lillehaugen, Brook Danielle & Sonnenschein, Aaron Huey (eds.). 2012a. *Expressing location in Zapotec*. Munich: Lincom Europa.

Lillehaugen, Brook Danielle & Sonnenschein, Aaron Huey. 2012b. Expressing location in Zapotec: An introduction. In Lillehaugen, Brook Danielle & Sonnenschein, Aaron Huey (ed.), *Expressing location in Zapotec*, 1–34. Munich: Lincom Europa.

Longacre, Robert. 1955. *Proto-Mixtecan*. Philadelphia: University of Pennsylvania. (Doctoral dissertation.)

Longacre, Robert. 1957. Proto-Mixtecan. *International Journal of American Linguistics* 23(4). 1–195.

Longacre, Robert. 1962. Amplification of Gudschinsky's proto-Popolocan-Mixtecan. *International Journal of American Linguistics* 28(4). 227–242.

Longacre, Robert. 1968. Comparative reconstruction of indigenous languages. In Thomas Sebeok (ed.), *Current trends in linguistics*, vol. 4, 320–360. The Hague: Mouton.

Lopez, Felipe H. & Lillehaugen, Brook Danielle (trans.). 2018. Liaza chaa and Valley Zapotec poems with translations. *Latin American Literature Today*. Online. (www.latinamericanliteraturetoday.org/en/2018/august) (Accessed 2018-28-07.)

Macaulay, Monica. 1996. *A grammar of Chalcatongo Mixtec*. Los Angeles: University of California Press.

Mak, C. & Longacre, R. 1960. Proto-Mixtec phonology. *International Journal of American Linguistics* 26(1). 23–40.

Marks, Donna. 1976. *Zapotec verb morphology: Categories and tonomechanics with special attention to Sierra Juárez Zapotec*. Arlington: University of Texas. (Master's thesis.)

Marlett, Stephen A. 1993. Zapotec pronoun classification. *International Journal of American Linguistics* 59(1). 82–101.

Marlett, Stephen A. & Pickett, Velma B. 1987. The syllable structure and aspect morphology of Isthmus Zapotec. *International Journal of American Linguistics* 53(4). 398–422.

Matsukawa, Kosuke. 2005. *Preliminary reconstruction of Proto-Trique*. Albany: State University of New York. (Master's thesis.)

McIntosh, Justin Daniel. 2015. *Aspects of phonology and morphology of Teotepec Eastern Chatino*. Austin: University of Texas. (Doctoral dissertation.)

McKendry, Inga. 2013. *Tonal association, prominence and prosodic structure in South-Eastern Nochixtlán Mixtec*. Edinburgh: University of Edinburgh. (Doctoral dissertation.)

Merrifield, William R. 1963. Palantla Chinantec syllable types. *Anthropological Linguistics* 5(5). 1–16.

Miranda, Francisco de. 1759. *Catecismo breve en lengua otomi*. Mexico City: Imp. De la Bibliotheca mexicana.

Mock, Carol C. 1982. Los casos morfosintácticos del chocho. *Anales de Antropología* 19(2). 345–378.

Mugele, Robert Louis. 1982. *Tone and ballistic syllable in Lalana Chinantec*. Austin: University of Texas. (Doctoral dissertation.)

Munro, Pamela & Lillehaugen, Brook Danielle & Lopez, Felipe H. 2007. *Cali Chiu? A course in Valley Zapotec*, vols. 1–4. Lulu Publishing. (www.lulu.com) (Accessed 2018-28-07.)

Munro, Pamela & Lopez, Felipe H. & Méndez, Olivia V. & Garcia, Rodridgo & Galant, Michael R. 1999. *Di'csyonaary x: tèe'n dìi'zh sah sann Lu'uc; San Lucas Quiaviní Zapotec dictionary*, 2 vols. Los Angeles: UCLA Chicano Studies Research Center.

Munro, Pamela & Sonnenschein, Aaron Huey. 2007. *Four Zapotec number systems*. Los Angeles: Ms.

Munro, Pamela & Terraciano, Kevin & Flores-Marcial, Xóchitl M. & Galant, Michael & Lillehaugen, Brook Danielle & Ornelas, Maria & Sonnenschein, Aaron Huey & Sousa, Lisa. 2018. The Zapotec language testament of Sebastiana de Mendoza, c. 1675. *Tlalocan XXIII*. 187–211.

Nájera Yanguas, Diego. 1637. *Doctrina y enseñança en la lengua maçahua de cosas muy utiles y prouechosas para los ministros de doctrina, y para los naturales que hablan la lengua maçahua*. Mexico City: Por Iuan Ruyz.

Nellis, Niel & Nellis, Jane Goodner. 1983. *Diccionario Zapoteco: Zapoteco de Juárez*. Mexico City: Instituto Linguistico de Verano.

Newman, Stanley & Robert Weitlaner. 1950a. Central Otomian I: Proto-Otomi reconstructions. *International Journal of American Linguistics* 16(1). 1–19.

Newman, Stanley & Robert Weitlaner. 1950b. Central Otomian II: Primitive Central Otomian reconstructions. *International Journal of American Linguistics* 16(2). 73–81.

Núñez Pérez, Fr. Juan. 1631. *Sermones de doctrina en lengua chiapaneca*. Biblioteque nacional de France, manuscript Américain 36.

Operstein, Natalie & Sonnenschein, Aaron Huey (eds.). 2015. Valence changes in Zapotec: Synchrony, diachrony, typology. In *Typological Studies in Language*, 110. Amsterdam: John Benjamins.

Oudijk, Michel R. 2003. Espacio y escritura. El Lienzo de Tabaá I. In Romero Frizzi, María de los Angeles (ed.), *Escritura Zapoteca: 2,500 años de historia*, 341–392. México: Conaculta, INAH.

Oudijk, Michel R. 2008. El texto más antiguo en zapoteca. *Tlalocan* 15. 227–240.

Oudijk, Michel R. 2012. Lienzo de San Lucas Yatau y Lienzo de Yatini. *Arqueología Mexicana* 42. 30–33. (https://mroudyk.weebly.com/uploads/5/1/1/2/5112023/art-arqmex-yatao.pdf) (Accessed 2018-28-07.)

Oudijk, Michel R. & Miceli, Iván. 2015. *Diccionario Zapoteco-Español, Español- Zapoteco basado en el 'Vocabulario en lengva çapoteca' de Fray Juan de Córdova (1578)*. Mexico City: Universidad Nacional Autónoma de México. (http://www.iifilologicas.unam.mx/cordova) (Accessed 2018-28-07.)

Palancar, Enrique L. 2004. Middle voice in Otomi. *International Journal of American Linguistics* 70(1). 52–85.

Palancar, Enrique L. 2009. *Gramática y Textos del Hñöñhö: Otomí de San Ildefonso Tultepec, Querétaro*, 2 vols. Madrid: Plaza y Valdez, S.A. de C.V.

Palancar, Enrique L. 2016. A typology of tone and inflection: A view from the Oto-Manguean languages of Mexico. In Palacar, Enrique L. & Léonard, Jean Léo (ed.), *Tone and inflection: New facts and new perspectives*, 109–140. Berlin: De Gruyter Mouton.

Palancar, Enrique L. 2018. Clefts in Otomi: Extended uses of the copular construction. *International Journal of American Linguistics* 84(1). 93–145.
Palancar, Enrique L. & Amith, Jonathan D. & Castillo García, Rey. 2016. Verbal inflection in Yoloxóchitl Mixtec. In Palancar, Enrique L. & Léonard, Jean Léo (eds.), *Tone and inflection: New facts and new perspectives*, 295–336. Berlin: De Gruyter Mouton.
Palancar, Enrique L. & Feist, Timothy. 2015. Agreeing with subjects in number: The rare split of Amuzgo verbal inflection. *Linguistic Typology* 19(3). 337–383.
Pascacio Montijo, Etna T. 2014. Reconstrucción morfológica y fonológica de los pronombres personales independientes del protoatzinca. *Cuadernos de Lingüística* 2. 239–285.
Pérez, N. L. 2007. *Synchronic and diachronic Matlatzinkan phonology*. Ann Arbor: University of Michigan. (Doctoral dissertation.)
Rasch, Jeffrey Walker. 2002. *The basic morpho-syntax of Yaitepec Chatino*. Houston: Rice University. (Doctoral dissertation.)
Regino, Juan Gregorio. 2015. Mazatec [Poetry]. In Terán & Shook (eds.): 1–38.
Rensch, Calvin R. 1968. Proto Chinantec phonology. In *Papeles de la Chinantla VI*. Mexico: Museo Nacional de Antropología.
Rensch, Calvin R. 1976. *Comparative Otomanguean phonology*. (Language Science Monographs, 14). Bloomington: Indiana University.
Rensch, Calvin R. 1977. *Classification of the Oto-Manguean languages and the position of Tlapanec*. In Oltrogge, David & Rensch, Calvin (eds.), *Two studies in middle American comparative linguistics*, 53–108. Dallas: Summer Institute of Linguistics.
Rensch, Calvin. R. 1989. *An etymological dictionary of the Chinantec languages*. (Studies in Chinantec languages 1). Dallas: Summer Institute of Linguistics.
Reyes, Antonio de los, O. P. 1593. *Arte en lengua mixteca*. Mexico: Casa de Pedro Balli. (https://archive.org/details/arteenlenguamixt00reye) (Accessed 2018-28-07.)
Roldán, Bartolomé, O. P. 1580. *Cartilla y Doctrina Christiana, breve y compendiosa, para enseñar los niños: y ciertas preguntas tocantes a la dicha Doctrina: traduzida, compuesta, ordenada, y romançada en la lengua Chuchona del pueblo de Tepexic de la Seda, por el muy Reuerendo Padre Fray Bartholome Roldan, de la orden del glorioso Padre Sancto Domingo*. Mexico: Casa de Pedro Ocharte.
Romero, Odilia & Sonnenschein, Aaron Huey. 2016. *Nuevos esfuerzos para el mantenimiento del zapoteco en Los Ángeles, California*. (Presented at the Coloquio sobre lenguas otomangues y vecinas VII: Juan José Rendón Monzón, Oaxaca).
Sapir, Edward. 1925. The Hokan affinity of Subtiaba in Nicaragua. *American Anthropologist* 27. 402–435.
Schmidt, P.W. 1977 [1926]. *Die Sprachfamilien und Sprachenkreise der Erde: Atlas von 14 Karten*. Hamburg: Helmut Buske Verlag.
Shields, Jäna K. 1988. A syntactic sketch of Silacayoapan Mixtec. In Bradley, C. Henry & Hollenbach, Barbara E. (eds.), *Studies in the syntax of Mixtecan languages*, 305–449. Dallas: Summer Institute of Linguistics; Arlington: University of Texas.
Silverman, Daniel. 1997a. Tone sandhi in Comaltepec Chinantec. *Language* 73(3). 473–486.
Silverman, Daniel. 1997b. Laryngeal complexity in Otomanguean vowels. *Phonology* 14. 235–261.
Simons, Gary F. & Fennig, Charles D. (eds.) 2018. *Ethnologue: Languages of the world*, 20th edn. Dallas: SIL International. Online (www.ethnologue.com) (Accessed 2018-28-07.)
Smith Stark, Thomas C. 2002. Las clases verbales del zapoteco de Chichicapan. In Estrada Fernández, Zarina & Ortiz Ciscomani, Rosa María (eds.), *VI Encuentro Internacional de Lingüística en el Noroeste: Memorias vol. 2*, 165–212. Hermosillo, Mexico: Universidad de Sonora.
Smith Stark, Thomas C. 2007. Algunos isoglosas zapotecas. In Christina Buenrostro et al. (eds.), *Clasificaci.n de las lenguas ind.genas de M.xico: Memorias del III Coloquio Internacional del Lingüística Mauricio Swadesh* 69–134. Mexico City: UNAM and Instituto Nacional de Lenguas Ind.genas.
Smith Stark, Thomas C. & López Cruz, Áurea & Montes de Oca Vega, Mercedes & Rodríguez Cano, Laura & Sellen, V. & Torres Rodríguez, Alfonso & Marcial Cerqueda, Vicente & Rosas Camacho, Rolando. 2008. Tres documentos zapotecos coloniales de San Antonino Ocotlán, In van Doesburg, Sebastián (ed.), *Pictografía y estcritura alfabética en Oaxaca*, 287–350. México: Instituto Estatal de Educación Pública de Oaxaca.
Smith Stark, Thomas C. & Tapia García, Fermín. 2002. El amuzgo como lengua activa. In Levy, Paulette (ed.), *Del cora al maya yucateco: Estudios lingüísticos sobre algunas lenguas indígenas mexicanas*, 81–129. Mexico City: Universidad Nacional Autónoma de México.
Smith, Mary Elizabeth. 1973. *Picture writing from Ancient Southern Mexico: Mixtec place signs and maps*. Norman: University of Oklahoma Press.
Soustelle, Jacques. 1937. *La Famille Otomi-Pame du Mexique Central*. Paris: Institut d'Ethnologie.
Stark, Sharon & Luna Villanueva, Verónica. 2011. *Gramática del Ngigua de San Marcos Tlacoyalco*. México: Instituto Lingüístico de Verano.

Stewart, Cloyd & Stewart, Ruth. 2000. *Diccionario amuzgo de San Pedro Amuzgos Oaxaca*. México: Instituto Lingüístico de Verano.

Suárez, Jorge A. 1973. On Proto-Zapotec phonology. *International Journal of American* Linguistics 39(4). 236–249.

Suárez, Jorge A. 1983. *The Mesoamerican Indian languages*. Cambridge: Cambridge University Press.

Suárez, Jorge A. 1986. Elementos gramaticales otomangues en tlapaneco. In Elson, Benjamin F. (ed.), *Language in global perspective: Papers in honor of the 50th anniversary of the Summer Institute of Linguistics 1935–1985*, 267–284. Dallas: Summer Institute of Linguistics.

Sullivant, J. Ryan. 2016. Reintroducing Teojomulco Chatino. *International Journal of American Linguistics* 82(4). 393–423.

Swadesh, Morris. 1947. The phonemic structure of Proto-Zapotec. *International Journal of American Linguistics* 13(4). 220–230.

Swadesh, Morris. 1960. The Oto-Manguean hypothesis and Macro Mixtecan. *International Journal of American Linguistics* 26(2). 79–111.

Swanton, Michael W. 2001. El texto Popoloca de la historia Tolteca-Chichimeca. *Relaciones* 86(22). 117–140.

Swanton, Michael W. 2016. *A history of Chocholetc alphabetic writing*. Leiden: University of Leiden. (Doctoral dissertation.)

Terán, Víctor. 2015. Isthmus Zapotec [Poetry]. In Terán, Víctor & Shook, David (eds.), *Like a new sun: New indigenous Mexican poetry*, 128–167. Los Angeles: Phoneme Media.

Terraciano, Kevin. 2001. *The Mixtecs of Colonial Oaxaca: Ñudzahui history, sixteenth through eighteenth centuries*. Stanford, CA: Stanford University Press.

Toledo, Natalia & Sullivan, Clare. 2015. *The black flower and other Zapotec poems*. Los Angeles: Phoneme Media.

Upson, B. W. & Longacre, R. E. 1965. Proto-Chatino phonology. *International Journal of American Linguistics* 31(4). 312–322.

van der Auwera, Johan. 1998. Revisiting the Balkan and Meso-American linguistic areas. *Language Sciences* 20(3). 259–270.

Vargas, Fr. Melchor de. 1576. *Doctrina cristiana muy útil y necesaria en castellano, mexicano y otomí: traducida em lengua otomí*. México: En casa de Pedro Balli. (http://primeroslibros.org/detail.html?lang=en&work_id=303960) (Accessed 2018-28-07.)

Veerman-Leichsenring, Annette. 1995. Un document popoloca del siglo XVIII, un studio preliminar. *Amerindia* 19–20. 163–169.

Veerman-Leichsenring, Annette. 2000. Popolocan independent personal pronouns: Comparison and reconstruction. *International Journal of American Linguistics* 66(3). 318–359.

Veerman-Leichsenring, Annette. 2004. Popolocan noun classifiers: A reconstruction. *International Journal of American Linguistics* 70(4). 416–445.

Velasco Casimiro, Filogonio. 2016. The rider. In Moctezuma, Lino Santacruz (ed.), *Potslom: Cuentos de los pueblos indígenas de México*. Berlin: Álamos.

Villard, Stéphanie. 2015. *The phonology and morphology of Zacatepec Eastern Chatino*. Austin: University of Texas. (Doctoral dissertation.)

Weitlaner, Roberto J. 1953. *Proto-otomi-matlatzinca: Reconstrucciones del proto-otomi III. Memorias del Congreso Científico Mexicano XII: Ciencias Sociales IV*, 199–206. México: Centenario de la Universidad de México.

Weitlaner, Roberto J. & Smith, Pablo. 1962. Detalles de la fonología del idioma Proto- Chinanteco. *Revista Mexicana de Estudios Antropológicos* 18. 117–123.

Wichmann, Søren. 2009. Case relations in a head-marking language: Verb-marked cases in Tlapanec. In Malchukov, Andrej & Spencer, Andrew (eds.), *The handbook of case*, 797–807. Oxford: Oxford University Press.

Wichmann, Søren (ed.). In press. *Languages and linguistics of Middle and Central America*. Berlin: DeGruyter Mouton.

Zavala, Lauro (ed.) & Cata, Victor (trans.). 2014. *Ti be'za'diidxa'ndahui sti'binni Zaguita (XX-XXI): Antología de cuento Mexicano en Zapoteco (Diidxazá)*. México: Ediciones del Ermitaño.

Zylstra, Carol F. 1991. A syntactic sketch of Alacatlatzala Mixtec. In Bradley, C. Henry & Hollenbach, Barbara E. (ed.), *Studies in the syntax of Mixtecan languages*, vol. 3, 1–178. Dallas: Summer Institute of Linguistics; Arlington: University of Texas.

16
MAYAN LANGUAGES

Lauren Clemens

1. Introduction

The Mayan language family consists of roughly 30 different languages spoken by at least six million people mainly in Guatemala and Mexico, but also in Belize, Honduras, and diaspora communities in North America. Census data for speakers of Mayan languages is unreliable for geographic, social, and political reasons, and so it should be assumed that population estimates are quite low. Present-day Mayan languages share a common ancestral language, Proto-Mayan, which was spoken over 4,000 years ago in the Western Highlands of Guatemala (Kaufman 1976). Today, the same region of Guatemala is the most linguistically diverse area of the Mayan speaking world. As many as 50% of the population of Guatemala are speakers of Mayan languages, and this number approaches 100% in some areas of the Highlands.

Although there are many fewer Mayan languages spoken in Mexico, nearly half of all speakers of Mayan languages live in Southern and Southeast Mexico, predominantly in Chiapas and Yucatan. Fleeing ethnic violence in Guatemala, speakers of Mayan languages formed diaspora communities in Florida, California, and Texas in the 1970s and 1980s but have since settled in more northern areas of the United States and Canada as well (Burns 1993; Morrison & May 1994; Loucky 2000). For more on the ancient, classic, and modern geographic distribution of Mayan languages as well as specific population estimates, see Fischer and McKenna Brown (1996), England (2003), Richards (2003), and Law (2014).

The names of the modern Mayan languages are listed in (1), mostly following conventions established by the Academia de Lenguas Mayas de Guatemala (ALMG) and the Instituto Nacional de Lenguas Indígenas (INALI). Alternative names in common use are also listed in parentheses. The exact number of Mayan languages depends on how the boundaries between languages are drawn. Achi is considered to be a dialect of K'iche', and Akatek is considered to be a dialect of Q'anjob'al by some speakers and researchers. Here, Chalchitek is subsumed under Awakatek; other sources treat Awakatek and Chalchitek as closely-related, but distinct languages. (Country name abbreviations are: BZ = Belize; HN = Honduras; GT = Guatemala; and MX = Mexico.)

(1) The Mayan languages

Language	*Subgroup*	*Region*
ACHI	Central K'ichean	Highlands GT
AKATEK	Q'anjob'alan	Highlands GT
AWAKATEK	Mamean	Highlands GT

†CHICOMUSELTEC (Kabil)	Huastecan	Southern MX
CHONTAL (de Tobasco)	Ch'olan	Southern MX
CHUJ	Chujean	Highlands GT; Southern MX
CH'OL	Ch'olan	Southern MX
†CH'OLTI'	Ch'olan	Lowlands GT; Southern BZ
CH'ORTI'	Ch'olan	Eastern GT, HN
HUASTEC (Teenek)	Huastecan	Southern; Northeast MX
ITZAJ (Itza')	Yucatecan	Lowlands GT
IXIL	Mamean	Highlands GT
KAQCHIKEL	Central K'ichean	Highlands, Pacific GT
K'ICHE'	Central K'ichean	Highlands, Pacific GT
LANCANDON (Lakantun)	Yucatecan	Southern MX; Lowlands GT
MAM	Mamean	Highlands, Pacific GT; Southern MX
MOCHO' (Qato'k)	Q'anjob'alan	Southern MX
MOPAN	Yucatecan	Southern BZ
POQOMAM	Poqom	Eastern GT
POQOMCHI	Poqom	Highlands GT
POPTI' (Jakaltek)	Q'anjob'alan	Highlands GT; Southern MX
Q'ANJOB'AL	Q'anjob'alan	Highlands GT
Q'EQCHI'	K'ichean	Low- & Highlands GT; Southern BZ
SAKAPULTEK	Central K'ichean	Highlands GT
SIPAKAPENSE	Central K'ichean	Highlands GT
TOJOLABAL (Tojol-ab'al)	Chujean	Southern MX
TSELTAL	Tseltalan	Southern MX
TSOTSIL	Tseltalan	Southern MX
TZ'UTUJIL	Central K'ichean	Highlands, Pacific GT
TEKITEK	Mamean	Lowlands GT
USPANTEK	K'ichean	Highlands GT
YUCATEC (Maya)	Yucatecan	Southeast MX; Northern BZ

As indicated by the '†' symbol in (1), two modern languages, Chicomuseltec and Ch'olti', have no living speakers. Two other languages, Itzaj and Mocho', have fewer than 100 speakers each (England 2017). In contrast, a number of Mayan languages have between 500,000 and one million speakers, including Kaqchikel, K'iche', Mam, Q'eqchi', and Yucatec. K'iche' also has a sizable population of L2 speakers. Nonetheless, all Mayan languages are under threat, as younger generations shift to Spanish for economic and sociopolitical reasons (England 2003).

Only the most basic genetic affiliation is given in (1), following Campbell and Kaufman (1985). See Bennett et al. (2016) and Aissen et al. (2017) for a more detailed overview of subgrouping in the family. Together the Ch'olan and Tseltalan languages form a subgroup of the Western branch, as do the Q'anjob'alan and Chujean languages. The Poqom and Central K'ichean languages are subgroups of K'ichean, which comprises the Eastern branch, along with the Mamean languages. Finally, each language's approximate geographic region is shown in (1). Highlands refers to Guatemala's Western and Central Highlands, but not Pacific Highlands, which is labeled Pacific. Southern Mexico refers to the states of Chiapas, Tabasco, and Veracruz, and Southeast Mexico refers to the Yucatan Peninsula.

The orthography for Mayan languages largely corresponds to the IPA, although there are exceptions. An umlaut marks a vowel as lax, e.g., ï = [ɨ]. Ejective consonants are digraphs consisting of the relevant stop plus an apostrophe, e.g., k' = [kʔ]. The velar nasal [ŋ] is written as nh. The palatal nasal [ɲ] is written as ñ and other palatalized consonants are digraphs that represent palatalization with y; e.g., ky = [kj]. In other contexts, y = [j]. Affricates are represented as follows: ch = [tʃ], tx = [tʂ], and tz = [ts] (in Guatemala) and ts = [ts] (in Mexico). For languages that do not have retroflex consonants, x = [ʃ], otherwise xh = [ʃ] and [x] = [ʂ]. Finally, j = [h], [x], or [χ].

The purpose of this chapter is to introduce the core linguistic phenomena shared by members of the Mayan language family, while highlighting some of the family's internal variation. The chapter includes a phonology section (§2) that covers consonant and vowel inventories, aspects of Mayan sound systems, root phonotactics, and basic suprasegmental phonology. The morphology section (§3) introduces Mayan word classes and focuses on the derivational and inflectional morphology associated with nominal and verbal roots. Voice, valency, and embedded structures are covered in the syntax section (§4), as are word order, topic, focus, and Mayan's famous restriction on ergative argument extraction.

2. Phonology

Proto-Mayan's vowel inventory consisted of five different vowel qualities and a length contrast. Its consonant system was richer and included plain and glottalized stops at seven places of articulation (Fox 1978; Kaufman & Norman 1984; Campbell & Kaufman 1985). The reconstructed phoneme inventory for Proto-Mayan is shown in (2):

(2) PROTO-MAYAN phoneme inventory

Consonants										*Vowels*	
Plain	*p	*t	*tʲ	*ts	*tʃ	*k	*q	*ʔ		*i(:)	*u(:)
Glottalized	*ɓ	*tˀ	*tʲˀ	*tsˀ	*tʃˀ	*kˀ	*qˀ			*e(:)	*o(:)
Fricative		*s			*ʃ		*χ	*h		*a(:)	
Nasal	*m	*n				*ŋ					
Approximant	*w	*l *r			*j						

This section focuses on the most common phonological properties of modern Mayan languages, including vowels, consonants, root phonotactics, and stress and intonation, with reference to Proto-Mayan. For more detailed overviews of Mayan phonology see Bennett (2016) and England and Baird (2017).

2.1. Vowels

Most Eastern and Yucatecan languages retain Proto-Mayan's vowel inventory (2), yielding a ten-vowel system as exemplified by Sipakapense in (3):

(3) SIPAKAPENSE vowel inventory

a.	/i/	[kˀiʃ]	*k'ix*	'shame'	b.	/i:/	[kˀi:ʃ]	*k'iix*	'thorn'
c.	/e/	[kˀeʃ]	*k'ex*	'pain'	d.	/e:/	[kˀe:ʃ]	*k'eex*	'collateral'
e.	/a/	[tʃaχ]	*chaj*	'pine'	f.	/a:/	[tʃa:χ]	*chaaj*	'ashes'
g.	/o/	[ʔoχ]	*oj*	'us'	h.	/o:/	[ʔo:χ]	*ooj*	'avocado'
i.	/u/	[ʔus]	*us*	'fly'	j.	/u:/	[pu:s]	*puus*	'mold'

(Barrett 1999: 17–20)

For many languages, Proto-Mayan's length contrast has been reinforced by the centralization of short vowels (Baird 2010; England 2011a; Bennett 2016), as in Mam (4):

(4) MAM vowel inventory

a.	/i/	[ʔɪtʃˀ]	*ich'*	'mouse'	b.	/i:/	[ʔi:tʃ]	*iich*	'chili'
c.	/e/	[tʃɛʔw]	*che'w*	'cold'	d.	/e:/	[ɓe:]	*b'ee*	'road'

e.	/a/	[tʃap]	*chap*	'crab'	f.	/aː/	[kʲaː]	*kyaa*	'grindstone'
g.	/o/	[pɔtʃʔ]	*poch'*	'bedbug'	h.	/oː/	[χoːχ]	*jooj*	'crow'
i.	/u/	[kʊtsʔ]	*kutz'*	'hummingbird'	j.	/uː/	[ʔuːts]	*uutz*	'cradle'

(England 2011a: 32)

A related process of short vowel centralization has completely or partially replaced the historic length contrast in some cases. For example, different varieties of Kaqchikel (5), as well as some varieties of K'iche', now have a tense-lax contrast instead of a long-short one (Campbell 1977; Majzul et al. 2000; England 2001; Bennett 2016).

(5) Kaqchikel vowel inventories

a.	Tecpán, Patzicía	6-Vowels:	/i, ɨ, e, a, o, u/
b.	San Miguel Pachuta	7-Vowels:	/i, ɨ, e, ə, a, o, u/
c.	Santa María de Jesús	9-Vowels:	/i, ɯ, e, ə, a, o, ɔ, u, ʊ/
d.	Sololá, Patzún	10-Vowels:	/i, ɪ, e, ɛ, ə, a, o, ɔ, u, ʊ/

(Majzul et al. 2000: 35–40)

A handful of other languages have split */a/ into /a/ and /ɨ/, rendering either an 11-vowel system, as in Itzaj, or a 6-vowel system, as in Ch'ol, depending on whether or not length is contrastive in the language (Fisher 1973; Kaufman & Norman 1984; Law 2014).

Like Ch'ol, most languages in the Western branch show a complete merger of Proto-Mayan's length contrast. However, some Western branch languages (e.g., Akatek) have lost and subsequently reintroduced long vowels from historically *[CVʔC], *[CVxC], and *[CVhC] contexts (Kaufman 1974; Raymundo González et al. 2000). *[CVʔC] and *[CVhC] are also environments that have famously given rise to tonogenesis in Yucatec, as well as a handful of other languages dispersed among the Yucatecan, Western, and Eastern branches. See Bennett and Henderson (2013), Bennett (2016), and England and Baird (2017) for more on tone in Mayan languages.

A somewhat thornier area of Mayan vowel inventories concerns the status of rearticulated vowels, which are commonly described as a vowel interrupted by a glottal stop followed by an echo vowel ($V_\alpha ʔV_\alpha$). Most of what is known about these vowels in Mayan comes from the Yucatecan and Ch'olan branches (Pike 1946; Fisher 1973; Lacadena & Wichmann 2004; Vázquez Álvarez 2011). Phonetic work on Yucatec in particular demonstrates that, instead of being truly rearticulated, these are a subtype of long vowel realized with a period of glottalization (Frazier 2009; 2011; Avelino et al. 2011).

Phonologically speaking, it is fairly clear that rearticulated vowels in Yucatec are complex nuclei and are not literally composed of a series of two short vowels flanking a glottal stop (Orie & Bricker 2000; Bennett 2016): (i) they have a high-falling tonal pattern disallowed in short vowels, which are usually specified as mid-tone or tone-less; and (ii) they surface in roots (see §2.3) – which generally take the shape CV(:)C – so a trisegmental analysis does not conform to Yucatec's root phonotactics. Similar arguments can be made for the status of rearticulated vowels in Ch'ol (Vázquez Álvarez 2011; Coon 2017), a language that is usually described as having a 6-vowel inventory. The existence of non-derived, monosegmental vowels with internally complex nuclei suggests that Mayan vowel inventories may be more elaborate than is typically acknowledged.

2.2. Consonants

All Mayan languages have stops at the labial, dental/alveolar, and velar places of articulation in addition to phonemic glottal stop. Only the Eastern branch and Q'anjobalan in the Western branch have retained Proto-Mayan's uvular stops, although Q'anjob'al and Akatek may be losing theirs (Zavala Maldonado 1992). Plain stops are typically aspirated in final position (syllable-, word-, or phrase-final, depending on the language), except for /q/, which is more frequently realized as [qᵡ] in this environment.

Proto-Mayan's palatalized stops were lost in all Mayan languages, but they were reintroduced in Mamean, K'ichean and Ch'ol, as shown in (6). The palatalization of velar consonants is phonemic in Mamean, but allophonic in K'ichean. Ch'ol has a series of palatalized coronals without plain counterparts, likely borrowed from a neighboring Zoquean language (Vázquez Álvarez 2011).

(6) Palatalized consonants

a.	MAM	/tʃikʲl/	[tʃɪkʲl]	*ch'ikyl*	'vertical'
		/tʃiːkl /	[tʃiːkl]	*chiikl*	'gum'
b.	TZ'UTUJIL	/k'im/	[kʲˀim̥]	*k'im*	'straw'
		/k'aam/	[kˀaːm̥]	*k'aam*	'twine'
c.	CH'OL	/tʲiɲɨm/	[tʲiɲɨm̥]	*tyiñäm*	'cotton'
		/tʲatʲ-mutʲ/	[tʲatʲmutʲ]	*tyatymuty*	'rooster'

(England 2011a: 31; Dayley 1985: 17; Bennett 2016: 482)

Most languages have coronal affricates /ts tʃ ts' tʃ'/ and plain fricatives at the same place of articulation /s ʃ/. For the most part, Proto-Mayan's distinction between */h/ and */x/ has merged to /h/, /x/, or /χ/, depending on the language (Law 2014; Bennett 2016). A subset of the Q'anjob'alan and Mamean languages have a larger inventory of sibilants that include the innovative retroflex series /ʂ tʂ tʂˀ/, as illustrated by Q'anjob'al of Santa Eulalia in (7).

(7) Q'ANJOB'AL plain and ejective sibilants by place

a.	/s/	[sik]	*sik*	'cold'				
	/ts/	[tsu]	*tzu*	'Tecomate'	/tsˀ/	[tsˀikin]	*ts'ikin*	'bird'
b.	/ʂ/	[ʂaχaw]	*xajaw*	'moon'				
	/tʂ/	[tʂamex]	*txamej*	'nose'	/tʂˀ/	[tʂˀiʔ]	*tx'i'*	'dog'
c.	/ʃ/	[χalu]	*xhalu*	'pitcher'				
	/tʃ/	[tʃaneχ]	*chanej*	'skirt'	/tʃˀ/	[tʃˀim]	*ch'im*	'straw'

(Raymundo et al. 2000: 33)

Most languages have the sonorants /m n l j w/, although /w/ also surfaces as [v] or [β] depending on the language and context. The phoneme /r/ is only robustly attested in K'ichean; elsewhere, the reflexes of Proto-Mayan */r/ are /t j tʃ/. Proto-Mayan */ŋ/ is found in Chuj, Popti', and Mocho'; for other languages, it merged with /n/ or /x/ (Campbell & Kaufman 1985; Justeson et al. 1985; Law 2014). Final sonorant devoicing is widespread in the family. This is especially true for oral sonorants, but nasals can also be affected, as shown in (8) for Ch'ol:

(8) CH'OL sonorant devoicing

a.	/l/	[lum̥]	*lum*	'earth'	/l/	[ʃtʃil̥]	*xchil*	'grasshopper'
b.	/m/	[mutʲʰ]	*muty*	'chicken'	/m/	[lum̥]	*lum*	'earth'
c.	/ñ/	[ɲetʲˀ]	*ñety'*	'between'	/ñ/	[tʲuɲ̥]	*tyuñ*	'stone'
d.	/w/	[wiɲikʰ]	*wiñik*	'man'	/w/	[xoɲow̥]	*joñow*	'bumblebee'

(Vázquez Álvarez 2011: 39–40)

A defining feature of Mayan's consonant inventory is the contrast between plain voiceless and 'glottalized' stops (commonly Cˀ), which are monosegmental and contrast with Cʔ and ʔC sequences. The nature of glottalization depends on the language, segment, and context, although glottalized consonants are most frequently realized as either ejective or implosive (DeChicchis 1989; Zavala Maldonado 1992; Majzul et al. 2000; Zocal Chayax et al. 2001; Baquiax Barreno et al. 2005; Polian 2013; England & Baird 2017). Bennett (2016) warns that the extensive variation shown in (9) – some of which is allophonic in a given language – may reflect methodological differences, e.g., instrumental vs. impressionistic, as opposed to genuine phonetic variation. (See also Rice, this volume, for general discussion of various problems in phonemic and segmental analysis for many languages of North America.)

(9) Glottalized Cs in approx. order of prevalence with one example language

a.	b’	[ɓ]	ITZAJ	[pˀ]	POPTI’	[ɓ̥]	KAQCHICKEL var.	[b]	HUASTECO
		[mˀ/wˀ]	POQMOCHI’	[ˀb]	TSELTAL	[f/ɸ]	HUASTECO		
b.	t’	[tˀ]	*most languages*	[ɗ]	MAM var.				
c.	k’	[kˀ]	*reliably across languages*						
d.	q’	[qˀ]	Q’EQCHI’	[ʛ]	MAM	[kˀ]	Q’ANJOB’AL var.	[ʔ]	AKATEK
		[ʛ̥]	KAQCHIKEL var.						

Other phonemic contrasts involving glottalization include /p, pˀ, b/ in Yucatecan and Tseltalan (Campbell 1977; Kaufman & Norman 1984) and /t, tˀ, ɗ/ in Mopan (Hofling 2011).

2.3. Root Phonotactics

While syllable structure is typically more varied, roots in Mayan languages (see §3.1) conform to a basic CVC pattern (Kaufman 1990), which may be extended to include CV:C and CV’VC roots, depending on whether a particular language has a length contrast and/or rearticulated vowels. Complex syllable margins on roots are nonetheless attested, especially in derived roots, loanwords, and cases of diachronic vowel deletion (see Bennett 2016 for examples and references).

While underlying VC roots are attested in most Mayan languages; they typically surface with [ʔ] in initial position. Q’anjob’al and Chuj stand out in the family (and cross-linguistically) for contrasting vowel-initial and [ʔ]-initial words, as illustrated in (10); but see Bennett (2016) for an argument that [ʔ] in the non-possessed forms is nonetheless epenthetic.

(10) QANJOB’AL V-initial and [ʔ]-initial words

a.	[ʔiʂim]	*ixim*	‘corn’	b.	[iʂim]	*hixim*	‘your corn’
c.	[ʔun]	*un*	‘paper’	d.	[un]	*hun*	‘your paper’
e.	[ʔon]	*on*	‘avocado’	f.	[on]	*hon*	‘your avocado’

(England 2001: 28)

Finally, co-occurrence restrictions on stops and sibilants are prevalent in Mayan roots. Root-internal restrictions on stops focus on the intersection of laryngeal specification and place of articulation. As shown in (11), two versions of the restriction are found: a basic restriction that applies to all Mayan languages, and an extended version that applies to a smaller subset.

(11) Co-occurrence restrictions on stops

a. BASIC: If a CVC root contains two glottalized stops ($T^ʔ$ & $T^ʔ$), they must be homorganic.

b. EXTENDED: If a CVC root contains two homorganic stops (T_α & T_α), they must have the same laryngeal specification.

For languages with the basic restriction, well-formed roots include all of those shown in (12) (e.g., see Barrett 1999 and Bennett et al. 2017 for K'ichean); for languages with the extended version, well-formed roots are limited to examples a–d in (12) (e.g., see Straight 1976 for Yucatecan). No Mayan language allows roots of the form Tʔ$_{\alpha}$VTʔ$_{\beta}$.

(12) Possible roots

a.	Tʔ$_{\alpha}$ V Tʔ$_{\alpha}$	b.	T$_{\alpha}$ V T$_{\alpha}$
c.	Tʔ$_{\alpha}$ V T$_{\beta}$	d.	T$_{\alpha}$ V Tʔ$_{\beta}$
e.	Tʔ$_{\alpha}$ V T$_{\alpha}$	f.	T$_{\alpha}$ V Tʔ$_{\alpha}$

Mayan languages show similar co-occurrence restrictions on the place, manner, and laryngeal features of sibilants, but restrictions on these segments are more varied and less frequent (Edmonson 1988; Gallagher & Coon 2009; Bennett 2016).

2.4. Stress and Intonation

Mayan languages show a variety of lexical stress patterns including both fixed and mobile systems. The K'ichean branch and Western Mam has fixed final stress, whereas Southern Mam has fixed penultimate stress (Kaufman 1990; England 2001). Mobile systems include quantity sensitive stress, as found in Huastecan and Northern Mam, and phrasally conditioned lexical stress, as found in the Q'anjob'alan and Tseltalan branches (Day 1973; Kaufman 1990; Hofling 2000; Polian 2013). Stress variation in varieties of Mam is illustrated in (13).

(13) MAM stress patterns

a.	Tacaná	[laʔˈʛeʔ]	*la'q'e'*	'advance'
	Final	[keʔiˈχi]	*ke'iji*	'seen'
		[laˈχoχ]	*lajoj*	'ten'
b.	Cajolá	[ˈʔaʔtsˀin]	*a'tz'in*	'salt'
	Penultimate	[ˈχaʔlin]	*ja'lin*	'now'
		[ʔoːˈʂeχe]	*ooxeje*	'three days ago'
c.	Ixtahuacán	[ˈspikʲˀa]	*spiky'a*	'clear'
	Weight sensitive	[puʔˈlaʔ]	*pu'la'*	'dipper'
		[ʔaˈʛuːntl]	*aq'uuntl*	'work'

(Godfrey 1981: 4; England 2001: 43; Bennett 2016: 495)

The status of lexical stress and its interaction with lexical tone is debated in the Yucatecan literature, although these languages are generally considered to have quantity sensitive word-level stress (e.g., Bricker et al. 1998; Gussenhoven & Teeuw 2008; Herrera Zendejas 2011). Work on the acoustic correlates of stress includes Kidder (2013) and Baird (2015).

Turning to intonation, declarative clauses in a number of Mayan languages are realized with a rising contour, which is a fairly uncommon pattern cross-linguistically (see Berinstein 1991 for Q'eqchi'; Shklovsky 2011 for Tseltal; Palosaari 2011 for Mocho'). The more typical association between falling intonation and declarative clauses is also found in the family (see Nielsen 2005 and Baird 2010 for K'iche'; Knowles 1984 for Chontal; Larsen & Pike 1949 for Huastec). Both polar and constituent questions are typically realized with a final rise.

Most work on sentence-level phonology in the Mayan family addresses the prosody of utterances with one of the following constituent types: preverbal topic, preverbal focus, and in situ focus. Aissen (1992) reports that preverbal topics are separated from the rest of the clause by an intonational boundary in Jakaltek, Tsotsil, and one type of topicalized structure in Tz'utujil, but constituents focused in preverbal position are not delimited by a similar boundary. Analogous phrasing has been reported for K'iche' (Can Pixabaj & England 2011), Yucatec (Avelino 2011), and Tseltal (Shklovsky 2011). Research on the prosodic phrasing of preverbal and in situ focus in K'iche' can be found in Velleman (2014), Burdin et al. (2015), and Yasavul (2017).

Kügler et al. (2007), Kügler & Skopeteas (2007), and Gussenhoven & Teeuw (2008) report that lexical tone does not interact with focus or sentence-level intonation in Yucatec, which is an uncommon finding cross-linguistically. However, the distribution of pauses does set off focused constituents from the rest of the clause (Kügler & Skopeteas 2007; Avelino 2011). Lesure and Clemens (2015) and Clemens and Coon (2018b) report on the acoustic correlates of phrasing at the level of the phonological phrase for Ch'ol. Based in part on these findings, Clemens and Coon (2018a) develop an account of word order for Ch'ol with prosodic predictions for extension to the rest of the family.

3. Morphology

Mayan languages have rich systems of inflectional and derivational morphology. They are highly synthetic, agglutinative, and predominantly head-marking. The Sakapultek example in (14) exemplifies these properties. Notice the large morpheme-to-word ratio, the easily differentiated morphemes, and the fact that syntactic relationships are indicated on the phrase head with Set A (ergative) and Set B (absolutive) markers. For more on the distribution of Set A and Set B markers, see §3.3.[1]

(14) . . . x-Ø-a-r-siky'-o'-l juun, Ø -r-xub'u-j-poon l-aj-laab' . . .
CPL-B3-LAT-A3-pick.up-DEP-DIR one B3-A3-whistle.to-SS-DIR DET-DIM-boy
' . . . one went and picked it up, he whistled to the boy. . .'

(Du Bois 2006: 205)

The family's morphological processes are mostly concatenative, e.g., suffxation, prefixation, and compounding, although non-concatenative patterns are also found, e.g., reduplication, vowel alternation, and tone alternation. See Coon (2016) and Polian (2017a) for recent overviews of common and less common morphological phenomena in Mayan languages and Grinevald and Peake (2012) for verbal morphology in particular.

3.1. Root and Word Classes

Mayan languages have root classes, e.g., transitive, intransitive, and nominal, that do not necessarily correspond to surface lexical categories, e.g., verbs and nouns. Nominal roots can often serve directly as nouns (see also §3.2 on nominal morphology). Other roots, e.g., intransitive roots, must combine with certain functional morphology to form a stem before becoming a word, e.g., an intransitive verb or a derived transitive verb (see also §3.3 on verbal morphology). Other root classes include adjectives, positionals, and ideophones. See Haviland (1994), Lois and Vapnarsky (2006), Lois (2011), and Coon (2019) for further discussion on the roots, stems, and words in Mayan languages.

The number of adjectival roots in the family is limited, but there are a number of strategies for deriving adjectives and other modifiers, some of which are regularly occurring, e.g., partial reduplication (England 2004; Polian 2017a). Other strategies are unique to a particular language, e.g., the addition of the relative clause marker *=bä* in Ch'ol (Vázquez Álvarez 2011). Adverbs are typically particles, i.e., morphologically simplex, although some are derived from number terms, as shown in (15) for Tsotsil.

(15) TSOTSIL adverbs derived from numerals

a.	*cha'*	'two'	b.	*ox*	'three'
c.	*cha'-ej*	'in two days'	d.	*ox-ej*	'in three days'
e.	*chab-je*	'two days ago'	f.	*ox-je*	'three days ago'

(Cowan 1969: 42)

All Mayan languages have a class of roots known as positionals for their unique semantic properties, often having to do with position, configuration, and shape (Kaufman 1977). Positionals are alternatively classified as a distinct word class, adjective-type, or participle, depending on the language and the author (Haviland 1994; Coon 2016; Polian 2017a and sources therein; Henderson 2018). The examples in (16) show nonverbal predicates formed from positional roots; positionals never surface independently.

(16) Positional stems

a.	TSELTAL	*nak-al*	'seated'
		sep-el	'in circular form'
b.	CHUJ	*chot-an*	'crouched'
		jenh-an	'outstretched'
c.	YUCATEC	*och-okbal*	'stooped, bent'
		bech'-ekbal	'sprawled'

(Bricker et al. 1998: 15, 29; Polian 2013: 54, 576; Coon 2019)

Mayan languages also have a class of roots known as ideophones (alternatively affect words or expressives) that employ sound symbolism often in the form of onomatopoeia (Barrett 2014; Henderson 2016; Polian 2017b). Examples from Yucatec (Pérez González 2012) and Tseltal (Le Guen 2014) are given in (17).

(17) YUCATEC and TSELTAL ideophones

a. Tso'oj bey u máan kitam, jaaleb, kéej.
IDPH.crush thus A3 pass wild.boar paca deer
'tso'oh is how wild boar, paca, or deer pass.'

(Le Guen 2014: 22)

b. Pura ch'il-bil, tsok' x-chi ta mantekat.
puro frito-ASP IDPH.fry CPL-say PREP manteca
'Completely fried, they go tsok' in the fat.'

(Pérez González 2012: 154)

Closed class words include demonstratives, determiners, classifiers, pronouns (see §3.2), interrogatives, negatives, conjunctions, and discourse participles. Mayan languages have few if any true prepositions. Instead, they rely on a class of obligatorily possessed nominals called 'relational nouns' (Larsen 1988; England 2017) to express both spatial and thematic relations. The Akatek example in (18) shows relational nouns introducing the agent of a passive and an instrument.

(18) X-i-le el yin an lima **y-uu** naj in-c'aal=an **y-etoj** ch'en nawa...
CPL-take-PASS DIR peel CL orange A3-by CL A1-son=1P A3-with CL knife
'The orange was peeled by my son with a knife...'

(Peñalosa 1987: 283)

Mayan languages have two sets of person markers known as SET A and SET B. Set A markers index the complement of relational nouns, as in (18), possessors, the subject of transitive clauses, and the subject of some intransitive clauses (see §3.3). Set B markers index the object of transitive clauses, the subject of most intransitive clauses, and the subject of nonverbal predicates (see §3.3); they are also related to freestanding pronouns in many languages.

3.2. Nominal Morphology

Functional morphology associated with the nominal phrase includes demonstratives and determiners, both of which typically precede the head noun. For many languages, demonstratives and determiners can co-occur.

Western branch languages also display a variety of classifier systems. For example, in Ch'olan languages, hundreds of different numeral classifiers, often derived from verbs, combine with numerals to make nouns countable. Numeral classifiers are typically used only with smaller numbers and are never used with the higher numbers that are typically borrowed from Spanish (Knowles 1984; Bale & Coon 2014).

(19) CHONTAL numeral classifiers

a.	*-tu*	people and animals	*un-tu ahlo'*	'one boy'
			cha'-tu wichu'	'two dogs'
b.	*-k'e*	flat, leaf-like objects	*un-k'e pop*	'one sleeping mat'
			cha-k'e wah	'two tortillas'
c.	*-ch'it*	long, slender objects	*un-ch'it*	'one candle'
			cha-ch'it bih	'two roads'

(Knowles 1984: 201)

Q'anjobalan languages use only a handful of numeral classifiers, if any, but they have rich systems of noun classifiers. Noun classifiers are typically derived from nouns that are semantically bleached in their functional use (see Buenrostro 2009 for Chuj; Craig 1986 for Popti'; Zavala Maldonado 2000 for Akatek). A subset of Chuj's nominal classifiers are given in (20).

(20) CHUJ nominal classifiers

a.	*ix*	feminine	b.	*winh*	masculine
c.	*anh*	plant	d.	*nok'*	animal
e.	*ixim*	grain	f.	*a'*	liquid
g.	*te'*	wood	h.	*k'en*	metal

(Buenrostro et al. 1987: 1229)

Noun classifiers also have a pronominal function, as shown for the Chuj example in (21).

(21) Ø-s-wo' ixim wa'il ix malin. Ø-s-wo' ixim ix.
B3-A3-make CL:grain tortilla CL:FEM Maria B3-A3-make CL:grain CL:FEM
'Maria made the tortillas. She made them.'

(Buenrostro et al. 1987: 1230)

Otherwise, independent personal pronouns in Q'anjob'alan languages and the family more widely are related to a language's Set B markers (see §3.3). This is shown for K'iche' in (22).

(22) K'ICHE' Pronouns and Set B (absolutive) suffixes

in	1SG	*-in*	B1SG	*oj*	1PL	-oj	B1PL
at	2SG FAM	*-at*	B2SG FAM	*ix*	2PL FAM	-ix	B2PL FAM
laal	2SG FOR	*-laq*	B2SG FOR	*alaq*	2PL FOR	-alaq	B2PL FOR
are'	3SG	-Ø	B3SG	*a're'*	3PL	-e'~ ee	B3PL

(Larsen 1988: 100, 105)

Although Mayan languages are predominantly head-initial, the most common type of nominal compound is formed with a modifier that precedes the nominal head. Many Mayan languages also have nominal dvandvas, in which the resulting compound is an agglomeration of nouns conjoined without an overt conjunction. Examples of both head-final and dvandva compounds are given in (23):

(23) Nominal compounds

a.	K'ICHE'	*saq-wach*	'potato'	lit.: white-face
		qati't-qamaam	'our grandparents'	lit.: our grandma-our grandpa
b.	TSELTAL	*mak-te'*	'fence, corral'	lit.: close-stick
		cham-balam	'animals'	lit.: snake-jaguar

(Wälchli 2005: 239; Polian 2017a: 206)

The primary inflectional processes applying to Mayan nouns involve possession and plurality. The basic structure of possession is fairly uniform across the family. If there is an overt possessor, it follows the possessum, unless it is a *wh*-possessor, in which case it precedes the possessum. The possessum is marked with a Set A prefix that cross-references the possessor. In most languages, certain noun classes are obligatorily possessed, while others may not be directly possessed. Inalienable nouns – e.g., body parts, clothing, and kinship terms – typically require special morphology, such as a distributive or abstract noun suffix, in order to surface in their unpossessed form. The possession of nouns belonging to the natural world – e.g., wild animals and weather phenomena – is either disallowed or restricted to certain contexts. Examples from Uspantek are given in (24).

(24) USPANTEK possession

a.	Alienable	*tz'i'*	'my dog'	***ín**-tz'i*	'my dog'
		tiko'n	'sowing'	***a**-tiko'n*	'your sowing'
b.	Inalienable	*q'u'-**niik***	'jacket'	***ín**-q'u'*	'my jacket'
		*ji'-**xeel***	'son-in-law'	***a**-jii'*	'your son-in-law'
c.	Natural world	*koj*	'lion'	***ín**-koj*	'my lion (toy, etc.)'
		jaab'	'rain'	***qa**-jaab'*	'our rain (ceremonial)'

(Can Pixabaj 2006: 64–66; 106)

Plural marking on lexical nouns takes the form of a suffix or enclitic that is optional or disallowed for non-human referents. Distributional patterns for plural marking on human nouns vary: for some languages, plural human nouns are obligatorily marked (e.g., England 2011b for K'iche'; Polian 2013 for Tseltal). For other languages, plural human nouns are only usually marked (e.g., Butler 2011 and England 2011b for Yucatec). Even in cases of non-obligatory marking of plural human nouns, a tendency has been noted to mark animate plural nouns with either a plural suffix or via agreement with the predicate (Aissen 1987; England 2011b).

3.3. Verbal Morphology

Most of the family's morphological complexity is found in the verbal domain. This section addresses the core elements of the Mayan verb stem, indicated in (25), except for the voice category, which will be addressed in §4.

(25) Elements of the Mayan verb stem

TAM · {ABS} · ERG · **VERB ROOT** · VOICE · STATUS SUFFIX/MOOD · {ABS}

England (2017) observes that the verb stem's preverbal elements are mostly inflectional, while postverbal morphemes are predominantly derivational. Variation in verbal morphology within the family is mostly found in the postverbal, derivational domain. Another feature of Mayan verbal morphology is allomorphy driven by an opposition between transitive vs. intransitive roots and whether a stem's valency is derived or underlying.

Preverbal TAM markers are either represented as independent words or part of the verb, depending on factors ranging from the distribution of second-position clitics to orthographic convention. The primary function of preverbal TAM markers is to mark aspectual properties of the event; tense is indicated periphrastically, and mood is predominantly marked with postverbal suffixes. Minimally, preverbal TAM markers in Mayan languages show a distinction between the completive and incompletive aspects, but they may also mark the progressive and secondarily encode mood differences as well.

Postverbal mood markers are less uniform across the family and may include irrealis, perfect, and imperative. Some of Q'anjob'al's aspect and mood distinctions are illustrated in (26). The potential, exhortative, and optative moods are formed with the irrealis suffix *-oq*, which combines with the reportative *-ab'* in the optative.

(26) Q'ANJOB'AL Tense-Aspect-Mood

		Intransitive		*Transitive*	
a.	CPL	***x***=*ach way-i*	'You slept.'	***x***=*ach y-il-a'*	'S/he saw you.'
b.	ICPL	***ch***=*ach way-i*	'You sleep.'	***ch***=*ach y-il-a'*	'S/he sees you.'
c.	POT	***q***=*ach way-**oq***	'You will sleep.'	***q***=*ach y-il-a'*	'S/he will see you.'
d.	EXH	*way-**oq**=on*	'Let's sleep.'	*j-il=eq (ix)*	'Let's see her.'
e.	OPT	*way-**oq-ab'**=i*	'S/he may sleep.'	y-*il-**oq-ab'**=hach*	'S/he may see you.'

(Mateo Toledo 2017: 539)

In (26), the irrealis *-oq* suffix is used in the exhortative and optative moods with intransitive verbs, but not transitive ones. As mentioned earlier, the opposition between transitive and intransitive verbs is observed in Mayan languages in a number of ways, including inflectional allomorphy, derivational strategies, and person marking on the verb. (See Law & Stuart 2017 for a discussion of differences between transitive and intransitive verbs in Classic Mayan.)

One or both person markers follow preverbal TAM markers. All Mayan languages have an ergative alignment pattern where ergative person markers (Set A markers) index the subjects of transitive clauses, and absolutive person makers (Set B markers) index the objects of transitive clauses and the subjects of intransitive clauses.

Proto-Mayan's ergative and absolutive markers are shown in (27). Note that the Set A/ergative markers include distinct forms for affixing to vowel- vs. consonant-initial stems. This phonologically determined allomorphy remains present across the family. The third-person singular Set B marker is null in all languages as well.

(27) PROTO-MAYAN person markers

	Set A/ERG		Set B/ABS
	__V	*__C*	
1SG	**inw-*	**in-*	**iin*
2SG	**aaw-*	**a-*	**at*
3SG	**r-*	**u-*	*Ø
1PL	**q-*	**q-*	**o'nh*
2PL	**eer-*	**iw-*	**ix*
3PL	**k-*	**k-*	**eb'*

(Kaufman 1990: 71–72)

As shown in (27), both the Set A and Set B series encode person and number. The number distinction has been most faithfully maintained in the languages of the Eastern branch. Other languages mark number with a generalized plural enclitic, e.g., *=o'ob* in Yucatec, or a plural person enclitic, e.g., *=aq* in Uspantek, in combination with Set A markers that encode person but not number.

Languages differ with respect to the location of the absolutive person marker. Eastern branch languages, with the exception of Ixil, are described pretheoretically as 'high' absolutive languages: the absolutive maker is preverbal and follows the TAM marker. Yucatecan and Ch'olan-Tseltalan languages are described as 'low' absolutive languages, because the absolutive marker surfaces at the end of the verb stem. This positional variation is illustrated for Achi and Ch'ol in (28).

(28) High and low absolutive markers

	ACHI	CH'OL	
a.	*x-**in**-u-laq'apuuj*	*tyi i-mek'ey-**oñ***	'S/he hugged me.'
b.	*x-**at**-u-laq'apuuj*	*tyi i-mek'ey-**ety***	'S/he hugged you.'
c	*x-**Ø**-u-laq'apuuj*	*tyi i-mek'e-**Ø***	'S/he hugged him.'

(Lóopez & Sis Iboy 1992: 77)

Languages in the Q'anjob'alan branch, with the exception of Tojolabal, utilize both positions depending on the context, e.g., whether or not the clause includes an overt preverbal TAM marker. When there is a TAM marker present, the absolutive marker cliticizes there, as in (26a–c), otherwise, it surfaces in the low position, following the verb stem, as in (26d–e). Based on arguments such as their variable position in some languages, absolutive makers are typically considered to be clitics instead of affixes. In contrast, ergative person markers are prefixes in every Mayan language except those in the Yucatecan branch.

Mayan languages show a number of other alignment patterns in addition to the strictly ergative pattern introduced previously (see Zavala Maldonado 2017 for a more complete overview of morphological alignment in Mayan languages). Whereas the completive aspect is strictly associated with morphological ergativity across the family, the incompletive and potential trigger a tripartite system for Ch'orti' (Quizar 1979) and accusative alignment patterns in Yucatecan, Ch'olan, and Poqom languages. Compare (29a) to (29b) for the ergative pattern in Yucatec and (29a) to (29c) for the accusative pattern in Yucatec.

(29) YUCATEC alignment

a. T-**in** w-il-aj-**ech**
   CPL-A1.SG see-PERF-B2.SG
   'I saw you.'

b. J-k'uch-**ech**
   CPL-arrive-B2.SG
   'You arrived.'

c. Táan **in** k'uch-ul.
   DUR A1.SG arrive-IMPERF
   'I am arriving.'

(Bricker 1981: 83–84)

Split ergative patterns like the one shown for Yucatec in (29) likely developed from bi-clausal structures consisting of a matrix verb and an embedded nominalization (Bricker 1981; Kaufman 1990). Coon (2010a; 2013) develops a related, synchronic account of Ch'ol's apparent accusative alignment pattern, in which the imperfect and progressive markers are treated as intransitive predicates that select nominalized complements. On this account, the Set A marker indexes a possessor, not the subject of an intransitive verb as it would in the opposing absolutive analysis.

In addition to person markers that indicate whether a stem is intransitive or transitive, most Mayan languages also have a series of inflectional suffixes known as status or thematic suffixes that vary according to certain properties of the verb stem, including the number of arguments it selects. The status suffixes that have been reconstructed for Proto-Mayan most closely resemble those found in K'iche' (Kaufman & Norman 1984; Kaufman 1990; Robertson 1992), which have different forms depending on whether the stem is transitive or intransitive and whether it is an independent clause. Depending on the language, status suffixes might also reinforce aspectual or derivational distinctions. The table in (30) represents some of the variation found in status suffix morphology.

(30) Status suffixes

a.	K'ICHE'	INTRANS	*-ik*	*k-at-b'iin-**ik***	'You are walking.'
		TRANS	*-o/-u*	*x-Ø-at-k'ex-**o***	'You changed it.'
		DEP INTRANS	*-oq/-a*	*k-at-b'iin-**oq***	'Walk!'
		DEP TRANS	*-V'/V*	*cha-Ø-k'ex-**a'***	'Change it!'
b.	MOPAN	ICPL INTRANS	*-Vl*	*walak a-jok'-**ol***	'You go out.'
		ICPL TRANS	*-ik*	*walak 'aw-il-**ik**-en*	'You see me.'
		CPL INTRANS	*-Ø*	*jok'-**Ø**-eech*	'You went out.'
		CPL TRANS	*-aj*	*aw-il-**aj**-en*	'You saw me.'
		DEP INTRANS	*-Vk*	*ka'-jok'-**ok**-ech*	'that you go out'
		DEP TRANS	*-V'*	*ka'aw-il-**a'**-een*	'that you saw me.'
c.	CH'OL	ICPL CVC TRANS	*-Ø*	*mi i-tyaj-**Ø***	'S/he finds it.'
		CPL CVC TRANS	*-V*	*tyi i-tyaj-**a***	'S/he found it.'
		ICPL DERIVED TRANS	*-Vñ*	*mi k-il-**äñ***	'I see it.'
		CPL DERIVED TRANS	*-V*	*tyi k-il-**ä***	'I saw it.'

(Larsen 1988: 194; Vázquez Álvarez 2011: 188; Hofling 2017: 709)

One final note about status suffixes is that, for some languages, whether or not they surface, or the particular form in which they surface, depends on whether or not they are located in the final position of the phrase. If the K'iche' examples in (30) were followed by an adverb, e.g., *iwiir* 'yesterday', the status suffix would drop in both examples of independent clauses and it would surface as *-a* for the dependent intransitive and *-V* for the dependent transitive (Larsen 1988; Can Pixabaj 2015). As such, status suffixes in languages displaying this type of distribution are described as 'phrase-final' suffixes (Mondloch 1978; Larsen 1988; Kaufman 1990; Can Pixabaj 2015); for a prosodic analysis see Aissen (1992) and Henderson (2012a).

4. Syntax

Mayan languages are robustly head-initial in all domains. In most languages, the order of the major sentential constituents in discourse-neutral context is verb-initial; however, when a constituent is questioned, focused, or topicalized, it surfaces before the verb. Many Mayan languages have restrictions on the extraction of ergative arguments, which condition the use of a special AGENT FOCUS construction. This section focuses on a description of a few core aspects of verbal and clausal syntax, but see Aissen (1996), Lois and Vapnarsky (2006), and Coon (2010b) for connections to the nominal domain. Data from Mayan languages have contributed to recent theoretical developments in a number of areas of syntactic research, including morphological ergativity and extraction restrictions (Coon et al. 2014; Assmann et al. 2015; Deal 2016; Polinsky 2016; 2017; Douglas et al. 2017); φ-feature agreement (Preminger 2014); and split ergative systems (Coon 2013; Coon & Preminger 2017).

4.1. Voice and Valency

Mayan languages have complex grammatical voice systems with both valency-increasing and valency-decreasing operations that include dedicated suffixes for causative, applicative, passive, anticausative, and antipassive constructions. Grammatical voice is a particularly well-studied area of Mayan linguistics; overviews include Dayley (1981), Grinevald and Peake (2012), Coon (2016), England (2017), Polian (2017a), and Zavala Maldonado (2017).

4.1.1. Increasing Valency

Causative suffixes in Mayan languages offer a productive means to increase the valency of both verbal and nonverbal predicates. Tojolabal stands out among Mayan languages for relying primarily on periphrasis to form causative constructions (Curiel 2017, cf. Gómez 2017), which is a strategy that other languages use only with root transitives. For more on the topic of syntactic causatives, see Aissen (1987) and Coon (2010a).

In K'iche', the morphological causative *-isa* combines with intransitive verb roots (Larsen 1988; Can Pixabaj 2017), whereas in Q'anjob'al, the morphological causative *-ne* combines with adjectival and nominal roots (Mateo Toledo 2008; 2017). In Tseltal, *-(t)es* applies to both verbal and nonverbal predicates (Polian 2013, 2017b). Causative suffixes that apply to positional roots typically take a different form than those that apply to other types of predicates, e.g., *-ab'aa* in K'iche', *-b'a* in Q'anjob'al, and *<h/j>-an* in Tseltal. Examples of morphological causatives are given in (31).

(31) Causative suffixes

		Root			*CAUS stem*	
a.	K'iche'	*kam*	'die'	INTR	*kam-**isa***	'kill'
		b'iin	'walk'	INTR	*b'iin-**isa***	'drive'
		tzay	'hanging'	POS	*tzay-**ab'aa***	'hang'
b.	Q'anjob'al	*miman*	'big'	ADJ	*miman-**ne***	'make big'
		winaq	'man'	NOM	*winaq-**ne***	'make a man'
		tel	'lying'	POS	*tel-**b'a***	'lay s.o. down'
c.	Tseltal	*lok'*	'exit'	INTR	*lok'-**es***	'take out'
		ejch'en	'wound'	NOM	*ejch'en-**tes***	'hurt'
		ban	'lying'	POS	*ba<**h**>n-**an***	'set down'

(Larsen 1988: 185; Mateo Toledo 2017: 541; Polian 2017b: 627)

Many Mayan languages can increase the valency of a root transitive with an applicative suffix that is cognate with Proto-Mayan **-b'e*. Huastec is an exception for having non-cognate applicative suffixes *-chi~-tsiy* and *-na'*, and Yucatecan languages lack a morphological applicative construction entirely (Mora-Marín 2003). In the Western branch, the applicative's third argument is typically a benefactive that is treated like a direct object, as evident from Set B agreement. In the Eastern branch, the applicative suffix is used only when an instrument is focused, questioned, or relativized. Otherwise, the applicative is expressed in an oblique phrase. Languages in this group vary as to whether the instrument is indexed on the verb, as in K'iche', or the direct object is, as in Tz'utujil (Dayley 1981; Mora-Marín 2003).

Ixil is the only Mamean language that has reflexes of Proto-Mayan **-b'e*. In the example in (32) (from Mora-Marín 2003), the instrument is licensed by the applicative *-b'e* when it undergoes focus-fronting but is introduced by a relational noun when it surfaces in postverbal position. In both cases, the person features of the direct object are indexed on the verb.

(32) IXIL applicative constructions

a. A-k'oni=in t-a'n uula.
A2SG-shoot=B1SG A3SG-RN sling
'You shot me with a sling.'

b. Uula a-k'oni-**b'e**=in.
sling A2SG-shoot-APL= B1SG
'With a sling, you shot me.'

(Ayres 1983: 42)

For more on the syntax of applicative constructions in Mayan languages see Henderson (2007) for Kaqchikel and Coon (2016) for a comparative perspective.

4.1.2. Decreasing Valency

Turning to valency-decreasing operations, Mayan languages often have multiple passive constructions. Passive verbs in Mayan languages show intransitive person marking. The patient is promoted to the subject position and the agent, or canonical subject, may either be unexpressed, as in (34b), or surface as an oblique, as in (33b) and (38b).

Passive voice, and voice morphology more generally, is an area where nonconcatenative morphology arises in Mayan languages. In Yucatec, a vowel alternation marks the passive for certain root classes. As shown in (33), the difference between the root transitive *jek'* 'break' and the passive stem *jé'ek* is one of vowel quality (Bricker et al. 1998; Avelino et al. 2011; Lois 2011). In K'iche', the root vowel is lengthened in the passive (Larsen 1988), which is one of the many reflexes of Proto-Mayan's *<*h*> infix found in Mayan languages today (Campbell 1977; 2017; Law & Stuart 2017).

(33) YUCATEC passive

a. T=in jek'-ah=Ø.
CPL-A1SG break-SS=B3SG
'I broke it.'

b. **Je'ek'**-Ø=Ø tuméen teen.
break<PASS>-SS=B3SG because 1SG
'It was broken by me.'

(Bricker 1978: 8)

Mamean languages have particularly rich passive inventories, in which a particular passive voice suffix may change the semantics of the event by adding, e.g., an iterative, durative, achievement, or purpose meaning (England 1988; 2011a; Pérez Vail & Jiménez 1997; Pérez Vail 2014). The iterative and durative passives, two of seven distinct forms, are shown for Cajolá Mam in (34):

(34) Two CAJOLÁ MAM passives

a. In Ø=q'maa-**njtz**.
ICPL B3SG=say-PASS
'It is said (non-stop).'

b. In Ø=q'um-**li**.
ICPL B3SG=say-PASS
'It is said (repeatedly).'

(Pérez Vail 2014: 104)

As in the passive, the subject of the anticausative construction is the semantic patient. Polian (2017b: 626) describes the effect of the anticausative in Tseltalan as allowing "the event to be presented from the viewpoint of the patient". Also called the mediopassive or middle voice construction, analogues are found in each of the major branches. Depending on the language, authors report that agents are (i) disallowed in the anticausative; (ii) less likely to appear in the anticausative as compared to the passive; or (iii) expressed in the anticausative in order to add a particular meaning to the event, e.g., an abilitative sense, as in (35).

(35) TSELTAL anticausative

a. La j-mak-Ø te ti'nah=e.
CPL A1-close-B3 ART door=ENC
'I closed the door.'

b. Ma<**h**>k-Ø te ti'nah=e.
close<ANTIC>-B3 ART door=ENC
'The door closed.'

c. Ma<**h**>k-Ø k-u'un te ti'nah=e.
close<ANTIC>-B3 A1-RN ART door=ENC
'I was able to close the door.'

(Polian 2017b: 626)

Wichmann (1999) discusses three anticausatives in Ch'orti: *-p*, which involves motion, as in *chok-p* 'to become lost' from *chok* 'to throw away', *-tz'*, which involves a change of appearance, as in *nam-tz'* 'to vanish' from *nam* 'to hide', and *-k'*, which involves a change of state, as in *b'ax-k'* 'to become pulled up' from *b'ax* 'to pull up'.

In addition to the passive and anticausative constructions that detransitivize the verb by demoting the actor, most Mayan languages also have a morphologically indicated antipassive construction that detransitivizes the verb by demoting the patient. In the most common type of antipassive construction, often referred to as the absolutive antipassive, the person features of the actor are co-indexed on the verb with Set B morphology and the theme is unexpressed or realized in an oblique phrase, depending on the context and the language. For example, in Sipakapense (36), only third-person singular patients may be overt in this construction.

(36) SIPAKAPENSE absolutive antipassive

a. Ri q'iij xib'al k-Ø-por-n.
DET sun much ICPL-B3-burn-ANTIP
'The sun burns a lot.'

b. Wiixa k-Ø-chom-r-s-n-ik ri r-kuch Mariy.
Wiixa ICPL-B3-fat-VERS-CAUS-ANTIP-PFM DET A3SG-pig Mary
'Wiixa is fattening up Mary's pig.'

(Barrett 1999: 243–244)

In addition to the absolutive antipassive, Q'anjob'alan languages also have an incorporation antipassive construction, in which a non-referential and nonspecific object unaccompanied by functional structure, e.g., demonstratives, determiners, or classifiers, must immediately follow the verb (Maxwell 1976; Craig 1979; Zavala Maldonado 1992; Mateo Toledo 2008; Coon 2019). Thus, incorporation antipassives in Q'anjob'alan languages are a rare instance of VOS order in what are typically VSO languages.

(37) Q'ANJOB'AL antipassive

a. Max- Ø s-tzok' naq winaq te' si'.
CPL-B3 A3-chop CL man CL wood
'The man cut the wood.'

b. Max- Ø s-tzok' si' naq winaq.
CPL-B3 chop-ANTIP-SS wood CL man
'The man cut wood.'

(Clemens & Coon 2018a)

One final note about voice and argument structure in Mayan languages is that saliency hierarchies often determine whether an event is expressed in a particular voice. For example, detransitivizing voices are commonly used to avoid inanimate ergative arguments (Craig 1977; Berinstein 1985; Aissen 1997), to express events with obviate actors and proximate patient, or third-person actors and speech-act-participant patients (Aissen 1997; 1999b; Zavala Maldonado 2007). An example from Tsotsil is given in (38).

(38) TSOTSIL passive

a. *I-Ø-x-poxta Xun li pox=e.
ICPL-B3SG-A3SG-cure Juan DET medicine= ENC
('The medicine cured Juan.')

b. I-Ø-poxta-**at** ta pox li Xun=e.
ICPL-B3SG-cure-PASS by medicine DET Juan=ENC
'Juan was cured by the medicine.'

(Aissen 1997: 727)

The reverse is also true: detransitivizing voices are disallowed or dispreferred for events in which an actor is ranked higher than the patient. An example from Ch'ol is given in (39).

(39) CH'OL passive

a. Tyi i-mel-e-Ø waj k-ña'jel.
CPL A3-make-SS-B3 tortilla A1-aunt
'My aunt prepared the tortilla.'

b. *Tyi me<**j**>l-i-Ø waj tyi k-ña'jel.
CPL A3-make<PASS>SS-B3 tortilla PREP A1-aunt
('The tortilla was prepared by my aunt.')

(Zavala Maldonado 2007: 297)

4.2. Embedded Clauses

Embedded clauses in Mayan languages vary according to how much they resemble matrix clauses. Finite embedded clauses may be introduced by a complementizer, as in (40a), in which case they are extraposed in many languages. Embedded clauses without a complementizer, as in (40b), do not necessarily have this requirement (Aissen 2017a).

(40) TSOTSIL finite embedded clauses

a. I-y-il ti s-me' un-e [ti muk'bu ta s-sa' y-ajnil
CPL-A3-see DET A3-mother PAR-ENC COMP never ICPL A3-seek A3-wife
ti. s-krem un-e].
DET A3-son PAR-ENC
'His mother saw that his son was never going to find a wife.'

b. Mu s-kan [ch-k-uch'-be-tik] li yajval=balamil-e.
NEG A3-want ICPL-A1-drink-APPL-1PL.INCL DET lord=earth-ENC
'The Earth Lord didn't want us to drink it.'

(Aissen 2017a: 261)

Verbs in finite embeddings have the full range of aspectual marking and person marking, and so they must project at least as high as IP. Predicate negation in embedded clauses is only possible when the clause is introduced by an overt complementizer. Because negation is higher than IP in Mayan languages (e.g., see (44a) and (47)) where negation precedes the aspectual marker, embedded clauses without an overt complementizer must project only as high as IP (Aissen 2017a).

Nonfinite embedded clauses in Mayan languages do not surface with preverbal TAM markers, but variation occurs with respect to whether or not arguments are indexed on the verb stem. Nonfinite embedded clauses with intransitive verbs often show no person marking, as in the Q'eqchi' and Ch'ol examples from Coon (2016) in (41).

(41) Q'EQCHI' and CH'OL embedded nonfinite intransitives

a. N-inw-aj [xik sa' li k'ayil].
ASP-A1SG-want go into DET market
'I want to go to the market.'

(Kockelman 2003: 30)

b. K-om [wäy-el].
A1-want sleep-NML
'I want to sleep.'

(Coon 2016: 545)

In nonfinite embeddings of transitive verbs, person marking varies. Consider the Q'eqchi' example in (42a), in which the person marking indexes the third-person singular object *ch'op* 'pineapple', whereas in the Ch'ol example in (42b), person marking on the verb is first-person singular, indexing the subject.

(42) Q'EQCHI' and CH'OL embedded nonfinite transitives

a. T-inw-aj [x-loq'-bal li ch'op].
ASP-A1SG-want A3SG-buy-NML DET pineapple
'I want to buy the pineapple.'

(Kockelman 2003: 32)

b. K-om [k-mäñ jiñi pajch'].
A1-want A1-buy DET pineapple
'I want to buy the pineapple.'

(Coon 2016: 545)

In cases like (42a), derivational morphology transparently indicates that embedded clauses are nominalizations. Examples like (42b), in which the nonfinite embedding does not bare nominal morphology, are also analyzed as involving nominalization on the basis of syntactic characteristics (Coon 2013). See Aissen (2017a) for cases of nonfinite embedded clauses that resist a nominalization analysis. For more on embedded clauses in individual languages and from a cross-linguistic perspective, see Craig (1977), Dayley (1981), Mateo Toledo (2008), Coon (2013), Vázquez Álvarez (2013), Imanishi (2014), and Can Pixabaj (2015), among others.

4.3. Word Order

Although 'basic' word order is an ill-fitting concept for many languages, including those in the Mayan family (Quizar 1979; Brody 1984; Larsen 1988; England 1991; Robinson 2002; Clemens & Coon 2018a), Mayan languages typically exhibit verb-initial word order in discourse-neutral contexts. Non-verb-initial word orders arise in information-structural configurations that involve topic and focus, both of which are associated with preverbal positions across the family. For some

Mayan languages, all six possible permutations are attested: VSO, VOS, SVO, SOV, OVS, and OSV (Brody 1984; Hofling 1984; Can Pixabaj 2006).

4.3.1. Discourse-Neutral Word Order

The Mayan family is described as verb-initial, because VSO and VOS order are associated with discourse-neutral contexts for many languages. A more specific statement about 'basic' word order in individual Mayan languages is more challenging, in part because core-arguments are often not realized as full lexical nominal phrases. A K'iche' corpus example is provided in (43), in which the person and number features of the subject and object are marked on the verb, but only the oblique argument is expressed lexically.

(43) K-Ø-in-tzijo-j chi k-e konojeel l=a'k'al-aab'.
ICPL-B3SG-A1SG-tell-SS PREP A3PL-RN all DET=child-PL
'I tell it to all children.'

(Can Pixabaj 2017: 480)

Drawing heavily on Tseltsal data, Norman and Campbell (1978) argue that Proto-Mayan word order alternated between VOS and VSO. In the following Tseltal corpus examples, the subject precedes the object in (44a), while in (44b), the object precedes the subject.

(44) TSELTAL verb-initial clauses

a. Ma' ba s=tak' xlok' **j=k'atin** [s jo'tik]
NEG A3=be.possible AUX A1=take.warmth.from 1PL.PRON
[o te j=ch'ul-tat-tik=e].
DET A1=holy-father-1PL=ENC
'It is not possible for us to get out and warm ourselves in the sun.'

b. Ja' nax laj jich, la laj **s=ta** [o alchaxiltik]
EMPH only HS thus PFV HS A3=find orange.orchard
[s te winik=e].
DET man=ENC
'Thus it was, the man found an orange orchard.'

(Robinson 2002: 61, 76)

Word order in the family is often categorized as: (i) strictly VSO; (ii) strictly VOS; or (iii) VSO/VOS alternating. More accurately, languages in the family differ with respect to the availability and frequency of VOS word order; however, all Mayan languages allow VSO order in some contexts (England 1991: 484; Clemens & Coon 2018a). In languages with fully transitive VOS clauses, postverbal argument order is often determined by definiteness or D^0-level material on the object, e.g., a determiner or demonstrative, but not typically a numeral classifier (England 1991; Coon 2010b; Clemens & Coon 2018a). VSO is found with DP objects, as in (44a), whereas VOS is found with NP objects, as in (44b) and (45a).

Phonological weight and/or syntactic complexity also contributes to determining the relative order of postverbal arguments; heavy arguments tend to surface towards the end of the clause (Larsen 1988; England 1991). Word order examples from San Mateo Chuj are given in (45). Note the heavy object in (45b).

(45) SAN MATEO CHUJ verb-initial clauses

a. **Ix=Ø=y-il** [o waj Xun] [s ix Malin].
PFV=A3=B3-kill CL Juan CL Maria
'Maria saw Juan.'

b.	**Ix=s=milcham** [s	eb'	winak] [o	cha'-wan	eb'	winh	k-et'	b'ey-um].
	PFV=A3=kill	PL	man	two-CL	PL	CL	A1P-RN	walk-NML

'The men killed two of our companions.'

(Buenrostro 2013: 108–109)

A frequent claim, especially in the early literature on Mayan word order, is that the relative animacy of the subject and object determines the order of postverbal elements. While certain combinations of animate and inanimate arguments are licit only with certain predicate types (see §4.1), animacy probably does not contribute more directly to word order alternations (Minko 2000; Robinson 2002; Skopeteas & Verhoeven 2005; Clemens & Coon 2018a).

There are a variety of accounts for verb-initial word order in Mayan languages that include: (i) generating the subject in a right-side specifier to derive VOS (Aissen 1992); (ii) raising the VP into a position above the subject to derive VOS and evacuating the object in advance of VP-raising to derive VSO (Coon 2010b); and (iii) cyclically X^0-raising the verb into $Infl^0$ in all clauses, which results in VSO, and deriving VOS via prosodic reordering of bare NP objects, right-side topicalization, and heavy-NP shift (Clemens & Coon 2018a). Also see Chung (2017) and Clemens and Polinsky (2017) for overview articles on the derivation of verb-initial structures in Mayan and other languages.

4.3.2. Topic and Focus

Subject-initial word order also occurs frequently across the family and is argued by some to be the canonical word order for varieties of Ch'orti', Yucatec, and Kaqchikel (Quizar 1979; Gutiérrez Bravo & Monforte y Madera 2008; Gutiérrez Bravo 2011; Clemens 2013). SVO order is most commonly the result of a specific information-structural configuration, e.g., when the grammatical subject is a designated topic, as in (46a), or when the subject undergoes constituent focus, as in (46b).

(46) CH'OL SVO clauses

a.	[TOP	(A)	li	aj-Wañ=i	] **tsa'=bi**	**kej-i-Ø**	tyi	troñel.
		(TOP)	DET	CL-Juan=ENC	CPL=REP	start-SS-B3	PREP	work

'As for Juan, it is said that he started to work.'

b.	[FOC	Jiñ=bi	aj-Wañ]	**tyi**	**kej-i-Ø**	tyi	troñel.
		FOC=REP	CL-Juan	CPL	start-SS-B3	PREP	work

'It is said that it is Juan who started working.'

(Vázquez Álvarez 2011: 325)

Topicalized constituents in Mayan languages are characterized as either 'external' or 'internal' depending on how well integrated they are into the main clause (Aissen 1992, 2017c). The Ch'ol example in (46a) exemplifies Mayan's external topic construction (Vázquez Álvarez 2011); the topic is followed by the intonational enclitic *=i*, which is typically found in clause-final position. Also note the placement of the reportative marker *=bi* in (46a) as compared to (46b): unlike the focused subject, the topicalized subject in (46a) is skipped by second position clitics. In contrast, the Tz'utujil example in (47) exemplifies Mayan's internal topic construction, in which the topic is more fully integrated into the clause. For an overview of the differences between the two types of topics in different Mayan languages see Aissen (2017c), who analyzes external topics as adjoining to CP and internal topics as generated in the specifier of CP.

(47) [TOP	Ja	ch'ooy] ma	**x-uu-tij**	ta	ja	kéeso.
	DET	rat NEG	CPL- A3SG-eat	IRR	DET	cheese

'The rat didn't eat the cheese.'

(Dayley 1985: 321)

Clauses in many languages can surface with two preverbal arguments yielding both OSV and SOV orders. The topic position precedes the focus position, as shown in (48) for Itzaj.

(48) ITZAJ SOV and OSV clauses

a. [TOP In-tech-ej] [FOC b'a'ax] **k-a-kiix-t-ik** wa'yej?
EMPH-2SG-TOP what ICPL-A2-seek-TR-SS here
'You, WHAT are you seeing here?'

b. [TOP U-meyaj-ej] [FOC in-ten] **k-inw-il-ik** ti'i.
A3-work-TOP EMPH-1SG ICPL-A1-see-SS 3SG.IO
'His work, I look after it for him.'

(Hofling 2000: 196)

Topicalized constituents can also occur on the right periphery of the clause, in which case the resulting word order might be verb-initial (Can Pixabaj 2004; Curiel 2007). An example of a VOS clause with a topicalized subject is given in (49) for Tojolabal.

(49) **S-mak'-unej** [O ja jorje] [TOP ja jwano='i].
A3-hit-PERF DET Jorge DET Juan=TOP
'Juan hit Jorge.'

(Curiel 2007: 74)

Discussing topic and focus in the context of word order provides only the most basic introduction to the phenomena. For more on the syntax and semantics of these constructions and the morphosyntactic realization of information structure more generally, see the works cited in this subsection as well as Can Pixabaj and England (2011), Gutiérrez Bravo and Monforte y Madera (2010), Vázquez Álvarez and Zavala Maldonado (2013), and Velleman (2014).

4.4. Syntactic Ergativity

As introduced in §3.3, all Mayan languages are morphologically ergative, but the absolutive person marker can occur in one of two positions. In high absolutive languages, the absolutive marker is preverbal and precedes the ergative marker. In low absolutive languages, the absolutive marker surfaces at the end of the verb stem. The position of the absolutive person marker is a good predictor for whether or not the language in question is syntactically ergative. For a syntactic explanation of this correlation, see Tada (1993) and Coon et al. (2014); for a historical, diffusion-based explanation, see Aissen (2017b).

High absolutive languages display ergative patterns in their syntax; i.e., transitive subjects are treated differently from objects and intransitive subjects in certain syntactic contexts. For Mayan languages, ergative patterns in the syntax are found mostly in focus constructions, relative clauses, and *wh*-questions, i.e., constructions that involve A'-movement. For a broader discussion of syntactic ergativity in Mayan languages, see Zavala Maldonado (2017).

In Ch'ol, a low absolutive language (28), the structure of subject and object *wh*-questions is comparable. In Ch'ol, the object of the transitive clause can be questioned directly (50a), as can the subject of the transitive clause (50b).

(50) CH'OL constituent questions

a. Chuki tyi i-k'ux-u-Ø jiñi ts'i'?
what PFV A3-eat-SS-B3 DET dog
'What did the dog eat?'

b. Maxki tyi i-k'ux-u-Ø jiñi waj ?
who PFV A3-eat-SS-B3 DET tortilla
'Who ate the tortilla?'

In Achi, a high absolutive language (28), the structure of the object *wh*-question (51a) looks quite similar to that of the Ch'ol object *wh*-question (50a): the *wh*-word precedes the aspect marker, the verb shows transitive person marking, and the subject follows the verb. In contrast, Achi uses an intransitive, antipassive construction to question the semantic agent (51b). In (51b), the verb lacks the ergative, Set A marker that is present in the object *wh*-question (51a). In addition, the theme in (51b) is introduced in an oblique phrase. Finally, the antipassive suffix *-ow* appears on the verb. Thus, in order to form a *wh*-question targeting the thematic agent, the thematic agent must first be placed in a grammatical context in which it is the subject of a formally intransitive clause.

(51) ACHI constituent questions

a. Sa' x-Ø-u-tij ri ts'i' ?
what PFV-B3.SG-A3.SG-eat DET dog
'What did the dog eat?'

b. Chinaa x-Ø-tij-**ow** r-e ri wa?
who PFV-B3.SG-eat-ANTIP A3.SG-RN DET tortilla
'Who ate the tortilla?'

(López & Sis Iboy 1992: 163)

While the thematic patient is introduced by a relational noun in Achi (51b), it can be introduced directly in other syntactically ergative languages, such as Q'anjob'al, in the context of agent focus (also known as agent voice or the focus antipassive). Agent focus circumvents the transitive subject extraction restriction without relegating the object to an oblique phrase.

(52) Q'ANJOB'AL agent focus

a. Miman-Ø jun no' ch-ach xib'te-**n**-i.
big-B3 one animal CPL-B2sg frighten-AF-SS
'An animal that frightens you is big.'

b. A naq unin max-Ø tayene-**n** te na.
FOC CL child PFV-A3SG take.care-AF CL house
'It is the child who took care of the house.'

(Mateo Toledo 2008: 79; 2017: 558)

Agent focus constructions have a notionally dyadic predicate with intransitive person marking. In many Mayan languages, the agent focus marker (*-n* in the Q'anjob'al examples presented in (52)) is found in other types of constructions including antipassives and embedded transitives. Agent focus constructions in individual languages differ with respect to a number of properties, including (i) whether the thematic agent or patient controls person marking on the verb, and (ii) whether or not the person hierarchy (1/2 > 3PL > 3SG) plays a role in the use and form of agent focus constructions. Furthermore, the use of an agent focus construction is nonobligatory in some cases; e.g., see Heaton et al. (2016) for Kaqchikel.

In some languages, including Q'eqchi', the semantic agent always agrees with the Set B marker on the verb (Berinstein 1985). In contrast, in Q'anjo'bal, the thematic patient always determines the form of the Set B marker (Mateo Toledo 2008). For other languages, including K'iche' (Larsen 1988; Davies & Sam-Colop 1990), whether or not the thematic agent or patient is marked on the verb depends on which argument is highest ranked according to the person hierarchy. Person hierarchies are also important in determining whether an agent focus construction is even necessary. In Q'anjob'al, agents freely extract when they are speech act participants (Mateo Toledo 2008), and in Tsotsil, agents freely extract when the agent is higher on the person hierarchy than the object (Aissen 1999a). When these conditions are not met, the agent focus construction is required.

Mayan's agent focus construction has received a good deal of attention in the theoretical literature. Formal analyses of agent focus constructions have been developed on the basis of case-assignment (Ordoñez 1995; Coon et al. 2014), person features (Stiebels 2006; Aissen 1999a), and anti-locality (Erlewine 2016; but see Henderson & Coon 2018). See Aissen (2017b) for more on Mayan's agent focus construction and Zavala Maldonado (2017) for syntactic ergativity in Mayan languages more generally.

5. Conclusion

The Mayan language family is one of the best-documented and well-studied language families in the Americas. This chapter focused on core aspects of Mayan phonology, morphology, and syntax, but the variety of topics covered in the literature is considerably more extensive (see the Further Reading section in this chapter). Our understanding of the structure of Mayan languages is enriched by a long history of linguistic research, many native speaking linguists, and interest from around the world. Despite this rich tradition, research on Mayan languages continues to be time sensitive, as speakers in many communities shift to Spanish at increasing rates. Speakers of Mayan languages have faced centuries of marginalization that continues to the present day. Yet, with the rise of the ethnopolitical Pan-Maya Movement in Guatemala and Mexico in the late 1980s, language shift has been met with language activism that has made sizable gains in areas including language ideology, Mayan-medium primary school education, community-based radio, and digital technologies (Brody 2000; Barrett 2008; Maxwell 2011; Cru 2017).

Acknowledgments

Thanks to Scott AnderBois, Ryan Bennett, Jessica Coon, Jason Haugen, Brook Danielle Lillehaugen, Carol-Rose Little, Carolyn O'Meara, Verónica Pérez Rodríguez, and Rodrigo Ranero for commenting on previous versions of this chapter. Any remaining errors are my own.

Further Reading

Mayan languages are among the most well-studied languages of North America. Major works in the phonology, morphology, and syntax of Mayan languages were named in this chapter, but also see England and Zavala Maldonado (2013) for a comprehensive bibliography. Other reference works on Mayan languages include England (1988; 2001; 2017), the papers in Bennett et al. (2015), and the chapters in Aissen et al. (2017). Beyond phonology, morphology, and syntax, research on the semantics and pragmatics of Mayan languages – see Henderson (2016) for an overview – covers topics such as pluractionality (Henderson 2012b; 2017); focus and questions (Tonhauser 2003a; 2003b; Brown 2010; AnderBois 2012; Velleman 2014; AnderBois 2017); the organization of space (Hanks 1990; Bohnemeyer 2017); and discourse and conversational interaction (Datz 1980; Hofling 1982; Haviland 2017). There have also been a number of studies on the acquisition of Mayan languages, including Pye (1980); Mateo Pedro (2015); and sources cited in Pye et al. (2017). Major works on the sociolinguistics of Mayan languages include Romero (2006), Caz Cho (2007), Law (2014), and other sources cited in Romero (2017). Finally, for further reading on the topic of language shift and revitalization, see the papers cited in §5 as well as Fischer and McKenna Brown (1996), Richards and Richards (1998), England (2003), and Collins (2005).

Note

1. Abbreviations used in glosses are as follows: A = Set A (ergative, possessive), ABS = absolutive, ADJ = adjective, AF = agent focus, ANTIC = anticausative, ANTIP = antipassive, APL = applicative, ART = article, ASP = aspect, AUX = auxiliary, B = Set B (absolutive), CL = classifier, CPL = completive, DEM = demonstrative, DEP = dependent, DET = determiner, DIR = directional, DUR = durative, ENC = enclitic, EMPH = emphatic, EXH = exhortative, FAM = familiar, FOC = focus, FOR = formal, HS = hearsay, ICPL = incompletive, IDPH = ideophone, IMPERF = imperfect, INTR = intransitive, IRR = irrealis, LAT = lative, NEG = negation, NML = nominalizer, NOM = nominal, OPT = optative, P = person, PAR = particle, PASS = passive, PERF = perfect, PFV = perfective, PFM = phrase-final marker, PL = plural, POS = positional, POT = potential, PREP = preposition, PRON = pronoun, REP = reportative, RN = relational noun, SG = singular, SS = "status suffix", TOP = topic, TR = transitive. In some cases, glosses and transcriptions have been modified from the original source for consistency and in accordance with revised conventions (see discussion in Mateo Toledo 2003 and Bennett et al. 2016).

References

Aissen, Judith. 1987. *Tzotzil clause structure*. Dordrecht: Reidel.

Aissen, Judith. 1992. Topic and focus in Mayan. *Language* 68. 43–80.

Aissen, Judith. 1996. Pied-pipping, abstract agreement, and functional projections in Tzotzil. *Natural Language and Linguistic Theory* 14. 447–491.

Aissen, Judith. 1997. On the syntax of obviation. *Language* 73. 705–750.

Aissen, Judith. 1999a. Agent focus and inverse in Tzotzil. *Language* 75. 451–485.

Aissen, Judith. 1999b. External possessor and logical subject in Tz'utujil. In *External poessession*, vol. 68, 451–485. Amsterdam: John Benjamins.

Aissen, Judith. 2017a. Complement clauses. In Aissen, Judith & England, Nora C. & Maldonado, Roberto Zavala (eds.), *The Mayan languages*, 259–292. (Routledge Language Family Series). London: Routledge.

Aissen, Judith. 2017b. Correlates of Ergativity in Mayan. In Coon, Jessica & Massam, Diane & de Mena Travis, Lisa (eds.), *The Oxford handbook of ergativity*, 737–758. Oxford: Oxford University Press.

Aissen, Judith. 2017c. Information structure in Mayan languages. In Aissen, Judith & England, Nora C. & Maldonado, Roberto Zavala (eds.), *The Mayan languages*, 293–324. (Routledge Language Family Series). London: Routledge.

Aissen, Judith & England, Nora C. & Maldonado, Roberto Zavala (eds.). 2017. *The Mayan languages*. (Routledge Language Famliy Series). London: Routledge.

AnderBois, Scott. 2012. Focus and uninformativity in Yucatec Maya questions. *Natural Language Semantics* 20. 349–390.

AnderBois, Scott. 2017. Focus, interrogation, and indefinites. In Aissen, Judith & England, Nora C. & Maldonado, Roberto Zavala (eds.), *The Mayan languages*, 348–361. (Routledge Language Family Series). London: Routledge.

Assmann, Anke & Georgi, Doreen & Heck, Fabian & Müller, Gereon & Weisser, Philipp. 2015. Ergatives move too early: On an instance of opacity in syntax. *Syntax* 18. 343–387.

Avelino, Heriberto. 2011. Intonational patterns of topic and focus constructions in Yucatec Maya. In Avelino, Heriberto (ed.), *New perspectives in Mayan linguistics*, 56–79. Cambridge, MA: MIT Working Papers in Linguistics.

Avelino, Heriberto & Shin, Eurie & Tilsen, Sam. 2011. The phonetics of Laryngealization in Yucatec Maya. In Avelino, Heriberto (ed.), *New perspectives in Mayan linguistics*, 1–20. Newcastle: Cambridge Scholars Publishing.

Ayres, Glenn. 1983. The antipassive 'Voice' in Ixil. *International Journal of American Linguistics* 49. 20–45.

Baird, Brandon O. 2010. Un analisis acustico de las vocales de K'ichee' [An acoustic analysis of vowels in K'ichee']. In *Proceedings of the Conference on Indigenous Languages of Latin America*. Austin: The Center for Indigenous Languages of Latin America at the University of Texas.

Baird, Brandon O. 2015. Acoustic correlates of stress in K'ichee': A preliminary investigation. In Clemens, Lauren & Henderson, Robert & Mateo Pedro, Pedro (eds.), *Proceedings of formal approaches to Mayan linguistics* (FAMLi 2), 21–34. Cambridge: MIT Working Papers in Linguistics.

Bale, Alan & Coon, Jessica. 2014. Classifiers are for numerals, not nouns: Evidence from Mi'gmaq and Ch'ol. *Linguistic Inquiry* 45. 695–707.

Baquiax Barreno, Modesto & Mateo, Rigoberto Juárez & Mejía, Fernando Rodríguez & Pérez, María Magdalena. 2005. *Yaq'b'anil stxolilal ti' Q'anjob'al: Gramática descriptiva Q'anjob'al*. Academia de Lenguas Mayas de Guatemala.

Barrett, Rusty. 1999. *A grammar of Sipakapense Maya*. Austin: University of Texas. (Doctoral dissertation.)

Barrett, Rusty. 2008. Linguistic differentiation and Mayan language revitalization in Guatemala. *Journal of Sociolinguistics* 12. 275–305.

Barrett, Rusty. 2014. Ideophones and (non-) arbitrariness in the K'iche' poetry of Humberto Ak'abal. *Pragmatics and Society* 5. 406–418.

Bennett, Ryan. 2016. Mayan phonology. *Language and Linguistics Compass* 10. 469–514.

Bennett, Ryan & Coon, Jessica & Henderson, Robert. 2015. Special issue: Mayan linguistics. *Language and Linguistics Compass* 10. 453–588.

Bennett, Ryan & Coon, Jessica & Henderson, Robert. 2016. Introduction to Mayan linguistics. *Language and Linguistics Compass* 10. 453–454.

Bennett, Ryan & Henderson, Robert. 2013. Accent in Uspanteko. *Natural Language and Linguistic Theory* 31. 589–645.

Bennett, Ryan & Tang, Kevin & Ajsivinac, Juan. 2017. *Laryngeal co-occurrence restrictions as constraints on sub-segmental articulatory structure*. Santa Cruz: University of California. (Unpublished Ms.)

Berinstein, Ava. 1985. *Evidence for multiattachment in K'ekchi Mayan*. New York: Garland.

Berinstein, Ava. 1991. The role of intonation in K'ekchi Mayan discourse. In *Texas linguistic forum 32: Discourse*. Austin: Department of Linguistics and the Center for Cognitive Science, The University of Texas.

Bohnemeyer, Jürgen. 2017. The organization of space. In Aissen, Judith & England, Nora C. & Maldonado, Roberto Zavala (eds.), *The Mayan languages*, 327–347. (Routledge Language Family Series). London: Routledge.

Bricker, Victoria Reifler. 1978. Antipassive constructions in Yucatec Maya. In England, Nora C. (ed.), *Papers in Mayan linguistics*, 3–24. (Number 2 in Studies in Mayan Linguistics). Columbia: University of Missouri Miscellaneous Publications in Anthropology.

Bricker, Victoria Reifler. 1981. The source of the ergative split in Yucatec Maya. *Journal of Mayan Linguistics* 2. 83–127.

Bricker, Victoria Reifler & Po'ot Yah, Eleuterio & de Po'ot, Ofelia Dzul. 1998. *A dictionary of the Maya language: As spoken in Hocaba, Yucatan*. Salt Lake City: University of Utah Press.

Brody, Jill. 1984. Some problems with the concept of basic word order. *Linguistics* 22. 711–736.

Brody, Jill. 2000. Spatilab'il sk'ujol 'tell them "hey" for me': Traditional Mayan speech genre goes multimedia. In *Texas linguistics forum*, vol. 43, 1–14. Austin: University of Texas.

Brown, Penelope. 2010. Questions and their responses in Tzeltal. *Journal of Pragmatics* 42. 2627–2648.

Buenrostro, Cristina. 2009. *Chuj de San Mateo Ixtatán*. Mexico: El Colegio de México.

Buenrostro, Cristina. 2013. *La voz en Chuj de San Mateo Ixtatán*. Mexico: El Colegio de México. (Doctoral dissertation.)

Buenrostro, Cristina & Díaz, José Carmen & Maldonado, Roberto Zavala. 1987. Sistema de clasificación nominal del chuj. In *Memorias del segundo coloquio internacional de mayistas*. México: Universidad Nacional Autónoma México.

Burdin, Rachel & Phillips-Bourass, Sara & Turnbull, Rory & Yasavul, Murat & Clopper, Cynthia G. & Tonhauser, Judith. 2015. Variation in the prosody of focus in head and head/edge-prominence languages. *Lingua* 165. 254–276.

Burns, Allan F. 1993. *Maya in exile: Guatemalans in Florida*. Philadelphia, PA: Temple University Press.

Butler, Lindsay Kay. 2011. *The morphosyntax and processing of number marking in Yucatec Maya*. Tucson: University of Arizona. (Doctoral dissertation.)

Campbell, Lyle. 1977. *Quichean linguistic prehistory*. (Volume 81 of University of California Publications in Linguistics). Berkeley: University of California Press.

Campbell, Lyle. 2017. Mayan history and comparison. In Aissen, Judith & England, Nora C. & Maldonado, Roberto Zavala (eds.), *The Mayan languages*, 43–61. (Routledge Language Family Series). London: Routledge.

Campbell, Lyle & Kaufman, Terrence. 1985. Mayan linguistics: Where are we now? *Annual Review of Anthropology* 14. 187–198.

Can Pixabaj, Telma A. 2004. *La topicalización en K'ichee': Una perspectiva discursiva*. (BA thesis.)

Can Pixabaj, Telma. 2006. *Gramática descriptiva Uspanteka*. Oxlajuuj Keej Maya' Ajtz'iib' (OKMA).

Can Pixabaj, Telma A. 2015. *Complement and purpose clauses in K'iche'*. Austin: University of Texas. (Doctoral dissertation.)

Can Pixabaj, Telma A. 2017. K'iche'. In Aissen, Judith & England, Nora C. & Maldonado, Roberto Zavala (eds.), *The Mayan languages*, 461–499. (Routledge Language Family Series). London: Routledge.

Can Pixabaj, Telma A. & England, Nora C. 2011. Nominal topic and focus in K'iche'. In Bravo, Rodrigo Gutiérrez & Mikkelsen, Line & Potsdam, Eric (eds.), *Representing language: Linguistic essays in honor of Judith Aissen*, 15–30. Santa Cruz: Linguistics Research Center, University of California.

Caz Cho, Sergio. 2007. *Variación dialectal en Q'eqchi'*. Guatemala City: Cholsamaj.

Chung, Sandra. 2017. Properties of VOS languages. In Everaert, Martin & van Riemsdijk, Henk C. (eds.), *The Wiley Blackwell companion to syntax*, 2nd edn. Hoboken, NJ: Wiley Blackwell.

Clemens, Lauren Eby. 2013. V2 in a V1 language: Kaqchikel SVO. In Kenstowicz, Michael (ed.), *MIT working papers in linguistics volume on Kaqchikel*. MIT Working Papers in Linguistics. MIT Press.

Clemens, Lauren Eby & Coon, Jessica. 2018a. Deriving verb-initial word order in Mayan. *Language* 94(2). 237–280.

Clemens, Lauren Eby & Coon, Jessica. 2018b. Prosodic constituency of verb-initial clauses in Ch'ol. In Keough, Megan & Weber, Natalie & Anghelescu, Andrei & Chen, Sihwei & Guntly, Erin & Johnson, Khia & Reisinger, Daniel & Tkachman, Oksana (eds.), *Proceedings of the 21st workshop on structure and constituency in languages of the Americas*, 88–100. Vancouver: The University of British Columbia Working Papers in Linguistics.

Clemens, Lauren Eby & Polinsky, Maria. 2017. Verb-initial word orders, primarily in Austronesian and Mayan languages. In Everaert, Martin & van Riemsdijk, Henk C. (eds.), *The Wiley Blackwell companion to syntax*, 2nd edn. Hoboken, NJ: Wiley Blackwell.

Collins, Wesley. 2005. Code-switching avoidance as a strategy for Mam (Maya) linguistic revitalization. *International Journal of American Linguistics* 71. 239–276.

Coon, Jessica & Mateo Pedro, Pedro & Preminger, Omer. 2014. The role of case in A-bar extraction asymmetries: Evidence from Mayan. *Linguistic Variation* 14. 179–242.

Coon, Jessica & Preminger, Omer. 2017. Split ergativity is not about ergativity. In Coon, Jessica & Massam, Diane & Travis, Lisa (eds.), *Oxford handbook of ergativity*, 226–252. Oxford: Oxford University Press.

Coon, Jessica. 2010a. *Complementation in Chol (Mayan): A theory of split ergativity*. Cambridge: Massachusetts Institute of Technology. (Doctoral dissertation.)

Coon, Jessica. 2010b. VOS as predicate fronting in Chol Mayan. *Lingua* 120. 345–378.

Coon, Jessica. 2013. *Aspects of split ergativity*. Oxford: Oxford University Press.

Coon, Jessica. 2016. Mayan morphosyntax. *Language and Linguistics Compass* 10. 515–550.

Coon, Jessica. 2017. Ch'ol. In Aissen, Judith & England, Nora C. & Maldonado, Roberto Zavala (eds.), *The Mayan languages*, 648–684. (Routledge Language Family Series). London: Routledge.

Coon, Jessica. 2019. Building verbs in Chuj: Consequences for the nature of roots. *Journal of Linguistics* 55.1. 35-81.

Cowan, Marion M. 1969. *Tzotzil grammar*. (SIL International Publications in Linguistics 18). Norman: Summer Institute of Linguistics of the University of Oklahoma.

Craig, Colette. 1977. *The structure of Jacaltec*. Austin: University of Texas Press.

Craig, Colette Grinevald. 1979. The antipassive and Jacaltec. In Martin, Laura (ed.), *Papers in Mayan linguistics*, vol. 1, 139–164. Lucas Brothers.

Craig, Colette Grinevald. 1986. Jacaltec noun classifiers. *Lingua* 70. 241–284.

Cru, J. 2017. Language revitalisation from the ground up: Promoting Yucatec Maya on Facebook. *International Journal of Bilingual Education and Bilingualism* 20. 481–496.

Curiel, Alejandro. 2007. *Estructura de la información, enclíticos y configuración sintáctica en tojol'ab'al*. Mexico: CIESAS (Master's thesis.)

Curiel Ramírez del Prado, Alejandro. 2017. Tojolabal. In Aissen, Judith & England, Nora C. & Maldonado, Roberto Zavala (eds.), *The Mayan languages*, 570–609. (Routledge Language Family Series). London: Routledge.

Datz, Margaret. 1980. *Jacaltec syntactic structure and the demands of discourse*. Boulder: University of Colorado. (Doctoral dissertation.)

Davies, William & Sam-Colop, Luis Enrique. 1990. K'iche' and the structure of antipassive. *Language* 66. 522–549.

Day, Christopher. 1973. *The Jacaltec language*. Bloomington: Indiana University.

Dayley, Jon. 1981. Voice and ergativity in Mayan languages. *Journal of Mayan Linguistics* 2. 3–82.

Dayley, Jon Philip. 1985. *Tzutujil grammar*. Berkeley: University of California Press.

Deal, Amy Rose. 2016. Syntactic ergativity: Analysis and identification. *Annual Review of Linguistics* 2. 165–185.

DeChicchis, Joseph Edmond II. 1989. *Q'eqchi' (Kekchi Mayan) variation in Guatemala and Belize*. Philadelphia: University of Pennsylvania. (Doctoral dissertation.)

Douglas, Jaime & Ranero, Rodrigo & Sheehan, Michelle. 2017. Two kinds of syntactic ergativity in Mayan. In Yoshitaka Erlewine, Michael (ed.), *Proceedings of GLOW in Asia XI*. Cambridge, MA: MIT Working Papers in Linguistics.

Du Bois, John W. 2006. The pear story in Sakapultek Maya: A case study of information flow and preferred argument structure. In Sedano, Mercedes & Bolívar, Adriana & Shiro, Martha (eds.), *Haciendo lingüística: Homenaje a Paola Bentivoglio*, 191–221. Caracas: Universidad Central de Venezuela.

Edmonson, Barbara. 1988. *A descriptive grammar of Huastec (Potosino dialect)*. New Orleans, LA: Tulane University. (Doctoral dissertation.)

England, Nora C. 1988. Mam voice. In Shibatani, Masayoshi (ed.), *Passive and voice*, 525–545. Amsterdam: John Benjamins.

England, Nora C. 1991. Changes in basic word order in Mayan languages. *International Journal of American Linguistics* 57. 446–486.

England, Nora C. 2001. *Introducción a la gramática de los idiomas mayas*. Ciudad de Guatemala, Guatemala: Cholsamaj.

England, Nora C. 2003. Mayan language revival and revitalization: Linguists and linguistic ideologies. *American Anthropologist* 105. 733–743.

England, Nora C. 2004. Adjectives in mam. In Dixon, R. M. W. & Aikhenvald, Alexandra Y. (eds.), *Adjective classes: A cross-linguistic typology*, 125–146. Oxford: Oxford University Press.

England, Nora C. 2011a. *A grammar of mam, a Mayan language*. Austin: University of Texas Press.

England, Nora C. 2011b. Plurality agreement in some Eastern Mayan languages. *International Journal of American Linguistics* 77. 397–412.

England, Nora C. 2017. Mayan languages. In *Oxford research encyclopedia of linguistics*. Oxford: Oxford University Press. (http://linguistics.oxfordre.com/view/10.1093/acrefore/9780199384655.001.0001/acrefore-9780199384655-e-60) (Accessed 2018–01–10.)

England, Nora C. & Baird, Brandon O. 2017. Phonology and phonetics. In Aissen, Judith, England, Nora C. & Maldonado, Roberto Zavala (eds.), *The Mayan languages*, 175–200. (Routledge Language Family Series). London: Routledge.

England, Nora C. & Maldonado, Roberto Zavala. 2013. Mayan languages. In Aronoff, Mark (ed.), *Oxford bibliographies in linguistics*. Oxford: Oxford University Press.

Erlewine, Michael Yoshitaka. 2016. Anti-locality and optimality in Kaqchikel agent focus. *Natural Language and Linguistic Theory* 35. 429–479.

Fischer, Edward & Brown, Robert McKenna (eds.). 1996. *Maya cultural activism in Guatemala*. Austin: University of Texas Press.

Fisher, William. 1973. *Towards the reconstruction of Proto-Yucatec*. Chicago, IL: University of Chicago. (Doctoral dissertation.)

Fox, James. 1978. *Proto-Mayan accent, morpheme structure conditions, and velar innovation*. Chicago, IL: University of Chicago. (Doctoral dissertation.)

Frazier, Melissa. 2009. *The production and perception of pitch and glottalization in Yucatec Maya*. Chapel Hill: University of North Carolina. (Doctoral dissertation.)

Frazier, Melissa. 2011. Tonal dialects and consonant-pitch interaction in Yucatec Maya. In Avelino, Heriberto (ed.), *New perspectives in Mayan linguistics*, 21–55. Newcastle: Cambridge Scholars Publishing.

Gallagher, Gillian & Coon, Jessica. 2009. Distinguishing total and partial identity: Evidence from Chol. *Natural Language and Linguistic Theory* 27. 545–582.

Godfrey, Thomas James. 1981. *Grammatical categories for spatial reference in the western Mam dialect of Tacana*. Austin: University of Texas. (Doctoral dissertation.)

Gómez Cruz, José. 2017. *Estructuras morfosintácticas del tojol-ab'al en perspectiva comparativa: el caso de una lengua maya mixta*. Centro de Investigaciones y Estudios Superiores en Antropología Social. (Doctoral dissertation.)

Grinevald, Colette & Peake, Marc. 2012. Ergativity and voice in Mayan: A functional-typological approach. In Authier, Gilles & Haude, Katharina (eds.), *Ergativity, valency and voice*, 15–49. Berlin: Mouton de Gruyter.

Gussenhoven, Carlos & Teeuw, Renske. 2008. A moraic and a syllabic H-tone in Yucatec Maya. In Zendejas, Esther Herrera & Butragueño, Pedro Martiín (eds.), *Fonología instrumental: patrones fónicos y variacion*. Mexico: El Colegio de México.

Gutiérrez Bravo, Rodrigo. 2011. External and internal topics in Yucatec Maya. In Bravo, Rodrigo Gutiérrez & Mikkelsen, Line & Potsdam, Eric (eds.), *Representing language: Linguistic essays in honor of Judith Aissen*, 105–119. Santa Cruz: Linguistics Research Center, University of California.

Gutiérrez Bravo, Rodrigo & Monforte y Madera, Jorge. 2008. La alternancia sujeto inicial/verbo inicial y la teoría de la optimidad. In Gutiérrez Bravo, R. & Herrera Zendejas, Y. E. (eds.), *Teoría de optimidad: Estudios de sintaxis y fonología*, 61–90. México: El Colegio de México.

Gutiérrez Bravo, Rodrigo & Monforte y Madera, Jorge. 2010. On the nature of word order in Yucatec Maya. In Camacho, José & Gutiérrez Bravo, Rodrigo & Sánchez, Liliana (eds.), *Information structure in indigenous languages of the Americas*, 139–170. Berlin: Mouton de Gruyter.

Hanks, William. 1990. *Referential practice: Language and lived space among the Maya*. Chicago, IL: University of Chicago Press.

Haviland, John. 1994. 'Te xa setel xulem' (the buzzards were circling): Categories of verbal roots in (Zinacantec) Tzotzil. *Linguistics* 32. 691–741.

Haviland, John. 2017. Mayan conversation and interaction. In Aissen, Judith & England, Nora C. & Zavala Maldonado, Roberto (eds.), *The Mayan languages*, 401–432. (Routledge Language Family Series). London: Routledge.

Heaton, Raina & Deen, Kamil & O'Grady, William. 2016. The status of syntactic ergativity in Kaqchikel. *Lingua* 170. 35–46.

Henderson, Robert. 2007. Observations on the syntax of adjunct extraction in Kaqchikel. In *Proceedings of the Conference on Indigenous Languages of Latin America*. Austin: The Center for Indigenous Languages of Latin America at the University of Texas.

Henderson, Robert. 2012a. Morphological alternations at the intonational phrase edge: The case of K'ichee. *Natural Language and Linguistic Theory* 30. 741–787.

Henderson, Robert. 2012b. *Ways of pluralizing events*. Santa Cruz: University of California. (Doctoral dissertation.)

Henderson, Robert. 2016. Mayan semantics. *Language and Linguistics Compass* 10. 551–588.

Henderson, Robert. 2017. Pluractionality in Mayan. In Aissen, Judith & England, Nora C. & Zavala Maldonado, Roberto (eds.), *The Mayan languages*, 362–376. (Routledge Language Family Series). London: Routledge.

Henderson, Robert. 2018. *The roots of measurement*. University of Arizona. (Unpublished Ms.)

Henderson, Robert & Coon, Jessica. 2018. Adverbs and variability in Kaqchikel agent focus: A reply to Erlewine (2016). *Natural Language and Linguistic Theory* 36. 149–173.

Herrera Zendejas, Esther. 2011. Peso silábico y patron acentual en Huasteco. In Shklovsky, Kirill & Mateo Pedro, Pedro & Coon, Jessica (eds.), *Proceedings of formal approaches to Mayan linguistics* (FAMLi), 135–146. Cambridge: MIT Working Papers in Linguistics.

Hofling, Charles A. 1982. *Itza Maya morphosyntax from a discourse perspective*. St. Louis, MO: Washington University. (Doctoral dissertation.)

Hofling, Charles A. 1984. On Proto-Yucatecan word order. *Journal of Mayan Linguistics* 4. 35–64.

Hofling, Charles A. 2000. *Itzaj Maya grammar*. Salt Lake City: University of Utah Press.

Hofling, Charles A. 2011. *Mopan Maya-Spanish-English dictionary*. Salt Lake City: University of Utah Press.

Hofling, Charles A. 2017. Comparative Maya (Yucatec, Lacandon, Itzaj, and Mopan Maya). In Aissen, Judith & England, Nora C. & Maldonado, Roberto Zavala (eds.), *The Mayan languages*, 685–760 (Routledge Language Family Series). London: Routledge.

Imanishi, Yusuke. 2014. *Default ergative*. Cambridge: Massachusetts Institute of Technology. (Doctoral dissertation.)

Justeson, John & Norman, William M. & Campbell, Lyle & Kaufman, Terrence S. 1985. *The foreign impact on Lowland Mayan language and script*. New Orleans: Middle American Research Institute, Tulane University.

Kaufman, Terrence S. 1974. *Idiomas de Mesoamerica*. Guatemala City: Seminario de Integración Social Guatemalteca.

Kaufman, Terrence S. 1976. Archaeological and linguistic correlations in Mayaland and associated areas of Meso-America. *World Archeology* 8. 101–118.

Kaufman, Terrence. 1977. Areal linguistics and Middle America. In Sebeok, Thomas A. (ed.), *Native languages of the Americas*, vol 2. 63–87. Boston, MA: Springer.

Kaufman, Terrence S. 1990. Algunos rasgos estructurales de los idiomas mayances con referencia especial al k'iche'. In England, Nora C. & Elliott, Stephen (eds.), *Lecturos sobre la Lingüística Maya*, 59–114. Antigua, Guatemala: Centro de Investigacione Regionales de Mesoamérica.

Kaufman, Terrence S. & Norman, William M. 1984. An outline of Proto-Cholan phonology, morphology, and vocabulary. *Phoneticism in Mayan Hieroglyphic Writing* 77–166.

Kidder, Emily. 2013. *Prominence in Yucatec Maya: The role of stress in Yucatec Maya words*. Tucson: University of Arizona. (Doctoral dissertation.)

Knowles, Susan Marie. 1984. *A descriptive grammar of Chontal Maya (San Carlos dialect)*. New Orleans, LA: Tulane University. (Doctoral dissertation.)

Kockelman, Paul. 2003. The interclausal relations hierarchy in Q'eqchi' Maya. *International Journal of American Linguistics* 25–48.

Kügler, Frank & Skopeteas, Stavros. 2007. On the universality of prosodic reflexes of contrast: The case of Yucatec Maya. In *Proceedings of the 16th International Congress of Phonetic Sciences*. Saarbrücken.

Kügler, Frank & Skopeteas, Stavros & Verhoeven, Elisabeth. 2007. Encoding information structure in Yucatec Maya: On the interplay of prosody and syntax. In Ishihara, S. & Jannedy, S. & Schwarz, A. (eds.), *Interdisciplinary studies on information structure*, vol. 8, 187–208. Potsdam: Universitätsverlag Potsdam.

Lacadena, Alfonso & Wichmann, Soren. 2004. On the representation of the glottal stop in Maya writing. In Wichmann, Soren (ed.), *The linguistics of Maya writing*, 103–162. Salt Lake City: University of Utah Press.

Larsen, Raymond & Pike, Eunice. 1949. Huasteco intonations and phonemes. *Language* 25. 268–277.

Larsen, Thomas. 1988. *Manifestations of ergativity in Quiche grammar*. Berkeley: University of California. (Doctoral dissertation.)

Law, Danny. 2014. *Language contact, inherited similarity and social difference: The story of linguistic interaction in the Maya lowlands*. Amsterdam: John Benjamins.

Law, Danny & Stuart, David. 2017. Classic Mayan: An overview of language in ancient hieroglyphic script. In Aissen, Judith & England, Nora C. & Zavala Maldonado, Roberto (eds.), *The Mayan languages*, 128–172. (Routledge Language Family Series). London: Routledge.

Le Guen, Olivier. 2014. Expressive morphology in Yucatec Maya. In Léonard, Jean-Léo & Khim, Alain (eds.), *Patterns in Mesoamerican morphology*, 178–211. Paris: Michel Houdiard.

Lesure, Cora & Clemens, Lauren Eby. 2015. Prosodic boundary marking in Ch'ol: Acoustic indicators and their applications. In *Proceedings of the conference on indigenous languages of Latin America*, vii. Austin: The Center for Indigenous Languages of Latin America at the University of Texas.

Lois, Ximena. 2011. Roots and patterns in Yucatecan languages. In Shklovsky, Kirill & Mateo Pedro, Pedro & Coon, Jessica (eds.), *Proceedings of formal approaches to Mayan linguistics*. Cambridge: MIT Working Papers in Linguistics.

Lois, Ximena & Vapnarsky, Valentina. 2006. Root indeterminacy and polyvalence in Yukatekan Mayan languages. In Lois, Ximena & Vapnarsky, Valentina (eds.), *Lexical categories and root classes in Amerindian languages*, 69–116. Berlin: Peter Lang.

López, Manuel Antonio & Iboy, Juliana Sis. 1992. *Gramatica del idioma Achi*. Antigua, Guatemala: Proyecto Lingüístico Francisco Marroquin.

Loucky, James. 2000. *Maya diaspora: Guatemalan roots, new American lives*. Philadelphia, PA: Temple University Press.

Majzul, Filiberto Patal & García Matzar, Pedro Oscar & Serech, Carmelina Espantzay. 2000. *Rujunamaxik ri kaqchikel chi': variación dialectal en kaqchikel*. Ciudad de Guatemala, Guatemala: Cholsamaj.

Mateo Pedro, Pedro. 2015. *The acquisition of inflection in Q'anjob'al Maya*. Amsterdam: John Benjamins.

Mateo Toledo, Eladio. 2003. The use of languages' names: The Mayan case. *International Journal of American Linguistics* 69. 151–153.

Mateo Toledo, Eladio. 2008. *The family of complex predicates in Q'anjob'al (Maya): Their syntax and meaning*. Austin: University of Texas. (Doctoral dissertation.)

Mateo Toledo, Eladio. 2017. Q'anjob'al. In Aissen, Judith & England, Nora C. & Maldonado, Roberto Zavala (eds.), *The Mayan languages*, 533–569. (Routledge Language Family Series). London: Routledge.

Maxwell, Judith M. 1976. Chuj intransitives: Or when can an intransitive verb take an object? *Journal of Mayan Linguistics* 1. 128–140.

Maxwell, Judith M. 2011. Bilingual bicultural education: Best intentions across a cultural divide. In Little, Walter E. & Smith, Timothy J. (eds.), *Mayas in postwar Guatemala: Harvest of violence revisited*. Tuscaloosa: University of Alabama Press.

Minkoff, Seth. 2000. Animacy hierarchies and sentence processing. In Carnie, Andrew & Guilfoyle, Eithne (eds.), *The syntax of verb initial languages*, 201–212. Oxford University Press.

Mondloch, James. 1978. *Basic Quiche grammar*. Albany, NY: Institute for Latin American Studies, State University of New York.

Mora-Marín, David F. 2003. Historical reconstruction of Mayan applicative and antidative constructions. *International Journal of American Linguistics* 69. 186–228.

Morrison, Andrew R. & May, Rachel A. 1994. Escape from terror: Violence and migration in post-revolutionary Guatemala. *Latin American Research Review* 29. 111–132.

Nielsen, Kuniko Y. 2005. Kiche intonation. *UCLA Working Papers in Phonetics* 104. 45–60.

Norman, William M. & Campbell, Lyle. 1978. Toward a Proto-Mayan syntax: A comparative perspective on grammar. In England, Nora C. (ed.), *Papers in Mayan linguistics*. (Volume University of Missouri Miscellaneous Publications in Anthropology, No. 6; Studies in Mayan Linguistics, No. 2). Columbia: University of Missouri.

Ordoñez, Francisco. 1995. The antipassive in Jacaltec: A last resort strategy. In *Catalan working papers in linguistics* (CatWPL), vol. 4, 329–343. Barcelona, Spain: Autonomous University of Barcelona.

Orie, Olanike Ola & Bricker, Victoria. 2000. Placeless and historical laryngeals in Yucatec Maya. *International Journal of American Linguistics* 66. 283–317.

Palosaari, Naomi. 2011. *Topics in Mocho' phonology and morphology*. Salt Lake City: University of Utah. (Doctoral dissertation.)

Peñalosa, Fernando. 1987. Major syntactic structures of Acatec (Dialect of San Miguel Acatan). *International Journal of American Linguistics* 53. 281–310.

Pérez González, Jaime. 2012. *Predicados expresivos e ideófonos en tseltal*. Centro de Investigaciones y Estudios Superiores en Antropología Social. (Master's thesis.)

Pérez Vail, Eduardo Gustava. 2014. *La inversión y obviación en el mam de Cajolá*. Centro de Investigaciones y Estudios Superiores en Antropología Social. (Master's thesis.)

Pérez Vail, Eduardo Gustava & Jiménez, Odilio. 1997. *Ttxoolil qyool mam: Gramática mam*. Ciudad de Guatemala, Guatemala: Cholsamaj.

Pike, Kenneth. 1946. Phonemic pitch in Maya. *International Journal of American Linguistics* 12. 82–88.

Polian, Gilles. 2013. *Gramática del tseltal de Oxchuc*. (Publicaciones de la Casa Chata). México: Centro de Investigaciones y Estudios Superiores en Antropología Social.

Polian, Gilles. 2017a. Morphology. In Aissen, Judith & England, Nora C. & Maldonado, Roberto Zavala (eds.), *The Mayan Languages*, 201–225. (Routledge Language Family Series). London: Routledge.

Polian, Gilles. 2017b. Tseltal and Tsotsil. In Aissen, Judith & England, Nora C. & Maldonado, Roberto Zavala (eds.), *The Mayan languages*, 610–657. (Routledge Language Family Series). London: Routledge.

Polinsky, Maria. 2016. *Deconstructing ergativity: Two types of ergative languages and their features*. Oxford: Oxford University Press.

Polinsky, Maria. 2017. Syntactic ergativity. In Everaert, Martin & van Riemsdijk, Henk C. (eds.), *The Wiley Blackwell companion to syntax*, 2nd edn. Hoboken, NJ: Wiley Blackwell.

Preminger, Omer. 2014. *Agreement and its failures*. Cambridge, MA: MIT Press.

Pye, Clifton. 1980. *The acquisition of grammatical morphemes in Quiche Mayan*. Pittsburgh, PA: University of Pittsburgh. (Doctoral dissertation.)

Pye, Clifton & Pfeiler, Barbara & Mateo Pedro, Pedro. 2017. Mayan language acquisition. In Aissen, Judith & England, Nora C. & Maldonado, Roberto Zavala (eds.), *The Mayan languages*, 19–42. (Routledge Language Family Series). London: Routledge.

Quizar, Robin. 1979. *Comparative word order in Mayan*. Boulder: University of Colorado. (Doctoral dissertation.)

Raymundo González, Sonia & Pascual, Adan Francisco & Mateo Pedro, Pedro & Toledo, Eladio Mateo. 2000. *Sk'exkixhtaqil yallay koq'anej: Variación dialectal en q'anjob'al*. Ciudad de Guatemala, Guatemala: Cholsamaj.

Richards, Julia & Richards, Michael. 1998. Persistencia del idioma kaqchikel de 1524 a la actualidad. *Mesoamérica* 35. 27–48.

Richards, Michael. 2003. *Atlas Lingüistico de Guatemala*. Guatemala City: Universidad Rafael Landívar.

Robertson, John. 1992. *The history of tense/aspect/mood/voice in the Mayan verbal complex*. Austin: University of Texas Press.

Robinson, Stuart. 2002. Constituent order in Tenejapa Tzeltal. *International Journal of American Linguistics* 68. 51–80.

Romero, Sergio. 2006. *Sociolinguistic variation and linguistic history in Mayan: The case of K'iche*. Philadelphia: University of Pennsylvania. (Doctoral dissertation.)

Romero, Sergio. 2017. The labyrinth of diversity: The sociolinguistics of Mayan. In Aissen, Judith & England, Nora C. & Maldonado, Roberto Zavala (eds.), *The Mayan languages*, 379–400. (Routledge Language Family Series). London: Routledge.

Shklovsky, Kirill. 2011. Petalcingo Tseltal intonational prosody. In Shklovsky, Kirill & Mateo Pedro, Pedro & Coon, Jessica (eds.), *Proceedings of formal approaches to Mayan linguistics*. Cambridge: MIT Working Papers in Linguistics.

Skopeteas, Stavros & Verhoeven, Elisabeth. 2005. Postverbal argument order in Yucatec Maya. *Sprachtypologie und Universalienforschung* 58. 347–373.

Stiebels, Barbara. 2006. Agent focus in Mayan languages. *Natural Language and Linguistic Theory* 24. 501–570.

Straight, H. Stephen. 1976. Decompositional structure in Yucatec verbs. *Mayan Linguistics* 1. 189–198.

Tada, Hiroaki. 1993. *A/A-bar partition in derivation*. Cambridge: Massachusetts Institute of Technology. (Doctoral dissertation.)

Tonhauser, Judith. 2003a. F-constructions in Yucatec Maya. In Anderssen, Jan & Menendez-Benito, Paula & Werle, Adam (eds.), *The Proceedings of Sula*-2, 203–223. Amherst: Graduate Linguistic Student Association, University of Massachusetts.

Tonhauser, Judith. 2003b. On the syntax and semantics of content questions in Yucatec Maya. In Castillo, Juan (ed.), *Proceedings of the 6th workshop on American Indian languages*, 106–122. Santa Barbara, CA: Santa Barbara Papers in Linguistics.

Vázquez Álvarez, Juan Jesus. 2011. *A grammar of Chol, a Mayan language*. Austin: University of Texas. (Doctoral dissertation.)

Vázquez Álvarez, Juan Jesus. 2013. Dos tipos derepasulas no finitas en ch'ol. In Palancar, Enrique & Maldonado, Roberto Zavala (eds.), *Estudios sintácticos en lenguas de Mesoamerica*. México: Centro De Investigaciones Y Estudios Superiores En Antropologia Social.

Vázquez Álvarez, Juan Jesus & Maldonado, Roberto Zavala. 2013. La estructura argumental preferida en el chol, una lengua agentiva. In *Proceedings of the conference on indigenous languages of Latin America*. Austin: The Center for Indigenous Languages of Latin America at the University of Texas.

Velleman, Leah. 2014. *Focus and movement in a variety of K'ichee'*. Austin: University of Texas. (Doctoral dissertation.)

Wälchli, Bernhard. 2005. *Co-compounds and natural coordination*. (Oxford Studies in Typology and Linguistic Theory). Oxford: Oxford University Press.

Wichmann, Soren. 1999. *A Ch'orti' morphological sketch*. Unpublished Ms. Seminar für Sprachwissenschaft, Eberhard Karls Universität Tübingen.

Yasavul, Sevket Murat. 2017. *Questions and answers in K'iche'*. Columbus: Ohio State University. (Doctoral dissertation.)

Zavala Maldonado, Roberto. 1992. *El Kanjobal de San Miguel Acatán*. Mexico: UNAM.

Zavala Maldonado, Roberto. 2000. Multiple classifier sytems in Akatek (Mayan). In Senft, Gunter (ed.), *Systems of nominal classification*, 114–146. Cambridge: Cambridge University Press.

Zavala Maldonado, Roberto. 2007. Inversion and obviation in Mesoamerica. In Austin, P. K. & Simpson, Andrew (eds.), *Endangered languages*. Hamburg: Helmut Buske Verlag.

Zavala Maldonado, Roberto. 2017. Alignment patterns. In Aissen, Judith & England, Nora C. & Maldonado, Roberto Zavala (eds.), *The Mayan languages*, 226–258. (Routledge Language Family Series). London: Routledge.

Zocal Chayax & Aj'Otoniel & IxBerta Huez Chan & IxTomasa Chan Tesucún & AjMarlen Cohuoj Chayax & Aj'Alfonso Tesucún & Aj'Edgar Canté Cohuoj & IxPetrona Vitzil. 2001. *Alb'ál xokna'at t'an: Gramática descriptiva itza'*. Guatemala City: Academia de Lenguas Mayas de Guatemala.

17
MUSKOGEAN LANGUAGES

George Aaron Broadwell

1. Languages and Locations

Muskogean is the largest group of Indigenous languages in the southeastern United States. All the Muskogean languages are endangered. Muskogean languages were originally spoken in a wide region that includes most of Georgia, Alabama, and Mississippi, along with nearby portions of Florida, Tennessee, and Louisiana. Most people speaking Muskogean languages were displaced from their original territories due to European and American colonialism and expansion. The Choctaw, Chickasaw, Creek, and Seminole tribes were victims of Indian Removal in the 1830s, and were forced from their homelands to Indian Territory, now Oklahoma. (Mississippi Choctaws and Florida Seminoles are descended from those who managed to resist removal.) Alabama, Koasati, and Mikasuki speakers (as well as speakers of non-Muskogean languages such as Natchez and Yuchi) were part of the Creek Confederacy, and some of these language communities were also affected by Indian Removal.

The six Muskogean languages still spoken are

- Choctaw [cho], spoken in Mississippi and Oklahoma by several thousand people.
- Chickasaw [cic], spoken in Oklahoma by fewer than 20 people.
- Alabama [akz], spoken in Texas by about 200–300 people.
- Koasati [cku], spoken in Louisiana by about 200 people. The language is also known as Coushatta.
- Mikasuki [mik], spoken in Florida by a few thousand people. The language is also known as Miccosukee.
- Creek [mus] is spoken in Oklahoma and Florida by several thousand people. The language is also known as Muskogee.

Choctaw and Chickasaw show many overall similarities, and together are known as Western Muskogean.

In addition to these languages, we have records of three other Muskogean languages, which are no longer spoken. Apalachee was spoken in western Florida, and is only attested in one 17th-century document (Kimball 1987; 1988). Hitchiti was spoken in tribal towns within the Creek Confederacy in Georgia and, after removal, in Oklahoma. It is generally regarded as the same language as Mikasuki (Martin 2004: 75). Finally, Mobilian Jargon was a pidgin language, used in the Gulf of Mexico, whose vocabulary was based primarily on Choctaw (Crawford 1978; Drechsel 1997).

Many aspects of Proto-Muskogean phonology and morphology have been reconstructed in works such as those by Haas (1940; 1946; 1947; 1977), Booker (1980), Broadwell (1993), and Martin and Munro (2005). Haas (1951; 1951; 1956) proposed that Muskogean was part of a larger language family called Gulf, which included Muskogean, Natchez [ncz], Tunica [tun], Atakapa [aqp], and Chitimacha [ctm]. This larger family is no longer widely accepted, but the relationship of Muskogean and Natchez is still widely accepted by Muskogeanists, e.g., Kimball (2005). Other possible connections to Yuki [yuk]-Wappo [wao] (Munro 1994) and to Timucua [tjm] (Crawford 1988; Broadwell 2015) have also been proposed in the literature.

2. Phonetics, Phonology, and Orthographies

2.1. Phoneme Inventories

Muskogean languages have rather small phonemic inventories. All the languages have a vowel system with three contrastive vowel qualities and a two-way length contrast, as in Table 17.1.

Creek also has three diphthongs: /ey/, /oy/, and /aw/.[1] In many of the languages, there is a tendency for short vowels to be more centralized ([ɪ, ə, ʊ]), while long vowels are more peripheral ([i, e, o]) (Gordon et al. 2001; Martin 2011).

In addition to the three contrastive oral vowels, all the Muskogean languages also have three contrastive nasalized equivalents to these vowels. In Choctaw, all nasal vowels are long (Broadwell 2006). Length contrasts for nasal vowels are possible, but unusual, in Creek (Martin 2011).

The consonant inventory of Alabama, shown in Table 17.2, is typical of many Muskogean languages.

Western Muskogean languages additionally contrast alveolar and postalveolar sibilants [s] vs. [ʃ]. There is a voicing distinction for labial stops but not for other stops in all the Muskogean languages except Creek. Haas (1947) argues that this is the result of variable realizations of Proto-Muskogean *kʷ.

All the Muskogean languages distinguish single consonants from geminates, as Table 17.3 illustrates with regard to contrasts in Creek.

Table 17.1 Vowel Phonemes of Creek

	Front	*Back*
Non-low	i, iː	o, oː
Low	a, aː	

Table 17.2 Consonant Inventory of Alabama

	Labial	*Alveolar*	*Post-alveolar*	*Labiovelar*	*Velar*	*Glottal*
Stops	p, b	t			k	
Fricatives	f	s, ɬ				h
Affricate			tʃ			
Nasal	m	n				
Glide			y (= IPA [j])	w		
Lateral		l				

In several Muskogean languages, the glottal stop has a marginal phonemic status. Glottal stop is frequently contrastive in a subset of the environments in which other consonants contrast. For example, glottal appears only in word-final position in most dialects of Choctaw, and its occurrence in this position is not entirely predictable, as Broadwell (2006) and Ulrich (1986) argue. In Koasati, Kimball (1991: 24–25) shows that glottal stop appears contrastively only in two demonstratives and in the formation of verbal aspectual grades (discussed in §3.2.3).

2.2. Pitch and Stress

Muskogean languages have pitch-accent, which works somewhat differently in nouns and verbs.

For nouns, the placement of the pitch accent is largely, but not entirely, predictable in many Muskogean languages. Kimball (1991: 27) writes that in Koasati,

> Every noun must have an accented syllable. The vast majority of root (i.e. underived) nouns have regular accentuation based on the shape of the penultimate syllable of the word; if the penultimate syllable has a long vowel, that syllable bears the accent; if the penult syllable does not have a long vowel, then the ultima bears the accent.

Kimball mentions a small number of exceptions to this rule. In Creek, syllables are grouped from left to right into bimoraic feet, with stress signaled by high pitch on the last syllable of each foot. The bimoraic foot can be composed of two CV syllables or one heavy syllable. High pitch begins on the first stressed syllable and extends to the final stressed syllable, and initial H is slightly lowered before another H (designated below by H↓) (Martin 2011: 76–78). Consider the examples from Creek in Table 17.4, which demonstrate the system.

For verbs, the placement of the accent is generally an effect of the verb grade. Different grades of the verb change the location of the accent, as in the following Choctaw verbs:

(1) a. *Taloowá-h.*
[cho] sing-TNS
'[3rd person] sings'
b. *Talohṍwa-h*
sing:HNGR-TNS
'[3rd person] keeps on singing.'

Table 17.3 Creek Plain Versus Geminate Consonants

Plain	*Geminate*
hafáp-i: 'weedy'	*kasápp-i:* 'cold'
hotop-itá 'to barbecue'	*hottop-íta* 'to be itchy'

Table 17.4 Iambic Stress in Creek

Creek	*Tonal Pattern*	*Gloss*
(i.fá)	[H$^{\downarrow}$H]	dog
(no.kó)si	[H$^{\downarrow}$HL]	bear
(no.kó)(so.cí)	[H$^{\downarrow}$HHH]	bear cub
(sók)ha	[HL]	hog
(ho.nán)wa	[H$^{\downarrow}$HL]	man
(í:)(ka.ná)	[H$^{\downarrow}$HH]	land

c. *Tálloowa-h*
sing:GGR-TNS'
[3rd person] finally sang.'

In the first example (1a), the plain form of the verb takes pitch on its final syllable. In the hn-grade (iterative) aspect of the verb shown in (1b), the accent appears on the penult, and in the g-grade of the verb in (1c), the accent is on the antepenult.

The Creek accent placement rule shown in Table 17.4 is sensitive to iambic feet. Iambic stress processes are also visible in the Western Muskogean languages, Chickasaw, and Choctaw, in a rule referred to in the literature as rhythmic lengthening. Rhythmic lengthening is a type of a more widespread phenomenon known as iambic lengthening (Buckley 1998).

In Choctaw, rhythmic lengthening works to lengthen the vowel of a nonfinal CV syllable when preceded by another CV syllable. The Choctaw rule is restricted to a particular morphological domain within the noun or verb stem. For nouns, it applies to the noun stem plus a possessor agreement prefix from the II (accusative)[2] set. For verbs, it applies to the verb stem + its derivational suffixes (stative /-a/, transitive /-li/, causative /-chi/) + the 1sg set I (nominative) suffix /-li/. Among the prefixes, only the set II (accusative) agreement prefixes are within the domain of rhythmic lengthening. Consider the examples in Table 17.5.

The rule does not apply to other kinds of prefixes or suffixes, even when they would otherwise appear to meet the environment for the rule. For example, the III prefix *im-*, used for alienable possession on nouns and a dative argument on verbs, cannot be resyllabified to create rhythmic lengthening environments. Table 17.6 shows the cases in which rhythmic lengthening does not apply.

Table 17.5 Rhythmic Lengthening in Choctaw

Choctaw (Underlying)	*After Lengthening*	*Translation*
salaha liver	(sa.la:)ha	liver
sa-salaha 1:s:II-liver	(sa.sa:)(la.ha)	my liver
pisa-li-h see-1:s:I-TNS	(pi.sa:)li	I see [3rd per.].
chi-pisa-li-h 2:s:II-see-1:s:I-TNS	(chi.pi:)(sa.li)	I see you.
pisa-chi-h see-caus-TNS	(pi.sa:)chi	[3rd per.] causes [3rd per.] to see
chi-pisa-chi-h 2:s:II-see-caus-TNS	(chi.pi:)(sa.chi)	[3rd per.] causes you to see.
chi-pisa-chi-li-h 2:s:II-see-caus-1:s:I-TNS	(chi.pi:)(sa.chi:)li	I cause you to see.
habina-h receive-TNS	(ha.bi:)na	[3rd per.] receives [3rd per.].
chi-habina-h 2:s:II-receive-TNS	(chi.ha:)(bi.na)	[3rd per.] receives [3rd per.] from you.
chi-habina-li-h 2:s:II-receive-1:s:I-TNS	(chi-.ha:)(bi.na:)-li	I receive a present from you.
habina-chi-h receive-CAUS-TNS	(ha.bi:)(na.chi)	[3rd per.] causes [3rd per.] to receive [3rd per.]
chi-habina-chi-h 2:s:II-receive-CAUS-TNS	(chi.ha:)(bi.na:)chi	[3rd per.] causes [3rd per.] to receive a present from you.

Table 17.6 Non-application of Rhythmic Lengthening in Choctaw

Choctaw (Underlying)	*Lack of Lengthening*	*Translation*
abo:ha room	(a.bo:)ha	room
am-aboha 1:s:III-room	(am)(a.bo:)ha [*(a.ma:)(bo.ha)]	my room
achifa-tok wash-tns	(a.chi:)(fa.tok)	[3rd per.] washes [3rd per.].
im-achifa-tok III-wash-tns	(im)(a.chi:)(fa.tok) [*(i.ma:)(chi.fa:)tok]	[3rd per.] washes [3rd per.] for [3rd per.].

2.3. Orthographies

Some of the Muskogean languages (Choctaw, Creek) have been written since the 19th century and have traditional orthographies that are used in New Testament translations and hymnals. In 19th-century Oklahoma, after removal, there were newspapers and pamphlets in Choctaw and Creek, and speakers wrote letters to each other in these languages. See Pitchlynn (2013) and Martin (2016) for examples of native writers in these languages.

The representation of consonants is mostly unproblematic in traditional orthographies, but the lateral fricative /ɬ/ and the affricate /tʃ/ are spelled differently in different languages. Choctaw traditional orthography uses <hl> and <lh> for /ɬ/, while Creek uses <r> for /ɬ/. Choctaw also uses <ch> for /tʃ/, while Creek uses <c> for /tʃ/. Choctaw uses <sh> for /ʃ/. Neither traditional orthography shows gemination very consistently.

Representation of vowels is more problematic. The traditional orthographies for both Choctaw and Creek reflect the 19th-century missionaries' difficulty in hearing and understanding vowel length distinctions in the language. In both these languages, the traditional orthography uses all five of the traditional vowels <a, e, i, o, u> in orthographies based on the Roman alphabet plus a sixth vowel, written <v> in Creek and <ʋ> in Choctaw.

In Creek, the most general correspondence is that in traditional spelling, <a, o> are used to represent the long vowels /a:, o:/, while <v, u> represent the corresponding short vowels /a, o/.[3] Choctaw shows a similar tendency, where <a, e, o> are primarily used for long vowels /a:, i:, o:/ and <ʋ, i, u> represent /a, i, o>. In both languages, there is some inconsistency in the traditional spelling.

Nasal vowels in Choctaw traditional orthography are indicated with either an underline or use of a homorganic nasal. Creek traditional orthography seldom marks vowel nasalization but sometimes also uses the underline and sometimes the nasal hook (ogonek) (Martin 2011: 102).

Despite their difficulties, many speakers strongly favor use of traditional orthographies for these languages. Hymnals and other religious materials using traditional orthographies are in regular use in churches, and some 19th-century literature also used these orthographies.

Consider the following examples of Creek (2a–b) and Choctaw (3a–b) words written in traditional orthographies, along with their phonemic representations:

(2) a. *<vm efv>*
[mus] *am-ifa*
1:s:DAT-dog
'my dog'

b. *<cukohvmēcvlke>*
tʃoko *hami:tʃ-âlki*
house all-PL
'family'

(3) a. *<vm ofi>*
[cho] *am-ofi?*
1:S:DAT -dog
'my dog'
b. *<chukachvfa>*
tʃokka *(a)tʃaffa*
house one
'family'

Much modern linguistic literature uses adaptations of traditional orthography to match speaker preferences. Thus, literature on Choctaw and Chickasaw typically uses <lh> for /ɬ/ and underlines for vowel nasalization, while most literature on Creek uses <r> for /ɬ/.

3. Morphology

From a typological perspective, Muskogean languages are highly agglutinative, with large numbers of prefixes, suffixes, and infixes. The languages show a mixture of head-marking and dependent-marking properties. At the nominal level, Muskogean languages mostly show head-marking, with agreement for the possessor marked on the head of the noun phrase (see §3.1.2). At the clausal level, however, there is both dependent-marking (since there is nominal case-marking (see §3.1.1)) and head-marking (since there is extensive verbal indexing of arguments). While words in Muskogean languages tend to have elaborate morphology, Muskogean languages are not usually classified as highly agglutinative, rather than polysynthetic, since they do not have productive noun incorporation.[4]

Muskogean languages generally have multiple criteria that show a distinction between nouns and verbs. The existence of most other part-of-speech categories is a matter of debate. For example, Munro (2005) argues that there are no postpositions in Chickasaw, and their equivalents are relational nouns. Broadwell (2006) argues that postpositions show a mix of categorial properties in Choctaw but are more similar to verbs than to nouns. All Muskogean languages have complex nominal and verbal morphology.[5]

3.1. Nominal Morphology

Nouns in Muskogean languages typically inflect for possession, case, and various discourse categories such as topic and focus.

3.1.1. Case Morphology

The simplest case systems are like those found in Choctaw, Chickasaw, and Creek, which show a distinction between nominative case and accusative case. Nominative case appears on subject, and accusative case appears on objects and obliques. Table 17.7 shows the most neutral forms of these case markers.

Alabama and Koasati have more complex case systems. Kimball (1991: 388–403) describes Koasati as having seven cases, shown in Table 17.8. The form that Kimball labels 'autonomous' is the unsuffixed noun, and the locative and inessive forms seem to show the incorporation of postpositional material into the noun.

In all the languages, there are also other versions of the case markers that signal special discourse statuses, such as topic, previous mention, contrast, and focus. Consider the following examples from Chickasaw:

Table 17.7 Two-way Case Distinctions

	NOMINATIVE	ACCUSATIVE
Choctaw	-at	-a̱ [-ã]
Chickasaw	-at	-a̱ [-ã]
Creek	-it	-in

Table 17.8 Koasati Cases

CASE	MARKER
nominative	*-k*
accusative	*-n* or vowel nasalization
autonomous	-ø
locative	*-fa*
allative	*-fon*
inessive	*-hayó*
vocative	deletion of final vowel or -ka

(4) a. *Shiiki-ako̱*
[cic] buzzard-CON:ACC
'the buzzard (contrastive)
b. *Shiiki-aash-oot*
buzzard-PREV-FOC:NOM
'The (aforementioned) buzzard (nom.)

(Munro [2005: 130–131])

Some of the suffixes which signal discourse status co-occur with case marking, while other suffixes suppress normal case marking, as is the case for Koasati *-p* 'topic' Kimball (1991: 411) and Creek *-ta:t(i)* 'focus of attention' (Martin 2011: 340). While most linguists working on Muskogean languages treat these nominal suffixes as case markers, see Davis and Hardy (1984) and Hardy and Davis (1988) for a dissenting view, which argues that the nominal suffixes show a central vs. peripheral distinction based on discourse status.

3.1.2. Possession

All Muskogean languages have a contrast between two types of possession, which correspond approximately to the alienable/inalienable distinction; consider the paradigm for Koasati in Table 17.9 (Kimball 1991: 432–434). Table 17.10 displays paradigms for 'wife' and 'dog' that show the contrast between the two types of nouns.

Although the contrast between nouns taking the two different agreement types is like the semantic distinction between alienable and inalienable possession, in (apparently) all Muskogean languages, there are unpredictable contrasts in possession type. Some body parts and kinship terms take agreement from the Accusative/II set and others take agreement from the Dative/III set. Consider the following contrasts from Koasati (Table 17.11). Some of these differences are partially explicable from history and etymology. In all the Muskogean languages, the Dative/III set is the productive set used with new words, such as loans from English or other languages. So loanwords like Koasati *má:ma* 'mother' and *tá:ta* 'father' show Dative/III agreement because of their origin. Native words, such as Koasati *hiłi* 'seed, semen', that have an origin outside the kinship or body part class also often take Dative/III agreement.

Table 17.9 Koasati Possessive Markers

	Accusative/II Agreement	Dative/III Agreement
1sg	*ca-*	*am-*
2sg	*ci-*	*cim-*
3rd	--	*im-*
1pl	*ko-*	*kom-*
2pl	*haci-*	*hacim-*

Table 17.10 Koasati Alienable and Inalienable Possession

	halki 'wife'	ifá 'dog'
1sg	*ca-halki* 'my wife'	*am-ifá* 'my dog(s)'
2sg	*ci-halki* 'your wife'	*cim-ifá* 'your dog(s)'
3rd	*halki* 'his wife/their wives'	*im-ifá* 'his/her/their dog(s)'
1pl	*ko-halki* 'our wives'	*kom-ifá* 'our dog(s)'
2pl	*haci-halki* 'y'all's wives'	*hacim-ifá* 'their dog(s)'

Table 17.11 Koasati Possession Contrasts

Accusative/II Agreement	Dative/III Agreement
ippokó:si 'grandchild'	*łakfósi* 'brother of a woman'
cofosí 'great uncle'	*awó* 'grandfather'
hakcó 'outer ear'	*cokbí* 'navel'
ihiłicí ' testicles'	*bonká* 'scrotum'

However, in general, such explanations are only partial, and there is an irreducible amount of lexical idiosyncrasy in the system. See Martin (1993) for discussion of the synchronic and diachronic origins of this system in Creek.

3.2. Verbal Morphology

Verbs show extensive derivational and inflectional morphology in Muskogean. The following subsections give an overview of the major types of derivational morphology (valence, causative, applicative, aspectual) and the major types of inflectional morphology (agreement, tense, mood, evidentiality, and switch-reference).

3.2.1. Verbal Derivation – Valence

All the Muskogean languages make a division between simple and derived verb stems. Simple verb stems are monomorphemic and may be either transitive or intransitive, as in the following examples from Choctaw and Mikasuki.[6]

(5) a. *illi-h*
[cho] die-TNS
[3rd per.] died.
b. *abi-h*
kill-TNS
[3rd per.] killed [3rd per.].

(6) a. *coko:l-om*
[mik] sit:SG-AUX
[3rd per.] sits.
b. *hic-om*
see-AUX
[3rd per.] sees [3rd per.].

(Boynton [1982: 65])

Simple verb stems contrast with derived stems. Derived verb stems consist of a bound verbal root + a marker of transitivity or a causative. Many derived verbs come in pairs, where one member of the pair is intransitive and the other is transitive. Tables 17.12 and 17.13 show examples of such pairs from Chickasaw (Munro 2005) and Creek (Martin 2011). As these tables show, there are a variety of morphological operations visible in such pairs.

First, it is important to recognize that many of the verbal roots here (e.g., Choctaw *tah* 'finish', Creek *acca*: 'lean against') cannot appear alone; they require an additional affix which shows their transitivity. Second, there is substantial variation in whether the transitive is derived from the intransitive (the 'causative' pattern), the intransitive is derived from the transitive (the 'anticausative' pattern), or whether both forms involve different affixes (the 'equipollent' pattern).

The pattern labeled equipollent here, where there is a single root which takes one suffix (Chickasaw *-a*, Creek *-k-*) for the intransitive and a different suffix for the transitive (Chickasaw *-li*, Creek *-y-*), probably dates back to Proto-Muskogean. Haas (1946) has reconstructed two 'classifying suffixes' for Proto-Muskogean, where **ka* is an intransitive classifier and **li* is a transitive classifier. In Haas's reconstruction, verbs like those shown in (5) and (6) were inflected directly, while other verbs required the **ka* or **li* classifying suffix. In somewhat more modern terms, we might think of reflexes of **ka* 'intransitive' and **li* 'transitive' as like auxiliaries (Martin & Munro 2005) or perhaps as heads of some projection like *v*P or VoiceP in the syntax.

The type of complex agreement system seen in Alabama and Koasati (§3.2.4) is considered to be reflective of the Proto-Muskogean contrast between direct inflection and inflection via auxiliary, while Haas (1946) and Martin and Munro (2005) suggest that Western Muskogean languages have simplified the system into a single direct inflectional paradigm.

Table 17.12 Chickasaw Verb Pairs[7]

ALTERNATION TYPE	INTRANSITIVE	TRANSITIVE
equipollent (-a 'intr' vs. -li 'trans')	*tah-**a*** 'be finished'	*tah-**li*** 'finish'
equipollent (-a 'intr' vs. -li 'trans')	*kolof-**a*** 'be cut'	*kolof-**fi*** 'cut'
equipollent (-a 'intr' vs. -li 'trans')	*tiw-**a*** 'open (intr.)'	*tiw-**wi*** 'open (tr.)'
l-infix for intransitive	*a<**l**>bi* 'be smeared'	*aabi* 'smear'
l-infix for intransitive	*oksh<**il**>itta* 'be closed'	*okshitta* 'close'
l-infix + -a 'intr' for intransitive, -li for trans	*a<**l**>tah-**a*** 'be ready'	*atah-**li*** 'get ready (tr.)'

Table 17.13 Creek Verb Pairs

ALTERNATION TYPE	INTRANSITIVE	TRANSITIVE
equipollent (-k 'intr' vs. -y 'trans')	*acca:-**k**-itá* 'lean against (intr.)'	*acca:-**y**-ita* 'lean (sg obj.) against'
equipollent (-k 'intr' vs. -y 'trans')	*ka:-**k**-itá* 'to sit (dual subj.)'	*ka:-**y**-itá* 'to set (dual obj.)'
-ic for transitive	*il-itá* '*die* (sg. subj)'	*il-**i:c**-itá* 'kill (sg. obj.)'
-eyc for transitive	*hic-itá* 'see'	*hic-**eyc**-itá* 'show'
-k- for intransitive	*tał-**k**-i:´* 'woven, knitted'[8]	*tał-ita* 'weave'
-k- for intransitive	*i:h-**k**-itá* 'hide (oneself)'	*i:h-itá* 'hide (something)'

Muskogean languages show other valence-changing morphology as well. An l-infix derives intransitives in Choctaw, Chickasaw, Alabama, and Koasati. Creek frequently shows a *-k* affix for intransitives that does not correspond to any morpheme in the corresponding transitive.

3.2.2. Verbal Derivation – Causatives and Applicatives

All languages have a causative and various applicatives. The causative is reconstructed for Proto-Muskogean as **-chi*, and this form is retained in Western Muskogean, Alabama, and Koasati in examples like those shown in (7) and (8).

(7) a. *taloowa-h*
[cho] sing-tns
'[3rd per.] sing(s)'
b. *taloowa-**chi**-h*
sing-CAUS-TNS
'[3rd per.] causes [3rd per.] to sing'

(8) a. *halokpa*
[akz] sharp
'be sharp, pointed'
b. *halokpa-**chi***
sharp-CAUS
'to sharpen, hone'

(Sylestine et al. 1993: 108)

The addition of a causative has effects on the verbal agreement, as examined in detail for Choctaw (Davies 1986; Ulrich 1986) and Creek (Martin 1991). Causative verbs will typically show Nominative/I agreement with the causer, but the agreement type of the causee and any other arguments show a number of complexities.

All of the languages also have applicative prefixes, which add instrumental, comitative, and various kinds of locative arguments to the verb. Consider the following examples:

(9) a. Choctaw comitative *ibaa-* 'with'
*Sa-**baa**-washooha-h!*
1:S:ACC-COM-play-TNS
'Play with me'
b. Creek locative *oh(h)-* 'on, over, at, toward'
***Ohh**-ahkpon-itá*
on-play-INF
'play on (a road, etc.)'

(Martin 2011: 162)

c. Alabama instrumental *ist-* 'with'
***ist**-achitìi-li*
INS-tie-TR
'button up with, fasten onto with, tie onto with'

(Sylestine et al. 1993: 206)

There are substantial syntactic and lexical complications associated with the applicative prefixes. See Munro (2000), Ulrich (1986), and Martin (2011) for further discussion.

3.2.3. Verbal Derivation – Aspectual Grades

All Muskogean languages have verb roots with infixed morphology. Within modern grammars of Muskogean languages, the various infixed forms of a verb are usually referred to as the verbal 'grades'. Although aspectual information is often inflectional in other languages of the word, this is less clear-cut in Muskogean languages, where some grades have limited productivity and there are often considerable lexical restrictions on the use of grades. Thus they are listed here as a kind of derivational morphology, though not all linguists working on Muskogean languages would necessarily agree on this characterization.[9]

The most basic form of the verb, with no infix, is often called the zero-grade of the verb. It has no special aspectual semantics (apart from those provided by discourse or other affixes). The other grades of the verb are typically associated with special aspectual semantics. For example, the hn-grade in Choctaw and Chickasaw is associated with repetitive or durative actions and is typically translated as 'all the time' or 'over and over', while the y-grade is used with events that have a delayed inception and is typically translated as 'finally':

(10) a. Zero grade
habishko-tok
sneeze-PT
'[3rd per.] sneezed.'

b. Y-grade
habíyyishko
sneeze:ygr-PT
'[3rd per.] finally sneezed.'

c. HN-grade
habihĩ́shko-tok.
Sneeze:hngr-PT
'[3rd per.] keeps sneezing over and over.'

In very general terms, all of the grades insert phonological material into the penult of the verb stem. For example, the Choctaw y-grade accents the penult, and infixes a geminate /y/ before a copy of the penult vowel.

Nevertheless, there are often complications that depend on phonological properties of the verb stem, such as whether the penult is open or closed. It is challenging to come up with a complete phonological account of grade formation in any Muskogean language.

Verb grades also require consideration of the morphological unit that counts as a verb stem for the purposes of the infixation rule. Because grades involve lengthening or infixing material in particular syllables of the verb stem, it is important to understand which affixes count as part of the stem and which do not. In the Muskogeanist literature, affixes which are within the domain of grade infixes are often called 'stem-forming'. Consider the following contrasts in Creek between the stem-forming suffix *-ak-* 'plural', and the non-stem-forming suffix *-ak* 'impersonal agent'.

(11) a. *awṓ:l-os-i:-t* *ô:-s* *[má:k-a:k]-i:-s*
close:NGR-DIM-DUR-SS be:FGR-IND say-PL:LGR-DUR-IND
'They [specific people] say it's very close.'

b. *awṓ:l-os-i:-t* *ô:-s* *[ma:k]-**ak**-i:-s*
close:NGR-DIM-DUR-SS be:FGR-IND say:LGR-IMPERS:AGT-DUR-IND
'One could say its very close.'

(Martin [2011: 231])

Table 17.14 Chickasaw Verb Grades

	Typical Semantics	kosoma 'be smelly'	fatabli 'have dandruff'	oklhilili 'be dark'
hn-grade	repetitive, habitual	*kosohǒ́ma*	*fatahámbli*	*oklhihį́li*
n-grade	durative, resultative	*kosǒ́ma*	*fatámbli*	*oklhį́li*
y-grade	delayed inception, intensive	*kosóyyoʔma*	*fatáyyabli*	*oklhíyyiʔli*
g-grade	delayed inception, intensive	*kóssoʔma*	*fáttabli*	*oklhíʔli*
h-grade	intensive	*kosóhhoʔma*	*fatáhhabli*	*oklhíhhiʔli*
glottal-form	none	*kosoʔma*	*fatabli*	*oklhiliʔli*

Table 17.15 Creek Verb Grades

	Typical Semantics	hic- 'see'
lengthened grade	eventive	*hi:c-is* '[3rd per.] is looking at it'
falling grade	resultative	*hî:c-is* '[3rd per.] sees it'
aspirating (h-)grade	perfective	*híhc-is* '[3rd per.] saw it (today/last night)'
expressive (n-)grade	expressive	*hį́:c-is* '[3rd per.] keeps looking at it'

Because the plural affix *-ak-* is inside the verb stem for purposes of the grades, in (11a) the lengthened grade applies to the stem [*ma:k-ak*] to yield [*má:k-a:k*]. However, in (11b), the impersonal agent affix is outside the stem, so the lengthened grade applies only to [*ma:k*].

For various detailed accounts of Western Muskogean grades and their analysis, see Ulrich (1986; 1994), Lombardi and McCarthy (1991), and Weeda (1992). Tables 17.14 and 17.15 provide an idea of the types of grades and their associated semantics by showing verb forms from Chickasaw (Munro 1985) and Creek (Martin 2011: 241).[10] As Martin (2011) notes, some of the grades have many uses in addition to the semantics shown in Table 17.15.

The grades vary considerably in their productivity and intersect with aktionsart in ways that are not very well understood. It is typical for positional, stative, and active verbs to have somewhat different interpretations in different grades. Thus the Choctaw hn-grade typically shows repeated events for punctual verbs but prolonged duration for non-punctual verbs, and the h-grade shows sudden inception for punctual verbs but a comparative for adjectival stative verbs (Broadwell 2006: 164–165).

Due to the variable productivity of the grades, the Chickasaw dictionary of Munro and Willmond (1994) lists all the grades available for each verb. It might be possible to predict many aspects of grade productivity if we had a more detailed understanding of the lexical semantics of Muskogean verbs, and this area in particular might benefit from careful semantic fieldwork.

3.2.4. Verbal Inflection – Agreement

All Muskogean languages have agreement systems with several different types of argument agreement. Table 17.16 shows the agreement morphology of Choctaw. Where two alternatives are shown in this table, the first is before a vowel and the second is before a consonant. The 1st sg I affix -li is the only suffix in the system; all the other agreement is via prefix.

The labels for these agreement sets vary from grammar to grammar. The Roman numeral system (I/II/III) is originally due to Munro and Gordon (1982) and is used in other work on Western Muskogean as well (Broadwell 2006). The virtue (and perhaps the weakness) of this system is that it does not make any prediction about how these agreement sets are used in the grammar. As a result, some accounts label them as Nominative, Accusative, Dative agreement (Davies 1986;

Table 17.16 Choctaw Agreement Morphology

	Nominative/I	Accusative/II	Dative/III	Negative/N
1sg	*-li*	*sa-*	*(s)am-/(s)ã-*	*ak-*
2sg	*ish-*	*chi-*	*chim-/chĩ-*	*chik-*
1pl paucal	*il-/ii-*	*pi-*	*pim-/pĩ-*	*kil-/kii-*
1pl multiple	*il-/ii-*	*hapi-*	*hapim-/hapĩ-*	*kil-/kii-*
2pl	*hash-*	*hachi-*	*hachim-/hachĩ-*	*hachik-*
default			*im-/ĩ-*	*ik-*

Ulrich 1986). Although these labels are suggestive of their uses, they create a conflict between the terms used for verbal morphology and the case morphology which occurs on overt noun phrases. As discussed in §3.1.1, no matter what kind of agreement a verb takes, its subject has nominative case.

There are many possible linkages between grammatical function and agreement type. Intransitive subjects in Choctaw, for example, can take any of the three kinds of agreement.

(12) a. I subject
[cho] *(An-akoosh)* *baliili-**li**-tok.*
1:S-CON:NOM run-1:S:I-PST
'I ran.'
b. II subject
(An-akoosh) ***sa**-niya-h.*
1:S-CON:NOM 1:s:II-fat-TNS
'I am fat.'
c. III subject
(An-akoosh) *a̱-ponna-h.*
1:S-CON:NOM 1:s:III-skilled-TNS
'I am skilled.'

Despite the different verb agreement, an overt subject for any of these clauses will be nominative. Transitive verbs also fall into several classes, depending on the sort of agreement with subjects and objects. The most frequent types of transitive show I agreement for the subject and either II or III agreement for object.

(13) a. I subject and II object
***Chi**-pi̱sa-**li**-h*
2:s:II-see:NGR-**1:s:I**-TNS
'I see you.'
b. I subject and III object
***Chi̱**-pa̱ya-**li**-h.*
2:s:III-call-**1:s:I**-TNS
'I call you.'

A much smaller number of transitive verbs trigger II or III agreement for their subjects:

(14) a. II subject and II object
[cho] ***Chi-sa**-banna-h*
2:s:II-1:s:II-want-TNS
'I want you'

b. II subject and III object
***Chi̱-sa**-noklhaka̱cha-h*
2:s:III-1:s:II-be:startled-TNS
'I was startled by you.'

In Choctaw, subjects of negative and hortative verbs show agreement from the N set instead of their normal agreement. For verbs with a I subject, the N prefix substitutes for the I.

(15) a. *pi̱sa-**li**-h*
[cho] see:NGR-1:s:I-TNS
'I see'
b. ***ak**-píis-o-h*
1:s:N-see:LGR-NEG-TNS
'I don't see.'
c. ***ak**-pisa-h*
1:s:N-see-TNS
'Let me see'

For verbs with a II or III subject, the default N precedes the II or III agreement.[11]

(16) a. ***sa**-banna-h*
[cho] 1:s:II-want-TNS
'I want.'
b. ***ik-sa**-bánn-o-h.*
DEF:N-1:s:II-want:LGR-NEG-TNS
'I don't want.'

Although the agreement morphology for Choctaw is relatively complex, the most complex agreement systems in the family are found in Alabama and Koasati. Alabama has six morphological subclasses that correspond to verbs taking Nom/I agreement. Consider the data in Table 17.17, paying attention to the location of the agreement morphology. An ongoing issue in the grammar of Muskogean languages is the extent to which the agreement type associated with a verb is predictable.

Some facts about the agreement system are obviously idiosyncratic to lexical items. For example, there is nothing about the semantics of Alabama *ipa* 'eat' and *isko* 'drink' that predicts that they belong to verb types 1a and 1b in Table 17.17.

On the other hand, the choice of Nominative/I, Accusative/II, and Dative/III agreement is not completely arbitrary. Verbs whose subjects deliberately control actions consistently use the Nominative/I markers, and verbs whose subjects lack control use Accusative/II marking. Verbs whose subjects can be either in control or out of control show a 'fluid' agreement pattern in many Muskogean languages. Table 17.18 displays contrasts in Creek Martin (2011: 171–174).

However, most of the languages also have verbs whose agreement type is difficult to predict. Among intransitives, the difference between verbs that take Accusative/II and Dative/III agreement is the hardest to understand. Table 17.19 shows examples from Choctaw of intransitive verbs with differing agreement types.

There are similar difficult contrasts between transitive verbs. Some verbs take Nominative/I agreement for the subject and Accusative/II agreement for their object (I/II or Nom/Acc verbs), and some verbs take Nominative/I agreement for the subject and Dative/III agreement for their object (I/III or Nom/Dat verbs). Examples of these contrasts appear in Table 17.20.

Table 17.17 Alabama Agreement

VERB TYPE	ROOT	INFLECTED FORMS
1a	*ipa* 'eat'	*ipa*-**li** 'I eat' **is**-*pa* 'you eat' **il**-*pa* 'we eat'
1b	*isko* 'drink'	*isko*-**li** 'I drink" *is*<**is**>*ko* 'you drink' *is*<**il**>*ko* 'we drink'
1c	*liphachi* 'crush'	*liphachi*-**li** 'I crush' *liphach*-**iska** 'you crush' *liphach*-**ilka** 'we crush'
1d	*hosso* 'write'	*hosso*-**li** 'I write' *ho*<**chi**>*sso* 'you write' *ho*<**li**>*sso* 'we write'
1e	*batli* 'hit (repeatedly)'	*batli*-**li** 'I hit' *bat*-**chi** ' you hit' *bat*-**hili** 'we hit'
1f	*paapa* 'carry'	*paapa*-**li** 'I carry' *paa*<***s***>*pa* 'you carry' *paa*<***l***>*pa* 'we carry'

Table 17.18 Creek Nominative vs. Accusative Agreement

NOMINATIVE/I AGREEMENT	ACCUSATIVE/II AGREEMENT
*i:sk-**ey**-s* 'I'm drinking'	***aca**-col-í:-s* 'I'm old'
*ta:sk-**éy**-s* 'I'm jumping'	***acá**-poyc-ís* 'I'm dreaming'
*fikhom-**éy**-s* 'I'm stopping'	***cá**-fikwánh-i:-s* 'I'm out of breath'
*latêyk-**ey**-s* 'I fell (on purpose)'	***ca**-latêk-s* 'I fell (by accident)'

Table 17.19 Choctaw II vs. III Agreement

	ACCUSATIVE/II	DATIVE/III
Psychological states	***sa**-ba̱shkah* 'I am friendly'	***am**-ahchibah* 'I am tired, bored'
	***sa**-komootah* 'I am fearful'	***a̱**-chiloosah* 'I am lonesome'
	***sa**-hoofahyah* 'I am embarrassed'	***a̱**-takohbih* 'I am lazy'
Body states	***sa**-chokfollih* 'I am dizzy'	***a̱**-kapassah* 'I feel cold'
	***sa**-biikowah* 'I have a nosebleed'	***am**-oklhiliikah* 'I faint'
	***sa**-hottoopah* 'I am hurt'	***a̱**-palammih* 'I suffer'

Table 17.20 Choctaw I/II vs. I/III Agreement

	I/II (NOM/ACC)	I/III (NOM/DAT)
Verbs of contact	*ahpalih* 'kiss'	*i̱-tokoowah* 'kiss'
	apaatah 'sit beside'	*i̱-bili̱kah* 'be close to'
	hammih 'rub'	*im-atiilichih* 'massage'
Verbs of emotion	*ahnichih* 'like, love'	*i̱-hichaalih* 'hate'
	holiitoblih 'value, respect'	

See Heath (1977), Munro and Gordon (1982), Davies (1986), Broadwell (2006), Martin (2011), and Hardy and Davis (1993) for contrasting opinions on the predictability of agreement type in Muskogean languages.

3.2.5. Verbal Inflection – Tense, Mood, and Evidentiality

All Muskogean languages allow large numbers of verbal suffixes, which indicate tense, mood, evidentiality, and a number of adverbial notions. Broadwell (2006) gives the following template for suffixes in Choctaw:

VERB-(Adverb$_1$)-(Modal)-(Adverb$_2$)-Tense-(Adverb$_3$)-Evidential/IllocutionaryForce

The modal position in Choctaw includes affixes such as *-aachi̠* 'irrealis', *-ahii* 'irrealis2', and *-ahi̠la* 'possible'. Future events in Choctaw are indicated through use of one of two modals – *-aachi̠* 'irrealis' or *-ahii* 'irrealis2'. These are subtly different; in general, the irrealis2 suffix refers to a future event that is more definite, but more careful semantic work is needed to completely understand the difference between the two.

Creek has a similar distinction between two suffixes that Martin (2011: 269–271) calls 'prospective' and 'future'. The prospective *-aha:n-* is 'used for casual propositions regarding intention or predication, often in the near future', while the future *-áɬl* is used for 'promises, pledges, or proposals'. Given the rather similar meanings of the two Creek suffixes, it is surprising that they show quite different morphological patterns. Subject agreement follows the prospective, but precedes the future:[12]

(17) a. *wanáy-**aha:n**-íck-is*
[mus] tie-PROSP-2:S:NOM-IND
'You are going to tie it.'
b. *wanáy-ick-**áɬi**-s*
tie-2:S:NOM-FUT-IND
'You will tie it.'
(Martin 2011: 430)

Choctaw has three-way distinction in tense among *-ttook* 'distant past', *-tok* 'recent past', and *-h* default, where the default tense marker receives its interpretation from discourse, aktionsart, and sentence adverbials.

Tense marking is sometimes conflated with marking of various kinds of evidence. Thus, Koasati has four past-like tense suffixes Kimball (1991: 207–210). There is a distinction between immediate past, recent past, and distant past. But the set of suffixes in this position also includes *:sa-*, which indicates an event 'out of the experience of the hearer'. It is typically, but not necessarily, interpreted as referring to past events.

In the same way, the first-hand evidential suffix *-hli/-hnik-hlik*[13] in Choctaw is used with events that the speaker has witnessed. These will almost always be in the past, but sentences that use the evidential cannot be explicitly marked for tense.

(18) a. *O̠ba-tok*
[cho] rain-PST
'It rained (evidence not stated)'
b. *O̠ba-**hli***
rain-**EVID**
'It rained (I saw it).'

c. *Oba-tok-hli
rain-PT-evid
(Intended: 'It rained.')

(Broadwell 2006: 187–88)

Creek has the most elaborate tense system in the family, with five past tenses in the earliest documented forms of the language. One of these tenses is no longer in use, but the modern language still uses four past tenses (Martin 2010). Creek shows a complex interaction between the grade of the verb, the tense-marking affix, and the perfectivity of the event. As Martin (2011: 257–259) explains, the future verb typically appears in the zero grade, Past 2 and Past 3 are typically in the falling grade, and the Past 1 imperfective, Past 4, and Past 5 are typically in the lengthened grade. The Past 1 perfective is in the h-grade. Consider the following examples, which illustrate this.

(19) a. Present, l-grade
[mus] *ni:s-ís*
buy<LGR>-IND
'[3rd per.] is buying it, bought it (up to a few seconds ago)'

b. Past 1, perfective, h-grade
*ni**h**s-ís*
buy<HGR>-IND
'[3rd per.] bought it (sometime between today and last night)'

c. Past 1, imperfective, l-grade
*ni:s-**êy**-s*
buy<LGR>-past1:IMPF-IND
'[3rd per.] was buying it (sometime between today and last night)'

d. Past 2, f-grade
*nî:s-**ank**-s*
buy<FGR>-past2-IND
'[3rd per.] bought it (sometime between yesterday and several weeks ago)'

e. Past 3, f-grade
*nî:s-**imát**-s*
buy<FGR>-past3-IND
'[3rd per.] bought it (sometime between several weeks and about a year ago)'

f. Past 4, l-grade
*ni:s-**ánt(a)**-s*
buy<LGR>-past4-IND
'[3rd per.] bought it (long ago, at least several years)'

g. Past 5, l-grade
*ni:s-**ati:**-s*
buy<LGR>-past5-IND
'[3rd per.] bought it (very long ago)'

h. Future, zero-grade
*nis-**ali**:-s*
buy-FUT-IND
'[3rd per.] will buy it'

All the Muskogean languages appear to allow various adverbial elements to appear among the suffixes. From a diachronic point of view, one can see that formerly independent words have become auxiliaries or affixes in various languages, and there are some disagreements among linguists about what counts as an affix. Munro (1984) discusses the various items that function either as auxiliaries or as affixes in Chickasaw.

3.2.6. Verbal Inflection – Switch-Reference

All the Muskogean languages have switch-reference systems, which mark whether the subject of a given clause has the same or different subject as some other clause.

Booker (1980) reconstructs the Proto-Muskogean switch-reference markers as *-t and *-k 'same-subject' and *-n 'different subject'.[14] Consider the following example from Creek, which shows multiple instances of same-subject marking.

(20) *'S-a-tóccina-n* *'m-a-tipk-itá-n* *kôn-**t** o:m-êys* *,ma*
[mus] INS-LOC-three-ACC DAT-LOC-slap-INF-ACC try:FGR-SS be:LGR-even that
hiłkináka-ta:t *ká:pa-n* *káhy-**it*** *a:-itipóhy-**t***
preacher-ATN coat-ACC take:off:DU:HGR-SS DIR-fight:HGR-SS
*ti:ⁿpk-**it*** *mi:c-ati:-s.*
slap:LGR-SS do:LGR-past5-IND'

[The man$_j$] tried to slap [the preacher$_i$] a third time, but the preacher$_i$ pulled off his coat, and (he$_i$) fought him$_j$ back, and (he$_i$) really whipped him$_j$, he$_i$ did.'

(Martin 2011:345–6)

In this passage, the initial clause describes the actions of the man who is fighting against the preacher. The initial clause has the man as its subject and ends with the verb *kô:n-t o:m-êys* 'tried', ends with a suffix *-êys* 'even though', which never takes switch-reference. The next four clauses (headed by *káhy-it* 'take off', *a:-itipóhy-t* 'fought', *ti:ⁿpk-it* 'whipped', and *mi:c-ati:-s* 'did') describe the actions of the preacher. Thus, there is change of subject from 'the man' to 'the preacher', which is not explicitly ambiguous in the morphology. In the sequence of clauses describing the preacher's actions, only the final verb 'did' is fully marked for tense (*-ati:* 'past 5') and illocutionary force (*-s* 'declarative'). The verbs that precede 'did' have th– same-subject suffix *-(i)t*, showing that they all have the preacher as subject.

The following passage, also from Creek, shows different subject marking describing the actions of two agents in a fight:

(21) *a:-oséyy-**in*** *halâ:t-ey-**n*** *an-ciyall-**in***
[mus] DIR-come:out:HGR-DS hold:FGR-1:S:Agt-DS 1:S:DAT-struggle:against:LGR-DS
*ti-weyk-êy-**n*** *hola:n-**it**. . .*
RECP-throw:LGR-1:S:AGT-ds defecate:LGR-SS

'[Rabbit] came out, I grabbed him, and he struggled against me, I threw him down, and he crapped, and (he went in there).'[15]

(Martin 2011: 346)

Here the alternating actions of the two agents are signaled by the use of the different subject markings.

As (20) and (21) also show, typical discourse in Muskogean languages is very 'verb-heavy', with limited use of overt nouns and no overt pronouns. Thus switch-reference plays an important functional role in allowing the hearer to follow referential continuity and change in natural discourse.

The definition of switch-reference given at the start of this subsection is intentionally vague about the syntactic relationship between the two clauses that are involved in switch-reference. Following Haiman and Munro (1983), we may call the clause in which switch-reference is marked as the 'marking clause', and the clause with reference to which it is marked as the 'reference clause'. The most frequent instances in Muskogean languages are typically of the type shown in (20) and (21), where the marking clause precedes the reference clause, and the event of the marking clause precedes the event of the reference clause.

It is also possible for other, more complex, patterns to arise. For example, the marked clause is occasionally separated from the reference clause by several other verbs, or after the reference clause. Consider example (22) from Chickasaw, which illustrates the possibility of non-adjacency in switch-reference:

(22) *Kolo'fa-**na*** *im-pállammi-**cha*** *tí'wa-**na*** *kaniya'-mat*
[cic] be:cut:LGR-DS DAT-be:serious:LGR-SS lie:LGR-DS someone-INDEF:NOM
im-alikch-a'ni-ką *hoyo-**kat*** *áyya'sha.*
DAT-doctor:LGR-POT-COMP:DS look:for-COMP:SS be:there:TPL:YGR
'[Rabbit$_i$] was wounded and he$_i$ had it so bad that he$_i$ was lying [in bed], so they$_j$ were looking for someone$_k$ to doctor him$_i$.'

(Munro 2005: 115)

As Munro (2005) explains, the different subject marking on the marked clauses headed by 'be cut', 'lie', and 'doctor' is due to the fact that the reference clause is the final verb + auxiliary 'be looking for'. However, the verb 'be serious' is marked for same subject because its reference clause is the immediately following the verb 'lie'.

Chickasaw also allows the possibility of a marked clause after the reference clause, as in example (23):[16]

(23) *Rabbit* *m-at* *foni'* *illa-at* *áyya'sha-ttook* *miya,* *apa-t*
rabbit that-NOM bone only-NOM be:there:TPL:YGR-DPAST HSAY eat-PRT
*tahli-**na**.*
finish:GLGR-DS
'Only Rabbit's bones were there (they say), [because] they had eaten him all up.'

(Munro 2005: 120)

In this example, the final verb sequence 'they had eaten him all up' is marked for different subject, but its reference clause is '(the bones) were there'.

Switch-reference occurs on a number of different kinds of clauses in Muskogean languages – in clause-linking constructions of the 'and then' variety, as well as on many other adverbial clauses, most complement clauses, and relative clauses. The occurrence of switch-reference on complement clauses, as in the Chickasaw example in (24), is problematic for approaches to switch-reference, which try to reduce it to coordination.

(24) *[Ishno'* *sa-ya* *ki'yo-**kat**]* *ithą́na-li.*
you 1:s:I-be not-COMP:SS know:NGR-1:S:I
'I know that I'm not you.'

(Munro [2016])

The view that switch-reference marking primarily shows change of subject, rather than change of event or topic, appears to be the majority view among scholars working on Muskogean languages (e.g., Munro & Gordon 1982; Kimball 1991; Broadwell 2006; Martin 2011; Munro 2016). However, for the dissenting view, see Davis and Hardy (1984) and Rising (1990).

4. Syntax

4.1. Word Order Typology

All Muskogean languages show a predominantly head-final word order. Within clauses, the regular order is Subject-Object-Verb, and within noun phrases, the possessor precedes the possessed. Consider the following examples from Alabama and Chickasaw:

(25) a. *Naani-k* *ifa* *ak-o-n* *ib-o*
[akz] man-NOM dog that-DET-ACC kill-PFV
'The man killed that dog.'
(Lupardus [1982:213])

b. *Wanda* *im-iisa*
Wanda DAT-house
'Wanda's house'
(Hardy [2005])

(26) a. *Shiiki* *yamm-at* *chokfi* *yamm-a̠* *im-alikchi.*
[cic] buzzard that-NOM rabbit that-ACC DAT-doctor
'Buzzard doctored Rabbit'
(Munro [2005:117])

b. *ofi'* *in-chokka'*
dog DAT-house
'the dog's house'
(Munro and Willmond [2008:94])

As examples (25a) and (26a) show, subjects receive nominative case and objects, and obliques receive accusative case. Muskogean languages differ somewhat in whether an overt case marker is obligatory. For the Western Muskogean languages, nominative is normally obligatory on the subject and optional on the object. For Creek, both overt nominative and accusative are optional, and their appearance is related to the discourse status and possible ambiguity of the sentence (Martin 2011: 339–343).

4.2. Noun Phrases

Adjectives follow nouns in Muskogean languages.

(27) a. [mus] *isti* *cáati*
person red
'Indian (red person)'
b. [cho] *oklah* *homma'*
people red
'Indians (red people)'

Languages vary on the position of determiner/demonstrative words. In Western Muskogean, demonstratives follow the noun. In other languages, the demonstratives precede the noun.

(28) a. [cku] *ma* *í:sa* *má:t-on*
that house other-FOC:ACC
'that other house'

(Kimball [1991]: 487)

b. [cho] *hattak-m-at*
man-DEM-NOM
'that man (nom.)'

As shown in (25b) and (26b), the possessor precedes the possessed.

Muskogean languages have various ways to form relative clauses. One structure found in all the languages is the internally headed relative clause.[17] Consider the following examples.

(29) a. [mus] *móhm-in* *a:tami* *[halw-i:* *isti* *aháa:ka* *i:m-ati:]*
be:so:HGR-DS Adam high-DUR person law give:LGR-past5
aca:yi:c-ika:t *omi:ceyec-i:-n. . .*
obey-not-REF because-DUR-DS
'Because Adam didn't obey the law that the angels gave him, . . .'

(Martin 2011: 395)

b. [cho] *Ofi-it* *[John-at* *kaah* *chǫpa-tok]-ą* *notaaka'* *aa-nosi-tok*
dog-NOM John-NOM car buy-PST-ACC under LOC-sleep-PST
aachiini-tok.
EVID-PST
'The dog apparently sleeps under the car that John bought.'

(Broadwell 2006: 297)

c. [cku] *Am-tá:ta-k* *tayyi* *hí:ca-:say-ok*
1:S:DAT-father-NOM woman see-PRES:PART-FOC:NOM
ci-halk-ók *óm*
2:S:DAT-wife-foc:NOM be
'The woman that my father saw is your wife.'

(Kimball 1991: 525)

Though internally headed relative clauses are possible in Creek, Martin (2011: 395) reports that modern speakers generally prefer left headed relative clauses like the following:

(30) *asêy* *ifá* *[wo:hk-i:]* *[a:-hôyl-a:t]* *lopéyc-i:-t* *ô:s.*
[mus] that dog bark:LGR-DUR DIR-stand:FGR-REF nice-DUR-SS be:FGR-IND
'That dog standing over there barking is nice.'

(Martin 2011: 392)

In this example, 'that dog' is modified by two relative clauses, 'barking' and 'standing over there'.

4.3. Case and Switch-Reference

A difficult problem in the syntax of most Muskogean languages is the partial homophony of the case affixes discussed in §3.1.1 and the switch-reference suffixes discussed in §3.2.6. We expect case affixes to appear on nouns and switch-reference markers to appear on verbs, but there are many cases where it is difficult to decide if a particular affix should be considered a case marker or a switch-reference marker. Consider the following Choctaw example:

(31) *Hattak* *toklo-kat* *am-ofi'* *hǫkopa-tok.*
[cho] man two-COMP:SS?:NOM? 1:S:DAT-dog steal-PST
'Two men stole my dog.'

Is the *-t* on the end of the word *toklokat* best treated as nominative case or a switch-reference? Under the first analysis, 'two' is adjectival and modifies 'man', so nominative case appears on the end of the noun phrase. Under the second analysis, 'be two' is a verbal element, and 'man' is its subject, so that the structure of (31) is literally something like 'The men are two and they stole my dog.' The *-t* is thus a marker of same-subject.

In this particular example, the second analysis, in which *-t* is a same-subject marker, is probably correct. The reason is that the suffix *-ka,* which appears on the predicate *toklo* 'be two', is normally a complementizer suffix for verbs. There is no nominal *-ka* suffix in Choctaw, so the word it is attached to must be a verb.

However in other cases, both analyses seem plausible, and it is hard to find a way to determine which is correct. Consider the following Choctaw relative clause (repeated from (29b)):

(32) a. *Ofi-it* *[John-at* *kaah* *chǫpa-tok]-ą* *notaaka'* *aa-nosi-tok*
[cho] dog-NOM John-NOM car buy-PST-ACC under LOC-sleep-PST
aachiini-tok.
EVID-PST
'The dog apparently sleeps under the car that John bought.'
(Broadwell 2006: 297)

Here the final *-ã* on the relative clause 'the car that John bought' has been glossed as accusative, which appears at the end of the internally headed relative clause. It is also possible that it could be interpreted as a different-subject marker, in which case the structure of (32a) is more like 'John bought a car and the dog apparently sleeps under it'. Determining which of these analyses is correct requires extensive knowledge of the language, and there are many uncertainties of analysis.

Synchronically, it is clear that the case and switch-reference systems are not completely the same. Choctaw and Chickasaw have two switch-reference markers, *-cha* 'and then (same subject)' and *-na* 'and then (different subject)', which do not correspond to any case markers. Similarly, the Koasati case marking system shown in Table 17.8 does not include a nominal suffix *-t,* but Koasati does have a switch-reference marker *-t* Kimball (1991: 527–528).

Some authors have tried to treat the nominal suffixes as derived from switch-reference markers, and some have tried to treat the switch-reference markers as derived from the case markers. For further discussion of how to best treat the overlap between the two types of morphology, see Camacho (2010), Munro (2016), and Gordon and Munro (2017), inter alia.

Because many instances of final -t, -k, and/or -n are ambiguously interpreted as either case or switch-reference, some authors (Martin 2011) do not provide a grammatical gloss for them, but only a gloss such as -T or -N.

5. Conclusion

Studies of Muskogean languages have contributed substantially to linguistic theory. The languages show many fascinating phonological, morphological, and syntactic properties that are typologically unusual. For example, Muskogean data have informed theories of unaccusativity (Davies 1986; Harris 1992; Levin & Hovav 1995), internal and external possession (Munro & Gordon 1982; Martin 1993), voice and causatives (Martin 1991; Hardy 1994), internally headed relative clauses (Bonneau 1994; Basilico 1996; Gordon & Munro 2017), switch-reference (Munro & Gordon 1982; Broadwell 1997; Camacho 2010; Keine 2013; Munro 2016), lexical categories Haag (1997), inflectional morphology Anderson (1992), morphological truncation (Weeda 1992; Broadwell 1993; Kosa 2008), stress systems (Hammond 1993; Hayes 1995; Buckley 1998; Gordon 2004), and prosodic morphology (Lombardi & McCarthy 1991). Documentation of these languages has advanced very substantially in the last 30 years, and there are now good grammars and dictionaries of most of the languages. There are fewer good collections of oral or spoken texts in most of these languages, with the notable exceptions of Creek (Gouge 2004; Haas et al. 2015) and Koasati (Kimball 2010).

All the Muskogean languages are now endangered, but there are still opportunities to do fieldwork on these languages. To do so requires careful consideration of the needs of the communities and speakers of Choctaw, Chickasaw, Alabama, Koasati, Mikasuki, and Creek. Many people in these tribes are working to preserve and revitalize their native languages, and they can benefit from the work of linguists who are concerned with the needs of the communities where these languages are spoken.

Acknowledgments

I thank Jane Hill, Jack Martin, and an anonymous reviewer for valuable comments on this chapter. I also thank the many speakers of these languages who have worked in collaboration with linguists on the documentation of their languages.

Further Reading

An excellent collection, containing sketches of several Muskogean languages (Chickasaw, Choctaw, Alabama, and Creek), as well as discussion of Proto-Muskogean phonology and morphology, can be found in Hardy and Scancarelli (2005). Goddard (2005) is valuable for understanding the position of Muskogean languages in the larger linguistic landscape of the Southeast. An older, classic, overview of research is Haas (1979). Valuable pedagogical information for those trying to learn or learn about Muskogean languages can be found in textbooks co-authored by linguists and native speakers, such as Willmond and Munro (2012) on Chickasaw, Haag and Willis (2001; 2007) on Choctaw, and Innes et al. (2004; 2009) on Creek.

Notes

1. Martin (2011) notes that Creek formerly had a contrast between /ay/ and /ey/, but that for most speakers this has been neutralized to /ey/.
2. The following abbreviations are used in this chapter: 1 = first person, 2 = second person, I = agreement from the I set, II = agreement from the II set, III = agreement from the III set, ACC = accusative, AGT = agent-type agreement, ATN = focus of attention, AUX = auxiliary, CAUS = causative, COM = comitative, COMP = complementizer, CON = contrastive, DAT = dative, DEF = definite, DEM = demonstrative, DET = determiner, DIR = directional, DPAST = distant past, DS = different subject, DU = dual, DUR = durative, EVID = evidential, FGR = falling grade (in Creek), FOC = focus, FUT = future, GLGR = glottal-grade (in Chickasaw), GGR = g-grade (verbal form with gemination of penult-initial onset), HGR = h-grade (verbal form with infixed h), HNGR = hn-grade (verbal form with infixed hṼ), HSAY = hearsay evidential, IMPERS = impersonal, IMPF = imperfective, IND = indicative, INDEF = indefinite, INF = infinitive, INS = instrumental, LGR = lengthened grade, LOC = locative, N = neuter, NEG = negation, negative, NGR = nasalized grade, NOM = nominative, PART = participle, PFV = perfective', PL = plural, POT = potential, PRES = present', PREV = previous mention, PROSP = prospective, PRT = participle, PST = past, RECP = reciprocal, REF = referential clitic (Creek), S = single argument of canonical intransitive verb, SG = singular, SS = same subject, TNS = default tense (in Choctaw), TPL = triplural, TR = transitive, YGR = y-grade

3. As Martin (2011: 101–103) explains, traditional Creek spelling does not show a very clear distinction between representations of /i/ and /i:/. Martin and Mauldin (2000) add a macron <ē> to distinguish /i:/.
4. However, see Haas (1941) for discussion of archaic instances of incorporation in Proto-Muskogean.
5. See also Fitzgerald (2015) for another recent overview of morphology in Muskogean.
6. Martin and Munro (2005) make the same distinction, referring to the monomorphemic stems as 'neutral' verbs, and the polymorphemic verb stems as 'voiced verbs'.
7. The transitive suffix -li in Chickasaw (and Choctaw) assimilates to the preceding consonant when the consonant is /b, f, ɬ, m, n, w/.
8. In some cases, the -k- form is primarily seen in a derived adjectival form.
9. The first detailed description of this system is due to Haas (1940), who referred the system as 'ablaut'. Although grade morphology in Muskogean does bear some resemblance to Indo-European ablaut alternations, the term ablaut is not particularly appropriate. The Muskogean grade system does not alter vowel qualities, but involves infixing laryngeals, /y/, and nasals, and geminating various consonants.

   There are also some intriguing similarities between Muskogean grades and the Semitic system of *binyanim* or stem templates (see Arad 2006 and Bat-El 1994, inter alia).
10. I have combined in this table the forms that Munro (1985) calls "grades" as well as the "glottal" form of the root. Munro argues that because the glottal form is far more productive than other forms, fails to change the pitch accent, and has no independent semantics, it is substantially different from the other grades and ought to be considered a different kind of infixing morphology.
11. Choctaw negative verbs also have an -o(k) suffix and appear in the l-grade, which places an accent on the penult, and lengthens the vowel of the penult if the syllable is open. See Broadwell (2006: 148–152) for further discussion.
12. The translation of one verb with English 'going to' and the other with 'will' follows Martin (2011), but the Creek distinction is clearly not exactly the same as the English distinction.
13. Different dialects or idiolects of Choctaw have different variants of this affix.
14. In Choctaw and Chickasaw, the reflex of different subject marking is typically nasalization of the final vowel.
15. The example is taken from a longer text Haas et al. (2015: 514). The final verb 'defecate' has SS marking because it has the same subject as the following verb.
16. The narrator used the English word 'rabbit' instead of the Chickasaw *chokfi'* in this clause.
17. Some authors (Kimball 1991: 525–526) have argued that these constructions are not truly subordinate clauses, but that an example like (29c) should be interpreted as coordination, along the lines of 'My father saw the woman and she is your wife'.

References

Anderson, Stephen. 1992. *A-morphous morphology*. Cambridge: Cambridge University Press.

Arad, Maya. 2006. *Roots and patterns: Hebrew morpho-syntax*. Berlin: Springer.

Basilico, David. 1996. Head position and internally headed relative clauses. *Language* 498–532.

Bat-El, Outi. 1994. Stem modification and cluster transfer in modern Hebrew. *Natural Language and Linguistic Theory* 12(4). 571–596.

Bonneau, José. 1994. *The structure of internally headed relative clauses: Implications for configurationality*. Montreal: McGill. (Doctoral dissertation.)

Booker, Karen. 1980. Comparative Muskogean: *Aspects of Proto-Muskogean verb morphology*. Lawrence: University of Kansas. (Doctoral dissertation.)

Boynton, Sylvia. 1982. *Mikasuki grammar in outline*. Gainesville: University of Florida. (Doctoral dissertation.)

Broadwell, George Aaron. 1993. Subtractive morphology in Southern Muskogean. *International Journal of American Linguistics* 416–429.

Broadwell, George Aaron. 1997. Binding theory and switch-reference. In Bennis, Hans & Pica, Pierre & Rooryck, Johan (eds.), *Atomism and binding*, 31–50. Dordrecht: Foris.

Broadwell, George Aaron. 2006. *A Choctaw reference grammar*. Lincoln: University of Nebraska Press.

Broadwell, George Aaron. 2015. Timucua -ta: Muskogean parallels. In Picone, Michael D. & Davies, Catherine Evans (eds.), *New perspectives on language variety in the South: Historical and contemporary approaches*, 72–81. Tuscaloosa: University of Alabama.

Buckley, Eugene. 1998. Iambic lengthening and final vowels. *International Journal of American Linguistics* 64. 179–223.

Camacho, José. 2010. On case concord: The syntax of switch-reference clauses. *Natural Language and Linguistic Theory* 28. 230–274.
Crawford, James M. 1988. On the relationship of Timucua to Muskogean. In Shipley, William (ed.), *In honor of Mary Haas*. Berlin: Walter de Gruyter.
Crawford, James. 1978. *The mobilian trade language*. Knoxville: University of Tennessee Press.
Davies, William. 1986. *Choctaw verb agreement and universal grammar*. Dordrecht: Reidel.
Davis, Philip & Hardy, Heather. 1984. Nominal-sentential morphology in Alabama. *Southwest Journal of Linguistics* 7. 87–101.
Drechsel, Emmanuel. 1997. *Mobilian jargon: Linguistic and sociohistorical aspects of a Native American pidgin*. Clarendon Press.
Fitzgerald, Colleen. 2015. Morphology in the Muskogean languages. *Language and Linguistics Compass* 10. 681–700.
Goddard, Ives. 2005. The indigenous languages of the Southeast. *Anthropological Linguistics* 47(1). 1–60.
Gordon, Lynn & Munro, Pamela. 2017. Relative clauses in Western Muskogean languages. *Glossa* 2. 1–18.
Gordon, Matt. 2004. A phonological and phonetic study of word-level stress in Chickasaw. *International Journal of American Linguistics* 70(1). 1–32.
Gordon, Matt & Munro, Pamela & Ladefoged, Peter. 2001. Chickasaw. *Journal of the International Phonetic Association* 31(2). 287–290.
Gouge, Ernest. 2004. *Totkv Mocvse/new fire: Creek folktales*. Martin, Jack B. & Mauldin, Margaret McKane & McGirt, Juanita (trans.). Norman: University of Oklahoma Press.
Haag, Marcia. 1997. Continuous and discrete adjectival scales. *Lingua* 103. 113–126.
Haag, Marcia & Willis, Henry. 2001. *Choctaw language and culture: Chahta anumpa*, vol. 1. Norman: University of Oklahoma.
Haag, Marcia & Willis, Henry. 2007. *Choctaw language and culture: Chahta anumpa*, vol. 2. Norman: University of Oklahoma.
Haas, Mary. 1940. Ablaut and its function in Muskogee. *Language* 16. 141–150.
Haas, Mary. 1941. Noun incorporation in the Muskogean languages. *Language* 17. 311–315.
Haas, Mary. 1946. A Proto-Muskogean paradigm. *Language* 22(4). 326–332.
Haas, Mary. 1947. Development of Proto-Muskogean *k^w. *International Journal of American Linguistics* 13(3). 135–137.
Haas, Mary. 1951. The Proto-Gulf word for 'water' (with notes on Siouan-Yuchi). *International Journal of American Linguistics* 17(2). 71–79.
Haas, Mary. 1956. Natchez and the Muskogean languages. *Language* 32(1). 61–72.
Haas, Mary. 1977. From auxiliary verb phrase to inflectional suffix. In Li, Charles (ed.), *Mechanisms of syntactic change*, 525–537. Austin: University of Texas.
Haas, Mary. 1979. Southeastern languages. In Campbell, Lyle & Mithun, Marianne (eds.), *The languages of Native America: Historical and comparative assessment*. Austin: University of Texas.
Haas, Mary & Hill, James H. & Martin, Jack. 2015. *Creek (Muskogee) texts*. Berkeley: University of California Press.
Haiman, John & Munro, Pamela. 1983. *Switch reference and universal grammar: Proceedings of a symposium on switch reference and universal grammar, Winnipeg, May 1981*. John Benjamins Publishing.
Hammond, Michael. 1993. Heavy trochees in Choctaw morphology. *Phonology* 10(2). 325–336.
Hardy, Don. 1994. Middle voice in Creek. *International Journal of American Linguistics* 60(1). 39–68.
Hardy, Heather. 2005. Alabama. In Hardy & Scancarelli (eds.).
Hardy, Heather & Davis, Philip. 1988. Comparatives in Alabama. *International Journal of American Linguistics* 54. 209–231.
Hardy, Heather & Davis, Philip. 1993. The semantics of agreement in Alabama. *International Journal of American Linguistics* 59. 453–472.
Hardy, Heather & Scancarelli, Janine (eds.). 2005. *Native languages of the Southeastern United States*. Lincoln: University of Nebraska Press.
Harris, Alice. 1992. Georgian and the unaccusative hypothesis. *Language* 58(2). 290–306.
Hayes, Bruce. 1995. *Metrical stress theory: Principles and case studies*. Chicago, IL: University of Chicago Press.
Heath, Jeffrey. 1977. Choctaw cases. (Paper presented at the Berkeley Linguistics Society, Berkeley, CA.)
Innes, Pamela Joan & Alexander, Linda & Tilkens, Bertha. 2004. *Beginning Creek*, vol. 1. Norman: University of Oklahoma.
Innes, Pamela Joan & Alexander, Linda & Tilkens, Bertha. 2009. *Intermediate Creek: Mvskoke Emponvkv Hokkolat*. Norman: University of Oklahoma.

Keine, Stefan. 2013. Deconstructing switch-reference. *Natural Language and Linguistic Theory* 31(3). 767–826.

Kimball, Geoffrey. 1987. A grammatical sketch of Apalachee. *International Journal of American Linguistics* 53. 136–174.

Kimball, Geoffrey. 1988. An Apalachee vocabulary. *International Journal of American Linguistics* 54. 387–398.

Kimball, Geoffrey. 1991. *Koasati grammar*. Lincoln: University of Nebraska Press.

Kimball, Geoffrey. 2005. Natchez. In Hardy, Heather & Scancarelli, Janine (eds.), *Native languages of the Southeastern United States*. Lincoln: University of Nebraska Press.

Kimball, Geoffrey. 2010. *Koasati traditional narratives*. Lincoln: University of Nebraska Press.

Kosa, Loredana Andreea. 2008. *An argument for process-based morphology: Subtractive morphology in Tohono O'odham*. Vancouver: Simon Fraser. (Doctoral dissertation.)

Levin, Beth & Hovav, Malka Rappaport. 1995. *Unaccusativity: At the syntax-lexical semantics interface*. Cambridge, MA: MIT Press.

Lombardi, Linda & McCarthy, John. 1991. Prosodic circumscription in Choctaw morphology. *Phonology* 8. 37–72.

Lupardus, Karen. 1982. *The language of the Alabama Indians*. Lawrence: University of Kansas. (Doctoral dissertation.)

Martin, Jack B. 1991. Lexical and syntactic aspects of Creek causatives. *International Journal of American Linguistics* 57. 194–229.

Martin, Jack B. 1993. 'Inalienable possession' in Creek (and its possible origin). *International Journal of American Linguistics* 59. 442–452.

Martin, Jack B. 2004. Languages. In Fogelson, Raymond D. (ed.), *Handbook of North American Indians. Vol. 14. Southeast*, 68–86. Washington, DC: Smithsonian.

Martin, Jack B. 2010. How to tell a Creek story in five past tenses. *International Journal of American Linguistics* 76. 43–70.

Martin, Jack B. 2011. *A grammar of Creek (Muskogee)*. Lincoln: University of Nebraska Press.

Martin, Jack B. 2016. *Pum Mvhayv Toyetskat: Creek letters to Ann Eliza Worcester Robertson, 1878–1905*. Mauldin, Margaret McKane (trans.), Martin, Jack B. (ed.). (http://muskogee.blogs.wm.edu/letters/) (Accessed 2017-04-01.)

Martin, Jack B. & Mauldin, Margaret McKane. 2000. *A dictionary of Creek/Muskogee*. Lincoln: University of Nebraska Press.

Martin, Jack B. & Munro, Pamela. 2005. Proto-Muskogean morphology. In Hardy, Heather & Scancarelli, Janine (eds.), *Native languages of the Southeastern United States*. Lincoln: University of Nebraska Press.

Munro, Pamela. 1984. Auxiliaries and auxiliarization in Western Muskogean. In Fisiak, Jacek (ed.), *Historical syntax*, 332–62. Berlin: Mouton.

Munro, Pamela. 1985. Chickasaw accent and verb grades. In Pieper, U. & Stickel, G. (eds.), *Studia linguistica, diachronica, et synchronica: Werner Winter sexagenario anno MCMLXXXIII*, 581–591. Amsterdam: Mouton de Gruyter.

Munro, Pamela. 1994. Gulf and Yuki-Gulf. *Anthropological Linguistics* 36(2). 125–222.

Munro, Pamela. 2000. The leaky grammar of the Chickasaw applicatives. In Okrent, A. & Boyle, J. P. (eds.), *Proceedings from the main session of the Chicago Linguistics Society*, vol. 36, 285–310. Chicago, IL: Chicago Linguistics Society.

Munro, Pamela. 2005. Chickasaw. In Hardy, Heather & Scancarelli, Janine (eds.), *Native languages of the Southeastern United States*. Lincoln: University of Nebraska Press.

Munro, Pamela. 2016. Chickasaw switch-reference revisited. In van Gijn, Rik & Hammond, Jeremy (eds.), *Switch-reference 2.0*. Amsterdam: John Benjamins.

Munro, Pamela & Gordon, Lynn. 1982. Syntactic relations in Western Muskogean: A typological perspective. *Language* 81–115.

Munro, Pamela & Willmond, Catherine. 1994. *Chickasaw: An analytical dictionary*. Norman: University of Oklahoma Press.

Munro, Pamela & Willmond, Catherine. 2008. *Let's speak Chickasaw Chikashshanompa' Kilanompali'*. Norman: University of Oklahoma Press.

Pitchlynn, Peter Perkins. 2013. *A gathering of statesmen: Records of the Choctaw council meetings*. Norman, OK: University of Oklahoma Press.

Rising, David. 1990. *Koasati switch-reference in discourse*. Arlington, TX: University of Texas. (MA thesis.)

Sylestine, Cora & Hardy, Heather & Montler, Timothy. 1993. *Dictionary of the Alabama language*. Austin: University of Texas Press.

Ulrich, Charles. 1986. *Choctaw morphophonology*. Los Angeles: UCLA. (Doctoral dissertation.)

Ulrich, Charles. 1994. A unified account of Choctaw intensives. *Phonology* 11. 325–339.

Weeda, D.S. 1992. *Word truncation in prosodic morphology*. Austin: University of Texas. (Doctoral dissertation.)

Willmond, Catherine & Munro, Pamela. 2012. *Let's speak Chickasaw: Chikashshanompa'kilanompoli'*. Norman: University of Oklahoma.

18
IROQUOIAN LANGUAGES

Michael Barrie and Hiroto Uchihara

1. Introduction

The Iroquoian languages are spoken in south central Canada (Ontario and Quebec) and the eastern and southern United States (New York, Wisconsin, Oklahoma, North Carolina, and Arkansas). The family is divided into two branches: Southern Iroquoian and Northern Iroquoian, which are discussed in detail in this chapter. The split between Southern and Northern Iroquoian is thought to have taken place 3,500–4,000 years ago (Lounsbury 1978), giving rise to a great number of divergent properties between the two branches; for instance, cognates between the two branches are not numerous. Common notable properties of all Iroquoian languages include the lack of labial consonants, a certain kind of accent which can be reconstructed as a penultimate accent (§2), fusional morphophonology (§3), polysynthesis (§3 and §5), and the overall template of the verb is strikingly similar (§3). Thus, despite outstanding differences between the two branches to be discussed in this chapter, the genetic relation between the two branches is evident (Hewitt 1887; Haas 1961; Lounsbury 1961).

This chapter is structured as follows. We begin with a discussion of the historical development of the Iroquoian family (this section). We then discuss the phonological (§2) and morphological (§3) properties of Iroquoian languages. Next, we discuss lexical categories (§4) and noun incorporation (§5), followed by a discussion of syntax (§6).

The Proto-Iroquois were a people living near water and relying heavily on fishing, probably centered around current New York State, central and northwestern Pennsylvania, and northeastern Ohio (Lounsbury 1978), based on cultural reconstructions from lexical materials (Mithun 1984b). Southern Iroquoian (Cherokee [chr]) first split from the rest of the family (Northern Iroquoian) and migrated to the Southeast (see Figure 18.1). As Cherokee is the only member of Southern Iroquoian, we will use Cherokee hereafter to refer to this branch. Within Northern Iroquoian, Tuscarora [tus] and Nottaway [ntw] split first, followed by Huron [no code] from the rest of the family (Five Nations Iroquoian and Susquehannock; cf. Mithun 1981). Scholars have different views on the position of Cayuga [cay] within Northern Iroquoian (Chafe & Foster 1981). Cherokee was spoken in the mountainous region of Southern Appalachia. After the "Trail of Tears" in 1838, the majority of Cherokee people were relocated to northeastern Oklahoma, while a small portion remained in western North Carolina.

Several languages are extinct (Susquehannocks [sqn], Laurentian [lre], Huron, Nottoway, Wyandot [wya]), while those that remain are severely endangered. Revitalization efforts are underway for some Iroquoian languages. Mohawk [moh] revitalization began as early as 1979 and is

Iroquoian
- Southern
  - Cherokee
- Northern
  - Tuscarora-Nottaway
  - Huron
  - Five Nations
    - Seneca-Cayuga
    - Onondaga
    - Susquehannock
    - Oneida-Mohawk

Figure 18.1 Iroquoian Language Family

discussed in Hoover and Center (1992). Revitalization efforts also exist for Cayuga and are discussed in Hinton (2008).

The Iroquoian languages are all largely oral languages with strong oral traditions. Cherokee does have a syllabary developed by Sequoya in the 19th century, which is mainly used in the Cherokee Bible and by traditional Cherokee doctors (Walker 1969).

2. Phonology

2.1. Segmental Phonology

The phoneme inventories of Iroquoian languages are small. Proto-Iroquoian consonant phonemes are the following: *s, *t, *k, *kw, *ts, *h, *ʔ, *y, *w, *n, and *r (Lounsbury 1978: 337; Mithun 1979a: 162). Labial plosives (*p* and *b*) are not found in Iroquoian languages, and thus in loanwords from other languages these sounds are replaced by *k*, *kw*, or *w*: e.g., [chr] *gwa:gwu* 'Bob', *wǐ:li* 'Bill'. The labial nasal *m* is found in some words in Cherokee (*dla:me:ha* 'bat', *kama:ma* 'butterfly, elephant'), which could be from a sequence of *w* and a nasal vowel or from loanwords. In Wyandot, *m* appears as an allophone of *w* next to a nasal vowel. Mohawk [moh] and some dialects (such as in Sallisaw, Oklahoma) of Cherokee have *f*, which results when *w* is adjacent to *h* or *ʔ*. There is no contrast between *l* and *r*, and the realization of the liquid varies according to the language, or to dialects within the same language, as in Mohawk (Bonvillain 1973) or in Cherokee (Mooney 1900/1992: 188). Phonologically, most languages do not contrast voiced vs. voiceless or unaspirated vs. aspirated. However, phonetically unaspirated and aspirated plosives are found as a result of juxtaposition of a plosive and *h*: e.g., [chr] *ada* /ata/ 'wood' vs. *ǎ:ta* /ǎ:tha/ 'young woman'. In some languages (such as Seneca [see]) the aspirated series are considered phonologized, while in others, such as in Oklahoma Cherokee, the Voice Onset Time of the *Ch* sequences is very short (Uchihara 2013: Chapter 2) and gives the impression that they are units, rather than sequences, despite their phonological sequence status. In orthographic conventions, some languages (Onondaga [ono], Cayuga, Seneca, and Cherokee) employ *k* vs. *g*, *t* vs. *d*, etc. while others (Mohawk, Oneida, Tuscarora, and Huron) employ phonemically based systems (*kh* vs. *k*, *th* vs. *t*). In this chapter, the first line of the examples, or the examples in the text, respect the orthographic conventions, and the segmentation lines (if present) are in phonologically based representations.

Proto-Iroquoian is reconstructed with four oral vowels, *a, *e, *i, and *o, and two nasalized vowels, *ę and *ǫ (Lounsbury 1978: 337; Mithun 1979a: 162). Another vowel phoneme, *æ* [æ], has developed in Onondaga and Seneca conditioned by *r and its subsequent loss (Chafe & Foster 1981; Michelson 1986; Michelson 1988: Chapter 7; Woodbury 1981). Vowel length is not reconstructed for Proto-Northern Iroquoian (but see Rudes 1995 for an opposing view). Nevertheless, a vowel is lengthened in an open accented syllable (§2.2), and some languages (such as Seneca) have further developed other vowel lengthening processes. Vowel length is contrastive in Cherokee, as is evident from the existence of (near-)minimal pairs.

(1) Cherokee

a. *ama*
'water'

b. *á:ma*
'salt'

(Feeling 1975: 43)

(2) Cherokee

a. *ji-go:lǐ:yéʔ-a*
1SG.AG-examine:PRES-IND[1]
'I'm examining it'

b. *ji:-go:lǐ:yéʔ-a*
1SG>AN-examine:PRES-IND
'I'm examining him'

(Feeling 1975: 18)

The source of contrastive vowel length in Cherokee is no longer recoverable from internal reconstruction, although one source of a long vowel can be from a laryngeal consonant here. Long vowels could also be the regular reflexes of the short vowels.

Consonant clusters are common both in Northern Iroquoian and Cherokee: e.g., [see] *saʔswat* 'put out the fire!', [chr] *ksladí* 'you are roping me'. Some sequences are parsed as heterosyllabic, while others as tautosyllabic; this difference is in some cases crucial in accent assignment (§2.2) since some languages rely on the syllable weight in assigning accent (Michelson 1988).

Vowel sequences are not reconstructed for Proto-Iroquoian but are attested in Seneca and Cayuga due to the loss of *r and intervocalic *h, and in Oneida and Mohawk in the possessive prefixes ([one] *laó:slet* 'his car') and in combinations involving the optative pre-pronominal prefix ([one] *yah thau:tú:* 'it's not possible, can't') (Karin Michelson, p.c.). In Cherokee, when a vowel sequence would result due to the loss of a consonant (such as *k), two adjacent vowels are fused into one to avoid a vowel sequence (the reconstructed forms are justified internally and externally).

(3) Cherokee

a. *e:-do:t*
< *aki-to:ta
1SG.PAT-father
'my father'

(Junior Scraper, speaker)

b. *à:hyvhté:ʔa*[2]
< *à:-hyvhthakiʔ-a
3SG.AG-kick:PRES-IND
'he is kicking him'

(Feeling 1975: 29)

Various phonological processes obscure underlying structures, such as vowel epenthesis in Northern Iroquoian (Michelson 1988: Chapter 5; Michelson 1989; Dyck 1990), laryngeal metathesis/vowel deletion in Cayuga and Cherokee (Foster 1982; Flemming 1996; Uchihara 2016: Chapter 3), and various processes that apply to the final syllable of the word, observed in Oneida in the utterance final positions (Lounsbury 1942; Michelson 2000) and in Cherokee in general (Bender & Harris 1946: 17; Feeling 1975: xii; Uchihara 2016: §2.3.1). Such processes can obscure the relation between inflectionally related forms, as in (4). In (4a), the vowel *v* is deleted due to vowel deletion, while in (4b), vowel deletion is not applied but the final syllable is omitted:

(4) Cherokee

a. *kdǐ:ya*
k-(v)ht-ǐ:y-a
3SG.AG-use-PRES-IND
'He is using it'

b. *sdvhdí*
st-vht-ǐ:(y-a)
2DU-use-PRES-IND
'You two are using it'

(Junior Scraper, speaker)

2.2. Word-Prosody

A penultimate accent is reconstructed for Proto-Northern Iroquoian and is preserved almost intact in some languages (such as Tuscarora or Mohawk), but each language has developed complex accentual systems due to interactions with the laryngeal consonants and epenthetic vowels (Chafe 1977a; Foster 1982; Michelson 1989; Melinger 2002). Additionally, in Onondaga, Cayuga, and Seneca, even-odd syllable counting from the right edge of the word also plays a role; this has a remnant in Cherokee with a modal function (Uchihara 2016: Chapter 10). The following example from Seneca illustrates complex interactions of these phonological factors. In Seneca, the accent is assigned to the last nonfinal even syllable that is either closed itself or followed by a nonfinal closed syllable (Michelson 1988: 111), and thus in (5), the accent is assigned to the second syllable. The lengthening of the penultimate syllable is the reflex of the earlier penultimate accent:

(5) Seneca

oʔtíswatenyę:toh
oʔ-ti-sw(a)-at-nyęt-o-h
FACT-DU-2AG-MID-shin-put.in.water-PUNC
'You waded'

(Chafe 1967: 74; Michelson 1988: 111)

Cherokee has morphologized the original penultimate accent (superhigh accent, represented as *a̋:*), and now it has morphosyntactic functions, such as subordination or nominalization, among others (Uchihara 2016: Chapter 11).

(6) Cherokee

jà:lsdâ:yv̋:hvsk
c-Ø-alistâ:(ʔ)yv:hvsk-(i)
REL-3SG.AG-have.meal:IMPF-NOM/SH
'the one who is having a meal'

(Uchihara 2016: 220)

Cherokee has further developed a complex tonal system: a syllable with a long vowel in Oklahoma Cherokee can carry the following pitch patterns, in addition to the superhigh accent (*a̋*): low (*a*), high (*á*), low-high (*ǎ:*), high-low (*â:*), and lowfall (*à:*). The form in (7) has a low, high, and lowfall tone in addition to the superhigh accent:

(7) Cherokee

yisgwahtv́:dà:sdǐ:ha
yi-skw-ahthv́:dà:(ʔ)sti:h-a
IRR-2SG>1SG-listen:PRES-IND/SH
'if you listen to me'

(Uchihara 2016: 3)

The historical source of the lowfall tone and one class of high tone is a glottal stop (Lindsey 1985; Uchihara 2009; Uchihara 2016). The even-odd syllable counting observed in Onondaga, Cayuga, and Seneca may have given rise to a floating high tone associated with a pre-pronominal prefix in Cherokee (Uchihara 2016: Chapter 10). See also Buckley (this volume) for further discussion of Cherokee in the context of word-prosody in North American languages in general.

3. Morphology

Iroquoian languages in general are polysynthetic and fusional. Polysynthesis refers to the fact a single word can contain a large number of morphemes. Consider the following Mohawk example.

(8) Mohawk

Enwá:ton'ensenikaratónnion'.

en-w-aton-'	en-seni-kar-aton-nion-'
FUT-3SG.NT.AG-be.possible-PUNC	FUT-2DU.AG-story-tell-DIST-PUNC
it will be possible	you two will converse

'It will be possible for you two to carry on a conversation.'

(Mithun 2009: 54)

The fusional nature of Iroquoian is manifested in several ways. First, some morphemes are portmanteau, such as the pronominal prefixes (e.g., [chr] *kv:(y)-* 1SG agent acting on 2SG patient, not analyzable into two parts) or a combination of a derivational suffix + an aspect suffix (e.g., [chr] *-uʔk-* AND.PUNC). Secondly, many morphemes have complex allomorphy, and the distribution of allomorphs is conditioned by phonological and morphological factors. For instance, the 3SG.NEUT pronominal prefix in Oneida has allomorphs *ka-*, *kʌ-*, *w-*, *y-*, *u-*, or *h-* depending on the initial sound of the following stem (Michelson & Doxtater 2002); the iterative pre-pronominal prefix in Oklahoma Cherokee has allomorphs *v:-/vʔ-* or *i:-/iʔ-* (or simply a high tone on the first vowel of the pronominal prefix), first conditioned by the modal suffix and then the phonological environment (Pulte & Feeling 1975: 254). In some cases, two (or more) adjacent morphemes can be fused. For instance, in Oklahoma Cherokee, a sequence of the irrealis (*y(i)-*) and translocative (*w(i)-*) pre-pronominal prefixes can fuse to form *yu:-* (Pulte & Feeling 1975: 244); the cislocative pre-pronominal prefix (*ta(y)-*) and the 3SG.A pronominal prefix (*a-*) can fuse to form *tv:-* (Cook 1979: 74). In Onondaga (as well as in other Northern Iroquoian languages), the pre-pronominal prefixes often partially fuse. For example, the repetitive often fuses with other pre-pronominal prefixes as in *s+waʔ* > *sa-*, repetitive, and factual (Barrie 2015a: 32), although an analysis is possible in which /a/ is an allomorph of /waʔ/. We do not pursue any kind of analysis here, but merely note that reduced forms such as the one shown here are quite common in Northern Iroquoian when more than one pre-pronominal prefix appears.

Morphology is further complicated by stem alternation processes found in Cherokee. One is Laryngeal Alternation (Cook 1979; Munro 1996; Uchihara 2007), in which the first *h* of the stem is replaced by a glottal stop when the stem takes certain pronominal prefixes, such as 1SG.AG. In (9b), the *h* of the stem as is observed in (9a) alternates with a glottal stop:

(9) Cherokee

a. *go:ho:sga*	b. *goʔo:sga*[3]
k-o:ho:-sk-a	k-o:ho:-sk-a
3SG.AG-fall-PRES-IND	1SG.AG-fall-PRES-IND
'He is falling'	'I am falling'

(Feeling 1975: 121)

3.1. Nouns

The general morphological template for nouns is as follows. (PPP stands for pre-pronominal prefix, PP for pronominal prefix, and NFS for noun forming suffix. The morphemes in parentheses are not obligatory.)

(10) (PPP-)(PP-)ROOT(-NFS)

In Northern Iroquoian, nouns rarely occur with pre-pronominal prefixes, but in Cherokee, many nouns can take the distributive pre-pronominal prefix to mark plurality ([chr] *ahnawo* 'shirt', *di-:-hnawo* DIST-3SG.AG-shirt 'shirts'), and some nouns lexically take the partitive pre-pronominal prefix ([chr] *í̋:-g-ati* PART-3SG.AG-size 'size'). In Northern Iroquoian almost all nouns take pronominal prefixes, while in Cherokee in general, only human root nouns, body parts, clothing, and kinship terms take pronominal prefixes (Scancarelli 1987; Montgomery-Anderson 2015: Chapter 6). Pronominal prefixes can encode a possessor (11) or a copula subject (12).

(11) Cherokee

aw-à:salě:ni
1SG.PAT-coat
'my coat'

(Ed Jumper, speaker)

(12) Cherokee

jì:-sgaya
1SG.AG-man
'I am a man'

(Pulte & Feeling 1975: 323)

As mentioned, in Northern Iroquoian, almost all nouns take a pronominal prefix. There is a very small number of monomorphemic nouns such as [one] *é:lhal* ('dog'). In addition to the possessive and copular uses as shown earlier for Cherokee, Northern Iroquoian uses a third-person neuter prefix for non-possessed inanimate nouns. The choice between the agentive and patientive series (§3.2.2) on inanimate nouns is often arbitrary in most Northern Iroquoian languages (on non-possessed nouns – see later in this section for possessed nouns), but in Onondaga, the choice is predictable. Nouns referring to man-made items bear the third-person agent prefix, and nouns referring to naturally occurring items bear the third-person patient prefix (Woodbury 2003).

(13) Onondaga

oyǫ́:daˀ

o-	yǫt-	aˀ
3NT.SG.PAT-	beak-	NFS

'beak'

(Woodbury 2003: 937)

(14) Onondaga

ganákdaˀ

ka-	nakt-	aˀ
3NT.SG.AG	bed-	NFS

'bed'

(Woodbury 2003: 677)

Alienability is distinguished both in Northern Iroquoian and Cherokee, but in different ways. In Northern Iroquoian, agentive pronominal prefixes indicate inalienable possession, while patientive pronominal prefixes indicate alienable possession (Mithun 1996a; 2001). In addition, the external locative suffix is often strongly preferred (Seneca; Chafe 2015: 89) or obligatory (Mohawk; Mithun 1996a: 638) with the alienable nouns, depending on the language. In Cherokee, on the other hand, the selection of pronominal prefixes is lexically conditioned but is not conditioned by alienability. Instead, inalienability of body part terms is encoded by nominal suffixes (*-ni, -ke, -o:li, -ǐ:ʔi*, etc.), which are cognate with the external locative suffixes in Northern Iroquoian (Pulte & Feeling 1975: 312f; Chafe 1996: 570; Uchihara 2014: 27):

(15) Cherokee

a. *a-sgv:dage*
3SG.AG-shin
'his shin (alienable)'

b. *a-sgv:dagě:-ni*
3SG.AG-shin-NFS
'his shin (inalienable)'

(Feeling 1975: 312)

(16) Cherokee

a. *u:-sgwǒ:la*
3SG.PAT-stomach
'his stomach (alienable)'

b. *u:-sgwo:hl-ǐ:i*
3SG.PAT-stomach-NFS
'his stomach (inalienable)'

(Feeling 1975: 313)

Kinship nouns appear with transitive or reciprocal agreement in Northern Iroquoian. As the patterns are quite complex, we do not deal with them here. The grammars of the individual languages in the Further Reading section provide details. An analysis on kinship noun in Oneida can be found in Koenig & Michelson (2010).

In Northern Iroquoian languages, a nominal suffix, called the *noun forming suffix* (NFS) is typically required, while in Cherokee it is absent: [one] *ka-nasti-ʔ* 3SG.NT.AG-ROOT-NFS 'pail/pot'. Nouns can be derived from other nouns with suffixes or enclitics (in many cases unproductive). The following Cherokee examples show the locative *-ʔi/-hi*, 'real/pure' *-ya:ʔi*, and diminutive *-u:ca*, respectively.

(17) Cherokee

a. *goʔǐ:-ʔi*
grease-LOC
'greasy'

(Mongomery-Anderson 2015: 370)

b. *ani:-yv:wi-yǎ:ʔi*
3PL.AG-person-real
'Indians'

(Feeling 1975: 66)

c. *a-wi:n-ǔ:ja*
3SG.AG-young.man-DIM
'adolescent boy'

(Feeling 1975: 62)

The following Northern Iroquoian examples illustrate the internal locative *-kǫwah* in Onondaga, the external locative *-ke* in Oneida, and the internal locative *-aku* in Oneida, respectively. The internal locative refers to the internal surface of the noun it attaches to, while the external locative refers to the external surface of the noun it attaches to. Note, however, that there are a variety of locative suffixes in Northern Iroquoian languages, and the discussion here merely scratches the surface.

(18) a. Onondaga

gahǫwagǫ́:wah
ka-hǫw-a-kǫwah
3SG.NT.AG-boat-A-INT.LOC
'in the boat'

(Barrie 2015a: 24)

b. Oneida

kanatá:ke
ka-nat-aʔ-ke
3SG.NT.AG-settlement-NSUF/A-EXT.LOC
'in town'

(Abbott 2000: 49)

c. Oneida

kálhaku
ka-lh-aku
3SG.NT.AG-woods-INT.LOC
'in the woods'

(Abbott 2000: 49)

Observe that the internal locative supplants the noun forming suffix, while the situation for the external locative is less clear. On one analysis, the external locative is attached to the right of the noun suffix (NSUF); on another analysis, it supplants the noun suffix (as the internal locative does). Under this analysis, the epenthetic /a/ is the joiner A vowel discussed in the section on noun incorporation (§5). Karin Michelson (p.c.) suggests the latter analysis is on the right track based on the behavior of noun suffixes other than /-aʔ/.

3.2. Verbs

Since the details on verbal morphology are covered in great detail in so many other works on Iroquoian, we review just the basic facts here. Northern Iroquoian and Cherokee share a strikingly similar verbal template. The only major difference between the two is the modal suffixes in Cherokee. The general morphological templates for the two branches are as follows. In (19) and (20), the morphemes in parentheses are optional, and the raised N indicates that the morpheme in question can occur more than once. A raised N in brackets indicates additional instances of the morpheme in question may simply be the result of historical re-analysis. Again, PPP stands for pre-pronominal prefixes, PP pronominal prefix, REFL/MID reflexive and middle, IN incorporated noun, DERIV derivational suffix, and ASP aspect suffix.

(19) Verbal template for Northern Iroquoian
(PPP^{N}-)PP-(REFL/MID-)(IN$^{(N)}$-)ROOT$^{(N)}$-(DERIV^{N}-)ASP-(EXPANDED ASP)(=CLITICS^{N})

(20) Verbal template for Cherokee
(PPP^{N}-)PP-(REFL/MID-)(IN-)ROOT$^{(N)}$-(DERIV^{N}-)ASP-(DERIV^{N})-MOD(=CLITICS^{N})

Examples illustrating the verbal templates are shown in (21) and (22), respectively.

(21) Mohawk

waʔkenuhwarorókhsiʔ
waʔ-k-nuhwar-orok-hsy-ʔ
FACT-1SG.AG-head-cover-REV-PUNC
PPP-PP-IN-ROOT-DERIV-ASP
'I took off my hat'

(Michelson 1988: 53)

(22) Cherokee

yu:dáwoʔḗ:na
y-u:-(a)ta-wo(:)ʔ-e:-n-a
IRR-3SG.PAT-MID-bathe-AND-PUNC-IND/SH
PPP-PP-MID-ROOT-DERIV-ASP-MOD
'When he goes swimming'

(Ed Jumper, speaker)

Scholars are not in agreement whether the Iroquoian verbal template is flat (Lounsbury 1953), that is, the verbs do not have any internal structure and morphemes are categorized into position classes; or layered (Chafe 1960; Dyck 2009), that is, the verbs are internally organized into hierarchical structure. The issue has not been resolved, but Cherokee prosody is better accounted for if a layered structure is assumed (Uchihara 2018); see also Dyck (2009) for Cayuga.

3.2.1. *The Base*

The verb base may consist simply of a verb root ([chr] *-k-* 'eat', *-v:-* 'weave', *-hwahth-* 'find, etc.); compounding of two verb roots ([one] *-yena-waʔku-* take-hold 'hold on to'; [chr] *-kiʔ-st-* eat-crush 'chew'), which is not productive; or an incorporated noun root plus a verb root (see §5).

Iroquoian verbs can be augmented by derivational suffixes. In Cherokee, some derivational suffixes are directly attached to the verb base, and others to the perfective stem (cf. §3.2.5) of the verb. In Northern Iroquoian, derivational suffixes, if present, always appear between the verb base and the aspect suffix. Some derivational suffixes manipulate the argument structure, e.g., instrumental and applicative (see §6.1). Other derivational suffixes are aspectual or modal. In Cherokee, for instance, the following suffixes are attested: repetitive (*-i:lo:-*), completive (*-ohv-/-ohn-*), duplicative (*-i:s-*), multiplicative (*-vhv-/-vhn-*), and inceptive (*-i:t-*). Some derive motion verbs: andative (*-e:-*), ambulative (*-i:to:-*), and venitive (*-i:h-*). Note that these aspectual and modal suffixes are not the same as those that appear in the PPP or Aspect slot in the template, even though their semantic contribution aligns with standard notions of aspect and mood. This is partly due to standard nomenclature in the Iroquoianist tradition, but is also due to the formation of the verbal complex in Iroquoian. The slot labeled "Aspect" in the templates above are obligatorily filled, as is the PPP slot, depending on which obligatory aspect appears in the Aspect slot. In contrast, the aspectual and modal suffixes discussed here are typically always optional. Below are examples with the repetitive (23) and ambulative (24) suffixes in Cherokee, and progressive (25) and reversative (26) in Onondaga.

(23) Cherokee

dà:jì:sgv:dv:ní:lo:ja
t-aci:-skv:tv:n-í:lo:-c-a
DIST-UNSP-hit.in.shin-REPET-PUNC-IND
'He hit him in the shin repeatedly.'

(Pauline Glass, speaker)

(24) Cherokee

à:ganá:di:dó:ha
a-kana:t-(ʔ)-i:t-o:(ʔ)h-a
3SG.AG-lick-PFT-AMB-PRES-IND
'He is licking here and there.'

(Robert Bushyhead, speaker)

(25) Onondaga

ahgaʔtcyųhá:dyeʔ
wak-kaʔtcy-ųh-atye-ʔ
1SG.PAT-take.apart-STAT-PROG-PURP
'I am undoing it as I go.'

(Woodbury 2003: 450)

(26) Onondaga

hayę̨thwá:gwas
ha-yę̨thw-kw-as
SG.M.AG-plant-REV-HAB
'He harvests.'/'He picks.'

(Woodbury 2003: 13)

3.2.2. Pronominal Prefixes

Pronominal prefixes encode the sole argument of an intransitive verb, and transitive pronominal prefixes index both the agent and patient. Note that inanimate arguments appear only with agreement in Northern Iroquoian if there are no animate arguments on the verb. (Note that we are using agreement in a very general sense, referring to a morphological reflex on the verb that co-varies with the event participant.) Thus, *John saw Mary* has agreement with both John and Mary on the verb, whereas *John saw a tree* has intransitive agreement, referencing *John* only, and *The tree fell* has intransitive agreement referencing *the tree*. Hereafter we refer to all predicates that agree with only one argument as monovalent, regardless of the number of semantic participants in the event. There exist detailed studies on pronominal prefixes to which the reader is referred. On the pronominal prefixes in Northern Iroquoian in general, see Koenig and Michelson (2015) and Michelson (2016), as well as Abrams (2006) for Onondaga and Deer (2011) for Cayuga in particular. For the historical development of the pronominal prefixes, see Chafe (1977b; 1984), Mithun (1993; 1996b) and Sasse (1995).

Both Northern Iroquoian and Cherokee exhibit a distinction between agentive and patientive marking. Semantically transitive predicates with two animate arguments index the subject with an agentive pronominal prefix and the object with a patientive pronominal prefix (typically portmanteaux, as mentioned earlier). The sole argument of monovalent verbs can be encoded either with the agentive or patientive series of pronominal prefixes, conditioned lexically. Regardless of which series of pronominal prefixes a verb lexically employs, when monovalent verbs appear with the stative/perfective aspect, they employ the patientive pronominal markers. Only two animate arguments can be referenced on any given verb. Thus, a ditransitive must contain at most two animate participants. One participant must be inanimate, recalling that inanimate arguments do not trigger agreement. Northern Iroquoian languages have complex gender agreement for third-person arguments. The languages differ in precise details. Oneida, for instance, encodes two kinds of feminine agreement, in addition to one masculine agreement type (Abbott 1984; Michelson 2015).

In Cherokee, the number of categories distinguished is reduced. Thus, gender is not distinguished, except for the distinction between third-person animate and inanimate. The number of allomorphs for each pronominal prefix is also significantly reduced. Another difference between the Northern and the Southern branch is the inverse use of the patientive series of the third-person pronominal prefixes (Scancarelli 1987); when both the agent and patient of a transitive verb are third person, the patientive series is employed when the patient is pragmatically more salient than the agent.

Table 18.1 lists all the pronominal prefixes in Oklahoma Cherokee, partly adapted from Scancarelli (1987). The agentive intransitive series is found under the column 'Ø/3SG', which can

Table 18.1 Pronominal Prefixes in Oklahoma Cherokee

PATIENT AGENT	*1SG*	*1DU.EX*	*1PL.EX*	*1DU.IN*	*1PL.IN*	*2SG*	*2DU*	*2PL*	*Ø/3SG*	*3SG.AN*	*3PL.INAN*	*3PL.AN*
1SG	REFL					kv:(y)*	stv:(y)*	i:cv:(y)*	ci/k *	ji:(y)*	DIST+ ci/k*	kaci:(y)*
1DU.EX		REFL				stv:(y)*	stv:(y)*	i:cv:(y)*	o:st(i:)	o:sd(i:)*	DIST+ o:st(i:)	DIST+ o:st(i:)
1PL.EX			REFL			i:cv:(y)*	i:cv:(y)*	i:cv:(y)*	o:c(i:)	o:c(i:)*	DIST+ o:c(i:)	DIST+ o:c(i:)
1DU.IN				REFL					i:n(i:)	e:n(i:)*	DIST+ i:n(i:)	DIST+ i:n(i:)
1PL.IN					REFL				i:t(i:)	e:t(i:)*	DIST+ i:t(i:)	DIST+ i:t(i:)
2SG	ski/skw	skin(i:)*	(i:)ski:(y)*			REFL			h(i)	hi:(y)*	DIST+ h(i)	kahi:(y)*/ DIST+h(i)
2DU	skin(i:)*	skin(i:)*	(i:)ski:(y)*				REFL		st(i:)	e:st(i:)*	DIST+ st(i:)	DIST+ st(i:)
2PL	(i:)ski:(y)*	(i:)ski:(y)*	(i:)ski:(y)*					REFL	i:c(i:)	e:t(i:)*	DIST+ i:c(i:)	DIST+ i:c(i:)
Ø/3SG	aki /akw	o:kin(i:)	o:k(i:)	kin(i:)	i:k(i:)	c(a)	st(i:)	i:c(i:)	act. a/Ø /k(a)	inv. u:/uw	act. DIST+ a/Ø/ka	inv. u:n(i:)
3PL	kv:ki /kv:kw	ko:kin(i:)	ko:k(i:)	ke:kin(i:)	ke:k(i:)	ke:c(a)	ke:st(i:)	ke:c(i:)	act. an(i:)	inv. kv:w(a)	act. DIST+ an(ii)	inv. kv:wan(i:)
UNSP	v:ki /v:kw	o:kin(i:)	o:k(i:)	e:kin(i:)*	e:k(i:)*	e:c(a)	e:st(i:)*	e:c(i:)*	aci/ak*	aci/ak*	ke:ci/ke:k*	ke:ci/ke:k*

Source: Excerpt from Scancarelli (1987: 71), with orthographical modification.

also indicate combinations with 3SG inanimate patient, and the patientive pronominal prefixes are found in the row Ø/3SG. The lighter gray cells are pronominal prefixes of the agentive series, while the darker gray cells are pronominal prefixes of the patientive series. For transitive prefixes, the agent component of the prefix is shown at the left of Table 18.1, and the patient component of the prefix is shown at the top of the table. Some pronominal prefixes show phonologically conditioned alternations (such as the deletion of the final vowel or the final glide), and those elements which are deleted are in parentheses. Some pronominal prefixes show suppletive alternations ('weak' or 'strong') according to the phonological environment; in such cases, the allomorph occurring before a consonant is listed first, and the allomorph occurring before a vowel is listed after a slash (/). Pronominal prefixes with an asterisk (*) require the glottal grade forms of Laryngeal Alternation, which was discussed on page 428. The abbreviations 'act.' and 'inv.' stand for pronominal prefixes used in active construction and inverse construction, respectively. 'REFL' indicates that a reflexive prefix is employed (§3.2.3). 'DIST' indicates that the distributive pre-pronominal prefix is employed (cf. §3.2.4).

3.2.3. Reflexive/Middle Prefixes

The reflexive and middle (also called semireflexive) prefixes occur immediately before the verb base and after the pronominal prefix. The prefixes have various allomorphs conditioned by phonological and lexical environments; for instance, in Oklahoma Cherokee, reflexive has the allomorphs *ata:t-/ata(:)-/at-*, while middle has *ata(:)-/at-/ali-*. Despite its denomination, the core function of the reflexive prefix appears to be that of defocusing the object (§6.1). One of the functions derived from this core use is the reflexive function, where the agent that is performing the action is the same as the patient that is being affected by the action. The middle prefix indicates that the action of the verb is affecting the person or thing that is the agent of the verb. In many cases, the middle forms appear to be lexicalized. It appears with verbs of grooming and inherently reflexive verbs. Lounsbury (1953) first noticed the similarity between the middle and the Romance SE morpheme. The difference in functions between the reflexive and middle prefix can be illustrated in the following examples:

(27) Cherokee

a. *dà:da:wó:ʔa*
t-Ø-ata:-wo:-́ʔ-a
DIST-3SG.AG-REFL-bathe-PRES-IND
'He is performing baptism.'
(Feeling 1975: 67)

b. *à:dawó:ʔa*
Ø-ata-wo:-́ʔ-a
3SG.AG-MID-bathe-PRES-IND
'He is bathing.'
(Feeling 1975: 9)

c. *gawó:ʔa*
k-awo:-́ʔ-a
3SG.AG-bathe-PRES-IND
'He is bathing him.'
(Feeling 1975: 117)

(28) Tuscarora

wahrathrę̨hwá:kuʔ
wa-hra-at-hrę̨-hw-a-kuʔ
FACT-3SG.M.AG-MID-put.up-CAUS-EPEN-REV.PUNC
'He turned around.'

(Rudes 1999: 59)

(29) Onondaga

a. *wa?gadadaehsęthwa?*
wa?-k-atat-aehsęthw-a?
FACT-1SG.AG-REFL-kick-PUNC
'I kicked myself.'
(Barrie 2015a: 61)

b. *wahadya?dohae?*
wa?-ha-at-ya?t-ohae-?
FACT-3SG.M.AG-MID-body-wash-PUNC
'He washed (himself).'
(Barrie 2015a: 62)

Traditionally, the reflexive and middle prefixes have been assumed to belong to the base (Lounsbury 1953: §6.2). However, a couple of pieces of evidence support the view that they are outside of the domain of the base and belong to the same domain as the pronominal prefixes (§3.2.2). First, reflexive and middle prefixes (along with the pronominal prefixes) are outside of the domain of a phonological process that applies within the base in Oklahoma Cherokee: H1 Spreading (Uchihara 2016: §6.5.2.4). Secondly, the principal function of the reflexive prefix is not reflexive, but rather defocusing the object argument without changing the thematic structure, at least in Cherokee (§6.1); in this sense, the reflexive prefix behaves the same way as the pronominal prefixes in encoding the syntactic argument structure of the verb.

3.2.4. Pre-Pronominal Prefixes

The pre-pronominal prefixes are a set of morphemes that occur before the pronominal prefixes. They encode a range of semantic and grammatical categories (Abbott 1981). For more details on the pre-pronominal prefixes, the readers are referred to Pulte and Feeling (1975) and Montgomery-Anderson (2015: Chapters 5 and 16) for Cherokee, and Lounsbury (1949) for Northern Iroquoian. Pre-pronominal prefixes exemplify a case of a morphological template, where the order of each morpheme appears to be arbitrary and have no functional motivation, and prefixes which appear to be semantically compatible cannot co-occur because they belong to the same slot (such as Irrealis and Relative in Cherokee). Table 18.2 shows the positions of pre-pronominal prefixes in Cherokee.

In Oklahoma Cherokee, sequences of up to four pre-pronominal prefixes are attested:

(30) Cherokee

wundo:dagv̂:ndé:si
wi-n(i)-to:-ta-k-v:(?)nhté:-(?)s-i
TRNSL-PART-DIST-CISL-1SG.AG-take.off-PFT-MOT
'I will take them off from there.'

(Ed Jumper, speaker)

The conditioning factors for allomorphy of pre-pronominal prefixes can be extremely complex and idiosyncratic, in some cases involving long-distance dependencies. For instance, in Oklahoma Cherokee, the alternation of the partitive prefix is conditioned by whether the verb is in the nominal form or not; alternation of cislocative and iterative is conditioned by the modal suffix; alternation of negative is conditioned by whether the pronominal prefix involves a second-person agent.

Similar facts hold of the pre-pronominal prefixes in Northern Iroquoian. Complex allomorphy and fusion among the forms hinders a simple agglutinative analysis. Nevertheless, generalizations

Table 18.2 Pre-pronominal Prefixes in Cherokee

Irrealis	Translocative	Partitive	Distributive	Cislocative	Iterative	Negative
Relative						

Table 18.3 Pre-pronominal Prefixes in Seneca

Negative	Coincident Contrastive	Translocative	Partitive	Dualic	Iterative Cislocative

on affix ordering can be gleaned. Table 18.3 contains the template for Seneca, and an example is in (31).

(31) Seneca

dedwadigá:ne:ʔ
te-t-wati-kan-eʔ
DUC-CISL-3PL.F.AG-look.for-STAT
'They (fem.) are looking for it again.'

(Chafe 2015: 45)

3.2.5. Aspect Suffixes

Northern Iroquoian languages have four aspect categories (punctual, habitual, stative, and purposive), while Cherokee has five (present, imperfective, perfective, punctual, and infinitive). For the terminology in Northern Iroquoian, see Foster (1985; 1986). See Lounsbury (1949) for a description of the aspect suffixes in Northern Iroquoian, as well as the individual grammars listed in the Further Reading section in this chapter. The stative in Northern Iroquoian has two readings, as discussed in Chafe (1980) for Seneca. It can have either a progressive reading or a reading akin to the English present perfect, depending on the verb root. In Cherokee, present indicates a present event or state; imperfective, ongoing action; perfective, completed action; punctual, an immediate past or future event. The infinitive appears only in embedded clauses. Punctual can also be used as imperative, sometimes with the difference in tone (Uchihara 2016: Chapter 9). See also Cook (1979: Chapter 4) and Montgomery-Anderson (2015: Chapter 4) on Cherokee, for more details of the use of each aspect. While the aspect suffix is obligatory, an optional expanded aspect suffix may appear to give rise to a larger range of tense/aspect distinctions. See the grammars listed in the Further Reading section.

In both Northern and Southern branches, aspect suffixes have numerous allomorphs, and their selection is unpredictable. For instance, Table 18.4 shows sample paradigms of five verbs in Oklahoma Cherokee, each belonging to different verb classes and thus taking different allomorphs of the aspect suffixes. The aspect suffixes are in boldface. All the forms except for punctual are in the 3SG form and take the 3SG.AG pronominal prefix in present and imperfective and the 3SG.PAT pronominal prefix in perfective and infinitive. The punctual aspect is represented by the imperative

Table 18.4 Verb Classes by Aspect Suffixes in Oklahoma Cherokee

	-Y- 'PICK UP LG'	*-LO:-* 'PASS'	*-O:LI-* 'UNDERSTAND'	*-AWO:-* 'BATHE'	*-LO:NU:-* 'CHEAT'
PRES	*à:-y-**íh**-a*	*ga-lo:-**sg**-a*	*g-o:l(i)-**hg**-a*	*g-awó:-**ʔ**-a*	*ga-lo:nu:-**hě:h**-a*
IMPF	*à:-y-**ǐ:sg**-óʔi*	*ga-lo:-**sg**-ó:ʔi*	*g-o:l(i)-**hg**-ó:ʔi*	*g-awó-(ʔ)**sg**-ó:ʔi*	*ga-lo:nu:-**hě:sg**-óʔi*
PFT	*ù:-y-**v:h**-v̌:ʔi*	*ù:-lo:-**s**-v̌:ʔi*	*ù:w-o:l(i)-**hj**-v̌:ʔi*	*ù:-wó:-**ʔ**-v̌:ʔi*	*ù:-lo:nu:-**hě:hl**-v̌:ʔi*
PUNC	*hi-y-**Ø**-a*	*hi-lǒ:-**h**-i*	*h-o:l(i)-**hg**-i*	*hi:y-awǒ:-**j**-a*	*hi-lo:nu:-**hv̌:l**-a*
INF	*u:-y-**(v)ht**-i*	*u:-lo:-**hist**-i*	*uw-o:l(i)-**híst**-i*	*u:-wò:-**(ʔ)sd**-i*	*u:-lo:nu:-**hehd**-i*

Source: From Feeling (1975).

form with the 2SG.AG or 2SG>AN pronominal prefix (since this is the form available in Feeling (1975)). Aspect suffixes are followed by modal suffixes (§3.2.6): indicative *-a* or *-i*, habitual *-ó(:)ʔi*, assertive *-v̌:ʔi*, and nominal *-i*.

For Northern Iroquoian, based on such allomorphy, Lounsbury (1953) proposes five conjugation classes with subclasses, Michelson and Doxtater (2002) eight classes with subclasses, and Woodbury (2003) eight classes with subclasses; for Cherokee, both Cook (1979) and Uchihara (2016) propose eight classes with subclasses.

3.2.6. Modal Suffixes

Cherokee verbs obligatorily take one of the modal suffixes, which serve as evidential and mood markers. Modal suffixes in Oklahoma Cherokee include indicative *-a/-i*, assertive *-v̌:ʔi*, reportative *-é(:)ʔi*, habitual *-ó:ʔi*, and motion *-i* (see Table 18.4 for examples). Evidentiality is not a grammatical category in Northern Iroquoian (Mithun 1986a), but the distinction is obligatory in Cherokee (Pulte 1985).

4. Lexical Categories

All Iroquoian languages have nouns, verbs, and particles. Nouns and verbs are inflected (§4.1), while particles are not. The category of adjectives is lacking in Northern Iroquoian (not distinguishable from verbs) while its existence is controversial in Cherokee (§4.2). Northern Iroquoian further has a fourth lexical category, kinship terms (Koenig & Michelson 2010; Chafe 2015). Even though the lexical category is unambiguous at the root level, a full inflected verb can function as a noun in Northern Iroquoian, while nominalization and adjectivalization strategies are rich in Cherokee (§4.3).

4.1. Nouns and Verbs

Most Iroquoianists agree that the lexical category is a property of the root, and a root cannot function both as a verb root and a noun root (Mithun 2000b). That is, there are no category-neutral roots akin to English *drink* that can appear either as a noun or as a verb. Note, however, that some verb roots can be nominalized with a lexically selected nominalizer to be used as nouns. See Sasse (2001) for an opposing view in favor of category neutrality. Another complicating factor is that a fully inflected verb can function as a noun, and thus the distinction between nouns and verbs can be obscure (Mithun 2000b; Koenig & Michelson 2010). Here is an example of such a deverbal noun. Mithun (1979b) discusses several syntactic and semantic diagnostics showing that such forms are indeed nouns.

(32) Onondaga

gayaˀdá:gä:s

ka-	yaˀt-	akä-	s
3SG.NT.AG-	body-	smell-	HAB

'goat' (lit. 'it has a smelly body')

(Woodbury 2003: 443)

4.2. Adjectives

There is no distinct lexical category of adjectives in Northern Iroquoian languages (Chafe 2012), rather, one finds a distinction between stative and active verbs. On the other hand, Lindsey and Scancarelli (1985) argue that adjectives do exist as an independent lexical category in Cherokee. Their arguments are that adjectives in Cherokee differ from verbs in that: (i) the verbs are inflected for negation or aspect or mood while the 'adjectives' are not; (ii) the pronominal prefix is obligatory with verbs while it is not for adjectives; and (iii) a superhigh accent is always assigned to the adjectives but not always to the verbs. Lindsey and Scancarelli (1985) also argue that adjectives are different from nouns in that: (iv) the adjectives are always marked for the number while the nouns are not; and (v) adjectives precede nouns they modify while nouns follow another noun when they modify it. It is indeed the case that Cherokee adjectives are distinct from verbs, unlike in the case of Northern Iroquoian, but they have many properties in common with nouns. In fact, all the characteristics listed above as the properties of adjectives also apply to deverbal nouns. First, negation or mood is not marked on deverbal nouns, but rather they require a copula. In (33), 'spirits' (lit. 'we midnight walkers') is a deverbal noun derived from the verb root *-e:t-* 'walk around', and cannot take the irrealis pre-pronominal prefix *yi-*, which verbs can.

(33) Cherokee

sv:nǒ:yi *o:je:dő:hi yígi,*
sv:nǒ:yi o:c-e:tő:h-i yí-ki
midnight 1PL.EX-walk.around:IMPF-NOM/SH IRR-COPULA/SH
'if we were spirits of the night,'

(Montgomery-Anderson et al. 2010)

On the other hand, some 'adjectives' can take pre-pronominal prefixes directly: [chr] *yi-gá-nv:hi* IRR-3SG.AG-long 'if it is long'. Thus, the inflection for negation, aspect, or mood is not a good criterion for distinguishing adjectives from other lexical categories. The second characteristic which deverbal nouns share with the 'adjectives' is that the pronominal prefix is optional in some cases for the deverbal nouns: in [chr] *(a-)ko:dě:sg-i* (3SG.AG-) shovel:IMPF-NOM/SH 'spade', the pronominal prefix *a-* is optional (Feeling 1975: 145). Third, a superhigh accent is assigned to deverbal nouns in most cases (Uchihara 2016: Chapter 11), as for the 'adjectives'. Lastly, plurality is always marked on deverbal nouns, as with 'adjectives': [chr] *a-hyv:dladì:sdí:sg-i* 3SG.AG-cool.down:IMPF-NOM/SH 'refrigerator' vs. *di:-hyv:dladì:sdí:sg-i* DIST.3SG.AG-cool.down:IMPF-NOM/SH 'refrigerators' (Feeling 1975). These facts suggest that the so-called 'adjectives' in Cherokee are in fact a class of nouns, particularly a type of deverbal nouns.

4.3. Nominalization

In Northern Iroquoian languages, the full inflected verb can be used as a noun, as we saw in §4.1. Additionally, many verb roots can be nominalized to form freestanding nouns or to undergo noun incorporation.

(34) a. Onondaga

adę:náʔtshäʔ
atęnaʔt-shR-aʔ
take.provisions-NZLR-NSUF
'groceries'

(Woodbury 2003: 139)

b. Oneida

kahyatúslaʔ
ka-hyatu-hsl-aʔ
3SG.NT.AG-write-NZLR-NSUF
'paper/book'

(Michelson & Doxtator 2002: 43)

Noun incorporation is discussed in the next section, so we leave the relevant illustrations until then.

Cherokee is rich in nominalization strategies. Not only does it have a special infinitive form derived from the causative-instrumental suffix, which itself may be related to the verb root *-vht-* 'use' (Cook 1979: 138; Mithun 2000b), but also agentive nouns, event nouns, and location nouns (Cook 1979: 148; Scancarelli 1987: 299; Montgomery-Anderson 2015: Chapter 12). No verbalization process is reported in Iroquoian languages. Northern Iroquoian languages do, however, have a number of verbs which require noun incorporation. Although such forms are not traditionally considered verbalizers, they do have in common with verbalizers the fact that they cannot appear on their own. Consider the following examples. Observe that the form *a* ('grab') obligatorily incorporates a noun.

(35) Oneida

a. *waʔshakohnyá:saʔ*

waʔ-	shako-	hnyaʔs-	a-	ʔ
FACT-	3SG.M>3SG.F-	neck-	grab-	PUNC

'He put his arms around her neck.'

(Barrie 2011: 101ff.)

b.* *yenyalá:ke wa:sháko?*

ye-nyal-ake	waʔ-shako-a-ʔ
3SG.F-neck-LOC	FACT-3SG.M>3SG.F- grab-PUNC

'He put his arms around her neck.'

5. Noun Incorporation and Classificatory Verbs

A notable difference between Northern Iroquoian and Cherokee is the availability of noun incorporation (NI) in these two branches. While NI is quite robust and productive across the Northern Iroquoian languages, its distribution is significantly restricted in Cherokee. We begin with a discussion of the properties of NI in Northern Iroquoian.

5.1. Noun Incorporation in Northern Iroquoian

NI constructions are prototypically formed from a verbal root and a nominal root or base that thematically stands in a verb-direct object relation or a verb-theme relation with intransitive verbs typically described as unaccusative, although incorporation of adjuncts is also available as we will discuss later. Consider first the following Onondaga example with a non-incorporated DP.

(36) Onondaga

waˀkhnínú: neˀ ganakdaˀ

waˀ-	k-	hninu-	꞉	neˀ	ka-**nakt**-aˀ
FACT-	1SG.AG-	buy-	PUNC	NE	3SG.NT.AG-**bed**-NFS

'I bought the/a bed.'

(Gloria Williams and Nora Carrier, speakers)

Notice that the freestanding object DP contains functional morphology that is absent when the nominal root meaning *bed* undergoes NI, as shown in the following example. The absence of nominal morphology on the incorporated root is a hallmark of NI (Mithun 1984a; 2000a; Baker 1988; Massam 2009).

(37) Onondaga

waˀgenakdahnínú:

waˀ-	k-	**nakt-**	hninu-	´:
FACT-	1SG.AG-	**bed-**	buy-	PUNC

'I bought a bed.'

(Gloria Williams and Nora Carrier, speakers)

Note, however, that the incorporated noun (IN) is not necessarily a bare root. In some languages, including Onondaga, a nominalizer is found in instances where a deverbal root is incorporated. Consider the following examples.

(38) Onondaga

a. *agatgų̨ˀtshé:hwih*

ak-	[atkų̨-	*(ˀtshR)]-	ohw	-ih
1SG.PAT-	[be.poisonous-	NZLR]-	put.in.water	-STAT

'I have poisoned it with liquid poison.'

(Woodbury 2003: 278)

b. *agadę̨naˀtshähninų́h*

ak-	[atę̨naˀt-	*(shR)]-	hninų̨	-´h
1SG.PAT-	[take.provisions-	NZLR]-	buy	-STAT

'I have bought groceries.'

(Woodbury 2003: 139)

Also, as mentioned, while the incorporated noun is often the theme or direct object of the verb, other elements can incorporate, such as locations and instruments (Mithun 2005; Barrie & Li 2013). Here are some Onondaga examples.

(39) Onondaga

a. *Honathahidákheˀ.*

hon-	at-	hah-	itakhe	-ˀ
3PL.M.AG-	MID-	path-	run	-PUNC

'They are walking on a path.'

(Woodbury 2003: 282)

b. *Waˀhageˀnhyayę́hdaˀ.*

waˀ-	hak-	ˀnhya-	a-	yę̨ht	-aˀ
FACT-	3SG.M>1SG.PAT-	stick-	JOIN-	hit	-PUNC

'He hit me with a stick.'

(Woodbury 2003: 928)

Although it is not the place here to delve into the details of the analysis of NI (see Barrie & Mathieu, this volume), Iroquoian languages have, nevertheless, played an integral role in the theoretical analysis of noun incorporation. There are two competing analyses for NI. In the syntactic analysis, NI (in addition to word formation in general) is done in the syntax. This analysis is developed by Baker (1988; 1996), but see also Barrie (2015b) for recent discussion. The lexicalist analysis claims that the NI forms are either stored lexically or are put together in a pre-syntactic module. This view is explored in Mithun (1984a; 1986b) and Rosen (1989). There are, of course, many other references dealing with this topic, but the references mentioned here deal in particular with Iroquoian languages. We leave the reader to consider these references further. Note, though, that noun incorporation is typically distinguished from verb compounding (see the next section) in that noun incorporation is productive, while verb compounding is not.

5.2. Noun Incorporation and Classificatory Verbs in Cherokee

In Cherokee, the instances of noun incorporation are much more limited than in Northern Iroquoian, and all of these cases are lexicalized. All the instances of lexicalized noun incorporation involve body part terms or few other nouns such as 'water' (Uchihara 2014). In (40), the last verb 'hit in the stomach' lexically incorporates the body part term 'stomach' (*-skwo:h-lí̋:ʔi*).

(40) Cherokee

gi:hli dù:ktĭ:lé̋:na, gansda gv̋hdi ù:sgwo:halv̌:nî:lv̌:ʔi

ki:hli	t-ù:-k(a)hthĭ:lé̋:n-a,	kansta	kv̋hti	ù:-skwo:halv:nî:(ʔ)l-v̌:ʔi
dog	DIST-3SG.PAT-attack:PFT-IND/SH	stick	with	3SG.PAT-hit.in.stomach:PFT-ASR

'When a dog attacked him, he hit it in the stomach with a stick.'

(Montgomery-Anderson et al. 2010)

In this case, the incorporated element 'stomach' has resemblance to the free noun form, *-skwo:h-lí̋:ʔi* (which requires the patientive pronominal prefixes), and also the hosting verb root is clearly related to the independent form of the verb 'hit', *-lv:ʔn-*. However, the incorporated element does not always have a clear relation with its independent form; for instance, the element *-as-* is found in some verbs having to do with 'hand' (*-asihthat-* 'place hand on', *-asihthv:n-* 'slap', *-asu:l-* 'wash hands'), but its free noun form is *-oʔy-*.

Some speakers consider verbs incorporating body part terms, like (40), to be obsolete and thus prefer analytic expressions, as in (41) (Scancarelli 1994: 157; Uchihara 2014: 25):

(41) Cherokee

jasgwo:hli:ʔi	*dagv:yv́:nì:li*
ca-skwo:hlí̋:ʔi	ta-kv:y-v:nì:(ʔ)l-i
2SG.PAT-abdomen	CISL-1SG>2SG-hit:PFT-MOT

'I'm going to hit you in the stomach.'

(Montgomery-Anderson et al. 2010)

To compensate for the lack of noun incorporation, Cherokee has a system of classificatory verbs which has been described in a number of sources (Haas 1948; Reyburn 1954: 50ff.; Pulte & Feeling 1975: 302ff.; King 1978; Cook 1979: Chapter 9; Blankenship 1997; Uchihara 2014). There are around three dozen sets of classificatory verbs in Cherokee according to King (1978: 40), such as 'have', 'set', 'give', 'leave', 'find', 'hang', and 'hide', and each set has the following five distinct categories: compact (CMP), long (LG), liquid (LQ), flexible (FL), and animate (AN). These classificatory verbs classify for intransitive agent and transitive patient or theme arguments. In (42), the verb 'have' has different forms according to the category of the theme argument:

(42) Cherokee

a.

kalsě:ji	*à:giha*
khalsě:ci	aki-h-a
candy	1SG.PAT-have.CMP-IND

'I have candy.'

(Montgomery-Anderson 2015: 83)

b. *galò:gwe* *à:gwv̌:ya*
kalò:kwe akw-v̌:y-a
gun 1SG.PAT-have.LG-IND
'I have a gun.'

(Montgomery-Anderson 2015: 83)

c. *ǔ:gáma* *à:ginéha*
ǔ:káma aki-néh-a
soup 1SG.PAT-have.LQ-IND
'I have soup.'

(Montgomery-Anderson 2015: 83)

d. *à:su:lo à:ginάʔa*
à:su:lo aki-náʔ-a
pants 1SG.PAT-have.FL-IND
'I have pants.'

(Montgomery-Anderson 2015: 83)

e. *sǒ:gwíli* *à:gikáha*
sǒ:kwíli aki-kháh-a
horse 1SG.PAT-have.AN-IND
'I have a horse.'

(Montgomery-Anderson 2015: 83)

Noun incorporation in modern Cherokee is limited in semantic domain and in productivity, but various authors have argued that noun incorporation is reconstructable for Proto-Iroquoian, arguing that vestiges of noun incorporation is found in three domains of modern Cherokee grammar: classificatory verbs, clothing verbs, and verbs incorporating body part terms (King 1978: 43; Lounsbury 1978: 337; Mithun 1984a: 883–884; Rudes 1984: 502–504; Blankenship 1997: 99–104; among others). On the other hand, Uchihara (2014) argues that the only solid evidence for reconstructing productive noun incorporation for an earlier stage of Cherokee is found solely for incorporation of body part terms, and that this is not sufficient evidence for reconstructing productive noun incorporation (cf. Chafe 2000). The argument is based on the analysis that the main source of classificatory verbs is verb compounding rather than noun incorporation, and that clothing verbs are instances of incorporation of body part terms rather than incorporation of clothing terms.

6. Syntax

Word order in Iroquoian languages is strongly dictated by pragmatic and discourse factors rather than by grammatical roles (Mithun 1992; 1995). As such, they are typically labeled discourse-configurational languages (an updating of the term *non-configurational*) after Hale's landmark study on configurationality (Hale 1983). Although we attempt to eschew any kind of theoretical analysis in this chapter, Hale's theoretical analysis of (non-)configurationality informs the description of major properties of Iroquoian syntax. Specifically, three properties of discourse-configurational languages are identified, all of which are found in Iroquoian. These are, namely, (i) free word order, (ii) discontinuous constituency, and (iii) massive pro-drop (meaning simply that an overt noun/noun phrase is not required to refer to the discourse participants). These are well established properties of Iroquoian languages, which we will discuss in detail. This section will end with a brief discussion of other less-studied aspects of Iroquoian syntax.

On the first property, Iroquoian languages have been shown to have rather free word order by a number of researchers (Baker 1996; Mithun Williams 1974). Consider the following constructed examples. Speakers typically remark that there is no appreciable or easily detectable difference in meaning in an out-of-the-blue context (though see below after example (45)).

(43) Onondaga

a. *Mary waʔek swahyó:nah*
Mary she.ate.it apple
'Mary ate an apple.'

(Barrie 2015a: 85)

b. *Mary swahyó:nah waʔek*
c. *waʔek Mary swahyó:nah*
d. *waʔek swahyó:nah Mary*
e. *swahyó:nah Mary waʔek*
f. *swahyó:nah waʔek Mary*

Like many discourse-configurational languages, Iroquoian languages exhibit discontinuous constituency. Note, though, that the discontinuous constituency in Iroquoian is more constrained than in the Australian language Warlpiri (Pama-Nyungan), the language studied by Hale in his proposal for non-configurationality. See Baker (1996) for more details and a theoretical proposal for the observed patterns. The following Mohawk example shows the putative nominal phrase *all the leather* split into two components: *akwé:kon* and *ne óhnaʔ*.

(44) Mohawk

Akwé:kon	*kʌ*	*wá-hs-atst-eʔ*	*ne*	*óhnaʔ*
all	Q	FACT-2SG.AG-use-PUNC	NE	leather

'Did you use all of the leather?'

(Deering & Delisle 1976: 388)

Massive pro-drop is witnessed by the fact that many utterances consist of just a verb with no noun phrases. Iroquoianists have often made the observation that sentences with more than one nominal phrase are quite rare in spontaneously produced speech (Koenig & Michelson 2015: 23):

(45) Oneida

khe-nú·weh-seʔ
1SG>3.NM-like-HAB
'I like her or them.'

(Koenig & Michelson 2015: 6)

We mentioned previously that word order is relatively free in Iroquoian languages. Mithun (1995) explores various semantic properties that shape word order in Tuscarora. We review some of these here, noting that this is a vastly underexplored area in Iroquoian linguistics in general. Mithun notes that preverbal nominals tend to be focused, contrastive, or somehow newsworthy, while postverbal nominals tend to be old or backgrounded information. The following two examples describe a group of starving people traveling across the ice. In the first example, the head man had not been mentioned before in the text, so that is new information. This nominal appears preverbally.

(46) Tuscarora

haʔ	*uhą̂ʔnąh*	*ruʔą̂ʔąh*	*wahrą̂hrąʔ . . .*
the	head	man	he.said

'The head man said, ". . ." '

(Mithun 1995: 408)

Later in the narrative, a question is asked about the head man. Now, the head man is old information and appears postverbally.

(47) Tuscarora

ąwœh	*tihruyą́hwʔąh*	*hœní:ką:*	*uhą́ʔnąh*	*ruʔą́ʔąh?*
where	he.has.learned.it.from	that	head	man

'Where had he learned it, that head man?'

(Mithun 1995: 408)

6.1. Voice Operations

Mithun (2006) and Koenig and Michelson (2015) argue that all voice operations in Northern Iroquoian are morpholexical (i.e., transparently change a verb's thematic structure and subcategorization), and that there is no morphosyntactic voice operation in these languages (i.e., one that changes the subcategorization and the linking properties of the verb to adapt it to a particular information perspective in discourse, while leaving its thematic structure intact). Thus, there is nothing corresponding to a passive construction in Northern Iroquoian (there is a special series of pronominal prefixes to defocus agents instead). There are, however, numerous benefactive and causative constructions. These are lexically conditioned, and these authors argue that they are essentially stored in the lexicon.

(48) Onondaga

a. *oˀsehdaná:węh*

o-	ˀseht-	a-	nawę-	h
3SG.NT.PAT-	car-	EPEN-	wet-	STAT

'The car is wet.'

(Barrie 2015a: 65)

b. *waˀeˀsehdanawęhadˀ neˀ Meri*

waˀ-	e-	ˀseht-	a-	nawę-	ht-	aˀ	neˀ Meri
FACT-	3SG.F.AG-	car-	JOIN-	wet-	CAUS-	PUNC	NE Mary

'Mary got the car wet.'

(Barrie 2015a: 65)

However, at least in Cherokee, there is a candidate for a morphosyntactic voice operation: the object-defocusing prefix *ataat-/at-/ataa-*, which is traditionally labeled as the reflexive prefix (Scancarelli 1987: 85ff.; Montgomery-Anderson 2015: §9.7). The Cherokee object-defocusing prefix is employed as a reference tracking device; it is used when the object of the inexplicit clause is coreferential to an argument of the referentially explicit clause, whether to the subject or object (Scancarelli 1987: 89, 148ff.; Montgomery-Anderson 2015: §14.3.2):

(49) Cherokee

jă:n dù:nv́:ne:le mě:li ani:jilv̋:sgi

că:n	t-u:-nv́:(ʔ)ne:l-e	mě:li	ani:-cilv̋:ski
John	DIST-3SG.PAT-give.CMP:PFT-REP	Mary	3PL.AG-flour

mě:líhno	*dú:da:nv́:ne:lv̌:ʔi*
mě:lí=hno	t-ǿ-u:-ata:-nv́:(ʔ)ne:l-v̌:ʔi
Mary=and	DIST-ITER-3SG.PAT-REFL-give.CMP.PFT-ASR

'John gave Mary some flowers, and Mary gave them right back to him.'

(Scancarelli 1987: 88; Montgomery-Anderson 2015: 414)

In (49), the object-defocusing prefix on the last verb serves to equate the object of this verb to the referent in the previous context, namely *John* or *Mary*. This function of object-defocusing affix, that of adapting the verb to a particular information perspective in discourse, while leaving its thematic structure, is the hallmark of a *morphosyntactic* voice operation. Furthermore, this process should be productive in theory, since any transitive verbs should be able to provide this form whenever the discourse structure requires this construction.

6.2. Wh-*Movement*

Finally, we discuss *wh*-movement in Iroquoian. Northern Iroquoian languages exhibit fairly ordinary *wh*-movement to the front of the clause.

(50) Cayuga

Dę'ho'dę' a'ehni:nǫ' ne' sanǫ:ha'?

dę'ho'dę'	a'-	e-	hninǫ	-'	ne'	sanǫ:ha'
what	FACT-	3SG.F.AG-	buy	-PUNC	NE	your.mother

'What did your mother buy?'

(Barrie et al. 2014: 5)

The question word *dę'ho'dę'* ('what') appears at the left edge of the clause. It is possible for other elements to appear to the left of the *wh*-phrase. Such elements appear to be interpreted as topics; however, more research is needed in this area. In no case can the *wh*-phrase appear to the right of the verb.

(51) Cayuga

a. *Sanǫ:ha' dę'ho'dę' a'ehni:nǫ'?*

sanǫ:ha'	dę'ho'dę'	a'-	e-	hninǫ	-'
your.mother	what	FACT-	3SG.F.AG-	buy	-PUNC

'What did your mother buy?'

(Barrie et al. 2014: 5)

b.* *A'ehni:nǫ' dę'ho'dę' ne' sanǫ:ha'?*

a'-	e-	hninǫ	-'	dę'ho'dę'	ne'	sanǫ:ha'
FACT-	3SG.F.AG-	buy	-PUNC	what	NE	your.mother

'What did your mother buy?'

Baker (1996: 66ff.) made similar observations for Mohawk. Baker also showed that Mohawk has long-distance questions and indirect questions:

(52) Mohawk

a. *Oh nahótʌ í-hs-ehr-e? Sak wa-ha-tshʌ́ri-??*

Oh nahótʌ	í-hs-ehr-e?	Sak	wa-ha-tshʌ́ri-??
what	I-2SG.AG-think-HAB	Sak	FACT-3SG.M.AG-find-PUNC

'What do you think Sak found?'

(Baker 1996: 69)

b. *Wa-hake-rihwanútu?s-e oh nahótʌ Uwári wa?-e-tshʌ́ri-?.*

Wa-hake-rihwanútu?s-e	oh nahótʌ	Uwári	wa?-e-tshʌ́ri-?.
FACT-3SG.M>1SG-ask-PUNC	what	Mary	FACT-3SG.F.AG-find-PUNC

'He asked me what Mary found.'

(Baker 1996: 69)

7. Conclusion

In this chapter, we have discussed the major issues in phonology, morphology, and syntax in the Iroquoian languages. Iroquoian languages are polysynthetic and discourse-configurational. They have complex aspect, mood, and agreement systems, and, in Northern Iroquoian, productive noun incorporation. Crucial areas for future research in the Iroquoian family include dialectal variation, prosody, and intonation (see Williams 2013 for some preliminary work), and first and second language acquisition (see Mithun 1989 for an early study).

Acknowledgments

We are grateful to the speakers of Iroquoian languages who provided us with data: Ed Jumper, Junior Scraper, Eda Scraper, DJ McCarter, and Durbin Feeling for Oklahoma Cherokee; Nora Carrier and Gloria Williams for Onondaga; and Barb Garlow and Amos Keye for Cayuga. We would also like to thank Karin Michelson and the reviewers for this chapter – Lisa Matthewson, Mark C. Baker, and Jason Haugen – for their insightful feedback. All errors and shortcomings rest with the authors.

Further Reading

There exist other overview chapters on the Iroquoian language family: Lounsbury (1978), Michelson (2011; 2016), and Mithun (2017). For an overview of historical and comparative Iroquoian, see Mithun (1979a), Campbell (1997), and Julian (2010).

Grammars and dictionaries of each language include the following: Onondaga (Woodbury 2003; 2018; Barrie 2015a), Oneida (Abbott 2000; Michelson & Doxtator 2002), Cayuga (Froman et al. 2002), Tuscarora (Williams 1976; Rudes 1999), Seneca (Chafe 1996; 2015), Mohawk (Bonvillain 1973; Deering & Delisle 1976), Wyandot (Kopris 2001), and Cherokee (Feeling 1975; Pulte & Feeling 1975; Cook 1979; Montgomery-Anderson 2015).

Notes

1. The following abbreviations are used: A = joiner vowel /a/, AG = agent, AMB = ambulative, AN = animate, AND = andative, ASR = assertive, CAUS = causative, CISL = cislocative, CMP = compact, DAT = dative, DIM = diminutive, DIST = distributive, DU = dual, DUC = dualic, E = epenthetic, EX = exclusive, EXT = external, F = feminine, FACT = factual, FL = flexible, FUT = future, HAB = habitual, I = prothetic vowel /i/, IMPF = imperfective, IN = inanimate, IND = indicative, INF = infinitive, INT = internal, IRR = irrealis, ITER = iterative, LG = long, LOC = locative, LQ = liquid, M = masculine, MID = middle, MOT = motion, NE = a nominal particle related to definiteness and specificity in Iroquoian languages, NFS = noun forming suffix, NM = non-masculine, NMS = non-masculine singular, NOM = nominative, NT = neuter, NZLR = nominalizer, PART = partitive, PAT = patient, PFT = perfective, PL = plural, PRES = present, PROG = progressive, PUNC = punctual, PURP = purposive, Q = interrogative, REFL = reflexive, REL = relative, REP = reportatve, REPET = repetitive, REV = reversative, SG = singular, SH = superhigh, STAT = stative, TRNSL = translocative, UNSP = unspecific.
2. *v* is a mid-central unrounded [ɘ] or a mid-back unrounded [ʌ], with an optional nasalization.
3. The alternation of the vowel length of *o:* is due to a general phonological constraint against a sequence of a long vowel followed by a glottal stop (*V:ʔ). The pronominal prefixes of the 3SG.AG and 1SG.AG have the same form here (*k-*) due to the phonological context (see Table 18.1).

References

Abbott, Clifford. 1981. Here and there in Oneida. *International Journal of American Linguistics* 47. 50–57.
Abbott, Clifford. 1984. Two feminine genders in Oneida. *Anthropological Linguistics* 26. 125–137.
Abbott, Clifford. 2000. *Oneida*. Munich: Lincom Europa.
Abrams, Percy. 2006. *Onondaga pronominal prefixes*. Buffalo: State University of New York. (Doctoral dissertation.)

Baker, Mark C. 1988. *Incorporation: A theory of grammatical function changing*. Chicago, IL: University of Chicago Press.

Baker, Mark C. 1996. *The polysynthesis parameter*. Oxford: Oxford University Press.

Barrie, Michael. 2011. *Dynamic antisymmetry and the syntax of noun incorporation*. Dordrecht: Springer.

Barrie, Michael. 2015a. *A grammar of Onondaga*. Berlin: Lincom.

Barrie, Michael. 2015b. Two kinds of structural noun incorporation. *Studia Linguistica* 69. 237–271.

Barrie, Michael & Chung, Inkie & Deer, Roronhiakehte. 2014. Clitics and the left periphery in Cayuga. *Studies in Generative Grammar* 24. 1–26.

Barrie, Michael & Yen-Hui, Audrey Li. 2013. The semantics of (Pseudo)incorporation and case. (Paper presented at the The Syntax and Semantics of Pseudo-Incorporation Workshop, DGfS, 2013), Potsdam, Germany.

Bender, Ernest & Harris, Zellig S. 1946. The phonemes of North Carolina Cherokee. *International Journal of American Linguistics* 12. 14–21.

Blankenship, Barbara. 1997. Classificatory verbs in Cherokee. *Anthropological Linguistics* 39. 92–110.

Bonvillain, Nancy. 1973. *A grammar of Akwasasne Mohawk*. Hull and Gatineau, QC: National Museum of Man and Nature.

Campbell, Lyle. 1997. *American Indian languages: The historical linguistics of Native America*. Oxford: Oxford University Press.

Chafe, Wallace L. 1960. Seneca morphology III: Expanded pronominal prefixes. *International Journal of American Linguistics* 26. 224–23

Chafe, Wallace L. 1967. *Seneca morphology and dictionary*. Smithsonian Contributions to Anthropology 4. Washington, DC: Smithsonian Press.

Chafe, Wallace L. 1977a. Accent and related phenomena in the five nations Iroquois languages. In Hyman, L. (ed.), *Studies in stress and accent*, 169–181. (Southern California Occasional Papers in Linguistics, 4). Los Angeles: UCLA Department of Linguistics.

Chafe, Wallace L. 1977b. The evolution of third person verb agreement in the Iroquoian languages. In Li, C. (ed.), *Mechanisms of syntactic change*, 493–524. Austin: University of Texas Press.

Chafe, Wallace L. 1980. Consequential verbs in the Northern Iroquoian languages and elsewhere. In Klar, K. & Langdon, M. & Silver, S. (eds.), *American Indian and Indoeuropean studies: Papers in honor of Madison S. Beeler*, 43–49. The Hague: Mouton.

Chafe, Wallace L. 1984. How to say “they drank” in Iroquois. In Foster, M. K. & Campisi, J. & Mithun, M. (eds.), *Extending the rafters; interdisciplinary approaches to the Iroquois*, 301–311. Albany: Suny Press.

Chafe, Wallace L. 1996. Sketch of Seneca, an Iroquoian language. In Goddard, I. (ed.), *Handbook of North-american Indians. Volume 17: Languages*, 551–579. Washington, DC: Smithsonian Institute.

Chafe, Wallace L. 2012. Are adjectives universal? The case of Northern Iroquoian. *Linguistic Typology* 16. 1–39.

Chafe, Wallace L. 2015. *A grammar of the Seneca language*. Oakland: University of California Press.

Chafe, Wallace L. & Foster, Michael K. 1981. Prehistoric divergences and recontacts between Cayuga, Seneca, and the other Northern Iroquoian languages. *International Journal of American Linguistics* 47. 121–142.

Cook, William H. 1979. *A grammar of North Carolina Cherokee*. New Haven, CT: Yale University. (Doctoral dissertation.)

Deer, Roronhiakehte. 2011. *Dwasgohowá: naht: Towards a feature structure of Cayuga pronominals*. University of Western Ontario. (MA thesis.)

Deering, N. & Delisle, Helga H. 1976. *Mohawk: A teaching grammar*. La Macaza, QC: Manitou Community College.

Dyck, Carrie. 1990. *Cayuga syllable structure and epenthesis*. University of Toronto. (MA thesis.)

Dyck, Carrie. 2009. Defining the word in Cayuga (Iroquoian). *International Journal of American Linguistics* 75. 571–605.

Feeling, Durban. 1975. *Cherokee-English dictionary*. Tahlequah: Cherokee Nation of Oklahoma.

Flemming, Edward. 1996. Laryngeal metathesis and vowel deletion in Cherokee. (Cherokee Papers from UCLA, P. Munro, ed.), 23–44. Los Angeles: University of California.

Foster, Michael K. 1982. Alternating weak and strong syllables in Cayuga words. *International Journal of American Linguistics* 48. 59–72.

Foster, Michael K. 1985. The language of tense, mood, and aspect in Northern Iroquoian descriptions. *International Journal of American Linguistics* 51. 403–405.

Foster, Michael K. 1986. Updating the terminology of tense, mood and aspect in Northern Iroquoian descriptions. *International Journal of American Linguistics* 52. 65–87.

Froman, Frances & Keye, Alfred J. & Keye, Lottie & Dyck, Carrie. 2002. *English-Cayuga/Cayuga-English dictionary*. Toronto: University of Toronto Press.

Haas, Mary R. 1948. Classificatory verbs in Muskogee. *International Journal of American Linguistics* 14. 244–246.

Haas, Mary R. 1961. Comment on Floyd G. Lounsbury's, Iroquois-Cherokee linguistic relations. In Fenton, W. & Gulick, J. (eds.), *Symposium on Cherokee-Iroquois culture*, 21–23. Bureau of American Ethnology.

Hale, Ken. 1983. Warlpiri and the grammar of non-configurational languages. *Natural Language and Linguistic Theory* 1. 5–47.

Hewitt, J. N. B. 1887. *The Cherokee an Iroquoian language*. Washington, DC: B.o.A. Ethnology.

Hinton, Leanne. 2008. Languages and language programs. In Sturtevant, W. C. (ed.), *Handbook of North American Indians*, vol. 2, 351–391. Washington, DC: Government Printing Office.

Hoover, Michael J. & The Kanien'kehaka Raotitiohkwa Cultural Center. 1992. The revival of the Mohawk language in Kahnawake. *Canadian Journal of Native Studies* 12. 269–287.

Julian, Charles. 2010. *A history of the Iroquoian languages*. Winnipeg: University of Manitoba. (Doctoral dissertation.)

King, Duane. 1978. Cherokee classificatory verbs. *Journal of Cherokee Studies* 3. 40–44.

Koenig, Jean-Pierre & Michelson, Karin. 2010. Argument structure of Oneida Kinship terms. *International Journal of American Linguistics* 76. 169–205.

Koenig, Jean-Pierre & Michelson, Karin. 2015. Invariance in argument realization: The case of Iroquoian. *Language* 91. 1–47.

Kopris, Craig. 2001. *A grammar and dictionary of Wyandot*. Buffalo: University of New York at Buffalo. (Doctoral dissertation.)

Lindsey, Geoffrey. 1985. *Intonation and interrogation: Tonal structure and the expression of a pragmatic function in English and other languages*. Los Angeles: University of California. (Doctoral dissertation.)

Lindsey, Geoffrey & Scancarelli, Janine. 1985. Where have all the adjectives come from? The case of Cherokee. (Paper presented to the annual meeting of the Berkeley Linguistic Society 11, 1985).

Lounsbury, Floyd Glenn. 1942. *Phonology of the Oneida language*. University of Wisconsin. (MA thesis.)

Lounsbury, Floyd Glenn. 1949. *Iroquoian morphology*. New Haven, CT: Yale University (Doctoral dissertation.)

Lounsbury, Floyd Glenn. 1953. *Oneida verb morphology*. New Haven, CT: Yale University.

Lounsbury, Floyd Glenn. 1961. Iroquois-Cherokee linguistic relations. In Fenton, W. & Gulick, J. (eds.), *Symposium on Cherokee and Iroquois culture*, 11–17. Bureau of American Ethnology.

Lounsbury, Floyd Glenn. 1978. Iroquoian languages. In Trigger, B. G. (ed.), *Handbook of North American Indians, vol. 15: Northeast*, 334–343. Washington, DC: Smithsonian Institute.

Massam, Diane. 2009. Noun incorporation: Essentials and extensions. *Language and Linguistics Compass* 3. 1076–1096.

Melinger, Alissa. 2002. Foot structure and accent in Seneca. *International Journal of American Linguistics* 68. 287–315.

Michelson, Karin. 1986. Ghost r's in Onondaga: An autosegmental analysis of *r-stems. In Wetzels, L. & Sezer, E. (eds.), *Studies in compensatory lengthening*, 147–166. Dordrecht: Foris.

Michelson, Karin. 1988. *A comparative study of Lake-Iroquoian accent*. Dordrecht: Kluwer.

Michelson, Karin. 1989. Invisibility: Vowels without a timing slot in Mohawk. In Gerdts, D. & Michelson, K. (eds.), *Theoretical perspectives on native American languages*, 38–69. Albany: Suny Press.

Michelson, Karin. 2000. Utterance-final phenomena in Oneida. In Fujimura, O. & Joseph, B. & Palek, B. (eds.), *Item order in language and speech, proceedings of LP '98*, 31–45. Prague: Charles University Press.

Michelson, Karin. 2011. Iroquoian languages. In Aronoff, M. (ed.), *Oxford bibliographies online: Linguistics*. New York: Oxford University Press.

Michelson, Karin. 2015. Gender in Oneida. In Hellinger, M. & Motschenbacher, H. (eds.), *Gender across languages*, 277–302. Amsterdam and Philadelphia: John Benjamins Publishing Company.

Michelson, Karin. 2016. *Iroquoian languages*. Oxford University Press.

Michelson, Karin & Doxtator, Mercy. 2002. *Oneida-English/English-Oneida dictionary* Toronto: University of Toronto Press.

Mithun, Marianne. 1979a. Iroquoian. In Campbell, L. & Mithun, M. (eds.), *The languages of native America: A historical and comparative assessment*, 133–212. Austin: University of Texas Press.

Mithun, Marianne. 1979b. Some semantics of polysynthesis. (Paper presented to the The Fifth LACUS Forum, New York).

Mithun, Marianne. 1981. Stalking the susquehannock. *International Journal of American Linguistics* 47. 1–26.

Mithun, Marianne. 1984a. The evolution of noun incorporation. *Language* 60. 847–894.

Mithun, Marianne. 1984b. The Proto-Iroquoians: Cultural reconstruction from lexical materials. In Campisi, J.& Foster, M. K. & Mithun, M. (eds.), *Extending the rafters*, 259–282. Albany: Suny Press.

Mithun, Marianne. 1986a. Evidential diachrony in Northern Iroquoian. In Chafe, W. & Nichols, J. (eds.), *Evidentiality: The linguistic coding of epistemology*, 89–112. Norwood, NJ: Ablex.

Mithun, Marianne. 1986b. On the nature of noun incorporation. *Language* 62. 32–37.

Mithun, Marianne. 1989. The acquisition of polysynthesis. *Journal of Child Language* 16. 285–312.

Mithun, Marianne. 1992. Is basic word order universal? In Payne, D. L. (ed.), *Pragmatics of word order flexibility*, 15–62. Amsterdam: John Benjamins.

Mithun, Marianne. 1993. Reconstructing the unidentified. In Aertsen, H. & Jeffers, R. (eds.), *Historical linguistics 1989*, 329–347. Amsterdam: Benjamins.

Mithun, Marianne. 1995. Morphological and prosodic forces shaping word order. In Downing, P. & Noonan, M. (eds.), *Word order in discourse*, 387–423. Amsterdam: John Benjamins Publishing Co.

Mithun, Marianne. 1996a. Multiple reflections of inalienability in Mohawk. In Chappell, H. (ed.), *The grammar of inalienability: A typological perspective on body part terms and the part whole relation*, 633–649. Berlin: Mouton de Gruyter.

Mithun, Marianne. 1996b. New directions in referentiality. In Fox, B. (ed.), *Studies in Anaphora*, 413–435. Amsterdam, Netherlands: Benjamins.

Mithun, Marianne. 2000a. Incorporation. In Booij, G. & Lehmann, C. & Mugdan, J. (eds.), *Morphology*, 916–928. Berlin: deGruyter.

Mithun, Marianne. 2000b. Noun and verb in Iroquoian languages: Multicategorisation from multiple criteria. In Vogel, P-M. (ed.), *Approaches to the typology of word classes*, 397–420. Berlin, Germany: Mouton de Gruyter.

Mithun, Marianne. 2001. The difference a category makes in the expression of possession and inalienability. In Baron, I. (ed.), *Dimensions of possession*, 285–310. Amsterdam, Netherlands: Benjamins.

Mithun, Marianne. 2005. Beyond the core: Typological variation in the identification of participants. *International Journal of American Linguistics* 71. 445–472.

Mithun, Marianne. 2006. Voice without subjects, objects or obliques: Manipulating argument structure in agent/patient systems. In Tsunoda, T. & Nishimitsu, Y. & Kageyama, T. (eds.), *Voice and grammatical relations*, 195–216. Amsterdam: John Benjamins.

Mithun, Marianne. 2009. *Re(e)volving complexity: Adding intonation*. In Givon, T. & Shibatani, M. (eds.), *Syntactic complexity: Diachrony, acquisition, neuro-cognition, evolution*, 53–80. Amsterdam: John Benjamins.

Mithun, Marianne. 2017. The Iroquoian language family. In Aikhenvald, A. Y. & R. M. W. Dixon (eds.), *The Cambridge handbook of linguistic typology*, 747–781. Cambridge Handbooks in Language and Linguistics. Cambridge: Cambridge University Press.

Mithun Williams, Marianne. 1974. *Word order in Tuscarora*. Foster, M. K. (ed.). *Papers in linguistics from the 1972 Conference on Iroquoian Research*, 27–35. Ottawa: National Museum of Man.

Montgomery-Anderson, B. 2015. *Cherokee reference grammar*. University of Oklahoma Press.

Montgomery-Anderson, B. & Yamamoto, Akira & Sixkiller, Anna & Jumper, Ed & Trihus, Greg & Bryson, Beth & Sikora, Andrew. 2010. *Cherokee electronic dictionary: Cherokee nation foundation*. University of Oklahoma Press.

Mooney, James. 1900/1992. *James Mooney's history, myths, and sacred formulas of the Cherokees*. Asheville, NC: Historical Images.

Munro, Pamela (ed.). 1996. *The Cherokee Laryngeal alternation rule*, 3–7. (Cherokee Papers from UCLA). Los Angeles: University of California Press.

Pulte, William. 1985. The experienced and non experienced past in Cherokee. *International Journal of American Linguistics* 51. 543–544.

Pulte, William & Feeling, Durban. 1975. *Outline of Cherokee grammar: Cherokee-English dictionary* (Pulte, W., Ed.), 235–255. Tahlequah: Cherokee Nation of Oklahoma.

Reyburn, William D. 1954. Cherokee verb morphology III. *International Journal of American Linguistics* 20. 44–64.

Rosen, Sara Thomas. 1989. Two types of noun incorporation: A lexical analysis. *Language* 65. 294–317.

Rudes, Blair. 1984. Reconstructing word order in a polysynthetic language: From SOV to SVO in Iroquoian. In Fisiak, J. (ed.), *Historical syntax*, 471–508. Berlin: Walter de Gruyter.

Rudes, Blair. 1995. Iroquoian vowels. *Anthropological Linguistics* 37. 16–69.

Rudes, Blair. 1999. *Tuscarora-English English-Tuscarora dictionary*. Toronto: University of Toronto Press.

Sasse, Hans Jürgen. 1995. *The evolution of person prefixes in the Iroquoian languages and its functional background. Language and culture in Native North America*. Dürr, M. & Renner, E. & Oleschinski, W. (eds.). Munich: Lincom Europa.

Sasse, Hans Jürgen. 2001. *Scales between nouniness and verbiness. Language typology and language universals/Sprachtypologie und sprachliche Universalien/La Typologie des langues et les universaux linguistiques: An international handbook/Ein internationales Handbuch/Manuel international*, 1–2. Haspelmath, M. (ed.), 495–509. Berlin, Germany: de Gruyter.

Scancarelli, Janine. 1987. *Grammatical relations and verb agreement in Cherokee*. Los Angeles: University of California. (Doctoral dissertation.)

Scancarelli, Janine. 1994. Another look at a "primitive language". *International Journal of American Linguistics* 60. 149–160.

Uchihara, Hiroto. 2007. Laryngeal Alternation, Laryngeal Metathesis and Aspirated Consonants in Oklahoma Cherokee. *Tokyo University Linguistic Papers* 26. 49–72.
Uchihara, Hiroto. 2009. High tone in Oklahoma Cherokee. *International Journal of American Linguistics* 75. 317–336.
Uchihara, Hiroto. 2013. *Tone and accent in Oklahoma Cherokee*. University at Buffalo, The State University of New York. (Doctoral dissertation.)
Uchihara, Hiroto. 2014. Cherokee noun incorporation revisited. *International Journal of American Linguistics* 80. 5–38.
Uchihara, Hiroto. 2016. *Tone and accent in Oklahoma Cherokee*. Oxford: Oxford University Press.
Walker, Willard. 1969. Notes on native writing systems and the design of native literacy programs. *Anthropological Linguistics* 11. 148–166.
Williams, Lana. 2013. *Pitch accent and intonation in Cayuga: An acoustic analysis and ToBI recommendations: Memorial University of newfoundland.* (MA thesis.)
Williams, Marianne Mithun. 1976. *A grammar of Tuscarora*. New York: Garland Press.
Woodbury, Hanni. 1981. The loss of a phoneme. *International Journal of American Linguistics* 47. 103–120.
Woodbury, Hanni. 2003. *Onondaga-English/English-Onondaga dictionary*. Toronto: University of Toronto Press.
Woodbury, Hanni. 2018. *A reference grammar of the Onondaga language*. Toronto: University of Toronto Press.

19

SALISH LANGUAGES

Henry Davis

1. Introduction

The Salish language family comprises 23 languages, spoken or formerly spoken in northwest North America in a more or less contiguous zone from northwestern Montana in the southeast to southeastern Vancouver Island in the northwest, with outliers on the northern coast of Oregon (Tillamook) and central coastal British Columbia (Bella Coola).

The languages, their principal dialects, and the average age of their remaining L1 speakers as of 2018 are shown in (1). Language names given here are the traditional (anglicized) versions used in the Salishan linguistics literature. Many Salish speech communities have adopted different names, often employing community orthographies: these are given in parentheses. Principal dialects are given below language names. Language status is given at the right: † = no first language speakers, 60+ = nearly all L1 speakers over 60, etc.[1]

(1) Salish languages

A. BELLA COOLA	
Bella Coola (Nuxalk)	80+ (?)
Bella Coola	
Kimsquit	
Tallio	
B. COAST SALISH	
i. Central Salish	
Comox-Sliammon (ʔayʔaǰuθəm)	
Island Comox	†
Mainland Comox	65+
Pentlatch	†
Sechelt (Shashishalhem)	90+
Squamish (Sk̲wx̲wú7mesh)	90+
Halkomelem	
Island/Cowichan (hul̓q̓umin̓um̓)	75+
Downriver/Musqueam (hən̓q̓əmin̓əm̓)	†
Upriver/Chilliwack (halq̓emeylem)	90+
Nooksack (Lhéchalosem)	†
Twana	†

Lushootseed (dəx^{w}ləšucid, x^{w}ələšucid)	
Northern	90+?
Southern	†
(a) STRAITS DIVISION	
Northern Straits	
Sooke (T'sou-ke)	†
Saanich (SENĆOŦEN)	85+
Songhees/Songish (Lekwungen)	†
Semiahmoo	†
Samish	80+?
Lummi (Xwlemi'chosen)	†
Klallam	†
ii. TSAMOSAN	
(a) INLAND DIVISION	
Upper Chehalis	†
Satsop	
Tenino	
Oakville	
Cowlitz	†
(b) MARITIME DIVISION	
Quinault	†
Lower Chehalis (Łəw̓ál̓məš)	†
iii. TILLAMOOK	†
Tillamook	
Tillamook	
Siletz	
Nehelem	
C. INTERIOR SALISH	
i. SOUTHERN INTERIOR	
Moses Columbia (nxaʔamxcín)	90+
Columbia	
Wenatchi	
Coeur D'Alene (snchitsu'umshtsn)	90+
Salish-Spokane-Kalispel	
Spokane	90+
Kalispel (Q̓lispé)	90+ (?)
Montana Salish/Flathead (Séliš)	80+
Okanagan (Nsyílxcen)	
Northern/Lakes	60+
Southern/Colville	75+
ii. NORTHERN INTERIOR	
Shuswap (Secwepemctsín)	
Western	70+
Eastern	80+ (?)
Thompson (River) (nłeʔkepmxcín)	
Lytton/Canyon	70+
Nicola Valley	80+
Lillooet (St'át'imcets)	
Upper/Fountain/Fraser River	70+
Lower/Mount Currie	65+

The integrity of the Salish family has been recognized at least since Powell (1891) and is uncontroversial. While there is still uncertainty about the precise relationship of Bella Coola to the other members of the family – in particular, whether it should be grouped into a Greater Coast Salish branch (Kuipers 2002), or treated as a sister to the Coast and Interior branches (Kinkade 1990b) – most of the primary divisions in the family are well established.

As far as the relationship of Salish to other language families is concerned, the Mosan Hypothesis of Sapir (1921) and Swadesh (1953), which grouped Salish into a super-family along with the neighboring Chimakuan and Wakashan families, has been effectively debunked: there is little or no lexical evidence for a relationship between the three families, and grammatical resemblances appear to be features of a northwestern *Sprachbund* rather than evidence for a remote genetic relationship. At the present, there is no convincing evidence for a relationship between Salish and any other language family

2. Current Status of Salish Languages

At the time of writing, no Salish language has more than a hundred fluent L1 speakers, and most have considerably fewer; more than half are no longer spoken as first languages. In practical terms, linguistic fieldwork with fluent L1 speakers is currently possible for only a handful of languages, nearly all of them spoken in Canada. However, several languages are showing renewed signs of life as second languages, with fluent L2 speakers emerging from various programs and initiatives, increasingly under the direction of Salish speech communities themselves. For reasons of space, I am able to mention only a couple of these initiatives here.

In British Columbia, the First Peoples' Cultural Council has taken a lead role in coordinating language revival efforts at the community level. Besides publishing the *Report on the Status of B.C. First Nations Languages*, now in its third edition (First Peoples' Cultural Council 2018), which has the most up-to-date language assessment for BC Salish languages, the organization has either spearheaded or supported a number of other important initiatives in language documentation and pedagogy, including language nests, a mentor-apprentice program, and the *First Voices* electronic archive, located at www.firstvoices.com. The latter comprises a suite of web-based tools for language documentation and pedagogy, including electronic dictionaries (with associated sound files) for 13 BC Salish speech communities.

Across the border, the Salish School of Spokane in eastern Washington State (www.salishschoolofspokane.org) has been particularly active in language revitalization efforts for the four Southern Interior Salish languages. Aside from running language programs for both children and adults, the school has produced extensive curriculum materials, which are widely used on both sides of the border. Another fulcrum for language revitalization is the Celebrating Salish Conference, which is held annually on the territory of the Kalispel Tribe in Montana, and which brings together speakers, teachers, and learners of Southern Interior Salish languages (see www.kalispeltribe.com/ourtribe/language/celebrating-salish-conference). Community language education efforts in Salish territory have been supported and supplemented by institutions of higher education: many Salish languages are now accredited at the university level, and several partnerships exist between universities and Salish-speaking communities, in both Canada and the United States. Overall, while the challenges of language education in Salish-speaking territory should not be underestimated, particularly given the small size of the speech communities and the fragmentation of resources that this entails, there is reason for cautious optimism: a generation of trial and error has largely dispelled the "magic bullet" approach to language education in Salish communities and, in doing so, has produced a realistic and committed cadre of teachers and students, who are both highly conscious of the critical role of language in the survival of Indigenous culture and identity, and determined to ensure that Salish languages will not pass away with the last of their fluent L1 speakers.

3. History of Linguistic Work on Salish

As the largest language family confined to the Pacific Northwest of North America, Salish has a long history of linguistic research and documentation, dating from the start of contact between European colonizers and the Indigenous inhabitants of the area. The earliest records, however, largely consist of word lists recorded by explorers, missionaries, and amateur ethnographers with little or no phonetic training, and are of limited utility today; systematic linguistic work really began at the end of the 19th century with Franz Boas and his associates.[2] Boas did fieldwork on a surprisingly large number of Salish languages, both on the coast and in the interior; his influence remains strong in Salish linguistics, not least because his unpublished field notes yield the most comprehensive data available for several languages and dialects which disappeared during the early to middle 20th century, including Tillamook, Upper Chehalis, Pentlatch, and Island Comox. Kinkade (1990a) gives an excellent account of the early history of linguistics on the northwest coast.

Fieldwork on Salish in the mid-20th century suffered something of a hiatus, with a couple of notable exceptions in the Southern Interior. Boas's student Gladys Reichard did field research on Coeur D'Alene; both her (1938) grammar and Hans Vogt's (1940) grammar of neighboring Kalispel (written on the basis of six weeks of fieldwork!) remain standard references for those languages. In the early 1950s, Morris Swadesh drew on this work as well as earlier comparative Salish lexical data from Boas and Haeberlin to provide a revised model of Salish-internal relationships based on lexico-statistical methodology. The later part of the decade saw the beginnings of a resurgence in fieldwork on Salish, led by the anthropologists William W. Elmendorf (Tsamosan, Tillamook, Central Salish, and Interior Salish) and Wayne Suttles (Central Salish). Both emphasized the role of language in cultural continuity and change; Suttles in particular paved the way for contemporary Salish linguistics through his commitment to Salish speech communities as well as to their languages, and his monumental grammar of Musqueam (published in 2004) remains one of the best descriptive accounts of any Salish language.

However, the modern era really began with the establishment of the International Conference on Salish Languages (ICSL) in 1965. Subsequently renamed the International Conference on Salish and Neighbo(u)ring Languages (ICSNL) to reflect its broader influence on northwest linguistics, the conference quickly became a clearing house for linguistic research under the leadership of Laurence C. and M. Terry Thompson, M. Dale Kinkade, and Aert H. Kuipers, who effectively dominated the field for a quarter of a century. Aside from the primary research they conducted on more than half a dozen languages, including Klallam, Thompson and Tillamook (the Thompsons), Upper Chehalis, Cowlitz, and Moses Columbia (Kinkade), and Squamish and Shuswap (Kuipers), their work on comparative and historical Salish provides a benchmark for all subsequent research on the subject (see in particular L.C. Thompson 1979 and Kuipers 1981; 2002). Both Kuipers and the Thompsons were also active in recruiting graduate students, many of whom who went on to write grammars and dictionaries for other Salish languages. Prominent Salishanists trained by the Thompsons include Barry Carlson (Spokane), Steve Egesdal (Thompson, Montana Salish, Tillamook), Thom Hess (Lushootseed), Anthony Mattina (Okanagan), and Timothy Montler (Straits Salish); those trained by Kuipers include Hank Nater (Bella Coola) and Jan van Eijk (Lillooet).

Though the Kinkade-Kuipers-Thompson School of Salishan linguistics was largely rooted in the Bloomfieldian structuralist tradition and eschewed the generative revolution taking place elsewhere (sometimes vociferously so, as in the case of Kuipers), it is also fair to say that it set the agenda for some important theoretical debates which have continued to engage the field ever since. Seminal contributions include L.C. Thompson's work on agent control (L.C. Thompson 1985) and Kuipers and Kinkade's provocative contributions to the noun-verb controversy (Kuipers 1968; Kinkade 1983). In addition – and unusually, for that era – the organizers of the ICSNL made a conscious attempt to foster collaboration between Salish linguists and speakers: particularly prominent long-term attendees included legendary language activists and educators Laurence Nicodemus

(Coeur D'Alene) and Vi Hilbert (Lushootseed). That tradition has continued: the ICSNL is held regularly in Salish-speaking communities and has always featured presentations by community language groups in addition to linguists.

The late 1970s and early 1980s saw the first stirrings of a new interest in the syntax of northwest coast languages from a theoretical perspective. Two pioneers of this trend were Thomas Hukari, who in the late 1970s was the first to explore a generative approach to Central Salish, and Donna Gerdts, whose 1981 dissertation on Island Halkomelem, written in the framework of Relational Grammar, represents the first comprehensive theoretical treatment of argument structure in a Salish language (Gerdts 1988). Gerdts and Hukari have continued to investigate the grammar of Island Halkomelem, both individually and collaboratively: their cumulative contributions represent perhaps the most sustained investigation of the syntax of any Salish language (see, e.g., Gerdts & Hukari 2006; 2008), and their ongoing work on language education in Cowichan-speaking communities puts the results of their linguistic research directly to practical use in revitalization efforts.

At around the same time, Eloise Jelinek began a collaboration with Richard A. Demers at the University of Arizona on the Lummi dialect of Northern Straits Salish. Jelinek's ability to draw out the consequences of earlier descriptive work and to present it in a way that emphasized its theoretical implications had a dramatic impact on the place of Salish in the field as a whole and paved the way for much subsequent research on Salish syntax and semantics; see in particular Jelinek and Demers (1994) and Jelinek (1995).

The 15 years from about 1990 to 2005 represent perhaps the most active period in Salish linguistics. Accurate descriptive coverage of the languages increased dramatically, with the publication of a string of grammars, dictionaries, and texts. This in turn led to refined historical and comparative work, including Paul Kroeber's (1999) landmark volume on comparative morphosyntax. In the areas of phonology and phonetics, new theoretical models led to more sophisticated phonological analyses of phenomena such as stress (Czaykowska-Higgins 1993a) and reduplication (Urbanczyk 2001), while technological advances in phonetics facilitated the first serious instrumental investigations, including Nicola Bessell's (1992) pioneering research on the acoustics of post-velars in Interior Salish, and Carlson et al.'s (2004) laryngoscopic analysis of Thompson. Research in syntax greatly expanded, addressing a wide range of topics, including lexical categories, aspect and argument structure, configurationality, A'-dependencies, and binding and coreference; see the annotated bibliography on syntax and semantics in Davis and Matthewson (2009). Of particular importance during this period was the emergence of serious work on formal semantics, marked by Lisa Matthewson's seminal work on determiners and quantifiers (Matthewson 1998). Work on these topics has continued, and semantic inquiry has expanded to tense, aspect, and modality, intersecting with earlier analyses of control and argument structure.

More recent years have seen a consolidation of earlier work, with a focus on areas that had not been previously investigated in detail. Partly, this is in response to the diminishing opportunities to work with fluent L1 speakers, and a realization among both Salish linguists and speech communities that in the very few years left where primary fieldwork is possible, it is important to fill in gaps in documentation that cannot be gleaned from existing resources. At the same time, there have been intensive efforts to digitize, transcribe, and translate as much of the large stockpile of recorded textual material as possible, and there has been a renewed interest in lexicography, driven by advances in electronic archiving and dissemination.

4. Phonetics and Phonology

A composite phonemic inventory for Salish consonants is given in Table 19.1. Symbols in bold represent those which can be reconstructed to Proto-Salish; symbols in parentheses are only marginally present, either because they are limited to one or two languages or because they are present only as allophones rather than full phonemes.[3]

Table 19.1 Salish Consonants

	BILABIAL	CORONAL	POST-ALVEOLAR	PALATAL	VELAR	UVULAR	PHARYNGEAL	LARYNGEAL
Stop	**p** **p̓**	**t** **t̓**			**k** **k**^{w} **k̓** **k̓**^{w}	**q** **q**^{w} **q̓** **q̓**^{w}		**ʔ**
(Voiced stop)	b	d			g (g^{w})			
Affricate		**c** ç (t$^{\theta}$) **c̓** t$^{\theta̓}$ **ƛ̓** (ƛ)	č č̓					
(Voiced affricate)		(d^{z})	ǰ ǰ̓					
Fricative		**s** ş θ **ɬ**	š	(x^{y})	**x** **x**^{w}	**x̌** **x̌**^{w}	(ħ ħ^{w})	**h**
Nasal	**m** **m̓**	**n** **n̓**			ŋ ŋ̓			
Liquid		**l** ḷ r **l̓** ḷ̓ r̓						
Glide		z z̓		**y** **y̓**	**ɣ** **w** **ɣ̓** **w̓**		**ʕ** **ʕ**^{w} **ʕ̓** **ʕ̓**^{w}	

As is typical of northwest North America, Salish languages are characterized by fairly large and typologically unusual consonant inventories, with a primary phonological opposition between resonants on the one hand (including liquids, nasals, and glides, as well as glottal stop and /h/) and obstruents (stops, affricates and fricatives) on the other.[4] This opposition is particularly important for syllable structure, which strictly follows the sonority hierarchy, with resonants always closer to the syllabic nucleus than obstruents: violations of the hierarchy generally lead to schwa epenthesis.

Throughout the family, both obstruents (stops and affricates) and resonants show a plain-glottalized contrast. However, while glottalized obstruents are always realized as ejectives with complete glottal closure, glottalized resonants (and glottal stop) are often realized as creaky voice on adjacent vowels; furthermore, the timing of glottalization on resonants is variable both within and between languages (see Bird et al. 2008 on Lillooet and Thompson). Unlike in other parts of the NW *Sprachbund*, glottalized obstruents and resonants do not pattern together phonologically: both synchronically and diachronically, glottalized resonants frequently decompose into sequences of glottal stop and plain consonant (particularly in Central Salish), while ejectives never do.

Voiced stops and affricates have developed in several languages, either from nasals (in Lushootseed and Twana) or glides (Lushootseed, Comox-Sliammon, and Coeur D'Alene), but continue to pattern phonologically as resonants rather than obstruents.[5] More generally, resonants appear to be particularly unstable in Salish: separate sound changes across the family have changed nasals to vowels and liquids, liquids to glides, and glides into affricates and stops.

Six to eight places of primary articulation are distinguished, with post-velar consonants being particularly well represented. Secondary labialization is contrastive on velar and post-velar consonants except before rounded vowels, where it is neutralized. Non-labialized velars are often palatalized: Proto-Salish *k, *k̓ and *x have become č, č̓, and š, respectively, at least three separate times in the history of Salish.[6] The first of these changes affected coastal languages (including Tillamook but excluding Tsamosan and Bella Coola), with further modification of č, č̓ to c, c̓ in Halkomelem and to s, c̓ in Northern Straits. (A distinct but overlapping innovation in the Georgia Strait area of southwestern British Columbia saw Mainland Comox-Sliammon, Pentlatch, the Saanich dialect of Northern Straits, and Halkomelem develop t$^{\theta}$/θ and t$^{\theta̓}$ from c and c̓, leading to a particularly complex set of conditioned sound changes.) A second palatalization process took place in the Southern Interior languages Coeur D'Alene and Salish-Spokane-Kalispel, and a third (which was still in progress for the last generation of L1 speakers) in the Tsamosan languages Upper Chehalis and Cowlitz.

Interior Salish has velar (ɣ, ɣ̓) and post-velar (ʕ, ʕ̓, ʕʷ, ʕ̓ʷ) resonant series, both missing on the coast. Post-velars are most highly developed in Moses Columbia, which has innovated voiceless pharyngeal (ħ ħʷ) to complement the voiced ones present elsewhere in the Interior. In her extensive acoustic investigation of post-velar articulation, Bessell (1992) found that post-velar resonants were true pharyngeals in all the Southern Interior languages as well as in Shuswap, but that in Thompson they were sometimes articulated as uvular trills. Employing laryngoscopal technology, Carlson et al. (2004) confirmed this finding for Thompson; subsequently, Namdaran (2006) used ultrasound to show that post-velar resonants in Lillooet also have uvular rather than pharyngeal articulation. The absence of uvular-pharyngeal resonants on the coast raises the question of whether they were present in the proto-language and subsequently lost, or arose as innovations in the Interior: current views sway towards the former position.

Interior languages also exhibit contrastive tongue root retraction on certain coronal consonants, conventionally represented with an under-dot as [ḷ ḷ̓, ṣ c̣]; retraction is also present on adjacent vowels and is often taken to be a property of roots rather than individual segments. In some languages, retraction may spread from roots to affixes: compare Lillooet *ʔama-wílx̌* (√good-become) 'get better' with *qəḷ-wíḷx̌* (√bad-become) 'get worse', the first with a non-retracted and the second with a retracted root. Historical reflexes of a 'darkened' /ḷ/ are realized as /r/ in the Southern Interior, which is always articulated with tongue root retraction. Retraction probably arose as the result of the loss of a conditioning pharyngeal, which originally retracted adjacent vowels: retracted vowels then spread to adjoining consonants (Kuipers 1981; 2002).

In contrast to the consonant system, there are comparatively few distinctive vowels in Salish: the basic pattern is a four-vowel system consisting of the cardinal vowels *i, u,* and *a*, together with schwa, though in several languages a further distinction between *a* and *e* has arisen: for example, in Halkomelem and Northern Straits, Proto-Salish *u has lowered to /a/, /a/ has raised to /e/, and then /u/ has been borrowed back or developed from /əw/ sequences, leading to a five-vowel system. The phonological status of schwa is still uncertain: while most Salishanists treat it as present in underlying representations, in many languages its distribution is (almost) entirely predictable from syllable structure constraints and stress requirements, which has led to attempts to eliminate it from the underlying inventory. Bella Coola notoriously lacks schwa, with a concomitant increase in the complexity of its syllable structure, such that resonants and even fricatives may constitute syllabic nuclei (Bagemihl 1992).

Vowel quality in all Salish languages is heavily influenced by surrounding consonants, most strongly by a following consonant, but also by a preceding one. Vowels are typically raised by adjacent high (particularly palatal) consonants, retracted by post-velar consonants, and rounded by labialized consonants, with these effects particularly obvious on schwa. Variability in the realization of vowels means that their pronunciations can overlap: for example, a raised /a/ is sometimes phonetically indistinguishable from a retracted /i/.

In Interior Salish, the phenomenon of root retraction potentially complicates the vowel system. If vowels in retracted roots are contrastive (as argued by, e.g., Kuipers 1981), then in Lillooet, Thompson, and Moses Columbia, each of the four modal vowels has a retracted counterpart /ị/, /ụ/, /ạ/, /ə̣/. If, on the other hand, vowel retraction is always triggered by an underlying retracted coronal consonant, as argued by Czaykowska-Higgins (1990) for Moses Columbia, then it is possible to maintain a simpler vowel system by complicating the consonant system to include retracted /ṣ/, /c̣/, /ḷ/, and /ḷ̓/. A third possibility is to treat retraction as a property of an entire root rather than any particular set of segments, simplifying the phonemic inventory but introducing an extra suprasegmental feature. At least in Lillooet, there is evidence against the latter two positions: there are retracted roots, including √*pə̣m*, as in *pə̣m-p* 'fast', *p(ə̣)m-ị́lx* 'hurry' with no triggering coronals, and there are roots with only partial retraction, such as *c̓əḷs* 'kingfisher' (cf. Lower Lillooet *ʔạ́ḷṣəm* 'sick'), arguing against a root-based account.

Vowel length in Salish is not generally contrastive, though both Upriver Halkomelem and the Tsamosan languages (separately) appear to have been developing a length contrast from vowel plus glottal stop sequences. The same is true of tone, with tonal contrasts emerging recently from historically glottalized segments separately in Upriver Halkomelem and Comox-Sliammon.

Stress in Salish languages was probably originally trochaic, though the PS system is obscured in many languages, and complicated by the fact that both roots and suffixes may contain lexically specified stress (prefixes are unstressed). Particularly in the Interior, morphemes are often classified into "strong" (lexically stressed), "weak" (stressless), and "variable". Post-tonically, vowels often delete and consonants undergo various types of truncation, with this tendency most pronounced in the Southern and Eastern Interior.

Canonical syllable structure is CVC. No Salish language permits onsetless syllables (with epenthetic *h* used to resolve vowel hiatus). Apparent vowel-initial words actually contain initial glottal stop: this is readily demonstrated by reduplication, as in Lillooet *ʔímač* 'grandchild', *ʔəm•ʔímač* 'grandchildren', *ʔí•ʔ•mač* 'little grandchild', *ʔəm•ʔí•ʔ•mač* 'little grandchildren'.[7] Most languages allow complex onsets and codas, with three- or four-consonant clusters common. Bella Coola represents an extreme in this respect, tolerating vowel-less syllables quite freely (a local trait shared by neighboring Heiltsuk-Oowekyala, a Northern Wakashan language). At the other extreme, Comox-Sliammon lacks complex onsets altogether, again under the influence of a neighboring Northern Wakashan language (this time, Kwak'wala).

5. Morphology

Salish languages are predominantly suffixing, exclusively so in the case of lexical affixes, transitivity, and voice. The prefixal domain consists of a small number of fixed slots: several prefixes may compete for the same slot, leading to coalescence or deletion of morphemes. Non-concatenative morphology is widespread: reduplication is particularly common, but infixation and ablaut are also present.

Clitics are also very common and include subject pronouns as well as a range of tense, modal, and discourse particles. In Central and Northern Interior languages, these elements form a second position "clitic string" following the first prosodic word (either the main predicate or an associated auxiliary). In the Southern Interior, the clitic string generally precedes the predicate rather than following it, but Moses Columbia provides an interesting transitional system, with clitics both preceding and following the predicate. Articles throughout the family are proclitics. Some morphemes (notably, the nominalizer **s*- and associated possessive pronouns) can either act as affixes or clitics, depending on their syntactic environment.

Descriptive work on Salish typically makes a basic morphological distinction between inflected words and "particles". Inflected words consist of an obligatory root plus a variable number of derivational and inflectional affixes, while particles are invariant, and forming a small closed class of adverbs, conjunctions, and interjections. In the following section, I give a brief overview of the structure of inflected words, beginning with the root and working outwards to the stem and the inflectional domain.

5.1. Roots

There has been a long-running debate in Salish linguistics as to whether roots are categorially specified (as nouns, verbs, and adjectives) or are category-neutral; see Kinkade (1983) for an exposition of the category-neutral hypothesis and van Eijk and Hess (1986) for morphological arguments for a noun-verb distinction. In the morphology, the issue hinges on the selectivity of affixation. On the one hand, advocates of category-neutrality point to morphological processes which apply cross-categorially (e.g., plural and diminutive reduplication, as well as lexical suffixation), and argue that apparently category-sensitive processes (e.g., aspectual marking on verbs) are sensitive to lexical semantics rather than morphosyntax (Wiltschko 2005). On the other hand, advocates of categorial distinctions adduce evidence based on processes which appear to target morphosyntactic categories independently of semantics. The dominant current view is that at least nouns and verbs must be distinguished morphologically. One well-known argument to this effect (van Eijk & Hess 1986) comes from the interaction of possessive pronominal affixes with the nominalizer **s-*. This prefix is found across the family on a significant proportion of otherwise underived nouns, as well as on a productive class of nominalized intransitive verbs. On nouns, whether "nominalized" or not, possessive affixes are optional: for example, in Lillooet both the non-nominalized noun *kʷtamč* 'husband' and the nominalized noun *s-kíxzaʔ* 'mother' may optionally take possessive affixes, as in *n-kʷtamč* 'my husband' and *n-s-kíxzaʔ* 'my mother', respectively. However, nominalized verbs *must* be prefixed with the nominalizer, and when nominalized, *must* take possessive affixation, as in *n-s-məlyíh* 'the one I married', where both *#s-məlyíh* and *#n-məlyíh* are ill-formed.

In every Salish language, a subset of bare roots may surface with appropriate inflection but without further derivational morphology. Bare roots may be nominal, adjectival, or verbal; however, since any root lacking a transitivizing suffix is treated as morphologically intransitive, even semantically transitive verbs surface as intransitive in bare root form. The majority of such semantically transitive but syntactically intransitive verbs are "patient-oriented" – that is, like unaccusatives in better-studied languages, they license a single internal argument; see, for example, (Island) Halkomelem *pas* 'get hit with something thrown', *tᶿəx̌ʷ* 'get washed', *ləʔ* 'get put away', Lillooet *qʷəz* 'get used', *ʔus* 'get thrown out', and *łap* 'get forgotten'. However, a smaller subset of bare verb roots, known as *control roots* in the Salish literature following L.C. Thompson (1985), patterns like unergatives in selecting an external (agentive) argument: these include Halkomelem *łak̓ʷ* 'fly', *qʷal* 'speak', *yays* 'work', Lillooet *matq* 'walk', *paqʷ* 'look', and *ʔúqʷaʔ* 'drink'. There has been controversy as to how to represent verb root classes. At one extreme, Davis (1997) and Davis and Matthewson (2009) propose to treat *all* verbs as lexically intransitive and unaccusative, with both transitives (overtly) and control roots (covertly) derived by affixation. At the other, Gerdts and Hukari (2012) claim that verb roots are lexically represented as transitive, unergative, or unaccusative, with (in)transitivizing morphology treated as a kind of inflection that appears on bases already specified for transitivity. One morphological argument in favor of the first position is that there is a cross-Salishan asymmetry in the direction of derivational morphology: whereas a number of suffixes derive agentive (unergative) intransitives from unaccusative roots, there are *no* affixes that derive unaccusative verbs from unergative roots.

5.2. Root-Level Morphology

Salish roots may be modified by a number of non-concatenative morphological processes, including reduplication, infixation, and ablaut.[8] Across the family there are four common types of reduplication. The first has the shape C_1(V)- and is productive in Central Salish, where it marks imperfective/progressive aspect on verbs, as in Squamish *wə•włqʷ-əm* 'boiling' from √*w(ə)łqʷ*, *ʔi•ʔłən* 'eating' from √*ʔiłən*. Elsewhere, it is less productive and compositional, with various idiosyncratic and/or archaic uses (e.g., to mark the 'human' forms of numbers).

The second common Salish reduplicant has the shape C_1(V)C_2; it marks plurality on nouns and pluractionality on verbs, and in that function is often referred to as 'augmentative', but it is also commonly found without plural semantics on 'stative' (likely, adjectival) roots, where it is termed 'characteristic'. These two functions may be phonologically as well as semantically distinct: Czaykowska-Higgins (1993b) argues that in Moses Columbia, stress patterns as well as alternations between full vowels and schwa provide evidence that augmentative reduplication is prefixal, as in *ħəy•ħúy-n* 'bother somebody (tr.)', while characteristic reduplication is suffixal, as in *ħúy•ħuy-t* 'bothersome person'.

The third common reduplication pattern involves a (V)C_1 reduplicant, variously treated either as a prefix or an infix, and often associated with a vowel change and/or glottalization. It is used productively throughout the family with a broadly diminutive denotation, with the precise meaning dependent on the category of the root class to which it attaches, as can be seen in the (Upper)

Lillooet examples *s-m•ə́m̓ɬac* 'girl', from the noun *s-múɬac* 'woman', *n-q̓s•ə́sn̓ək* 'giggle' from the verb *n-q̓san̓k* 'laugh', and *kək•ə́kəw̓* 'a little further' from the adjective *kəkáw̓* 'far' (which is itself lexically reduplicated from √*kaw*).

Finally, we find a suffixal reduplicant -(V)C_2 marking inchoative aspect on verbs in Interior Salish, often with a secondary 'out-of-control' connotation, as in Okanagan *k̓ul̓•(ə)l̓* 'be born' and *nik̓•(ə)k̓* 'get cut'. It is also found in Tillamook, Lushootseed, and Comox-Sliammon, in the last marking inchoative aspect on 'stative' (adjectival) roots, as in *tih•ih* 'get big' from *tih* 'big' and *pəs•əs* 'get numb' from *pəs* 'numb' (Kroeber 1988).

Common infixes include a glottal stop which marks inchoative aspect on strong roots in Interior Salish, as in Lillooet *za-ʔ-x̌ʷ* 'melt', *lí-ʔ-əʕ̓ʷ* 'collapse', *su-ʔ-ƛ̓* 'drain out', and (one allomorph of) imperfective (a.k.a. 'actual') aspect in Halkomelem and Straits Salish, as in Saanich *ʔé-ʔ-əy̓əl̓* 'to be borrowing' from *ʔey̓əl̓* 'to borrow', *x̌í-ʔ-q̓ət* 'to be scratching something (an itch)' from *x̌íq̓ət* 'to scratch something'. Another prominent infix is an *-l-* or *-l̓-*, which marks (one allomorph of) plurality in a number of Central Salish languages, as in Downriver Halkomelem *sqələwθ* 'potatoes' from *sqəwθ* 'potato', and *k̓ʷal̓əxʷaʔ* 'boxes' from *k̓ʷaxʷaʔ* 'box'.

Ablaut is attested quite widely though sporadically across the family, usually with a plural or pluractional function, as in Moses Columbia *ciq* 'split (pl.)' from *c̣əq* 'split', *ciʕ* 'tear (pl.)' from *cəʕ* 'tear', Comox-Sliammon *k̓ʷəqʷəxwas* 's/he has split it' versus *k̓ʷiqʷəxwas* 's/he has split all of them', *həkʷʔəmθasuɬ* 's/he hung it for me' versus *hakʷʔəmθasuɬ* 's/he hung many things for me'. Urbanczyk (2004) suggests that ablaut might result from vowel infixation rather than vowel change per se, on the basis of the fact that it almost always involves a full vowel (either *i* or *a*) alternating with schwa or zero.

In addition to internal modification of the root, a number of suffixes and prefixes are attached at the root level. On verbs, root-level affixes are typically aspectual; they include the inchoative suffix *-p*, which attaches to weak roots in Interior Salish, as in Lillooet *ʕʷəl-p* 'burn', *cəs-p* 'stretch', *ɬəʕʷ-p* 'bounce' (cf. the Lillooet inchoative examples above with *-ʔ-* on strong roots), as well as reflexes of the pan-Salish 'stative' or 'resultative' prefix **ʔac-*, missing only in Comox-Sliammon; see, e.g., Squamish *ʔəs-x̌awƛ̓* 'broken' from √*x̌awƛ̓* 'break', Thompson *ʔes-n-ɬem̓* 'on board' from √*ɬem̓* 'get in or on'.

Following the root and associated morphology, we find *lexical suffixes*. These form a large set of bound nominal roots (in some languages, containing a hundred or more members) with "substantive" meanings. Many lexical suffixes denote body parts (and are therefore sometimes termed "somatic" suffixes), but they may also denote common or culturally prominent notions (e.g., 'net', 'canoe/vessel', 'plant/tree', 'house'), as well as locations and instruments. The basic meaning of somatic suffixes is frequently extended to related concepts or locations: for example, **-ucin* 'mouth' is used for openings including doors and river mouths, food and drink, and language, and **-us* 'face' is used for round objects (berries, money) as well as eyes, mirrors, windows, and facing locations (Hinkson 1999). Lexical suffixes almost certainly developed historically from compounds, as evidenced by the frequent presence of a relic compound connector *-al-* or *-aɬ-*, as well as stress patterns and the presence – albeit sporadically – of independent roots with related shape and meaning, as in, e.g., Sechelt *cúcin*, Saanich *θáθən* 'mouth', Upper Chehalis *mus*, Twana *bus* 'face' (Kinkade 1998).

There are two main approaches to the grammatical analysis of lexical suffixes, which are themselves partly based on how roots are represented. The first approach analyzes them as root modifiers, added at a level prior to the specification of transitivity (see, e.g., Wiltschko 2009); the second, based on the assumption that roots are underlyingly specified for transitivity, treats them as cases of (lexical) incorporation (Gerdts 2003). Broadly, the former approach predicts that lexical suffixation will have no effect on valency, while the latter predicts the opposite. In general, the effects of (in-) transitivizing suffixes are the same whether or not a lexical suffix is present on a root, supporting the first hypothesis: compare, for example, Lillooet *sək=kán* 'I got whipped', with the unaccusative verb *sək* 'get hit (with something long)', to *sək-ákaʔ=ɬkan* 'I got whipped on the hand' with the same root and a somatic lexical suffix. However, somatic suffixes do yield a distinctive "medio-reflexive" interpretation when combined with reflexes of the pan-Salish middle suffix **-m*, as in Lillooet *šúp-ləqš-aṁ* 'scratch one's (own) nose', Comox-Sliammon *t̓ᶿək̓ʷ-us-əm* 'wipe one's (own) face': this constitutes a potential argument for an incorporation analysis, on the assumption that the middle suffix here is signaling detransitivization of a transitive verb root by the lexical suffix.

While most lexical suffixes do not affect the morphosyntactic category of the root to which they attach, there is a subclass of nominalizing lexical suffixes, including the pan-Salish instrumental suffixes **-tən* and **-min*, and the Central Salish suffix **-iṅaq* 'person'. Given their bleached semantics and categorial signature, it is possible that these form a separate class altogether: in at least some languages (e.g., Lillooet, Halkomelem), they occur following intransitive and even transitivizing suffixes, indicating they are added at the stem rather than the root level.

5.3. Stem-Level Morphology

Stem-level affixes clearly differentiate between nouns and verbs (with adjectives being negatively distinguished by the lack of either distinctive nominal or verbal morphology). On nouns, the most important stem-level morpheme is the lexical nominalizer **s-*, found throughout the family on about a third of otherwise underived nouns.[9] Given a root-level distinction between nouns and verbs, the nominalizer poses something of a puzzle: it cannot be treated simply as part of the root, because it consistently acts as a prefix for the purpose of root-level morphological operations such as reduplication. Wiltschko (2005; 2009) argues that it is a head of category *n*, thereby reinstating category neutrality at the root level; obviously, this hypothesis depends on all apparently category-sensitive root-level processes (including aspectual marking as well as reduplication and lexical suffixation) being reanalyzed as semantically rather than syntactically constrained.

The most important verbal(izing) morphemes at the stem level are transitive and intransitive markers. All formally transitive verbs are suffixed with a transitivizer, which licenses either a following object or a reflexive or reciprocal suffix. (Bella Coola, which has fused transitivity marking with object suffixes, is the only exception.)

Each language has a small set of transitivizers: choice is partially lexicalized, partially morphologically conditioned (e.g., verbs with aspectual marking take the causative transitivizer in Interior Salish), and partially semantically determined. In the latter case, the most important factor is what is known in the Salish literature as *(agent) control*, which may be defined as the degree to which an agent is able to influence the outcome of an event. For example, most transitive verbs in Central Salish languages allow either a "full control" transitivizer (derived from Proto-Salish **-n-t*) or a "limited control" transitivizer (derived from Proto-Salish **-nəxʷ*). The alternation between them is conditioned jointly by properties of the agent and of the event. With a full control transitivizer, the event is under the control of an agent but does not necessarily have to culminate. With a limited control transitivizer, the event either has no agent or an agent not fully in control of its outcome (either because it is accidental or achieved with difficulty); culmination, however, is entailed. A third transitivizer, the "causative" (from Proto-Salish **-stəxʷ*) is unspecified for control and often acts as a default in environments where the other two are blocked (e.g., on derived intransitives). There is ongoing debate about whether the aspectual effects of transitivizers can be derived from their control properties, or vice versa: see Jacobs (2011) for a recent discussion of the issue in Squamish.

The transitivizer may be preceded by an applicative suffix, which specifies the thematic role of the direct object. Each language has from two to six applicatives, with the greatest number being found in the Tsamosan and Southern Interior branches. They fall into two types, termed "redirective" and "relational" in the Salish literature: as a rule, redirectives mark recipients and beneficiaries as direct objects, while relationals specify a variety of roles, including instrument, source, and theme. Kiyosawa and Gerdts (2010), in a detailed study of applicatives across the family, argue that relationals attach to intransitive and redirectives to transitive bases, thus providing an indirect argument that transitivity is a lexical property of roots rather than being supplied directly by transitivizing morphology.

Aside from transitivizers, every Salish language also has a set of suffixes which mark semantically transitive verb stems as formally *in*transitive: as such, they cannot take object or ergative suffixes. There are two basic types, which we might term "patient-oriented" and "lexical reflexive". The first type backgrounds a patient argument, which may however still be expressed as an oblique DP: for this reason, these suffixes are sometimes referred to as "antipassives", though "active intransitive" is perhaps more apt, because unlike passives, they do not detransitivize a formally transitivized stem. Typical examples include Lillooet *-xal* and Comox-Sliammon *-ʔəm*, as in *xáƛ̓-xal, gət^θ-ʔəm* 'unload (something) from a canoe' and *ƛ̓úč-xal'*, *t̓ikʷ-ʔəm* 'chop (wood)', respectively.

The second type of intransitive marker creates lexical reflexives: its most widespread exponent is the "autonomous" suffix **-iləx* (more common in the Interior than in Central Salish, where it is partially replaced by lexicalized variants of the reflexive suffix **-sut*). Typical autonomous-marked predicates include Lillooet *xáƛ̓-ləx̧* 'disembark from a canoe', *tát-ləx* 'stand (oneself) up', and Comox-Sliammon *θap-iš* 'bathe', *k̓ʷiʔ-iš* 'stand (oneself) up'. The ubiquitous pan-Salish middle marker **-m* has *both* of these uses, depending on the predicate to which it attaches: for example, 'search' in Lillooet is *xʷíl̓-əm*, with a patient-oriented meaning, and 'take a bath' is *šáxʷ-əm*, with a lexical reflexive meaning, while in Comox-Sliammon, 'search' is *t^θiy-əm* (patient-oriented) and 'disembark' is *t̓ikʷ-um* (lexical reflexive).

Intransitive-marked verbs may in turn be retransitivized, most typically by reflexes of causative **-stəxʷ*. Examples of causativized active intransitives include Lillooet *məc-xál-s* 'let or make someone write', Comox-Sliammon *yəq-ʔem-sxʷ* 'make someone buy something'; examples of causativized autonomous-marked intransitives include Lillooet *wəq̓ʷ-ílx-s* 'let something or someone drift' and Comox-Sliammon *təx̌ʷ-iš-sxʷ* 'put someone's legs out straight'; and examples of causativized middles include Lillooet *ʔumík-əm-s* 'take something up stream' and Comox-Sliammon *č̓it-im-sxʷ* 'make someone dance'. Significantly, control roots are also transitivized with the causative transitivizer rather than the usual full control transitivizer. In fact, the latter is generally in complementary distribution with intransitive markers, providing evidence that control intransitives are affixed with a covert intransitive marker, as originally proposed by Davis (1997). Examples include Lillooet *ʔítən-s*, Comox-Sliammon *ʔíttən-sxʷ* 'to feed someone or something', from *ʔítən* and *ʔíttən* 'to eat', respectively; and Lillooet *ʔutxʷ-s*, Comox-Sliammon *ʔuttu-sxʷ* 'let or make someone enter', from *ʔutxʷ* and *ʔuttxʷ* 'enter', respectively.

Stem-level morphology also includes a miscellaneous set of affixes which typically attach outside all other derivational morphemes, but inside inflectional morphology. The most widespread outer prefixes are denominal, with meanings such as 'go to', 'ingest', 'obtain', and 'have'; the last of these is particularly common across the family, which largely lacks the lexical verb 'have'. There is evidence that some denominal prefixes may in fact be proclitics, since they attach to a noun phrase (including prenominal modifiers) rather than to its nominal head: see Gerdts and Hukari (2008) on Halkomelem. Outer suffixes are often termed "abstract" suffixes in the literature; they are semantically quite diverse, encompassing aspectual, desiderative, and intensifying meanings, but are phonologically and syntactically distinctive. Unlike most other affixes, they tend to be phonologically strong (inherently stressed), and are notably unselective with respect to syntactic category, attaching rather freely to nouns, adjectives, and intransitive verbs. Both these properties are illustrated by the Lillooet intensifying suffix *-ʔúl*, which means 'real/authentic' on nouns (as in *sk̓əḷ-ʔúl* 'buckskin', i.e., 'real leather') and 'really' or 'so (much)' on adjectives and verbs (as in *ƛ̓əp-ʔúl* 'so deep', *ʔalkst-ʔúl* 'work too much').

5.4. Inflectional Morphology

Inflectional morphology in Salish largely consists of person marking (neither tense nor number are inflectional categories; see Wiltschko 2008).[10] Every language has a possessive paradigm on nouns, one or two object paradigms on transitive verbs, and up to four different subject paradigms, in addition to a set of "independent" (predicative) pronouns; see Kroeber (1999), Davis (2000), and references therein.

In most of the family, intransitive predicates of all categories take one of three sets of subject clitics, whose syntactic distribution is determined by clause type: indicative clitics occur in most main clauses, subjunctive clitics (often referred to as "conjunctive" in the Salish literature) in optative and irrealis clauses, and possessive subject clitics (homophonous with possessive affixes on NPs) in nominalized clauses, which include most types of declarative subordinate clause.

The three Proto-Salish series are given in Table 19.2, based on Davis (2000) and building on important earlier work by Newman (1979a).

In Central and Northern Interior Salish, subject clitics generally form part of the second position clitic string, and therefore attach to the end of the first prosodic word, which may either be an auxiliary or the main predicate; however, in several languages (including Lillooet, Squamish, Halkomelem, and Comox-Sliammon), indicative clitics may also occur initially, often with a concomitant difference in tense/aspect. In Southern Interior languages (which lack auxiliaries), subject clitics generally precede the predicate.

Though a three-way opposition between clitic series is clearly the original pattern, it has been reconfigured in more peripheral parts of Salish territory. In the Southern Interior, the subjunctive series has been lost, except for a relic in Coeur D'Alene; in Lower Chehalis, Upper Chehalis, and Cowlitz of the Tsamosan branch, the indicative and either the possessive or subjunctive series have been repurposed to mark perfective and imperfective aspect, respectively; and in Bella Coola, a single suffixal paradigm consisting of forms borrowed from the possessive, indicative, and independent pronoun series is used for both intransitive subjects and possessors in noun phrases.

The inflection of transitive verbs is more complex than that of intransitive predicates, consisting of object suffixes and transitive subject (ergative) suffixes, in that order, with the latter either supplanting, supplementing, or alternating with subject clitics, depending on language, clause type, and person (see discussion in Table 19.4).

Transitivizers are obligatorily followed by object suffixes except when the latter are replaced by a reflexive or a reciprocal suffix, although throughout the family the most common third person object is *-Ø*. Most languages have at least remnants of two object paradigms, one 'plain' and one 'causative': the distinction between them is a formal one, triggered by the shape of the preceding transitivizer, with control transitivizers usually selecting plain objects and limited control and causative transitivizers selecting causative objects. The Proto-Salish object paradigms are given in Table 19.3, from Newman (1979b).[11]

Table 19.2 Proto-Salish Subject Clitic Series

	*1*SG	*2*SG	*3*	*1*PL	*2*PL
INDICATIVE	**=kan*	**=kaxʷ*	**=Ø*	**=kat*	**=kap*
SUBJUNCTIVE	**=wan*	**=waxʷ*	**=was*	**=wat*	**=wap*
NOMINALIZED	**n=*	**ʔn=*	**=s*	**=(a)ł*	**=lap*

Table 19.3 Proto-Salish Object Series

	*1*SG	*2*SG	*3*	*1*PL	*2*PL
PLAIN	**-c (< ł-s)*	**-ci (< ł-si)*	**-Ø*	**-al*	**-ulm*
CAUSATIVE	**-mx*	**-mi*	**-Ø*	**-muł*	**-muł*

Table 19.4 Proto-Salish Transitive Subject (Ergative) Suffixes

	1SG	2SG	3	1PL	2PL
ERGATIVE	**-an*	**-axʷ*	**-as*	**-at*	**-ap*

In most of Interior Salish, object suffixes are obligatorily followed either by an ergative suffix or a passive suffix. The Proto-Salish ergative suffixes are given in Table 19.4: they clearly form the basis of both the indicative and subjunctive clitic series given in Table 19.2.

In Central Salish (and Lillooet), ergative suffixes have been partially or wholly supplanted by subject clitics, which originally marked only intransitive subjects (and still do in other Interior languages). In Lillooet and most of Central Salish, the old ergative system has been retained in third person and (variably) in subordinate clauses, and in these contexts the two subject inflections may co-occur, with the clitic attaching to a pre-predicative auxiliary and the suffix to the main verb. However, in Lushootseed and Twana, subject suffixes have been entirely replaced by clitics (Davis 2000).

Languages at the periphery of the family have reshaped the original transitive system more drastically. In the Southern Interior, the original subject suffix series has been retained in transitive contexts, but has been supplemented by additional paradigms based historically on formally *in*transitive verbs and introduced by combinations of the nominalizer **s-* with either the stative prefix **ʔac-* ("continuative") or the irrealis prefix **kaɬ-* ("irrealis"). In both these cases, subject clitics are then used to mark *objects* (giving them an absolutive distribution), with possessive affixes employed to mark (transitive) subjects. In Tillamook, at the extreme south of Salish territory, the original transitivity distinction has been lost altogether, with all indicative subjects being marked by suffixes and all subjunctive subjects by clitics. And finally, at the extreme northwestern periphery, Bella Coola has created an innovative set of transitive subject suffixes which combine recognizable parts of the Proto-Salish subject suffix paradigm with elements of the object and intransitive subject paradigms.

Passives in Salish usually involve a reflex of **-m* (main clauses and/or first and third persons) or **-t* (subordinate clauses and/or second persons). In most of the family, passives are non-promotional, in that although the agent is demoted and may generally only surface as an oblique, object suffixes are retained. However, promotional passives have developed in both the Central and Tsamosan branches of the family, with pronominal patients represented by subject clitics rather than object suffixes.

Nominal inflection is much simpler than that of verbs: in addition to taking subject clitics when acting as predicates, nouns (whether nominalized or not) occur optionally with possessive affixes in both predicate and argument positions.

6. Syntax

All Salish languages are basically predicate-initial, though many languages permit subjects to precede the predicate with varying degrees of freedom. A typical Salish clause consists of an inflected predicate followed optionally by one – or more rarely, two – direct arguments, each obligatorily introduced by an article, with oblique arguments and adjuncts introduced additionally by one of a small set of proclitic prepositions (varying from one in most of Central Salish to about ten in Tsamosan).

Neutral word order for intransitive clauses is usually Predicate-Intransitive Subject-Other (PSX), and for transitive clauses typically Verb-Transitive Subject-Object-Other (VAOX), with VOAX also quite common, particularly in Interior Salish. Order of A and O arguments is generally flexible (though more rigidly VAOX in contemporary Comox-Sliammon and Bella Coola), with neutral word order easily overridden by a range of syntactic and pragmatic factors. Many languages also allow alternate SPX/AVOX orders: in Central and Northern Interior Salish, subject-initial orders show syntactic and semantic restrictions, suggesting they involve topicalization rather than base-generation; but in the Southern Interior they are less restricted, and may be becoming unmarked.

In transitive clauses with a single non-oblique DP, all languages aside from those in the Southern Interior show an effect known as the *One Nominal Interpretation Condition*, following Gerdts (1988): in clauses with two third-person arguments, a single (non-oblique) post-predicative DP must be interpreted as O, never as A. Passive is usually employed in order to circumvent this condition, allowing an A argument to surface overtly as an oblique-marked DP with a zero-marked O. Some Central Salish languages have extended this condition: in Lushootseed and Twana, non-oblique overt DP A arguments are banned in all transitive clauses with two third-person arguments, while in contemporary Comox-Sliammon, they are banned altogether, and passive is consequently obligatory whenever an overt DP A argument is present (see Davis & Huijsmans 2017 and references therein).

Two areas have been particularly prominent in discussions of Salish syntax: category neutrality and non-configurationality. The hypothesis that Salish languages (and those of the neighboring Wakashan family) lack any syntactic (as opposed to morphological) distinction between nouns, verbs, and adjectives rests on two empirical observations. The first is that any lexical category can be the main predicate of a sentence. Salish languages lack predicational copulas, so there is no formal syntactic distinction between predicative nouns, adjectives, and intransitive verbs: compare, for example, Lillooet *šmúłač ti?* 'That one's a woman', *lə́x̌ləx̌ ti?* 'That one's smart', *ƛ̓iq ti?* 'That one arrived'. The second observation is almost the inverse of the first: when preceded by an article, any lexical category can act as an argument. Compare, for example, Lillooet *ta=šmúłač=a* 'the/a woman' with *ta=lə́x̌ləx̌=a* 'the/a smart one' and *ta=ƛ̓íq=a* 'the one who arrived'. Together, these two properties yield what is sometimes referred to as "predicate-argument flexibility": that is, the existence of truth-conditionally equivalent pairs of sentences with predicate and argument reversed. Compare, for example, Lillooet *ƛ̓iq ta=šmúłač=a* 'The woman arrived' with *šmúłač ta=ƛ̓íq=a* 'The one who arrived is a woman'.

Obviously, one way to understand these facts is simply to treat predicates as undifferentiated for syntactic category, as explicitly proposed by Kinkade (1983) and Jelinek and Demers (1994). However, other evidence clearly points to syntactic differences between lexical categories in Salish languages. The syntax of modification, for example, provides a three-way distinction between nouns, adjectives, and verbs, as shown schematically in Table 19.5.

Note that this particular set of diagnostics is purely syntactic, thus avoiding the charge that lexical category distinctions may be merely morphological, as argued by Van Eijk and Hess (1986); see also Demirdache and Matthewson (1995), Davis and Matthewson (1999), Montler (2003), and Davis (2011).

Turning to configurationality, Salish languages have attracted attention in the typological and theoretical literature ever since Jelinek's claim that Northern Straits Salish is a *pronominal argument* language (Jelinek & Demers 1994). The basic idea behind this claim is that in languages such as those of the Salish family with "very rich" agreement morphology (i.e., where agreement is obligatorily specified for all person-number combinations) and optional lexical DPs, the agreement

Table 19.5 Lexical Category Distinctions in Salish

	May Directly Modify	May Be Directly Modified
NP	√	√
AP	√	*
VP	*	*

morphology directly saturates argument variables on the predicate, with the DPs acting as coindexed adjuncts. Though this hypothesis is superficially attractive for Salish, there are compelling empirical arguments against it: first, not all argument DPs are licensed by agreement morphology, which is problematic if agreement directly saturates argument variables; second, A'-extraction is allowed out of argument CPs but not adjunct CPs, an unexpected result if arguments *are* adjuncts; and third, in at least some Salish languages, standard constituency tests such as ellipsis and coordination argue for the presence of a VP constituent, which is predicted to be absent if all DPs are sentential adjuncts. See Davis and Matthewson (2009) and references therein.

Nevertheless, investigation of the pronominal argument hypothesis has provided an important stimulus to work on Salish syntax, uncovering some unexpected results. One of the most striking is the existence of systematic violations of Condition C of the binding theory: it has now been shown for several languages in Central and Northern Interior Salish that pronouns may c-command their referential antecedents across clausal boundaries (Davis 2009 and references therein). This property is almost certainly an intra-sentential reflection of the ability of pronouns to precede their antecedents in discourse, which is in turn likely linked to the broader absence of familiarity presuppositions throughout the grammar: see the next section.

7. Semantics and Pragmatics

In recent years, Salish has been influential in the emerging discipline of cross-linguistic semantics. An initial boost was provided by Jelinek's (1995) radical claim concerning the lack of generalized quantifiers in Northern Straits Salish, which stimulated empirical investigation across the family, including Matthewson's pioneering research on the semantics of determiners and quantifiers in Lillooet (Matthewson 1998; 1999; 2001). This in turn inspired further semantic work on determiners in Squamish (Gillon 2006) and Okanagan (Lyon 2013). One of the most significant results of this work has been the discovery that determiners (i.e., articles) in Salish languages are not only non-quantificational, but also indefinite. More broadly, familiarity presuppositions are systematically missing throughout the family, not only in the determiner system but also in clefts, pronouns, and even with such standardly presuppositional elements as (the Salish equivalents of) 'again'; see Matthewson (2008). As for quantifiers, though it has been shown, contra Jelinek's initial claim, that Salish languages (including Northern Straits) do have D-type (though not determiner!) quantifiers, it appears that at least Lillooet may indeed lack generalized quantifiers: see Matthewson and Davis (this volume).

Another area of intensive investigation in Salish semantics has centered around the representation of tense and aspect. Salish languages do not encode tense distinctions inflectionally: instead, the aspectual properties of predicates, together with auxiliaries, adverbial phrases, temporal particles, and even "absent" determiners on argument DPs (Demirdache 1996) jointly conspire to situate utterances in time. This has led to claims that Salish languages are "tenseless", in the sense that tense specification is absent from the compositional semantics: see in particular Wiltschko (2003) on Upriver Halkomelem. Matthewson (2006), on the other hand, argues that in Lillooet, tense is present as an (abstract) functional head, but that it is semantically underspecified, being marked only for a future versus non-future distinction; she provides evidence that future interpretations must be overtly encoded via a modal enclitic or aspectual auxiliary, in contrast to past and present, which may be contextually determined.

In contrast to tense, overt aspect marking is pervasive in Salish; however, serious investigation of its formal semantics (as opposed to its morphology) has been a relatively recent development: see in particular Bar-el (2005) on Squamish. One phenomenon which has attracted a great deal of interest is the existence of *non-culminating accomplishments* (Bar-el et al. 2005). These are the equivalents of transitive accomplishment verbs like 'build', 'roast', or 'devour', which in English entail culmination of the event which they denote. In Salish languages, culmination is only a (cancelable) implicature, accounting for the well-formedness of e.g., Lillooet *máysənɬkan ta q̓láx̌ana, ƛ̓uʔ xʷʔạy ƛ̓uʔ kʷ smaysc*, in contrast to its literal English translation #'I fixed the fence but it didn't get fixed'. Here, the unaccusative root *mays* 'get fixed' in the second clause entails culmination, but its transitivized counterpart *mạ́ysən* (with the control transitivizer *-ən*) in the first clause does not.

A third area in which Salish has made contributions to cross-linguistic semantics is in the study of evidentials, mood, and modality. One important finding is that some Salish modal systems encode different dimensions of meaning from those in more familiar European systems: rather than distinguishing modal force (existential versus universal), they distinguish modal base (epistemic versus circumstantial). Thus in Lillooet, *k̓a* means either 'may' or 'must' relative to a speaker's knowledge, whereas *ka* means 'may' or 'must' relative to permission or obligation: see Matthewson et al. (2007), Rullmann et al. (2008).

Finally, there has been a growing recent interest in information structure, particularly since Koch (2008) showed that focus has no intonational correlates in Thompson but instead is regulated by word order, with focus systematically associating with the predicate at the left edge of the clause. It is unclear how widespread this typologically unusual pattern is in Salish: it remains an active area of current investigation

Acknowledgments

Many thanks to Heather Bliss, Carrie Gillon, Lisa Matthewson, Gloria Mellesmoen, and Suzanne Urbanczyk for comments which have much improved this chapter.

Further Reading

The most valuable single resource for students of Salish is the archive of *Papers for the International Conference on Salish and Neighbo(u)ring Languages*, housed online at http://linguistics.ubc.ca/overview-publications/icsnl/. The (pre-circulated) *Papers* constitute an invaluable documentary resource as well as representing the cumulative efforts of three generations of Salish linguists.

As indicated earlier, there is a rich tradition of excellent descriptive work in Salish: most languages have grammars and dictionaries, and for many languages there are also quite extensive textual resources. The best way to locate them is via Jan van Eijk's (2008) *Bibliography of Salish Linguistics* (www.sfu.ca/nwjl/Articles/V002_N03/VanEijkSalishBiblio.pdf).

There are several important surveys of topics in Salish linguistics written by authorities in the field. These include Thompson (1979) (general, with a focus on historical phonology), Thompson and Kinkade (1990) (coastal languages), Kinkade et al. (1998) (plateau languages), Czaykowska-Higgins and Kinkade (1998) (general), and Davis and Matthewson (2009) (syntax and semantics, with an annotated bibliography). Kuipers (2002) is an authoritative etymological dictionary of the family.

Three volumes stand out as landmarks in Salish syntax and semantics. The first is Donna Gerdts' *Object and Absolutive in Halkomelem Syntax* (1988), the second is Paul Kroeber's *Reconstructing Syntax: The Salish Language Family* (1999), and the third is Lisa Matthewson's (1998) *Determiner Systems and Quantificational Strategies: Evidence from Salish.*

Notes

1. The choice has been made here to gauge language status by the average age of the remaining L1 speakers rather than by giving absolute numbers, because the latter measure is notoriously difficult to judge. There are two main reasons for this: first, assessment measures for linguistic competence used by speech communities are usually based on self-evaluation, which can be unreliable; and second, even L1 status (based on "natural" exposure in the home) is gradient. Since this chapter is specifically concerned with the analysis of Salish languages as first languages, I do not include the increasing number of fluent second-language

speakers here; this should in no way discount their critically important role in language revitalization efforts.

2. An exception is the Jesuit missionary Father Gregorio Mengarini, who wrote a full grammar of Montana Salish ("Flathead"), one of the three major dialects of the Salish-Spokane-Kalispel language, published in Latin in 1861.
3. Phonemic representations are given here in the "northwestern" version of the Americanist Phonetic Alphabet (APA) standardly employed by Salishanists.
4. The term "resonant" is the one traditionally used in Salish linguistics, but "sonorant" might be more appropriate, given the inclusion of glides. Even that term, however, does not extend to *ʔ* and *h*, which are phonetically a stop and a fricative, respectively, but group phonologically with the sonorants (in terms of phonotactics, for example).
5. The Coast Salish outlier Tillamook appears to be an exception, having developed a set of unaspirated (voiced) stops which contrast with the regular aspirated (voiceless) and ejective stop series.
6. I use the asterisk * throughout to indicate a proto-form; unacceptability (both syntactic and semantic) is indicated by #.
7. A bullet (•) is used throughout to mark reduplication, in contrast to a dash for (-) for affixation or an equals sign (=) for cliticization.
8. Certain types of reduplication (particularly -VC_1- and -VC_2) may be sensitive to phonological rather than morphological constituency, and therefore may copy non-root material. This possibility seems to be cross-linguistically variable across Salish; see, e.g., van Eijk (1990).
9. It is important to distinguish lexical nominalization from two other types of nominalization, both of which also involve reflexes of Proto-Salish **s*, but which apply above the word-level. Predicate nominalization with the prefix *s-* forms NPs from extended projections of the VP, with an obligatory possessive-marked agent; clausal nominalization with the proclitic *s=* derives nominalized subordinate clauses, with an obligatory possessive-marked subject. See Kroeber (1999) and J. Thompson (2012).
10. Lillooet, however, marks number obligatorily in its determiner system.
11. While Newman's reconstruction of the Proto-Salish singular object forms is straightforward, his reconstruction of the plural forms is much less so, as pointed out by Kroeber (1999). Both across and within languages, there is much overlap in the plural part of the paradigm between first and second persons and between the plain and causative series, and the persistent presence of a vowel + l/ɬ sequence (*-al, -ul, -uɬ*) is suspiciously reminiscent of the compound connector also found fused to many lexical suffixes. It is possible, in fact, that there may originally have been no plural object forms at all, with contemporary languages having innovated them by borrowing and repurposing fragments of other morphemes.

References

Bagemihl, Bruce. 1992. Syllable structure in Bella Coola. *Linguistic Inquiry* 22. 589–646.

Bar-el, Leora. 2005. *Aspectual distinctions in Sḵwx̱wú7mesh*. Vancouver: University of British Columbia. (Doctoral dissertation.)

Bar-el, Leora & Davis, Henry & Matthewson, Lisa. 2005. On non-culminating accomplishments. In *Proceedings of the 35th annual meeting of the North East Linguistics Society*, 87–102. Amherst: Graduate Linguistic Student Association, University of Massachusetts.

Bessel, Nicola. 1992. *Towards a phonetic and phonological typology of post-velar articulation*. Vancouver: University of British Columbia. (Doctoral dissertation.)

Bird, Sonya & Caldecott, Marion & Campbell, Fiona & Gick, Bryan & Shaw, Patricia. 2008. Oral-laryngeal timing in glottalized resonants. *Journal of Phonetics* 36. 492–507.

Carlson, Barry & Esling, John & Harris, Jimmy G. 2004. A laryngoscopic phonetic study of Nla'kapamux (Thompson) Salish glottal stop, glottalized resonants, and pharyngeals. In Gerdts, Donna & Matthewson, Lisa (eds.), *Studies in Salish in honor of M. Dale Kinkade*, 58–71. Missoula: University of Montana Occasional Papers in Linguistics 17.

Czaykowska-Higgins, Ewa. 1990. Retraction in Moses Columbia Salish. In *Papers for the 25th International Conference on Salish and Neighbouring Languages*, 89–95. Vancouver: University of British Columbia.

Czaykowska-Higgins, Ewa. 1993a. Cyclicity and stress in Moses-Columbia Salish (Nxa'amxcin). *Natural Language and Linguistic Theory* 11. 197–278.

Czaykowska-Higgins, Ewa. 1993b. The phonology and semantics of CVC-reduplication in Moses-Columbian Salish. In Mattina, Anthony & Montler, Timothy (eds.), *American Indian linguistics and ethnography in honor of Laurence C. Thompson*, 47–72. Missoula: University of Montana Occasional Papers in Linguistics 10.

Czaykowska-Higgins, Ewa & Kinkade, M. Dale. 1998. Introduction. In Czaykowska-Higgins, Ewa & Kinkade, M. Dale (eds.), *Salish languages and linguistics: Theoretical and descriptive perspectives* (Trends in Linguistics: Studies and Monographs 107), 1–68. Berlin: Mouton de Gruyter.

Davis, Henry. 1997. Deep unaccusativity and zero syntax in St'át'imcets. In Mendiko-Etxea, Andrea & Uribe-Etxebarria, Myriam (eds.), *Theoretical issues at the morphology-syntax interface*, 55–96. Bilbao: Supplements of the International Journal of Basque Linguistics and Philology.

Davis, Henry. 2000. Remarks on proto-Salish subject inflection. *International Journal of American Linguistics* 66. 499–520.

Davis, Henry. 2009. Cross-linguistic variation in anaphoric dependencies: Evidence from the Pacific Northwest. *Natural Language and Linguistic Theory* 27. 1–43.

Davis, Henry. 2011. Stalking the adjective in St'át'imcets. *Northwest Journal of Linguistics* 5. 1–60.

Davis, Henry & Huijsmans, Marianne. 2017. Changes in the alignment of arguments in transitive clauses in ʔayʔaǰuθəm (Comox-Sliammon). In *Papers for the 52nd international conference on Salish and neighbouring languages*, 13–46. Vancouver: UBCWPL 43.

Davis, Henry & Matthewson, Lisa. 1999. On the functional determination of lexical categories. *Revue Québécoise de Linguistique* 27. 27–67.

Davis, Henry & Matthewson, Lisa. 2009. Issues in Salish syntax and semantics. *Language and Linguistics Compass* 3–4. 1097–1166.

Davis, Henry & Matthewson, Lisa. This volume. Quantification.

Demirdache, Hamida. 1996. The chief of the United States sentences in St'át'imcets (Lillooet Salish): A cross-linguistic asymmetry in the temporal interpretation of noun phrases and its implications. In *Papers for the 31st International Conference on Salish and Neighbouring Languages*, 79–100. Vancouver: University of British Columbia.

Demirdache, Hamida & Matthewson, Lisa. 1995. On the universality of syntactic categories. In *Proceedings of the 25th annual meeting of the North East Linguistics Society*, 79–94. Amherst: Graduate Linguistic Student Association, University of Massachusetts.

First Peoples' Cultural Council. 2018. *Report on the status of B.C. first nations languages*, 3rd edn. (www.fpcc.ca/language/status-report/2018) (Accessed 2018-05-06.)

Gerdts, Donna B. 1988. *Object and absolutive in Halkomelem Salish*. New York: Garland.

Gerdts, Donna B. 2003. The morphosyntax of Halkomelem lexical suffixes. *International Journal of American Linguistics* 69. 345–356.

Gerdts, Donna B. 2006. Argument realization in Halkomelem: A study in verb classification. In *Proceedings of the 11th workshop on structure and constituency in languages in the Americas*, 61–81. Vancouver: UBCWPL 19.

Gerdts, Donna B. & Hukari, Thomas E. 2008. Halkomelem denominal verb constructions. *International Journal of American Linguistics* 74. 489–510.

Gerdts, Donna B. & Hukari, Thomas E. 2012. A closer look at Salish intransitive/transitive alternations. In *Proceedings of the 32nd annual meeting of the Berkeley Linguistics Society*, 503–514. Berkeley: University of California.

Gillon, Carrie. 2006. *The semantics of determiners: Domain restriction in S<u>k</u>wx<u>w</u>ú7mesh*. Vancouver: University of British Columbia. (Doctoral dissertation.) (Published 2013 by Cambridge Scholars Publishing, Newcastle Upon Tyne.)

Hinkson, Mercedes Q. 1999. *Salishan lexical suffixes: A study in the conceptualization of space*. Burnaby, BC: Simon Fraser University. (Doctoral dissertation.)

Jacobs, Peter. 2011. *Control in S<u>k</u>wx<u>w</u>ú7mesh*. Vancouver: University of British Columbia. (Doctoral dissertation.)

Jelinek, Eloise. 1995. Quantification in straits Salish. In Bach, Emmon & Jelinek, Eloise & Kratzer, Angelika & Partee, Barbara (eds.), *Quantification in natural languages*, 487–540. Dordrecht: Kluwer.

Jelinek, Eloise & Demers, Richards A. 1994. Predicates and pronominal arguments in Straits Salish. *Language* 70. 697–736.

Kinkade, M. Dale. 1983. Salish evidence against the universality of 'noun' and 'verb.' *Lingua* 60. 25–39.

Kinkade, M. Dale. 1990a. History of research in linguistics. In Suttles, Wayne (ed.), *Handbook of North American Indians, vol. 7, Northwest Coast* (William C. Sturtevant, general editor), 98–106. Washington, DC: Smithsonian Institution.

Kinkade, M. Dale. 1990b. Prehistory of Salishan languages. In *Papers for the International Conference of Salish and Neighbouring Languages*, vol. 25, 197–208. Vancouver: University of British Columbia.

Kinkade, M. Dale. 1998. Origins of Salishan lexical suffixes. In *Papers for the International Conference of Salish and Neighboring Languages*, vol. 33, 266–295. Seattle: University of Washington.

Kinkade, M. Dale & Elmendorf, William W. & Rigsby, Bruce & Aoki, Haruo. 1998. Languages. In Walker Jr., Dewald E. (ed.), *Handbook of North American Indians, vol. 12, plateau* (William C. Sturtevant, general editor), 49–72. Washington, DC: Smithsonian Institution.

Kiyosawa, Kaoru & Gerdts, Donna B. 2010. *Salish applicatives*. Leiden: Brill.
Koch, Karsten. 2008. *Intonation and focus in nłeʔkepmxcín (Thompson River Salish)*. Vancouver: University of British Columbia. (Doctoral dissertation.)
Kroeber, Paul D. 1988. Inceptive reduplication in Comox and interior Salishan. *International Journal of American Linguistics* 54. 141–167.
Kroeber, Paul D. 1999. *The Salish family: Reconstructing syntax*. Lincoln: University of Nebraska Press.
Kuipers, Aert H. 1968. The categories verb-noun and transitive-intransitive in English and Squamish. *Lingua* 21. 610–626.
Kuipers, Aert H. 1981. On reconstructing the proto-Salish sound system. *International Journal of American Linguistics* 47. 323–335.
Kuipers, Aert H. 2002. *Salish etymological dictionary*. Missoula: University of Montana Occasional Papers in Linguistics 16.
Lyon, John. 2013. *Predication and equation in Okanagan Salish: The syntax and semantics of determiner phrases*. Vancouver: University of British Columbia. (Doctoral dissertation.)
Matthewson, Lisa. 2008. Pronouns, presuppositions and semantic variation. In Friedman, T. & Ito, S. (eds.), *Proceedings of semantics and linguistic theory XVIII*, 527–550. Ithaca, NY: Cornell University.
Matthewson, Lisa. 1998. *Determiner systems and quantificational strategies: Evidence from Salish*. The Hague: Holland Academic Graphics.
Matthewson, Lisa. 1999. On the interpretation of wide-scope indefinites. *Natural Language Semantics* 7. 79–134.
Matthewson, Lisa. 2001. Quantification and the nature of cross-linguistic variation. *Natural Language Semantics* 9. 145–189.
Matthewson, Lisa. 2006. Temporal semantics in a supposedly tenseless language. *Linguistics and Philosophy* 29. 673–713.
Matthewson, Lisa & Davis, Henry & Rulmann, Hotze. 2007. Evidentials as epistemic modals in St'át'imcets. *Linguistic Variation Yearbook* 7. 201–254.
Montler, Timothy. 2003. Auxiliaries and other categories in Straits Salishan. *International Journal of American Linguistics* 69. 103–134.
Namdaran, Nahal. 2006. *Retraction in St'át'imcets: An ultrasonic investigation*. Vancouver: University of British Columbia. (Master's thesis.)
Newman, Stanley. 1979a. A history of the Salish possessive and subject forms. *International Journal of American Linguistics* 45. 207–223.
Newman, Stanley. 1979b. The Salish object forms. *International Journal of American Linguistics* 45. 299–308.
Powell, John W. 1891. Indian linguistic families of America north of Mexico. In *Seventh annual report, Bureau of American Ethnology*, 1–142. Washington, DC: Government Printing Office.
Reichard, Gladys.1938. Coeur D'Alene. In Boas, Franz (ed.), *Handbook of American Indian languages*, vol. 3, 517–707. Glückstadt: J. J. Augustin Inc.; New York: Columbia University Press.
Rullmann, Hotze & Matthewson, Lisa & Davis, Henry. 2008. Modals as distributive indefinites. *Natural Language Semantics* 16. 317–357.
Sapir, Edward. 1921. *Language: An introduction to the study of speech*. New York: Harcourt, Brace and Co.
Suttles, Wayne. 2004. *Musqueam reference grammar*. Vancouver: University of British Columbia Press.
Swadesh, Morris. 1953. Mosan I: A problem of remote common origin. *International Journal of American Linguistics* 19. 26–44.
Thompson, James. 2012. *Syntactic nominalization in Halkomelem syntax*. Vancouver: University of British Columbia. (Doctoral dissertation.)
Thompson, Laurence C. 1979. Salishan and the Northwest. In Campbell, Lyle & Mithun, Marianne (eds.), *The languages of Native America: Historical and comparative assessment*, 692–765. Austin: University of Texas Press.
Thompson, Laurence C. 1985. Control in Salish grammar. In Plank, Frans (ed.), *Relational typology* (Trends in Linguistics: Studies and Monographs 28), 391–428. Berlin: Mouton de Gruyter.
Thompson, Laurence C. & Kinkade, M. Dale. 1990. Languages. In Suttles, Wayne (ed.), *Handbook of North American Indians, vol. 7, Northwest Coast* (William C. Sturtevant, general editor), 30–51. Washington, DC: Smithsonian Institution.
Urbanczyk, Suzanne. 2001. *Patterns of reduplication in Lushootseed*. New York: Garland.
Urbanczyk, Suzanne. 2004. Plurality and ablaut in Central Salish. In Gerdts, Donna & Matthewson, Lisa (eds.), *Studies in Salish in Honor of M. Dale Kinkade*, 429–453. Missoula: University of Montana Occasional Papers in Linguistics 17.
Van Eijk, Jan. 1990. VC reduplication in Salish. *Anthropological Linguistics* 32. 228–262.
Van Eijk, Jan. 2008. A bibliography of Salish linguistics. *Northwest Journal of Linguistics* 3. 1–128.
Van Eijk, Jan & Hess, Thom. 1986. Noun and verb in Salish. *Lingua* 69. 319–331.
Vogt, Hans. 1940. *The Kalispel language*. Oslo: Det Norske Videnskaps-Akademi.

Wiltschko, Martina. 2003. On the interpretability of tense on D and its consequences for case theory. *Lingua* 113. 659–696.
Wiltschko, Martina. 2005. The syntax of precategorial roots. In Armoskaite, Solveiga & Thompson, James (eds.), *Proceedings of workshop on the structure and constituency of the languages of the Americas*, vol. 10, 100–113. Vancouver: UBCWPL.
Wiltschko, Martina. 2008. The syntax of non-inflectional plural marking. *Natural Language and Linguistic Theory* 26. 639–694.
Wiltschko, Martina. 2009. √Root incorporation: Evidence from lexical suffixes in Halkomelem Salish. *Lingua* 119. 199–223.

20
THE NA-DENE LANGUAGES

Alessandro Jaker, Nicholas Welch, and Keren Rice

1. Background and Genetic Relationships

The term *Na-Dene* refers to the language family that includes the Dene languages proper (also known as Athapaskan/Athabaskan/Athabascan), plus Eyak and Tlingit (also referred to as Athapaskan-Eyak-Tlingit or AET). It is one of the largest families in North America, comprising about 50 languages in the western part of the continent. The Dene languages proper have been conventionally divided geographically: the Northern group, distributed across Alaska and northwestern Canada; the Pacific Coast group, along the west coast of the United States; and the Apachean (or Southern) group, in the southwestern United States and northwestern Mexico. It is widely acknowledged that this division does not reflect diachronic relationships: the genetic picture is much more complex, especially in the northern part of the Dene area, where extended, pervasive contact between languages makes establishing precise relationships challenging.

The taxonomy of the family is a matter of active debate. The tree in (1) represents a picture of the genetic relationships based on the work of Keren Rice, and described in Goddard (1997), Mithun (1999), and Tuttle and Hargus (2004). Individual language names are in italics, language groups in plain text. Names largely reflect those in use by linguists in the 1990s.[1]

(1) The Na-Dene family (Rice-Goddard-Mithun classification)

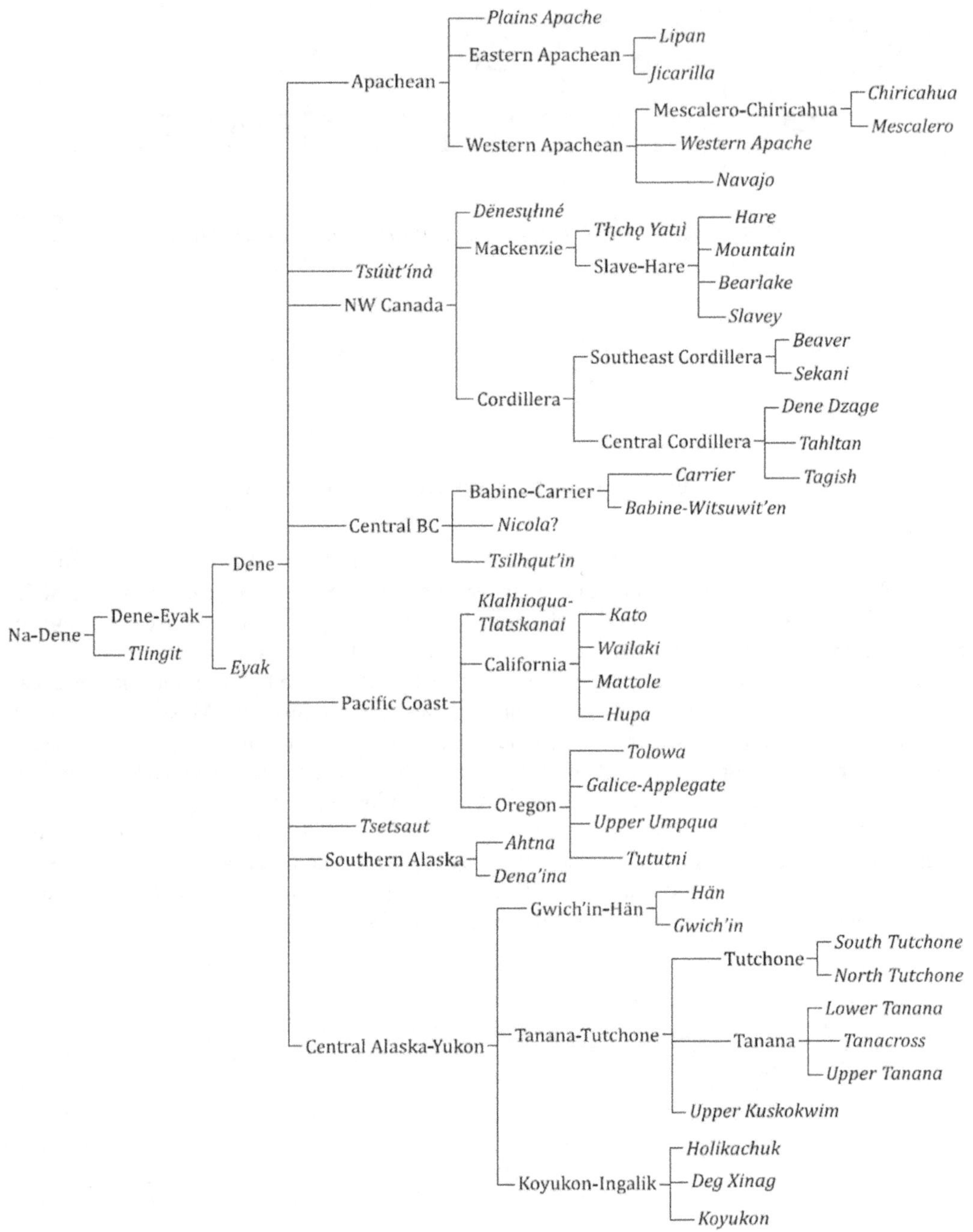

A different classification by Jeff Leer (Tuttle & Hargus 2004: 72–74) groups Ts'úùt'ínà, the Pacific Coast and Apachean branches together, contrasting them with Alaskan, Yukon, British Columbian, and Eastern branches. A dialectometric treatment by Snoek and Cox (2013), applying statistical methods to quantify phonological divergence, suggests closer relationships between the Apachean, Pacific Coast, and Canadian groups than any of these has with the Alaskan languages. It has been recognized since Boas (1917) that Tlingit, in coastal Alaska and British Columbia, is related. Krauss (1964) established a connection with Eyak (Southern Alaska) as well. The resulting grouping is called alternatively Na-Dene or Athapaskan-Eyak-Tlingit (AET). A relationship between Dene and Haida has been postulated numerous times since Sapir (1915), but no rigorous evidence has been adduced. Trombetti (1923) first proposed a link between Na-Dene and the Yeniseian languages of central Siberia, based largely upon verb morphology. Vajda (2010; 2016; 2018) revisited this proposal, supporting it with verbal morphological evidence and sound correspondences that can be derived from comparisons of nonverbal lexica. This DENE-YENISEIAN HYPOTHESIS has met widespread (Kari & Potter 2010) but not universal (L. Campbell 2011) acceptance. The tree in (2) represents the relationships proposed by Vajda.

(2) The Dene-Yeniseian hypothesis

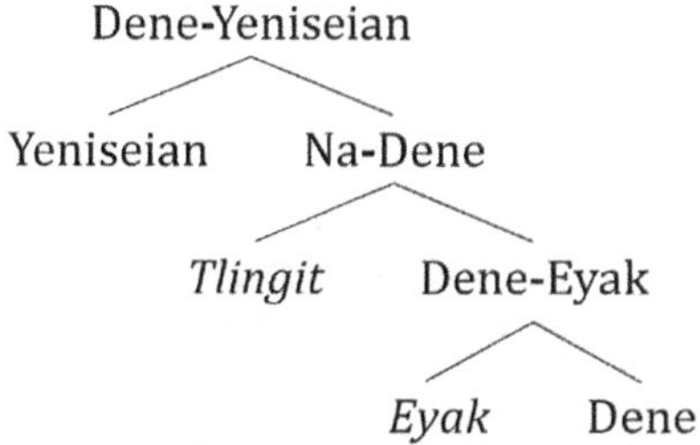

2. Formal Properties

The bulk of this chapter details formal morphological and syntactic properties of the family. The phonetic and phonological side of things we leave alone strictly for reasons of space; for a comprehensive review of the phonological literature, see Hargus (2010).

2.1. Morphology and Verb Structure

Na-Dene languages are morphologically complex. Their verbal morphology has proven especially challenging, since they seem to counter-exemplify many typological generalizations. As Rice notes, "It often appears as if any generalization that one draws about morphosyntax is falsified by the verb of some Athapaskan language" (Rice 2000: 1). This difficulty ultimately stems from the fact that the languages exhibit several different dimensions of structure – phonological, morphological, and semantic – which are (or appear to be) non-isomorphic: phonological constituency seems to have little to do with morphological constituency, and linear order of morphemes seems to bear little relation to semantic compositionality. It is thus difficult to classify them typologically – for example, between so-called 'template morphology' and 'layered morphology' (Simpson & Withgott 1986) – since Dene verb morphology seems layered from a phonological perspective, yet templatic from a morphological perspective.

As a result of these fundamental mismatches, Dene morphology has been approached from several perspectives. The main difference between the models is which dimension of structure they prioritize. The TEMPLATE model and its extension, the INTERRUPTED SYNTHESIS model (Kari 1989; 1992), are good at capturing paradigmatic relations between inflectionally and derivationally related sets of verbs, and capture compositional semantic relations at an abstract level. The LEXICAL PHONOLOGY model (Hargus 1988; Rice 1989; Jaker & Kiparsky, in preparation) is successful in describing the morphophonemic alternations, while the SCOPE HYPOTHESIS (Rice 2000) provides a principled account of morpheme order. However, there is not a unified model which explains the various dimensions of structure. Our goal in this section is to introduce the models and highlight some of their relative strengths and weaknesses, and also to make these models more accessible to interested readers who wish to consult the original sources.

2.1.1. The Dene Verbal Template

A template is a formal ordering device, consisting of a fixed number of 'positions' or 'slots'. Each prefix is assigned a template position as part of its lexical entry, and in most cases only one prefix at a time can go in each slot. The exact number of positions proposed varies, ranging from 10 positions assumed for Navajo (Diné Bizaad; Young & Morgan 1987) to 11 positions and over 30 sub-positions for Ahtna (Kari 1990; 1992). It is not clear to what extent these differences in the number of positions reflect actual differences in the languages, or differences of analysis. In this section, we assume the set of 13 positions proposed for Slavey by Rice (1989) as a general description of the verbal morphology of the Northwest Canada branch of the family.

(3) Northwest Canada verbal template

adverbial$_1$ – distributive$_2$ – iterative$_3$ – incorporate$_4$ – number$_5$ – object$_6$ – deictic subject$_7$ – qualifier$_8$ – aspect$_9$ – conjugation$_{10}$ – mode$_{11}$ – subject$_{12}$ – classifier$_{13}$ – stem

(Based on Rice 1989)

The structural positions of (3) were later re-interpreted as functional projections as part of the Scope Hypothesis (Rice 2000) and given new labels, as in (4) and (5). Under the Scope Hypothesis, certain positions which had been assumed to be arbitrary verb class markers are re-interpreted as semantically meaningful: thus 'conjugation' is re-interpreted situation aspect, while the 'classifiers' are re-interpreted as voice/valence markers (as long recognized in the Dene literature).

(4) Terminological correspondences

TRADITIONAL DESCRIPTIVE	TERM FROM RICE
thematic	lexical
aspect	subsituation aspect
conjugation	situation aspect
mode	viewpoint aspect
classifier	voice/valence

While the Scope Hypothesis does not recognize template position numbers as such, the corresponding position numbers are provided for comparison with (3).

(5) Structural positions in the Dene verb, under the Scope Hypothesis

preverb$_1$ – quantificational elements$_{2,3}$ – incorporate$_4$ – object$_{5,6}$ – number subject$_7$ – qualifier$_8$ – subsituation aspect$_9$ – situation aspect$_{10}$ – viewpoint aspect$_{11}$ – 1st/2nd person subject$_{12}$ – voice/valence$_{13}$ – stem

(Rice 2000)

The template model dates to the American Structuralist era, in works of Sapir (Sapir & Hoijer 1967), Whorf (1932), Hoijer (1946a; 1946b), and Li (1946). This model forms the point of departure for later models, which refer to the template directly or replicate its function by other means (in the case of the Scope Hypothesis). However, even during the American Structuralist era, there were different interpretations of the template emerging. Whereas Li divided the template positions into 'conjunctive', 'disjunctive', and 'in-between' prefixes to account for their phonological patterning (1946: 410) in a way which could be characterized as 'layered morphology' and which anticipated later work in Lexical Phonology, Whorf (1932) explored discontinuous dependencies – his 'split semantemes' – in ways which prefigured work on verb theme categories (Kari 1979) and derivational strings (Kari 1992).

2.1.2. Interrupted Synthesis

The term 'interrupted synthesis' first appears in print in the following quote from Whorf (Kari 1979: 3):

> This trait of split semantemes, of making the expression of an idea depend upon a binary compound that is readily interrupted by the expression of auxiliary ideas or by some of the interrupted parts of auxiliary expressions likewise binomially composed – "interrupted synthesis", to use Sapir's term for it – is the outstanding peculiarity of Athabaskan. The interlocking of a number of interrupted semantemes into a firmly knit structure seems to be a leading principle of coherence in these languages. . . . Athabaskan languages present the appearance of intricate highly patternized combinations of small elements having independent and discernible meanings, but used largely in formula-like combinations. . . . There is, however, much phonetic interaction and contraction between the elements of a combination.
>
> (Whorf 1932: 17–19)

The elements of the verb which most often appear discontinuously are the VERB THEME, which carries the basic lexical meaning of the verb, MODE (consisting of a mode prefix plus a suffix or special stem allomorph),[2] and DERIVATION. In this section, we focus on the most important set of concepts in the traditional (interrupted synthesis) approach to verb morphology – VERB THEME, VERB BASE, DERIVATIONAL STRING, INFLECTION, and VERB THEME CATEGORY.

We begin with VERB THEME, the combination of morphemes which express the basic lexical meaning of the verb – for example, 'eat', 'live', 'speak', etc. While the theme can consist of prefixes from almost any template position, most commonly it consists of a root and a classifier (position 13). An example of a verb theme in Tetsǫ́t'ıné (a dialect of Dënesųłıné) is given in (6).

(6) Verb theme *ya*$_4$*# . . . ł*$_{13}$*-tı yałtı* 'speak' (Tetsǫ́t'ıné)

Verb Theme Inflection

ya$_4$ ne$_{12}$ ł$_{13}$ tı

yanełtı 'you (sg) speak' (IPFV)

Verb Theme Inflection

ya$_4$ he$_7$ ł$_{13}$ tı

yahełtı 'they speak' (PFV)

In Dene languages, INFLECTION is generally understood to include the categories of subject number and person (positions 7, 12) (Rice & Saxon 1994), object (position 6), and mode (position 11). The category of 'mode' includes imperfective, perfective, and optative, categories which Rice interprets as viewpoint aspect (2000: 246–251). Other types of aspectual prefixes, such as that which is called 'conjugation' in the Dene linguistics literature (Rice calls this situation aspect, position 10) or simply 'aspect' (Rice calls this subsituation aspect, position 9), are treated as derivational in the Dene literature because they select different sets of inflectional prefixes, and thus must be added earlier in the morphological derivation (Kari 1992), although Rice treats these as functional. In (6), a discontinuous verb theme is shown, with inflectional information between pieces of the theme. The theme *yałtı* 'speak' consists of an incorporated *ya#* 'speech' (position 4), the *ł-* classifier (position 13), and the root *=tı*.

The semantics of themes is non-compositional – a theme is a basic lexical entry. For example, while *yałtı* 'speak' may have meant something like 'place words', synchronically, *ya#* does not exist as an independent noun in the language, *=tı* does not exist independently as a root, and although the *ł-* classifier can function as a valence marker which adds an argument, it is not obvious in what sense an argument is added synchronically, as this verb is syntactically intransitive. Themes are best thought of as a single, discontinuous morpheme underlyingly, realized as several separate morphs, whose linear position must be lexically specified. One of several DERIVATIONAL STRINGS can be added to the theme (Kari 1979; 1989; 1990; 1992). Examples include the so-called terminative in (7a), translated here as 'up to a point' and *ná#* conclusive-progressive derivational string in (7b) added to the theme *yałtı* 'speak'. Note that the derivational prefix is treated as consisting of two parts, an adverbial and what is called a conjugation pattern. We simplify the conjugation pattern here, showing only the conjugation marker in the perfective.

(7) Two derivational strings based on *yałtı* 'speak' (Tetsǫ̨t'ıné)

a. Terminative *ní$_1$# . . . ne$_{10}$*-derivational string, used with *yałtı* 'speak'

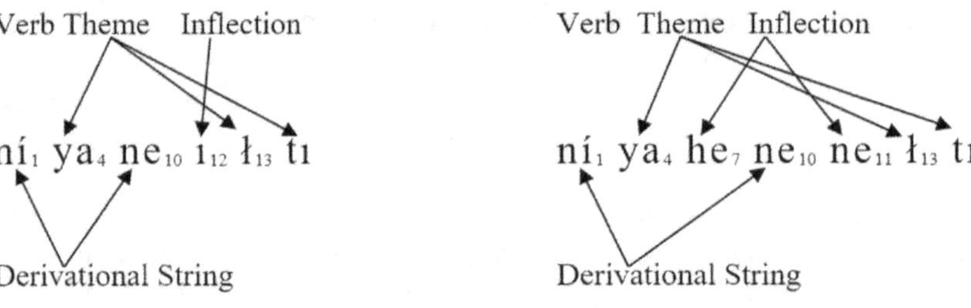

níyaıłtı 'I spoke up to a point' (IPFV) *níyahı̨łtı 'they spoke up to a point' (PFV)*

b. *Ná#* conclusive-progressive *ná$_1$# . . . the$_{10}$*-derivational string, used with *yałtı* 'speak'

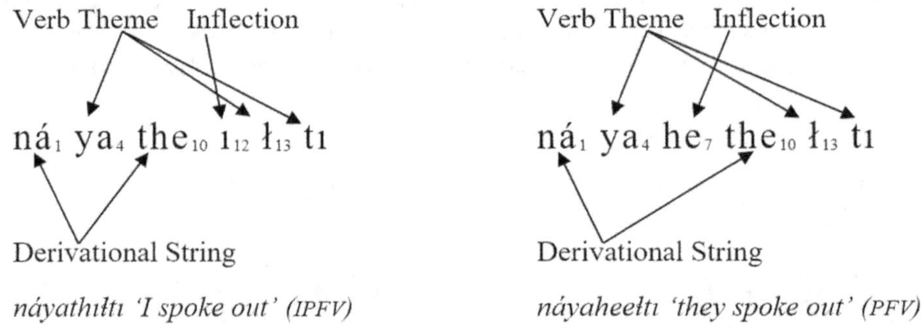

náyathıłtı 'I spoke out' (IPFV) *náyaheełtı 'they spoke out' (PFV)*

The terminative suggests stopping an action or performing an action up to a specific time or place; the *ná#* conclusive-progressive in this case changes the lexical meaning from 'speak' to 'speak up/out'. Both of these derivational strings consist of a preverb (position 1), plus a conjugation pattern. A conjugation pattern describes the set of conjugation markers which a verb uses in the imperfective, perfective, and optative modes. For example, the semelfactive (*hí, the, hí*) conjugation pattern uses *hí-* in the imperfective, *the-* in the perfective, and *hí-* in the optative, while the momentaneous (*ne, ne, ne*) pattern uses *ne-* in all three modes. Derivational strings which require a particular conjugation pattern are called ASPECTUAL DERIVATIONS, while those strings which have no effect on the conjugation pattern are called NON-ASPECTUAL DERIVATIONS (Kari 1992). At least at the level of underlying representations, the verb theme, derivational strings, and inflection are interleaved – this is what is meant by 'interrupted synthesis'.

We are now in a position to understand word formation under the Interrupted Synthesis model. Under this model, we start with the verb theme, add one or more derivational strings to arrive at the VERB BASE, and finally add inflection to arrive at the complete underlying form, which is the input to the phonological derivation. The primary motivation for proceeding in this order is morphological selection: each theme has a set of derivational strings with which it may be used, and the derivational strings, in turn may be used with some inflectional prefixes but not others.

To illustrate, let us consider the first-person singular perfective forms *níyaıłtı* 'I spoke up to a point' from (7a) and *náyathıłtı* 'I spoke out' from (7b), and how these forms could be derived under the Interrupted Synthesis model. A sample derivation is given in (8). Both forms begin with the same verb theme, *ya*$_4$*#. . . ł*$_{13}$*=tı* 'speak', as shown in (8a). However, *níyaıłtı* adds the terminative derivational string, while *náyathıłtı* adds the conclusive-progressive derivational string, as in (8b). This results in two different verb bases (8c). To both of these verb bases, we then add the first-person singular perfective prefix *ı*$_{12}$ as shown in (8d), and we also select the perfective conjugation markers *ne-* and *the-* from the (*ne, ne, ne*) and (*ghe, the, Ø*) conjugation patterns, respectively, resulting in the underlying forms in (8e). Finally, the application of phonological rules to these underlying forms results in the surface forms in (8f). Under some versions of the Interrupted Synthesis model (e.g., Kari 1990; 1992), the structure of the template also includes different phonological boundary symbols, in between template positions belonging to different position classes (i.e., *disjunct #, conjunct –, stem =*). This results in prefixes in different positions having different boundary symbols following them (e.g., *ya#, ne–, ł=*), and these boundary symbols can, in turn, condition different sets of phonological rules. In this way, the Interrupted Synthesis model can also describe many of the phonological patterns which are accounted for by level ordering in the Lexical Phonology model (see §2.1.3).

(8) Example of derivation under the Interrupted Synthesis model

a.	VERB THEME	*ya*$_4$*#. . . ł*$_{13}$ *= tı* 'speak'	*ya*$_4$*#. . . ł*$_{13}$ *= tı* 'speak'
b.	DERIVATIONAL STRING	*ní*$_1$*# . . . (ne, ne, ne)*$_{10}$*-* TERMINATIVE	*ná*$_1$*#. . . (ghe, the, Ø)*$_{10}$*-* CONCLUSIVE-PROGRESSIVE
c.	VERB BASE	***ní*$_1$*#. . . ya*$_4$*#. . .(ne, ne, ne)*$_{10}$** *-. . .ł*$_{13}$ *= tı* 'speak up to a point' 'speak up to a point'	***ná*$_1$*#. . . ya*$_4$*#. . .(ghe, the, Ø)*$_{10}$** *-. . .ł*$_{13}$ *= tı* 'speak out' 'speak out'
d.	INFLECTION	***ı*$_{12}$*-*** PFV.1SG	***ı*$_{12}$*-*** PFV.1SG
e.	UNDERLYING FORM	*ní*$_1$*#ya*$_4$*#ne*$_{10}$*-ı*$_{12}$*-ł*$_{13}$ = tı 'I spoke up to a point'	*ní*$_1$*#ya*$_4$*#the*$_{10}$*-ı*$_{12}$*-ł*$_{13}$ *= tı* 'I spoke out'
f.	SURFACE FORM	***níyaıłtı***	***náyathıłtı***

The set of derivational strings which a verb theme is allowed to take is to some extent idiosyncratic, but is also to some extent governed by a system of verb theme categories (Kari 1979; 1992; Rice 1989). This system roughly corresponds to lexical aspects of verbs – that is, situation aspect (Rice 2000: 251–323). The basic verb theme categories are given in (9), along with the situation aspect category to which they correspond.

(9) Verb theme categories and situation aspect in Tetsǫ́t'ıné

VERB THEME CATEGORY (Kari 1979; Rice 1989)	SITUATION ASPECT (Rice 2000)	*PRIMARY ASPECTUAL STRING* (IPFV, PFV, OPT)
operative	activity	*Ø, ghe, Ø*
conversive	accomplishment	*Ø, the, Ø*
successive	semelfactive	*hi, the, hi*
motion	achievement	*ne, ne, ne*

The term PRIMARY ASPECTUAL STRING refers to the conjugation pattern selected for a verb of a particular verb theme category if no derivational strings are present. In addition to explaining default conjugation patterns, the verb theme category system predicts a verb theme's DERIVATIONAL POTENTIAL – or the set of derivational strings with which a given verb theme may be used. For example, while successive (semelfactive) verbs may be freely used with the operative (activity) conjugation pattern, to express repeated action (e.g., ***th****ılk'éth* 'I shot [once] vs. ***h****ılk'éth* 'I shot [repeatedly]'), the reverse is not true: the verb 'work' is an operative verb and may not be used with the successive (semelfactive) conjugation pattern. Thus, one can only say *ʔeghálaasna* 'I work [for an extended period of time]', not **ʔeghálaísna* 'I work [suddenly]'.

The strength of the interrupted synthesis model is in providing a descriptively adequate account of the highly complex morphological patterns of Dene languages. It provides an account of derivational potential – that is, the ability of verbs in certain verb theme categories to take certain derivational strings productively – as well as a means by which to describe idiosyncratic patterns and irregular verbs. It can easily describe discontinuous dependencies within the Dene verb. Finally, this model provides an elegant account of how the lexicon is organized: a single verb theme can have several verb bases (i.e., with different derivational strings), and each verb base can have a whole paradigm of inflected forms. This model is useful for practical purposes such as lexicography, documentation, and revitalization.

Two main types of phenomena are largely unexplained under this model. The first is phonological constituency. While it is true that the Interrupted Synthesis model can describe the differing phonological behavior of prefixes in different positions through the use of different boundary symbols, as shown in (8), the use of these symbols seems unrelated to any other structural property of the verb under this model. That is, while the purely morphological structure of the verb seems to involve discontinuous constituents – an observation captured elegantly by the Interrupted Synthesis model – from a phonological perspective, the verb seems to be built up inside-out, from right to left. It was this other type of evidence – evidence suggesting a right-branching tree structure – which motivated the Lexical Phonology model, described in the next section. The other main unexplained phenomenon is morpheme order itself: while the Interrupted Synthesis model provides a descriptively adequate account of which prefixes appear in which positions, it does not provide an explanation of why the prefixes occur in the order they do. It was the search for an answer to the latter question that led to the development of the Scope Hypothesis.

2.1.3. Lexical Phonology and the Stem-Core Model

The Lexical Phonology or 'Stem-Core' model views the verb as constructed through several successive layers of prefixation, inside-out, from right to left. This model was anticipated by the early-20th-century work of Fang-Kuei Li (Li 1930b; 1946), who grouped verbal prefixes into 'conjunctive', 'disjunctive', and 'in-between' categories, based on their phonological behavior.

The terms 'conjunctive' and 'disjunctive' suggest being more closely bound and more loosely bound to the stem. Li observes that there are phonological rules of contraction undergone by the CONJUNCT PREFIXES, but not the DISJUNCT PREFIXES, which suggests a certain serialism: the disjunct prefixes are added 'after' these rules have applied. These observations can be translated into Lexical Phonology (Kiparsky 1982; 1985), where – generally speaking – the conjunct and disjunct prefixes can be re-interpreted as STEM LEVEL and WORD LEVEL affixes. In fact, however, Dene languages require more lexical levels; researchers in lexical phonology argue for four or five levels (plus a postlexical level) (Rice 1982; 1989; Hargus 1988; Jaker 2012; Jaker & Kiparsky, in preparation). This model has been referred to as the STEM-CORE MODEL (Halpern 1992).

(10) The Stem-Core model

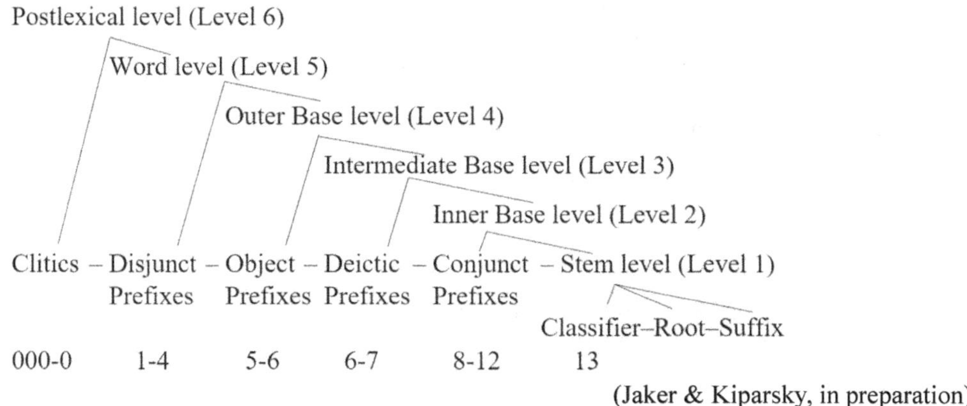

(Jaker & Kiparsky, in preparation)

Two main principles are used to assign a prefix to a level. The first is *linear order*: the word is built outwards from the root, from right to left. If B is to the left of A, then B will always be added either at the same level as A, or later than A. The second is *participation in phonological processes*. A Level 1 morpheme will participate in phonological processes of Levels 1–6, a Level 2 prefix will participate in the phonological processes of Levels 2–6 but not 1, etc.

The Lexical Phonology (LP) model, with its use of level ordering and a right-branching sublexical constituent structure, is successful in providing a phonological explanation for the complex and opaque morphophonemic alternations in Dene languages – alternations which, in other frameworks, require extensive use of morphologically conditioned phonology (e.g., Coleman 1976; Ackroyd 1982), or of lexically listed allomorphy (e.g., McDonough 1990; Holden 2013). The LP model also relates phonological patterning to morphological structure. The LP model, when applied to Dene languages, is an extension of the template model, in that it assumes position-class information as its point of departure: it is assumed that each prefix contains, as part of its lexical entry, a specification for the template position to which it belongs, and prefixes are grouped together into levels based on their template positions. In this sense, both the interrupted synthesis model and the LP model are template-based, although they build different types of structure off of this common representational basis.

There are two major disadvantages of the LP model. One is that the type of morphological structure assumed under the model, i.e., a right-branching tree, bears no relation to the system of verb theme, verb bases, aspects, derivational strings, and verb theme categories described by the Interrupted Synthesis model. The LP model offers no account of morphological productivity or derivational potential, and discontinuous strings have no formal status. At best, it might be possible to reconcile the LP model with the Interrupted Synthesis model by supposing that the LP model operates on the output of the Interrupted Synthesis model (that is, the phonological derivation begins after all of the prefixes have been selected and arranged in order, by an independent word-formation procedure). The other disadvantage to the LP model is that, like the Interrupted Synthesis model, the LP model assumes a set of template positions as a formal ordering device, without any principled explanation for morpheme order. These shortcomings of the LP model led to the development of a third model, the Scope Hypothesis.

2.1.4. The Scope Hypothesis

The primary motivation for the Scope Hypothesis model is to explain morpheme order. This model dispenses with the template as a formal device, seeking to derive surface morpheme order from principles of SEMANTIC SCOPE. The verb is represented structurally as a syntactic tree, and morphemes higher in the tree c-command, and therefore take scope over, morphemes lower in the tree.

A (simplified) illustration of the syntactic structure assumed by Rice is given in (11). Templatic positions corresponding to those in (3) and (5) are given in angle brackets; the model posits that the verb stem is raised to a position right of position <12> before spell-out, leaving positions <1> and <2,3> linearly adjacent.

(11) Syntactic representation of Dene verb structure

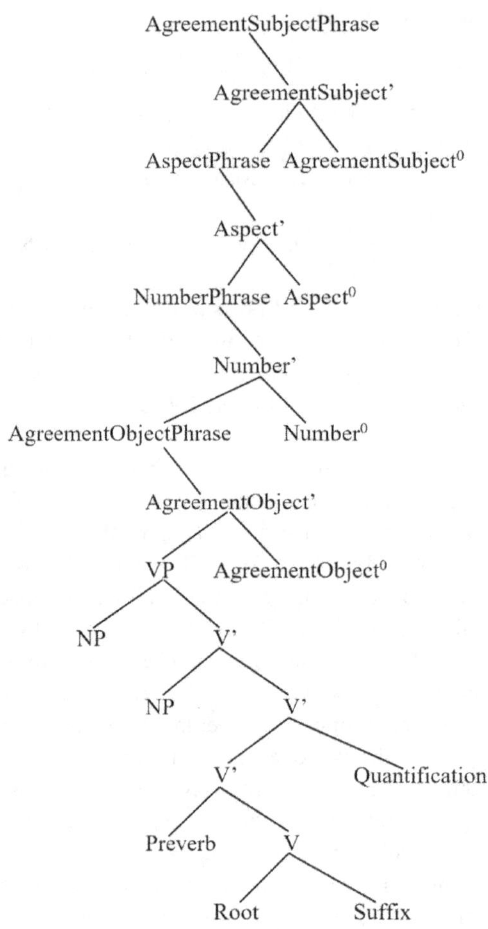

(Based on Rice 2000: 28)

The representation in (11) provides an explanation of morpheme order generally and brings our understanding of the Dene verb in line with well-established typological generalizations about syntax, to which it would otherwise be a counterexample. For example, the MIRROR PRINCIPLE (Baker 1985; 1988) predicts that, whether a language is prefixing or suffixing, subject agreement should occur outside of object agreement. Dene languages appear to counterexemplify this generalization, since they are prefixing with object agreement appearing to the left of subject agreement. Under the Scope Hypothesis, Dene languages are actually not a counterexample: at a deep level of structure, the root and suffix actually originate at the bottom of the tree and raise to the right edge of the clause before spell-out. In other words, the verbal root + suffix (i.e., the 'stem') appears to be in the 'wrong place' on the surface, as a result of syntactic movement: "The verb stem originates as a sister to the preverbs. . . . Given this position, the Athapaskan verb is, at a deep level, not a counterexample to the generalization that inflection is outside derivation" (Rice 2000: 78).

Syntactic movement of the stem can also account for some of the discontinuous dependencies observed by the Interrupted Synthesis model. For example, verb themes may include the verbal root, a classifier, and a preverb. Under the Scope Hypothesis, the classifiers are sisters to V. Thus, at a deep level of structure, the preverb, classifier, and verbal root all form a syntactic constituent, and are not discontinuous.

The Scope Hypothesis can account for the derivational potential of the different verb theme categories by appealing to situation aspect. The operative, conversive, successive, and motion verb theme categories in the traditional Dene literature are re-interpreted as activities, accomplishments, semelfactives, and achievements, respectively – in terms of the default lexical aspect of particular verb themes. The fact that certain derivational strings may be used with some verb theme categories, but not others, is accounted for by this model in terms of semantic compatibility or coherence (Rice 2000: 284–295). It should be noted, however, that the number of derivational strings in Dene languages is quite large – in some cases several dozen or more – and so it remains to be investigated how many of these derivational strings can have their distribution explained on semantic grounds.

The Scope Hypothesis is successful in accounting for morpheme order, as well as at least some discontinuous dependencies, and some facts regarding derivational potential. Rice (2011: 182–184) offers an account of some of the phonological problems, proposing that scope can be overridden by phonological factors, with phonologically small affixes attaching closer to the verb stem in scopal order.

Apart from the classifier-root-suffix complex, which forms a constituent under both the LP and Scope Hypothesis models, the structures proposed by the two models seem largely contradictory: the LP model assumes a structure which is uniformly right-branching, while the Scope Hypothesis assumes a structure which is, to a large extent, left-branching.

2.1.5. Summary

In this section, we have reviewed three models of Dene word formation: the Interrupted Synthesis model, the Lexical Phonology model, and the Scope Hypothesis. Each has strengths and weaknesses, and each model was intended to account for a certain aspect of Dene verb structure: the Interrupted Synthesis model focuses on explaining derivational potential and discontinuous dependences, the LP model focuses on morphophonemics, and the Scope Hypothesis focuses on morpheme order. To the extent that these different models propose contradictory representations of verb structure, this can ultimately be attributed to the Dene verb itself: this is a language family in which phonological structure, semantic scope, and morphological dependencies are all, to a large degree, non-isomorphic – at least on the surface. Thus, any formal theory of Dene verb structure is faced with the challenge of attempting to reconcile often conflicting evidence from morphophonology, morphotactics, and morpho-semantics, in trying to construct a coherent model of Dene verb morphology. Although we do not expect a single, unified model to emerge any time soon, each of these models has served to advance our understanding of Dene languages and Dene verb structure, and we hope that work in each of these models and others that have not yet been proposed will encourage additional descriptive fieldwork in Dene languages, while this is still possible.

2.2. Constituent Order

Dene languages, as well as Eyak, are typically described as exhibiting subject-object-verb constituent order, as in (12).

(12) SOV order

a. Tłı̨chǫ Yatıı̀

Dǫ	wehdaà	ekwǫ̀	nıgeet'à.
dǫ	wehdaà	ekwǫ̀	nı-ge-e-t'à
people	some	caribou	LEX-3PL.SBJ-IPFV-cut.up.IPFV

'Some people are butchering the caribou.'

(Saxon & Siemans 1996: 81)

b. Tsúùt'ínà

Nick	Violet	ʔuwà	Gerald	yiʔí.
Nick	Violet	ʔuwà	Gerald	yi-Ø-ʔí
Nick	Violet	and	Gerald	PFV-3.SBJ-see.PFV

'Nick saw Violet and Gerald.'

(VM 2013)

c. Gwich'in

Tr'iinin	nichìh	leii	įį'àl'.
child	rosehip	lots	PFV.3.SBJ.eat

'The child ate lots of rosehips.'

(Yukon Native Language Centre 2003: 146)

d. Eyak

Lila:'	'Aw	ts'iyuh	shAshehL.
man	DET	black.bear	killed

'That man killed a black bear.'

(Krauss 2012: 605)

Adjunctive elements most typically occur between subject and predicate (hence the designation *SXOV* by Saxon (1986: 3)).

(13) Adjunct placement in Tłįchǫ Yatıì

Mıshè	**taa**	**sadzeè**	**t'à**	dzǫ	hoònǫ	ıhk'è	įlè.
Mıshè	**taa**	**sadzeè**	**t'à**	dzǫ	hoònǫ	ı-Ø-h-k'è	įlè
Michel	**three**	**hour**	**in**	muskrat	ten	PFV-3.SBJ-VOICE-shoot.PFV	ANT

'Michel shot ten muskrats in three hours.'

(MLBW 2012)

Tlingit requires SOV in embedded clauses (Crippen 2012: 1), but exhibits much freer order within main clauses (Leer 1991).[3]

(14) Tlingit constituent orders[4]

a. SOV

John	ƛiʿẏ	ʔasʔí·
John	dleey	as.ée
John	meat	3.is.cooking.3

'John is cooking meat.'

(Leer 1991: 25)

b. SVO

John-ǯ	saʔí·	wé	ƛiʿẏ
John-j	sa.ée	wé	dleey
John-ERG	3.is.cooking.3	that	meat

'John is cooking the meat.'

(Leer 1991: 25)

c. OVS

ƛiʿẏ	ʔasʔí·	John
dleey	as.ée	John
meat	3.is.cooking.3	John

'John is cooking the meat.'

(Leer 1991: 26)

Even within the Dene branch of the family, it is common for the final element in the clause to be nonverbal, for several reasons. First, there are postverbal particles that typically express categories such as emphasis (15a),[5] interrogative (15b), speaker attitude (15c), temporal categories (15d–e), and evidentiality (15e).[6]

(15) Postverbal particles

a. Upper Tanana

Jan	Nedzeegn	**ha'**.
this	Nedzeegn	EMPH

'This is Nedzeegn.'

(Lovick 2012)

b. Gwich'in

Zhòh	gòonlìi	**lèe**?
wolf	be.many	Q

'Are there many wolves?'

(Yukon Native Language Centre 2003: 217)

c. Tsilhqut'in

Nick	hejin	**lanh**.
Nick	Ø-Ø-jin	**lanh**
Nick	IPFV-3.SBJ-sing.IPFV	ATT

'Nick is singing (oh no!/darn it!).'

(LS 2006)

d. Hupa

tin	miq'i[t]	xo'ch	na[']diɬ-**te**
road	on	safely	they.HUMAN.travel-**will**

'People will travel the trails in safety.'

(A. Campbell et al., n.d.)

e. Tłįchǫ Yatıì

Dedıı	wıhk'è	**ha**	dehwhǫ	**įłè,**
dedıı	wı-h-h-k'è	**ha**	de-Ø-h-whǫ	**įłè**
moose	OPT-1SG.SBJ-VOICE-shoot.OPT	FUT	LEX-IPFV-1SG.SBJ-want.IPFV	ANT
tłįcho	hǫt'e	**nǫǫ̀!**		
tłįcho	ha-į-Ø-t'e	**nǫǫ̀**		
horse	LEX-IPFV-3.SBJ-be.IPFV	EVID		

'I had wanted to shoot a moose, but it turned out it was a horse!'

(AW 2012)

Further, constituents may be preposed (16a) and postposed (16b) for what appear to be information-structural reasons.

(16) Information-structural ordering[7]

a. Tłįchǫ Yatıì

Eyı	tįch'aà dìı,	Mıshè	yełaįdè.
eyı	**tıch'aàdìı**	Mıshè	ye-eła-į-Ø-dè
DEM	**animal**	Michel	4.OBJ-LEX-PFV-3.SBJ-kill.PFV

'Those animals, Michel killed them.'

(AW 2012)

b. Dene Dzage
Ghanje tū zedlé' dehbéts lî, eskukāni.
Canada.goose broth only he.boiled before **white.man**
'The white man had boiled a Canada goose.'
(Moore 1999: 247)

It is also common for complex adjuncts to be postposed:

(17) Postposed adjuncts

a. Tlingit
Ch'áakw, tléi náx̱ ch'aak k̲wáan a̲an-k̲áawu,
long.ago one NUM eagle community nobleman
du Anóoshi goox̱ k̲a du káani yaa
3.POSS Russian slave and 3.POSS brother-in-law along
has nak̲úx̱ **yú a̲an-k̲áawu dáax-i kalé yík-t.**
3PL went.by.vehicle **DET nobleman canoe-PNS grand inside-at**
'Long ago, a nobleman of the Eagle clan, his Russian slave and his brother-in-law went paddling in the nobleman's grand canoe.'
(Velten 1944: 174)

b. Tsúùt'ínà
Sisàghá xànítìì ilí náts'idiyitlíshdí.
si-sàghá xànítìì Ø-Ø-lí **ná-ts'i-di-yi-tlí-sh-dí**
1SG-grandson buffalo IPFV-3.SBJ-be.IPFV **ITER-0.SBJ-INC-PFV-PLAY-ITER-REL**
'My grandson is a buffalo in the play.'
(VM 2012)

c. Dene Dzage
I ts'įh gādéli dugusādi.
that from they.walked **far**
'From then, they walked and walked, traveling far. . .'
(Moore 1999: 189)

The question of constituent order directly relates to headedness. It has often been assumed, explicitly (Rice & Saxon 2005) or implicitly, that languages of the family are right- headed, at least in the clausal domain. For departures from this assumption, see Speas (1991), who adduces data to argue that Navajo functional phrases are left-headed, and lexical, right- headed. Crippen (2015, p.c.; 2017) argues that Tlingit verbal morphosyntax is entirely left-headed on the basis of verb morphology, and that postverbal elements are adverbial. Welch (2015a) claims on the basis of the obligatoriness of postverbal particles that Tłįchǫ clausal structure is right-headed. Given the time-depth of separation as reflected in trees (1) and (2), and the typological differences between Tlingit and the Dene languages, it is possible that both the latter views are correct. Whether functional phrases are left- or right-headed, or whether this property is subject to intra-family variation, is not yet clear. The fact that different diagnostics for headedness yield opposite results suggests the question deserves more research.

2.3. Nominal Inflection

Na-Dene languages are famous for the complexity of their verbal morphology. By contrast, nouns are much less complex, inflecting only to show that they are possessed or modified, and (in some languages of the family) for plurality.

2.3.1. Possessors

Nouns show prefixation indicating the person and number of their possessor. In most languages, these are similar or identical to the markers of direct and indirect object inflection and postpositional agreement. Certain nouns, including at least body parts and most kinship terms, are inalienably possessed: they are ungrammatical without a possessor. The examples in (18) show Tsúùt'ínà possession paradigms for 'foot' and 'knife'; note while *más* 'knife' exists as an independent word, the *-ká* 'foot' examples have no independent counterpart; the closest is the form *guká* 'someone's foot'.

(18) Possession in Tsúùt'ínà

POSSESSOR	*'foot'*	*'knife'*
NONE		más
1SG	siká	simázà
2SG	niká	nimázà
3	miká	mimázà
3 REFL	diká	dimázà
4	yiká	yimázà
1PL	niháká	nihámaàzà
2PL	niháká	nihámázà
3PL	gimiká	gimimázà
3PL REFL	gidiká	gidimázà
3PL RECIP	atłiká	atłimázà
4PL	giyiká	giyimázà
ANIM UNSPEC	guká	gumázà
INAN UNSPEC		imázà

(Based on Starlight & Donovan 2008)

The forms labeled "4" represent the DISJOINT ANAPHOR (Saxon 1986: 99ff.), which in Tsúùt'ínà, as in most (though not all) Dene languages, marks non-coreference between a third-person non-subject argument and a third-person subject; it has also been called fourth person and obviative (Aissen 2000) (although its syntax and interpretation differ somewhat from those of obviatives in, e.g., the Algonquian languages).[8] Morphosyntactic and semantic factors in the alternations between the forms labeled "4" and "3" differ among the various Dene languages. This is the famous *yi-/bi-* alternation, which has an extensive literature in Dene studies; cf. Hale (1973), Speas (1982), Sandoval (1984), Thompson (1989), Gunlogson (2001), Rice and Saxon (2005), and Webster (2006).

2.3.2. The Possessed Noun Suffix

Possessed nouns may be doubly inflected, with prefixes indicating the person and number of the possessor and suffixes (which may be tonal, moraic, and/or segmental) the fact of possession. However, the function of the latter is not limited to possession; the POSSESSED NOUN SUFFIX (PNS) occurs more broadly in modificational contexts as in the minimal pair in (19). The presence and form of the PNS depends upon several different factors; this topic is treated at length by Saxon & Wilhelm (2016), who analyze the PNS as one of several nominalizing functional heads (little *n* in Distributed Morphology; Halle & Marantz 1993).

(19) Possessed noun suffix and modification in Tłı̨chǫ Yatıı̀

a. dzę̨
dzę̨
'day'

b. sedzę̀ę̀
se-dzę-ɹ̀
1SG-day-PNS
'my birthday'

c. dıı dzę̀ę̀
dıı dzę-ɹ̀
DEM day-PNS
'today'

(Tłı̨chǫ Community Services Agency 2007)

2.3.3. Plural

Nominal plurality is marked on the noun in many Na-Dene languages; in others, only in verb agreement. In most languages, the verbal marking of plurality occurs in two distinct domains: in the stem alternations of the classificatory verb system (see §3.1) and in inflectional agreement (20a–b). The former system includes plurality as one of the many criteria for stem selection, regardless of the animacy of the argument. The latter shows agreement only with animate arguments (only sentient/human in some languages), and the same is generally true for plural marking on the noun in languages that exhibit it.

(20) Plurality on noun and verb in Tsúùt'ínà

a. Dináka tsís ʔaginisdál-là
diná-**ka** tsís a-**gi**-ni-s-**dál**-là
person-**PL** hill LEX-**3PL**.SBJ-TERM-PFV-**walk.PFV.PL**-ANT
'The people reached the hill.'

b. Tsá(***ka**) nàda(***gi**)yíkáás.
tsá(-***ka**) nà-da-(***gi**-)yí-**káás**
rock(-***PL**) ITER-down-***3PL**-PFV-**fall.PFV.PL**
'The rocks fell down.'

(BRS 2014)

2.4. Postpositions

Postpositions inflect to show agreement with their objects. In some languages, this affixation co-occurs with overt nominal objects; in others, it is in complementary distribution with them. For in-depth treatment of the syntax of postpositions in Dene languages, see Saxon (1986), Thompson (1989), Willie (1991), and the various reference grammars (Morice 1932; Golla 1970; Ackroyd 1982; Cook 1984; 2004; 2013; Young & Morgan 1987; Rice 1989; de Reuse & Goode 2006; Hargus 2007; Boraas 2010; Krauss 2015; Begay 2017).

2.5. Temporal Grammar

All Na-Dene languages encode aspect inflectionally in the verb word. Many also encode further temporal categories such as modality or tense, whether inflectionally or periphrastically.

2.5.1. Aspect

Every language of the family marks temporal categories in verbal inflection, including at least perfective/imperfective (VIEWPOINT ASPECT: Smith 1991; Rice 2000). Individual languages mark further categories, such as optative, future, etc. Typically, this information is marked twice: in affixal morphology in the conjunct-prefix domain, and additionally in alterations to the verb stem. In the protolanguage, these alterations involved suffixation (Krauss 1965), and suffixes are still traceable in some of the modern languages, such as Tsúùt'ínà perfective *-n* (21).[9] Stem changes also may involve unpredictable patterns of tonal (22) and vocalic ablaut and suppletion.

(21) Tsúùt'ínà TAM suffixation

a. ʔásaàt'í
ʔá-saà-t'í
LEX-IPFV.1PL.SBJ-do.IPFV
'We are doing it.'

b. ʔáyaàt'ìn
ʔá-yi-aà-t'ì-**n**
LEX-PFV-1PL.SBJ-do.PFV-**PFV**
'We did it.'

(Starlight & Donovan 2008: 353, 224)

(22) Tłıchǫ Yatıì TAM tonal ablaut

a. Mısè Madlę̀ wemǫ eʔı̨̀.
Mısè Madlę̀ we-mǫ Ø-Ø-**ı̨̀**
Michel Madeleine 3-mother IPFV-3.SBJ-**see.IPFV**
'Michel sees Madeleine's mother.'

b. Dǫ Madlę̀ wemǫ eʔı̨.
dǫ Madlę̀ we-mǫ a-Ø-**ı̨**
person Madeleine 3-mother PFV-3.SBJ-**see.PFV**
'The person saw Madeleine's mother.'

(ANON 2013)

In addition, most languages show similar patterns in the marking of situation aspect, also known as inner aspect, lexical aspect, or Aktionsart, and in the Dene linguistic literature typically divided into aspect, super-aspect, and subsituation aspect, and including distinctions such as iterativity, stativity, durativity, telicity, and so forth.[10]

Markers of viewpoint aspect (often called 'mode' in the Dene literature) are sometimes separable from markers of situation aspect.

(23) Separable viewpoint aspect and situation aspect prefixes

a. Dënesųłıné (situation aspect *ni-*, viewpoint aspect *n-*)
ts'ɛnı̨dher
ts'ɛ-**nı-n**-Ø-dher
LEX-**MOM-PFV**-3.SBJ-wake.PFV
'S/he woke up.'

(Li 1946: 414–415)

b. Tsúùt'ínà (situation aspect *ni-*, viewpoint aspect *yi-*)
Sikolà moghàná niyiskó.
si-kolà mo-ghà-ná ni-yi-s-kó
1SG-husband 3-TO-**ITER-COMPL-PFV**-1SG.SBJ-give.container.PFV
'I gave the plate back to my husband.'

(VM 2012)

In less phonologically transparent examples, common in the languages of the Mackenzie and Apachean branches, it can be challenging to distinguish whether the result is true morphological fusion between markers of viewpoint aspect and situation aspect (Aktionsart), or phonology that spells out separate morphemes in phonologically merged forms. The forms in (24) are representative.

(24) Fusion of viewpoint aspect and situation aspect prefixes

a. Navajo
bisééłdá
bi-**sé**-ł-dá
3.OBJ-**STAT.PFV.1SG.SBJ**-VOICE-sit.ANIM.PFV
'I have an animate object in sitting position.'

(Chee 2017: 45)

b. Tłįchǫ Yatıì
dèhtła
de-wh-Ø-tła
INC-PFV-3SG.SBJ-walk.PFV
'S/he started off.'

(Ackroyd 1982: 29)

For further discussion of this issue, see the introduction to Holden (2013) on the challenges of morphological glossing in Dënesųłıné.

2.5.2. Tense

Tense is an area of current research in Na-Dene languages. As an ANCHORING category, that is a grammatical category whose marking is obligatory for the interpretation of a clause (Enç 1987), tense appears to be rare in this family, as morphosyntactic marking of the relation between the speech time and the reference time (Reichenbach 1947; Klein 1994; Demirdache & Uribe-Etxebarria 2000; and much subsequent research) is often optional (Smith et al. 2003). Welch (2015b) argues for an obligatory future/non-future distinction in Tłįchǫ Yatıì.

2.5.3. Modality and Mood

As mentioned in §2.1.2, the traditional descriptive label "mode" in the Dene literature refers to a morphological category that includes both perfective and imperfective, which in syntactic theory are considered viewpoint aspects, as well as optative (a mode) and future (a tense). However, many languages of the family appear to mark additional modal distinctions with postverbal particles:

(25) Modal auxiliaries

a. Tłįchǫ Yatıì

Dıı	nàowo	ładįį̀	ats'ele	**welè**!
dıı	nàowo	ładįį-µ̀	a-ts'e-Ø-le	**we-Ø-lè**
DEM	law	different-ADV	LEX-1PL.SBJ-IPFV-do.IPFV	**OPT-3.SBJ-COP$_2$.OPT**

'Let's change this law!'

(AW 2012)

b. Dënesųłıné

hoʔą́zį́	dúé	**walí**
hoʔą́zį́	dúé	**wa-Ø-lí**
be.bad.situation	really	**OPT-3.SBJ-COP$_2$.OPT**

'It will be much worse.'

(Elford & Elford 1998: 448)

c. Dene Dzage

... dene	kā	kīndāí	dents'ek	**ulḗ**	t'é'.
people	for	you.watch	you.listen	**it.will.be**	then

'Watch and listen carefully for people.'
(Lit.: 'Let it be that you watch and listen for people.')

(Moore 1999: 213)

Whether these mark the same modal categories that are marked by verbal inflection is unresolved. What seems to be quite separate is the marking of ILLOCUTIONARY FORCE, often referred to as *mood* in Indo-Europeanist grammatical traditions. This tends to be marked by postverbal particles in Dene languages.

(26) Marking of illocutionary force

a. Dënesųłıné

nuhdzédułtth'ı	**sánɛ́**
nuh-dzé-du-Ø-ł-tth'ı	**sánɛ́**
2PL-heart-INC.OPT-3.SBJ-VOICE-trouble	**PROH**

'Do not let your heart be troubled.'

(Elford & Elford 1998: 447)

b. Tsúùt'ínà

John	mòò	nilín	**ìla**?
John	m-òò	Ø-ni-lí	**ìla**
John	3-mother	IPFV-2SG.SBJ-COP_2.IPFV	**Q**

'Are you John's mother?'

(VM 2012)

2.6. Complex Clauses

2.6.1. Embedded Clauses

Clausal embedding in Dene languages can be marked by overt complementizers (often derived from postpositions) (27a–b) or not (28a–b). Complementizers may embed purposive clauses in many languages:

(27) Overt complementizers

a. Navajo

Jáan	nitsaaz	si-Ø-lį́į́	**gi'**	á -Ø-Ø-t'é.
Jáan	nitsaaz	si-Ø-lį́į́	**gi'**	á -Ø-Ø-t'é.
John	3.SBJ.large	PFV-3.SBJ-become.PFV	**at**	LEX-IPFV-3.SBJ-BE.IPFV

'It looks like John got bigger/fatter.'

(Willie 1996: 334)

b. Tłįchǫ Yatıì

Setà	xawèehsį	**gha**	nàtomǫehjà.
se-tà	xa-wèe-h-sį	**gha**	nà-tomǫ-e-h-jà
1SG-father	LEX-PFV-1SG.SBJ-tell.PFV	**COMP**	ITER-LEX-PFV-1SG.SBJ-run.PFV

'I ran back in order to tell my father.'

(ANON 2013)

(28) Embedding without complementizers

a. Dena'ina
Ida qut'ana nach' ghedeł iq'qit'a.
chum people toward.us are.coming it.sounds.like
'Chum, it sounds like people are coming toward us.'
(Tenenbaum 1976a: 39)

b. Tłı̨chǫ Yatıì
Ası̨ı̨ wek'èı̨zǫ Yamoòzha wets'èke
ası̨ı̨ we-k'è-ı̨-zǫ Yamoòzha we-ts'èke
Q 3-LEX-IPFV.2SG.SBJ-know Yamoòzha 3-wife
tsà hǫt'e ahxò?
tsà ha-ı̨-Ø-t'e ahxò
beaver LEX-IPFV-3.SBJ-COP$_1$.IPFV maybe
'Do you know Yamoòzha's wife might be a beaver?'
(ANON 2016)

2.6.2. Direct Discourse

Direct discourse quotations are embedded without complementizers in multiple languages, e.g., Slavey (Rice 1989), Dene Dzage (Moore 2002), Koyukon (Jetté et al. 2000), San Carlos Apache (de Reuse & Goode 2006), and Navajo (Schauber 1979; Speas 2000; Bogal-Allbritten 2016). This family is known for direct discourse constructions being employed for what in many languages would be expressed by indirect discourse (Speas 2000). In such constructions, in which the matrix verbs include quotative (29a), hortative (29b), and psych verbs (30–31), the embedded verb is finite, and shows person and number marking consistent with the perspective of the matrix verb's subject.

(29) Direct discourse constructions

a. Tłı̨chǫ Yatıì
Dǫzhìa wenahdì-le dı.
dǫzhì-a we-na-Ø-h-dì-le dı
man-DIM 3.OBJ-LEX-IPFV-1SG.SBJ-remember.IPFV-NEG say
'The little boy said he didn't remember.'
(Lit: 'The little boy said I don't remember.')
(Blondin et al. 2007: 2)

b. Navajo
Jáan Mary chidí neidiyoołnih yó'ní.
John Mary car 3.OBJ.IPFV.2SG.SBJ.buy 3.IOBJ.3.SBJ.say.PFV
'John told Mary to buy a car.'
(Lit: 'John told Mary you buy a car.')
(Speas 2000: 20)

A cross-linguistically consistent property of clauses embedded under what Bogal-Allbritten (2014; 2016) refers to as the ATTITUDINAL VERB is that the interpretation of this verb depends chiefly upon the temporal and modal properties of the embedded clause. The way in which this compositional interpretation is derived is language-specific. In Navajo, when the embedded clause is future or irrealis, as in (30a), the matrix verb *nizin* is interpreted 'want'. When it is non-future realis but headed by a counterfactual indicator such as *laanaa*, as in (30b), the matrix is interpreted 'wish'. Otherwise, it is interpreted 'think', 'believe', 'suspect' (30c).[11]

(30) Interpretation of attitudinal verb in Navajo[12]

a. Háídíígíísh binideeshnish
háídíígíísh bi-ni-de-e-sh-nish
which.one 3.OBJ-on-FUT-IPFV-1SG.SBJ-work.IPFV
nínízin?
ní-Ø-ní-**zin**
LEX-IPFV-2SG.SBJ-**ATT**.IPFV
'Which one do you want to work on?'

b. **Háájółyį́įh** **laanaa** nisin.
háájółyııḥ **laanaa** ni-Ø-sh-**zin**
IPFV.1SG.SBJ.rest.IPFV **wishful** LEX-IPFV-1SG.SBJ-**ATT**.IPFV
'I wish I could rest.'

c. NAME t'aa hó ajít'į́ nisin. . .
NAME t'aa hó a-**jí**-Ø-t'į́ ni-Ø-Ø-sh-**zin**
NAME FOC thus LEX-**0.SBJ**-do.PFV LEX-IPFV-1SG.SBJ-**ATT**.IPFV
'I suspect that NAME did it.'

(Binaltsoos 1997: 76, 82, 105)

Tłįchǫ Yatıì shows very similar patterns. In this language, when the embedded clause is irrealis (31a), the matrix verb is interpreted 'want'. When it is realis but headed by *(nı)dè* 'if', as in (31b), the matrix is interpreted 'wish'. Otherwise, it is interpreted 'think' or 'believe' (31c).

(31) Interpretation of attitudinal verb in Tłįchǫ Yatıì

a. Seagı̨ą nìgııdè dehwhǫ.
se-agı̨ą nì-ge-**we**-dè de-Ø-h-**wǫ**
1SG-friend LEX-**3PL.SBJ-OPT**-arrive.OPT LEX-IPFV-1SG.SBJ-**ATT**.IPFV
'I want my friends to arrive.'

b. Seagı̨ą nìgı̨įde **dè** dehwhǫ.
se-agı̨ą nì-**ge**-į-de **dè** de-Ø-h-**wǫ**
1SG-friend LEX-3PL.SBJ-**PFV**-arrive **if** LEX-IPFV-1SG.SBJ-**ATT**.IPFV
'I wish my friends would arrive.'

c. Nǫ̀gha yı̨ʔà sǫnı gııwǫ.
nǫ̀gha ye-**ı**-Ø-ʔà sǫnı ge-į-wǫ
wolverine 4.OBJ-**PFV**-3.SBJ-eat DUB 3PL.SBJ-IPFV-ATT.IPFV
'They think maybe a wolverine ate it.'

(ANON 2016)

2.6.3. Relative Clauses

Dene languages employ various relativization strategies. A nominal element, the "head", within the clause may either be extracted, as in English *the people$_i$* [*whom$_i$ I saw e$_i$ yesterday*], or remain in situ.[13] Both are common cross-linguistically, the latter especially in head-final languages such as Japanese (Hoshi 1995; Shimoyama 1999; 2000), Korean (Kim 2007), and Quechua (Cole 1987; Hastings 2004). Like some other head-final languages, some Dene languages, including Tłįchǫ Yatıì, appear to contain both head-external (32a) and head-internal (32b–c) relative clauses. Tlingit (Crippen 2012) differs from the Dene languages in having only head-external relative clauses: the presence of a semantic head noun is obligatory for a relative clause interpretation.

(32) Relative clauses

a. Ts'èko amèe ʔelà nàelı xa dìi-lee sìı hazhǫ̀ǫ̀
Ts'èkoᵢ **amèe**ᵢ ʔelà nàelı xa dìi-le-µ sìı hazhǫ̀ǫ̀
woman **who** boat 3.sews FUT impossible-NEG-REL FOC all
gıgà nìgohwho.
gıga nìgohwho
4.beside 3SBJ.arrive.PL
'The women who can sew canoes all rush to it.'

b. ʔı̨łèh kǫ̀ gozìı dǫ taı, dǫ dı̨ hanì
ʔı̨łèh kǫ̀ go-zìı **dǫ** **taı** **dǫ** **dı̨** hanì
one house AR-inside **person** **three** **person** **four** like
nàdèe gıghǫ ʔehts'adı dè . . .
nà-Ø-Ø-dè-µ gı-ghǫ ʔeh-ts'a-Ø-Ø-dı dè
LEX-IPFV-3.SBJ-live-REL 4-about RECIP-IPFV-3.SBJ-help if
'If the three or four people or so who live in one house help each other with it, . . .'

c. Dǫ Madlę̀ wı̨de hǫt'ee welaedì?
dǫ Madlę̀ wı̨-de ha-ı̨-Ø-t'e-µ we-laedì
person Madeleine 3-elder.brother LEX-IPFV-3.SBJ-COP1-REL 3-where.is
'Where's the man who is Madeleine's elder brother.'

(Tłı̨chǫ Yatıì; Saxon 2000: 104, 94; ANON 2016)

(33) Relativizing morphemes

a. Tsúùt'ínà
náhagiyínoʔì
náha-gi-yí-no-**ʔì**
1PL.OBJ-3PL.SBJ-IPFV-look.after.IPFV-**REL**
'someone who looks after us'

(VM 2013)

b. Tłı̨chǫ Yatıì
Eyı dǫ tìa baà wheda ı̨lèe
eyı dǫ tìa baà whe-Ø-da ı̨lè-**µ**
DEM person lake beside IPFV-3.SBJ-sit.IPFV ANT-**REL**
weehʔı̨.
we-e-h-ʔı̨
3.OBJ-PFV-1SG.SBJ-see.PFV
'I saw the person who was sitting beside the lake.'

(ANON 2016)

c. Dena'ina
"Aa', yagheli," qetni łu ghuna chik'dałyuq**na**.
yes it's.okay they.said ANT those killers
'"Yes, it's okay", the killers said.'

(Tenenbaum 1976b: 34)

Head-internal relative clauses may occur with the semantic head in either clause-initial or clause-final position. In at least some languages, these appear to correspond to stage-level (roughly, transient) (34a) or individual-level (roughly, defining or characterizing) (34b) interpretations, respectively.[14]

(34) Relative clause configurations

a. Tłı̨chǫ Yatıì
dǫ nàzèe
dǫ nà -Ø-Ø-zè-µ
person LEX-IPFV-3.SBJ-hunt.IPFV-REL
'person who is hunting'

b. Tłı̨chǫ Yatıì: nàzèe-dǫǫ̀
nà -Ø-Ø-zè-µ-**dǫ**-µ̀
LEX-IPFV-3.SBJ-HUNT.IPFV-REL-**person**-PNS
'hunter'

(AW 2012)

A feature of all languages of the family is that relativization resembles nominalization. In fact, nominalization of clauses is a major source of nominal vocabulary in many Na-Dene languages.

(35) Lexicalized nominalizations

a. Tłı̨chǫ Yatıì:

tı̨ch'aàdìı	<	tı̨lı	ch'a	nàdèe
tı̨ch'aàdìı	<	tı̨lı	ch'a	nà-Ø-Ø-dè-µ
animal	<	trail	away.from	LEX-IPFV-3.SBJ-live-REL
'animal'	<	'one that lives off the trail'		

b. Tsúùt'ínà:
michàdikodí
mi-chà-di-Ø-Ø-kòd-í
3-tail-LEX-IPFV-3.SBJ-be.broad.IPFV-REL
'beaver' < 'one whose tail is broad'

(Starlight & Donovan 2008)

However, Crippen (2012: 8) argues that in Tlingit, relativization and nominalization are distinct processes and result in syntactic objects with differing properties. Nominalizations have no external nominal head and may be possessed, while relative clauses may not. Hucklebridge (2016) points out that relative clauses in Tłı̨chǫ Yatıì may occur as arguments of verbs and in possessive constructions, suggesting that they are nominalizations, a conclusion also argued by Wilhelm (2014) for Dënesųłıné, and by Saxon and Wilhelm (2016) for Tłı̨chǫ Yatıì and Dënesųłıné. Languages like Dena'ina (33c) and Navajo (Perkins 1982), where different kinds of relativizations and nominalizations are distinguished by distinct morphology, are an obvious place to investigate the degree of variation in this area of Na-Dene morphosyntax.

2.7. Nonverbal Predication

Nonverbal predicates in Na-Dene languages include at least nominal and postpositional phrases. These typically occur as complements of copular verbs. A robust property of the Dene languages is the existence of at least two copular verbs that introduce predicates of differing interpretations (Welch 2017). One copula generally introduces individual-level predicates (36). The other introduces both stage-level predicates (37a) and predicates of role or profession (37b).[15]

(36) Copula 1

a. Tsúùt'ínà

Nùwí	dimádzi	**át'à.**
nùwí	dimádzi	á-Ø-Ø-**t'à**
DEM	circle	LEX-IPFV-3.SBJ-**COP$_1$**.IPFV

'This is a circle.'

(VM 2012)

b. Tłı̨chǫ Yatıı̀
Eyı ts'ı edzǫ **hǫt'e**.
eyı ts'ı edzǫ ha-ı̨-Ø-**t'e**
DEM tree black.spruce LEX-IPFV-3.SBJ-**COP₁**.IPFV
'That tree is a black spruce.'

(MLBW 2011)

(37) Copula 2

a. Tsúùt'ínà
Diyí ʔichí góh **ilí**
Diyí ʔichí góh Ø-Ø-**lí**
DEM stick spruce IPFV-3.SBJ-**COP₂**.IPFV
gùnàgugiwátí.
gù-nà-gu-gi-Ø-wá-t-í
LEX-ITER-AR-3PL.SBJ-IPFV-play.IPFV-ITER-REL
'That stick is a spruce tree in the play.'

(VM 2012)

b. Tłı̨chǫ Yatıı̀
Madlę̀ Mıshè wets'èkeè elı̨.
Madlę̀ Mıshè we-ts'èke-µ̀ Ø-Ø-**lı̨**
Madeleine Michel 3-wife-PNS IPFV-3.SBJ-**COP₂**.IPFV
'Madeleine is Michel's wife.'

(MLBW 2011)

There has been comparatively little analysis of this phenomenon compared to the somewhat similar systems attested in Romance and Celtic languages. Willie (2000) examines the stage-/individual-level distinction in the Navajo classificatory verb system without reference to the copula system. Welch (2012; 2018) analyzes the copula system of Tłı̨chǫ Yatıı̀ as dependent upon the presence or absence of an external argument in either *v* or Voice. However, the latter is almost certainly an oversimplification, and there remain puzzling unexplained areas of the pattern, such as Navajo's use of a form of the individual-level copula to mark an optional past tense, the nearly universal use of the same copula in stage-level questions such as "How are you?", and language-specific interactions with animacy, humanness, and sentience.

2.7.1. Minor Lexical Categories

A number of Dene languages have an adjectival category: nonverbal property descriptors, whether attributive or predicative. These lack inflection for aspect, modality, or agreement. In predicative position, the marking of non-default values of these categories[16] may require a copula, as in (38).

(38) Copula insertion with adjectival predicates in Tłı̨chǫ Yatıı̀

a. Sı̨là eya.
sı̨-là eya
1SG-hand painful
'My hand hurts.'

b. Sı̨là eya welì.
sı̨-là eya **we-Ø-lì**
1 SG-hand painful **OPT-3.SBJ-COP₂.OPT**
'My hand might hurt.'

(ANON 2016)

In most Na-Dene languages, adverbs are non-inflecting and tend to be either morphologically simplex or derived from relative clauses. Saxon (2015) has argued that adverbs may serve as complements of certain verbs in Tłı̨chǫ Yatıì, and similar patterns appear to occur in other languages of the family.

3. Semantics

The semantics of various Na-Dene languages have been investigated by Axelrod (1993), Bogal-Allbritten (2016), Fernald (2000), and Willie (1991; 1996; 2000), among others. Here we give only a brief sketch of classificatory verb systems, one of the most fascinating areas of Na-Dene conceptual categorization.

Classificatory verbs have stems whose semantics encode information about their inmost argument: the subjects of intransitive verbs and the objects of transitives. These systems are thus ergative in alignment, though apart from Tlingit (Crippen 2012), the Na-Dene languages are accusative in their inflectional system. The classificatory verbs are a lexico-semantically defined subset of the inventory of verbs, a typologically unusual situation in which to find split ergativity. Depending upon the language, they may fall into subclasses: typically, verbs of motion, location, and handling may involve classificatory suppletion. The stem (occasionally along with the classifier) conveys information about the countability, number, animacy, and shape/consistency of the argument, as demonstrated by the Tłı̨chǫ Yatıì examples in (39). The number of categories in the system varies widely cross-linguistically; some languages have more or fewer productive categories than Tłı̨chǫ Yatıì.

(39) Examples of imperfective of classificatory verbs in Tłı̨chǫ Yatıì (third-person arguments)

category	'fall'	'lie'	'pick up'
default entity	daè**kw'ı**	whe**ʔǫ**	nıì**tsı**
container	daè**htǫ**	whe**htǫ**	nıì**kà**
sticklike entity	daè**tǫ**	whe**tǫ**	nıì**tı̨**
clothlike entity	daè**chı**	whe**chı**	nıì**chıh**
ropelike entity	daè**tł'ì**	whe**la**	nıì**la**
plural inanimate entities	daè**tł'ì**	whe**la**	nıì**la**
animate entity	daè**kw'ıh**	whe**tı̨**	nıì**tı̨**
plural animate entities	da**geètł'ı̨**	**geèhte**	nıì**te**

(Based on Ackroyd 1982; Tłı̨chǫ Community Services Agency 2007)

4. Vitality

At least one Na-Dene language, Eyak, has recently become dormant with the death of the last native speaker in 2008 (Holton 2012). The remainder are all at risk to varying degrees, from Navajo, with tens of thousands of speakers but a declining number of children acquiring the language, to Hän, with fewer than a dozen speakers. The latter situation is closer to typical of the family. Aside from Navajo, the languages with the highest vitality appear to be Dënesųłıné, with several thousand speakers and a number of communities where children are still acquiring it (Statistics Canada 2011), and Tłı̨chǫ Yatıì, with around 2,000 speakers but few new first-language learners.

There are numerous efforts toward revitalization. Various methodologies are in use, depending on local circumstances. Navajo is taught at the college and university levels; Dënesųłıné is now on the curriculum of University Blue Quills in northern Alberta (Holden 2018). In some communities, efforts have concentrated on child learning. Language immersion programs exist for at least Tłı̨chǫ Yatıì (Mantla & Mantla 2014), Dënesųłıné (Jessie Sylvestre p.c., 2016), Navajo (Johnson & Wilson 2005), and probably others. Mentor-apprentice programs, where a fluent speaker is paired with a small number of learners for extended, intensive learning, are in use for Tsúùt'ínà (Steven Crowchild p.c., 2015) and Tolowa (Loren Me'-lash-ne Bommelyn p.c., 2016), as this method has shown great promise for languages with few first-language speakers.

Further Reading

The overview papers on Dene offer an excellent starting point on understanding this language family. These include Krauss (1973), Leer (1994), and Rice and de Reuse (2017). There are a number of excellent grammars of Dene languages: in addition to those mentioned in §2.4, see Kari (1976 for phonology of Navajo) and Li (1930a for Mattole; 1946 for Chipewyan). The Navajo dictionaries (Young & Morgan 1987; Young et al. 1992) and the Koyukon dictionary (Jetté & Jones 2000) are important contributions to lexicography.

Kari (1975; 1979; 1992), McDonough (1999), Rice (2000), and Holden (2013) include in-depth discussion of verb structure. Important works on syntax and semantics include Hale (1973), Perkins (1978), Platero (1978), Saxon (1986), Willie (1991), Bogal-Allbritten (2016), Saxon and Wilhelm (2016), and Wilhelm (2006); Sapir (1936) and Witherspoon (1977) offer perspectives.

Notes

1. In addition to the conventions of the Leipzig Glossing Rules (Comrie, Haspelmath, & Bickel n.d.), we use the following abbreviations in this chapter: ANT = anterior, ATT = attitudinal, EVID = evidential, INC = inceptive, IOBJ = indirect object, ITER = iterative, LEX = lexical affix (or thematic, in the Dene literature), MOM = momentaneous, OPT = optative; PNS = possessed noun suffix, STAT = stative, 0.SBJ = impersonal (unspecified) subject. Examples are cited by source, by author and date for previously published sources, or by initials for fieldwork consultants (ANON for consultants who prefer not to have their names published): AW = Archie Wedzin, BRS = Bruce R. Starlight, LS = Linda Smith, MLBW = Marie-Louise Bouvier White, VM = Violet Meguinis. The data are generally drawn from the Dene group, with a few examples from Tlingit and Eyak; most are from languages that we have worked on and/or that are under-represented in the literature. We use transcription conventions from the sources.
2. In the Dene literature, the term *mode* often refers to a shared templatic position where viewpoint aspect alternates with future, irrealis modes, or both, depending on the language. For further discussion, see §2.5.
3. SVO in main clauses may require case marking on the subject, as well as verb allomorphy, as in (14b).
4. The first line of each example is Leer's transcription; the second is the Tlingit practical orthography, based on examples in Crippen (2012). Further Tlingit examples in this chapter are presented only in the practical orthography.
5. This is perhaps equivalent to clausal focus (Welch 2015a).
6. Or mirativity; these two categories are often marked identically.
7. It is not always clear whether this ordering signals topicalization or focalization. More research is needed on this subject.
8. The third person and disjoint forms are not labeled "singular" as those that are not explicitly plural may have, contextually, either singular or plural interpretations.
9. Note that these suffixes are not universally productive, and co-exist with ablaut and suppletion.
10. These concepts are also discussed in §2.1.2 and §2.1.4.
11. This is a simplification. For full details on this rather subtle topic, see Bogal-Allbritten (2016).
12. The morphological glosses in these examples are our own.
13. Note that the term "head" in this terminology is a *semantic* one, referring to the relativized verb's salient argument, rather than to a syntactic head. Hence, the statement that head-internal relative clauses are common in head-final languages uses the word "head" in two different and unrelated ways.

    Typically, though not universally, relative clauses are formed by the addition of a relativizing morpheme to a clause-level constituent, as in (33), whether attached to the verb, as in (33a), or a postverbal element (33b). In some languages, relativizations and nominalizations are formed with a variety of markers. Hence, in Dena'ina, *-na* marks a plural human agent, as in (33c), and *-i* an inanimate (Boraas 2010: 17).
14. The stage-/individual-level predicate distinction has a large cross-linguistic literature; see especially Carlson (1977), Kratzer (1995), and Roy (2013).
15. The latter, termed CHARACTERIZING predicates by Roy (2013), are individual-level predicates that allow temporal gaps or agentivity, and pattern in some respects like stage-level predicates.
16. That is, perfective aspect, irrealis mode, or non-third-person-singular subject agreement.

References

Ackroyd, Lynda. 1982. *Dogrib grammar*. Toronto: University of Toronto. (Ms.)
Aissen, Judith. 2000. *Yi-* and *bi-*: Proximate and obviative in Navajo. In Carnie, Andrew & Jelinek, Eloise & Willie, Mary Ann (eds.), *Papers in honor of Ken Hale*, 129–150. Cambridge, MA: MIT Press.
Axelrod, Melissa. 1993. *The semantics of temporal categorization: The aspectual system of Koyukon Athabaskan*. Lincoln: University of Nebraska Press.
Baker, Mark C. 1985. The mirror principle and morphosyntactic explanation. *Linguistic Inquiry* 16(3). 373–415.
Baker, Mark C. 1988. *Incorporation: A theory of grammatical function changing*. Chicago, IL: University of Chicago Press.
Begay, Kayla Rae. 2017. *Wailaki grammar*. Berkeley: University of California. (Doctoral dissertation.)
Binaltsoos, Irene. 1997. *Interactional Navajo*. Division of Diné Education.
Blondin, George & Blondin, John. 2007. *Ekwǫ̀ dǫzhìa wegondı* [*The legend of the caribou boy*]. Penticton: Theytus Books.
Boas, Franz. 1917. *Grammatical notes on the language of the Tlingit Indians*. Philadelphia: University of Pennsylvania Press.
Bogal-Allbritten, Elizabeth. 2014. The decomposition of belief and desire. (Paper presented at SULA 8, Vancouver.)
Bogal-Allbritten, Elizabeth. 2016. *Building meaning in Navajo*. Amherst, MA: University of Massachusetts. (Doctoral dissertation.)
Boraas, Alan. 2010. *An introduction to Dena'ina grammar: The Kenai (Outer Inlet) dialect*. Soldotna, AK: Kenai Peninsula College. (Ms.)
Campbell, Amy & Carpenter, Kayla & Escamilla, Ramon & Garrett, Andrew & Newbold, Lindsey & Pycha, Anne & Risling Baldy, Cutcha & Spence, Justin. n.d. *Hupa online dictionary and texts*. (http://nalc.ucdavis.edu/hupa/hupa-lexicon.html) (Accessed 2019-07-08.)
Campbell, Lyle. 2011. Review of *The Dene-Yeniseian Connection* by James Kari and Ben A. Potter. *International Journal of American Linguistics* 77(3). 445–451.
Carlson, Gregory N. 1977. *Reference to kinds in English*. Amherst: University of Massachusetts. (Doctoral dissertation.)
Chee, Melvatha. 2017. *A longitudinal cross-sectional study on the acquisition of Navajo verbs in children aged 4 years 7 months through 11 years 2 months*. Albuquerque: University of New Mexico. (Doctoral dissertation.)
Cole, Peter. 1987. The structure of internally headed relative clauses. *Natural Language & Linguistic Theory* 5(2). 277–302.
Coleman, Phyllis. 1976. *Dogrib phonology*. Ann Arbor: University of Michigan. (Doctoral dissertation.)
Comrie, Bernard & Haspelmath, Martin & Bickel, Balthasar. n.d. *Leipzig glossing rules*, vol. 2012.
Cook, Eung-Do. 1984. *A Sarcee grammar*. Vancouver: University of British Columbia Press.
Cook, Eung-Do. 2004. *A grammar of Dëne Sųłıné (Chipewyan)*. Winnipeg: Algonquian and Iroquoian Linguistics.
Cook, Eung-Do. 2013. *A Tsilhqút'in grammar*. Vancouver: University of British Columbia Press.
Crippen, James. 2012. *Exploring Tlingit relative clauses: Morphology and syntax*. (Ms., University of British Columbia.)
Crippen, James. 2015. *Stem variation in Tlingit*. (Ms., University of British Columbia.)
de Reuse, William J. & Goode, Phillip. 2006. *A practical grammar of the San Carlos Apache language*. München: LINCOM Europa.
Demirdache, Hamida & Uribe-Etxebarria, Myriam. 2000. The primitives of temporal relations. In Martin, Roger & Michaels, David & Uriagereka, Juan & Keyser, Samuel Jay (eds.), *Step by step: Essays on Minimalist syntax in honor of Howard Lasnik*, 157–186. Cambridge, MA, and London: MIT Press.
Elford, Leon W. & Elford, Marjorie. 1998. *Dene (Chipewyan) dictionary*. Prince Albert: Northern Canada Mission Distributors.
Enç, Mürvet. 1987. Anchoring conditions for tense. *Linguistic Inquiry* 18(4). 633–657.
Fernald, Theodore B. 2000. Generalizations in Navajo. In Fernald, Theodore & Platero, Paul (eds.), *The Athabaskan languages: Perspectives on a Native American language family*, 51–72. Oxford: Oxford University Press.
Goddard, Ives. 1997. *Handbook of North American Indians*, vol. 17. Washington, DC: Smithsonian Institution.
Golla, Victor K. 1970. *Hupa grammar*. Berkeley: University of California. (Doctoral dissertation.)
Gunlogson, Christine. 2001. Third-person object prefixes in Babine-Witsuwit'en. *International Journal of American Linguistics* 67(4). 365–395.
Hale, Kenneth. 1973. A note on subject-object inversion in Navajo. In Kachru, Braj (ed.), *Issues in linguistics: Papers in honor of Henry and Renée Kahane*, 300–309. Urbana: University of Illinois Press.

Halle, Morris & Marantz, Alec. 1993. Distributed Morphology and the pieces of inflection. In Hale, Kenneth & Keyser, Samuel Jay (eds.), *The view from building 20: Essays in linguistics in honor of Sylvain Bromberger*, 111–176. Cambridge: MIT Press.

Halpern, A. 1992. *Topics in the placement and morphology of clitics*. Stanford, CA: Stanford University. (Doctoral dissertation.)

Hargus, Sharon. 1988. *The lexical phonology of Sekani*. New York: Garland.

Hargus, Sharon. 2007. *Witsuwit'en grammar: Phonetics, phonology, morphology*. Vancouver: University of British Columbia Press.

Hargus, Sharon. 2010. Athabaskan phonetics and phonology. *Language and Linguistics Compass* 4(10). 1019–1040.

Hastings, Rachel E. 2004. *The syntax and semantics of relativization and quantification: The case of Quechua*. Ithaca, NY: Cornell University. (Doctoral dissertation.)

Hoijer, Harry. 1946a. The Apachean verb, part III: The classifiers. *International Journal of American Linguistics* 12. 51–59.

Hoijer, Harry. 1946b. Chiricahua Apache. In Osgood, Cornelius (ed.), *Linguistic structures of native America*, 55–85. New York: Viking Fund.

Holden, Josh. 2013. *Benasní – I remember: Dëne Sųłıné oral histories with morphological analysis*. Leiden: Brill.

Holden, Josh. 2018. Pedagogies for Cree and Dene language programs. (Paper presented at the Symposium on American Indian Languages, Ottawa.)

Holton, Gary. (2012). Potentials of language documentation: Methods, analyses, and utilization. In Seifart, Frank & Haig, Geoffrey & Himmelmann, Nikolaus P. & Jung, Dagmar & Margetts, Anna & Trilsbeek Paul (eds.), *Language archives: They're not just for linguists any more*, 111–117. Honolulu: University of Hawai'i Press.

Hoshi, Koji. (1995). *Structural and interpretive aspects of head-internal and head-external relative clauses*. Rochester: University of Rochester. (Doctoral dissertation.)

Hucklebridge, Sherry. (2016). *Internally-headed relative clauses in Tłı̨chǫ Yatıì*. Toronto: University of Toronto. (Master's thesis.)

Jaker, Alessandro. (2012). *Prosodic reversal in Dogrib (Weledeh dialect)*. Stanford, CA: Stanford University. (Doctoral dissertation.)

Jaker, Alessandro & Kiparsky, Paul. in preparation. *Conjugation tone mapping in Tetsǫ́t'ıné (Yellowknife): Level ordering and opacity*. Stanford, CA: Stanford University (Ms.)

Jetté, Jules & Jones, Eliza & Kari, James M. (2000). *Koyukon Athabaskan dictionary*. Fairbanks: Alaska Native Language Center.

Johnson, Florian Tom & Wilson, Jennifer. (2005). Navajo immersion in the Navajo Nation. In Reyner, Jon (ed.), *Indigenous Bilingual Education*. 30–31.

Kari, James M. 1975. The disjunct boundary in the Navajo and Tanaina verb prefix complexes. *International Journal of American Linguistics* 41. 330–346.

Kari, James M. 1976. *Navajo verb prefix phonology*. New York: Garland.

Kari, James M. 1979. *Athabaskan verb theme categories: Ahtna*, vol. 2. Fairbanks: Alaska Native Language Center.

Kari, James M. 1989. Affix position and zones in the Athapaskan verb complex: Ahtna and Navajo. *International Journal of American Linguistics* 55(4). 424–454.

Kari, James M. 1990. *Ahtna Athabaskan dictionary*. Fairbanks: Alaska Native Language Center.

Kari, James M. 1992. Some concepts in Ahtna Athabaskan word formation. In Aronoff, Mark (ed.), *Morphology now*, 107–132. Albany: Suny Press.

Kari, James M. & Potter, Ben A. (eds.). 2010. *The Dene-Yeniseian connection*. Fairbanks: Alaska Native Language Center.

Kim, Min-Joo. 2007. Formal linking in internally headed relatives. *Natural Language Semantics* 15(4). 279–315.

Kiparsky, Paul. 1982. Lexical phonology and morphology. In Linguistics Society of Korea (ed.), *Linguistics in the morning calm*. Seoul: Hanshin Publishers.

Kiparsky, Paul. 1985. Some consequences of lexical phonology. *Phonology Yearbook* 2. 85–138.

Klein, Wolfgang. 1994. *Time in language*. London: Routledge.

Kratzer, Angelika. 1995. Stage-level and individual-level predicates. In Carlson, Gregory & Pelletier, F. Jeffry (eds.), *The generic book*, 125–175. Chicago, IL: University of Chicago Press.

Krauss, Michael. 1964. Proto-Athapaskan-Eyak and the problem of Na-Dene: The phonology. *International Journal of American Linguistics* 30(2). 118–131.

Krauss, Michael. 1965. Proto-Athapaskan-Eyak and the problem of Na-Dene II: Morphology. *International Journal of American Linguistics* 31(1). 18–28.

Krauss, Michael. 1973. Na-Dene. In Sebeok, Thomas A. (ed.), *Linguistics in North America*. The Hague: Mouton.

Krauss, Michael. 2012. *Eyak dictionary*. Alaska Native Language Center (Ms.)

Krauss, Michael. 2015. *Eyak grammar*. Alaska Native Language Center (Ms.)

Leer, Jeffry. 1991. *The schetic categories of the Tlingit verb*. Chicago, IL: University of Chicago. (Doctoral dissertation.)

Leer, Jeffry. 1994. Na-Dene languages. In Asher, R. & Simpson, J. (eds.), *The encyclopedia of languages and linguistics*, 2665–2666. Oxford: Pergamon Press.

Li, Fang-Kuei. 1930a. *Mattole, an Athabaskan language*. Chicago, IL: University of Chicago Press.

Li, Fang-Kuei. 1930b. A study of Sarcee verb-stems. *International Journal of American Linguistics* 6(1). 3–27.

Li, Fang-Kuei. 1946. Chipewyan. In Osgood, Cornelius (ed.), *Linguistic structures of native America*, 398–423. New York: The Viking Fund.

Lovick, Olga. 2012. The identification of narrative genres in Upper Tanana Athabascan: A preliminary study. *Northwest Journal of Linguistics* 6(1). 1–29.

Mantla, Rosa & Mantla, Therese. 2014. An immersion kindergarten program for Tłı̨chǫ Yatıì. (Paper presented at the Dene Verb Paradigm Workshop, Toronto.)

McDonough, Joyce. 1990. *Topics in the phonology and morphology of Navajo verbs*. Amherst: University of Massachusetts. (Doctoral dissertation.)

McDonough, Joyce. 1999. On a bipartite model of the Athabaskan verb. In Fernald, T. B. & Platero, P. R. (eds.), *Athabaskan language and linguistics*, 1–32. Oxford: Oxford University Press.

Mithun, Marianne. 1999. *The languages of native North America*. Cambridge: Cambridge University Press.

Moore, Patrick. 1999. *Dene gudeji*. Kaska Tribal Council, Integraphics.

Moore, Patrick. 2002. *Point of view in Kaska historical narratives*. Bloomington: Indiana University. (Doctoral dissertation.)

Morice, Adrien Gabriel. 1932. *The Carrier language (Déné family): A grammar and dictionary combined*, vol. 1. Vienna: Anthropos.

Perkins, Ellavina. 1978. *The role of word order and scope in the interpretation of Navajo sentences*. Albuquerque: University of New Mexico. (Doctoral dissertation.)

Perkins, Ellavina. 1982. Extraposition of relative clauses in Navajo. *International Journal of American Linguistics* 48(3). 277–285.

Platero, Paul. 1978. *Missing noun phrases in Navajo*. Cambridge, MA: MIT. (Doctoral dissertation.)

Reichenbach, Hans. 1947. *Elements of symbolic logic*. New York: Macmillan.

Rice, Keren. 1982. On stems and lexical phonology: An Athapaskan example. (Paper presented at the Canadian Linguistics Association annual meeting.)

Rice, Keren. 1989. *A grammar of Slave*. Berlin and New York: Mouton de Gruyter.

Rice, Keren. 2000. *Morpheme order and semantic scope: Word formation in the Athapaskan verb*. Cambridge and New York: Cambridge University Press.

Rice, Keren. 2011. Principles of affix ordering: An overview. *Word Structure* 4(2). 169–200.

Rice, Keren & de Reuse, William J. 2017. Athabaskan (Dene) language family. In Aikhenvald, Alexandra Y. & Dixon, R. M. W. (eds.), *Cambridge handbook of linguistic typology*, 683–706. Cambridge: Cambridge University Press.

Rice, Keren & Saxon, Leslie. 1994. The subject position in Athapaskan languages. In Harley, Heidi & Phillips, Colin (eds.), *The morphology-syntax connection*, vol. 2, 173–195. Cambridge: MIT Press.

Rice, Keren & Saxon, Leslie. 2005. Comparative Athapaskan morphosyntax: Arguments and projections. In Cinque, Guglielmo & Kayne, Richard S. (eds.), *The Oxford handbook of comparative syntax*, 698–774. New York: Oxford University Press.

Roy, Isabelle. 2013. *Nonverbal predication: Copular sentences at the syntax/semantics interface*. Oxford: Oxford University Press.

Sandoval, Merton. 1984. The syntactic function of the *yi-/bi-* alternation in Jicarilla Apache. In *Coyote papers: Working papers in linguistics from A–Z, studies on Native American languages, Japanese and Spanish*, 153–190. Tucson: University of Arizona.

Sapir, Edward. 1915. The Na-Dene languages: A preliminary report. *American Anthropologist* 17(3). 534–558.

Sapir, Edward. 1936. Internal linguistic evidence suggestive of the Northern origin of the Navaho. *American Anthropologist* 38.

Sapir, Edward & Hoijer, Harry. 1967. *The phonology and morphology of the Navaho language*, vol. 40. Berkeley and Los Angeles: University of California Press.

Saxon, Leslie. 1986. *The syntax of pronouns in Dogrib (Athapaskan): Some theoretical consequences*. San Diego: University of California. (Doctoral dissertation.)

Saxon, Leslie. 2000. Head-internal relative clauses in Dogrib (Athapaskan). In Carnie, Andrew & Jelinek, Eloise & Willie, Mary Ann (eds.), *Papers in honor of Ken Hale*, 93–108. Cambridge: MIT Press.

Saxon, Leslie. 2015. The Tłı̨chǫ syntactic causative and non-nominal CPs. (Paper presented at the Dog Days Syntax Workshop, Toronto, 12 August 2015.)
Saxon, Leslie & Siemens, Mary. 1996. *Tłı̨chǫ yatıì enıhtł'è: A Dogrib dictionary*. Rae-Edzo: Dogrib Divisional Board of Education.
Saxon, Leslie & Wilhelm, Andrea. 2016. The 'possessed noun suffix' and possession in two Northern Dene (Athabaskan) languages. *International Journal of American Linguistics* 82(1). 35–70.
Schauber, Ellen. 1979. *The syntax and semantics of Navajo questions*. New York: Garland.
Shimoyama, Junko. 1999. Internally headed relative clauses in Japanese and e-type anaphora. *Journal of East Asian Linguistics* 8(2). 147–182.
Shimoyama, Junko. 2000. *Wh-constructions in Japanese*. Amherst: University of Massachusetts. (Doctoral dissertation.)
Simpson, Jane & Withgott, Meg. 1986. Pronominal clitic clusters and templates. In Borer, Hagit (ed.), *Syntax and semantics 19: The syntax of pronominal clitics*. New York: Academic Press.
Smith, Carlotta S. 1991. *The parameter of aspect*, vol. 43. Dordrecht and Boston: Kluwer Academic Publishers.
Smith, Carlotta S. & Perkins, Ellavina T. & Fernald, Theodore B. 2003. Temporal interpretation in Navajo. *The proceedings of SULA2 (Semantics of Underrepresented Languages of the Americas 2)*, 175–192.
Snoek, Conor & Cox, Christopher. 2013. Measuring linguistic distance in Athapaskan. *Proceedings of the Berkeley Linguistics Society 2013* 245–258.
Speas, Peggy. 1982. Navajo verbal prefixes in current morphological theory. In *Coyote papers: Working papers in linguistics from A–Z, studies on Native American languages, Japanese and Spanish*, 115–144. University of Arizona Linguistics Circle.
Speas, Peggy. 1991. Functional heads and the mirror principle. *Lingua* 84. 181–214.
Speas, Margaret. 2000. Person and point of view in Navajo direct discourse complements. In Carnie, Andrew & Jelinek, Eloise & Willie Mary Ann (eds.), *Papers in honor of Ken Hale*, 19–38. Cambridge: MIT Working Papers in Linguistics.
Starlight, Bruce & Donovan, Gary. 2008. *Tsúùt'ínà pedagogical dictionary in printed and digital format*. Tsúùt'ínà Gunaha Instıtute. (Ms.)
Statistics Canada. 2011. *2011 Census of Canada: Topic-based tabulations: Languages spoken most often at home*, vol. 2014; Tech. Rep. Ottawa: Statistics Canada.
Tenenbaum, Joan M. (ed.). 1976a. *Dena'ina sukdu'a*, vol. II. Fairbanks: Alaska Native Language Center.
Tenenbaum, Joan M. (ed.). 1976b. *Dena'ina sukdu'a*, vol. I. Fairbanks: Alaska Native Language Center.
Thompson, Chad L. 1989. Pronouns and voice in Koyukon Athapaskan: A text-based study. *International Journal of American Linguistics* 55(1). 1–24.
Tłı̨chǫ Community Services Agency. 2007. *Tłı̨chǫ yatıì multimedia dictionary*. Behchokǫ̀: Author. (http://tlicho.ling.uvic.ca) (Accessed 2019-07-08.)
Trombetti, Alfredo. 1923. *Elementi di glottologia*. Bologna: Nicola Zanichelli.
Tuttle, Siri & Hargus, Sharon. 2004. Explaining variability in affix order: The Athabaskan areal and third person prefixes. *Working Papers in Athabaskan Languages: Alaska Native Language Center Working Papers* 4. 70–98.
Vajda, Edward. 2010. A Siberian link with Na-Dene languages. In Kari, James M. & Potter, Ben A. (eds.), *The Dene-Yeniseian connection*, 33–99. Fairbanks: Alaska Native Language Center.
Vajda, Edward. 2016. Dene-Yeniseian. In Aronoff, Mark (ed.), *Oxford research encyclopedia of linguistics*. Oxford: Oxford University Press.
Vajda, Edward. 2018. Dene-Yeniseian: Progress and unanswered questions. *Diachronica* 35(2). 277–295.
Velten, H. V. 1944. Three Tlingit stories. *International Journal of American Linguistics* 10(4). 168–180.
Webster, Anthony K. 2006. On speaking to him (Coyote): The discourse functions of the *yi-/bi-* alternation in some Chiricahua Apache narratives. *Southwest Journal of Linguistics* 25(2). 143–160.
Welch, Nicholas. 2012. *The bearable lightness of being: The encoding of coincidence in two-copula languages*. Calgary: University of Calgary. (Doctoral dissertation.)
Welch, Nicholas. 2015a. Deducing clause structure from the right periphery in Tłı̨chǫ Yatıì. *International Journal of American Linguistics* 81(2). 261–291.
Welch, Nicholas. 2015b. Obligatory future in a Dene language. *International Journal of American Linguistics* 81(1). 41–81.
Welch, Nicholas. 2017. *Structures et interprétations des phrases copulaires en langues dénées*. Toronto: University of Toronto. (Ms.)
Welch, Nicholas. 2018. *Differential grammaticalization of copulas in two Dene languages*. Toronto: University of Toronto. (Ms.)
Whorf, Benjamin L. 1932. *The structure of the Athabascan languages*. Sterling Memorial Library, Yale University. (Ms.)
Wilhelm, Andrea. 2006. *Telicity and durativity: A study of aspect in Dëne Sųłıné (Chipewyan) and German*. New York: Routledge.

Wilhelm, Andrea. 2014. A radically [+arg, -pred] language. (Paper presented at SULA 8 (Semantics of Underrepresented Languages of the Americas).)
Willie, Mary Ann. 1991. *Pronouns and obviation in Navajo*. Tucson: University of Arizona. (Doctoral dissertation.)
Willie, Mary Ann. 1996. On the expression of modality in Navajo. In Jelinek, Eloise & Midgette, Sally & Rice, Keren & Saxon, Leslie (eds.), *Athabaskan language studies: Essays in honor of Robert W. Young*, 331–348. Albuquerque: University of New Mexico Press.
Willie, Mary Ann. 2000. Individual and stage level predication and the Navajo classificatory verbs. In Carnie, Andrew & Jelinek, Eloise & Willie, Mary Ann (eds.), *Papers in honor of Ken Hale*, 39–50. Cambridge: MIT Press.
Witherspoon, Gary. 1977. *Language and art in the Navajo universe*. Ann Arbor: University of Michigan Press.
Young, Robert W. & Morgan, William. 1987. *The Navajo language: A grammar and colloquial dictionary*, rev. edn. Albuquerque: University of New Mexico Press.
Young, Robert W. & Morgan, William & Midgette, Sally. 1992. *Analytical lexicon of Navajo*, 1st edn. Albuquerque: University of New Mexico Press.
Yukon Native Language Centre. 2003. *Gwich'in listening exercises*. Nenana: Yukon College.

21
ALGONQUIAN LANGUAGES

Will Oxford

The Algonquian family consists of a large number of closely related languages spoken over a broad area stretching from the Great Plains to the Great Lakes and the eastern seaboard. Because they were the first languages of North America encountered by French and English colonists, many Algonquian languages have a long history of written documentation and have been the source of numerous English loanwords (e.g., *caribou, moose, pecan, toboggan, moccasin, wigwam*) and placenames (e.g., *Mississippi, Illinois, Quebec, Saskatchewan, Winnipeg, Manhattan*). This chapter outlines the members of the Algonquian family (§1) and sketches their phonology (§2), syntax (§3), and morphology (§4).

1. The Algonquian Family

Algonquian languages are often divided into Central, Eastern, and Plains groups, but only the Eastern group is a genetic unit (Goddard 1980). The areal Central and Plains groupings do correlate to a degree with linguistic differences, however, as the Central languages are generally more conservative than the Plains languages. Approximate historical locations of the languages are shown in Figure 21.1, based on Goddard (1996). The following paragraphs outline the languages in each group (Goddard 1996; Mithun 1999).

The Central Algonquian languages, spoken in a large area centered on the Great Lakes, fall into six groups: (1) Meskwaki-Sauk-Kickapoo, (2) Miami-Illinois, (3) Shawnee, (4) Menominee, (5) Ojibwe-Potawatomi, and (6) Cree-Innu-Naskapi. The latter two groups are large and internally diverse (Rhodes & Todd 1981). The Ojibwe-Potawatomi group consists of the Potawatomi language and several Ojibwe (Anishinaabemowin) varieties, including Southwestern Ojibwe, Saulteaux, Oji-Cree, Nishnaabemwin (Odawa and Eastern Ojibwe), and Algonquin. The Cree-Innu-Naskapi group is a language continuum whose members, from west to east, are Plains Cree, Woods Cree, Swampy Cree, Moose Cree, Atikamekw, East Cree, Innu, and Naskapi; also related is Michif, a Cree-French mixed language. Current speakers number in the tens of thousands for Ojibwe and Cree-Innu-Naskapi and in the hundreds for Meskwaki-Sauk-Kickapoo, Shawnee, and Michif. Only a handful of native speakers of Menominee and Potawatomi remain. Miami-Illinois has been without native speakers since the 1960s.

The Eastern Algonquian languages were historically spoken along much of the eastern seaboard. The best-documented Eastern language groups are (1) Mi'gmaq (Micmac); (2) Maliseet-Passamaquoddy; (3) Abenaki, consisting of Western and Eastern branches; (4) Southern New

Figure 21.1 Historical Distribution of Major Algonquian Languages

Source: Author, based on Goddard (1996).

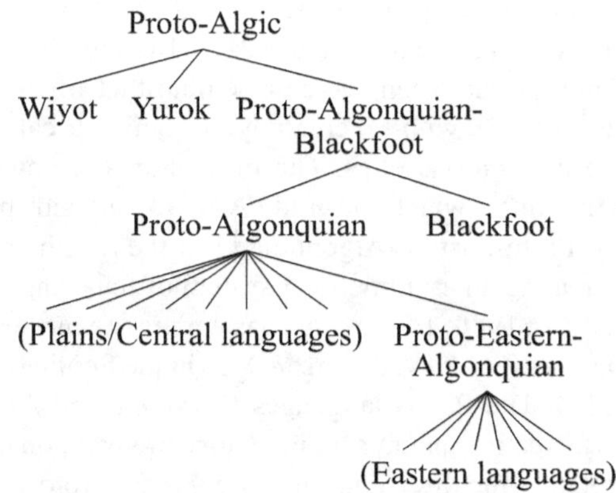

Figure 21.2 Algonquian Genetic Relationships

England Algonquian, a language continuum whose members include Massachusett (Wampanoag), Narragansett, Mohegan-Pequot-Montauk, and Quiripi; (5) Mahican; and (6) the Delaware (Lenape) languages Munsee and Unami. Several other poorly attested Eastern languages existed, including Etchemin, Nanticoke, Powhatan, and Pamlico. Current speakers number in the thousands for Mi'gmaq and the hundreds for Maliseet-Passamaquoddy. All other Eastern languages have become extinct, recently in some cases (Delaware) and centuries ago in others (Powhatan).

The three Plains Algonquian language groups are (1) Blackfoot, (2) Cheyenne, and (3) the Arapahoan languages, which include Arapaho, Gros Ventre (Atsina), and Nawathinehena. Current speakers number in the low thousands for Blackfoot and Cheyenne and in the hundreds for Arapaho. No native speakers of Gros Ventre or Nawathinehena remain.

The genetic relationships of the Algonquian languages are illustrated in Figure 21.2. Proto-Algonquian is distantly related to the Wiyot and Yurok languages spoken in California, forming a larger Algic family (Haas 1958). It is thought that Proto-Algonquian was spoken c. 1000–500 BCE (Pentland 1979: 329), most likely in the area immediately west of Lake Superior (Goddard 1994a: 207). Within the Algonquian family, the deepest division is between Blackfoot and the remaining languages, to the extent that Blackfoot is likely a sister rather than a daughter of Proto-Algonquian (Goddard 2015). Among the daughters of Proto-Algonquian, the only large genetic subgroup is Eastern Algonquian (Goddard 1980). Among the (non-Blackfoot) Plains and Central languages, there are no large genetic subgroups, but evidence from shared archaisms suggests that Cree-Innu-Naskapi and Arapahoan were the first of these languages to split off from the Proto-Algonquian core, followed by Cheyenne and Menominee, and followed later by a split between the "Core Central" languages (Meskwaki-Sauk-Kickapoo, Miami-Illinois, Shawnee, Ojibwe-Potawatomi) and Proto-Eastern-Algonquian (Goddard 1994a). The fact that the oldest splits are in the west while the most recent splits are in the east is consistent with a west-to-east migration of Algonquian peoples (Goddard 1994a: 203).

2. Phonology

This section surveys vowel inventories (§2.1), consonant inventories (§2.2), phonotactics (§2.3), processes (§2.4), and suprasegmental phonology (§2.5).

2.1. Vowel Inventories

Proto-Algonquian (PA) had four vowel qualities plus a length contrast (marked with a middle dot), giving the symmetrical eight-vowel system in Figure 21.3 (Bloomfield 1946: 86).

The vowel systems of most Central languages resemble that of PA. Cree-Innu-Naskapi and Ojibwe-Potawatomi merged short **e* with **i*, creating an asymmetrical seven-vowel system; further mergers have occurred in some varieties. The most dramatic vowel change in the Central languages took place in Menominee, which lowered PA **e·* to /æ·/ and split PA **i·* and **o·* into /i·, e·/ and /u·, o·/, respectively. Proto-Eastern-Algonquian lost the length contrast in the high vowels and shifted short **e* to **ə*, creating an asymmetrical system of four long vowels **i· *e· *a· *o·* and two short vowels **ə *a* (Goddard 1980: 149), which has undergone further changes in most Eastern languages including the chain shift of **a·* > *ã·* and **e·* > *a·* in the Southern New England languages and Mahican (Goddard 1971). The Plains languages Cheyenne and Arapaho merged **o(·)* with **i(·)* (Goddard 1974a; 1988), creating an unusual inventory of vowel qualities (**i, *e, *a*) that was resolved in Cheyenne by rotating the three qualities into a more prototypical arrangement (**i, *e, *a* > *e, a, o*) and in Arapaho by adding a fourth quality, high back *u*.

2.2. Consonant Inventories

The consonant phonemes of Proto-Algonquian are shown in Figure 21.4 (Bloomfield 1946: 87; Goddard 1979: 71). Note the absence of a voicing contrast among obstruents and the lack of a labial fricative. Two protophonemes are of marginal status: **ʔ* occurred only as the first member of

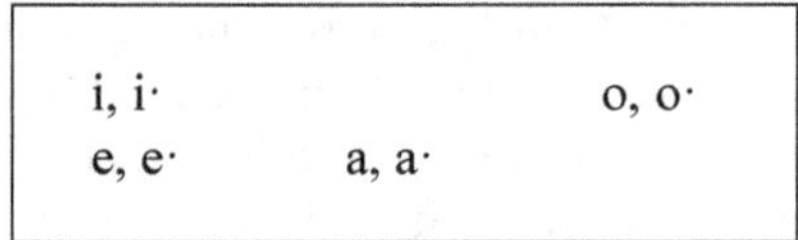

Figure 21.3 Proto-Algonquian Vowels

p		t	č	k	ʔ
	θ	s	š		h
m		n			
w		r	y		

Figure 21.4 Proto-Algonquian Consonants (*č, š, y* = IPA [tʃ, ʃ, j])

a consonant cluster and *_č_ was mostly in complementary distribution with *_t_. PA *_r_ was symbolized as *_l_ by Bloomfield (1946) but its most likely phonetic value was a trill or tap (Pentland 1979: 351; Goddard 1994a: 204–205).

The consonant that changes most often in the daughter languages is *_θ_, which is retained as /θ/ only in Arapaho. The other languages merge *_θ_ with either *_t_ (Cree, Gros Ventre) or *_r_ (all other languages). The next most frequently changed consonant is *_r_, which often merges with either *_n_ (Meskwaki, Menominee, Ojibwe, Swampy Cree, Massachusett, Proto-Arapaho-Gros Ventre), *_t_ (Cheyenne, Nawathinehena), or *_y_ (Plains Cree, Mohegan-Pequot-Montauk). Among the languages that retain *_r_ as a distinct phoneme, many shift it phonetically to [l], but Woods Cree unusually has [ð]. Also susceptible to change is *_š_, which merges with *_s_ in Menominee, some Cree dialects, and many Eastern languages. The Plains languages Cheyenne and Arapaho have both undergone rapid sequences of dramatic sound changes, such as, in Arapaho, the merger of initial *_s_ with *_n_ and the shift of *_p_ to _k_ after original *_k_ was lost without a trace (Goddard 1974a). The resulting phonological system shares little with that of PA.

2.3. Phonotactics

The Proto-Algonquian syllable template is (C)(G)V(:)(C), where C is a non-glide consonant and G is a glide. Coda consonants occur only word-medially, where they are always followed by an onset consonant; word-final syllables are always open (Bloomfield 1946: 93). Table 21.1 exemplifies the 16 possible PA syllable types using vocabulary from Hewson (1993).

Many languages retain the (C)(G)V(:)(C) template. Changes in syllable structure are most often driven by syncope of unstressed short vowels, which, when phonologized, can create new types of consonant clusters such as _mk_ and _zn_ in Odawa _mkiznan_ 'shoes'; cf. non-syncopated Southwestern Ojibwe _makizinan_ (Rhodes & Todd 1981: 58). Another common change involves word-final syllables, which always ended with a vowel in PA. Final vowels have been lost in all languages except Meskwaki-Sauk-Kickapoo, Miami-Illinois, Shawnee, and Blackfoot, creating many words with a final consonant (PA *_mesesa·hka_ 'horsefly' > Cree _misisa·_**_hk_**). Two-syllable words with short vowels are typically exempt from final vowel deletion (PA *_nex_**_ka_** 'goose' > Cree _nis_**_ka_**), although some languages delete final vowels even here (Innu _ni_**_šk_**).

Table 21.1 Proto-Algonquian Syllable Types

V	*__e__._wa_	's/he says'	CV	*__ma__._či_	'bad'
V·	*__e·__._he_	'yes'	CV·	*__ma·__._ma.wi_	'together'
VC	*__eh__._kwa_	'louse'	CVC	*__maθ__._kwa_	'bear'
V·C	*__e·h__._sa_	'clam'	CV·C	*__ma·n__._θeh.si_	'flint'
GV	*__wa__._to·.wa_	'clot'	CGV	*__kwe__._či_	'try to'
GV·	*__wa·__._ši_	'den'	CGV·	*__kwi·__._θa.wi_	'impatiently'
GVC	*__waʔ__._šaš.kwa_	'muskrat'	CGVC	*__kweʔ__._ta.mwa_	's/he fears it'
GV·C	*__wa·ʔ__._se·.ya·.wi_	'there is light'	CGV·C	*__kwe·θ__._ki_	'other side'

Table 21.2 Proto-Algonquian Clusters

C_1 (Coda)	C_2 (Onset)								
	k	*p*	*t*	*č*	*s*	*š*	*θ*	*r*	*m*
ʔ~x	xk	xp	ʔt	ʔč	ʔs	ʔš	ʔθ	ʔr	Hm
h	hk	hp	ht	hč	hs	hš	hθ	(hr)	
m~n	nk	mp	nt	nč	ns	nš	nθ	nr	
š	šk	šp	(št)						
θ	θk	θp							
ç	çk								

As stated previously, a PA coda consonant is always followed by an onset consonant, creating a C_1C_2 cluster. The composition of such clusters is restricted: only the combinations in Table 21.2 are permitted (Goddard 1979: 71).[1] Particularly striking is the limited range of contrasts that can be expressed in C_1 (coda) position, which is never occupied by a plosive, affricate, or **s*.

Coda consonants (C_1) have been highly susceptible to change in the daughter languages and the changes that affect a given consonant in coda position often differ from its treatment elsewhere (e.g., Miami-Illinois **θ* > *l* but **θk* > *hk*). Particularly common changes include merger of **ʔ* and **h* (PA **ʔt, *ht* > Delaware *ht*), debuccalization of nasals (PA **nt* > Cheyenne *ht*), and complete loss of particular coda consonants (PA **nt* > Massachusett *t*). Because of such changes, the set of possible clusters in many daughter languages is even smaller than that of PA. Meskwaki, for example, only has clusters of the form *h*C or *š*C.

In many Ojibwe dialects, the contrast between a single obstruent C and an *h*C cluster (e.g., *p* vs. *hp*) has shifted to a lenis-fortis contrast (*p* vs. *pp*) or even a voicing contrast (*b* vs. *p*) (Rhodes & Todd 1981: 58), thereby adding a new series of obstruents to the inventory.

2.4. Phonological Processes

The most prominent phonological process in Proto-Algonquian is the palatalization of **t* →**č* and **θ* →**š* before **i, *i·, *y*, a phonologically regular process that has been morphologized in various ways in the daughter languages due to independent phonological changes (Goddard 1977; see analyses in Kaye & Piggott 1973 and Russell 1992). All other regular processes in PA involve sandhi in CC, VV, and (V)GV sequences that arise at morpheme boundaries. Some languages have developed new processes such as the palatalization of *k* in Innu-Naskapi and Southern New England Algonquian. The vowel shift that took place in Menominee (§2.1) created a vowel harmony alternation that has attracted theoretical attention (e.g., Archangeli & Pulleyblank 1994) due to its interesting conditioning: the raising of /e, o/ to /i, u/ is blocked by an intervening /æ/ but not by an intervening /a/. The dramatic sound changes that occurred in Cheyenne and Arapaho created a complex synchronic phonology (Goddard 1974a) that is not yet fully understood.

2.5. Stress and Tone

Many of the languages have alternating stress patterns. According to Rhodes (1985), stress in Proto-Algonquian falls on even-numbered syllables counting from left to right; syllables with long vowels, however, are always stressed, with the alternating pattern restarting to their right. In terms of metrical stress theory (Hayes 1995), this is a quantity-sensitive left-to-right iambic pattern. Similar left-to-right iambic patterns are found in Menominee, Ojibwe, Potawatomi, and Delaware, and right-to-left iambic patterns are reported for Meskwaki and Cree; the languages vary in whether heavy syllables must be stressed, whether a coda consonant makes a syllable heavy, and whether final material is extrametrical (Hayes 1995: 211–221; Milligan 2005). Trochaic patterns are reported for Passamaquoddy (LeSourd 1993: 101ff.) and Mi'gmaq (Olson 2012).

Contrastive tone has developed in Cheyenne, Kickapoo, and Western Innu; pitch accent systems, sometimes described as tonal, have developed in Blackfoot, Arapaho, Maliseet-Passamaquoddy, and Penobscot.

3. Syntax

This section describes the typological status of Algonquian syntax (§3.1) as well as the grammatical categories (§3.2) and grammatical functions (§3.3) that are typically distinguished.

3.1. Syntactic Type

Algonquian syntax can be described as non-configurational: word order is flexible, null anaphora is common, and constituents may be discontinuous. This section illustrates these properties and discusses evidence that the underlying syntax may nevertheless be configurational.

3.1.1. Word Order

Most or all possible orders of S, V, and O are typically grammatical, with pragmatic factors determining which order is used. Dahlstrom (1995: 3) proposes that Meskwaki word order follows the template in (1), with dedicated preverbal positions for Topic, Focus, and Oblique; the verb may be followed by one or more other phrases (indicated by "XP*").

(1) [$_{S'}$ (Topic) [$_{S}$ (Neg) (Focus) (Oblique) V (XP*)]]

Although this template has not been shown to hold for the entire family, the association of preverbal positions with topical or focal constituents is widespread. In the East Cree sentences in (2) (Junker 2004: 354), SVO order is used when S is the focus while OVS order is used when O is the focus.[2]

(2) a. ***Awaash*** *miyeyim-eu* *atim-h.* (SVO order)
child like-3SG>3OBV dog-OBV
'The CHILD likes dogs.' (as answer to 'Who likes dogs?')
b. ***Atim-h*** *miyeyim-eu* *uu awaash.* (OVS order)
dog-OBV like-3SG>3OBV this child
'This child likes DOGS.' (as answer to 'What does this child like?')

In the absence of a topic or focus, the unmarked order is verb-initial in Ojibwe (Rhodes 1994: 436–438) and East Cree (Junker 2004: 349), as predicted by the template in (1).

3.1.2. Pronominal Arguments

A verb's arguments are usually identified by rich agreement inflection (§4), which allows subject and object nominals to be freely omitted. The sentence in (3), for example, consists simply of two verb forms.

(3) *Ni-tshissenim-âu* *menuât-ât.*
1-know-1SG>3SG IC.like-3SG>3OBV
'I know he likes her.'

(Innu; Clarke 1982: 138)

The argument-indexing affixes on Algonquian verbs are sometimes regarded as bound pronominal arguments rather than agreement markers (e.g., Mithun 1999: 339). However, LeSourd (2006) provides several arguments against a pronominal argument analysis of Passamaquoddy, most of which are applicable across the family.

3.1.3. Constituency

Evidence for a VP constituent is elusive, but most languages have clear NP/DP constituents (Kathol & Rhodes 1999; LeSourd 2004), illustrated for Passamaquoddy in (4); some languages also have PP constituents (Oxford 2011; LeSourd 2014).

(4) *Nopal* $[_{NP}$ ***yùt*** $[_{N'}$ ***pilèy layyektákon***$]]$ *milkiyàn.*
if.only **this** **new** **toy** give.X>1SG
'I wish I would be given this new toy.'
(LeSourd 2004: 261)

NPs and PPs can surface discontinuously. Many languages have a construction in which the initial element of a phrase immediately precedes the verb while the remainder of the phrase follows the verb (Kathol & Rhodes 1999; Reinholtz 1999; LeSourd 2004; 2014). The Passmaquoddy NP in (4), for example, can alternatively straddle the verb as in (5).

(5) *Nopal* ***yùt*** *milkiyàn* [***pilèy*** ***layyektákon***].
if.only **this** give.X>1SG **new** **toy**
'I wish I would be given this new toy.'
(LeSourd 2004: 261)

The Passamaquoddy examples in (4) and (5) appear to have the same meaning, but in Swampy Cree, the construction equivalent to (5) focuses the preverbal element (Reinholtz 1999: 208).

3.1.4. Underlying Configurationality

Although the properties described earlier have been considered hallmarks of non-configurationality (Hale 1983), many specialists now reject a non-configurational analysis of Algonquian syntax due to the discovery of structural asymmetries akin to those in configurational languages. Russell and Reinholtz (1995: 434), for example, show that in Swampy Cree, preverbal NPs c-command postverbal NPs: a preverbal negative NP licenses the polarity-sensitive reading of *kêkwân* 'something' as 'anything', as in (6a), but when the order is reversed, the polarity-sensitive reading is not licensed, as in (6b).

(6) a. [*Namôna awiyak*] *ta-wâpaht-am* ***kêkwân-iniw.***
not anyone FUT-see-3SG>INAN **anything-OBV.INAN**
'Nobody will see **anything.**'
b. ? ***Kêkwân-iniw*** *ta-wâpaht-am* [*namôna awiyak*].
something-OBV.INAN FUT-see.it.3SG>INAN not anyone
'There is **something** that nobody will see.' (* 'Nobody will see **anything.**')

Similarly, Bruening (2001: 31) shows that in Passamaquoddy, a subject quantifier can bind a pronominal variable within an object, as in (7a), but an object quantifier cannot bind a pronominal variable within a subject, as shown in (7b).

(7) a. *Katolu* **psi=te** **wen** *'-koselom-al* *wikuwoss-ol.*
of.course **all=EMPH** **someone** 3-love-3SG>3OBV 3.mother-OBV
'Of course **everyone**$_i$ loves **his**$_i$ mother.'

b. *Skitap* *musqitaham-acil* *'-koti-tqon-al* **psi=te** **wen-il.**
man hate-3SG>3OBV 3-FUT-arrest-3SG>3OBV **all=EMPH** **someone-OBV**
'A man that **he**$_{*i}$ hates will arrest **everyone**$_i$.'

3.2. Grammatical Categories

Four broad parts of speech are traditionally distinguished: nouns, pronouns, verbs, and particles, the latter a cover term for all items that do not inflect (Bloomfield 1946).

Nouns fall into two syntactic classes: dependent nouns, which must occur with a possessor, and independent nouns, which can occur with or without a possessor. Most dependent nouns denote kin (PA **-kwiʔs-* 'son') or body parts (PA **-te·h-* 'heart').

Pronouns come in various types. A typical language has an emphatic personal pronoun paradigm, a demonstrative paradigm, various indefinite and interrogative pronouns, and an inflecting noun substitute (e.g., Maliseet *iyok* 'the ones; what's-their-name'; LeSourd 2003).

Verbs fall into four morphological classes determined by the derivational FINAL suffix that ends the verb stem (§4.2). Morphologically intransitive stems end with a final that expresses the animacy of the actor (Animate Intransitive, Inanimate Intransitive) while morphologically transitive stems end with a final that expresses the animacy of the patient (Transitive Inanimate, Transitive Animate). These classes are exemplified in Table 21.3. The TA class includes ditransitive verbs that take a theme and an animate recipient, known as TA+O verbs (PA **mi·r-* 'give X to someone'); in such stems the final marks the animate recipient rather than the theme.

The morphological verb classes align only roughly with syntactic patterning, as illustrated by the following examples from Delaware (O'Meara 1990). AI verbs are prototypically intransitive, but a subclass of "AI+O" verbs can appear with an object, either optionally (*məne·-* 'drink (it)') or obligatorily (*awe·he-* 'use it'). Conversely, TI verbs are prototypically transitive, but some, known as OBJECTLESS TI VERBS, can appear without an object, either optionally (*ni·ske·lənt-* 'be angry (about it)') or obligatorily (*wi·niht-* 'be annoying').

Particles, a heterogeneous class, include items that function as quantifiers, numerals, adjectives, adverbs, prepositions, and conjunctions. Certain particles may immediately precede and modify a stem, as shown for Ojibwe in (8) (Nichols 1980: 101, 264); particles in this position are known as PREVERBS or PRENOUNS.

(8) a. *ni-* **kii=** **nanta=** *kikkentaan*
1- **PAST=** **seeking=** know.it.1SG
'I sought to know it'

b. **kicci=** **misko=** *waapooyaan*
big= **red=** blanket
'big red blanket'

Table 21.3 Morphological Verb Classes

VERB CLASS		*DEFINITION*	*PA EXAMPLE (ROOT *PANK- 'FALLEN')*
AI	Animate Intransitive	Final marks anim. actor	**pank-**ihšin-*** 'to fall (animate)'
II	Inanimate Intransitive	Final marks inan. actor	**pank-**ihθen-*** 'to fall (inanimate)'
TI	Transitive Inanimate	Final marks inan. patient	**pank-**ihšim-*** 'to drop an animate'
TA	Transitive Animate	Final marks anim. patient	**pank-**ihθet-*** 'to drop an inanimate'

Preverb meanings range from concrete (*nanta* 'seeking') to grammatical (*kii* 'past'). Prenouns such as *misko* 'red' may be the structural equivalent of attributive adjectives (Rosen 2016), which do not form a grammatically distinct part of speech in most Algonquian languages. Aside from prenouns, adjective-like meanings can also be expressed by intransitive verbs (Delaware *wələsi·*- 'be good, pretty', *kato·pi·*- 'be hungry').

3.3. Grammatical Functions

There are three core grammatical functions for clausal arguments: (1) actor (Bloomfield 1962) or subject (Goddard 1969); (2) primary object; and (3) secondary object. All verbs take an actor/subject; transitive verbs additionally take a primary and/or secondary object. Table 21.4 shows the grammatical functions selected by each class of verbs and the thematic roles that correspond to each grammatical function.

The two types of objects differ in various ways (Rhodes 1990a): primary objects can be first, second, or third person while secondary objects can only be third (a Person-Case Constraint effect, as noted for Ojibwe in Lochbihler 2012: 118); the animacy of a primary object is selected by the verb stem while that of a secondary object is not; and primary objects are more likely than secondary objects to be indexed by verb inflection. The Delaware transitive forms in (9) (Goddard 1969) both involve a primary object 'them', which is obligatorily animate (selected by the stems *ne·w*- 'see someone', *mi·l*- 'give to someone') and is indexed inflectionally (*-ak* 3.AN.PL). The ditransitive form in (9b) also has a secondary object, 'something/someone', which can be animate or inanimate and is not indexed inflectionally.

(9) a. ***nə*-*ne·w-a·*-*w*-*ak***
1-see-DIR-1SG-3.AN.PL
'**I** see them (anim.).'

b. ***nə*-*mi·l-a·*-*w*-*ak***
1-give-DIR-1SG-3.AN.PL
'**I** give something/someone to them (anim.).'

Algonquian ditransitives show secundative rather than indirective alignment (Haspelmath 2005): monotransitive patients and ditransitive recipients pattern together (as primary objects) while ditransitive themes are treated distinctly (as secondary objects) (Dryer 1986).

Although most Algonquianists refer to the external argument of a transitive verb as the subject, the notion of subjecthood is complicated by the existence of an inverse construction. Compare, for example, the Menominee sentences in (10) (Bloomfield 1962: 39), which both involve a more topical PROXIMATE argument, 'the man', and a less topical OBVIATIVE argument, 'the woman' (see §4.3 for more on obviation). In DIRECT forms like (10a), proximate acts on obviative, while in INVERSE forms like (10b), obviative acts on proximate.

Table 21.4 Core Grammatical Functions

VERB CLASS	*FUNCTIONS*	*Θ-ROLES*
Intransitive (AI, II)	actor/subject	any role
Transitive (TA, TI)	actor/subject primary object	agent/experiencer patient/theme
Ditransitive (TA+O)	actor/subject primary object secondary object	agent/experiencer recipient patient/theme
AI+O	actor/subject secondary object	agent/experiencer patient/theme

(10) a. *nɛ·w-ɛ·-w* [*enoh* *enɛ·niw*] [*anenoh* *metɛ·mohs-an*].
see-DIR-**3.PX** **that.PX** **man.PX** this.OBV woman-OBV
'**The man (PROX)** sees the woman (OBV).'

b. *nɛ·w-ek-w*[3] [*enoh* *enɛ·niw*] [*anenoh* *metɛ·mohs-an*].
see-INV-**3.PX** **that.PX** **man.PX** this.OBV woman-OBV
'The woman (OBV) sees **the man (PROX)**.'

Despite the reversal of thematic relations, the proximate enjoys the same morphosyntactic prominence in both sentences: it consistently precedes the obviative and is agreed with by the verb (*-w* 3.PROX.SG). Rhodes (1994) and Bruening (2001) provide additional evidence that proximates occupy a more prominent structural position than obviatives. A possible conclusion is that the proximate is in fact the structural subject in both (10a) and (10b), as Bloomfield (1962: 45) suggests. The direct-inverse alternation can then be understood as a split-ergative pattern (Déchaine 1999: 50–51): direct forms like (10a) show accusative alignment, as the nominative/absolutive role is assigned to the actor, while inverse forms like (10b) show ergative alignment, as the nominative/absolutive role is assigned to the theme.

Nominals may appear in two additional non-core grammatical functions: RELATIVE ROOT COMPLEMENT and OBLIQUE (Rhodes 2010), exemplified for Ojibwe in (11). Both functions have oblique semantics, but a relative root complement is selected by a verb-internal lexical morpheme known as a RELATIVE ROOT (e.g., Ojibwe *in-~izh-* 'to, like', *ond-* 'from, because of') while an oblique is not selected. For example, in (11a), the relative root *izh-* 'to' selects the complement 'upstairs', while in (11b) nothing selects the oblique 'one year'.

(11) a. *Gii=* ***izh**-aa* ***ishpimisagong**.*
PAST= **to**-go.3SG **upstairs**
'He went **(to) upstairs**.' (relative root complement)

(Rhodes 2006: 18)

b. ***Ningo=*** ***biboon*** *ni-gii=* *ayaa* *iwidi*.
one= **winter** 1-PAST= be.at.1SG there
'I was there **for one year**.' (oblique)

(Rhodes 2010: 308)

4. Morphology

This section describes the typological status of Algonquian morphology (§4.1) and the basic properties of stem formation (§4.2), noun inflection (§4.3), and verb inflection (§4.4).

4.1. Morphological Type

In terms of form, Algonquian morphology lies between agglutinative and fusional: nouns and verbs can appear with many affixes, some expressing a single feature (PA *ne- 'first person') and others expressing multiple features (PA *-*aki* 'animate proximate plural'); most affixes are suffixal. In terms of the locus of marking, Algonquian morphology is strongly head-marking: possessed nouns inflect to index their possessor (§4.3) and verbs inflect to index their subject and object (§4.4); nominals are not marked for structural case. In terms of function, Algonquian morphology is polysynthetic: a single verb can express a richly descriptive sentence, as in the Cree example in (12a), and can include an incorporated noun, as in the Oji-Cree example in (12b).

(12) a. *Sâkihisosihkâsoskiw*

sâkih	-iso	-isi	-hkâso	-iski	-w
love	-self	-DIM	-pretend	-habitual	-3SG

'He's in the habit of pretending to love himself a little bit.'

(Dahlstrom 1991: 135)

b. *Kiih-kisiipiikipahpaapiwine*

kiih=	kisiipiik	-pahpaapiwin	-e	-w
PAST=	wash	-window	-do	-3SG

'S/he has washed the windows.'

(Slavin 2015: 384)

4.2. Stem Formation

As (12) illustrates, Algonquian stems are morphologically complex. Two types of stem derivation are distinguished: PRIMARY DERIVATION, in which a stem is formed from components that cannot stand alone as a stem, and SECONDARY DERIVATION, in which a stem is derived from an existing stem by the addition of a SECONDARY FINAL suffix (Bloomfield 1946: 104; Goddard 1990). Of these two types, it is secondary derivation that corresponds to what is known simply as "derivation" in Indo-European languages. Tables 21.5 and 21.6 exemplify the secondary derivation of noun and verb stems in Ojibwe (data from Nichols 1980). Secondary derivation is highly prominent in the lexicon: even many basic nouns are secondary derivatives of verb stems (e.g., Delaware *təmah-* 'to sever by tool', *təmah-i·kan-* 'axe', lit. 'tool for severing'; O'Meara 1990). Successive layers of secondary derivation may apply, producing a string of secondary finals as in (12a).

In contrast to secondary derivation, primary derivation is an Algonquian-specific process. Primary stems are formed from three components, none of which can stand alone as a stem: an INITIAL, which expresses the core lexical meaning of the stem, an optional noun-like MEDIAL, and a FINAL, which marks

Table 21.5 Secondary Noun Stem Derivation in Ojibwe

STEM TYPE	*EXAMPLE (PRIMARY STEM, SECONDARY NOUN STEM)*
diminutive	*makkw-* 'bear', *makkoo-**nss-*** 'bear cub'
instrument nominalization	*nipaa-* 'sleep', *nipaa-**kan-*** 'bed'
process nominalization	*nakamo-* 'sing', *nakamo-**win-*** 'singing'
product nominalization	*nakamo-* 'sing', *nakamo-**n-*** 'song'

Table 21.6 Secondary Verb Stem Derivation in Ojibwe

STEM TYPE	*EXAMPLE (PRIMARY STEM, SECONDARY VERB STEM)*
verb of being	*ciipay-* 'ghost', *ciipay-**iwi-*** 'be a ghost'
verb of making	*anaakkan-* 'mat', *anaakkan-**ikke-*** 'make mats'
verb of possession	*šiiššiip-* 'duck', ***o**-šiiššiip-**imi-*** 'have ducks'
causative	*mintito-* 'be big (anim.)', *mintito-**h-*** 'enlarge someone'
benefactive of intrans.	*anokkii-* 'work', *anokkii-**taw-*** 'work for someone'
benefactive of trans.	*naat-* 'fetch it', *naat-**amaw-*** 'fetch it for someone'
reciprocal	*noontaw-* 'hear someone', *noontaa-**ti-*** 'hear each other'
reflexive	*noontaw-* 'hear someone', *noontaa-**tiso-*** 'hear oneself'
detransitive	*takkon-* 'hold it', *takkon-**ike-*** 'hold things'
lexical passive	*piit-* 'bring it', *piic-**ikaate-*** 'be brought'
mediopassive	*noontaw-* 'hear someone', *noontaa-**ikosi-*** 'make noise'

Table 21.7 Primary Verb Stem Derivation in Meskwaki

STEM	COMPONENTS
sanakesi- 'be difficult (anim.)'	Initial *sanak-* 'difficult' Abstract final *-esi* 'be', forms AI verb
sanakat- 'be difficult (inan.)'	Initial *sanak-* 'difficult' Abstract final *-at* 'be', forms II verb
išiki- 'grow in such a way (anim.)'	Initial *iši-* 'thus' Concrete final *-ki* 'grow', forms AI verb
išiken- 'grow in such a way (inan.)'	Initial *iši-* 'thus' Concrete final *-ken* 'grow', forms II verb
pi·tike·- 'enter a dwelling'	Initial *pi·t-* 'into' Medial *-wik-* 'dwelling' Abstract final *-e·*, forms AI verb
pema·hkwisen- 'lie lengthwise on/as a solid'	Initial *pem-* 'along' Medial *-a·hkw-* 'wood, solid' Concrete final *-isen* 'lie', forms II verb

the grammatical category of the stem. Verb finals usually also mark the animacy of one of the verb's arguments, as discussed in §3.2, and thus typically come in animate-inanimate pairs. On semantic grounds, two types of finals may be distinguished: ABSTRACT FINALS, which serve only to categorize the stem and mark animacy, and CONCRETE FINALS, which also make a tangible semantic contribution (though see Denny 1984 for an argument that even abstract finals have semantic import). Table 21.7 gives examples of primary verb stem derivation in Meskwaki (Bloomfield 1946).

Although the conventional description of primary derivation is Algonquian-specific, there is a striking similarity between the Initial+Final template and the Root+*v* structure posited in Distributed Morphology, and much recent work has investigated Algonquian stem structure from a syntactic perspective (e.g., Brittain 2003; Hirose 2003; Branigan et al. 2005; Mathieu 2007; Slavin 2012).

Stems undergo reduplication at their left edge to convey meanings such as repetition and distributivity: Menominee *a·čemow* 's/he narrates', ***a·ya***·*čemow* 's/he keeps narrating'; *ni·s* 'two', ***na·***ni·s* 'two each' (Bloomfield 1946: 122). Formal and semantic details vary across the family.

4.3. Noun Inflection

Two layers of inflection appear on nouns. All nouns take a word-final suffix that marks animacy, number, and obviation, exemplified for Meskwaki in Table 21.8 (Dahlstrom forthcoming). In most languages, the animate and inanimate singular suffixes have become null due to final vowel loss, and several languages have neutralized the number contrast for animate obviatives (e.g., Menominee *-an* 'AN.OBV.SG/PL'). The nominal suffix position may alternatively be occupied by a locative suffix, which converts the noun into an oblique expression of location. Some languages also have vocative nominal suffixes, as shown for Meskwaki in Table 21.8. The Eastern languages have a parallel paradigm of absentative nominal suffixes, which indicate absence or death: Munsee *nó·xw* 'my father', *nó·xw**aya*** 'my late father' (Goddard 1979: 100).

Possessed nouns, exemplified for Meskwaki in (13) (adapted from Dahlstrom forthcoming), add an inner layer of inflection that marks the person and number of the possessor using a prefix (for singular possessors, (13a)) or circumfix (for plural possessors, (13b)). Some noun stems must be augmented by a "possessed theme" suffix (Bloomfield 1946: 95) before possessor inflection can be added, as in (13c).

Table 21.8 Meskwaki Nominal Suffixes

FEATURES	EXAMPLE	
animate proximate singular	*ineniw-**a***	'man'
animate proximate plural	*ineniw-**aki***	'men'
animate obviative singular	*ineniw-**ani***	'(other) man'
animate obviative plural	*ineniw-**ahi***	'(other) men'
inanimate singular	*či·ma·n-**i***	'canoe'
inanimate plural	*či·ma·n-**ani***	'canoes'
locative	*či·ma·n-**eki***	'in the canoe(s)'
vocative singular	*ni·hka·n-**e***	'O friend!'
vocative plural	*ni·hka·n-**etike***	'O friends!'

Table 21.9 Meskwaki Possessor Inflection and Personal Pronoun

	POSSESSOR INFLECTION	PERSONAL PRONOUN	
1SG	*ne-*	*ni·na*	'I/me'
2SG	*ke-*	*ki·na*	'you (sg.)'
3SG	*o-*	*wi·na*	's/he, him/her'
1PL	*ne- . . . -ena·n*	*ni·na·na*	'we/us (excl.)'
21PL	*ke- . . . -ena·n*	*ki·na·na*	'we/us (incl.)'
2PL	*ke- . . . -wa·w*	*ki·nwa·wa*	'you (pl.)'
3PL	*o- . . . -wa·w*	*wi·nwa·wa*	'they/them'

(13) a. ***ne**-ta·nes-aki*
1-daughter-AN.PL
'my daughters'

b. ***ne**-ta·nes-**ena·n**-aki*
1-daughter-**1PL**-AN.PL
'our daughters'

c. ***ne**-ši·ši·p-em-**ena·n**-aki*
1-duck-POSS-**1PL**-AN.PL
'our ducks'

Freestanding personal pronouns strongly resemble possessed noun forms due to the diachronic origin of the former as a possessed noun meaning 'one's body' (Goddard 2007: 218). Both paradigms distinguish exclusive (1PL) and inclusive (21PL) first-person plural, as shown for Meskwaki in Table 21.9 (Dahlstrom forthcoming).

Two nominal features, animacy and obviation, warrant special comment. The division of nouns into animate and inanimate grammatical genders has a partial semantic basis, as all nouns that denote sentient beings are grammatically animate, but the animate gender also includes many nouns that denote non-living entities (Cree *cistêmâw* 'tobacco', *apoy* 'paddle'). The classification of such nouns is ultimately arbitrary. For some nouns, gender shift expresses semantic contrasts such as individuation: Meskwaki *šo·niya·h-**i*** IN.SG 'money', *šo·niya·h-**a*** AN.SG 'a coin, a bill' (Goddard 2002: 213).

When a clause contains multiple third-person referents, one, normally the most topical, is designated as proximate (notated **3** or PROX); any others must be obviative (notated **3′** or OBV) (for discussion and analysis see, among others, Thomason 2003; Quinn 2006; Muehlbauer 2012). Obviation is obligatory in transitive clauses with multiple third-person arguments, where either the agent or the patient may be marked obviative (see (10)). Obviation is also obligatory when a noun has a third-person possessor; in such cases, the noun can only be obviative, while the possessor may be either proximate or obviative, as shown in (14) for Cree (Wolfart 1978: 257). The additional obviative morpheme *-iyiw* in (14b) is sometimes said to mark a second degree of obviation (**3″**) but is better understood simply as obviative possessor agreement (Wolfart 1978: 258–260).

(14) a. [*okimâw*] *o-têm-a*
chief.3 3-horse-3′
'[the chief's.PROX] horse.OBV'

b. [*okimâw o-kosis-a*] *o-têm-iyiw-a*
chief.3 3-son-3′ 3-horse-OBV.POSS-3′
'[the chief's.PROX son's.OBV] horse.OBV'

In addition to its pragmatic association with topicality, obviation marks disjoint reference. For example, in the Oji-Cree sentences in (15) (author's fieldwork), the proximate possessor in (15a) must be interpreted as coreferent with the proximate subject while the obviative possessor in (15b) must be disjoint.

(15) a. *Tepit o-waapam-aa-n o-tayihsh-an.*
David.3 3-see-DIR-3′ 3-dog-3′
'David.PROX sees **his.PROX** dog.OBV.' (his = David)

b. *Tepit o-waapam-aa-n o-tayihsh-iniw-an.*
David.3 3-see-DIR-3′ 3-dog-OBV.POSS-3′
'David.PROX sees **his.OBV** dog.OBV.' (his = not David)

Obviation is not marked in the inflection of inanimate nouns in most languages (see, e.g., Table 21.8), but there is evidence that inanimate nouns are covertly obviative in the same contexts where animate nouns are overtly obviative (Wolfart 1978: 259; Rhodes 1990b: 103).

4.4. *Verb Inflection*

There exist three parallel sets of verb inflection known as the INDEPENDENT, CONJUNCT, and IMPERATIVE ORDERS, which express mostly the same contrasts but use different morphology, as shown by the Plains Cree 2PL>3SG forms in (16) (Wolfart 1973: 41–43).

(16) a. INDEPENDENT
ki**-wâpam-â-**wâw
2-see-DIR-**2PL**
'you (pl.) see him/her'

b. CONJUNCT
*wâpam-â-**yêk***
see-DIR-**2PL**
'you (pl.) see him/her'

c. IMPERATIVE
*wâpam-**ihk***
see-**2PL>3**
'look (pl.) at him/her!'

The independent and conjunct inflections are used canonically in main and subordinate clauses, respectively, although the details are subtle and variable (see e.g., Brittain 2001 and Cook 2014 for Cree-Innu-Naskapi). The conjunct is normally required in all *wh*-questions, whether subordinate or not; the traditional explanation is that *wh*-questions are clefts and thus the verb is always in a subordinate clause (Bloomfield 1946: 116). In some contexts, typically those involving *wh*-extraction, conjunct forms are affected by an ablaut process called INITIAL CHANGE, which alters the first vowel of the verb or a preceding preverb: Innu ***pimûtê-*** 'walk' → ***pêmûtê-***; ***uî**-pimûtê-* 'want to walk' → ***uâ**-pimûtê-* (Clarke 1982: 85).

Simplified independent and conjunct inflectional templates are given for Ojibwe in Figures 21.5 and 21.6 (Nichols 1980). The agreement slots in these templates pattern as follows:

- The innermost layer of agreement, the THEME SIGN, appears only in transitive forms. The theme sign normally marks person/animacy agreement with the logical object: *-i* '1OBJ', *-in* '2OBJ', *-aa* '3.AN.OBJ' (or 'DIRECT'), *-am* 'INAN.OBJ'.[4] However, a special INVERSE theme sign *-ikw* appears instead when the logical object outranks the logical subject on a construction-specific person hierarchy. In the independent, the hierarchy is 1/2 > X > 3 > 3′ > 0. Since 1 outranks 3 on this hierarchy, an independent 3-on-1 form such as 'they see us' will be marked with the inverse theme sign, as in Figure 21.5. In the conjunct, the hierarchy is just 3 > 3′ > 0 (Rhodes 1994: 432). Since this hierarchy establishes no ranking between 1 and 3, a conjunct 3-on-1

Prefix	Stem	Theme sign	Negation	Central suffix	Mode	Peripheral suffix
ni-	*waapam*	*-ikw*	*-ssii*	*-naa*	*-token*	*-ak*
1	see	INV	NEG	1PL	DUB	3PL

Figure 21.5 Ojibwe Independent Inflection Template

Exemplified by *niwaapamikossiinaatokenak* 'they might not see us'.

Stem	Theme sign	Negation	Central suffix	Mode
waapam	*-i*	*-ssiiw*	*-ankit-waaw*	*-en*
see	1OBJ	NEG	-3>1PL-3PL	DUB

Figure 21.6 Ojibwe Conjunct Inflection Template

Exemplified by *waapamissiiwankitwaawen* 'they might not see us'.

form such as 'they see us' will not be marked as inverse and will instead show the default pattern of object agreement in the theme sign slot (*-i* '1OBJ'), as in Figure 21.6.

- The next layer is the CENTRAL AGREEMENT, which is a prefix-suffix combination in the independent (*ni- . . . -naa* '1PL', similar in form to nominal possessor agreement) and an entirely unrelated suffix in the conjunct (*-ankit* '3 > 1PL', here augmented by *-waaw* '3PL'). The central agreement indexes whichever argument ranks highest on the person hierarchies given earlier. When the relevant hierarchy does not establish a ranking between the arguments (as in a conjunct 3-on-1 form, for example), a portmanteau suffix indexing both arguments may be realized (*-ankit* '3>1PL' in Figure 21.6) or finer-grained morphological hierarchies may come into play, such as a 2>1 hierarchy for the prefix and a 1PL > 2 hierarchy for the central suffix (Zúñiga 2008; Macaulay 2009).
- The outermost layer, present only in the independent, is the PERIPHERAL SUFFIX, which marks third persons only and is similar in form to the word-final suffix on nouns.

Similar inflectional templates apply in most of the languages, although the functions of negative and modal suffixes are sometimes taken over by preverbs or particles, and some languages have made the conjunct inverse hierarchy more like that of the independent (see e.g., Dahlstrom 1989 for Plains Cree).

In most languages the inflection of TA verbs distinguishes animate third-person actors, inanimate actors (notated **0** or INAN) and impersonal actors (notated **X** and functionally equivalent to a passive), as shown for Meskwaki in (17) (Goddard 1994b: 191).

(17)	a. *ne-wa·pam-ekw-a*	b. *ne-wa·pam-ekwi*	c. *ne-wa·pam-eko·-pi*
	1-see-INV-3.AN.SG	1-see-INV.INAN	1-see-INV-X
	's/he sees me' (3>1)	'it sees me' (0>1)	'people see me' (X>1)

A verb that takes a clausal complement may show default inanimate object agreement, as in the Plains Cree sentence in (18a), or it may enter a long-distance agreement relationship with an argument in the complement clause, as in (18b) (Dahlstrom 1991: 67), a fact that has attracted much theoretical interest (e.g., Branigan & MacKenzie 2002).

(18) a. *Ni-kiskêyiht-ên* *ê=nôhtê-sipwêhtê-t.*
1-know.TI-1SG>**INAN** COMP=want-leave-3SG
'I know (**it**) that he wants to leave.'

b. *Ni-kiskêyim-âw* *ê=nôhtê-sipwêhtê-t.*
1-know.TA-1SG>**3.AN.SG** COMP=want-leave-3SG
'I know (**him**) that he wants to leave.'

Some Eastern languages distinguish parallel ABSOLUTE and OBJECTIVE independent forms. An absolute form leaves the features of some third-person argument unspecified while an objective form specifies them. The Delaware objective 3SG > 3′ verb form in (19a), for example, inflects for both its 3SG subject and its 3′ object, while the parallel absolute 3SG > 3′ verb form in (19b) inflects only for its 3SG subject (Goddard 1979: 88).

(19) a. ***wə****-nihl-a·-****w****-al* *máxkw-al*
3-kill-DIR-**3SG**-3′ bear-3′
'He killed the bear.'

b. *máxkw-al* *nihl-e·-****w***
bear-3′ kill-DIR-**3SG**
'He killed a bear.'

Where this contrast is retained, it functions as a type of differential object marking conditioned by definiteness, as in (19). Most languages, however, have lost the contrast and uniformly use either a (19a)-type form (Ojibwe, Passamaquoddy) or a (19b)-type form (Cree, Menominee).

The independent inflection closely resembles the inflection of possessed nouns (see (13)); compare the Plains Cree verb and noun forms in (20) (Wolfart 1973: 31, 41). This resemblance reflects the diachronic origin of the independent, which arose when possessed deverbal nouns were reanalyzed as full-fledged verbs (Goddard 1974b: 325–327).

(20) a. ***ni****-wâpam-â-****nân****-ak*
1-see-DIR-**1PL**-3.AN.PL
'we (excl.) see them'

b. ***ni****-têm-****inân****-ak*
1-horse-**1PL**-3.AN.PL
'our (excl.) horses'

Some languages have a special CONJUNCT PARTICIPLE form, which functions as a relative clause headed by an argument of the verb. Compare, for example, the Ojibwe conjunct form in (21a) with the conjunct participle in (21b) (Nichols 1980: 201). As its translation indicates, the participle functions syntactically as a 3PL noun. Its inflection resembles that of a 3PL noun as well: plurality is marked by a peripheral suffix *-ik* 'AN.PL', related to the nominal plural suffix *-ak* 'AN.PL' in (20b), rather than the usual conjunct central suffix pluralizer *-waa* in (21a).

(21) a. *waapamaawaat*
waapam -aa **-waa** -t
see -DIR **-PL** -3
'**they (PROX)** see him/her (OBV)'

b. *wayaapamaacik*
wayaapam -aa -t **-ik**
IC.see -DIR -3 **-AN.PL**
'**they (PROX)** who see him/her (OBV)'

The conjunct participle form, bleached of its participial meaning, has been generalized to additional contexts in several languages. In Cree (Goddard 1995: 129), the conjunct participle has replaced the plain conjunct, while in Mi'gmaq, the conjunct participle has become the default main-clause verb form, completely replacing the independent indicative (Goddard 1967: 78).

Further Reading

The classic work in comparative Algonquian linguistics, Bloomfield's sketch is both a reconstruction of Proto-Algonquian and a concise grammar of Meskwaki, Ojibwe, Cree, and Menominee.

Bloomfield, Leonard. 1946. Algonquian. In Hoijer, Harry (ed.), *Linguistic structures of Native America*, 85–129. Viking Fund Publications in Anthropology 6. New York.

This grammar is the fullest and most refined presentation of Bloomfield's framework for the analysis of Algonquian languages.

Bloomfield, Leonard. 1962. *The Menomini language*. New Haven, CT: Yale University Press.

This book is a pioneering study of foundational issues in Algonquian morphosyntax. Dahlstrom develops a variety of diagnostics to investigate the syntactic status of direct-inverse morphology and obviation.

Dahlstrom, Amy. 1991. *Plains Cree morphosyntax*. New York: Garland.

Although nominally about Delaware, this work takes a pan-Algonquian view of the inflectional system and codifies much of the terminology that is now standardly used.

Goddard, Ives. 1969. Delaware verbal morphology: A descriptive and comparative study. Cambridge, MA: Harvard University. (Doctoral dissertation.) Published 1979, New York: Garland.

This lengthy study of Nishnaabemwin, an Ojibwe variety, is perhaps the most complete reference grammar of any Algonquian language.

Valentine, J. Randolph. 2001. *Nishnaabemwin reference grammar*. Toronto: University of Toronto Press.

Notes

1. **H* represents the neutralization of **h* and **ʔ*. The symbols **x* and **ç* are placeholders for segments whose phonemic identity is obscure (Bloomfield 1946: 88) and should not be read with their IPA values. The reconstruction of the two clusters in parentheses is tenuous.
2. Abbreviations in glosses follow the Leipzig Glossing Rules, with the following additions: 0 = inanimate third person, 3 = animate proximate third person, 3′ = animate obviative third person, AN = animate, DIM = diminutive, DIR = direct, DUB = dubitative, EMPH = emphatic, IC = initial change, INAN = inanimate, INV = inverse, OBV = obviative, PX = proximate, X = impersonal actor. Derivational suffixes are not segmented out in glosses. In some examples a string of inflectional suffixes is given a single combined gloss, such as '3SG>3OBV' for the *-eu* ending in (2a), which could be more exhaustively segmented as *-e* 'DIR' + *-u* '3' + -Ø 'AN.SG'.
3. Underlying *nɛ·w-ek-w* surfaces as *niak* due to regular phonological rules (Bloomfield 1962: 155).
4. The theme sign *-aa* may be analyzed as either an animate third-person object marker (e.g., Rhodes 1994) or a special DIRECT marker that contrasts minimally with the inverse marker, appearing when the logical subject outranks the logical object (e.g., Wolfart 1973).

References

Archangeli, Diana & Pulleyblank, Douglas. 1994. *Grounded phonology*. Cambridge: MIT Press.

Bloomfield, Leonard. 1946. Algonquian. In Hoijer, Harry & Bloomfield, L. & Haas, M. R. & Halpern, A. M. & Li, F. K. & Newman, S. S. & Swadesh, M. & Trager, G. L. & Voegelin, C. F. & Whorf, B. L. (eds.), *Linguistic structures of Native America*, 85–129. (Viking Fund Publications in Anthropology 6). New York: Viking Fund.

Bloomfield, Leonard. 1962. *The Menomini language*. New Haven, CT: Yale University Press.

Branigan, Phil & Brittain, Julie & Dyck, Carrie. 2005. Balancing syntax and prosody in the Algonquian verb complex. In Wolfart, H. C. (ed.), *Papers of the 36th Algonquian conference*, 75–93. Winnipeg: University of Manitoba.

Branigan, Phil & MacKenzie, Marguerite. 2002. Altruism, A-bar-movement, and object agreement in Innu-aimûn. *Linguistic Inquiry* 33. 385–407.

Brittain, Julie. 2001. *The morphosyntax of the Algonquian conjunct verb: A Minimalist approach.* New York: Garland.

Brittain, Julie. 2003. A Distributed Morphology account of the syntax of the Algonquian verb. In Somesfalean, Stanca & Burelle, Sophie (eds.), *Proceedings of the 2003 annual conference of the CLA*, 25–39. Montreal:

Département de linguistique et de didactique des langues, Université du Québec à Montréal. Bruening, Benjamin. 2001. *Syntax at the edge: Cross-clausal phenomena and the syntax of Passamaquoddy*. Cambridge, MA: MIT. (Doctoral dissertation.)

Clarke, Sandra. 1982. *North-West river (Sheshâtshît) Montagnais: A grammatical sketch*. (Mercury Series). Ottawa: National Museum of Man.

Cook, Clare. 2014. *The clause-typing system of plains Cree: Indexicality, anaphoricity, and contrast*. Oxford: Oxford University Press.

Dahlstrom, Amy. 1989. Morphological change in plains Cree verb inflection. *Folia Linguistica Historica* 9(2). 59–71.

Dahlstrom, Amy. 1991. *Plains Cree morphosyntax*. New York: Garland.

Dahlstrom, Amy. 1995. *Topic, focus and other word order problems in Algonquian*. (The Belcourt Lecture). Winnipeg: Voices of Rupert's Land.

Dahlstrom, Amy. forthcoming. *A grammar of Meskwaki, an Algonquian language*.

Déchaine, Rose-Marie. 1999. What Algonquian morphology is really like: Hockett revisited. *MIT Occasional Papers in Linguistics* 17. 25–72.

Denny, J. Peter. 1984. Semantic verb classes and abstract finals. In Cowan, William (ed.), *Papers of the 15th Algonquian Conference*, 241–271. Ottawa: Carleton University.

Dryer, Matthew S. 1986. Primary objects, secondary objects, and antidative. *Language* 62. 808–845.

Goddard, Ives. 1967. The Algonquian independent indicative. In DeBlois, A. D. (ed.), *Contributions to anthropology, linguistics I (Algonquian)*, 66–106. Ottawa: National Museum of Canada Bulletin 214.

Goddard, Ives. 1969. *Delaware verbal morphology: A descriptive and comparative study*. Cambridge, MA: Harvard University. (Doctoral dissertation.) (Published 1979 by Garland, New York.)

Goddard, Ives. 1971. More on the nasalization of PA *a·in Eastern Algonquian. *International Journal of American Linguistics* 37. 139–145.

Goddard, Ives. 1974a. An outline of the historical phonology of Arapaho and Atsina. *International Journal of American Linguistics* 40. 102–116.

Goddard, Ives. 1974b. Remarks on the Algonquian independent Indicative. *International Journal of American Linguistics* 40. 317–327.

Goddard, Ives. 1977. The morphologization of Algonquian consonant mutation. *Berkeley Linguistics Society (BLS)* 3. 241–250.

Goddard, Ives. 1979. Comparative Algonquian. In Campbell, Lyle & Mithun, Marianne (eds.), *The languages of Native America*, 70–132. Austin: University of Texas Press.

Goddard, Ives. 1980. Eastern Algonquian as a genetic subgrouping. In Cowan, William (ed.), *Papers of the 11th Algonquian Conference*, 143–158. Ottawa: Carleton University.

Goddard, Ives. 1988. Pre-Cheyenne *y. In Shipley, William (ed.), *In honor of Mary Haas: From the Haas festival conference on native American linguistics*, 345–360. Berlin: Mouton de Gruyter.

Goddard, Ives. 1990. Primary and secondary stem derivation in Algonquian. *International Journal of American Linguistics* 56. 449–483.

Goddard, Ives. 1994a. The west-to-east cline in Algonquian dialectology. In Cowan, William (ed.), *Actes du 25e Congrès des Algonquinistes*, 187–211. Ottawa: Carleton University.

Goddard, Ives. 1994b. *Leonard Bloomfield's Fox lexicon: Critical edition*. Winnipeg: Algonquian and Iroquoian Linguistics.

Goddard, Ives. 1995. Notes on Fox (Mesquakie) inflection: Minor modes and incompletely described morphemes. In Pentland, David H. (ed.), *Papers of the 26th Algonquian conference*, 124–150. Winnipeg: University of Manitoba.

Goddard, Ives. 1996. The classification of the native languages of North America. In Goddard, Ives (ed.), *Handbook of North American Indians, volume 17: Languages*, 290–323. Washington, DC: Smithsonian.

Goddard, Ives. 2002. Grammatical gender in Algonquian. In Wolfart, H. C. (ed.), *Papers of the 33rd Algonquian conference*, 195–231. Winnipeg: University of Manitoba.

Goddard, Ives. 2007. Reconstruction and history of the independent indicative. In Wolfart, H. C. (ed.), *Papers of the 38th Algonquian conference*, 207–271. Winnipeg: University of Manitoba.

Goddard, Ives. 2015. Blackfoot and core Algonquian inflectional morphology: Archaisms and innovations. (Paper presented at the 47th Algonquian Conference, Winnipeg, October 23.)

Haas, Mary R. 1958. Algonkian-Ritwan: The end of a controversy. *International Journal of American Linguistics* 24. 159–173.

Hale, Ken. 1983. Warlpiri and the grammar of non-configurational languages. *Natural Language and Linguistic Theory* 1. 5–47.

Haspelmath, Martin. 2005. Argument marking in ditransitive alignment types. *Linguistic Discovery* 3. 1–21.

Hayes, Bruce. 1995. *Metrical stress theory: Principles and case studies*. Chicago, IL: University of Chicago Press.

Hewson, John. 1993. *A computer-generated dictionary of Proto-Algonquian*. Hull: Canadian Museum of Civilization.

Hirose, Tomio. 2003. *Origins of predicates: Evidence from plains Cree*. New York: Routledge.

Junker, Marie-Odile. 2004. Focus, obviation and word order in East Cree. *Lingua* 114. 345–365.

Kathol, Andreas & Rhodes, Richard A. 1999. Constituency and linearization of Ojibwe nominals. In Caldecott, Marion & Gessner, Suzanne & Kim, Eun-Sook (eds.), *Proceedings of WSCLA 4*, 75–91. Vancouver: UBCWPL.

Kaye, Jonathan D. & Piggott, Glyne L. 1973. On the cyclical nature of Ojibwa t-palatalization. *Linguistic Inquiry* 4. 345–362.

LeSourd, Philip S. 1993. *Accent and syllable structure in Passamaquoddy*. New York: Garland.

LeSourd, Philip S. 2003. The noun substitute in Maliseet-Passamaquoddy. In Rudes, Blair A. & Costa, David J. (eds.), *Essays in Algonquian, Catawban and Siouan linguistics in memory of Frank T. Siebert, Jr.*, 141–163. Winnipeg: Algonquian and Iroquoian Linguistics.

LeSourd, Philip S. 2004. The internal structure of the noun phrase in Maliseet-Passamaquoddy. In Wolfart, H. C. (ed.), *Papers of the 35th Algonquian conference*, 239–263. Winnipeg: University of Manitoba.

LeSourd, Philip S. 2006. Problems for the pronominal argument hypothesis in Maliseet-Passamaquoddy. *Language* 82. 486–514.

LeSourd, Philip S. 2014. Prepositional phrases in Maliseet-Passamaquoddy. *International Journal of American Linguistics* 80. 209–240.

Lochbihler, Bethany. 2012. *Aspects of argument licensing*. Montreal: McGill. (Doctoral dissertation.)

Macaulay, Monica. 2009. On prominence hierarchies: Evidence from Algonquian. *Linguistic Typology* 13. 357–389.

Mathieu, Éric. 2007. Petite syntaxe des finales concrètes en ojibwe. In Wolfart, H. C. (ed.), *Papers of the 38th Algonquian Conference*, 295–321. Winnipeg: University of Manitoba.

Milligan, Marianne. 2005. *Menominee prosodic structure*. Madison: University of Wisconsin. (Doctoral dissertation.)

Mithun, Marianne. 1999. *The languages of Native North America*. Cambridge: Cambridge University Press.

Muehlbauer, Jeffrey. 2012. The relation of switch-reference, animacy, and obviation in plains Cree. *International Journal of American Linguistics* 78. 203–238.

Nichols, John D. 1980. *Ojibwe morphology*. Cambridge, MA: Harvard University. (Doctoral dissertation.)

O'Meara, John. 1990. *Delaware stem morphology*. Montreal: McGill. (Doctoral dissertation.)

Olson, Erin. 2012. Describing the accent system of Listuguj Mi'gmaq. Paper presented at the 44th Algonquian Conference, University of Chicago, October 27.)

Oxford, Will. 2011. The syntax of Innu-aimun locatives. In Black, Alexis & Louie, Meagan (eds.), *Proceedings of WSCLA 16*, 135–150. Vancouver: UBCWPL.

Pentland, David H. 1979. *Algonquian historical phonology*. Toronto: University of Toronto. (Doctoral dissertation.)

Quinn, Conor M. 2006. *Referential-access dependency in Penobscot*. Cambridge, MA: Harvard University. (Doctoral dissertation.)

Reinholtz, Charlotte. 1999. On the characterization of discontinuous constituents: Evidence from Swampy Cree. *International Journal of American Linguistics* 65. 201–217.

Rhodes, Richard A. 1985. The consequential future in Cree and Ojibwa. *International Journal of American Linguistics* 51. 547–549.

Rhodes, Richard A. 1990a. Ojibwa secondary objects. In Dziwirek, Katarzyna & Farrell, Patrcik & Mejías-Bikandi, Errapel (eds.), *Grammatical relations: A cross theoretical perspective*, 401–414. Stanford, CA: CSLI.

Rhodes, Richard A. 1990b. Obviation, inversion, and topic rank in Ojibwa. *Berkeley Linguistics Society (BLS)* 16(supplement). 101–115.

Rhodes, Richard A. 1994. Agency, inversion, and thematic alignment in Ojibwe. *Proceedings of BLS 20*. 431–446.

Rhodes, Richard A. 2006. *Clause structure, core arguments and the Algonquian relative root construction*. Winnipeg: Voices of Rupert's Land.

Rhodes, Richard A. 2010. Relative root complement: A unique grammatical relation in Algonquian syntax. In Wohlgemuth, Jan & Cysouw, Michael (eds.), *Rara & rarissima*, 305–324. Berlin: De Gruyter Mouton.

Rhodes, Richard A. & Todd, Evelyn M. 1981. Subarctic Algonquian languages. In Helm, June (ed.), *Handbook of North American Indians, volume 6: Subarctic*, 52–66. Washington, DC: Smithsonian.

Rosen, Bryan. 2016. On attributive adjectives in Ojibwe and Cinque's phrasal movement analysis of adjective orders. *Linguistic Inquiry* 47. 158–168.

Russell, Kevin. 1992. Palatalization and epenthesis in Plains Cree. In Dyck, Carrie & Ghomeshi, Jila & Wilson, Tom (eds.), *Proceedings of the 1992 annual conference of the Canadian Linguistic Association*, 269–284. Toronto: Department of Linguistics, University of Toronto.

Russell, Kevin & Reinholtz, Charlotte. 1995. Hierarchical structure in a non-configurational language: Asymmetries in Swampy Cree. *West Coast Conference on Formal Linguistics (WCCFL)* 14. 431–455.
Slavin, Tanya. 2012. Phonological and syntactic evidence for stem structure in Oji-Cree. *International Journal of American Linguistics* 78. 497–532.
Slavin, Tanya. 2015. Possessive noun incorporation in Oji-Cree. *International Journal of American Linguistics* 81. 379–408.
Thomason, Lucy. 2003. *The proximate and obviative contrast in Meskwaki*. Austin: University of Texas. (Doctoral dissertation.)
Wolfart, H. C. 1973. *Plains Cree: A grammatical study*. (Transactions of the American Philosophical Society, n.s.), vol. 63, part 5. Philadelphia: University of Pennsylvania.
Wolfart, H. C. 1978. How many obviatives: Sense and reference in a Cree verb paradigm. In Cook, Eung-Do & Kaye, Jonathan D. (eds.), *Linguistic structures of Native Canada*, 255–272. Vancouver: UBC Press.
Zúñiga, Fernando. 2008. How many hierarchies, really? Evidence from several Algonquian languages. In Richards, Marc & Malchukov, Andrej L. (eds.), *Scales*, 277–294. (Linguistische Arbeits Berichte 86). Universität Leipzig.

22

ESKIMO-ALEUT

Alana Johns

1. Introduction

The Eskimo-Aleut language family (sometimes called Eskaleut or Inuit-Yupik-Unangan) stretches geographically from Kalaallit Nunaat[1] (Greenland) to Siberia. The languages within this family are spoken along the coastlines of the Beaufort Sea, the Arctic Ocean, Hudson Bay, the Labrador Sea, etc. The speakers of these languages harvest from both land and sea, so their traditional lands extend from the tree line to the coast. These languages vary in vitality and all are under stress from outside languages, predominantly English.

1.1. Language Family

There are three main divisions within the language family, shown in (1), which is based on information from Dorais (2010). We must keep in mind that definitions between language and dialect

(1)[2]

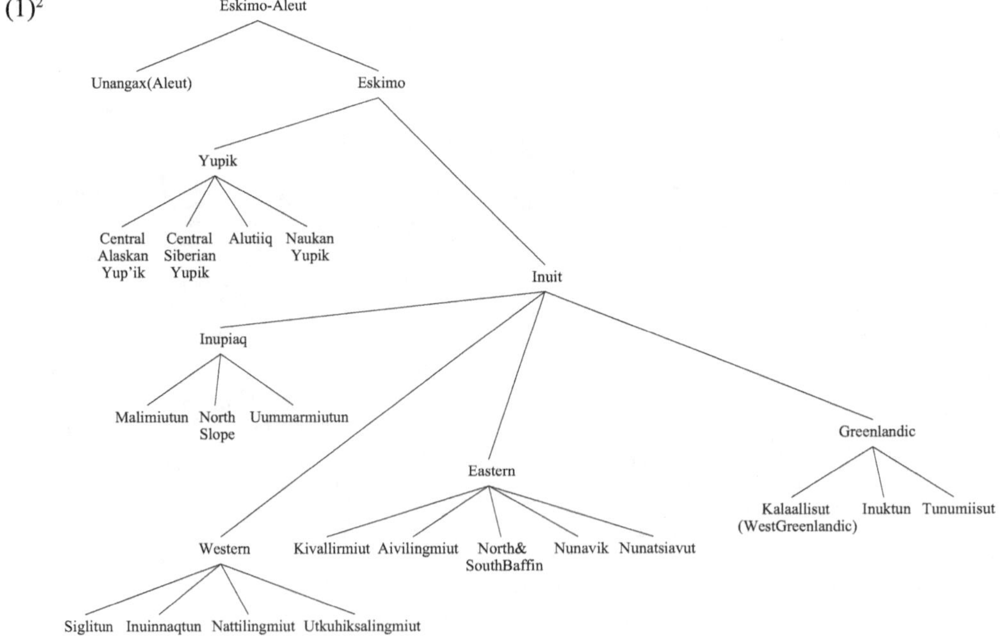

are not precise. It is also relevant to be aware of when communities have viewpoints about language groupings that differ from a purely linguistic perspective.

Unangax̂ or Aleut is an independent language within this family and differs the most from the others, having broken off the earliest. The name Aleut is an exonym based on the name of the volcanic islands (Aleutian) where the language was traditionally spoken. Recent endonyms are Unangax̂ or Unangam Tunuu.

Unangax̂ is related but distinct from the branch of languages referred to as Eskimo, which consist of Yupik languages and the Inuit language. The term Eskimo is an exonym and is still used in Alaska in English as a term to refer to both Alaska Inuit (Inupiat) and/or to Yupit people. In contrast, the term Eskimo is no longer considered acceptable in other Inuit areas.[3] These generally use the term Inuit for the people but often prefer local group labels. For example, in the Northwest Territories of Canada (NWT), the term for the Inuit people in that region is Inuvialuit, and their group of dialects is called Inuvialuktun, while in Kalaallit Nunaat, the people refer to themselves as Kalaallit.

Within the Eskimo group there are two divisions. The Yupik division consists of four languages. The one with the largest number of speakers is Central Alaskan Yup'ik (see Jacobson 1995; 2012). Central Siberian Yupik is the next largest language in this group and is spoken both in Siberia and St. Lawrence Island, Alaska. Alutiiq (known also as Sugpiaq or Pacific Gulf Yupik) is spoken in southern Alaska. Finally, the smallest language is Naukan Yupik, which is spoken in Siberia.

The second division within the Eskimo group is the Inuit language, which stretches from Alaska through Inuit Nunangat (Canadian Inuit regions) to Kalaallit Nunaat. The many dialects are frequently mutually intelligible to varying degrees. A study examining in detail mutual intelligibility across the Inuit language would be both interesting and useful (see Fortescue 1985 for a linguistic perspective). The dialects of the Inuit language are divided into four main clusters: Inupiaq, Western, Eastern, and Greenlandic.[4]

Inupiaq consists of Malimiutun and North Slope, which are spoken in Alaska, USA, as well as Uummarmiutun. Since Uummarmiutun is spoken within the NWT, Canada, people there usually refer to it as Inuvialuktun. This is a regional term for the three NWT Inuit dialects, even though they are not closely related.

The Western cluster consists of Siglitun (NWT), Inuinnaqtun (NWT and Nunavut), Nattilingmiut (Nunavut), and Utkuhiksalingmiut (Nunavut). Siglit and the variety of Inuinnaqtun within the NWT[5] are also called Inuvialuktun. Nattilingmiut is spoken along the Arctic coast and Utkuhiksalingmiut is spoken along the Arctic coast and in Qamani'tuaq (Baker Lake).[6]

The Eastern cluster consist of dialects spoken on the west coast of Hudson Bay (Kivallirmiut, Aivilingmiut), through Baffin Island (North and South Baffin) through Nunavik (Northern Québec) dialects, and finally to Nunatsiavut (northern Labrador) dialects.[7]

The Inuit of Canada now use the name Inuktut to encompass all Inuit dialects within Canada.

The Greenlandic cluster consists of Kalaallisut (West Greenlandic), Inuktun (Polar or Thule), and Tunumiisut (East Greenlandic).

An excellent overview of the Eskimo-Aleut language family, focusing especially on Inuit dialects, is Dorais (2010), which includes an extensive set of references. See also Johns (2010) for a general introduction to morphosyntactic linguistic issues. Fortescue et al. (2010) provide an invaluable historical perspective of the entire language family with comparative examples (both lexical and inflectional) from many languages and dialects.

1.2. Vitality

Unangax̂ is the most severely endangered of the three languages, and is critically endangered according to the categories provided on UNESCO's Atlas of the World's Languages in Danger (Moseley 2010). Central Alaskan Yup'ik is reasonably healthy, with children still learning the language as a first language. In the NWT and in western Nunavut, the language has mostly older fluent speakers (definitely endangered), while in the rest of Nunavut the language is reasonably strong, though varying widely depending on the community (vulnerable). In Nunavik, the language is quite strong (vulnerable) and in Nunatsiavut it is definitely endangered, with one dialect (Rigolet) effectively extinct. In Greenland, Kalaallisut is vulnerable, while the other dialects are definitely endangered.

2. Phonology

Across the language family we find a set of three or four vowels, in addition to a length contrast. The main three vowels are /i/, /u/, and /a/ with a fourth vowel, /ə/, appearing in Yupik. Unangax̂, and all Inuit dialects, except for some varieties of Inupiaq, have collapsed /i/ and /ə/ to [i].[8] Nevertheless, other Inuit dialects still maintain the distinction in a more abstract form. In these dialects "strong i" triggers palatalization on following alveolar consonants, but "weak i" does not. Compton and Dresher (2011) argue that these dialects effectively maintain a four-vowel contrast, and that the other dialects have a genuine three-vowel system. Under their analysis, the single /i/ within the three-vowel varieties is predicted not to trigger palatalization, since palatalization was originally a contrastive feature [coronal] within the four-vowel system. The loss of contrast between the two i's resulted in loss of the single contrastive feature, thus loss of palatalization.

In terms of consonant inventory, the language family is known for its voiceless uvulars, which occur either as stops (most Inuit dialects) or fricatives (Unangax̂).

The uvular stop in onset position has changed to uvular/velar fricative in some Eastern Inuit dialects (for example, see Smith 1975). Unangax̂ has lost bilabial stops (Taff et al. 2001). The language family also has a voiced velar fricative /ɣ/. Most varieties also have a voiceless lateral fricative /ɬ/, with the exception of Inuinnaqtun, the Nunavik dialect, and some Baffin dialects. In these, it has merged with /h/ or /s/, respectively. In Kalaallisut, only geminate /l/ is voiceless. All varieties have a voiced uvular continuant /ʁ/.[9] Some Western dialects also have a distinct phoneme /ɹ/. A number of Western dialects also have [h] where other dialects have [s] (see Dyck & Briggs 2005).

Members of the language family uniformly do not allow consonant clusters in either coda or onset position.[10] As a result, clusters appear only when there is a single coda followed by a single onset. The more phonologically conservative dialects in the west permit a wider range of cluster combinations (while also allowing geminates) than the eastern ones. The latter have undergone a great deal of assimilation to the extent than many mixed clusters have become (near) geminates. The examples in (2) illustrate differences across dialects.[11] Notice that the Yup'ik words often have more syllables, so shortening of some sort seems to have taken place to produce the more eastern cognates.

(2)		*Yup'ik*[12]	*Kangiryuarmiut*	*Labrador*	*Gloss*
	a	[qa**vl**uq]	[qablu]	[χa**ll**uk]	'eyebrow'
	b.	[up**n**I**ʁk**aq]	[upi**nŋ**aaq]	[upi**ŋŋ**aak]	'springtime'
	c.	[piʧI**ʁt**uk]	[pI**qt**ʊq]	[pi**tt**uk]	'blizzard' 'drifting snow'
	d.	[nI**vk**oq]	[mi**pk**u]	[ni**kk**uk]	'dried meat (or fish)'
	e.	[nI**ŋ**I**lv**a**ɣ**toq]	[ni**ɣl**aqtʊq]	[ni**ll**avuk]	'It got colder.'
	f.	[uta**q**al**ɣ**i**ʁ**toq]	[uta**qq**ijʊq]	[uta**kχ**ijuk]	'He/she is waiting.'

The varying degrees of consonant cluster assimilation across Inuit dialects are examined in Dorais (1986) and Bobaljik (1996).

Some Inuit dialects exhibit a cluster reduction rule that operates left to right across the word, referred to as Schneider's Law or the Law of Double Consonants. This phenomenon reduces a cluster of consonants from complex (two consonants) to simple (one consonant) if a syllable containing a complex cluster immediately precedes. Some examples are in (3) from the Nunavik dialect spoken in Québec. Note that the negative morpheme is *-nngit-*, i.e., geminate /ŋŋ/. Deleted consonants are in parentheses.

(3) Nunavik

a. *aulla-(n)ngi-mmi-junga*
leave-NEG-also-PART.1SG
'I am also not going.'

b. *qanui-nngi-(m)mi-junga*
not.well-NEG-also-PART.1SG
'I am also fine.' [Lit. 'not doing badly']

(Mahieu 2017: 60)

We see in (3) that whether or not the geminate in the negative is simplified depends on whether or not the preceding stem contains a complex consonant cluster. What happens to the geminate in the negative in turn has consequences for the initial geminate of the morpheme *-mmi-* meaning 'also.' Rose et al. (2012) argue that this rule is a remnant of an older iambic metrical process which now produces trochaic patterning at the syllable level (for related phonological processes, see Kaplan 1985). Kaplan (2016) calls these underlying factors *nunataks*, after the geological term borrowed from the Inuit language to refer to protrusions or uncovered parts of mostly unseen geological forms, e.g., a ridge.

2.1. Prosody

Important to a linguistic understanding of these languages is the examination of prosody. The prosodic word can group together more units than are normally found in single words in other languages, resulting in polysynthesis (see Sadock 1980). The word in this language family is a continuous stretch of utterance, normally without pauses or corrections. It forms a domain for phonological processes that do not occur across words. Foundational work on prosody can be found for Yupik in Kraus (1985) and for Kalaallisut in Rischel (1974) and Fortescue (1983a; 1984). The only varieties which have been shown to have stress are Unangax̂ and Yupik/Yup'ik. Arnhold (2014), in an experimental study of Kalaallisut, describes the language as having no lexically specified tones, stress, or pitch accent. Prosody consists of tones attached to moras, creating tonal contours over the phonological word. The word ends in a HLH pattern, which sometimes is not fully realized. Yes/no questions end in a falling pitch. Arnhold proposes an additional intonation phrase which can connect short sequences of words and allows for other processes such as downstep. She examines focus contexts and finds pitch reset on focused words. Arnhold's study does not need a phonological phrase, but she acknowledges this might be the result of limitations of her data set. Research on prosodic hierarchies in Canadian varieties is needed.

2.2. Writing Systems

The use of many different writing systems across the language[13] family unfortunately obscures similarities. In Inuit Nunangat, there are at least five writing systems in use, two syllabic and three roman-based. A task force of Inuit Tapiriit Kanatami called Atausiq Inuktut Titirausiq is developing a proposal for a single writing system for Inuit Nunangat so that the educational system can produce more shared resources, and so that the writing system helps to strengthen unity across varieties (see Patrick et al. 2018).

The written symbol *r*, which represents uvular [ʁ], poses a problem in a few communities where Inuit believe it can represent only English sound r. Although the letter r is not used in the modern Labrador Inuttut writing system, one can hear [ʁ] in speech, although it may no longer be phonemic.[14] In the current Labrador system, both [ʁ] and [ɣ] are written as g.

Within Baffin dialects, there is a need to pay special attention to [N] (see Bobaljik 1996), which results from voicing and nasal assimilation of /q/ when it immediately precedes a nasal. While in other dialects this is written as r (based on voicing), some Baffin speakers prefer to write this sound as ng, based on the nasality of [N]; however, ng is how velar nasals [ŋ] are written, so learners could easily make pronunciation mistakes based on this usage. The sequence N+nasal vs. ŋ+nasal is still contrastive. One solution would be to explicitly insist on the written use of an r, e.g., *qajar-mut* kayak-to 'to the kayak' (rather than the misleading *qajang-mut*), regardless of the nasalization of the final consonant of *qajaq* 'kayak' before a nasal.

3. Morphology

The languages in this family are very rich in morphology, and most of what we view as grammar is done via morphology. The components of a word are a root or stem, followed on the right by any derivational morphemes, followed by inflection (which is discussed in §4), and sometimes followed by clitics. More comprehensive works are Bergsland (1997) for Unangax̂; de Reuse (1994) for Siberian Yupik; Woodbury (1981; 2017), Jacobson (1995), and Miyoaka (2012) for Central Yup'ik; Lanz (2010) and MacLean (2014) for Inupiaq; Dorais (1988) for Nunavik Inuktut; and Fortescue (1984) for Kalaallisut. The derivational morphemes are the elements which make the word more complex, in fact the basis of polysynthesis. Within the Eskimo-Aleut literature, the roots are often referred to as bases and the derivational morphemes as postbases. Both verbs and nominals can be complex, as in (4) (see §3.2 for examples with just base and inflection).

(4) Labrador

a. *ilinnia-tit-si-Katau-gialla-nia-mmi-junga*
learn-CAUSATIVE-SEMTR-do.with.another-again-N.FUT-also-PART.1SG
'I will also teach with someone else'

b. *ilinnia-tit-si-Katta-lau-nni-ga-ni*
learn-CAUSATIVE-SEMTR-habitual-D.PAST-NMLZ-POSS.1SG/SG-LOC
'at the place where I taught before'

(Sara Townley, p.c.)

The base and final inflection are obligatory elements. Postbases are added to effect grammatical changes or to express additional meaning. Postbases are a finite set of elements essential for full grammatical expression, since they include negation, passive, quantity, etc. (see Fortescue 1983b for comparative list across some dialects). In some Eastern Inuktut dialects, bases may be dropped, similar to ellipsis (Swift & Allen 2002). Bases can be nominal, verbal, and sometimes demonstrative or pronominal.

3.1. *Morphophonology*

A morpheme joins to the right of another with a variety of phonological effects. These include no change, as in (5); deletion of the preceding consonant (6); assimilation of the preceding consonant (7); or fusion/coalescence (8), etc. Which process is triggered is a property of the attaching morpheme.

(5) Inupiaq

kaŋiq-siuq-
source-seek
'to investigate/study/ask questions about/ inquire about'

(MacLean 2014)

(6) Utkuhiksalingmiutut Inuktut

nutaraugama
nutaraq-u-gama
child-be-CAUS.1SG
'when I was a child'

(Briggs et al. 2015)

(7) Unangax̂

axtuĝ-
aĝ-tuĝ-
pût/gîve-several
'to put several; to give to several'

(Bergsland 1994)

(8) N. Baffin

isirumajuq
isiq-juma-juq
enter-want-PART.3SG
'He wants to enter.'

(Harper 1979)

Yupik has even more complex processes, as in (9) where the postbase *-(u)sigh* deletes any final /gh/ if it is preceded by any vowel but schwa. The resulting two vowels assimilate.

(9) Siberian Yupik

igaasiq
igagh-(u)sigh
write-instrument.for.Ving
'pen/pencil'

(de Reuse 1994: 22)

Fortescue (1992) argues that these morphophonological alternations effectively maintain morpheme boundaries through increased salience.

There is also a consonant mutation process which is termed consonant gradation (Kaplan 1982). This is found in western varieties of Inuit (see Kaplan 1981; Lowe 1985b) and Kalaallisut. Eastern Inuktut dialects do not exhibit this, except in occasional frozen forms. Typical examples are triggered by suffixation, as in (10).

(10) Inupiaq 'raven' [ABS]

a.	tulugaq	singular
b.	tulukkak	dual
c.	tulukkat	Plural

(Kaplan 1981: 169)

In (10) we see that the consonant is geminated and devoiced in the environment preceding a dual *-k* or plural *-t* suffix.

3.2. Bases (Roots)

Every word must have a base, verbal, nominal, dummy or even antecedent.

Verbal bases can be divided into stative (11a), durative (or atelic) (11b), or non-durative (or punctual) (11c). See Bohnemeyer and Swift (2004) and Spreng (2012) for discussion of verb classes.

(11) Uummarmiut (Inupiaq)

a. *ilihima-r̂uq*
know-PART.3SG
'She knows.'

b. *niri-r̂uq*
eat-PART.3SG
'He is eating.'

c. *tikit-chuq*
arrive-PART.3SG
'She arrived.'

(Lowe 1984)

Note that the non-durative class is translated into English as immediate past, as in (11c).

A second important property of a verbal stem (based on a verbal base or verbal postbase) is whether or not it requires both subject and object inflection on the verb. Subject-only inflection is often termed "intransitive" and subject/object inflection is "transitive". This terminology is somewhat misleading because the object may appear in the utterance without inflection on the verb (in the antipassive/semi-transitive construction). I therefore use the terminology of Dorais (1988), who labels this distinction single person vs. double person. Examples from the Nunavik dialect are shown in (12).

(12) Nunavik (Eastern)

a. *puibjuraq-tuq*
swim-PART.3SG
'She is swimming.'

b. *kailla-paa*
encourage-INDIC.3SG/3SG
'He encourages him.'

c. tikip-paa
arrive-INDIC.3SG/3SG
'He reaches it.' ('He arrives there.')

(Schneider 1985)

Many intransitive verbs that do not allow an object in English readily allow double person inflection in Inuktut, as in (12c).

Non-adjectival verb bases are inherently eventive relating to the speech act, and morphology must be added to make them habitual, as in (13).

(13) Labrador

immu-mik imi-Katta-tuk
milk-MOD.SG drink-often-PART.3SG
'He drinks milk.'

As a result, the example in (12a) cannot be interpreted habitually. Compton (2012) shows that there is a distinct adjectival class which behaves differently from verbs in subtle ways. For example, in some dialects, if a modal is added, adjectival bases require an intervening participial plus copula, as in (14).[15]

(14) S.Baffin

a. *sanngi-junga*
strong-PART.1SG
'I am strong.'

(Compton 2012: 26)

b. *sanngi-ju-u-gunnaq-tunga*
strong-PART-be-can-PART.1SG
'I can be strong.'

(Compton 2012: 41)

Nominals bases are strikingly uniform in properties; however, Gillon (2012) shows that subtle differences can be found to differentiate between individuated (count) vs. non-individuated (mass) noun bases.

3.3. Postbases

While bases are an open class, postbases are a closed class, consisting of a few hundred elements which either expand on the meaning of the stem, as in (15), or alter the valency of the stem by adding extra arguments, as in (16).

(15) Inupiaq

ii-qqayaq-
swallow-almost-
'to almost swallow'

(MacLean 2014)

(16) Kalaallisut

sana-ap-paa
sana-ut-paa
work.on-APPL-INDIC.3SG/3SG
'He made something for him.'

(Fortescue 1984)

Postbases can be higher matrix predicates, such as in (17).

(17) Central Alaskan Yupik

angun kaig-ni-uq
man[ABS.SG] hungry-say-3SG
'The man says that he is hungry.'

(Jacobson 1995)

Specific postbases change the category of the stem from nominal to verbal or vice versa.

(18) Tunumiisut (East Greenlandic)

kamik-taaq-puq
boot-get-INDIC.3SG
'He has new boots.'

(Tersis 2008)

(19) Uummarmiut (Inuktut)

nirri-vik
eat-place.for[ABS.SG]
'a place to eat; a table'

(Lowe 1984)

Although the addition of postbases is the source of lengthy word/sentences (see §5.4 on polysynthesis), limitations on processing apply. The result is that long words usually do not contain more than six postbases.

4. Inflection

Both verbs and nouns have obligatory inflection. Inflectional paradigms are the main components of most traditional grammars, as they are numerous and form the building blocks of the syntax. Woodbury (2004) says that Central Alaska Yupik has 1,500 inflectional endings.

4.1. Nominal Inflection

Nominal inflection consists of number, possession, and case. There is no gender distinction in this language family. Number consists of singular, plural. Most varieties of Inuit also have dual, with the exception of Kalaallisut and Tunumiisut (East Greenlandic), which have lost dual altogether. There is possessive inflection on both possessors and possessees. Possessors are marked with relative case (see (23b)), while possessees are marked for some combination of possessor/possessee features. A small number of nominal bases exhibit a property similar to inalienable possession. These are not body parts or individual family members, but bases indicating position in the form of a part/whole relation (20).

(20) Aivilingmiut

sivuni-a
front-POSS.3SG/3SG
'its front/in front of it'

(Spalding 1998)

Examples in (21) from Kangiryuarmiut show possessive marking followed by case. The combination is often treated as portmanteau morphemes.

(21) Kangiryuarmiut

a. *iglu-mnun*
house-POSS.1SG/SG;DU;PL.ALL
'to my house/houses'

(Lowe 1985a)

b. *iglu-ingnun*
tent-POSS.3SG/DU.ALL
'to his houses (two)'

(Lowe 1985a)

The example in (21a) shows a stem *iglu* 'house' followed by inflection *-mnun*. Although we might be tempted to break up this inflection into *-m-* POSS.1SG/SG;DU;PL + *-nun-* allative case, the situation is more complicated, since 'my 2 houses' in absolutive case is *iglu-kka*, where *-kka* is POSS.1SG/DU[ABS.SG].

Dialects in the east often have innovative forms, probably resulting from the ambiguities produced from consonant cluster assimilation. For example, the Labrador version of (21a) is *illo-kka-nut* (illuu-kka-nut). This form shows the dual triggering lengthening of the last vowel of the stem *illu* 'house', followed by 1SG/N.SG possessive marking *-kka*, followed by allative case. The innovative Labrador form is more agglutinative than the conservative form in (21a), since the features are more transparently spread across the morphemes.

4.1.1. Number

Number pervades the nominal, verbal, and pronominal/demonstratives systems but, as in most languages, it often undergoes syncretism when multiple features interact. We see this in the Kangiryuarmiut dialect in (22). There is no distinction in (22c) between first-person singular with singular, dual, or plural possessee in ablative case (see also (21a)), even though it makes distinctions in absolutive case (22a) and (22b).[16]

(22) Kangiryuarmiut

a. *iglu-kka*
house-POSS.1SG/DU[ABS.SG]
'my (two) tents'

b. *iglu-tka*
house-POSS.1SG/PL[ABS.SG]
'my (many) tents'

c. *iglu-mnin*
house-POSS.1SG/SG;DU;PL.ABL.SG
'from my (two) houses' or 'from my (many) houses'

(Lowe 1985a)

Inuit educators have voiced concern over the loss of the dual in younger generations of speakers. Its use has never been thoroughly studied in the natural speech of older generations (Alorut & Johns 2016).

4.1.2. Person

Nouns and verbs in this family have first, second, and third person, and a second third person which is called either reflexive third person or fourth person. Reflexive third person in nominals marks possessors that are obligatorily coindexed to a higher, not necessarily preceding, third person, as in the Uummarmiutun example in (23), where *-ni* indicates that the possessor is the identical to the subject of the verb.

(23) Uummarmiutun

irñi-ni	*apiqȓu-raa*
son-POSS.3R[ABS.SG]	ask-PART.3SG/SG

'He$_i$ asked his$_{i/*j}$ son'

(Lowe 1985b)

In principle, two third persons within a single clause/utterance would be expected to be interpreted as disjoint in reference (see Baker and de Souza on switch-reference, this volume). In reality, syncretism, dialect change, etc., often result in two co-indexed third persons not being marked with 3R, especially in eastern dialects (see Mauro 2018). In the Labrador dialect, possessive third-person reflexive is entirely absent on nominals in absolutive case, as in (24a). In this configuration, third person is ambiguous as disjoint or same person. Nonetheless, in oblique case contexts, the 3/3R distinction is maintained, as seen in (24b).

(24) Labrador

a. *anguti-up* *taku-janga* *inni-nga*/*inni-ni
man-REL.SG see-PART.3SG/SG son-POSS.3SG/SG[ABS.SG]/-3R[ABS.SG]
'The man saw his$_{i/j}$ son.'

b. *angutik* *inni-mi-nik* *taku-juk*
man[ABS.SG] son-POSS.3R-MOD see-PART.3SG
'The man sees his$_{i/*j}$ son.'

(Johns 1996a)

4.1.3. Case

There are eight nominal cases in Inuit (seven in Yupik). The linguistic terminology is not consistent across grammars, nor is it particularly transparent. Inuktut terminology of grammatical terms would be very helpful (see, for example, Dorais 1988). In (25), we see examples of the cases in Labrador Inuttut.

(25) Labrador Inuttut

a. Absolutive (phonetically null in singular)
naujak *nigi-juk*
seagull[ABS.SG] eat-PART.3SG
'The seagull is eating.'

b. Relative (sometimes called ergative on subjects of double person verbs)
nauja-up *mikKu-nga*
seagull-REL.SG feather-POSS.3SG/SG[ABS.SG]
'the seagull's feather'

c. Modalis (also called instrumental, comitative, or even accusative)
nauja-mik *taku-kKau-vunga*
seagull-MOD.SG see-N.PAST-INDIC.SG
'I saw a seagull (today).'

d. Allative (also called terminalis or dative)
kakivam-mut *iKalunnia-juk*
fish.spear-ALL.SG trout.fishing-PART.SG
'He is after trout with a spear.'

(Jeddore 1976)

e. Ablative
KakKa-mit *taku-tsak*
hill-ABL.SG see-POT
'It can be seen from the hill.'

(Jeddore 1976)

f. Locative
Kaittu-mi *situgangua-jut*
rock.bank-LOC.SG play.slide-PART.3PL
'They are sliding down the rock bank.'

(Jeddore 1976)

g. Translative (also called vialis or perlative)
nuvuja-kkut *tingi-juk*
cloud-TRAN.SG fly-PART.SG
'It is flying through the clouds.'

(Jeddore 1976)

h. Simulative (also called similaris)
uvat-tut *pi-kasâ-vuk*
1s.PRO-SIM.SG dummy-almost-INDIC.3SG
'He nearly did what I did.'

(Jeddore 1976)

Like other case languages, each case often serves multiple purposes. For example, the allative case is also found on agents of passive in Labrador Inuttut. The Kangiryuarmiut dialect uses the ablative case for agents of passive.

Note that the /m/ forms of singular case morphemes become /n/ when they attach directly to inflection or pronouns, as in (24b) and (21).

While Yupik has merged (combined) ablative with modalis, South Baffin has merged modalis with ablative.[17]

4.2. Verbal Inflection

Verbs do not have infinitive forms. All verbs that are not derived through postbases into nominals must end in a mood. Mood is followed by person/number of subject for single person stems and subject/object for double person stems. Whether the stem is single or double person depends on the verb and whether postbases have affected its valency.

4.2.1. Moods

Verbal moods also have many alternative names, which will be given in parentheses. Again, a language-based set of terminology would be welcome. Moods divide into two types: main moods and dependent moods. Main moods are usually stand-alone propositions, while dependent moods are propositions that co-occur with or seem to imply a main proposition. I will first provide an outline of the main moods.

Statement moods are indicative, as in (26a), or participial,[18] as in (26b), or either, depending on the language variety.[19]

(26) Nunavik

a. *taku-vaatit*
see-INDIC.3SG/2SG
'He/she/it sees you.'

b. *taku-jaatit*
see-PART.3SG/2SG
'He/she/it sees you.'

c. *taku-juq*
see-PART.3SG
'He/she/it sees' or 'the one who sees'

(Dorais 1988: 58–59)

Participial forms often can be found with nominal interpretations, as shown in (25c). When it is nominal, it has the interpretation translated into English as a relative clause. The indicative mood is never nominal. The change in the status of the participial across varieties is fascinating (Johns 1996b; Berge 2017). As Berge (2017) discusses, the participial mood becomes more restricted in eastern dialects and is generally not used in main clauses in Greenlandic varieties. In the Labrador dialect, person and grammatical function interact with the use of participial/indicative so that the participial is optional in some contexts but prohibited in others. For example, the participial is generally prohibited in first or second person single person contexts in Labrador Inuttut (Smith 1977; Johns 1996a; 1996b);[20] nonetheless, it can appear after *-mmi* 'also', as in (4a) in §3.

Interrogative mood is used for questions, as in (27a), but questions can also be formed with the participial mood plus phonological processes, as in (27b).

(27) Labrador Inuttut

a. *nigi-vâ* [â=aa]
eat-INTERR.3SG
'Is she eating?'

b. *nigi-jong* [o=uu][21]
eat-PART.3SG
'Is she eating?'

The imperative mood is closely related to the optative mood. Both moods serve to exhort the listener to an action. As we see in (28c), the optative mood exhorts the listener to refrain from an unspecified action that would prevent someone else's specified action (Mackenzie 2016). This produces the English translation 'Let X. . .'.

(28) Kalaallisut

a. *niri-guk*
eat-IMP.3SG
'Eat it'

b. *qaa-git*
come-IMP.2SG
'Come'

c. *urnil-li-sigut*
come.to-OPT.3SG-1PL
'Let him come to us.'

d. *patin-nanga*
hit-NEG.CONJ.1SG
'Don't hit me.'

(Fortescue 1984: 25–26)

Cross-linguistically, a negative form of the imperative often triggers an alternative mood, such as the example in (28d). In this case, it is the conjunctive mood (see Cook & Isac 2014; Mackenzie 2016).

The dependent moods consist of the conjunctive (contemporative; appositional; participial), the causative (perfective),[22] and the conditional. One observes many instances of dependent moods on a single verb of an utterance, as in (28d). This topic of dependent mood marking on main verbs has not been fully investigated. In some Baffin dialects, the causative mood is used in questions (29).

(29) Baffin

kina-u-gavit
who-be-CAUS.2SG
'Who are you?'

The conjunctive mood is one of the most important moods of the language. Its primary use is to link clauses to main clauses through temporality, the default being simultaneity, as in (30a). It can also link clauses in terms of preceding or following the time of the main clause, similar to the meanings conveyed in English by prepositions 'before' and 'after'.

(30) S. Baffin

a. *miali* *niri-tillugu* *jaan* *pisu-lauq-tuq*
Mary[ABS.SG] eat-DJ.CONJ.3SG John[ABS.SG] walk-D.PAST-PART.3SG
'While Mary was eating, John was walking.'

b. *iglu-ga*[23] *salummaqsar-niaq-tunga*
house-POSS.1SG/SG[ABS.SG] clean-N.FUT-PART.1SG
naulaq *qai-lau-nngi-tillugu*
Naulaq[ABS.SG] come-D.PAST-NEG-DJ.CONJ.3SG
'I will clean my house before Naulaq comes.'

c. *ullumi* *silalu-lauq-tillugu* *jaan* *qai-niaq-tuq*
today rain-D.PAST-DJ.CONJ.3SG John[ABS.SG] come-N.FUT-PART.3SG
'Today after it rains John will come.' or
'Today when it has rained, John will come.'

(Hayashi 2011)

The causative mood is normally used in dependent clauses which either encode reason pertaining to the main clause event (31), or temporal linking ('when X'), as in (32).

(31) Nunavik

tikim-mat *aliasut-tunga*
arrive-CAUS.3SG glad-PART.1SG
'Because he arrives, I am glad.'

(Dorais 1988, 63)

(32) Kangiryuarmiut

tikin-mata *hinik-tugut*
arrive-CAUS.3PL sleep-PART.1PL
'When they arrived, we were sleeping.'

(Lowe 1985a: 168)

The closely related conditional mood encodes 'if X' (33) or 'when X' (34), with respect to the main clause.

(33) Kangiryuarmiut

taku-gupku *apiri-niaq-tara*
see-COND.1SG/3SG ask-N.FUT-PART.3SG
'If I see him I will ask him.'

(Lowe 1985a: 153)

(34) N. Baffin

audla-ruvit *quviasu-jja-nngit-tunga*
depart-COND.2SG happy-def-NEG-PART.1SG
'When you go away, I will be unhappy.'

(Harper 1974: 20)

4.2.2. Person and Number Inflection on Verbs

One of the common distinctions found across the language family is that between single vs. double person, as in (35).

(35) Alaska Inupiaq

a. *niġi-gaa*
eat-PART.3SG/3SG
'She is eating it.'

b. *niġi-ruq*
eat-PART.3SG
'She is eating.'

(MacLean 2014: 761)

Double person marking is the lynchpin factor pertaining to what are called ergative constructions in the Inuit language (see §5.2).[24]

Most moods can be followed by either by single or double agreement, but the conjunctive mood has single agreement with either the subject or the object, but usually not both.[25] In the conjunctive mood, single subject correlates with intransitives and antipassive subjects (36), while single object correlates with transitive objects (with the non-agreeing subject understood as the subject of the verb of the main clause), as in (37).

(36) Uummarmiut (Inuktut)

naniriaqtuq-tillunuk *Iñuuvik-tuaq*
trap-DJ.CONJ.1DU Inuvik-3SG
'While we were trapping, she went to Inuvik.'

(Lowe 1985b: 200)

(37) Siglit (Inuktut)

ani-llugu *angivi-tara*
go.out-CONJ.3SG take.apart-PART.1SG/3SG
'I put it outside and took it apart.'

(Lowe 1985c: 229)

Note the disjoint marker *til* preceding the conjunctive mood in (35). This form is obligatory when the subject of the conjunctive is not the same as the subject of the verb of the main clause. Johns and Smallwood (1999) show that in some dialects, this morpheme is optionally found even when subjects of the two clauses are the same (see also Mauro 2018). The conjunctive mood has allomorphs sensitive to the tense of the higher clauses[26] and to negation. This mood varies in use across dialects in complex and interesting ways that have not been fully studied. Although a widely used and core mood within the grammar, this is one of the least-studied sets of verbal inflection in Inuktut and the language family from a theoretical perspective.

One main difference between inflection on independent and dependent moods is that only dependent moods are able to mark third-person reflexive on verb forms, similar to what we saw with respect to the possessive forms in §4.1.2.

(38) Kangiryuarmiut (Inuktut)

a. *qinmiq* *qakutaq* *tigu-ngmagu* *qirnarik-tuq*
dog[ABS.SG] white[ABS.SG] take-CAUS.3SG/3SG black-PART[ABS.SG]
put-tuq
cower-PART.3SG
'When he grabbed the white dog, the black one cowered.'

(Lowe 1985a: 168–169)

b. *nanuq* *hiqqura-pqar-mani* *ulru-yuq*
polar.bear[ABS.SG] shoot-barely-CAUS.3SG/3R fall.over-PART.3SG
'As soon as he shot at the polar bear, it fell over.'

(Lowe 1985a: 168–169)

In (38a) the object of the dependent clause and the subject of the main clause are different, but in (38b) they are the same. Again, dialects vary in this property; Eastern dialects inflect for reflexive subject but rarely inflect for reflexive objects.

5. Syntax and Semantics Issues

There have been a number of linguistic threads of debate and discussion surrounding topics in the Eskimo-Aleut languages. Some of these include the nature of tense/aspect in the languages, what syntactic or semantic properties lie behind the double transitive (ergative) construction, and how to analyze noun incorporation, where nominals are morphologically part of the verb. I provide a brief discussion of each of these issues.

5.1. Aspect/Tense

The languages of this family are rich in tense and aspectual distinctions. Verb roots have inherent aspect, as demonstrated in §3.2 where no marking on a durative base results in present progressive (not habitual) meaning. In contrast, no marking on a non-durative base results in immediate past interpretation (see analyses in Bohnemyer & Swift 2004; Hayashi 2011).

Trondhjem (2012; 2016; 2017) provides discussion of the types of aspectual distinctions found in Kalaallisut (see Mithun & Ali 1996 for Central Alaskan Yup'ik). She describes how the base aspect may be modified through the addition of postbases, as in (39).

(39) Kalaallisut

iser-uma-voq
enter-want-INDIC.3SG
's/her wants to come in'

(Trondhjem 2017: 68)

In this example the base verb is non-durative verb *iser-* 'enter' (termed perfective by Tronhjem 2017). The construction becomes a state through the addition of the postbase meaning *-(j)uma* 'want', which itself has aspectual properties. In addition to postbases which carry aspect along with lexical meaning, there are postbases that only convey aspect, as in (40).

(40) Kalaallisut

ise-qattar-ta-ler-poq
enter-repeatedly-HABITUAL-begin-INDIC.3SG
'He begins to have the habit to enter repeatedly', e.g., several times a week because of a certain girl.

(Trondhjem 2017: 84)

Trondhjem points out that the sequence of three postbases in this example seems to act like a single unit with respect to the verb stem (see also Sadock 2017). This contrasts to the more general case, where each postbase scopes over the stem to its left (see Fortescue 1980 for a seminal analysis of postbase scope and interaction). We see very similar effects in Central Alaskan Yup'ik, shown in (41).

(41) Central Alaskan Yup'ik

uit-aurar-tur-a-lria
remain-continue-DURATIVE-repeatedly-PART.3SG
'He continued to stay still.'

(Mithun & Ali 1996: 121)

The Inuit language is sometimes said to lack a past tense distinction (Bittner 2005). Others argue that there is tense (Trondhjem 2009; Hayashi 2011). Western varieties within the language family appear to obligatorily mark only future. As Trondhjem (2009) discusses, Kalaallisut has an obligatory future marking, but past time is optionally marked. Time adverbs can serve to convey past tense, as in (42).

(42) Kalaallisut

ippassaq	*Piitaq*	*arpap-poq*
yesterday	Peter[ABS.SG]	run-INDIC.3SG

'Yesterday Peter was running.'

(Trondhjem 2009: 173)

Trondhjem reports that younger Kalaallisut speakers are obligatorily using various aspect markers to mark past tense, e.g., *-nikuu-* marked in parentheses in (43), where older speakers would not have marked anything.

(43) Kalaallisut

1996-mit	*1998-mut*	*Nuum-mi*	*suli-(nikuu)-vunga*
-ABL.SG	-ALL.SG	Nuuk-LOC.SG	work-(PRETERITE)-INDIC.1SG

'From 1996 to 1998 I worked in Nuuk.'

(Trondhjem 2009: 179)

In contrast, as Hayashi (2011) discusses, a number of eastern Inuit dialects must obligatorily mark past tense – compare Kalaallisut (42) with (44).

(44) S. Baffin

* *jaan*	*mumiq-tuq*	*ippatsaq*
John[ABS.SG]	dance-PART.3SG	yesterday

'John danced/was dancing yesterday.'

(Hayashi 2011)

In addition, these dialects display gradient tense distinctions, e.g., between past today (near past) and past before today (distant past), as in the examples in (45).

(45) S. Baffin

a. *	*jaan*	*tiki-qqau-juq*	*ippatsaq*
	John[ABS.SG]	arrive-N.PAST-PART.3SG	yesterday
	'John arrived yesterday.'		
b.	*jaan*	*mumiq-laut-tuq*	*ippatsaq*
	John[ABS.SG]	dance-D.PAST-PART.3SG	yesterday
	'John danced/was dancing yesterday.'		

(Hayashi 2011)

In (45a), there is near past tense marking on the verb, but this form is restricted to the day of the utterance. In (45b), we see the appropriate distant past marking on the verb, which is compatible with the external adverbial. Gradient tense markers vary across dialects, and their use even varies within a single dialect (Hayashi 2011; Hayashi & Oshima 2015). In particular, dependent mood clauses sometimes lack distinctions found in main mood clauses.

5.2. Ergativity

Ergativity is a syntactic issue that has been the topic of much attention. Transitive agents have a special pattern, while intransitive subjects and transitive objects pattern the same. The examples are from the Kangiryuarmiut dialect (Lowe 1985a). The first example (46a) is an intransitive verb (single person), and the second example is a transitive verb (double person).

(46) Kangiryuarmiut

a. *nutaqqa-t* *ulapqiuyaq-tut*
child\INFL-PL[ABS.SG] play-PART.3PL
'The children are playing.'

(Lowe 1985a: 36)

b. *iqaluk* *qinmi-m* *niri-yaa*
fish[ABS.SG] dog\INFL-REL.SG eat-PART.3SG/SG
'The dog ate the fish.'

(Lowe 1985a: 114)

We see that in (46a), the subject *nutaqqat* 'children' is in absolutive case, but in (46b), the subject *qinmi-m* 'dog' is in relative case. Moreover, the object *iqaluk* 'fish' in (46b) is also in absolutive case. This patterning has been analyzed by numerous syntacticians and semanticists (Bok-Bennema 1991; Johns 1992; Murasugi 1992; Bittner & Hale 1996a; 1996b; Wharram 2003; Spreng 2012; Yuan 2018; among others). For an overview, see Compton (2017).

The assumption that the double person construction in (43b) is the canonical transitive clause in these languages is somewhat misleading. The Inuit language typically shows a larger proportion of single person (intransitive) verbs compared to intransitive verbs in other languages (Berge 2011; Allen 2013). Intransitives can result from passivization and noun incorporation. Equally intransitives (single person) result from another object construction in the language. This is the so-called antipassive or semi-transitive, the latter a more neutral term. An object with this type of verb is shown in another Kangiryuarmiut example in (47).

(47) Kangiryuarmiut

tuktu-mik *taku-yuq*
caribou-MOD.SG see-PART.3SG
'He saw a caribou.'

(Lowe 1985a: 60)

This alternative to the double person object construction varies across dialects. While in Western varieties of Inuit it is restricted to themes of ditransitives or to indefinites, in Eastern dialects it is much less restricted and appears to be almost the default object construction, appearing on proper names, etc. (Johns 2001; 2006).

Johns (2017), Johns and Kučerová (2017), and Yuan (2018) propose that some elements of double person agreement are clitic in nature, thus accounting for dialects where it appears to be in complementary distribution with overt nominals. These authors, as well as Woolford (2017), also examine striking similarities between Inuit dialects and Unangax̂. Finally, Carrier (2017) provides the first real evidence that ergativity is decreasing in an Inuit dialect, using a quantitative methodology across speakers of different ages in one community. Previously, this change had been argued to have taken place based solely on comparative evidence.

5.3. Noun Incorporation

Noun incorporation involves issues that straddle morphology, syntax, and semantics. In the Eskimo-Aleut languages, it is an obligatory process involving specific verbal affixes that attach exclusively to a nominal root or other lexical material, as in (48), and others that, in addition, can attach to an inflected nominal, as in (49).

(48) Mittimatalik (North Baffin)

ulu-iruti-junga
ulu-lack-PART.1SG
'I'm out of ulus (type of knife).'

(Johns 2007: 549)

(49) Kalaallisut

Palasi-p	*illu-a-nu-kar-poq*
priest-REL.SG	house-POSS.SG/SG-ALL-go-INDIC.3SG

'He went to the priest's house.'

(Sadock 1980: 315)

Noun incorporation has attracted a great deal of attention because the object forms a unit within the complex predicate. Sadock (1980) shows convincingly that it cannot be a lexical process. The question is how to derive the construction. Van Geenhoven (1998) argues that it is derived by a process whereby predicative indefinites (incorporated nominals) undergo semantic incorporation with the verbal predicate, thus accounting for obligatory narrow scope. If there is an external discourse referent seemingly referring to the incorporated nominal, this results from properties of the verbal predicate, not the nominal.

Johns (2007) proposes a syntactic analysis, relying on the key fact that the postbases involved are not a random set of affixes. Instead, they consist of what linguists term light verbs. The nominal stem provides critical root material to the complex verb.

Sherkina-Lieber and Murasugi (2015) find in a morphosyntactic study that heritage speakers of Inuktut do not prefer non-incorporated constructions over incorporated alternants, and that they display reasonable knowledge of the syntactic properties of noun incorporation. Nevertheless, this knowledge is clearly not as good or as stable as that of fluent speakers.

5.4. Polysynthesis

As discussed in §3, members of the Eskimo-Aleut family exhibit polysynthesis, where the word may express not just a complete sentence but one that can contain adverbial modifiers, expressive elements, causatives, etc. Woodbury (2017: 536) describes Central Arctic Yupik as "exhuberantly polysynthetic". An example is shown in (50).

(50) Central Arctic Yupik

ane-ngnaq-saaqe-llru-ngat-aq-ua
go.out-try-alas!-in.the.past-seem-would-INDIC.1SG
'I would seem to have tried, to no avail, to go out.'

(Woodbury 2017: 554)

Fortescue (1980) is the first to formalize the word internal domain in detail, and many of the valuable proposals and insights of this paper have yet to be fully explored (see also Woodbury 1981). Compton and Pittman (2010) provide a novel explanation for a number of issues involving complex words. They argue, based on Chomsky (1999), that the only syntactic phases for the Inuktitut word are the clause and nominal (CP/DP). While DP words are similar to other languages, the lack of *v*P phase, etc., entails that adverbial, aspectual, tense, and even subject-oriented material will continue to be added to the word complex until the final clause end is reached. More recently, see Fortescue et al. (2017), which contains a number of papers pertaining to polysynthesis of Inuit and Yupik languages.

5.5. Other Areas

There is a lack of detailed study in other areas of syntax. Questions in Inuktut have been examined in Gillon (2000) and Sherkina-Lieber (2005). Höltl (2018) provides a typological overview of questions within the language family. Modals in Uummarmiutun have been examined in Berthelin (2017). Maria Bittner has done extensive formal semantics analyses of Kalallisut. Her webpage (Bittner, n.d.) provides a full list, as well as texts.

6. Conclusion

Although this language-family has received quite a bit of linguistic attention, there are topics which bear further formal investigation, and others which have been barely studied at all. In the former category is the third-person reflexive agreement, as well as the syntax of dependent clauses. In the latter is narrative structure (but see Woodbury 1985). Community linguistics issues are increasingly on the forefront, and linguists both in the academy and the communities are sharing efforts in producing materials and training.

Acknowledgments

My thanks to reviewers for many corrections and suggestions. I also thank Sarah Townley and other Nunatsiavummiut for examples from Labrador Inuttut. This research was supported by the Social Sciences and Humanities Research Council of Canada.

Further Reading

Beach, Matthew David. 2011. *Studies in Inuktitut grammar*. Buffalo, NY: University of Buffalo. (Doctoral dissertation.)

Berge, Anna. 2016. Eskimo-Aleut. In Brown, Keith (ed.), *Encyclopedia of language and linguistics*, 219–223. Amsterdam: Elsevier.

Fortescue, Michael. 2017. The Eskimo-Aleut language family. In Aikhenvald, Alexandra Y. and Dixon, R. M. W. (eds.), *The Cambridge handbook of linguistic typology*, 683–706. Cambridge: Cambridge University Press.

Johns, Alana. 2014. Eskimo-Aleut. In Lieber, Rochelle & Štekauer, Pavol (eds.), *The Oxford handbook of derivational morphology*, 702–724. Oxford: Oxford University Press.

Johns, Alana. 2017. Noun incorporation. In Everaert, Martin & van Riemsdijk, Henk (eds), *The Wiley-Blackwell companion to* syntax, 2nd edn., 2731–2757. New York, NY: Wiley-Blackwell.

Johns, Alana & Massam, Diane & Ndayiragije, Juvenal (eds.). 2006. *Ergativity: Emerging issues*. Dordrecht: Springer.

Kaplan, Lawrence D. & Berge, Anna (eds.). 2017. *Studies in Inuit linguistics in honor of Michael Fortescue* (Alaska Native Language Center Research Papers). Fairbanks: University of Alaska.

Lowe, Ronald. 1978. Le mythe de l'ergatif en Inuktitut. *Etudes/Inuit/Studies* 2. 108–115.

Lowe, Ronald. 1988. La forme declarative et l'alternance des suffixes -VU- et -JU- dans les dialects inuit d'Arctique canadien de l'Est. *Revue Quebecoise de linguistique* 17. 137–164.

Sadock, Jerrold. 2003. *A grammar of Kalaallisut* (*West Greenlandic Inuttut*). (Languages of the World/Materials 162.) Muenchen: LINCOM.

Sherkina-Lieber, Marina & Helms-Park, Rena. 2015. A prototype of a receptive lexical test for a polysynthetic heritage language: The case of Inuttitut in Labrador. *Language Testing* 32. 419–442.

Sammons, Mary Susan. 1985. *Inuktitut in Rankin Inlet*. Ann Arbor: University of Michigan. (Doctoral dissertation.)

Nagai, Tadataka. 2006. *Agentive and patientive verb bases in North Alaskan Inupiaq*. Fairbanks: University of Alaska. (Doctoral dissertation.)

Woodbury, Anthony C. 1985. Noun phrase, nominal sentence, and clause in Central Alaskan Yupik Eskimo. In Nichols, Johanna & Woodbury, Anthony C. (eds.), *Grammar inside and outside the clause: Some approaches to theory from the field*, 61–88. Cambridge: Cambridge University Press.

Notes

1. (i) *Kalaall-it* *Nuna-at*
   Greenlander-PL land- POSS.3PL/SG
   'Greenlanders' land'
2. Some glosses were added to examples that did not have any, and others were modified to make them consistent. Those not in or used differently from the Leipzig glossing rules are as follows: / = subject/object or possessor/possessee, caus = causative mood, cond = conditional mood, conj = conjunctive mood, dj. conj = disjoint conjunctive mood, d.past = distant past, imp = imperative mood, indic = indicative mood, \infl = stem has undergone phonological change because of following affix, inter = interrogative mood, mod = modalis, n.fut = near future, n.past = near past, n.sg = non-singular, opt = optative mood, part = participial mood, pot = potentiality (nominalizer), pro = pronoun, r = reflexive, rel = relative, semtr = semi-transitive, sim = simulative, tran = translative.
3. In 2010 the Inuit Circumpolar Council made a resolution that the term Eskimo should be replaced by Inuit in communities and science.
4. There is not enough space here to give a finer breakdown of these many varieties (see Dorais 2010).
5. Innuinaqtun within the NWT is also called Kangiryuarmiut (see Lowe 1985a; Kudlak & Compton 2018).
6. Quite a number of different dialect groups settled in Qamani'tuaq, which have presumably undergone dialect amalgamation, a natural consequence of close dialect contact.
7. The Labrador dialect has long been called Inuttut, although many also use Inuttitut or even Inuktitut when referring to the language in English.
8. Or to [a] before another vowel (Dorais 2010: 56).
9. The Labrador dialect is thought to be an exception.
10. It is therefore interesting that derivational morphemes exist which have two consonants initially. The first consonant forms the coda of the element to which it attaches, e.g., the negative affix /ŋŋit/ in Inuktut.
11. Yup'ik examples are phonetic renditions based on Jacobson (2012), Kangiryuarmiutun examples are based on Kudlak and Compton (2018), and Labrador Inuttut examples are based on Jeddore (1976).
12. The apostrophe in Yup'ik indicates a number of features. Here (after a consonant and before a vowel) it indicates that the p is geminated, but it has other uses as well (see Jacobson 2012).
13. The numerous writing systems derive from different contact histories (see Harper 1983 on the Canadian ones).
14. In the Rigolet dialect, uvular and velar alternants are conditioned by vowels (Dresher & Johns 1996).
15. Labrador Inuttut requires a copula on adjectives in first/second person but not on verbs:

    (i) *naittovunga*
    naittu-**u**-vunga
    short-be-INDIC.1SG
    'I am short.'

    but

    (ii) *nigi-vunga*
    eat-INDIC.1SG
    'I am eating.'
16. This is oversimplified. Other roots allow gradation, which affords further distinctions.
17. Some dialects in Nunavik are undergoing this merge also (Richard Compton, p.c.). In South Baffin, this change is likely related to an Eastern dialect process of word-final consonant deletion (Murasugi & Christie 2012). This process also manifests as consonant merger.
18. Participial is sometimes termed declarative.
19. I use indicative or participial mood to refer to particular sets of morphological forms (i.e., not function).
20. This restriction on first and second person looks to be a PCC (Person-Case Constraint; see Johns & Kučerová 2017).

21. In this example, the third-person singular participial ending *-juk* has been lengthened and nasalized to *-jong*. This process turns it into a question.
22. Note that the terms used for this mood are somewhat misleading, as there is no necessary causativization, and if it is indeed perfective, it would only be one small aspect of its meaning.
23. As far as I know, modalis case should be on the object here.
24. Double person is also relevant in the debate about whether or not the Inuit language involves possessor raising (Van Geenhoven 2002; Woolford 2017) since the "raised possessor" will be marked on the verb with double person.
25. This is for first/second person. Third-person reflexive may create double person inflection in some dialects (see Dorais 1988: 95–96 for double person conjunctive in Nunavik).
26. The conjunctive mood makes a morphological distinction between past/present and future forms, except in the disjoint form.

References

N.B.: Quite a number of the older materials are out of print.

Allen, Shanley E. M. 2013. The acquisition of ergativity in Inuktitut. In Bavin, Edith L. & Stoll, Sabine (eds.), *The acquisition of ergativity*, 71–106. Amsterdam: John Benjamins.

Alorut, Raigelee & Johns, Alana. 2016. The use of the dual in some Inuit dialects: The importance of *tirliaq*. *Amerindia* 38. 111–128.

Arnhold, Anja. 2014. Prosodic structure and focus realization in West Greenlandic. In Jun, Sun-Ah (ed.), *Prosodic typology II*, 216–251. Oxford: Oxford University Press.

Berge, Anna. 2011. *Topic and discourse structure in West Greenlandic agreement constructions*. Lincoln: University of Nebraska Press.

Berge, Anna. 2017. Is the participial and independent or a dependent mood? In Kaplan, Lawrence D. & Berge, Anna (eds.), *Studies in Inuit linguistics in honor of Michael Fortescue*, 123–134. (Alaska Native Language Center). Fairbanks: University of Alaska.

Bergsland, Knut. 1994. *Aleut dictionary: Unangam tunudgusii*. (Alaska Native Language Center). Fairbanks: University of Alaska.

Bergsland, Knut. 1997. *Aleut grammar: Unangam tunuganaan achixaasix̂* (Alaska Native Language Center Research Papers no. 10). Fairbanks: Alaska Native Language Center, University of Alaska.

Berthelin, Signe Rix. 2017. *The semantics and pragmatics of Uummarmiutun modals*. Trondheim: Norwegian University of Science and Technology. (Doctoral dissertation.)

Bittner, Maria. 2005. Future discourse in a tenseless language. *Journal of Semantics* 22. 339–387.

Bittner, Maria & Hale, Ken. 1996a. The structural determination of case and agreement. *Linguistic Inquiry* 27. 1–68.

Bittner, Maria & Hale, Ken. 1996b. Ergativity: Towards a theory of a heterogenous class. *Linguistic Inquiry* 27. 531–604.

Bittner, Maria. n.d. (https://sites.google.com/view/maria-bittner/home) (Accessed 2019-06-08.)

Bobaljik, Jonathan David. 1996. Assimilation in the Inuit languages and the place of the uvular nasal. *International Journal of American Linguistics* 62. 323–350.

Bohnemeyer, Jürgen & Swift, Mary. 2004. Event realization and default aspect. *Linguistics and Philosophy* 27. 263–296.

Bok-Bennema, Reineke. 1991. *Case and agreement in Inuit*. Berlin: Foris.

Briggs, Jean & Johns, Alana & Cook, Conor. 2015. *Utkuhikšalingmiut uqauhiitigut uqauhiliurut: Dictionary of Utkuhiksalingmiut Inuktitut postbase suffixes*. Iqaluit, NWT: Nunavut Arctic College Media.

Carrier, Julien. 2017. The ergative-antipassive alternation in Inuktitut: Analyzed in a case of new-dialect formation. *Canadian Journal of Linguistics/Revue Canadienne de Linguistique* 62. 661–684.

Chomsky, Noam. 1999. *Derivation by phase*. (MIT Occasional Papers in Linguistics 18). Cambridge, MA: MIT Press.

Compton, Richard. 2012. *The syntax and semantics of modification in Inuktitut: Adjectives and adverbs in a polysynthetic language*. Toronto: University of Toronto. (Doctoral dissertation.)

Compton, Richard. 2017. Ergativity in Inuktitut. In Coon, Jessica & Massam, Diane & Travis, Lisa (eds.), *The Oxford handbook of ergativity*, 832–850. Oxford: Oxford University Press.

Compton, Richard & Dresher, B. Elan. 2011. Palatalization and 'strong i' across Inuit dialects. *Canadian Journal of Linguistics/Revue Canadienne de Linguistique* 56. 203–228.

Compton, Richard & Pittman, Christine. 2010. Word formation by phase in Inuit. *Lingua* 120. 2167–2192.

Cook, Conor & Isac, Daniela. (2014). Shades of imperative force in Inuktitut. (Paper presented at MOLTH Syntax Workshop, McGill University, 22–23 March 2014.)

de Reuse, Willem J. 1994. *Siberian Yupik Eskimo: The language and its contacts with Chukchi*. Salt Lake City: University of Utah Press.

Dorais, Louis-Jacques. 1986. Inuktitut surface phonology: A trans-dialectal survey. *International Journal of American Linguistics* 52. 20–53.

Dorais, Louis-Jacques. 1988. *Tukilik: An Inuktitut grammar for all*. (Inuit Studies Occasional Papers 2/Cahiers d'Etudes Inuit 2). Québec: Association Inuksiutiit Katimajiit.

Dorais, Louis-Jacques. 2010. *The language of the Inuit: Syntax, semantics and society in the Arctic*. Montreal: McGill-Queen's University Press.

Dresher, Elan & Johns, Alana. 1996. Rigolet and phonological change in Labrador. *Études/Inuit/Studies* 20. 113–121.

Dyck, Carrie & Briggs, Jean. 2005. Historical antecedents of /h/, /s/, and /j/, and /ř/ in Utkuhiksalik (Inuktitut). *Études/Inuit/Studies* 29. 307–340.

Fortescue, Michael. 1980. Affix ordering in West Greenlandic derivational processes. *International Journal of American Linguistics* 46. 259–278.

Fortescue, Michael. 1983a. Intonation contours across Inuit dialects. *Études/Inuit/Studies* 7. 113–124.

Fortescue, Michael. 1983b. *A comparative manual of affixes for the Inuit dialects of Greenland, Canada and Alaska*. Copenhagen: Meddelelser om Grønland.

Fortescue, Michael. 1984. *West Greenlandic*. London: Croom Helm.

Fortescue, Michael. 1985. The degree of interrelatedness between Inuit dialects as reflected by percentages of shared affixes. *International Journal of American Linguistics* 51. 188–221.

Fortescue, Michael. 1992. Morphophonemic complexity and typological stability in a polysynthetic language family. *International Journal of American Linguistics* 58. 242–248.

Fortescue, Michael & Jacobson, Steven & Kaplan, Lawrence D. 2010. *Comparative Eskimo dictionary: With Aleut cognates*. 2nd edn. (Alaska Native Language Center Research Papers no. 9). Fairbanks: University of Alaska.

Fortescue, Michael & Mithun, Marianne & Evans, Nicholas. 2017. *The Oxford handbook of polysynthesis*. Oxford: Oxford University Press.

Gillon, Carrie. 2000. Multiple movement and wh-in-situ in Inuktitut. In *Proceedings of the West Coast conference on formal linguistics 19*, 111–124. Somerville, MA: Cascadilla Press.

Gillon, Carrie. 2012. Evidence for mass and count in Inuttut. *Linguistic Variation* 12. 211–246.

Harper, Kenn. 1974. *Some aspects of the grammar of the Eskimo dialects of Cumberland Peninsula and North Baffin Island*. (Mercury Series). Ottawa, ON: Museum of Man. (https://press.uottawa.ca/series/french-and-canadian-studies/mercury-series.html) (Accessed 2019-06-08.)

Harper, Kenn. 1979. *Suffixes of the Eskimo dialects of Cumberland Peninsula and North Baffin Island*. (Mercury Series). Ottawa, ON: Mercury Series, Museum of Man. (https://press.uottawa.ca/series/french-and-canadian-studies/mercury-series.html) (Accessed 2019-06-08.)

Harper, Kenn. 1983. Writing in Inuktitut: An historical perspective. *Inuktitut* 53. 3–84. (https://www.itk.ca/inuktitut-issue-53/) (Accessed 2019-06-08.)

Hayashi, Midori. 2011. *The structure of multiple tenses in Inuktitut*. Toronto: University of Toronto. (Doctoral dissertation.) (Accessed 2019-06-08.)

Hayashi, Midori & Oshima, David Y. 2015. How multiple past tenses divide the labor: The case of South Baffin Inuktitut. *Linguistics* 53. 773–808.

Höltzl, Andreas. 2018. *A typology of questions in Northeast Asia and beyond*. Berlin: Language Science Press.

Inuit Circumpolar Council. n.d. *The use of the term Inuit*. (https://www.inuitcircumpolar.com/wp-content/uploads/2019/01/iccexcouncilresolutiononterminuit.pdf) (Accessed 2019-06-08.)

Jacobson, Steven A. 1995. *A practical grammar of the Central Alaskan Yup'ik Eskimo language* (Alaska Native Language Center). Fairbanks: University of Alaska. (Also available through University of Chicago Press.)

Jacobson, Steven A. 2012. *Yup'ik Eskimo dictionary*. Fairbanks: Alaska Native Language Center, University of Alaska. (www.uaf.edu/anla/collections/search/resultDetail.xml?id=CY972J2012) (Accessed 2019-06-08.)

Jeddore, Rose. 1976. *Labrador Inuit uqausingit*. Nain, NL: The Labrador Committee on Literacy.

Johns, Alana & Kučerová, Ivona. 2017. On the morphosyntactic reflexes of the information structure in the ergative patterning of the Inuit language. In Coon, Jessica & Massam, Diane & Travis, Lisa (eds.), *The Oxford handbook of ergativity*, 397–418. Oxford: Oxford University Press.

Johns, Alana. 1992. Deriving ergativity. *Linguistic Inquiry* 23. 57–87.

Johns, Alana. 1996a. The occasional absence of anaphoric agreement in Labrador Inuttut. In Black, James R. & Motapanyane, Virginia (eds.), *Micro-parametric syntax and dialect variation*, 121–143. (Current Issues in Linguistic Theory 139). Philadelphia: John Benjamins.

Johns, Alana. 1996b. On some mood alternations in Labrador Inuttut. In Burgess, Clifford S. & Dziwirek, Katarzyna & Gerdtsm Donna (eds.), *Grammatical relations: Theoretical approaches to empirical questions*, 131–151. Stanford, CA: Center for the Study of Language and Information. (Also available through University of Chicago Press.)

Johns, Alana. 2001. Ergative to accusative: Comparing evidence from Inuktitut. In Faarlund, Jan Terje (ed.), *Grammatical relations change*, 205–221. Amsterdam: John Benjamins.

Johns, Alana. 2006. Ergativity and change in Inuktitut. In Johns, Alana & Massam, Diane & Ndayiragije, Juvenal (eds.), *Ergativity: Emerging issues*, 293–311. Dordrecht: Springer.

Johns, Alana. 2007. Restricting noun incorporation: Root movement. *Natural Language and Linguistic Theory* 25. 535–576.

Johns, Alana. 2010. Eskimo-Aleut languages. *Language and Linguistics Compass* 4. 1041–1055.

Johns, Alana. 2017. Anaphoric arguments in Unangax̂ and Eastern Canadian Inuktitut. In Kaplan, Lawrence D. & Berge, Anna (eds.), *Studies in Inuit linguistics in honor of Michael Fortescue*, 91–103. (Alaska Native Language Center). Fairbanks: University of Alaska.

Johns, Alana & Smallwood, Carolyn. 1999. On (non-)finiteness in Inuktitut. *Toronto Working Papers in Linguistics* 17. (http://twpl.library.utoronto.ca/index.php/twpl/article/view/6260) (Accessed 2019-06-08.)

Kaplan, Lawrence D. 1981. *Phonological issues in North Alaska Inupiaq*. (Alaska Native Language Research Papers no. 6). Fairbanks: University of Alaska.

Kaplan, Lawrence D. 1982. Consonant alternation in Inupiaq Eskimo. *International Journal of American Linguistics* 48. 385–393.

Kaplan, Lawrence D. 1985. Seward Peninsula Inupiaq consonant gradation and its relationship to prosody. In Krauss, Michael (ed.), *Yupik Eskimo prosodic systems: Descriptive and comparative studies*, 191–210. (Alaska Native Language Center Research Papers Number 7). Fairbanks: University of Alaska.

Kaplan, Lawrence D. 2016. Western Alaska: Inuit-Yupik language homeland and borderland. (Paper presented at 20th Inuit Studies conference, Memorial University of Newfoundland, 7–10 October 2016.)

Krauss, Michael (ed.). 1985. *Yupik Eskimo prosodic systems: Descriptive and comparative studies* (Alaska Native Language Center Research Papers no. 7). Fairbanks: University of Alaska.

Kudlak, Emily & Compton, Richard. 2018. *Kangiryuarmiut Inuinnaqtun Uqauhiitaa Numiktitirutait–Kangiryuarmiut Inuinnaqtun dictionary*. Iqaluit, NWT: Nunavut Arctic College Media.

Lanz, Linda A. 2010. *A grammar of Iñupiaq morphosyntax*. New Haven, CT: Yale University. (Doctoral dissertation.)

Lowe, Ronald. 1984. *Uummarmiut uqalungiha mumikhitchiȓutingit: Basic Uummarmiut Eskimo dictionary*. Inuvik, NWT: Committee of Original Peoples Entitlement.

Lowe, Ronald. 1985a. *Kangiryuarmiut uqauhingita ilihautdjutikhangit: Basic Kangiryuarmiut Eskimo grammar*. Inuvik, NWT: Committee of Original Peoples Entitlement.

Lowe, Ronald. 1985b. *Ummarmiut uqalungiha ilihauȓȓutikrangit: Basic Uummarmiut Eskimo grammar*. Inuvik, NWT: Committee of Original Peoples Entitlement.

Lowe, Ronald. 1985c. *Siglit Inuvialuit uqausiita ilisarviksait: Basic Siglit Inuvialuit Eskimo grammar*. Inuvik, NWT: Committee for Original Peoples Entitlement.

Mackenzie, Zoë. 2016. *A syntactic account of imperatives in Labrador Inuttut*. Toronto: University of Toronto. (MA Forum paper.)

MacLean, Edna Ahgeak. 2014. *Iñupiatun uqaluit taniktun sivuninit: Iñupiaq to English dictionary*. Fairbanks: University of Alaska Press. (Also available through University of Chicago Press.)

Mahieu, Marc-Antoine. 2017. Description du morphophonologique du l'inuktitut du Nunavik. In Kaplan, Lawrence D. & Berge, Anna (eds.), *Studies in Inuit linguistics in honor of Michael Fortescue*, 41–66. (Alaska Native Language Center). Fairbanks: University of Alaska.

Mauro, Christophe. 2018. *Le statut de la troisième personne en Inuktitut*. Montreal: Université du Québec à Montréal. (Mémoire.)

Mithun, Marianne & Ali, Elizabeth. 1996. The elaboration of aspectual categories: Central Yup'ik. *Folia Linguistica Europaea* 30. 111–128.

Miyaoka, Osahito. 2012. *A grammar of Central Alaskan Yupik: An Eskimo language*. (Mouton Grammar Library). Berlin: De Gruyter Mouton.

Moseley, Christopher (ed.). 2010. *Atlas of the world's languages in danger*. 3rd edn. Paris: UNESCO Publishing. (www.unesco.org/culture/en/endangeredlanguages/atlas) (Accessed 2017-10-26.)

Murasugi, Kumiko. 1992. *Crossing and nested paths: NP movement in accusative and ergative languages*. Cambridge, MA: MIT. (Doctoral dissertation.)

Murasugi, Kumiko & Christie, Elizabeth. 2012. Word-final consonant deletion in Inuktitut speakers. (Paper presented at the 18th Inuit Studies Conference, Washington, DC, 24–29 October 2012.)

Patrick, Donna & Kumiko Murasugi & Jeela Palluq-Cloutier. 2018. Standardization of Inuit languages in Canada. In Lane, Pia & Costa, James & De Korne, Haley (eds.), *Standardizing minority languages: Competing ideologies of authority and authenticity in the global periphery*, 135–153. (Critical Studies in Multilingualism). New York: Routledge.

Rischel, Jørgen. 1974. *Topics in West Greenlandic phonology*. Copenhagen: Akademisk Forlag.

Rose, Yvan & Pigott, Paul & Wharram, Douglas. 2012. Schneider's Law revisited: The syllable-level remnant of an older metrical rule. *McGill Working Papers in Linguistics* 22. (www.mcgill.ca/mcgwpl/archives/volume-221-2012) (Accessed 2019-06-08.)

Sadock, Jerrold. 1980. Noun incorporation in Greenlandic: A case of syntactic word formation. *Language* 56. 300–319.

Sadock, Jerrold. 2017. Affix clusters and the lexicon in Kalaallisut. In Kaplan, Lawrence D. & Berge, Anna (eds.), *Studies in Inuit linguistics in honor of Michael Fortescue* (Alaska Native Language Center), 1–25. Fairbanks: University of Alaska.

Schneider, Lucien. 1985. *Ulirnaisigutiit: An Inuktitut-English dictionary of Northern Quebec, Labrador and Eastern Arctic dialects.* Laval, QC: Les Presses de l'Université Laval.

Sherkina-Lieber, Marina. 2005. Fronting of wh-words in Inuktitut as focus movement. In *Proceedings of the 10th workshop on structure and constituency in languages of the Americas*, 191–202. Vancouver: University of British Columbia Working Papers in Linguistics.

Sherkina-Lieber, Marina & Murasugi, Kumiko. 2015. Noun incorporation and case in heritage Inuktitut. *Proceedings of the annual conference of the Canadian Linguistics Association.* (http://cla-acl.ca/wp-content/uploads/SherkinaLieber_Murasugi-2015.pdf) (Accessed 2019-06-08.)

Smith, Lawrence R. 1975. Labrador Inuttut surface phonology. *International Journal of American Linguistics* 41. 97–105.

Smith, Lawrence R. 1977. *Some grammatical aspect of Labrador Inuttut (Eskimo): A survey of the inflectional paradigms of nouns and verbs.* (Mercury Series no. 37). Ottawa, ON: National Museum of Man. (https://press.uottawa.ca/series/french-and-canadian-studies/mercury-series.html) (Accessed 2019-06-08.)

Spalding, Alex & Kusugaq, Thomas. 1998. *Inuktitut – A multi-dialectal outline dictionary (with an Aivilingmiutaq base).* Iqaluit: Nunavut Arctic College. (www.inuktitutcomputing.ca/Spalding/index.php?lang=en) (Accessed 2019-06-08.)

Spreng, Bettina. 2012. *Viewpoint aspect in Inuktitut: The syntax and semantics of antipassives.* Toronto: University of Toronto. (Doctoral dissertation.)

Swift, Mary D. & Allen, Shanley E. M. 2002. Verb base ellipsis in Inuktitut conversational discourse. *International Journal of American Linguistics* 68. 133–156.

Taff, Alice & Rozelle, Lorna & Cho, Taehong & Ladefoged, Peter & Dirks, Moses & Wegelin, Jacob. 2001. Phonetic structures of Aleut. *Journal of Phonetics* 29. 231–271.

Tersis, Nicole. 2008. *Formes et sens des mots Tunumiisut.* Paris: Peeters.

Trondhjem, Naja Blytmann. 2009. Marking of past time in Kalaallisut, the West Greenlandic language. In Mahieu, Marc-Antoine & Tersis, Nicole (eds.), *Variations on polysynthesis: The Eskaleut languages*, 171–182. Amsterdam: John Benjamins.

Trondhjem, Naja Blytmann. 2012. Repetitive, iterative and habitual aspectual affixes in West Greenlandic. *Acta Linguistica Hafniensia* 44. 64–76.

Trondhjem, Naja Blytmann. 2016. Distributive and collective aspect in Kalaallisut. *Amerindia* 38. 129–144.

Trondhjem, Naja Blytmann. 2017. Verbal aspects in West Greenlandic – Lexical and grammatical aspects. In Kaplan, Lawrence D. & Berge, Anna (eds.), *Studies in Inuit linguistics in honor of Michael Fortescue* (Alaska Native Language Center), 67–90. Fairbanks: University of Alaska.

Van Geenhoven, Veerle. 1998. *Semantic incorporation and indefinite descriptions: Semantic and syntactic aspects of noun incorporation in West Greenlandic.* Stanford, CA: CSLI Publications.

Van Geenhoven, Veerle. 2002. Raised possessors and noun incorporation in West Greenlandic. *Natural Language and Linguistic Theory* 20. 759–821.

Wharram, Douglas. 2003. *On the interpretation of (un)certain indefinites in Inuktitut and related languages.* Storrs: University of Connecticut. (Doctoral dissertation.)

Woodbury, Anthony C. 1981. *Study of the Chevak dialect of Central Yup'ik Eskimo.* Berkeley: University of California. (Doctoral dissertation.)

Woodbury, Anthony C. 1985. The functions of rhetorical structure: A study of Central Alaskan Yupik Eskimo discourse. *Language in Society* 14. 153–190.

Woodbury, Anthony C. 2004. Morphological orthodoxy in Yupik-Inuit. *BLS* 30. 151–171.

Woodbury, Anthony C. 2017. Polysynthesis in Central Alaskan Yupik (Eskimo-Aleut): A sketch of morphologically orthodox polysynthesis. In Fortescue, Michael & Mithun, Marianne & Evans, Nicholas (eds.), *The Oxford handbook of polysynthesis*, 536–559. Oxford: Oxford University Press.

Woolford, Ellen. 2017. Mainland Scandinavian object shift and the puzzling ergative pattern in Aleut. In Bailey, Laura & Sheehan, Michelle (eds), *Order and structure in syntax I: Word order and syntactic structure*, 117–133. Berlin: Language Science Press.

Yuan, Michelle. 2018. *Dimensions of ergativity in Inuit: Theory and microvariation.* Cambridge, MA: MIT. (Doctoral dissertation.)

23

EVALUATING PROPOSALS FOR LONG-DISTANCE GENETIC RELATIONSHIPS

Uto-Aztecan vs. Plateau Penutian

Jason D. Haugen

1. Introduction

The historical linguistics of Native North America has been a bit of a mixed bag. On one hand, the application of standard historical linguistic methodologies has led to many successful proposals for genetic relationships among these languages, and many proposed language families have long been accepted by scholars as legitimate. Indeed, historical linguistic research on the languages of the Americas helped to establish that the methods that had previously been used to make connections among other, better-known language families (e.g., Indo-European) could also be applied effectively elsewhere in the world. Campbell and Poser (2008) note, for example, that Edward Sapir's definitive establishment of the Uto-Aztecan language family in the early 20th century was "one of the first systematic demonstrations of the applicability of the comparative method to languages without long traditions of writing" (p. 118).

On the other hand, there has also been a long-standing, controversial tradition of efforts to link established language families to even older 'super-families' (also called 'stocks', or 'macro-families', or 'phyla', etc.). The same Edward Sapir who is rightly credited for definitively establishing the Uto-Aztecan family in the 1910s is also blamed for feeding a 'reductionist frenzy' with his 'Super-Six' classification in the 1920s, which sought to reduce a large number of independent language families and isolates of North America into a very few macro-families (see Campbell 1997: 74–76). Two of Sapir's proposed phyla, Hokan and Penutian, are still in common usage today, even though they remain controversial as genetic classifications. There is controversy because it remains possible that the affinities demonstrated among the various languages within these groupings result not from descent from a common ancestor but, rather, from descent from a very old language contact, diffusion, or spread zone. (Campbell 1997 strongly critiques Hokan and Penutian as genetic groupings; see Golla 2011 for a recent overview and more sympathetic treatment. Hill, this volume, provides further discussion of the Hokan and Penutian languages in the larger context of the California Sprachbund.)

In a notable few cases, some larger phylum proposals have actually proven to be successful. The prototypical case in point is Algic, a language family connection again credited originally to Sapir in the 1910s but not actually firmly and finally established until more than half a century later. The Algic macrofamily links two Pacific coastal California languages, Wiyot and Yurok (collectively referred to as Ritwan), to the quite large and geographically diffuse Algonquian language family of more easterly regions of the United States and Canada. In a classic paper applying the traditional comparative method, Goddard (1975) shows that there are certain systematically corresponding idiosyncratic elements shared between the Ritwan languages and the accepted system reconstructed for Proto-Algonquian. These correspondences pertain both to the morphological system (specifically, the set of pronominal agreement prefixes) as well as to a large number of lexical items (stems). As Goddard notes, there are two crucial steps needed in order to prove that languages share a common ancestor:

> it is necessary to show not only that the resemblances are so numerous and detailed as to exclude the possibility of chance as an explanation but also that they are so tightly woven into the basic fabric of the languages that they cannot be explained simply as borrowings. (Goddard 1975: 249)

This high bar sets the minimal threshold that modern mainstream historical linguists use to gauge genetic relationships (see Campbell & Poser 2008 for detailed discussion of this point, and clear demonstration that this bar has been set for historical linguistics for well over a century).

At the opposite end of the spectrum is Joseph Greenberg's (1987) proposal of 'Amerind', an effort to reduce dozens of independent language families and isolates, including the aforementioned controversial clades of Hokan and Penutian, into one giant megastock (or a macro-macro-phylum, if you will). With no support for such a clade coming from traditional historical linguistic methodology, and in particular not from the careful application of the comparative method to identify for these languages systematic correspondences in form and meaning (as Goddard had done for Algic), Greenberg sought to introduce a new method: multilateral comparison. This method was supposed to enable an analyst to avoid the rigors associated with the comparative method by spotting, through simple inspection and intuition, linguistic genetic relationships of greater and greater antiquity. The results of this method suffered under the close scrutiny of experts on many of the languages and language families subsumed under the Amerind label, and the Amerind proposal met with a vociferous rejection (see Campbell 1988 for a classic, scathing review, the gist of which is repeated in even more gory detail by Campbell 1997 and again by Campbell & Poser 2008). The Amerind proposal, and multilateral comparison as 'method' specifically, have become textbook examples of how *not* to do historical linguistics.

The most important point to bear in mind when evaluating proposals for long-distance linguistic genetic relationships is that the methods needed to firmly establish such relationships are, in principle, no different from those used to establish more recent familial relationships. Specifically, the comparative method must be used to establish systematic correspondences in form and meaning between two languages, and from these systematic sound changes can be inferred to explain the discrepancies between languages. Such changes are posited as 'sound laws' to explain alterations of phonological systems from the reconstructed ancestral language. Languages can often be grouped together into sub-families based on the shared innovations encapsulated by the sound laws; this is particularly the case when a given sound change or set of sound changes is cross-linguistically unusual (or 'marked'). A famous example is Grimm's Law, a consonantal chain shift that altered the entire system of plosives that Germanic languages inherited from Proto-Indo-European, thus defining Germanic as a subgroup of Indo-European (i.e., the daughters of a presumed intermediate ancestor language, Proto-Germanic).

Because of loanwords and other kinds of borrowing that can happen at all levels of grammar, shared grammatical 'aberrancies' (such as the 'strong verb' paradigms of Germanic) are also useful in establishing genetic relationships. The logic is straightforward: because the connection between the form and meaning of linguistic signs (such as words, roots, stems, and morphemes) are largely arbitrary, they are not expected to be similar across languages unless one of three factors is in play: (i) language contact and borrowing from one language to another; (ii) chance coincidence; or (iii) shared descent from a common ancestor. Thus, Goddard's entreaty that examples be both 'numerous' and 'detailed' (with the detail involving systematic correspondences rather than mere surface resemblances) and grammatically 'woven into the fabric' of the languages in question; these help to rule out contact and chance, leaving shared common descent as the most reasonable explanation for the correspondences.

With these caveats in mind, this chapter will revisit a proposal for a long-distance genetic relationship, Rude's (2000) connection of the Plateau-Penutian (PP) languages to the Uto-Aztecan (UA) language family, as a case study in presenting and evaluating evidence for long-distance relationships. We will examine the arguments for Rude's UA-PP proposal and show that they do not meet the bar for establishing a genetic relationship. Along the way, we will develop a comparative look into the grammatical structures of UA and PP, especially in regard to phonology and morphology.

This chapter is structured as follows. Section 2 briefly introduces the two language families under review (UA and PP), and then Section 3 reviews Rude's arguments for proposing a distant genetic relationship. Section 4 provides a detailed comparison of various aspects of the PP and UA languages, and Section 5 concludes that this proposal does not pass muster for definitively establishing a genetic relationship, distant or otherwise.

2. The Uto-Aztecan and Plateau Penutian Language Families

2.1. Uto-Aztecan

Although there still remains some debate about a few of the particulars of family-internal subgrouping, the Uto-Aztecan (UA) language family has been firmly established as a legitimate genetic unit since Edward Sapir used the comparative method to establish the fact a century ago. UA languages are spread through a vast territory spanning much of the western and southwestern United States; northwestern, western, and central Mexico; and as far south as Nicaragua. The traditional geographical division of languages into Northern and Southern groups (i.e., Northern Uto-Aztecan/NUA and Southern Uto-Aztecan/SUA, corresponding roughly to what became the international border between the United States and Mexico) have also been claimed to be genetic groups. While the ongoing debates about UA family-internal subgrouping will not play a role in this chapter (see Merrill 2013 and Haugen forthcoming for recent discussion), it is important to note that features widespread in both NUA and SUA are generally considered to be likely candidates for reconstruction back to Proto-Uto-Aztecan (PUA). The languages and major subgroups included in UA are shown in (1); question marks indicate the more uncertain groupings.

(1) Uto-Aztecan languages and subgroups

I. Northern Uto-Aztecan

A. Numic

Western Numic

Mono, Northern Paiute

Central Numic

Comanche, Shoshone, Timbisha (=Panamint)

Southern Numic

Kawaiisu, Southern Paiute—Ute—Chemehuevi

B. Takic

Serran

Serrano, Kitanemuk

Gabrielino-Cupan

Gabrielino

Cupan

Cupeño, Cahuilla, Luiseño

C. *Tübatulabal*
D. *Hopi*
II. Southern Uto-Aztecan (?)
E. Tepiman
Piman
Upper Piman
Pima, Tohono O'odham
Lower Piman
Pima Bajo, Nevome
Tepehuan
Northern Tepehuan, Southern Tepehuan, Tepecano
F. Taracahitan (?)
Cahitan
Hiaki (Yaqui), Mayo
Opata-Eudeve
Tarahumara, Guarijío
G. *Tubar*
H. Corachol-Aztecan
Corachol
Cora, Huichol
Aztecan
Pochutec
General "Aztec": *Nahuatl* (many varieties), *Pipil*
(Adapted from Haugen forthcoming)

2.2. *Plateau Penutian*

As discussed previously, the 'Penutian' stock was one of several macrofamily proposals put forth by Sapir in the 1920s. Like Hokan, this supposed family is associated with the California culture area and Sprachbund (see Hill, this volume). The Penutian languages are spread from central California to the Pacific Northwest of the United States and Canada. Major proposed subgroups of Penutian include, in addition to Plateau Penutian (to be discussed in more detail in this section): Tsimshianic; Coastal Oregon Penutian (Alsea; Siuslaw; Coosan); Kalapuya-Takelma; Maiduan; Wintuan; and Yok-Utian (Yokutsan and Miwok-Costanoan) (Golla 2011: 129). As is also the case with Hokan, the nature of the relationships amongst the Penutian languages remains controversial and subject to ongoing research. It is conceivable that many of the shared affinities between these languages derive from a very old areal contact zone; no definitive account of shared sound changes or morphological innovations has yet been given for Penutian, and there is no universally accepted account of Proto-Penutian.

That said, the proposed grouping of Plateau Penutian consists of two main subgroups: Sahaptian (consisting of two languages: Nez Perce and Sahaptin) and Klamath (a singleton). Some scholars also include the Molala language in the PP group, but since Rude does not include Molala data in his discussion, we will likewise avoid discussion of it here. The proposal of Plateau Penutian as a genetic unit seems to be much more accepted than the much larger "Penutian" (see Rude 1987; DeLancey 1996; Campbell 1997; among others). For the purposes of our discussion, we will assume that PP is a legitimate language family (whether or not it may also form a subgroup within the larger Penutian group). Of course, if the PP languages are later shown to be not as closely related as presently thought, then this would even further problematize any PP-UA connection beyond what we will be discussing here. Larger connections of Rude's PP-UA with other supposed Penutian languages will not be considered here.

3. Arguments for a Link Between Plateau Penutian and Uto-Aztecan

Rude's (2000) proposal to link PP to UA is quite unique – even Edward Sapir kept the two families distinct in his "Super Six" classification scheme (with PP in Penutian and UA in a stock he labeled as Aztec-Tanoan, which included UA, Kiowa-Tanoan, and Zuni).[1] It is important to note at the outset that Rude acknowledges that his proposal does not meet the high evidentiary bar for definitively establishing genetic relations that were discussed earlier. Specifically, Rude does not identify for these languages any specific systematic correspondences in form and meaning that would require an explanation of descent from a common ancestor, nor does he point to particular grammatical resemblances "so tightly woven into the basic fabric of the languages that they cannot be explained simply as borrowings", as Goddard (1975: 249) had done when linking Ritwan to Algonquian.

Rude's arguments for a genetic relationship fall into several categories, which we will review in turn: evidence from pronouns (§3.1); adverbial prefixes on verbs (§3.2); morpheme resemblances (§3.3); and lexical resemblances (§3.4).

3.1. Evidence From Pronouns

Rude provides the following table presenting his proposed correspondences involving 'pronominal formants' between PP and UA. (Note: Rude's discussion of PUA comes strictly from Langacker 1977, who provided the reconstructed forms; within PP, the languages are abbreviated as follows: Klamath = Kl; the Sahaptian languages are NzP = Nez Perce, S = Sahaptin.)

(2) Pronominal formants

	Klamath	*Proto-Sahaptian*	*Proto-Uto-Aztecan*
1st	*ni*	**n*, **ne-*	**nɨ*
2nd	*mi* 'your(s)'	**m*, **me-*	**mɨ*
	ʔi	**ʔe* (NzP only)	**ʔɨ*
3rd	*bi*	**pi* (NzP), **pɨn*	**pɨ*
		ʔe- 'absolutive' (from obviative pronominal?)	*ʔa* 'non-human' (from obviative pronominal?)
1stPL	*/naa-d/*	*=*ne-te-š* (S only) Other plural: **né-s-* (NzP PL ACC)	*=*ta*, *(*ʔi*)*ta*(*mɨ*) **na-* 'reflexive, reciprocal' (human)
Pluralizer		*-me	*-mɨ

(Rude 2000: 311 [Table 1])

First, note the *n-/m-* alternation in the first- and second-person pronouns, which are familiar to many linguists from the famous Greenbergian pronoun system associated with 'Amerind' where formants for first-person singular are associated with morphemes involving *n* and second person with morphemes involving *m*. There has been a huge debate about these pronouns in the literature, but a reasonable conclusion is that they seem not to be good evidence for shared inheritance from a common ancestor (as Greenberg had proposed for Amerind). Nichols and Peterson (1996) argue that these pronouns are areally limited within so-called 'Amerind' (specifically, Western-ish Amerind, relevant to PP and UA, but also appearing along the Pacific Rim, especially in Melanesia). However, Nichols and Peterson do agree that there is likely a shared history of some kind (even if non-genetic) for the languages with these pronouns. Campbell (1997), though, points to some problems with Nichols and Peterson's typological sample (as well as their methods) and concludes that the distribution is not necessarily so limited, and that it is not surprising to see nasals appearing in pronominals after all.

It may be worth revisiting Langacker's (1977) pronominal reconstructions, which were clearly not originally presented as definitive at the time they were published – his original PUA paradigm was presented as "but a first guess at what the P-UA system may have been like" (p. 24). A couple of Rude's PP forms are apparently not even derived from Proto-Sahaptian (i.e., they are from Nez Perce or Sahaptin only), much less older PP, and the connections between the semantic functions of some of the others are relatively loose (e.g., absolutive case vs. marking 'non-human'). Perhaps the most promising evidence here is the putative pluralizing suffix, but it is not clear that there really is a vowel correspondence in Sahaptian *e and UA *ɨ. Indeed, it appears that there is not, since even in the very small set of comparisons in (2), there are correspondence sets relating examples of PP *e* with UA examples with both *ɨ* and *a*, and PP *i* with UA *ɨ*! These plural suffixes are most likely similar due to chance, as we will suggest for other morphological correspondences. (And, interestingly, other language families have similar morphology for the plural, e.g., Semitic, indicating clear independent development by coincidence.)

Shaul (2014: 91) reviews the pronominal similarities and concludes that they derive from contact and borrowing between distinct sub-groups of UA and PP: specifically, the Numic subgroup of UA and the Sahaptian sub-group of PP (as well as Molala). All of the above considerations cast much doubt on the pronominal evidence for a distant genetic connection between PP and UA.

3.2. Adverbial Prefixes on Verbs

Rude also points to similarities between UA and PP in the usage of adverbial prefixes on verbs; these are usually referred to in the UA literature as 'instrumental prefixes'. Some examples are given in (3).

(3) Adverbial ("instrumental") prefixes on verbs

	PUA		*Plateau Penutian*
a.	**ca-*	'Adv. with the hand'	Kl *ča-* 'act upon a handful of granular objects'
b.	**ci-*	'Adv. with a pointed object'	PS **cú-* 'with a long object, with a pointed or pole-like object'
c.	**kɨ-*	'Adv. with the mouth'	PS **ke-* 'with the teeth or mouth'
d.	**ta-*	'Adv. with the foot'	PS [*tɨx-*] or [*tɨ-*] 'with the foot/legs' PS **tuné* 'with the foot'
e.	**wɨ-*	'Adv. with a long object'	PS **we-* 'with an implement'

(Rude 2000: 312–313)

Although there are some clear resemblances here that could be due to factors other than chance, instrumental and adverbial prefixes of this kind are well-known elements of a widespread areal pattern cross-cutting families and stocks (including both Hokan and Penutian) – i.e., what DeLancey (1996) has called "the bipartite stem belt". DeLancey points out that Plateau Penutian is one of the core groups in this areal spread (which includes non-UA languages), and says that contact among these languages must have occurred very early in the development of these systems. The Numic languages of UA do make more extensive use of instrumental prefixes than most other languages within the family, but the other non-UA languages in this 'belt' have much more robust systems and more functional integration of many of these elements than does Numic (see DeLancey 1996 for discussion). Further, the development of IPs could proceed by analogy rather than direct borrowing (see Thornes 2011 for discussion), so even resemblant forms in this domain could be due to chance even if the same grammatical mechanism of deriving complex verb forms was borrowed.

This clearly areal feature is not a good indicator of a genetic connection between PP and UA.

3.3. Morpheme Resemblances

Most of Rude's discussion is focused on connecting various individual morphemes in PP languages with what Langacker (1977) had proposed for PUA. A lot of comparative UA work has been done in the decades since Langacker's foundational work, so it would be worth revisiting his original reconstructions to see what holds up and what may need to be reconsidered.

Nevertheless, a general critique of Rude's proposed PP-UA connections has to do with the high likelihood that even the best of his cases could be due to chance (if not to borrowing). As Ringe's (1999) work in computational historical linguistics has demonstrated, it is surprisingly easy to match short roots (CVC) by chance/coincidence alone; this should be even easier to do with affixes of even shorter form: C, V, CV, etc.

Connecting spurious forms is particularly likely if a good deal of semantic latitude is allowed. For examples of semantic latitude, consider some of Rude's proposed connections from the domain of interrogatives, indefinites, reciprocals, and reflexives: e.g., PUA *ta- 'unspecified subject' ~ PP *t/*d 'non-human interrogative'; PUA *te- 'unspecified object' ~ Proto-Sahaptian (PS) **tú* and Klamath *dwaa* ('what?', 'something', 'anything'); PUA *na- 'indefinite human reflexive' ~ PS *ne ('speech act participants in general'). One particularly interesting comparison from this set is the compounding process used to derive the numeral 'four', which involves a reciprocal prefixed onto the word for 'two': i.e., PUA *na-*wo Recip-'two' = 'four' ~ PS *pi-*nep Recip -'two' = 'four'. The forms are clearly non-cognate, but the similar formula is striking. On the other hand, such formulas (aka calques) are not unknown to transfer through contact. Indeed, Epps et al. (2012) find areal patterns specifically in the formation of words for 'four', with derivation of 'four' from 'two' being common in Australia as well as California and the Great Basin of North America, but not in Africa or South America.

Another interesting case presented by Rude involves 'bahuvrihi' constructions, which involves deriving possession constructions from nominals. Rude relates Langacker's 'general stative suffix', *-ka, itself thought to originate from a copula (*ka BE), to the Klamath stativizer /-dk/. In the Taracahitan language Hiaki (Yaqui), for example, possessive verbs can be derived by suffixing the possessed noun with any of the suite of tense, aspect or mood suffixes (including the perfective -*(e)k*):

(4) Hiaki bahuvrihi

*Peo kar-**ek***	'Peo has (a) house(s)'
Peo kar-ekan	'Peo had houses'
Peo kari-ne	'Peo will have houses'
Peo kari-su-kan	'Peo used to have houses'
Peo kari-pea	'Peo feels like owning houses'
Peo kari-vae	'Peo is gonna have houses'
Peo kari-maci	'Peo should have houses'
Peo kari-'ean	'Peo should have (had) houses'

(Escalante 1990 [16])

Klamath supposedly has a similar construction, but the (morpho)syntax here is quite different. In Klamath, the resemblant suffix attaches to the copula, not the possessed noun:

(5) Klamath bahuvrihi

dom-dwaa *gi-**tk*** *hoot*
many-what be-**PP** that(he)
'He has many things.' (Lit. 'He [is] been many things.')

(Rude 2000: 314 [11]; Barker 1963: 141)

Table 23.1 UA Affixes Used to Generate Denominal Verbs of Possession in UA

	Example	Affix	Proposed PUA Source	Proposed PUA Source Function
	Gosiute Shoshone			
a.	*Nɨ kahni-**kantin***	*-ka*	-*ka	'HAVE (alienable)'
	1.sg house-**have**			
	'I have (rent) a house' (Miller 1996b: 706)			
	Gosiute Shoshone			
b.	*Nɨ kahni-**pai***	*-pai*	-*pV	'HAVE (inalienable)'
	1.sg house-**have**			
	'I have (own) a house' (Miller 1996b: 706)			
	Guarijío			
c.	*puhkú-**e*** or *puhku-**é***	*-e*	*-ɨ	Postposition (Locative?)
	'pet'-**have**			
	'tener animal'/'have an animal' (Miller 1996a: 149)			
	Cupeño			
d.	*ash-**lyu***	*-tu*	*-tu	Active Possession (GET, ACQUIRE)
	'pet'-**have**			
	'have a dog' (*-ash* 'pet', *achi-ly* 'cow') (J. Hill 2005: 279 [45a])			
	Tepecano			
e.	*viv-**ga**-d*	*-ga*	*-wa	Attributive Possession ('possessed thing')
	tobacco-POSSD-his			
	'his tobacco' (Langacker 1977: 89 [32])			

Source: Haugen (2017: 164–165).

Interestingly, most of the UA languages employ some kind of denominal verb suffix to create possessive verbs from nouns. These come from a variety of historical sources; see Table 23.1 for a sampling from across the family.

The Hiaki case is interesting, and apparently unusual within UA, in that this language seems to have reanalyzed its reflex of the inherited suffix *-k(a) as the perfective (*-(e)k*), and then, by analogy, allowed *any* TAM suffix to mark possession. In short, while perhaps superficially similar in form to one possessive-marking verbalizing suffix in Hiaki, the Klamath stativizer is different enough in syntax that it seems quite distinct from what is more typical in UA.

In sum, although Rude has made some interesting suggestions regarding possibly related morphemes in PP and UA, he has not ruled out the possibility that many (and possibly most) of these are coincidental or due to contact.

3.4. Lexical Resemblances

Rude presents about 50 UA cognate sets with potential affinities with Nez Perce, Sahaptin, and/or Klamath. His UA data come from Miller (1967) and Langacker (1977). Because lexical items are generally thought to be the most easily borrowed aspects of language, Rude acknowledges that this is his weakest evidence, and he sets up these comparisons knowing that some will likely be spurious.

It may prove interesting to delve more deeply into these comparisons in light of updated versions of the comparative UA lexicon, as with Stubbs (2011) and Hill (2014). If there were systematic correspondences between the languages, then it may be possible to do two crucial things: (i) separate loanwords from inherited vocabulary; and (ii) identify layers of borrowing (i.e., establish a 'linguistic stratigraphy', wherein vocabulary may be shown to come into a language after certain sound changes but before other ones). At the very least, it would be interesting to see if there are specific vocabulary items in common to languages or subgroups in close proximity (most likely, NUA languages nearest to PP), which could indicate areal contact.

This deeper comparative work remains to be done, however, and, until criteria are established to distinguish loanwords from cognates inherited from a common ancestral language, a list of resemblant vocabulary cannot be taken as definitive evidence for a genetic relationship.

3.5. Interim Conclusion

In this section we have reviewed Rude's arguments for a PP-UA connection, and found that none preclude non-genetic explanations such as coincidence or contact. In the next section we will search the PP languages for some grammatical phenomena that are more closely tied to UA, ubiquitous in the family and likely descended from PUA. We will argue that these areas of grammar are "more tightly woven into the basic fabric of the UA languages" (in Goddard's words) than the random assortment of morpheme resemblances identified by Rude, so if connections could be made between PP and UA in these domains, then this would constitute *even better* evidence for a PP-UA genetic relationship.

4. A Closer Comparison of Uto-Aztecan and Plateau Penutian Grammar

In this section we will review some of the most striking grammatical phenomena common to the UA languages to see if they can be connected to corresponding phenomena in the PP languages. Our focus will be on cross-linguistically marked patterns of grammar (phonology and morphology), and especially ones that are ubiquitous to the UA languages and which therefore likely derive from shared common ancestry from PUA, rather than from contact or through independent developments. If it can be shown that the PP languages do indeed have corresponding elements to the UA-ubiquitous grammatical domains under review, then this could form a much stronger argument for a deep genetic relationship among these languages than was proposed by Rude. Section 4.1 will look at comparative phonology, and then Section 4.2 will look at comparative morphology. Section 4.3 will conclude with a review of some common aspects of UA morphology and syntax which are *not* good candidates for drawing larger conclusions about genetic relationships, i.e., areas of comparative UA grammar that involve elements that are *not* "tightly woven into the basic fabric of [these] languages".

Let's now turn to see how the PP languages fare when we consider some of the most characteristic aspects of UA grammar. Since there is no reconstruction of Proto-PP, we will use the relatively well-described Nez Perce language (NzP) as our representative example in most of this discussion, with supplementary information from Sahaptin and/or Klamath in key places. The major (relatively) full grammatical descriptions available for PP are Aoki (1970; 1994) for Nez Perce, Jacobs (1931) and Rigsby and Rude (1996) for Sahaptin, and Barker (1964) for Klamath.

4.1. Comparative Phonology

As discussed earlier, the classic way to demonstrate solid linguistic genetic relationships has always been the discovery of sound laws by means of the comparative method (Campbell & Poser 2008). Rude (2000) clearly acknowledges that his proposed link between UA and PP does not meet this criterion. Still, it is worth contrasting the phoneme systems of these languages, both to highlight the differences between the systems and to indicate what would require placement into correspondence in order to make an argument for reconstruction of any kind of Proto-Plateau-Aztecan (PPA) macrofamily (§4.1.1). We will also consider the important domain of word-level prominence marking, including stress and accent systems in these languages (§4.1.2).

4.1.1. Comparative Vowel and Consonant Inventories

With respect to vowel inventories, the attested UA languages can vary in number from four vowels, as with Classical Nahuatl (an Aztecan language with *i, e, a,* and *o*) to as many as seven, as found in Serrano (a Takic language with *a, i, ɨ, u,* plus three rhotic (retroflexed) vowels: *a˞* , *ɨ˞* , *o˞* ; Serrano also has *o* and *e*, but these are mostly found in Spanish loanwords). These vowel contrasts usually also accompany contrastive vowel length. The 'typical' UA vowel system is probably five vowels (plus contrastive length), which is what is usually reconstructed for PUA (6).

(6) PUA vowel inventory

*i(:)	*ɨ(:)	*u(:)
		*o (:)
	*a(:)	

(Langacker 1970; Haugen, forthcoming)

The vowels *i, *u, *o, and *a are universally agreed upon. There is some uncertainty as to the quality of the fifth vowel, given here as *ɨ (high central unrounded), as its pronunciation can be highly variable according to language, dialect, or speaker. Most of the Tepiman languages have not altered the system reconstructed in (6), while for other UA languages the quality of the fifth vowel can be high, back, and unrounded (*ɯ*), or more mid-central (like schwa). Most of the SUA languages (excepting Tepiman) have shifted this vowel to the mid front vowel *e*.

To contrast with the UA vowel inventory situation, consider representative vowels systems from the PP languages Nez Perce (7a) and Sahaptin (7b).

(7) a. Nez Perce vowels

i(:)		u(:)
		o(:)
æ(:)	a(:)	

b. Sahaptin Vowels

i(:)	ɨ	u(:)
	a(:)	

(Aoki 1994: xi–xii; Rigsby & Rude 1996: 671)

Both of these systems fall into the range that we see in UA languages. The Nez Perce five-vowel system resembles, superficially at least, the five-vowel system of PUA, while Sahaptin has four vowels, which happen to be four of the five vowels reconstructed for PUA. However, many (and possibly most) languages of the world have vowel systems very near the ranges seen here. Maddieson's (2013) survey of vowel quality inventories reveals that around two-thirds of the languages of the world have either small (two to four vowels) or average (five or six vowels) inventories.[2] Similarly, the quality and location of the vocalic phonemes in these systems are typical and expected given cross-linguistic tendencies towards dispersion within the articulatory vowel space. (See Rice, this volume, for discussion of vowel inventories across North America.) So, in lieu of specific identification of actual sound correspondences for these languages and proposals for sound laws to explain deviations from the ancestral system, mere resemblance is not sufficient to draw any kind of conclusion about linguistic genetic relationships between these languages.

Turning to consonant inventories, UA languages once again show a good deal of variation, but the correspondences within the family are relatively well understood and sound laws have largely been worked out (see J. Hill 2011 for a review). One version of the proposed consonant inventory for PUA is given in (8):

(8) PUA consonant inventory

*p	*t		*k	*k^{w}	*ʔ
	*s				*h
		*c			
*m	*n		*ŋ		
	*-L				
*w		*y			

(Haugen forthcoming, largely following Merrill 2013)

Most of these segments are uncontroversial. The PUA liquid is a bit of a mystery, since some UA languages have *l*, some have *r*, some have both, and some have neither; *-L here indicates for PUA the reconstruction of a non-word-initial liquid of uncertain articulation. A second question is whether PUA had the third nasal, *ŋ, which would have been lost in many languages, or whether reflexes of *ŋ show innovations in the extant UA languages that have them (see Merrill 2013 for arguments in favor of reconstructing it). There was a single affricate, represented here as *c* (probably pronounced as *ʦ* or *ʧ* in PUA). The extant UA languages generally have consistent variations on this basic system.

While UA languages tend to have 'small' to 'moderately small' consonant inventories (with the consonantly robust Takic languages falling into the crosslinguistically 'average' category), PP languages have 'moderately large' inventories (see Rice, this volume) with many more consonantal contrasts than what we see in UA. Consider Nez Perce as a case in point (see Rice, this volume, for the Sahaptin consonant inventory):

(9) Nez Perce consonants

p	t			k	k^{w}	q	q^{w}	ʔ
p’	t’			k’	k^{w}’	q’	q^{w}’	
	s	ʃ	ɬ	x		χ		h
	ts							
	ts’		*tɬ’					
m	n		l		j	w		
m’	n’		l’		j’	w’		

(Aoki 1994: xi–xii)

Not only are there more distinctions made in place of articulation in Nez Perce than what we typically see in UA (including uvular and rounded uvular consonants, and fricatives at many more places of articulation), there are more kinds of manner used to make consonants, including extensive use of ejectives in stops, affricates, and sonorants. The Nez Perce system is more than twice the size of that reconstructed for PUA. Klamath has an even larger consonantal system (with a series of distinctively aspirated consonants in addition to the plain and ejective sets), so we can conclude that the prototypical PP consonant inventory is quite unlike what we find in UA. Indeed, the complex PP consonantal systems are much more like other large consonant inventories found in the Pacific Northwest Sprachbund (Beck 2000), making the PP languages look a lot more like other languages in that linguistic area than they do languages in UA.

It is conceivable that PP developed a radically larger consonant inventory than what was inherited from a prospective PPA, either through independent developments or through contact with the languages of the Pacific Northwest. Under either scenario, identification of specific sound correspondences with UA languages and sound laws to explain changes from the PPA system would need to be proposed. Without such correspondences, the evidence from comparative UA and PP phoneme inventories does not support connecting the two language families.

4.1.2. Comparative Stress (and Other Prominence-Marking) Systems

Buckley (this volume) overviews the many different ways that Native American languages mark prosodic prominence at the level of the word. Many of Buckley's illustrative examples come from UA languages, which illustrate a wide variety of patterns. UA prominence-marking can be left-edge oriented (on the first or second syllable or mora) or right-edge oriented (e.g., on the penultimate or final syllable); it can be regular or lexical; it can involve stress, or pitch accent, or tone(s), or some combination (see Haugen forthcoming for a more thorough overview and discussion of UA prominence marking). The wide array of prominence-marking in the UA family clearly demonstrates that a good deal of change must have occurred in various subgroups and in individual languages over time. However, PUA is generally reconstructed as having regular stress on the first or second syllable (or mora) (e.g., Munro 1977; Manaster Ramer 1993). A truly decisive long-range connection to PUA would need to address the supposed fit of the other groups to the general historical picture for UA.

Stress in Nez Perce shows a complex interaction of phonology and morphology, where a regular trend towards rightwardness can be superseded by various lexical and morphological factors (including lexical stress on prefixes). See Crook (1999) and Bjorkman (2010) for details of the interplays of morphology with the phonology of underlying long vowels, stress, etc. (Buckley, this volume, also provides some examples and discussion.) While long vowels in NzP surface only when they are stressed, accent is quantity-sensitive in Klamath – i.e., stress is attracted to long vowels if one appears in a word, but it is otherwise usually initial (antepenultimate for three-syllable words or penult for disyllables). See Hayes (1995: 279–281) for more details, discussion, and analysis. As far as I know, no reconstruction of prominence marking for PP exists.

Suffice it to say at this point that there is currently no evidence from stress or prominence-marking to link PP to UA. (Indeed, in general, issues of stress and other word-level prominence are relatively sparsely discussed in comparative and historical linguistics; this domain would be an interesting one to develop further in future research.)

4.2. Comparative Morphology

In using morphological comparisons to make claims about genetic relationships, the popularization of employing 'shared aberrancy' in morphological systems as a criterion has been attributed to Antoine Meillet (Campbell & Poser 2008: 181–182). Rather than appealing to broad typological categories which might be found in many different languages and language families, linguists appealing to morphological innovations can most clearly do so by finding cross-linguistically unusual (marked) patterns, or what Meillet referred to as "local morphological peculiarities", "anomalous forms", "singular facts", and the like (p. 182). In this section we will consider a number of "morphological peculiarities" that seem to be "local" to the UA language family in the sense that they are cross-linguistically unusual ("peculiar"), and because they occur across the family, they have been argued to be reconstructable to PUA. In a sense, then, these ubiquitous morphological phenomena are particularly "Uto-Aztecan-y", and as such may form a more solid basis on which related language families may be compared to assess the likelihood that they may share these features (and thus, potentially, a very old shared common ancestor).

The morphological domains that we will consider in this section include the so-called absolutive suffix in the nominal domain (§4.2.1); suppletion for plural number agreement in the verbal domain (§4.2.2); and multiple contrasting patterns of reduplication (§4.2.3).

4.2.1. Reflexes of the PUA 'Absolutive' Suffix?

A universally agreed-upon aspect of PUA morphosyntax is that the language would have had a nominal suffix that UA scholars call the 'absolutive'. This suffix has nothing to do with the better-known absolutive case-marking suffix in ergative-absolutive languages like Nez Perce, but rather would have marked non-possessed nouns and was in complementary distribution with possessor-marking prefixes; there was also a marker, *-wa, for possessed nouns (at least for some noun class(es)). Prototypical uses of the UA absolutive suffix are shown in (10a) for Classical Nahuatl (Aztecan) and (10b) for Luiseño (Takic).

(10) Usage of the UA absolutive suffix

a. Classical Nahuatl

cihuātl	*icihuāuh*
cihuā-tl	*i-cihuā-w*
woman-ABS	3.SG.POSS-woman-PSSD
'woman'	'his woman (wife)'

(Launey 2011: 88)

b. Luiseño

huu-la	*no-huu*
arrow-ABS	1.SG.POSS-arrow
'arrow'	'my arrow'

(Steele 1979: 463)

This PUA suffix has developed in different ways in different languages, and different phonological forms can serve this purpose. Classical Nahuatl, for example, had two suffixes: *-tli/-tl/-li* for most nouns, and the suffix *-in* used for some animal and plant names. The function of marking non-possessed nouns remains relatively robust in several UA subgroups, including Aztecan, Numic, Takic, and Tübatulabal. In some other UA languages, however, the function of the original PUA nominal suffix has been reanalyzed as an accusative case marker, as in Hopi, Numic, and Taracahitan, where in Hiaki, for example, the accusative marker is *-ta*.

The reconstructed phonological form of the PUA absolutive is not uncontested. Langacker (1977) reconstructs the absolutive suffix as *-tɨ, which could take on an additional suffix *-a in the accusative case (hence, the accusative case marker *-ta* in Hiaki). However, Hill and Hill (2017) reconstruct two suffixes relevant to the PUA absolutive: *-ta for accusative non-singulars and *-tɨ marking plurals. Despite Langacker's reconstruction of a decompositional analysis of the PUA absolutive morpheme, then, there is no current consensus that *-a was a productive accusative marker in PUA. In his connection of PP to UA, however, Rude (2000) refers to an *-a accusative in PP, but makes no connection to *-tɨ or the nominal/adjective accusative distinction seen in UA. A convincing argument for connecting a language family to the PUA nominal morphology would need to account for the *t element in the absolutive.

4.2.2. Verbal Suppletion for Ergative Number Agreement?

The UA languages are known to contain a variety of paradigms which employ radically different verb forms for marking number agreement. This shared pattern of verbal suppletion according to an ergative agreement pattern (where intransitive verbs agree with their subjects and transitive verbs agree with their objects) has been attributed to shared common descent from PUA (Langacker 1977), but not until very recently has an effort been made to reconstruct the actual phonological forms of specific morphs back to the protolanguage (Haugen & Everdell 2015). It turns out that many of the suppletive verb forms serving the function of marking agreement are apparently not themselves cognate, although the meanings of the verbs are the same or similar across the languages. This can be seen by comparing and contrasting the suppletive verbs of Hopi (NUA singleton) and Hiaki (from the SUA group Taracahitan).

(11) Suppletive verbs in Hopi and Hiaki – number agreement with intransitive subjects

	Gloss	*Hopi*		*Hiaki*	
		SG./DL SUBJ.	PL.SUBJ.	SG. SUBJ.	PL.SUBJ.
a.	'arrive'	*pitu*	*öki*	*yepsa*	*yaha*
b.	'be dancing'	*wunima*	*tiiva*	—	—
c.	'be eating'	*tuumoyta*	*noonova*	—	—
d.	'be lying down' (pres.) —	—	*vo'ote*	*to'ote*	
e.	'descend'	*haawi*	*haani*	—	—
f.	'die'	***mooki***	***so'a***	***muuke***	***koko***
g.	'enter'	*paki*	*yungya*	*kivake*	*kiimu*
h.	'fall'	*pòosi*	*löhö(k-)*	*weche*	*watte*
i.	'get up'	—	—	*yehte*	*hoote*
j.	'go, leave (pres.)'	—	—	*siime*	*saka*
k.	'go, walk'	—	—	***weye***	*kaate*
l.	'go out'	*yama(k-)*	*nönga(k-)*	—	—
m.	'run'	*wari(k-)*	*yùutu(k-)*	*vuite*	*tenne*
n.	'sit, dwell'	*qatu*	***yeese***	***yeesa***	*hooye*
o.	'sleep'	*puuwi*	*tookya*	—	—
p.	'stand up'	—	—	*kikte*	*hapte*
q.	'walk around'	***waynuma***	*yakta*	***weama***	*rehte*

(Haugen & Siddiqi 2013: 499–501)

(12) Suppletive verbs in Hopi and Hiaki – number agreement with transitive objects

	Gloss	*Hopi*		*Hiaki*	
		SG./DL. OBJ.	PL.OBJ.	SG. OBJ.	PL.OBJ.
a.	'bring along'	*wiiki*	*tsaama*	—	—
b.	'bring in, put into'	*pana*	*tangata*	*kivacha*	*kiima*
c.	'kill'	*niina*	***qöya***	*me'a*	***sua***
d.	'put, place'	*tavi*	*oya*	*yecha*	*hoa*
e.	'put on top'	*tsokya*	*kwapta*	—	—
f.	'stand (s.t.) up'	—	—	*kecha*	*ha'abwa*

Lexical replacement of material seems to be endemic to such cases of strong suppletion (Juge 2000), so reconstruction of forms back to PUA is difficult for most verb forms. However, there is enough to consistency in the forms of a few paradigms that reconstructions can be made, as with the verb forms for 'die' and 'kill':

(13) PUA suppletive verb paradigm for 'die' and 'kill'

	SG	PL
'DIE'	*muku-	*ko(i)-
'KILL'	*mɨʔa	*ko-ya
		die.PL-CAUS

(Haugen & Everdell 2015: 244)

Other semantic functions commonly found across the family are considered as being 'high likelihood' or 'medium likelihood' for reconstruction to PUA, based on how frequently they appear in different subgroups.

(14) Possible PUA glosses for suppletive verbs – high likelihood (4+ subgroups)

a.	ARRIVE	g.	LIE/LIE DOWN
b.	BRING/CARRY	h.	PUT/PLACE
c.	DIE	i.	RUN
d.	FALL	j.	SIT
e.	GO	k.	STAND/STAND UP/STAND SOMETHING UP
f.	KILL		

(Haugen & Everdell 2015: 274)

(15) Possible PUA glosses for suppletive verbs – medium likelihood (3 subgroups)

a.	DWELL	d.	GO UP
b.	ENTER	e.	WALK AROUND
c.	GO OUT		

(Haugen & Everdell 2015: 274)

Do verbs with similar meanings also supplete for number agreement in PP? It appears that the answer is generally not. A survey of Aoki's (1994) Nez Perce dictionary comes up short, as summarized in (16) (where the symbol × indicates a lack of suppletion, and forms marked with question marks are clarified immediately below).

(16) Suppletive verbs in PP?

	NZ		NZ
ARRIVE	×	PUT/PLACE	×
BRING/CARRY	×	RUN	?†
DIE	×	SIT	?‡
FALL	×	STAND/STAND S.T. UP	×
GO	×	ENTER	×
KILL	×	WALK	×
LIE/LIE DOWN	×		

Two meanings from this semantic set at first seem promising: RUN (†) and SIT (‡). Aoki (1994) lists *'iyem* as 'run (pl.)', but in the entry for *ke'éy* 'move, change location or position', he states that this initial element is "often plural" (p. 217), and he gives a non-plural form, *'iyemíke'ykse* 'I am going to run', which seems to indicate that *'iyem* can be used for singulars. Regarding the word for 'sit', Aoki (1994: 710) lists two words of form *temé·*. The first is *temé·* 'to sit, settle, lie down, assume a stationary position (often in reference to plural)' and related forms glossed are 'encircle', 'be stuck next to', etc. There second is *temé·* 'to throw (a singular object); shoot' (p. 64). This form used with singular objects is contrasted, though, with a very phonologically similar form *té·m-* 'throw (plural object)'. A similar contrast is found for the causative, which appears in two forms: *sé·p* 'causative (plural object)' and *sepé·* 'causative (singular object)'. Whatever is going on with these contrasting forms seems like (at least semi-) productive morphology and not the kind of strong suppletion, where there exist totally unrelated forms in paradigmatic relation, that we find across UA.

One PP language that does have a similar pattern of suppletion is Klamath. Barker (1963) reports suppletive pairs for both 'die' and 'kill'. These are: *gḷeg* 'die (sg.)' vs. *č̓o·q̇* 'die (pl.)', and *siwg* 'kill (sg.)' vs. *h̲e̲sč̓o·q̇a* 'kill (pl.)'. (Note that the plural version of 'kill' involves a causative prefix, *h̲e̲s-*, attached to the plural form for 'die', *č̓o·q̇*.) There are few other examples as well, such as singular/plural contrasting verb pairs for 'run', 'stand', 'fall', and 'lie down', each of which are of relatively high frequency across UA and thought to be likely retentions from PUA (Haugen & Everdell 2015: 274).

It might seem that this similar pattern of suppletion should provide suggestive support for a shared common descent between UA and PP (or between UA and Klamath, at least). The kind of 'maximal irregularity' that is associated with suppletion is often assumed to be less amenable to transfer by contact than other linguistic features like words (lexicon) or more superficial aspects of grammar (see, e.g., Dixon 1997: 22). That said, other linguists maintain that, given a deep enough social contact situation, pretty much *any* aspect of language can be borrowed (e.g., Thomason & Kaufman 1988). Previous scholars have found that suppletion is an areal feature of the southwest US (especially the Pueblos; cf. Bereznak 1995) and, more generally, the Greater Southwest (including northwest Mexico, cf. Everdell 2013), and it seems to be much reduced in UA languages, like Nahuatl and Pipil, which are associated with a Sprachbund, Mesoamerica, that is not noted for verbal suppletion (Haugen & Everdell 2015). So, although Klamath has a suppletive pattern for 'die', 'kill', and some motion verbs, similar in function but not in form to what is typical of UA, such suppletion does not seem to be a general trait of PP languages, and this singular Klamath trait does not constitute a definitive argument in favor of an old genetic relationship with UA.

Finally, it is interesting to further note that Nez Perce has many verbs for motion and location that vary depending on what one is talking about: e.g., humans vs. four-footed animals vs. plants/trees, etc. The language appears, therefore, to have had ample opportunities to have grammaticalized or analogized (or retained) suppletion for number agreement for these and similar functions, but has not done so. The contrast with what is ubiquitous in the UA languages is therefore quite striking, and the lack calls into question a genetic link between the two groups.

4.2.3. Multiple Contrasting Patterns of Reduplication?

Many languages of the Americas employ reduplication and other types of prosodic morphology to indicate various semantic functions; see Urbanczyk (this volume) for an overview and many examples. The UA languages are especially interesting because they often have multiple contrasting reduplication patterns. A case in point is Tohono O'odham (Tepiman), which allows nouns to take two different types of reduplication to mark two different meanings: one is a light syllable (CV) reduplicant to indicate 'plural', and the other is a heavy syllable reduplicant, which induces gemination at the morpheme boundary with the base to form a CVC, to indicate 'distributive' (17). There is also a class of nouns which take a different kind of heavy syllable reduplicant, a CVV, for plurality (thus contrasting with both unmarked plurals and distributives), as in (18).

(17) Tohono O'odham plural vs. distributive reduplication

Singular	*Plural*	*Distributive*	*Gloss*
a. nówiu	**nó**nowiu	**nón**nowiu	'ox'
b. náhagio	**ná**nhagio	**nán**nhagio	'earring'
c. hódai	**hó**hodài	**hoh**hodai	'rock, stone'
d. ʔá:g	**ʔá**ʔag	**ʔáʔ**ʔag	'a pair of animal horns'

(Fitzgerald 2012: 456)

(18) Tohono O'odham special plurals (heavy syllable with long vowel)

Singular	*Plural*	*Gloss*	
a. ban	**ba:**ban	'coyote'	(p. 18)
b. taḍ	**ta:**taḍ	'foot'	(p. 9)
c. ñem	**ñe:**ñem	'liver'	(p. 9)
e. ṣon	**ṣo:**ṣon	'trunk of a plant'	(p. 22)

(Hill & Zepeda 1998)

Although UA languages vary in detail, many of them have similar contrasting patterns where a heavy syllable reduplicant is formed to contrast with a different light syllable reduplicant. (The formation of the heavy syllable can vary from gemination or vowel-lengthening, as in Tohono O'odham, or epenthesis of an unmarked consonant, usually a laryngeal (glottal stop or *h*).) This unusual, 'marked' pattern has been argued to be a retention from PUA rather than individual innovations in the different languages and subgroups that have the pattern (Haugen 2008a).

Reduplication is also a feature of the PP languages, although it is not clear that there is a light- vs. heavy-syllable contrast in these languages. Nez Perce has reduplication for nominals and adjectives, including bare roots/stems (19a) as well as those inflected by/compounded with thematic prefixes (19b). Reduplication in both nouns and verbs are regarded by Aoki as 'distributive' in meaning:

(19) Nez Perce nominal reduplication

	Stem Form			*Distributive Form*	
a.	há·cwal	'son'	→	**ha**hácwal	'son (distributive)' (p. 57)
b.	RED + peH + néqe redup + 'each'+ 'half'		→	**pi**pennéqe	'half-breeds' (p. 61)

(Aoki 1970)

(20) Nez Perce adjectival reduplication

	Stem Form			*Distributive Form*	
a.	wepcú·k	'intelligent'	→	**wi**wé·pcux	'intelligent (distributive)' (p. 57)
b.	néx̣sep	'different'	→	**ni**néx̣sep	'different (distributive)' (p. 65)

(Aoki 1970)

I have not found find any mention of secondary reduplication processes discussed by Aoki (1970). Jacobs (1931) mentions multiple reduplication patterns for nouns and adjectives in Northern Sahaptin, but the details are quite different from what is found in UA. Jacobs contrasts *duplication* with *reduplication*, with the distinction being full vs. partial copying. Regular full 'duplication' can mean 'distributive plural' (21):

(21) 'Distributive plural' duplication in Northern Sahaptin

Nouns: "the entire word or noun complex is duplicated, the accent falling within the first half" (p. 135).

a. i′lkwas 'stick'	>	i′lkwasilkwas	'many sticks'
b. əni·′ᴅ 'house'	>	əni·′ᴅəni·ᴅ	'many houses' (p. 136)

Verbs: "the verb root or root complex is duplicated" (p. 135).

b. –tiya- 'laugh'	>	iti·′yat·iyaᴅna	'he laughed and laughed'

(Jacobs 1931: 135–138)

The formation of the diminutive usually involves full duplication concomitant with some kind of consonant or vowel mutation:

(22) "Diminutive duplication, with concomitant C- and V- changes"

a.	a′tca·c	'eyes'	>	atsa′yatsai	'little eyes'
b.	əni·′ᴅ	'house'	>	əli·′ᴅəli·ᴅ	'little house' (p. 137)
b'.	əni·′ᴅ	'house'	>	əni·′ᴅəni·ᴅ	'a small house'

(Jacobs 1931: 136–137)

According to Jacobs, partial reduplication is only occasionally used, for distributive plural in nouns, adjectives, and pronouns. It involves what has since been dubbed 'bare consonant' reduplication (copying the initial C):

(23) Northern Sahaptin partial reduplication for distributive plural

a. tma′i	'unmarried girl'	>	ttmayi·′ma	'unmarried girls'
b. tə′x̣c	'willow'	>	ttə′x̣c	'willows'

(Jacobs 1931: 137–138)

Neither full copy reduplication nor bare consonant reduplication feature very strongly (if at all) within UA.

In sum, although reduplication is productive in both PP and UA languages, the details are different enough that there is no particular evidence for shared common inheritance of specific reduplication patterns in these groups. The semantic similarities involved in the reduplication in these languages (plurality, pluracationality, distributivity) are cross-linguistically common, semi-iconic functions of reduplication (Moravcsik 1978).

4.2.4. Other Cross-UA Features to Think About

There are a variety of productive derivational morphemes which are near ubiquitous in UA, and to which one might want to make connections if proposing a long-distance genetic connection. For example, PUA had valence-increasing suffixes, which results in cognates across the family similar to *-tua* (for causative) and *-ria/-lia* (for applicative). PP has morphological causatives but they are prefixal, and not at all similar in form to UA: Sahaptian *hii- and *-šeep-, and Klamath *s-*, *sne-*, and *hes-* (Rude 1987: 78). PUA also had valency-decreasing morphology, with the most common being some reflex of passive *-wa*; see Jacobs (1975) for extensive discussion. Many UA languages also show reflexes of a variety of denominal verb-forming suffixes (i.e., creating verbs from nouns), such as *-ta 'make' and *-tu 'inceptive' (Langacker 1977; Haugen 2008b), a number of which are implicated in various ways in creating denominal verbs of possession in various UA languages and subgroups. These have been reconstructed as *-ka 'have (alienable)'; *-pV 'have (inalienable)'; *-tu 'active possession (get, acquire)'; *-wa 'attributive possession'/'possessed thing'; and a postposition, *-ɨ, which was most likely a locative (Haugen 2017).

4.3. Grammatical Comparisons that Constitute Weak Evidence for Genetic Relations

In this section we will briefly overview some areas of comparative syntax and morphosyntax that constitute very weak (and possibly counter-)evidence for long-distance genetic relationships for UA and PP. These include basic word order (§4.3.1); case-marking on nominals and agreement-marking pronominal affixes on verbs (§4.3.2); and a second position clitic complex (§4.3.3).

4.3.1. Basic Word Order

First, let us consider basic word order. Most UA languages are straightforwardly SOV, which is what is reconstructed for PUA. However, there is variation across the family, with some languages taking on a basic non-final word order (such as most of the languages of the Aztecan branch, well ensconced in the Mesoamerican Sprachbund where verb non-finality is an areal feature) or even displaying characteristics of non-configurationality (e.g., Tohono O'odham). Even these languages have the remnants of an earlier verb-finality, however, including productive derivational suffixes.

The PP languages do not show basic verb-final word order. The Nez Perce case has been analyzed in different ways. While Aoki (1979) considers the preferred word order to be VSO, Rude's (1992) text analysis leads him to conclude that it is a free word order language, with word order determined by discourse factors. Deal (2010), however, presents an argument from subject and object asymmetry in binding that there is an underlying configurationality. Sahaptin has also been described as being a free word order language (Rigsby & Rude 1996: 673).

Basic word order (or the lack thereof) is a notoriously thorny topic in historical linguistic reconstruction, but the basic facts of PP and UA seem to be quite different. Although some languages in UA are free word order, this is likely an independent development long after the break-up of PUA.

4.3.2. Case on NPs/DPs and Argument-Marking Pronominal Affixes on Verbs

Most UA languages are nominative/accusative, with unmarked nominative case on subject NPs/DPs and a marked accusative case on object NPs/DPs. UA languages also frequently employ pronominal marking on the verb. Interestingly, there is wide variation across the family in this regard, so different subgroups seem to have grammaticalized these bound pronominals at different times, and in some cases, in different orders. Sometimes the marking is obligatory, sometimes it is optional, and sometimes it is conditional (e.g., dependent on tense, as in the Takic language Cupeño). A summary of some this variation in the morphological verb complex is given in (24) (where S = subject-marker; O = object marker; parentheses = optionality):

(24) Subject and object marking on the transitive verb across UA

Language	*Subgroup*	*Order of Verbal Inflection*
Classical Nahuatl	Aztecan	S-O-V
Cahuilla	Takic	O-S-V
Cupeño	Takic	(O)-S-$V_{\text{(past tense)}}$
Tohono O'odham	Tepiman	O-V
Hopi	NUA singleton	O-$V_{\text{(for a small closed class of verbs)}}$, (O)-$V_{\text{(elsewhere)}}$
Hiaki	Taracahitan	(O)-V

(Haugen forthcoming)

The facts of agreement and case-marking in PP are much more complex. First, these languages tend to have much more extensive case marking (for example, Rigsby & Rude 1996: 673 compare case-marking in Sahaptin to the well-known complex systems of Finnish and Turkish). These languages also employ ergative-absolutive case alignment, unlike typical UA languages. Deal (2010) presents a comprehensive discussion of the situation in Nez Perce, where (usually prefixal) verbal agreement interacts in various ways with overt case-marking on nominals.

The severe differences between the PP and UA languages in regard to nominal case-marking and verbal agreement-marking are not knock-down arguments against a genetic relationship, but they hardly constitute an argument for a relation.

4.3.3. A Second Position Clitic Complex

Many UA languages have a second position clitic complex, composed of all or some of the following: markers of mood, tense, and/or pronominal subject. Steele (1979) reconstructs the full clitic complex back to PUA, but Haugen (2007) argues that subject pronominal marking, at least, was probably variable in PUA (being available for second position, or optionally preverbal). Considering the geographic distribution of the second position clitic complex within the family, Hill (2005) regards it as being likely an areal development since the break-up of PUA.

Second position clitics are also relevant in PP. Crook (1999) examines different classes of agreement morphology in complementary distribution; namely, first- and second-person clitics suffix to certain clause-initial particles, while third-person clitics prefix to verbs. Crook suggests that the former may have developed from second position clitics. Sahaptin has an even more complex system of productive second position clitics and affixal agreement morphology in the verb complex.

Again, while there may seem to be some superficial similarities, the details of the phenomena at hand are different enough that they do not directly support positing an old genetic link between the families.

5. Conclusion

In this chapter we have reviewed a long-standing propensity for Americanists to attempt to connect well-established language families to ever more remote relations. Such proposals need to be held to the same standard as non-remote familial proposals. Specifically, (i) the comparative method must be used to establish systematic correspondence in both form and meaning, and (ii) typologically unusual grammatical phenomena ('shared aberrancies') should be identified in order to rule out other sources of similarity, such as coincidental independent development or transfer through contact. These criteria have not been met in the case of Rude's (2000) proposed connection between PP and UA, so we regard his proposed PP-UA macro-family as being both unproven and quite unlikely. The larger theme is that any proposed long-range macrofamily proposal should be held to the same standards as established families.

Acknowledgments

Many thanks to the audience at the 2017 Friends of Uto-Aztecan Conference, held at Boise State University, for helpful discussion of this material, as well as to Jane Hill, Dan Siddiqi, and Michael Everdell for comments on the manuscript. The usual disclaimers apply.

Further Reading

There are many very good historical linguistics textbooks on the market, any of which can provide useful introductions to theories and methods of historical linguistics. Campbell's (2013) textbook pays particularly close attention to the languages of the Americas (among many others). Campbell (1997) reviews the general history of the classification of the languages of the Americas (including North, Central, and South America), with extensive discussion and evaluation of various proposals of long-distance genetic relations in the so-called 'New World'. Campbell and Poser (2008) offer a global overview of the history of historical linguistics and review proposals for legitimate language families, as well as provide criticisms of many proposed long-distance genetic relationships, from all over the world. Many descriptive reference works (grammars and dictionaries) for individual languages in both the Uto-Aztecan and Plateau Penutian families are cited in this chapter. The classic work on comparative Uto-Aztecan grammar is Langacker (1977), and, for the comparative UA lexicon, see Stubbs (2011).

Notes

1. Greenberg (1987) follows suit by putting these language families into distinct sub-groups of his controversial "Amerind". Like Sapir, Greenberg places PP in Penutian (which in Greenberg's proposal is a larger stock than Sapir originally proposed), while UA is clustered with Kiowa-Tanoan and Oto-Manguean in a branch he calls "Central Amerind". While Penutian still maintains some proponents, none of these Greenbergian classifications are accepted by mainstream linguists.
2. The specific numbers from Maddieson's (2013) survey of a sample of 564 languages are: 93 'small' (2–4 vowels, = 16.5%); 287 'average' (5–6 vowels, = 51%); and 184 'large' (7–14 vowels, = 33%).

References

Aoki, Haruo. 1970. *Nez Perce grammar*. (University of California Publications in Linguistics 62). Berkeley: University of California Press.

Aoki, Haruo. 1979. *Nez Perce texts*. (University of California Publications in Linguistics 90). Berkeley: University of California Press.

Aoki, Haruo. 1994. *Nez Perce dictionary*. (University of California Publications in Linguistics 122). Berkeley: University of California Press.

Barker, M. A. R. 1963. *Klamath dictionary*. (California Publications in Linguistics 31). Berkeley: University of California Press.

Barker, M. A. R. 1964. *Klamath grammar*. (California Publications in Linguistics 32). Berkeley: University of California Press.

Beck, David J. 2000. Grammatical convergence and the genesis of diversity in the Northwest Coast Sprachbund. *Anthropological Linguistics* 42 (2). 147–213.

Bereznak, Catherine Christine. 1995. *The Pueblo region as a linguistic area: Diffusion among the indigenous languages of the Southwest United States*. Baton Rouge: Louisiana State University. (Doctoral dissertation.)

Bjorkman, Bronwyn M. 2010. Morphology and stress in Nez Perce verbs. In Rogers, Beth & Szakay, Anita (eds.), *Papers for WSCLA 15: The fifteenth workshop on structure and constituency in the Americas*, 70–84. (UBC Working Papers in Linguistics 29).

Campbell, Lyle. 1988. Review article: Language in the Americas by Joseph H. Greenberg. *Language* 64(3). 591–615.

Campbell, Lyle. 1997. *American Indian languages: The historical linguistics of Native America*. Oxford: Oxford University Press.

Campbell, Lyle. 2013. *Historical linguistics: An introduction*, 3rd edn. Cambridge, MA: MIT Press.

Campbell, Lyle & Poser, William J. 2008. *Language classification: History and method*. Cambridge: Cambridge University Press.

Crook, Harold D. 1999. *The phonology and morphology of Nez Perce stress*. Los Angeles: UCLA. (Doctoral dissertation.)

Deal, Amy Rose. 2010. Ergative case and the transitive subject: A view from Nez Perce. *Natural Language and Linguistic Theory* 28. 73–120.

DeLancey, Scott. 1996. The bipartite stem belt: Disentangling areal and genetic correspondences. *Berkeley Linguistics Society* 22.

Dixon, R. M. W. 1997. *The rise and fall of languages*. Cambridge: Cambridge University Press.

Epps, Patience & Bowern, Claire & Hansen, Cynthia A. & Hill, Jane H. & Zentz, Jason. 2012. On numeral complexity in hunter-gatherer languages. *Linguistic Typology* 16. 41–109.

Escalante, Fernando. 1990. *Voice and argument structure in Yaqui*. Tucson: University of Arizona. (Doctoral dissertation.)

Everdell, Michael. 2013. *Reconsidering the Puebloan languages in a Southwestern areal context*. (Oberlin College Honors thesis.) (http://rave.ohiolink.edu/etdc/view?acc_num=oberlin1368021379)

Fitzgerald, Colleen M. 2012. Prosodic inconsistency in Tohono O'odham. *International Journal of American Linguistics* 78(4). 435–463.

Goddard, Ives. 1975. Algonquian, Wiyot, and Yurok: Proving a distant genetic relationship. In Kinkade, M. Dale & Hale, Kenneth L. & Werner, Oswald (eds.), *Linguistics and anthropology in honor of C.F. Voegelin*, 249–262. Lisse: Peter de Ridder Press.

Golla, Victor. 2011. *California Indian languages*. Berkeley: University of California Press.

Greenberg, Joseph H. 1987. *Language in the Americas*. Stanford, CA: Stanford University Press.

Haugen, Jason D. 2007. On the development of pronominal clitics and affixes in Uto-Aztecan. *Southwest Journal of Linguistics* 26(1). 39–60.

Haugen, Jason D. 2008a. *Morphology at the interfaces: Reduplication and noun incorporation in Uto-Aztecan*. Amsterdam: John Benjamins Publishing.

Haugen, Jason D. 2008b. Denominal verbs in Uto-Aztecan. *International Journal of American Linguistics* 74(4). 439–470.

Haugen, Jason D. 2017. Derived verbs of possession in Uto-Aztecan: Reconstructions and paths of change. *Anthropological Linguistics* 59(2). 163–204.

Haugen, Jason D. Forthcoming. Uto-Aztecan. In Wichmann, Søren (ed.), *The languages and linguistics of middle and Central America: A comprehensive guide*. To be published in the World of Linguistics series by Mouton de Gruyter.

Haugen, Jason D. & Everdell, Michael. 2015. 'To kill' & 'to die' (and other suppletive verbs) in Uto-Aztecan. *Language Dynamics and Change* 5(2). 227–281.

Haugen, Jason D. & Siddiqi, Daniel. 2013. Roots and the derivation. *Linguistic Inquiry* 44(3). 493–517.

Hayes, Bruce. 1995. *Metrical stress theory: Principles and case studies*. Chicago, IL: University of Chicago Press.

Hill, Jane H. 2005. *A Grammar of Cupeño*. (University of California Publications in Linguistics Vol. 136). Berkeley: University of California Press.

Hill, Jane H. 2011. Subgrouping in Uto-Aztecan. *Language Dynamics and Change* 1. 241–278.

Hill, Jane H. & Zepeda, Ofelia. 1998. Tohono O'odham (Papago) plurals. *Anthropological Linguistics* 40(1). 1–42.

Hill, Kenneth C. 2001. Comments on Hopi and comparative Uto-Aztecan. In Moctezuma Za-marrón, José Luis & Hill, Jane H. (eds.), *Avances y balances de lenguas yutoaztecas*, 293–312. México: Instituto Nacional de Antropología e Historia.

Hill, Kenneth C. 2014. *Wick Miller's Uto-Aztecan cognate sets* (Kenneth C. Hill, revised and expanded). Tucson, AZ: Tshwanelex Data File.

Hill, Kenneth C. & Hill, Jane H. 2017. Comparative Takic: Vocalism of the absolutive suffixes. (Paper presented at the Friends of Uto-Aztecan Conference; Boise State University, Boise, ID, 21 October 2017).

Jacobs, Melville. 1931. A sketch of northern Sahaptin grammar. *University of Washington Publications in Anthropology* 4(2). 85–292. Seattle: University of Washington.

Jacobs, Roderick A. 1975. *Syntactic change: A Cupan (Uto-Aztecan) case study*. Berkeley: University of California Publications in Linguistics 79.

Juge, Matthew. 2000. On the rise of suppletion in verbal paradigms. In Chang, Steve S. & Liaw, Lily & Ruppenhofer, Josef (eds.), *Proceedings of the twenty-fifth annual meeting of the Berkeley Linguistics Society, 12–15 February 1999*, 183–194. Berkeley, CA: Berkeley Linguistics Society.

Langacker, Ronald W. 1970. The vowels of Proto Uto-Aztecan. *International Journal of American Linguistics* 36(3). 169–180.

Langacker, Ronald W. 1977. *Studies in Uto-Aztecan grammar I: An overview of Uto-Aztecan grammar*. Dallas, TX: Summer Institute of Linguistics.

Launey, Michel. 2011. *An introduction to classical Nahuatl*. (Christopher Mackay, trans.) Cambridge: Cambridge University Press.

Maddieson, Ian. 2013. Vowel quality inventories. In Dryer, Matthew S. & Haspelmath, Martin (eds.), *The world atlas of language structures online*. Leipzig: Max Planck Institute for Evolutionary Anthropology. (http://wals.info/chapter/2) (Accessed 2018-06-01.)

Manaster Ramer, Alexis. 1993. Blood, tears, and murder: the evidence for Proto-Uto-Aztecan syllable-final consonants. In van Marle, Jaap (ed.), *Historical linguistics 1991: Papers from the 10th International Conference on Historical Linguistics*, 199–209. Amsterdam: John Benjamins Publishing Company.

Merrill, William L. 2013. The genetic unity of Southern Uto-Aztecan. *Language Dynamics and Change* 3. 68–104.

Miller, Wick R. 1967. *Uto-Aztecan cognate sets*. (University of California Publications in Linguistics 48). Berkeley: University of California Press.

Miller, Wick R. 1996a. Sketch of Shoshone, a Uto-Aztecan language. In Ives Goddard (ed.), *Handbook of North American Indians*, vol. 17, *Languages*, 693–720. Washington, DC: Smithsonian Institution Press.

Miller, Wick R. 1996b. *Guarijío: Gramática, textos y vocabulario*. Mexico City: Universidad Nacional Autónoma de México.

Moravcsik, Edith. 1978. Reduplicative constructions. In Greenberg, Joseph H. (ed.), *Universals of human language vol. 3: Word structure*, 297–334. Stanford, CA: Stanford University Press.

Munro, Pamela. 1977. Towards a reconstruction of Uto-Aztecan stress. In Hyman, Larry M. (ed.), *Studies in stress and accent*, 303–326. (Southern California Occasional Papers in Linguistics 4). Los Angeles: Department of Linguistics, USC.

Nichols, Johanna & Peterson, David A. 1996. The Amerind personal pronouns. *Language* 72(2). 336–371.

Rigsby, Bruce & Rude, Noel. 1996. Sketch of Sahaptin, a Sahaptian language. In Goddard, Ives (ed.), *Handbook of North American languages, vol. 17 (languages)*, 666–692. Washington, DC: Smithsonian Institution.

Ringe, Don. 1999. How hard is it to match CVC- roots? *Transactions of the Philological Society* 97(2). 213–244.

Rude, Noel. 1987. Some Sahaptian-Klamath grammatical correspondences. *Kansas Working Papers in Linguistics* 12. 67–83.

Rude, Noel. 1992. Word order and topicality in Nez Perce. In Payne, Doris (ed.), *Pragmatics of word order flexibility*, 193–208. Amsterdam: John Benjamins.

Rude, Noel. 2000. Some Uto-Aztecan-Plateau grammatical comparisons. In *Uto-Aztecan: Structural, temporal, and geographic perspectives: Papers in memory of Wick R. Miller by the friends of Uto-Aztecan*, 309–318. Hermosillo, Sonora: Editorial Unison.

Shaul, David Leedom. 2014. *A prehistory of Western North America: The impact of Uto-Aztecan languages*. Albuquerque: University of New Mexico Press.

Steele, Susan. 1979. Uto-Aztecan: An assessment for historical and comparative linguistics. In Campbell, Lyle & Mithun, Marianne (eds.), *The languages of native America: Historical and comparative assessment*, 444–544. Austin: University of Texas Press.

Stubbs, Brian D. 2011. *Uto-Aztecan: A comparative vocabulary*. Blanding, UT: Rocky Mountain Books and Productions.

Thomason, Sarah Grey & Kaufman, Terrence. 1988. *Language contact, creolization, and genetic linguistics*. Berkeley: University of California Press.

Thornes, Tim. 2011. Dimensions of Northern Paiute multi-verb constructions. In Muysken, P. & Aikhenvald, A. (eds.), *Multi-verb constructions: A view from the Americas*, 27–61. Leiden: Brill.

24

AREAL LINGUISTICS AND LINGUISTIC AREAS IN CALIFORNIA

Jane H. Hill

1. Introduction

Indigenous Californians spoke at least 78 distinct languages, representing at least five large language families and two smaller ones. The distribution of these across the landscape (see Figure 24.1) is modeled by Golla (2011) as the product of a layered accretion of languages that have spread across the region over at least 10,000 years of history.

Yukian and Chumashan languages (and Waikuri in Baja California) may represent the most ancient Californians. The diverse "Hokan" groups, including both isolated languages and small families,[1] constitute a complex second layer of settlement and radiation. The radiations and spreads of the "Penutian" families: successively, Utian, Wintun, Maiduan, and Yokutsan,[2] in the Central Valley pushed Hokan languages into their historic distribution around its mountainous margins. The Yuman languages, also linked to Hokan, persist in extreme Southern California and Baja California, divided from their probable relatives by the spread of the Uto-Aztecan Takic subgroup into Southern California. The last layers include, in northwestern California, the Algic languages Yurok and Wiyot and the cluster of Pacific Coast Athabaskan languages; and in the east, the expansion of Western Mono, from another Uto-Aztecan subgroup, Numic, west across the Sierra Crest into the western foothills of the range.[3]

This complex history of language spreads was accompanied by changes in social organization that must have continually reshaped networks of interaction and language contact. For instance, Bettinger (2015) argues that a generalized hunter-gatherer economy, focused on hunting by highly mobile groups, was replaced by around 600 AD by an economy focused on intensive management and privatization of plant resources, especially acorns. Mobile hunting bands were replaced by small territorial groups that controlled these resources. The very small size of these social groups meant that 'language' had little socio-political relevance: close relatives might speak different languages (Conathan 2004), and, as Golla (2011: 3) points out, "some of your most dangerous enemies" might speak yours. In the far northwest, individual villages were the fundamental units of social organization. The larger Yokuts, Chumashan, Takic, and Yuman groups, with relatively larger territories and relatively closer alignments between political organization and language boundaries, created a different context for language contact.

The webs of language contact that were woven and unwoven during this long history have left an intricate palimpsest of shared traits[4] in every dimension of language structure, attesting to a long history of exchanges among the languages. Attempts to penetrate the layers of the palimpsest and to untangle the webs, especially with the goal of distinguishing signals of contact from those of

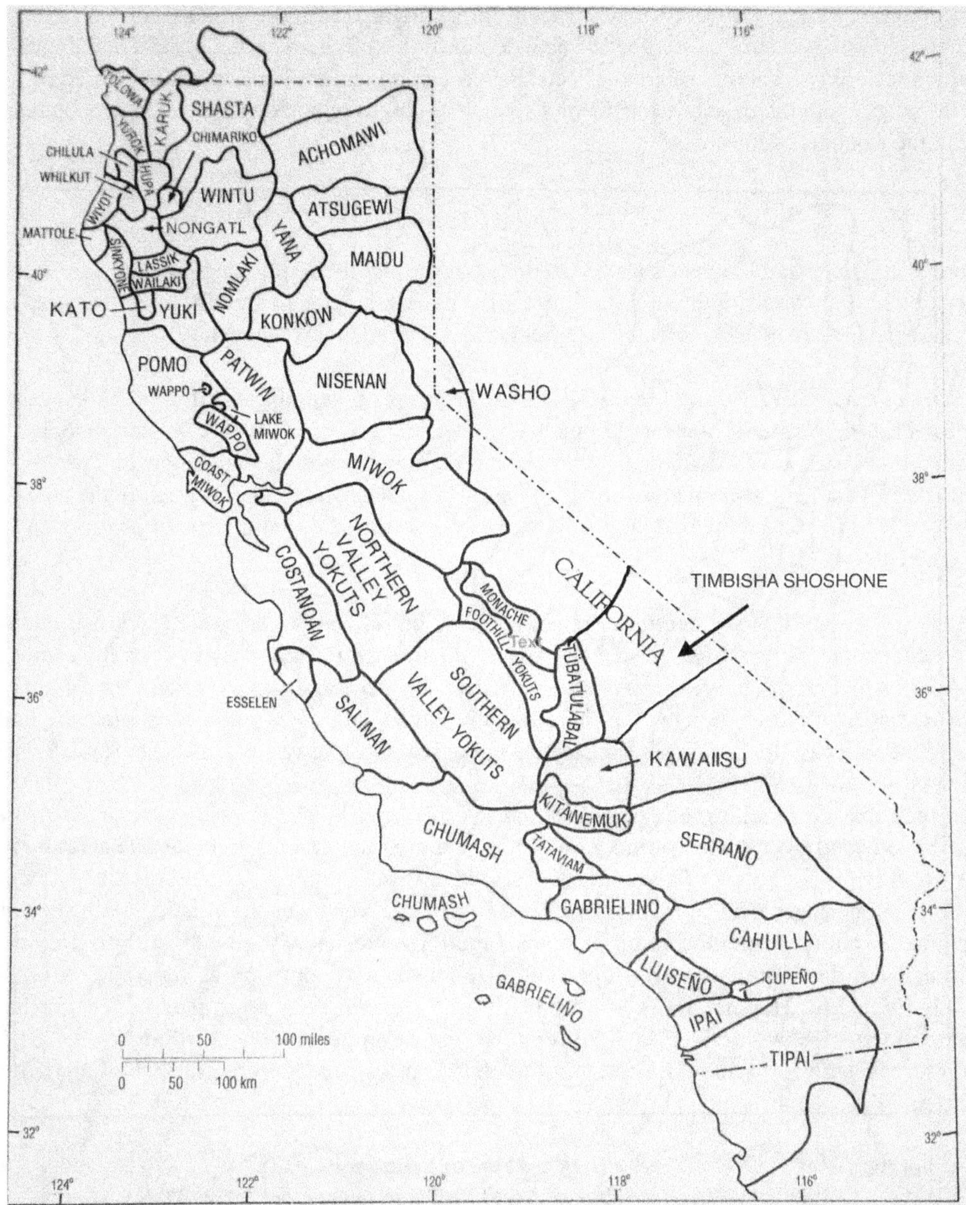

Figure 24.1 California Native Languages Map
Source: Campbell (1997: 357).

genetic inheritance, have made Californianist studies something of a hotbed of areal linguistics. Areal linguistic analysis has contributed to our understanding of California prehistory, uncovering evidence of ancient contact between language groups that by the time of white invasion were widely separated, as well as to the reconstruction of ancient networks of trade and exchange.

The sections of this chapter include, first, a discussion of linguistic areas (or "language areas") that have been proposed for California languages. I then turn to recent critiques of the concept, and to examples of work in California that represent "areal linguistics" more broadly, through attention to spreads of linguistic traits and the historical details of these dynamics, both social and linguistic. Finally, I look at two sources of areal effects: the case of an underlying substratum shared by several languages, and the case of traits from a spreading language borrowed into diverse languages around the frontiers of the spread.[5]

2. Linguistic Areas

Dating from Dixon and Kroeber's (1903) finding that the distribution of language traits in California exhibited "territorial continuity", Californianists have attempted to identify linguistic areas and their associated traits, at diverse scales. Enfield (2005: 190) defines "linguistic area" as

> a geographical region in which neighboring languages belonging to different language families show a significant set of structural properties in common, where the commonalities in structure are due to historical contact between speakers of the languages, and where the shared structural properties are not found in languages immediately outside the area (ideally where these include languages belonging to the same families as those spoken inside the area).

Enfield observes that the definition raises as many questions as it answers. The restriction to "historical contact" means that chance and shared inheritance must be ruled out as the source of the shared structural properties. The more – and deeper – genetic diversity among the languages, the more coherent the geography, the more traits involved, and the typologically rarer the traits, the stronger the case for areality is considered to be, but absolute values for these characteristics cannot be specified.

At the most far-reaching geographical scale, California languages with *n/m* pronoun systems[6] have been linked to a "Pacific Rim" linguistic area that stretches as far as Australia and New Guinea (J. Nichols & Peterson 1996, 1998, 2013a; Bickel & J. Nichols 2006). Many languages in northern California can be linked to a larger Northwest linguistic area, especially by phonetic traits that include complex consonantal inventories with plain vs. glottalized contrasts and the development of multiple lateral phonemes (Thompson & Kinkade 1990: 42; Mithun 1999: 314; Haynie 2012). Within California, several sub-areas, seen in (1)–(5), have repeatedly been acknowledged in the literature (e.g., Campbell 1997; Mithun 1999; 2017).[7] The references given include original arguments and more recent work on phenomena within the area.

(1) Northern

Hokan: Karuk, Shasta, Chimariko, Yana, Pomoan, Achomawi-Atsugewi, Yana, Washo; Penutian: Wintun, Lake Miwok, Southern Sierra Miwok, Maidu; Algic: Yurok, Wiyot; Athabaskan: Tolowa, Hupa, Mattole, Kato; Yukian; Wappo

(Haas 1976; Campbell 1997; Mithun 1999; Jany 2009; Haynie 2012)

(2) Northwest California[8]

Wiyot, Yurok, Karuk, Hupa

(Conathan 2004; O'Neill 2008)

(3) Clear Lake

Pomoan, Yuki, Wappo, Lake Miwok, Patwin

(Callaghan 1964; 1987; 2014; Mithun 1999)

(4) South Coast Range
Esselen, Salinan, Chumashan

(Hinton 1991; Campbell 1997)

(5) Southern California–Western Arizona
Yuman, Takic Uto-Aztecan

(Sproat 1981; Hinton 1991; Elliott 1994; Hill 2017)

3. Beyond Linguistic Areas to "Areal Linguistics"

The concept "linguistic area" continues to be used by Californianists. Golla identified a California linguistic area within North America defined by the trait mentioned in the introduction: "the absence of a congruence between the linguistic and the sociopolitical" (Golla 2011: 2). However, this trait itself is gradient, being most striking in the far northwest. Furthermore, examination of the on-the-ground distribution of languages and traits in any of the areas listed in (1) will show that they have rough edges and complex distributions of traits. Some languages are marginal, some strikingly lack expected traits, and languages well outside any reasonable notion of geographical continuity; for instance Washo in the Northern California linguistic area list in (1) may be included in an area.[9]

These problems challenge the utility of the concept of linguistic area – one that has never been defined to the satisfaction of all linguists. An important recent critique is that of Campbell (2006; 2017). Campbell reviews the history of theorization of "language area", including in other terminological guises, the most famous probably being Sprachbund (Trubetskoy 1928). He concludes that the search for a satisfactory definition is bound to fail, and that the many cases, at multiple scales, that have been identified in the literature do not constitute a coherent set of objects.[10] Furthermore, Campbell argues that linguistic areas too frequently are proposed on the basis of "circumstantialist" evidence that assumes that lists of common traits speak for themselves as evidence of language contact. In his view, scholarly attention should turn from "*post hoc* attempts to impose geographical order on varied conglomerations of . . . borrowings" toward "historicist" accounts of "individual historical events of diffusion" (Campbell 2017: 19). The historicist approach seeks "concrete evidence that the shared traits are diffused" (Campbell 2017: 24). Campbell (2017) proposes that the appropriate unit of analysis is not the 'language area', but what he calls the "trait sprawl area", the distribution across languages of individual traits. The focus should be on "what changes took place, rather than on defining some geographical area itself" (Campbell 2017: 28). He distinguishes the "trait sprawl area" from the "language area *sensu stricto*", where the focus is on "traits mostly continued within and shared across the languages of a clearly delimited geographical space" (Campbell 2017: 28).

A brief survey of a single case can illustrate the distinction between circumstantialist and historicist accounts. Golla's (2011) survey of the distribution of typological markers in California languages – in which Golla uses the term "cluster" for possible examples of trait sprawl areas – shows complex overlaps and intersections, with different markers picking up different clusters of languages, some of them widely separated in space, illustrating clearly the difficulties of identifying a "language area *sensu stricto*". As pointed out by Thomason (2001), at such a large scale historicist accounts are probably unachievable, so Golla's discussion is unavoidably "circumstantialist". But it does provide examples of trait spreads which offer a scale that enables a historicist approach.

One of the most important questions for a historicist account is, is a trait a conservative retention in a language or language family, or is it an innovation? And if a trait is an innovation, to what degree is the innovation determined by language-internal dynamics, versus borrowing? An example of the problem involves the contrast between pre-velar *k* and back velar *q*, which Golla (2011: 206) locates in "three clusters":

> a northwestern cluster including California Athabaskan, Chimariko, Northern Wintuan, Pomo, and Lake Miwok; (2) a northeastern cluster including Klamath-Modoc and Palaihnihan; and (3) a southwestern cluster including Chumash, Takic, and Yuman.

The following offers a historical approach to the distribution of the *k/q* contrast in Golla's southwestern cluster. The contrast is reconstructed for Proto-Chumashan (Klar 1977: 32) and Proto-Yuman (Langdon 1970: 542). It is often assumed that, before the arrival of the Takic languages in Southern California, Chumashan (an isolate family, unrelated to Hokan Yuman) and Yuman probably shared a frontier, although Bright and Bright (1976 [1969]) observe that an investigation of non-Uto-Aztecan vocabulary in the Takic language Gabrielino/Tongva suggests the presence in the Los Angeles Basin of a substratum language or languages that were neither Chumashan nor Yuman.

The *k/q* contrast in the Takic languages is not due to contact between those languages and Chumashan or Yuman. The *q* of the Takic languages is inherited from Proto-Northern Uto-Aztecan (PNUA), where it replaced Proto-Uto-Aztecan *k before low vowels. PNUA *k* and *q* were in complementary, not contrastive, distributions. In Mono and Southern Paiute, two Numic languages, the complementary distribution remains (although in Southern Paiute, *q* has replaced *k* before all vowels except *i*).[11] In Hopi, the distribution remains largely complementary, but the original high vowel/low vowel environments have been obscured by innovations in the vowel system yielding *ko* from *ku, and *qe*, usually from **qai*. In Serrano, a Takic language, only a few words disturb the complementary distribution.

The development of *q* as an allophone of **k* before low vowels in PNUA may have involved influence from Yuman. A word for "mesquite" (*Prosopis* spp.) can be reconstructed for PNUA, so the PNUA speech community is unlikely to have been located farther west than the lower Virgin or Mojave Rivers, in the northwestern-most corner of the range of mesquite at the time depth of PNUA, ca. 4000–3500 BP. That is much too far east for contact with Chumashan. But in that region, PNUA could have been in contact with speakers of Yuman languages. Yuman languages have both *k* and *q* before reflexes of all three Proto-Yuman vowels. While Yuman *q* may have provided an external phonetic prototype for PNUA speakers (see the discussion later in this section of Blevins's work on this point), the high-vowel/low-vowel allophony of the PNUA split of PUA *k into *k* and *q* shows that the distribution of the innovation was shaped by structural determinants internal to that language.

Only in the Cupan subgroup of Takic did a series of vowel shifts yield a definite *k/q* contrast. The merger of *o and *i to *i* in Cupeño and Cahuilla produced many near-minimal pairs like Cupeño *qiŋiʃ* 'ground squirrel', *kiŋʔi* 'to burn (intr.)'. Interestingly, Gabrielino/Tongva, in intimate contact with *k/q* contrasting speakers of Chumashan languages, appears to have entirely lost *q*. The raising of **o* to *i* was part of a chain shift that led to the loss of the Proto-Uto-Aztecan central vowel in Luiseño, Cahuilla, and Gabrielino/Tongva (in the last case, the change probably did not take place until the historic period).[12] An early stage of Yuman, with a Proto-Yuman system with only three vowels (Langdon 1976), might have influenced the loss of the central vowel in Luiseño and Cahuilla. However, this seems unlikely, because the Yuman languages in closest contact with the Cupan group, Iipay 'Aa and Tiipay 'Aa (Northern and Southern Diegueño), actually developed a central vowel,[13] elaborating the Proto-Yuman three-vowel system, which remains in Cocopa, Diegueño's nearest relative. In this case, if there was diffusion, it was surely from Cupan into the Diegueño languages, perhaps from a pre-Cupan stage predating the vowel shifts and the loss of the central vowel in Luiseño, or perhaps simply from Cupeño, which retained the central vowel. In summary, there is indeed a "cluster" of languages in Southern California where *k* contrasts with *q*, but the approach sketched here suggests a much more complex history of this trait sprawl than a simple "diffusion" across the boundaries between Chumashan, Yuman, and Takic.

Areal scholarship on California languages in the last few decades has anticipated Campbell's call for historicist approaches to the spread of individual traits. An example is the work of Langdon and Silver (1994) on the distribution of contrasts between a more fronted versus a more retracted pronunciation of *t*, for which they use the symbols *t/ṭ*. Their unit of investigation is the trait itself, not a geographical unit: "For our purposes, . . . we do not wish to exclude a priori any languages of the present state of California" – or languages around its borders (Langdon & Silver 1994: 140). They conclude that the sprawl area for the trait is ancient, since the *t/ṭ* contrast reconstructs to all of the proto-languages in their survey except Yuman. However, they suggest directionality for only part of the trait sprawl area, a zone where the backed variant is realized as *tṣ* in Costanoan, Esselen and Salinan, Yokutsan, and the Serran languages (Serrano and Kitanemuk) within Takic. Since Serran is the only Takic group with the contrast, they conclude that the innovation entered Serran from Yokutsan after the radiation of Takic. This case raises an interesting paradox. One of the criteria that Langdon and Silver suggest for evaluating the antiquity of a trait in a language is "installation": whether the trait appears only in lexical items, or in grammatical morphemes, especially affixes, as well. In Serran, Proto-Uto-Aztecan noun suffixes *-*ta* 'genitive' and *-*ti* 'absolutive' have split into two allomorphs, with /t/ preserved where the noun stem was originally consonant-final, and /tṣ/ where it was vowel-final. The absolutive suffix appears on every non-possessed noun, and the genitive suffix is also frequent. The same split appears in the very productive suffix -*tuʔa* ~ -*tṣuʔa* ~ -*tʃuʔa*, which derives verbs from nouns. The contrast also appears in stems, e.g., Serrano *kʷɨ·tṣ*- 'get up', *rɨwɨt*- 'disappear'. Thus, at least in this case, "installation" and "antiquity" are not correlated.

The Northwest California linguistic area has interested anthropologists from an early date, due to the contrast between its relative cultural homogeneity and the genetic diversity of the languages, which include languages of Hokan, Athabaskan, and Algic affiliation. Three recent studies of convergence and divergence among the languages, by Juliette Blevins, Lisa Conathan, and Sean O'Neill, can illustrate some current directions in areal linguistics, with attention to the details of the linguistic and sociolinguistic processes that advance or restrict trait sprawl.

Blevins's (2002; 2003; 2017) work on the spread of an "areal sound pattern" into the Algic language Yurok examines the psycholinguistic processes involved in the incorporation of borrowed traits into a language. The Northwest California linguistic area is located at the edge of the larger Northwest area where having a glottalized series of consonants is a very widespread trait. Yurok, the only Algic language with glottalized consonants, shares this structural development. Blevins points out that the trait is not rare globally, and might have emerged in Yurok as a natural phonetic development, yielding a chance resemblance to the glottalized consonants in the Athabaskan languages Hupa and Tolowa and in Hokan Chimariko. This is a concern because most examples of Yurok glottalized consonants appear in inherited vocabulary as reductions of old consonant clusters, a kind of change well attested in other languages. However, Blevins (2017) argues that language contact was "catalytic" in creating a favorable environment for this sound change in Yurok. Glottalized consonants in nearby languages provide "an external phonetic prototype" that has a "perceptual magnet effect" that pulls similar Indigenous Yurok sounds – especially, clusters of Cʔ and Ct – toward a realization as C' (99). Interestingly, some details of "installation" of the Yurok glottalized series suggest the relative recency of this change. The glottalized obstruents are of more limited distribution than their plain counterparts. The glottalized sonorants cannot appear in word-initial position, and syllabify as a glottal stop coda and a sonorant onset in intervocalic position. However, they behave as unit phonemes under truncation (Blevins 2003). Blevins emphasizes that loanwords are not a major source for glottalized consonants in Yurok. New sounds do enter languages in loan vocabulary (for instance, *f* from Spanish words like *fósforo* 'match' in many Mesoamerican languages), but Yurok has very few loans. The exception to internal development appears in only ten loanwords with word initial *t'* and *c'* (Blevins 2002).

Conathan (2004; 2006) reviewed archival evidence, including field notes from the earliest workers on six languages of the Northwest California area, in order to detail the sociocultural processes that have favored the spread of traits. These sources report a number of multilingual individuals, although they also record the limits of multilingualism, which required that translators often had to be provided for visitors to ceremonies. Certain frontier areas were known to be dominantly bilingual. Consultants for the early fieldworkers were often bilingual and spoke of relatives who were bilingual as well, or who spoke a different language. Martha Horn, who was apparently of Karuk origin, provided materials for A.L. Kroeber in Karuk, Tolowa, and Shasta. None of the languages was dominant over another. All were considered to be of equal utility, all had approximately the same number of speakers (roughly, 2,000 to 3,000), and there was no pressure to shift (except apparently among the Chimariko, who were shifting to Hupa and Wintu). Most bilinguals were the offspring of mixed marriages (which accounted for up to 20% of unions), and had learned both languages in early childhood. In spite of bilingualism, there was no code-switching and almost no borrowing of lexical items. In their lexicon and most of their structural features the languages remain quite divergent, although the contact zone is probably a thousand years old. However, a culture of language was shared, exhibiting "functional convergence", where quite different formal means were used to express the semantic and pragmatic functions shared in all the communities.

O'Neill (2008) includes three of the languages – Hupa (Athabaskan), Yurok (Algic), and Karuk (Hokan) – in his study of the "different structural means" found in each of them at loci where functional convergence is obvious. Among his many examples is spatial and directional reference. The three languages share a semantic space defined by four directions: upstream and downstream, and uphill and downhill. These directions shift depending on where the speaker is, taking into account the direction of flow of the twisting river and the angles of the surrounding mountains, so deep local knowledge is required to understand their reference in context. Among the many details of structural difference are the following. Karuk directionals are obligatory affixes on verbs. In an elaboration on the basic system, speakers must distinguish "coming from" and "going in" a direction (such as upstream or uphill), as well as coming from and going toward across water or with reference to the centers of water. The other languages do not require attention to goal versus source of motion. Hupa has its own elaboration of the system, with directional adverbs that refer to midway paths that split the angle between stream direction and mountain direction. In Hupa, uphill and downhill can be expressed by (optional) directional modifiers on verbs, but the stream flow directions are expressed by adverbs. Yurok has only one verbal affix relating to directionality, for "across the stream". Yurok has directional adverbs for each of the major directions, and these are inflected with additional elements that narrow down the space of reference. In Hupa and Yurok, all these resources are optional for speakers, not required as in Karuk. O'Neill finds that these differences are carefully maintained; there is no convergence in how direction is expressed, in spite of multilingualism. Attention to distinction is driven by a local shared ideology of languages that values their distinctiveness, power, and their time depth in the places to which they are linked.

4. Loanwords and Areal Distributions

Scholarship in areal linguistics has mainly focused on structural typological variables, and not on the distribution of lexical resources. However, loanwords also can constitute areal traits and may be revealing about the circumstances of trait sprawl for variables in other dimensions of language structure. The languages of the Northwest California linguistic area share relatively few loanwords, given the intensity of contact among the languages. Golla (2011: 227) suggests that this is typical of California. Even in the case of Lake Miwok, very much assimilated into the system of shared traits in the Clear Lake linguistic area (see (3)), quite different from other Miwokan languages, and with a number of identifiable borrowings, "fewer than a hundred probable loan words can be identified" (Golla 2011: 227).[14] Bowern et al. (2011) found that in a sample of 42 languages from California, the Great Basin, and the lower Colorado River Yuman languages, most have fewer than 5% of loanwords in basic vocabulary (although rates are higher in other domains; for instance, borrowing in the domain of flora and fauna has a mean of 11% in the sample (Bowern et al. 2014)). Californianists have argued that areal patterns in the region show that phonological and grammatical convergence is more prominent than lexical borrowing, challenging the usual understanding that lexical items are universally more "borrowable", needing less intense language contact than is required for convergence of traits of grammar and phonology (Thomason & Kaufman 1988). That is, where we find the latter type of convergence, we expect to find high rates of loan vocabulary as well.[15]

Although Californianists find lexical borrowing to be sparsely attested, there are some notable suites of loans. Words for 'dog' were widely borrowed, and sort roughly into four sets that have considerable geographical coherence (Golla 2011: 227).[16] Words for 'tobacco' are widely diffused (Hill 2011), and there are widespread loans in other domains as well. A spectacular *Wanderwort* (Haynie et al. 2014) appears in (6).[17] Its distribution extends along the entire eastern edge of California into the Great Basin as far as Hopi (where the form is probably a loan from a Southern Numic language). The spread of this item is probably at least 1,500 years old, pre-dating the regular sound change PUA *l > Numic *n*, contrasting with PUA *l retained in Takic (Merrill 2013).

(6) <əl- ~ al> 'bad, evil, ugly, ghost':[18] Klamath *-alla* (with verbs) 'V for an evil purpose, wickedly, immorally'; Achomawi *ʔeleʔwo·qoji·* 'bad'; Northern Yana *ʔal* 'taboo', *ʔalʔalai* 'ugly', *ʔalc'ilaa(na)* 'nightmare, dead person seen in dream'; Proto-Eastern Miwok *ʔəl·i- 'ghost, reflection (in mirror)'; Palewyamni Yokuts *el-lít* 'evil spirit, ghost'; Proto-Numic *ɨnɨ (Mono *ɨnɨʔ* 'anything dangerous or harmful, European person'; Timbisha Shoshone *ɨnɨ* 'dangerous'; Southern Paiute *ɨnɨ* 'evil spirit, ghost'); Hopi *ɨnaʔ-* 'dangerous, to do with bad intentions' (a compounding element with verbs); Takic (Cupan): Cahuilla *elélema* 'bad', Cupeño *əlálʔish* 'bad', Luiseño *alaxish* 'evil'.

Sometimes loanwords are the most important spreading traits. This is the case for the Western Mono convergence with Yokutsan languages, where phonological and grammatical trait spread is apparently absent. Western Mono (Monache) spread from the Owens Valley east of the Sierra Nevada into its historic territory west of the Sierra Crest between 300 and 600 years ago (Morgan 2010). The expansion displaced Sierra Miwok and Yokutsan groups, and gained the Mono a reputation as fierce warriors. Gayton (1948) suggests that communities with members of both Yokuts and Mono heritage did not form until the 1860s, and trade and communication between the two groups was still contaminated by "an undercurrent of hostility" (Gayton 1948: 56) well into the early 20th century. In spite of this maintenance of social distance, Mono subsistence and religious/political systems are heavily Yokuts-ized, and Western Mono dialects have many Yokuts loanwords. The figures in (7) come from counts of vocabularies for flora and fauna collected by C.H. Merriam, a zoologist whose notes provide reliable information on the meaning of words for animals and plants.[19] The percentage of loans in the flora-fauna domain in (7) is considerably higher than the mean of 11% found for the sample of 42 languages mentioned previously.

(7) Percentages of Yokuts loans in C.H. Merriam's flora-fauna materials in three Western Mono varieties of the Upper San Joaquin River region

a. Northfork Mono: 38 Yokuts loans in 225 items: 17%
b. Wobonuch Mono: 32 Yokuts loans in 172 items: 19%
c. Entembich Mono: 93 Yokuts loans in 239 items: 39%

Gayton (1948: 254) found the Entembich Mono to be "partially Yokuts-ized or formerly Yokuts", perhaps reflecting a shift of Yokuts to Mono. However, this proposal is not supported by a wider range of data. The frequency of Yokuts loans in the flora-fauna domain in Entembich Mono is far lower than in Merriam's data on Bankalachi, a variety of Tübatulabal whose speakers were definitely shifting to Yokuts, with 72 Yokuts words in a list of 88 flora-fauna terms. Furthermore, varieties of Yokuts in contact with Western Mono have almost no Mono loans. For instance, Merriam's Chukchansi Yokuts list has only two such items, a word for 'piñon nuts' and a word for 'cedar'. No Mono loans appear in Merriam's Wukchamni Yokuts word lists, although Wuksachi Mono as recorded by Gayton (1948) has many loans from Wukchamni Yokuts in all domains.

While the spread of Mono speakers downhill, in contrast with the spread of Yokuts linguistic resources uphill into their communities, is a relatively recent phenomenon, it may provide a model for more ancient processes. During the Mono spread, temperature minima in western North America associated with the Little Ice Age occurred at about 1450 and again at about 1850 (Mann 2002).[20] The relationship between downhill Yokuts and uphill Mono and Bankalachi thus conforms perfectly to J. Nichols's generalization, derived from her work in the Caucasus, about the dynamics of Alpine language spreads: "Isoglosses and language spreads move downhill during warm periods and uphill during cold periods. Population movements go in the opposite direction" (J. Nichols 2004: 129). This suggests a model for more ancient areal patterns elsewhere around the margins of the Central Valley, perhaps permitting us to distinguish cold-period language spreads from those due to warm-period events such as the "Great Drought" in the 12th and 13th centuries, potentially permitting us to (at least roughly) date various spreads.

5. Areal Effects From Substratum Languages

While areal traits can be shared because of networks of intercommunication among many languages, some California areal phenomena may reflect a different source: a common substratum language has supplied the same traits to more than one superstratum language.[21] The widespread loan in (6) may represent the influence of a substratum language now lost. Such effects arise when members of a substratum population are incorporated into communities of a spreading language and pass on features of the substratum to their children in the form of "interferences" – which may reflect conscious choice by speakers – in their usage of the new language. Substratum effects in California have been documented by several scholars. Klar (2002) argues that "residue vocabulary" in Island Chumash reflects a lost language of the northern Channel Islands, replaced by a Central Chumash language from the mainland. Bright and Bright (1976 [1969]) made a similar argument for words in Gabrielino/Tongva that are not found in any other Uto-Aztecan languages and could not be traced to Chumashan or Yuman. Among these mystery words are the terms for "fire" and "blood", items that are generally very stable in Uto-Aztecan languages and, respectively, numbers 1 and 7, that is, of the highest stability, on the Leipzig-Jakarta vocabulary list of the 100 most stable vocabulary items (Haspelmath & Tadmor 2009). While the source of the Gabrielino/Tongva words is unknown, sometimes the substratum can be identified: Callaghan (2014) details evidence of an Esselen substratum in Costanoan and Miwokan languages.

An example of a possible substratum effects from a language of the Central Valley, perhaps Yukian or Hokan but now lost, may be illustrated by the loan sets in (8)–(15).

(8) <taat> 'person' : Proto-Northern Yukian **ʔahtat* 'people' (Yuki *ʔa·ṭát* 'man'), Proto-Pomo *ʔaká·kʔ*, Lake Miwok *ṭaih*, Proto-Yokutsan **ṭʰaʔṭʰ*, Tübatulabal *taatwal*[22]

(9) <tʃay-> 'sifting basket': Lake Miwok *c'ájwa* 'a large basket used for shaking, *cáajaka* 'sifter", Yawdanchi Yokuts *tʃaiji* 'seed beater', Obispeno Chumash *tşaja* 'chaya, traste, basket in general', Ventureño Chumash *caya* 'kind of basket', Cupeño *tʃaymal* 'coarse, scoop-shaped basket', Lu. *tʃaayit* 'type of basket', *tʃaayilaʃ* 'sifter'

(10) <mamil> 'Blackberry"; Proto-Yukian *mam 'berry', Proto-Nim-Yokuts *mamil 'blackberry', Southern Sierra Miwok *mamla* 'blackberry', Tubatulabal *mamil* 'blackberry', Timbisha Shoshone *mamil* 'blackberry'.

(11) <sVkV-> 'Soaproot (*Chlorogalum pomeridianum*)': Wintu *sa·q'as*, Lake Miwok *ṣikíiti*, Proto-Western Miwok *hak·a-ṣ, Proto-Eastern Miwok *sakani, Proto-Nim-Yokuts *t̪ʰoxot̪ʰ, Antoniano Salinan *ṣátala* 'brush', Migueleño Salinan *ṣk'aləh*, Ineseño Chumash *kot'*, Cupeno *suxuxul*; Gabrielino *ṣuuhar* 'soap plant, brush'

(12) <saw-> 'Acorn bread': Proto-Wintun *sa·w, Wappo *ʃáwo* (from Patwin); Central Yana *sau(na)*, Yowlumne Yokuts *sah-sah*, Yawdanchi Yokuts *ṣaṣa-ñitṣ*; Cupan *ṣaw-

(13) <mah> 'dogbane, Indian hemp (*Apocynum cannabinum*)': Proto-Yukian *mah*, Proto-Pomo **mahxá*, Migueleño Salinan *t'mahn'*

(14) <to> 'head, hair': Proto-Pomo **hoʔt'ó* 'brains, head', Wappo *t'ol* 'hair', Northern Wintun *tómoy* 'hair', Patwin *doL* 'head', Proto-Eastern Miwok *tolo-, Cruzeño Chumash *tohol* 'head', Obispeño Chumash *tʃoʔ, ʃoʔ* 'head, hair', Proto-general Yokuts **ʔoṭ'ow* 'head' < **ʔoṭ'aw* (Utian *uṭ'u), Proto-general Yokuts **to'ol* < **toʔal* 'hair'

(15) <kaw->, <haw> 'Gray Fox':[23] Chimariko *haw'*, Proto-Pomo *haq'áw, PWintun *ha:w 'fox', Proto-Maiduan *haw 'gray fox', Marin Miwok *Ah-wah-ke*, Proto-Nim-Yokuts *ʔawtʃʰaʔ, Ventureno Chumash *haw*, Cahuilla *qáwisiʃ*, Cupeno *kawísiʃ*; Proto-Yuman *p-rxa·w/m-rxa·w

6. Areal Effects at the Margins of a Language Spread

When speakers of a spreading language come into contact with speakers of diverse other languages along the new frontiers, an areal cluster of traits may be created that does not reflect intercommunication among all the languages involved. For instance, the spread of Yokutsan left a trail of Yokutsan loanwords in languages on both sides of the San Joaquin Valley and south into the Takic languages, as seen in the word for 'tobacco' in (16) in Chumash and Gabrielino in the west and Tübatulabal on the east, which was then borrowed from Tübatulabal into two Numic languages, Timbisha Shoshone and Kawaiisu.

(16) Proto-Yokutsan *so·kon < **so·kan 'to smoke tobacco', Central Chumash *ʃow ~ sow'* 'tobacco', Gabrielino *ṣuukiy* 'tobacco', Tübatulabal *ṣoʔogonht* 'tobacco', Timbisha *soka* 'chaw of tobacco', Kawaiisu *soʔo(n)dɨ* 'Nicotiana bigelovii'

A controversial case that has been advanced as an example of this type is the spread of Uto-Aztecan languages into California. Sherzer (1968) suggested Uto-Aztecan (U-A) influence as the source for nine of the traits he examined for California languages, diffused from Uto-Aztecan into the following languages (not all traits appear in all of them): Achomawi-Atsugewi, Maidu, Eastern Miwok, Costanoan, Esselen, Chumash, Yokuts, and Diegueño. Examples of traits include the presence of a schwa vowel, the presence of the phoneme *ŋ*, and reduplication for distributive or plural.[24] A few scholars have suggested that the Central Valley might have been the Proto-Uto-Aztecan homeland. M. Nichols (1981) identified possible U-A loanwords as far north as Yuki and Hupa that he argued attested to contact with "Old California Uto-Aztecan". Several other scholars took up this question in the 1980s (e.g., Klar 1980; Shaul 1982; Turner 1983). Shaul (2014) revived the hypothesis, presenting loanword evidence from Esselen and Costanoan languages in support of the Central Valley of California as the Proto-Uto-Aztecan homeland. However, evidence from the U-A ethnobiological lexicon developed by Fowler (1983) made this hypothesis extremely unlikely. Furthermore, the loanword evidence offered by M. Nichols (1981) and Shaul (2014) exhibits many problems and uncertainties (Hill 2014; 2015). The secure examples of loanwords all come from Numic or Takic, and thus date to a period after the radiation of Northern Uto-Aztecan. Nonetheless, there is a good deal of evidence (see (9), (11), (12), and (15)) that some Takic peoples once lived within or near the southern margins of the Central Valley, and may have been pushed southward into their historic territories by the spread of Yokuts. However, ethnobiological evidence locates the Takic homeland in the Mojave and Colorado Deserts of southeastern California, not in the Central Valley (Hill 2015).

7. Conclusions

The great diversity and density of the languages of Indigenous California has attracted linguists to apply areal linguistic approaches for over a century, and inspired them to develop improved methods for identifying interesting patterns and sorting these out. Advances in linguistic typology have identified many linguistic traits that were not recognized by the pioneers in the field, which can be a foundation for new work. As our understandings of the historical development of the California language families improve, areal-linguistic questions and conclusions can be refined. California should remain a valuable laboratory for research in areal linguistics.

Further Reading

Hickey, Raymond (ed.). 2017. *The Cambridge handbook of areal linguistics*. Cambridge: Cambridge University Press.

Matras, Yaron, April McMahon, and Nigel Vincent (eds.). 2006. *Linguistic areas: Convergence in historical and typological perspective*. Houndsmills, Basingstoke, UK: Palgrave MacMillan.

Muysken, Pieter (ed.). 2008. *From linguistic areas to areal linguistics*. Amsterdam and Philadelphia: John Benjamins Publishing Company.

Thomason, Sarah G. 2001. *Language contact: An introduction*. Edinburgh: Edinburgh University Press.

Notes

1. Most linguists suspect – and some are sure – that these "Hokan" languages are genetically related. However, the common ancestor, if it existed, was very ancient, and the trajectories of radiation of the family are obscure. Golla (2011: 242–243) advances some proposals for grouping the California Hokan languages based on areal linguistic evidence. I use scare quotes around "Penutian" for the same reason. The California "Penutian" families (Yok-Utian, Wintun, Maiduan) do not form a single clade within the phylum.
2. Utian (with two subgroups, Miwokan and Costanoan) and Yokutsan probably constitute a single clade, Yok-Utian (Callaghan 1997; 2001; 2014). However, while Utian ancestors were probably in the Central Valley by about 4,500 years ago, the Yokutsan spread appears to be no more than about 1,500 years old (Golla 2011).
3. Tübatulabal, perhaps distantly related to Takic, is another Uto-Aztecan language that has been located in the southernmost Sierra Nevada for about 2,500 years (Garfinkel 2007).
4. A linguistic "trait" is a structural feature (sometimes a cluster of features) at any level of organization, from patterning in discourse to phonetic realizations.
5. Thomason (2001) has an excellent summary of the diverse processes that yield areality.
6. These are pronoun systems where the first person has *n* as its prominent (or only) consonant, and the second person has *m*; for example, the Kitanemuk (Uto-Aztecan, Takic subgroup) independent pronouns *niʔ* 'I', *imiʔ* 'you (singular)'. Such systems contrast with *m/t* systems (e.g., French *moi, tu*) that are widespread in Eurasia (Nichols & Peterson 2013b).
7. Interestingly, Mithun (2017) does not include in her list – headed by the words "such as" – perhaps the best-known proposal of a "Northern California linguistic area" (Haas 1967; 1976). Haynie's (2012) statistical analysis shows that many of the languages that Haas includes are better understood as the southernmost members of a Northwest Coast linguistic area rather than as constituting a coherent linguistic and geographical unit in their own right. Haas's proposal reaches out to include languages as far south as Sierra Miwok; in Campbell's (2017) terms, it combines half a dozen different "trait sprawl areas" to create a sort of Venn diagram, which Haas then calls an "area".
8. I use "Northwest California" to distinguish this area from the larger Northwest linguistic area that extends as far north as Alaska.
9. The assumption, of course, is that geographical links between Washo, a Hokan language, and the more northern Hokan languages were broken in relatively recent times by the spread of Maiduan. Areal linguists

often appeal to this sort of non-geographical understanding (Donohue & Whiting 2011 argue that this is appropriate and necessary).

10. Bickel and Nichols (2006), Donohue and Whiting (2011), and Haynie (2012) propose statistical methods that can test for areality.
11. Note that the *k/q* contrast is not reconstructed for Proto-Numic (Iannucci 1973; M. Nichols 1974). So it is possible that the *k/q* allophony in Mono and in Southern Paiute represents two independent developments, and not an inheritance of the PNUA allophony.
12. The vowel shift in Gabrielino-Tongva is probably quite recent. The Fernandeño dialect retains the central vowel, and several of Harrington's Gabrielino speakers often had schwa instead of *o* as reflexes of the UA central vowel. The shift of *ə* to *o*, and the shift of *o to *e*, both exactly as in the Cupan language Luiseño, may reflect the influence of the latter language during the historic period. Contrary to Hinton's (1991) claim that there is no influence from Yuman in Gabrielino-Tongva, the language does have *kʷaho·xaʔ* 'red', from Yuman 'blood', and *aşa·wt* 'eagle', from Yuman 'bird', with a Takic augmentative suffix. Both of these loans are widespread in Takic.
13. The central vowel, ə, is the only one of the Diegueño vowels that does not have a corresponding long vowel, hinting that it is not wholly integrated into the system. Langdon (1976: 129) observes that "The underlying system is . . . clearly a three-vowel one".
14. Golla interprets this as a low number. In fact, Lake Miwok has 11.4% loanwords in a 205-word list of basic vocabulary (Bowern et al. 2011). In a sample of 42 California languages, only three had a higher rate: Wappo (also in the Clear Lake area), Tübatulabal, and Bankalachi, a variety of Tübatulabal. Most California languages have no more than 5% of loan words in basic vocabulary. It must be recalled that documentation of the lexicon for most California languages is sparse; we might recognize many more loanwords if we had dictionaries of a size comparable to those for better known languages.
15. It must be noted that this characterization of the reversed borrowing hierarchy in California is impressionistic. While there are quantitative studies of lexical borrowing in comparative perspective (e.g., Haspelmath & Tadmor 2009), I am not aware of similar exercises for typological traits, so we have no standard for their relative importance. In addition, it is possible that much of the loanword signal from early stages of language contact in California is invisible to us due to sound change and vocabulary replacement.
16. 'Dog', at (84) on the Leipzig-Jakarta list of basic vocabulary (Haspelmath & Tadmor 2009), is one of the least stable words on the list; that is, it is easier for a language to replace the word for "dog" than it is to replace 83 other items on the list.
17. While the resemblances here include only a very short phonetic sequence, their geographical coherence argues that they may be of historical significance, constituting a trait sprawl rather than a chance resemblance.
18. The brackets < > indicate that the shape assigned to the *Wanderwort* is not a formal reconstruction, but merely a rough estimate of the shape of the item. The German word *Wanderwort* is usually applied to lexical items with exceptionally extensive distribution; modern examples include the forms that show up in English as 'tea', 'coffee', 'tobacco', and 'sugar'.
19. C. Hart Merriam Papers, Volume 1. Papers relating to work with California Indians 1850–1974. The Bancroft Library, University of California, Berkeley. Unfortunately, rather than adopting the standards for phonetic transcription suggested to him by linguists, Merriam preferred to use an English-based system of his own invention where, for instance, *e* stands for [i], and *i* stands for [ai]. In spite of this eccentricity, the Merriam materials are very useful. They often provide our only attestation for lexical items in the languages.
20. Recall that the Donner Party attempted to cross the Sierras in 1846 and was stranded in heavy early snowfall. The survivors resorted to cannibalism.
21. A "substratum" language is a historic mother tongue of a speech community that has adopted a new language, the "superstratum", which replaces, either partially or completely, the substratum language.
22. Manaster-Ramer (1992) links Tubatulabal *taatwal* to Numic *taNwa forms, but this requires us to recognize reduplication in a singular. A link to Yokutsan is equally plausible. Regarding the Pomoan form, McLendon (1973: 53) observes that Proto-Pomoan *k "seem[s] to have been characterized by a rather palatal, pre-velar articulation in at least some environments". I thank Eugene Buckley for contributing this example.
23. Campbell (1997: 307) notes forms with *kaw-* meaning 'bark' in Koasati and Natchez, and suggests that the form is onomatopoetic, so these resemblances may be due to chance, not diffusion. I give (15) because it has a geographical distribution similar to the examples in (8)–(14). The similar forms in Chimariko and Yuman hint that it may be a Hokan word.
24. Recent research shows that several of Sherzer's proposals are clearly wrong. For instance, Proto-Yuman has *kʷ, and Diegueño *kʷ* is a reflex of that sound, not diffused from Takic. Incorporation is not a family trait of Uto-Aztecan, although it does appear in several of the languages.

References

Bettinger, Robert L. 2015. *Orderly anarchy: Sociopolitical evolution in aboriginal California*. Berkeley and Los Angeles: University of California Press.

Bickel, Balthasar & Nichols, Johanna. 2006. Oceania, the Pacific Rim, and the theory of linguistic areas. In *Proceedings of the Berkeley linguistic society 32*, 3–12. Berkeley, CA: Berkeley Linguistics Society.

Blevins, Juliette. 2002. Notes on sources of Yurok glottalized consonants. In Buszaard-Welcher, Laura & Hinton, Leanne (eds.), *Proceedings of the meeting of the Hokan-Penutian workshop: Survey of California and other Indian languages report*, vol. 11, 1–18. Berkeley: University of California Press.

Blevins, Juliette. 2003. The phonology of Yurok glottalized sonorants: Segmental fission under syllabification. *International Journal of American Linguistics* 69. 371–396.

Blevins, Juliette. 2017. Areal sound patterns: From perceptual magnets to stone soup. In Hickey, Raymond (ed.), *The Cambridge handbook of areal linguistics*. Cambridge University Press.

Bowern, Claire & Epps, Patience & Gray, Russell & Hill, Jane & Hunley, Keith & McConvell, Patrick & Zentz, Jason. 2011. Does lateral transmission obscure inheritance in hunter-gatherer languages? *PLoS One* 6(9). e25195.

Bowern, Claire & Haynie, Hannah & Sheard, Catherine & Alpher, Barry & Epps, Patience & Hill, Jane & McConvell, Patrick. 2014. Loan and inheritance patterns in hunter-gatherer ethnobiological systems. *Journal of Ethnobiology* 34(2). 195–227.

Bright, William & Bright, Marcia. 1976 [1969]. Archaeology and linguistics in prehistoric Southern California. In Dil, Anwar S. (ed.), *Variation and change in language: Essays by William Bright*, 189–205. Stanford, CA: Stanford University Press.

Callaghan, Catherine A. 1964. Phonemic borrowing in Lake Miwok. In Bright, William (ed.), *Studies in California linguistics*, 46–53. (University of California Publications in Linguistics 34). Berkeley and Los Angeles: University of California Press.

Callaghan, Catherine A. 1987. Lake Miwok naturalization of borrowed phonemes. In Joseph, Brian & Zwicky, Arnold (eds.), *A festschrift for Ilse Lehiste*, 84–93. (Working Papers in Linguistics, vol. 35). Columbus: Ohio State University Department of Linguistics.

Callaghan, Catherine A. 2001. More evidence for Yok-Utian: A reanalysis of the Dixon-Kroeber sets. *International Journal of American Linguistics* 67. 313–345.

Callaghan, Catherine A. 2014. *Proto Utian grammar and dictionary*. (Trends in Linguistics: Documentation 31). Berlin and Boston, MA: De Gruyter Mouton.

Campbell, Lyle. 1997. *American Indian languages: The historical linguistics of native America*. New York: Oxford University Press.

Campbell, Lyle. 2006. Areal linguistics: A closer scrutiny. In Matras, Yaron & McMahon, April & Vincent, Nigel (eds.), *Linguistic areas: Convergence in historical and typological perspective*, 1–31. Houndmills and Basingsoke: Palgrave Macmillan.

Campbell, Lyle. 2017. Why is it so hard to define a linguistic area? In Hickey, Raymond (ed.), *The Cambridge handbook of areal linguistics*, 19–39. Cambridge University Press.

Conathan, Lisa. 2004. *The linguistic ecology of Northwestern California: Contact, functional convergence and dialectology*. Berkeley: University of California. (Doctoral dissertation.)

Conathan, Lisa. 2006. Recovering sociolinguistic context from early sources: The case of Northwestern California. *Anthropological Linguistics* 48. 209–232.

Dixon, Roland B. & Kroeber, Alfred L. 1903. The native languages of California. *American Anthropologist* 5. 1–26.

Donohue, Mark & Bronwen, Whiting. 2011. Quantifying areality: A study of prenasalization in Southeast Asia and New Guinea. *Linguistic Typology* 15. 101–121.

Elliott, Eric B. 1994. 'How' and 'thus' in UA Cupan and Yuman: A case of areal influence. *1993 Hokan Penutian Workshop* 145–169.

Enfield, Nicholas J. 2005. Areal linguistics and mainland Southeast Asia. *Annual Review of Anthropology* 34. 181–206.

Fowler, Catherine S. 1983. Lexical cues to Uto-Aztecan prehistory. *International Journal of American Linguistics* 49. 224–257.

Garfinkel, Alan. 2007. *Archaeology and rock art of the Eastern Sierra and Great Basin frontier*. (Maturango Museum Publication Number 22). Ridgecrest, CA: Maturango Museum.

Gayton, Anna H. 1948. Yokuts and Western mono ethnography I: Tulare Lake, Southern Valley, and Central Foothill Yokuts. *Anthropological Records* 10(1). 1–142.

Golla, Victor. 2011. *California Indian languages*. Berkeley and Los Angeles: University of California Press.

Haas, Mary, R. 1967. Language and taxonomy in Northwestern California. *American Anthropologist* 69: 358–362.

Haas, Mary R. 1976. The Northern California linguistic area. In Margaret Langdon & Shirley Silver (eds.), *Hokan Studies*, 347–359. The Hague: Mouton.

Haspelmath, Martin & Tadmor, Uri (eds.). 2009. *Loan words in the world's languages: A comparative handbook*. Berlin and Boston, MA: De Gruyter Mouton.

Haynie, Hannah Jane. 2012. *Studies in the history and geography of California languages*. Berkeley: University of California Press. (Doctoral dissertation.)

Haynie, Hannah Jane & Bowern, Claire & Epps, Patience & Hill, Jane H. & McConvell, Patrick. 2014. Wanderwörter in languages of the Americas and Australia. *Ampersand* 1. 1–18.

Hill, Jane H. 2011. Borrowed names and indexical function in the Northern Uto-Aztecan botanical lexicon. In Whallon, Robert & Lovis, William & Hitchcock, Robert K. (eds.), *Information and its role in hunter-gatherer bands*, 167–180. Los Angeles, CA: UCLA Cotsen Institute of Archaeology Press.

Hill, Jane H. 2014. 'Old California Uto-Aztecan': A re-evaluation. In Dakin, Karen & Moctezuma Zamarrón, José Luís (eds.), *Lenguas yuto-aztecas: Acercamiento a su diversidad lingüística*, 191–248. (Serie: Estudios sobre lenguas Americanas 8.). México: Seminario de Lenguas Indígenas, Instituto de Investigaciones Filológicas, Universidad Nacional Autónoma de México.

Hill, Jane H. 2015. New California Uto-Aztecan: Chronological and cultural coherence in the evaluation of evidence for prehistoric language contact. *Journal of Anthropological Research* 71. 327–358.

Hill, Jane H. 2017. Historical linguistics. In Mills, Barbara & Fowles, Severin (eds.), *Oxford handbook of Southwest archaeology*, 121–135. Oxford University Press.

Hinton, Leanne. 1991. Takic and Yuman: A study in phonological convergence. *International Journal of American Linguistics* 57. 133–157.

Iannucci, David Edmund. 1973. *Numic historical phonology*. Ithaca, NY: Cornell University. (Doctoral dissertation.)

Jany, Carmen. 2009. *Chimariko grammar: Areal and typological perspective*. (University of California Publications in Linguistics 142). Berkeley: University of California Press.

Klar, Kathryn. 1977. *Topics in historical Chumash grammar*. Berkeley: University of California. (Doctoral dissertation.)

Klar, Kathryn. 1980. Northern Chumash numerals. In Klar, Kathryn A. & Langdon, Margaret & Silver, Shirley (eds.), *American Indian and Indoeuropean studies: Papers in honor of Madison S. Beeler*, 113–119. The Hague: Mouton.

Klar, Kathryn. 2002. The Island Chumash language: Implications for interdisciplinary work. In Browne, David W. & Mitchell, Kathryn L. & Chaney, Henry W. (eds.), *Proceedings of the fifth California Islands symposium*, 654–658. Santa Barbara, CA: Santa Barbara Museum of Natural History.

Langdon, Margaret. 1970. Review of Alan Campbell Wares. *A Comparative Study of Yuman Consonantism. Language* 46. 533–544.

Langdon, Margaret. 1976. The proto-Yuman vowel system. In Langdon, Margaret & Silver, Shirley (eds.), *Hokan studies*, 129–148. (Janua Linguarum Series Practica 181). The Hague and Paris: Mouton de Gruyter.

Langdon, Margaret & Silver, Shirley. 1994. California t/ṭ. *Journal of California and Great Basin Anthropology Papers in Linguistics* 4. 139–165.

Manaster-Ramer, Alexis. 1992. Tübatulabal 'man' and the subclassification of Uto-Aztecan. *California Linguistic Notes* 23(2). 30–31.

Mann, Michael E. 2002. Little ice age. In McCracken, Michael C. & Perry, John S. (eds.), *Encyclopedia of global environmental change Volume I: The earth system. Physical and chemical dimensions of environmental change*, 504–509. Chichester: John Wiley and Sons.

McLendon, Sally. 1973. *Proto-Pomo*. (University of California Publications in Linguistics 71). Berkeley and Los Angeles: University of California Press.

Merrill, William L. 2013. The genetic unity of Southern Uto-Aztecan. *Language Dynamics and Change* 3. 68–104.

Mithun, Marianne. 1999. *The languages of native North America*. Cambridge: Cambridge University Press.

Mithun, Marianne. 2017. Native North American languages. In Hickey, Raymond (ed.), *The Cambridge handbook of areal linguistics*. Cambridge University Press.

Morgan, Christopher. 2010. Numic expansion in the southern Sierra Nevada. *Journal of California and Great Basin Anthropology* 30. 157–174.

Nichols, Johanna. 2004. The origin of the Chechen and Ingush: A study in Alpine linguistic and ethnic geography. *Anthropological Linguistics* 46. 129–155.

Nichols, Johanna & Peterson, David A. 1996. The Amerind personal pronouns. *Language* 72(2). 336–371.

Nichols, Johanna & Peterson, David A. 1998. Amerind personal pronouns: A reply to Campbell. *Language* 74(3). 605–614.

Nichols, Johanna & Peterson, David A. 2013a. N-M Pronouns. In Dryer, Matthew S. & Haspelmath, Martin (eds.), *The world atlas of language structures online*. Leipzig: Max Planck Institute for Evolutionary Anthropology. (http://wals.info/chapter/137) (Accessed 2017-04-30.)

Nichols, Johanna & Peterson, David A. 2013b. M-T Pronouns. In Dryer, Matthew S. & Haspelmath, Martin (eds.), *The world atlas of language structures online*. Leipzig: Max Planck Institute for Evolutionary Anthropology. (http://wals.info/chapter/136) (Accessed 2017-04-30.)

Nichols, Michael P. 1974. *Northern Paiute historical grammar*. Berkeley: University of California. (Doctoral dissertation.)

Nichols, Michael P. 1981. Old California Uto-Aztecan. In Schlichter, Alice & Chafe, Wallace L. & Hinton, Leanne (eds.), *Survey reports 1981*, 5–41. (Survey of California and Other Indian Languages, Report 1). Berkeley: Department of Linguistcs, University of California Press.

O'Neill, Sean P. 2008. *Cultural contact and linguistic relativity among the Indians of Northwestern California*. Norman: University of Oklahoma Press.

Shaul, David Leedom. 1982. Esselen linguistic prehistory. In *Proceedings of the eighth annual meeting of the Berkeley Linguistic Society*, 205–218. Berkeley, CA: Berkeley Linguistics Society.

Shaul, David Leedom. 2014. *A prehistory of Western North America: The impact of Uto-Aztecan languages*. Albuquerque: University of New Mexico Press.

Sherzer, Joel. 1968. *An areal-typological study of the American Indian languages North of Mexico*. Philadelphia: University of Pennsylvania. (Doctoral dissertation.)

Sproat, Richard. 1981. Southern California reflexives: An example of translation borrowing? *Journal of California and Great Basin Anthropology Papers in Lingusitics* 3. 77–94.

Thomason, Sarah G. 2001. *Language contact: An introduction*. Edinburgh: Edinburgh University Press.

Thomason, Sarah G. & Kaufman, Terrence. 1988. *Language contact, creolization, and genetic linguistics*. Berkeley: University of California Press.

Thompson, Laurence D. & Kinkade, M. Dale. 1990. Languages. In Suttles, Wayne (ed.), *Handbook of North American Indians, Volume 7: Northwest coast*. Washington, DC: Smithsonian Institution.

Trubetzkoy, Nikolai Sergeevich. 1928. Proposition 16. *Acts of the First International Congress of Linguists* 17–18.

Turner, Katherine. 1983. Areal and genetic affiliations of the Salinan. *Kansas Working Papers in Linguistics* 8(2). 215–246.

LANGUAGES INDEX

Note: Page numbers in *italics* indicate a figure on the corresponding page and page numbers in **bold** indicate a table on the corresponding page.

SUBJECT INDEX

Note: Language families appear here. Specific languages appear in the Languages Index. Page numbers in *italics* indicate a figure on the corresponding page and page numbers in **bold** indicate a table on the corresponding page.

For Product Safety Concerns and Information please contact our EU
representative GPSR@taylorandfrancis.com
Taylor & Francis Verlag GmbH, Kaufingerstraße 24, 80331 München, Germany

www.ingramcontent.com/pod-product-compliance
Lightning Source LLC
Chambersburg PA
CBHW081353090726
47908CB00011B/2652

* 9 7 8 1 0 3 2 4 7 5 2 0 2 *